"Sophisticated, well researched . . .
fun and useful at all levels of scholarship."
—*Choice*

The words we use reveal as much about our culture and ourselves as they do about the objects and acts described. Etiquette has in the past tended to discourage the uttering, writing, and studying of certain prohibited words and subjects—usually associated with sex and bodily functions. For this reason, dictionaries of the standard language have for the most part been careful to omit these terms.

Now, at last, this indispensable resource book fills this vast linguistic gap by cataloging and explaining these prohibited words and subjects, thus opening the way out of polite society and into a world of free and innovative speech, rich in metaphor and unabashed in its vulgarity and directness.

RICHARD A. SPEARS began collecting words at the age of eight and dictionaries at fourteen. This love of language eventually led to a Ph.D. from Indiana University. Formerly a professor in the Department of Linguistics at Northwestern University, he has written on West African languages and nonstandard English, including pidgins and creolized languages. He has compiled and authored more than three dozen dictionaries, primarily for students of English as a second language. Currently, he is Editor Director, Dictionaries and Reference, McGraw-Hill/Contemporary.

SLANG AND EUPHEMISM

A dictionary of oaths, curses,
insults, ethnic slurs, sexual slang and
metaphor, drug talk,
college lingo, and related matters

THIRD REVISED
AND ABRIDGED EDITION
Richard A. Spears

A SIGNET BOOK

SIGNET
Published by New American Library, a division of
Penguin Putnam Inc., 375 Hudson Street,
New York, New York 10014, U.S.A.
Penguin Books Ltd, 27 Wrights Lane,
London W8 5TZ, England
Penguin Books Australia Ltd, Ringwood,
Victoria, Australia
Penguin Books Canada Ltd, 10 Alcorn Avenue,
Toronto, Ontario, Canada M4V 3B2
Penguin Books (N.Z.) Ltd, 182–190 Wairau Road,
Auckland 10, New Zealand

Penguin Books Ltd, Registered Offices:
Harmondsworth, Middlesex, England

First published by Signet, an imprint of New American Library,
a division of Penguin Putnam Inc. Published by arrangement with Jonathan David
Publishers, Inc.

First Printing, Abridged Edition, November 1982
First Printing, Second Revised and Abridged Edition, September 1991
First Printing, Third Revised and Abridged Edition, July 2001
10 9 8 7 6 5 4 3 2

 REGISTERED TRADEMARK—MARCA REGISTRADA

Printed in the United States of America

Library of Congress Card Catalog Number 00-050491

For Jack Berry

ACKNOWLEDGMENTS

My heartfelt thanks go to:

Sally Reyering for proofreading various stages of the manuscript for the last two years.

Nancy Spears for her help with proofreading.

Professor Morris Goodman for his help with the material in French, Hebrew, and Yiddish.

Professor B. Claude Mathis for providing space for this project in its early stages.

Professors Rae Moses, Robert Gundlach, and James Wertsch for reading parts of the manuscript.

Alice Thompson, Manager, Language Laboratories, for a painstaking check of the entries.

And to M. Dwass, P. Heller, B. Litowitz, N. N. New, J. L. Wagner, J. Yozallinas.

SLANG AND
EUPHEMISM

INTRODUCTION TO THE
THIRD ABRIDGED EDITION

Unlike when the first edition of this volume appeared, in the early part of the twenty-first century, the traditional varieties of taboo language are much in evidence on cable television, most movies, the stage, and certainly in magazines and novels. Newspapers and church bulletins seem to be the most notable holdouts. Restrictions on the kinds of vocabulary, visual imagery, and subject matter that can be put before the public continue to decline. No one seems interested in avoiding giving offense either to persons who object to this matter or those who seek to protect impressionable children from images of the most violent, lawless, and lewd aspects of modern society. The innocent television sitcoms of the 1950s, such as *Father Knows Best,* have grown into those containing openly sexual dialog, as with the friendly young people on the syndicated show *Friends.* At the same time, there are still millions of people who observe strong restrictions on the vocabulary that they use in everyday social interactions and utter strong condemnation of the frequent public use of foul language, as well as the imagery of violence, lawlessness, and lewdness.

One seemingly harmless and entertaining aspect of the age of increasing naughtiness is the vocabulary used. It's typically humorous and represents a centuries-old practice in the English-speaking world: the use of clever slang and euphemism to talk about the things we are not supposed to mention in public. The very fact that the categories of slang and euphemism still exist proves that there are still some standards of public behavior regarding our choice of words.

Old Trends and New

In this sea of open sexuality and scatological references, is there anything new? Yes, lots. And there are about 1,800 of them included in this new edition. The area of human activity that has produced the most fanciful English terms over the centuries is still drunkenness. (See **woofled** in the dictionary for the full list.) In the last decade, the outpouring of these terms continued. Many are simply patterned on previous terms or themes, but the amount of creativity and humor incorporated in these expressions is obvious. A sample of really good terms for **drunk** includes:

bladdered (from the drinker's frequently full bladder)
fitshaced (from "shitfaced")
giffed (from *TGIF,* "Thank God it's Friday")
honking (from *honking,* or vomiting drunk)
maggoty (based on "rotten")
putrid (again from "rotten")

One of the newest areas of joking and creativity seems to be male masturbation. Stand-up comedians seem to delight their audiences with colorful discussions of their own masturbatory practices and skills, complete with clever vocabulary. *Burping one's worm* is the absolute top choice for cleverness in this subject area. See **waste time** in the dictionary for a long list. Other new ones include:

arm the cannon (based on the action of pounding a charge into a cannon)
audition the finger puppets (from the use of the hand)
buff the helmet (the *helmet* is the glans)
shake hands with the governor (the *governor* is the boss)
spank the monkey (from the action)

The female variety, at long last, is moving toward parity with the activity of the jerky gender:

brush the beaver (*beaver* is an old term for the female pubic hair and genitals)
jill off (parallel to the male "jack off")
paddling the pink canoe (*canoe* is a reference to the labia)
tickle the tack (the *tack* is the clitoris)

Drinking is still a major activity on college campuses, along with its occasional vomitous results. Vomiting itself is still a hot topic, although creativity seems to be waning here. See **york** in the dictionary for a long list. Some new additions are:

decorate one's shoes and
shout at one's shoes (both seem to represent a lack of projection)
hork (onomatopoeia at its best)
laugh at the lawn (contrived for the alliteration)
lose one's guts (from the point of view of the vomiter)
woof one's custard (focusing both on onomatopoeia and texture)

What About the Future?

At the beginning of this new century, an enormous amount of vocabulary that can be identified as rude, vulgar, and derogatory is in common usage. Although this kind of language is still banned from many spheres of human activity, its use continues. Moreover, this is no longer a trend, but a way of life for many. Those who oppose all this have not yet thrown in the towel. All of the reasons for avoiding rude language that were discussed in the introduction to the first edition of this book are still alive and well. There will always be new children to protect, there will always be upwardly mobile people who tidy up their language as part of their transformation, and there will always be people who seek moral superiority for themselves as reflected in their views on language. These attitudes will serve to keep things in balance in the future just as they have in the past.

How much farther can things go? The pendulum has been swinging in one direction for a very long time now. Our experience with human history suggests that the pendulum will eventually reverse course and the public use of taboo language will be limited once again. Until that occurs, we will continue to document its use and try to make sense out of it.

GUIDE TO THE DICTIONARY

The Entry

Each entry consists of an entry word and its variants, followed by a definition or other identification. Parts of the definition or identification are separated by commas or semicolons and definitions or identifications are followed by a period. Following the definition, there may be statements concerning the derivation of the word (if it is English) and cross-referencing directions. The last part of the entry, which is enclosed in brackets, gives information such as location of use, foreign language etymology, type of use, period of use, and a source for the entry word.

Main Entry Words

Main entries and their variants appear in boldface roman type. Foreign words which are often italicized in written English are followed by an asterisk. Variants and closely related synonyms which apply to the entry and all of its senses follow the main entry in parentheses, for example, **phooey** (also **fooey**). Spelling variants applicable to only one sense of a word with numerous senses are listed after the applicable sense. Whenever main entries or their variants are cited elsewhere, they appear in small capitals. Some of the words that appear in the long lists of synonyms are not entry words in the abridged edition.

Definitions, Identifications, and Senses

Each main entry is followed by one or more definitions or identifications. Definitions are synonyms or phrasal equivalents of the main entry. Identifications are translations of foreign words, the spelling out of acronyms and initialisms, and indications of broad areas of meaning or function, such as oath, curse, or nickname.

Where there is more than one sense to a word, the senses are numbered if they appear to have distinct periods of usage or otherwise need to be referred to separately. Where a word has a range of related meanings, those meanings are separated by semicolons rather than numerals. Numbered senses are often listed in chronological order, but this is not an implication that the senses were derived in that order or are necessarily related unless that fact is specifically stated.

Parts-of-Speech

Part-of-speech is indicated by the grammatical form of the definition or identification. Where words, compounds, or phrases have uses or restrictions which are not evident from the definition, an example of usage is given. It should be noted that a lack of rigidity in the use of words in their usually assigned part-of-speech is a major characteristic of slang and jargon.

Pronunciation

There are no standards of pronunciation for slang, colloquial, or jargon. Much of the slang and colloquial material gathered before 1900 did not have its pronunciation recorded in any form. Where pronunciation must be indicated, it is done either with rhyming words (for example, "tear," which rhymes with "bear" or with "beer") or with phonetic respelling ("jee-ho-suh-fat").

Source and Etymology

Due to the limitations of space, the dictionary contains only very brief etymological notes. Some of the entry words are borrowed from languages other than English, but most slang, colloquial, and euphemistic words are reinterpretations of existing English words. When an entry word has as its source a foreign language or a specific dialect of English, that information is included in brackets at the end of the entry. When slang, colloquial, and euphemistic terms are derived from other slang, colloquial, or euphemistic terms, that fact is stated explicitly or is indicated through the cross-referencing. Many of the words have extremely long and complex etymologies, and many of those etymologies are in doubt. The exact origin of some of the dialect terms is totally unknown.

The final element in the bracketed material is sometimes a book title or an author's name. These titles and names refer to material listed in the bibliography. Where a title or author's name appears in parentheses, that means that the word in question was used rather than defined in the work listed. In a few instances, a listed source is the sole source for an entry. In most cases it is difficult if not impossible to tell what the very first attestation of a word is. The locations and dates listed in the bracketed material are not necessarily the same as those given by the source cited.

Geographical Domains

The specification of a country within the brackets at the end of an entry indicates the location(s) where an entry word has been recorded in its greatest use, or where it originated. It should be assumed that the knowledge and usage of many words extend beyond the country mentioned. It should not be assumed that all speakers in a particular country know a particular word. People sometimes think of slang as known on a national basis, but most slang is used locally and regionally. It is impossible to know where, when, and how frequently much of the colloquial and slang terms are used. The geographical domains listed are based on information found in the works listed in the bibliography.

It should be assumed that "British" refers to England and various parts of the Empire or Commonwealth (depending on the date specified). "British use, 1600s-1700s" includes the thirteen American colonies. The "1700s-1800s" could include the English spoken in Africa, Australia, India, and the United States. "British dialect" refers only to England. It can be assumed that "U.S." refers to North American use in general. It is certain that much of the twentieth-century slang listed as "British" or "U.S." is known and used in Australia and Canada. It is certain that there has been a far greater exchange of slang between Great Britain and the United States than is indicated here and that the U.S. and Canada share a far greater vocabulary than is indicated here. Since the World Wars, the exchange of slang in the English-speaking world has increased at a high rate.

The term "widespread" is used instead of a geographical location to indicate that the word probably has global distribution in English-speaking countries.

When no country is named, that indicates that no conclusive evidence exists as to whether the term is of British or U.S. origin.

In most such instances, the word can be assumed to be common to both countries to some degree at one time or another.

Periods of Usage and Dates

The dates shown are in some cases speculative and in a few cases educated guesses. The dating period specified for a word is intended to mark the outside boundaries of the period of "greatest usage" of the word. No claim is made that the word was universally known during the period or when a period of "lesser usage" might have begun or ended. The dating period means that "during the period specified, the available attestations indicate that the word was created by someone, used by a large population or one of its subgroups, or known to, or remembered by, one or more persons." Most of the words with only one (early) date listed are still preserved in some fashion.

"Recurrent nonce" refers to a word that has probably been "coined" hundreds or even millions of times over the centuries. In phallic nomenclature alone, metaphorical nicknames such as "carrot," "post," "snake," and "rod" have been created independently by millions of persons. Such words are certainly older than their earliest attestations. The study of ancient languages indicates that this type of naming is extremely old.

In assigning dates, each century is divided into thirds. Even these divisions may be interpreted generously. It is quite certain that word use is in no way keyed to the turn of the century. Therefore, early 1900s could be 1890-1940 or 1910-1925; late 1700s could be 1775-1810. Mid 1800s could be a period as long as 1820-1880.

Usage Domains

Many words have more than one class of usage, and many of the older words were not recorded with any indication of usage domains. The terms used are explained in the section Terms and Abbreviations.

All of the labels are very broad and must be interpreted carefully. For instance, "prostitute's argot" means that the word is attested as having been used by prostitutes. It does not mean that it is known to all prostitutes, and there is also a high probability that the word is known to persons other than prostitutes.

Virtually all of the sexual metaphors, swear words, and drinking terms are in the domain of male usage. Many of the definitions reflect this. Explanations and definitions assume an orientation of traditional sex roles and attitudes. Definitions of sexual matters should be assumed to refer to heterosexual matters unless indicated otherwise.

Punctuation and Spelling

Most of the spelling up to the 1700s has been modernized. Most of the British spelling has been Americanized if the term is known in the U.S.

Acronyms and other initialisms are regularized. Acronyms appear capitalized and do not have a period after each letter, for example, **AWOL,** pronounced "ay-wall." Other initialisms are capitalized, and each letter is followed by a period, for example, **A.W.O.L.,** pronounced "ay-double-u-oh-ell." This applies only to entry words in this dictionary and is not necessarily the way the acronyms and initialisms are found in writing.

The problem of hyphenization is one which plagues even the standard orthography. Many compound words could appear in any one of three ways, for example, **blubber brain, blubber-brain, blubberbrain.** The hyphenization of nonstandard material in written attestations is completely chaotic. In general, words like "housepainter" are hyphenated; beyond that, the chaotic hyphenation and spacing found in written attestations is used here. If written attestations were not available, words of the compound are separated by a space. Although this has been done "carefully," it has not been done "authoritatively"; that is, this dictionary is not the ultimate authority on the hyphenation and spacing of compounds, and indeed it contradicts standard dictionaries in some cases.

Oaths and exclamations and other entries which constitute complete sentences begin with a capital letter and end with the appropriate punctuation.

Main entry words which often appear italicized when used in written English are printed in boldface roman type and are followed by an asterisk.

CROSS-REFERENCING

There are four terms used in cross-referencing: *cf., q.v.,* "see," and "see also." *Cf.* means "consider the following word as you ponder the meaning of the entry word." The word following *cf.* may be a synonym of the entry word or simply a related form. *Q.v.* after a word or series of words is used here as a stylistic variant of *cf.* For instance, HOUSE (*q.v.*) is the same as *cf.* HOUSE. When one is referred to a specific sense of a word, the *q.v.* is omitted; thus, HOUSE (sense 3) is the same as HOUSE (*q.v.*, sense 3). In both cases one is not obliged to look up the word or words in question if one is satisfied with one's understanding of the definition. "See," on the other hand, indicates that one should look up the word after "see" in order to have all of the information available concerning the entry word. In some cases, "see" will lead to the definition, the date, or some other relevant piece of information.

A variant of "see" is "see also," which refers to *unrelated* entries which are similar in some way to the entry word in question. These references are for convenience and do not lead one to any additional information pertaining to the entry in which they occur.

Many of the topics covered in this work have generated long lists of synonyms or related subjects. Generally, cross-referencing will lead the reader to the appropriate list. Some are to be found at familiar terms. Others are to be found at euphemisms. Here is a directory of the main entry where these lists can be found. Note that for the interest of the reader, the lists include words that may have appeared in earlier editions of this book but which are no longer included as main entries in this edition.

alcohol	**booze**
amphetamines	**amp**
anus	**anus**
backside	**duff**
barbiturates	**barb**

bastard .... **accident**
belly... **belly**
black (person) .... **ebony**
bloody .... **bloody**
booze (strong) .... **embalming fluid**
break wind .... **gurk**
breasts.. **bosom**
brothel .... **brothel**
bull .... **bull**
bull (nonsense)... **bullshit**
butt.. **duff**
castrate .... **castrate**
Caucasian .... **peckerwood**
cemetery.. **cemetery**
cocaine .... **nose-candy**
coffin .... **coffin**
condom... **eel-skin**
copulate with .... **occupy**
copulation.. **smockage**
corpse .... **corpse**
crazy.. **daft**
cunnilingus .... **cunnilingus**
dame .... **bird**
damn .... **damn**
damned .... **damned**
dead... **done for**
death .... **demise**
defecate .... **ease oneself**
deflower... **deflower**
delirium tremens.. **ork-orks**
devil.. **fiend**
diarrhea .... **quickstep**
die.. **depart**
doctor.. **doc**
drunk.. **woofled**
drunkard .... **alchy**
dung (animal) .... **droppings**
dung .... **dung**
effeminate male .... **fribble**
ejaculate .... **melt**
erection.. **erection**
fellator .... **piccolo-player**

fondling... **firkytoodle**
fool .... **oaf**
gadget .... **gadget**
gay (noun) .... **epicene**
genitals... **genitals**
gin .... **ruin**
gonorrhea .... **gonorrhea**
groping... **firkytoodle**
group sex .... **group sex**
hang (verb) .... **nub**
hell... **hell**
heroin .... **heroin**
high (drugs) .... **tall**
homosexual (noun)... **epicene**
hymen .... **bean**
impregnate .... **stork**
Irishman .... **harp**
Jew .... **five and two**
L.S.D.. **acid**
lecher .... **lecher**
lesbian... **lesbyterian**
lewd.. **lewd**
lust... **lust**
marijuana .... **mari**
marijuana cigarette .... **mezzroll**
masculine woman .... **Amazon**
masturbate .... **waste time**
menses .... **floods**
Mexican .... **Mex**
mistress.. **spare rib**
morphine .... **morph**
mulatto .... **mahogany**
naked .... **starkers**
Negro .... **ebony**
nonsense... **animal**
oaths.. **'Zounds**
obscene .... **lewd**
opium.. **ope**
outhouse.. **ajax**
pederast .... **pederast**
pederast (young)... **bronco**
pederasty... **pederasty**

penis.. yard
period.. floods
physician... doc
pimp... pimp
police officer.. flatfoot
pregnant .... fragrant
prostitute... harlot
pubic hair (female)............................... Downshire
pudendum .... monosyllable
rape.. assault
rascal.. snoke-horn
scrotum .... tool bag
semen... mettle
sexually aroused.. humpy
syphilis............................... specific stomach
sodomite.. sodomite
sodomy .... sodomy
stupid .... stupid
sycophant .... acquiesce-man
testicles .... whirlygigs
toilet .... W.C.
trousers... galligaskins
underwear .... nether garments
urinate.. retire, whiz
urine.. tea
V.D. .... social disease
vagina................................... passage, monosyllable
vomit.. york
vulva.. monosyllable
whorehouse............................... house, brothel
wife... warden
woman as sex .... lay, tail

TERMS AND ABBREVIATIONS

The following terms and abbreviations are used in the dictionary. Cross-referencing refers to terms in this section.

abbreviation a shortening of a word or phrase by cutting the word(s) down to one syllable or initial(s), *e.g.*, A., meaning "amphetamine." See ACRONYM, INITIALISM.

acronym an abbreviation of a phrase where the initial letters are pronounced as if they were a single word. Acronyms are capitalized, but the letters are not followed by periods, *e.g.*, **AWOL**, meaning "absent without leave." See INITIALISM.

all senses when introducing a comment, this means the comment applies to all of the senses listed above the comment in a particular entry. See BOTH SENSES.

also 1. "also" enclosed in parentheses immediately after the entry word introduces spelling variants and closely related synonyms which correspond to all senses of the entry. **2.** "also" followed by a word or phrase in boldface type introduces a spelling variant or closely related synonym corresponding only to the numbered sense in which the "also" appears.

Anglo-Saxon a language spoken in England from about 800-1300; the basic Germanic component of English. Also called OLD ENGLISH.

argot the French equivalent of CANT (*q.v.*). Also, any slang or jargon. See CANT, JARGON, SLANG.

asterisk (*) indicates an entry word which is usually italicized in written English.

attested as introduces a location, date, or usage domain which may appear to be questionable.

backslang refers to the reversal of the letters of a word, *e.g.*, "mur" for "rum."

based on means that the entry word is related semantically or formally to the form or forms specified after "based on."

B.E. the initials of the author of a cant dictionary printed in about 1690. His full name is unknown.

because some entry words and their definitions constitute a riddle. For instance, "Because she is open to all parties" explains why the entry **public ledger** means "prostitute."

black slang refers to words which are currently or originally American Negro slang.

black use refers to words which are currently or originally used by black people.

Boontling a collection of slang, jargon, and catch phrases spoken by the population of Boonville, California, between 1880 and 1920.

both senses refers to a comment which applies to the two senses listed immediately above the comment in a particular entry. See ALL SENSES.

cant British criminal and underworld jargon which flourished from the 1600s to the 1800s. See ARGOT, JARGON.

catch phrase a frequently repeated phrase which attracts attention to the speaker or some activity being performed.

center slang a type of permutation where the spelling of a word is turned inside out, *e.g.,* "oolfoo" for "fool."

cf. an abbreviation of Latin *confer,* "compare." The word following *cf.* should be considered as one ponders the meaning of the entry word. It does not mean that one must look the word up in order to understand the meaning.

Cockney pertains to the pronunciation and dialect of the working class residing in the East End of London.

cognate related in form to the specified word or the ancestor of the specified word.

coit See COIT in the dictionary. The term is borrowed from the works of Eric Partridge where it is used as a transitive or intransitive verb. It replaces cruder terms such as "fuck" or "screw" for the actions of the male in copulating with a female. Standard English lacks a transitive verb for this action.

college slang a word or phrase typical of the very informal colloquial patter used on campus among college students.

colloquial pertains to words which are used every day in informal speech but which are not written as formal English. Some taboo words are traditionally considered colloquial. SLANG (*q.v.*) and colloquial are similar, and a word may be used as slang in some domains and colloquial in others.

corruption pertains to words which have been formed by either accidentally or purposefully distorting another word. *E.g.,* **Cheese and Crust!** is a corruption of "Jesus Christ!" See MINCED OATH.

costermonger's slang the jargon of the London pushcart hawker of fruits and vegetables.

derogatory pertains to terms of address or words derived therefrom which are deliberately insulting to the addressee.

dialect pertains to nonstandard words used in a specific region of a country.

double entendre refers to ambiguous words or phrases which have at least one taboo or indelicate meaning in addition to the standard meaning.

drug culture pertains to a word or phrase which is typical of the jargon of drug users and addicts since the mid 1900s.

dysphemism pertains to a word which has been deliberately degraded to having unpleasant or taboo connotations.

Egan's Grose refers to Pierce Egan's version of Grose's *A Classical Dictionary of the Vulgar Tongue.*

elaboration a word or phrase which is built on another expression, *e.g.,* **Bessie Smith** is an elaboration of **B.S.,** both signifying "bullshit."

euphemism a relatively mild or vague phrase substituted for a harsh or specific word or phrase, or the process of making such substitutions.

eye-dialect the use of spelling to signify dialect pronunciation, *e.g.,* "shore" for "sure," or illiteracy, *e.g.,* "sez" for "says."

fad word a word which quickly becomes known in a specific geographical area and becomes disused or obsolete just as quickly.

from 1. derived from; borrowed from a foreign language. **2.** derived from a particular sense of an English word.

generic pertains to a term for a group or type as applied to an individual or used as a nickname.

homosexual use pertains to terms originated by or used primarily by homosexuals.

initialism an abbreviation consisting of the initial letter(s) of a word or phrase in which each letter is pronounced separately and followed by a period, *e.g.,* **A.W.O.L.,** "absent without leave."

jargon a specialized vocabulary used by a well-defined group of people. See ARGOT, CANT, SLANG.

jocular deliberately humorous; joking.

juvenile pertains to terms typically used by children or adults speaking to children.

literary pertains to any writings in standard English regardless of merit.

malapropism a ridiculous misuse of a word. Usually a deliberate misuse.

medical pertains to words used primarily in the physical health sciences.

military pertains to a term originated in or primarily or originally used in any military organization.

minced oath a disguised or euphemized profane oath.

mock an imitation of a particular language or style. Typically "mock-Chinese" or "mock-Latin."

nickname a familiar name substituted for the proper name of a group or of an individual.

nonce pertains to a word which was made up for use on a particular occasion. See RECURRENT NONCE.

Old English See ANGLO-SAXON.

onomatopoetic pertains to a word whose phonological form is suggested by the sound of the thing for which it stands, *e.g.,* YORK, meaning "vomit."

orthography the standard spelling system.

phonological refers to the actual sounds (not the spelling) of words or to characteristic sound patterns of words.

Pig Latin a type of play language used in the U.S., *e.g., air-chay,* "chair."

play on punning on; based on in a jocular fashion.

pres. the present time.

q.v. an abbreviation of Latin *quod vide,* "which see." The word preceding *q.v.* should be considered as one ponders the meaning of the entry word. It does not mean that one must look the word up in order to understand it. "Both *q.v.*" means consider both of the preceding words or phrases.

recurrent nonce pertains to a word or phrase which has been coined afresh numerous times by different individuals over the years.

reinforced by pertains to the semantics of a word or phrase. Indicates a secondary or supporting etymology. For example, the word **bomphlet,** meaning "propaganda leaflet dropped from the air," is a blend of **bumf** (from **bumfodder**) and "pamphlet," reinforced by "bomb."

rhyming slang the word represented by a and b (or just a) in the pattern a and b = c, *i.e.,* needle and pin means gin (a = needle, b = pin, c = gin). Also called "Cockney rhyming slang."

rural pertains to farming and country life. See also DIALECT.

see indicates that the reader should look up the word which follows it in order to have all of the available information about the entry word.

see also refers to unrelated entries which share a key word with the entry in which the "see also" appears. This cross-referencing does not lead to any new information about the entry word.

slang pertains to a word or phrase which is known to always be used as slang, has been observed to be used as slang, or appears to have all of the characteristics of a slang word or phrase. Slang and COLLOQUIAL (*q.v.*) are similar, and a word may be used as slang in some domains and colloquial in others.

spoonerism pertains to an exchange of initial consonants in a pair of words, such as "blushing crow" for "crushing blow."

synonym a word or phrase having essentially the same meaning as another.

taboo pertains to an expression which has prohibitions against its utterance under certain situations.

truncation refers to a shortening of a word or phrase. Technically, abbreviations are truncations.

ultimately from refers to the probable original language source regardless of the route taken into the English language.

underworld pertains to the specialized vocabulary used by thieves, convicts, prostitutes, con-artists, and tramps. It is sort of a twentieth-century cant. Terms relating to mid 1900s dope use and the youth-drug cult are classified as DRUG CULTURE. (*q.v.*).

widespread indicates that the entry word probably has global distribution in English-speaking countries. It usually indicates attestations for Australia, England, and the U.S. with the assumption that it occurs elsewhere.

word-of-choice pertains to a word or phrase which is the most likely expression used in a given setting.

SLANG AND
EUPHEMISM

A

A. 1. an abbreviation of AMPHET-
AMINE (*q.v.*). *Cf.* AMP (sense 2). **2.** the
drug L.S.D. (*q.v.*); an abbreviation of
ACID (*q.v.*). [both senses, U.S. drug
culture, mid 1900s-pres.]

Aaron's rod the penis. *Cf.* STAFF OF
LIFE. For synonyms see YARD. ["Aar-
on's rod" is from the Old Testament
(Numbers); British, 1800s]

abbess the procuress or madam of a
brothel. *Cf.* ABBOT. [British, late 1700s]

Abbie (also **Abe, Abie**) a nickname
for a Jewish male. From the proper
name "Abraham." Derogatory when
used as a generic term. For synonyms
see FIVE AND TWO. [U.S. slang and colloquial, 1900s and before]

abbot 1. a PONCE (*q.v.*), an abbess's
favorite man. [British slang and cant,
1800s] **2.** Nembutal (trademark), a barbiturate. From the manufacturer's
name, "Abbott Laboratories." [U.S.
drug culture, mid 1900s-pres.]

A.B.C. See ACE BOON COON.

Abe a nickname for a Jewish male.
See ABBIE.

A-bomb a marijuana cigarette containing heroin or opium. [U.S. drug
culture, mid 1900s]

A-bomb juice MOONSHINE (sense 2);
inferior or strong liquor. [U.S. slang,
mid 1900s]

aborts Absolut vodka and port, mixed
together. For synonyms see BOOZE,
EMBALMING FLUID. [U.S., late 1900s-
pres.]

about gone intoxicated with alcohol.
For synonyms see WOOFLED. [U.S.
slang, early 1900s-pres.]

about right (also **about done**) intoxicated with alcohol [U.S. slang, mid
1900s-pres.]

about to find pups pregnant; about
to give birth. *Cf.* CAST (sense 2), DROP

(sense 1), FIND. [U.S., 1900s and
before]

Abraham 1. the penis. For synonyms
see YARD. **2.** the female genitals. For
synonyms see MONOSYLLABLE. [both
senses, 1900s and before]

abso-bloody-lutely (also **abso-bally-
lutely**) absolutely; emphatically. [wide-
spread slang, 1800s-1900s]

abso-fucking-lutely absolutely; without a doubt. [U.S. slang, 1900s]

abuse 1. to cheat; to make a cuckold
of. From an earlier sense meaning
"cheat." [late 1400s] **2.** to ABUSE ONE-
SELF (*q.v.*); to masturbate. See SELF-
ABUSE. [since the late 1500s] **3.** masturbation. A truncation of SELF-ABUSE
(*q.v.*). [since the late 1500s]

abuse oneself to masturbate. [wide-
spread euphemism]

academician a prostitute; an inmate
of an ACADEMY (*q.v.*). [cant, 1800s or
before]

academy a bawdy house; a brothel.
[British, late 1600s, B.E.]

Acapulco gold (also **Acapulco**) high-
quality marijuana grown in Mexico. *Cf.*
GOLD. [U.S. drug culture, mid 1900s-
pres.]

accident 1. a bastard. [colloquial and
nonce since the early 1900s or before]
Synonyms: ADULTERINE, ADULTERINE
BASTARD, ADULTEROUS BASTARD, AVE-
TROL, BABE OF LOVE, BACHELOR'S
BABY, BACHELOR'S SON, BANTLING, BAR
STEWARD, BASE-BEGOTTEN CHILD, BASE-
BORN, BASE-SON, BAST, BASTARD, BAS-
TARDA, BASTRICH, BELL-BASTARD,
BLANKARD, BORN OUT OF WEDLOCK,
BRAT, BUSH CHILD, BUSH COLT, BY-CHOP,
BYE-BLOW, BY-SCAPE, BY-SLIP, BY-SPELL,
CATCH-COLT, CHANCE-BAIRN, CHANCE-
BORN, CHANCE-CHILD, COME-BY-CHANCE,
FILIUS NULLIUS, FILIUS POPULI, GRASS
COLT, HASTY PUDDING, HYBRID, ILLEGIT-

IMATE, INCIDENT, LOVE-BEGOTTEN CHILD, LOVE-BRAT; LOVE-CHILD, MERRY-BEGOTTEN CHILD, MISBEGOTTEN, MOMZER, MONGREL, NATURAL, NATURAL-CHILD, NEPHEW, NIECE, NON-WED-LOCK, NULLIUS FILIUS, OFF-GIRL, OF UNKNOWN BIRTH, OLD FIELD COLT, OUT-CHILD, OUTSIDE, OUTSIDE CHILE, OUT-SIDER, SIDE-SLIP, SIDE-WIND, SIDE-WIPE, SINGLE CHILD, SON OF A BACHELOR, SON OF A BITCH, SQUEAKER, STALL WHIMPER, UNLAWFULLY BEGOTTEN, WHORE'S-KITTLING, WHORESON, WOODS-COLT, YARD-CHILD. **2.** an unplanned conception, specifically a failure of a birth control device. [U.S., mid 1900s-pres.] **3.** a loss of control of the bowels or bladder, said primarily of young children.

accommodate to copulate; to fit oneself to another; to serve another person sexually. For synonyms see OCCUPY. [colloquial since the 1800s]

accommodation house a brothel. [British slang, early 1800s]

A.C.-D.C. (also **A.C./D.C.**) **1.** BISEXUAL (sense 2). [U.S. slang, mid 1900s-pres.] **2.** pertaining to a homosexual male who is ambivalent to the choice of male or female sex roles. [slang, mid 1900s-pres.]

A.C.-D.C. bar a bar offering sexually oriented entertainment appealing to both male and female sexual interests. Usually considered appealing to a BISEXUAL (sense 3) person. [U.S., mid 1900s-pres.]

ace 1. a marijuana cigarette. [U.S. drug culture, mid 1900s-pres.] **2.** the female genitals. From ACE OF SPADES (sense 1) and the darkness of the pubic hair. For synonyms see MONOSYLLABLE. [British slang, late 1800s] **3.** a sarcastic term for an oaf or jerk. [U.S. slang, mid 1900s]

ace boom-boom one's good and loyal black friend. Akin to ACE BOON COON. For synonyms see EBONY. [U.S. mid 1900s-pres.]

ace boon coon (also **A.B.C.**) one's best and most dependable friend. Typically said about a [male] black's best male friend. For synonyms see EBONY. [U.S., primarily black use, late 1900s]

ace of spades 1. the female genitals. From the color or shape of the pubic hair. [British slang, late 1800s, Farmer and Henley] **2.** a Negro. Potentially derogatory. Also in the phrase "as black as the ace of spades," referring to a very dark Negro. For synonyms see EBONY. [U.S. before mid 1900s]

achers, the the testicles. The same as ACRES, THE. For synonyms see WHIRLYGIGS. [British, late 1900s-pres.]

achieve to achieve coition with a woman. Also "win the heart of." *Cf.* SCORE. [from *Othello* (Shakespeare)]

acid lysergic acid diethylamide, the drug L.S.D. [U.S. drug culture, mid 1900s-pres.] Synonyms: A., ANIMAL CRACKERS, BART SIMPSONS, BATTERY ACID, BIG D, BLACK SUNSHINE, BLACK TABS, BLOTTER, BLUE ACID, BLUE CHEER, BLUE FLAG, BLUE HEAVEN, BLUE MIST, BLUE SPLASH, BROWN DOTS, CALIFORNIA SUNSHINE, CANDY, CHERRY TOP, CHOCOLATE CHIPS, CID, CLEAR LIGHT, COFFEE, CONTACT LENS, CUBE, DELYSID, DOMES, DOTS, FLAKE ACID, FLATS, GELATIN, HAZE, INSTANT ZEN, L., L.S.D., LUCY IN THE SKY WITH DIAMONDS, LUGGAGE, MELLOW-YELLOW, MICRODOTS, ORANGE MUSHROOMS, ORANGE SUNSHINE, ORANGE WEDGES, OUTER, OWSLEY, PAPER ACID, PEARLY GATES, PINK, PINK SWIRL, PURPLE FLATS, PURPLE HAZE, PURPLE MICRODOTS, RAGGEDY ANN, ROYAL BLUE, SID, SID, STRAWBERRY FIELDS, SUGAR, SUGAR LUMP, SUNSHINE, SWISS PURPLE, T., TEE, THE CHIEF, THE HAWK, TICKET, WEDDING BELLS ACID, WEDGES, WHITE LIGHTNING, WINDOW PANE, YELLOW, YELLOW SUNSHINE, ZEN.

acid-head (also **acid-dropper, acid-freak**) One who uses the drug L.S.D. regularly and is frequently under its influence. [U.S. drug culture, mid 1900s-pres.]

acid pad a place to consume the drug L.S.D. in safety and seclusion. [U.S. drug culture, mid 1900s-pres.]

ackers money. From Egyptian *akka*. [British, mid 1900s-pres.]

acne an inflammation of the skin of the face and sometimes the back and chest, usually with noticeable pustules.

A truncation of ACNE VULGARIS. [since the early 1800s]

acquiesce-man a sycophant. Punning on "yes-man." [U.S. slang, mid 1900s] Synonyms: ARSE-CRAWLER, ASS-KISSER, ASS-SUCKER, ASS-WIPE, BOOT-LICK, BOOT-LICKER, BROWN-NOSE, BROWN-TONGUE, BUM-LICKER, BUM-SUCKER, BUTT-WIPE, CATCH-FART, CLAWBACK, COCK-SUCKER, CRAWL, EGG-SUCKER, FARTLICKER, FART-SUCKER, FOOTLICKER, GRAECULUS ESU-RIENS, GREASE-BOY, GREASER, HAIRY BELLY, KISS-ASS, LICKDISH, LICKSPIT, LICKSPITTLE, PAPELARD, PICKTHANK, SCRAPE-SHOE, SLAP-SAUCE, SOAP-CRAWLER, SPANIEL, STROKER, SUCK, SUCK-ASS, SYCOPHANT, TOAD-EATER, TOADY, TRUCKLER, TUFT-HUNTER, YES-MAN.

acres, the testicles. See ACHERS, THE. For synonyms see WHIRLYGIGS. [Australian and British, mid 1900s-pres.]

act, the copulation. A truncation of "the sexual act." For synonyms see SMOCKAGE. [euphemistic since the 1600s or before]

action 1. coition; sexual activity; intrigue with the opposite sex. [since the 1600s or before; U.S. euphemism and slang, early 1900s-pres.] **2.** excitement, especially from gambling. [U.S., early 1900s-pres.]

activated tipsy; alcohol intoxicated. For synonyms see WOOFLED. [U.S. slang, 1900s, Dickson]

active citizen a louse. Usually in the plural. [British and U.S. slang, early 1800s]

activity booster an amphetamine tablet; a PEP PILL (*q.v.*). [U.S. slang and drug culture, mid 1900s-pres.]

act of androgynation a euphemism for "copulation." For synonyms see SMOCKAGE. [mid 1600s (Urquhart)]

act of generation (also **act of sport**) a euphemism for "copulation." [British, late 1800s]

act of kind a euphemism for "copulation." *Cf.* DEED OF KIND. [British, 1800s]

act of love a euphemism for "copulation." [1800s-1900s]

A.D. an abbreviation of "drug addict." [U.S., mid 1900s-pres.]

Adam methylenedioxy-methamphetamine; Ecstasy, a hallucinogen similar to L.S.D. [British and U.S., late 1900s-pres.]

Adam, the old 1. original sin; male and female lust; human sexuality. [from *Henry V* (Shakespeare)] **2.** the penis. *Cf.* ADAM'S ARSENAL. [both senses, British, 1800s, Farmer and Henley] **3.** lust; male sex drive and potency.

Adam-and-Eve it 1. to copulate. *Cf.* WHAT EVE DID WITH ADAM. [British slang, late 1800s, Farmer and Henley] **2.** to be in a state of nudity; to practice nudism. [U.S., mid 1900s]

Adam and Eve's togs (also **Adam and Eve's clothes**) nakedness; nudity. [British and U.S., early 1900s]

Adamatical naked; nude. For synonyms see STARKERS. [implied in the 1600s, *Oxford English Dictionary*]

Adamize to copulate, from the male point of view. *Cf.* PHALLICIZE. [British, 1800s]

Adam's arsenal the male genitals, the penis and testicles. For synonyms see VIRILIA. [British, late 1800s, Farmer and Henley]

Adam's own the female genitals. [British, 1800s]

Adonis a fop or dandy; an extremely good-looking or "pretty" male. [from the proper name "Adonis" in Greek mythology; U.S., early 1900s-pres.]

adrip sated and intoxicated with alcohol. [U.S. colloquial, 1900s]

adultery an act of sexual intercourse where at least one partner is married to someone else. [since the 1300s] Synonyms: COMARITAL SEX, CONJUGAL INFIDELITY, EWBRICE, FLESHLY TREASON, FOUL PLAY, INFIDELITY, MARRIAGE-BREACH, SMOCK-TREASON, SPOUSE-BREACH, TREASON.

a--e "arse," the posteriors; the anus. See ARSE, ASS. [British, late 1700s, (Grose)]

affair 1. a romantic or sexual relationship of a brief duration, especially an illicit one. [U.S., 1900s or before] Synonyms and related terms: AFFAIRE D'AMOUR, AFFAIRE DE COEUR, AMORETTE, AMOUR, AMOURETTE, CARRY ON, ENTANGLEMENT, EXTRA-CURRICULAR ACTIVITIES, FLING, FOOL AROUND, INTRIGUE, SMOCK-SECRET, TRYST. **2.** the male or female genitals. Sometimes in the plural. Used jokingly in double entendre. [since the late 1500s]

affaire d'amour* a "love affair"; an AFFAIR (sense 1). [French]

affaire de coeur* an "affair of the heart"; a love affair as opposed to a purely sexual matter. [French]

afflicted intoxicated with alcohol. For synonyms see WOOFLED. [slang since the early 1700s]

affy lustful. [U.S. slang, 1900s, Berrey and Van den Bark]

afgani the alcohol extract of CANNABIS SATIVA (q.v.). For synonyms see OIL. [U.S. drug culture, mid 1900s-pres.]

afgay a homosexual male. From AGFAY (q.v.), which is Pig Latin for FAG (sense 2). For synonyms see EPICENE. [British backslang, early 1900s, Dictionary of the Underworld]

afloat intoxicated with alcohol; drunk. Cf. AWASH. [British and U.S., late 1800s-1900s]

African black a variety of marijuana said to be from Africa. [U.S. drug culture, mid 1900s-pres.]

Afro 1. an American Negro. [U.S., early 1900s-pres.] **2.** a hairstyle worn mostly by blacks of both sexes. [U.S., mid 1900s-pres.] **3.** Negroid; African. [U.S., early 1900s-pres.]

Afro-American 1. an American Negro. For synonyms see EBONY. [U.S., early 1900s-pres.] **2.** pertaining to the American Negro. [both senses, U.S., early 1900s-pres.]

Afro-Saxon a Negro who behaves like or aspires to be like Caucasians. Cf. OREO. [U.S., mid 1900s-pres.]

after hair chasing after women, especially for sexual purposes. Refers to the pubic hair. Cf. HAIR. [since the 1800s]

after one's greens in pursuit of sexual release or satisfaction, usually said of men. [British, 1800s]

ag-fay a homosexual male. Pig Latin for FAG (sense 2). Cf. AFGAY. [U.S., early 1900s-pres.]

aggro (also **agro**) **1.** aggravation. [widespread, mid 1900s-pres.] **2.** great; awesome. [U.S., late 1900s-pres.]

agots testicles. For synonyms see WHIRLYGIGS. [Australian, late 1900s-pres.]

A.H. a really wretched person, male or female; an abbreviation for ASS-HOLE. Also a provocative term of address. For synonyms see SNOKE-HORN. [U.S. and elsewhere, late 1900s]

A-head a frequent user of amphetamines. A. (sense 1) refers to amphetamines. [U.S., mid 1900s-pres.]

A-hole 1. the anus. **2.** a term of contempt. Both are from ASS-HOLE (q.v.). [both senses, U.S., 1900s]

a-ight all right. [U.S., late 1900s-pres.]

airborne copulation a FLYING-FUCK as found in GIVE A FLYING-FUCK and GO TAKE A FLYING-FUCK. A jocular elaboration. [U.S. military, 1900s, Soldier Talk]

airbrain (also **airhead**) a silly, giddy person of either sex. [widespread slang, late 1900s]

airheaded stupid; giddy. [U.S. slang, late 1900s]

air one's belly to vomit. For synonyms see YORK. [U.S. slang, 1900s]

air one's pores to be naked; to become naked, partially or completely. [British, 1900s]

airs, in one's intoxicated with alcohol. [U.S. slang, early 1700s, Ben Franklin]

aitch heroin; a spelling-out of H. For synonyms see HEROIN. [U.S. drug culture, mid 1900s-pres.]

ajax a PRIVY (q.v.). A jocular variation of "a JAKES" (q.v.), an outhouse. From The Metamorphosis of Ajax, by Sir John Harington. [British, late 1500s; U.S. slang, 1900s] Synonyms: BACK, BACKHOUSE, BACKY, BANK, BOG, BOGGARD, BOG-HOUSE, BOG-SHOP, CACATO-

RIUM, CAN, CHAPEL, CHAPEL OF EASE, CHIC SALE, CLOSET, CLOSET OF EASE, COFFEE HOUSE, COFFEE-SHOP, COMMONS, COMPOST HOLE, COTTAGE, COUNTING-HOUSE, CRAP-HOUSE, CRAPPER, CRAP-PERY, CRAPPING-CASA, CRAPPING-CASE, CRAPPING CASTLE, CRAPPING-KEN, CROP-PING-KEN, DILBERRY CREEK, DONAGHER, DONEGAN, DONIGAN, DRAUGHT, DUNA-GAN, DUNNAKEN, DUNNAKIN, DUNNY, DUNNYKEN, FORAKERS, FORICA, GAR-DEN-HOUSE, GONG, GONG HOUSE, HONEY-HOUSE, HOOSEGOW, HOPPER, HOUSE OF EASEMENT, HOUSE OF OFFICE, IVY-COVERED COTTAGE, JACQUE'S, JAKE, JAKE-HOUSE, JAKES, JAQUES, JOHN, KYBO, LEAK-HOUSE, LIBRARY, LITTLE HOUSE, NECESSARIUM, NECESSARY, NEC-ESSARY HOUSE, NECESSARY VAULT, OFFICE, OUTDOOR PLUMBING, PARLIA-MENT, PETTY-HOUSE, PLACE, PLACE OF CONVENIENCE, PLACE OF EASEMENT, PLACE OF RESORT, PLACE WHERE YOU COUGH, PREP CHAPEL, PRIVATE OFFICE, PRIVY, QUAKER'S BURYING-GROUND, REAR, RELIEF STATION, SCOTCH ORDI-NARY, SHACK, SHIT-HOLE, SHIT-HOUSE, SHITTER, SHOUSE, SIEGE, SIEGE-HOLE, SIEGE-HOUSE, SIR HARRY, SMOKE-HOUSE, SPICE-ISLAND, STOOL OF EASE, TEMPLE, THE PATH, UNCLE, UNFLUSH-ABLE, VANDYKE, WARDROBE.

A.K. 1. an "ass-kisser." **2.** an ALTE KACKER (*q.v.*), an old man; an "old shitter." [possibly from German *alte Knacker*, "old fogey"; both senses, U.S., early 1900s-pres.]

alchy (also **alki, alky**) **1.** alcoholic beverages; any kind of alcohol. [U.S., mid 1800s-1900s] **2.** a drunkard. [U.S., early 1900s-pres.] The following terms apply to men unless indicated otherwise: AFTER DINNER MAN, ALCOHOLIC, ALE-KNIGHT, ALE-WISP, ALKI STIFF, ALKY BUM, BANG-PITCHER, BAR-FLY, BARREL-HOUSE BUM, BAT, BEER-JERKER, BEER MONSTER, BEER-SLINGER, BEER-SWIPER, BELCH-GUTS, BEZ-ZLER, BIB-ALL-NIGHT, BIBBLER, BILED OWL, BILLY-BORN-DRUNK, BIMMY, BINGO-BOY, BINGO-MORT (female), BLACK POT, BLOAT, BLOATER, BLOKE, BLOMBOLL, BLOTTER, BOOSE-HOUND, BOOSEY-COCK, BOOZE ARTIST, BOOZE-FIGHTER, BOOZE-FREAK, BOOZEGOB, BOOZEHEIS-TER, BOOZE-KING, BOOZER, BOOZICIAN,

BOOZINGTON, BORACHIO, BOTTLE-BABY, BOTTLE-MAN, BOTTLE-SUCKER, BRANDY-FACE, BREW DOGGER, BREWER'S HORSE, BREW-HOUND, BREWSTER, BROTHER-WHERE-ART-THOU?, BUBBER, BUBBING-CULL, BUBSTER, BUDGER, BUDHEAD, BUM-BOOZER, BUMPER, BURSTER, BUST-HEAD, CADGER, CAGER, CATERPILLAR, COD, COMPOTATOR, COPPER-NOSE, CROCK, CROW, DEHORN, DIPS, DIPSO, DISTILLERY STIFF, DRAINIST, DRAMSTER, DRINKSTER, DRUNKARD, D-T-IST, ELBOW-BENDER, ELBOW-CROOKER, EN-SIGN-BEARER, FIDDLE-CUP, FLUFFER, FUDDLE-CAP, FUDDLER, FUDDLING-FEL-LOW, FUNNEL, GARGLER, GEEK, GIN DIS-POSAL UNIT, GIN-HEAD, GLOWWORM, GRAPE-MONGER, GRAVEL-GRINDER, GROG-HOUND, GULLION, GUTTLE, GUZZLE-CUTS, GUZZLER, HAIL-FELLOW-ALL-WET, HAMMER-HEAD, HISTER, HOISTER, HOOCH-HOUND, HOOTCHER, INEBRIATE, JAG, JAR-HEAD, JERKER, JICK-HEAD, JOB, JOLLY NOSE, JUGHEAD, JUICEHEAD, KENNEDY ROT, KENNURD, LAPPER, LAPPY CULL, LARGE-HEAD, LEANAWAY, LICK-SPIGOT, LICK-WIMBLE, LOVE-POT, LUG-POT, LUSH, LUSHCOVE, LUSHER, LUSHING MAN, LUS-HINGTON, LUSH MERCHANT, LUSHY, LUSHY-COVE, MALT-BUG, MALT-HORSE, MALT-WORM, MOIST 'UN, MOONER, MOP, NAZY-COVE, NAZY-NAB, OENOPHILIST, OILER, ONE OF THE FAITHFUL, PEGGER, PHILISTINE, PINT POT, PISS ARTIST, PISS-HEAD, PISS-MAKER, PISSO, PISSY-PAL, PITCHER-MAN, PLONK-DOT, PLONKO, POT, POT-FURY, POT-KNIGHT, POWER DRINKER, PRETZEL-BENDER, PUB-ORNAMENT, QUARTER POT, REEL-POT, ROB-POT, RUM-BAG, RUM-DUMB, RUMMY, RUMPOT, RUM-SUCKER, SCHICKER, SCOWRER, SHAKER, SHICK, SHIFTER, SHIKKER, SIPSTER, SLUSH HOG, SNORTER, SOAK, SOAKER, SOD, SOD-DEN BUM, S.O.T., SOT, SOUSE, SPIGOT-SUCKER, SPONGE, SPUD, SQUIFF, STEADY-LAPPER, STEW, STEW BUM, STEWIE, SUCK-BOTTLE, SUCK-PINT, SUCK-SPIGOT, SWAL-LOWER, SWELL-HEAD, SWILL-BOWL, SWILLER, SWILL-POT, SWILL-TUB, SWIPER, SWIPPINGTON, SWIZZLE-GUTS, TAVERNER, THIRSTINGTON, TICKLE-BRAIN, TICKLE-PITCHER, TID, TIGHT SKIRT (female), TIP-PLE-ARSE, TIPPLER, TOAST, TODDYCASK, TOOTER, TOPE, TOPER, TOSS-POT, WAS-SAILER, WET-HAND, WET-QUAKER, WETS-

TER, WET-SUBJECT, WET-'UN, WHIPCAN, WINEBAG, WINEBIBBER, WINO.

Al Cohol alcohol; alcohol personified. *Cf.* JOHN HALL. [U.S. slang, early 1900s]

alcoholized saturated with alcohol; drunk. For synonyms see WOOFLED. [U.S. slang, early 1900s or before]

alcove the female genitals. *Cf.* CRANNY, NICHE-COCK. [British, late 1800s]

alecie (also **alecy**) intoxicated with ale. A play on "lunacy" and an old nonce word preserved in dictionaries. [late 1500s]

aled(**-up**) intoxicated due to drink or drugs. For synonyms see TALL, WOOFLED. [British, late 1900s-pres.]

ale-knight (also **pot-knight**) a tippler; a drunkard. For synonyms see ALCHY. [British, late 1500s-1800s]

ale-wisp a drunkard. [British slang, 1800s or before, Farmer and Henley]

Alice B. Toklas a BROWNIE (sense 4) with marijuana baked into it. Named for Gertrude Stein's companion in the 1920s who is said to have devised the recipe for brownies containing marijuana. [U.S., mid 1900s-pres.]

alien sex fiend strong powdered P.C.P. mixed with heroin. [U.S., late 1900s-pres.]

A little more choke and he would have started. a catch phrase said upon hearing a man break wind. [Australian, mid 1900s-pres.]

Al K. Hall a jocular nickname for liquor based on "alcohol." [U.S. slang, 1900s]

alkied-up (also **alkied**) intoxicated with alcohol. For synonyms see WOOFLED. [U.S., 1900s]

alki hall alcohol. [U.S. slang, early 1900s]

alki stiff a hobo drunkard; any drunkard. [U.S. underworld, early 1900s]

alky bum a hobo drunkard; any drunkard. [U.S., 1900s]

all at sea intoxicated with alcohol. [nautical, 1900s or before]

alley apple 1. a piece of horse manure. *Cf.* HORSE APPLE, ROAD APPLE. [U.S. slang, early 1900s] **2.** a stone used as a missile. [U.S. slang, 1900s]

alley cat 1. a prostitute, especially one who prowls in the night. *Cf.* MOON-LIGHTER. [U.S., early 1900s] **2.** any person who is loose in sexual matters. *Cf.* TOMCAT. [U.S. slang, mid 1900s-pres.]

all face naked; nude. [British and U.S. slang, late 1800s]

all gone intoxicated with alcohol. For synonyms see WOOFLED. [U.S. slang, 1900s]

alligator bait 1. poor-quality food or disliked food **2.** a Negro, especially a Negro child. Derogatory and jocular. [both senses, U.S. slang, early 1900s or before]

alligator bull nonsense; BULLSHIT (*q.v.*). A play on "bull alligator," the mature male alligator.

all mouth and trousers making a useless commotion. [British, late 1900s-pres.]

all over one, be to be in close bodily contact, *i.e.*, fighting, necking, or fondling. [U.S. slang, mid 1900s-pres.]

all pink elephants alcohol intoxicated. For synonyms see WOOFLED. [U.S. slang, 1900s, Dickson]

all piss and wind making a noisy and useless commotion. [British, mid 1900s-pres.]

alls-bay nonsense; BALLS (sense 4). Pig Latin. [U.S., 1900s]

all's not quiet on the waterfront a catch phrase pertaining to a woman's state when menstruating.

all the way copulation, especially in "go all the way." *Cf.* LIMIT, THE. [U.S. slang, mid 1900s-pres.]

almanach the female genitals. Possibly having something to do with MONTHS (*q.v.*). For synonyms see MONOSYLLABLE.

almond rock (also **almond**) the penis. Rhyming slang for COCK (sense 3). *Cf.*

DICKORY DOCK. For synonyms see YARD. [British, late 1800s]

altar a toilet; the water-flush toilet bowl; a chamber pot. [U.S. slang, early 1900s-pres.]

altar of Hymen the female genitals. *Cf.* TEMPLE OF LOW MEN. [Brtish, late 1800s]

altar of love the female genitals. For synonyms see MONOSYLLABLE. [British, late 1800s]

altar room a W.C.; a bathroom. *Cf.* ALTAR. [U.S. slang, early 1900s-pres.]

alte kacker* (also **alter cocker, alter kocker, alter kucker**) a dirty old man; a seasoned lecher. [possibly from German *alte Knacker*, "old fogey"; U.S., early 1900s]

alter to castrate a male animal. *Cf.* CHANGE. [U.S. colloquial, late 1800s-pres.]

altitudes, in one's intoxicated with alcohol and in an elevated mood. [British colloquial, 1600s-1700s]

altogether, in the naked; nude. [colloquial, late 1800s-pres.]

altogethery intoxicated with alcohol. For synonyms see WOOFLED. [British slang]

amateur night 1. refers to an instance of copulation involving a woman who is casual about sex but not a prostitute. **2.** a specified night at an entertainment establishment featuring nude entertainment in which the patrons are invited to participate. [both senses, U.S. slang, mid 1900s-pres.]

Amazon 1. a mythical, warlike woman found in Greek mythology. The notion that the word is from the Greek for "without a breast" is doubted. (Amazons were supposed to have cut off their right breasts in order to facilitate drawing the strings of their bows.) [in English by the 1300s] **2.** an extremely masculine woman; a virago. [since the mid 1700s] Synonyms for sense 2: ANDROGYNE, BELDAME, BOON-DAGGER, BOY, BRIMSTONE, BULL BITCH, COTQUEAN, HORSE-GODMOTHER, JEZE-BEL, MUSCLE MOLL, OGRESS, QUEER QUEEN, VIRAGO.

amber fluid beer. For synonyms see BOOZE. [Australian, mid 1900s-pres.]

ambidextrous bisexual. See AMBISEX-TROUS. [British, early 1900s, *Dictionary of Slang and Unconventional English*]

ambisextrous pertaining to a bisexual person. A jocular play on AMBIDEX-TROUS (*q.v.*). [U.S., early 1900s]

ambulance-chaser a lawyer who seeks out clients from persons who are in trouble or injured. [U.S., early 1900s-pres.]

amen-snorter a religious person, especially a clergyman. For synonyms see SKY-PILOT. [since the late 1800s]

American letter See FRENCH LETTER.

American sock a condom. For synonyms see EEL-SKIN. [British, mid 1900s-pres.]

A.M.F. "Adios mother fucker!"; "Aloha mother fucker!"; "Good-bye and good riddance!" [U.S. military, 1900s, *Soldier Talk*]

amies See AMY.

ammunition 1. toilet tissue. [British and U.S. slang, 1800s-pres.] **2.** a perineal pad, sanitary pad, or napkin. For synonyms see MANHOLE COVER. [slang, early 1900s, *Dictionary of Slang and Unconventional English*]

amoeba phencyclidine, the drug P.C.P., an animal tranquilizer. For synonyms see P.C.P. [U.S. drug culture, late 1900s]

among one's frills copulating; the act of copulating. *Cf.* FRILLS. [British, 1800s, Farmer and Henley]

amorous congress an old euphemism for "sexual intercourse." For synonyms see SMOCKAGE. [late 1700s]

amorous rites lovemaking; coition. [from *Romeo and Juliet* (Shakespeare)]

amp 1. an ampule of a drug. **2.** an amphetamine tablet or capsule. Usually in the plural. [both senses, U.S. drug culture, mid 1900s-pres.] Synonyms for sense 2: A., AMPHETAMINE, AMPHETS, BAM, BLACK BEAUTIES, BLACKBIRD, BLACK MOLLIES, BOTTLE, BROWNS, BUMBLEBEE, CARTWHEEL, CHALK, CHICKEN POWDER, COASTS-TO-

COASTS, COCKLE BURR, CO-PILOTS, CRANKS, CROSSROAD, CRYSTAL, DOLL, DOUBLE-CROSS, EYE-OPENER, FIVES, FOOTBALLS, FORWARDS, GREEN DRAGON, GREENIE, JELLY BABY, JELLY BEAN, JOLLYBEAN, JUG, L.A. TURNABOUTS, LID-POPPERS, LIGHTNING, LIQUID BAM, METH, MINIBENNIES, NUGGETS, PEACH, PEP PILL, RHYTHMS, ROAD DOPE, ROOT, ROSAS, ROSES, SKYROCKET, SPARKLE PLENTY, SPECKLED BIRD, SPEED, SPLASH, SWEET, TENS, THRUST, THRUSTERS, TRUCK-DRIVER, TURNABOUTS, UP, UPPER, UPPIE, WAKE-UP, WEST-COAST TURNAROUNDS, WHITE CROSS, WHITES, WHITEY, ZOOM.

amped intoxicated with amphet-amines. From AMP (*q.v.*) with rein-forcement from "ampere." For synonyms see TALL. [U.S. drug culture, mid 1900s-pres.]

ampersand the posteriors; the but-tocks. A compressed form consisting of "and-per-se-and," represented by the symbol "&" (which is the last symbol in children's alphabets, thus "the end"). This was a way of indicating that one was talking about the word "and" and not using it as a conjunc-tion. Whenever letters were recited or words were spelled out, they were cited in the form "a per se a," and "o per se o," (Nares). [British, 1800s and before]

amphets amphetamines. For syn-onyms see AMP. [U.S. drug culture, 1900s, DeSola]

amy 1. an amyl nitrite ampule. This appears frequently as "amyl nitrate"; the plural is "amies" or "amys." *Cf.* PEARL (sense 2), SNAPPER (sense 5). **2.** an Amytal sodium (trademark) tablet or capsule, one of the barbiturates. [both senses, U.S. drug culture, mid 1900s-pres.]

Amy-John a masculine lesbian. A play on AMAZON (*q.v.*). *Cf.* JOHN-AND-JOAN (sense 2). [U.S., mid 1900s]

amyl amyl nitrite. See AMY (sense 1).

anal applause the breaking of wind. Jocular. For synonyms see GURK. [U.S., late 1900s-pres.]

anal astronaut a pederast. For syn-onyms see PEDERAST. [U.S., late 1900s-pres.]

anal avenger a pederast. For syn-onyms see PEDERAST. [U.S., late 1900s-pres.]

anatomical a euphemism for "lewd" or "sexually oriented"; explicit about the breasts or genitals. *Cf.* ADULT. [early 1900s-pres.]

anchored in Sot's Bay intoxicated with alcohol. For synonyms see WOOFLED. [nautical, 1900s or before]

angel 1. a male homosexual pederast; an INSERTOR (*q.v.*) who supports one or more other homosexuals. *Cf.* SUGAR-DADDY. [U.S. slang, early 1900s] **2.** a passive pederast; a RECEIVER (*q.v.*); a catamite. *Cf.* ANGELINA. For synonyms see BRONCO. [U.S. slang, 1900s] **3.** co-caine. For synonyms see NOSE-CANDY. [U.S. drug culture, mid 1900s-pres.]

angel dust (also **angel hair**) **1.** pow-dered P.C.P. (*q.v.*), an animal tranquil-izer. *Cf.* HEAVEN DUST. **2.** synthetic heroin. [both senses, U.S. drug culture, mid 1900s-pres.]

angel hair See ANGEL DUST.

angelina a hobo's catamite or any passive pederast; a RECEIVER (*q.v.*). *Cf.* ANGEL (senses 1 and 2). [U.S., 1900s]

angel lust the source of an erection in a corpse. [U.S., late 1900s-pres.]

angel mist (also **angel puke**) phency-clidine; the drug P.C.P., an animal tranquilizer. For synonyms see P.C.P. [U.S. drug culture, late 1900s]

angel poke P.C.P. [U.S., late 1900s-pres.]

angel tears liquid L.S.D. [U.S., late 1900s-pres.]

angie cocaine. From ANGEL (sense 3). [Australian, mid 1900s, Baker]

angle the penis. *Cf.* YARD. [British slang, late 1800s]

Anglo-Saxon pertaining to words (usually "dirty words") which are as-sumed to be Old English. See PARDON MY FRENCH.

angry erect. Said of the penis. [U.S. euphemism, late 1900s]

anilingism See ANILINGUS.

anilingus (also **anilingism**) the use of the mouth or tongue to stimulate the anus of another person.

animal 1. a euphemistic nickname for a bull. [U.S. rural colloquial, 1900s] **2.** nonsense, *i.e.,* BULLSHIT (*q.v.*). [U.S. slang, 1900s] Synonyms for sense 2: ALLIGATOR BULL, ALLS-BAY, AP-CRAY, APPLESAUCE, ARGLE-BARGLE, BALDER-DASH, BALDUCTUM, BALLOCKS, BALLOON JUICE, BALLS, BALLYHOO, BALLY HOOEY, BALONEY, BATSHIT, BEANS, BIBBLE-BABBLE, BILGE, BIRDSHIT, BIRD-TURD, BLAH, BLARNEY, BLATHER, BOSH, BOVRIL, B.T., BULL, BULL-FEATHERS, BULL-FODDER, BULLO, BULLONEY, BULLISH, BULLSHIT, BULL'S WOOL, BUM-FLUFF, BUNCOMBE, BUNK, BUNKUM, BURMA SHAVE, CHAFF, CLACK, CLAPTRAP, CLISH-CLASH, COBBLER'S AWLS, COBBLER'S STALLS, COCK, CODDING, COD'S WALLOP, CORRAL DUST, COW-CONFETTI, COWSH, COWSHIT, COW-YARD CONFETTI, CRAP, CRAPOLA, DRIP, DRIVEL, DURHAM, EYEWASH, FADOODLE, FALDERAL, FIBLE-FABLE, FIDDLE-CUM-FADDLE, FIDDLEDEEDEE, FIDDLE-FADDLE, FIDDLESTICKS, FLAMDOODLE, FLAPDOODLE, FLAP-SAUCE, FLUMMADIDDLE, FLUMMYDIDDLE, FOLDEROL, FOOEY, FOR THE BIRDS, FUDGE, GAMMON, GAS, GIBBER-GABBER, GIBBERISH, GILHOOLEY, GOBBLEDYGOOK, GUFF, GUMF, HOKUM, HOOEY, HORNSWOGGLE, HORSE, HORSE APPLE, HORSE FEATHERS, HORSERADISH, HORSESHIT, HORSH, HOT AIR, HOT COCK, HUMBUG, JACK SHIT, KIBOSH, LOAD OF CODS (WALLOP), LOAD OF CRAP, LOAD OF GUFF, LOAD OF OLD COBBLERS, MACARONI, MALARKY, LIP GLOSS, MEADOW DRESSING, MEADOW-MAYONNAISE, MIFF-MAFF, MOONSHINE, MUMBO-JUMBO, MUSH, NERTS, NURTS, OIL OF TONGUE, PALAVER, PARSLEY, PHOOEY, PIFFLE, PIGSHIT, PIG-WASH, PILE OF SHIT, PISS AND WIND, POPPYCOCK, PRIZE BULL, RATS!, RIMBLE-RAMBLE, ROT, SHIT FOR THE BIRDS, SHUCK, SKIMBLE-SCRAMBLE, SLOBBER, SLUDGE, SONG AND DANCE, TITOTULAR BOSH, TOMMY-ROT, TRIPE, WHANGDOODLE, WHIFFLE-WHAFFLE, YAWP. **3.** a term of contempt for a person implying nonhumanness. **4.** a fool; an oaf. [since the late 1500s] **5.** an athlete, especially if big, clumsy, ugly, or smelly. *Cf.* JOCK (sense 5). [U.S., mid 1900s-pres.] **6.** a sexually aggressive male; a STUD (sense 2) or an extremely uncouth male. [U.S., mid 1900s-pres.] **7.** a prostitute. Essentially a contemptuous term for any person of low character and habits. [U.S. underworld, 1900s] **8.** phencyclidine, the drug P.C.P. For synonyms see P.C.P. [U.S. drug culture, late 1900s] See also PARTY ANIMAL.

animal crackers small, animal-shaped cookies impregnated with the drug L.S.D. For synonyms see ACID. [U.S. drug culture, late 1900s, DeSola]

animal tranquilizer the drug P.C.P. (*q.v.*). *Cf.* ELEPHANT. [U.S. slang, mid 1900s-pres.]

ankle an attractive young woman or girl. [U.S. slang, mid 1900s] See also SPRAIN ONE'S ANKLE.

annihilated very drunk; intoxicated with a drug. For synonyms see TALL, WOOFLED. [U.S. slang, late 1900s]

answer nature's call to retire to the W.C., specifically to defecate or urinate. [colloquial euphemism, 1900s and before]

answer the final summons to die. For synonyms see DEPART. [late 1800s-pres.]

ansy-pay a homosexual male. Pig Latin for PANSY (*q.v.*). *Cf.* AG-FAY. [U.S., 1900s]

antifreeze 1. liquor. For synonyms see BOOZE. [U.S., 1900s] **2.** heroin. From sense 1. [U.S. drug culture, mid 1900s-pres., Wentworth and Flexner]

antifreezed alcohol intoxicated. For synonyms see WOOFLED. [U.S. slang, 1900s]

antipodes, the the female genitals; the "exact opposite" of the male genitals. For synonyms see MONOSYLLABLE. [British, 1800s or before]

antiseptic alcohol intoxicated. Clean and sterilized from excessive alcohol use. For synonyms see WOOFLED. [U.S. slang, 1900s]

anus the posterior opening of the alimentary canal. [since the mid 1600s] Synonyms: A—E, A-HOLE, ARS, ARSE, ARS MUSICA, A-S, ASS-HOLE, BACKDOOR, BACKDOOR TRUMPET, BACK-WAY, BAZOO,

BLIND-EYE, BLOT, BOGEY, BOGY, BOODY, BOTTLE AND GLASS, BROWN, BROWN BUCKET, BROWNIE, BRUNSWICK, BUCKET, BUM, BUNG, BUNG HOLE, BUNKEY, BUTTHOLE, CHUFF, CORN HOLE, CRACK, CRACKER, CULO, DATE, DEADEYE, DILBERRY-MAKER, DINGER, DIRT-CHUTE, DIRT-ROAD, DOPEY, DOT, ELEPHANT AND CASTLE, EXHAUST PIPE, FARTING-CLAPPER, FEAK, FRECKLE, FUDGEPOT, FUGO, FUN, FUNDAMENT, GARY GLITTER, GAZOO, GIG, GIGI, GLORY HOLE, GONGA, GOOSEBERRY-GRINDER, HIND-BOOT, HINDER-ENTRANCE, HOLE, JACKSIE, KAZOO, KEESTER, KHYBER PASS, MEDLAR, MONOCULAR-EYEGLASS, NOCKANDRO, NORTH POLE, PERVY, PODEX, POOPCHUTE, PORT-HOLE, RINCTUM, RING, RIP, ROUNDEYE, ROUND-MOUTH, SERVANT'S ENTRANCE, SEWER, SHIT-HOLE, SIEGE, SLOP-CHUTE, SPICE-ISLAND, STANK, TANTRACK, TEWEL, THE BROWN WINDSOR, TIB, TOKUS, TRILL, WHERE THE SUN DON'T SHINE, WIND MILL, WINDWARD PASSAGE.

ap-cray nonsense. Pig Latin for "crap." For synonyms see ANIMAL. [U.S. slang, 1900s]

ape 1. a derogatory nickname for a Negro. [U.S., 1900s or before] **2.** a hoodlum or strong-arm man. [1900s] **3.** any ugly man, especially if large. *Cf.* BABOON. [U.S. slang, 1900s]

aped intoxicated with alcohol. For synonyms see WOOFLED. [U.S., early 1900s-pres.]

ape-shit the state of being obsessed with a person or thing, as in the expression "go ape-shit" or "be apeshit." [U.S., mid 1900s]

ape wild intoxicated with alcohol; wildly drunk; APED. See APE-SHIT, GO APE-SHIT OVER SOMEONE OR SOMETHING. For synonyms see WOOFLED. [U.S. collegiate, late 1900s, Eble]

aphrodisiacal tennis court the female genitals. [1600s (Urquhart)]

apparatus the male genitals; the VIRILIA (*q.v.*). *Cf.* EQUIPMENT. [U.S. slang, 1900s]

apple and pip urine; to urinate; an act of urination. Rhyming slang for "sip," which is backslang for "piss."

[British, 1800s, *Dictionary of Rhyming Slang*]

apple dumpling shop a woman's breasts, especially if fat and partially exposed. [British slang, late 1700s-1800s]

apple-jack 1. brandy made from apples. **2.** any alcoholic liquor. For synonyms see BOOZE. [both senses, U.S., early 1800s-pres.]

apple jacks crack cocaine. For synonyms see NOSE-CANDY. [U.S., late 1900s-pres.]

apple palsy drunkenness from APPLEJACK (*q.v.*). [U.S., late 1800s-early 1900s]

apples 1. a woman's breasts. See CAT HEADS. [U.S., 1900s or before] **2.** the testicles; the same as LOVE-APPLES (*q.v.*). For synonyms see WHIRLYGIGS. [slang, 1800s-1900s] See also ALLEY APPLE.

apple-squire (also **apron-squire**) **1.** a kept man. **2.** a pimp. [both senses, British, 1500s-1700s]

apps drug use apparatus. [U.S. drug culture, mid 1900s-pres.]

appurtenances a woman's breasts. For synonyms see BOSOM. [U.S., 1900s]

apricots testicles. For synonyms see WHIRLYGIGS. [Australian, mid 1900s-pres.]

apron-up pregnant in "have one's apron-up." Refers to the bulge of the abdomen. *Cf.* SHORT-SKIRTED. [British, late 1800s, Farmer and Henley]

ap-say an oaf; a dullard. Pig Latin for SAP (*q.v.*). [U.S., 1900s]

aquatic water-grown marijuana. For synonyms see MARI. [U.S., late 1900s-pres.]

arbor vitae* "tree of life," the penis, especially when erect. *Cf.* STAFF OF LIFE. For synonyms see YARD. [Latin; British, 1700s-1800s]

ard hot; sexually aroused. From ARDOR (*q.v.*), possibly reinforced by HARD (sense 1). [British, 1600s-1800s]

ardor (also **ardour**) very strong lust; heated passion. [1300s-pres.]

arf an arf 1. "half and half," lightly

intoxicated with alcohol. For synonyms see WOOFLED. [early 1800s] **2.** an equal mixture of ale and porter. [British slang, 1800s]

arfarfanarf "half, half, and half," very drunk. [Cockney, late 1800s-early 1900s, Ware]

argle-bargle the throwing about of words; nonsense. [British, 1800s]

arm the penis. *Cf.* SHORT-ARM, SMALL-ARM. For synonyms see YARD. [U.S., mid 1900s-pres.]

armour a condom. For synonyms see EEL-SKIN. [late 1700s, Grose]

armour, in angry and fighting drunk; courageous due to liquor. *Cf.* POT-VALIANT. [British, 1600s-1700s, B.E.]

arm the cannon to masturbate. For synonyms see WASTE TIME. [late 1900s]

army form blank toilet paper. For synonyms see T.P. [British military, mid 1900s]

aroma of men butyl nitrite. See also LOCKER-ROOM. [U.S., late 1900s-pres.]

around the world a variety of sexual acts performed with the tongue and lips, including licking and sucking the penis, testes, and anus of a man, or licking the entire body. [originally prostitute's argot; U.S. slang, 1900s]

arrange to castrate. [U.S. euphemism, 1900s]

arse (also **a- -e, ars, a-s**) **1.** the posteriors or the anus. *Cf.* BOTTOM (sense 1). [since *c.* 1000, *Oxford English Dictionary*] **2.** the bottom of anything. [British dialects, 1800s and before] See also ASS.

arse about face facing in the wrong direction. [Australian and British, mid 1900s-pres.]

arse bandit a pederast. For synonyms see PEDERAST. [British, mid 1900s-pres.]

arse-end the rear or last part of something. [British, early 1900s-pres.]

arseholed very drunk. For synonyms see WOOFLED. [British, late 1900s-pres.]

arse-king a pederast, especially one who is notably proficient. For synonyms see SODOMITE. [British, early

1900s, *Dictionary of Slang and Unconventional English*]

arse-licker an obsequious person. [British, mid 1900s-pres.]

arse-opener the penis. For synonyms see YARD. [British slang, 1800s, Farmer and Henley]

arse over elbow head over heels. [British, mid 1900s-pres.]

arse over tit(s) head over heels. U.S. ASS OVER TIT. [Australian and British, mid 1900s-pres.]

arse-rug trousers; breeches. For synonyms see GALLIGASKINS. [British, 1800s, Farmer and Henley]

arse something up to ruin something; to bungle something. [British, mid 1900s-pres.]

arse-wedge the penis. For synonyms see YARD. [British, 1800s, Farmer and Henley]

arsey-versey (also **arsey-varsy, arsy-varsey**) topsy-turvy, head over heels. *Cf.* BASSACKWARDS. [British dialects, mid 1500s-pres.]

ars musica* the anus, specifically when it is crepitating, *i.e.*, when one is breaking wind. [a play on *ars musica*, Latin for "art of music"; British, 1700s, Grose]

arsworm (also **arseworm**) a small or insignificant fellow; an oaf. For synonyms see OAF. [British slang, 1600s, B.E.]

arsy-farcy ass-ended; vice-versa. *Cf.* ARSEY-VERSEY. [British colloquial, 1700s or before]

arsy-tarsy backwards; ass-ended; BASSACKWARDS (*q.v.*). *Cf.* ARSEY-VERSEY. [British]

artichoke **1.** a debauched old woman, especially a hideous old prostitute. [underworld slang, 1800s-pres.] **2.** a hanging, *i.e.*, a "hearty choke." [British, 1800s]

article **1.** a wench, woman, or prostitute. *Cf.* LEADING ARTICLE. [British, 1800s] **2.** a CHAMBER POT (*q.v.*). For synonyms see POT. [British, 1800s] See also ARTICLES.

article of virtue a virgin, usually said of a female. [British, mid 1800s, Farmer and Henley]

artillery man a drug addict who injects narcotics directly into a vein; one who shoots (drugs). [U.S. underworld and drug culture, mid 1900s-pres.]

artsy-fartsy arty; having an affinity for arty things. [U.S. slang, mid 1900s]

a-s "arse," the posteriors; the anus. *Cf.* ARSE, ASS. [British, mid 1700s]

as busy as a cat burying shit very busy. [Australian, mid 1900s-pres.]

as camp as a row of tents very gay. [Australian, late 1900s-pres.]

as cunning as a shithouse rat very cunning. [Australian, mid 1900s-pres.]

as dry as a dead dingo's donger 1. very dry as from a dry climate. [Australian, mid 1900s-pres.] **2.** very thirsty. [Australian, mid 1900s-pres.]

as dry as an Arab's fart very dry. [Australian, late 1900s-pres.]

as dry as a nun's nasty very dry, indeed. [Australian, mid 1900s-pres.]

as dry as a pommy's towel very dry. Pommy=Englishman, who is thought not to bathe often. [Australian, late 1900s-pres.]

as easy as spearing an eel with a spoon not easy; extremely difficult. [Australian, late 1900s-pres.]

as fine as wine good-looking and well dressed. [U.S., late 1900s-pres.]

as full as a fairy's phone book drunk. For synonyms see WOOFLED. [Australian, late 1900s-pres.]

as keen as mustard very keen; enthusiastic. [1900s or before]

ashes marijuana. For synonyms see MARI. [U.S. drug culture, 1900s]

asleep in Jesus a euphemism for "dead." For synonyms see DONE FOR. [U.S., late 1800s-1900s)

as loose as a cock in a sock very loose. [Australian, mid 1900s-pres.]

aspro an experienced male homosexual, especially a pederast; a male homosexual prostitute. From "ass prostitute." *Cf.* ARSE-KING. [British slang, mid 1900s, *Dictionary of Slang and Unconventional English*]

ass 1. a donkey. Sometimes taboo in this sense. *Cf.* JOHNNY BUM. [since the 1200s, *Oxford English Dictionary*] **2.** the rectum, anus, or posteriors. For synonyms see DUFF. [U.S. from a British dialect variation, 1800s and long before] **3.** the female genitals; women considered sexually. [1800s-pres.] **4.** a fool; an oaf. See also ARSE.

ass!, My a vulgar oath and an exclamation; an expression of complete disbelief. [U.S., 1900s]

ass, on one's 1. depressed; broken; down-and-out. [U.S., 1900s] **2.** intoxicated with alcohol. [U.S., mid 1900s-pres.]

assault 1. to ravish or rape forcibly. A truncation of "sexual assault" or of "an assault with intent to commit rape." **2.** an act of forcible rape. These synonyms for both senses refer to women unless indicated otherwise; AN-AGRIF, ATTACK, BREAK, CONSTUPRATE, DEBAUCH, MAN-RAPE (male), OUTRAGE, PLOW, RAVAGE, RAVISH, SHORT-ARM HEIST, SKIN-HEIST, STATUTORY OFFENSE.

ass-backwards in reverse; in an awkward or jumbled fashion. *Cf.* BACKASS-WARDS, BASSACKWARDS. [U.S., mid 1900s-pres.]

ass boy a male homosexual. For synonyms see EPICENE. [British, mid 1900s-pres.]

ass(ed) out broke; penniless. [U.S., late 1900s-pres.]

asseroonie the anus; the posteriors. [U.S. slang, mid 1900s]

assface a stupid person. [U.S. slang, late 1900s]

ass-fuck 1. to copulate anally, usually between males. *Cf.* BUTT-FUCK. [U.S., mid 1900s-pres.] **2.** an act of PEDER-ASTY. For related subjects see PEDER-ASTY. [U.S. slang, late 1900s] **3.** someone who practices PEDERASTY. [U.S. slang, late 1900s] **4.** a disliked and annoying person. [U.S. slang, late 1900s]

ass-hammer a motorcycle with reference to the jolts suffered while operating it. [U.S., mid 1900s-pres.]

ass-hole 1. the anus. [since the 1400s or before] **2.** bad; rotten. [U.S., 1900s] **3.** a contemptible person. [U.S. slang, early 1900s-pres.] **4.** a very good pal or buddy. *Cf.* ASS-HOLE FRIEND. [U.S., mid 1900s-pres.]

assholed fucked up. [U.S., late 1900s-pres.]

ass-hole friend (also **ass-hole buddy**) a good friend or buddy. [U.S., mid 1900s-pres.]

asskash (also **asscache**) a supply of drugs hidden in the rectum. A linguistic blend of ASS and *cache*. For related subjects see STASH. [U.S. drug culture, mid 1900s]

ass-kicker someone who gets things done; a pushy or demanding person. *Cf.* KICK SOME ASS (AROUND), BUTT-KICKER. [U.S. slang, late 1900s]

ass-kisser (also **ass-licker**) a sycophant; an A.K. (sense 1). *Cf.* ASS-SUCKER. [U.S. slang, early 1900s-pres.]

ass-man 1. a sexually active man; one who is able to SCORE (*q.v.*) frequently. For synonyms see LECHER. [U.S., early 1900s-pres.] **2.** a man who is sexually aroused by shapely feminine buttocks; a man who is attracted to a particular woman because of her shapely buttocks. [U.S., mid 1900s-pres.]

ass-master an oaf; a disliked person. For synonyms see OAF. [U.S., late 1900s-pres.]

ass over head head over heels, especially when falling. *Cf.* ARSEY-VERSEY, TOPSY-TURVY. [U.S., 1800s, Green]

ass over tit head over heels. The same as ARSE OVER TITS [U.S., late 1900s-pres.]

ass-peddler 1. a pimp; a procurer. [U.S., 1900s] **2.** a prostitute. [U.S., 1900s]

ass pirate a pederast. For synonyms see PEDERAST. [U.S., late 1900s-pres.]

ass-sucker a sycophant; a BUM-SUCKER (*q.v.*). *Cf.* ASS-KISSER, EGG-SUCKER. [U.S., mid 1900s-pres.]

assteriors the buttocks. A blend of ASS and POSTERIORS (both *q.v.*). [U.S., 1900s] See also CATASTROPHE.

ass up mess up; BUGGER UP or FUCK UP (both *q.v.*). [U.S., 1900s]

ass-wipe 1. toilet paper. **2.** a real jerk; a sycophant; someone who would wipe

someone else's anus if asked to. *Cf.* BUM-SUCKER. [both senses, U.S., 1900s].

assy uppity, overbearing, or brash. [U.S., early 1900s-pres.]

as thick as pigshit very stupid; mentally dense. For synonyms see STUPID. [British, mid 1900s-pres.]

as ugly as a hatful of arseholes very ugly. [Australian, mid 1900s-pres.]

as useful as tits on a bull totally useless. [Australian, mid 1900s-pres.]

as useless as an ashtray on a motorbike completely useless. [Australian, late 1900s-pres.]

ate up intoxicated on drugs. For synonyms see TALL. [U.S., late 1900s-pres.]

athenaeum the penis. For synonyms see YARD. [British, late 1800s-early 1900s]

atomic atmosphere air sullied by the breaking of wind. [U.S. collegiate, late 1900s, Munro]

atshitshi marijuana. For synonyms see MARI. [U.S., late 1900s-pres.]

attitude-adjuster a club; a police officer's night stick. Euphemistic. [U.S. black use, late 1900s]

audition the finger puppets to masturbate. For synonyms see WASTE TIME. [late 1900s]

Auld Hornie 1. Satan. [Scots, 1700s-pres. (Robert Burns)] **2.** the penis. Not usually capitalized in this sense. [Scots, 1800s-1900s]

au naturel* 1. naked; nude; raw. Occasionally (and erroneously) "in the au naturel." *Cf.* NATURAL, IN THE. **2.** undoctored or untreated, as with undiluted liquor. [both senses, French, 1900s]

aunt 1. a prostitute, especially an old prostitute. [since the early 1600s] **2.** the madam of a brothel; a procuress. [slang, 1900s] **3.** an aged sodomist. [U.S., 1900s] **4.** an aged fellator. *Cf.* AUNTIE. [U.S., 1900s, Goldin, O'Leary, and Lipsius] **5.** the woman's restroom, especially "the aunt." *Cf.* UNCLE (sense 1). [slang, 1900s]

Aunt Annie the vagina. Rhyming slang for FANNY=vagina. For synonyms see GENITALS, MONOSYLLABLE. [British, late 1900s-pres.]

aunteater a homosexual male. A play on CANNIBALL. *Cf.* AUNT. For synonyms see EPICENE. [U.S. slang, 1900s and recurrent nonce]

Aunt Emma morphine. Based on the letter "M." *Cf.* MISS EMMA. [U.S. drug culture, mid 1900s]

Aunt Flo a woman's menstrual period. *Cf.* VISIT FROM FLO. From *flow*. For synonyms see FLOODS. [attested as U.S. collegiate, late 1900s, Munro]

Aunt Hazel heroin. *Cf.* H. [U.S. drug culture, mid 1900s-pres.]

auntie an elderly homosexual male. Also a homosexual male past his prime period of desirability. [U.S. homosexual use, 1900s]

Aunt Jane a black woman who is a traitor to her race; a black woman who adopts aspects of a Caucasian lifestyle. Based on UNCLE TOM (*q.v.*). [U.S., mid 1900s]

Aunt Tom a woman who does not cooperate with or who works against Women's Liberation movements. Based on UNCLE TOM (*q.v.*). [U.S., mid 1900s]

aural sex telephone sex. [U.S., late 1900s-pres.]

aurora borealis phencyclidine, the drug P.C.P. For synonyms see P.C.P. [U.S. drug culture, late 1900s, Abel]

Aussie Wuzzie a dark-skinned person native to New Guinea. [Australian, 1900s]

author a drug addict known to be able to write acceptable prescriptions as a means of obtaining drugs. The same as SCRIBE. [U.S. drug culture, late 1900s, Kaiser]

autobate to masturbate while thinking of oneself. For synonyms see WASTE TIME. [U.S., late 1900s-pres.]

awash intoxicated with alcohol. For synonyms see WOOFLED. [1900s]

away from one's desk a phrase sometimes meaning that an office worker has gone to the W.C. [U.S., mid 1900s-pres.]

awkward euphemistic for "pregnant," especially applicable in the later months of pregnancy. For synonyms see FRAGRANT. [colloquial, 1800s-1900s]

awning over the toyshop, the a man's beer belly. For synonyms see BELLY. [Australian, mid 1900s-pres.]

awry-eyed intoxicated with alcohol; cockeyed drunk. *Cf.* HOARY-EYED, ORIE-EYED. [U.S. slang, early 1900s]

Aztec two-step diarrhea, specifically that contracted in Mexico or South America. *Cf.* MONTEZUMA'S REVENGE, TOURISTAS. For synonyms see QUICK-STEP. [U.S., mid 1900s-pres.]

B

B. "Benzedrine" (trademark), an amphetamine. For synonyms see BENZ. [U.S. drug culture, mid 1900s-pres.]

B.A. the naked BUTTOCKS; a bare ASS. For synonyms and related terms see DUFF. [U.S. slang, late 1900s] See also HANG A B.A.

babaloos the [female] human breasts. For synonyms see BOSOM. [U.S. slang, 1900s, Lewin and Lewin]

babe-magnet something that attracts women, especially a fancy car. [U.S., late 1900s-pres.]

babe of love an illegitimate child; a bastard. [euphemistic, early 1700s]

baboon an oaf or a jerk. Especially in the expression "big baboon." [British and U.S., 1900s]

baby 1. marijuana. [U.S. drug culture, mid 1900s-pres.] **2.** a woman or a girlfriend. *Cf.* BABE. [U.S. slang and colloquial, early 1900s-pres.] **3.** a homosexual male. From sense 2. [U.S. underworld, early 1900s, Monteleone] **4.** a prostitute's customer. [British, 1900s, *Dictionary of the Underworld*]

baby batter semen. For synonyms see METTLE. *[U.S., late 1900s-pres.]*

baby-bound pregnant. *Cf.* BOUND (sense 1). For synonyms see FRAGRANT. [U.S. slang, early 1900s]

baby catcher an obstetrician. [U.S., late 1900s-pres.]

baby-juice semen. For synonyms see METTLE. [recurrent nonce; attested as British slang, 1800s]

baby-maker 1. the penis. **2.** the female genitals. [both senses, slang, 1800s-1900s]

baby pillows the breasts. *Cf.* PILLOWY. [U.S. slang or colloquial, 1900s]

baby shit mustard. [U.S. and elsewhere, military dysphemism, mid 1900-pres., *Soldier Talk*]

baby slits M.D.M.A.; ecstasy. [U.S., late 1900s-pres.]

baby T crack. [U.S., late 1900s-pres.]

bachelor-mother an unwed mother. [U.S. slang, mid 1900s, Wentworth and Flexner]

bachelor's baby (also **bachelor's son**) an illegitimate child. *Cf.* SON OF A BACHELOR. [since the late 1700s]

bachelor's wife 1. a real or imagined "perfect wife." **2.** a prostitute. **3.** a mistress. For synonyms see LAY. [all senses, U.S., 1900s]

back a privy. A truncation of BACKHOUSE (*q.v.*). *Cf.* BACKY, REAR. [British, 1800s]

backassed pertaining to something that is backwards, awkward, or roundabout. [widespread, 1900s if not before]

backasswards backwards; pertaining to something done very badly. From ASS-BACKWARDS (*q.v.*). *Cf.* BASSACKWARDS. [U.S. slang and colloquial, 1900s]

backdoor 1. the anus in anal intercourse. *Cf.* BACK-DOOR WORK. **2.** the anus in general. [both senses, U.S., 1900s]

back-door trots (also **back-door trot**) diarrhea. Refers to the use of the back door to get to the privy or refers to the anus. See BACKDOOR (sense 2). The plural form is most prevalent in the U.S., analogous to other terms for diarrhea. For synonyms see QUICKSTEP. [British and U.S., 1800s-1900s]

back-door trumpet the anus considered as a musical instrument in the breaking of wind. *Cf.* ARS MUSICA. [British, mid 1800s, *Dictionary of Slang and Unconventional English*]

back-door work PEDERASTY (*q.v.*). *Cf.* BACKDOOR (sense 1). [cant or slang, 1800s-1900s]

backed-up intoxicated with drugs. For synonyms see TALL. [U.S. drug culture, mid 1900s-pres.]

backfire to break wind. For synonyms see GURK. [British and U.S., mid 1900s-pres.]

backhouse a privy. Cf. BACK, BACKY. [U.S. colloquial, mid 1800s-1900s]

back-land the buttocks. Cf. BACKSIDE. [since the 1600s]

back-parts the posteriors; the buttocks. Cf. PARTS BELOW, UNDERPARTS. [U.S. euphemism, 1800s]

backra See BUCKRA.

back-scuttle (also **back-scull**) 1. PEDERASTY (q.v.). 2. to commit pederasty. 3. to coit woman from the rear, presumably anally. Cf. SCUTTLE. [all senses, British, 1800s, Dictionary of Slang and Unconventional English]

backside the buttocks. In some parts of the world euphemistic, and in others extremely vulgar. [since the 1500s]

back-talk. 1. an impertinent remark; sauciness. [U.S., 1900s or before] 2. flatulence; a release of intestinal gas. For synonyms see GURK. [U.S. jocular colloquial, 1900s]

back-way the anus; the anus in anal copulation. Cf. BACKDOOR. [U.S., early 1900s]

backy a privy. Cf. BACK. [U.S. colloquial, 1900s and before]

backyard the buttocks or the rear end. For synonyms see DUFF. [U.S., mid 1900s-pres.]

bacon 1. a country bumpkin; a rustic oaf. [from Henry IV, Part One (Shakespeare)] 2. a police officer. For synonyms see FLATFOOT. [U.S. black use, late 1900s] See also LARD, PIG, PORK.

badass (also **bad-ass**) 1. really bad. An elaboration of bad. [U.S. slang, late 1900s] 2. a tough guy. [U.S. slang, late 1900s] 3. really good. An elaboration of the intensifier bad, which means good. [U.S. collegiate, late 1900s, Munro]

badger a smelly prostitute; a low whore. For synonyms see HARLOT. [British slang, 1800s, Farmer and Henley]

bad hair day a bad day in general. [British and U.S., late 1900s-pres.]

badical really good; excellent. Bad plus radical. [U.S., late 1900s-pres.]

bad shape, in 1. injured or debilitated in any manner. 2. pregnant. From sense 1. [U.S. slang, 1900s] 3. intoxicated with alcohol. From sense 1. [U.S. slang, 1900s]

bad shit 1. a rotten person, usually a male. Cf. SHIT (sense 9). [U.S. slang, 1900s] 2. bad luck. Possibly from "bad shot." Cf. TOUGH SHIT! [U.S., 1900s] 3. a bad event; bad luck; evil practices. [widespread, late 1900s]

bad-time to be unfaithful to one's spouse or lover. [U.S. slang, mid 1900s-pres.]

bad trip 1. a bad experience with drugs. 2. any bad experience. From sense 1. [U.S. drug culture and general slang, mid 1900s-pres.]

baffle someone with bullshit to confuse or impress someone with a lengthy, confusing, complex, but meaningless explanation. [British and U.S., late 1900s-pres.]

bag 1. an udder or a breast. See BAGS (sense 2). [colloquial, mid 1500s] 2. a low and despicable person. A truncation of DOUCHE BAG (q.v.). [U.S. slang, 1900s] 3. an old hag; any old woman. Usually "old bag." 4. a prostitute, especially an old one. Probably from sense 3. Cf. BAGNIO. [British and U.S. slang and colloquial, late 1800s-pres.] 5. the female genitals. [U.S. slang, mid 1900s] 6. the scrotum. For synonyms see TOOL BAG. [colloquial and nonce, 1900s and certainly long before] 7. a condom. Cf. BAGGIE, JO-BAG, JOY-BAG. [U.S., 1900s] 8. a contraceptive diaphragm. [U.S., 1900s, Wentworth and Flexner] 9. a sexual talent or preference. See WHAT'S YOUR BAG? 10. a quantity or package of drugs. [U.S. drug culture, mid 1900s-pres.] 11. to copulate [with] someone. For synonyms see OCCUPY. [U.S., late 1900s-pres.]

bag, in the drunk. Cf. BAGGED. For synonyms see WOOFLED. [U.S. slang, late 1900s if not before]

bag ass to depart in a hurry. Cf. BAR-

REL ASS, CUT ASS, DRAG ASS, HAUL ASS, SHAG ASS. [U.S. slang, mid 1900s-pres.]

bagel-bender a derogatory nickname for a Jew. Compare to SPAGHETTI-BENDER. For synonyms see FIVE AND TWO. Derogatory. [British and U.S. slang, late 1900s]

bag 'em and tag 'em "put the body in a bag and tag it to be sent to the morgue." [U.S., late 1900s-pres.]

baggage 1. a flirtatious young woman. **2.** a prostitute; a woman of bad character. For synonyms see HARLOT. [both since the late 1600s, B.E.]

bagged 1. pregnant. [since the 1400s] **2.** intoxicated with alcohol. [U.S. slang, 1900s] **3.** arrested. [British and U.S., late 1900s-pres.]

bagger See ONE-BAGGER.

baggie a condom. From the trademarked name of a food packaging product. *Cf.* BAG (sense 7), SCUMBAG (sense 1). For synonyms see EEL-SKIN. [U.S. slang, 1900s]

bagging using a paper bag to deliver inhalant drugs. [U.S., late 1900s-pres.]

bag lady a female narcotics pusher. *Cf.* BAGMAN. [U.S. drug culture, mid 1900s-pres.]

bagman 1. a tramp. From the bundle with which he travels. [Australian, 1800s, Baker] **2.** a seller of marijuana or illicit drugs. From the bags or packages in which drugs are sold. *Cf.* BAG (sense 10), SWING MAN. **3.** any racketeer. [U.S. underworld, early 1900s-pres.]

bag of tricks the male genitals, especially the scrotum. *Cf.* PAWPAW TRICKS. [British, 1800s and nonce elsewhere]

bagpipe 1. an act of PENILINGUS (*q.v.*). According to Grose, "a lascivious practice too indecent for explanation." **2.** to perform an act of PENILINGUS (*q.v.*). *Cf.* FLUTE, PICCOLO, SILENT FLUTE. [British, late 1700s] **3.** the penis. *Cf.* BAG (sense 6), PIPE (sense 1). [nonce]

bags 1. trousers. *Cf.* HAM-BAGS, RICE-BAGS. [British and U.S., mid 1800s-

1900s] **2.** the breasts. *Cf.* BAG (sense 1). [since the late 1500s]

bag-shanty a brothel. *Cf.* BAG (sense 4), BAGNIO. [British naval slang, 1900s]

Bag your face! "Go away!"; "Drop dead!"; "You are so ugly, you need a bag over your face." *Cf.* BAGGER. California teens. [U.S. slang, late 1900s]

bake to smoke marijuana. [U.S., late 1900s-pres.]

baked intoxicated with drugs. *Cf.* FRIED (sense 2). [U.S. drug culture, mid 1900s-pres.]

baker a bitch; a bastard. An elaboration of Baker, which is the "phonetic" name for "B" in international signalling. *Cf.* S.O.B. [U.S. military, World War II]

balcony 1. a protruding bosom. [Australian, early 1900s, *Dictionary of Slang and Unconventional English*] **2.** protruding buttocks. [U.S., 1900s]

balderdash 1. adulterated wine; a jumbled mix of different types of alcoholic drink. [1600s-1800s] **2.** nonsense. From sense 1. [since the late 1600s]

bald-headed hermit the penis. This "hermit" lives in a CAVE (sense 1), the vagina. *Cf.* HERMIT. [British, 1800s, Farmer and Henley]

bald-headed mouse the penis. From the "baldness" of the glans. [U.S., mid 1900s]

bale a pound or kilogram of marijuana. Literally, "a full bale of marijuana." [U.S. drug culture, mid 1900s-pres.]

ball 1. a testicle. See BALLS. For synonyms see WHIRLYGIGS. **2.** to copulate. [both senses, British and U.S. slang, mid 1900s-pres.] **3.** to absorb narcotics through the mucous membranes of the genitals. [U.S. drug culture, mid 1900s-pres.] **4.** to leave, possibly from *bail* which has the same meaning. [U.S., late 1900s-pres.]

ball and chain 1. a wife or sweetheart. The woman who restrains a man. For synonyms see WARDEN. [British and U.S., 1900s] **2.** marriage. From sense 1. **3.** a tramp's catamite. From sense 1. [U.S. underworld, early 1900s, Monteleone]

ball-bearing mousetrap a tomcat. A play on "ball-bearing." *Cf.* BALLS (sense 1). [mid 1900s]

ball-bearing stewardess (also **ball-bearing hostess**) a [male] steward on an airplane. [U.S. jocular slang, late 1900s, Chapman]

ball-bearing WAC a male soldier who does woman's work (as determined during the period of usage of this expression). [U.S. military, World War II, *Soldier Talk*]

ball-breaker (also **ball-buster**) 1. a difficult situation demanding hard work or effort. 2. a hard taskmaster. 3. a female who is threatening to males. [all senses, U.S. slang, mid 1900s-pres.]

ball-buster (also **ball-breaker, ball-wracker**) 1. a difficult task. 2. the person who assigns difficult tasks; a hard taskmaster. 3. a sexually attractive woman. 4. a castrating woman. [all senses, U.S. slang, mid 1900s-pres.]

ball-busting 1. very difficult or challenging. 2. very obnoxious and threatening. [both senses, U.S. slang, mid 1900s-pres.]

ball-dozed intoxicated with liquor. A play on BULL-DOZED (*q.v.*). [Australian, mid 1900s, Baker]

baller 1. an athlete. Someone who plays with footballs, basketballs, baseballs, etc. [U.S., late 1900s-pres.] 2. a person who is sexually attractive. [U.S., late 1900s-pres.]

ball-face a derogatory term for a Caucasian, used by Negroes. For synonyms see PECKERWOOD. [attested as U.S. (Salem, Mass.), 1810-1820, Farmer and Henley]

ballhead an athlete. Perhaps a stupid one. [U.S., late 1900s-pres.]

ball is in someone's court it is someone else's move, play, or turn. [U.S., mid 1900s-pres.]

ball maul a woman who hates men. *Ball*=testicle. [U.S., late 1900s-pres.]

ballock (also **ballick, ballok, balluk, balok**) 1. a testicle. See BALLOCKS. 2.

to coit a woman. See BALL (sense 2). [British slang, 1800s-1900s]

ballock-cod the scrotum. *Cf.* BALLOCKS, COD. [mid 1400s]

ballocker a lecher; a whoremonger. [British colloquial, 1800s]

ballock-naked stark naked with the genitals uncovered, said of both males and females. *Cf.* STARK-BALLOCK-NAKED. [British, 1900s or before]

ballocks (also **ballicks, balloks, balluks, ballux, bolaxe, bollix, bolloks, bollox**) 1. the testicles of a man or animal. For synonyms see WHIRLYGIGS. 2. the scrotum and its contents. [senses 1 and 2 since *c.* 1000] 3. a nickname for a whoremonger. [British, 1800s] 4. an exclamation, "Ballocks!"; the same as BALLS (sense 4), an expression of surprise or disbelief. [primarily British and Australian with U.S. dialect use]

ballocky naked. *Cf.* BALLOCK-NAKED. [British, early 1900s, *Dictionary of Slang and Unconventional English*]

ball off to masturbate, said of a male. From BALL (sense 2). For synonyms see WASTE TIME. [primarily British, 1900s]

ball of fire an energetic and ambitious person; a go-getter. [British and U.S., mid 1900s-pres.]

balloon 1. a condom. *Cf.* BAGGIE, SCUMBAG. [U.S. slang, 1900s] 2. a bag or toy balloon used for carrying heroin or other drugs. [U.S. drug culture, mid 1900s-pres.]

balloon juice 1. soda water. [British slang, late 1800s, Ware] 2. nonsense; the same as GAS (sense 2). For synonyms see ANIMAL. [U.S., since 1900]

balloons the breasts. [U.S. slang, 1900s]

ballot heroin. For synonyms see HEROIN. [U.S., late 1900s-pres.]

balls 1. the testicles. For synonyms see WHIRLYGIGS. 2. courage; virility. [both senses, U.S., 1900s or before] 3. masculine behavior in a female. 4. "nonsense" when used as an exclamation, "Balls!" *Cf.* BALLOCKS (sense 4). [senses 3 and 4 are U.S., 1900s] Disguises: COBBLER'S AWLS, COBBLER'S STALLS, COFFEE STALLS.

ballsack 1. the scrotum. For synonyms see TOOL BAG. [U.S., late 1900s-pres.] **2.** a very brief men's swimsuit. [U.S., late 1900s-pres.]

balls and bat the male genitals; the same as BAT AND BALLS (q.v.). Cf. STICK AND BANGERS. [U.S. euphemism, early 1900s-pres.]

balls-out very fast. Based on general slang *flat-out*. [U.S. slang, late 1900s]

Balls to you! a curse and a rude exclamation. Cf. ORCHIDS TO YOU!, TESTICLES TO YOU! [British, 1800s-1900s]

balls-up a mess or mistake. [Australian, mid 1900s-pres.]

ballsy 1. courageous; daring; foolhardy. Usually said of a male. [U.S., late 1900s-pres.] **2.** aggressive; masculine. Said of a female, especially a masculine female. [U.S., late 1900s-pres.]

ball up (also **balls up**) **1.** a man's underwear flap. Also **ball-lap**. [British dialects, c. 1600, Halliwell] **2.** to confuse; to mess up. **3.** a mess; a confused situation. Usually hyphenated in this sense. [senses 2 and 3 are primarily U.S., 1900s]

bally 1. BLOODY (q.v.). [British euphemism, early 1800s-1900s] **2.** exceedingly; very. Essentially the same as sense 1. [1900s]

balmed alcohol intoxicated. This is a play on BOMBED derived from EMBALMED. For synonyms see WOOFLED. [U.S. slang, late 1900s]

balmy 1. crazy; giddy and aloof. [colloquial, 1900s or before] **2.** intoxicated with alcohol. [U.S. slang, mid 1800s-pres.]

baloney (also **bologna, boloney**) **1.** a woman of loose morals. [U.S. underworld, early 1900s, Goldin, O'Leary, and Lipsius] **2.** nonsense. [senses 1 and 2 are U.S., mid 1900s-pres.] **3.** the penis. From its shape. Cf. LIVE SAUSAGE, SAUSAGE (sense 1). [U.S. slang, 1900s]

baloney-pony the penis considered as something to be ridden sexually. For

synonyms see GENITALS, YARD. [U.S., late 1900s]

baloobas the [female] human breasts, especially if notably large or shapely. For synonyms see BOSOM. [British slang, 1900s, McDonald]

bam 1. a mixture of barbiturates and amphetamines. **2.** amphetamines. [both senses, U.S. drug culture, mid 1900s-pres.]

Bama an oaf; a jerk. From *Alabama*. For synonyms see OAF. [U.S., late 1900s-pres.]

bambalacha marijuana. For synonyms see MARI. [U.S. drug culture, mid 1900s]

bamboo an opium pipe in expressions such as SUCK BAMBOO (q.v.). [U.S. drug culture, 1900s]

bamboozled intoxicated with alcohol. [U.S. slang and colloquial, mid 1800s-pres.]

banana 1. a sexually attractive mulatto or light black woman. From the yellow color. Cf. YELLOW (sense 1). [U.S. slang, mid 1900s] **2.** the penis in expressions such as "have one's banana peeled." [slang and nonce, 1800s-1900s] **3.** a person of East Asian descent who acts "too much" like a Caucasian. Yellow on the outside, but white on the inside. Compare to OREO. [U.S. slang, late 1900s]

bananas and cream male masturbation. Sexual references to the male are probably widespread recurrent nonce. For synonyms and related subjects see WASTE TIME. [U.S. slang, late 1900s, Lewin and Lewin]

banana hammock a very brief men's swimsuit. [U.S., late 1900s-pres.]

banana-head a stupid person. For synonyms see OAF. [U.S., late 1900s-pres.]

banana with cheese a marijuana cigarette doctored with FREE BASE. Named for the odor. For synonyms see MEZZROLL. [U.S. drug culture, late 1900s, Abel]

band 1. a woman of easy morals; a prostitute. Cf. BELT (sense 3). [British and U.S., early 1900s] **2.** a brothel. [Australian, mid 1900s, Baker]

bandage a sanitary napkin; a PERI-NEAL PAD (*q.v.*). For synonyms see MAN-HOLE COVER. [widespread jocular colloquial; attested as British, 1800s, Farmer and Henley]

B. and B. "breast and buttock," pertaining to magazines featuring female nudity. *Cf.* T. AND A. [U.S. slang, mid 1900s]

B. and D. "bondage and discipline," a form of sadism and masochism. See BONDAGE, SADISM. [U.S. slang, mid 1900s-pres.]

bandit a sadistic homosexual male. *Cf.* LEATHER (sense 2), WOLF (sense 3). [U.S. slang, mid 1900s-pres., Wentworth and Flexner]

B. and T. female bodies and sexuality. Also BUM AND TIT. [British, late 1900s-pres.]

bang 1. narcotics in general. [U.S. drug culture, mid 1900s-pres.] **2.** an injection of a narcotic; a puff of a marijuana cigarette. *Cf.* HIT (sense 2). [U.S. drug culture, early 1900s-pres.] **3.** to inject narcotics intravenously. [U.S. underworld and drug culture, early 1900s-pres.] **4.** "Damn!" [U.S. euphemism, early 1900s] **5.** a brothel. [Australian, early 1900s, Baker] **6.** to coit a woman; to copulate. For synonyms see OCCUPY. **7.** an act of human copulation. [senses 6 and 7 are British and U.S. slang, 1900s]

banged up pregnant. For synonyms see FRAGRANT. [Australian and U.S., mid 1900s-pres.]

bangin' excellent. [U.S., late 1900s-pres.]

bangles 1. the female breasts. For synonyms see BOSOM. [British, late 1900s-pres.] **2.** the testicles. For synonyms see WHIRLYGIGS. [British, late 1900s-pres.]

bang like a shithouse door [for a woman] to indulge in sexual intercourse eagerly. [British, late 1900s-pres.]

bangs like a dunny door copulates easily and frequently. a *dunny* is an outhouse. [Australian, mid 1900s-pres.]

bangster 1. a sexually loose woman; a prostitute. *Cf.* BANG (sense 7). [British, 1800s] **2.** one who injects drugs. Modeled on "gangsters." [U.S. underworld, early 1900s, Rose]

banjaxed alcohol intoxicated; destroyed by alcohol. For synonyms see WOOFLED. [U.S. slang, 1900s]

banji marijuana. Said to be a word from an African language. [U.S. drug culture, mid 1900s-pres.]

bank 1. a privy, the place where one makes a DEPOSIT (sense 2). For synonyms see AJAX. [U.S. slang, 1900s] **2.** the female genitals. *Cf.* DEPOSIT (sense 1). [British slang, 1800s] **3.** money; cash. [U.S., late 1900s-pres.]

banner the female pubic hair. For synonyms see DOWNSHIRE. [British slang or nonce, 1800s, Farmer and Henley]

baps the breasts. For synonyms see BOSOM. [British, late 1900s-pres.]

baptized 1. drowned. [Australian, early 1800s] **2.** pertaining to adulterated liquor. [U.S. slang, early 1900s] **3.** saturated with alcohol; intoxicated with alcohol. [U.S. slang or nonce, mid 1900s]

barb a barbiturate tablet or capsule. Usually in the plural. [U.S. drug culture, mid 1900s-pres.] Synonyms and related terms: BLOCK-BUSTER, BLUNT, CANDY, CHRISTMAS TREE, COURAGE PILLS, DOUBLE-TROUBLE, DOWNER, FENDER-BENDER, GANGSTER PILLS, G.B., GOOF-BALL, GOOFER, GORILLA PILLS, GREEN DRAGON, HORS D'OEUVRES, IDIOT PILLS, KING KONG PILLS, MARSHMALLOW REDS, MEXICAN RED, PEANUT, PHENNIES, PINK LADY, PURPLE HEART, RED AND BLUE, SECONAL, SEX, SLEEPER, STUM, STUMBLER, THRILL PILLS, TUIE, TUS, TWOS.

barbecue an attractive female; a woman who looks good enough to EAT (*q.v.*). *Cf.* GOOD-EATING, TABLE-GRADE. [U.S. slang, early 1900s-pres.]

barclay to masturbate. On *bank* which is rhyming slang for WHANK. For synonyms see WASTE TIME. [British, late 1900s-pres.]

bare-assed 1. naked; completely nude with the buttocks uncovered. **2.** immature; pertaining to a young male whose buttocks are not hairy. *Cf.* HAIRY-ASSED. [both senses, U.S. slang, 1900s]

bareback pertaining to an act of copulation performed without a condom. *Cf.* ROUGH-RIDING. [U.S. slang, 1900s, Wentworth and Flexner]

barley broth (also **barley juice, barley water**) beer. *Cf.* OIL OF BARLEY. [British and U.S. slang, late 1700s-pres.]

bare-naked naked. [U.S. colloquial, 1900s]

barf 1. to vomit. For synonyms see YORK. **2.** vomit. [both senses, U.S. colloquial, mid 1900s-pres.]

Barf City anything totally disgusting or undesirable. Teenage use. *Cf.* BARF. [U.S. slang, late 1900s]

bar-fly a drunkard, especially one who lingers around bars. [U.S. colloquial, early 1900s-pres.]

barge-arse 1. markedly protruding buttocks. **2.** a nickname for a person with markedly protruding buttocks. [both senses, British, 1800s]

barking spider (also **trumpet spider**) a release of intestinal gas, especially if loud. *Cf.* STEP ON A FROG. [U.S. collegiate, late 1900s]

barley-corn beer or ale. See JOHN BARLEYCORN. [British dialect, 1800s or before]

barleycorn sprints diarrhea caused by drinking whisky. *Cf.* JOHN BARLEYCORN. [colloquial, 1900s and before]

barley pop beer. [U.S. slang, 1900s, Lewin and Lewin]

barnacle 1. a prostitute. For synonyms see HARLOT. [U.S. underworld, early 1900s, Goldin, O'Leary, and Lipsius] **2.** a pickpocket. [cant, mid 1800s]

Barney a desirable male. [U.S., late 1900s-pres.]

barrack-hack a soldier's prostitute; a camp follower. [British, 1800s]

barrel 1. to drink to excess; to consume "barrels" of drink [U.S. slang, 1900s] **2.** the drug L.S.D. (*q.v.*). [U.S. drug culture, mid 1900s-pres.]

barrel ass to move or drive carelessly and rapidly. *Cf.* BAG ASS, DRAG ASS,

HAUL ASS, SHAG ASS. [U.S. slang or colloquial, 1900s]

barreled-up (also **barreled**) intoxicated with alcohol. *Cf.* BARREL (sense 1). [U.S. slang, 1900s]

barrel-fever 1. intoxication with alcohol. **2.** a HANGOVER (*q.v.*). **3.** the DELIRIUM TREMENS (*q.v.*). For synonyms see ORK-ORKS. **4.** a name for the cause of death when a lethal dose of alcohol has been ingested. [widespread, 1800s-1900s]

barrel-house bum a beggar-drunkard. [U.S., mid 1900s]

barrel-house drunk heavily intoxicated with alcohol. [U.S. slang, early 1900s]

Bart Simpsons L.S.D. For synonyms see ACID. [U.S., late 1900s-pres.]

base 1. FREE BASE. For synonyms see FREE BASE. **2.** to use FREE BASE. [both senses, U.S. and elsewhere, drug culture, late 1900s] **3.** to argue with someone; to attempt to deceive someone. From sense 1 or from *debase*. [U.S. slang, late 1900s]

baseballing the use of FREE BASE (*q.v.*), a form of pure cocaine. See BALL (sense 3). [U.S. drug culture, late 1970s-pres.]

base-begotten child a bastard; an illegitimate child. [U.S. colloquial, 1900s or before]

base binge a drug-use session using FREE BASE. [U.S. drug culture, late 1900s, Abel]

basehead a FREE BASE user. [U.S. drug culture, late 1900s]

baseman someone who is using FREE BASE; someone who is "on base." A **first baseman** gets the first puff of FREE BASE, then the **second baseman**, etc. [U.S. drug culture, late 1900s, Abel]

bashys cool; excellent. [U.S., late 1900s-pres.]

basing using FREE BASE. [U.S. drug culture, late 1900s]

basket 1. the stomach, as in BREAD-BASKET (*q.v.*). [U.S., 1900s] **2.** the female genitals. *Cf.* BOX (sense 2), PANNIER. [U.S. slang, 1900s, Monteleone] **3.** the male genitals considered as a package; the bulging shape of the VIRI-LIA (*q.v.*) when contained in any garment constructed like an athletic supporter. [U.S. homosexual use, mid 1900s-pres.] **4.** the scrotum or the scrotum and its contents. [U.S. slang, 1900s]

basketball a 250 milligram capsule of Placidyl™. From the size of the capsule. [U.S. drug culture, late 1900s, Kaiser]

basket days warm weather when clothing revealing the outline of the male genitals is likely to be worn. See BASKET (sense 3). [U.S. homosexual use, mid 1900s-pres., Farrell]

basket for days a catch phrase describing large male genitals. Based on MEAT FOR DAYS (*q.v.*). *Cf.* MENTULATE. [U.S. homosexual use, mid 1900s-pres.]

basket-making copulation. For synonyms see SMOCKAGE. [British, late 1700s, Grose]

bassackwards (also **basackwards, bassackards**) done the wrong way. Based on "ass backwards." *Cf.* ASS-BACKWARDS, BACKASSWARDS. [U.S. colloquial and slang, early 1900s-pres.]

bastard 1. a child born of unlawful sexual intercourse; a child conceived in haste, *e.g.*, on a bed-roll or pack-saddle (French *bast*). [since the 1200s, *Oxford English Dictionary*] **2.** a despicable male or any male buddy. [U.S. slang, 1900s or before]

basted 1. intoxicated with alcohol. Refers to having liquid poured over oneself. For synonyms see WOOFLED. [U.S. slang, early 1900s-pres.] **2.** drug intoxicated. From sense 1. *Cf.* BAKED, FRIED (sense 2). For synonyms see TALL. [U.S. drug culture, mid 1900s-pres.]

bastrich a curse and a nickname for a despised person. A blend of "bastard" and "bitch" modeled on "ostrich." [U.S., 1900s or before]

bat 1. a low prostitute; one who moves about at night. *Cf.* NIGHT-HAWK. [British and U.S., 1800s-pres.] **2.** any unattractive young woman. For synonyms see BUFFARILLA. [U.S. slang, 1900s] **3.** a drunken spree. [U.S. slang, mid 1800s-1900s] **4.** a drunkard. [U.S. slang,

1900s, Wentworth and Flexner] **5.** to masturbate. From "bachelor." For synonyms see WASTE TIME. [U.S. dialect (Boontling), late 1800s-early 1900s, Charles Adams] **6.** the penis, especially the erect penis. [U.S. slang, early 1900s-pres.] **7.** in the plural, crazy.

bat and balls (also **balls and bat**) the VIRILIA (*q.v.*). [U.S. slang and nonce, 1900s]

bath 1. a BATHROOM (*q.v.*) regardless of the presence or absence of bathing facilities. The essential piece of equipment in a bathroom is a water-flush toilet bowl. [U.S., 1900s or before] **2.** "hell" in "Go to Bath!" [British colloquial, 1800s]

bathroom a W.C., a small room set aside for elimination, bathing, and personal grooming. The primary function of the bathroom is to provide privacy. A bathroom in a public building is usually referred to as a restroom. The term bathroom is most often used in the home by the family members and is out of place in public. [colloquial]

baths, the the gay steam baths. [British and U.S., mid 1900s-pres.]

bathtub scum a totally despised person. *Cf.* POND SCUM. For synonyms see SNOKE-HORN. [U.S. slang, late 1900s]

batshit nonsense. A variation of BULL-SHIT (*q.v.*). [U.S. slang, mid 1900s-pres.]

batted intoxicated with alcohol. For synonyms see WOOFLED. [U.S. slang, 1900s, Berrey and Van den Bark]

batter to coit a woman. *Cf.* CANE (sense 1). [British, 1900s, *Dictionary of Slang and Unconventional English*]

battered intoxicated. For synonyms see TALL, WOOFLED. [British and U.S., mid 1900s-pres.]

battering-piece the penis, especially when erect. [British slang, 1800s, Farmer and Henley]

battery acid L.S.D. For synonyms see ACID. [U.S., late 1900s-pres.]

battle cruiser a bar; a PUB. Rhyming slang for BOOZER. For related subjects see BAR. [British slang, 1900s, Pratt]

bauble (also **bawble**) **1.** the penis.

[from *Romeo and Juliet* (Shakespeare)]
2. a testicle. See BAUBLES.

baubles (also **bawbels, bobbles**) the
testicles. *Cf.* BOBBLES. For synonyms
see WHIRLYGIGS.

bawd (also **baud**) a male or female
keeper of a brothel. Originally a procurer, later a MADAM (sense 3). [since
the 1300s]

bawdry (also **baudy**) **1.** bad or obscene language. [British, 1800s, Halli-
well] **2.** illegal copulation. [mid 1400s-
1600s]

bawdy 1. to make dirty; to defile. [ob-
solete, 1300s] **2.** lewd; obscene. [since
the early 1500s]

bawdy basket 1. a member of one of
the orders of thieves in England in the
1500s. Usually women who sold obscene materials from innocent-looking
cloth-covered baskets. [cant, mid 1500s]
2. a prostitute. [cant, late 1500s]

bawdyhouse (also **bawd's house**) a
brothel. [since the 1600s]

bayonet the penis. [British slang, 1800s,
Farmer and Henley]

bazonkers the breasts. For synonyms
see BOSOM. [British slang, late 1900s,
McDonald]

bazoo 1. a jeer; a raspberry [U.S.
slang, 1900s] **2.** the female genitals, especially the vagina. For synonyms see
MONOSYLLABLE. [U.S. slang, mid 1900s-
pres.] See also WAZOO. **3.** the human
mouth. **4.** the stomach or belly. For
synonyms see BELLY. **5.** the anus. For
synonyms see ANUS. [all senses, U.S.
slang, mid 1900s-pres.]

bazooka 1. a marijuana cigarette
laced with cocaine. For synonyms see
MEZZROLL. [U.S. drug culture, late
1900s] **2.** the penis, especially the erect
penis. For synonyms see ERECTION,
YARD. [U.S. slang, 1900s] **3.** cocaine;
crack. For synonyms see NOSE-CANDY.
[U.S., late 1900s-pres.]

bazooms (also **bazoom**) the human
breasts. From BOSOM (*q.v.*). [U.S.
slang, mid 1900s-pres.]

bazoongies (also **bazongas**) the
human breasts, especially if large and

shapely. For synonyms see BOSOM.
[U.S. slang, mid 1900s-pres.]

B.B. 1. a "bloody bastard." [British,
1900s] **2.** a "blue bomber," a ten-
milligram tablet of Valium (trademark). [U.S. drug culture, mid 1900s-
pres.] **3.** "base burnout," debilitation
from the excessive use of FREE BASE.
[U.S. drug culture, late 1900s, Abel]

B-B-brain an oaf; a person with a
brain the size of shot. [U.S. slang,
mid 1900s]

B.C. "birth control," usually in the
form of conception control. [U.S.,
1900s] Specific terms for birth control
devices or methods: BIRTH CONTROL,
COIL, COITUS INTERRUPTUS, CONTRA-
CEPTION, DIAPHRAGM, FAMILY PLAN-
NING, I.C.U.D., I.U.D., JELLY, LOOP, PILL,
PUSSY BUTTERFLY, RHYTHM METHOD,
RING, RUBBER, RUBBER RING, SANITARY
SPONGE, SHOWER-CAP, TABLET, VATICAN
ROULETTE. See EEL-SKIN for condom
synonyms.

B./D. "bondage and discipline." Activities involve restraint and domination of an individual by another,
producing sexual gratification in one or
both. *Cf.* B. AND D. [U.S., mid 1900s-
pres.]

B.D.T.s "back-door trots," diarrhea.
[colloquial, 1800s-1900s]

beached whale a very fat person.
[U.S., late 1900s-pres.]

beach whistle a tampon insertor
found washed up on a public beach.
[U.S. nonce or slang, late 1900s]

bead-puller (also **bead-counter**) a derogatory term for a Roman Catholic.
[colloquial, 1800s-1900s]

beak the penis. *Cf.* STROP ONE'S BEAK.
[British slang, 1800s, Farmer and
Henley]

beam the buttocks or hips, especially
if wide. *Cf.* KEEL. [colloquial, 1800s-
pres.]

beamer a user of crack. [U.S., late
1900s-pres.]

beaming intoxicated with marijuana.
For synonyms see TALL. [U.S. drug culture, mid 1900s-pres.]

beam up 1. to die. From the *Star Trek*

television program, where characters are beamed up to the space ship from the planet below. For synonyms see DEPART. [U.S. collegiate, late 1900s, Eble] **2.** to get intoxicated on CRACK cocaine. [U.S. drug culture, late 1900s]

bean 1. a capsule or tablet of Benzedrine (trademark), an amphetamine. [U.S. drug culture, mid 1900s-pres.] **2.** as an exclamation, "Bean!" meaning "Damn!" [U.S., early 1900s] **3.** a derogatory term for a Mexican. See also BEANER. [U.S. slang, mid 1900s-pres.] **4.** the hymen. Cf. CHERRY (sense 1). [U.S. slang, early 1900s, Goldin, O'Leary, and Lipsius] Synonyms for sense 4: BUG, CHERRY, CLAUSTRUM VIRGINALE, FLOWER, MAIDEN GEAR, MAIDENHEAD, MAID'S RING, ROSE, TAIL-FEATHERS, THAT, TOY, VIRGINAL MEMBRANE, VIRGINHEAD, VIRGIN-KNOT. **5.** the penis. Cf. BEAN-TOSSER. [British, 1900s or before] **6.** a PEYOTE BUTTON (q.v.). [U.S. drug culture, mid 1900s-pres.] **7.** in the plural, nonsense. See BEANS.

bean-eater 1. a Bostonian. From "Boston baked beans." **2.** a derogatory term for a Mexican, especially a poor Mexican. [both senses, U.S., 1900s and before]

beaner (also **bean**) a derogatory term for a Mexican or a Mexican-American. From BEAN-EATER (q.v.). [U.S. slang, 1900s]

bean flicker a lesbian; a female masturbator. BEAN=the clitoris. For synonyms see LESBYTERIAN. [British, late 1900s-pres.]

beanhead an oaf. From the small size of the brain. [U.S. slang, early 1900s-pres.]

bean-tosser the penis. Cf. BEAN (sense 5). [British slang, 1800s, Farmer and Henley]

bear a hairy, beefy gay male. [British and U.S., late 1900s-pres.]

beard the female pubic hair. For synonyms see DOWNSHIRE. [since the 1600s if not before]

bearded axe wound, the the vulva. For synonyms see MONOSYLLABLE. [British, late 1900s-pres.]

bearded clam the female genitals; the

vulva. The BEARD is the pubic hair. For synonyms see GENITALS, MONOSYLLABLE. [U.S. and elsewhere, slang, late 1900s]

beard-jammer a whoremonger. [U.S. underworld, early 1900s, Irwin]

beard-splitter. 1. a whoremonger. Cf. WHISKER-SPLITTER. For synonyms see LECHER. [cant, late 1600s-1700s] **2.** the penis. [cant, 1800s or before]

bearskin the female pubic hair. Cf. TWAT-RUG. [British slang, 1800s, Farmer and Henley]

beast 1. a low prostitute. Cf. ANIMAL (sense 7). [U.S., early 1900s, Goldin, O'Leary, and Lipsius] **2.** an ugly woman. [U.S. slang, mid 1900s-pres.] **3.** a Caucasian. For synonyms see PECKERWOOD. [U.S. black use, 1900s] **4.** the drug L.S.D. (q.v.). [U.S. drug culture, mid 1900s-pres.]

beat having to do with marijuana ashes or marijuana after the smokable substance is exhausted. [U.S. drug culture, late 1900s]

beat off to masturbate, said of a male. For synonyms see WASTE TIME. [U.S. slang, mid 1900s-pres.]

beat one's hog (also **belt one's hog**) to masturbate. For synonyms and related subjects see WASTE TIME. [British slang, late 1900s, J. Green]

beat one's mongrel to masturbate. For synonyms see WASTE TIME. [Australian, late 1900s-pres.]

beat seven shades of shit out of someone to beat someone severely. [British, mid 1900s-pres.]

beat sheets pornographic magazine pages. Refers to *beating off*. [British and U.S., late 1900s-pres.]

beat someone with an ugly stick to COIT someone, presumably a woman. The stick is the penis. For synonyms see OCCUPY. [U.S. collegiate, late 1900s, Munro]

beat the bishop to masturbate. Compare the shape of the glans penis to a bishop's miter. Cf. BOX THE JESUIT AND GET COCKROACHES, POLICEMAN'S HELMET. [U.S. underworld, early 1900s, Goldin, O'Leary, and Lipsius]

be at the curb to be vomiting; to be where one can vomit. For synonyms see YORK. [U.S. collegiate, late 1900s, Munro]

beat the dummy to masturbate, said of a male. *Cf.* DUMMY (sense 3). [U.S. slang, 1900s]

beat the meat (also **beat one's meat**) to masturbate, said of a male. *Cf.* POUND THE MEAT. [U.S. slang, 1900s]

beat the pup to masturbate, said of a male. For synonyms see WASTE TIME. [U.S., early 1900s]

beat the shit out of to strike very hard; to beat some sense into someone. [U.S., 1900s]

beautiful boulders crack cocaine. For synonyms see NOSE-CANDY. [U.S., late 1900s-pres.]

beauty-spot 1. the female genitals. [British slang, 1800s, Farmer and Henley] **2.** a mole or a wart. [euphemistic, 1900s or before]

beaver 1. the female pubic region. From the fur of a beaver and a play on a nickname for a beaver, "flat tail." [U.S., early 1900s-pres.] **2.** the female genitals, specifically the vagina. [U.S. slang, early 1900s-pres.] **3.** any woman. From sense 2. [primarily citizens band radio slang; U.S., mid 1900s-pres.]

beaver base a brothel. *Cf.* BEAVER (sense 3). [U.S. citizens band radio slang, mid 1900s-pres.]

beaver-flick a pornographic film featuring sexual activity with women. *Cf.* BEAVER. [U.S. slang, mid 1900s-pres.]

beaver hunt (also **beaver patrol**) keeping a lookout for women while traveling; watching for women drivers, especially those whose skirts are pulled up while they drive. [U.S. citizens band radio slang, mid 1900s-pres.]

beaver page a picture of a woman, usually nude or partially nude, with her legs spread in a manner that will expose her genitals. See BEAVER (sense 1). [1900s]

beaver-retriever a lecher. For synonyms see LECHER. [U.S. collegiate, late 1900s]

beaver-shot a view, possibly a photo-graph of a woman's pubic area. *Cf.* BEAVER POSE. [U.S. slang, mid 1900s-pres.]

bebe crack cocaine. For synonyms see NOSE-CANDY. [U.S., late 1900s-pres.]

become a lady to begin the menses; to reach the MENARCHE (*q.v.*). [colloquial, 1900s or before]

become ill to vomit; to become sick. [U.S. euphemism]

bed 1. to take a woman to bed and copulate with her. *Cf.* CHAMBER (sense 1), COUCH. [since the 1500s] **2.** afterbirth. [1600s]

bed-bunny (also **bed-bug**) a woman easy to get into bed. *Cf.* CONY, CUDDLE-BUNNY. [U.S. slang, mid 1900s]

beddy a female whom a male would like to copulate with. Possibly based on BETTY. For synonyms see TAIL. [U.S. collegiate, late 1900s, Munro]

bed-fellow (also **bed-mate**) **1.** any person with whom one shares a bed. **2.** a concubine. [since the late 1400s]

bed-ready sexually aroused; ready to copulate. [U.S. slang, late 1900s]

bed-rite copulation. For synonyms see SMOCKAGE. [1600s]

bed stick a state wherein you really want to stay in bed. [U.S., late 1900s-pres.]

bed suck something a bed seems to be doing in order to keep you in it. [U.S., late 1900s-pres.]

bedtime story coition. *Cf.* DO THE STORY WITH. [U.S. slang, 1900s]

bedworthy pertaining to a desirable woman or one who is sexually aroused for copulation. *Cf.* FUCKABLE, FUCKSOME, PUNCHABLE, ROMPWORTHY, SHAFTABLE. [British, early 1900s, *Dictionary of Slang and Unconventional English*]

bee-bites See MOSQUITO BITES.

Beecham's Pills the testicles. Rhyming slang for "testi-kills." From the name of a patent medicine. [British, 1800s, *Dictionary of Rhyming Slang*]

beef 1. the female genitals; women considered sexually; a prostitute. *Cf.* MEAT (sense 2). [since the 1600s, (Shakespeare)] **2.** the penis. *Cf.* MEAT (sense 4), MUTTON (sense 5). [slang and nonce, 1800s-1900s] **3.** any large and muscular male. [colloquial, mid 1800s-pres.] **4.** to coit a woman. [U.S. slang, mid 1900s-pres.] **5.** a popular and sexually attractive young woman. *Cf.* MUTTON (sense 4). [U.S. slang, mid 1900s-pres.] **6.** to break wind; to release intestinal gas audibly through the anus. From the rhyming slang BEEF-HEARTS. For synonyms see GURK. **7.** an act of breaking wind. For synonyms see GURK. [both senses, U.S. slang, late 1900s]

beef-a-roni a well-built male. A play on BEEF (sense 3) and *macaroni*. [U.S. collegiate, late 1900s, Eble]

beef bayonet the penis. For synonyms see GENITALS, YARD. [British slang or nonce, 1900s, McDonald]

beefcake 1. a display of the male physique, usually in photographs; a well-built or muscularly handsome male. Based on CHEESE CAKE (senses 1 and 2). *Cf.* BEEF (sense 3). **2.** a male on display in some degree of undress. [both senses, U.S., mid 1900s-pres.]

beef curtains 1. the female breasts. For synonyms see BOSOM. [British, late 1900s-pres.] **2.** the female genitals. For synonyms see GENITALS, MONOSYLLABLE. [British and U.S., late 1900s-pres.]

beef-head an oaf; a MEATHEAD (*q.v.*). For synonyms see OAF. [colloquial, 1700s-1900s]

beef-hearts 1. beans. Because they cause intestinal gas. Rhyming slang for "farts," breakings of wind. See BREAK WIND. [British, 1800s] **2.** audible releases of intestinal gas through the anus. Also from rhyming slang. For synonyms see GURK. [U.S. slang, late 1900s]

beef injection See MEAT INJECTION.

beefsteak a prostitute who works for a pimp. *Cf.* BEEF (sense 1), based on "grubsteak." [British, early 1900s, *Dictionary of Slang and Unconventional English*]

beef-witted (also **beef-headed**) oafish, stupid, and bovine. *Cf.* BEEF-HEAD. [primarily British; late 1500s-1800s]

beehive the female genitals. *Cf.* HONEY, HONEY-POT. [British slang, 1800s, Farmer and Henley]

beejer an act of fellatio. From B.J.= BLOW JOB. [U.S., late 1900s-pres.]

been at an Indian feast intoxicated with alcohol. [U.S., early 1700s, Ben Franklin]

been bobbing for fries to have an ugly face as if it had been boiled in oil. [U.S., late 1900s-pres.]

been had 1. cheated. **2.** deflowered. [both senses, U.S. slang and colloquial, 1900s]

been in the sun intoxicated with alcohol. For synonyms see WOOFLED. [late 1800s, Ware]

been in the sun too long crazy. For synonyms see DAFT. [colloquial, 1900s]

been playing tricks pregnant. *Cf.* BAG OF TRICKS, PAW-PAW TRICKS. [British slang, 1800s]

been there 1. experienced sexually, said of a woman. **2.** experienced in general, said of either sex. [both senses, 1800s-pres.]

been to France intoxicated with alcohol. [U.S. slang, early 1700s, Ben Franklin]

beer semen. For synonyms see METTLE. [U.S., late 1900s-pres.]

beer goggles a case of blurred vision from beer drinking. [U.S. collegiate, late 1900s]

beerified intoxicated with alcohol. For synonyms see WOOFLED. [U.S. slang, 1900s, Berrey and Van den Bark]

beer-jerker 1. a tippler; a drunkard. For synonyms see ALCHY. [U.S. slang, mid 1800s, Farmer and Henley] **2.** a bartender. Based on "soda jerk" and "tear-jerker." [U.S. slang, 1900s, Berrey and Van den Bark]

beer monster a heavy beer drinker. For synonyms see ALCHY. [British, late 1900s-pres.]

beerslinger 1. a bartender. [U.S. slang, late 1800s] **2.** a beer-drinker. [slang, late 1800s-1900s]

beer-swiper a drunkard. For synonyms see ALCHY. [Australian, Baker]

beery (also **beer, in**) intoxicated with alcohol. [since the mid 1800s]

beetle 1. a loose girl; a sexually loose woman. *Cf.* BUG (sense 3). [U.S. slang, 1900s] **2.** marijuana. Compare to ROACH. For synonyms see MARI. [U.S. drug culture, late 1900s]

beetle-brain an oaf; a stupid person with a small brain. [U.S., 1900s]

beetle-head a dull oaf. *Cf.* BEETLE-BRAIN. [British and U.S. slang, early 1800s-1900s]

beezie-weezies the DELIRIUM TREMENS. [U.S. slang, 1900s if not before]

befuddle to intoxicate with alcohol. See FUDDLED. [U.S. slang and colloquial, 1900s and before]

begonias the breasts. For synonyms see BOSOM. [U.S. euphemism, 1900s]

behind the posteriors. The first syllable is usually accented. [colloquial since the 1700s or before]

behind-door work copulation, especially that among the household servants. [from *A Winter's Tale* (Shakespeare)]

behind the cork intoxicated with alcohol. Patterned on "behind the eight-ball." [U.S. slang, 1900s]

be in someone's crack about something (also **be up someone's ASS about something**) **1.** to be deeply involved in someone's business. **2.** to be harassing someone about something. [both senses, U.S., late 1900s]

bejonkers the [female] breasts. For synonyms see BOSOM. [British slang, late 1900s, McDonald]

belch 1. to bring up stomach gas. [since *c.* 1000] **2.** an eructation; a burp; an upwards release of stomach gas. [since the late 1500s] Synonyms for both senses: BERP, BREAK WIND UPWARDS, BRING UP GAS, BURP, ERUCT, ERUCTATE, GROWL, GRUNT, MAKE A RUDE NOISE, REPROVE, RETURN, RIFT, RUCT. **3.** beer, especially inferior beer. For synonyms see SUDS. [since the late 1600s]

belch-guts a drunkard. For synonyms see ALCHY. [British and U.S. slang, 1800s]

Belgeek a Belgian. *Cf.* GEEK (sense 1). [from the French pronunciation *Belgique;* British and U.S., World War II]

belle (also **bell**) **1.** an attractive young woman. [since the early 1600s] **2.** an attractive, effeminate homosexual male. [U.S. homosexual use, 1900s]

bell-end the glans penis. From its shape. *Cf.* BELL-ROPE, BELL-TOPPED, BLUNT-END. For synonyms see HEAD. [British, 1900s, *Dictionary of Slang and Unconventional English*]

belligerent drunk. For synonyms see WOOFLED. [U.S., late 1900s-pres.]

bell-rope the penis. *Cf.* BELL-END. [U.S. slang, mid 1900s-pres.]

belly 1. the abdomen or a large paunch. [since the 1500s] Synonyms: ABDOMEN, ALVUS, AUNTIE NELLY, AWNING OVER THE TOYSHOP, BASKET, BAY WINDOW, BAZOO, BINNY, BREAD-BASKET, DEEP CHEST, ELLY-BAY, EPIGASTRIUM, GERMAN GOITER, GUT-BUCKET, GUTS, KEG, LITTLE MARY, MIDDLE, MIDSECTION, NED KELLY, SHIT-BAG, SHIT LOCKER, TABLE-MUSCLE, TUMMY, TUM-TUM, VENTER. **2.** a person's guts or intestines. [U.S., 1900s] **3.** the penis. *Cf.* LAP. [attested as U.S. (New York), early 1900s]

bellyache 1. a stomachache; the colic. [since the mid 1500s] **2.** to complain. [widespread colloquial, late 1800s]

belly-bound constipated. [since the mid 1600s]

belly-bristles the female pubic hair. *Cf.* BELLY-THICKET, BELLY-WHISKERS. [British slang, 1800s, Farmer and Henley]

belly-bumper a lecher; a whoremonger. [late 1600s]

belly-bumping coition. For synonyms see SMOCKAGE. [1600s (Urquhart)]

belly-button the navel. [U.S. colloquial, 1800s-1900s]

belly-cork the navel. [colloquial, 1900s or before]

belly-dale (also **belly-dingle, belly-entrance**) the female genitals. [British slang, 1800s. Farmer and Henley]

belly-full pregnant, as in "have a belly-full." [colloquial, 1700s-1800s]

belly-naked completely nude. [1500s]

belly-ride an act of copulation. [U.S. slang, 1900s or before, Read]

belly-thicket the female pubic hair. Cf. BELLY-BRISTLES, BELLY-WHISKERS. [British slang, 1800s, Farmer and Henley]

belly-up 1. (also **bellied-up**) pregnant. [British and later, U.S. colloquial, 1600s-1900s] **2.** alcohol intoxicated. A synonym of DEAD. For synonyms see WOOFLED. [1900s, Dickson]

belly-warmer an act of copulation. [British colloquial, 1800s, Farmer and Henley]

belly-wash 1. weak or inferior liquor or any liquor. [British and U.S. slang, 1800s-pres.] **2.** lemonade; any sweet, nonalcoholic or noncarbonated drink. [British and U.S. slang and colloquial, late 1800s-1900s]

belly-whiskers the female pubic hair. Cf. BELLY-BRISTLES, BELLY-THICKET. For synonyms see DOWNSHIRE. [British slang, 1800s, Farmer and Henley]

belsh beer and ale. As if one were saying "belch" while under the influence of alcohol. Cf. BELCH (sense 3). For synonyms see SUDS. [British slang, 1600s, B.E.]

belswagger 1. a pimp. **2.** a whoremonger; a lecher. A truncation of "bellyswagger." [both senses, late 1500s]

belt 1. to coit, said of the male. [British, 1800s] **2.** an act of copulation. [British, 1900s or before, *Dictionary of Slang and Unconventional English*] **3.** a prostitute. Cf. BELTER, ENDLESS BELT. [Australian, 1900s, Baker] **4.** a marijuana cigarette. **5.** the CHARGE (sense 1) from narcotics or from a marijuana cigarette. [senses 4 and 5 are U.S. drug culture, 1900s] **6.** a drink or shot of alcohol. [U.S. slang and colloquial, 1900s]

belted 1. intoxicated with alcohol. Cf. BELT (sense 6). For synonyms see WOOFLED. **2.** intoxicated with drugs or marijuana. Cf. BELT (sense 5). For synonyms see TALL. [both senses, U.S., 1900s]

belter a prostitute. Cf. ENDLESS BELT. [British dialect, 1800s or before, Halliwell]

belt one's hog See BEAT ONE'S HOG.

belt the grape to drink heavily. Refers to the grapes from which wine is made. [U.S. slang, mid 1900s]

Belushi cocaine and heroin, referring to the drug mixture that killed John Belushi. For synonyms see NOSE-CANDY. [U.S., late 1900s-pres.]

bemused intoxicated with alcohol. From a word meaning "confused." [slang, 1700s-1800s]

bend down for 1. to position oneself for and submit to anal copulation. Cf. BEND ONE OVER. [since the 1800s] **2.** to submit to someone's domination, not necessarily sexual domination. [both senses, U.S., late 1900s]

bender 1. a drunken binge. [U.S. colloquial, early 1800s-pres.] **2.** a catamite. For synonyms see BRONCO. [U.S. underworld, early 1900s, Goldin, O'Leary, and Lipsius]

bend one over to position someone for pederasty; to dominate or humiliate someone, usually said of a male. Cf. BEND DOWN FOR. [U.S. underworld, early 1900s, Goldin, O'Leary, and Lipsius]

Benjamin a one-hundred dollar bill. [U.S., late 1900s-pres.]

benny (also **bennie**) **1.** a Benzedrine (trademark) tablet or capsule. [U.S. slang and drug culture, early 1900s] **2.** a state of intoxication from Benzedrine (trademark); the same as BENNY JAG (*q.v.*). [U.S. slang, mid 1900s-pres.]

benny jag intoxication from Benzedrine (trademark). Cf. JAG (sense 5). [U.S. slang, mid 1900s]

bent 1. intoxicated with alcohol. Also **bent out of shape.** Cf. CURVED. [U.S., early 1800s-1900s] **2.** drug or marijuana intoxicated. From sense 1. [U.S. drug culture, mid 1900s-pres.] **3.** homosexual; pertaining to a homosexual male. The opposite of STRAIGHT (sense 2). Reinforced by the positioning for pederasty. Cf. BEND DOWN FOR, BENDER (sense 2). [U.S. slang, mid 1900s-pres.]

bent and broken alcohol intoxicated. An elaboration of BENT. For synonyms see WOOFLED. [1900s, Dickson]

bent as a nine-bob note quite gay. For synonyms see EPICENE. [British, late 1900s-pres.]

benz Benzedrine (trademark), an amphetamine. [U.S. drug culture, mid 1900s-pres.] Synonyms: BEAN, BENNY, BROTHER BEN, CO-PILOT BEN, HI-BALL, PEP PILL, WHITES.

be on someone's ass to harass someone constantly. Cf. BE UP SOMEONE'S ASS ABOUT SOMETHING. [U.S. slang, late 1900s]

be on someone's jock [for a female] to pursue a male for sex or romance. Cf. JOCK. [U.S. collegiate, late 1900s, Munro]

be on someone's tit [for a male] to pursue a female, presumably for sex. [U.S. collegiate, late 1900s]

berk (also **birk**) the female genitals. For synonyms see MONOSYLLABLE.

Berkeley Hunt (also **Berkeley, Sir Berkeley, Sir Berkeley Hunt**) 1. the female genitals. Rhyming slang for "cunt." Cf. BERKSHIRE HUNT, BIRK, LADY BERKELEY. 2. a fool or an oaf; a CUNT (sense 4). [both senses, British, 1800s-pres.]

berker a brothel. Cf. BERK. [British military slang, World War II]

berks (also **berkeleys, burks**) the human breasts. For synonyms see BOSOM. [said to be from a Gypsy word, *berk* or *burk* (Farmer and Henley); British, 1800s]

Berkshire Hunt 1. the female genitals. Rhyming slang for "cunt." Cf. BERKELEY HUNT. 2. a fool. Cf. CUNT FACE, JOE ERK, JOE HUNT. For synonyms see OAF. [both senses, British, 1800s, *Dictionary of Rhyming Slang*]

bernice (also **bernies, burnese**) cocaine. Sometimes capitalized. [U.S. underworld and drug culture, 1900s]

berp (also **burp**) an (upward) release of stomach gas; a belch. See BURP. [U.S. colloquial, 1900s or before]

berps (also **burps**) alcoholic liquor. Cf. BERPWATER. [U.S. slang, 1900s]

berpwater beer, ale, and sometimes champagne; the same as BERPS (*q.v.*). Because it causes belching.

berries 1. the testicles. Cf. JINGLE-BERRIES. For synonyms see WHIRLY-GIGS. [U.S. slang, 1900s, Berrey and Van den Bark] 2. wine. Originally black. See also GRAPES. [U.S., mid 1900s-pres.]

best buy a sexually loose woman. For synonyms see BIRD. [U.S., late 1900s-pres.]

best leg of three the penis. Cf. MIDDLE LEG, THIRD LEG. [British slang, 1800s]

best piece 1. one's girlfriend. 2. one's wife. [both senses, U.S. slang, mid 1900s-pres.]

better half one's wife; the majority, more than one-half of the marital union. Cf. BITTER HALF. [colloquial since the late 1500s]

better than a poke in the eye with a blunt stick better than something else. [Widespread, late 1900s-pres.]

better than a poke in the eye with a sharp stick better than something worse. [Widespread, late 1900s-pres.]

Betty 1. a homosexual male. For synonyms see ETHEL. [U.S. slang, mid 1900s] 2. a generic term for a good-looking girl. Cf. BEDDY. [U.S. slang, late 1900s]

be up someone's ass about something See BE IN SOMEONE'S CRACK ABOUT SOMETHING.

bevvy (also **bevie, bevy, bivvy**) 1. beer. From "beverage." 2. to drink; to drink beer. [both senses, British and U.S. slang, 1900s]

bewitched intoxicated with alcohol. [U.S. slang, early 1700s-pres.]

bewottled alcohol intoxicated. For synonyms see WOOFLED. [1900s if not before, Dickson]

Beyond, the (also **Great Beyond, the**) heaven; death; the afterlife. [U.S. euphemism, late 1800s-pres.]

bezongas the [female] breasts. For synonyms see BOSOM. [U.S. slang, late 1900s if not before]

bezzle (also **beezzle**) to drink greedily. [British dialect, early 1600s]

bezzler a tippler; a drunkard. *Cf.* BEZZLE. [late 1500s]

B.F. **1.** a "bloody fool." [British, 1900s] **2.** a "boyfriend." [U.S., 1900s]

B.F.A. "butt-fucking Africa," a long way off. *Cf.* B.F.E. [U.S. collegiate, late 1900s, Munro]

B.F.D. "Big fucking deal!"; "So what?" [U.S. slang, late 1900s]

B.F.E. "butt-fucking Egypt," a long way off. *Cf.* B.F.A. [U.S. collegiate, late 1900s, Munro]

B-girl 1. a "bar-girl" who solicits drinks from male customers. **2.** a semi-professional prostitute who works in bars. **3.** a nickname for any sexually promiscuous woman. [all senses, U.S. slang, 1900s]

B.H. "bloody hell" in oaths and curses. [British, 1900s]

bhang 1. the leaves and stems of the marijuana plant; Indian hemp. Usually a liquid extract of marijuana, which is drunk. [since the mid 1500s] **2.** any commonly available marijuana. [U.S. drug culture, mid 1900s-pres.] See also BONG (sense 2).

bhang ganjah marijuana. *Cf.* GANJAH. [U.S. drug culture, mid 1900s-pres.]

bhong See BONG (sense 2).

bi 1. a BISEXUAL (*q.v.*) person. Someone capable of homosexual or heterosexual acts. [U.S. slang, mid 1900s-pres.] **2.** pertaining to a bisexual person; having to do with bisexuality. [both senses, U.S., mid 1900s-pres.]

bibble to drink often or much; to tipple. [late 1500s, *Oxford English Dictionary*]

bibbler a tippler; a drunkard. *Cf.* BIBBLE. [mid 1500s]

Bible-pounder (also **Bible-banger, Bible-basher, Bible-puncher, Bible-thumper**) a clergyman; a chaplain. For synonyms see SKY-PILOT. [colloquial and slang, 1800s-1900s]

bicho the penis. [from Spanish; U.S. slang, mid 1900s-pres.]

bicycle a prostitute; something to RIDE (sense 2). *Cf.* BARBER'S CHAIR, FERRY. [British slang, early 1900s, *Dictionary of Slang and Unconventional English*]

biddy magnet a male who attracts females easily. [British, late 1900s-pres.]

biffda a fat marijuana cigarette. For synonyms see MEZZROLL. [British, late 1900s-pres.]

biffer a sexually loose woman. For synonyms see LAY. [attested as "rare," (Wentworth and Flexner), possibly nonce; U.S., 1900s]

biffy (also **bif**) **1.** a W.C. [British and U.S. slang, 1900s] **2.** intoxicated with alcohol. A variant of BUFFY (*q.v.*). [British slang, 1900s, *Dictionary of Slang and Unconventional English*]

bigass big, important, or overly important. [U.S. slang, mid 1900s]

big bloke cocaine. Rhyming slang for "coke." [U.S. underworld and drug culture, early 1900s-pres.]

big brown eyes the breasts. The EYES (*q.v.*) are the nipples. For synonyms see BOSOM. [U.S. slang, early 1900s-pres.]

big-C. 1. cancer. [U.S., mid 1900s-pres.] **2.** cocaine. *Cf.* C. (sense 1). [U.S. drug culture, mid 1900s-pres.]

big chief MESCALINE (*q.v.*). [U.S. drug culture, 1900s]

big-D. 1. Dilaudid (trademark) tablets, an analgesic taken as a RECREATIONAL DRUG (*q.v.*). [U.S. drug culture, mid 1900s-pres.] **2.** the drug L.S.D. (*q.v.*). [U.S. drug culture, mid 1900s-pres.] **3.** damn. [euphemistic, 1800s-1900s]

big daddy 1. HEROIN. For synonyms see HEROIN. [U.S. drug culture, late 1900s] **2.** the penis. For synonyms see YARD. [U.S., late 1900s-pres.]

big-H. heroin. *Cf.* BIG-C. (sense 2). [U.S. drug culture, mid 1900s-pres.]

big Harry heroin; the same as HARRY (*q.v.*). A reinterpretation of BIG-H. (*q.v.*). [U.S. drug culture, mid 1900s-pres.]

big-juice a gangster; a powerful gangster. [U.S. underworld, black use, late 1900s]

big kahuna the important person; the knowledgeable authority on some matter. From the Hawaiian language. [U.S., mid 1900s-pres.]

big-O. 1. opium. *Cf.* BIG-C., BIG-H. [U.S. drug culture, mid 1900s-pres.] **2.** an orgasm. [U.S. euphemism, late 1900s]

big one a bowel movement (compared to urination). For synonyms see EASEMENT. [U.S. juvenile, 1900s]

big potty a bowel movement. *Cf.* BIG ONE. [U.S. juvenile, 1900s]

big shit 1. an exclamation of surprise or disbelief, "Big shit!" *Cf.* SHIT (sense 8). [U.S. slang, mid 1900s] **2.** a dysphemism for "big shot." [U.S. slang, mid 1900s]

big time copulation (compared to petting and kissing). For synonyms see SMOCKAGE. [U.S. slang, mid 1900s-pres.]

big-time operator a big shot; a lecher; a real HUSTLER (sense 5). [U.S. slang, mid 1900s-pres.]

big twenty 1. a twenty-dollar fee for a prostitute. **2.** a promiscuous female; a prostitute. *Cf.* GUINEA-HEN. [both senses, U.S. slang, mid 1900s-pres.]

big willy the penis. See WILLY. For synonyms see YARD. [British, late 1900s-pres.]

big with child pregnant. Based on GREAT WITH CHILD (*q.v.*). For synonyms see FRAGRANT. [U.S. colloquial, 1900s]

bike a sexually loose woman. *Cf.* BICYCLE. [Australian, 1900s, Baker]

bike boys cops; the police. For synonyms see FLATFOOT. [U.S., late 1900s-pres.]

bike dyke a female motorcycle police officer. For synonyms see FLATFOOT. [U.S., late 1900s-pres.]

bikini stuffers female breasts. For synonyms see BOSOM. [U.S., late 1900s-pres.]

biled owl (also **boiled owl**) a drunkard. *Cf.* BOILED AS AN OWL, DRUNK AS A BOILED OWL. [U.S., late 1800s-1900s]

billie paper money; a bill. Also BILLY. [U.S., late 1900s-pres.]

bim 1. a sexually loose girl. *Cf.* BIMBO (sense 1). For synonyms see LAY. [U.S. slang, early 1900s-pres.] **2.** the posteriors. *Cf.* BOM, BUM (sense 1). [Scots, 1900s, *Dictionary of Slang and Unconventional English*]

bimbette a teenage BIMBO. For synonyms see BIRD. [British, late 1900s-pres.]

bimbo 1. a young woman or a girl. [U.S. slang, 1900s] **2.** a sexually loose woman. [U.S. slang, early 1900s] **3.** the female genitals. Probably a variant of BUMBO (sense 1). [British, mid 1900s, *Dictionary of Slang and Unconventional English*] **4.** a woman considered sexually. [British and U.S., 1900s] **5.** a tramp's catamite. For synonyms see BRONCO. [Australian, mid 1900s, Wilkes]

bimmy a prostitute, especially a habitually drunken one. *Cf.* BIM (sense 1), BIMBO (sense 2). [U.S. underworld, early 1900s, Goldin, O'Leary, and Lipsius]

bimph toilet paper. *Cf.* BUMF. [British slang, 1800s]

bindle-boy a tramp's CATAMITE (*q.v.*); a young BINDLE-MAN (*q.v.*); a young hobo. For synonyms see BRONCO. [U.S. underworld, early 1900s, Goldin, O'Leary, and Lipsius]

bindle-man a tramp; a "bundleman."

bindle-stiff 1. a hobo who carries a bundle or bedroll. [U.S. slang, early 1900s] **2.** a drug addict. From sense 1. [U.S. underworld, 1900s]

binged intoxicated with alcohol; having been on a BINGE (*q.v.*). Rhymes with "cringed." [U.S. slang, early 1900s, Rose]

bingle 1. a drug-peddler. **2.** drugs; a large supply of drugs. [both senses, U.S. underworld, 1900s]

bingo brandy; any alcoholic drink. Possibly a (linguistic) blend of "brandy" and "stingo." [originally cant; since the 1600s]

bingo-boy a drunkard. For synonyms see ALCHY. [slang since the 1800s]

bingoed intoxicated with alcohol, having drunk too much BINGO (*q.v.*). [British and U.S., early 1900s]

bingy the penis. One of many diminutives for the male member. [attested as Anglo-Irish juvenile (nursery), 1800s-1900s, *Dictionary of Slang and Unconventional English*]

bint 1. a young woman or girlfriend. *Cf.* GIPPY BINT. **2.** a prostitute. [World War I] **3.** to girl; to seek a woman for sexual purposes. [all are from the Arabic word for "girl" or "daughter"; all senses, British and U.S., World War I]

bip-bam-thank-you-ma'am pertaining to a rapid and unemotional sexual encounter. *Cf.* WHAM-BAM-THANK-YOU-MA'AM. [U.S. slang, 1900s or before]

bird 1. a girl or woman. [in various senses, occasionally derogatory, since the 1300s] Synonyms: ANKLE, BABE, BABY, BACHELOR-GIRL, BAGGAGE, BAIT, BARBECUE, BEAVER, BEEF, BEETLE, BEST BUY, BEST PIECE, BIDDY, BIM, BIMBETTE, BIMBO, BINT, BIRDEEN, BITCH, BIT OF JAM, BIT OF MUSLIN, BIT OF NONSENSE, BIT OF SPARE, BIT OF SKIN, BIT ON THE SIDE, BLINT, BOB MY PAL, BOFFER, BONNET, BRA-BUSTER, BRIDE, BROAD, BROAD BOD, BROOD, BRUSH, BUFF, BUNCH OF CALICO, BUTTERCUP, CABBAGE, CANARY, C.D., CEILING INSPECTOR, CHARITY-BANG, CHARLEY WHEELER, CHERRY, CHERRY PIE, CHICK, CHICK-A-BIDDY, CHICKEN, CHIPPY, COVER GIRL, CRACK, DELL, DIRTBIKE, DISH, DOBASH, DOE, DOLL, (ENTHUSIASTIC) AMATEUR, FAIRY, F.B., FEMME, FILLY, FINIE, FLAPPER, FLOOSEY, FLY GIRL, FLY MINK, FOX, FRILL, FRISGIG, FUCK NUGGET, GAL, GLUTZ, HOOD RAT, HOTTIE, HUNK OF HEAVEN, LUSH BINT, MINI-SKIRT, MINK, MOUSE, MUFF, MUFFET, OCEAN PEARL, PIECE, SKINZ, SQUIRREL, SURFBOARD, SWEET YOUNG THING, TART, TIT, TITTER, TITTY, TOMATO, TOWN BIKE, TWIRL, TWIST, TWIST AND TWIRL, WENCH, YUMMY PANTS. For terms for sexually loose women see LAY. **2.** the penis. A play on COCK (sense 3). [slang, 1800s-pres.] **3.** the female genitals. A play on COCK (sense 6). [U.S. slang, 1900s] **4.** the FINGER

(*q.v.*); a particular obscene gesture made with the middle finger. *Cf.* FLIP THE BIRD. [U.S. slang, mid 1900s-pres.] **5.** a Bronx cheer. [U.S. slang, mid 1900s-pres.] **6.** a prostitute. [British slang, 1800s, Farmer and Henley] **7.** any odd person, as in "odd bird." [U.S. slang, 1900s]

birdie a homosexual male. From BIRD (sense 1, 6, or 7). [U.S. slang, early-mid 1900s, Rose]

birdie stuff any kind of powdered drug. For synonyms see COTICS. [U.S. drug culture, early 1900s, Berrey and Van den Bark]

bird's-eggs the testicles. For synonyms see WHIRLYGIGS. [British slang, 1800s, Farmer and Henley]

birdshit (also **bird-turd**) **1.** bird dung. For synonyms see DROPPINGS. [1900s and before] **2.** an obnoxious person; a total JERK. For synonyms see OAF. [U.S. slang, late 1900s] **3.** worthless. *Cf.* CHICKEN SHIT. [U.S. slang, late 1900s] **4.** nonsense; BULLSHIT. For synonyms see ANIMAL. [U.S. slang, late 1900s]

bird-turd 1. nonsense. Based on BULLSHIT (*q.v.*). *Cf.* COWSH, FROGSH. **2.** to BULLSHIT (*q.v.*); to talk nonsense. [both senses, U.S., 1900s]

bird-washing CUNNILINGUS (*q.v.*); mutual cunnilingus. *Cf.* BIRD (sense 3). [U.S. homosexual use, mid 1900s-pres., Farrell]

birdwood marijuana. For synonyms see MARI. [U.S. slang, mid 1900s-pres.]

birk an oaf; a dullard. Rhyming with "jerk." *Cf.* BERK, BERKELEY HUNT. [U.S. slang, mid 1900s-pres.]

birthday suit nakedness; one's bare skin. The term is from the name of a suit worn for the king's birthday celebration (early 1700s). *Cf.* SUNDAY SUIT. [since the late 1700s]

birth-naked nude; naked as at birth. [colloquial, 1900s and before]

biscuit 1. a sexually loose woman or a prostitute. *Cf.* BUN (sense 4), CAKE (sense 3). For synonyms see LAY. [U.S. slang, mid 1900s, Rose] **2.** a tablet of METHADONE. [U.S. drug culture, late 1900s] **3.** a piece of PEYOTE; peyote cactus. A truncation of DOG BISCUITS. [U.S. drug culture, late 1900s, Kaiser]

biscuit bitches American Red Cross woman volunteers. [U.S. military, (Vietnamese War) late 1900s, *Soldier Talk*]

biscuit, in the 1. in the head. **2.** in the anus. *Cf.* BUN (sense 2). [both senses, U.S. slang, early 1900s]

bish 1. a bishop. **2.** a ship's clergyman. [both senses, 1900s]

bishop 1. a large condom used as a package to carry other condoms. *Cf.* BALLOON. [British, late 1700s, Grose] **2.** a CHAMBER POT (*q.v.*). For synonyms see POT. [British slang, 1800s, Farmer and Henley] **3.** a bustle. [U.S. slang, mid 1800s] **4.** the penis. In phrases such as BOX THE BISHOP (*q.v.*). For synonyms see GENITALS, YARD. [U.S. and elsewhere, 1900s and long before]

bishop-beating male masturbation. *Cf.* BEAT THE BISHOP, BISHOP. For synonyms and related subjects see WASTE TIME. [U.S. slang, late 1900s, Lewin and Lewin]

bison to vomit. See comments at YAK. To BISON is more severe than to YAK. *Cf.* WATER BUFFALO, which is the biggest and worst vomiting of all. For synonyms see YORK. [U.S. collegiate, late 1900s, Munro]

bit 1. the female genitals. **2.** copulation. **3.** women considered sexually. [all senses, primarily British slang, 1800s-1900s, Farmer and Henley]

bitch 1. a female dog. No negative connotations. [since *c.* 1000, *Oxford English Dictionary*] Synonyms: BRACHE, DOGGESS, DOG'S LADY, DOG'S WIFE, LADY-DOG, PUPPY'S MAMMA, SHE-DOG. **2.** a derogatory term for a woman. The derogation comes from comparing a woman to a female dog in heat and suggesting that the woman acts out of carnal lust. Refers primarily to sexual appetite. [since the 1400s] **3.** a derogatory term for a male; a "dog." [British, 1500s-1700s] **4.** a blatant or BITCHY (*q.v.*) male homosexual. [U.S. homosexual use, mid 1900s-pres.] **5.** a derogatory term for any woman; a woman with vicious tendencies; any rude

woman. Refers primarily to temperament. For synonyms see BUFFARILLA. [U.S. slang, 1900s] **6.** a prostitute. [colloquial, 1900s and before] **7.** the queen at cards and at chess. [U.S., 1900s] **8.** to womanize; to whore. [British slang, 1800s, Farmer and Henley] **9.** to complain. [U.S. slang, mid 1900s-pres.] **10.** one who complains or is in a BITCHY (*q.v.*) mood, either a male or a female. [U.S. slang, mid 1900s-pres.] **11.** a difficult thing or person. [U.S. slang, 1900s] **12.** a CATAMITE (*q.v.*). From sense 5. [U.S. underworld, early 1900s, Monteleone] **13.** copulation. [British slang, 1800s, Farmer and Henley] **14.** to botch something up; to mess it up. [U.S., 1900s] **15.** a "bitch lamp," a can of grease with a wick. [U.S., early 1900s]

(bitchen-)twitchen very fine; excellent. From California. [U.S. slang, late 1900s]

bitchin' (also **bitchen**) excellent; great; classy. [U.S. slang, late 1900s]

bitch magnet a male who attracts females easily. [U.S., late 1900s-pres.]

bitch of a person or thing a very difficult or unpleasant person or thing. [U.S. and elsewhere, mid 1900s-pres.]

bitch out to complain. [U.S., late 1900s-pres.]

bitch's blind a wife or girlfriend who is a "cover" for the sexual activities of a homosexual male. *Cf.* BITCH (sense 4). [U.S. homosexual use, 1900s]

bitch session an informal gathering where people air their grievances. [U.S., mid 1900s-pres.]

bitch slammer a women's prison. [U.S., late 1900s-pres.]

bitch slap a slap across the face by a woman. [U.S., late 1900s-pres.]

bitch someone off to make someone very angry. [U.S. slang, late 1900s]

bitch something up to mess something up; to ruin or spoil something. [U.S. and elsewhere, slang, mid 1900s-pres.]

bitch tits gynecomastia; visible breast tissue in the male. Bodybuilding. [U.S., late 1900s-pres.]

bitchy 1. pertaining to a mood wherein one complains incessantly about anything. Although this applies to men or women, it is usually associated with women, especially when they are menstruating. **2.** sexy; in the manner of a dog in heat. [U.S. slang, 1900s] **3.** spiteful, hateful, and rude. [widespread, 1900s]

bite 1. the female genitals. [British, late 1600s] **2.** a rascal; a rogue. For synonyms see SNOKE-HORN. [British, late 1600s, B.E.] **3.** a fool; an oaf; a dupe. Perhaps like a fish which bites the bait. [Australian, early 1900s, Baker] **4.** to steal something. [U.S. black use, late 1900s]

biter 1. a woman who is so sexually aroused that her genitals are "ready to bite her a-se" (Grose). "A-se" is ARSE (*q.v.*). [British, late 1700s] **2.** a thief. *Cf.* BITE (sense 2). [U.S. black use, late 1900s]

bite the big one to die. For synonyms see DEPART. [U.S. slang, late 1900s]

bite the brown to commit ANILINGUS. *Cf.* BROWN. [U.S. slang, late 1900s]

bite the dust to die. *Cf.* KISS THE DUST. [originally U.S. slang and colloquial, late 1800s-pres.]

Bite the ice! "Go to hell!" [U.S., late 1900s-pres.]

Bite your bum! "Go away!" [Australian, mid 1900s-pres.]

bit for the finger a digital investigation of a woman's vagina. *Cf.* FINGER-FUCK, TIP THE MIDDLE FINGER. [British, 1800s, *Dictionary of Slang and Unconventional English*]

bit of black velvet copulation with a black woman. Also refers to an Australian aborigine woman. *Cf.* BLACK VELVET. [British military, late 1800s, *Dictionary of Slang and Unconventional English*]

bit of blink any alcoholic beverage. Rhyming slang for "drink." [British slang, late 1800s, Ware]

bit of Braille the sexual groping for a woman by a man. [British, late 1900s-pres.]

bit of brown pederasty. *Cf.* BROWN (sense 1), "anus." [British, 1800s, *Dictionary of Slang and Unconventional English*]

bit of cauliflower copulation. *Cf.* CAULIFLOWER. [British slang, 1800s]

bit of fish an act of copulation. *Cf.* FISH (sense 1). [British slang, 1800s]

bit of flat copulation. *Cf.* FLAT COCK. [British slang, 1800s, Farmer and Henley]

bit of front-door work copulation. [primarily British slang, 1800s]

bit of hair copulation. *Cf.* AFTER HAIR, HAIR. [British slang, 1800s, Farmer and Henley]

bit of hard (also **bit of stiff**) **1.** the erect penis. For synonyms see ERECTION. **2.** copulation from the female point of view. [both senses, British slang, 1800s]

bit of hard for a bit of soft copulation. The "hard" is the penis; the "soft" is the vagina. [British slang, 1800s, Farmer and Henley]

bit of jam 1. a sexually loose young woman, especially a wanton woman. [British slang, late 1800s, Ware] **2.** the female genitals. **3.** copulation. [both senses, British slang, 1800s, Farmer and Henley]

bit of meat 1. a prostitute. **2.** an act of copulation. *Cf.* MEAT (sense 2). [both senses, British slang, 1800s]

bit of mutton a prostitute. *Cf.* LACED-MUTTON, MUTTON. [British slang, 1800s or before]

bit of nifty (also **nifty**) copulation. [British slang, 1800s-1900s, *Dictionary of Slang and Unconventional English*]

bit of nonsense, a a mistress; an illicit girlfriend. For synonyms see BIRD. [British, mid 1900s-pres.]

bit of pork the female genitals; an act of copulation. *Cf.* MEAT (sense 1), PORK (sense 1). [British slang, 1800s]

bit of rough copulation. [British slang, 1800s, Farmer and Henley]

bit of skin a sexually loose young woman; a woman considered sexually. [British slang, 1900s]

bit of snug 1. copulation from the female point of view. *Cf.* SNUG (sense 1). **2.** the penis. [both senses, British slang, 1800s, Farmer and Henley]

bit of snug for a bit of stiff 1. the vagina. For synonyms see PASSAGE. **2.** copulation from the female point of view. [both senses, British slang, 1800s, Farmer and Henley]

bit of a spare, a a married man's mistress. For synonyms see BIRD. [British, mid 1900s-pres.]

bit of the goose's-neck copulation from the female point of view. *Cf.* GOOSE'S-NECK. [British slang, 1800s, Farmer and Henley]

bit of the other coition. *Cf.* ANTIPODES, THE. [British slang, early 1900s, *Dictionary of Slang and Unconventional English*]

bit on, a intoxicated with alcohol. [British and U.S., 1800s-1900s]

bit on a fork 1. the female genitals. **2.** copulation, getting into the fork of the female's body. [both senses, British slang, 1800s]

bit on the side, a an illicit girlfriend. For synonyms see BIRD. [British, mid 1900s-pres.]

bi-trade 1. the bisexual sex business. *Cf.* BI. **2.** persons seeking prostitutes of either sex. [both senses, U.S. slang, late 1900s]

bitter half one's wife. A play on BETTER HALF (*q.v.*). For synonyms see WARDEN. [U.S. slang, mid 1900s]

bizatch a bitch. [U.S., late 1900s-pres.]

biznitch a bitch. [U.S., late 1900s-pres.]

B.J. a BLOW-JOB (*q.v.*), an act of PENILINGUS (*q.v.*).

black bart marijuana. For synonyms see MARI. [U.S., late 1900s-pres.]

black beauties amphetamine capsules; Biphetamine (trademark), which comes in black or black-and-white capsules. From the name of a horse in children's fiction. For synonyms see AMP. [U.S. drug culture, mid 1900s-pres.]

black Bess the female genitals. [British slang, 1800s, Farmer and Henley]

blackbird 1. a Negro. Mildly derogatory and jocular. [slang, late 1800s-early 1900s] **2.** an amphetamine capsule. *Cf.* BLACK BEAUTIES, BLUEBIRD, REDBIRD, SPECKLED BIRD. [U.S. drug culture, mid 1900s-pres.]

black death coffee; bad coffee; strong coffee. [British dysphemism, World War I, *Soldier Talk*]

black dog the delirium tremens. For synonyms see ORK-ORKS. [British and U.S. slang, 1800s-1900s]

black gungeon (also **gungeon**) a type of marijuana from Africa or Jamaica. From GANJAH (*q.v.*). [U.S. drug culture, mid 1900s-pres.]

black gunny a type of marijuana. From BLACK GUNGEON (*q.v.*). Reinforced by "gunny" of a HEMP (*q.v.*) gunny sack. [U.S. drug culture, mid 1900s-pres.]

black-hole the female genitals. A reinterpretation of the "black hole of Calcutta." [British slang, 1800s, Farmer and Henley]

black-jock (also **brown-jock, grey-jock**) the female genitals. The color refers to the color of the pubic hair. *Cf.* BLACK JOKE. [British slang, 1800s, Farmer and Henley]

black joke the female genitals. From a popular song of the times. [British slang, early 1800s]

Black-Man, the 1. the devil. **2.** a bugbear to frighten children. [both senses, colloquial, 1500s-1900s]

black moat (also **black mo**) a type of marijuana. [U.S. drug culture, mid 1900s]

black mollies an amphetamine capsule. From the name of a popular tropical fish, *Mollienisia latipinna*. *Cf.* BLACK BEAUTIES. [U.S. drug culture, mid 1900s-pres.]

black oil an alcohol extract of hashish. For synonyms see OIL. [U.S. drug culture, mid 1900s-pres.]

black pearl opium. For synonyms see OPE. [U.S., late 1900s-pres.]

black pills opium. *Cf.* BLACK STUFF. For synonyms see OPE. [U.S. drug culture, 1900s]

black-pot a drunkard. Originally from the name for a beer mug. Rhyming slang for "sot." [British slang, 1500s-1800s]

black-ring the female genitals. *Cf.* RING (sense 1). [British slang, 1800s, Farmer and Henley]

black rock crack cocaine. For synonyms see NOSE-CANDY. [U.S., late 1900s-pres.]

Black Russian HASHISH (*q.v.*). For synonyms see HASH. [U.S. drug culture, mid 1900s-pres.]

black smoke (also **black silk**) opium. For synonyms see OPE. [1900s]

black sunshine L.S.D. For synonyms see ACID. [U.S., late 1900s-pres.]

black tabs L.S.D. For synonyms see ACID. [U.S., late 1900s-pres.]

black whack the drug phencyclidine, P.C.P. For synonyms see P.C.P. [U.S. drug culture, late 1900s, Abel]

bladdered drunk. For synonyms see WOOFLED. [British, late 1900s-pres.]

blade the penis. *Cf.* BRACMARD. [British, 1800s, Farmer and Henley]

blakes See COW-BLAKES.

blanco a white person; a Caucasian. From Spanish. For synonyms see PECKERWOOD. [U.S., mid 1900s-pres.]

blankard a bastard. [Australian euphemism, mid 1900s, Baker]

blanked 1. damned. *Cf.* BLANK. [colloquial, 1800s-1900s] **2.** intoxicated with alcohol. [from French *vin blanc;* British and U.S., World Wars]

blanket drill 1. a night's sleep. No negative connotations. **2.** copulation. **3.** masturbation. [all senses, British with some U.S. use, early 1900s, *Dictionary of Slang and Unconventional English*]

blanket hornpipe copulation. For synonyms see SMOCKAGE. [British slang, early 1800s, *Lexicon Balatronicum*]

blanks heroin. [U.S. drug culture, mid 1900s-pres.]

blast 1. an exclamation or a curse, "Damn!" Now a euphemism for BLOODY (*q.v.*). [colloquial, late 1600s-pres.] **2.** to smoke marijuana. *Cf.*

BLASTED (sense 3). [U.S. drug culture, mid 1900s-pres.] **3.** to use any narcotic. [U.S. drug culture, mid 1900s-pres.] **4.** a release of intestinal gas. For synonyms see GURK. [U.S. slang, 1900s; much older as nonce]

blasted 1. damned; BLOODY (*q.v.*). *Cf.* BLAST (sense 1). [British and later, U.S., late 1600s-pres.] **2.** intoxicated with alcohol. [U.S. slang, early 1900s-pres.] **3.** intoxicated with drugs, especially marijuana. [U.S. drug culture, early 1900s-pres.]

blast party a session of marijuana smoking. *Cf.* BLAST (sense 2). [U.S. drug culture, mid 1900s-pres.]

blatherskite (also **blatherskate, bletherskite**) a boaster; someone who speaks nonsense. Literally, "a dung-talker." *Cf.* BULLSHITTER, SKITE (sense 2). For synonyms see BULLER. [from Scots dialect; British and U.S. colloquial, late 1800s-pres.]

blatts diarrhea. For synonyms see QUICKSTEP. [British, late 1900s-pres.]

blaze to smoke marijuana. [U.S., late 1900s-pres.]

blazed intoxicated on marijuana. For synonyms see TALL. [U.S., late 1900s-pres.]

blazes "hell" in expressions such as "Go to blazes!" "Like blazes!" "What in blazes!" "What the blazes!" Refers to the flames of hell. [colloquial since the early 1800s]

blazing really good; really good-looking. [U.S., late 1900s-pres.]

bleary-eyed intoxicated with alcohol. [U.S. slang, early 1900s-pres.]

blech 1. a belch. **2.** to belch. A play on BELCH (*q.v.*). *Cf.* ERUCTATE. [both senses, U.S., mid 1900s-pres.]

blighter a contemptible fellow; someone who causes a blight of unpleasantness. For synonyms see SNOKE-HORN. [British slang, late 1800s-pres.]

Blimey! a disguised oath or exclamation, "May God blind me!" *Cf.* BLARM ME! [originally Cockney; British, 1800s-pres.]

blimp 1. a fat prostitute; a sexually loose woman. [U.S. underworld, early

1900s, Monteleone] **2.** any fat person. [U.S. slang and colloquial, early 1900s-pres.]

blimp boat an obese person. Possibly patterned on *shrimp boat*. [U.S. collegiate, late 1900s, Eble]

blimped intoxicated with alcohol; gorged and swollen with drink. [U.S. slang, mid 1900s-pres.]

blimp out to overeat. [U.S., late 1900s-pres.]

blind 1. intoxicated with alcohol. See BLIND DRUNK. [since the early 1600s] **2.** intoxicated with marijuana or other drugs. From sense 1. For synonyms see TALL. [U.S. drug culture, mid 1900s-pres.] **3.** uncircumcised. Because the EYE-HOLE (*q.v.*) is covered. [U.S. homosexual use, mid 1900s]

blind Bob, old the penis. Because it has only one eye, which does not see. *Cf.* BOB TAIL (sense 3). [British (Cockney), 1900s]

blind cheeks the posteriors. *Cf.* CHEEKS. [British, late 1600s, B.E.]

blind cupid the posteriors. For synonyms see DUFF. [British slang, early 1800s, Egan's Grose]

blind drunk deeply intoxicated with alcohol. *Cf.* BOOZEBLIND. [British and U.S., 1700s-pres.]

blinded intoxicated with alcohol. For synonyms see WOOFLED. [U.S. slang, 1900s]

blinders intoxicated with alcohol. [British slang, early 1900s]

blind-eye 1. the anus. *Cf.* ROUNDEYE (sense 2). [British, 1800s or before] **2.** the female genitals with reference to the vulva and the vagina. In expressions such as GET A SHOVE IN ONE'S BLIND-EYE (*q.v.*). *Cf.* LONG-EYE, SQUINT.

blind fart an inaudible but nevertheless potent release of intestinal gas. For synonyms see GURK. [British, 1800s, *Dictionary of Slang and Unconventional English*]

blindo 1. intoxicated with alcohol. [British and U.S., 1800s] **2.** a drunken spree. [British, 1800s, *Dictionary of Slang and Unconventional English*] **3.**

to die. Farmer and Henley show this as a verb. [British military, 1800s]

blind squid ketamine. [U.S., late 1900s-pres.]

blind staggers intoxication with alcohol. [widespread slang, 1900s or before]

blind tiger strong or inferior alcoholic drink. [U.S. slang, 1900s]

blink (also **blinking**) damn; bloody. From BLANK (*q.v.*). [U.S., 1900s and before]

blinky FREE BASE cocaine. Origin unknown. For synonyms see FREE BASE. [U.S. drug culture, late 1900s, Abel]

blint a sexually loose young woman; a prostitute. *Cf.* BINT. [U.S., 1900s, Berrey and Van den Bark]

blips cocaine. For synonyms see NOSE-CANDY. [U.S., late 1900s-pres.]

Bliss 1. See MICKEY BLISS. **2.** marijuana. For synonyms see MARI. [U.S., late 1900s-pres.]

blissed out alcohol or drug intoxicated. For synonyms see TALL, WOOFLED. [U.S. drug culture, late 1900s]

bliss out to become euphoric by taking Quaaludes or by smoking marijuana. [U.S. drug culture, late 1900s]

blister an annoying person. [British, late 1900s-pres.]

blistering bloody; damned. See BLISTER (sense 2). [British and U.S., 1900s]

blithered intoxicated with alcohol. For synonyms see WOOFLED. [Australian, early 1900s, Baker]

blitzed 1. intoxicated with alcohol. [U.S. slang, mid 1900s-pres.] **2.** drug intoxicated. From sense 1. [U.S. drug culture, mid 1900s-pres.]

blitzkrieged alcohol intoxicated. For synonyms see WOOFLED. [U.S. slang, late 1900s]

blixed mildly drug or marijuana intoxicated. For synonyms see TALL. [U.S. drug culture, late 1900s, Kaiser]

blizzie a marijuana cigarette; a BLUNT. For synonyms see MEZZROLL. [U.S., late 1900s-pres.]

bloat 1. a drunkard. [British and U.S.

slang, 1800s] **2.** a drowned corpse. For synonyms see CORPSE. [U.S., 1800s]

bloated 1. intoxicated with alcohol; overfilled with drink. [U.S. slang, early 1900s-pres.] **2.** bloody; damned. [British, early 1900s]

bloater a drunkard; the same as BLOAT (sense 1). [U.S., 1900s]

blob, be on to be sexually aroused, said of men. Possibly related to LOB (sense 2). Cf. BLOTTY, BE. For synonyms see HUMPY. [British, 1900s, *Dictionary of Slang and Unconventional English*]

block 1. an oaf; a blockhead. [early 1500s] **2.** to copulate with a woman. For synonyms see OCCUPY. [British and U.S. slang, 1800s-pres.]

blockbuster a Nembutal (trademark) capsule; amphetamines in general. From the nickname of a powerful bomb used in World War II. [U.S. drug culture, mid 1900s-pres.]

blocked 1. intoxicated with alcohol. [British and U.S., mid 1900s] **2.** intoxicated with drugs. From sense 1. [U.S. drug culture, mid 1900s-pres.]

blockhead a stupid oaf. Cf. BLOCK (sense 1). [since the mid 1500s]

blodgie a hoodlum; a punk. [Australian, 1900s]

bloke (also **bloak**) **1.** a mildly contemptuous term for a man, especially a stupid man. [British and some U.S. use, 1800s-pres.] **2.** a drunkard. Cf. BLOAT (sense 1). [U.S., 1900s] **3.** cocaine. Rhyming slang for "coke." From BIG BLOKE (q.v.). For synonyms see NOSE-CANDY. [U.S. drug culture, mid 1900s-pres.]

blomboll a drunkard. [British slang, 1800s, Farmer and Henley]

blond (or blonde) 1. hashish. A truncation of BLOND HASHISH (q.v.). For synonyms see HASH. [U.S. drug culture, 1900s] **2.** marijuana. For synonyms see MARI. [US., late 1900s-pres.]

blond hashish (also **blond hash**) a mild form of hashish. Cf. HASHISH. [U.S. drug culture, 1900s]

blond Lebanese a type of strong, light-colored HASHISH. For synonyms

see HASH. [U.S. drug culture, late 1900s]

blooch 1. to masturbate. For synonyms see WASTE TIME. **2.** a state of mental retardation erroneously attributed to excessive masturbation. [both senses, U.S. dialect (Boontling), late 1800s-early 1900s, Charles Adams]

blood 1. a fop; a dandy; a high-spirited male, as in "noble-blood" or "blue-blood." [British, mid 1500s-1900s] **2.** a Negro; one's fellow black. From "blood brother." [U.S. black use, mid 1900s-pres.] **3.** catsup. A dysphemism. For similar terms see DOG'S VOMIT. [U.S., 1900s]

blood-box an ambulance. Cf. BONE-BOX. [U.S. slang, 1900s]

blood-bucket an ambulance; the same as BUCKET OF BLOOD (q.v.). [U.S. slang, 1900s]

blood disease syphilis. Cf. BAD DISEASE. [U.S. euphemism, early 1900s-pres.]

blood of a bitch a term of contempt meaning the blood descendent of a bitch. Cf. S.O.B. [U.S., 1900s or before, Wentworth]

blood-tub an ambulance. Cf. BLOOD-BUCKET. [British military, 1900s]

blood-wagon an ambulance. [British military, early 1900s]

bloody damned; cursed. In the 1800s, the British equivalent of U.S. "fucking." The word was originally a very low-class "decoration" for almost any utterance. The immense impact of the word is attributable to its low-class origins rather than its "real" meaning. The utterance of such a rude lower-class term was itself the source of shock. See BLOOD (sense 1) for the most likely source. Before it became symbolic as a marker of the Cockney, the word had numerous uses. Many etymologies have been proposed to account for the intense power this word once had when uttered in polite society. It has been suggested that it is a corruption of "By our Lady!" [primarily Australian and British, 1800s-pres.] Synonyms and related terms: BALLY, BLANKITY, BLASTED, BLEEDING,

BLIGHTED, BLISTERING, BLOATED, BLOOM-
ING, BLUGGY, BLURRY, BLUSHING, CRIM-
SONEST OF ADJECTIVES, GREAT
AUSTRALIAN ADJECTIVE, HEMATOID,
IM-BLOODY-POSSIBLE, N.B.G., N.B.L.,
PINK, PLURRY, Q.B.I., RUDDY, SAN-
GUINARY.

bloody Mary 1. the menstrual period.
From the name of an alcoholic mixed
drink and Queen Mary 1 (Mary
Tudor). [U.S. slang, 1900s] **2.** catsup.
[U.S. slang, 1900s]

blooming bloody; damned. [used as
an intensifier as early as the early
1700s; British and some U.S. use, late
1800s-pres.]

blootered drunk. For synonyms see
WOOFLED. [British, late 1900s-pres.]

blorphs a drug called BLUE MOR-
PHONE. Possibly the elixir of morphine
sulfate, which is blue. [U.S. drug culture, late 1900s, Kaiser]

blort cocaine. A blend of BLOW and
SNORT. For synonyms see NOSE-CANDY.
[U.S. drug culture, late 1900s]

blot the posteriors; the anus. For synonyms see DUFF. [Australian, 1900s,
Baker]

blot someone out to kill someone.
Underworld. [U.S., mid 1900s-pres.]

blotter 1. a drunkard. From the way
a drunkard soaks up alcohol. [U.S.,
1900s and before] **2.** the drug L.S.D.
(q.v.). From the practice of ingesting
bits of blotter saturated with L.S.D.
[U.S. drug culture, mid 1900s-pres.]

blotto 1. intoxicated with alcohol;
dead drunk. [British and U.S., early
1900s-pres.] **2.** any strong alcoholic
beverage. For synonyms see BOOZE.
[British military, early 1900s, Dictionary of Slang and Unconventional
English]

blotty, be sexually aroused, said of
men. Cf. BLOB, BE ON. For synonyms
see HUMPY. [British, 1900s, Dictionary
of Slang and Unconventional English]

blow 1. a prostitute, mistress, or con-
cubine. [cant, late 1700s or before,
Grose] **2.** a drunken spree. See also
BLOW-OUT. [British and U.S., early
1800s-1900s] **3.** to perform penilingus.
See BLOW-JOB. [U.S., early 1900s-pres.]

4. to perform CUNNILINGUS (q.v.).
[U.S., mid 1900s-pres.] **5.** cocaine. Cf.
SUPERBLOW. [U.S. drug culture, mid
1900s-pres.] **6.** to SNORT (sense 2)
drugs. [U.S. drug culture, mid 1900s-
pres.] **7.** to smoke marijuana. [U.S.
drug culture, mid 1900s-pres.]

blow a fart to release a burst of intestinal gas through the anus. For synonyms see GURK. [1900s if not before]

blow a stick (also **blow gage, blow
hay, blow jive, blow pot, blow tea**) to
smoke marijuana. [U.S. drug culture,
mid 1900s-pres.]

blow beets to vomit. Cf. BLOW
LUNCH. For synonyms see YORK. [U.S.
slang, mid 1900s-pres.]

blow-boy 1. a man who plays the
bugle. Not necessarily with negative
connotations. [U.S., 1900s] **2.** a fellator.
From sense 1. For synonyms see PIC-
COLO-PLAYER. [mid 1900s, Dictionary
of the Underworld]

blow chow to vomit. For synonyms
see YORK. [U.S. slang, late 1900s]

blowed-away 1. intoxicated with alcohol. For synonyms see WOOFLED. **2.**
drug intoxicated. Cf. BLOWN-AWAY.
For synonyms see TALL. [both senses,
U.S. slang, mid 1900s-pres.]

blow grits to vomit. For synonyms see
YORK. Southern. [U.S. slang, late
1900s]

blow-hole a hole made in a men's
bathroom partition allegedly for PENI-
LINGUS (q.v.), but more likely to en-
able the male seated in a stall to
observe the penis of a man who is
standing at a urinal. From the term for
a whale's nostril. See GLORY HOLE.
[U.S. slang, mid 1900s-pres.]

blow-job 1. an act of FELLATIO or
PENILINGUS (both q.v.). Cf. B.J., BLOW
(sense 3). For synonyms see PENILIN-
GUS. [U.S. slang, mid 1900s-pres.] **2.** an
act of cunnilingus. Less common than
sense 1. For synonyms see CUNNILIN-
GUS. [U.S. slang, mid 1900s-pres.]

blow lunch (also **blow one's lunch**) to
vomit. Cf. BLOW BEETS. [U.S. slang,
mid 1900s-pres.]

blow monkey somone who performs

fellatio. For synonyms see PICCOLO-PLAYER. [U.S., late 1900s-pres.]

blown-away 1. dead; killed. [U.S. colloquial, 1900s] **2.** deeply drug intoxicated. *Cf.* BLOWED-AWAY. [U.S. slang, mid 1900s-pres.]

blown-out intoxicated with drugs. *Cf.* BLOWN-AWAY. [U.S. drug culture, mid 1900s-pres.]

blown-up (also **blown**) intoxicated with alcohol. Refers to the pressure in one's head and to being bloated with drink. [U.S. slang, mid 1800s-pres.]

blow off 1. to ejaculate; to have an orgasm. [cant or slang, 1600s-1700s] **2.** to break wind; to release intestinal gas audibly. [British colloquial, 1900s] **3.** to masturbate. **4.** to goof off; to waste time; to procrastinate. **5.** a time-waster; a procrastinator. Usually hyphenated in this sense. **6.** to perform fellatio on someone. **7.** to cheat, deceive, or lie to someone. [senses 2-7, U.S. current slang] **8.** a release of intestinal gas. For synonyms see GURK. [British, mid 1900s-pres.]

blow one's cookies to vomit. For synonyms see YORK. *Cf.* DROP ONE'S COOKIES, SNAP ONE'S COOKIES, WOOF COOKIES. [U.S. slang, late 1900s]

blow one's doughnuts to vomit. For synonyms see YORK. [U.S. slang, late 1900s]

blow one's groceries to vomit. For synonyms see YORK. [U.S. slang, late 1900s]

blow one's roof to smoke marijuana. *Cf.* BLOW (sense 7). For synonyms see SMOKE. [U.S. drug culture, mid 1900s-pres.]

blow-out a drinking spree. From a colloquial term for a feast or a period of gluttony. [U.S., 1900s or before]

blow smoke up someone's ass to deceive or impress someone. [U.S. slang, late 1900s]

blow snot rockets to blow a mass of nasal mucus from a nostril by blocking off the other with the thumb. [U.S., late 1900s-pres.]

blow someone away 1. to kill someone; to shoot someone. Underworld. [U.S., late 1900s-pres.] **2.** to overwhelm someone; to amaze someone. [U.S., late 1900s-pres.]

blow someone's doors off to defeat someone; to surpass someone. As if someone were going by another vehicle on the highway at such a high speed that the doors would be blown off in passing. [U.S., late 1900s-pres.]

blow someone's mind 1. to impress someone; to overwhelm someone. [U.S., late 1900s-pres.] **2.** [for a drug] to intoxicate someone. [U.S., late 1900s-pres.]

blow the coke (also **blow coke**) to SNORT (sense 2) or inhale cocaine. [U.S. underworld, 1900s]

blow the horn to release intestinal gas audibly. *Cf.* ARS MUSICA, TRUMP. [British slang, 1800s, Farmer and Henley]

blowtorch the penis. *Cf.* TORCH of CUPID. Possibly in reference to PENILINGUS (*q.v.*). See BLOW (sense 3). [attested as U.S. underworld (tramps), early 1900s, Monteleone]

blow up 1. to ejaculate. *Cf.* THROW UP (sense 3). [a vague reference occurring in *Pericles* and other plays (Shakespeare)] **2.** to become pregnant. In reference to a woman's swollen abdomen. [colloquial, 1900s]

blubber gut(s) a fat person. Also a rude term of address. [U.S., mid 1900s-pres.]

blubbers the breasts. *Cf.* CHUBBIES, SPORT BLUBBER. [British and U.S. slang, late 1800s-1900s]

bludgeon the penis, especially the erect penis. *Cf.* WEAPON. For synonyms see ERECTION. [British slang, 1800s, Farmer and Henley]

bludger a lazy oaf. For synonyms see OAF. [Australian, late 1900s-pres.]

blue 1. lewd; obscene. *Cf.* PURPLE. [colloquial, 1800s-1900s] **2.** intoxicated with alcohol. *Cf.* BLUE DEVILS (sense 2). [U.S. and elsewhere, early 1800s-1900s] **3.** a Negro. [U.S., 1900s or before] **4.** the drug L.S.D. **5.** depressed. See BLUE DEVILS (sense 1). [colloquial, 1900s and before] **6.** gay [males]. For synonyms see EPICENE. [U.S., late 1900s-pres.]

blue acid the drug L.S.D. [U.S. drug culture, mid 1900s-pres.]

blue angel an Amytal (trademark) capsule. Refers to jet planes flying in formation, *i.e.*, the Blue Angels. *Cf.* BLUEBIRD, BLUE HEAVEN. [U.S. drug culture, mid 1900s-pres.]

blue balls venereal disease, especially gonorrhea. *Cf.* HOT ROCKS, STONE-ACHE. [U.S. slang, mid 1900s]

blue bomber a (blue) ten-milligram tablet of Valium (trademark). Abbreviated as B.B. (sense 2). [U.S. drug culture, mid 1900s-pres.]

blue cheer the drug L.S.D. (*q.v.*). From the trademarked brand name of a laundry detergent. *Cf.* BLUE (sense 4). [U.S. drug culture, mid 1900s-pres.]

bluecoat a policeman; any man in a blue uniform. For synonyms see FLAT-FOOT. [slang, mid 1600s-pres.]

blue collar crack the cleavage at the top of the buttocks appearing when a man bends over and his pants scoot down. [U.S., late 1900s-pres.]

blued (also **blewed**) intoxicated with alcohol. [British and U.S. slang, 1800s-1900s]

blue devils 1. very low spirits up to and including severe clinical depression. [colloquial, late 1700s-1800s] **2.** the DELIRIUM TREMENS (*q.v.*). Blue devils and red monkeys are typical hallucinations seen while having the delirium tremens. *Cf.* PINK ELEPHANTS. [slang since the early 1800s] **3.** capsules of Amytal (trademark), a barbiturate. *Cf.* RED DEVIL. [U.S. drug culture, mid 1900s-pres.]

blue-eyed intoxicated with alcohol. For synonyms see WOOFLED. [U.S. slang, mid 1800s, Wentworth and Flexner]

blue-eyed devil 1. a Caucasian. *Cf.* DEVIL (sense 3). [U.S. black use, mid 1900s-pres.] **2.** a person who is overtly kind and as innocent as a lamb, but is evil underneath. [U.S., 1900s]

blue flag the drug L.S.D. (*q.v.*). *Cf.*

BLUE (sense 4), ROYAL BLUE. [U.S. drug culture, mid 1900s-pres.]

bluehair an old lady, especially one whose hair is tinted blue. [U.S., mid 1900s-pres.]

blue heaven 1. an Amytal (trademark) capsule. Usually in the plural. [U.S. drug culture, mid 1900s-pres.] **2.** the drug L.S.D. (*q.v.*). *Cf.* HEAVENLY BLUE. [U.S. drug culture, mid 1900s-pres.]

blue horrors (also **horrors**) the DE-LIRIUM TREMENS (*q.v.*). *Cf.* BLUE DEV-ILS (sense 2), HORRORS. [U.S. slang, mid 1800s]

blue jeans and T-shirts a mixture of Talwin™ and Pyribenzamine™. [U.S. drug culture, late 1900s]

blue Johnnies the DELIRIUM TRE-MENS (*q.v.*). [Australian, 1800s, Farmer and Henley]

blue mist the drug L.S.D. (*q.v.*). [U.S. drug culture, mid 1900s-pres.]

blue morphone morphine or a derivative of morphine. Possibly elixir of morphine, which is blue. *Cf.* BLORPHS. [U.S. drug culture, late 1900s, Kaiser]

blues 1. despondency; depression. *Cf.* BLUE (sense 5). **2.** the DELIRIUM TRE-MENS (*q.v.*). A truncation of BLUE DEV-ILS (*q.v.*). [colloquial since the 1800s] **3.** Amytal (trademark) capsules. [U.S. drug culture, mid 1900s-pres.]

blue sage a marijuana cigarette. For synonyms see MEZZROLL. [drug culture, mid 1900s]

blueskin 1. a Negro. [U.S., early 1800s] **2.** the child of a black woman and a white man. [Caribbean, 1800s] **3.** the penis. [British slang, 1800s, Farmer and Henley]

blue splash L.S.D. on a bit of blotter paper. For synonyms see ACID. [U.S. drug culture, late 1900s, Abel]

blue star morning glory seeds used as a mild hallucinogenic. From the color name. For synonyms see SEEDS. [U.S. drug culture, mid 1900s-pres.]

blue stone inferior gin or whisky. "Blue stone" is an old term for "copper sulfate." [British slang, mid 1800s, Farmer and Henley]

blue suit a police officer. For synonyms see FLATFOOT. [U.S. slang, late 1900s]

blue steeler a very hard erection. For synonyms see ERECTION. [U.S., late 1900s-pres.]

blue tape gin. For synonyms see RUIN. [British and U.S. slang, 1700s-1900s]

blue-veined custard chucker the penis; an erection. For synonyms see ERECTION, YARD. [late 1900s]

bluff a female homosexual who assumes either the active or passive sexual role. A blend of "bitch" and "fluff." [U.S. homosexual use, mid 1900s, Stanley]

bluggy bloody. A euphemism of disguise for "bloody" in the sense "gory." [allegedly mock baby talk; U.S. late 1800s]

blunt 1. barbiturates in general. For synonyms see BARB. **2.** a capsule of Seconal (trademark), a barbiturate used as a recreational drug. [both senses, U.S. drug culture, mid 1900s-pres.] **3.** a marijuana cigarette rolled in the tobacco-leaf wrapper of a Phillies Blunt cigar. For synonyms see MEZZROLL. [U.S., late 1900s-pres.]

blunted intoxicated with marijuana. For synonyms see TALL.

blunted out having smoked many BLUNTS of marijuana. For synonyms see TALL. [U.S., late 1900s-pres.]

blunt end the glans penis. Cf. BELL-END. [British military, 1900s, *Dictionary of Slang and Unconventional English*]

blushing bloody. [British euphemism, late 1800s-early 1900s]

B.M. 1. a "bowel movement," an act of defecation. **2.** a disgusting and annoying person. A way of calling a person a SHIT. [U.S. slang, late 1900s] **3.** BLUE MORPHONE. Cf. BLORPHS. [U.S. drug culture, late 1900s, Kaiser]

B.N. a "bloody nuisance." [British slang, 1900s]

bo 1. Colombian marijuana. Cf. COLUMBIAN RED, LIMBO (sense 4), LUMBO. [U.S. drug culture, mid 1900s-pres.] **2.** a tramp's catamite or "boy." Rein-

forced by "beau." For synonyms see BRONCO. [U.S. underworld, early 1900s, Weseen]

B.O. 1. "body odor," a sweaty or other unpleasant body odor. [used euphemistically in advertising and U.S. slang, mid 1900s-pres.] **2.** "HBO," the Home Box Office cable television channel. [U.S. dysphemism, late 1900s]

boag to vomit. Probably from BOGUE. For synonyms see YORK. [U.S. slang, late 1900s]

boat and oar a prostitute. Rhyming slang for "whore." Cf. BROKEN OAR. [U.S. slang, 1900s or before]

BOB "big old bitch." [British, late 1900s-pres.]

bob (and dick) 1. unwell. Rhyming slang on *sick*. [British, mid 1900s-pres.] **2.** the penis. Rhyming slang on PRICK. For synonyms see YARD. [British, mid 1900s-pres.]

bobbers the breasts. Cf. BLUBBERS. [attested as British slang, mid 1900s, *Dictionary of Slang and Unconventional English*]

bobbles the testicles. From a dialect word meaning "stones." Cf. BAUBLES. [British, 1800s, Barrère and Leland]

Bob Hope marijuana. Rhyming for DOPE. For synonyms see MARI. [British, late 1900s-pres.]

bobo drunk. For synonyms see WOOFLED. [U.S. collegiate, late 1900s, Munro]

bo-bo bush marijuana. [U.S. underworld, mid 1900s]

bob squirt a worthless fellow. Cf. SQUIRT (sense 1). [British, 1800s]

bob tail 1. a lewd woman; a woman who masturbates herself. [British, late 1600s-1800s] **2.** an impotent man; a eunuch. As if his penis had been bobbed. [British, 1800s, *Lexicon Balatronicum*] **3.** the penis. Cf. CUTTY-GUN, SHORT-ARM, TAIL (sense 3). **4.** a worthless oaf; a jerk. [since the early 1600s]

bod 1. a body of any type, living or dead. [U.S., 1900s] **2.** an especially good male or female body. Cf. ANTI-BOD. [U.S. slang, mid 1900s-pres.]

bodacious tatas very impressive

breasts. For synonyms see BOSOM. [U.S. collegiate, late 1900s, Munro]

bodewash buffalo chips; dried cattle dung used for fuel. Also some use as BULLSHIT (*q.v.*). For synonyms see COW-CHIPS. [from the French *bois-de-vache*, literally, "wood from the cow"]

bodice ripper a romantic novel aimed at female readers. [British, late 1900s-pres.]

bod squad a group of attractive males or females in a group. Patterned on *Mod Squad*. [U.S., late 1900s-pres.]

body-naked naked. [U.S., 1800s, Wentworth]

body-packer (also **body-carrier**) someone who does BODY-PACKING by swallowing packets of drugs in order to smuggle them into the U.S. [U.S. drug culture, late 1900s]

body queen a male homosexual who is aroused by men with muscular bodies. See QUEEN for similar topics. [U.S. homosexual use, mid 1900s, Stanley]

body's captain, my a man's penis. From the notion that the male is totally controlled by his sexual urges. [British euphemism, 1800s, Farmer and Henley]

body wax dung; human feces. [U.S., early 1900s]

B.O.F. a "boring old fart." [British, late 1900s-pres.]

boff 1. to obtain sexual relief through copulation. [U.S., 1900s] **2.** to vomit. A disguise of BARF (*q.v.*). For synonyms see YORK. [U.S., 1900s, Wentworth and Flexner] **3.** to masturbate, usually said of a male. [U.S., 1900s] **4.** to punch someone. [U.S., late 1900s-pres.] **5.** to break wind. For synonyms see GURK. [British, late 1900s-pres.] **6.** the buttocks. For synonyms see DUFF. [British, mid 1900s-pres.]

boffed alcohol intoxicated. For synonyms see WOOFLED. [U.S. slang, late 1900s]

boffer 1. a sexually willing girl. For synonyms see BIRD. [British, late 1900s-pres.] **2.** a male who masturbates habitually. [British, late 1900s-pres.]

boffing copulating. For synonyms see SMOCKAGE. [British, late 1900s-pres.]

boffo great; excellent. [late 1900s]

bog 1. a W.C.; a restroom. **2.** to retire to the W.C. **3.** to urinate or use the W.C.; to defile with excrement. [current colloquial use; some senses since the 1500s or 1600s]

Bogart to linger with a marijuana cigarette before passing it on to another person; to get more than one's share of marijuana smoke. From the proper name "Humphrey Bogart," who did this with a tobacco cigarette in a movie. [U.S. drug culture, mid 1900s-pres.]

bog-ignorant very ignorant; stupid. For synonyms see STUPID. [British, late 1900s-pres.]

Bog off! "Go away!" [British, mid 1900s-pres.]

bog queen a gay male who visits public toilets for sex. For synonyms see EPICENE. [U.S., mid 1900s-pres.]

bog-roll a roll of toilet paper. [British, mid 1900s-pres.]

bog seat a toilet seat. [British, late 1900s-pres.]

bog standard boring; typical; normal. [British, late 1900s-pres.]

bog-up 1. to make a mess of things. **2.** a mess. [British, late 1900s-pres.]

bohunk (also **bohak, bohawk, boho**) **1.** any low-class southern European; any immigrant laborer. A blend of "bohemian" and "Hungarian." **2.** any of the languages of low-class southern Europeans. **3.** any stupid or awkward person. [all senses, U.S. slang and colloquial, late 1800s-1900s] **4.** a Caucasian from the point of view of a Negro. See HONKY, HUNK (sense 3). For synonyms see PECKERWOOD.

boiled intoxicated with alcohol. *Cf.* PAR-BOILED. [slang, late 1800s-1900s]

boiled as an owl intoxicated with alcohol. *Cf.* BILED OWL, DRUNK AS A BOILED OWL, OWLED. [British and U.S., late 1800s-1900s]

boiler an unattractive or stupid woman, especially an older one. As with an old hen suitable only for boiling. [British, mid 1900s-pres.]

boilermaker 1. a virile male; a rough caveman. **2.** beer with a shot of whisky in it. **3.** a very hard punch or blow to the body. [all senses, U.S. slang, 1900s]

boiling drunk heavily intoxicated with alcohol. Based on "boiling mad." [U.S. slang, 1900s]

boink to copulate; to COIT someone. For synonyms see OCCUPY. [U.S. slang, late 1900s]

boinkable very sexually attractive. [U.S., late 1900s-pres.]

Bo Jimmy marijuana. For synonyms see MARI. [U.S. drug culture, late 1900s]

B.O. juice a deodorant; an underarm deodorant. [U.S., mid 1900s-pres.]

Bolivian marching powder cocaine. For synonyms see NOSE-CANDY. [U.S. drug culture, late 1900s]

bollix up (also **bollix**) to foul something up; to ball something up. From BALLOCKS (q.v.), but not usually recognized as such. Cf. BALL-UP. [U.S. slang, mid 1900s] Synonyms: ASS UP, BALLIX, BALLS-UP, BALL-UP, BUGGER, BUGGER UP, COCK UP, FRIG-UP, FUCK UP.

bollocky starkers absolutely naked. For synonyms see STARKERS. [British, mid 1900s-pres.]

bolt an erect penis; an erection of the penis. For synonyms see ERECTION. [Australian, mid 1900s-pres.]

bomb-biggity excellent. [U.S., late 1900s-pres.]

bombed 1. intoxicated with alcohol. [U.S. slang, early 1900s-pres.] **2.** drug intoxicated. From sense 1. [U.S. drug culture, mid 1900s-pres.]

bomber (also **bomb**) a thick marijuana cigarette. Cf. TORPEDO. [U.S. drug culture, mid 1900s-pres.]

bombo 1. a cheap wine. [Australian slang, early 1900s] See also BUMBO (sense 3). **2.** the female genitals; the same as BIMBO (sense 3). see BUMBO (sense 1).

bombosity the posteriors. [U.S., early 1900s]

bommy (or **bomby**) excellent; as good as DA BOMB. [U.S., late 1900s-pres.]

bone 1. the FINGER (q.v.). **2.** the penis, especially the erect penis. Cf. HAM-BONE, MARROW-BONE. **3.** a trombone. No negative connotations. **4.** a marijuana cigarette. [all senses, U.S. slang, colloquial, and nonce, 1900s and before] **5.** to COIT someone, presumably a woman. For synonyms see OCCUPY. [U.S. slang, late 1900s]

bone-ache (also **bone-ague**) syphilis. Cf. BONE (sense 2). [late 1500s-1600s]

bone addict a female who is obsessed with copulating with males. Cf. BONE. [U.S. slang, late 1900s]

bone-bender (also **bone-breaker**) a nickname for a physician. For synonyms see DOC. [U.S., 1900s, Wentworth and Flexner]

bone-box 1. a coffin. **2.** an ambulance. Cf. BLOOD-BOX. [both senses, U.S., 1900s] Synonyms: BLOOD-BOX, BLOOD-BUCKET, BLOOD-TUB, BLOOD-WAGON, BONE-BOX, BUCKET OF BLOOD, MEAT-WAGON. **3.** the mouth. [1900s]

bonecrusher crack cocaine. For synonyms see NOSE-CANDY. [U.S., late 1900s-pres.]

boned intoxicated with alcohol. For synonyms see WOOFLED. [British, early 1900s, Dictionary of Slang and Unconventional English]

bone dance copulation; an act of copulation. Cf. BONE. For synonyms see SMOCKAGE. [U.S. collegiate, late 1900s, Eble]

bone dome a protective helmet, as worn by motorcyclists. [British, late 1900s-pres.]

bonehead a stupid-acting person. For synonyms see OAF. [U.S., early 1900s-pres.]

bone-on 1. an erection in "have a bone-on." Cf. BONE (sense 2). For synonyms see ERECTION. **2.** lustful; to be sexually aroused. For synonyms see HUMPY. [both senses, U.S. slang, 1900s and before]

bone-orchard a graveyard. Cf. BONE-YARD, MARBLE ORCHARD. [British and U.S. colloquial, 1900s]

bone out to leave. [U.S., late 1900s-pres.]

boner 1. the erect penis. *Cf.* BONE (sense 2). **2.** a mistake; a silly or serious error. [both senses, U.S. slang, mid 1900s-pres.]

bones crack cocaine. For synonyms see NOSE-CANDY. [U.S., late 1900s-pres.]

bones, on the pregnant. [British slang, 1800s, Farmer and Henley]

bone-yard a cemetery. *Cf.* BONE-ORCHARD, MARBLE ORCHARD. [U.S. colloquial, late 1800s-pres.]

bonfire the penis. *Cf.* BLOWTORCH. [British slang, 1800s, Farmer and Henley]

bong 1. dead. Possibly from an Australian aboriginal language. [attested as Australian Pidgin, 1800s, Barrère and Leland] **2.** a device used in smoking marijuana. Also **bhong.** [U.S. drug culture, 1900s]

bong-breath an annoying person. [U.S. collegiate, late 1900s, Eble]

bongoed (also **bongo, bongo'd**) intoxicated with alcohol. *Cf.* BINGOED. [U.S. slang, mid 1900s-pres.]

bonk to COIT someone, presumably a woman. *Cf.* BOINK. For synonyms see OCCUPY. [British and U.S. slang, late 1900s, McDonald]

bonkers 1. insane; crazy. For synonyms see DAFT. [U.S. slang, 1900s] **2.** slightly intoxicated with alcohol. [British military, early 1900s, Granville]

bonus breast enhancements, including implants. [U.S., late 1900s-pres.]

boo (also **bu**) **1.** marijuana. [U.S. drug culture, early 1900s] **2.** a derogatory nickname for a Negro. From JIGABOO (*q.v.*).

boob 1. a gullible oaf; a bumpkin. A truncation of BOOBY (sense 2). [U.S. slang, early 1900s-pres.] **2.** a breast. See BOOBIES, BOOBS.

boobies (also **boobys**) the human breasts. See the much older form, BUB-BIES. [U.S. slang and colloquial, 1900s]

boobiferous having very large breasts. [U.S., late 1900s-pres.]

boob job a breast augmentation [surgical] operation. [U.S. slang, late 1900s] See also TIT JOB.

boo-boo 1. a derogatory nickname for a Negro. A reduplication of BOO (sense 2). [U.S. slang, 1900s] **2.** the posteriors. [British, 1800s, *Dictionary of Slang and Unconventional English*] **3.** feces; human feces. [primarily juvenile, U.S. colloquial, 1900s] **4.** a testicle. Usually in the plural. [U.S., 1900s (Truman Capote)] **5.** an error. [U.S., mid 1900s-pres.] **6.** the buttocks. For synonyms see DUFF. [British, late 1900s-pres.]

boobs the breasts. *Cf.* BOOBIES, BUB-BIES. [U.S. slang and colloquial, mid 1900s-pres.]

boob tube a woman's tight strapless dress top. [British, late 1900s-pres.]

boody (also **bootie**) **1.** the buttocks. **2.** a young woman with particularly well-proportioned buttocks; women considered sexually. **3.** the female genitals, specifically the vagina. **4.** coition, especially in the expression "get some boody." Senses 1-4 are synonymous with ASS (*q.v.*). **5.** male coition *per anum.* From sense 4. [all senses, U.S. slang, mid 1900s-pres.]

booed and hissed drunk. Rhyming slang for PISSED. For synonyms see WOOFLED. [British, mid 1900s-pres.]

boofa a total JERK; a despised person. Probably related to BUFU. For synonyms see OAF. [U.S. collegiate, late 1900s, Munro]

boofhead an oaf; a fool. For synonyms see OAF. [Australian, mid 1900s-pres.]

booger mucus; a glob of nasal mucus removed from the nose. [1900s if not before]

booger juice cocaine. For synonyms see NOSE-CANDY. [U.S. drug culture, late 1900s]

boogie 1. syphilis. [U.S. slang, mid 1900s, Deak] **2.** a derogatory nickname for a Negro. Also **boog.** [U.S. slang, early 1900s] **3.** nasal mucus; a glob of nasal mucus. [U.S. colloquial, 1900s] Synonyms and related terms: BUBU, BUGABOO, BUGGER, CATARRH,

PHLEGM, SNOB, SNOT, SNOTTER. **4.** to copulate; to have sex. [U.S. slang, originally black use, late 1900s]

boo-hog a very fat girl or woman. [U.S. collegiate, late 1900s, Eble]

booly-dog copulation. For synonyms see SMOCKAGE. [U.S. slang, 1900s or before]

boom-boom 1. a bowel movement. For synonyms see EASEMENT. [U.S. juvenile, 1900s] **2.** copulation; an act of copulation. Possibly nonce. For synonyms see SMOCKAGE. [U.S. slang, late 1900s]

boomin(g) having large BUTTOCKS. [U.S. black use, late 1900s]

boom the census to impregnate a woman. For synonyms see STORK. [British slang, 1900s, *Dictionary of Slang and Unconventional English*]

boon-dagger a virago; a masculine lesbian. *Cf.* BULL-DAGGER, BULLDIKER. [U.S. slang, mid 1900s-pres.]

boor an illiterate oaf or rustic; an uncouth man. For synonyms see OAF. [from Dutch Boer, "peasant"; since the early 1900s]

boosey cock (also **boosy cock**) a drunkard. [British, 1700s-1800s]

boosiasms a woman's breasts. Patterned on *enthusiasm*. For synonyms see BOSOM. [U.S. slang, mid 1900s]

boost to copulate; to COIT someone. Possibly from the general slang sense "to shoplift." For synonyms see OCCUPY. [U.S. collegiate, late 1900s, Munro]

boot 1. an instrument of torture which encases the lower leg. Also **bootikins.** [Scots, late 1500s] **2.** to vomit. For synonyms see YORK. [U.S. slang, mid 1900s, *Current Slang*] **3.** a derogatory nickname for a Negro. A truncation of BOOTLIPS (*q.v.*). [U.S. slang, mid 1900s-pres.]

bootie call an instance of the sexual urge. [U.S., late 1900s-pres.]

bootie drought a lack of sex; a sexual famine; a period of sexual abstinence. *Cf.* BOODY. [U.S. collegiate, late 1900s, Munro]

bootie food food that goes straight to the buttocks. [U.S., late 1900s-pres.]

boot the gong to smoke marijuana. [U.S., mid 1900s-pres.]

booty call sexual arousal. Also BOOTIE CALL. [U.S., late 1900s-pres.]

booze (also **boose, bowse, bowze**) **1.** to drink alcohol; to spree. [since the 1300s] **2.** alcohol; liquor. [since the 1300s; cant by the 1600s; widespread slang, 1800s-pres.] Synonyms, names of specific beverages, and related terms for sense 2: A-BOMB JUICE, ABORTS, ALCHY, AL COHOL, AL K. HALL, ALKI HALL, AMBER FLUID, ANTIFREEZE, APPLE-JACK, AQUA VITAE, ARDENT SPIRITS, BARLEY BROTH, BARLEY JUICE, BARLEY WATER, BATHTUB GIN, BELCH, BELLY-VENGEANCE, BELLY-WASH, BELSH, BERPS, BERPWATER, BEVVY, BITCHES' WINE, BIT OF BLINK, BIVVY, BLOTTO, BLUE BLAZER, BLUE BLAZES, BLUE PIG, BLUE RIBBON, BLUE RUIN, BLUE STONE, BLUE TAPE, BOB, BOILER-MAKER, BOMBO, BOOTLEG, BREAKY-LEG, BRIAN O'LINN, BUB, BUBBLE-WATER, BUBBLY, BUCKET OF SUDS, BUDGE, BUG JUICE, BUMBO, CACTUS JUICE, CANEBUCK, CAPER-JUICE, CATGUT, CAT'S WATER, CHAIN LIGHTNING, CHALK, CHAM, CHILLY, CHOC, CHOKE-DOG, CLAP OF THUNDER, COCK-ALE, COFFIN VARNISH, COLD COFFEE, COLDIE, COLORADO COOLAID, CONK-BUSTER, CORN, CORN-JUICE, CORN-MULE, COUGAR-MILK, CRAZY WATER, DIDDLE, DIDO, DOCTOR, DOCTOR HALL, DONK, DRAFTY, DRAIN, DRUDGE, DUTCH COURAGE, EMBALMING FLUID, EYEWASH, EYE-WATER, FAMILY DISTURBANCE, FAR AND NEAR, FINGER AND THUMB, FIREWATER, FIZZ, FLASH OF LIGHTNING, FOAM, FOGRAM, FOX-HEAD, FROTH, GARGLE, GAS, GATOR SWEAT, GAUGE, GAY AND FRISKY, GIDDY-WATER, GIGGLE GOO, GIGGLE-JUICE, GIGGLE-WATER, GIGGLE G, GOLDEN CREAM, GRAPE(S), GRAPES OF WRATH, GRAVE-DIGGER, GREEK FIRE, GROWLER, GUT-ROT, HAPPY JUICE, HARD LIQUOR, HARD STUFF, HEART STARTER, HIGHLAND FRISKY, HOGWASH, HOOCH, JACK-A-DANDY, JACKY, JOHN BARLEYCORN, JOHN HALL, JOLLOP, JOY JUICE, JOY-WATER, JUICE, JUNGLE-JUICE, JUNIPER-JUICE, KILL-DEVIL, KILL-GRIEF, KINGDOM COME, KNOCK-ME-DOWN, KOOL-

AID, LAGE, LAUGHING SOUP, LIGHT-NING, LIGHT WET, LIQUID AMBER, LIQUID BREAD, LIQUID-FIRE, LIQUOR, LONDON MILK, LOTION, LUBE, LUBRICATION, LUSH, MAX, MEDICINE, MEXICAN MILK, MISERY, MOONSHINE, MOTHER'S MILK, MOUNTAIN-DEW, MUR, MYRRH, NANNY-GOAT SWEAT, NANTZ, NEAR BEER, NECK-OIL, NELSON'S BLOOD, NEVER-FEAR, NIG, NOSE PAINT, O-BE-JOYFUL, OIL OF BARLEY, OLD TOM, PAIN-KILLER, PALEFACE, PANTHER JUICE, PANTHER PISS, PANTHER PIZEN, PANTHER SWEAT, PHYSIC, PIG'S EAR!, PIG SWEAT, PINE-TOP, PISH, PISS, PISS-MAKER, PIZEN, PLINK, PLONK, PLUCK, PONG, PONGELOW, POP-SKULL, POTATO SOUP, PRAIRIE-DEW, PRECIOUS JUICE, PRUNE JUICE, PURGE, QUEER BEER, RAG-WATER, RED-EYE, RED NED, REEB, RIGHT-SORT, ROT-GUT, ROTTO, RUIN, SATIN, SAUCE, SCAMPER JUICE, SCOOCH, SCREECH, SHAM, SHAMPOO, SHEEPWASH, SHICKER, SHINE, SILKEN TWINE, SILLY MILK, SILO DRIPPINGS, SISSY BEER, SKEE, SKIT, SKY, SKY BLUE, SLOSH, SNAKE, SNAKEBITE MEDICINE, SNAKE-JUICE, SNAKE MEDICINE, SNAKE-POISON, SPIRITS, SPIRITUS FRUMENTI, SQUAW PISS, STAGGER-JUICE, STAGGER-SOUP, STAGGER-WATER, STARK NAKED, STINGO, STINKIBUS, STINKIOUS, STREAK OF LIGHTNING, STRIP-ME-NAKED, STRONG AND THIN, STRONG WATERS, STUMP-LIKKER, SUCK, SUDS, SUGAR-CANDY, SUPER SUDS, SWIG, SWILL, SWIPES, SWIZZLE, TANGLEFOOT, TANGLE-LEG, TAPE, TARANTULA-JUICE, TEA, THE DEMON RUM, THIMBLE AND THUMB, TICKLE-BRAIN, TIGER JUICE, TIGER MILK, TIGER PISS, TIGER SWEAT, TINNIE, TIPPLE, TITLEY, TITTERY, TOM THUMB, TONSIL BATH, TONSIL PAINT, TWANKAY, UNSWEETENED, VARNISH-REMOVER, WANKS, WATER OF LIFE, WHISTLE-BELLY VENGEANCE, WHITE, WHITE COFFEE, WHITE LIGHTNING, WHITE LINE, WHITE MULE, WHITE PORT, WHITE SATIN, WHITE STUFF, WHITE TAPE, WHITE VELVET, WHITEWASH, WHITE WINE, WHOOPEE-WATER, WILD MARE'S MILK, WITCH-PISS, WHOOZLE-WATER, YARD OF SATIN.

boozeblind intoxicated with alcohol. *Cf.* BLIND DRUNK.

booze bus a police van used for ran-dom breath-testing for alcohol use. [Australian, mid 1900s-pres.]

boozed (also **boozed-up, bowzed**) in-toxicated with alcohol. [widespread slang, mid 1800s-pres.]

booze-fighter a drunkard; an alco-holic. [Australian and U.S. 1900s]

booze-freak a drunkard. [U.S., slang, mid 1900s-pres.]

boozefuddle liquor; alcohol. A play on "befuddle," meaning "confuse." [U.S. dialect, 1900s or before]

boozegob a drunkard. "Gob" is a cant word for "mouth." [U.S. slang, 1900s, Weseen]

booze-hound a drunkard; a heavy drinker. [U.S. slang, early 1900s-pres.]

booze-hustler a bootlegger; a seller of illegal alcohol during Prohibition. [U.S. slang, early 1900s]

booze-king a drunkard. [Australian, 1900s, Baker]

boozer (also **bouser**) **1.** a drunkard. [since the 1500s or before] **2.** a tavern; a saloon. [British slang, late 1800s, Ware]

boozician a drunkard. For synonyms see ALCHY. [Australian, 1900s, Baker]

boozington a drunkard; the same as LUSHINGTON (*q.v.*). [Australian and British, 1800s-1900s]

boozle coition. For synonyms see SMOCKAGE. [mid 1900s, *Dictionary of Slang and Unconventional English*]

boozy (also **boosy, bousey, bousy, bowsy**) intoxicated with alcohol. [since the early 1500s]

bop 1. copulation; an act of copula-tion. For synonyms see SMOCKAGE. [U.S. slang, late 1900s] **2.** to COIT some-one, presumably a woman. For syn-onyms see OCCUPY. [U.S. slang, late 1900s] **3.** a drug or narcotic in pill form; a dose of a drug. [U.S. drug cul-ture, late 1900s] **4.** to masturbate. Said of the male. *Cf.* SHE-BOP. For synonyms and related subjects see WASTE TIME. [U.S. slang, late 1900s]

bop one's baloney (also **bop the bologna**) to masturbate. Said of the male. *Cf.* BOP. For synonyms and related subjects see WASTE TIME. [U.S. slang, late 1900s]

bopped copulated with; LAID. [U.S. slang, late 1900s]

bore 1. the female genitals, specifically the vagina. *Cf.* CYLINDER, PISTON ROD. **2.** to copulate. [both senses, British slang, 1800s, Farmer and Henley]

boring old fart any older person, especially a male. B.O.F. [British, mid 1900s-pres.]

bosh to copulate [with] a woman. For synonyms see OCCUPY. [British, late 1900s-pres.]

boshy intoxicated with alcohol. From BOSKY (*q.v.*), pronounced as if one were intoxicated. [British underworld, early 1900s, *Dictionary of the Underworld*]

bosiasm the bosom; a woman's breasts. [U.S. slang, mid 1900s-pres.]

bosko absoluto intoxicated with alcohol. *Cf.* BOSKY. [mock-Latin; British (Kipling)]

bosky almost drunk; nearly intoxicated with alcohol. From "bosk," a thicket. *Cf.* BOSHY. [slang since the early 1700s]

Bosnia an erection. For synonyms see ERECTION. [U.S., late 1900s-pres.]

bosom 1. the breasts. Also **bosoms.** [U.S. euphemism, 1800s-1900s] Synonyms: APPLE DUMPLING SHOP, APPLES, APPURTENANCES, BABALOOS, BABY PILLOWS, BABY'S PUBLIC HOUSE, BAGS, BALCONY, BALLOONS, BALOOBAS, BANGLES, BAPS, BAZONGAS, BAZONKERS, BAZOOMS, BAZOONGIES, BEAUSOM, BEAUTS, BEE-BITES, BEEF CURTAINS, BEGONIAS, BEJONKERS, BERKS, BEZONGAS, BIG BROWN EYES, BIKINI STUFFERS, BLUBBERS, BOBBERS, BODACIOUS TATAS, BOOBIES, BOOBS, BOOSIASMS, BOSIASM, BOSOMS, BOULDERS, BOUNCERS, BRA-BUSTER, BREASTWORKS, BREESTS, BRISTOL CITIES, BRISTOLS, BUBBIES, BUBBLES, BUCKETS, BUFFERS, BULBS, BUMPERS, BUMPS, BUST, BUTTER-BAGS, BUTTER-BOXES, CABMAN'S RESTS, CANS, CAT AND KITTIES, CAT HEADS, CATS AND KITTIES, CHARLIES, CHARMS, CHE-CHEES, CHEST AND BEDDING, CHESTNUTS, CHESTY, CHUBBIES, COKER-NUTS, CREAMJUGS, CUPCAKE, DAIRIES, DIDDIES, DIGS, DINNERS, DROOPERS, DUBBIES, DUMPLINGS, DUMPLING-SHOP, EAST AND WEST, EASTS AND WESTS, EYES, FAINTING FITS, FEEDING-BOTTLES, FIGURE, FLIGHT DECK, FLIP-FLAPS, FORE-BUTTOCKS, FRANKENTITS, FRIED EGGS, FRONT, FUNBAGS, GARBANZOS, GAZONGAS, GAZUNGAS, GLOBES, GOONAS, GRAPEFRUITS, GRAPES, GROWTHS, HANDS, HAND-WARMERS, HANGERS, HEADLIGHTS, HEMISPHERES, HOGANS, HOG JAWS, HONEYDEW MELONS, HONKERS, HOOTERS, JAMBOREE BAGS, JELLY-ON-SPRINGS, JERSEY CITIES, JUBBIES, JUBLIES, JUGS, JUJUBES, KAJOOBIES, KETTLEDRUMS, KNOCKERS, LEMONS, LEWIS AND WITTIES, LOLLOS, LOVE-BUBBLES, LOVE TIPS, LUNGS, LUNG WARTS, MAE WEST, MAMMETS, MANCHESTER CITY, MANCHESTERS, MARACAS, MARSHMALLOWS, MASOB, MEAT, MEAT-MARKET, MELONS, MILK-BAR, MILK-BOTTLES, MILKERS, MILKSHOP, MILK-WALK, MILKY-WAY, MOSQUITO BITES, MOUNTAINS, MOUNT OF LILIES, MUFFINS, MURPHIES, NATURE'S FONTS, NICK-NACKS, NINNIES, NINNY-JUGS, NORGIES, NORMA SNOCKERS, NUBBIES, NUGGETS, OOJAHS, ORANGES, OTHER PARTS, PAIR, PANTERS, PANTRY SHELVES, PAPS, PEACHES, PELLETS, PIGGIES, PLAYGROUND, PRIZE FAGGOTS, PUMPS, RACK, RACKS, RIB CUSHIONS, RIPPLES FOR NIPPLES, SACKS, SHOCK ABSORBERS, SNORBS, STONKERS, STRUCTURAL ENGINEERING, SUPERDROOPERS, SWEATER FULL, SWINGERS, TEACUPS, THE PERSON, THOUSAND PITTIES, THREEPENNY BITS, TIG BITTIES, TITSKIS, TONSILS, TOP, TOP BALLOCKS, TOP ONES, TORALOORALS, TORPEDO, TOWNS AND CITIES, TREASURE, TREMBLERS, TREY BITS, TWIN LOVELINESS, TWINS, UDDER, UPPER-DECK, UPPER-WORKS, VEILED TWINS, VOOS, WALLOPIES, WAMMERS, WARTS, WATERMELONS, WHAMDANGLERS, WHAMMERS. **2.** a woman's upper thorax; the bust. **3.** the center of one's feelings.

bosom chums 1. lice. For synonyms see WALKING DANDRUFF. [British and U.S., 1900s] **2.** rats. [U.S. slang, early 1900s, Rose]

bosom friend 1. a louse. Usually in the plural. *Cf.* BOSOM CHUMS. [British, 1700s] **2.** alcohol. [U.S. slang, 1900s]

bosom of the pants the posteriors.

Cf. FORE-BUTTOCKS. [U.S. slang, mid 1900s]

boss excellent. [U.S., late 1900s-pres.]

boss pimp a powerful pimp with a large collection of prostitutes. [U.S. prostitute's argot, James]

botch to release intestinal gas with fluid, causing a stain. For synonyms see GURK. [U.S. collegiate, late 1900s, Munro]

botcher a wet release of intestinal gas that stains. For synonyms see GURK. [U.S. collegiate, late 1900s, Munro]

both sheets in the wind intoxicated with alcohol. *Cf.* THREE SHEETS IN THE WIND, TWO SHEETS TO THE WIND. [U.S. and elsewhere, 1900s and before]

bottle-ache 1. a hangover. See WINE-ACHE. [British and U.S., 1800s-1900s] **2.** the DELIRIUM TREMENS (*q.v.*). [British slang, 1800s, Farmer and Henley]

bottle and glass the anus; the posteriors. Rhyming slang for "ass." [slang, 1900s]

bottled intoxicated with alcohol. For synonyms see WOOFLED. [British and U.S., 1900s]

bottle-sucker a drunkard. [British and U.S. slang, 1800s-early 1900s]

bottom 1. the buttocks. [British and U.S. colloquial euphemism since the 1700s] **2.** the female genitals; the female genital area including the PERINEUM (*q.v.*). [colloquial, 1900s or before]

bottomless-pit 1. the female genitals, specifically the vagina. *Cf.* DEAD-END STREET, HELL (sense 2). [British and later, U.S., early 1800s-pres.] **2.** hell. [usually attributed to a Biblical source (Revelations); British and U.S. euphemism]

bottoms a nickname for a catamite. For synonyms see BRONCO. [U.S. slang, mid 1900s-pres.]

bottom's up 1. copulation wherein the male enters the vagina from the rear. **2.** anal heterosexual copulation. From the drinking toast. [both senses, U.S. slang, 1900s]

botty boy a pederast. For synonyms see PEDERAST. [British, mid 1900s-pres.]

boulder a big piece of crack cocaine. For synonyms see NOSE-CANDY. [U.S., late 1900s-pres.]

boulders breasts, especially large or pendulous breasts. *Cf.* OVER-THE-SHOULDER-BOULDER-HOLDER. [U.S. slang, 1900s]

bounce 1. to copulate with a woman; to coit a woman. [slang, late 1800s-1900s] **2.** to leave; to depart. [U.S., late 1900s-pres.]

bounce refrigerators to copulate. As if the motion would shake the furniture. [U.S. collegiate, late 1900s, Eble]

bouncers the breasts, especially if large and active. For synonyms see BOSOM. [British slang and probably nonce elsewhere, 1900s, McDonald]

bouncing-powder cocaine. Because it makes you HIGH (sense 2). [nonce, early 1900s, *Dictionary of the Underworld*]

bouquet of ass-holes something extremely contemptible; an excess of something extremely contemptible. [U.S. slang, 1900s]

bovine excrement 1. cattle dung. **2.** a jocular euphemism for BULLSHIT (*q.v.*). [both senses, U.S. slang, mid 1900s]

bovine excrescence the same as BOVINE EXCREMENT (*q.v.*).

bovril nonsense; BULLSHIT (*q.v.*). From the brand name of a beef extract. [Australian, early 1900s, Baker]

bow the penis. For playing the FIDDLE (sense 2), the vagina. *Cf.* FIDDLE-BOW. [slang, 1800s-1900s]

bowel movement 1. an act of defecation. For synonyms see EASEMENT. **2.** feces; human feces. Both are abbreviated "B.M." [both senses, U.S. euphemism, 1900s]

bowel off to have diarrhea. [U.S. dialect (Ozarks), Randolph and Wilson]

bowling pin an obese female shaped like a bowling pin. [U.S. black use, late 1900s]

bow to the porcelain altar (also **bow to the porcelain god**) to vomit.

For synonyms see YORK. [U.S. slang, late 1900s]

bow-wow an ugly person; a DOG of a person. Usually in reference to a woman. [U.S. slang, late 1900s]

box 1. coffin. [U.S., 1800s and probably before] **2.** the female genitals, specifically the vagina. [widespread slang, 1900s] **3.** the male or female genitals. [U.S. homosexual use, mid 1900s] **4.** the male genitals, especially as made visible in revealing clothing. Cf. BASKET (sense 3). [U.S. homosexual use, mid 1900s, Farrell] **5.** to copulate with a woman. [U.S. slang, mid 1900s-pres.]

box, in copulating; having the penis in the vagina. Cf. BOX (sense 2). [U.S. slang, mid 1900s]

boxed dead; died. For synonyms see DONE FOR. [U.S. slang, late 1900s]

boxed on the table died on the table. Said of a patient who has died on the operating table. For synonyms see DONE FOR. [U.S. medical slang, late 1900s]

boxed-up (also **boxed**) **1.** intoxicated with alcohol. [U.S. slang, mid 1900s, Wentworth and Flexner] **2.** drug intoxicated. From sense 1. [U.S. drug culture, mid 1900s-pres.]

boxing copulation. For synonyms see SMOCKAGE. [U.S., late 1900s-pres.]

box lunch CUNNILINGUS (q.v.). Based on the colloquial term for a picnic lunch. Cf. BOX (sense 2). [U.S. slang, mid 1900s-pres.]

boxmaster a male who is a good sexual partner. [U.S., late 1900s-pres.]

box tonsils to kiss deeply. Cf. GIVE SOMEONE A TONSILLECTOMY. [U.S. collegiate, late 1900s, Eble]

box-unseen the female genitals. Cf. BOX (sense 2). [vague references from *All's Well That Ends Well* (Shakespeare)]

boy 1. a derogatory term for a Negro male of any age. [U.S. 1800s-1900s] **2.** a catamite. [U.S. underworld, mid 1900s] **3.** heroin. Cf. GIRL (sense 9). [U.S. drug culture, mid 1900s-pres.] **4.** an effeminate male homosexual. Similar to sense 2. [U.S. slang, 1900s, Went-

worth and Flexner] **5.** a masculine woman. Cf. TOM (sense 6). For synonyms see AMAZON. [U.S., 1900s, Berrey and Van den Bark]

boy-in-the-boat the clitoris. Cf. LITTLE MAN IN THE BOAT, TALK TO THE CANOE DRIVER. [British, 1800s, *Dictionary of Slang and Unconventional English*]

boys in blue, the the police. For synonyms see FLATFOOT. [Australian, mid 1900s-pres.]

bozack the penis. For synonyms see YARD. [U.S., late 1900s-pres.]

bra a brassiere. [U.S. colloquial, early 1900s-pres.] Synonyms: BRASSIERE, DOUBLE-BARRELLED CATAPULT, DOUBLE-BARRELLED SLING-SHOT, FLOPPER-STOPPER, FRONT-SUSPENSION, HAMMOCK FOR TWO, OVER-THE-SHOULDER-BOULDER-HOLDER, SOUNDPROOF BRA, TIT-BAG, TIT-HAMMOCK.

bra-burner a nickname for a woman who supported the women's liberation movement of the 1960s and 1970s. [British and U.S., late 1900s-pres.]

bra-buster 1. a shapely female; a woman with large or extremely large breasts. [U.S. slang, mid 1900s-pres.] **2.** a very large breast. Usually plural. For synonyms see BOSOM. [U.S. slang, 1900s]

brace and bit a girl; woman considered sexually. Rhyming slang for TIT (sense 2). [U.S., 1900s, *Dictionary of Rhyming Slang*]

Brahms and Liszt drunk. Rhyming slang on PISSED. For synonyms see WOOFLED. [British, mid 1900s-pres.]

brain bucket a bike or motorcycle helmet. [U.S., late 1900s-pres.]

brain-dead stupid. [U.S. slang, late 1900s]

Brainfart! said when blanking out and forgetting; said when one is BRAIN-DEAD. [U.S. collegiate, late 1900s, Munro]

brainiac a studious student. [U.S., late 1900s-pres.]

brains fellatio. Akin to HEAD. [U.S., late 1900s-pres.]

brakes the female pubic hair. "Brakes"

refers to a thicket. [double entendre from *A Midsummer Night's Dream* (Shakespeare)]

brandle to masturbate. From a term meaning "shake." [early 1600s]

brass nail a prostitute. Rhyming slang for TAIL (sense 6). [British, early 1900s, *Dictionary of Rhyming Slang*]

brass nob a prostitute. Possibly rhyming slang for JOB (sense 2 or 3). [British, early 1900s, *Dictionary of the Underworld*]

brat-getting place the female genitals. For synonyms see MONOSYLLABLE. [British slang, 1800s, Farmer and Henley]

bread the female genitals. *Cf.* BUN (sense 3), JELLY-ROLE (sense 1), YEAST-POWDER BISCUIT. [U.S. slang, 1900s, Wentworth and Flexner]

bread-basket the belly; the stomach. [since the mid 1700s]

bread-winner the female genitals, specifically the vagina. [British prostitute's slang, 1800s, Farmer and Henley]

break a lance with to copulate with a woman. *Cf.* LANCE. [British slang, 1800s, *Dictionary of Slang and Unconventional English*]

break a leg 1. to get pregnant; to get seduced and pregnant. **2.** to copulate with a woman. [both senses, U.S. slang, late 1800s-early 1900s, Barrère and Leland]

break one's ass (to do something) See BUST (ONE'S) ASS (TO DO SOMETHING).

break one's balls (also **bust one's nuts**) to suffer adversity or discomfort to accomplish something. *Cf.* BALL-BUSTER. [U.S. slang, mid 1900s-pres.]

break someone's balls to wreck or ruin someone; to overwork someone; to overwhelm someone, usually a male. [U.S. slang, late 1900s]

break up 1. to separate; to divorce; to cease going steady. **2.** a separation; a divorce. Usually hyphenated when used as a noun. [U.S. colloquial, mid 1900s-pres.] Synonyms and related terms for both senses: DEWIFE, GREAT DIVIDE, HOLY DEADLOCK, MATCHRUPT-CY, RENOVATE, SPLIT THE BLANKETS, SPLIT UP.

breed to copulate; to have sex. For synonyms see OCCUPY. [U.S., late 1900s-pres.]

breeder an adult heterosexual person who may be of a mind to have children, as opposed to a homosexual. In a homosexual context. [U.S. slang, late 1900s]

breeze a release of intestinal gas. For synonyms see GURK. [U.S. slang, 1900s]

breezer a breaking of wind; a BREEZE. For synonyms see GURK. [U.S. slang, 1900s]

breezy intoxicated with alcohol. Refers to the drinker's alcohol-laden breath. [U.S. slang, mid 1800s, Wentworth and Flexner]

brew dog a beer. [U.S. collegiate, late 1900s, Eble]

brew dogger a beer drinker; a beer drunkard. For synonyms see ALCHY. [U.S. collegiate, late 1900s, Eble]

brewed alcohol intoxicated. For synonyms see WOOFLED. [U.S. slang, late 1900s]

brewer's droop impotence brought on by too much alcohol. [British slang, 1900s if not before, J. Green] See also WHISKY DICK.

brew-ha (also **brew-ha-ha**) beer; a beer. [U.S. slang, late 1900s]

brew-hound a heavy drinker; a prodigious beer-drinker. For synonyms see ALCHY. [U.S. slang, late 1900s]

brews brothers beer-drinking college boys. Based on the movie *The Blues Brothers*. [U.S. slang, late 1900s]

brewski (also **brewsky**) a beer; a can of beer. [U.S. slang, late 1900s]

brewster 1. a beer drinker; a beer drunkard. For synonyms see ALCHY. [U.S. slang, late 1900s] **2.** beer; a can of beer. [U.S. collegiate, late 1900s, Eble]

brick 1. opium. [U.S. underworld, early 1900s] **2.** a pound or a kilogram of marijuana molded in the shape of a brick. *Cf.* KEY, KI [U.S. drug culture, mid 1900s-pres.]

brickhouse a full-breasted, well-shaped woman. From BUILT LIKE A BRICK SHIT-HOUSE. [U.S. collegiate, late 1900s]

brickies the cleavage at the top of the buttocks appearing when a man bends over and his pants scoot down. [Australian, late 1900s-pres.]

bridgey intoxicated with alcohol. [U.S. slang, early 1700s, Ben Franklin]

bright 1. a dandy; a fop. See BLOOD (sense 1). **2.** a mulatto. A truncation of BRIGHT MULATTO (q.v.). For synonyms see MAHOGANY. [U.S. slang, 1800s-1900s]

brightened drug intoxicated; HIGH on marijuana. Cf. ON THE BEAM. For synonyms see TALL. [U.S. drug culture, late 1900s, Kaiser]

bright in the eye tipsy; intoxicated with alcohol. [British slang, late 1800s, Farmer and Henley]

bright mulatto an OCTOROON or a QUADROON. Cf. BRIGHT (sense 2). [U.S., 1900s, Berrey and Van den Bark]

Brighton Pier a homosexual male. Rhyming slang for "queer." For synonyms see EPICENE. [British slang, early 1900s, *Dictionary of Slang and Unconventional English*]

bring down by hand to abate an erection by masturbating to ejaculation, accomplished by oneself or someone else. The opposite of BRING UP BY HAND (q.v.). Cf. BRING OFF BY HAND, TAKE DOWN. [British slang, 1800s, Farmer and Henley]

bring off by hand to cause orgasm in oneself or another person by masturbation. [British, 1800s]

bring out to introduce or initiate (someone) into homosexual activities; to cause someone to COME OUT OF THE CLOSET (q.v.). Cf. DAUGHTER, MOTHER (sense 3). [U.S. homosexual use, mid 1900s-pres., Stanley]

bring someone off to induce an orgasm in someone. [British, mid 1900s-pres.]

bring someone on to excite someone sexually. [British, mid 1900s-pres.]

bring up 1. to vomit; to vomit some-thing. **2.** to cough up something, as in "bring up blood." [both senses, U.S. colloquial, 1900s or before]

bring up by hand to produce an erection (one's own or someone else's) through manual stimulation. A play on the expression describing the careful nurturing of a living thing. Cf. BRING DOWN BY HAND. [British slang, 1800s, Farmer and Henley]

Bristol cities (also **Bristol city**) the human breasts. Rhyming slang for "tit-ties," usually seen as BRISTOLS (q.v.). Cf. JERSEY CITIES, MANCHESTER CITY. For synonyms see BOSOM. [British slang, early 1900s-pres.]

Bristols the human breasts. From BRISTOL CITIES (q.v.). Cf. MANCHES-TERS. [British slang, early 1900s-pres.]

britton peyote. [U.S., late 1900s-pres.]

Brixton briefcase a ghettoblaster. [British, late 1900s-pres.]

broad 1. a mistress or a prostitute. [U.S. underworld use and general slang, early 1900s-pres.] **2.** any woman. Mildly derogatory. [U.S. slang, mid 1900s-pres.]

broad-jumper 1. a rapist. Cf. BROAD (sense 2), JUMP. [early 1900s] **2.** a thief who leaves (jumps out on) his woman; a jilter. [U.S. underworld, early 1900s]

broccoli marijuana. For synonyms see MARI. [U.S. drug culture, mid 1900s-pres.]

broiler an attractive female; a sexually tempting or seductive female. Based on the "heat" of passion and on a "broiler" chicken. From CHICK (sense 1). [U.S. slang, early 1900s, Berrey and Van den Bark]

broke high on marijuana. For syn-onyms see TALL. [U.S., late 1900s-pres.]

broken her teacup to have been de-flowered. See DEFLOWER. Cf. CRACK A JUDY'S TEACUP. [British euphemism, 1800s, Farmer and Henley]

broken oar a prostitute. Rhyming slang for "whore." Cf. BOAT AND OAR. [British, 1900s, *Dictionary of Rhyming Slang*]

broken-rib a divorced woman. *Cf.* RIB, SPARE RIB.

broken-wrist a homosexual male; the same as LIMP-WRIST (*q.v.*). For synonyms see EPICENE. [U.S. slang, mid 1900s-pres.]

bronco (also **bronc, bronk**) a CATAMITE (*q.v.*). [from a Spanish word for a "rough" horse; U.S. underworld, early 1900s, Monteleone] Synonyms: ANGELINA, AUNT, BALL AND CHAIN, BENDER, BIMBO, BINDLE-BOY, BITCH, BO, BOONG-MOLL, BOTTOMS, BOXER, BOY, BRAT, BROWN, BRUNSER, BUM-BOY, CATCH, CHERRY-PICKER, CHUFF, CINAEDUS, COMFORT FOR THE TROOPS, FAG, FAIRY, FRUIT, GAL-BOY, GANYMEDE, GASH, GAY-CAT, GAZOOK, GAZOONEY, GAZOONY, GINCH, GONSEL, HAT, HIDE, HUMP, INGLE, KID LAMB, KIFE, LAMB, LAY, LILYWHITE, LITTLE LADY, MALE VARLET, MASCULINE WHORE, MISS NANCY, MUSTARD-POT, NAN-BOY, NANCE, NEPHEW, NIGH ENOUGH, ONE OF THE BROWN FAMILY, ONE OF THOSE, PAINTED-WILLIE, PANSY, PASSIVE PARTICIPANT, PATHIC, PEDDLE-SNATCH, PEG BOY, PIECE OF SNATCH, PINK PANTS, POGER, POSSESH, POUFTER, PRESHEN, PRUSHUN, PUNCE, PUNK, PUNK KID, RECEIVER, RING-TAIL, RING-TAIL WIFE, ROAD KID, ROUNDEYE, SNATCH-PEDDLER, TRUG, TWIDGET, WIFE, WILLIE, YOUTHFUL VICTIM OF DEGENERATE.

broom-handle (also **broomstick**) the penis. *Cf.* BROOM (sense 1). [harlot's use (Farmer and Henley); British slang, 1800s]

brotel a hotel that is also a BROTHEL. For synonyms see BROTHEL. [U.S. slang, 1900s, DeSola]

brothel a house of prostitution; a place where prostitutes perform their services; a brothelhouse. Originally a good-for-nothing man (1300s), and then a prostitute (1400s). Now used in the "house" sense exclusively. Currently the U.S. polite word-of-choice for this topic. These synonyms refer to female brothels unless indicated otherwise: ACADEMY, ACCOMMODATION HOUSE, ASSIGNATION HOUSE, BAGNIO, BAG-SHANTY, BAND, BAND-BOX, BANDHOUSE, BANG, BAT HOUSE, BAWD'S HOUSE, BAWDYHOUSE, BEAUTY PARLOR, BEAVER BASE, BED-HOUSE, BERKER, BIRD-CAGE, BODIKIN, BORDEL, BORDELLO, BROTEL, BROTHEL-HOUSE, BULL-RING CAMP (male), BUTTON-HOLE FACTORY, CAB, CAB-JOINT, CAKE-SHOP, CALL-HOUSE, CAMP, CAN HOUSE, CASA, CAT-FLAT, CAT-HOUSE, CAVAULTING SCHOOL, CHAMBER OF COMMERCE, CHIPPY-HOUSE, CHIPPY-JOINT, CORINTH, COUPLING-HOUSE, COW-BAG, CREEP-JOINT, CRIB, CRIB-HOUSE, DIRTY SPOT, DISORDERLY HOUSE, DIVE, DOSS, DOSS HOUSE, DRESS-HOUSE, DRUM, FANCY HOUSE, FAST HOUSE, FISH-MARKET, FLASH-CASE, FLASH-CRIB, FLASH-DRUM, FLASH-HOUSE, FLASH-KEN, FLASH-PANNY, FLEA AND LOUSE, FLESH-FACTORY, FLESH-MARKET, FLESH-POT, FLESH-SHAMBLES, FORNIX, FRANZY HOUSE, FUCKERY, FUCK-HOUSE, GARDEN-HOUSE, GAY HOUSE, GIRLERY, GIRL SHOP, GOAT-HOUSE, GOOSEBERRY-RANCH, GOOSING-RANCH, GOOSING-SLUM, GRINDING-HOUSE, HEIFER BARN, HEIFER DEN, H. OF I.F., HOOK-SHOP, HOT-HOLE, HOT-HOUSE, HOUSE IN THE SUBURBS, HOUSE OF ALL NATIONS, HOUSE OF ASSIGNATION, HOUSE OF CALL, HOUSE OF CIVIL RECEPTION, HOUSE OF ENJOYMENT, HOUSE OF ILL-DELIGHT, HOUSE OF ILL-FAME, HOUSE OF ILL-REPUTE, HOUSE OF JOY, HOUSE OF LEWDNESS, HOUSE OF PROFESSION, HOUSE OF RESORT, HOUSE OF SALE, HUMMUMS, ICE PALACE, JACKSIE, JAG-HOUSE (male), JAZZ JOINT, JOINT, JOY HOUSE, JUKE-HOUSE, KIP, KIP SHOP, KNOCKING-HOUSE, KNOCKING-JOINT, KNOCKING-SHOP, LADIES' COLLEGE, LEAPING-HOUSE, LEWD HOUSE, LOOSE-LOVE CENTER, LUPANAR, MEAT HOUSE, MOLL-SHOP, MOLLY-HOUSE (male), MONKEY-HOUSE, NANNY-HOUSE, NANNY-SHOP, NAUGHTY-HOUSE, NAUTCH-JOINT, NOTCHERY, NOTCH-HOUSE, NOTCH-JOINT, NUGGING-HOUSE, NUGGING-KEN, NUNNERY, OCCUPYING-HOUSE, ONERY-HOUSE, PARLOR HOUSE, PEG-HOUSE (male), PHEASANTRY, POON-TANG PALACE, PUNCH-HOUSE, PUSHING SCHOOL, RED LAMP, RED LIGHT, RED-LIGHT HOUSE, RIB-JOINT, SCHOOL OF VENUS, SERAGLIETTO, SERAGLIO, SHANTY, SLAUGHTER-HOUSE, SLUT HUT, SMOONGY, SMUGGLING-KEN, SNAKE RANCH, SNOOZING-KEN, SPINTRY (male), SPORTER, SPORTING-HOUSE, SPORTING-TAVERN, STEW, TEMPLE OF VENUS, THE STEWS, TIMOTHY, TOUCH-CRIB, TRUG-

GLING-KEN, VAULTING-HOUSE, VAULTING-SCHOOL, VROW-CASE, WALK-UP, WARM SHOP, WARREN, WHOREHOUSE, WHORE-SHOP, WINDOW TAPPERY, WOPSHOP.

brothel sprouts a venereal disease, especially GONORRHEA. Jocular and contrived. [U.S. slang, late 1900s, Lewin and Lewin]

brother 1. heroin. *Cf.* BOY (sense 3). [U.S. drug culture, mid 1900s-pres.] **2.** a black man. A term of address used by blacks. *Cf.* BLOOD (sense 2). [U.S. slang, mid 1900s-pres.]

brother Ben an amphetamine, Benzedrine. See CO-PILOT BEN. [U.S. drug culture, mid 1900s-pres.]

brown 1. the anus. A truncation of "brown asshole" or similar expression. [British and U.S., 1800s-1900s] **2.** to perform anal intercourse as a receiver or an insertor. [U.S., 1900s or before] **3.** a CATAMITE (*q.v.*). [U.S. underworld, early 1900s, Goldin, O'Leary, and Lipsius] **4.** pertaining to the anus or to human feces. [U.S., 1900s] Senses 1-4 refer to the color of feces. **5.** a Mexican or a Puerto Rican. Derogatory. [U.S. slang, mid 1900s-pres.] **6.** heroin. *Cf.* BROWN SUGAR (sense 2). [U.S. drug culture, mid 1900s-pres.] **7.** a mulatto. Derogatory. [U.S., 1900s] **8.** to butter someone up in order to win a favor. [British, late 1900s-pres.]

brown bag it to copulate with someone so ugly that it can only be accomplished by putting a bag over the other person's head. For synonyms see OCCUPY. [U.S., late 1900s-pres.]

brown bag special a woman with an ugly face and a sexually attractive body. [U.S., late 1900s-pres.]

brown bottle flu a hangover or other sickness from drinking. [U.S. journalistic slang, late 1900s]

brown boy a male who obtains sexual gratification through COPROPHILIA (*q.v.*). See FECAL-FREAK, KITCHEN-CLEANER, POUND-CAKE QUEEN. [U.S. slang, mid 1900s-pres.]

brown bread dead. Rhyming slang. For synonyms see DONE FOR. [British, late 1900s-pres.]

brown-eye 1. (also **eye**) anal copulation; an act of anal copulation. Usually said of males. *Cf.* BROWN (sense 2). [U.S. slang, 1900s] **2.** to flash one's rump and anus. [Australian, late 1900s-pres.]

brown-eyed mullet a fecal mass floating in the sea. For synonyms see DUNG. [Australian, mid 1900s-pres.]

brown-hatter a pederast. *Cf.* BROWN (sense 2), BUD SALLOGH. [British naval slang, early 1900s, *Dictionary of Slang and Unconventional English*]

brown hole 1. to commit or permit anal sexual intercourse. [both homosexual and heterosexual use] **2.** anal copulation; pederasty. For synonyms see SODOMY. [both senses, U.S. slang, mid 1900s]

brownie 1. ECSTASY, a hallucinogen similar to L.S.D. [U.S., late 1900s-pres.] **2.** a male homosexual. For synonyms see EPICENE. [British, late 1900s-pres.]

brown-noser a sycophant; one who flatters for self-serving motives. [British and U.S., mid 1900s-pres.]

brownie queen a pederast; the "passive" partner; a RECEIVER (*q.v.*). *Cf.* BROWNIE KING. [U.S. homosexual use, mid 1900s, Farrell]

browning copulating anally. *Cf.* BROWN (sense 2). [U.S. homosexual use, 1900s]

brown-job ANILINGUS (*q.v.*). *Cf.* ANILINGISM, EAT POUND-CAKE, REAM, RIM, RIM-JOB, TONGUE-FUCK.

brown-jock See BLACK-JOCK.

brown-nose 1. to curry favor; to be a sycophant. **2.** a sycophant. Both refer to the BROWN (sense 4) of feces. *Cf.* BROWN-TONGUE. [both senses, U.S. slang, 1900s]

browns amphetamines. Both Benzedrine (trademark) and Dexedrine (trademark) are sold in capsules which are half brown and half some other color. [U.S. drug culture, mid 1900s-pres.]

brown sugar 1. a Negro, especially one's black boyfriend or girlfriend. [U.S. slang, 1900s] **2.** heroin. [U.S. drug culture, mid 1900s-pres.]

bruised intoxicated with alcohol. For

synonyms see WOOFLED. [U.S. slang, mid 1800s-1900s]

brush 1. the female pubic hair. For synonyms see DOWNSHIRE. [widespread slang, mid 1800s-pres.] **2.** a woman considered sexually. [Australian and British, 1800s-1900s] **3.** coition. [British, mid 1800s, Barrère and Leland] **4.** to coit a female. [British and U.S. slang, mid 1800s-pres.]

brush-ape a hillbilly; a rural oaf. [U.S. slang, 1900s and before, Wentworth]

brush teeth to perform fellatio. [U.S., late 1900s-pres.]

brush the beaver to masturbate (female). For synonyms see WASTE TIME. [U.S., late 1900s-pres.]

brute 1. the bull. Cf. ANIMAL (sense 1). [U.S. dialect, 1900s or before] **2.** an edible brown paste made from coca leaves (the source of cocaine). From Colombia. [U.S. drug culture, late 1900s, Abel]

B.S. 1. "bullshit," nonsense. [U.S. euphemism, 1900s] **2.** a "bad situation." A reinterpretation of the initials in sense 1. [U.S., 1900s]

B.T. BIRD-TURD (sense 4); BULLSHIT. Based on B.S. (q.v.). For synonyms see ANIMAL. [U.S. slang, late 1900s]

bu See BOO.

bub 1. strong beer or any alcoholic beverage. [British, late 1600s, B.E.] **2.** a breast; a BUBBY (sense 1). Usually in the plural. For synonyms see BOSOM. [British slang, 1800s, Farmer and Henley]

bubber 1. a drunkard; a beer-drinker. Cf. BUB (sense 1). [British, late 1600s] **2.** an old woman with extremely large breasts or "bubs." [U.S., mid 1800s, Farmer and Henley]

bubbies the human breasts. See BOOBIES, BOOBS. [British and U.S. colloquial, 1800s-1900s]

bubble butt 1. a large posterior; a big BOTTOM. For synonyms and related terms see DUFF. **2.** a person with a large posterior. [both senses, U.S. collegiate, late 1900s, Munro]

bubbled alcohol intoxicated. For synonyms see WOOFLED. [1900s, Dickson]

bubble-pipe a water pipe for smoking marijuana or some other drug. Cf. BONG. [U.S. drug culture, late 1900s]

bubbles the human breasts. From the roundness and from BUB (sense 2). Cf. LOVE-BUBBLES. [U.S. slang, 1900s]

bubby 1. a human breast. Usually in the plural. Cf. BOOB (sense 2). [widespread colloquial English since the late 1600s] **2.** intoxicated with alcohol. From BUB (sense 1). [British slang, 1600s]

bubo a swelling of a lymph node in the groin, as with syphilis or the bubonic plague. Cf. BLUE BOY. [since the late 1300s] Synonyms: ADEN, BLUE BOY, CHANCRE, CHANK, DUMB WATCH, FRENCH PIG, GOOSE, HARD SORE, IRISH BUTTON, PEARL, PIMPLE, PINTLE-BLOSSOM, POULAIN, WART, WINCHESTER-GOOSE, WINCHESTER-PIGEON.

buckage money. [U.S., late 1900s-pres.]

bucket 1. the female genitals. Despite the dates, probably from sense 2. [British slang, 1800s, Farmer and Henley] **2.** the anus or buttocks. Cf. BROWN BUCKET. [U.S. slang since the early 1900s or before] **3.** jail; prison. [U.S. underworld (tramps), mid 1900s-pres.]

buckets the female breasts. For synonyms see BOSOM. [U.S., late 1900s-pres.]

buckskin a condom. For synonyms see EEL-SKIN. [U.S. slang, 1900s]

bucks' night a bachelor party the night before the wedding. [Australian, mid 1900s-pres.]

buck snort an audible release of intestinal gas. For synonyms see GURK. [U.S. slang, mid 1900s]

buddah marijuana. For synonyms see MARI. [U.S., late 1900s-pres.]

Buddha head (also **buddhahead**) someone of East Asian descent who wears a turban or other distinctive cloth headdress. [U.S. slang, late 1900s]

buddha stick a marijuana cigarette. Cf. THAI STICKS. For synonyms see MEZZROLL. [U.S. drug culture, mid 1900s-pres.]

budget the female genitals. From a

term for a leather bottle. See LEATHER (sense 1). [British slang, 1800s, Farmer and Henley]

budgy intoxicated with alcohol. [British and U.S. slang, late 1800s-early 1900s]

budhead a beer drinker; a beer drunkard. From the Budweiser™ brand name. For synonyms see ALCHY. [U.S. slang, late 1900s]

budwiper a Budweiser™ beer; any beer. [U.S. collegiate, late 1900s, Eble]

buff 1. the bare skin; nudity. [colloquial, mid 1600s-pres.] **2.** to strip naked. Primarily in "to buff it." [British, mid 1800s] **3.** an oaf; a jerk. [U.S., 1900s or before] **4.** a girl or woman. A truncation of BUFFALO (sense 2). [U.S. slang, 1900s] **5.** a movie containing nudity. From sense 1. [U.S. slang, mid 1900s-pres.] **6.** to dilute or buffer a powdered drug. [U.S. drug culture, late 1900s]

buff, in the (also **buff, in**) naked; nude. *Cf.* BUFF (sense 1). [since the early 1600s]

buffalo chick a fat woman. [U.S., late 1900s-pres.]

buffalo chips dried buffalo (or cattle) dung used as fuel. *Cf.* BODEWASH, PRAIRIE COAL, SURFACE FUEL. For synonyms see COW-CHIPS. [U.S. colloquial, mid 1800s-1900s]

buffarilla an ugly young woman. A blend of "buffalo" and "gorilla." *Cf.* BUFFALO (sense 2). [U.S. slang, mid 1900s] Synonyms: BAT, BEAR, BEAST, BITCH, BOWZER, BURNT, BUSHBITCH, BUSHPIG, CHEESE, COOLER, DRACK, GRODDESS, HOG, MACKABROIN, MIVVY, PIG, PILL, PITCH, PORKER, SCAG, SCUZZ, SNAG, WITCH, ZELDA.

buff-bare naked; nude. *Cf.* buff (sense 1). [U.S., 1900s or before]

buffers the breasts. For synonyms see BOSOM. [British slang, 1800s-1900s, *Dictionary of Slang and Unconventional English*]

buff the helmet to masturbate (male). For synonyms see WASTE TIME. [U.S., late 1900s-pres.]

buffy intoxicated with alcohol. For synonyms see WOOFLED. [British and U.S. slang, mid 1800s-1900s]

bufu 1. a homosexual male. From BUTT-FUCK. For synonyms see EPICENE. [U.S. slang, late 1900s] **2.** having to do with male homosexuality; in the manner of a male homosexual. [U.S. slang, late 1900s] **3.** to COIT someone anally. For related subjects see PEDERASTY. [U.S. slang, late 1900s, Munro] **4.** any despised person. For synonyms see SNOKE-HORN. [U.S. slang, late 1900s]

bug-fucker 1. a male with a small penis. For synonyms see GENITALS, YARD. **2.** a small penis. For synonyms see GENITALS, YARD. **3.** an insignificant and worthless male. For synonyms see OAF. [all senses U.S., late 1900s]

bugger 1. a heretic. From "Bulgar." Sexual perversion of all types was ascribed to these early heretics. [1300s-1500s] **2.** someone who practices forms of sexual perversion; a sodomist. [since the mid 1500s] **3.** a PEDERAST (*q.v.*). [British and U.S., early 1700s-pres.] **4.** to perform PEDERASTY (*q.v.*) or other nonorthogenital sexual activities. [primarily British, since the early 1600s] **5.** a fellow or pal. No negative connotations. [British 1800s or before to the present] **6.** a small person or thing, especially in the expression "little bugger." **7.** as an oath, "Bugger!", a strong exclamation. The equivalent of U.S. "Oh, fuck!" [Australian and British, 1900s and before] **8.** a ghost. [U.S. dialect] **9.** to mess up. A truncation of BUGGER UP (*q.v.*). **10.** a bad situation or difficult task. *Cf.* BITCH (sense 11). [1900s]

buggered exhausted. [Australian, mid 1900s-pres.]

buggerlugs a pejorative term of address sometimes used as a friendly greeting. [British, late 1900s-pres.]

Bugger Me! "I'll be damned!" For synonyms see 'ZOUNDS. [British, mid 1900s-pres.]

Bugger me backwards! an expression of astonishment. For synonyms see 'ZOUNDS. [British, late 1900s-pres.]

Bugger me dead! "I am totally shocked!" For synonyms see 'ZOUNDS. [Australian, mid 1900s-pres.]

Bugger off! a curse or an exclamation, "Get the hell out of here!" The equivalent of FUCK OFF (sense 4). [British, 1900s]

bugger's muddle, a a mess; a confused situation. [British, mid 1900s-pres.]

bugger up (also **bugger**) to mess something up. Cf. FUCK UP. [British and later U.S. via the World Wars]

buggery 1. the act of sodomy; anal intercourse. For synonyms see SODOMY. [British, 1800s-pres.] **2.** ruination; oblivion; destruction. [British, early 1900s-pres.]

bugly BUTT-UGLY; really ugly. [U.S., late 1900s-pres.]

Buick to vomit. Onomatopoetic, on the automobile name. Cf. RIDE THE BUICK. For synonyms see YORK. [U.S. slang, late 1900s]

builder's bum the buttocks' cleavage visible above the beltline of the jeans worn by laborers. [British, late 1900s-pres.]

built like a brick shit-house 1. pertaining to a well-built woman. Referring to the curves of an unevenly laid brick wall. **2.** pertaining to a sturdily-built male. Cf. STACKED LIKE A BRICK SHIT-HOUSE. [both senses, U.S., 1900s]

bulbs the human breasts. From "electric light bulb." [U.S. slang, mid 1900s]

bull 1. for a cow to desire copulation with a bull. **2.** for a bull to copulate with a cow. It is sense 2 which caused speakers of American English to use euphemisms for "bull" such as GENTLEMAN COW (q.v.). [British and later U.S. colloquial and dialect, 1300s-pres.] Terms for the bull (animal) that are avoidances for these senses are: ANIMAL, BIG ANIMAL, BRUTE, BUTTERMILK COW, COW-BRUTE, COW'S SPOUSE, CRITTER, GENTLEMAN COW, GENTLEMAN OX, HE-COW, HE-THING, JONATHAN, MALE BEAST, MALE BRUTE, MALE COW, MAN-COW, OX, ROGER, SEED-OX, STOCK BEAST, STOCK BRUTE, STOCK COW, SURLY, TOP COW. **3.** nonsense. This sense was recorded without reference to "bullshit" and appears to have developed independently from the coarser term, although it is now regarded as a truncation of

BULLSHIT (q.v.). [the form may be from Medieval Latin meaning "bubble," i.e., "as fleeting as a bubble," or perhaps cognate with Icelandic bull, "nonsense," or a Middle English term for a joke or a jest; since the early 1600s] **4.** a lecher. Cf. TOWN BULL. [1600s-1700s] **5.** to cheat or lie; to BULLSHIT (sense 2). [British and U.S. slang, 1900s] **6.** a lesbian; a masculine lesbian. Cf. BULLDIKER. [U.S. slang mid 1900s-pres.] **7.** to copulate with a woman. From sense 2. [British and U.S. slang, late 1700s-pres.] **8.** an officer of the law. [originally and primarily underworld (tramps), U.S., 1900s or before]

bull ants (also **bull's aunts**) trousers; pants. Rhyming slang for "pants." Cf. INSECTS AND ANTS. [British and U.S., 1900s, Dictionary of Rhyming Slang]

bull bitch a masculine female or a virago. From the name for a female bulldog and from BULLDIKER (q.v.). [U.S. slang, mid 1900s]

bull-dagger a lesbian. See BULLDIKER. [U.S. slang, mid 1900s]

bulldiker (also **bulldike**) a masculine woman or a masculine lesbian. Usually considered quite deragotory. Cf. DIKE (sense 2). [U.S. slang, early 1900s-pres.]

bull-dozed intoxicated with alcohol. Cf. HALF-BULLED. From "dose of the bull," a beating with a strip of cowhide. [Australian, early 1800s-1900s]

bull-dust (also **bull-fodder**) **1.** nonsense. **2.** to talk nonsense; to deceive. Both are euphemisms for BULLSHIT (q.v.). [both senses, Australian, 1900s, Baker]

bull-dust artist a BULLSHIT ARTIST. [Australian, mid 1900s-pres.]

bulldyker (also **bulldyke**) a variant of BULLDIKER (q.v.).

bulletproofed alcohol intoxicated. For synonyms see WOOFLED. [U.S. slang, late 1900s]

bullets 1. the testicles. **2.** semen. Cf. I.O.F.B., SHOOT (sense 1). [widespread recurrent nonce since at least the 1600s]

bullet stopper a U.S. Marine. From the Persian Gulf War. [U.S., mid 1900s-pres.]

bull-fodder nonsense; a euphemism for BULLSHIT (*q.v.*). *Cf.* BULL-DUST. [Australian, 1900s, Baker]

bull fuck 1. a thick gravy with chunks of meat. A dysphemism based on "bull semen." *Cf.* FUCK (sense 3). **2.** a custard. [attested as Canadian, early 1900s, *Dictionary of the Underworld*]

bull gravy a thick cream gravy. Probably means "bull semen." See BULL FUCK. [U.S. dialect, 1900s]

bullo nonsense; BULLSHIT (*q.v.*). [Australian, mid 1900s, Baker]

bullock's heart a release of intestinal gas. Rhyming slang for "fart." *Cf.* BEEF-HEARTS. [British, late 1800s, *Dictionary of Rhyming Slang*]

bull-ring camp a brothel offering virile males for male and female customers. [U.S. underworld, early 1900s, Goldin, O'Leary, and Lipsius]

bull-roar nonsense; BULLSHIT (*q.v.*). [slang, 1900s]

bullsh (also **bulsh**) nonsense. A truncation of BULLSHIT (*q.v.*). [attested as Boontling, late 1800s-early 1900s; otherwise attested as Australian, World Wars]

bullshartist a boaster and talker of nonsense; a teller of tall tales. *Cf.* BULLSH, BULLSHIT ARTIST. [Australian, 1900s, Baker]

bullshit 1. nonsense. **2.** to utter nonsense; to lie or deceive. Based on BULL (sense 5), of which it is an elaboration. [U.S. slang, 1900s] Disguises and synonyms for both senses: ALLIGATOR BULL, BATSHIT, BESSIE SMITH, BIRD SEED, BOVINE EXCREMENT, BOVINE EXCRESCENCE, BOVRIL, B.S., BULL, BULL-DUST, BULL-FEATHERS, BULL-FODDER, BULLO, BULL-ONEY, BULL-ROAR, BULLISH, BULLSHOT, BULLSKATE, BULL'S WOOL, BULSH, BURMA SHAVE, BUSHWAH, CORRAL DUST, COW-CONFETTI, COWSH, COWYARD CONFETTI, FROGSH, HOGWASH, HORSE, HORSE APPLE, HORSE FEATHERS, HORSERADISH, HORSESHIT, HORSH, TAURI EXCRETIO. See ANIMAL for other terms for nonsense. **3.** angry; mad. [U.S. collegiate, late 1900s, Munro]

bullshit artist a well-known teller of tall tales; a liar; a cheat. *Cf.* BULLSHART-

IST. For synonyms see BULLER. [U.S. slang, mid 1900s]

bullshitter a liar; a teller of tale tales; a boaster. For synonyms see BULLER. [U.S. slang and colloquial, 1900s]

bullshot nonsense. A euphemism for BULLSHIT (*q.v.*). [U.S. slang, 1900s, Wentworth and Flexner]

bum 1. the posteriors. [colloquial, late 1300s-pres.] **2.** a prostitute in the sense of TAIL (sense 6). **3.** the female genitals. *Cf.* ASS (sense 3), BUTT (sense 3). **4.** a hobo; an oaf. [early 1500s-pres.] **5.** a SPREE (sense 2). [U.S., 1900s and before] **6.** bad. The opposite of "rum," meaning "good." [British and U.S. slang and colloquial, 1900s]

bum and tit female bodies and sexuality. Also B. AND T. [British, late 1900s-pres.]

bum bag a small bag attached by a belt around the waist, a [U.S.] fanny pack. [British, late 1900s-pres.]

bum bandit a pederast. For synonyms see PEDERAST. [British, mid 1900s-pres.]

Bumblefuck 1. a primitive and rural place; podunk. **2.** typically primitive and rural. [both senses, U.S., late 1900s]

bumbo 1. the female genitals. *Cf.* BUM (sense 3). [attributed to various West African languages; British, 1700s] **2.** the buttocks. *Cf.* BUM (sense 1). [Caribbean (Jamaican), Cassidy and Le Page] **3.** a rum drink. [from Italian; British, mid 1700s]

bum-boozer a drunkard. *Cf.* ALKY BUM.

bum cleavage the buttocks' cleavage. [British, late 1900s-pres.]

bumf toilet paper. From BUM-FODDER (*q.v.*). For synonyms see T.P. [British, 1600s-1900s]

Bumfay! (also **Bum-lady!, Bum-troth!**) an oath and an exclamation, "By my fay!" or "By my faith!" For synonyms see 'ZOUNDS! [late 1500s]

bum-fodder 1. toilet paper. [colloquial, mid 1600s-pres., (Urquhart)] **2.** obscene reading material; cheap, trashy reading material. From sense 1. [British slang, mid 1700s]

bumhole engineer a pederast. For synonyms see PEDERAST. [British, late 1900s-pres.]

bummer 1. a bad drug experience. [U.S. drug culture, mid 1900s-pres.] **2.** any bad experience. From sense 1. [U.S. slang, mid 1900s-pres.] **3.** an idle loafer; a worthless BUM (sense 4). [British, 1800s] **4.** a sodomite; a person who participates in anal copulation. Usually said of a male. [slang, 1900s]

bum nuts eggs. [Australian, mid 1900s-pres.]

bump 1. to coit and impregnate a woman. [U.S. slang, 1900s] **2.** a pimple. See BUMPS (sense 1). [U.S. colloquial, 1900s] **3.** a baby's bottom. [U.S. juvenile, 1900s] **4.** a jolt, charge, or RUSH from a dose of drugs, especially cocaine FREE BASE. [U.S. drug culture, late 1900s]

bumpers the human breasts. [British and U.S. slang, mid 1900s]

bumpkin (also **bumkin**) a country oaf; a dull rustic. [since the late 1500s] Synonyms: BACON, CHAW-BACON, CHURL, CLOD-HOPPER, CLOWN, CLUMPERTON, CLUNCH, CLUNK, COUNTRY JAKE, DUNG-FORK. See OAF for similar terms.

bump monkies to copulate. For synonyms see OCCUPY. [U.S., late 1900s-pres.]

bumpsy (also **bumpsie**) intoxicated with alcohol. [British, early 1600s]

bump tummies to copulate. For synonyms see OCCUPY. [British, mid 1900s-pres.]

bum-sucker a sycophant; a toady. Cf. EGG-SUCKER, KISS-ASS, SUCK-ASS. [British slang, mid 1800s-pres.]

bumtags bits of fecal material clinging to the anal hairs. Cf. DINGLEBERRY. [British slang, 1900s, McDonald]

bum-tickler the penis. [British slang, 1800s, Farmer and Henley]

bum wad toilet paper. Cf. BUMF. For synonyms see T.P. [slang, mid 1900s]

bun 1. the tail of a hare. No negative connotations. Cf. SCUT (sense 1). [early 1500s] **2.** a buttock. See BUNS (sense 1). Also used for the buttocks. **3.** the female genitals. See TOUCH BUN FOR

LUCK. [British slang and cant, 1600s-1700s] **4.** a prostitute. From sense 3 or from TART (q.v.). [British slang, late 1800s, Barrère and Leland] **5.** a drunk; a buzz. Cf. HAVE A BUN ON. [U.S. slang, 1900s or before]

bunch-punch the legendary GANG-BANG (q.v.), serial copulation of one person by a number of males. See similar terms at GROUP SEX. [U.S. slang, mid 1900s-pres.]

bung 1. the anus. [since the 1600s] **2.** intoxicated with alcohol. Cf. BUNGED. [British, early 1700s]

bunged intoxicated with alcohol. Cf. BUNG (sense 2). For synonyms see WOOFLED.

bung-eyed intoxicated with alcohol. [British, 1800s, Sinks of London Laid Open]

bung-fodder toilet paper. Cf. BUM-FODDER, BUNG (sense 1). [U.S. colloquial, 1800s-1900s]

bungfu intoxicated with alcohol. A truncation of "bungfull." [U.S. slang, 1900s or before]

bung hole 1. anal intercourse. Cf. BUNG (sense 1). **2.** to permit or perform anal sexual intercourse. **3.** the anus. [all senses, U.S., 1900s] **4.** the female genitals, specifically the vagina. [slang, 1800-pres.] **5.** the mouth. [Australian, mid 1900s-pres.]

bunker 1. a pederast; the INSERTOR (q.v.). [U.S. underworld, early 1900s, Irwin] **2.** to commit pederasty; to perform anal copulation. [U.S. slang, early 1900s]

bunk-up a secretive act of sexual intercourse. For synonyms see SMOCK-AGE. [British, mid 1900s-pres.]

bunned intoxicated with alcohol. Cf. BUN (sense 5), HAVE A BUN ON. [U.S. slang and colloquial, 1900s or before]

bunny 1. the female genitals. Cf. CONY. [British, 1700s] **2.** a sexually loose woman. Cf. BED-BUNNY. [U.S. slang, mid 1900s-pres.] **3.** a male or female prostitute. [senses 2 and 3 are U.S., mid 1900s-pres.]

bunny-fuck very rapid sexual intercourse; an act of sexual intercourse involving very rapid thrusting by the male. [U.S. slang, mid 1900s-pres.]

bunny hugger an environmental activist. [U.S., late 1900s-pres.]

buns 1. the posteriors. From the shape of the buttocks and the gluteal furrow. Cf. BUN (sense 2). [U.S. slang, mid 1900s-pres.] **2.** formed lumps of horse dung. From the shape. [U.S., 1900s]

buoyant (also **buoyed**) alcohol intoxicated. For synonyms see WOOFLED. [U.S. slang, 1900s, Dickson]

buppie a black yuppie. For synonyms see EBONY [U.S., late 1900s-pres.]

burble a PIMPLE (sense 1) or a boil. [mid-1500s] Synonyms are related terms: ACNE, ACNE-TYPE SURFACE BLEMISH, ACNE VULGARIS, BLACKHEAD, BLAIN, BLEMISH, BLOB, BOIL, BUBUKLE, BULLA, BUMP, CARBUNCLE, COMEDO, FURUNCLE, GOOB, GUBERS, HICKIE, HICKY, JERK BUMPS, MACULATION, PIMGINNIT, ROSY-DROP, RUM-BLOSSOM, SPOTS, ZIT.

burese cocaine. [U.S. underworld and drug culture, 1900s]

burglar 1. a pederast; the INSERTOR (q.v.). Cf. BACK-DOOR WORK, USHER. [U.S. underworld, early 1900s] **2.** a Bulgarian. [military, Fraser and Gibbons]

Burma Shave a reinterpretation of "B.S.," BULLSHIT (q.v.). A euphemism of disguise. Cf. BESSIE SMITH, B.S. [U.S. slang, mid 1900s]

burn 1. to lust after someone. [since c. 1000, Oxford English Dictionary] **2.** to infect someone with a venereal disease, probably gonorrhea. [since the early 1500s] **3.** an exclamation or a curse, "Go to hell!" [U.S. colloquial, early 1900s]

burnese (also **bernese**) cocaine. Sometimes capitalized. Cf. BERNICE, BURESE. [U.S. underworld, early 1900s]

burning having an S.T.D., probably gonorrhea. [U.S., late 1900s-pres.]

burn one's poker to contract a venereal disease. Cf. BURN (sense 2). [British slang, 1800s, Dictionary of Slang and Unconventional English]

burnt (also **burned**) infected with a venereal disease. [since the late 1600s]

burnt cheese 1. a foul-smelling release of intestinal gas. Cf. BURN BAD POWDER, CHEEZER, CUT ONE'S FINGER, CUT THE CHEESE. **2.** an extremely ugly young woman. [U.S. slang, mid 1900s-pres.]

burn the grass to urinate outdoors on the grass, usually said of males. Cf. KILL A TREE. [Australian, 1900s, Baker]

burp one's baby to masturbate. For synonyms see WASTE TIME. [U.S., late 1900s-pres.]

burp one's worm to masturbate. For synonyms see WASTE TIME. [U.S., late 1900s-pres.]

burrito the penis. For synonyms see GENITALS, YARD. [U.S. collegiate, late 1900s, Munro]

bury a quaker to defecate. Cf. QUAKER'S BURYING-GROUND. [originally Anglo-Irish, British slang, 1800s]

bury one's wick to copulate. [British slang, mid 1800s, Dictionary of Slang and Unconventional English]

bury the weenie See PLAY HIDE THE SALAMI.

bus a fat person. Someone as big as a bus. [U.S. collegiate, late 1900s, Eble]

bush 1. the female genitals. Refers to the pubic hair. Cf. HAIR. [U.S. slang, 1900s] **2.** pubic hair, especially female pubic hair. [U.S. slang, 1900s] **3.** a substantial patch of hair on a man's chest. Cf. MOSS ON THE BOSOM. **4.** an Afro-style hairdo; any head of hair. [U.S. slang, 1900s] **5.** a woman considered sexually. For synonyms see TAIL. **6.** marijuana. Cf. BO-BO BUSH, WEED (sense 1). [U.S. drug culture, early 1900s-pres.]

bush-beater the penis. Cf. BUSH (sense 2), BUSHWHACKER. [British slang, 1800s, Farmer and Henley]

bushbitch (also **bushpig**) a real ugly girl or woman. One from the bush or the jungle. For synonyms see BUFFARILLA. [U.S. collegiate, late 1900s, Munro]

bush boogie someone of African descent. Derogatory. For synonyms see EBONY. [U.S., late 1900s-pres.]

bush colt a bastard; an illegitimate

child. For synonyms see ACCIDENT. [U.S. colloquial, 1900s or before]

bush pig an ugly woman. [Australian and elsewhere, late 1900s-pres.]

bushwah (also **booshwa, booshwah, boushwa, bushwa**) **1.** dried cattle or buffalo dung used as fuel. *Cf.* BODE-WASH. [from the French *bois-de-vache*, "wood from the cow"; U.S. colloquial, 1900s and before] **2.** nonsense. A disguise of and avoidance for BULLSHIT (*q.v.*). [U.S. slang, 1900s]

bushwhacker 1. originally a rural feller of trees. By extension, an outlaw who resides in the bush and is not to be trusted; a guerrilla. In Australia, one who lives in the bush. In the U.S., a Civil War deserter. [1800s–1900s] **2.** the penis. *Cf.* BUSH (sense 1), TALLY-WHACKER. [British slang, 1800s, Farmer and Henley] **3.** a marijuana smoker. *Cf.* BUSH (sense 6). [U.S. drug culture, mid 1900s-pres.]

business class pertaining to huge buttocks. [U.S., late 1900s-pres.]

business girl a prostitute, especially one who is independent and not connected with a pimp or a brothel. *Cf.* WORKING GIRL. [British, early 1900s]

busk the penis. From the name of whalebone or wooden stiffeners for corsets. [British slang, 1800s]

buss 1. a kiss. **2.** to kiss. [both since the mid 1700s] Synonyms of both senses: MOUSE, MOUSLE, MOUTH, MOW, MUCKLE ON, MUZZLE, OSCULATION.

bust 1. a woman's bosom; the breasts; the general shape or outline of the breasts. Also in the plural meaning "breasts." [euphemistic since the early 1700s] **2.** as an oath and an exclamation, "Bust!" meaning "Damn!" **3.** a drunken spree. *Cf.* BURST. [British and U.S., mid 1800s-pres.] **4.** to ejaculate prematurely. [U.S. slang, mid 1900s-pres.] **5.** an arrest for shoplifting or drug possession. [U.S. slang and drug culture, mid 1900s-pres.] **6.** to arrest; to raid and arrest. [U.S. underworld and general slang, mid 1900s-pres.] **7.** a failure; a disastrous mess. [U.S. slang, mid 1900s-pres.]

busta a punk; a jerk. From the nick-

name *buster*. For synonyms see SNOKE-HORN. [U.S., late 1900s-pres.]

bust a cap to take a narcotics capsule. *Cf.* CAP, CAP OUT. [U.S. drug culture, mid 1900s-pres.]

bust a gut 1. to strain oneself physically, perhaps sufficiently to produce a hernia. **2.** to strain oneself mentally. [both senses, U.S. slang, mid 1900s-pres.]

bust ass to make a valiant physical effort. *Cf.* BUST A GUT. [U.S. slang, mid 1900s-pres.]

busted ugly. [U.S., late 1900s-pres.]

busted and dusted arrested and fingerprinted. [U.S., late 1900s-pres.]

busted in drunk. For synonyms see WOOFLED. [U.S., late 1900s-pres.]

buster a loud release of intestinal gas. *Cf.* TRUMP. [U.S. slang, mid 1900s-pres.]

bustle (also **bustler**) a pad, a roll of fabric, or a wire frame worn under the skirts and over the buttocks of a woman. It was worn to emphasize the smallness of the waist. [British and U.S., late 1700s-pres.] Synonyms: ARSE-COOLER, BACK-STAIRCASE, BIRD-CAGE, BISHOP, CANARY CAGE, DRESS-IM-PROVER, FALSE HEREAFTER, JOHNNY RUSSELL, LORD JOHN RUSSELL, RAT-TRAP, RUMP-ROLL, SCOTCH BUM, TOUR-NURE.

bust (one's) ass (to do something) (also **break one's balls to do something, bust one's butt to do some thing, bust one's nuts to do something**) to work very hard to do something; to work very hard at something. Said typically of a male. [U.S. slang, colloquial, 1900s]

bust one's nuts 1. to ejaculate. *Cf.* BUST (sense 4), GET ONE'S NUTS CRACKED, POP A NUT. [U.S. slang, mid 1900s-pres.] **2.** the same as BREAK ONE'S BALLS (*q.v.*), to suffer adversity or discomfort to accomplish something.

busty said of a woman with large breasts. [British and U.S., early 1900s-pres.]

busy-bee the animal tranquilizer

phencyclidine, the drug P.C.P. Rhyming slang for P.C.P. For synonyms see P.C.P. [U.S. drug culture, late 1900s]

butch 1. a masculine lesbian; a lesbian in the male role. For synonyms see LESBYTERIAN. **2.** a virile homosexual male. [both senses, U.S. homosexual use, mid 1900s-pres.] **3.** for a homosexual (male or female) to act more masculine than is customary. Found in the expression "butch it up." [U.S. homosexual use, mid 1900s-pres., Farrell] **4.** a physician. From "butcher." [U.S. nautical, Berrey and Van den Bark]

butcher's shop the female genitals. [British slang, 1800s, Farmer and Henley]

Butchski a derogatory nickname for a Czechoslovakian. [U.S., 1900s]

butler's revenge a silent release of intestinal gas, as might be done by an angry butler before leaving the room. For synonyms see GURK. [U.S. slang, 1900s]

butt 1. the bottom or thicker end of anything. Sometimes taboo even in this sense. [since the mid 1400s] **2.** the posteriors. Originally impolite, but now used more freely. For synonyms see DUFF. [U.S. colloquial, 1800s1900s] **3.** women considered sexually. Cf. ASS, FANNY, RUMP. [U.S. slang, 1900s] **4.** copulation. [U.S. slang, 1900s]

buttboy 1. a homosexual male. Possibly patterned on *bat boy.* For synonyms see EPICENE. **2.** a total JERK. For synonyms see OAF. [both senses, U.S., late 1900s, Munro]

butter 1. semen in compound words, BUTTERED-BUN, DUCK-BUTTER, MELTED-BUTTER (all *q.v.*). For synonyms see METTLE. [British slang, 1800s, Farmer and Henley] **2.** a woman. From BUTT. [U.S. slang, mid 1900s-pres.]

butter-bags the human breasts. Cf. BUTTER-BOXES. [British slang, 1800s, Farmer and Henley]

butter-boat the female genitals. Cf. BUTTER. [British slang, 1800s, Farmer and Henley]

butterbox (also **butterbag**) a derogatory term for a Dutchman. [slang, 1600s-1900s] Synonyms: BUTTER-MOUTH, CABBAGEHEAD, CHEESE-EATER, FROGLANDER, NIC FROG, OFFAL-EATER.

butter-boxes the human breasts. Cf. BUTTER-BAGS. [British slang, 1800s, Farmer and Henley]

buttered bun 1. a woman's vagina containing semen from a recent ejaculation. Said of prostitutes who have repeated or serial coition. Cf. BUN (sense 3), WET DECK. **2.** a mistress; a prostitute. [both senses, British, 1600s-1800s]

butter flower marijuana. [U.S. drug culture, mid 1900s-pres.]

butterfly queen a homosexual male who prefers mutual FELLATIO (*q.v.*). For synonyms see QUEEN. [U.S. homosexual use, mid 1900s, Farrell]

butter-knife the penis. Refers to spreading the BUTTER on the BUN (both *q.v.*). [British, mid 1600s]

buttermilk semen. Cf. BUTTER, CREAM (sense 1), HOT MILK, MILK (sense 2). [British slang, 1800s, Farmer and Henley]

buttermilk cow a bull. BUTTERMILK (*q.v.*) is a jocular reference to semen. [U.S. jocular, early 1900s]

butter-queen (also **butter-whore**) a scolding woman; a shrew. [British, mid 1600s]

buttfloss a string bikini. [U.S., late 1900s-pres.]

butt-fuck 1. anal copulation. **2.** to practice anal copulation. [both senses, U.S. slang, mid 1900s-pres.]

buttfucker a sodomist. For synonyms see EPICENE. [widespread, 1900s]

butt-fucking Egypt a place that is very far away. [U.S., mid 1900s-pres.]

butthead a stupid or obnoxious person of either sex. [U.S. slang, late 1900s]

butthole the anus. For synonyms see ANUS. [widespread, 1900s if not before]

butt itch something that is irritating [U.S., late 1900s-pres.]

butt-kicker a person really good at something. Someone who really kicks butt. [U.S. slang, late 1900s]

buttlick 1. an ASS-KISSER; a sycophant. **2.** any worthless JERK. For synonyms see OAF. [both senses, U.S. collegiate, late 1900s, Munro]

buttload a great amount; a SHITLOAD. [U.S. slang, late 1900s]

buttly very ugly; BUTT-UGLY. [U.S. collegiate, late 1900s, Munro]

butt naked totally nude. For synonyms see STARKERS. [U.S. slang, mid 1900s-pres.]

buttock 1. one of the prominences formed by the gluteal muscles. Usually in the plural. [since the 1300s] **2.** a common strumpet; a harlot. Cf. ASS (sense 3), BUTT (sense 3), FANNY (sense 1), RUMP (sense 2). [British, 1600s–1800s]

buttock-broker a madam or a pimp. Cf. FLESH-PEDDLER. [British slang, late 1600s, B.E.]

buttocks the posteriors. See BUTTOCK (sense 1).

buttock-stirring copulation. Cf. BUTTOCK (sense 2). [British slang, 1800s, Farmer and Henley]

button 1. the clitoris. [colloquial, 1800s–1900s] **2.** a baby's penis. [British, 1800s, *Dictionary of Slang and Unconventional English*] **3.** an opium pellet. [underworld, early 1900s, *Dictionary of the Underworld*] **4.** a PEYOTE BUTTON (*q.v.*). [U.S. drug culture, mid 1900s-pres.]

button-hole the female genitals. Cf. BUTTON (sense 1). [British slang, 1800s, Farmer and Henley]

button-hole factory a brothel. Cf. BUTTON (sense 1). [British slang, 1800s]

button-hole-worker 1. a whoremonger. **2.** the penis. [both senses, British, 1800s]

buttons 1. the testes of animals. **2.** the dung of a hare, sheep, or other animals with similar small, pellet-shaped feces. [British, mid 1700s] **3.** tips of the Peyote cactus. See PEYOTE BUTTON. [U.S. drug culture, mid 1900s-pres.]

butt-peddler 1. a pimp. **2.** a prostitute. Cf. ASS-PEDDLER. [both senses, U.S., early 1900s]

butt pirate a PEDERAST. [U.S. collegiate, late 1900s, Munro]

butt rash something that is irritating. [U.S., late 1900s-pres.]

butt-thong the string or thin band of cloth running between the BUTTOCKS, connecting the "belt" and the crotch of a tiny swimming suit or similar costume. [U.S. slang, late 1900s]

butt-ugly very ugly. [U.S. slang, late 1900s]

butt-wipe 1. toilet paper. For synonyms see T.P. **2.** a sycophant. Cf. ASS-WIPE. [both senses, U.S. slang, mid 1900s-pres.]

buxom 1. pertaining to a healthy, plump girl or woman. [since the late 1500s] **2.** pertaining to a large or full-breasted woman. [since the 1800s or before]

buy the big one to die. For synonyms see DEPART. [U.S., mid 1900s-pres.]

buy the farm (also **buy it**) to die. [U.S. slang, early 1900s-pres.]

buzz 1. an audible release of intestinal gas. For synonyms see GURK. [widespread recurrent nonce, 1900s and before] **2.** the mellowness of alcohol or drug intoxication in "to have a buzz on." **3.** a sexual thrill or feeling. [senses 2 and 3 are U.S. slang, 1900s]

buzz crusher something that puts an end to pleasure. [U.S., late 1900s-pres.]

buzzed (also **buzzed-up**) slightly intoxicated. Cf. BUZZ (sense 2). [U.S. slang, mid 1900s-pres.]

buzzer 1. a homosexual male. For synonyms see EPICENE. [U.S. homosexual use, mid 1900s] **2.** a pickpocket. [underworld, early 1900s or before]

buzzey intoxicated with alcohol. [U.S. slang, early 1700s, Ben Franklin]

buzzing drunk. Cf. HAVE A BUZZ ON. For synonyms see WOOFLED. [U.S. slang, late 1900s]

buzz the brillo to copulate. "Brillo" is the trademarked brand name of a metallic wool scourer. Refers to the female pubic hair. [U.S. slang, mid 1900s, *Current Slang*]

C

C. 1. "cocaine." *Cf.* H., M. [U.S. underworld and drug culture, early 1900s-pres.] **2.** women considered as sexual objects. From "cunt." [U.S. slang, mid 1900s]

caballo heroin. *Cf.* HORSE. [from the Spanish word for "horse"; U.S. drug culture, mid 1900s-pres.]

cabbage-garden (also **cabbage-field, cabbage-patch**) the female genitals. [British and U.S., 1800s-1900s]

cabbagehead 1. an oaf or fool. [British and U.S. slang and colloquial, mid 1800s-1900s] **2.** a derogatory nickname for a German or a Dutchman. For synonyms see GERRY. [U.S., mid 1800s-1900s]

caboose 1. the human posteriors. From the name of the car at the end of a railroad train. [U.S. colloquial and slang, 1900s or before] **2.** a nickname for the last male to copulate in a group sex act. See PULL A TRAIN. [U.S. slang, mid 1900s-pres.]

ca-ca (also **caca, ka-ka**) **1.** heroin; sometimes false or adulterated heroin. See SHIT (sense 5). [from Spanish via U.S. Mexican and Puerto Rican slang; U.S. drug culture and slang, mid 1900s-pres.] **2.** to defecate. [Caribbean (Jamaican), 1900s, Cassidy and Le Page] **3.** feces; dung. [slang, 1900s and certainly much older] **4.** defecation. [slang, 1900s or before]

cacafuego literally, "shit-fire," a very difficult or devilish person. *Cf.* SPITFIRE (sense 1). [British, 1600s-1900s]

cack 1. dung; feces. **2.** to eliminate. [both since the early 1400s] **3.** to vomit. *Cf.* BARF, SHIT (sense 6). [U.S. colloquial, 1900s] **4.** to kill someone. [U.S. underworld, late 1900s]

cackling fart a hen's egg. [British jocular slang or cant, late 1600s]

cactus dead. For synonyms see DONE FOR. [Australian, late 1900s-pres.]

cactus juice tequila. A Mexican liquor. For synonyms see BOOZE. [U.S., mid 1900s-pres.]

cadet a condom. For synonyms see EEL-SKIN. [U.S., late 1900-pres.]

Cadillac 1. cocaine. *Cf.* C. (sense 1). **2.** the drug P.C.P. (*q.v.*). [both senses, U.S. drug culture, mid 1900s-pres.]

cadger See CAGER.

caged intoxicated with alcohol. [U.S. slang, 1900s]

cage of anger, the a prison. [U.S., late 1900s-pres.]

cager (also **cadger**) a drunkard; someone who sponges drinks. [U.S. slang, 1900s]

cake 1. the female genitals. For synonyms see MONOSYLLABLE. [U.S. slang, 1900s] **2.** the buttocks of a woman, especially if well-formed. *Cf.* ASS (senses 2 and 3). [British and U.S. slang, mid 1900s] **3.** a sexually desirable woman. *Cf.* PIE, TART. [U.S. slang, 1900s] **4.** a prostitute. For synonyms see HARLOT. [Australian, early 1900s]

cake-eater an effeminate male; one who is quite comfortable at fussy tea parties. [U.S. slang, early 1900s]

cake-hole the mouth. [Widespread, mid 1900s-pres.]

cakes the buttocks. For synonyms see DUFF. [U.S., late 1900s-pres.]

cake whore a woman who uses vast amounts of makeup. [U.S., late 1900s-pres.]

caking selling drugs. [U.S., late 1900s-pres.]

California cornflakes cocaine. *Cf.* JOY FLAKES. [U.S. slang, mid 1900s-pres.]

California sunshine the drug L.S.D. (*q.v.*). [U.S. drug culture, mid 1900s-pres.]

called to straw pertaining to a woman who has gone into LABOR (*q.v.*). Refers to a cow giving birth. [U.S. dialect, 1900s and before]

call Earl to vomit. Onomatopoeia. For synonyms see YORK. [British and U.S. slang, late 1900s]

call (for) Hughie to vomit; to CRY HUGHIE. For synonyms see YORK. [British and U.S. slang, late 1900s]

call-girl 1. a prostitute who makes appointments by telephone or a prostitute who can be called on (visited) for her services. **2.** any prostitute. *Cf.* C-GIRL. [both senses, U.S., early 1900s-pres.]

call-house (also **call-joint**) a brothel. Proposed origins include: a place where someone makes a call to find the telephone number of a prostitute, a brothel where prostitutes make appointments by telephone, and a brothel where you can call on prostitutes to do anything. *Cf.* HOUSE OF CALL. [U.S. slang, 1900s]

call Ruth to vomit. The same as CRY RUTH. For synonyms see YORK. [British slang, late 1900s, McDonald]

Cambo a Cambodian. Not necessarily derogatory. [U.S. slang, late 1900s]

camel jockey an Arab or person from any country where camels might be found. Derogatory. [U.S. slang, late 1900s]

camel toes the shape of the vulva seen through tight clothing. [British and U.S., late 1900s-pres.]

camp 1. a brothel. **2.** a residence or gathering place for male homosexuals. [both senses, U.S. slang or nonce, Monteleone] **3.** pertaining to obvious and open or exaggerated male homosexual behavior. Also **campy.** [U.S. and British slang and underworld, early 1900s-pres.] **4.** to display one's homosexual behavior openly or in an exaggerated manner. *Cf.* CAMP IT UP. [U.S. homosexual use, mid 1900s-pres.]

camp it up to overdo effeminacy. Refers to behavior in theatrical roles (Partridge) or in the public behavior of a homosexual. [British and U.S. slang, early 1900s-pres.]

campy the same as CAMP (sense 3).

can 1. a restroom or toilet. In addition to referring to the receptacle, "can" may have been reinforced by the "gan" or "ken" of "donegan" or "dunnaken." See DONIKER. [U.S. slang and colloquial, 1900s if not before] **2.** a jail; a prison. For synonyms see COW. [U.S. slang, 1900s] **3.** the female genitals. [British slang, 1800s] **4.** a breast. See CANS. **5.** the buttocks; the bottom. [U.S. slang and colloquial, 1900s or before] **6.** one ounce of marijuana. From a tobacco "can" (in which the plant was commonly transported) and from "Cannabis." [U.S. drug culture, mid 1900s]

Canadian black a type of marijuana said to be grown in Canada. [U.S. drug culture, mid 1900s-pres.]

Canadian quail methaqualone, specifically Quaalude.™ [U.S. drug culture, late 1900s, Abel]

canary 1. a young woman or girl, especially a female vocalist; a BIRD (sense 1) who sings. [U.S., 1900s and before] **2.** a Chinese. From the yellow color of a canary. For synonyms see JOHN CHINAMAN. [Australian, 1900s and before, Baker]

cancer-stick a dysphemism for "cigarette." *Cf.* COFFIN-NAIL. [U.S. slang, 1900s]

candle the penis. A mate to the CANDLESTICK (*q.v.*). See CANDLE-BASHER. [British slang, 1800s, Farmer and Henley]

candle-basher a spinster; a female masturbator. *Cf.* BASHER, CANDLE. [British, early 1900s or before, *Dictionary of Slang and Unconventional English*]

candlestick the female genitals. *Cf.* CANDLE. [British slang, 1800s, Farmer and Henley]

C. and M. a mixture of "cocaine and morphine." For similar terms see HOT AND COLD. [U.S. drug culture, mid 1900s-pres.]

candy 1. intoxicated with alcohol. For synonyms see WOOFLED. [British slang, early 1800s, Egan's Grose] **2.** any drug. Usually refers to hard drugs, specifically cocaine, hashish, L.S.D., and barbiturates. Originally only cocaine. *Cf.* CANDY MAN, NEEDLE-CANDY, NOSE-CANDY. [U.S. drug culture, early 1900s-pres.]

candy-ass a coward; a timid and helpless person. *Cf.* PUCKER-ASSED. [U.S. slang, mid 1900s-pres.]

candy-ass(ed) timid; habitually frightened; cowardly. [U.S. slang, late 1900s]

candycane cocaine. For synonyms see NOSE-CANDY. [U.S. drug culture, black use, late 1900s]

candyflip 1. to use L.S.D. and Ecstasy together [U.S., late 1900s-pres.] **2.** a session of using L.S.D. and Ecstasy together. [U.S., late 1900s-pres.]

candyhead (also **candy fiend**) a cocaine user. [U.S. drug culture, early 1900s]

candy man a seller of hard drugs. *Cf.* CANDY (sense 2) for examples. [U.S. drug culture, 1900s]

cane 1. to copulate with a woman in the sense of "beat." [British slang, 1900s, *Dictionary of Slang and Unconventional English*] **2.** the penis in the expression VARNISH ONE'S CANE (*q.v.*). [British, 1800s] **3.** cocaine. For synonyms see NOSE-CANDY. [U.S. drug culture, late 1900s])

caned drunk; drug intoxicated. For synonyms see TALL, WOOFLED. [British, late 1900s-pres.]

can house a brothel. See CAN (sense 3). [U.S., 1900s or before]

canister The female genitals. British slang for "hat," which is slang for the female sexual organ. See HAT, OLD. *Cf.* CAN (sense 3). [British slang, 1800s, Farmer and Henley]

cannibal a fellator, specifically a homosexual male. *Cf.* MANEATER (sense 1). For synonyms see PICCOLO-PLAYER. [U.S. underworld, 1900s]

cannon balls the testicles. *Cf.* BULLETS (sense 1). [British slang and nonce, late 1800s, Farmer and Henley]

can-paper toilet paper. For synonyms see T.P. [U.S. slang or colloquial, 1900s]

cans the breasts. Usually in the plural. For synonyms see BOSOM. [U.S., 1900s] See also CAN (sense 4).

can't see a hole in a ladder a catch phrase pertaining to a person who is heavily intoxicated. Occurs in numerous variants. [British and U.S. slang, 1800s-1900s]

canyon the female genitals; the vagina. Especially in YODEL IN THE CANYON. For synonyms see GENITALS, MONOSYLLABLE. [U.S. black use, late 1900s]

canyon yodeling CUNNILINGUS (*q.v.*). *Cf.* YODEL. [U.S. slang, 1900s]

cap 1. to buy or use narcotics. Originally from "capsule," now refers to various forms of drugs. *Cf.* CAP OUT. [U.S. drug culture, mid 1900s-pres.] **2.** to destroy someone's kneecaps, especially as a punishment. [U.S. underworld, late 1900s]

Cape Horn the female genitals. The HORN (sense 3) is the penis. [British slang, 1800s, Farmer and Henley]

Cape of Good Hope the female genitals. For synonyms see MONOSYLLABLE. [British slang, 1800s, Farmer and Henley]

capernoited intoxicated with alcohol. [from a Scots word meaning "muddle-headed"; U.S., 1800s]

capon 1. a castrated male bird. No negative connotations. [since the late 1500s] **2.** a eunuch. [since the 1600s] **3.** a homosexual male; a pederast; an effeminate male. [U.S. slang, mid 1900s]

capoop 1. to defecate. **2.** dung. *Cf.* POOP (senses 3 and 7). [both senses, U.S. dialect (Ozarks), 1900s or before, Randolph and Wilson]

cap out to pass out from the use of marijuana or drugs. *Cf.* CAP. [U.S. drug culture, mid 1900s-pres.]

captain is at home a catch phrase indicating that a woman is menstruating. *Cf.* ENTERTAINING THE GENERAL. [British colloquial, late 1700s-1800s]

Captain Standish the erect penis. *Cf.* BODY'S CAPTAIN, MY. [British slang, 1800s, Farmer and Henley]

cardboard box veneral disease. Rhyming slang for *pox*. [British, late 1900s-pres.]

cark the penis. From a British dialect term for "load" or possibly from a similar term meaning "stiff" (Halliwell). It seems to be but is not a dialect pronunciation of "cock." [attested as U.S. slang, mid 1900s]

cark (it) to die. For synonyms see DEPART. [Australian, mid 1900s-pres.]

carnal 1. pertaining to fleshly, as opposed to spiritual, matters. In particular, sexual matters or desires. [mid 1400s-pres.] **2.** to copulate. *Cf.* CARNALIZE. [mid 1600s; rare then and obsolete now]

carnal acquaintance copulation. An early euphemism. *Cf.* CARNAL KNOWLEDGE, KNOWLEDGE.

carnal connection (also **carnal engagement**) sexual intercourse. A euphemism for "copulation." [1800s or before]

carnal copulation sexual intercourse. Now "copulation" alone carries the full meaning. [euphemistic, 1500s-1800s]

carnal enjoyment sexual pleasure; presumably a euphemism for "copulation."

carnal intercourse copulation, now usually "intercourse."

carnal parts the genitals of a male or female; the sexual parts. [early 1700s]

carnal stump the penis. *Cf.* MIDDLE STUMP. [written nonce; late 1600s]

carob chips HASHISH. *Cf.* CHOCOLATE. Compare to CHOCOLATE CHIPS. For synonyms see HASH. [U.S. drug culture, late 1900s]

carpet muncher a person who performs cunnilingus. [British, late 1900s-pres.]

carpet patrol crack smokers searching the floor for crack. [U.S., late 1900s-pres.]

Carrie a reinterpretation of the initial "C" of "cocaine." From the proper name. Not always capitalized. *Cf.* C. [U.S. drug culture, mid 1900s-pres.]

carrot the penis, especially the penis

of a child. [slang, nonce, or juvenile since the 1600s or before]

carrying a flag having a menstrual period. For synonyms see FLOODS. [U.S. slang, 1900s]

carrying something heavy intoxicated with alcohol, as if the drinker's difficulty in moving were due to carrying a heavy load. [U.S. slang, early 1900s]

carrying two red lights (also **carrying three red lights**) intoxicated with alcohol. Based on the signal for a ship out of control. Refers to the uncontrolled gait of a drunkard. [British and U.S., nautical and World War II]

carsey (also **carsi**) **1.** a house, den, or crib. *Cf.* CASA (sense 1). [cant, 1800s or before] **2.** a restroom, toilet, or JOHN (*q.v.*). Also **carzy, karzy.** *Cf.* CASA (sense 2). [possibly from the Hindi word *khazi*; primarily Cockney, British, late 1800s-pres.]

cartwheel an amphetamine tablet marked on one side with cross-scoring to make it easy to break. *Cf.* CROSSROAD, DOUBLE-CROSS. [U.S. drug culture, mid 1900s-pres.]

carving-knife one's own wife; anyone's wife. Rhyming slang for "wife." For synonyms see WARDEN. [British, 1900s, *Dictionary of Rhyming Slang*]

casa 1. a brothel, a HOUSE (*q.v.*). Also **case.** [British, 1600s] **2.** a toilet; a W.C. See CARSEY. [British slang or cant, 1800s or before]

cascade to vomit. [slang and colloquial, late 1700s-1900s]

case 1. the female genitals. See CAZE. *Cf.* BOX (sense 2), KEESTER (sense 3). [British, 1600s-1800s] **2.** a W.C.; a toilet. Originally "house." *Cf.* CARSEY, CASA. [cant, 1600s]

cashed 1. having to do with a portion of marijuana that has had all the active principle smoked out of it. *Cf.* CASHED. [U.S. drug culture, late 1900s] **2.** exhausted; worn out. [U.S. slang, late 1900s] **3.** dead. Supported by CASH IN ONE'S CHIPS. For synonyms see DONE FOR. [U.S. slang, late 1900s]

cash in one's chips (also **cash in**

one's checks) to die. [British and U.S., late 1800s-pres.]

casket 1. a coffin. Recognized as an American euphemism in the late 1800s, now the word-of-choice for "coffin." [U.S., late 1800s-pres.] **2.** to place a corpse in a coffin. [U.S. funeral trade, 1900s]

Casper the ghost crack cocaine. For synonyms see NOSE-CANDY. [U.S., late 1900s-pres.]

cast 1. to vomit. Also **cast up.** *Cf.* THROW UP ONE'S ACCOUNTS. [British slang or cant, early 1600s] **2.** to bear young, as in "cast kittens." [late 1500s-1800s] **3.** to excrete; to cast dung. Said mostly of animals in avoidance of more direct terms. [British, early 1700s] **4.** drunk; very drunk. For synonyms see WOOFLED [British slang or colloquial, early 1900s]

casting-couch a legendary couch found in the offices of casting directors for use in seducing young women by offering them acting roles in theatrical productions. The legend has been extended to include homosexual favors. [U.S. slang, 1900s]

castrate 1. to remove the testicles by cutting. Synonyms: ALTER, ARRANGE, CAPSIZE, CHANGE, DEHORN, DESEXUALIZE, DEVIRILIZE, DOCTOR, DOMESTICATE, FIX, GELD, GLIB, KNACKER, LIB, MAIM, MARK, MUTILATE, NUT, THROW, TRIM, UN-MAN, UNSEX, WORK ON. **2.** to remove the ovaries surgically. Rare if not obsolete. [both since the early 1600s] **3.** to expurgate a book. [since the early 1600s]

cast up one's accounts to vomit. See CAST (sense 1). From a phrase meaning "balance the books." For synonyms see YORK.

cat 1. a prostitute. [British, early 1400s-pres.] **2.** intoxicated with alcohol. [U.S., early 1700s, Ben Franklin] **3.** a gossip; a shrewish woman. [late 1700s-pres.] **4.** a male; a buddy. [U.S. slang, 1900s] **5.** to seek women for sex; to chase women. From TOMCAT (sense 2). [U.S., 1900s or before] **6.** the female genitals. "Cat" is a nickname for a lady's MUFF (sense 1), which refers to the female genitals, and it is further

reinforced by PUSSY (sense 1). [British and U.S., mid 1800s-pres.] **7.** to vomit. *Cf.* SHOOT THE CAT. For synonyms see YORK. [British and U.S. slang, 1800s-1900s] **8.** heroin. *Cf.* BOY (sense 3), BROTHER (sense 1). [U.S. drug culture, mid 1900s-pres.]

cat and kitties (also **cats and kitties**) the breasts. Rhyming slang for "titties." For synonyms see BOSOM. [U.S., early 1900s, *Dictionary of Rhyming Slang*]

catastrophe the posteriors. From the "ass" in the second syllable. Sometimes pronounced "cat-ass-trophy." [nonce and slang since the late 1500s]

catch 1. in male homosexual intercourse, the male receiving the phallus and the semen. *Cf.* INSERTOR, PASSIVE PEDERAST, RECEIVER. [U.S. homosexual use, 1900s] **2.** to become pregnant *Cf.* KETCHED, TAKE (sense 2). [British and U.S. colloquial and dialect, 1800s-1900s] **3.** a matrimonially desirable male or female. [British and U.S., late 1500s-pres.]

catch a buzz to begin to feel the effects or BUZZ of alcohol or drugs. [U.S. drug culture, late 1900s]

catch an oyster coition from the point of view of the woman. OYSTER (sense 3) refers to semen. [British slang, 1800s, Farmer and Henley]

catch a packet to catch a venereal disease. The expression generally means to get into trouble, to be reprimanded, or to be disciplined. [British military, early 1900s]

catcher's mitt a contraceptive diaphragm. From the shape and function. [U.S. slang, late 1900s]

catch-'em-alive-O the female genitals. From a nickname for a type of sticky flypaper used in the mid 1800s. British slang, mid 1800s, Farmer and Henley]

catch-fart a page or footboy who follows closely behind his master. [British, late 1600s-1700s]

catch shit to get into trouble; to get bawled out. [U.S. colloquial, late 1900s]

caterpillar a drunkard; someone drunk

enough to crawl. For synonyms see ALCHY. [Australian, early 1900s, Baker]

cat-flat a brothel. *Cf.* CAT (sense 1), CAT-HOUSE. [U.S. underworld, early 1900s]

catgut inferior liquor; rotgut. For synonyms see EMBALMING FLUID [U.S. slang, 1900s]

cat heads (also **cat's heads**) the breasts. From a popular species of very large apples. [British slang, early 1800s or before, *Lexicon Balatronicum*] See also CAT'S-HEAD-CUT-OPEN.

catholic bagel a non-traditional bagel made or flavored with cinnamon, blueberries, strawberries, etc. [U.S., late 1900s-pres.]

cat-house a brothel. [U.S. slang, mid 1900s-pres.]

cat's-head-cut-open the female genitals, especially the vulva. Refers to a cross section of a large apple. *Cf.* CUT CABBAGE, RED ONION. [British slang, early 1900s, *Dictionary of Slang and Unconventional English*] See also CAT HEADS.

cat-skin the female pubic hair. See CAT (sense 6). For synonyms see DOWNSHIRE. [British slang, 1800s, Farmer and Henley]

cat's meat the female genitals. For synonyms see MONOSYLLABLE. [British slang, 1800s, Farmer and Henley]

cattle-truck an act of copulation; to coit. Rhyming slang for "fuck." [slang, 1900s, *Dictionary of Rhyming Slang*]

cat valium ketamine. [U.S., late 1900s-pres.]

caucasian waste a worthless white person. A play on *white trash* [U.S., late 1900s-pres.]

caught pregnant. *Cf.* CATCH (sense 2), KETCHED, TAKE (sense 2). [U.S. colloquial and dialect, 1900s or before]

caught in a snowstorm intoxicated with cocaine. See SNOW and the entries which follow it for additional expressions on the SNOW-CAINE (*q.v.*) theme. [U.S. slang, mid 1900s]

cauliflower the female genitals. *Cf.* CABBAGE and see the explanation at

RED ONION. [British slang, 1800s or before]

caulk to copulate. With reference to forcing material between the planks of a ship's hull. A play on COCK (sense 4). [British, 1800s, Farmer and Henley]

cavalier an uncircumcised male. [British, late 1900s-pres.]

cavaulting (also **cavolting**) copulation. From horses and horseback-riding. *Cf.* PRIG (sense 1), RIDE. [British, 1800s or before]

cave 1. the female genitals, specifically the vagina and especially if large. **2.** women considered solely as sexual objects. *Cf.* CAVE OF HARMONY. For synonyms see TAIL. [both senses, U.S. slang, 1900s and earlier as nonce]

cave man a strong, virile man, especially one bearing much body hair or body hair in unusual places. [British and U.S., late 1800s-pres.]

cave of harmony the female genitals. *Cf.* CAVE. [1800s and probably much earlier]

caviar crack cocaine. For synonyms see NOSE-CANDY. [U.S., late 1900s-pres.]

caze (also **case, kaze**) the female genitals. *Cf.* CASE (sense 1), KAZE. [British, late 1800s, Farmer and Henley]

C.B. an abbreviation of COCK-BLOCK (*q.v.*), an attempt to interfere with another man's woman. Punning on the initials of citizens band radio. [U.S. slang, mid 1900s-pres.]

C.D. a sexually loose woman. See CUM DUMPSTER. For synonyms see BIRD. [U.S., late 1900-pres.]

Cecil cocaine. *Cf.* C. (sense 1). From the proper name. Not always capitalized. [U.S. underworld, mid 1900s-pres.]

cee cocaine. *Cf.* C. (sense 1). [U.S. underworld, mid 1900s]

ceiling inspector a willing or frequent female sexual partner. For synonyms see BIRD. [British, late 1900s-pres.]

cellar the female genitals, specifically the vagina. *Cf.* BOTTOMLESS-PIT (sense

1). [British slang, 1800s, Farmer and Henley]

cellar-door the female genitals; probably also the hymen. For synonyms see MONOSYLLABLE. [British, 1800s, Farmer and Henley]

cemetery a place for the interment of the dead. Originally for Roman catacombs and later for the land surrounding a Christian church. [from Greek; in English since the 1300s] Synonyms: BONE-ORCHARD, BONE-YARD, BOOT HILL, CHURCHYARD, CITY OF THE DEAD, COLD STORAGE, DEAD CENTER, FINAL RESTING PLACE, GOD'S ACRE, GRAVEYARD, HEADSTONE CITY, LAND-YARD, LAST HOME, MARBLE CITY, MARBLE ORCHARD, MEMORIAL PARK, NECROPOLIS, OSSUARY, PERMANENT REST CAMP, POLYANDRION, POLYANDRIUM, POTTER'S FIELD, REST CAMP, SAINT TERRA.

center of attraction the female genitals. *Cf.* POINT-OF-ATTRACTION. [U.S. slang, 1800s]

center of bliss the female genitals. [1800s or before]

central furrow the female genitals, especially the PUDENDAL CLEAVAGE (*q.v.*). [British, 1800s, Farmer and Henley]

central office the female genitals. [British, 1800s, Farmer and Henley]

cess marijuana. For synonyms see MARI. [U.S., late 1900s-pres.]

C.F. an act of group rape, a "cluster fuck." [U.S., late 1900s-pres.]

C.F.M. "come-fuck-me," referring to sexually suggestive actions, words, or dress. [U.S. collegiate, late 1900s, Munro]

C-girl a prostitute; a CALL-GIRL (*q.v.*). *Cf.* B-GIRL. [U.S. slang, 1900s]

C-habit a "cocaine-habit." *Cf.* C. (sense 1). [U.S. drug culture, 1900s]

chain gang a DAISY CHAIN. [British slang, late 1900s, McDonald]

chain-jerk See CIRCLE-JERK.

chain lightning inferior whisky or other liquor. For synonyms see EMBALMING FLUID. [U.S. slang or colloquial, 1800s]

chair the electric chair. [U.S. underworld and stereotypical gangster talk, 1900s] Synonyms: DEATH CHAIR, FLAME CHAIR, HOT CHAIR, HOT SEAT, HOT SQUAT, JUICE CHAIR, OLD MONKEY, OLD SMOKY, OLD SPARKY, SMOKY SEAT.

chalk 1. liquor. The same as CHOC (*q.v.*). For synonyms see BOOZE. [U.S., early 1900s] **2.** amphetamines. From the color and texture of powdered chalk. For synonyms see AMP. [U.S. drug culture, mid 1900s-pres.]

cham (also **chammy**) champagne. [British slang, late 1800s]

chamber of commerce 1. a brothel. See SEXUAL COMMERCE. [U.S. underworld, Monteleone] **2.** a chamber pot or toilet; a restroom. [U.S. slang and colloquial, 1800s-1900s]

chamber pot a vessel kept in bedrooms for the reception of urine during the night. This eliminated the necessity of transporting oneself to an outdoor privy. A truncation of "bedchamber pot." For synonyms see POT. [since the 1500s]

chanticleer the penis. From a nickname for the rooster. See COCK (sense 1). [British jocular euphemism, 1800s]

chapel of ease (also **chapel**) a privy; a W.C. From a term for a chapel of worship located on the outskirts of a parish. [British slang, mid 1800s]

charge 1. a thrill or jolt produced by drugs. See JOLT (sense 2). [U.S. underworld, 1900s] **2.** marijuana. [U.S., 1900s] **3.** a burst of sexual excitement or an experience of sexual excitement. [U.S., mid 1900s-pres.] **4.** an erection of the penis. For synonyms see ERECTION. [U.S., 1900s]

charge like a wounded bull to charge very high prices. [Australian, late 1900s-pres.]

charity-bang a woman providing free sex; a woman who "gives it away." For synonyms see BIRD. [British, late 1900s-pres.]

charity dame (also **charity girl, charity moll**) a woman who is sexually accommodating but not a prostitute, who charges a fee. She gives it away. In wartime, a girl who yields charitably to servicemen. [widespread slang, 1900s]

Charles 1. cocaine, a euphemistic disguise based on the initial "C" of "cocaine." Not always capitalized. [U.S. drug culture, 1900s] **2.** a Caucasian. See CHARLIE.

Charley Coke 1. cocaine. **2.** a heavy user of cocaine. [both senses, U.S. underworld, mid 1900s]

Charley Frisky Scotch whisky; any whisky. Rhyming slang for "whisky." *Cf.* GAY AND FRISKY. [British slang, mid 1800s]

Charley Hunt (also **Charley**) the female genitals. Rhyming slang for CUNT (*q.v.*). *Cf.* BERKELEY HUNT. [British slang, late 1800s, *Dictionary of Slang and Unconventional English*]

Charlies (also **Charleys**) **1.** the breasts. [British and U.S., late 1800s-pres.] **2.** the testicles. [British slang, 1900s, *Dictionary of Slang and Unconventional English*]

charras (also **charas, churrus**) marijuana, especially refined marijuana; resin from marijuana flowers. [from Hindi; U.S. drug culture, mid 1900s-pres.]

chaste 1. pertaining to a virgin and to virginity. **2.** pertaining to someone (now usually a woman) who has never voluntarily had sexual intercourse unlawfully. [since the 1200s, *Oxford English Dictionary*]

chat the female genitals. *Cf.* PUSSY. [from the French *chat*, "cat"; British slang, 1800s, Farmer and Henley]

châteaued drunk. As from the wine of a particular house or château. For synonyms see WOOFLED. [British slang, 1900s, J. Green]

cheater a condom. For synonyms see EEL-SKIN. [slang, mid 1900s]

cheaters 1. false breasts; FALSIES (*q.v.*). [U.S., mid 1900s] **2.** any padding to make the body more attractive by increasing the size of or improving the shape of the hips or buttocks. [U.S. slang, 1900s]

che-chees the breasts. *Cf.* CHICHI (sense 4). [U.S., 1900s]

check one's oil to mastrubate. For synonyms see WASTE TIME. [U.S., early 1900s]

check the ski rack to retire to urinate, usually said by a male. Based on WATER THE HORSES (*q.v.*). For synonyms see RETIRE. [probably nonce; U.S. slang, mid 1900s]

chedda money. From CHEDDAR. [U.S., late 1900s-pres.]

cheddar money. See also CHEESE. [U.S., late 1900s-pres.]

cheese 1. SMEGMA (sense 2). *Cf.* CROTCH-CHEESE. [British and U.S. slang, 1800s-1900s] **2.** an attractive young woman. From "cheesecake." [U.S., mid 1900s] **3.** cocaine FREE BASE. *Cf.* BANANAS AND CHEESE. For synonyms see FREE BASE. [U.S. drug culture, late 1900s, Abel] **4.** marijuana. For synonyms see MARI. [U.S. drug culture, late 1900s] **5.** to ejaculate semen. For synonyms see MELT. [British slang, 1900s, J. Green] **6.** to break wind; to emit a CHEEZER. [British slang, late 1900s] **7.** to vomit. For synonyms see YORK. [U.S. slang, late 1900s] **8.** cannabis resin. [U.S., late 1900s-pres.] **9.** money. [U.S., late 1900s-pres.]

cheesecake 1. pictures of scantily clad girls. Usually not totally nude and usually not shown in unusual sex acts or in the process of excreting. [U.S. slang, early 1900s-pres.] **2.** a scantily clad young woman with the restrictions listed in sense 1. Occasionally a nickname for a cute young woman. Also used for a group of such women. [U.S. slang, early 1900s-pres.] **3.** photographs of virile men. From sense 1 and not common. *Cf.* BEEFCAKE. [U.S., mid 1900s-pres.]

cheesed-off angry; disgusted. [U.S., late 1900s-pres.]

cheese dong a stupid social outcast. *Cf.* DONG. [U.S. collegiate, late 1900s, Munro]

cheese-eater 1. a derogatory nickname for a Dutchman. [Australian, Baker] **2.** a term of address directed at non-Catholics who call Catholics "fish-eaters." See FISH-EATER. [jocular and derogatory, 1800s-1900s]

cheese-head an oaf; a dullard. [U.S. slang, early 1900s]

cheesing posing with a smile; smiling very obviously. [U.S., late 1900s-pres.]

cheezer a very bad-smelling breaking of wind. *Cf.* BURNT CHEESE, CUT THE CHEESE. For synonyms see GURK. [slang since the early 1800s, *Lexicon Balatronicum*]

cherry 1. the hymen. [widespread slang and colloquial, 1900s] **2.** a woman's nipple. Often in the plural. **3.** virginity. [widespread slang, 1900s] **4.** a virgin, male or female. [U.S., 1900s, Monteleone] **5.** pertaining to a virgin or to virginity; virginal. [widespread slang, 1900s] **6.** a girl or young woman. [British and U.S. slang, mid 1800s-1900s]

cherry leb an alcohol extract of marijuana. [U.S. drug culture, mid 1900s-pres.]

cherrylets (also **cherrilets**) a woman's nipples. This may include other feminine charms such as the lips. *Cf.* CHERRY (sense 2). [late 1500s-1600s]

cherry-merry mildly intoxicated with alcohol; tipsy. For synonyms see WOOFLED. [slang since the early 1700s]

cherry-picker an effeminate man; a passive male homosexual. For synonyms see FRIBBLE, EPICENE. [British, late 1900s-pres.]

cherubimical intoxicated with alcohol. [U.S. and elsewhere, early 1700s, Ben Franklin]

Cheskey a derogatory nickname for a Czechoslovakian. [U.S. slang, 1900s, or before]

chest and bedding the breasts. For synonyms see BOSOM. [British nautical slang, late 1700s, Grose]

Chester Molester a lecherous or sexually aggressive male. Also a rude term of address. For synonyms see LECHER. [U.S. collegiate, late 1900s, Munro]

chestnuts 1. the breasts, the nuts on the chest. **2.** the testicles. *Cf.* NUTS (sense 1). [both senses, U.S. slang, 1900s, Landy]

chesty [said of a woman] possessing large breasts. For synonyms see BOSOM. [British and U.S., late 1900s-pres.]

chewed abused. [U.S., late 1900s-pres.]

chew face to kiss; to FRENCH KISS. *Cf.* SUCK FACE. [U.S. slang, late 1900s]

chew someone's ass out to berate someone; to scold someone severely. [U.S. slang, mid 1900s-pres.]

chew someone's ball(ocks) off to scold someone severely. [British, mid 1900s-pres.]

chew the cheese to vomit. *Cf.* CHEESE. For synonyms see YORK. [U.S. collegiate, late 1900s, Munro]

Chicago green a variety of marijuana. *Cf.* ILLINOIS GREEN. For synonyms see MARI. [U.S. drug culture, mid 1900s-pres.]

chichis the breasts. For synonyms see BOSOM. [U.S. slang, mid 1900s-pres.]

chick 1. any female. *Cf.* SLICK-CHICK. [U.S. slang, early 1900s-pres.] **2.** heroin. [U.S. drug culture, mid 1900s-pres.] **3.** a male prostitute for males. *Cf.* CHICKEN (senses 1 and 2). [mid 1900s, *Dictionary of Slang and Unconventional English*]

chicken 1. a homosexual teenage boy. [U.S. underworld and slang, early 1900s-pres.] **2.** a teenage boy considered as a sex object by male homosexuals. [U.S. homosexual use, mid 1900s-pres.] **3.** a coward. [U.S. slang, 1900s] **4.** a cute young woman or any female. *Cf.* CHICK (sense 1). [U.S. slang and colloquial, 1900s] **5.** the penis in expressions such as CHICKEN-CHOKER (*q.v.*). A play on COCK (sense 3).

chicken-breasted pertaining to a FLAT-CHESTED (*q.v.*) woman. [British slang, early 1800s, Egan's Grose]

chicken-choker a male masturbator. [well-known euphemism used on citizens band radio; U.S., mid 1900s-pres.]

chickendick a male with a small penis. [U.S., late 1900s-pres.]

chicken-grabbing pertaining to a despised man; masturbating. A euphemistic disguise. See CHICKEN (sense 5). [U.S. slang, 1900s]

chicken-hawk a male homosexual who is particularly attracted to teenage boys; the same as CHICKEN QUEEN (*q.v.*). [U.S. slang, mid 1900s-pres., Wentworth and Flexner]

chicken-milking (also **lizard-milking**) male masturbation. *Cf.* MILK THE CHICKEN. For synonyms and related subjects see WASTE TIME. [U.S. slang, late 1900s, Lewin and Lewin])

chicken powder amphetamines. With the implication that a person is a coward to use amphetamines rather than stronger drugs. *Cf.* KIDSTUFF. [U.S. drug culture, mid 1900s-pres.]

chicken queen a homosexual male who is strongly attracted to adolescent males; the same as CHICKEN-HAWK (*q.v.*). *Cf.* CHICKEN (sense 2). See QUEEN for similar subjects. [U.S. slang and homosexual use, mid 1900s-pres.]

chicken scratching searching on hands and knees for crack. [U.S., late 1900s-pres.]

chicken-shit 1. any thing or person which is unpleasant. **2.** to boast and to lie; to BULLSHIT (sense 2). [both senses, U.S. slang, 1900s] **3.** anything that is small or worthless. [U.S. slang, mid 1900s-pres.] **4.** military decorations, especially the type which appears on the shoulders of the uniform. [U.S. military slang, World War II]

chickory (also **chickery**) intoxicated with alcohol. For synonyms see WOOFLED. [U.S. slang, early 1700s, Ben Franklin]

chicks with dicks transvestities. [U.S., late 1900s-pres.]

chief, the the drug L.S.D. (*q.v.*). [U.S. drug culture, mid 1900s-pres.]

child-getter the penis. [British slang, 1800s, Farmer and Henley]

chilly a beer. For synonyms see BOOZE. [U.S., late 1900s-pres.]

chimney the female genitals, specifically the vagina. In the expressions GET ONE'S CHIMNEY SWEPT OUT, MAKE THE CHIMNEY SMOKE (both *q.v.*). For synonyms see MONOSYLLABLE. [British slang, 1800s]

China white heroin as compared to

opium, which is black. [U.S. drug culture, mid 1900s-pres.]

Chinee a Chinese. A jocular and erroneous singular form of "Chinese." [U.S. slang and colloquial, late 1800s]

Chinese white (also **China white**) very potent heroin. [U.S., 1900s]

chingus the penis. *Cf.* DINGUS. For synonyms see YARD. [U.S. slang, mid 1900s, Berrey and Van den Bark]

Chinky (also **chinky**) **1.** a derogatory nickname for a Chinese. For synonyms see JOHN CHINAMAN. [Australian and U.S., late 1800s] **2.** pertaining to a Chinese or any Oriental. Derogatory. [slang, late 1800s-pres.]

chinless wonder a foolish upper-class person, usually male. [British and U.S., late 1900s-pres.]

Chino a derogatory nickname for a Chinese. [U.S. slang, early 1900s]

chip to use drugs occasionally and not addictively. *Cf.* CHIPPER, CHIPPY (sense 3). [U.S. drug culture, mid 1900s-pres.]

chipper an occasional heroin user. *Cf.* CHIP. [U.S. drug culture, mid 1900s-pres.]

chippy (also **chippie**) **1.** a woman, especially a sexually loose woman. **2.** an amateur prostitute who works only occasionally. For synonyms see HARLOT. [both senses, slang, 1900s] **3.** a person who uses strong drugs only occasionally; the same as CHIPPER (*q.v.*). [U.S. drug culture, mid 1900s-pres.] **4.** mild narcotics. [U.S. slang, 1900s]

chippy around to be sexually promiscuous. *Cf.* CHIPPY (sense 2). [U.S. underworld and slang, mid 1900s-pres.]

chippy-chaser a male who chases sexually loose women and girls. For synonyms see LECHER. [U.S. slang, 1900s]

chippy on to CHEAT ON (*q.v.*); to be sexually unfaithful to someone; to step out with a CHIPPY (sense 1), said of a male. [U.S. slang, 1900s]

chit 1. an obnoxious person; a worthless person. From a term for a child or a brat. Probably cognate with "kit" and "kitten." [colloquial, 1600s] **2.** a SHIT (sense 9); an obnoxious person; a deliberate disguise of "shit." [U.S. slang, mid 1900s]

choad (or **chode**) **1.** the penis. For synonyms see YARD. [British and U.S., late 1900s-pres.] **2.** a stupid person, usually male, a PRICK. [British and U.S., late 1900s-pres.]

choad smoker someone who performs fellatio. For synonyms see PICCOLO-PLAYER. [U.S., late 1900s-pres.]

chocha the female genitals. Farmer and Henley list **chocho**, *c.* 1900. [from Spanish; in U.S. slang, mid 1900s-pres.]

chocolate 1. hashish. [U.S. drug culture, mid 1900s-pres.] **2.** (also **chocolate drop**) an American black of African descent. For synonyms see EBONY. Mildly derogatory. [British and U.S. slang, mid 1900s-pres.] **3.** Negroid; having to do with American blacks of African descent. [U.S. slang, 1900s]

chocolate-bandit a pederast. See ARSE-BANDIT. For synonyms see PEDERAST. [British, late 1900s-pres.]

chocolate cha cha anal copulation. For synonyms see PEDERASTY. [Australian and British, late 1900s-pres.]

chocolate chips the drug L.S.D. (*q.v.*). [U.S. drug culture, mid 1900s-pres.]

chocolate ecstasy crack manufactured with cocoa. [U.S., late 1900s-pres.]

chocolate highway the anus in anal intercourse. [U.S. slang, mid 1900s-pres.]

chode the area between the scrotum and the anus. See also CHOAD. [U.S., late 1900s-pres.]

choke the chicken to masturbate. *Cf.* CHICKEN (sense 5), CHICKEN-CHOKER. For synonyms see WASTE TIME. [U.S. slang, mid 1900s-pres.]

chokey a prison. [British, mid 1900s-pres.]

Cholly cocaine. A pronunciation variant of CHARLIE (sense 3). [U.S. drug culture, mid 1900s-pres.]

chompers the teeth. Also **choppers**. [1900s, if not before]

chones 1. the testicles. For synonyms see WHIRLYGIGS. **2.** bravado. Both

from Spanish COJONES = testicles. [both senses, U.S., late 1900s]

choo-choo (also **chuga-chuga**) a series of copulations performed by a number of males and one female. *Cf.* PULL A TRAIN. [U.S. slang, mid 1900s-pres.]

choof to smoke marijuana. [U.S., late 1900s-pres.]

chooms the testicles. For synonyms see WHIRLYGIGS. [U.S. late 1900s-pres.]

chopper the penis. See MARROW-BONE-AND-CLEAVER. [British, 1900s, *Dictionary of Slang and Unconventional English*]

choriza the penis. The name of a sausage. For synonyms see YARD. [U.S., late 1900s-pres.]

chow box to perform cunnilingus. [British, late 1900s-pres.]

Christmas cheer liquor; drinking. [U.S. and elsewhere, 1900s if not before]

chrome a gun. [U.S., late 1900s-pres.]

chronic marijuana. For synonyms see MARI. [U.S., late 1900s-pres.]

chrons CHRONC; marijuana. For synonyms see MARI. [U.S., late 1900s-pres.]

chub a penis. For synonyms see YARD. [U.S., late 1900s-pres.]

chubbies large and well-proportioned breasts. *Cf.* BLUBBERS. For synonyms see BOSOM. [U.S. slang, mid 1900s-pres.]

chubbo a fat person. [U.S., late 1900s-pres.]

chubby an erection. For synonyms see ERECTION. [U.S., late 1900s-pres.]

chubbychasers someone who finds fat people sexually appealing. [British, late 1900s-pres.]

chubbychops a chubby or fat person. [U.S., late 1900s-pres.]

chubster a penis. For synonyms see YARD. [U.S., late 1900s-pres.]

chuck to vomit. For synonyms see YORK. [Australian, late 1900s-pres.]

chuck a dummy to vomit. For synonyms see YORK. [U.S. slang, late 1900s]

chuck a tread to coit a woman. [British slang, 1800s, Farmer and Henley]

chuck a turd to defecate. For synonyms see EASE ONESELF. [British slang, 1800s, Farmer and Henley]

chucked 1. intoxicated with alcohol. *Cf.* SCREWED (sense 1). [British slang, late 1800s] **2.** sexually aroused and therefore copulating very rapidly. Said by prostitutes of their more amorous customers. For synonyms see HUMPY. [British, 1800s, Farmer and Henley]

chuck up to vomit. *Cf.* THROW UP (sense 1), UPCHUCK [attested as Australian, 1800s-1900s, Brophy and Partridge]

Chuck you, Farley! (also **Buck you, Fuster!**) a disguise of "Fuck you, Charley!" and "Fuck you, Buster!" [British and U.S. slang, 1900s]

CHUD a Cannibalistic Humanoid Underground Dweller, a zombie-like character in the movie *C.H.U.D.* [U.S. collegiate, late 1900s]

chuff 1. a pelvic thrust in the act of copulation. **2.** a CATAMITE (*q.v.*). For synonyms see BRONCO. [British underworld, mid 1900s, *Dictionary of Slang and Unconventional English*] **3.** to masturbate. Also **chuffer**. [British slang, 1800s, Farmer and Henley] **4.** the posteriors or the anus. [Australian, Baker] **5.** a churl, oaf, or bumpkin. [British dialect, 1800s or before] **6.** an anal release of intestinal gas. For synonyms see GURK. [British, late 1900s-pres.]

chuff box the female genitals, specifically the vagina. See CHUFF (sense 1).

chuffer a disliked person. For synonyms see SNOKE-HORN. [U.S., late 1900s-pres.]

chuff-nut fecal matter clinging to anal or pubic hairs. From CHUFF (sense 4). *Cf.* DINGLEBERRY, FARTLEBERRY.

chuga-chuga See CHOO-CHOO.

chug nuts bits of dung stuck to body hair around the anus. [British, late 1900s-pres.]

chum 1. the female genitals. **2.** a man's own penis. **3.** a louse. See BOSOM CHUMS. [all senses, British slang, 1800s, Farmer and Henley]

chummy to vomit. For synonyms see YORK. [U.S. collegiate, late 1900s, Munro]

chum the fish to vomit, especially to vomit overboard. For synonyms see YORK. [U.S. slang, late 1900s]

chunder 1. to vomit. **2.** vomitus. For synonyms see YORK. [both senses, Australian, early 1900s-pres., Wilkes]

chunk 1. copulation. Similar to PIECE (sense 5). [U.S. slang, early 1900s-pres.] **2.** to do badly; to blunder. [U.S. slang, late 1900s] **3.** to vomit. *Cf.* BLOW CHUNKS. For synonyms see YORK. [U.S. collegiate, late 1900s]

chunky fat. [U.S., late 1900s-pres.]

churn the female genitals. Refers to the action of the churn-dasher. See BUTTER, which is the semen. [British slang, 1800s, Farmer and Henley]

churrus marijuana. See CHARRAS.

chutney ferret a pederast. For synonyms see PEDERAST. [British, late 1900s-pres.]

cid (also **Sid**) the hallucinogenic drug L.S.D. From ACID. For synonyms see ACID. [U.S. drug culture, late 1900s]

Cidin Coricidin™, a cough medicine. [U.S., late 1900s-pres.]

ciga-weed marijuana. For synonyms see MARI. [U.S., late 1900s-pres.]

circed pertaining to a circumcised penis. Rhymes with "jerked." [U.S. slang, late 1900s]

circle the female genitals. For synonyms see MONOSYLLABLE. [euphemistic, 1600s-1700s]

circle-jerk (also **chain-jerk, ring-jerk**) **1.** real or imagined mutual masturbation in a circle. It may involve males and females or males alone. See GROUP SEX for similar subjects. [U.S. slang, mid 1900s-pres.] **circle-jerk 2.** [for CIRCLE-JERK only] a boring or time-wasting meeting or other event. [U.S. slang, late 1900s]

circus love a real or imagined sexual orgy. See similar subjects at GROUP SEX. [U.S. slang, mid 1900s]

C.J. an abbreviation of "crystal joint," i.e., P.C.P. (q.v.). P.C.P. is often consumed by smoking it with tobacco or other burnable vegetable substances. See JOINT (sense 2). [U.S. drug culture, mid 1900s-pres.]

C-jam cocaine. See JAM (sense 5). [U.S. drug culture, mid 1900s-pres.]

claff the female genitals. An obsolete form of CLEFT (q.v.). For synonyms see MONOSYLLABLE. [British dialect, 1800s, Farmer and Henley]

clagnuts fecal material adhering to the anal hairs or the fur of an animal. [British, mid 1900s-pres.]

clam smackers lesbians. For synonyms see LESBYTERIAN. [U.S., late 1900s-pres.]

clangers the testicles. Cf. CLAPPERS. [British, 1900s or before]

clanks the delirium tremens. Cf. TRIANGLES. [U.S. slang, early 1900s]

clap (also **clapp**) **1.** venereal disease, usually gonorrhea but occasionally (in error) for syphilis. [since the late 1500s] **2.** to infect with gonorrhea. [since the mid 1600s]

clap-checker a medical officer who inspects soldiers for venereal disease. [U.S. military, 1900s, *Soldier Talk*]

clapped (also **clapt**) infected with gonorrhea. Cf. CLAP (sense 2).

clappers the testicles. Like the swinging clapper in a bell. Cf. CLANGERS. [probably written nonce; British, early 1900s, *Dictionary of Slang and Unconventional English*]

clapster a male who is infected with gonorrhea. [British slang, 1800s, Farmer and Henley]

clapt infected with gonorrhea; the same as CLAPPED (q.v.).

claptrap 1. nonsense; something introduced solely to get applause. [colloquial since the 1800s] **2.** a sexually loose woman presumed to be infected with gonorrhea. A reinterpretation of sense 1.

clarabelle tetrahydrocannabinol, (T.H.C.), i.e., synthetic marijuana, the "active ingredient" in marijuana. Cf. CLAY. [U.S. drug culture, mid 1900s-pres.]

clear 1. intoxicated with alcohol. [slang, late 1600s-pres.] **2.** totally and exclusively homosexual. For synonyms see EPICENE. [Australian, late 1900s-pres.]

clear light the drug L.S.D. [U.S. drug culture, mid 1900s-pres.]

click a gun. [U.S., late 1900s-pres.]

climax the end of any activity, specifically orgasm; the end of the sexual act. A euphemism and the polite word-of-choice for "orgasm." [U.S., 1900s]

climb to copulate with a woman; to mount and coit a woman. Cf. BOARD, MOUNT. [since the 1600s]

climb the golden staircase to die. For synonyms see DEPART. [U.S. colloquial, late 1800s-1900s]

clinchpoop (also **clinchpoup**) a term of contempt for an oaf; a dunce. [colloquial, mid 1500s]

clings like shit to a shovel (also **sticks like shit to a shovel**) a catch phrase describing the adherence of a sticky substance or a clingy person. [colloquial since the 1800s]

clinker fecal or seminal matter adhering to the anal or pubic hairs. Cf. CHUFF-NUT, DINGLEBERRY, FARTLEBERRY. [British slang, 1800s]

clinkerballs balls of dried dung in sheep's wool. Cf. CHUFF-NUT, CLINKER, DINGLEBERRY, FARTLEBERRY. [British dialect, 1800s or before]

Clinton to smoke marijuana without inhaling. [U.S., late 1900s-pres.]

clipped circumcised [British, early 1900s-pres.]

clipped-dick a derogatory nickname for a Jewish man. Refers to circumcision. Cf. CUTCOCK. For synonyms see FIVE AND TWO. [U.S. slang, 1900s, Wentworth and Flexner]

clit the clitoris. Cf. CLITTY. [U.S. slang, mid 1900s-pres.]

clit lit a feminist literature college course. [U.S., late 1900s-pres.]

clitoris the erectile sensory organ which is part of the female genitals.

[since the early 1600s] Synonyms: BOY-IN-THE-BOAT, BUTTON, CLIT, CLITTY, LITTLE MAN IN THE BOAT, MAN IN THE BOAT, MEMBRUM MULIEBRE, PENIS EQUIVALENT, PENIS FIMINEUS, PENIS MULIEBRIS, SLIT.

clitty the clitoris. A playful nickname similar to CLIT (*q.v.*). [U.S. slang, mid 1900s-pres.]

clitty litter secretions found in women's underpants. [U.S., late 1900s-pres.]

clobbered intoxicated with alcohol. For synonyms see WOOFLED. [U.S. slang, 1900s]

clock the female genitals. [British slang, 1800s, Farmer and Henley]

clock-weights the testicles. [British slang, 1800s, Farmer and Henley]

closet queen 1. a homosexual male who keeps his homosexuality a secret. *Cf.* CLOSET CASE. **2.** a LATENT HOMOSEXUAL (*q.v.*). For related subjects see QUEEN. [both are originally homosexual use and now are U.S. slang, 1900s]

closet queer the same as CLOSET QUEEN (*q.v.*) [U.S. slang, mid 1900s]

clothes prop the penis, especially when erect. For synonyms see ERECTION. [British slang, 1800s]

clouted arrested. [U.S., late 1900s-pres.]

clover-field the female pubic hair. [British, 1800s]

club 1. the penis. For synonyms see YARD. [widespread recurrent nonce since the 1600s or before] **2.** to coit a woman; to use the CLUB (sense 1) on a woman. For synonyms see OCCUPY. [British slang, 1800s, Farmer and Henley]

club sandwich a type of real or imaginary sexual intercourse for three. See CLUB (sense 1). See GROUP SEX for similar subjects. [U.S. slang, mid 1900s-pres.]

cluck (also **kluck**) **1.** a stupid oaf; a DUMB CLUCK (*q.v.*). [U.S. colloquial, 1900s] **2.** a very dark Negro. Derogatory. For synonyms see EBONY. [U.S. slang, Monteleone]

clucked intoxicated. For synonyms

see TALL, WOOFLED. [U.S., late 1900s-pres.]

clucky 1. pregnant. Refers to a brooding hen. [Australian, early 1900s, Baker] **2.** stupid; oafish. *Cf.* DUMB CLUCK. [U.S. colloquial, 1900s]

cluster, the the testicles. For synonyms see WHIRLYGIGS. [British, late 1900s-pres.]

cluster fuck 1. an act of gang rape. [U.S. military, late 1900s, *Soldier Talk*] **2.** any event as riotous as an act of group rape. [U.S. slang, late 1900s]

clyde a stupid person. From the proper name, sometimes capitalized. For synonyms see OAF. [U.S. slang, 1900s]

Clydesdale a sexually attractive male, as with a STUD or a STALLION. [U.S., late 1900s-pres.]

coachman on the box a venereal disease. Rhyming slang for POX (*q.v.*). In this case, syphilis or other venereal diseases. [British, 1900s, *Dictionary of Rhyming Slang*]

coagulated alcohol intoxicated. For synonyms see WOOFLED. [U.S. slang, late 1900s, Dickson]

coals syphilis. *Cf.* WINTER COALS. For synonyms see SPECIFIC STOMACH. [British slang, 1800s, Farmer and Henley]

coasting intoxicated with drugs. For synonyms see TALL. [British and U.S., late 1900s-pres.]

coast n' toast a drive-by shooting. [U.S., late 1900s-pres.]

coast-to-coasts amphetamine tablets or capsules. Referring to the use of amphetamines by cross-country truck drivers. *Cf.* L.A. TURN-ABOUTS. [U.S. slang and drug culture, mid 1900s-pres.]

coax the cojones to masturbate. Said of the male. For synonyms and related subjects see WASTE TIME. [U.S. collegiate, late 1900s]

cob 1. a male swan. [late 1500s] **2.** to GOOSE (sense 6) a person or to commit pederasty upon a person. **3.** a testicle. See COBS.

cobbler's awls (also **cobbler's**) the human testicles; nonsense. Possibly an elaboration of COBS (*q.v.*), "testicles." Rhyming slang for "balls." [British, 1900s]

cobbler's stalls the human testicles; nonsense. Possibly an elaboration of COBS (*q.v.*), "testicles." Rhyming slang for "balls." See ORCHESTRA STALLS. [British, 1900s, *Dictionary of Rhyming Slang*]

cobics heroin. *Cf.* COBY. [U.S. drug culture, mid 1900s-pres.]

cobra the penis. See also CROTCH COBRA. For synonyms see YARD. [U.S., late 1900s-pres.]

cobs (also **cobbs**) the testicles. The colloquial term for any stone, pebble, or pit. [British colloquial, early 1800s]

coby morphine. Usually in the plural, "cobies." *Cf.* COBICS. [U.S. drug culture, mid 1900s-pres.]

cocaine bugs See COKEROACHES.

cocaine crash severe anxiety or a depression following a heavy session of cocaine use. [U.S. drug culture, late 1900s]

cocainized under the influence of cocaine. [U.S., early 1900s]

cocanut(s) (also **coconut(s)**) cocaine. For synonyms see NOSE-CANDY. [U.S. drug culture, late 1900s]

cock 1. a male chicken. No negative connotations. [since the 800s, *Oxford English Dictionary*] **2.** a spout or tap, such as in a barrel. No negative connotations. [since the late 1400s] **3.** the penis. A nickname based on sense 2. Some etymologies suggest that the erectile cock's comb is a reinforcing factor. This is the most widespread nickname for the penis and is considered quite vulgar in some parts of the world. *Cf.* CHICKEN (sense 5), ROOSTER (sense 1), ROOSTERED. [widespread English since the early 1700s] **4.** to copulate with a woman, from the male point of view. [numerous written attestations, since the 1800s] **5.** any male; the equivalent of "buddy" or "chum." Also in compounds such as "turkeycock." [since the 1600s] **6.** the female genitals. In much of the Southern U.S. and Caribbean, "cock" refers to the female organs exclusively. Possibly

related to COCKLES (*q.v.*). *Cf.* sense 2. [U.S. dialect and Negro usage, 1800s and before] **7.** women considered solely as sexual objects. From sense 6. **8.** to receive a man in copulation, said of a woman. [British, 1800s, Farmer and Henley] **9.** nonsense. A truncation of POPPYCOCK (*q.v.*).

cock-ale beer or ale, allegedly with an aphrodisiac quality. Also due to its diuretic qualities. [British, late 1600s]

cock-alley the female genitals. For synonyms see MONOSYLLABLE. [British slang or cant, late 1700s, Grose]

cock-bite a castrating woman; an extremely hateful young woman or girl; a BITCH (sense 5). Refers to COCK (sense 3), the penis. [U.S. slang, mid 1900s-pres., Landy]

cock-block to interfere with a man's sexual activity with a woman. Abbreviated C.B. (*q.v.*). [U.S. black use, mid 1900s-pres.]

cock-cheese SMEGMA (sense 2). *Cf.* CHEESE (sense 1), CROTCH-CHEESE. [British slang, 1800s-1900s]

cock-doctor a doctor who treats venereal disease. [British slang, 1900s]

cocked 1. intoxicated with alcohol. *Cf.* ROOSTERED. For synonyms see WOOFLED. [U.S. and elsewhere, early 1700s, Ben Franklin] **2.** having been copulated with (said of a woman), or having copulated (said of a man). [British, 1800s, Farmer and Henley]

cocked-up pregnant. From COCK (sense 4). For synonyms see STORKED. [British slang, 1800s, Farmer and Henley]

cock-eyed slightly intoxicated due to drink or drugs. For synonyms see TALL, WOOFLED. [1900s.]

cock-fighter a whoremonger; a notorious copulator. For synonyms see LECHER. [British slang, 1700s-1800s]

cock-happy pertaining to a girl or woman who desires to be copulated with. [U.S., 1900s]

cock-holder the female genitals. *Cf.* COCK (sense 3). [slang, 1800s-1900s]

cocking 1. copulation; the use of the COCK (sense 3), "penis." [British and

U.S. colloquial and slang, 1800s-1900s] **2.** a euphemism for "fucking." *Cf.* COCK (sense 4).

cock-inn the female genitals. *Cf.* COCK-ALLEY. [British slang, 1700s-1800s]

cock jocks men's brief swimming trunks. [Australian, late 1900s-pres.]

cock-lane the female genitals. *Cf.* COCK-ALLEY. [British slang, late 1700s, Grose]

cockle burr an amphetamine tablet or capsule. [U.S. slang, mid 1900s-pres.]

cockles the labia minora. Possibly the origin of or an elaboration of COCK (sense 6). [British slang, 1700s]

cock-loft the female genitals. From the name of the place where chickens are kept. [British slang, 1700s-1800s]

cock-pipe a penis-shaped pipe for smoking marijuana. The smoke is sucked out of the "glans." [U.S. drug culture, mid 1900s-pres.]

cockpit the female genitals; the vagina. *Cf.* BOTTOMLESS-PIT. [recurrent nonce; British slang, 1700s-1800s]

cock pox a veneral disease. [British, late 1900s-pres.]

cock-quean 1. a female cuckold, a woman whose husband copulates with other women. [British slang, 1800s or before, Barrère and Leland] **2.** a beggar or a con man. [British, 1800s or before, Halliwell]

cock's eggs 1. a name for imaginary or nonexistent items; the equivalent of "hen's teeth," which are nonexistent. [British colloquial, 1800s] **2.** rooster droppings. [British, 1900s, *Dictionary of Slang and Unconventional English*]

cockshire the female genitals. *Cf.* MEMBER FOR THE COCKSHIRE. [British slang, 1800s, Farmer and Henley]

cocksman (also **cockhound, cocksmith**) a notorious woman-chaser; a lecher. [U.S. slang, 1900s]

cocksmoker a fellator. For synonyms see PICCOLO-PLAYER. [U.S., late 1900s-pres.]

cock sock a condom. For synonyms see EEL-SKIN. [U.S., late 1900s-pres.]

cock someone up to copulate [with] someone. For synonyms see OCCUPY. [U.S., late 1900s-pres.]

cock-stand an erection of the penis. *Cf.* CUNT-STAND. [primarily British; colloquial, 1700s-1900s]

cocksucker (also **cock-sucker**) **1.** a male and sometimes a female who performs fellatio. *Cf.* CORK-SACKING. [widespread slang, 1800s-pres.] **2.** a toady; a sycophant. [U.S. slang, 1800s-pres.] **3.** a strong term of contempt used by one male to another. The equivalent of calling a man a homosexual. [U.S. slang, 1900s]

cocksucking despicable; contemptible. [U.S. and elsewhere, mid 1900s-pres.]

cock swap a penile implant as a cure for impotence. [U.S., late 1900s-pres.]

cocktail 1. a prostitute. For synonyms see HARLOT. [British slang, 1800s] **2.** a coward. For synonyms see YELLOW-DOG. [British slang or colloquial, 1800s] **3.** a cigarette which is a mixture of marijuana and tobacco. [U.S. drug culture, mid 1900s]

cocktails diarrhea. [Australian, 1900s, Baker]

cock-teaser (also **cock-tease**) a woman who leads a man on sexually but who refuses to permit copulation. *Cf.* COCK-CHAFER, C.T. (sense 3), PRICK-TEASER. [British and U.S., 1800s-1900s]

cock up 1. to beat; to beat up. **2.** a mess. Usually hyphenated in this sense. [both senses, British colloquial, 1900s, and both senses taboo in some parts of the world] **3.** copulated with; impregnated. For synonyms see OCCUPY. See also COCKED-UP.

cock-wagon See SIN-BIN.

Cocoa Puffs a mixture of cocaine and marijuana. The name of a breakfast cereal. For synonyms see NOSE-CANDY. [U.S., late 1900s-pres.]

coconut(s) See COCANUT(S).

cod 1. a husk, shell, or bag. No negative connotation [c. 1000, *Oxford English Dictionary*] **2.** the scrotum and the testicles; sometimes the VIRILIA (q.v.). [1300s] **3.** a fool; an oaf. [British slang, 1600s-1900s] **4.** a drunkard. [British slang, 1800s]

codger a mean and unpleasant old man; now just an old man. [British and U.S. colloquial, 1700s-pres.]

cod-hopper a harlot; a sexually loose woman. Patterned on "clod-hopper." See COD (sense 2).

codpiece 1. a baglike flap in the crotch of the trousers which covers or contains the male genitals. Popular in England in the 1400s. [mid 1400s-pres.] **2.** something similar to a CODPIECE (sense 1) worn about the breast by a woman. [1500s, *Oxford English Dictionary*] **3.** the penis or the VIRILIA (q.v.). [British, late 1700s and before]

cods the testicles. Cf. COBS. [since the 1800s or before]

codys (also **cods**) codeine tablets. [U.S. drug culture, late 1900s, Kaiser]

coffee the drug L.S.D. (q.v.). [U.S. drug culture, mid 1900s-pres.]

coffee house 1. a privy; an outhouse. For synonyms see AJAX. **2.** the vagina in the expression "make a coffee house of a woman's cunt," to "go in and out and spend nothing" (Grose). [both senses, British slang or cant, 1700s, Grose]

coffee-shop 1. a euphemism for "coffin." [British slang, 1800s, Barrère and Leland] **2.** a privy; a W.C.; the same as COFFEE HOUSE (sense 1). [both senses, British slang, 1800s]

coffee stalls the testicles. Rhyming slang for "balls." Cf. ORCHESTRA STALLS. [British, 1900s, *Dictionary of Rhyming Slang*]

coffin a burial case for a corpse. [since the early 1500s] Synonyms: BIER, BONE-BOX, BONE-HOUSE, BOX, BURIAL CASE, CASKET, CATAFALQUE, CHICAGO-OVER-COAT, COFFEE-SHOP, COLD-MEAT BOX, ETERNITY-BOX, FERETORY, MAN BOX, PAINTED-BOX, PINE-OVERCOAT, PLANT-ING CRATE, SARCOPHAGUS, SCOLD'S CURE, SIX-FOOT BUNGALOW, THREE PLANKS, TREE SUIT, WOODEN-COAT, WOODEN-KIMONA, WOODEN-OVERCOAT, WOODEN-SUIT, WOODEN-SURTOUT.

coffin-nail (also **coffin-tack**) a dysphe-

mism for "cigarette." Cf. CANCER-STICK. [British and U.S., late 1800s-pres.]

coffin varnish any inferior alcoholic beverage, especially bad whisky. For synonyms see EMBALMING FLUID. [U.S. slang, 1900s]

cognacked intoxicated with alcohol. Cf. INCOG. [U.S. slang, early 1900s]

coil up one's ropes to die. [British naval slang, Fraser and Gibbons]

coin op a totally passive sexual partner. [U.S., late 1900s-pres.]

coin(s) money. [U.S., late 1900s-pres.]

coit 1. an act of copulation; copulation and impregnation; a sexual union of animals or of humans. Probably in use only as a scientific term. [from the Latin *coire*, late 1600s] **2.** to SCREW (sense 1); to PHALLICIZE (q.v.) a woman. Used here and elsewhere (e.g., *Dictionary of Slang and Unconventional English*) as a euphemism for less polite terms for sexual intercourse from the male point of view. There is no "polite," single-syllable, transitive verb for the male act of penetration and thrusting in copulation.

coition (also **coitus**) **1.** the act of moving the penis inward past the opening formed by the vulva. This degree of penetration constitutes sufficient contact to support a charge of rape. In the narrowest definition, the act of penetration completes the act of coition. Usually, however, it is interpreted in the following sense. **2.** the act of penetrating (as in sense 1) with sufficient movement on the part of one or both parties to produce orgasm in one or both parties. See COIT.

coitu, in* "in the act of copulating"; during sexual intercourse; the same as ACTUS COITU, IN (q.v.). [Latin; English use by the 1300s, *Oxford English Dictionary*]

coitus the same as COITION (q.v.). For synonyms see SMOCKAGE. [from Latin]

cojones the testicles. The "j" is pronounced as an "h." For synonyms see WHIRLYGIGS. [from Spanish; U.S. slang, 1900s]

coke 1. cocaine. [U.S. underworld and

drug culture, early 1900s-pres.] **2.** to use cocaine. [U.S. drug culture, late 1900s]

coked intoxicated with or under the effects of cocaine. [U.S. underworld, early 1900s]

coked out (also **coked up**) HIGH on cocaine. For synonyms see TALL. [U.S. drug culture, early 1900s-pres.]

coke-freak a frequent user of cocaine. Cf. SPEED-FREAK. [U.S., 1900s]

coke-head a heavy user of cocaine. For synonyms see USER. [U.S. drug culture, early 1900s-pres.]

coke-party a gathering where cocaine is consumed as the primary activity. From the nickname for a party where carbonated soft drinks are served. [U.S. drug culture, early 1900s-pres.]

cokeroaches (also **cocaine bugs, coke bugs**) imaginary bugs crawling on or under the skin of someone who is deranged by a cocaine binge. A play on *cockroach*. [U.S. drug culture, late 1900s]

coker-nuts the breasts, especially if well-developed. From the size and shape of the coconut. For synonyms see BOSOM. [British slang, late 1800s-early 1900s, Ware]

coke-smoke a cocaine smoker; someone who smokes cocaine in some form. [U.S. drug culture, late 1900s]

coke whore a cocaine user who begs for cocaine, or buys it with sexual acts. [U.S. drug culture, late 1900s]

cokey (also **cokie**) a heavy user of cocaine. [British and U.S. underworld and drug culture, early 1900s-pres.]

cold biscuit a cold, unresponsive woman. Cf. BISCUIT, YEAST-POWDER BISCUIT. [U.S. slang, early 1900s-pres.]

colder than a polar bear's behind very cold. [Australian, mid 1900s-pres.]

colder than a well-digger's ass very cold. [Australian, mid 1900s-pres.]

colder than a witch's tit in a brass bra very cold. [Australian, mid 1900s-pres.]

coldie a cold beer. For synonyms see BOOZE. [Australian, late 1900s-pres.]

cold meat a corpse. Cf. DEAD-MEAT. [British and U.S. colloquial, 1700s-1900s]

cold-meat box a coffin. Cf. COLD MEAT. [colloquial, early 1800s]

cold-meat cart a hearse, specifically a horsedrawn hearse. Cf. COACH. [British and U.S. colloquial, 1800s-1900s]

cold-meat party a funeral. [U.S. colloquial, 1800s-1900s]

cold-meat ticket a military identification disc; a "dog-tag" used to identify dead military personnel. [British and U.S. wartime slang, 1900s]

cold mud a grave. [U.S. slang, 1900s]

cold pop beer. Euphemistic or a disguise. [U.S. slang, late 1900s]

cold storage a grave; the cemetery; death. [U.S. slang, 1900s]

coli marijuana; Colombian marijuana. For synonyms see MARI. [U.S. drug culture, mid 1900s-pres.]

collar and cuff (also **collar**) an effeminate male; a homosexual male. Rhyming slang for PUFF (sense 2), a homosexual male. [British slang, early 1900s, *Dictionary of Slang and Unconventional English*]

Colleen Bawn an erection of the penis. Rhyming slang for "horn." [British, mid 1800s, *Dictionary of Rhyming Slang*]

collywobbles (also **gollywobbles**) **1.** a stomachache; an upset stomach; a rumbling, growling stomach. From the colloquial term "colly-wobble," meaning "uneven." Cf. MULLIGRUBS, WIFFLE-WOFFLES. [British and U.S., 1800s-pres.] Synonyms: GOLLYWOBBLES, GRIPES, MULLIGRUBS, WIFFLE-WOFFLES. **2.** the menses and the accompanying uterine cramps. [colloquial, 1800s-pres.]

Colombian gold See COLUMBIAN GOLD.

Colombian roulette the smuggling of cocaine from Colombia. A very risky activity. [U.S. drug culture, late 1900s]

colon cowboy a pederast. For synonyms see PEDERAST. [U.S., late 1900s-pres.]

colonial puck an act of copulation; to coit. Rhyming slang for FUCK (*q.v.*). [U.S., 1900s, *Dictionary of Rhyming Slang*]

color, in intoxicated with alcohol. For synonyms see WOOFLED. [U.S. slang, mid 1900s-pres.]

color, of pertaining to a person who has dark skin as a racial characteristic. In expressions such as "man of color," "person of color," or "woman of color." [euphemistic and polite, 1900s and before]

Colorado coolaid (also **Colorado Kool-aid**) beer, especially Coor's Beer (trademark), a brand of beer brewed in Colorado. From the trademarked brand name of a flavored drink mix, "Kool-aid." [U.S. slang, mid 1900s-pres.]

Columbian gold (also **Colombian gold**) marijuana grown in Colombia. Based on ACAPULCO GOLD (*q.v.*). *Cf.* GOLD. Appears in a variety of spellings. U.S. drug culture, mid 1900s-pres.]

Columbian red (also **bo, coli, Colombian red, Colombo, Columbian, Columbia red, Columbo, limbo, lumbo**) marijuana grown in Colombia. *Cf.* GOLD COLUMBIAN. Appears in a variety of spellings. [U.S. drug culture, mid 1900s-pres.]

comatose(d) very drunk; drug intoxicated. For synonyms see TALL, WOOFLED. [U.S. collegiate, late 1900s]

comboozelated intoxicated with alcohol. From BOOZE (*q.v.*). [U.S. slang, mid 1900s]

come (also **cum**) 1. in the male, to ejaculate during orgasm. 2. in the female, to experience orgasm. [both senses, colloquial, 1800s-pres.] 3. semen. From sense 1 [slang and colloquial, 1900s or before]

come aloft 1. to coit a woman. [British slang, 1800s, Farmer and Henley] 2. to get an erection. [both senses are nautical in origin, British, 1500s-1700s]

come around 1. to acquiesce to something, particularly copulation; to agree to copulate after a long time spent holding out. *Cf.* COME ACROSS.

[U.S., 1900s] 2. to begin the menses later than expected, relieving built-up fears of pregnancy. [U.S., 1900s] 3. to enter into HEAT (*q.v.*), said of livestock. [U.S., 1900s]

come-by-chance a bastard; an illegitimate child. For synonyms see ACCIDENT. [British and U.S. colloquial, late 1700s-1900s]

come off to ejaculate; to have an orgasm, said of the male. [British and U.S., 1800s-pres.]

come-on a flirt; a male or female who initiates or encourages advances. [U.S. slang, 1900s]

come one's cocoa to ejaculate. For synonyms see MELT. [British slang, 1900s, *Dictionary of Slang and Unconventional English*]

come one's mutton (also **come one's turkey**) to masturbate, said of the male. *Cf.* GOOSE'S-NECK, MUTTON. [British slang, 1800s, *Dictionary of Slang and Unconventional English*]

come on to someone to give someone the come-on; to lure someone sexually. [U.S. and elsewhere, late 1900s]

come out of the closet (also **come out**) 1. to begin to participate in homosexual social and sexual life. See CLOSET CASE. *Cf.* BRING OUT, GO OVER. [originally homosexual use, mid 1900s-pres.] 2. to bring any practice or belief out into the open. [U.S. colloquial, mid 1900s-pres.]

comfortable pleasantly intoxicated with alcohol. For synonyms see WOOFLED. [U.S. colloquial, 1900s]

comfort for the troops a CATAMITE (*q.v.*). A jocular reinterpretation of a term for any type of comfort or treat for military personnel. [military slang, early 1900s]

comings semen or semen and natural vaginal lubrication. *Cf.* COME (sense 3), SPENDINGS. [British colloquial, 1800s-1900s, *Dictionary of Slang and Unconventional English*]

COMMFU a "complete monumental military fuck-up." For synonyms see SNAFU. [U.S. military, early 1900s]

commode 1. a chamber pot built into

a chair for comfort and disguise; a CLOSE STOOL *(q.v.)*. [since the mid 1800s] 2. a toilet; a water-flush toilet bowl. From sense 1. [U.S. dialect (Southern), 1900s and before]

commode-hugging drunk very drunk; drunk and vomiting. For synonyms see WOOFLED, YORK. [U.S. slang, mid 1900s-pres.]

commodity 1. the female genitals. *Cf.* WARE (sense 2). 2. women considered solely as sexual objects and objects of sexual commerce, *i.e.,* prostitutes. [both senses, late 1500s-1800s]

common-jack a prostitute for military men. [British, 1800s, Farmer and Henley]

common sewer a low prostitute. With reference to her reception of just anyone's DIRTY WATER *(q.v.)*. *Cf.* DRAIN, SCUPPER. [British slang, late 1800s]

company girl a prostitute; a CALL-GIRL *(q.v.)*. For synonyms see HARLOT. [U.S. slang, early 1900s, Deak]

con 1. a trickster or swindler. 2. a homosexual male. See GONIF. [both senses, U.S., mid 1900s-pres.]

concern the male or female genitals. Often pluralized when referring to the male genitals. [British, mid 1800s]

concerned intoxicated with alcohol. For synonyms see WOOFLED. [British and U.S. colloquial, late 1800s-pres.]

condensed corn whisky; rotgut. [U.S. military, mid 1800s, *Soldier Talk*]

Coney Island Whitefish a used condom found on the beach, such as on the Coney Island beach. For synonyms see EEL-SKIN. [U.S. slang, late 1900s]

conflummoxed intoxicated with alcohol. For synonyms see WOOFLED. [U.S. slang, 1900s or before]

Congo hash a type of strong marijuana, presumably from Africa. For synonyms see MARI. [U.S. drug culture, late 1900s]

coning performing fellatio. [U.S., late 1900s-pres.]

conjure it down to make an erect penis flaccid by causing an orgasm in

the male. *Cf.* BRING DOWN BY HAND. [from *A Winter's Tale* (Shakespeare)]

conk-buster inferior liquor. The "conk" is the head. For synonyms see EMBALMING FLUID. [U.S., 1900s, Wentworth and Flexner]

connect to purchase drugs. See CONNECTION.

connection 1. a seller of drugs. 2. established traffic in drugs, as in the "French connection." [both senses, U.S. drug culture and slang, early 1900s-pres.] 3. copulation. See CARNAL CONNECTION.

construction worker crack the cleavage at the top of the buttocks appearing when a man bends over and his pants scoot down. [U.S., late 1900s-pres.]

continuations trousers; breeches. For synonyms see GALLIGASKINS. [British and U.S. slang, 1800s-early 1900s]

contrapunctum the female genitals, "the opposite of the point." "Point" here means "penis." *Cf.* ANTIPODES, THE; POINT. [based on Latin; British slang, 1800s, Farmer and Henley]

conundrum the female genitals. *Cf.* WHAT (sense 2). [written nonce, British, early 1600s]

convenience 1. a CHAMBER POT *(q.v.)*. For synonyms see POT. [British euphemism, 1800s] 2. a public restroom; a PUBLIC CONVENIENCE *(q.v.)*. [British and U.S., 1900s]

convenient a mistress or a prostitute. For synonyms see HARLOT. [cant or slang, late 1600s, B.E.]

cony the female genitals. From the colloquial term for a rabbit. [British slang or cant, late 1500s-1700s]

cooch 1. the female genitals. 2. women considered sexually. [both senses, U.S. slang, 1900s]

coochie cutters very tight shorts worn by girls so that the inseam visibly pushes between the lips of the vulva. [U.S., late 1900s-pres.]

cook 1. to prepare opium for smoking. [U.S. underworld, early 1900s or before] 2. to be electrocuted in the electric chair; the same as FRY (*q.v.*). [U.S. slang, early 1900s]

cooked 1. intoxicated with alcohol. *Cf.* FRIED (sense 1). [U.S. slang, 1900s or before] **2.** intoxicated with marijuana. *Cf.* FRIED (sense 2). [U.S. drug culture, mid 1900s-pres.]

cookie 1. a black who adopts a white lifestyle. A derogatory term used by a Negro for a Negro. From OREO (*q.v.*), the trademarked brand name of a cookie. **2.** the female genitals. *Cf.* BUN (sense 3), CAKE (sense 1). [U.S. slang, 1900s] **3.** a place for smoking opium. *Cf.* COOK (sense 1). **4.** an opium addict. Also **cookee, cooky.** [senses 3 and 4 are U.S. underworld, early 1900s] **5.** cocaine. For synonyms see NOSE-CANDY. [U.S. drug culture, late 1900s]

cookies the male genitals. For synonyms see GENITALS, VIRALIA. [U.S., late 1900s-pres.]

cooler 1. an unattractive young woman who cools one's ardor in an anaphrodisiac manner. [U.S. slang, 1900s, Wentworth and Flexner] **2.** the buttocks. **3.** women considered as sexual objects; women used as a means of abating a man's sexual heat. [British slang or cant, 1600s-1800s]

coolie a cocaine and tobacco cigarette. [U.S. drug culture, late 1900s]

coolie-do the female genitals. For synonyms see MONOSYLLABLE. [U.S. slang, mid 1900s]

cool out to copulate. For synonyms see OCCUPY. [U.S. slang, mid 1900s-pres.]

coon 1. a highly derogatory term for a Negro. For synonyms see EBONY. **2.** pertaining to a Negro or to black culture. Both are derogatory. [both senses, U.S. colloquial, mid 1800s-pres.]

coon-box a portable stereo radio and tape player combination; a WOG-BOX. *Cf.* COON. [U.S. slang, late 1900s, Chapman]

coosie 1. a derogatory term for a Chinese. Possibly related to sense 2. [U.S. military World War II, Wentworth and Flexner] **2.** the female genitals. [slang, mid 1900s]

coot 1. the female genitals. *Cf.* COOCH. For synonyms see MONOSYLLABLE. **2.** coition. [both senses, U.S. slang, mid 1900s-pres.] **3.** an oaf; a worthless fellow, especially in "old coot." [U.S. colloquial, 1800s-1900s] See also DRUNK AS A COOT.

cooze (also **cooz, coosie, coozie**) **1.** women considered solely as sexual objects. **2.** the female genitals. *Cf.* COOCH, CUZZY. [Both senses, U.S. slang, mid 1900s-pres.]

coozey a sexual "pervert." Related to the previous entry. Possibly a CATA-MITE (*q.v.*). [U.S. underworld, mid 1900s, Goldin, O'Leary, and Lipsius]

cop 1. to purchase marijuana. [U.S. drug culture and slang, mid 1900s-pres.] **2.** a policeman. For synonyms see FLATFOOT. [U.S. slang, 1900s or before]

cop a bean to deflower a virgin. *Cf.* BEAN (sense 4), "hymen." [U.S. slang, early 1900s, Goldin, O'Leary, and Lipsius]

cop a buzz to become intoxicated with marijuana. *Cf.* BUZZ (sense 2). [U.S. drug culture, mid 1900s-pres.]

cop a cherry to deflower a virgin. *Cf.* CHERRY (sense 1), "hymen." [U.S. slang, early 1900s-pres.]

cop a feel to touch or feel a woman's sexual parts either as if it were an accident or quite blatantly. Usually refers to touching the breasts. [U.S. slang, mid 1900s-pres.]

cop a head to get drunk. [U.S. slang, late 1900s]

copilot Ben Benzedrine (trademark), an amphetamine. With reference to some long-distance trucker's dependence on amphetamines. See BROTHER BEN. [U.S. drug culture, mid 1900s-pres.]

copilots amphetamine tablets or capsules. From CO-PILOT BEN (*q.v.*). [U.S. slang and drug culture, mid 1900s-pres.]

cop it get pregnant. *Cf.* CATCH (sense 2), TAKE (sense 2). [Australian, early 1900s, *Dictionary of Slang and Unconventional English*]

copper-nose a drunkard. From the color of the nose. [British and U.S. colloquial, 1800s]

copperstick the penis. For synonyms see YARD. [British slang, 1800s, Farmer and Henley]

cop rock to get some CRACK or a similar form of cocaine. [U.S. drug culture, late 1900s]

cop the brewery to get drunk. [British slang, late 1800s, Ware]

Copulater! "See you later!"; Cop (=catch) you later. [Australian, mid 1900s-pres.]

coral branch the penis. See GARGANTUA'S PENIS [1600s-1800s]

cord, on the taking METHADONE treatment for heroin addiction. The addict being treated must take a daily dose of METHADONE. This cord is like an umbilical cord that ties the addict to the drug. [U.S. drug culture, late 1900s, Kaiser]

corey the penis. [British dialect (Cockney), 1900s-pres.]

Corine cocaine. Cf. C. (sense 1). [U.S. drug culture, early 1900s-pres.]

cork a tampon. [U.S., late 1900s-pres.]

cork-sacking a euphemistic disguise of "cocksucking." An adjective derived from COCKSUCKER (q.v.). [U.S. slang, mid 1900s-pres.]

corky (also **corkey**) intoxicated with alcohol. For synonyms see WOOFLED. [British slang, 1800s or before]

corn whisky distilled from corn or any home-distilled alcoholic liquor. Cf. MOONSHINE (sense 2). [U.S. slang, early 1900s or before to the present]

corned (also **corny**) intoxicated with any liquor or intoxicated with CORN (q.v.). Cf. PICKLED, PRESERVED, SALTED-DOWN. [British and U.S., 1700s-pres.]

cornelius marijuana. For synonyms see MARI. [U.S., late 1900s-pres.]

corner the female genitals. Cf. CRANNY, NICHE-COCK. [1600s]

cornered intoxicated with alcohol; to be in a (drunken) predicament. Possibly from CORN (q.v.). [colloquial, 1800s-1900s]

corn hole 1. the anus. May relate to the use of corn cobs for anal cleansing. [U.S. slang, 1900s] **2.** to push a real or imagined object up someone's anus; to GOOSE (sense 6). [U.S. slang, 1900s] **3.** to perform anal intercourse upon a male; to commit pederasty. [U.S. slang, early 1900s-pres.] **4.** to perform anal intercourse upon a woman. [U.S. slang, mid 1900s-pres.]

corn-holer a pederast, the INSERTOR (q.v.). Cf. CORN HOLE (sense 3). [British and U.S. slang, 1900s]

corpse 1. the deceased body of a person. [since the 1300s] Synonyms: BLOAT, CADAVER, CARRION, COLD MEAT, CORPUS, CROAKER, DEADER, DEAD MAN, DEAD-MEAT, DEAR DEPARTED, DECEDENT, DOCTOR'S MISTAKE, DUSTMAN, GONER, LANDOWNER, LATE-LAMENTED, LOVED ONE, MORGUE-AGE, PORK, REMAINS, SHOT, STIFF, STIFF ONE, STIFFY, THE DECEASED, THE DEPARTED, WORM-CHOW, WORM-FOOD. **2.** to kill a person; to turn a person into a corpse. [British slang or cant, late 1800s, Farmer and Henley]

corpse-provider a physician. For synonyms see DOC. [British slang, early 1800s, Farmer and Henley]

corpse ticket a military identification disc, a dog-tag. Cf. COLD-MEAT TICKET. [U.S. military slang, World Wars]

corral a group of prostitutes who work for the same pimp; the same as STABLE (sense 2). [U.S. underworld, mid 1900s-pres.]

corral dust nonsense, lies, and exaggeration. A jocular play on BULLSHIT (q.v.). Cf. BULL-DUST, HEIFER-DUST. [U.S., 1900s or before]

cotics a truncation of "narcotics." [U.S. slang, mid 1900s-pres.] Cf. BINGLE, BIRDIE STUFF, BOW-SOW, DRECK, DRY GROG, DUTCH COURAGE, DYNAMITE, MAHOSKA, MOJO, MOOCH, NEEDLE-CANDY, SCHLOCK, SCHMECK, SMECKER, SWEET STUFF.

cottage a urinal [British, late 1900s-pres.]

cottage of convenience (also **cot-**

tage) a privy; an outhouse. See CONVE-NIENCE. For synonyms see AJAX. [British colloquial, late 1800s, Ware]

cotton the female pubic hair. For synonyms see DOWNSHIRE. [U.S. slang, mid 1900s-pres.]

cotton-picker 1. a derogatory nickname for a Negro. For synonyms see EBONY. [U.S., 1900s or before] **2.** a chum or buddy. **3.** a damn fool; a SON OF A BITCH (sense 2). **4.** a jocular reference to a real or imagined woman who has broken the string on her sanitary tampon. [senses 2-4 are U.S., 1900s]

cotton-picking a euphemism for "damned" or "damnable," especially in the expression "cotton-picking hands." [U.S. slang, 1900s]

couch to copulate; essentially "lie down with." Cf. BED (sense 1), CHAMBER (sense 1). [from *Othello* (Shakespeare)]

couch potato (also **couch turkey**) a lazy person. Someone who sits on the couch and watches television. [U.S. slang, late 1900s]

cougar-milk strong liquor or inferior liquor. For synonyms see EMBALMING FLUID. [U.S., 1900s or before]

couldn't organize a pissup in a brewery not capable of even the simplest organization. [British, mid 1900s-pres.]

couldn't organize a root in a brothel not capable of even the simplest organization. A *root* is a session of sexual activity. [British, mid 1900s-pres.]

council-houses trousers; pants. Rhyming slang for "trousers." [British slang, early 1900s, *Dictionary of Slang and Unconventional English*]

counter a prostitute's term for an act of intercourse that "counts" against a quota which she must fulfill. Cf. SCORE (sense 3). [attested as British underworld, early 1900s, *Dictionary of Slang and Unconventional English*]

counting-house a privy; an outhouse. For synonyms see AJAX. [British slang or cant, mid 1800s]

country cousin the menses. One of a series of VISITORS (*q.v.*). For synonyms

see FLOODS. [U.S. colloquial, 1900s or before]

couple 1. to marry; to copulate in marriage. [since the 1300s] **2.** to copulate, especially in reference to animals. **3.** to cohabit; to live together as man and wife unmarried. [U.S. slang, 1800s-1900s]

coupler the female genitals, specifically the vagina. [British, 1800s, Farmer and Henley]

courage pills drugs. Usually in reference to a specific narcotic, *i.e.*, heroin or a barbiturate. Cf. DUTCH COURAGE. [U.S. underworld and drug culture, early 1900s-pres.]

courses the menses. In the expression "her courses." [British and U.S. euphemism, 1800s-pres.]

cousin sis urine; an act of urination; to urinate. Rhyming slang for "piss." [British, 1900s, *Dictionary of Rhyming Slang*]

cover one's ass (also **cover one's tail**) to protect oneself; to act in advance of some hazard to protect one's interests. Cf. C.Y.A. [U.S. slang, mid 1900s-pres.]

cover the waterfront 1. to wear a perineal pad at the time of the menses. Cf. ALL'S NOT QUIET ON THE WATER-FRONT. [jocular colloquial, 1900s] **2.** to work the dock districts. Said of a prostitute who frequents the waterfront soliciting sailors and dockworkers. [Australian, 1900s, Baker]

cow 1. a rude term for a woman. [since the mid 1600s] **2.** a jail. From HOOSEGOW (sense 1). [U.S. underworld slang, 1800s and early 1900s] Synonyms: CALABOOSE, CAN, COLLEGE, COOP, HOOSEGOW, HOUSE OF CORRECTION, HOUSE OF DETENTION, LIMBO. **3.** an old prostitute. From sense 1. [British slang, 1800s, Farmer and Henley] **4.** cow dung. [euphemistic, 1900s or before]

cow-blakes (also **blakes**) dried cow dung used as fuel. For synonyms see COW-CHIPS. [British dialect, 1800s or before, Halliwell]

cowboy a homosexual male, specifically a masculine male homosexual. Cf.

MIDNIGHT COWBOY, TRUCK-DRIVER. [U.S. slang, mid 1900s-pres.]

cowboy bra a brassiere. Because it "heads them up and moves them out." See also SHEEPDOG. [Australian, late 1900s-pres.]

cow-chips cow dung dried for use as fuel. Sometimes euphemistic for BULL-SHIT (*q.v.*). Cf. BODEWASH, BUFFALO CHIPS. [U.S. dialect and colloquial, 1800s-1900s] Synonyms: BLAKES, BODE-WASH, BOOSHWAH, BUFFALO CHIPS, CAS-INGS, COW-BLAKES, PRAIRIE COAL, PRAIRIE FUEL, SCHARN, SHARN, SIT-STILL-NEST, SKARN, SURFACE FUEL. Additional variants are listed at DROPPINGS.

cow-clap (also **cow-cake, cow-flop, cow-pat**) cow dung. [British dialect, 1800s]

cow-clod cow dung. [U.S. dialect and colloquial, 1900s or before]

cow-cod a whip or a club made from a dried bull's penis. [attested as Jamaican, Cassidy and Le Page]

cow-confetti nonsense; a euphemism for BULLSHIT (*q.v.*). Cf. MEADOW-MAY-ONNAISE. [Australian, early 1900s, Baker]

cow-cunted pertaining to a woman whose genitals have been deformed by giving birth or by "debauchery" (Farmer and Henley). [British slang, 1800s]

cow-dab cow dung. [U.S. dialect (Virginia), 1800s, Green]

cow-doot a mass of cow dung as found in a pasture. For synonyms see DROPPINGS. [U.S. slang, late 1900s]

cow-kissing kissing with much movement of the tongues and lips. [U.S. slang, mid 1900s]

cow-pie a mass of cow dung. [U.S. colloquial, 1900s]

cow-pucky cow dung. [colloquial, 1900s or before]

cowsh "cowshit"; nonsense; BULLSHIT (*q.v.*). Parallel to BULLSH (*q.v.*). Cf. FROGSH. [Australian, 1900s or before, Baker]

cow-shard (also **cow-plat, cow-sharn, cow-shern**) cow dung; a mass of cow

dung. [British dialect and colloquial, late 1500s-1900s]

cowshit 1. the dung of the cow. For synonyms see DROPPINGS. **2.** nonsense; BULLSHIT. For synonyms see ANIMAL. [both senses, 1900s if not before]

cowslip cow dung, especially fresh cow dung. From the flower name. [U.S. colloquial, 1900s, Berrey and Van den Bark]

cowyard confetti (also **farmyard confetti**) nonsense. A jocular euphemism for "bullshit." Cf. COW-CONFETTI, MEADOW-MAYONNAISE. [Australian, early 1900s, Baker]

coyote the female genitals. Cf. CAT (sense 6), PUSSY (sense 1). [British slang, 1800s or before]

coyote date a date who is COYOTE-UGLY = very ugly. [U.S. collegiate, late 1900s, Eble]

coyote-ugly extraordinarily ugly. If you woke up beside this person and this person were resting on your arm, you would chew your arm off—in the manner of a trapped coyote—rather than withdraw it. [U.S. slang, late 1900s]

cozmos the drug phencyclidine, P.C.P. From *cosmos*. For synonyms see P.C.P. [U.S. drug culture, late 1900s, Abel]

cozzer a policeman. For synonyms see FLATFOOT. [British, late 1900s-pres.]

cozzpot a policeman. For synonyms see FLATFOOT. [British, late 1900s-pres.]

c- -r a disguise of COCKSUCKER (*q.v.*). [U.S., 1900s]

crab marijuana. For synonyms see MARI. [U.S., late 1900s-pres.]

crabwalk the perineum. An area presumably traveled by lice when going from the anal to the pubic areas. [U.S. slang, 1900s]

crack 1. the female genitals. A term describing the PUDENDAL CLEAVAGE (*q.v.*). [widespread recurrent nonce since the 1500s or before] **2.** coition. [U.S., 1900s] **3.** a prostitute. [since the late 1600s] **4.** the anus; the gluteal furrow. [widespread and very old; attested as U.S. colloquial and slang, 1900s or before] **5.** women considered as sexual objects. [U.S. slang, 1900s and before] **6.** any young woman or any girl. [U.S. slang, 1900s] **7.** crystallized cocaine. For synonyms see NOSE-CANDY. [U.S. drug culture, late 1900s]

crack a fart to release intestinal gas. For synonyms see GURK. [U.S. and elsewhere, 1900s]

crack a fat to get an erection. [Australian, mid 1900s-pres.]

crack a Judy's teacup (also **crack a pitcher**) to DEFLOWER (q.v.) a girl. [British slang, 1800s-1900s]

crack a stiffie to get an erection. [British, mid 1900s-pres.]

crack a tinnie to open a can of cold beer. [Australian, mid 1900s-pres.]

crack a tube to open a can of beer. [U.S., late 1900s-pres.]

cracked 1. crazy. For synonyms see DAFT. [since the early 1600s] **2.** intoxicated with alcohol. [U.S., early 1700s, Ben Franklin] **3.** deflowered. See DEFLOWER. [British and U.S. slang or colloquial, 1800s-1900s]

cracked in the ring deflowered. See DEFLOWER. Cf. RING (sense 1). [derived from "cracked within the ring" from *Hamlet* (Shakespeare)]

cracked pitcher (also **cracked piece**) a prostitute or a sportive, nonvirgin young woman. For synonyms see LAY. [British slang, early 1700s]

cracker 1. a Caucasian; a Southerner. A truncation of GEORGIA CRACKER (q.v.). For synonyms see PECKERWOOD. [U.S. black colloquial, 1800s-1900s] **2.** the anus of the buttocks. [British, late 1600s, B.E.]

Cracker Jacks crack smokers. [U.S., late 1900s-pres.]

crackfart a boaster; someone whose words are just HOT AIR (q.v.). [British dialect, 1800s or before, Halliwell]

crack house an abandoned house where CRACK cocaine is sold and used. [U.S. drug culture, late 1900s]

crack-hunter (also **crack-haunter**) the penis. A pun on "crack-marksman." [British slang, 1800s, Farmer and Henley]

crackish pertaining to a woman who is wanton or behaves like a prostitute. Cf. CRACK (sense 1). [British slang, late 1600s, B.E.]

crack it to copulate; to SCORE (q.v.). [Australian, mid 1900s-pres., Wilkes]

crack salesman 1. a pimp. **2.** a prostitute. Cf. CRACK (sense 2). [both senses, U.S. underworld, 1900s]

cracksman the penis. Cf. CRACK (sense 2). A reinterpretation of a cant term meaning "house-breaker." [British, mid 1800s, Farmer and Henley]

crack snacker a lesbian. For synonyms see LESBYTERIAN. [U.S., late 1900s-pres.]

crack some suds to drink some beer. [U.S. collegiate, late 1900s, Eble]

crack troops female soldiers. Cf. CRACK. [U.S. military, 1900s, *Soldier Talk*]

cradle the female genitals. For synonyms see MONOSYLLABLE. [British slang, 1800s, Farmer and Henley]

cradle-custard a baby's feces, especially when soft. [U.S. colloquial, 1900s or before]

cramped intoxicated with alcohol. For synonyms see WOOFLED. [U.S., early 1700s, Ben Franklin]

crank 1. methamphetamine. [U.S. drug culture, late 1900s] **2.** the penis. Cf. YANK SOMEONE'S CRANK. For synonyms see GENITALS, YARD. [U.S. slang, late 1900s]

cranks amphetamine tablets or capsules. For synonyms see AMP. [U.S. drug culture, 1900s]

cranny the female pudendum. Cf. CORNER, NICHE-COCK. [widespread recurrent nonce, 1800s-1900s]

cranny-hunter the penis. Cf. CRACK-HUNTER. [British slang, 1800s]

crap 1. nonsense; lies. Cf. BULLSHIT, SHIT (sense 4). [British and U.S., 1800s-pres.] **2.** feces; dung. Lightly euphemistic for SHIT (sense 3). Occurs frequently in "take a crap." [U.S., 1900s] **3.** to defecate. [British and U.S., mid 1800s-pres.] **4.** heroin. Sometimes used for counterfeit heroin. Cf. CA-CA (sense 1), SHIT (sense 5). **5.** chaff; later junk or dregs; the dregs of beer or ale. [British and U.S. slang and colloquial, 1800s-pres.] **6.** the gallows. [cant, early 1800s, Vaux] **7.** to hang a man. [cant, 1800s] **8.** an exclamation somewhat milder than "Damn!" or "Shit!" but still objectionable to some people. [U.S. colloquial, 1900s]

crapbrain (also **craphead**) a despised person; a stupid-acting person. For synonyms see SNOKE-HORN. [U.S. slang, late 1900s]

crap-house a privy; an outhouse. Somewhat milder than SHIT-HOUSE (*q.v.*). For synonyms see AJAX. [U.S. colloquial and slang, 1900s]

crap-list a euphemism for "shit-list." [U.S. colloquial, 1900s]

crapola 1. dung. For synonyms see DUNG. **2.** nonsense; BULLSHIT. Both are variants of CRAP. For synonyms see ANIMAL. [both senses, U.S., mid 1900s-pres.]

crapped (out) dead; finished. From the game of craps [dice], not from the other senses of CRAP. For synonyms see DONE FOR. [1900s or before]

crapper 1. a toilet, privy, or restroom. [U.S. colloquial and slang since the early 1900s or before] **2.** a bragger; a teller of lies and nonsense. *Cf.* BULLSHITTER, SHITTER (sense 2). [U.S. slang, mid 1900s-pres.]

crappery a privy, outhouse, or restroom. [U.S. slang and colloquial, 1900s]

crapping-castle (also **crapping-casa, crapping-case, crapping-ken**) a privy; an outhouse. *Cf.* CARSEY. [cant and slang, 1800s]

crappy lousy; undesirable. A milder form of SHITTY. [1900s or before]

craps diarrhea; euphemistic for the SHITS (*q.v.*). [U.S. slang, 1900s]

crater-face (also **pizza-face, pizza-puss**) a person with acne or many acne scars. Also a rude term of address. Derogatory or hurtful. [U.S. slang, late 1900s]

crazy water alcoholic beverages. For synonyms see BOOZE. [U.S. slang, 1900s]

cream 1. semen. *Cf.* HOT MILK. For synonyms see METTLE. [British and U.S. slang and colloquial, 1800s-pres.] **2.** to ejaculate semen. For synonyms see MELT. [U.S., 1900s and before] **3.** to coit a woman; to impregnate a woman. For synonyms see STORK. **4.** to beat the opposite team in a sporting event. No negative connotations. [U.S. slang, mid 1900s-pres.] **5.** to kill someone. [U.S., 1900s] **6.** [for a woman] to become sexually excited. [British, late 1900s-pres.]

creamed intoxicated with alcohol. From CREAM. [U.S., mid 1900s-pres.]

creamed foreskins a dysphemism for creamed chipped beef. *Cf.* SHIT ON A SHINGLE. [U.S., mid 1900s, Berrey and Van den Bark]

creamie a sexually desirable female. Refers to CREAM = semen or to COIT. [British slang, late 1900s]

cream-jug 1. the female genitals, specifically the vagina. The receiver for CREAM (sense 1). [British slang, 1800s, Farmer and Henley] **2.** a breast. See CREAM-JUGS.

cream-jugs the breasts. *Cf.* DAIRIES, JUGS, MILK-BOTTLES, NINNY-JUGS. [British slang, 1800s, Farmer and Henley]

cream one's jeans to ejaculate semen in one's trousers. A catch phrase describing the intensity of sexual excitement or any excitement sufficient to cause a male to ejaculate. [U.S. slang, 1900s]

cream one's knickers for a male to have an orgasm into his underpants. [British, late 1900s-pres.]

cream puff 1. a woman. [U.S., 1900s] **2.** an effeminate male. For synonyms see FRIBBLE. [U.S. slang, early 1900s-pres.]

cream sauce semen. For synonyms see METTLE. [U.S., late 1900s-pres.]

creamstick the penis. From CREAM (sense 1). [British slang, 1800s]

crease the female genitals, specifically the vulva. *Cf.* PUDENDAL CLEAVAGE. [U.S. colloquial, 1900s]

create fuck to display anger or annoyance; to create an angry scene or cause others annoyance. [U.S. and elsewhere, 1900s]

credentials the male genitals; the VIR-ILIA (q.v.). Cf. TESTIMONIALS. [British, late 1800s]

creedle cocaine. For synonyms see NOSE-CANDY. [U.S., late 1900s-pres.]

creep a jerk; an unpleasant or slimy oaf. For synonyms see SNOKE-HORN. [U.S. slang, early 1900s-pres.]

creeper(bud) marijuana that "creeps up on you." For synonyms see MARI. [U.S., late 1900s-pres.]

creeping crud 1. a variety of skin diseases. Refers to fungi which attack the feet, groin, or anus, or refers to any skin disorder. [U.S. military, World War II] **2.** any kind of nastiness made even worse by implying that it is ambulatory. [U.S. slang, mid 1900s]

crested hen a lesbian. A [female] hen with a [male] rooster's comb. For synonyms see LESBYTERIAN. [U.S. slang, late 1900s]

crevice the female genitals. Cf. CRACK, CRANNY, CREASE. [used as slang and as a polite avoidance]

crib (also **crib-house**) a brothel. Cf. FLASH-CRIB at FLASH-CASE. [Australian and U.S. underworld, 1800s-1900s]

crimson-chitterling the penis; the penis of Gargantua. See GARGANTUA'S PENIS for additional terms. [mid 1600s (Urquhart)]

cringeworthy causing embarrassment or apprehension. [British, late 1900s-pres.]

crinkum-crankum the female genitals. [British slang or cant, 1700s-1800s]

crinkums (also **crincomes, crincum, crinkum**) venereal disease, probably syphilis. [British slang or cant, early 1600s, B.E.]

crips high quality marijuana. For synonyms see MARI. [U.S., late 1900s-pres.]

crisp intoxicated with marijuana. Cf. FRIED (sense 2). [U.S. drug culture, mid 1900s-pres.]

crispo (also **crispy**) a person who is mentally, socially, and physically burned out by marijuana use. [U.S. drug culture, late 1900s]

crispy drunk; hungover. For synonyms see WOOFLED. [U.S., late 1900s-pres.]

crispy-critter 1. a person who is intoxicated with marijuana. Cf. CRISP-FRIED (sense 2). [U.S. drug culture, mid 1900s-pres.] **2.** a person (usually Vietnamese) who has been burned with napalm. Both are from the trade-marked brand name of a breakfast cereal. [U.S., 1960s]

croak 1. a rumbling in the bowels. Also **croake.** [mid 1500s] **2.** to die. For synonyms see DEPART. [cant and slang, early 1800s-pres.] **3.** to murder someone; to hang a man. [British and U.S. underworld, 1800s-early 1900s] **4.** a variant form of CRACK cocaine that contains heroin. The same as MOON-ROCK (q.v.). For synonyms see NOSE-CANDY. [U.S. drug culture, late 1900s]

croaked hanged; murdered. From the sputtering and gurgling of a hanged man. Cf. CROAK (sense 3). [cant, early 1800s, Egan's Grose]

croaker 1. a physician in various realms; any medical officer; an M.D. known to write prescriptions for abused drugs; an M.D. known to treat criminals without reporting injuries caused by violence. [British and U.S., 1800s-1900s] **2.** a corpse, i.e., the result of a croaking. See CROAK (sense 3). [British slang, 1800s, Farmer and Henley]

crock 1. a worthless person. Compared to a chipped or cracked vessel or to a chamber pot. [British and U.S., late 1800s-pres.] **2.** a CHAMBER POT (q.v.). For synonyms see POT. [British colloquial, 1900s or before] **3.** a drunkard. [U.S. and elsewhere, 1900s] **4.** nonsense. See CROCK OF SHIT.

crocked intoxicated with alcohol. For synonyms see WOOFLED. [U.S. slang, early 1900s-pres.]

crocko intoxicated with alcohol. A variant of CROCKED (q.v.). [U.S. slang, 1900s, Berrey and Van den Bark]

crock of shit a mass of lies; bragging or nonsense; bullshit. Common in its shortened form, **CROCK** (sense 4). [U.S. slang, mid 1900s-pres.]

cromagnon an ugly male. [U.S., late1900s-pres.]

crook the penis. Cf. JOINT (sense 1).

cross 1. to bestride or mount a horse; to mount and copulate with a woman. **2.** to cheat or deceive. For both cf. BOARD, MOUNT, PRIG (sense 1), RIDE. [both senses, British, late 1700s-1800s]

crossbar hotel a jail; a prison. [U.S. slang, 1900s]

cross-eyed intoxicated with alcohol. [U.S. slang, 1900s or before]

cross over to die; to have "crossed over" is to be dead. Cf. PASS OVER. [U.S. euphemism, 1900s or before]

crossroad an amphetamine tablet or capsule. For synonyms see AMP. With reference to the X scoring on the tablet. [U.S. drug culture, mid 1900s-pres.]

cross the great divide Cf. CROSS OVER. For synonyms see DEPART.

crotch-cheese 1. smegma. Cf. CHEESE, COCK-CHEESE, DUCK-BUTTER (sense 2). [U.S. slang, 1900s or before] **2.** a real or imagined nasty and smelly substance found in unclean pubic areas. [U.S. slang, 1900s]

crotch-cobra the penis. For synonyms see GENITALS, YARD. [U.S. and probably elsewhere, late 1900s]

crotch-monkey a louse. [U.S., late 1900s-pres.]

crotch-pheasants lice. For synonyms see WALKING DANDRUFF. [U.S. slang, early 1900s]

crotch-rot a skin irritation or disease characterized by itching of the groin and scrotum. Cf. CREEPING CRUD, GALLOPING KNOB-ROT, JOCK-ITCH. [British and U.S. slang, 1900s]

crotch pong masturbation. For synonyms see WASTE TIME. [U.S., late 1900s-pres.]

crowbar hotel a jail; a prison. Cf. CROSSBAR HOTEL. [U.S. slang, 1900s]

crower a rooster. A euphemism for COCK (sense 1). See ROOSTER for similar avoidances. [U.S. colloquial and dialect, 1900s and before]

crown and feathers the female genitals. For synonyms see MONOSYLLABLE. [British slang, 1800s, Farmer and Henley]

crown jewels 1. gaudy jewels worn by male homosexuals in DRAG (q.v.). **2.** the male genitals. Cf. DIAMONDS, FAMILY JEWELS, ROCKS, STONES (sense 2). [both senses, homosexual use, mid 1900s-pres.]

crow-pee "dawn" in the expression "at crow-pee." This and SPARROW-FART (q.v.) are jocular plays and mock euphemisms based on "at cock-crow."

crud (also **crut**) **1.** an older British dialect form of "curd" dating from the 1300s with no early negative connotations. **2.** any junk or worthless matter. Cf. CRAP (sense 5). **3.** fecal matter; CRAP (sense 2); a euphemism for SHIT (sense 3). [U.S. slang, 1900s] **4.** dried semen as might be found on clothing or bedclothes some time after ejaculation. [U.S. military, 1900s, Wentworth and Flexner] **5.** venereal disease, especially syphilis. Cf. SCRUD. [U.S. slang, mid 1900s-pres.] **6.** a repulsive male; a creep or jerk. [U.S. slang, mid 1900s-pres.] **7.** any skin disease. Cf. CREEPING CRUD. [U.S. slang and colloquial, 1900s]

cruise 1. to stalk the streets in search of a homosexual or heterosexual sex partner. **2.** to size up someone as a potential sexual partner; to try to establish eye contact with a potential sex partner. [both senses, primarily homosexual use, U.S., early 1900s-pres.]

cruiser 1. a prostitute in search of a customer. [British and U.S., 1800s-1900s] **2.** a homosexual male searching for a sex partner. [U.S. slang, 1900s]

crumped dead. For synonyms see DONE FOR. [U.S. slang, 1900s]

crumped-out intoxicated with alcohol. For synonyms see WOOFLED. [U.S. slang, 1900s, Wentworth and Flexner]

crumpet 1. the female genitals. Cf. BISCUIT, BUN (sense 3). [British, early 1900s] **2.** copulation; women considered sexually. Reinforced by STRUMPET (q.v.). [British slang, 1800s-early 1900s, *Dictionary of Slang and Uncon-*

ventional English] **3.** the buttocks considered by a homosexual male for the purposes of pederasty. From sense 1.

crumpet run driving around, looking at women. [British, late 1900s-pres.]

crump-footed intoxicated with alcohol. From an old term meaning "clubfooted." In reference to the drinker's staggering gait. [U.S. slang, early 1700s, Ben Franklin]

crunch and munch crack cocaine. For synonyms see NOSE-CANDY. [U.S., late 1900s-pres.]

crushed drunk. For synonyms see WOOFLED. [U.S., late 1900s-pres.]

crusher a policeman. For synonyms see FLATFOOT. [British, late 1900s-pres.]

crutch 1. a crock or a jar used as a chamber pot. [British dialect and colloquial, 1800s or before] **2.** a holder for a marijuana cigarette. *Cf.* ROACH CLIP. [U.S. drug culture, mid 1900s-pres.] **3.** a car. [U.S., late 1900s-pres.]

cry Hughie to vomit. For synonyms see YORK. [widespread, late 1900s]

crying drunk intoxicated with alcohol and weeping. This is not a degree of drunkenness but a type of behavior peculiar to some drinkers. *Cf.* MAUDLIN DRUNK. [since the 1800s]

crying out loud!, For an oath and exclamation euphemistic for "For Christ's sake!" [U.S. colloquial, 1900s or before]

cry Ralph to vomit. Onomatopoetic. For synonyms see YORK. [widespread, late 1900s]

cry Ruth to vomit. Onomatopoetic. *Cf.* CALL RUTH. For synonyms see YORK. [widespread, late 1900s]

crystal 1. some form of amphetamine sulphate, *e.g.,* methedrine. [U.S. drug culture, mid 1900s-pres.] **2.** a toilet; a JOHN (sense 2). [U.S. slang, 1900s, Weseen] **3.** the drug P.C.P. See CRYSTAL JOINT. **4.** a testicle. Usually plural. From *crystal ball*. Probably nonce. For synonyms see WHIRLYGIGS. [U.S. slang, mid 1900s]

crystal joint (also **crystal**) the drug P.C.P. (*q.v.*). JOINT (sense 2) refers to

a marijuana cigarette. [U.S. drug culture, mid 1900s-pres.]

C.S.P. a "casual sex partner." [U.S. collegiate, late 1900s, Munro]

C-stick a cigarette. From CANCER-STICK (*q.v.*).

C.T. 1. "colored-time." **2.** CUNT-TEASER (*q.v.*). **3.** COCK-TEASER (*q.v.*).

cubes the testicles. For synonyms see WHIRLYGIGS. [U.S. slang, mid 1900s-pres.]

cuck 1. excrement. **2.** to excrete. *Cf.* CACK. For synonyms see EASE ONE-SELF. [both since the early 1400s] **3.** an obsolete abbreviation of CUCKOLD (*q.v.*). [British, early 1700s] See also KUCKY.

cuckle to commit adultery; to CUCK-OLD (*q.v.*). [British and U.S. dialect, 1600s-1700s]

cuckold 1. a man whose wife has committed adultery. [since the 1200s] **2.** to make a man a cuckold by seducing his wife. [late 1500s-pres.] Synonyms for both senses: ACTAEON, BUCK'S FACE, CHEAT ON, CHIPPY ON, CORNUTO, CUCKOL, CUCKOO, GRAFT, GREEN-GOOSE, HALF-MOON, HODDY-POLL, HORN, HORN-GROWER, HORN-MERCHANT, RAMHEAD.

cuckold the parson for a man to copulate with his intended wife before marriage. [British slang, late 1700s, Grose]

cuckoo 1. a fool; a dull oaf. [colloquial, 1500s-pres.] **2.** a cuckold. A corruption of "cuckold." [from *Love's Labour's Lost* (Shakespeare)] **3.** the penis. For synonyms see YARD. [British juvenile, 1800s, Farmer and Henley]

cuckoo's nest the female genitals. A place for the CUCKOO (sense 3). [British slang, 1800s, Farmer and Henley]

cuckquean 1. a female CUCKOLD (*q.v.*). **2.** to cause a woman to be a female cuckold. [both senses, mid 1500s]

cucumber the penis, especially the erect penis. For synonyms see ERECTION, YARD. [U.S. and probably elsewhere, 1900s and recurrent nonce]

cuddle 1. to pet and fondle. **2.** to copulate. [both senses, British and U.S., 1800s-1900s]

cuddle-bunny a sexually loose woman. *Cf.* BED-BUNNY. For synonyms see LAY. [U.S. slang, 1900s]

cues Quaalude tablets. [U.S. drug culture, late 1900s, Kaiser]

cuff one's governor to masturbate. Said of the male. For synonyms and related subjects see WASTE TIME. [U.S. slang, late 1900s]

cully-shangy coition. See CULLS. For synonyms see SMOCKAGE. [British slang and cant, 1800s, Farmer and Henley]

culver-head a fool or an oaf; a thick-headed fool. The adjective "culverheaded" appeared in the 1500s. From "culver," meaning "dove." [British colloquial, late 1800s, Ware]

cum See COME.

cum catcher a fellator who swallows semen. [U.S., late 1900s-pres.]

cum dumpster a fellator who swallows semen. [U.S., late 1900s-pres.]

cum freak a young woman interested only in copulating. *Cf.* COCK-HAPPY. [U.S. slang, mid 1900s]

cunnikin the female genitals. A diminutive form of CUNT (*q.v.*). [British, 1800s, Farmer and Henley]

cunnilinguist (also **cunnilingist**) one who performs cunnilingus. [originally medical] Synonyms: DIVER, GROWL-BITER, LICK-TWAT, LINGUIST, MUFF-DIVER.

cunnilingus the act of tonguing a woman on the vulva and clitoris. [Latin, both the form and the meaning] Synonyms and related terms: BIRD-WASHING, BLOW, BLOW-JOB, BOX LUNCH, CANYON YODELING, DIVE A MUFF, EAT OUT, FACE JOB, FRENCH TRICKS, FRENCH WAY, LARKING, LICKETY-SPLIT, MUFF-BARKING, MOUTH-MUSIC, PEARL-DIVING, SEAFOOD, SKULL-JOB, SNEEZE IN THE BASKET, SODOMY, SUCK, TALK TO THE CANOE DRIVER, TONGUE-FUCK, TUNA TACO, YODEL IN THE CANYON, YODEL IN THE GULLY.

cunny (also **cunni**) **1.** from CONY (*q.v.*), "female genitals." Reinforced by Latin CUNNUS (*q.v.*). [colloquial, 1600s] **2.** a diminutive of "cunt." [British, 1700s]

cunny-burrow the female genitals, especially the vagina. From a term for a rabbit-burrow. See CONY, CUNNY. [British slang, 1700s]

cunny-catcher the penis. [British slang, 1700s] See also RABBIT-CATCHER.

cunny-haunted lewd and lecherous. For synonyms see HUMPY. [British slang, 1700s]

cunny-hunter a lecher; a whoremonger. Literally, "a rabbit-hunter." [British, 1600s]

cunny-skin the female pubic hair. From a word for "rabbit-skin." *Cf.* CAT-SKIN. [British slang, 1700s]

cunt (also **c*nt, c**t, c***, ****, ----**) **1.** the female genitals, specifically the vagina. [said to be from Latin CUNNUS (*q.v.*)] **2.** women considered sexually. **3.** copulation. [in numerous spellings since the 1300s] The word was banned from print in much of the British Empire until the middle of this century, and it is the most elaborately avoided word in the English language. There are numerous dimunitives: CUNNICLE, CUNNIKIN, CUNTKIN, CUNTLET, CUNNY. Avoidances are: INEFFABLE, MONOSYLLABLE, NAME-IT-NOT, NAMELESS. Disguises are: GRUMBLE AND GRUNT, SHARP AND BLUNT, SIR BERKELEY HUNT, TENUC, UNTÇAY. See MONOSYLLABLE for additional synonyms. **4.** a rotten fellow; a low, slimy man. [colloquial, 1800s-pres.] **5.** to intromit the penis. [attested in a limerick, late 1800s] See also DECUNT.

cunt-ball a disliked person. For synonyms see SNOKE-HORN. [U.S., late 1900s-pres.]

cunt cap (also **cunt-hat**) the military cap with two points. [since World War I]

cunt-curtain the female pubic hair. For synonyms see DOWNSHIRE. [British slang, 1800s, Farmer and Henley]

cunt face a derogatory nickname or a description of an ugly person. *Cf.* CUNT (sense 4), GASH (sense 4). [British slang, 1800s, *Dictionary of Slang and Unconventional English*]

cunt fart See PUSSY FART.

cunt-hair the female pubic hair. [widespread nonce and U.S. slang, 1900s or before]

cunt-hat 1. a felt hat. Because it must be "felt" to be enjoyed. [British, early 1900s] **2.** the same as CUNT CAP (*q.v.*).

cunt-hooks (also ****** hooks**) the fingers. A rude play on "cant-hook," meaning "fingers." *Cf.* SHIT-HOOKS. [British slang or cant, late 1700s, Grose]

cunt-hound a lecher; a male who is a notorious whoremonger or woman-chaser. [U.S., mid 1900s]

cunting fucking. [British with some U.S. use, 1800s-1900s]

cunt-itch sexual arousal in the woman. *Cf.* COCK-HAPPY. [British slang, 1700s-1900s]

cunt-juice (also **juice**) natural vaginal lubrication; natural vaginal lubrication and ejaculated semen. For synonyms see FEMALE SPENDINGS. [since the 1800s or before]

cunt-lapper 1. a CUNNILINGUIST (*q.v.*). *Cf.* LAPPER. **2.** a LESBIAN (sense 2). For synonyms see LESBYTERIAN. **3.** any disliked person. *Cf.* COCKSUCKER. [all senses, slang, 1900s]

cuntlet a diminutive of CUNT (*q.v.*). A play on "cutlet," a portion of MEAT (sense 2). *Cf.* CUNTKIN. [British, 1700s]

cunt-rag a perineal pad. For synonyms see MANHOLE COVER. [slang or nonce, 1900s or before]

cunt-stand sexual arousal in the woman. Based on COCK-STAND (*q.v.*). [British slang, 1800s, Farmer and Henley]

cunt stretcher an erect penis. For synonyms see ERECTION. [U.S. slang, late 1900s and probably recurrent nonce]

cunt-struck 1. utterly fascinated with the sexual possibilities of a specific woman. **2.** sexually fascinated with all women. *Cf.* COCK-HAPPY. [both senses, British slang, 1700s-1900s]

cunt-sucker someone who practices

CUNNILINGUS. [U.S. slang, late 1900s or before]

Cuntsville home; the U.S. during the Vietnam war—where women and sex are available. [U.S. military, Vietnamese War, *Soldier Talk*]

cunt-teaser 1. a male who stimulates a woman sexually but refuses to copulate. **2.** a male who stimulates a woman but is unable to carry out the act because of impotence. **3.** a female who knowingly or unknowingly stimulates a lesbian sexually but will not participate in sexual relations. *Cf.* C.T. [all senses, U.S., 1900s]

cunt-wagon a SIN-BIN. [U.S. slang, late 1900s]

cup-cake 1. an effeminate male, possibly a homosexual. [U.S. slang, 1900s, Weseen] **2.** a cute young woman. **3.** a dose of L.S.D. [U.S. drug culture, mid 1900s-pres.] **4.** a breast, especially if small and well-formed. Usually plural. For synonyms see BOSOM. [British and U.S. slang, 1900s]

Cupid's arbor the female pubic hair. [British euphemism, 1800s or before]

Cupid's cave the female genitals, specifically the vagina. [British, 1800s or before]

Cupid's cloister the female genitals. For synonyms see MONOSYLLABLE. [British euphemism, late 1800s (Farmer)]

Cupid's corner the female genitals. *Cf.* CORNER, CRANNY. [British, 1800s, Farmer and Henley]

Cupid's hotel the female genitals. *Cf.* COCK-INN. [British, 1800s]

Cupid's itch venereal disease. [U.S. euphemism, early 1900s-pres., Irwin]

Cupid's kettle drums the breasts. For synonyms see BOSOM. [British slang, early 1800s or before, *Lexicon Balatronicum*]

Cupid's scalding-house a brothel where one is likely to get a SCALDER (*q.v.*), a case of gonorrhea. [late 1500s]

Cupid's torch (also **torch of Cupid**) the penis. *Cf.* BLOWTORCH. [British, 1800s or before]

cupped alcohol intoxicated. Disabled

by the cup. For synonyms see WOOFLED. [1900s or before, Dickson]

cups the breasts. Possibly from the cup-shaped supports of a brassiere. [U.S. slang, 1900s] See also TEACUPS.

cups, in one's intoxicated with alcohol. [since the late 1500s]

cup-shot intoxicated with alcohol. *Cf.* GRAPE-SHOT, POT-SHOT. [slang, 1600s-1900s]

cupshotten intoxicated with alcohol. An earlier form of CUP-SHOT (*q.v.*). [1300s-1500s]

curbie a smoker who must leave a building to smoke at the curb. [U.S., late 1900s-pres.]

cure for the horn copulation. *Cf.* HORN (sense 3), which is the erect penis. [British slang, 1800s, Farmer and Henley]

cure the horn 1. to coit a woman, said of a man. **2.** to copulate with a man, said of a woman. [1800s or before]

curlies the pubic hairs. From SHORT AND CURLY (*q.v.*). *Cf.* SHORT HAIRS. Sometimes euphemistically defined as "the shorter hairs at the back of the neck." For synonyms see PLUSH. [British, 1900s or before]

curp the penis. Backslang for PRICK. For synonyms see YARD. [British, late 1900s-pres.]

curry queen a gay male who is attracted to East Indian homosexuals. For synonyms see EPICENE. [British, late 1900s-pres.]

curse, the the menses. For synonyms see FLOODS. [British and U.S. colloquial, late 1800s-pres.]

curse of Eve the menses; the same as, or an elaboration of, "the curse." [since the 1800s or before]

curse rag a sanitary towel; a PERINEAL PAD (*q.v.*) for the menses. *Cf.* RAG. [British, early 1900s, *Dictionary of Slang and Unconventional English*]

curved intoxicated with alcohol; the same as BENT (sense 1). [U.S. slang, 1900s]

cushion the female genitals. See the following entry. [British, 1800s, Farmer and Henley]

cushion for pushing 1. the female genitals. **2.** women considered as sexual objects, as in "just a cushion for pushin'." For synonyms see TAIL. [both senses, U.S. slang, mid 1900s-pres.]

cushion-rumped See HOPPER-ARSED.

cuss 1. to curse; to swear. A dialect pronunciation of "curse." [British and U.S. colloquial, mid 1800s-pres.] **2.** a man, as in "old cuss." [U.S. colloquial, mid 1800s-pres.]

cuss-fired damned. An exclamation avoiding stronger terms such as HELL-FIRED (*q.v.*). [U.S. colloquial, 1900s]

custard a pimple. Usually in the plural. [Australian, early 1900s, Baker]

custard chucker an ejaculating penis [U.S., late 1900s-pres.]

cut 1. to castrate. [colloquial since the mid 1400s] **2.** intoxicated with alcohol. *Cf.* DEEP CUT. [colloquial and slang since the late 1600s] **3.** the female genitals with reference to the PUDENDAL CLEAVAGE (*q.v.*). *Cf.* GASH (sense 1), WOUND. [since the 1700s] **4.** a prostitute. [British slang, 1700s] **5.** to adulterate drugs or alcoholic beverages. [U.S. underworld slang and drug culture, 1900s] **6.** to coit a woman. [U.S. slang, early 1900s-pres.] **7.** a testis. **8.** excrement. [slang or colloquial, 1900s or before] **9.** circumcised. [British and U.S., mid 1900s-pres.]

cut a fart to break wind; to LET A FART. For synonyms see GURK. [U.S. slang, 1900s]

cut and come again the female genitals. See CUT (sense 3). From a catch phrase indicating that there will be second helpings of meat. [British slang, 1800s, Farmer and Henley]

cut ass to depart in a hurry, as in "cut ass out of here." *Cf.* DRAG ASS, HAUL ASS, SHAG ASS. [U.S. slang, mid 1900s-pres.]

cut ass (out of some place) See BAG ASS (OUT OF SOME PLACE).

cut cabbage the female genitals, especially of a black woman. With reference to the visual image suggested by the cross section of a cabbage. [U.S. dialect (Boontling), late 1800s-early 1900s, Charles Adams]

cut-cock a derogatory term for a Jewish man. With reference to circumcision. *Cf.* CLIPPED-DICK. For synonyms see FIVE AND TWO. [U.S. slang, mid 1900s or before]

cut in the leg (also **cut in the back**) very drunk. As if the drinker were unable to stand up or walk due to an injury. *Cf.* CUT (sense 2). [British slang, late 1600s, B.E.]

cutlass the penis. Reinforced by CUT (sense 6) and "lass," a girl. *Cf.* BLADE, BRACMARD. For synonyms see YARD. [British slang, 1800s, Farmer and Henley]

cut off the joint an act of copulation; some MEAT (sense 2), from the male point of view. *Cf.* CUT AND COME AGAIN. [British, 1900s]

cut one to release intestinal gas, perhaps loudly. *Cf.* LET ONE. [U.S. colloquial, 1900s]

cut one's finger (also **cut a finger**) to break wind. For synonyms see GURK. [British and U.S. euphemism, late 1800s-pres.]

cut one's leg to be drunk. [colloquial, 1600s-1900s]

cut out to be a gentleman circumcised. Adapted from the standard expression meaning "destined" to be a

gentleman. [British, 1900s, *Dictionary of Slang and Unconventional English*]

cut puss an effeminate male. Refers to a castrated cat. *Cf.* CUT (sense 1). [Caribbean (Jamaican), Cassidy and Le Page]

cuts the testicles. For synonyms see WHIRLYGIGS. [U.S. slang, 1900s]

cut the cake to deflower a virgin woman. [U.S. black use, 1900s]

cut the cheese (also **cut the mustard**) to break wind. With reference to the odor rather than the sound. *Cf.* BURNT CHEESE, CHEEZER. [U.S., 1900s]

cutty-gun the penis. Literally, SHORT-ARM (*q.v.*). Similar to CULTY-GUN (*q.v.*). [from the Scots term for a short tobacco pipe, 1800s]

cuz 1. a defecation. For synonyms see EASEMENT. 2. the W.C. [possibly from a Hebrew term for a refuse container; both senses, British, 1800s, *Dictionary of Slang and Unconventional English*]

cuzzy 1. copulation. 2. the female genitals. *Cf.* COOZE. [both senses, U.S. slang, early 1900s-pres., Wentworth and Flexner]

C.Y.A. "Cover your ass!"; protect yourself. See COVER YOUR ASS. [U.S., late 1900s]

cyclone a dose of the drug P.C.P. (*q.v.*). [U.S. drug culture, mid 1900s-pres.]

cylinder the vagina. *Cf.* PISTON ROD. [widespread recurrent nonce; attested as Australian, early 1900s, *Dictionary of Slang and Unconventional English*]

D

D. "Dilaudid" (trademark), a pain-killer used as a RECREATIONAL DRUG (*q.v.*). Cf. BIG-D. (sense 1). [U.S. drug culture, mid 1900s-pres.]

D.A. 1. "duck ass" or "duck's ass" as in "duck's ass haircut." [U.S. slang, mid 1900s] **2.** a "drug addict"; the same as A.D. (*q.v.*). [U.S. slang, mid 1900s] **3.** "domestic affliction," the menses. Usually in the plural. Cf. D.A.s, FLOODS. [British euphemism, late 1800s-1900s]

da bomb [something that is] excellent. [U.S., late 1900s-pres.]

daffodil an effeminate male, possibly a homosexual male. Cf. DAISY, PANSY. For synonyms see FLOWER. [British, mid 1900s, *Dictionary of Slang and Unconventional English*]

daft stupid; insane; silly. [since the 1300s] Synonyms: BATS, BATTY, BEEN IN THE SUN TOO LONG, BONKERS, BRAIN-SICK, CRACKED, CRACKERS, HALF-CRACKED, LOONY, MESHUGA, NUTS, OFF ONE'S NUT, PSYCHO, SCREWY, SICK, TOUCHED, WACKER.

dagged intoxicated with alcohol. Literally, "dewy." [since the 1600s]

dagger the penis. See similar words at BRACMARD. [British slang, 1800s, Farmer and Henley]

dairies the breasts. Cf. CREAM-JUGS, MILK-BOTTLES. For synonyms see BOSOM. [British slang, 1700s-1800s]

dairy the breasts filled with milk. [British slang, early 1800s and before, *Lexicon Balatronicum*]

dairy arrangements the breasts; the same as DAIRY (*q.v.*).

daisy an effeminate man; a passive male homosexual. For synonyms see EPICENE, FRIBBLE. [British, mid 1900s-pres.]

daisy chain homosexual males engaged in simultaneous, mutual sexual activity. The usual image is a line of pederasts and catamites copulating anally. [U.S. slang, mid 1900s-pres.] See also FUGITIVE FROM A DAISY CHAIN GANG.

daisy-pushing dead; the same as PUSHING UP DAISIES (*q.v.*). For synonyms see DONE FOR.

da kine marijuana; *the kind.* For synonyms see MARI. [U.S., late 1900s-pres.]

damaged intoxicated with alcohol. For synonyms see WOOFLED. [since the mid 1800s]

damaged goods a nonvirgin female. Cf. CRACKED PITCHER, UNDAMAGED GOODS. [U.S. slang, early 1900s]

damber-bush the female pubic hair. For synonyms see DOWNSHIRE. [British slang, 1800s, Farmer and Henley]

damsel morphine. Cf. GIRL (sense 9). For synonyms see MORPH. [U.S., 1900s]

dance 1. to be hanged. [U.S. slang and steroptypical cowboy jargon, 1900s] **2.** to phallicize; to thrust in copulation. Said of the male. See DANCE THE BUTTOCK JIG.

dance the buttock jig to coit. From the action of the male in coition. [British, 1800s]

dance the goat's jig to copulate. For synonyms see OCCUPY. [British, 1800s]

dance the married man's cotillion to copulate. [British, 1800s, Farmer and Henley]

dance the matrimonial polka to copulate. [British, 1800s]

dance the mattress jig to copulate. [British, 1800s or before]

dangle 1. to be hanged. [since the late 1600s] **2.** to hover longingly about a woman without initiating anything. [British and U.S. colloquial, since the early 1700s] **3.** a nickname for an act of male exhibitionism. *Cf.* DANGLER (sense 2). [U.S., 1900s] **4.** the penis. [recurrent nonce]

dangle, on the pertaining to a flaccid penis. See DANGLE-PARADE, DANGLER (sense 2). [U.S. slang, mid 1900s, *Current Slang*]

dangle-parade group military inspection of the genitals for venereal disease. *Cf.* POULTRY-SHOW, PRICK-PARADE, SHORT-ARM INSPECTION, SMALL-ARM INSPECTION. [attested as New Zealand, 1900s, *Dictionary of Slang and Unconventional English*]

dangler 1. a seducer of women. From DANGLE (sense 2). In error for sense 2. [a misinterpretation by Matsell, 1800s] **2.** an exhibitionist of the penis. *Cf.* DANGLE (sense 3). [U.S. underworld, early 1900s] **3.** the penis. For synonyms see YARD. [1900s or before]

danglers the testicles. For synonyms see WHIRLYGIGS. [British, 1800s, *Dictionary of Slang and Unconventional English*]

dangling participle the penis, especially if flaccid. For synonyms see GENITALS, YARD. [recurrent jocular nonce]

Daniel Boone Club an imaginary drinker's club one joins when one goes out and "shoots one's lunch." Referring to Daniel Boone as a self-sufficient hunter. [U.S. contrived nonce, late 1900s]

dank 1. excellent [U.S., late 1900s-pres.] **2.** [of marijuana] high quality. [U.S., late 1900s-pres.] **3.** the penis. For synonyms see YARD. [U.S., late 1900s-pres.]

dart of love the penis. *Cf.* DARD, LOVE-DART. [British, 1800s or before, Farmer and Henley]

D.A.s the DOMESTIC AFFLICTIONS (*q.v.*), the menses. *Cf.* D.A. [British colloquial, 1800s-pres.]

dasher 1. a showy or dashing prostitute. [British slang, 1700s] **2.** a dashing young man; the same as BLOOD (sense 1). [British, late 1700s] **3.** a masturbator. See DOODLE-DASHER.

date 1. the anus. [Australian slang, 1900s or before] See also DOT. **2.** a

prostitute's customer. [U.S. euphemism, 1900s]

daub of the brush 1. coition. **2.** pederasty. Referring to the actions of the INSERTOR (*q.v.*). From sense 1. [both senses, U.S. underworld, mid 1900s, Goldin, O'Leary, and Lipsius]

daughter a homosexual male introduced into homosexual society by another homosexual male who is called a MOTHER (sense 3). [U.S. homosexual use, mid 1900s, Stanley]

day the eagle shits payday. [U.S. military, mid 1900s-pres., if not before]

dead intoxicated with marijuana. For synonyms see TALL. [U.S. drug culture, mid 1900s-pres.]

dead-ass dull; stupid. [U.S. colloquial, late 1900s]

deadcat bounce a small knee-jerk rally in one of the financial markets. [U.S., late 1900s-pres.]

dead drunk heavily intoxicated with alcohol. *Cf.* DEAD. [since the late 1500s]

dead-end street the female genitals. *Cf.* BOTTOMLESS-PIT. [Canadian and U.S., 1900s, *Dictionary of Slang and Unconventional English*]

deader a corpse. [British and U.S. slang, mid 1800s-1900s]

deadeye the anus. The eye that cannot see. For synonyms see ANUS. [British slang, 1900s]

deadly nightshade a prostitute; a very low prostitute. From the plant name. For synonyms see HARLOT. [British slang, 1800s]

dead man empty liquor bottles. See DEAD SOLDIER (sense 2). [cant, late 1700s, Grose]

dead-meat a corpse. *Cf.* COLD MEAT. [colloquial, 1800s]

deads heavily intoxicated with alcohol; DEAD DRUNK (*q.v.*). See DEAD. [British Navy, early 1900s, *Dictionary of Slang and Unconventional English*]

deadshit an oaf. For synonyms see OAF. [Australian, mid 1900s-pres.]

dead soldier 1. a formed lump of excrement. *Cf.* TURD. **2.** an empty beer or liquor bottle. *Cf.* DEAD MAN. [U.S. slang, 1900s]

dead to the world 1. sleeping deeply. No negative connotations. **2.** intoxicated with alcohol. [both senses, U.S., late 1800s-pres.]

dead whore a very easy college course. [U.S. collegiate, 1900s]

dealer a seller of narcotics or marijuana. *Cf.* BAGMAN, PUSHER. [U.S. drug culture, mid 1900s-pres.]

dearest bodily part the female genitals. For synonyms see MONOSYLLABLE. [from *Cymbeline* (Shakespeare)]

dearest member the penis. *Cf.* DEAREST BODILY PART. [ultimately Scots, 1700s (Robert Burns)]

death wish phencyclidine, the drug P.C.P. For synonyms see P.C.P. [U.S. drug culture, late 1900s]

decayed intoxicated with alcohol. For synonyms see WOOFLED. [U.S. slang, mid 1900s]

deck a package of drugs, specifically a package of heroin. [U.S. underworld and drug culture, mid 1900s-pres.]

decks awash intoxicated with alcohol. [originally nautical; U.S. slang, early 1900s]

decorate one's shoes to vomit [on one's shoes]. For synonyms see YORK. [U.S., late 1900s-pres.]

decunt to withdraw the penis from the vagina. *Cf.* CUNT (sense 5). [British use, late 1800s (Farmer)]

Dedigitate! a command to PULL YOUR FINGER OUT! (*q.v.*), *i.e.,* "Take your finger out of your anus!" The camouflaged version is "Take your finger out of your mouth!" [from World War II, British and U.S. slang]

deep cut heavily intoxicated with alcohol. *Cf.* CUT (sense 2). [colloquial, 1900s or before]

deep shit, in in serious trouble. [U.S. slang, mid 1900s-pres.]

deep six 1. a grave. Referring to the customary six-foot depth of a grave. For synonyms see LAST ABODE. [U.S. colloquial, 1900s] **2.** to kill someone or bury someone or something; to throw

something away. [U.S., mid 1900s-pres.]

deep throat to perform oral sex on a penis. From the title of the famous pornographic movie. [U.S. slang, late 1900s]

dees Dilaudid tablets, ampules, or suppositories. [U.S. drug culture, late 1900s, Kaiser]

deflower to terminate a woman's virginity; to rupture the HYMEN (sense 2). [since the 1300s] Synonyms: BREAK, COP A BEAN, COP A CHERRY, CRACK A JUDY'S TEACUP, CRACK A PITCHER, DEFLORATION, DEVIRGINATE, DEVIRGINIZE, DOCK, DOUBLE-EVENT, EASE, GET THROUGH, PERFORATE, PICK HER CHERRY, PLUCK, PUNCH, PUNCTURE, RANSACK, RUIN, SCUTTLE, TRIM, TRIM THE BUFF, VIOLATE.

defood to vomit. For synonyms see YORK. [U.S. slang, 1900s, Berrey and Van den Bark]

dehorn 1. to castrate. *Cf.* HORN (sense 3). [U.S. dialect (Ozarks), Randolph and Wilson] **2.** to copulate, especially after a long wait. *Cf.* HORN (sense 3). [U.S. slang, mid 1900s] **3.** as a noun "de-horn," a drunkard. [U.S. slang, mid 1900s-pres.]

deknackered castrated; emasculated. *Cf.* KNACKERS.

deleerit intoxicated with alcohol. For synonyms see WOOFLED. [U.S. colloquial, 1900s or before]

Delhi belly diarrhea, a malady suffered by tourists in India. *Cf.* MONTEZUMA'S REVENGE. [U.S. slang, 1900s]

delicious jam semen. For synonyms see METTLE. [attributed to Walt Whitman by Farmer and Henley]

demis Demerol (trademark) tablets or capsules. [U.S. drug culture, mid 1900s-pres.]

demise. death. [euphemistic and cultured; since the early 1700s] Synonyms and related terms: COLD STORAGE, DIRT NAP, ETERNAL CHECKOUT, THE, EVERLASTING KNOCK, EXITUS, FINAL SLEEP, GREAT UNKNOWN, GREAT WHIPPER-IN, KINGDOM COME, KING OF TERRORS, KISS OFF, LAST MUSTER, LAST REWARD, LAST ROUNDUP, LEAD-POISONING, LIGHTS OUT.

LONG LIB, NEBRASKA SIGN, OLD OLD GRIM, OLD MR. GRIM, OLD STONY LONESOME, O-SIGN, Q-SIGN, QUIETUS, SWEET-BY-AND-BY, TAP CITY, THE GRIM REAPER, THE OLD, UNDERSIDE.

demi-veg a partial vegetarian [U.S., late 1900s-pres.]

dems Demerol.™ *Cf.* DEMIS. [U.S. drug culture, late 1900s, Kaiser]

den the female genitals. From an old term for "ravine." [vague innuendo from *King John* (Shakespeare)]

denes (also **deens, deines**) CODEINE. [U.S. drug culture, late 1900s, Kaiser]

depart to die. [since the early 1500s] Synonyms: ABIIT AD MAJORES, ABIIT AD PLURES, ANSWER THE FINAL SUMMONS, ANSWER THE LAST CALL, ANSWER THE LAST MUSTER, BEAM UP, BE NO MORE, BITE THE BIG ONE, BITE THE DUST, BLINDO, BREATHE ONE'S LAST, BUY ONE'S LUNCH, BUY THE BIG ONE, BUY THE FARM, CARK (IT), CASH IN ONE'S CHIPS, CLIMB THE GOLDEN STAIRCASE, COCK UP ONE'S TOES, COIL UP ONE'S ROPES, COME OVER, CROAK, CROSS OVER, CROSS THE GREAT DIVIDE, DEPART TO GOD, DROP OFF THE HOOKS, EXPIRE, FADE, FLATLINE, GIVE UP THE GHOST, GO, GO ALOFT, GO FORTH, GO HOME, GO OFF, GO ON TO A BETTER WORLD, GO THE WAY OF ALL FLESH, GO TITS UP, GO TO MEET ONE'S MAKER, GO TO SLEEP, GO UP, GO WEST, HAND IN ONE'S CHIPS, HOP OFF, JOIN THE ANGELS, JOIN THE GREAT MAJORITY, KARK, KICK OFF, KICK THE BUCKET, KISS THE DUST, K.O., LAY DOWN THE KNIFE AND FORK, OFF, PASS AWAY, PASS IN ONE'S CHIPS, PASS IN ONE'S MARBLE, PASS ON, PASS OUT, PASS OVER, PERISH, PIP OFF, POP OFF, POP OFF THE HOOKS, PULL A CLUCK, RAISE THE WIND, SHUFFLE OFF THIS MORTAL COIL, SKIP OUT, SLING ONE'S HOOK, SLIP ONE'S BREATH, SLIP ONE'S CABLE, SLIP ONE'S WIND, SNUFF IT, SQUIFF IT, STEP INTO ONE'S LAST BUS, STEP OFF, STEP OUT, STICK ONE'S SPOON IN THE WALL, SUCCUMB, SWELT, TAKE AN EARTH BATH, TAKE THE LONG COUNT, TAP OUT, TIP OVER, YIELD UP THE GHOST.

deposit 1. to ejaculate semen. See BANK (sense 2). For synonyms see

MELT. **2.** an act of defecation; dung; feces. *Cf.* BANK (sense 1), MAKE A DEPOSIT. [U.S. slang, 1900s]

desires of the flesh food, drink, and sex, usually the latter. [euphemistic and vague]

Detroit pink a "trade name" for P.C.P. For synonyms see P.C.P. [U.S. drug culture, late 1900s, Abel]

deuce, the (also **duece, dewce**) the devil in expressions such as "What the deuce?", meaning "What the devil?" For synonyms see FIEND. [since the late 1600s]

devil 1. Satan; the devil; the supreme being of evil. Usually seen capitalized in older writings. For synonyms see FIEND. [since *c.* 800, *Oxford English Dictionary*] **2.** any malevolent spirit, either a servant of the Prince of Devils or a minor deity. Usually conceived of as male. **3.** a Caucasian. *Cf.* BLUE-EYED DEVIL. [U.S. black use, mid 1900s-pres.]

devil dust a "trade name" for P.C.P. For synonyms see P.C.P. [U.S. drug culture, late 1900s]

Devil's dandruff crack cocaine. For synonyms see NOSE-CANDY. [U.S., late 1900s-pres.]

dexo Dexedrine (trademark).

dexy (also **dexie**) DEXEDRINE (trademark) (*q.v.*). [U.S. drug culture, mid 1900s-pres.] Synonyms: DEXEDRINE, ORANGE, PEACH, PEP PILL, PURPLE HEART.

diamonds the testicles. From ROCKS (*q.v.*), a nickname for diamonds and for testicles. *Cf.* FAMILY JEWELS, STONES (sense 2). [U.S. slang, 1900s]

diarrhea of the mouth (also **diarrhea of the jawbone**) an imaginary condition involving constant talking or a constant stream of nonsense. [U.S. colloquial, 1900s]

dibble 1. the penis. From the shape of a gardening dibbler. For synonyms see YARD. [originally Scots, British, 1800s] **2.** to coit a woman. From sense 1. [British, 1800s, Farmer and Henley] **3.** the devil. [colloquial, 1800s-1900s]

dick 1. the penis. Rhyming slang for

PRICK (sense 1). [British and U.S., 1800s-pres.] **2.** a dictionary. [British slang, 1800s] **3.** to cheat or deceive. See SCREW. **4.** to seduce and coit a woman. [senses 3 and 4 are U.S. (Boontling), late 1800s-early 1900s, Charles Adams] **5.** to coit a woman; to COCK (sense 4) a woman. [U.S. slang, mid 1900s-pres.] **6.** a detective. [U.S. underworld, early 1900s-pres.] **7.** nothing; zero. As in "not worth dick." [U.S. slang, late 1900s] **8.** a worthless oaf. For synonyms see OAF. [U.S. slang, late 1900s]

dick around to waste time; to goof off. *Cf.* FUCK AROUND. [U.S. slang, late 1900s]

dickbrained exceptionally stupid; oafish. For synonyms see STUPID. [British and U.S., late 1900s-pres.]

dickbreath a despised person. For synonyms see SNOKE-HORN. [U.S. slang, late 1900s]

dicked **1.** cheated, literally, "screwed." *Cf.* DICK (sense 3). [U.S. slang, mid 1900s-pres.] **2.** copulate with. [U.S. slang, late 1900s]

dickens (also **dickings, dickins, dickons**) the devil; hell. Found now in expressions such as "What the dickens?" and "Get the dickens out of here!" [since the late 1500s]

dick for a person dumb enough to ask the question: "What's a dick for?" [U.S. collegiate, late 1900s]

dick-head (also **pecker-head**) **1.** a jerk or an oaf; a despised man. [U.S. slang, mid 1900s-pres.] **2.** the head of the penis. [U.S. slang, late 1900s or before]

dickless Tracy a policewoman. For synonyms see FLATFOOT. [widespead, late 1900s-pres.]

dickless wonder a weak, do-nothing person of either sex. [U.S., mid 1900s-pres.]

dickory dock the penis. Rhyming slang for "cock." *Cf.* ALMOND ROCK, COCK (sense 3). [British, 1900s, *Dictionary of Rhyming Slang*]

dick peddler a male prostitute. [U.S. slang, 1900s]

dicksplash a worthless oaf. For syn-

onyms see OAF. [British, late 1900s-pres.]

dicksplat a worthless oaf. For synonyms see OAF. [British, late 1900s-pres.]

dick stickers men's brief swimming trunks. [Australian, late 1900s-pres.]

dick-sucker **1.** a male who performs fellatio. For synonyms see PICCOLO-PLAYER. [British and U.S., mid 1900s-pres.] **2.** a low and despicable male; a male who is despicable enough to perform fellatio. For synonyms see SNOKE-HORN. [British and U.S., mid 1900s-pres.]

dickwad **1.** a mass of ejaculated semen. *Cf.* WAD. For synonyms see METTLE. [U.S. slang, late 1900s] **2.** a total JERK; a social outcast. From sense 1. Also a term of address. For synonyms see OAF. [U.S. collegiate, late 1900s, Munro]

dickweed a total JERK; a social outcast. For synonyms see OAF. [U.S. collegiate, late 1900s, Munro]

dicky (also **dickey, dickie**) **1.** a thing; a gadget. [U.S. colloquial, 1900s, Berrey and Van den Bark] **2.** the penis. From DICK (sense 1). [British and U.S. slang and colloquial, late 1800s-pres.]

dicky-diddle urine or to urinate. Rhyming slang for PIDDLE (*q.v.*). [British, 1900s, *Dictionary of Rhyming Slang*]

dicky-dido (also **dickey-dido**) **1.** an idiot. [British slang, 1800s] **2.** the female genitals. [attested as Canadian, 1900s, *Dictionary of Slang and Unconventional English*]

dicky-dunk copulation. *Cf.* DICKY (sense 2). [slang, 1900s]

dicky-licker **1.** a fellator. **2.** a derogatory term for a homosexual male. *Cf.* COCKSUCKER, DICK-SUCKER. **3.** a derogatory nickname for any male. [all senses, U.S. slang, mid 1900s-pres.]

diddies (also **didds**) the breasts or nipples. The singular is "diddey" or "diddy." *Cf.* TIT, TITTY. [British, 1700s-1800s]

diddle **1.** alcoholic drink, especially gin. [since the early 1700s] **2.** to copulate; to coit a woman. [British and U.S. colloquial, 1800s-1900s] **3.** to masturbate oneself or another, said of a male. [U.S., 1900s] **4.** to masturbate a woman vaginally with the finger. [1900s] **5.** to perform any sexual act, ORTHOGENITAL or NONORTHOGENITAL (both *q.v.*). **6.** any sexual act. [senses 5 and 6 are U.S., mid 1900s-pres.] **7.** to cheat; to deceive. [since the early 1800s] **8.** to dawdle; to waste time. **9.** the penis. [British, late 1800s, Farmer and Henley] **10.** the female genitals. [British, 1800s, Farmer and Henley]

diddly-shit 1. worthless. **2.** a damn. Something very trivial, as in "I don't give a diddly-shit" [both senses, U.S. slang, mid 1900s-pres.]

diddy a breast. See DIDDIES.

dids Dilaudid,™ a potent painkiller. [U.S. drug culture, late 1900s, Kaiser]

Did you get any pieces? "Did you have any sex?" *Cf.* PIECE OF ASS. [U.S. collegiate, late 1900s, Munro]

die in the furrow to copulate without ejaculating; to become impotent while copulating. The "furrow" is the pudendal furrow. [British slang, 1800s, Farmer and Henley]

dies (also **dis, dyes**) Valium, a tranquilizer. From the chemical name *diazepam*. [U.S. drug culture, late 1900s, Kaiser]

diesel dyke a masculine lesbian; a BULLDIKER (*q.v.*). *Cf.* TRUCK-DRIVER (sense 1). For synonyms see LESBYTERIAN. [U.S. slang, mid 1900s-pres.]

die with one's boots on 1. to be hanged. *Cf.* DIE IN ONE'S SHOES. **2.** to die while (still) active, not of old age or illness. [U.S. colloquial and stereotypical cowboy jargon, 1800s-1900s]

differential the posteriors; the rear end. Named for the rear axle gearbox of a vehicle. [U.S. slang, mid 1900s-pres.] See also GEAR.

digithead a computer science student. [U.S., late 1900s-pres.]

dike (also **dyke**) **1.** a latrine; a privy. From an old dialect term for a hole, pit, or trench. [Australian slang, early 1900s-pres.] **2.** a lesbian or a virago. Also **dikey.** Possibly from the dialect

term for "trench." *Cf.* BULLDIKER. [U.S. slang, early 1900s-pres.]

dilberry (also **dillberry**) fecal matter caught in the pubic or anal hair. *Cf.* DINGLEBERRY, FARTLEBERRY. [British and U.S. slang, 1800s-1900s]

dilberry-bush the female pubic hair. [British slang, 1800s, Farmer and Henley]

dilberry creek a privy. For synonyms see AJAX. [British, 1800s]

dilberry-maker the anus. [British slang, early 1800s, *Lexicon Balatronicum*]

dildo (also **dildoe**) **1.** to arouse a woman sexually by fondling her sexual parts. [British, 1600s-1700s] **2.** an artificial penis made of various substances. (*e.g.*, wax, leather, horn) and used by women to obtain sexual gratification. It can be fastened to the body of a female homosexual who then functions as a male. They have occasionally been equipped with ribs and other appendages to heighten their effectiveness. *Cf.* FRENCH-TICKLER. [since the 1600s] **3.** the penis. **4.** an oaf or jerk. *Cf.* DIL. [since the 1600s] **5.** an effeminate male. [U.S., 1900s or before]

dillies tablets of Dilaudid (trademark), a habit-forming painkiller similar to morphine. [U.S. drug culture, mid 1900s-pres.]

DILLIGAF an irresponsible person. "Do I look like I give a fuck?" Also **DILLIGAS,** "Do I look like I give a shit?" [U.S. slang, Vietnamese War, *Current Slang*]

dimblefuck a worthless JERK; an oaf. For synonyms see OAF. [U.S. collegiate, late 1900s]

dimbo 1. a stupid female; a dumb BIMBO. [U.S. collegiate, late 1900s, Munro] **2.** a dull-witted person; a dimwit. For synonyms see OAF. [British, late 1900s-pres.]

dime (also **dime's worth**) a ten-dollar bag of drugs or marijuana. [U.S. drug culture, mid 1900s-pres.]

dimple the female genitals. For synonyms see MONOSYLLABLE. [British, 1800s]

dinero money. Spanish [U.S., mid 1900s-pres.]

dingbats 1. the male genitals. See DINGBAT (sense 1). [U.S. slang and colloquial, early 1900s-pres.] **2.** the DELIRIUM TREMENS (*q.v.*). [Australian, 1900s]

ding-dong 1. the penis. *Cf.* DING (sense 3), DONG [U.S. juvenile and colloquial, 1900s] **2.** a fool; an oaf. [U.S. slang, 1900s]

dinghead a stupid-acting person. [U.S. slang, late 1900s]

dingle the penis. *Cf.* DINGLE-DANGLE. For synonyms see GENITALS, YARD. [U.S. slang, 1900s]

dingleberry 1. fecal matter clinging to anal hair. *Cf.* CHUFF-NUT, FARTLEBERRY. [U.S. slang, 1900s] **2.** an oaf; a person stupid enough to ingest dingleberries while performing ANILINGUS (*q.v.*). [U.S. slang, 1900s]

dingle-dangle the penis. *Cf.* DANGLE-PARADE. [since the late 1800s; probably older as a nonce word]

dingus 1. a thing or gadget. **2.** the penis. *Cf.* CHINGUS. [both senses, colloquial, 1800s-pres.]

dink the penis. For synonyms see YARD. [British, late 1900s-pres.]

dinky dow a marijuana cigarette. [mock-Chinese; U.S. drug culture, mid 1900s]

dinners the human breasts. [U.S. colloquial (Ozarks), Randolph and Wilson]

dino a nickname for a Mexican or Italian laborer. Mildly derogatory. [U.S., 1900s]

dip 1. a drunkard. [U.S. slang, mid 1900s-pres.] **2.** a drug addict. From sense 1. [U.S. slang, 1900s] **3.** a stupid, sloppy oaf. See DIPSHIT. [Australian and U.S., mid 1900s-pres.]

dip in the fudge pot anal coition. [U.S. homosexual use, mid 1900s, Farrell]

dip one's wick (also **dip the wick**) to coit a woman. *Cf.* WET ONE'S WICK, WICK. [slang, 1800s-1900s]

dipped mulatto; having some Negro heritage; having been dipped in tar. [U.S. colloquial, 1900s, Wentworth]

dips a drunkard. See DIP (sense 1). [early 1900s, *Dictionary of the Underworld*]

dipshit a stupid jerk; an oaf. A rude elaboration of DIP (sense 3). [U.S. slang, mid 1900s-pres.]

dipso (also **dypso**) a drunkard. From "dipsomaniac." [British and U.S. slang, mid 1900s-pres.]

dipstick 1. a jerk; a stupid oaf. *Cf.* DIPSHIT. **2.** the penis in "put lipstick on his dipstick." Refers to a woman performing penilingus. [both senses, U.S. slang, mid 1900s-pres.]

dipwad a socially inept male; any social outcast. A blend of DIPSHIT and WAD (both *q.v.*). [U.S. slang, late 1900s]

dirk the penis. *Cf.* BRACMARD. [from a Scots word for a type of dagger, 1700s-1800s]

dirt 1. dung, especially animal dung, as in "horse-dirt." Also in the plural, as in "mouse dirts." [since the 1300s] **2.** filth; obscenity; gossip. [U.S. colloquial, 1900s] **3.** a sadistic man who beats homosexual males after having sex with them.

dirtbike a slut. For synonyms see BIRD. [U.S., late 1900s-pres.]

dirt-chute (also **dirt-road, poop-chute**) the rectum. *Cf.* SEWER, SLOPCHUTE. [U.S. slang, early 1900s]

dirt nap death. Refers to an earthen burial. For synonyms see DEMISE. [U.S. slang, 1900s if not before]

dirty-drunk heavily intoxicated with alcohol. *Cf.* SLOPPY-DRUNK. [British colloquial, 1900s]

dirty-leg a sexually promiscuous girl or woman. *Cf.* LEG (sense 3).

dirty mouth to slander someone. [U.S. slang, mid 1900s-pres.]

dirty old man 1. an old man who displays a childish interest in excrement and sex, especially NONORTHOGENITAL (*q.v.*) sexual matters. Usually considered psychopathological. **2.** a male of any age showing an extremely high degree of interest in sexual matters. Abbreviated

D.O.M. [both senses, U.S. slang, mid 1900s-pres.] **3.** an elderly homosexual male; an "old man" in the sense of DADDY (sense 1). *Cf.* AUNTIE. [U.S. slang or nonce, 1900s, Wentworth and Flexner]

dirty water semen in the expression GET THE DIRTY WATER OFF ONE'S CHEST (*q.v.*). The phrase itself is a common way of saying "make a clean breast of it." For synonyms see METTLE.

dis 1. Valium. Rhymes with *pies*. From *diazepam*. [U.S. drug culture, late 1900s, Kaiser] **2.** to disparage someone; to be disrespectful; to show disrespect to someone; to degrade someone. Rhymes with *kiss*. See DISH. Originally black use. [U.S. slang, late 1900s] **3.** an act of disparagement. [U.S. slang, late 1900s] **4.** a bad situation; a disappointment; an unfortunate occurrence. [U.S. slang, late 1900s]

discipline marijuana. For synonyms see MARI. [U.S. drug culture, late 1900s, Eble]

disco drug butyl nitrite, the vapors of which are used by some disco dancers. [U.S. drug culture, late 1900s]

discombobulated (also **discomboobulated**) alcohol intoxicated. For synonyms see WOOFLED. [1900s]

discouraged intoxicated with alcohol. [U.S. slang, 1900s]

discumfuddled intoxicated with alcohol. *Cf.* FUDDLED. [U.S. colloquial, 1900s]

disguised intoxicated with alcohol. For synonyms see WOOFLED. [since the early 1600s]

dish 1. damn; dash. [U.S. colloquial, 1900s] **2.** an attractive man or woman, said by a member of the opposite sex. Usually refers to a woman. [British and U.S., 1900s] **3.** to cheat or deceive. [U.S. dialect (Boontling), late 1800s-early 1900s, Charles Adams] **4.** to engage in gossip; to dish out gossip. [U.S. homosexual use, mid 1900s-pres.]

dish queen a homosexual male who delights in spreading rumors and gossiping. See DISH (sense 4). [U.S. homosexual use, mid 1900s, Stanley]

dishy sexy. See DISH (sense 2).

dispatch one's cargo to defecate. *Cf.* DISCHARGE (sense 2). [British, early 1900s]

distillery stiff a drunken tramp; a hobo-drunkard. *Cf.* STIFF (sense 7). [U.S. slang, 1900s or before]

ditch weed marijuana; low-grade marijuana. [U.S. drug culture, mid 1900s-pres.]

dithered intoxicated with alcohol. From "dither," which means "shake" or "quiver." [Australian, early 1900s]

dithers the DELIRIUM TREMENS (*q.v.*). *Cf.* DITHERED. [U.S. slang, 1900s]

ditty the penis. For synonyms see YARD. [U.S., late 1900s-pres.]

dive 1. a saloon; a low drinking establishment. **2.** a brothel. [both senses, U.S. slang, late 1800s-pres.] See also DO A DIVE IN THE DARK.

dive a muff to perform CUNNILINGUS (*q.v.*). See MUFF-DIVER. [U.S. slang, mid 1900s]

diver 1. a male. **2.** the penis. *Cf.* DIVING SUIT. [both senses, widespread nonce use]

divine monosyllable the female genitals. An avoidance for "cunt." See MONOSYLLABLE. [British euphemism, 1800s, Farmer and Henley]

divine scar the female genitals. *Cf.* CUT, GASH, SLIT, WOUND. [British, late 1800s, (Farmer)]

diving suit a condom. *Cf.* RAINCOAT. For synonyms see EEL-SKIN. [mid 1900s]

divining rod the penis; the erect penis. For synonyms see ERECTION, YARD. [U.S. slang, 1900s and probably recurrent nonce]

dizack a penis. For synonyms see YARD. [U.S., late 1900s-pres.]

dizzy as a goose (also **dizzy as a coot**) intoxicated with alcohol. [U.S. slang, early 1700s-pres., Ben Franklin]

dizzy queen a flamboyant gay male. For synonyms see EPICENE. [British, late 1900s-pres.]

do 1. to perform any sexual act. [in various uses both homosexual and heterosexual since the 1600s] **2.** to rob or cheat; to deceive. [British slang or cant, early 1800s, *Lexicon Balatronicum*] **3.** to use drugs. [U.S. drug culture and drug treatment, late 1900s]

D.O.A. 1. "dead on arrival," a notation indicating that a person was pronounced dead upon arrival at a hospital. [U.S., 1900s] **2.** the drug P.C.P. (*q.v.*), a strong and sometimes dangerous, illegal drug. From sense 1. [U.S. drug culture, mid 1900s-pres.]

do a bottom-wetter to copulate, said by a woman. [British slang, 1800s]

do a dive in the dark to coit a woman. *Cf.* DIVER. [British slang, 1800s]

doady wrap a condom. For synonyms see EEL-SKIN. [British, late 1900s-pres.]

do a flop to coit a woman. [British and U.S. slang, late 1800s-1900s]

do a fruit salad [for a male] to exhibit his genitals. *Cf.* FLASH. [U.S. collegiate, late 1900s, Munro]

do a good turn to someone to give a woman sexual pleasure. For synonyms see OCCUPY. [British, mid 1900s-pres.]

do a grind to copulate. *Cf.* GRIND. [widespread slang, 1800s-pres.]

do a grouse to find and copulate with a woman. *Cf.* GROUSE. [British slang, late 1800s, Farmer and Henley]

do a job (also **do the job**) **1.** to defecate. [colloquial, 1800s-1900s] **2.** to coit and impregnate or just coit a woman. [British and U.S., 1900s] **3.** to perform the job of undertaker. [British euphemism, 1800s, Hotten]

do a joint to smoke a marijuana cigarette. *Cf.* JOINT. [U.S. drug culture, mid 1900s-pres.]

do a kindness to to coit a woman. *Cf.* DO A RUDENESS TO. [British euphemism, early 1700s-1900s]

do a line 1. to take a dose of phencyclidine, P.C.P. **2.** to SNORT a dose of cocaine. [both senses, U.S. drug culture, late 1900s]

do a number on to mistreat someone very badly; to put someone in a very bad situation. Literally, "to urinate or defecate on someone." *Cf.* NUMBER ONE, NUMBER TWO. [U.S. slang, mid 1900s-pres.]

do a push to coit a woman. [British slang, 1800s]

do a put to coit a woman; to intromit the penis. *Cf.* PUT (sense 3). [British, 1800s]

do a rudeness to to copulate with a woman. *Cf.* DO A KINDNESS TO, DO ILL TO.

do a shoot up the straight to coit a woman. From horseracing jargon. *Cf.* SHOOT (sense 1). [British slang, 1800s, Farmer and Henley]

do a spread to coit, from the female point of view. *Cf.* PUT DOWN (sense 1). [slang, 1800s-1900s]

do away with to kill. *Cf.* PUT AWAY (sense 5), PUT DOWN (sense 2).

do a woman's job for her to coit a woman; to stimulate a woman until she has an orgasm. [slang since the 1800s]

doc a physician. A truncation of "doctor." [colloquial, mid 1800s-pres.] The following synonyms usually refer to males unless indicated otherwise: BOLUS, BONE-BENDER, BONE-BREAKER, BONES, BUTCHER, CASTOR OIL ARTIST, CORPSE-PROVIDER, CROAKER, CROCUS, DOCTORINE (female), FEMME D. (female), FIXEMUP, FLESH-TAILOR, HEN MEDIC (female), MEDICINER, MEDICO, PILL-PUSHER, PINTLE-SMITH, PISS-PROPHET, PRICK-SMITH, QUACK, SAW-BONES, SIPHOPHIL, SMALL-ARM INSPECTOR, STICK-CROAKER.

dock 1. to DEFLOWER (*q.v.*) a woman. **2.** to copulate with a woman. **3.** the posteriors. For synonyms see DUFF. [all senses, since the 1500s]

Doctor M.D.M.A. [U.S., late 1900s-pres.]

Doctor Johnson the penis. From the statement "There is no one that Dr. Johnson was not prepared to stand up to (Partridge)." An elaboration of JOHN (sense 6). See JOHNSON. [British, late 1700s-1800s]

Doctor White cocaine. *Cf.* LADY WHITE, OLD; WHITE STUFF (sense 2).

[U.S. underworld, early 1900s, Berrey and Van den Bark]

dodad 1. a gadget. For synonyms see GADGET. **2.** a testicle. Usually plural. For synonyms see WHIRLYGIGS. [both are U.S., 1900s]

dode an oaf; a PRICK. For synonyms see OAF. [U.S., late 1900s-pres.]

dodgy boiler a woman thought to carry S.T.D. see BOILER. [British, late 1900s-pres.]

dodo (also **dumb-dodo**) a stupid oaf. From the term for the awkward and extinct bird. [British and U.S. colloquial, 1800s-pres.]

do-do See DOO-DOO.

do drugs to take recreational drugs; to be addicted to drugs. [U.S. drug culture, mid 1900s-pres.]

dodunk a jerk or an oaf; a stupid person. [U.S. colloquial, 1800s-1900s]

do face time to kiss and neck. [U.S. slang, late 1900s]

do for trade to provide someone with some sexual activity. Cf. TRADE. [U.S. slang, mid 1900s]

dofunny (also **doofunny, dufunny**) **1.** a gadget. **2.** the penis. [both senses, U.S., early 1900s-pres.]

dog biscuits (also **biscuits**) PEYOTE; peyote buttons. Named for their appearance. [U.S. drug culture, late 1900s, Kaiser]

dog dirt dog feces. See DIRT (sense 1), PURE. [U.S. colloquial, 1900s]

dogess a bitch. [U.S., late 1900s-pres.]

dog juice very bad liquor. Refers to dog urine. Cf. TIGER PISS. [U.S. black use, late 1900s]

dog-log a rodlike section of a dog's feces. For synonyms see DUNG. [U.S. slang, late 1900s]

dog nuisance dog feces, especially dog feces deposited in urban public places. [euphemistic, U.S., 1970s]

dognutz a good friend. [U.S., late 1900s-pres.]

dog's bollocks, the something excellent. [U.S., late 1900s-pres.]

dog's lady a female dog. A euphe-

mism for BITCH (q.v.). Cf. DOGESS. [British, 1800s or before]

dog's mother (also **dog's mama**) a BITCH of a woman. Cf. DOG'S LADY, DOG'S WIFE. [U.S. slang, 1900s]

dog's stone a species of orchid named for the testicular shape of its tubers. [late 1500s]

dog's vomit very poor-quality food. [Australian, mid 1900s, Baker] Similar terms: BLOOD, BULL FUCK, CALF-SLOBBER, CATSUP, CHATTER-BROTH, CHOKE-DOG, CREAMED FORESKINS, FISH'S EYES, FROG'S EYES, FROGSPAWN, GISM, GNAT'S PISS, HEMORRHAGE, HORSECOCK, SCANDAL-BROTH. See EMBALMING FLUID for alcohol dysphemisms.

dog's wife a BITCH (sense 1 or 2). Cf. DOGESS, DOG'S LADY. [British euphemism, 1800s]

dohickies the male genitals. For synonyms see VIRILIA. [U.S. slang and colloquial, 1900s, Berrey and Van den Bark]

dohicky (also **dohickey, dohickie, dohickus, doohickey**) **1.** a gadget. **2.** the penis. [both senses, U.S. colloquial, 1900s] **3.** a testicle. Usually plural. Cf. DOHICKIES. For synonyms see WHIRLYGIGS. [U.S. colloquial, 1900s and nonce]

do ill to to copulate with a female. Cf. DO A RUDENESS TO. [from Scots, 1800s or before]

do in to kill. Cf. DO FOR (sense 1). [British and U.S., 1900s]

doink to copulate [with] someone. For synonyms see OCCUPY. [U.S., late 1900s-pres.]

do it to copulate. For synonyms see OCCUPY. [since the 1600s or before]

do-it-yourself 1. to masturbate. [double entendre and recurrent nonce; U.S., mid 1900s-pres.] **2.** masturbation. For synonyms see WASTE TIME. [British, late 1900s-pres.]

doje the penis. For synonyms see YARD. [U.S., late 1900s-pres.]

dojigger (also **dojiggie, dojiggum, dojiggus, dojiggy, doojigger**) **1.** a gadget. [U.S. colloquial, 1900s] **2.** the penis. See DOJIGGERS. *Cf.* JIGGER (sense 1). [U.S. colloquial, 1900s]

dojiggers 1. the testicles. For synonyms see WHIRLYGIGS. **2.** the male genitals. [both senses, colloquial and slang, 1900s]

dojohnnie the penis. *Cf.* JOHNNY (sense 1). [U.S., 1900s]

dokus the posteriors. For synonyms see DUFF. [from the Yiddish TOKUS (*q.v.*); U.S. slang, mid 1900s, Wentworth and Flexner]

do lines to SNORT cocaine or powdered methamphetamine. [U.S. drug culture, late 1900s]

doll 1. a person attractive to either sex. [U.S. slang, mid 1900s-pres.] **2.** any illicit drug in pill form. [from the novel *Valley of the Dolls*; U.S. drug culture, mid 1900s-pres.]

D.O.M. 1. an abbreviation of 2,5-Dimethoxy-4-methylamphetamine; the same as S.T.P. (*q.v.*). Possibly a reinterpretation of *Deo optimo maximo,* "to God the highest," or *datur omnibus mori,* "it is allotted to all who die." [U.S. drug culture, mid 1900s-pres.] **2.** "dirty old man." [U.S. slang, mid 1900s]

domes the drug L.S.D. (*q.v.*). [U.S. drug culture, mid 1900s-pres.]

domestic afflictions the menses. *Cf.* D.A.s. For synonyms see FLOODS. [British euphemism, mid 1800s-pres.]

donagher a W.C., privy, or restroom. See other forms at DONIKER. [British, early 1900s]

Donald Duck copulation Rhyming slang for FUCK. For synonyms see SMOCKAGE. [U.S., late 1900s-pres.]

done METHADONE. Rhymes with *bone.* [U.S. drug culture, late 1900s, Kaiser]

done for dead. *Cf.* DO FOR (sense 1). Synonyms: ASLEEP IN JESUS, AT REST, BACKED, BONG, BOXED, BOXED ON THE TABLE, BROWN BREAD, CACTUS, CASHED, COLD, CRAPPED OUT, CRUMPED, DAISY-PUSHING, EASY, ELIMINATED, FLATLINED, GONE, GONE FOR SIX, GONE TO GLORY, GONE TO MEET ONE'S MAKER, GONE TRUMPET-CLEANING, GONE UNDER,

GRAVED, GRINNING AT THE DAISY ROOTS, JACKED IT, LAID-OUT, LATE, OUTED, OUT OF MESS, PASSED, PUSHING UP DAISIES, PUT TO BED WITH A SHOVEL, RUN THE GOOD RACE, ROCKED TO SLEEP, SALTED, SCRAGGED, SENT TO THE SKIES, SHOULDERED, SMABBLED, SNABBLED, SNOTTERED, STONE DEAD, STONKERED, THREW SIXES, USED-UP, WAY OF ALL FLESH. See also the list at DEPART.

donegan a W.C.; a privy. See DONIKER. [U.S. slang and colloquial, early 1900s]

done-over 1. deflowered; copulated with. [British, 1700s] **2.** intoxicated with alcohol. [British colloquial, 1800s]

done up like a pox doctor's clerk overdressed; dressed in a fancy way. [Australian, late 1900s-pres.]

dong the penis. [U.S. colloquial and slang, mid 1900s-pres.]

dong(er) the penis. For synonyms see YARD. [widespread, late 1900s-pres.]

dong-flogging male masturbation. *Cf.* FLOG ONE'S DONG. For synonyms and related subjects see WASTE TIME. [U.S. slang, late 1900s, Lewin and Lewin]

do night laps to copulate, presumably at night. [U.S. collegiate, late 1900s, Eble]

donjem marijuana. For synonyms see MARI. [U.S. drug culture, mid 1900s]

donkey a man with a large penis. [nonce, 1900]

donkey dick a large sausage. [U.S. military, World War II, *Soldier Talk*]

donkey-rigged pertaining to a man with a notably long penis. Named for the male donkey, which is so equipped. See MENTULATE. [British, 1800s, *Dictionary of Slang and Unconventional English*]

donor a volunteer for sexual intercourse; a willing sexual partner, presumably or originally male. Like a sperm donor [U.S. collegiate, late 1900s, Munro]

Don't get any on you! a vague catch phrase of warning used between males. It is to be interpreted rather freely as: "Don't contract a venereal disease through your abundant sexual activity!" or "Don't dribble urine down your trouser-leg!" or "Don't get your semen on your body or clothing!" [U.S., mid 1900s]

don't give a rat's arse not to care. [Australian, late 1900s-pres.]

don't piss in my pocket not to tell me all your miseries. [Australian, late 1900s-pres.]

doob the penis. [there is an extremely remote possibility that this is related to Latin *dubius*, "moving alternately in two directions"; attested as Australian juvenile, 1900s, *Dictionary of Slang and Unconventional English*]

doobage (also **dubage**) a supply or stash of marijuana; marijuana. *Cf.* DUBICH. For synonyms see MARI. [U.S. drug culture, late 1900s]

doobie (also **dubee, duby**) a marijuana cigarette. [U.S. drug culture, mid 1900s-pres.]

doobious intoxicated with marijuana. A play on DOOBIE and *dubious.* For synonyms see TALL. [U.S. collegiate, late 1900s, Eble]

doodle-dasher a male masturbator. *Cf.* DASHER (sense 3). For synonyms see HUSKER. [British slang, 1800s]

doodle-sack the female genitals. Based on an old nickname for the bagpipes. [British slang, late 1700s, Grose]

doodly-shit the same as DIDDLY-SHIT.

doo-doo (also **do-do**) **1.** feces. For synonyms see DUNG. **2.** to defecate. For synonyms see EASE ONESELF. [both senses, British and U.S. juvenile, 1800s-pres.]

doody See DUTY.

doof (also **doofus**) an oaf; a fool. [U.S. slang, mid 1900s-pres., *Current Slang*]

dooflicker 1. a gadget. **2.** the penis. [U.S. slang, 1900s or before]

doogie (also **dogie, dojee, dojie, doojee, dooji, dujer, duji**) heroin. [U.S. drug culture, mid 1900s-pres.]

dooky fecal matter For synonyms see DUNG. [U.S., late 1900s-pres.]

do one's office to copulate with a woman. *Cf.* DO A WOMAN'S JOB FOR HER. [euphemistic since the 1600s]

door-keeper a prostitute; a prostitute who occupies a doorway waiting for clients. For synonyms see HARLOT. [cant, 1600s, Dekker]

doors (also **dors**) Doriden™ sedative in any form. [U.S. drug culture, late 1900s, Kaiser]

doover the penis. Possibly related to HOOVER. For synonyms see GENITALS, YARD. [Australian, 1900s]

dope fiend a drug addict or a drug user. [U.S. slang, early 1900s-pres.]

dopenik a drug addict. Patterned on "sputnik" and "beatnik." For synonyms see USER. [U.S. slang, mid 1900s]

doper 1. a drug user, addict, or seller. *Cf.* PUSHER. [U.S. slang, mid 1900s-pres.] **2.** having to do with marijuana or marijuana users. [U.S. drug culture, late 1900s]

dopestick a marijuana cigarette. [U.S. drug culture, late 1900s]

dories Doriden™ sedative in any form. *Cf.* DOORS. [U.S. drug culture, late 1900s, Kaiser]

dork 1. the penis. **2.** an odd or eccentric person. [both senses, U.S. slang, mid 1900s-pres.] **3.** to copulate; to COIT someone. For synonyms see OCCUPY. [U.S. slang, late 1900s]

dorkmeier a total JERK; a social outcast. For synonyms see OAF. [U.S. slang, late 1900s]

dorkmunder a total JERK; a social outcast. For synonyms see OAF. [U.S. collegiate, late 1900s, Munro]

dork off to waste time; to goof off. [U.S. slang, late 1900s]

dorkus maximus a simpleton or fool; a great fool. For synonyms see OAF. [U.S., late 1900s-pres.]

dorky 1. pertaining to a person, thing, or situation which is unpleasant, unfair, or strange. From DORK (sense 2). [U.S. slang, mid 1900s-pres.] **2.** tacky, stupid, or awkward. From DORK. For synonyms see STUPID. [U.S., late 1900s-pres.]

dormouse the female genitals. *Cf.* TYTMOSE. [British, 1800s, Farmer and Henley]

dors See DOORS.

dose 1. an infection of venereal disease. [British and U.S. slang, mid 1800s-pres.] **2.** to infect with venereal disease. [U.S. slang, mid 1900s-pres.] **3.** a LOAD (sense 4) of liquor or a drink of liquor. *Cf.* MEDICINE. [slang since the 1800s]

dose of claps a case of gonorrhea. [U.S. slang, 1900s]

do some good for oneself to copulate, said of a male. *Cf.* SCORE (sense 1). [Australian euphemism, 1900s, Baker]

do some stewing to drink some beers. *Cf.* STEW. [U.S. collegiate, late 1900s]

doss house (also **doss**) a low brothel. "Doss" is from "dorse." [since the late 1700s]

dot the anus. [Australian, 1900s, *Dictionary of Slang and Unconventional English*] See DOTS.

dothead an [East] Indian person who wears a red dot on the forehead. Derogatory. [U.S. slang, late 1900s]

do the bone dance to copulate. *Cf.* BONE. [U.S. collegiate, late 1900s, Munro]

do the bone throw to copulate. For synonyms see OCCUPY [U.S., late 1900s-pres.]

do the business to copulate. For synonyms see OCCUPY. [British, mid 1900s-pres.]

do the chores to copulate with a woman, especially in a perfunctory manner. Also euphemistic for "coition." *Cf.* DO A JOB (sense 2). [U.S., mid 1900s]

do the do to coit a woman. *Cf.* DO, DO IT. [U.S. slang, mid 1900s-pres.]

do the drink thing to drink alcohol heavily. [U.S., late 1900s-pres.]

do the horizontal boogie to copulate. For synonyms see OCCUPY. [U.S., late 1900s-pres.]

do the lateral lambada to copulate. For synonyms see OCCUPY. [U.S., late 1900s-pres.]

do the nasty to copulate. *Cf.* DO THE NAUGHTY. [U.S. slang, late 1900s]

do the naughty 1. to practice prostitution. **2.** to copulate, said of a woman. *Cf.* NAUGHTY (sense 2). [both senses, British, mid 1800s]

dots the drug L.S.D. (*q.v.*). *Cf.* BROWN DOTS, MICRODOTS. [U.S. drug culture, mid 1900s-pres.]

double-assed (also **double-arsed**) having very large or very fat posteriors. [British and U.S. slang, 1800s-1900s]

double-barrelled slingshot (also **double-barrelled catapult**) a brassiere. For synonyms see BRA. [the first entry is U.S. and the "also" is British; both senses, 1900s]

double-cross an amphetamine tablet, especially one with cross-scoring. *Cf.* CARTWHEEL, CROSSROAD. For synonyms see AMP. [U.S. drug culture, mid 1900s-pres.]

double-cunted pertaining to a woman with large genitals. *Cf.* COW-CUNTED. [British, 1800s, *Dictionary of Slang and Unconventional English*]

double dipper a bisexual person. [U.S., late 1900s-pres.]

double-sucker female genitals with very large *labia*. [British, late 1800s, Farmer and Henley]

double-trouble Tuinal (trademark), a barbiturate. [U.S. drug culture, mid 1900s-pres.]

douche 1. a shower bath. Rarely heard in the U.S., its meaning having been supplanted by sense 2. **2.** a vaginal douche or the instrument used to administer one. [U.S., mid 1900s-pres.] **3.** an obnoxious person. *Cf.* BAG (sense 2), DOUCHE BAG. [U.S. slang, mid 1900s-pres.]

douche bag 1. a device used to administer a DOUCHE (sense 2) **2.** a contemptuous term for a person of either sex; the same as DOUCHE (sense 3). *Cf.* LOUSE-BAG, SCUMBAG (sense 2). [both senses, U.S. slang, mid 1900s-pres.]

Douglas (Hurd) a fecal bolus. Rhyming slang for TURD. For synonyms see DUNG. [British, late 1900s-pres.]

down 1. to position a woman for copulation. [1800s-1900s] **2.** the female pubic hair. [British colloquial and nonce, 1800s] **3.** a barbiturate. See DOWNER. [U.S. drug culture, mid 1900s-pres.]

down among the dead men very intoxicated due to drink. For synonyms see WOOFLED. [British, late 1900s-pres.]

downer (also **down**) a depressant; a barbiturate. For synonyms see BARB. [U.S. drug culture, mid 1900s-pres.]

down-leg the penis. Cf. BEST LEG OF THREE. [British slang, 1800s, Farmer and Henley]

Downshire the female pubic hair. [British slang, 1800s, Farmer and Henley] See also MEMBER FOR THE COCKSHIRE. Synonyms: BANNER, BEARD, BEARSKIN, BELLY-BRISTLES, BELLY-THICKET, BELLY-WHISKERS, BOSKAGE OF VENUS, BROOM, BRUSH, BUSH, BUSHY PARK, CAT-SKIN, CLOVER-FIELD, COTTON, CUNT-HAIR, DAMBER-BUSH, DOWN, FEATHER, FLEECE, FLUFF, FOREST, FRONT-DOOR MAT, FUR, FURBELOW, FUR-PIE, FURZE-BUSH, GARDEN-HEDGE, GOOSE-BERRY-BUSH, GREEN GROVE, GROVE OF EGLANTINE, LADY'S LOW TOUPEE, MERKIN, MOSS, MOTT-CARPET, MOTTE, MUSTARD AND CRESS, NATURE'S VEIL, NETHER EYEBROW, NETHER EYELASHES, PARSLEY, PUMPKIN-COVER, QUIM-BUSH, QUIM-WHISKERS, QUIM-WIG, RUG, SCUT, SHAVING-BRUSH, SHRUBBERY, SILENT BEARD, STUBBLE, SWEETBRIAR, TAIL-FEATHERS, THATCH, TOUPEE, TUFTED-HONORS, TWAT-RUG, WHIN-BUSH. Many of the terms listed at MONOSYLLABLE also refer to the female pubic hair.

downtown heroin. The opposite of UPTOWN = cocaine. For synonyms see HEROIN. [U.S. drug culture, late 1900s, Abel]

doyburger a total JERK; a social outcast. For synonyms see OAF. [U.S. slang, late 1900s]

D'Oyly Carte an anal release of intestinal gas. Rhyming slang for FART. For synonyms see GURK. [British, late 1900s-pres.]

drab a sexually loose woman; a low

prostitute. [colloquial, early 1500s-1800s]

drabble-tail a slattern; a DRAGGLE-TAIL (q.v.); a woman who has dirtied the hem of her skirt. [British and U.S. colloquial, 1800s]

drafty a draft beer; beer. For synonyms see BOOZE. [U.S., late 1900s-pres.]

drag ass 1. to decamp; to get out in a hurry. Cf. CUT ASS, HAUL ASS. [U.S. slang, 1900s] **2.** pertaining to a person who is droopy and depressed. Usually hyphenated in this sense. [U.S. slang, 1900s]

drag-ball (also **drag-party**) a party for homosexual males who attend in drag. See DRAG. Cf. DRAG-PARTY. [U.S. homosexual use, mid 1900s]

dragged drunk; drug intoxicated. For synonyms see TALL, WOOFLED. [U.S., late 1900s-pres.]

draggle-tail 1. an untidy woman. **2.** a low, dirty slattern. For synonyms see TROLLYMOG. **3.** a filthy prostitute. Cf. DRABBLE-TAIL. [all senses, since the late 1500s]

drag king a woman dressed like a man. For synonyms see EPICENE. [U.S., late 1900s-pres.]

dragon 1. a wanton woman; a prostitute, especially an old prostitute. [British, 1600s] **2.** a scold; a battle-axe; a WAR-HORSE (q.v.). **3.** the penis in the expression DRAIN THE DRAGON (q.v.).

drag-party the same as DRAG-BALL (q.v.). [U.S. slang, mid 1900s-pres.]

drag the shag to copulate. For synonyms see OCCUPY. [U.S., late 1900s-pres.]

drain 1. to urinate. Cf. DRAIN THE DRAGON. For synonyms see WHIZ. [U.S. slang and nonce, early 1900s-pres.] **2.** gin. For synonyms see RUIN. [British slang, early 1800s, Lexicon Balatronicum] **3.** the female genitals. Because they receive a lot of DIRTY WATER (q.v.), "semen." Cf. COMMON SEWER, SCUPPER.

drain one's radiator (also **drain one's crankcase**) to urinate. For synonyms see WHIZ. [U.S., 1900s]

drain one's snake to urinate. See DRAIN (sense 1). [British slang, early 1900s]

drain the bilge to empty one's stomach; to vomit. For synonyms see YORK. [Australian and U.S., mid 1900s-pres.]

drain the crankcase to urinate. [U.S. slang, 1900s]

drain the dragon (also **water the dragon**) to urinate. Cf. DRAIN (sense 1). [Australian, 1900s or before]

drain the lizard to urinate. The LIZARD (q.v.) is the penis. [U.S. slang, mid 1900s]

drain the main vein to urinate. Typically said of a male. For synonyms see WHIZ. [U.S. collegiate, late 1900s, Munro]

drain the spuds to urinate. Based on a reason for leaving the room, i.e., to remove the water from boiling potatoes. See STRAIN ONE'S TATERS. [Australian, 1900s]

drain the suds to urinate after drinking beer. Cf. SUDS.

Drat! "Damn!" For synonyms see 'ZOUNDS. [British, late 1900s-pres.]

draw off to urinate, usually said of the male. [British euphemism, 1900s. Dictionary of Slang and Unconventional English]

Dr. Bananas a "brand name" for the inhalant drug amyl nitrite. [U.S. drug culture, late 1900s, Abel]

dream cocaine. Borrowed from a term for opium. See DREAMS [U.S. drug culture, mid 1900s-pres.]

dream beads opium pills or pellets. [U.S. drug culture, 1900s or before]

dream gum opium. For synonyms see OPE. [U.S. underworld, early 1900s or before]

dreams opium. Cf. DREAM. [U.S. underworld, 1900s or before]

dreamstick 1. a marijuana cigarette or any cigarette. [U.S. slang and drug culture, 1900s] 2. opium. [U.S., 1900s or before] 3. an opium pipe. For synonyms see GONGER. [U.S. underworld, 1900s or before]

dream wax opium. Cf. GREASE. [U.S. underworld, 1900s or before]

drenched intoxicated with alcohol. [U.S. slang, 1900s]

drill for Vegemite to have anal intercouse. For synonyms see PEDERASTY, OCCUPY. [Australian, mid 1900s-pres.]

dribbling dart of love the penis considered as one of Cupid's arrows. Cf. DART OF LOVE. [from Measure for Measure (Shakespeare)]

drin Benzedrine. [U.S. drug culture, mid 1900s]

drink, in intoxicated with alcohol. Cf. LIQUOR, IN. [colloquial, late 1500s-1900s]

drinkative alcohol intoxicated. A play on talkative. For synonyms see WOOFLED. [1900s, Dickson]

drinking intoxicated with alcohol. For synonyms see WOOFLED. [U.S. colloquial, 1900s]

drinkster a drunkard. For synonyms see ALCHY. [British slang, 1800s]

drinky intoxicated with alcohol. [British colloquial, 1800s or before]

drinkypoo a little drink of liquor. Mock-baby talk. [U.S. slang, late 1900s]

drip 1. an oaf; a dunce; a disliked male; the same as JERK (sense 3). [1900s] 2. nonsense. 3. to utter nonsense. [senses 2 and 3 are British, 1900s, Dictionary of Slang and Unconventional English]

dripper an old prostitute. For synonyms see HARLOT. [British, late 1900s-pres.]

dripping for it pertaining to a woman who is sexually aroused. Refers to vaginal secretions. [British slang, early 1900s]

dripping-tight intoxicated with alcohol. For synonyms see WOOFLED. [British slang, early 1900s]

drive-by a shooting of someone from a passing car. [British and U.S., late 1900s-pres.]

drive home to coit; to penetrate a woman [U.S. slang, mid 1900s-pres.]

drive into to coit; to intromit the penis. See DRIVE HOME. [British slang and colloquial, 1800s and nonce elsewhere]

drive the (porcelain) bus to vomit into a toilet. For synonyms see YORK. [U.S. slang, late 1900s]

droned intoxicated. A blend of *drunk* and STONED. For synonyms see WOOFLED. [U.S. collegiate, late 1900s, Eble]

drongo an oaf; a blockhead. For synonyms see OAF. [U.S., late 1900s-pres.]

droob (also **drube**) a dull person; an oaf. Cf. DOOB. [Australian, mid 1900s-pres., Wilkes]

drop a ballock (also **drop a ball, drop a clanger, drop a goolie, drop one's balls**) to make a very serious error. Cf. BALLOCKS, CLANGERS, GOOLIES, which all mean "testicles." [British, early 1900s, *Dictionary of Slang and Unconventional English*]

drop a bop to take a drug in pill form. [U.S. drug culture, late 1900s]

drop anchor to defecate. For synonyms see EASE ONESELF. [U.S., late 1900s-pres.]

drop a rose to release foul-smelling intestinal gas. Based on PLUCK A ROSE (*q.v.*), a euphemism for "retire to the garden privy." [U.S. slang, mid 1900s]

drop ass to flatulate. For synonyms see GURK. [U.S., late 1900s-pres.]

drop hairpins (also **drop one's beads**) to reveal one's homosexuality by dropping hints. [U.S. homosexual use, mid 1900s]

drop off the hooks to die. For synonyms see DEPART. [British euphemism, 1800s, Farmer and Henley]

drop one to break wind. For synonyms see GURK. [British, mid 1900s-pres.]

drop one's cookies to vomit. Cf. BLOW (ONE'S) COOKIES, SNAP ONE'S COOKIES, WOOF COOKIES. For synonyms see YORK. [U.S. slang, late 1900s]

drop one's guts (also **blow one's guts out**) to release foul-smelling intestinal

gas. [Australian and British slang, early 1900s]

drop one's load. 1. to ejaculate Cf. LOAD (sense 1). **2.** to defecate. Cf. LOAD (sense 5). [both senses, colloquial or slang, 1900s or before]

drop one's wax to defecate. Cf. BODY WAX. [slang, 1800s-1900s]

droppings the dung of birds; the dung of animals; any dung or fecal material. [since the late 1500s] Various kinds of droppings are: BILLETING, BIRDSHIT, BIRD-TURD, BLAKES, BODEWASH, BOOSH-WAH, BUFFALO CHIPS, BULL-SCUTTER, BUNS, BUTTONS, CASINGS, COCK'S EGGS, COW-BLAKES, COW-DOOT, COW DUNG, COW-PLAT, COWSHIT, CROTILES, DAG-LINGS, DOG DIRT, FEWMETS, FIANTS, FU-ANTS, FUMETS, FUMISHINGS, GUANO, GUBBINS, HEN-DOWN, HORSE APPLE, MEADOW MUFFIN, MOOSE BEANS, MOOSE NUGGETS, MOOSE PECANS, MUTING, NEST, POOH, POOP, PRAIRIE COAL, PRAIRIE FUEL, PURE, SCHARN, SHARN, SIT-STILL-NEST, SKARN, SPRAINTS, SURFACE FUEL, TANTADLIN TART, TREDDLE, TROTTLES, WAGGYING, WERDROBE. See related terms at DUNG.

drop some iron to spend a lot of money. [U.S., late 1900s-pres.]

drop someone in it to expose someone to danger It=SHIT. [British, mid 1900s-pres.]

drop someone in the shit to expose someone to danger. [British, mid 1900s-pres.]

drop the kids off at the pool to defecate. For synonyms see EASE ONE-SELF. [U.S., late 1900s-pres.]

drop them [for a woman] to make herself sexually available by dropping her pants. [British, late 1900s-pres.]

drube a dullard; an oaf. For synonyms see OAF. [U.S., late 1900s-pres.]

drug 1. a medicinal compound. [since the 1300s, *Oxford English Dictionary*] **2.** a medicine or chemical substance used solely for its effect on the mind and body aside from any prescribed therapeutic purposes. See DOPE. **3.** all substances which can be used to produce a CHARGE (sense 1) or a HIGH (sense 3) including alcohol, amphetamines, barbiturates, cocaine, heroin, L.S.D., marijuana, P.C.P., and S.T.P. For other drug names see COTICS. [U.S. colloquial and drug culture, mid 1900s-pres.]

drug abuse the habitual use of, overuse of, or addiction to a drug. The meaning has been broadened to include tranquilizers and aspirin to demonstrate societal dependence on drugs in the U.S. [U.S., mid 1900s-pres.]

druggy (also **druggie**) a drug user or addict. [U.S. drug culture, mid 1900s-pres.]

drug habit 1. the frequent or habitual use of drugs. **2.** addiction to drugs. See HABIT. [both senses, U.S. colloquial and euphemism, mid 1900s-pres.]

drughead a heavy drug user; an addict. For synonyms see USER. [U.S. drug culture, mid 1900s-pres.]

drug-store cowboy an effeminate male; a ladies' man. For synonyms see FOP. [U.S. slang, 1900s]

drug-store johnson an addiction to drugs normally used as medication; an addiction to a habit-forming medication such as codeine or morphine. JOHNSON = JONES, and both are general slang terms for *thing*. [U.S. drug culture, late 1900s, Kaiser]

drum 1. a virile black male. [U.S. slang, mid 1900s-pres.] **2.** a brothel. [Australian and possibly British use, 1900s, Wilkes]

drumstick the penis. [widespread recurrent nonce, British, 1800s]

drunk as a boiled owl heavily intoxicated with alcohol. [British and U.S., late 1800s-1900s]

drunk as a brewer's fart intoxicated with alcohol; drunk and reeking with alcohol. [British, 1800s]

drunk as a broom heavily intoxicated with alcohol; the same as DRUNK AS A BESOM (*q.v.*). [British, 1800s]

drunk as a coot heavily intoxicated with alcohol. Patterned on "crazy as a coot." *Cf.* DIZZY AS A GOOSE. [U.S. slang, early 1900s]

drunk as a cunt heavily intoxicated with alcohol. Patterned on "black as a

cunt." [British, *Dictionary of the Underworld*]

drunk as a fiddler intoxicated with alcohol; as drunk as a fiddler who is paid in drink. *Cf.* DRUNK AS A PIPER. [slang since the 1800s]

drunk as a fly intoxicated with alcohol. [British, 1800s]

drunk as a fowl intoxicated with alcohol. *Cf.* DRUNK AS A COOT. [Australian, early 1900s, Baker]

drunk as a lord (also **drunk as an earl**) intoxicated with alcohol. [since the late 1600s]

drunk as a mouse intoxicated with alcohol. From "drunk as a drowned mouse." *Cf.* DRUNK AS A RAT. [1300s-1500s]

drunk as a newt (also **tight as a newt**) heavily intoxicated with alcohol. As saturated as the amphibious newt. [British military, 1900s, *Dictionary of Slang and Unconventional English*]

drunk as an owl heavily intoxicated with alcohol. *Cf.* DRUNK AS A BOILED OWL. [widespread slang and colloquial, 1800s-1900s]

drunk as a piper (also **drunk as a tinker**) heavily intoxicated with alcohol. *Cf.* DRUNK AS A FIDDLER. [British slang, late 1700s]

drunk as a piss-ant intoxicated with alcohol; euphemistic for "drunk as piss." *Cf.* PIS-ANT. [Australian, early 1900s]

drunk as a rat heavily intoxicated with alcohol. Worse than being DRUNK AS A MOUSE (*q.v.*). From "drunk as a drowned rat." [mid 1500s]

drunk as a rolling fart (also **drunk as a brewer's fart**) intoxicated with alcohol. [British, mid 1800s]

drunk as a skunk intoxicated with alcohol. [U.S. colloquial, 1900s or before]

drunk as a tapster intoxicated with alcohol; as drunk as a bartender. [British, 1800s, Farmer and Henley]

drunk as a tick intoxicated with alcohol; as full of alcohol as a tick is full of blood. From TIGHT AS A TICK (*q.v.*). [U.S. colloquial, 1900s]

drunk as a top intoxicated with alcohol; wobbling like a top running down.

drunk as a wheelbarrow intoxicated with alcohol. [U.S. colloquial, 1900s]

drunk as Bacchus intoxicated with alcohol; extremely drunk. [British, 1800s, Farmer and Henley]

drunk as buggery extremely intoxicated with alcohol. [British, 1800s]

drunk as Chloe (also **drunk as Floey**) heavily intoxicated with alcohol. [widespread slang, 1800s-1900s]

drunk as David's sow (also **drunk as Davy's sow**) heavily intoxicated with alcohol. For synonyms see WOOFLED. [British, 1700s]

dry bob copulation without ejaculation, possibly due to impotence. Cf. DRY FUCK. [British slang, late 1700s, Grose]

dry fuck the motions of copulation performed without removing the clothing. [U.S. slang, mid 1900s]

dry goods a woman; a woman considered sexually. [U.S. colloquial, 1900s] Synonyms and related terms: BIT OF MUSLIN, BUNCH OF CALICO, CALICO, CRINOLINE, HUNK OF SKIRT, LIFT-SKIRTS, LIGHT SKIRTS, LOOSE-BODIED GOWN, MINI-SKIRT, MUSLIN, PETTICOAT, PIECE OF STUFF, PLACKET, SKIRT, SMOCK, SMOCK-TOY.

dry high marijuana. A nonalcoholic source of a HIGH (sense 3). Cf. DRY GROG. [U.S. drug culture, mid 1900s-pres.]

dry-hump to simulate sexual intercourse. [British and U.S., mid 1900s-pres.]

dry run coition with a condom. [U.S. slang, 1900s, Wentworth and Flexner]

dry spell 1. a period of time when no drugs are available; a period of abstinence from drugs. [U.S. drug culture, late 1900s] **2.** a period with no sex. [U.S., late 1900s-pres.]

D.s tablets of Dilaudid painkiller. [U.S. drug culture, late 1900s, Kaiser]

D/T dominance training. A type of [sexual] MASOCHISM. Cf. B/D. C/P. [U.S. slang, late 1900s]

D.T. 1. the DELIRIUM TREMENS (q.v.).

Usually D.T.s (q.v.). For synonyms see ORK-ORKS. [British, mid 1800s] **2.** a "dick-teaser"; the same as COCK-TEASER (q.v.). Cf. C.T. [U.S. slang, mid 1900s-pres.]

D-T-ist a drunkard. From D.T. (sense 1). [British slang, 1800s, Farmer and Henley]

D.T.s the DELIRIUM TREMENS (q.v.). [since the 1800s]

dubage See DOOBAGE.

dubbies the female breasts. For synonyms see BOSOM. [British slang, 1900s]

dubee See DOOBIE.

dubich marijuana; DOOBAGE. For synonyms see MARI. [U.S. drug culture, black use, late 1900s]

ducats money; dollars. [U.S. slang, late 1900s]

duc-ducs money; dollars. [U.S. black use, late 1900s]

duck 1. a male urinal bedpan. [U.S. slang, 1900s] **2.** a young woman; a woman considered sexually. Cf. QUAIL. For synonyms see LAY. [U.S. slang, 1900s] **3.** a total JERK; a social outcast. For synonyms see OAF. [U.S. collegiate, late 1900s, Munro]

duck-butt a short person, especially someone with large posteriors. [U.S. slang, mid 1900s-pres.]

duck-butter 1. semen. Cf. BUTTER, MELTED-BUTTER. For synonyms see METTLE. [U.S. dialect (Ozarks), Randolph and Wilson] **2.** SMEGMA (sense 2). Cf. GNAT-BREAD. [U.S. colloquial, 1900s]

duckleberry the penis. For synonyms see YARD. [U.S., late 1900s-pres.]

duckettes money. From DUCATS. [U.S., late 1900s-pres.]

duckies money. From DUCATS. [U.S., late 1900s-pres.]

ducy the penis. Cf. LUCY. [U.S. colloquial, 1900s]

dude 1. an affected male; a FOP (q.v.); a sissified male resident of a dude ranch. [U.S. slang, 1800s-pres.] **2.** any male buddy or chum. [U.S. slang, mid 1900s-pres.]

dudette a young woman. The mate for DUDE. [U.S. slang, late 1900s]

duff 1. the posteriors. *Cf.* JUFF. [U.S. slang, mid 1900s-pres.] Synonyms: AMPERSAND, ANATOMY, ASS, ASSTERIORS, B.A., BACK-LAND, BACK-PARTS, BACK-SIDE, BACKYARD, BALCONY, BEAM, BEHIND, BIM, BLIND CUPID, BLOT, BOGEY, BOGY, BOM, BOMBOSITY, BOO-BOO, BOODY, BOSOM OF THE PANTS, BOTTOM, BOTTY, BREECH, BUBBLE BUTT, BUCKET, BUM, BUMBO, BUM FIDDLE, BUMMY, BUMP, BUNCHY, BUNS, BUTT, BUTTOCKS, CABOOSE, CAKE, CAMERA OBSCURA, CAN, CANETTA, CATASTROPHE, CHEEKS, CHUFF, CLUNES, COOLER, CORYBUNGUS, CROUP, CRUMPET, CRUPPER, CULO, DERRIERE, DIFFERENTIAL, DISH, DOCK, DOKUS, DOUBLE JUGGS, DRODDUM, DUMMOCK, DUSTER, FANNY, FIFE AND DRUM, FLANKEY, FLESHY PART OF THE THIGH, FRANCES, FUD, FULL MOON, FUN, FUNDAMENT, FUNDAMENTAL FEATURES, GAZONGA, GAZOO, GLUTEAL REGION, GLUTES, GLUTEUS MAXIMUS, HAMS, HANDLEBARS OF LOVE, HANGOVER, HAUNCH, HEINIE, HIND, HIND-END, HINDER-END, HINDER PARTS, HINDSIDE, HINTERLAND, HUNKERS, JACKSY-PARDY, JEER, JERE, JIBS, JUBILEE, JUFF, JUTLAND, KEEL, KEESTER, LABONZA, LA-LA, LARD ASS, LATTER-END, LUDS, MOON, MOTTOB, MUD FLAPS, NANCY, NATES, NOCKANDRO, OIL BAGS, PARKING PLACE, PARTS BEHIND, PART THAT WENT OVER THE FENCE LAST, POD, PODEX, POOP, POOPER, POSTERIORS, POSTERN, PRATS, PRESSED-HAM, PROMONTORIES, QUOIT, REAR, REAR-END, ROBY DOUGLAS, RUMBLE-SEAT, RUMDADUM, RUMP, RUMPUS, RUSTY-DUSTY, SADDLE-LEATHER, SCUT, SEAT, SESS, SITTER, SITTING-ROOM, SNATCH, SPREAD, STERN, SUNDAY FACE, TAIL, TOBY, TOCKS, TOKUS, TOUTE, TWAT, UNDER-SIDE. **2.** a feminine lesbian. *Cf.* FLUFF (sense 4). [U.S. homosexual use, mid 1900s-pres.]

duffer a foolish oaf; a bumbler. [since the mid 1800s]

dugout 1. a burned-out addict. Refers to the veins of the arms which are pitted and dug out from many injections. [U.S. drug culture, early 1900s-pres.] **2.** a type of marijuana pipe. [U.S. drug culture, late 1900s]

duke to vomit. *Cf.* PUKE, YUKE. Probably onomatopoeic. For synonyms see YORK. [U.S. slang, late 1900s]

duker a fecal bolus. For synonyms see DUNG. [U.S., late 1900s-pres.]

dumbasskiss a dull and witless oaf. For synonyms see OAF. [U.S., late 1900s-pres.]

dumbfuck (also **dumb fuck**) a stupid JERK; an OAF. For synonyms see OAF. [U.S. slang, late 1900s]

dumb-glutton the female genitals. Possibly rhyming slang for MUTTON (*q.v.*). *Cf.* FEED THE DUMB-GLUTTON. For synonyms see MONOSYLLABLE. [British slang or cant, late 1700s]

dumbnuts an oaf. For synonyms see OAF. [British, mid 1900s-pres.]

dumbo a stupid oaf. For synonyms see OAF. [British and U.S., mid 1900s-pres.]

dummy 1. a stupid oaf. [since the late 1500s] **2.** the female genitals. Probably from "dumb-glutton." *Cf.* FEED THE DUMMY. For synonyms see MONOSYLLABLE. [British slang, 1800s] **3.** the penis. *Cf.* BEAT THE DUMMY. For synonyms see YARD. [U.S. slang, mid 1900s-pres.]

dummy dust the drug P.C.P. (*q.v.*). *Cf.* ANGEL DUST. [U.S. drug culture, mid 1900s-pres.]

dump 1. to defecate. **2.** an act of defecation. **3.** to vomit. [all senses, U.S. slang, mid 1900s-pres.]

dumplings the breasts. *Cf.* APPLE DUMPLING SHOP. British slang, 1800s]

dump on to defecate on; literally, "to shit on." *Cf.* DUMP (sense 1). [U.S. slang, mid 1900s-pres.]

dump one's load 1. to defecate. For synonyms see EASE ONESELF. [U.S. slang, mid 1900s-pres.] **2.** to vomit. For synonyms see YORK. [British and U.S. slang, mid 1900s-pres]

dung any fecal matter, usually animal excreta. [since the 1200s] Synonyms and related terms: ALLEY APPLE, ALVINE DEJECTIONS, B.M., BODY WAX, BOGSTUFF, BOO-BOO, BOWEL MOVEMENT, BOWELS, BROWN-EYED MULLET, CA-CA, CACK, CACKY, CARRION, CAS-

INGS, CLART, COMPOST, COW, COW-CAKE, COW-CLAP, COW-CLOD, COW-DAB, COW-FLOP, COW-PAT, COW-PIE, COW-PUCKY, COW-SHARD, COW-SHARN, COW-SHERN, COWSLIP, CRADLE-CUSTARD, CRAP, CRAPOLA, CUT, DANNA, DEAD SOLDIER, DEJECTA, DEJECTIONS, DEJECTURE, DIRT, DOG-DOO, DOG-LOG, DOODY, DOOKY, DOUGLAS (HURD), DRECK, DROPPINGS, DUKER, DUTY, EXCREMENTUM, FECAL MATTER, FECULENCE, GERRY, GONG, GRUNT, GUANO, HOCKEY, HORSE AND TRAP, HORSE DUMPLING, JANK, JOB, JOBBER, KA-KA, KITTY NUGGET, LAWN-DRESSING, MANURE, MEADOW DRESSING, MERD, MERDA, MOLLOCK, MUCK, MUTE, NIGHTSOIL, ORDURE, ORTS, PILGRIM'S SALVE, PONY AND TRAP, POO, POOH, POOP, POO-POO, QUAKER, RECREMENT, RECTAL EXCRETA, RESIDUUM, RICH DIRT, SCHARN, SCUMBER, SEWAGE, SHARN, SHIT, SIEGE, SIGN, SIRREVERENCE, SOFT AND NASTY, SOFT-STUFF, SOZZLE, SPRAINTS, STERCUS, STOOL, TAD, TANTADLIN, TART, TANTOBLIN TART, TAUNTY, TOOT, TOO-TOO, TURD, WASTE, WHOOPSIE, YACKUM.

dunk to copulate. For synonyms see LAY, TAIL. [British, late 1900s-pres.]

dunkie a woman viewed as a sex object. For synonyms see LAY, TAIL. [British, late 1900s-pres.]

dunny budgie a fly. A *dunny* is an outhouse. [Australian, late 1900s-pres.]

dupe a sucker or a patsy; a person who can be used as an unknowing tool in a ploy; a victim of a con artist. [since the 1600s or before] Synonyms: ÂME, BUZZARD, COLL, DAMNÉE, FRUIT, GAY, GORK, PIGEON, SUCKER.

durb fellatio. [U.S., late 1900s-pres.]

dust 1. cocaine. See HEAVEN DUST. **2.** a truncation of ANGEL DUST, which is P.C.P. (both *q.v.*). [both senses, U.S. drug culture, mid 1900s-pres.] **3.** to kill someone. [U.S. slang, late 1900s or before]

duster 1. the female genitals. [British slang, 1800s] **2.** the posteriors. *Cf.* RUSTY-DUSTY. [U.S. slang, mid 1900s-pres.] **3.** a cigarette combining tobacco and heroin. [U.S. drug culture, mid 1900s] **4.** a testicle. See DUSTERS.

dusters the testicles. For synonyms see WHIRLYGIGS. [British military, early 1900s, *Dictionary of Slang and Unconventional English*]

dusthead a user of phencyclidine, the drug P.C.P. [U.S. drug culture, late 1900s]

dust rage a period of intoxication or distraction from taking ANGEL DUST = P.C.P. [U.S. drug culture, late 1900s]

Dutch boys men, gay or straight, who like to be around lesbians-dykes.[U.S., late 1900s-pres.]

Dutch courage 1. alcoholic drink. *Cf.* POT-SURE, POT-VALIANT. [British and U.S., 1800s-1900s] **2.** narcotics. From sense 1. [U.S. underworld, early 1900s]

duty (also **doody**) feces; usually human feces. [U.S. juvenile, 1900s]

dweeb a fool; an idiot; an OAF. For synonyms see OAF. [U.S. collegiate, late 1900s]

dwindles, the the advancement of disabilities owing to age. [U.S., late 1900s-pres.]

dyke 1. the female genitals. See comments at DIKE. [British slang, 1800s, Farmer and Henley] **2.** a virile lesbian; an obvious lesbian. *Cf.* BULLDIKER. For synonyms see LESBYTERIAN. [U.S. slang, 1900s]

dykey in the manner of a DYKE (*q.v.*). *Cf.* BULLDIKER. [U.S. slang, mid 1900s-pres.]

dyls Placidyl™, a sedative-hypnotic drug. [U.S. drug culture, late 1900s, Kaiser]

dynamite 1. strong, hard drugs, *i.e.*, heroin or opium. **2.** marijuana. **3.** cocaine. [all senses, U.S. drug culture, mid 1900s-pres.]

dypso See DIPSO.

E

E ECSTASY, a hallucinogen similar to L.S.D. [British and U.S., late 1900s-pres.]

eager-beaver 1. a person who is very eager to obtain something; a person who is always on time or always early; someone who volunteers for everything. [U.S. colloquial, 1900s] **2.** a man or woman who is very eager for sexual activity. [U.S. slang, 1900s]

Earl to vomit. For synonyms see YORK. [U.S. slang, late 1900s]

early door a prostitute. Rhyming slang for "whore." *Cf.* BROKEN OAR. [British, 1800s, *Dictionary of Rhyming Slang*]

earp (also **urp**) **1.** vomit. **2.** to vomit. *Cf.* BARF, RALPH, YORK. [both senses, U.S. slang and colloquial, 1900s]

earsex telephone sex. [U.S., late 1900s-pres.]

earth a marijuana cigarette. For synonyms see MEZZROLL. [U.S., late 1900s-pres.]

earth biscuit an environmental activist. [U.S., late 1900s-pres.]

earth muffin an environmental activist. [U.S., late 1900s-pres.]

easement elimination, primarily defecation. Synonyms: BIG ONE, BIG POTTY, B.M., BOOM-BOOM, BOWEL MOVEMENT, DEJECTION, DISCHARGE, ELIMINATION, JOBBY, MAJOR NEED, MOTION, NATURE'S CALL, NUMBER TWO, PAUSE THAT REFRESHES, STOOL.

ease oneself 1. to defecate or urinate. [euphemistic since the 1600s] Synonyms for defecate: ALVUM EXONERARE, BIG HIT, B.M., BURY A QUAKER, CA-CA, CAPOOP, CAST, CHUCK A TURD, CLART, CUCK, DEPOSIT, DISPATCH ONE'S CARGO, DO A JOB, DROP ANCHOR, DROP ONE'S LOAD, DROP ONE'S WAX, DROP THE KIDS OFF AT THE POOL, DROP TURDS, DUMP, EASE NATURE, EVACU-

ATE THE BOWELS, FILL ONE'S PANTS, FOREST (GUMP), GEORGE, GIVE BIRTH TO A POLITICIAN, GIVE ONE'S BUM AN AIRING, GO, GO TO THE BATHROOM, GRUMP, GRUNT, HOCKEY, IRISH SHAVE, JOB, LOG IN, MAKE A DEPOSIT, PERFORM THE WORK OF NATURE, PICK A DAISY, PINCH ONE OFF, POOP, POO-POO, POST A LETTER, POTTY, QUAT, RELIEVE ONESELF, RUMP, SCUMBER, SHIT, SIEGE, SMELL THE PLACE UP, SOIL ONE'S LINENS, SQUAT, SQUEEZE THE CHEESE, STOOL, TAKE A CRAP, TAKE A DUMP, TAKE A SHIT, THROW MUD, UNFEED, UNLOAD, VOID. **2.** to copulate or ejaculate. [British colloquial, 1700s]

east and west the bosom; a human breast. Rhyming slang for "breast." [British slang, early 1900s]

easts and wests the female breasts. Rhyming slang for *breasts*. For synonyms see BOSOM. [British, late 1900s-pres.]

easy lay a woman who can be persuaded to copulate easily. Later this also refers to a man. [U.S. slang, 1900s]

easy make (also **easy mark, easy meat**) **1.** an EASY LAY (*q.v.*), a woman who can be persuaded to copulate easily. Later this also refers to a man. **2.** a dupe; an easy target for deception. [both senses, British and U.S. slang, 1900s]

easy-rider 1. a man who lives off the earnings of a prostitute. [U.S. slang, mid 1900s-pres.] **2.** a young woman who copulates on the first date. *Cf.* RIDE. For synonyms see LAY. [U.S. slang, mid 1900s]

eat to perform any type of oral sexual intercourse, usually PENILINGUS or CUNNILINGUS, but also ANILINGUS (all *q.v.*). *Cf.* MUNCH. [U.S. slang, mid 1900s-pres.]

eat a kipper feast to perform CUNNI-

LINGUS. *Cf.* FISH. [British slang, 1900s, McDonald]

eat at the Y to perform oral sex on a woman. [U.S. slang, late 1900s]

eat face to kiss; to neck and kiss deeply. *Cf.* CHEW FACE. [U.S. collegiate, late 1900s]

eating-stuff 1. a woman who looks delicious and desirable, *i.e.*, good enough to eat. **2.** a good-looking woman who inspires a male to perform CUNNILINGUS (*q.v.*). *Cf.* TABLE-GRADE. [U.S. slang, mid 1900s-pres.]

Eat it! a coarse remark; a curse. Literally, EAT SHIT! (sense 3) or "Eat me!", *i.e.*, "perform PENILINGUS (*q.v.*) on me." [U.S. slang, mid 1900s-pres.]

Eat my shorts! "GO TO HELL!"; "Beat it!" [U.S. collegiate, late 1900s]

eat out 1. to perform PENILINGUS or CUNNILINGUS (both *q.v.*). From the expression meaning "to dine out at a restaurant." **2.** to berate or verbally chastise someone. [both senses, U.S. slang, mid 1900s-pres.]

eat pound-cake to perform ANILINGUS (*q.v.*). *Cf.* POUND-CAKE QUEEN. [U.S. slang, 1900s]

eat shit 1. to put up with a lot of abuse; to knuckle under. **2.** to swallow or believe BULLSHIT (*q.v.*). **3.** an epithet, "Eat shit!" [all senses, U.S. slang, mid 1900s-pres.]

eat someone's lunch to best someone; to defeat, outwit, or win against someone. In the way that a school bully takes away children's lunches and eats them at recess. [U.S., late 1900s-pres.]

ebony 1. a man or woman of African descent. Synonyms and related terms: A.B.C., ACE BOOM-BOOM, ACE BOON COON, ACE OF SPADES, AFRAMERICAN, AFRO, AFRO-AMERICAN, ALLIGATOR BAIT, APE, BLACK, BLACKAMOOR, BLACK BEAN, BLACKBIRD, BLACK DIAMOND, BLACK FAY, BLACKFELLOW, BLACKHEAD, BLACKIE, BLACK IVORY, BLACKOUT, BLO-MAN, BLOOD, BLUE, BLUEGUM, BLUEGUM MOKE, BLUESKIN, BONEHEAD, BOO, BOO-BOO, BOOG, BOOGIE, BOOTLIPS, BOY, BROTHER, BROTHER IN BLACK, BROWN-SKIN, BUCK, BUCK NIGGER, BUFFALO, BUGGY, BUPPIE, BURRHEAD, BUSH BOOGIE, BUTTERHEAD, CHARCOAL, CHARCOAL NIGGER, CHIMNEY CHOPS, CHOCOLATE, CHOCOLATE DROP, CLINK, CLUCK, COLORED, COLORED FOLK, COON, CROW, CUFF, CUFFEE, CULLUD GEMMAN, DARK CLOUD, DARK GABLE, DARKY, DEWBABY, DINGE, DINGHE, DINGY, DINK, DOMINO, DRUM, EGGPLANT, EIGHT-BALL, EIGHT-ROCK, ETHIOPIAN, FIELD DARKY, FIELD NIGGER, FIELD SLAVE, FUZZY-WUZZY, GANGE, GAR, GEECHEE, GHETTO BIRD, GROID, GROUND APE, HANDKER-CHIEF-HEAD, HARDHEAD, HEADLIGHT TO A SNOWSTORM, HOCKEY PUCK, HOME BOY, HOOFER, INK, INKFACE, INKY-DINK, INTER-NATIONAL NIGGER, JACK, JAR-HEAD, JAYBEE, JAZZ-BO, JIBAGOO, JIG, JIGA, JIG-ABOO, JIGGABOO, JIM CROW, JIT, JUBA, JUNGLE-BUNNY, KELTCH, KINK, KINKY-HEAD, KINKY-NOB, LILYWHITE, LOAD OF COAL, MAU-MAU, MEMBER, MIDNIGHT, MOKE, MOOLIE, MOSE, MOSS, MOSSHEAD, MUNGO, NAP, NAPPY, NEGATIVE, NEGRO, NIG, NIGGRA, OREO, OXFORD, PICCA-NINNY (child), PICKANINNY (child), POS-SUM, POWDER BURN, QUASHIE, RAISIN, RASTUS, REGGIN, SAMBO, SCHVARTZA, SCHWARZ, SCUTTLE, SEAL, SEEDY, SHADE, SHAD-MOUTH, SHADOW, SHINE, SHINY, SHOOFLY, SKID MARK, SKILLET, SKUNK, SMEAR, SMIDGET, SMOKE, SMOKED-IRISHMAN, SMOKEY, SMUDGE, SMUT BUTT, SNOWBALL, SPADE, SPAGINZY, SPEAR-CHUCKER, SPILL, SPLIB, SPOOK, SQUASHO, STOVE-LID, SUEDE, SUPERSPADE, SWARTZY, SWEET CHOCOLATE, TAR BABY (child), TAR POT (child), TEAPOT, THICKLIPS, UNBLEACHED AMERICAN, UNCLE TOM, VELCRO HEAD, WACCOON, WILLIE, WOOLY-HEAD, ZIGABOO, ZIGGER-BOO, ZULU. **2.** pertaining to a Negro. [both senses, colloquial, mid 1800s-1900s]

eco warrior an ecological activist. [British, late 1900s-pres.]

Ecstasy (also **ecstasy**) a DESIGNER DRUG similar to the hallucinogenic L.S.D. The chemical name is 3,4-methylene-dioxymethamphetamine or M.D.M.A. [U.S. drug culture, late 1900s]

edged intoxicated with alcohol. For synonyms see WOOFLED. [U.S. slang, early 1900s]

eel the penis. *Cf.* EEL-SKIN. [widespread nonce since the 1600s or before]

eel-skin a condom. *Cf.* FISH-SKIN. [U.S. slang, early 1900s, Wentworth and Flexner] Synonyms: AMERICAN LETTER, AMERICAN SOCK, ARMOUR, BAG, BAGGIE, BALLOON, BISHOP, BUCKSKIN, CADET, CHEATER, CIRCULAR PROTECTOR, COCK SOCK, CONDOM, CONEY ISLAND WHITEFISH, CUNDUM, DIVING SUIT, DOADY WRAP, DREADNOUGHT, ENVELOPE, FEARNOUGHT, FISH-SKIN, F.L., FRANGER, FRENCH LETTER, FRENCH SAFE, FRENCHY, FROG, FROG-SKIN, GLOVE, GOSSY, HAPPY CAP, HORSE, ITALIAN LETTER, JIMMY HAT, JO-BAG, JOHNNIE, JOHNNY BAG, JOY-BAG, LATEX, LETTER, LIFEJACKET, LOVE GLOVE, LUBIE, MACHINE, MALE PESSARY, MALE SHEATH, MANHATTAN EEL, NIGHTCAP, ONE-PIECE OVERCOAT, PARTY HAT, PHALLIC THIMBLE, PORT SAID GARTER, PRO, PROPHO, PROPHYLACTIC, PURSE, RAINCOAT, ROUGH RIDER, RUBBER, RUBBER BOOT, RUBBER DUCKIE, RUBBER JOHNNY, SAFE, SAFETY, SAFETY-SHEATH, SCUMBAG, SHEATH, SHOWER-CAP, SKIN, SPANISH LETTER, SPECIALITIES, SPITFIRE SWEATER, UMBRELLA, WELLIE, WELLY, WIENER WRAP, WILLIE-WELLIE. See also EEL-SKINS.

eel-skinner the female genitals. *Cf.* EEL, "penis." [British slang, 1800s, Farmer and Henley]

eel-skins trousers; very tight trousers; any tight-fitting article of clothing. [British slang, early 1800s]

eer-quay pertaining to a homosexual male and sometimes a female. Pig Latin for QUEER (sense 3). [U.S., 1900s]

effing a disguise of F-ING (*q.v.*), "fucking." [British and U.S., 1900s]

effing and blinding swearing and cursing. [British, late 1900s-pres.]

Eff off! "Fuck off!" Euphemistic. [U.S. slang, late 1900s]

egg intoxicated with alcohol. For synonyms see WOOFLED. [Australian, 1900s, Baker]

eggs the testicles. Refers both to the shape and the fragility. [jocular and nonce, 1900s and before]

egg-sucker a sycophant; a flatterer. A euphemism for ASS-SUCKER (*q.v.*). [U.S. colloquial, 1900s, or before]

Egypt a W.C.; a toilet. See GO TO EGYPT. [U.S. slang and colloquial, 1900s]

elbow-bender a drunkard. For synonyms see ALCHY. [U.S. slang, mid 1900s]

elbow-crooker a drunkard. [British slang, 1800s, Farmer and Henley]

elder 1. an udder. **2.** a breast; a human breast. By extension from sense 1. Usually in the plural and usually derogatory when referring to human breasts. [both since the late 1600s]

electric cure electrocution in the electric chair. [U.S. underworld, early 1900s, Weseen]

electrified intoxicated with alcohol; stunned with alcohol. [British slang, 1800s, Farmer and Henley]

elephant the drug P.C.P. (*q.v.*). A truncation of ELEPHANT TRANQUILIZER (*q.v.*). *Cf.* HOG (sense 3). [U.S. drug culture, mid 1900s-pres.]

elephant and castle the anus; an oaf. Rhyming slang for ASS-HOLE (*q.v.*). The term is from the official crest of an ivory trading firm (1800s), and later the name of a pub. [British, 1800s, *Dictionary of Rhyming Slang*]

elephant's trunk (also **elephants, elephant's**) intoxicated with alcohol. Rhyming slang for "drunk." [British slang and some U.S. use, 1800s-1900s]

elephant tranquilizer the drug P.C.P. (*q.v.*). Refers to the potency of the drug. *Cf.* ELEPHANT, HORSE TRANQUILIZER, PIG TRANQUILIZER. [U.S. drug culture, mid 1900s-pres.]

elevated mildly intoxicated with alcohol. [British and U.S. slang, 1800s-pres.]

eleventh finger the penis. For synonyms see YARD. [U.S., late 1900s-pres.]

Elrod a total JERK; a social outcast. For synonyms see OAF. [U.S. collegiate, late 1900s]

els Elavil™ antidepressent tablets. [U.S. drug culture, late 1900s, Kaiser]

em an abbreviation of "morphine." A spelling-out of M. (*q.v.*). Cf. AUNT EMMA. [U.S. underworld, early 1900s, Irwin]

embalmed intoxicated with alcohol. [U.S. slang, 1900s]

embalming fluid inferior or strong liquor; any alcoholic liquor. [U.S. slang, early 1900s-pres.] Synonyms: ABORTS, BLUE PIG, BLUE STONE, BUG JUICE, BUST-HEAD, CAPER-JUICE, CATGUT, CHARLEY FRISKY, CHOKE-DOG, COFFIN VARNISH, CORN-MULE, DRUDGE, FAMILY DISTURBANCE, GAY AND FRISKY, GREEK FIRE, HIGHLAND FRISKY, JOHN BARLEYCORN, LIQUID-FIRE, MOUNTAIN-DEW, NANNY-GOAT SWEAT, NIGGER-GIN, PALEFACE, PINE-TOP, PISH, PIZEN, PRAIRIE-DEW, SCREECH, SKEE, SKY, SNAKE, SNAKEBITE MEDICINE, SNAKE-JUICE, SNAKE MEDICINE, SNAKE-POISON, TANGLE-LEG, TARANTULA-JUICE, TIGER SWEAT, WHITE LIGHTNING, WOOZLE-WATER.

Emma Freud's hemorrhoids. Rhyming slang. [British, mid 1900s-pres.]

empty the trash to copulate and ejaculate. Cf. HAUL ONE'S ASHES. For synonyms see MELT. [U.S. black use, 1900s]

emsel a nickname for "morphine." Cf. EM. For synonyms see MORPH. [U.S. drug culture, mid 1900s-pres.]

end 1. the penis. [since the 1600s or before] **2.** the foreskin. **3.** the glans penis. Cf. BELL-END. For synonyms see HEAD. [senses 2 and 3 are colloquial, 1800s-1900s]

ends 1. money. [U.S., late 1900s-pres.] **2.** shoes. [U.S., late 1900s-pres.]

enema bandit a pederast. For synonyms see PEDERAST. [U.S., late 1900s-pres.]

enforcer a bully; a thug or bodyguard. [U.S., mid 1900s-pres.]

English Channel eyes eyes that are bloodshot from marijuana smoking. [U.S. collegiate, late 1900s, Eble]

enhanced HIGH on marijuana. For synonyms see TALL. [U.S. drug culture, late 1900s, Kaiser]

enjoy to coit a woman. See ENJOY A WOMAN. [from *The Rape of Lucrece* (Shakespeare)]

enjoy a woman to copulate with a woman. [euphemistic, 1800s if not long before]

enns Darvon-N™ or Darvocet-N™ painkiller. [U.S. drug culture, late 1900s, Kaiser]

enob backslang for "bone," the erect penis. See BONE (sense 2). [U.S., 1900s, Wentworth and Flexner]

entertaining the general pertaining to a woman who is experiencing the menses. Cf. CAPTAIN IS AT HOME.

(enthusiastic) amateur a woman who provides sex freely. For synonyms see BIRD. [British, late 1900s-pres.]

envelope a condom. From FRENCH LETTER (*q.v.*). For synonyms see EEL-SKIN. [British, 1800s, *Dictionary of Slang and Unconventional English*]

epicene 1. pertaining to nouns which fall into the same grammatical gender regardless of the biological sex of the named phenomenon in the real world. Found in Latin and Greek. In the English language, "common gender." **2.** of indeterminate or indeterminable sex. This includes (colloquially) homosexual, hermaphroditic, and effeminate. **3.** a homosexual male. Euphemistic. [all senses, since the 1600s] Synonyms and related terms for senses 2 and 3: ACTIVE SODOMIST, AFGAY, AG-FAY, ANGEL, ANSY-PAY, ARSE-KING, ASPRO, ASS BOY, AUNTEATER, AUNTIE, BABY, BADLING, BAG, BANDIT, BARD-ACHE, BELLE, BENT, BENT AS A NINE BOB NOTE, BETTY, BIRDIE, BITCH, BLUE, BOG QUEEN, BOY, BRIGHTON PIER, BRO-KEN-WRIST, BROWN-HATTER, BROWNIE, BUFU, BUTCH, BUTTBOY, BUTTERCUP, BUTTFUCKER, BUZZER, CAMP, CANNIBAL, CAPON, CHARLIE, CHERRY-PICKER, CHICHI, CHICKEN, CHICKEN-HAWK, CLEAR, CLOSET QUEEN, CLOSET QUEER, CON, COWBOY, DAFFODIL, DAISY, DANDY, DAUGHTER, DINGE, DIRTY OLD MAN, DIZZY QUEEN, DOLL, DRAG KING, DUTCH BOY, DYNA, EER-QUAY, EFFEMINATE MALE, ETHEL, FAG, FAGGART, FAGGOT, FAIRY, FARG, FART-CATCHER, FEMBO, FEMME, FEY, FLAMER, FLOWER, FLUTE, FLUTER, FLY BALL, FOOPER,

FOUR-LETTER MAN, FOXY LADY, FREAK, FREEP, FRIENDS OF DOROTHY'S. FRIT, FRUIT, FRUITCAKE, FRUITER, FRUIT-FLY, FRUIT-PLATE, FUGITIVE FROM A DAISY CHAIN GANG, FUNNY, GAY, GAY-BOY, GAYLORD, GEAR, GEAR-BOX, GINGER BEER, GIRL, GOBBLER, GONSEL, GREEN AND YELLOW FELLOW, GYM QUEEN, HAIRBURGER, HAIRY-FAIRY, HAT, HESH, HE-SHE, HIM-HER, HIMMER, HOCK, HOMIE, HOMO, HOMOPHILE, HOMOSEX-UAL, HORSE'S HOOF, INSERTEE, IN-SERTOR, INSPECTOR OF MANHOLES, INVERT, JERE, JOTO, JOY-BOY, K., KING LEAR, KINKY, KISSER, KWEER, LACY, LARRO, LAVENDER, LAVENDER BOY, LEATHER, LIGHT-FOOTED, LIGHT ON HIS FEET, LILY, LIMP-WRIST, LUMBERJACK, MAN'S MAN, MARY, MEAT HOUND, MID-NIGHT COWBOY, MINCE; MINTIE, MO, MOTHER, MOUSER, MUSCLE MARY, MUZ-ZLE, NANCE, NANCY, NANCY HOMEY, NELLY, NEUTER GENDER, NICK-NACK, NIC NAC, NIGH ENOUGH, NIGHT-SNEAK-ERS, NOLA, NOT INTERESTED IN THE OP-POSITE SEX, ODD, ODDBALL, ONE OF THOSE, ORCHESTRA, OSCAR, OTHER SEX, PANSY, PATO, PERVERT, PETAL, PETER PANSY, PETER-PUFFER, PINEAPPLE, PIXY, POOD, POOF, POOFTER, POUFFE, PUFF, PUNCE, PUNK, PURE SILK, PUSSY NELLIE, Q., QUAEDAM, QUEAN, QUEEN, QUEER, QUEER AS A NINE BOB NOTE, QUEERVERT, QUIMBY, QUINCE, RENTER, RICE QUEEN, RIMADONNA, RUMP-RANGER, SCREAMING FAIRY, SECKO, SHIM, SHIRT LIFTER, SISSY, SISTER, SKIPPY, SNOW QUEEN, SPINTRY, SPURGE, SWEET, SWEETIE, SWISH, THAT WAY, THING, THIRD SEX, THIRD-SEXER, THREE-DOLLAR BILL, THREE-LEGGED BEAVER, THREE-LETTER MAN, TICKLE-YOUR-FANCY, TINKERBELLE, TRICK, TRUCK-DRIVER, TWANK, TWINK, UNDER-COVER MAN, URANIST, URNING, WEIRD, WILLIE, WONK.

epsom salts ECSTASY, the drug. [U.S., late 1900s-pres.]

equalizer a gun; a pistol. Underworld. [U.S., late 1900s-pres.]

equipment the male genitals. *Cf.* AP-PARATUS, GEAR, OUTFIT. [U.S. collo-quial, 1900s]

erase to kill someone. [U.S., mid 1900s-pres.]

erb marijuana. In error for "herb." *Cf.* HERB, YERBA. [U.S. drug culture, mid 1900s-pres.]

erection an erection of the penis. A truncation of PENILE ERECTION (*q.v.*). The word is seen in other senses in its verb form, but in the noun form it al-ways refers to the penis. Synonyms and related expressions: BAZOOKA, BIT OF HARD, BIT OF SNUG, BIT OF STIFF, BLUE STEELER, BLUE-VEINED CUSTARD CHUCKER, BOLT, BONE, BONE-ON, BONER, BOSNIA, CAPTAIN STANDISH, CHARGE, CHUBBY, COCK-STAND, COLLEEN BAWN, CONCOMITANT OF DESIRE, CRACK A FAT, CUCUMBER, CUNT STRETCHER, DISTEN-SION OF THE PHALLUS, DIVINING ROD, ERECTIO PENIS, FIXED BAYONETS, FULL, GOLDEN RIVET, HAIL SMILING MORN, HALF MOST, HANG A HARD, HARD, HARD BIT, HARD-ON, HAVE A BONE-ON, HAVE A HARD-ON, HAVE A HARD-UP, HAVE IT ON, HAVE THE HORN, HORN, HORN-COLIC, HORNIFICATION, IN ONE'S BEST CLOTHES, IN ONE'S SUNDAY BEST, IRISH TOOTHACHE, JACK, LANCE IN REST, LOB, LOB-PRICK, MARQUESS OF LORN, MATUTINAL ERECTION, MORNING PRIDE, MORNING WOOD, MOUNTAIN, OLD HORNINGTON, OLD HORNY, ON THE STAND, PENILE ERECTION, PENIS IN ERECTUS, PISS-PROUD, PRIAPISM, PRICK, PRICK-PRIDE, PROD, PROUD, PROUD BELOW THE NAVEL, RAIL, RAMROD, REAMER, RISE, RISE IN ONE'S LEVIS, ROARING HORN, ROARING JACK, ROCK PYTHON, ROD OF LOVE, ROOT, SEED-LING, SPIKE, STABLE, STALK, STAND, STANDARD, STANDING-MEMBER, STAND-ING-WARE, STIFF, STIFF AND STOUT, STIFF-DEITY, STIFF ONE, STIFF PRICK, STIFF-STANDER, STIFFY, STORK, TEMPO-RARY PRIAPISM, THE OLD ADAM, TOOTHACHE, TUMESCENT, UP, VIRILE MEMBER, VIRILE REFLEX, WOOD, WOODY, YASSER.

erth the drug phencyclidine, P.C.P. Probably eye-dialect for *earth*, or an illiterate spelling. For synonyms see P.C.P. [U.S. drug culture, late 1900s, Abel]

essence of pig-shit an exceptionally unattractive woman. [British, late 1900s-pres.]

Esso-B a SON OF A BITCH (*q.v.*).

E-tard people who use Ecstasy. Patterned on *retard*. [U.S., late 1900s-pres.]

eternal checkout, the death. For synonyms see DEMISE. [1900s or before]

eternal God!, By the (also **Eternal!, By the**) an oath and an exclamation. "Eternal" does not mean "damned" here. For synonyms see 'ZOUNDS!

eternity-box a coffin. [British and U.S., 1700s-pres.]

Ethel a derogatory nickname for an effeminate male or a homosexual male. [U.S. slang, mid 1900s] Similar names are: BETTY, DYNA, GUSSIE, JENNY, JENNY WILLOCKS, LIZZIE BOY, MARGERY, MARY, MARY ANN, MISS NANCY, NAN-BOY, NANCE, NANCY, NANCY DAWSON, NANCY HOMEY, NELLIE FAG, NELLY.

ethereal intoxicated on drugs or alcohol; HIGH. For synonyms see TALL, WOOFLED. [U.S. collegiate, late 1900s]

eunuch a male whose testicles or penis and testicles have been removed or whose testicles never developed. [from Greek; in English since the early 1400s] Synonyms: ABEILARD, ANDROGYNE, BOB TAIL, CAPON, CASTRATO, GELDING, RASCAGLION, SPADO, THIRD SEX, WETHER.

everhard pertaining to a very hard erection of the penis. [U.S. slang, mid 1900s-pres.]

everlasting knock death. [U.S. colloquial, late 1800s-1900s]

everlasting wound the female genitals, specifically the PUDENDAL CLEAVAGE (*q.v.*). *Cf.* CUT (sense 3), GASH (sense 1), SLIT, WOUND. [British slang, 1800s, Farmer and Henley]

ever-loving a disguise of "motherloving," which is a disguise of "mother-fucking." See MOTHERFUCKER. [slang, 1900s]

every Richard every single man (in a group of men). Richard = DICK. *Cf.* EVERY SWINGING DICK. [U.S. military, 1900s, *Soldier Talk*]

every swinging dick every single man (in a group of men). *Cf.* EVERY RICHARD. [U.S. military, 1900s, *Soldier Talk*]

everythingathon an orgy in which various types of sexual activity are performed. *Cf.* CIRCUS LOVE. See GROUP SEX for similar terms. [U.S. homosexual use, mid 1900s, Farrell]

Excaliber a priapism. [U.S., late 1900s-pres.]

exchange spits to kiss or to copulate. [British, 1800s-1900s]

exhaust pipe the anus. For synonyms see ANUS. [U.S., late 1900s-pres.]

excuse me, the a toilet; a bathroom; a restroom. Rhyming slang for W.C. [British and U.S. slang and euphemism, 1900s]

execution the carrying out of a judicial order of punishment. Now usually in reference to the death penalty. Extended from the notion of executing a sentence of death to the actual killing of a person. [since the 1300s] Synonyms and related terms: BURYING ALIVE, DEMEMBRATION, DISEMBOWEL, DRAWN AND QUARTERED, DROWNING, ELECTRIC CURE, EMPALEMENT, EVENTRATION, EXCARNIFICATION, EXENTERATION, GANCH, LAPIDATION.

exercise the armadillo (also **exercise the ferret**) to copulate. From the male point of view. [Australian, late 1900s, McDonald]

exercise the dog (also **walk the dog**) to accompany an urban dog when it goes out to eliminate. [1900s]

extract the urine from someone beat the piss out of someone. [British and U.S., early 1900s-pres.]

extracurricular activities adultery. [British and U.S. colloquial, 1900s]

eye 1. the anus in reference to anal copulation. **2.** anal copulation, usually PEDERASTY (*q.v.*). [both senses, U.S. slang, mid 1900s-pres.] **3.** a breast. See BIG BROWN EYES, EYES.

eyeball palace a homosexual bar; any place where homosexual males can meet one another. *Cf.* EYE SHOP. [U.S. homosexual use, mid 1900s-pres.]

eye doctor a sodomite. *Cf.* EYE (sense

2). [U.S. underworld, early 1900s, Monteleone]

eye-opener 1. the penis. [British slang, 1800s, Farmer and Henley] **2.** a PEDERAST (*q.v.*). *Cf.* BROWN-EYE, EYE (sense 2). [U.S. slang, 1900s] **3.** a substance which gives a charge or a jolt, such as a drink of alcohol, an amphetamine tablet, or even a cold shower. [U.S. drug culture and general slang, mid 1900s-pres.]

eyes the breasts; the nipples. A reference to the nipples. An obvious avoidance in expressions such as "And she's got two beautiful, big brown—uh—eyes." See BIG BROWN EYES. [U.S. slang, 1900s]

eye shop to shop with the eyes, to seek a homosexual partner through prolonged eye contact. *Cf.* EYEBALL PALACE. [U.S. homosexual use, mid 1900s, Farrell]

F

F. an abbreviation or a disguise for FUCK or FUCKING (both *q.v.*). [colloquial, 1900s and before]

face-ache an ugly person [British, late 1900s-pres.]

faced intoxicated with alcohol. A truncation of SHIT-FACED (*q.v.*). [U.S. slang, mid 1900s-pres., *Current Slang*]

face job an act of CUNNILINGUS. For synonyms see CUNNILINGUS. [U.S. slang, late 1900s or before]

face like a dropped pie, a a really ugly face. [Australian, mid 1900s-pres.]

face queen a homosexual male who is attracted to men's faces. See QUEEN for similar terms. [U.S. homosexual use, mid 1900s, Farrell]

face rape brutal kissing. [U.S. collegiate, late 1900s, Eble]

fachiva heroin. [U.S., late 1900s-pres.]

faded drunk; drug intoxicated. For synonyms see TALL, WOOFLED. [U.S., late 1900s-pres.]

fag 1. an effeminate male; a sissy. **2.** a homosexual male. [senses 1 and 2 are U.S. underworld and general slang, early 1900s-pres.] **3.** a CATAMITE (*q.v.*). Senses 1-3 are from FAGGOT (sense 6). [early 1900s-pres.] **4.** the penis. From FAGGOT (sense 1), *i.e.*, "a stick." [U.S. slang, 1900s, Berrey and Van den Bark] **5.** a pimp. An epithet referring to the effeminate attire of some pimps. [U.S., 1900s]

fag-bag a woman who consorts with a homosexual male. *Cf.* FAG-HAG. [U.S. slang, mid 1900s]

fag-busting See GAY-BASHING.

fag-factory a gathering place for male homosexuals. [U.S., early 1900s]

faggart a homosexual male; an obsessive practitioner of nonorthogenital sexual acts. For synonyms see EPICENE. [U.S., early 1900s]

faggerette a cigarette. [British, late 1900s-pres.]

faggot (also **faggit, fagot**) **1.** a term of contempt for a person. Literally, "a bag of sticks." [from French; 1300s] **2.** a strong term of contempt for a woman, especially an old or dissipated woman. [British, late 1500s-1800s] **3.** a prostitute. For synonyms see HARLOT. [British and U.S., 1800s-1900s]. **4.** to copulate with a woman. *Cf.* FAG (sense 4). [British slang, 1800s, Farmer and Henley] **5.** to womanize; to consort with sexually loose women. [British slang, 1800s] **6.** a male homosexual. Usually considered a strongly derogatory term. For synonyms see EPICENE. [U.S. slang, early 1900s-pres.] **7.** a derisive term of contempt for a nonhomosexual male. *Cf.* FAIRY (sense 4). [U.S., 1900s] **8.** an unattractive young woman. Possibly from sense 2. For synonyms see BUFFARILLA. [U.S. slang, mid 1900s, *Current Slang*]

faggotry homosexuality (usually male); the world of homosexuals. *Cf.* FAGGOT (sense 6). [U.S. slang, mid 1900s]

faggoty effeminate; in the manner of an effeminate male homosexual. [U.S. slang, early 1900s, Goldin, O'Leary, and Lipsius]

fag-hag a heterosexual female who consorts with homosexual males for sex or for safety. *Cf.* FAG-BAG. [U.S. slang, mid 1900s-pres.]

fag-hole the mouth. [British, mid 1900s-pres.]

fag-joint a meeting place for homosexual males. *Cf.* FAG-FACTORY. [U.S. slang, early 1900s-pres.]

fag-mag a magazine or other publication featuring male nudity for homosexual males. [U.S., mid 1900s-pres., Farrell]

fag stag a heterosexual who enjoys the company of homosexual males. [British, late 1900s-pres.]

Fag your face! "Go away!"; "Drop dead!" A play on BAG YOUR FACE! and FAG. California teens. [U.S. slang, late 1900s]

fail in the furrow to become impotent while copulating. *Cf.* FALL IN THE FURROW. [British, 1800s]

fainting fits a woman's breasts. Rhyming slang for TITS. For synonyms see BOSOM. [British, late 1900s-pres.]

fair play fornication; copulation where neither partner is married to anyone. *Cf.* FOUL PLAY. [British slang, 1800s, Farmer and Henley]

fairy 1. a jaded and debauched old woman. [British, 1800s, Ware] **2.** an effeminate male. [U.S. colloquial, early 1900s-pres.] **3.** a male homosexual or any male practitioner of nonorthogenital sexual acts. For synonyms see EPICENE. [U.S. and elsewhere, early 1900s-pres.] **4.** a term of contempt for a non-homosexual male; the same as FAGGOT (sense 7). [U.S., 1900s] **5.** a pretty young woman. [colloquial, 1900s or before]

fairy glen a public restroom used for sex by gay males. [British, late 1900s-pres.]

fairy lady a lesbian in the passive role. [U.S. slang, mid 1900s]

fall for it to become pregnant. [British, late 1900s-pres.]

falling-down drunk intoxicated with alcohol; drunk and stumbling. [colloquial, 1900s and before]

fall in the furrow to ejaculate, perhaps to ejaculate prematurely. *Cf.* DIE IN THE FURROW, FAIL IN THE FURROW. The furrow is the PUDENDAL CLEAVAGE (*q.v.*). [British slang, 1800s, Farmer and Henley]

fall off the roof to begin the menses. *Cf.* ROOF, OFF THE. [U.S. colloquial, early 1900s-pres.]

falsies 1. false breasts; pads or forms which have the effect of making the breasts appear larger and more shapely. *Cf.* NIAGARA FALSIES. **2.** false

buttocks or other body padding designed to make one's body more sexually attractive. [both senses, U.S. colloquial, early 1900s-pres.]

familiar-way pregnant. A jocular play on "family way." For synonyms see FRAGRANT. [British and U.S. colloquial, 1800s-1900s]

family jewels 1. the testicles. So named for their great value and their role in creating a family. *Cf.* DIAMONDS. [U.S. slang, 1900s] **2.** the male genitals. Less well-known than sense 1. [U.S. slang, 1900s]

family organ the penis. A euphemism of avoidance. *Cf.* FAMILY JEWELS. [U.S. colloquial, 1900s or before]

family way, in a pregnant. *Cf.* FAMILIAR-WAY. [widespread colloquial, 1800s-1900s]

famous dimes crack cocaine. For synonyms see NOSE-CANDY. [U.S., late 1900s-pres.]

fancy parts the male genitals. For synonyms see GENITALS, VIRILIA. [British, early 1900s-pres.]

fancy-work the male genitals and pubic area. [British, 1800s]

fang-carpenter a dentist. [Australian, 1900s, Baker]

fang-faker a dentist. [British slang or cant, 1800s, Farmer and Henley]

fang-farrier a dentist; a dental surgeon. *Cf.* FANG-CARPENTER. [nautical, 1900s or before]

fanny 1. the female genitals. [British slang, mid 1800s-pres.] **2.** the posteriors. The meaning "posteriors" occurs only in a secondary sense as with ARSE, ASS, RUMP (all *q.v.*). [U.S. colloquial, early 1900s-pres.]

fanny about to mess around. [British, late 1900s-pres.]

fan(ny) belt a very short miniskirt. [British, late 1900s-pres.]

fanny fart a noise created by the vagina during sexual intercourse. [British, mid 1900s-pres.]

fanny magnet something believed to attract females. [British, late 1900s-pres.]

farg an effeminate male homosexual. A permutation of FAG (sense 2). *Cf.* FAGGART. [British, 1900s, *Dictionary of the Underworld*]

farmed alcohol intoxicated. A play on PLOUGHED, PLOWED (*q.v.*). For synonyms see WOOFLED. [U.S. collegiate, late 1900s, Eble]

Farmer Giles hemorrhoids. Rhyming slang for "piles." [Australian, mid 1900s, *Dictionary of Slang and Unconventional English*]

farmyard confetti See COWYARD CONFETTI.

far-out excellent. [widespread, mid 1900s-pres.]

fart 1. to release intestinal gas. [since the 1200s] **2.** an audible or inaudible release of intestinal gas; a breaking of wind. [since the 1300s] **3.** a term of contempt implying that the addressee is worthless. [since the 1500s]

fart about to waste time; to goof off; the same as FART AROUND (*q.v.*). [British, 1800s-1900s]

fart around to waste time; to goof off. *Cf.* FART ABOUT. [U.S. colloquial, 1900s]

fart-arseing about wasting time moving about. [Australian and British, late 1900s-pres.]

fart artist someone who breaks wind well, loudly, or with a horrible odor. [Australian, mid 1900s-pres.]

fart-blossom an oaf; a stupid person; the equivalent of TURD (sense 2). [U.S. slang, mid 1900s]

fart-catcher 1. a footman; a servant who follows his master closely enough to be aware of his master's breaking of wind. *Cf.* CATCH-FART. [British, late 1700s, Grose] **2.** a PEDERAST (*q.v.*). From the position associated with coiting *per anum*. [written nonce; British, early 1900s, *Dictionary of Slang and Unconventional English*]

fart-Daniel the female genitals. For synonyms see MONOSYLLABLE. [British slang, 1800s, Farmer and Henley]

farting shot a breaking of wind to register one's contempt while departing. For synonyms see GURK. [British, late 1900s-pres.]

fartleberry fecal matter clinging to the anal hairs. *Cf.* CHUFF-NUT, DINGLE-BERRY. [British, late 1700s, Grose]

fartlicker a low rascal; a sycophant. [British, 1700s or before]

fart off to goof off. See FART ABOUT, FART AROUND. [U.S. slang, mid 1900s]

farts the "fine arts." [U.S. collegiate, late 1900s if not before]

fart sack a bedroll; any bed. [U.S. military, 1900s, *Soldier Talk*]

fart-sucker a sycophant; the same as BUMSUCKER (*q.v.*). [British slang, 1800s, Farmer and Henley]

farty small; insignificant. [British, late 1900s-pres.]

fast-fuck 1. a rapid act of copulation or one done very vigorously. **2.** a person who participates in rapid copulation. [both senses, slang and nonce, 1800s-1900s]

father-fucker a PEDERAST (*q.v.*); a contemptuous term of address; patterned on MOTHER-FUCKER (*q.v.*). [U.S. homosexual use, mid 1900s]

father-stuff the male seed in a figurative sense; semen. [not in general use; from "Song of Myself," *Leaves of Grass* (Walt Whitman)]

fat jay a fat joint; a fat marijuana cigarette. *Cf.* J. (sense 1). [U.S. drug culture, mid 1900s-pres.]

Fat Pappy a fat marijuana cigarette. For synonyms see MEZZROLL. [U.S., late 1900s-pres.]

fat skrill lots of money. [U.S., late 1900s-pres.]

fat-slags uncouth, fat women. [British, late 1900s-pres.]

fatty 1. a derogatory nickname for a fat person. [British and U.S. since the 1800s or before] **2.** a thick marijuana cigarette. [U.S. drug culture, mid 1900s-pres.]

fatty cake a young woman with a plump, well-rounded figure. Patterned on "patty cake," a children's game.

fat-un (also **fat-one**) an extremely loud and bad-smelling breaking of wind; a ROUSER (*q.v.*). *Cf.* CHEEZER, WET ONE. [British slang, 1800s, Farmer and Henley]

fatzilla a fat person. [U.S., late 1900s-pres.]

faucett the female genitals. *Cf.* COCK (sense 6). [British slang, 1800s, Farmer and Henley]

faunlet (also **faunet**) an attractive, postadolescent male viewed as a potential sexual partner by a homosexual male; a CHICKEN (sense 2). The opposite of a nymphet or NYMPH (sense 2). [U.S. slang, mid 1900s, Wentworth and Flexner]

favor, the copulation thought of as a gift granted by the female to the male; the same as the ULTIMATE FAVOR (*q.v.*). [1800s-1900s]

fay 1. a derogatory nickname for a Caucasian from the point of view of a Negro. *Cf.* BLACK FAY, OFAY. For synonyms see PECKERWOOD. **2.** a Caucasian who seeks the association of blacks. [both senses, U.S., 1900s]

F.B. a female who loves to copulate; a "FUCK BUNNY." For synonyms see BIRD. [U.S., late 1900s-pres.]

f-bomb to say *fuck* in front of the wrong audience. [U.S., late 1900s-pres.]

fearnought a condom. *Cf.* DREADNOUGHT. For synonyms see EEL-SKIN. [British, 1900s]

fears no man intoxicated with alcohol. *Cf.* DUTCH COURAGE. [U.S. slang, early 1700s, Ben Franklin]

feather-bed jig coition. *Cf.* DANCE THE MATTRESS JIG. For synonyms see SMOCKAGE. [British slang, 1800s or before]

feather brain an oaf. For synonyms see OAF. [U.S., mid 1900s-pres.]

featured intoxicated with alcohol. For synonyms see WOOFLED. [U.S., early 1900s]

fecal-freak a type of nonorthogenital sex practitioner who is sexually stimulated (possibly to orgasm) by fecal material. This may include the ingestion of fecal material. [U.S., 1900s]

feddies money; paper money. [U.S., mid 1900s-pres.]

federal diploma a U.S. bank note. [U.S., late 1900s-pres.]

federal jug a federal prison. [U.S., late 1900s-pres.]

fed(s) money. [U.S., late 1900s-pres.]

feel (also **feel-up**) to explore or stimulate the vagina, breasts, or virilia of another person. [since the 1700s]

feel fuzzy to be sexually aroused; a variant of FEEL HAIRY (*q.v.*). [U.S. slang, 1900s]

feel gay to feel sexually aroused. *Cf.* GAY (sense 1). [British, 1800s and before, Farmer and Henley]

feel hairy to be sexually aroused. *Cf.* FEEL FUZZY. For synonyms see HUMPY. [British and later, U.S. slang, mid 1800s-pres.]

feeling good intoxicated with alcohol. Recently, intoxicated with drugs or drugs and alcohol. [colloquial euphemism, mid 1800s-pres.]

feeling no pain intoxicated with alcohol, drugs, or both. [mid 1900s-pres.]

feel like a pork chop in a synagogue to feel very much out of place. [Australian, late 1900s-pres.]

feel-up (also **feel**) to caress sexually. [U.S. colloquial, 1900s]

fee-tops (also **fees, fe-ops**) the female tops of marijuana plants. *Cf.* TOPS. For synonyms see MARI. [U.S. drug culture, late 1900s, Kaiser]

felch 1. (also **feltch**) to perform ANILINGUS (*q.v.*) on a male. [U.S. homosexual use, mid 1900s, Farrell] **2.** to lick or suck one's recently deposited semen from the anus. [British and U.S., late 1900s-pres.]

felch queen (also **feltch queen**) **1.** one who obtains sexual gratification from coming into close contact with fecal matter. *Cf.* FECAL-FREAK. **2.** a homosexual male who specializes in performing ANILINGUS (*q.v.*). [both senses, U.S. homosexual use, mid 1900s]

fellate to perform PENILINGUS (*q.v.*). [nonce or a neologism; U.S., mid 1900s, (Humphreys)]

fellatio (also **fellation**) PENILINGUS (*q.v.*); the act of one person (a man or a woman) sucking, licking, kissing, or nibbling the penis of a man. The act may lead to orgasm, but the term is also used to refer to sexual stimulation of the male in preparation for other types of sexual activity. [from the Latin for "suck" in an obscene sense]

fellatrice 1. a MOUTH-WHORE (*q.v.*); a prostitute who performs FELLATIO (*q.v.*). **2.** a professional female CUNNILINGUIST (*q.v.*). [assumed to be in error; late 1800s, Farmer] **3.** a female performer of fellatio; a female RECEIVER (*q.v.*) in contexts other than in prostitution.

fellatrix 1. a male RECEIVER (*q.v.*) in fellatio. *Cf.* FELLATRICE. This is in the feminine form, but it appears in Stedmann in reference to a male. **2.** a female performer of FELLATIO (*q.v.*); the same as FELLATRICE (sense 3).

fellatrix of women a lesbian; a woman who performs CUNNILINGUS (*q.v.*). [late 1800s, (Farmer)]

fell of a hix a deliberate spoonerism of "hell of a fix." *Cf.* MELL OF A HESS. [U.S. colloquial and euphemistic, early 1900s, Weseen]

female spendings vaginal secretions or vaginal secretions and ejaculated semen. *Cf.* SPENDINGS. [British, 1800s (Farmer and Henley)] Synonyms: CONCOMITANT OF DESIRE, CUNT-JUICE, GOOSE-GREASE, GRAVY, OIL OF GIBLETS, OIL OF HORN, SEXUAL DISCHARGE, SEXUAL SECRETION, VAGINA-JUICE.

fembo a homosexual male. A blend of *female* and *boy*. For synonyms see EPICENE. [U.S. collegiate, late 1900s, Munro]

femme (also **fem**) **1.** any woman or girl. [from French; U.S. slang, early 1900s] **2.** a passive female homosexual. [U.S. slang, mid 1900s-pres.] **3.** a male homosexual in the passive role; a CATAMITE (*q.v.*) or the receiver in fellatio; an effeminate male homosexual. [U.S., 1900s]

femme D. a female medical doctor. Contrived rhyming slang for "M.D." [U.S. slang, mid 1900s]

femme fatale a vamp; a seductress. [from French; U.S., 1900s]

fen 1. a prostitute. For synonyms see HARLOT. [cant, 1600s, B.E.] **2.** fentanyl, the powerful painkiller Sublimaze™. *Cf.* DESIGNER DRUG. [U.S. drug culture, late 1900s, Kaiser]

fender-bender a barbiturate tablet or capsule, especially Seconal (trademark). From a slang term for a minor automobile collision. For synonyms see BARB. [U.S. drug culture, mid 1900s-pres.]

fe-ops See FEE-TOPS.

ferret 1. to coit a woman. **2.** the penis in expressions such as HIDE THE FERRET (*q.v.*). *Cf.* MOLE. [both senses, British slang, 1800s, Farmer and Henley]

feshnushkied alcohol intoxicated. For synonyms see WOOFLED. [U.S. slang, late 1900s]

fetch up to vomit. For synonyms see YORK. [U.S. slang, 1900s]

fettered intoxicated with alcohol. [U.S. slang, early 1700s, Ben Franklin] See also GOOD FETTLE, IN.

fetti(e) paper money. From *confetti*. [U.S., 1900s-pres.]

fettle to coit a woman. From a standard term meaning "scour." [British, 1800s, *Dictionary of Slang and Unconventional English*]

fey 1. a homosexual male. For synonyms see EPICENE. [U.S. slang, 1900s] **2.** a Caucasian. See FAY.

fiddle-cup a drunkard. For synonyms see ALCHY. [British slang, 1800s, Farmer and Henley]

fiddled intoxicated with alcohol. [U.S. slang, 1900s, Weseen]

fiddle-farting wasting time; messing around. Similar to MONKEY-FARTING (*q.v.*). A blend of "fiddling around" and "farting around." [U.S. slang, mid 1900s-pres.]

fiddlestick 1. the penis; the same as FIDDLE-BOW (*q.v.*). *Cf.* FIDDLE (sense 2). **2.** in the plural, nonsense. [since the mid 1800s]

fiend 1. the devil. [since *c.* 1000, *Oxford English Dictionary*] Synonyms: APOLLYON, ARCH-FIEND, AULD HOR-

NIE, AUTHOR OF EVIL, AVERNUS, BAD MAN, BEELZEBUB, BELIAL, BLACKGENTLEMAN, BLACK-SPY, BUGGAR-MAN, CLOOTS, DARBLE, DIABLO, DIABOLARCH, DIABOLUS, DIAVOLO, DIBBLE, DICKENS, DIVEL, DIVIL, D---L, FALLEN ANGEL, FATHER OF LIES, GENTLEMAN IN BLACK, GOODMAN, HIS SATANIC MAJESTY, HOBB, LORD HARRY, LUCIFER, MEPHISTOPHELES, MIFFY, NICHOLAS, NICKEY, OLD BENDY, OLD BILLY, OLD BLAZES, OLD BOOTS, OLD BOY, OLD CAIN, OLD CLOOTIE, OLD DAD, OLD DRIVER, OLD GENTLEMAN, OLD GOOSEBERRY, OLD HARRY, OLD HORNY, OLD LAD, OLD NED, OLD NICK, OLD NICK BOGEY, OLD POGER, OLD POKER, OLD ROGER, OLD ROUND-FOOT, OLD RUFFIN, OLD SCRATCH, OLD SERPENT, OLD SPLIT-FOOT, OLD TOAST, PRINCE OF DARKNESS, QUEED, RAGAMUFFIN, RAGMAN, RUFFIAN, SAINT NICHOLAS, SAM HILL, SATAN, SCRATCH, SKIPPER, TANTARABOBS, THE BLACKMAN, THE BLACK PRINCE, THE DARK ONE, THE DEUCE, THE EVIL ONE, THE NOSELESS ONE, THE OLD ONE, THE WICKED ONE, TITIVIL, TOAST, TOOT, WARLOCK. **2.** a person who is obsessed with specific things or activities. [U.S., late 1800s-pres.]

fight one's turkey to masturbate. *Cf.* GOOSE'S-NECK. For synonyms see WASTE TIME. [British slang, 1800s, Farmer and Henley]

FIGJAM "Fuck I'm good; just ask me." [Australian, mid 1900s-pres.]

filthy lucre money. [1900s, if not before]

final resting place a cemetery; one's grave. *Cf.* LAST HOME. For synonyms see LAST ABODE.

F-ing (also **effing**) a disguise of FUCKING (*q.v.*). [U.S. slang, mid 1900s-pres.]

F-ing around goofing off; FUCKING AROUND (*q.v.*). [U.S. slang, mid 1900s-pres.]

finger **1.** to caress a woman sexually. For synonyms see FIRKYTOODLE. [1800s-1900s] **2.** to masturbate the vagina. *Cf.* FINGER-FUCK. [since the 1600s] **3.** to give someone the finger. [U.S. slang, mid 1900s-pres.] **4.** "the

finger," a specific obscene gesture. See FINGER, THE. [U.S., mid 1900s-pres.]

finger-fuck to masturbate a woman by inserting a finger into the vagina. This may be done by a man, the woman, or another woman. *Cf.* FUCKFINGER. [British and U.S., 1800s-1900s]

finger-job an act of sexual play possibly leading to orgasm. The finger is used to stimulate the vagina or anus. [U.S., mid 1900s-pres.]

finger wave **1.** THE FINGER, (*q.v.*). *Cf.* BIRD (sense 4), BONE, ONE-FINGER SALUTE. [U.S., mid 1900s-pres.] **2.** a rectal examination. [U.S., late 1900s-pres.]

finie a sexually attractive female. For synonyms see BIRD. [U.S., late 1900s-pres.]

finkydiddle sexual play; sexual foreplay. See FIRKYTOODLE. [British, 1900s, *Dictionary of Slang and Unconventional English*]

Finnegans a type of drug that boosts the power of a METHADONE dose. Possibly akin to FEN. [U.S. drug culture, late 1900s]

fir HASHISH. For synonyms see HASH. [U.S. drug culture, late 1900s, Abel]

fire a line to sniff (SNORT) a LINE of cocaine. [U.S. drug culture, late 1900s]

fire a shot to ejaculate. *Cf.* SHOT (sense 2). For synonyms see MELT. [British slang, 1800s, Farmer and Henley]

fireball an energetic and ambitious person; a go-getter. [British and U.S., late 1900s-pres.]

fire blanks **1.** to coit to ejaculation but fail to impregnate. **2.** to ejaculate sterile semen. Occurs in joking about the seduction of a woman by a man who claims he is sterile. *Cf.* I.O.F.B. [U.S. slang, mid 1900s-pres.]

firebrand the penis. *Cf.* BLOWTORCH, TORCH OF CUPID. [British slang, 1800s, Farmer and Henley]

fired-up intoxicated with alcohol. For synonyms see WOOFLED. [since the mid 1800s]

fire in the air **1.** to have a premature ejaculation. **2.** to have any ejaculation outside the vagina, especially ejaculation from masturbation. *Cf.* SHOOT IN THE BUSH. [both senses, British slang, 1800s, Farmer and Henley]

firelock the female genitals. Named for an early rifle which required rubbing to produce sparks to ignite the primary. [British slang, 1800s, Farmer and Henley]

fireplace the genitals. *Cf.* FIRE (sense 1). For synonyms see GENITALS, MONOSYLLABLE. [U.S. slang, 1900s]

fire queen a sadist who burns other people to arouse sexual pleasure. [U.S. slang, 1900s]

firkin fucking. [British, late 1900s-pres.]

firkytoodle 1. sexual play; sexual foreplay. 2. to perform sexual play. *Cf.* FINKYDIDDLE. [both senses, British, 1700s-1800s] Synonyms and related terms for both senses: BRING ON, CANOE, CANOODLE, CARESS, CATERWAUL, CLITORIZE, CONTRECTATION, COP A FEEL, DALLY, DIDDLE, DILDO, FAM, FEEL, FEEL-UP, FIDDLE, FINGER, FINKYDIDDLE, FOREPLAY, FRISKING, FUDGE, FUMBLE, FUTZ AROUND, GET ONE'S HAND ON IT, GET OVER SOMEONE, GRABBLE, GRUBBLE, GUDDLE, HANDLE, HORN, LING-GRAPPLING, LOVE UP, MAKE LOVE, MEDDLE WITH, MESS ABOUT, MIRD, MOUSE, MUGGING-UP, NECK, NETHER-WORK, NUG, PADDLE, PAW, PET UP, PITCH HONEY, PLAY GRAB-ASS, PRACTICE IN THE MILKY-WAY, RUMMAGE, SAMPLE, SEXAMINATION, SEXUAL FOREPLAY, SPOON, SPRUNCH, SPUNK UP, STROKE, THUMB, TICKLE, TIP THE MIDDLE FINGER, TOUCH-UP, TOY.

first line morphine. For synonyms see MORPH. [U.S. drug culture, mid 1900s-pres.]

fish 1. a woman considered sexually; probably the same as FLESH (sense 2). [since the 1600s or before] 2. a prostitute; an easy woman. [U.S. slang, mid 1900s] 3. a heterosexual female. [U.S. homosexual use, mid 1900s-pres.] 4. as an oath and an exclamation, "Fish!" Probably "By God's flesh!" [British dialects, 1800s or before] 5. A Roman Catholic. Derogatory. A truncation of FISH-EATER (*q.v.*). [U.S. colloquial, 1900s or before] 6. an oaf. [U.S. slang, 1900s

or before] 7. the female genitals. Probably an extension of sense 4, *i.e.*, the use of "fish" in avoidance for "flesh." See FISH-MARKET. [British slang, 1800s, Farmer and Henley] 8. the penis. [late 1800s-pres.]

fish and shrimp a pimp; a PONCE (*q.v.*). Rhyming slang for "pimp." [U.S., early 1900s, Monteleone]

fish-eater a nickname for a Roman Catholic. Derogatory. From the practice of eating fish rather than meat on Fridays. *Cf.* MACKEREL-SNAPPER. [U.S. slang, early 1900s-pres.] Synonyms: BEAD-COUNTER, BEAD-PULLER, MICK, PAPIST.

fish scales crack. For synonyms see NOSE-CANDY. [U.S., late 1900s-pres.]

fish skin a condom. For synonyms see EEL-SKIN. [U.S., late 1900s-pres.]

fishwife the female wife or consort of a homosexual male. *Cf.* FISH (sense 3). Based on a term for an ill-tempered woman. [U.S. slang, mid 1900s-pres.]

fishy about the gills intoxicated with alcohol. *Cf.* GILLS, UP TO THE. [late 1800s-1900s, Ware]

fist-fuck 1. to masturbate, said of a male. The opposite of FINGER-FUCK (*q.v.*). *Cf.* FUCK ONE'S FIST. [British slang, 1800s, Farmer and Henley] 2. to insert a clenched fist into a rectum. [British and U.S., mid 1900s-pres.]

fist it to grasp a penis for masturbation or as a guide for intromission, performed by a man or a woman. [British slang, 1800s, Farmer and Henley]

fit equipment for injecting drugs. A truncation of OUTFIT. [U.S. drug culture, mid 1900s-pres.]

fitshaced drunk. For synonyms see WOOFLED. [U.S., late 1900s-pres.]

five against one masturbation. The "five" refers to the fingers. The "one" is the phallus. [jocular nonce, 1900s or before]

five and two (also **fives, five by two**) a Jewish man or woman. Rhyming slang for "Jew." Not necessarily derogatory. [British, early 1900s, *Dictionary of Rhyming Slang*] Synonyms and related terms: ABBIE, ABE, ABIE, BAGEL-

BENDER, BOX OF GLUE, BUCKLE, BUCKLE MY SHOE, CHRIST-KILLER, CLIPPED-DICK, CLOAK-AND-SUITER, DOLLY-MAN, EAGLE-BEAK, FIFTEEN AND TWO, FIVE BY TWO, FOUR-BY-TWO, FRONT-WHEEL SKID, GHETTO FOLKS, HEBE, HEEB, HOOK-NOSE, IKE, IZZY, JEWBOY, JEWEY, JEWIE, JEWY, KANGAROO, KIKE, KODGER, KOSHER CUTIE (female), KOSHIATOR, MOCKY, MOTZY, MOUCHEY, NON-SKID, PITCHY-MAN, PORK, PORKER, PORKY, POT O' GLUE, QUARTER-TO-TWO, REFF, REFFO, REFUJEW, SARAH SOO, SAUCE-PAN LID, SHEENY, SHONKY, SHONNICKER, SMOUSE, TEAPOT, LID, TEN-TO-TWO, THREE-BY-TWO, WEDGE, WOODEN-SHOE, YEHUDA, YID, YIDDLE, YIT.

five-H. man "hell how he hates himself." A sarcastic accusation of vanity based on FOUR-LETTER MAN (q.v.). [U.S. slang, early 1900s, Weseen]

five knuckle shuffle male masturbation. For synonyms see WASTE TIME. [British, late 1900s-pres.]

five-letter woman a BITCH. Based on FOUR-LETTER MAN (q.v.). [British, early 1900s, Dictionary of Slang and Unconventional English]

fives 1. an amphetamine capsule. From the strength as expressed in milligrams. See TENS. For synonyms see AMP. [U.S. drug culture, mid 1900s-pres.] **2.** a derogatory reference to Jews. See FIVE AND TWO.

fix 1. to castrate, said of animals or jocularly of a man. [U.S., 1900s or before] **2.** an injection or dose of a drug. [U.S. drug culture, early 1900s-pres.]

fix her plumbing to copulate with a woman. [euphemistic and double entendre; U.S., mid 1900s-pres.]

fix someone up 1. to get a date for someone. **2.** to secure a prostitute for someone. **3.** to copulate with a woman, said of a man. **4.** to impregnate a woman. For synonyms see STORK. [all senses, U.S., 1900s]

fizz champagne. For synonyms see WHOOPEE-WATER. [U.S. slang, mid 1900s]

fizzle to break wind inaudibly or

nearly so. For synonyms see GURK. [colloquial, 1500s-1900s]

F.L. a "French letter," a condom. For synonyms see EEL-SKIN. [British, 1800s-1900s]

flabbergasted alcohol intoxicated. For synonyms see WOOFLED. [U.S. slang, 1900s, Dickson]

flag 1. a jade; a wanton woman. Implying that she is worthy only a few pence. From an old term for a coin worth fourpence. [early 1500s] **2.** a menstrual cloth or perineal pad considered as a danger signal. A truncation of RED FLAG (q.v.). [British slang, 1800s] **3.** an effeminate male; a homosexual male. [U.S. underworld, early 1900s, Monteleone] **4.** to signal a prostitute that her services are desired. [U.S. colloquial, 1900s]

flag day menstruation time. [British, late 1900s-pres.]

flagged arrested. [U.S., late 1900s-pres.]

flagging an expression indicating that a woman is experiencing the menses. Cf. RED FLAG. [U.S., 1900s]

flag is up (also **flag is out**) an expression indicating that a woman is experiencing the menses. [British and U.S., mid 1800s-pres.]

flake 1. a dummy; an oaf. See FLEAK. [U.S. slang, mid 1900s-pres.] **2.** a male who practices FELLATIO (q.v.). [U.S. homosexual use, mid 1900s-pres.] **3.** cocaine. [U.S. drug culture, mid 1900s-pres.]

flake acid a diluted solution of L.S.D. on blotter paper that is cut up into small pieces. For synonyms see ACID. [U.S. drug culture, late 1900s, Abel]

flakers intoxicated with alcohol. A truncation of HARRY FLAKERS (q.v.). [Australian, mid 1900s, Dictionary of Slang and Unconventional English]

flame 1. lust; sexual passion. [since the 1300s] **2.** a venereal disease, probably gonorrhea. Cf. BURNER. [British slang, 1800s, Farmer and Henley] **3.** a girlfriend; a mistress. [U.S., early 1900s-pres.] **4.** [for a male homosexual] to project himself blatantly and obviously. [U.S. slang, late 1900s] **5.** to verbally attack someone via an E-mail. [British and U.S., late 1900s-pres.]

flamer 1. an obvious male homosexual. For synonyms see EPICENE. [U.S. slang, late 1900s] **2.** a gun. [U.S., late 1900s-pres.]

flamers the police. For synonyms see FLATFOOT. [U.S., late 1900s-pres.]

flaming obviously [male] homosexual. [U.S. slang, late 1900s]

flaming queen a very obvious and exaggerated effeminate male homosexual. *Cf.* SCREAMING QUEEN. [U.S. homosexual use, mid 1900s-pres.]

flange the vulva. For synonyms see MONOSYLLABLE. [British, late 1900s-pres.]

flap 1. the female genitals. **2.** to coit a woman. [both senses, British slang, 1800s, Farmer and Henley] **3.** a sexually loose woman. *Cf.* FLAPPER. [U.S., mid 1900s, Goldin, O'Leary, and Lipsius]

flapdoodle 1. the penis. For synonyms see YARD. [1600s] **2.** the female genitals. *Cf.* FLAP (sense 1). [mid 1600s (Urquhart)] **3.** nonsense. *Cf.* FLAM-DOODLE, FLAP-SAUCE (sense 2). [British and U.S., early 1800s-1900s]

flapper 1. the penis. *Cf.* FLAPDOODLE (sense 1). [British slang, 1800s, Farmer and Henley] **2.** a young prostitute; an immoral teenage girl. [British, late 1800s] **3.** a lively, active young woman, cynical about society and sexually free. From sense 2. [U.S. colloquial, early 1900s]

flaps the labia, the vulva. For synonyms see MONOSYLLABLE. [British, late 1900s-pres.]

flash 1. to vomit. From FLASH THE HASH (*q.v.*). For synonyms see YORK. [U.S. slang, mid 1900s] **2.** to exhibit the penis, especially if done fleetingly. [1900s] **3.** to exhibit any of the private parts of the body, *i.e.,* those which are usually covered. **4.** cant, the language or special vocabulary of thieves and prostitutes. [cant, 1700s-1800s] See also FLASH-CASE.

flasher a male exhibitionist. See FLASH (sense 2).

Flash Gordon a male exhibitionist; a male, who for psychopathological reasons, exhibits his penis to females. From the science fiction character's name. See FLASH, FLASHER. [U.S. slang, late 1900s]

flash in the pan a fast act of coition without ejaculation. *Cf.* PAN. [British nonce, 1700s, *Dictionary of Slang and Unconventional English*]

flash in the pants 1. a burst of sexual arousal. **2.** a brief sexual infatuation. Both are based on "flash in the pan." [both senses, U.S. jocular, 1900s]

flash one's gash to show one's vulva. [Australian, mid 1900s-pres.]

flash the hash (also **flash hash**) to vomit. See FLASH (sense 1) for U.S. survival or reintroduction. [cant, 1700s, Grose]

flash the red flag to indicate that one is experiencing the menses, said of women. [British slang, 1800s]

flash the upright grin to expose the vulva. The "grin" is made with the *labia majora,* and the PUDENDAL CLEAVAGE (*q.v.*). *Cf.* UPRIGHT GRIN, WEARING A SMILE. [British slang, 1800s, Farmer and Henley]

flat 1. FLAT-CHESTED (*q.v.*); pertaining to a girl or woman with little or no breast development. **2.** the female genitals. See BIT OF FLAT, FLAT COCK. [slang, 1900s and before] **3.** the drug L.S.D. See FLATS. [U.S. drug culture, mid 1900s-pres.] **4.** an oaf; a blockhead. [British, 1800s or before]

flat-ass absolutely; totally. Based on general slang *flat out.* [U.S. slang, late 1900s]

flat-back to act as a prostitute. *Cf.* GRASSBACK. [U.S. slang, mid 1900s-pres.]

flatbacker a prostitute who offers only regular intercourse in the *Figura Veneris Prima.* This is viewed as an amateurish limitation in the profession. [U.S. slang, mid 1900s-pres.]

flat-chested pertaining to a woman with little or no breast development. Pertains to little girls and men as well. [U.S., 1900s]

flat cock the female genitals as compared to the male. *Cf.* COCK (sense 6), FLAT (sense 2). [British slang, 1700s-1800s] See also FAT COCK.

flatfoot a policeman. [U.S. slang and colloquial, 1900s] The following synonyms usually refer to men unless indicated otherwise: ARM OF THE LAW, BACON, BEAT-POUNDER, BIKE BOYS, BIKE DYKE, BLUEBOTTLE, BLUECOAT, BLUE SUIT, BOBBY, BOTTLE-STOPPER, BOYS IN BLUE, BULL, CINDER BULL, CINDER DICK, CONSTABLE, COP, COPESS (female), COPPER, COZZER, COZZPOT, CRUSHER, DICKLESS TRACY, ESCLOP, FLAMERS, FLATHEAD, FLY, FRESH BULL, FROG, FUZZ, GENDARME, GIRLIE BEAR (female), GOLDIE LOCKS (female), GOON SQUAD, GUMSHOE, HARNESS-BULL, JOHNNY LAW, JOHNNIES, JURA, KOJAK, LADY BEAR (female), LARD, LITTLE BOY BLUE, LOBSTER, LONG ARM OF THE LAW, MALLET, MAMA BEAR (female), MAMA SMOKEY (female), MARIA, MORK, MULDOON, MUSKRA, NAILER, NAMESCLOP, OCCIFER, OFFICERETTE (female), OSSIFER, PADDY, PAVEMENT-POUNDER, PEELER, PERCENTAGE BULL, PIG, POPEYE, PO-PO, PORK, RAILROAD BULL, ROACH, SHAM, SHAMUS, SLOP, Smokey BEAVER (female), SNATCHER, STICK MAN, STRING AND TOP, THE MAN, TOY COP, UNCLE NAB, WOOLY BEAR (female).

flat-fuck 1. a sexual union of two lesbians rubbing their genitals together. *Cf.* FLAT COCK, PRINCETON RUB. **2.** to perform a FLAT-FUCK (sense 1). [both senses, British, 1800s, *Dictionary of Slang and Unconventional English*]

flatline to die. For synonyms see DEPART. [U.S., late 1900s-pres.]

flatlined 1. dead. Refers to the straight line on an EEG or other life monitoring system after life has ceased. *Cf.* NEBRASKA SIGN. For synonyms see DONE FOR. [U.S. medical, late 1900s] **2.** drunk. For synonyms see WOOFLED. [U.S., late 1900s-pres.]

flatophile a "lover of flatulence"; someone who gets pleasure out of creating, hearing, or smelling flatulence; a person, fascinated by loud releases of intestinal gas. [contrived and jocular, early 1900s]

flat peter a male who is so dumb, his penis is flat from being stepped on. [U.S. military, 1900s, *Soldier Talk*]

flats the drug L.S.D. (*q.v.*). *Cf.* BLOTTER (sense 2), CUBE (sense 2), PURPLE FLATS. [U.S. drug culture, mid 1900s-pres.]

flattened fauna road kill. [U.S., late 1900s-pres.]

flat tire 1. an impotent man; a worthless, powerless man. [early 1900s] **2.** a flaccid penis. [1900s] **3.** a fool; an oaf; a worthless man. *Cf.* RUBBER SOCK, WET SOCK. [U.S. slang, early 1900s]

flesh-peddler 1. a pimp. **2.** a prostitute. *Cf.* LOVE-PEDDLER. [both senses, U.S. slang, mid 1900s]

flesh-pot 1. a brothel. [Biblical (Exodus), "the flesh-pots of Egypt"] **2.** any district or establishment which caters to sexual desires and other physical needs. [colloquial since the 1500s] **3.** a harlot; a sexually loose woman. See SEXPOT.

flesh session a session of lovemaking and copulation. *Cf.* FLESH (sense 1). [U.S. slang, mid 1900s]

flicking fucking. A thin disguise of FRICKING (*q.v.*). [British and some U.S. use, 1900s]

flid a disliked person. From the mispronunciation of *thalidomide flidomide*, in reference to babies disfigured by the drug. For synonyms see SNOKEHORN. [British, late 1900s-pres.]

flight deck the female breasts. For synonyms see BOSOM. [British, late 1900s-pres.]

flimp 1. to coit a woman. [British slang, mid 1800s, Farmer and Henley] **2.** to cheat or deceive. **3.** a pickpocket. [senses 2 and 3 are U.S. underworld, early 1800s-early 1900s]

fling 1. a penile thrust in the sexual act. [early 1500s] **2.** a love affair. [U.S., 1900s]

fling up to vomit. For synonyms see YORK. [U.S. colloquial, early 1900s or before]

flip a bitch to make an illegal U-turn. [U.S. collegiate, late 1900s, Munro]

flip-flap 1. the penis. Rhymes with "watergap." See WATER-BOX, "genitals." Cf. FLAPDOODLE. [mid 1600s (Urquhart)] **2.** a flighty woman. Probably related to FLIP-FLAPS (q.v.). Cf. FLAPPER. [British slang, 1700s]

flip-flaps 1. the human breasts, especially bouncing and wobbling breasts. **2.** young women with jiggling and bouncing breasts. See FLOPPER-STOPPER. [both senses, Australian slang, early 1900s,. Dictionary of Slang and Unconventional English]

flip-flop mutual oral sexual intercourse involving males or females in any combination of two. Cf. LOOP-DE-LOOP, SIXTY-NINE. [U.S. slang, mid 1900s-pres.]

flipping an intensifier. A disguise of "fucking." Cf. FLICKING. [slang, early 1900s]

flit 1. an effeminate male homosexual. Cf. FRIT. [U.S. underworld and slang, early 1900s-pres.] **2.** pertaining to a homosexual male or to male homosexuality.

flitty homosexual; obviously effeminate. From FLIT (q.v.). See CAMP (sense 4). [U.S. slang, mid 1900s-pres.]

F.L.K. "funny looking kid." [U.S., late 1900s-pres.]

floating 1. intoxicated with alcohol. [U.S. slang, 1900s] **2.** drug intoxicated. [U.S. drug culture and slang, mid 1900s-pres.]

flob a mass of phlegm. [British, late 1900s-pres.]

flog to masturbate. Cf. FLOG ONE'S DONKEY. [Australian, 1900s, Dictionary of Slang and Unconventional English]

flog one's donkey (also **flog one's meat, flog one's sausage**) to masturbate. Cf. FLOG. [British slang, 1800s, Dictionary of Slang and Unconventional English]

flog the bishop to masturbate. The bishop's miter is compared here to the glans penis. Cf. BOX THE JESUIT AND GET COCKROACHES. [British, 1800s,

Dictionary of Slang and Unconventional English] See also BISHOP.

flog the dummy (also **flog one's dong**) to masturbate. Said of the male. Cf. BEAT THE DUMMY, FLONG ONE'S DONG. For synonyms and related subjects see WASTE TIME. [U.S. slang, late 1900s]

flog the log to masturbate. For synonyms see WASTE TIME. [Australian, British, U.S., late 1900s-pres.]

flong one's dong to masturbate. Patterned on other rhyming expressions for this matter, i.e., BEAT THE MEAT (q.v.). Cf. DONG. For synonyms see WASTE TIME. [U.S. slang, mid 1900s-pres.]

floods the menses. [U.S., 1900s] Synonyms and related terms: ALL'S NOT QUIET ON THE WATERFRONT, AT NUMBER ONE LONDON, AUNT FLO, BECOME A LADY, BLOODY MARY, CAPTAIN IS AT HOME, CARRYING A FLAG, CATAMENIA, CATAMENIAL DISCHARGE, CATAMENIAL STATE, CHINKERINGS, COLLYWOBBLES, COUNTRY COUSIN, COURSES, CURSE OF EVE, D.A.s, DOMESTIC AFFLICTIONS, DYSMENORRHEA, ENTERTAINING THE GENERAL, FEELING POORLY, FEELING UNWELL, FEMALE DISORDER, FIELD DAY, FLAGGING, FLAG IS OUT, FLAG IS UP, FLASH THE RED FLAG, FLOWERS, FLOWING, FLYING BAKER, FLYING THE RED FLAG, FLY THE FLAG, FRIENDS TO STAY, GOT THE RAG ON, HAMMOCK IS SWINGING, HAVE IT ON, THE FLOWERS, HAVE THE GATE LOCKED AND THE KEY LOST, HELL WEEK, HIGH TIDE, HOLY WEEK, INDISPOSED, KNOCKED-UP, LITTLE FRIEND, LITTLE SISTER IS HERE, LITTLE VISITOR, LOSE, MENO, MENSES, MICKEY MOUSE IS KAPUT, MONTHLIES, MONTHLY BILL, MONTHLY CYCLE, MONTHLY FLOWERS, MONTHLY FLUX, MONTHLY TERMS, MONTHS, MOTHER-NATURE, NATURE, OFF THE ROOF, ON THE MOON CYCLE, ON THE RAG, O.T.R., OUT OF ORDER, OUT OF THIS WORLD, PERIOD, RAGGING, RAGGING IT, RAG TIME, REALLY SLICK, RED FLAG, RED SAILS IN THE SUNSET, RED TUMMY-ACHE, RIDING THE COTTON BICYCLE, RIDE THE COTTON PONY, RIDING THE RAG, RIDING THE WHITE HORSE, ROAD-MAKING,

ROAD UP FOR REPAIRS, ROSES, SICK, SO, STREET UP FOR REPAIRS, STUB ONE'S TOE, TAIL-FLOWERS, TERMS, THAT TIME, THAT WAY, THE CURSE, THE NUISANCE, THE THING, THOSE DAYS OF THE MONTH, THOSE DIFFICULT DAYS, TURNS, TWITTERS, UNDER THE WEATHER, UNWELL, VAPORS, VISIT FROM FLO, VISITOR, WET SEASON, WOMAN'S HOME COMPANION.

flooey intoxicated with alcohol. For synonyms see WOOFLED. [U.S. slang, early 1900s] See also DRUNK AS FLOEY at DRUNK AS CHLOE.

floor fuck to copulate on the floor. [Australian, early 1900s, *Dictionary of Slang and Unconventional English*]

flop a woman to place a woman, literally or figuratively, in a position to perform sexual intercourse. Cf. LAY DOWN, PUT DOWN (sense 1), SPREAD (sense 2). [British, 1800s, *Dictionary of Slang and Unconventional English*]

flop in to penetrate the vagina. [British colloquial, 1800s]

flop in the hay 1. to go to bed with a person for sexual activity. Cf. ROLL IN THE HAY, TOSS IN THE HAY. **2.** a rapid act of sexual intercourse. [both senses, U.S. slang, early 1900s-pres.]

flopper-stopper a brassiere. [Australian, British, U.S., mid 1900s-pres.]

floral arrangement a DAISY CHAIN. Contrived word play. [British slang, 1900s, McDonald]

Florida snow a white powder anesthetic snorted like cocaine; cocaine. For synonyms see NOSE-CANDY. [U.S. drug culture, late 1900s]

flower 1. the hymen. Implied in DE-FLOWER (*q.v.*). For synonyms see BEAN. **2.** the female genitals. [British slang, 1800s, Farmer and Henley] **3.** in the plural, the menses. See FLOWERS. **4.** a homosexual male. Cf. PANSY. [U.S., 1900s] Synonyms for sense 4: ANSY-PAY, BUTTERCUP, DAFFODIL, DAISY, LILY, PANSY.

flowers and frolics the testicles. Rhyming slang for BALLOCKS (*q.v.*). [British, 1900s, *Dictionary of Rhyming Slang*]

fluff 1. the female pubic hair. Cf.

FLEECE. [widespread recurrent nonce since the 1800s] **2.** to release intestinal gas. For synonyms see GURK. [Australian, 1900s, Baker] **3.** a young woman. [U.S., early 1900s-pres.] **4.** a lesbian with feminine traits. [U.S. homosexual use, mid 1900s]

fluff one's duff to masturbate. For synonyms see WASTE TIME. [British, mid 1900s-pres.]

flurgle (also **flergle**) to copulate. For synonyms see OCCUPY. [U.S. slang, mid 1900s]

flute (also **one-holed flute, living flute, silent flute**) **1.** the penis. Cf. BAGPIPE, PICCOLO. [British slang, early 1700s or before] **2.** a homosexual male. Possibly a deliberate mispronunciation of FRUIT (sense 4). Cf. FLUTER, PICCOLO-PLAYER. [U.S., 1900s]

fluter the male homosexual receiver in fellation. Cf. PICCOLO-PLAYER. [U.S. underworld and slang, early 1900s-pres.]

fluzz dyke a passive lesbian; a feminine female homosexual. Cf. BULL-DIKER, FLUFF. For synonyms see LESBYTERIAN. [U.S. homosexual use, mid 1900s, Farrell]

fly 1. a policeman. [in various usages since the mid 1800s] **2.** a wanton woman; a prostitute. From FLY THE FLAG (sense 1). [British, late 1800s, Farmer and Henley] **3.** to take narcotics habitually. **4.** to experience a HIGH (sense 3) from narcotics. [senses 3 and 4 are U.S. drug culture and slang, mid 1900s-pres.]

fly girl a sexually attractive female. For synonyms see BIRD. [U.S., late 1900s-pres.]

fly mink a fine woman. For synonyms see BIRD. [U.S., late 1900s-pres.]

flying a state of drug intoxication. Cf. FLY (sense 4). For synonyms see TALL. [U.S. drug culture, mid 1900s-pres.]

flying Baker to be experiencing the menses. Flying is a transitive verb here. The "Baker" signalling flag is red. Cf. FLY THE FLAG. [1900s]

flying-fuck 1. "nothing" in expressions such as GIVE A FLYING-FUCK and GO TAKE A FLYING-FUCK (both *q.v.*).

[mid 1900s-pres.] **2.** an imaginary act of coition accomplished in the air, as in an airplane or at the end of a great leap made by the male.

flying the (red) flag experiencing the menses; having one's menstrual period. For synonyms see FLOODS. [U.S. and elsewhere, 1900s]

F.O. 1. a "fuck-off," a worthless do-nothing; a jerk. **2.** a masturbator. For synonyms see HUSKER. [both senses, U.S., 1900s] **3.** "FUCK OFF!"; "Get out!" *Cf.* F! [U.S. euphemism, late 1900s]

foam beer. For synonyms see BOOZE. [U.S., late 1900s-pres.]

foaming at the mouth about to ejaculate; extremely anxious to proceed with sexual activity. *Cf.* DRIPPING FOR IT, READY TO SPIT. [colloquial, 1900s]

foaming beef probe the penis in an act of copulation. For synonyms see YARD. [U.S. mock medical, late 1900s]

fog-matic intoxicated with alcohol. [U.S., mid 1800s, Wentworth and Flexner]

foin to copulate; to thrust. From an old word meaning "thrust with a pointed weapon." [late 1500s, Florio]

foist a breaking of wind. See FICE, FOYST.

folded intoxicated with alcohol; the same as BENT (sense 1). [U.S. slang, early 1900s, Weseen]

folding money U.S. paper bank notes, as opposed to coins. [1900s, if not before]

folding stuff U.S. paper bank notes, as opposed to coins. [U.S., mid 1900s-pres.]

fomp to fool around sexually; to copulate. [U.S. collegiate, late 1900s]

fondle 1. to caress sexually; to handle the breasts of a woman or the genitals of a male or female of any age. [since the 1600s] **2.** to copulate. For synonyms see OCCUPY. [British, 1800s, Farmer and Henley]

foodie someone who is particular about food or is interested in all the lastest food fads. [U.S., late 1900s-pres.]

fool around 1. to tease. **2.** to engage in sexual activity short of copulation. **3.** to engage in an extramarital romance. [all senses, since the late 1800s]

foolish powder 1. any powdered narcotic. [U.S. underworld, early 1900s, Irwin] **2.** heroin. [U.S. underworld, early 1900s, Weseen]

fool-sticker the penis. For synonyms see YARD. [British slang, 1800s, Farmer and Henley]

fool-trap 1. a harlot. **2.** the female genitals. *Cf.* FLY-TRAP. [both senses, British slang, 1800s]

foop to engage in homosexual practices. Possibly backslang for POOF (*q.v.*). [U.S. slang, mid 1900s-pres., Underwood]

fooper a homosexual male. *Cf.* FOOP. [U.S. slang, mid 1900s-pres., Underwood]

foot 1. to copulate. See FOUTRE!, FUT! [from an innuendo in *Merry Wives of Windsor* (Shakespeare)] **2.** an oath and an exclamation, "Foot!" and "My foot!" [1600s]

footfuck to put the penis between the feet of one's partner who strokes it. [U.S., late 1900s-pres.]

foot queen a homosexual male who derives sexual pleasure from fondling or kissing someone else's feet. *Cf.* SHRIMP QUEEN, TOE QUEEN. [U.S. homosexual use, mid 1900s, Farrell]

foozlified intoxicated with alcohol. For synonyms see WOOFLED. [British slang, late 1800s, *Dictionary of Slang and Unconventional English*]

fop 1. a fool. [since the mid 1400s, *Oxford English Dictionary*] **2.** a male who is excessively concerned about dress and appearance; an effeminate dandy. [since the late 1600s] Synonyms for sense 2: ADONIS, BEAU, BLOOD, BRIGHT, COXCOMB, DANDIPRAT, DINK, JACK-A-DANDY, JEMMY, LARDY-TARDY TOFF, POPIN-JAY, PRINCOCK, STRUT-NODDY.

forbidden fruit 1. a young girl; a virgin. *Cf.* JAIL BAIT. [U.S. slang, 1900s] **2.** sex in general. Based upon the fruit of the tree of knowledge in the Garden of Eden.

forecastle the female genitals. Based on the nautical term and its pronunciation, "f'c'sle," *i.e.,* "fuck-sle." [British slang, 1800s]

forefinger the penis. *Cf.* LITTLE FINGER, MIDDLE FINGER, THUMB OF LOVE. [from *All's Well That Ends Well* (Shakespeare)]

forehatch the female genitals. *Cf.* HATCHWAY. [British slang, 1800s, Farmer and Henley]

foreman the penis. *Cf.* FOREWOMAN. For synonyms see YARD. [British euphemism, mid 1600s]

foreskin skin which covers the glans penis or glans clitoridis. Usually refers to the male prepuce, a cylinder of loose epidermis which is an extension of the skin of the shaft of the penis. Synonyms: END, JEWISH NIGHTCAP, LACE CURTAINS, SHEATH, SNAPPER, WHICKERBILL.

foreskin-hunter a prostitute. [British slang, 1800s, Farmer and Henley]

forest the female pubic hair. [implied as early as the 1500s and repeated nonce use; colloquial since the early 1700s or before]

Forest (Gump) an act of defecation. Rhyming slang for DUMP. For synonyms see EASE ONESELF. [British, late 1900s-pres.]

forewoman the female genitals. *Cf.* FOREMAN. [British slang, 1800s]

For fucksake! an angry exclamation. For synonyms see 'ZOUNDS. [British and U.S., late 1900s-pres.]

fork and knife one's own wife; anyone's wife. Rhyming slang for "wife." [British, 1900s, *Dictionary of Rhyming Slang*]

Fork you! "Fuck you!" [euphemism of disguise; U.S., 1900s, Wentworth and Flexner]

fornicate 1. to copulate, said of an unmarried person copulating with anyone. [since the mid 1500s] **2.** to copulate, said (erroneously) of any illicit copulating. **3.** to tell lies; to invent tales. A jocular or ignorant error for "prevaricate." [British dialect, 1800s]

Fornicate the poodle! an oath and an exclamation; an elaboration of "Fuck a dog!" [British, 1900s, *Dictionary of Slang and Unconventional English*]

fort the female genitals. A truncation of FORTRESS (*q.v.*). [British, 1600s]

Fort Bushy the female genitals. [attested as Canadian, 1900s, *Dictionary of Slang and Unconventional English*]

fortress (also **fort**) the female genitals. [British slang, 1800s, Farmer and Henley]

forty-four a prostitute. Rhyming slang for WHORE (sense 1). [British, 1900s, *Dictionary of Rhyming Slang*]

forwards amphetamine tablets or capsules. *Cf.* PEP PILL. [U.S. drug culture, mid 1900s-pres.]

F.O.S. "full of shit," pertaining to a person who is phony or who lies and boasts constantly. [U.S. slang, mid 1900s-pres.]

fossilized alcohol intoxicated. *Cf.* OSSIFIED. A play on STONED. For synonyms see WOOFLED. [U.S. slang, 1900s]

four-F. method a juvenile male view of a masculine or hypermasculine approach to women and sex, "find 'em, feel 'em, fuck 'em, and forget about 'em." Also occurs in other variations. [since the late 1800s]

four-letter man a man whose character can be described by any one of a series of four-letter words, *e.g.,* HOMO, DUMB, SHIT. From the term used to describe an athlete who has received four letters in team sports. *Cf.* FIVE-LETTER WOMAN, THREE-LETTER MAN. [British and U.S., 1900s]

four-letter word one of the traditional "dirty words," most of which are spelled with four letters. These are known worldwide: COCK, CUNT, FART, FUCK, PISS, SHIT, TURD. Less widely known are ARSE, QUIM, TWAT. *Cf.* ANGLO-SAXON.

fours and doors (also **four-doors**) Tylenol No. 4 (with codeine) plus Doriden™. [U.S. drug culture, late 1900s]

four-sheets to the wind intoxicated with alcohol. *Cf.* BOTH SHEETS IN THE

WIND, THREE SHEETS IN THE WIND, TWO SHEETS TO THE WIND. [slang, 1800s-pres.]

fox an extremely attractive female. [originally black use; U.S. slang, mid 1900s-pres.]

fox-drunk intoxicated with alcohol; drunk and crafty or stinking drunk. [1500s]

foxed intoxicated with alcohol. From the red color of the fox or the "stinking" in "stinking drunk." [British and U.S. colloquial, early 1600s-1900s]

fox-head homebrewed alcohol; moonshine. [U.S. dialect (Ozarks), Randolph and Wilson]

fox magnet a male who attracts females easily. See FOX. [U.S., late 1900s-pres.]

foxy lady 1. a sexually attractive female. [U.S. slang, mid 1900s-pres.] **2.** a sexually attractive male homosexual. From sense 1. [U.S. homosexual use, mid 1900s-pres., Farrell]

foyst (also **fice, fust, fyst**) **1.** an inaudible release of intestinal gas. For synonyms see GURK. [mid 1600s-1700s] **2.** to copulate. For synonyms see OCCUPY. [mid 1600s (Urquhart)]

fractured 1. intoxicated with alcohol. For synonyms see WOOFLED. [U.S. slang, early 1900s-pres.] **2.** demolished by laughter. [U.S., late 1900s-pres.]

fragrant pregnant. A jocular avoidance. [U.S. colloquial, 1900s] Synonyms and related terms: ABOUT TO FIND PUPS, APRON-UP, AWKWARD, BABY-BOUND, BAGGED, BANGED UP, BEEN PLAYING TRICKS, BELLY-FULL, BELLY-UP, BIG WITH CHILD, BOUND, BROKEN-KNEED, BROKEN-LEGGED, CHILDING, CLUCKY, COCKED-UP, COMING, COMING FRESH, DELICATE CONDITION, DOUBLE-RIBBED, ENCEINTE, EXPECTING, FAMILIAR-WAY, FULL-IN-THE-BELLY, FULL OF HEIR, GONE, GONE TO SEED, GRAVID, GREAT WITH CHILD, HAVE A BUN IN THE OVEN, HAVE A DUMPLING ON, HAVE A HUMP IN FRONT, HAVE A NINE-MONTHS DROPSY, HAVE ONE IN THE OVEN, HAVE ONE'S CARGO ABOARD, HIGH-BELLIED, HOW-CAME-YOU-SO?, IN A FAMILY WAY, IN A FIX, IN AN INTERESTING CONITION, IN BAD SHAPE, IN DUTCH, IN FOR IT, IN POD, IN THE PUDDING CLUB, IN TROUBLE, IN YOUNG, IRISH TOOTHACHE, I.T.A., JUMBLED-UP, KETCHED, KIDDED, KNAPPED, KNOCKED-UP, LADY IN WAITING, LAP-CLAP, LIVING IN SEDUCED CIRCUMSTANCES, LOADED, LOOKING PIGGY, LUMPY, LUSTY, ON THE BONES, ON THE HILL, ON THE WAY, OTHERWISE, PARTURIENT, P.G., PILLOWED, PIZENED, PODDY, POISONED, PREGGERS, PREGGY, PREGO, PUMPED, RUN TO SEED, SEWED-UP, SHORT-SKIRTED, SHOT IN THE GIBLETS, SHOT IN THE TAIL, SO, SPRINGING, STORKED, STORK-MAD, STUNG BY A SERPENT, SWALLOWED A WATERMELON SEED, TEEMING, TOO BIG FOR HER CLOTHES, UP-AND-COMING, UP THE DUFF, UP THE POLE, UP THE SPOUT, UP THE STICK, WEARING THE BUSTLE WRONG, WEDGED-UP, WELL-ALONG, WITH CHILD, WITH SQUIRREL, WITH YOUNG.

franger a condom. For synonyms see EEL-SKIN. [Australian, mid 1900s-pres.]

frankentits enormous, artificially enhanced breasts. For synonyms see BOSOM. [U.S., late 1900s-pres.]

frankfurter the penis. *Cf.* WEENIE. For synonyms see GENITALS, YARD. [U.S. slang, 1900s and probably nonce]

franzy house a brothel. [U.S. colloquial or dialect, 1900s or before, Wentworth]

frat dick a typical fraternity member. See DICK (sense 8). [U.S. collegiate, late 1900s]

frat fag a typical fraternity member. Derogatory. [U.S. collegiate, late 1900s, Munro]

frazzled intoxicated with alcohol. For synonyms see WOOFLED. [U.S. slang, late 1800s-pres.]

freak 1. a male homosexual or a practitioner of nonorthogenital sex acts. *Cf.* SEX FIEND. **2.** a nymphomaniac. [Both senses, U.S. slang, mid 1900s-pres.]

freak daddy an attractive male; a sexually attractive male. [U.S. slang, late 1900s]

freaked-out (also **freaked**) under the influence of marijuana. For synonyms see TALL. [U.S. drug culture, mid 1900s-pres.]

freak-fuck any nonorthogenital sexual act. [U.S. slang, late 1900s]

freaking a disguise of "fucking." *Cf.* FLICKING. [U.S., mid 1900s-pres.]

freak mommy (also **freak mama**) a good-looking woman; a sexually attractive woman. [U.S. slang, late 1900s]

freak off to copulate in an unconventional manner. *Cf.* FREAK (sense 1). [U.S. slang, mid 1900s-pres.]

freak trick a customer who demands that a prostitute be the object of VOYEURISM (*q.v.*) or sadism. *Cf.* FREAK OFF, TRICK. [U.S., mid 1900s-pres.]

freckle the anus. For synonyms see ANUS. [Australian, mid 1900s-pres.]

Fred 1. a creep; a social outcast; an ELROD. **2.** to vomit. Possibly onomatopoetic. For synonyms see YORK. [both are U.S. collegiate, late 1900s, Munro]

freeballing [of a man] not wearing underwear. [U.S., late 1900s-pres.]

free base 1. cocaine separated from other chemical components. [U.S. drug culture, late 1970s-pres.] **2.** to use FREE BASE. [both senses, U.S. drug culture, late 1900s] Synonyms: BASE, BLINKY, CHEESE, UP-QUAALUDE, WHITE TORNADO.

free base party a place or event where FREE BASE is used. [U.S. drug culture, late 1900s]

freebaser a user of FREE BASE. [U.S. drug culture, late 1900s]

free basing (also **baseballing, basing**) using an ether extract of cocaine as a recreational drug. [U.S. drug culture, late 1900s]

French (also **french**) **1.** deviant, sensuous, lewd, KINKY (*q.v.*), syphilitic, or illicit. [widespread in reference to syphilis, since the 1500s] **2.** to kiss sensuously using the tongue to explore the mouth of the partner. [slang, 1900s] **3.** FELLATIO (*q.v.*) or any type of oral sexual intercourse. [U.S. slang, mid 1900s-pres.] **4.** dirty words or swear words in English, as in PARDON MY FRENCH (*q.v.*). [U.S. colloquial, 1900s]

French abortion the swallowing or spitting out of semen after fellatio.

"The oral disposition of the semen incidental to fellation" (Roback). See SNOWBALL (sense 4), SNOWBALL QUEEN.

French-crown syphilis. So named for baldness produced by advanced syphilis. Ultimately from the name of a French coin. For synonyms see SPECIFIC STOMACH.

French-disease syphilis. One of a very old series of nicknames for syphilis implying that syphilis is indigenous to a country other than England.

Frencher 1. a Frenchman. Not necessarily derogatory. [since the mid 1800s] **2.** a practitioner of FELLATIO (*q.v.*) or similar sexual acts. *Cf.* FRENCH (senses 1 and 3). [slang, 1900s or before]

French-fried intoxicated with marijuana. An elaboration of FRIED (sense 2). [U.S. slang, mid 1900s-pres.]

French-fried-fuck a contemptible bit of nothing; a damn. *Cf.* FLYING-FUCK.

French fries crack cocaine. For synonyms see NOSE-CANDY. [U.S., late 1900s-pres.]

French kiss 1. a kiss where the tongue is used. See FRENCH (sense 2). [British and U.S., 1900s] **2.** penilingus or cunnilingus. See FRENCH (sense 3). [U.S. slang, 1900s, Wentworth and Flexner]

French letter (also **American letter, Italian letter, Spanish letter**) a condom. See FRENCH (sense 1). Not necessarily capitalized. *Cf.* ENVELOPE, LETTER. For synonyms see EEL-SKIN. [British and U.S., 1800s-pres.]

French safe a condom. *Cf.* FRENCH LETTER, SAFE. For synonyms see EEL-SKIN. [attested as Canadian, early 1900s, *Dictionary of Slang and Unconventional English*]

French tackle the lips, as used for kissing. [U.S., late 1900s-pres.]

French-tickler a DILDO (sense 2) or a condom equipped with ridges or larger protuberances designed to increase vaginal stimulation. *Cf.* FRENCH (sense 1). [U.S. slang, mid 1900s-pres.]

Frenchy 1. a Frenchman. Not necessarily derogatory. *Cf.* FRENCHER (sense 1). [British and U.S., 1800s-1900s] **2.** sexually attractive; sexy. *Cf.* FRENCH (sense 1). [U.S. slang, 1900s] **3.** a condom. See FRENCH LETTER [widespread slang, 1900s]

fresh meat copulation; the same as FRESH BIT or FRESH GREENS (both *q.v.*). For synonyms see SMOCKAGE. [British and U.S. colloquial, 1900s]

fribble 1. a silly oaf. **2.** an effeminate male; a homosexual male; possibly a transvestite. *Cf.* FERBLET. [both senses, British, 1600s-1700s] Synonyms and related terms for sense 2: BADLING, BOY SCOUT, BUN-DUSTER, BUTTERCUP, CAKE-EATER, CHERRY-PICKER, CHORUS BOY, COCK-QUEAN, COLLAR, COLLAR AND CUFF, CREAM PUFF, DAFFODIL, DAISY, DILDO, DRUG-STORE COWBOY, DUCKEY, EFFEMINATE MALE, ETHEL, FAG, FAIRY, FLAG, FLIT, GENTLEMISS, GIRLIE, GUSSIE, HAIRY-FAIRY, HEN-HUSSY, JAISY, JENNY, JENNY WILLOCKS, JOEY, LAD-LASS, LISPER, LITHPER, LIZZIE BOY, MALKIN, MAMAPOULE, MARGERY, MARY ANN, MEA-COCKE, MILKSOP, MISS NANCY, MOLLYCODDLE, MOLLY-MOP, NAMBY-PAMBY, NAN-BOY, NANCE, NANCY, NANCY DAWSON, NANCY HOMEY, NELLIE FAG, NICE NELLIE, NO BULLFIGHTER, ONE OF THE BOYS, PANSIFIED, PANSY, PANTY-WAIST, PAP-MOUTH, PEE-WILLIE, PERCY, PETAL, POOD, POOF, POOFTER, POWDER PUFF, PRETTY-BOY, PUSS-GENTLEMAN, PUSSY, QUEAN, QUEANIE, QUEEN, QUIMBY, QUINCE, SHE-HE, SHE-MAN, SIS, SISSY-BRITCHES, SKIPPY, SOAPY, SOFTIE, SPURGE, THITHY, TINKLE-TINKLE, TIT, TONK, TWANK, TWIDDLE-POOP, TWIXTER, WEAK SISTER, WHOOPS BOY, WILLIE BOY, WOMAN. See similar terms at EPICENE.

Frick! Fuck! For synonyms see 'ZOUNDS. [U.S., late 1900s-pres.]

frick and frack a nickname for the testicles, left and right. For synonyms see WHIRLYGIGS. [U.S. black use, late 1900s]

fricking a phonological disguise of FUCKING (*q.v.*). *Cf.* FRIGGING. [British and U.S., 1900s]

fried 1. intoxicated with alcohol. [U.S. slang, early 1900s-pres.] **2.** intoxicated with marijuana. *Cf.* CRISP, CRISPY-CRITTER, FRENCH-FRIED. [U.S. slang, mid 1900s-pres.]

fried to the gills intoxicated with alcohol, an elaboration of FRIED (sense 1). A mixture of FRIED (sense 1) and "up to the gills." [U.S. slang, mid 1900s]

friend of Dorothy's, a a gay person. Refers to Judy Garland in the *Wizard of Oz*. For synonyms see EPICENE. *[U.S., late 1900s-pres.]*

frig 1. to masturbate oneself. From an old term originally meaning "rub" or "chafe," this sense has now replaced the original sense. [ultimately cognate with Latin *fricatus*, "rubbing"; since the 1500s] **2.** to waste time. See JACK OFF (sense 2). [British, 1700s-1800s] **3.** to copulate; a euphemism for FUCK (*q.v.*). [primarily U.S., 1900s]

frigging 1. masturbation. [since the 1500s] **2.** time-wasting; demanding too much time. Said of a person or a task. [British, 1700s] **3.** copulation. [U.S., 1900s, Berrey and Van den Bark] **4.** damned; "fucking." *Cf.* FREAKING. [U.S. slang, mid 1900s-pres.]

friggle to masturbate. From a term originally meaning "jerk" or "wiggle." [British slang, 1800s, Farmer and Henley]

frisking petting or groping. From the patting and pressing done by police searching for concealed weapons on arrested persons. For synonyms see FIRKYTOODLE. [U.S. slang, 1900s]

frisky powder cocaine. For synonyms see NOSE-CANDY. [U.S. drug culture, late 1900s]

frit a homosexual male. Possibly a blend of FRUIT and FLIT (both *q.v.*). For synonyms see EPICENE. [both senses, U.S. slang, mid 1900s, Wentworth and Flexner]

frito toes smelly feet. Refers to the odor of cheese-flavored Fritos™ corn chips. [U.S. collegiate, late 1900s, Munro]

frog 1. a Frenchman; a Parisian. From the *fleur-de-lis*, the boggy site of Paris and frog's legs eaten for food. *Cf.* FROGGY, OG-FRAY. [since the 1700s] **2.** a policeman. Because he pounces on criminals. [British, 1800s-1900s] **3.** an adolescent male whose voice is changing. [U.S., 1900s] **4.** a condom. From FRENCHY (senses 1 and 3). For synonyms see EEL-SKIN. [attested as Australian, 1970s, Wilkes] **5.** an addict who hops from city to city looking for good drugs. [U.S. drug culture, late 1900s, Kaiser]

frog-eater a derogatory nickname for a Frenchman. See FROGGY. [British and U.S. slang, mid 1800s-1900s] Synonyms: FRENCHER, FRENCHY, FROG, FROGGY, OG-FRAY, PARLEYVOO.

frog's eyes (also **fish's eyes, frog spawn**) tapioca. A dysphemism. For related terms see DOG'S VOMIT. [colloquial, 1900s]

frogsh nonsense. A jocular avoidance of BULLSHIT (*q.v.*), patterned on BULLSH, COWSH, HORSH (all *q.v.*). [Australian, military, 1900s, Baker]

frog-skin a condom. *Cf.* EEL-SKIN, FISH-SKIN. [Australian, early 1900s, Baker]

frog slicing biology class; a biology course. [U.S., late 1900s-pres.]

from hell annoying; terrifying; imposing. [U.S. slang, late 1900s]

front to confront someone or something, perhaps in anger. [U.S. black use, late 1900s if not before]

front bottom the vagina. For synonyms see GENITALS, MONOSYLLABLE. [British, mid 1900s-pres.]

front-door mat the female pubic hair. [British slang, 1800s]

front-garden the female genitals. *Cf.* FORE-COURT. [British slang, 1800s]

front-parlor (also **parlor**) the female genitals. [British, early 1800s]

front passage the vagina. For synonyms see GENITALS, MONOSYLLABLE. [British, mid 1900s-pres.]

front-suspension a brassiere. From the term for the devices which support the front wheels of an automobile. For synonyms see BRA. [Australian, early 1900s, *Dictionary of Slang and Unconventional English*]

frosty 1. cold; sexually unresponsive; frigid. [from *Venus and Adonis*

(Shakespeare)] **2.** a Caucasian. From "Frosty the Snowman." **3.** an OREO (*q.v.*), a black who prefers to act like a Caucasian. [senses 2 and 3 are U.S. black use, mid 1900s] **4.** a beer; a cold beer. *Cf.* CHILL, COLD ONE. [U.S. late 1900s] **5.** (also **frost, frosted**) under the influence of cocaine. For synonyms see TALL. [U.S. drug culture, mid 1900s] **6.** (also **Frosty the snowman**) a cocaine seller. Probably recurrent nonce. [U.S. drug culture, late 1900s]

froth beer. For synonyms see BOOZE. [U.S., late 1900s-pres.]

froze his mouth became intoxicated with alcohol. [U.S. slang, early 1700s, Ben Franklin]

frozen intoxicated with alcohol. [U.S. slang, early 1700s, Ben Franklin]

fruit 1. a woman of easy morals. This sense is related to "easy-picking," and it is the likely semantic ancestor of sense 3 via sense 2. [U.S. underworld, early 1900s, Goldin, O'Leary, and Lipsius] **2.** a dupe; an easy mark. *Cf.* sense 3. There are numerous terms which mean both "dupe" and "male homosexual." See GAY (sense 3). [U.S. underworld, early 1900s, Irwin] **3.** an effeminate male; a passive homosexual male. See sense 2 above. [U.S. underworld, mid 1900s, Goldin, O'Leary, and Lipsius] **4.** any male homosexual. A derogatory term used by homosexuals and others. This term and QUEER (*q.v.*) are among the most resented of all derogatory nicknames for homosexuals. They are also the most widespread. [U.S., early 1900s-pres.] **5.** any strange person. [U.S. colloquial, mid 1900s]

fruitcake 1. a homosexual male, an elaboration of FRUIT (sense 4). **2.** any jerk or oaf. From "nutty as a fruitcake." *Cf.* NUT (sense 1). [both senses, U.S. slang, mid 1900s-pres.]

fruiter a homosexual male. *Cf.* FRUIT (sense 4). For synonyms see EPICENE. [U.S. underworld, early 1900s]

fruit-fly 1. a homosexual male, an elaboration of FRUIT (*q.v.*). **2.** a heterosexual woman who associates with homosexual males for sex or for security. *Cf.* FAG-BAG, SCAG-HAG. Both are from the common name for drosophila, an insect. [both senses, U.S. slang, mid 1900s-pres.]

fruit-picker a male who has occasional homosexual experiences. *Cf.* FRUIT-FLY. [U.S. homosexual use, mid 1900s, Wentworth and Flexner]

fruit-plate a homosexual male. An elaboration of FRUIT (sense 4), perhaps a variant of DISH (*q.v.*). [U.S., 1900s]

fruit-stand a homosexual bar; a gathering place for homosexual males. [U.S., mid 1900s]

fu marijuana. For synonyms see MARI. [U.S., mid 1900s]

F.U. 1. a "foul-up" or a "fuck-up." 2. "to foul up" or "to fuck up." [both senses, British with some U.S. use, mid 1900s]

FUBAR "fucked-up beyond all recognition," pertaining to a horribly messed-up person or situation. For synonyms see SNAFU. [U.S. slang, mid 1900s]

FUBB "fucked-up beyond belief," pertaining to an inconceivably confused person, object, or situation. For synonyms see SNAFU. [U.S. slang, mid 1900s]

FUBIS "Fuck you, buddy, I'm shipping (off or out)," pertaining to a particular type of antisocial attitude in the military. For synonyms see SNAFU. [U.S. slang, mid 1900s]

FUCK a contrived acronym for an imaginary etymology of FUCK (*q.v.*), "for unlawful carnal knowledge," or perhaps, "fornication under the consent of the king." [U.S., 1900s]

fuck (also f*ck, f**k, f***, ****, f--k, f---) 1. to copulate. 2. a copulation. [both since the early 1500s] 3. semen. *Cf.* BULLFUCK. [since the 1500s] 4. any sex act leading to orgasm. This includes all homosexual acts and other practices which are covered by the term SODOMY (*q.v.*). [mid 1900s-pres.] 5. a woman considered as a sex object, as in the phrase "a good fuck." [British and U.S., 1900s] 6. a man considered as a sex object, as in the phrase "a good fuck." [British and U.S., 1900s] 7.

vigor, especially sexual vigor in males. From sense 3. [British and some U.S. use, 1900s] 8. to cheat, deceive, or ruin. *Cf.* FUCK UP. [U.S. slang, mid 1900s-pres.] 9. to confuse. *Cf.* FUCK UP, MIND FUCK. [U.S. slang, mid 1900s-pres.] 10. a damn, especially in expressions such as "don't give a fuck." [U.S., mid 1900s-pres.] 11. as an expletive or exclamation, "Fuck!" Note: This term is popularly regarded as the worst of the "dirty words" and as the most reviled word in the English language. The most likely source is German *ficken*, "strike." A less likely source is Latin *pungo*, "to prick," but the origin of the word cannot be demonstrated conclusively. The word originally and primarily referred to the male aspects of copulation, and referred to the penetration, thrusting, and ejaculating of any male animal which copulates. It should be noted that most English words that refer exclusively to that act are not to be uttered in polite company. In the 1972 supplement of the *Oxford English Dictionary*, "fuck" is listed as an entry with its origin unknown. Numerous etymologies have been proposed: a truncation of "fecund"; an acronym for "fornication under the consent of the king"; an acronym for "for unlawful carnal knowledge"; an acronym for "for the use of carnal knowledge." It is possibly a disguise of FOUTRE (*q.v.*), which is from Latin *futuere* via French. Both FOOT and FUT! (both *q.v.*) were used as disguises of *foutre*, and FUCK may have originally been a minced version of *foutre*. The word was probably in use by the 1400s and may have been Scots originally. The earliest attestations were in the North of England and dated from 1503. If the word were strongly tabooed, it may not have appeared in writing as early as it would have otherwise. Disguises are: ****, COLONIAL PUCK, F., F***, F---, F*CK, F**K, F--K, FRIAR TUCK, FRIG, FUDGE, FUG, FULKE, FURK, FUTZ, GOOSE AND DUCK, IM-FUCKING-POSSIBLE, IRRE-FUCKING-SPONSIBLE, JOE BUCK, LAME DUCK, MRS. DUCKETT!, MUCK, PUSH IN THE TRUCK, RUCK, RUSSIAN DUCK, TROLLEY

AND TRUCK, UCK-FAY. See list at OCCUPY.

fuckable 1. pertaining to a sexually desirable woman. *Cf.* APPROACHABLE, BEDWORTHY, PUNCHABLE, ROMPWORTHY, SHAFTABLE. [British and U.S. slang, 1800s-1900s] **2.** readily agreeable to copulation. **3.** suitable or acceptable for copulation. [both senses, 1900s or before]

Fuck a duck! (also **Fuck a dog!**) an exclamation. *Cf.* DUCK-FUCKER, FORNICATE THE POODLE! [U.S. slang, mid 1900s-pres.]

fuck around to waste time; to mess around. [U.S. and elsewhere, late 1900s if not before]

fuck around with someone (also **fuck someone around**) to harass or intimidate someone; to give someone a hard time. [U.S. slang, late 1900s]

fuck around with something to fiddle or toy with someone or something. [U.S. slang, late 1900s]

fuckathon an extended period of paired or group homosexual activity usually involving FELLATIO and PEDERASTY (both *q.v.*). *Cf.* EVERYTHINGATHON. [U.S. slang, mid 1900s-pres.]

fuck-book a pornographic book depicting copulation. [British slang, 1900s, J. Green]

fuck-brained 1. stupid; mindless. **2.** obsessed with sex; having sex on the brain constantly. [both senses, U.S., late 1900s]

fuck bunny (also **F.B.**) someone who just loves to copulate. Usually said of a female. [U.S. slang, late 1900s if not before]

fuck buttock to coit anally. *Cf.* ASS-FUCK, BUTT-FUCK, GUT-BUTCHER. Possibly also meant PEDERAST (*q.v.*). [British colloquial, 1800s, Farmer and Henley]

fucked-out (also **fucked**) **1.** worn-out as from excessive copulating. **2.** worn-down as from continual abuse. [both senses, British and U.S., 1900s and before] **3.** totally exhausted from doing anything. [U.S. slang, late 1900s]

fucked-up (also **fucked**) **1.** temporarily confused or seriously mentally disturbed. **2.** in trouble; malfunctioning. **3.** intoxicated with drugs. For synonyms see TALL. [all senses, U.S. slang, mid 1900s-pres.]

fucker 1. a male lover. [British and U.S. colloquial, 1800s or before] **2.** a chum or buddy. [British and U.S. slang, 1800s-1900s] **3.** the penis. For synonyms see YARD. [recurrent nonce use] See also GUT-BUTCHER. **4.** a rude nickname, usually for a male. **5.** a male who copulates frequently or well. [U.S. slang, late 1900s or before]

fuckery (also **fuck-house**) a brothel; a house of prostitution. For synonyms see BROTHEL. [U.S. slang, late 1900s]

fuckface a social outcast. [U.S. slang, late 1900s]

fuckfaced having a dismal-looking, half-awake facial expression. [British slang, late 1900s]

fuck-film a pornographic film which features explicit scenes of various types of copulation. *Cf.* SKIN-FLICK. [U.S. slang, mid 1900s-pres.]

fuck-finger a female masturbator. *Cf.* FINGER-FUCK, FRICATRIX. [British slang, 1800s, Farmer and Henley]

fuck-fist a male masturbator. A term of contempt. *Cf.* FIST-FUCK. For synonyms see HUSKER. [British slang, 1800s, Farmer and Henley]

fuck-freak a woman, especially a prostitute, who is obsessed with copulation. [U.S. slang, mid 1900s-pres.]

fuck-head an oaf or jerk. [U.S. slang, mid 1900s-pres.]

fuckheaded stupid; senseless. [U.S. slang, mid 1900s-pres.]

fuck-hole the female genitals, especially the vagina. [British and U.S. colloquial and nonce]

fuck-house See FUCKERY.

Fuckinaye! "Fucking absolutely"; FUCKING A. For synonyms see 'ZOUNDS. [U.S., late 1900s-pres.]

fucking 1. copulation. For synonyms see SMOCKAGE. **2.** an intensifier; the U.S. equivalent of "bloody." Also **fuckin'.**

Fucking A "Absolutely!" [U.S., late 1900s-pres.]

fucking around goofing off; playing and not attending to duty. [U.S. slang, mid 1900s-pres.]

fucking machine a legendary machine (most often seen in limericks) which provides a variety of sexual services tirelessly. [since the 1800s]

fucking-rubber a condom. An elaboration of RUBBER (*q.v.*), which might otherwise be construed as a rubber-band or an eraser. For synonyms see EEL-SKIN. [U.S., mid 1900s-pres.]

fuckish 1. sexually aroused. See FUCK-ABLE. **2.** pertaining to a sexually loose woman. [both senses, British slang, 1800s, Farmer and Henley]

Fuck it all! (also **Fuck all!, Fuck 'em all!, Fuck it!**) a rude exclamation, "Damn it!" or "Damn it all!" [British and U.S. 1800s-1900s]

fuckle to copulate. For synonyms see OCCUPY. [British slang, 1800s, Farmer and Henley]

fuck like a bunny to copulate very quickly in the manner of a rabbit; to copulate frequently. [U.S. and elsewhere, 1900s]

fuck like a rattlesnake to PHALLICIZE (*q.v.*) vigorously; to coit as vigorously as a rattlesnake shakes its tail. [Partridge suggests that it is of U.S. origin; attested as Australian, late 1800s, *Dictionary of Slang and Unconventional English*]

fuck Mary fist to masturbate. Said of the male. *Cf.* FIST-FUCK. For synonyms and related subjects see WASTE TIME. [U.S. slang, late 1900s]

Fuck me! "I'll be damned!" For synonyms see 'ZOUNDS. [British and U.S., mid 1900s-pres.]

fuck-me boots sexually suggestive high boots worn with a miniskirt. *Cf.* C.F.M. [U.S. collegiate, late 1900s, Munro]

Fuck me gently! (also **Fuck me pink!**) **1.** an exclamation, "I'll be damned!" [British and U.S., 1900s] **2.** "Destroy me or cheat me in a genteel

manner!"; "Screw me politely!" [U.S. slang, mid 1900s-pres.]

Fuck me harder! "Go ahead, see if you can devastate me further!" For synonyms see 'ZOUNDS. [British and U.S., late 1900s-pres.]

fuck nugget a sexually enticing female. For synonyms see BIRD. [U.S., late 1900s-pres.]

fucknut an oaf; one who messes up a lot. For synonyms see OAF. [U.S., late 1900s-pres.]

fuck off 1. to masturbate. **2.** to waste time; to GOOF OFF (*q.v.*). **3.** a person who wastes time; a goof-off. Usually hyphenated in this sense. **4.** "Get out!" or "Buzz off!" [all senses, U.S. slang, mid 1900s-pres.]

fuck one's fist to masturbate, said of a male. *Cf.* FIST-FUCK. [British slang, 1800s, Farmer and Henley]

fuck over 1. to work over; to beat up; to use physical violence to teach someone a lesson. **2.** to cheat or deceive someone. *Cf.* FUCK (sense 8). [both senses, U.S. slang, mid 1900s-pres.]

fuckpig a disgusting person, typically a female. For synonyms see SNOKE-HORN. [U.S., mid 1900s-pres.]

fucksauce gobbler a fellator who catches semen and swallows it. For synonyms see PICCOLO-PLAYER. [U.S., late 1900s-pres.]

fuck-shit a term of contempt for a despised person. [U.S., 1900s]

fucksome pertaining to a sexually desirable woman. Punning on BUXOM (*q.v.*). *Cf.* FUCKABLE. [British slang, 1800s, Farmer and Henley]

fuck someone or something up (also **fuck up someone or something**) to mess up someone or something; to damage or ruin someone or something. [U.S. slang, mid 1900s-pres.]

fuck someone over (also **fuck over someone**) to give someone a very hard time; to abuse someone physically or mentally. [U.S. slang, late 1900s]

fuck someone's mind to badger and confuse someone into behavior or a particular manner of thinking; to fuck someone up. *Cf.* FUCK (sense 9), FUCK UP. [U.S. slang, mid 1900s-pres.]

fuckster a lecher or a whoremonger; a man noted for his sexual prowess or interest in women. For synonyms see LECHER. [British, 1800s]

fuckstick the penis. For synonyms see YARD. [British and U.S., mid 1900s-pres.]

fuckstrated sexually frustrated. [U.S. slang, late 1900s]

fuckstress 1. a prostitute. **2.** a woman who is known to be sexually willing and satisfying. *Cf.* FUCK (sense 5). For synonyms see LAY. [both senses, British slang, 1800s, Farmer and Henley]

Fuck this for a game of soldiers! "Enough of this" For synonyms see 'ZOUNDS. [British, mid 1900s-pres.]

fuck up 1. to ruin; to mess up; to confuse. *Cf.* BUGGER UP. **2.** a mess; a confusion. Usually hyphenated in this sense. [both senses, U.S. slang, 1900s] **3.** someone who does everything wrong; someone who messes everything up; a loser; a total failure as a person. [widespread, mid 1900s-pres.]

fuckwit an oaf; an idiot. For synonyms see OAF. [widespread, 1900s if not before]

fuck with someone or something. 1. to meddle with someone or something. **2.** to cause trouble for someone or something; to threaten someone or something. [both senses, U.S., late 1900s]

Fuck you! a very strong curse. Stronger than "Damn you!" Occasionally "Fuck you, Charlie!" or something similar. [U.S., 1900s] See also FUBIS.

fudd the female sexual organ. For synonyms see MONOSYLLABLE. [British, mid 1900s-pres.]

fudge 1. nonsense. For synonyms see ANIMAL. [British and U.S. colloquial, 1700s-1900s] **2.** to masturbate someone to orgasm. From the colloquial sense "cheat." [U.S. slang, 1900s, Wentworth and Flexner] **3.** a phonological disguise of "fuck"; an exclamation, "Fudge!" [U.S. slang, mid 1900s-pres.]

fudge-packer (also **turd-packer**) a pederast. [U.S. slang, late 1900s]

fudgepot the anus. For synonyms see ANUS. [U.S., late 1900s-pres.]

fuel phencyclidine, the drug P.C.P. For synonyms see P.C.P. [U.S. drug culture, late 1900s, Abel]

fugitive from a daisy chain gang a homosexual male. Based on the expression "fugitive from a chain gang." *Cf.* DAISY CHAIN. [U.S. jocular, 1900s]

fugle (also **fugel**) to copulate. From a word meaning to cheat or trick. *Cf.* FUCKLE, FUG, HONEY-FUGGLE. [British slang, early 1700s]

fugly "FUCKING ugly," very ugly indeed. [U.S. slang, late 1900s]

FUJIAMA "Fuck you, Jack, I'm all right!" [British, mid 1900s-pres.]

full 1. intoxicated with alcohol. [widespread colloquial, 1700s-pres.] **2.** erect, said of the penis. [British slang, 1800s, Farmer and Henley]

full as a the basis of a series of terms for "drunk" most of which are from the 1800s or before: full as a boot, full as a bull, full as a fiddle, full as a goat, full as a goog, full as a lord, full as a tick. *Cf.* DRUNK AS A LORD, TIGHT AS A TICK.

full moon a large, fat set of buttocks. See MOON. For synonyms see DUFF. [U.S., late 1900s-pres.]

full of fuck 1. virile and full of masculine vigor. *Cf.* FUCK (sense 7). **2. sexually aroused; full of desire or full of semen.** *Cf.* FUCK (sense 3). For synonyms see HUMPY. [both senses, slang, 1900s]

full of gism the same as FULL OF FUCK (*q.v.*). [U.S. slang, 1900s]

full of heir pregnant. A pun based on the homonyms "air" (as in "full of hot air") and "heir." [U.S. jocular slang, 1900s]

full of shit (also **full of bull, full of crap**) deceitful; full of nonsense and lies. [U.S. slang, 1900s]

full-on sexually excited and desirous of copulation, the same as TURNED-ON (sense 2). *Cf.* FLAVOUR, FULL-FLEDGED, ON, SALT (sense 1).

full to the bung intoxicated with alcohol. *Cf.* BUNGEY. For synonyms see WOOFLED. [primarily British, 1800s-1900s]

FUMTU "fucked-up more than usual," pertaining to a state considerably more messed up than usual. For synonyms see SNAFU. [British and U.S., mid 1900s]

fun and frolics the testicles. Rhyming slang for "ballocks." For synonyms see WHIRLYGIGS. [British, 1800s, *Dictionary of Rhyming Slang*]

fun and games sexual play or intercourse. *Cf.* PLAY AROUND [U.S. slang, mid 1900s-pres.]

funbags the female breasts. For synonyms see BOSOM. [British and U.S., late 1900s-pres.]

funch (also **nooner**) a hasty act of copulation performed during the lunch hour. The main entry is a blend of FUCK and *lunch*. *Cf.* NOONER. For synonyms see SMOCKAGE. [U.S. slang, late 1900s]

funeral a ceremony or rites concerned with the burial or commemoration of a dead person. Synonyms: COLD-MEAT PARTY, MEMORIAL SERVICE, OBSEQUIES, PLANTING.

funny 1. intoxicated with alcohol. [colloquial since the 1700s] **2.** effeminate; homosexual. A vague euphemism for QUEER (sense 3). [U.S. slang, mid 1900s-pres.]

funny cigarette a marijuana cigarette. For synonyms see MEZZROLL. [U.S. slang, late 1900s]

funny stuff marijuana. For synonyms see MARI. [U.S. drug culture, mid 1900s-pres.]

fur 1. the female pubic hair. For synonyms see DOWNSHIRE. [British and U.S. colloquial, 1800s-1900s] **2.** the female genitals; women considered sexually. [U.S. slang, 1900s]

furball an obnoxious person. For synonyms see SNOKE-HORN. [U.S., late 1900s-pres.]

furbelow the female pubic hair. A reinterpretation of the name of a fur edge on a dress or petticoat. [British, 1600s]

furburger the female genitals and pubic hair. *Cf.* HAIRBURGER (sense 1). [U.S. slang, mid 1900s-pres.]

fur-pie the female genitals and pubic hair. *Cf.* FURBURGER. For synonyms see DOWNSHIRE, MONOSYLLABLE. [U.S. slang, mid 1900s-pres.]

furry frisbee road kill; an animal flattened by road traffic. [U.S., late 1900s-pres.]

future the scrotum and its contents; the testicles. That which a man needs to father his descendants. Also, when said of a boy, that upon which one's future sex life depends. *Cf.* FAMILY JEWELS. [U.S., mid 1900s-pres.]

futz 1. to coit. [U.S., 1800s-1900s] **2.** the female genitals. [U.S., 1900s] **3.** to cheat or deceive. From sense 1. See PHUTZ. A disguise of FUCK (sense 8). [U.S., mid 1900s-pres.]

futz around 1. to play sexually. **2.** to GOOF OFF (*q.v.*); to FUCK OFF (*q.v.*). [both senses, U.S. slang, 1900s]

futzed-up a disguise of FUCKED-UP (*q.v.*). [U.S., 1900s]

fuzzle to make someone or oneself drunk. *Cf.* FUDDLE. [British, early 1600s, *Oxford English Dictionary*]

fuzzled intoxicated with alcohol. *Cf.* FUDDLED. [since the early 1700s]

fuzzy intoxicated with alcohol. For synonyms see WOOFLED. [British and U.S. slang, late 1700s-pres.]

G

gab room a women's restroom. [U.S. slang, mid 1900s]

gadget 1. a thing or tool. Many of the following synonyms have also been used to mean "penis" and, in the plural, "testicles" or VIRILIA (*q.v.*). Synonyms for "gadget": DEEDEE, DICKY, DIDDENWHACKER, DIDDLEDYFLOP, DIDDLEHEIMER, DINGBAT, DINGLE, DINGUS, DINKUS, DINKY, DOBAUBLE, DOBOB, DOBOBBIS, DOBOBBLE, DOBOBBUS, DOBOBBY, DODAD, DODADDY, DODINGLE, DODINKUS, DOFLICKETY, DOFLOPPY, DOFUNNY, DOGADGET, DOHICKEY, DOHICKIE, DOHICKUS, DOHICKY, DOJIGGER, DOJIGGIE, DOJIGGUM, DOJIGGUS, DOLOLLY, DOMAGGUS, DOMAJIG, DOMAJIGGER, DOODAD, DOODLE, DOOFLICKER, DOOFUNNY, DOOHICKEY, DOOJIGGER, DOOMAJIG, DOOSENWHACKER, DOOWHISTLE, DOOWILLIE, DOOZANDAZZY, DOWHACKER, DOWHOPPER, DUDENWHACKER, DUFUNNY, FAKUS, FANDANGLE, FIRKIN, FOLDEROL, FRIGAMAJIG, FUMADIDDLE, GAZINKUS, GAZUNKUS, GEEGAW, GEWGAW, GIGAMAREE, GILGUY, GILHOOLEY, GIMCRACK, GIMIX, GINGAMBOB, GINKUS, GIZMO, GOOFUS, HICKEY, HICKIE, HICKUS, HICKY, HINKUS, HOOFEN-POOFER, HOOTMALIE, HOOTNANNY, JIGALORUM, JIGGAMY, JIGGER, JIGGIE, JIGGUM, JIGGUMBOB, JIGGUS, JIGGY, JINGUMBOB, JOBBER, JOBBY, KAJODY, KNACK, MAJIG, RIGAMAJIG, THINGABOB, THINGABOBBLE, THINGABOBBUS, THINGABOBBY, THINGAMABOB, THINGAMADING, THINGAMADOODLE, THINGAMAJIG, THINGAMAJIGGER, THINGAMAJINGIE, THINGAMAJOHN, THINGAMAREE, THINGDOODLE, THINGMAJIGGUS, THINGUMABOB, THINGUMBOB, THINGUMMIE, THINGUMTIBOB, THINKUMTHINKUM, THUMADOODLE, UNIT, WHACKER, WHAMDITTY, WHANGDOODLE, WHANGYDOODLE, WHATCHAMACALLEM, WHATCHAMACALLIT, WHATCHAMADAD, WHATCHAMADADDY, WHATCHAMADIDDLE, WHATCHAMA-DINGLE, WHATCHAMADOODLE, WHATCHAMAGADGET, WHATCHAMAHICKEY, WHATCHAMAJIGGER, WHATSIS, WHATSIT, WHATZIT, WHAZZIT, WHINGDING, WHOSERMY-BOB, WHOSERMYJIG, WIDGET, WINGDING, WINGDOODLE. 2. the penis. For synonyms see YARD. [both senses, U.S. slang and colloquial, mid 1900s-pres.]

gaffel bogus cocaine. [U.S., late 1900s-pres.]

gaffer 1. a rustic old man; an old bumpkin. Also **old gaffer**. A telescoping of "grandfather." [since the late 1500s] 2. to coit a woman. [British slang, 1800s, Farmer and Henley]

gaffle to steal something. [U.S., late 1900s-pres.]

gaffled arrested. [U.S., late 1900s-pres.]

gag 1. to retch, especially to retch noisily. 2. to choke on food or foreign matter in the throat. 3. to attempt to make oneself vomit by placing an object such as a finger far back in the throat. [all senses, U.S. colloquial, 1900s or before]

gag a maggot to discuss something completely disgusting. [Australian and U.S., mid 1900s-pres.]

gage a gun of some kind, probably a sawed-off shotgun of a certain gauge. [U.S. slang, late 1900s]

gaged (also **gauged**) intoxicated with alcohol. For synonyms see WOOFLED. [U.S. slang, early 1900s]

gagger a thing or a person that makes one gag. [U.S. collegiate, late 1900s, Munro]

gagging for it eager for sex. For synonyms see HUMPY. [British, late 1900s-pres.]

Gainesville green a variety of marijuana named for "Gainesville," Florida. [U.S. drug culture, mid 1900s-pres.]

gal 1. a prostitute. 2. a girl, especially a

girlfriend. [British and U.S. colloquial, 1800s-1900s]

gal-boy 1. a masculine woman. [U.S. slang, late 1900s, Farmer and Henley] **2.** a CATAMITE or a FELLATOR (both *q.v.*). [U.S. underworld, mid 1900s, Goldwin, O'Leary, and Lipsius]

galley-arsed suffering from the effects of bad food. [British, mid 1900s-pres.]

galligaskins (also **galigaskins**) **1.** a type of hose or breeches. One etymology is that this is from "galley gaskins," *i.e.*, the type of trousers worn in a ship's galley. The exact origin of the word is unknown. *Cf.* GASKINS. [in other spellings, 1500s; in this spelling since the 1800s] **2.** trousers. [British and U.S. colloquial, 1800s-1900s] Synonyms usually refer to men's trousers unless indicated otherwise: ARSE-RUG, ARTICLES, BAG, BELONGINGS, BLOOMERS (female), BREECH, BREECHES, BREEKS, BRITCHES, BROGUES, BULL ANTS, BULL'S AUNTS, BUM-BAGS, BUM-CURTAIN, CALF-CLINGERS, CONTINUATIONS, COUNCIL-HOUSES, DENIMS, DON'T-NAME-'EMS, DRUMSTICK CASES, DUNGAREES, EEL-SKINS, FARTING-CRACKERS, FLEAS AND ANTS, GALLYSLOPES, GAM-CASES, GASKINS, HAM-CASES, HAMS, HOLY-FALLS, INDESCRIBABLES, INDISPENSABLES, INEXPLICABLES, INEXPRESSIBLES, INNOMINABLES, INSECTS AND ANTS, IRREPRESSIBLES, JEANS, JOLLY ROWSERS, KICK, KICK-CLOY, KICKS, KICKSIES, KICKSTERS, KNICKER-BOCKERS, LEG-BAGS, LEG-COVERS, LEVI'S, LIMB-SHROUDERS, MARY-WALKERS, MUSTN'T-MENTION-'EMS, NETHER GARMENTS, NEVER-MENTION-'EMS, PAIR OF DRUMS, PANTALOONS, PANTS, PLUS FOURS, RAMMIES, RANK AND RICHES, RESWORT, RICE-BAGS, RIPS, RIPSEY ROUSERS, ROUND-ME-HOUSES, ROUND-MES, ROUNDS, ROUND-THE-HOUSES, SACKS, SCRATCHES, SIN-HIDERS, SIT-DOWN-UPONS, SIT-UPONS, SKILTS, SONG AND DANCE, SRES-WORT, STOVE-PIPES, STRIDERS, STRIDES, STROSSERS, THINGUMBOBS, TROLLY-WAGS, TROLLY-WOGS, TROU, TROUSERLOONS, TROUSIES, TRUCKS, UNCLES AND AUNTS, UNHINTABLES, UN-MENTIONABLES, UN-SPEAKABLES, UN-UTTERABLES, UNWHISPERABLES.

galloping dandruff lice. [U.S., mid 1900s-pres.]

galloping knob-rot a phallic itch, an itching in the male genital area. *Cf.* KNOB. [British military, mid 1900s, *Dictionary of Slang and Unconventional English*]

gallop one's antelope to masturbate, said of males. From "hand-gallop" in horsemanship, an easy gallop. [British, 1800s-1900s]

gallop one's maggot to masturbate, said of males. From "hand-gallop" in horsemanship, an easy gallop. [British slang, 1800s, *Dictionary of Slang and Unconventional English*]

gallows a framework from which a man could be hanged by the neck until dead. Synonyms: BOUGH, CHATES, CRAP, DEADLY NEVERGREEN, FORKS, FURCA, GIBBET, GOVERNMENT-SIGNPOST, HORSE FOALED OF AN ACORN, LEAFLESS TREE, MARE WITH THREE LEGS, MORNING DROP, NUBBING-CHEAT, PICTURE-FRAME, SCRAGGING-POST, SHERIFF'S PICTURE FRAME, SQUEEZER, STALK, STIFFLER, SWING, THE THREE TREES, THREE-LEGGED MARE, THREE-LEGGED STOOL, TOPPING CHEAT, TREE, TRIPLE-TREE, TURNING TREE, TWO-LEGGED TREE, WOODEN HORSE, WOODEN-LEGGED MARE.

galvanized alcohol intoxicated. For synonyms see WOOFLED. [1900s, Dickson]

gam fellatio. [British, late 1900s-pres.]

game-cock a whoremonger. Based on a term used for wildfowl. *Cf.* COCK (senses 3 and 5), GAME (sense 1). For synonyms see LECHER. [British, 1800s]

gamester a prostitute; any lewd woman. *Cf.* SPORT. [from *All's Well That Ends Well* (Shakespeare)]

gang-bang 1. a real or fantasized sexual activity where one person is coited by a group of males serially; group rape. [both heterosexual and homosexual use, mid 1900s] **2.** an activity similar to sense 1 where promiscuous copulation takes place within a group. This is the original model for a series of similar rhyming pairs. See GROUP SEX for a list. [U.S. slang, mid 1900s-pres.]

gangbanger a member of a street gang. [U.S., late 1900s-pres.]

gang fuck a group rape. [U.S. military, 1900s, *Soldier Talk*]

gang-shag (also **gang-shay**) group copulation; the same as GANG-BANG (*q.v.*), but usually heterosexual only.

gang splash a group rape. [Australia, 1900s, McDonald]

gangsta bitch a woman who hangs out with members of a gang. [British, late 1900s-pres.]

gangster 1. a hoodlum; a thug. [U.S., early 1900s-pres.] **2.** marijuana. **3.** a marijuana cigarette. [senses 2 and 3 are U.S. underworld, mid 1900s]

gangster pills barbiturate tablets or capsules. *Cf.* GANGSTER (senses 2 and 3). For synonyms see BARB. [U.S. drug culture, mid 1900s-pres.]

ganjah (also **ganja, gunja**) a potent variety of marijuana; a Jamaican term for marijuana. [from Handi; in English since 1800]

gank 1. marijuana. For synonyms see MARI. [U.S. black use, late 1900s] **2.** to steal something. [U.S., late 1900s-pres.]

gannet a greedy person. [British, late 1900s-pres.]

gap (also **gape**) **1.** the female genitals. See PUDENDAL CLEAVAGE. [recurrent nonce; attested as early 1700s] **2.** the space between the breasts. [slang, 1900s]

G.A.P.O. "giant armpit odor;" a bad underarm odor. [U.S., mid 1900s-pres.]

garbage mouth a user of obscene language. [U.S. slang, mid 1900s] Synonyms and related terms: BLACK MOUTH, BUCKET MOUTH, CUD-CASTER, FOUL MOUTH, FOUL-TONGUED, POTTY MOUTH, SEWERMOUTH, TOILET MOUTH.

garbage something down to gobble something up; to bolt something down. [U.S., late 1900s-pres.]

garbanzos a woman's breasts. From the name of the bean. For synonyms see BOSOM. [U.S. slang, late 1900s]

garden of Eden the female genitals. *Cf.* GARDEN. [British slang, 1800s, Farmer and Henley]

gargle 1. to drink alcohol. **2.** alcoholic drink; a drink of alcohol. [both senses, U.S. slang, 1900s]

Gary Glitter the anus. Rhyming slang for SHITTER. For synonyms see ANUS. [British, mid 1900s-pres.]

gas 1. intestinal gas. For synonyms see GURK. [colloquial, 1800s-1900s] **2.** nonsense. *Cf.* BALLOON JUICE. **3.** to talk nonsense. [senses 2 and 3 are British and U.S. colloquial, mid 1800s-pres.] **4.** liquor. For synonyms see BOOZE. [U.S., 1900s, Berrey and Van den Bark]

gash 1. the female genitals. *Cf.* SLIT. [widespread recurrent nonce and slang, 1700s-pres.] **2.** a sexually loose woman; women considered sexually. From sense 1. [widespread slang, 1900s or before] **3.** a CATAMITE (*q.v.*). From sense 2. For synonyms see BRONCO. **4.** an ugly male. From sense 1. **5.** to have sex; to copulate. [U.S. collegiate, late 1900s, Munro]

gash-bucket a refuse bucket; a bucket used as a urinal.

gash-hound a whoremonger; possibly also a PEDERAST (*q.v.*). *Cf.* GASH (sense 1). [U.S., mid 1900s]

gas-passer a jocular nickname for an anesthetist. Hospitals. [U.S., mid 1900s-pres.]

gassed (up) alcohol or drug intoxicated. For synonyms see TALL, WOOFLED. [U.S., mid 1900s-pres.]

gat a handgun; a revolver. Old. [U.S., early 1900s-pres.]

gate the female genitals, specifically the vulva. *Cf.* GARDEN-GATE, JANUA VITAE. [1800s and before]

gate-of-horn (also **gate-of-life, gate-of-plenty**) the female genitals. See HORN (sense 3), "penis." *Cf.* JANUA VITAE. [British, 1800s, Farmer and Henley]

gator sweat homebrewed whisky, especially that which is aged in earthen mounds. From the manner in which an alligator incubates its eggs, and patterned on PANTHER SWEAT (*q.v.*). [U.S. colloquial (Southern), 1900s or before]

gaubshite a filthy and slovenly man; the same word as GOBSHITE (*q.v.*). "Shite" is an old form of SHIT (*q.v.*). [British dialect, 1800s]

gaucho to MOON (sense 1); to expose the buttocks, usually in the window of a car as an insult to someone. *Cf.* HANG A B.A., PRESSED-HAM. [U.S. slang, mid 1900s, *Current Slang*]

gauge (also **gage**) **1.** a CHAMBER POT (*q.v.*). For synonyms see POT. [British, 1700s] **2.** cheap whisky; inferior whisky which might have come out of a chamber pot. For synonyms see EMBALMING FLUID. [U.S. slang, 1900s] **3.** marijuana. [U.S. drug culture, mid 1900s-pres.]

gauge-butt (also **gage-butt**) a marijuana cigarette. [U.S. slang, mid 1900s]

gay 1. sexually loose; dissipated. Originally pertaining only to a woman. [clearly implied in the 1300s (Chaucer); occurs in *Othello* (Shakespeare); used for a male, mid 1700s (Farmer and Henley); British slang and colloquial, early 1800s-1900s] **2.** intoxicated with alcohol. Refers primarily to one's uplifted spirits. [slang and nonce, 1800s-early 1900s] **3.** the dupe of a prostitute or of a con man. *Cf.* FRUIT (sense 2). **4.** pertaining to a homosexual, usually thought of as a male as in sense 5. Also used currently for a lesbian. [U.S. underworld and then slang, early 1900s-pres.; now widely known U.S. slang] **5.** a young, unattached, highly visible, and highly social homosexual male. The term preferred by homosexual males. [U.S. slang and later widespread, mid 1900s-pres.]

gay and frisky Scotch whisky; any whisky. Rhyming slang for "whisky."

gay as pink ink pertaining to an obvious homosexual person, usually a male. [U.S. homosexual use, mid 1900s-pres.]

gay bar a bar that caters to and serves as a meeting place for homosexual males. [U.S. slang and colloquial, mid 1900s-pres.]

gay-bashing (also **fag-busting**) verbal or physical abuse directed at homosexuals. [U.S. slang, late 1900s]

gay-boy a homosexual male. *Cf.* NAN-BOY. [Australian, early 1900s, *Dictionary of Slang and Unconventional English*]

gay-cat a young tramp; most likely a CATAMITE (*q.v.*). *Cf.* ANGELINA [U.S. underworld, early 1900s, Goldin, O'Leary, and Lipsius]

gaydar a radarlike ability to identify gay people. [U.S., late 1900s-pres.]

gay deceivers false breasts. No relation to GAY (*q.v.*). *Cf.* CHEATERS, FALSIES. [U.S. slang, mid 1900s]

gay dog a philanderer; a lecher. Ultimately from GAY (sense 1). [U.S. colloquial, 1900s]

gay-girl (also **gay-bit, gay-piece, gay-woman**) a prostitute. See GAY (sense 1). For synonyms see HARLOT. [British slang, early 1800s, Farmer and Henley]

gay house a brothel. [British and U.S. slang, 1800s-1900s]

gaying instrument the penis. *Cf.* GAY (sense 1). [British slang, early 1800s, *Lexicon Balatronicum*]

gay in the groin (also **gay in the arse, gay in the legs**) pertaining to a sexually loose woman. [British slang, 1800s, Farmer and Henley]

gay it to copulate, said of either sex. [British slang, 1800s, Farmer and Henley]

Gay Lib a political movement (patterned on the Women's Liberation movements) which advocates the establishment and guaranteeing of specific rights for homosexuals. A truncation of "Gay Liberation." [U.S., mid 1900s-pres.]

gay life an immoral life; a life of prostitution, said of women. [British, 1800s]

Gaylord a gay man. For synonyms see EPICENE. [U.S., late 1900s-pres.]

gay-man a whoremonger; a man who seeks GAY (sense 1) women. [British slang, 1800s, Farmer and Henley]

gay wench a prostitute; a sexually loose woman. *Cf.* GAY-GIRL. [U.S. slang, early 1900s]

gay-woman a prostitute. For synonyms see HARLOT. [British and U.S. slang, late 1800s-early 1900s]

gazonga the BUTTOCKS. For synonyms and related terms see DUFF. [U.S. slang, late 1900s, Lewin and Lewin] See also GAZONGAS.

gazongas the breasts; extremely well-shaped breasts. For synonyms see BOSOM. [U.S. slang, 1900s]

gazoo (also **kazoo**) the rectum or anus. For synonyms see ANUS. [U.S. slang, 1900s]

gazoony a bully or strong-arm man. Underworld [U.S., early 1900s-pres.]

gazungas the female breasts. A variant spelling of GAZONGAS. For synonyms see BOSOM. [U.S. slang, late 1900s]

G.B. 1. a mixture of cocaine and heroin. 2. a mixture of amphetamines and barbiturates. 3. barbiturates. All are from GOOF-BALL (*q.v.*). [all senses, U.S. drug culture, mid 1900s-pres.]

gear 1. the male genitals. *Cf.* APPARATUS, KIT, LOT. [colloquial and nonce, 1600s-1900s] 2. the female genitals. [1500s, Florio] 3. to coit a woman. [British slang, 1800s, Farmer and Henley] 4. a homosexual male. Rhyming slang for QUEER (*q.v.*). Also **gear-box.** [British, early 1900s, *Dictionary of Rhyming Slang;* U.S. attestation, 1970s]

geech 1. to copulate with a woman; to masturbate a woman. [U.S. dialect (Boontling), late 1800s-early 1900s, Charles Adams] 2. an unattractive person. [U.S. slang, mid 1900s, *Current Slang*]

geed-up intoxicated with alcohol. *Cf.* GEEZED-UP. [U.S. slang, mid 1900s]

geedus money. [U.S., early 1900s-pres.]

Gee-hollikens! a disguised oath used as an exclamation. See GEE-WHOLLIKER!

geek (also **geke**) 1. a disliked person. 2. a drunkard. 3. a sexual degenerate or a homosexual male; a practitioner of nonorthogenital sexual acts. [all senses, U.S. slang, early 1900s] 4. a devoted student; an eccentric and hard-studying student. [U.S. collegiate, late 1900s]

geekazoid a social outcast; a NERD. For synonyms see OAF. [U.S., late 1900s-pres.]

geek-chic stylish or fashionable only for social outcasts. [U.S., late 1900s-pres.]

geekdom the realm of the hard-studying GEEKS. [U.S. collegiate, late 1900s]

geeked high on cocaine. For synonyms see TALL. [U.S., late 1900s-pres.]

geek out to study hard. [U.S. collegiate, late 1900s, Eble]

geetis money. [U.S., early 1900s-pres.]

geetus money. [U.S., early 1900s-pres.]

geezed-up (also **geezed**) 1. intoxicated with alcohol. For synonyms see WOOFLED. 2. drug intoxicated. For synonyms see TALL. [both senses, U.S. slang, early 1900s-pres.]

geezer 1. a strange old man. [British and U.S. colloquial, late 1800s-pres.] 2. a drink of alcohol; strong alcoholic drink. 3. a shot of narcotics. [senses 2 and 3 are U.S. slang, early-mid 1900s]

gel to relax and let one's hair down. [U.S., late 1900s-pres.]

gender sex; the difference between male and female. A euphemism that swept the English-speaking world in the early 1990s. (Widespread English)

gender-bender 1. a device that changes electrical plugs or sockets to the opposite gender—male to female, female to male. [U.S., mid 1900s-pres.] 2. having to do with something that obscures male/female distinctions. [U.S., late 1900s-pres.]

generation tool the penis. *Cf.* TOOL (sense 1). [British slang, 1800s, Farmer and Henley]

generous 1. intoxicated with alcohol. [U.S. slang, early 1700s, Ben Franklin] 2. sexually willing.

genitals the male and female genitals. The term refers to the organs of reproduction, both internal and external, but is often used solely for the visible, external genitals of the male or female. Synonyms: APPARATUS UROGENITALIS, AREA, AUNT ANNIE, BOX, CARNAL PARTS, CONCERN, COOKIES, CROTCH, DODADS, EDEA, FANCY PARTS, FLESH, FRONT BOTTOM, FRONT PASSAGE, GADGETS, GENITALIA, HONEYPOT, LOINS, LOVE-FLESH, LOVE PURSE, NAKEDNESS, NATURA, NATURALIA, NATURAL PARTS, NATURAL PLACES, NATURALS, NATURE, NAUGHTY BITS, NETHERS, ORGAN OF GENERATION, PACKET, PARTS, PARTS BELOW, PINK PALACE IN THE BLACK FOREST, PLACE, PRIVATE PARTS, PRIVATE PROPERTY, PRIVATES, RHUBARB, RUDE BITS, SECRETS, SECRET WORKS, TACKLE, THE PERSON, UNDERPARTS, VITALS, WARE, WATER-BOX, WATERCOURSE, WATER-ENGINE, WATER-GAP, WATER-WORKS, WEDDING TACKLE, WORKS. See also MONOSYLLABLE and YARD.

george 1. to seduce and copulate. [U.S. slang, mid 1900s, Dahlskog] **2.** a bowel movement. For synonyms see EASEMENT. [British, 1900s, *Dictionary of Slang and Unconventional English*] **3.** to defecate. For synonyms see EASE ONESELF. [U.S. slang, mid 1900s]

geri an old person. From *geriatric*. [U.S., late 1900s-pres.]

gerk an elderly oaf. From *geriatric jerk*. [U.S., late 1900s-pres.]

gerks cocaine. For synonyms see NOSE-CANDY. [U.S., late 1900s-pres.]

German goiter a beer belly. For synonyms see BELLY. [U.S., mid 1900s-pres.]

get a can on to get drunk. [U.S., mid 1900s-pres.]

get a crumpet to coit. *Cf.* CRUMPET (senses 1 and 2). [British, mid 1900s, *Dictionary of the Underworld*]

get (a) hold of oneself to masturbate. For synonyms and related subjects see WASTE TIME. [U.S. jocular euphemism, mid 1900s and nonce]

Get any? a question addressed to one male by another after a date with a young woman, "Did you score?" or "Did you copulate?" *Cf.* GETTING ANY? [U.S. slang, mid 1900s-pres.]

get a pair of balls against one's

butt to copulate. From the female point of view. [British slang, 1800s, Farmer and Henley]

get a rise 1. to get someone to respond, either to laugh or to become angry. **2.** to cause an erection in the male. The ambiguity of senses 1 and 2 is the source of much jest. [frequent double entendre; British and U.S., 1800s-1900s]

get a shove in one's blind-eye to coit, from the woman's point of view. *Cf.* BLIND-EYE (sense 2). [British slang, 1800s, Farmer and Henley]

Get bent! "Drop dead!" For synonyms see DEPART. [U.S., late 1900s-pres.]

get blown to receive an act of FELLATIO (*q.v.*). Occasionally used in reference to CUNNILINGUS (*q.v.*). See BLOW (senses 3 and 4). [U.S. slang, mid 1900s-pres.]

get caught to get pregnant. *Cf.* CATCH (sense 2). [U.S. slang, early 1900s]

get cockroaches (also **eat cockroaches**) to masturbate. A truncation of BOX THE JESUIT AND GET COCKROACHES (*q.v.*). [British slang, 1800s, Farmer and Henley]

get down 1. to perform CUNNILINGUS (*q.v.*). See GO DOWN. [U.S. slang, mid 1900s-pres.] **2.** to get down to sex in general. [U.S. slang, late 1900s]

get down to it (also **get down to business**) to copulate. [British and U.S. slang, 1900s]

get henged to get drunk. From *Stonehenge*, an elaboration of STONED. [U.S., late 1900s-pres.]

get in(to) someone's pants to manage to copulate with a certain female. For synonyms see OCCUPY. [U.S., mid 1900s-pres.]

get it off to obtain sexual relief, preferably through coition, usually said of the male. Refers to ejaculation. *Cf.* GET THE DIRTY WATER OFF ONE'S CHEST. [U.S. slang, 1900s]

get it on 1. to become excited about anything. **2.** to become sexually excited. **3.** to get an erection. **4.** to copulate. [all senses, U.S. slang, mid 1900s-pres.]

get it up to get an erection. [U.S. slang, mid 1900s-pres.]

get Jack in the orchard to penetrate a woman. *Cf.* ORCHARD. [British slang, 1800s, Farmer and Henley]

Get knotted! "Get out!" [Australian, mid 1900s-pres.]

get layed to have sexual intercourse, said originally of the female, now of both sexes. [U.S. slang, 1900s or before]

get lip to get some kissing; to NECK. [U.S., late 1900s-pres.]

get lock-legged to get drunk. [U.S., late 1900s-pres.]

get looted to get drunk. [U.S., late 1900s-pres.]

get malty to get drunk. [U.S., late 1900s-pres.]

get naked 1. to party and get drunk. [U.S. collegiate, late 1900s] **2.** to enjoy oneself thoroughly; to relax and enjoy oneself. [U.S., late 1900s-pres.]

get narkied to inject drugs; to become addicted. [U.S., mid 1900s-pres.]

get nut to ejaculate. [U.S., late 1900s-pres.]

get off 1. to ejaculate. *Cf.* GET IT OFF. For synonyms see OCCUPY. [U.S. slang, mid 1900s-pres.] **2.** to become intoxicated with marijuana or other drugs. [U.S. drug culture, mid 1900s-pres.]

Get off my bumper! "Stop monitoring me!" [U.S., late 1900s-pres.]

get off (on something) 1. to get pleasure from something. [U.S., late 1900s-pres.] **2.** to take a drug and experience a RUSH. [U.S., mid 1900s-pres.] **3.** to do well on something. [U.S., late 1900s-pres.]

get off the nut to ejaculate. *Cf.* GET ONE'S NUTS OFF. For synonyms see MELT. [U.S. slang, mid 1900s]

get one's ashes hauled to copulate. *Cf.* HAUL ONE'S ASHES. [U.S. slang, 1900s]

get one's ass in gear to get oneself in order. [U.S. slang, mid 1900s-pres.]

get one's ass up to pull rank on someone; to act like an important person. [U.S. military, mid 1800s-pres., *Soldier Talk*]

get one's bowels in an uproar to get overly excited. [U.S. slang, mid 1900s-pres.]

get one's chimney swept out to be copulated with; to copulate. From the point of view of a woman. *Cf.* CHIMNEY. [British slang, 1800s, Farmer and Henley]

get one's cookies off to ejaculate. For synonyms see MELT. [U.S. slang, mid 1900s-pres.]

get one's end away to copulate; to intromit. For synonyms see OCCUPY. [British, mid 1900s-pres.]

get one's end in to copulate; to intromit. For synonyms see OCCUPY. [British, mid 1900s-pres.]

get one's knob polished to copulate or otherwise have sex. For synonyms see OCCUPY. [U.S., late 1900s-pres.]

get one's leg across to copulate with a woman; to master a woman. *Cf.* BOARD, MOUNT. [British and U.S., 1800s-1900s]

get one's nose cold to snort cocaine. [U.S., late 1900s-pres.]

get one's nuts cracked to achieve copulation, said of a man. [U.S. slang, mid 1900s-pres.]

get one's nuts off (also **get one's rocks off**) to ejaculate. [U.S. slang, mid 1900s-pres.]

get one's oats from someone to copulate with someone. *Cf.* SOW ONE'S WILD OATS. [Australian, mid 1900s, Baker]

get one's oil changed to copulate, said of a male. *Cf.* MAN OIL, OIL OF MAN. For synonyms see OCCUPY. [U.S. slang, mid 1900s]

get one's panties in a knot to become agitated and annoyed. [U.S., late 1900s-pres.]

get one's rocks off (on something) to enjoy something. [U.S., late 1900s-pres.]

get one's shorts in a knot to become agitated and annoyed. [U.S., late 1900s-pres.]

get on someone's tits to annoy someone. [British, mid 1900s-pres.]

get on someone's wick to annoy someone. [British, mid 1900s-pres.]

get on top of to copulate. *Cf.* MOUNT. [British and U.S., late 1800s-1900s]

get outside of (also **get outside of it**) to receive a man sexually, said of a woman. [British slang, 1800s, Farmer and Henley]

get over the garter to feel a woman's genitals; to manage to grope one's way above the garter line. [British slang, 1800s, *Dictionary of Slang and Unconventional English*]

get pissy-eyed to get drunk. [U.S. slang, late 1900s]

get small to use drugs; to have a session of drug use. [U.S. collegiate, late 1900s]

get some action to get some sex; to copulate. *Cf.* ACTION. [U.S. slang, mid 1900s-pres.]

get some ass (also **get some tail**) to achieve copulation; to SCORE (*q.v.*). *Cf.* ASS (sense 3). [U.S. slang, mid 1900s-pres.]

get some big leg to copulate with someone. Perhaps referring to the penis. [U.S. black use, late 1900s, Folb]

get some cold cock to copulate. For synonyms see MELT. [U.S. slang, mid 1900s-pres.]

get some cunt to achieve coition. [U.S. slang, mid 1900s-pres.]

get someone by the balls to have someone completely under one's control. [British and U.S., mid 1900s-pres.]

get someone by the short and curlies to have someone completely under one's control. [British and U.S., mid 1900s-pres.]

get some roundeye to perform PEDERASTY or ANILINGUS (both *q.v.*). *Cf.* ROUNDEYE. [U.S. slang, mid 1900s-pres.]

get stonkers to get drunk. [U.S. slang, late 1900s]

get stupid to get drunk or drug intoxicated. [U.S. slang, late 1900s]

get the dirty water off one's chest to ejaculate. [British, 1900s, *Dictionary of Slang and Unconventional English*]

get the horn to get an erection. [British, early 1900s-pres.]

Get the lead out of your ass! (also **Get the lead out!**) a command to hurry. [U.S. slang, mid 1900s-pres.]

get the upshoot to receive the ejaculation of a man, said of a woman. [from *Love's Labour's Lost* (Shakespeare)]

get through 1. to DEFLOWER (*q.v.*) **2.** to copulate with a woman. [both senses, British colloquial, 1800s-1900s]

Getting any? a friendly greeting question asked of one male by another. Literally, "Are you getting any sexual activity, especially sexual intercourse?" See GET ANY? [primarily Australian and U.S.; slang and colloquial, early 1900s-pres.]

getting off using drugs or alcohol. A truncation of "getting off on a high." See HIGH. [U.S. drug culture and slang, mid 1900s-pres.]

get tweaked to get drunk. [U.S., late 1900s-pres.]

get up the pole to copulate, said of a woman. *Cf.* POLE, UP THE. [since the 1600s]

get waxed to get drunk. [U.S., late 1900s-pres.]

G.F. a "girlfriend." *Cf.* B.F. (sense 2). [U.S. slang, 1900s]

G.F.U. "general fuck-up," a person who is a lazy good-for-nothing or a troublemaker; a confused situation. [World War II]

gherkin the penis in JERK ONE'S GHERKIN (*q.v.*). From the name of a small cucumber used in pickling. *Cf.* PUMP ONE'S PICKLE. [U.S. slang, 1900s]

gherkin-jerkin(g) male masturbation. From JERK ONE'S GHERKIN. For synonyms and related subjects see WASTE TIME. [U.S. slang, late 1900s, Lewin and Lewin]

ghetto bird 1. someone who hangs around the [black] neighborhood. For synonyms see EBONY. [U.S. slang, late 1900s-pres.] **2.** a police helicopter in Los Angeles. [U.S., late 1900s-pres.]

ghetto sled a ruined car as found in the ghetto. [U.S., late 1900s-pres.]

ghost turd a wad of lint as found under beds, etc. [U.S. military (West Point), 1900s, *Soldier Talk*]

G.I.B. See GOOD IN BED.

Gibraltar a type of strong CRACK cocaine. Based on ROCK of Gibraltar. For synonyms see NOSE-CANDY. [U.S. drug culture, late 1900s]

gick monster a crack monster. [U.S., late 1900s-pres.]

giffed alcohol intoxicated. From T.G.I.F., *Thank God It's Friday.* Said of people who celebrate the end of the workweek with liquor. For synonyms see WOOFLED. [U.S., late 1900s-pres.]

giggle goo liquor. For synonyms see BOOZE. [U.S., mid 1900s-pres.]

giggle-smoke (also **giggles-smoke**) marijuana. For synonyms see MARI. [U.S. drug culture, mid 1900s-pres.]

giggle-stick the penis. Rhyming slang for "prick." For synonyms see YARD. [U.S., 1900s, *Dictionary of Rhyming Slang*]

giggle-water (also **giggle-juice**) alcoholic drink, especially champagne. *Cf.* BUBBLE-WATER, JOY-WATER, LAUGHING SOUP. [U.S. slang, early 1900s-pres.]

giggle-weed marijuana. *Cf.* GIGGLE-SMOKE [U.S. drug culture, mid 1900s-pres.]

gills, up to the (also **gills, to the**) intoxicated with alcohol. The expression is frequently combined with other terms to indicate a high degree of intoxication. [U.S. colloquial, 1900s or before]

gin 1. a device for torturing; the rack. From "engine." [1200s, *Oxford English Dictionary*] **2.** fetters. From sense 1. [mid 1600s] **3.** a black prostitute. From "aborigine." [Australian and U.S. slang, early 1900s] **4.** cocaine. For synonyms see NOSE-CANDY. [U.S. drug culture, mid 1900s-pres.] See also GHIN, GINNEY.

ginch 1. a girl; a sexually loose woman. **2.** a prostitute. **3.** a CATAMITE (*q.v.*). **4.** copulation. **5.** women considered sexually. [all senses, U.S. slang, early 1900s-pres.]

gin disposal unit a gin drunkard. [British, jocular and nonce]

gingambobs (also **gingumbobs**) the testicles. For synonyms see WHIRLYGIGS. [British, 1700s-1800s]

ginger beer 1. an engineer. Rhyming slang. No negative connotations. **2.** a homosexual male. Rhyming slang for QUEER (*q.v.*). [both senses, British, 1900s, *Dictionary of Rhyming Slang*]

gink an oaf; a silly person. For synonyms see OAF. [Australian, mid 1900s-pres.]

gip to vomit. For synonyms see YORK. [British, mid 1900s-pres.]

girked intoxicated with heroin. For synonyms see TALL. [U.S., late 1900s-pres.]

girl 1. a prostitute; a harlot. [late 1700s-pres.] **2.** to wench; to WOMANIZE (*q.v.*); to pursue women for sexual purposes. [1700s-1900s] **3.** a mistress; a concubine. [since the 1800s] **4.** a servant girl. [British and U.S. colloquial, 1800s and before] **5.** to flirt and court a young woman; to date women. [1900s] **6.** a woman or a girl. Found quite objectionable by the members of some of the Women's Liberation movements. Otherwise in wide usage for females of all ages. [U.S. colloquial, early 1900s-pres.] **7.** a homosexual male. [U.S. homosexual use and slang, mid 1900s-pres.] **8.** a male whore. See SHE (sense 2). [British, early 1900s, *Dictionary of Slang and Unconventional English*] **9.** cocaine. *Cf.* HER. [U.S. drug culture, mid 1900s-pres.]

girlometer the penis. *Cf.* MANOMETER, YARD MEASURE. [British slang, 1800s, Farmer and Henley]

girl shop a brothel. [slang, 1800s-1900s]

girl street 1. women considered sexually. **2.** the female genitals. [both senses, British slang, 1800s, Farmer and Henley]

girl-trap a woman-chaser; a lecher. *Cf.* MANTRAP. [British slang, 1800s, Farmer and Henley]

gism (also **chism, jism**) **1.** any syrupy type of food. **2.** gravy. See BULL FUCK (sense 1). [U.S. colloquial, 1900s] **3.**

semen. For synonyms see METTLE. **4.** physical strength and vigor; male vigor and potency. [senses 3 and 4 are colloquial and slang, 1900s or before]

give to copulate anally. The opposite of TAKE (sense 3). From the point of view of the INSERTOR (q.v.). [U.S. underworld, mid 1900s, Goldin, O'Leary, and Lipsius]

give a dose to infect with a venereal disease. Cf. DOSE (sense 2). [U.S. underworld, 1900s]

give a flying-fuck to care not at all, as in "I don't give a flying-fuck." [U.S. slang, mid 1900s-pres.]

give a fuck (about someone or something) to care about someone or something; to be bothered about someone or something. [U.S. slang, mid 1900s-pres.]

give a hole to hide it in to grant copulation, said of a woman. [British slang, 1800s, Farmer and Henley]

give a shit to care. Usually in the negative, "don't give a shit," a stronger version of "don't give a damn." [U.S. colloquial, 1900s]

give a woman a shot to coit, specifically to ejaculate while copulating. Cf. SHOOT (sense 1). [British slang, 1800s]

give birth to a politician to defecate. For synonyms see EASE ONESELF. [Australian, late 1900s-pres.]

give cone to perform oral sex on a penis. Refers to licking an ice-cream cone. [U.S. slang, late 1900s]

give face to perform CUNNILINGUS. Compare to GIVE HEAD. [U.S. slang, late 1900s]

give hard for soft to coit, said of a man. See HARD. [British slang, 1800s, Farmer and Henley]

give head 1. to copulate with a woman; to INTROMIT (q.v.). **2.** to perform FELLATIO (q.v.). Cf. HEAD-JOB, SERVE HEAD. [both senses, U.S. slang, mid 1900s-pres.]

give juice for jelly to copulate with a woman. The "juice" is the semen; the "jelly" is the vagina. See JELLY

(sense 2), JUICE (sense 1). [British slang, 1800s, Farmer and Henley]

give mutton for beef to copulate; to permit copulation. Said of a woman. See BEEF, MUTTON. [British slang, 1800s, Farmer and Henley]

give one's bum an airing to defecate. For synonyms see EASE ONESELF. [British, mid 1900s-pres.]

give one's gravy to ejaculate. Cf. GRAVY (sense 1). For synonyms see MELT. [British slang, 1800s, Farmer and Henley]

give one the works to copulate with a woman roughly; to rape a woman. [U.S. slang, mid 1900s, Goldin, O'Leary, and Lipsius]

give someone a Melvin to jerk up someone's pants or underwear, drawing the fabric up sharply between the BUTTOCKS. It is assumed that some GEEK named Melvin habitually goes about with this arrangement. [U.S. collegiate, late 1900s, Munro]

give someone a perm to perform oral sex on someone, presumably a woman. Refers to wetting the female pubic hair. [U.S. collegiate, late 1900s]

give someone a tonsillectomy to kiss someone very hard. Cf. BOX TONSILS. [U.S. collegiate, late 1900s]

give someone the shits to frighten someone. [British and U.S., mid 1900s-pres.]

give standing-room for one to permit copulation, said of a woman. Cf. STAND. [British slang, 1800s, Farmer and Henley]

gizzum See JISM.

gizzy marijuana. For synonyms see MARI. [U.S. drug culture, late 1900s]

glad intoxicated with alcohol. Cf. GAY (sense 2), MERRY (sense 2). [U.S. slang, early 1700s, Ben Franklin]

glassy-eyed 1. intoxicated with alcohol. [U.S. slang, early 1900s-pres.] **2.** sexually aroused or sexually spent. [U.S., 1900s]

gleep a fool; an oaf. For synonyms see OAF. [U.S., late 1900s-pres.]

glick a strange person. [U.S. slang, late 1900s]

globber a glob of phlegm. [U.S. colloquial, late 1900s]

globes the breasts. *Cf.* BUBBLES, HEMISPHERES. [British and U.S. slang, mid 1800s-pres.]

globetrotter an addict who moves from place to place looking for the best quality drugs, usually heroin. *Cf.* FROG. For synonyms see HEROIN. [U.S. drug culture, late 1900s]

globular intoxicated with alcohol. [U.S. slang, early 1700s, Ben Franklin]

Glock a gun; a revolver. [U.S., late 1900s-pres.]

glom 1. to steal something. [U.S., early 1900s-pres.] **2.** to take a look at someone or something. [U.S., early 1900s-pres.]

glommed arrested. [U.S., early 1900s-pres.]

glorious intoxicated with alcohol; gloriously drunk. For synonyms see WOOFLED [Scots, late 1700s (Robert Burns)]

glory hole 1. any drawer, niche, locker, cubbyhole, or pigeonhole for the storage of odds and ends. [British and U.S. colloquial, 1800s-1900s] **2.** a church; a Salvation Army meeting hall. [British and U.S. slang and colloquial, late 1800s-1900s] **3.** a dugout. [British military, World Wars] **4.** a hole in a stall partition in a men's public restroom. Said to be used for fellatio, with the INSERTOR (*q.v.*) standing on one side of the partition and the RECEIVER (*q.v.*) on the other side. Observation (by Humphreys) has shown it to be used primarily for spying on the penis of a man urinating or for signalling to a potential sex partner. *Cf.* TEAROOM. [U.S. slang and homosexual use, mid 1900s-pres.] **5.** the anus. For synonyms see ANUS. [U.S. slang, late 1900s if not before]

glove a condom. For synonyms see EEL-SKIN. [U.S., late 1900s-pres.]

glowworm a drunkard; an alcoholic. For synonyms see ALCHY. [U.S., mid 1900s-pres.]

glued 1. infected with gonorrhea. [British slang, 1900s or before] **2.** intoxicated with alcohol. From the immobility experienced in heavy intoxication. [U.S. slang, 1900s, Wentworth and Flexner] **3.** arrested. [U.S., late 1900s-pres.]

glue sniffer someone, presumably a teenager, who sniffs glue containing toluene for a HIGH. [U.S. drug culture, late 1900s]

glutes the buttocks. From *gluteus maximus*. For synonyms see DUFF. [U.S., late 1900s-pres.]

glutton a man or woman with a large sexual appetite. A specialized use of the standard sense. *Cf.* DUMB-GLUTTON.

glutz a slut; a woman of low morals. For synonyms see BIRD. [U.S., late 1900s-pres.]

gnat-bread SMEGMA (sense 2). *Cf.* DUCK-BUTTER (sense 2). [U.S. colloquial, 1900s or before]

gnat's piss weak tea; any weak or inferior drink including alcoholic drinks. [slang, 1800s-1900s]

gnerts See NERTS.

go all the way to copulate; to participate in sex up to and including copulation. [widespread, 1900s]

go and catch a horse to depart to urinate; to urinate. [Australian, 1900s, Baker]

go ape-shit over someone or something to get very excited about someone or something; to become very enthusiastic about something or something. [U.S. slang, mid 1900s-pres.] See also APE-SHIT, APE WILD.

goat 1. a lecher; a lascivious man. [since the late 1500s] **2.** to act lecherously, said of a man. [British slang, 1800s, Farmer and Henley] **3.** body odor, especially underarm odor. *Cf.* FOXY (sense 1). [U.S. colloquial and slang, 1900s]

goat-drunk intoxicated with alcohol and lustful. *Cf.* TIGHT AS A GOAT. [since the early 1600s]

goat-house a brothel. *Cf.* GOAT (senses 1 and 2). [British, 1800s or before]

goatish 1. lecherous; sexually aroused. *Cf.* RAMMISH. [since the late 1500s] **2.**

pertaining to a person with strong underarm odor or to the odor itself. *Cf.* GOAT (sense 3). [colloquial, 1900s or before]

goat-milker 1. a prostitute. *Cf.* MILK. **2.** the female genitals. [both senses, British slang, 1800s, Farmer and Henley]

goat's jig (also **goat's gigg**) copulation. For synonyms see SMOCKAGE. [British slang, late 1700s, Grose]

gob 1. to spit. **2.** spittle. Both are from cant "gob," the "mouth." [both since the mid 1700s]

go ballistic to go mad with rage. [British and U.S., late 1900s-pres.]

gobbin an oaf. For synonyms see OAF. [British, 1900s or before]

go bitchcakes to go wild or crazy. [U.S., late 1900s-pres.]

gobble to commit FELLATIO (*q.v.*). *Cf.* GOBBLER, MUNCH. [British and U.S., 1800s-1900s]

gobblegoo a prostitute who does FELLATIO as a specialty. For synonyms see HARLOT. [U.S. slang, early 1900s]

gobble-prick a wanton and lewd woman. Possibly a reference to fellation. [British slang, late 1700s, Grose]

gobbler (also **gobler**) a FELLATOR (*q.v.*). *Cf.* MOUSER (sense 2), NIBBLER. For synonyms see PICCOLO-PLAYER. [U.S. slang, 1900s or before]

gob-job an act of oral sex performed on the penis. The *gob* is the mouth. [British slang, late 1900s if not before, J. Green]

gobsmacked amazed; astounded. [British, mid 1900s-pres.]

go down 1. For a woman to submit to copulation. **2.** for a man or woman to copulate. Extended from sense 1. *Cf.* GET DOWN. [both senses, U.S. slang, mid 1900s-pres.]

go down for the gravy to perform oral sex on someone. [British, late 1900s-pres.]

go down on 1. to perform PENILINGUS (*q.v.*) on a man or CUNNILINGUS (*q.v.*) on a woman. [both homosexual and heterosexual use, U.S., mid 1900s-pres.] **2.** for a man or woman to perform any NONORTHOGENITAL (*q.v.*) sexual act. **3.** to commit sodomy. Possibly referring to PEDERASTY (*q.v.*) exclusively. Also **get down on.** [U.S. slang, mid 1900s-pres.]

go down the line to SNORT A LINE of cocaine. [U.S. drug culture, late 1900s, Kaiser]

go drabbing to go coiting; to associate with a DRAB (*q.v.*). [British, 1600s-1800s]

go flat to lose an erection. *Cf.* FLAT TIRE. [U.S. colloquial, 1900s]

go for sushi to practice French kissing. [U.S. collegiate, late 1900s, Eble]

go for the drag off to SCORE (*q.v.*); to succeed in copulating a woman. [Australian, 1900s, Baker]

go goosing to go coiting. *Cf.* GOOSE (sense 3). [British slang, 1800s, Farmer and Henley]

go in the brown to commit PEDERASTY. For related subjects see PEDERASTY. [U.S. slang, late 1900s]

go home to die. [British and U.S. colloquial, late 1800s-1900s]

go in unto to copulate. [Biblical euphemism; since the 1600s]

go jottling to go coiting. *Cf.* JOTTLE. [British slang, 1800s, Farmer and Henley]

gold any high-powered (and expensive) variety of marijuana. The name comes from the color and the quality. *Cf.* ACAPULCO GOLD, GOLD COLUMBIAN. [U.S. drug culture, mid 1900s-pres.]

gold Columbian a nickname for marijuana from Colombia. *Cf.* COLUMBIAN RED. Appears in a variety of spellings. For synonyms see MARI. [U.S. drug culture, mid 1900s-pres.]

gold dust 1. cocaine. *Cf.* POWDERED DIAMOND. For synonyms see NOSE-CANDY. [U.S. underworld and later drug culture, early 1900s-pres.] **2.** heroin. Extended from sense 1. [U.S. drug culture, mid 1900s-pres.]

golden leaf marijuana, especially a high grade of marijuana. *Cf.* ACAPULCO GOLD, GOLD. [U.S. drug culture, mid 1900s-pres.]

golden shower a stream of urine directed on someone. Usually in the male homosexual context. [U.S. slang, late 1900s]

golden shower boy in male homosexuality, a sexual perversion wherein sexual gratification is obtained from being urinated on or from other close contacts with urine; the same as GOLDEN SHOWER QUEEN (*q.v.*). [U.S. homosexual use, mid 1900s-pres.]

golden shower queen (also **shower queen**) a homosexual male who obtains sexual gratification from being urinated on. See QUEEN for similar nicknames. [U.S. homosexual use, mid 1900s-pres.]

go like a shower of shit to go very fast. [Australian, mid 1900s-pres.]

gone for a slash gone out to urinate. For synonyms see RETIRE. [Australian, mid 1900s-pres.]

gone to glory dead. For synonyms see DONE FOR. [U.S. colloquial, 1900s or before]

gone trumpet-cleaning dead. [British military, World Wars, Fraser and Gibbons]

gone under 1. dead; dead and buried. See PUT DOWN. [euphemistic, mid 1800s-1900s] **2.** having succumbed to the effects of alcohol, drugs, or anesthetic. [U.S., 1900s]

gong 1. a privy. For synonyms see AJAX. **2.** dung in a privy. *Cf.* GONG HOUSE. [senses 1 and 2 since *c.* 1000, *Oxford English Dictionary*] **3.** opium. For senses 3-6, see SHIT (sense 5) and GONG (sense 2). [U.S. underworld, 1900s-pres.] **4.** an opium pipe. For synonyms see GONGER. [U.S. underworld, early 1900s, Irwin] **5.** an opium addict. [U.S. underworld, early 1900s, Irwin] **6.** to smoke opium. For synonyms see SMOKE. [U.S. underworld, early 1900s]

gonga 1. the anus. Possibly "gonger." See GONG (sense 2). [British, 1900s, *Dictionary of Slang and Unconventional English*] **2.** marijuana. *Cf.* GANJAH. [U.S. underworld, mid 1900s, Goldin, O'Leary, and Lipsius]

gong-beater an opium-smoker. [U.S.

underworld and drug culture, early 1900s-pres.]

gonged drug intoxicated. Originally on opium. For synonyms see WOOFLED. [U.S., late 1900s-pres.]

gonger 1. opium. **2.** an opium pipe. [both senses, U.S. underworld, 1900s or before] Synonyms: BAMBOO, CHINESE SAXOPHONE, GEE-STICK, GONG, GONGOLA, HOP-STICK, JOY-STICK, LOG, SAXOPHONE, STEM, WATER-PIPE.

gonger, on the to be smoking opium; addicted to opium. *Cf.* GONGER. [U.S. underworld, early 1900s]

gong house (also **gong**) a privy. *Cf.* GONG (sense 1). For synonyms see AJAX.

gong-kicker 1. an opium smoker. **2.** a marijuana smoker. From sense 1. [U.S. underworld and drug culture, mid 1900s]

gonk a prostitute's derogatory name for a client. [British, late 1900s-pres.]

gonorrhea a venereal disease. Greek for "flow of semen." The mucous discharge is not semen, but the more accurate term blennorrhea never replaced this term. [from Greek; since the mid 1500s] Synonyms: BLENNORRHEA, BUBE, BURNER, CLAP, DELICATE TAINT, DOSE OF CLAPS, G.C., GENTLEMAN'S COMPLAINT, GLEET, GLIM, GLUE, GONOBLENNORRHEA, HAT AND CAP, HORSE AND TRAP, LULU, NEISSERIAN INFECTION, OLD JOE, PISS PINS AND NEEDLES, PISS PURE CREAM, STRAIN, TEAR, V.D.G.

gonsel (also **gonsil, gonzel, guncel, gunsel, gunsil, guntzel, gunzel**) **1.** a tramp's CATAMITE (*q.v.*). **2.** any catamite. **3.** any young boy. *Cf.* PUNK. [senses 1-3 are U.S. underworld, early 1900s] **4.** any homosexual male. **5.** any slob or jerk. [senses 4 and 5 are U.S. slang, mid 1900s-pres.; all senses, from the German word for "gosling," via Yiddish]

goob a pimple. A truncation of GOOBER (sense 2). *Cf.* GUBERS. For synonyms see BURBLE. See also GOO.

goober 1. the penis. "Goober" is a name for the peanut. Possibly a play on PEE and NUT (both *q.v.*). For synonyms see YARD. **2.** a pimple. See GU-BERS. **3.** a very odd or eccentric person. [U.S. black use, late 1900s]

goober-grabber 1. a pea-picker; a person who picks peanuts. No negative connotations. **2.** a lascivious woman. *Cf.* FIST IT. For synonyms see LAY. [both senses, U.S. dialect (Ozarks), Randolph and Wilson]

good fettle, in (also **fine fettle, in**) intoxicated with alcohol. For synonyms see WOOFLED. [British and later, U.S. colloquial, 1800s-pres.]

good in bed (also **G.I.B.**) proven to copulate well or at least satisfactorily. [U.S. slang, late 1900s]

good lay 1. a passionate and satisfying man or woman. Originally said of a woman. **2.** a sexually easy woman; an easy target for sex. For synonyms see LAY. **3.** a satisfying act of copulation. [all senses, U.S. slang, early 1900s-pres.]

goof (also **goofer, goofus**) **1.** an oaf; a ridiculous jerk. [U.S. slang and colloquial, 1900s] **2.** marijuana. [U.S. underworld, mid 1900s, Goldin, O'Leary, and Lipsius]

goof-ball 1. marijuana. [U.S. slang, mid 1900s-pres.] **2.** a portion of narcotics, especially barbiturates in various forms. See G.B. [U.S. drug culture, mid 1900s-pres.] **3.** a jerk; an oaf. [U.S. slang, mid 1900s-pres.]

goof burner a marijuana smoker. [U.S. military, early 1900s, *Soldier Talk*]

goof-butt (also **goofy-butt**) a marijuana cigarette. For synonyms see MEZZ-ROLL. [U.S. drug culture, mid 1900s-pres.]

goofed-up 1. intoxicated with drugs. **2.** mentally confused; disoriented. [both senses, U.S. drug culture and slang, mid 1900s-pres.]

goofer 1. a jerk; the same as GOOF (sense 1). [U.S. slang, mid 1900s] **2.** a drug user. [U.S. drug culture, mid 1900s-pres.] **3.** a barbiturate capsule or tablet; the same as GOOF (sense 2). For synonyms see BARB. [U.S. drug culture, mid 1900s-pres.]

go off 1. to die. For synonyms see DE-

PART. [colloquial, 1600s] **2.** to ejaculate. For synonyms see MELT. **3.** to have an orgasm. [both senses, colloquial, 1800s-pres.]

go off half-cocked (also **go off at half-cock**) to ejaculate prematurely. A semantic play based on the misfiring of a gun. *Cf.* COCK (sense 3), GO OFF (sense 2). [British and U.S. slang and colloquial, mid 1800s-pres.]

goof off 1. to waste time; to play aimlessly when there is work to be done. **2.** a person who plays aimlessly. Usually hyphenated. [both senses, U.S. colloquial, mid 1900s-pres.]

goog beer; a glass of beer. [U.S. collegiate, late 1900s]

goolies the testicles. From the dialect term "gooly," meaning "stone." [British, Australian, and elsewhere, 1800s-1900s]

goombah a buddy; a trusted friend. From Italian. [U.S., late 1900s-pres.]

goonas the human breasts. For synonyms see BOSOM. [U.S. slang, mid 1900s, Berrey and Van den Bark]

gooned drunk. For synonyms see WOOFLED. [U.S. slang, late 1900s]

gooner 1. an odd or eccentric person; a GOON. [U.S. slang, late 1900s] **2.** a term for an East Asian. Derogatory. [U.S., late 1900s-pres.]

goon-platoon a platoon of misfits; a platoon that is noted for its errors. Military. [U.S., mid 1900s-pres.]

goon squad 1. the police, in general. For synonyms see FLATFOOT. [U.S. black use, late 1900s] **2.** any gang of rough and threatening males. [U.S. slang, mid 1900s-pres.] **3.** any collection of people. Jocular. [U.S. slang, late 1900s]

go on to a better world to die. *Cf.* LEAVE THIS WORLD. [euphemistic, 1900s or before]

goophead an inflamed pimple. Patterned on *blackhead*. [U.S., late 1900s-pres.]

goose 1. a prostitute. **2.** copulation; sexual release; women considered sexually. **3.** to GIRL (sense 2); to womanize. [all senses, British slang, 1800s] **4.** a syphilitic chancre. A truncation of WINCHESTER-GOOSE (*q.v.*). [British and U.S. slang, 1800s-1900s] **5.** a silly oaf; a silly goose. [since the 1500s] **6.** to poke something, perhaps a finger, in someone's anus. [U.S. slang, mid 1900s-pres.] **7.** to make something or someone give a sudden start, *e.g.*, to stamp down on the accelerator of a car. No negative connotations. [U.S. slang and colloquial, mid 1900s-pres.] **8.** PEDERASTY (*q.v.*); perhaps to perform pederasty. [U.S. underworld, early 1900s, Monteleone] **9.** a derogatory nickname for a Jewish man. Possibly from GONSEL (*q.v.*). [U.S. underworld, early 1900s, Monteleone]

gooseberries the testicles. *Cf.* JINGLE-BERRIES. [British slang, mid 1800s, Farmer and Henley]

goose girl a lesbian. For synonyms see LESBYTERIAN. [British, late 1900s-pres.]

gooser 1. the penis. *Cf.* GOOSE (sense 2). For synonyms see YARD. [British slang, 1800s, Farmer and Henley] **2.** a PEDERAST (*q.v.*). *Cf.* GOOSE (sense 8).

goose's-neck the penis. From the image of the skinned neck of a fowl. *Cf.* BIT OF THE GOOSE'S-NECK. [British slang, late 1800s, Farmer and Henley]

goot the penis. For synonyms see YARD. [U.S. slang, early 1900s]

goot-gobbler a fellator. For synonyms see PICCOLO-PLAYER. [U.S. slang, early 1900s]

goozlum any gummy, sticky substance: syrup, gravy, soup, etc. [U.S., 1900s]

go postal to become violent. [U.S., late 1900s-pres.]

gorey-eyed intoxicated with alcohol. *Cf.* ORIE-EYED. [U.S. slang, early 1900s, Weseen]

gorilla juice steroids. Bodybuilding. [U.S., late 1900s-pres.]

gorilla pills barbiturate tablets or capsules; the same as KING KONG PILLS (*q.v.*). For synonyms see BARB. [U.S. drug culture, mid 1900s-pres.]

gorilla pimp a brutal and cruel pimp. [U.S. slang, mid 1900s-pres.]

gorilla tabs the drug phencyclidine, P.C.P. For synonyms see P.C.P. [U.S. drug culture, late 1900s, Abel]

gorked anesthetized. [U.S., late 1900s-pres.]

gossy a condom. For synonyms see EEL-SKIN.

go star-gazing on one's back to copulate, from a woman's point of view. [British slang, 1800s, Farmer and Henley]

Go take a flying-fuck! "Get out!" "Go jump in the lake!" "Go take a long walk on a short pier!" From "flying-leap." See FLYING-FUCK. [U.S. slang, 1900s]

go tits up to die; to fail. Patterned on general slang *go belly up*. For synonyms see DEPART. [U.S. slang, late 1900s]

Go to buggery! "Get out!"; "Mind your own business!" For synonyms see 'ZOUNDS. [Australian, mid 1900s-pres.]

go to Egypt to depart to urinate; to urinate. For synonyms see WHIZ. [U.S. colloquial, early 1900s]

go to Europe with Ralph and Earl in a Buick to vomit. All the capitalized terms are onomatopoetic. For synonyms see YORK. [U.S. collegiate, late 1900s, Eble]

Go to Helen B. Happy! a contrived disguise of "Go to hell!" [U.S. colloquial, early 1900s]

Go to hell! "Beat it!"; "Drop dead!" [widespread, 1900s and long before]

go to it to copulate. Implying rapid movement. *Cf.* GO (sense 2), IT (sense 5). [colloquial since the 1600s]

go to meet one's maker to die. Seen often in the past tense. [U.S. euphemism, 1900s or before]

go to one's reward to die and go to heaven or hell. [U.S. colloquial, 1900s or before]

go to pay the water bill to urinate. For synonyms see WHIZ. [British, late 1900s-pres.]

go to sleep to die. *Cf.* PUT TO SLEEP. [U.S. colloquial euphemism, 1900s and before]

go to work with to copulate with a woman. *Cf.* WORK (sense 1). [since the 1600s]

got the gout intoxicated with alcohol. [U.S. slang, early 1700s, Ben Franklin]

got the rag on experiencing the menses. Occurs in a variety of additional forms. *Cf.* RAG, ON THE. For synonyms see FLOODS. [colloquial, late 1800s-pres.]

gouch off to pass out under the influence of drugs. [U.S., late 1900s-pres.]

goup an oaf. See GOOP.

go up the dirt road to commit PEDERASTY. For related subjects see PEDERASTY. [U.S. slang, late 1900s]

go up the mustard road to copulate anally. For related subjects see PEDERASTY. [U.S. slang, late 1900s]

government art collection money; paper money. [U.S., late 1900s-pres.]

government-inspected meat a gay man in the armed service. [U.S., late 1900s-pres.]

gozz to spit. [British, late 1900s-pres.]

G.Q. having to do with good-quality drugs or anything of good quality. [U.S. drug culture, late 1900s]

grapefruits the human breasts. For synonyms see BOSOM. [U.S. slang and colloquial, 1900s]

grape(s) 1. champagne; wine. For synonyms see BOOZE. [U.S., late 1900s-pres.] **2.** hemorrhoids. [U.S., late 1900s-pres.]

grapes the female breasts; a woman's nipples. For synonyms see BOSOM. [U.S. black use, 1900s, Folb] See also GRAPE(S) and BERRIES.

grape-shot intoxicated with wine. From the term "small shot." *Cf.* CUP-SHOT. [British and U.S. slang, late 1800s-1900s, Farmer and Henley]

grape smuggling an imaginary activity done by males, evidenced by the visibility of the outlines of the *glans penis* and testes through brief swimming trunks. See also PEANUT SMUGGLING. [U.S., late 1900s-pres.]

grapes of wrath wine; cheap wine.

For synonyms see BOOZE. [U.S., mid 1900s-pres.]

grass 1. marijuana. For synonyms see MARI. [U.S. drug culture, mid 1900s-pres.] **2.** straight hair; Caucasian hair. [U.S. black use, mid 1900s]

grassback a promiscuous young woman, one who spends quite a bit of time on her back. *Cf.* FLAT-BACK, GREEN GOWN. For synonyms see LAY. [U.S. slang, mid 1900s]

grasshead a marijuana smoker. [U.S. drug culture, mid 1900s]

grasshopper a marijuana smoker. From the common name of the insect and from GRASS (sense 1). [U.S. slang, mid 1900s-pres.]

grass party a marijuana-smoking party. [U.S., late 1900s-pres.]

grass trip a period of smoking marijuana; being HIGH on marijuana (as opposed to L.S.D.). [U.S. drug culture, late 1900s]

grass weed marijuana. *Cf.* GRASS, WEED. [U.S. drug culture, mid 1900s]

grave-dancer someone who profits over someone else's misfortune. [U.S., late 1900s-pres.]

gravel-pounder an infantry soldier. Military. [U.S., mid 1900s-pres.]

graveyard shift the night shift of work in a factory, usually starting at about midnight. [U.S., mid 1900s-pres.]

gravy 1. the sexual secretions of the male and female; sexual SPENDINGS (*q.v.*). *Cf.* BULL FUCK, BULL GRAVY. [British slang, late 1700s] **2.** a mixture of blood and heroin in a syringe used to inject heroin. [U.S. drug culture, mid 1900s-pres.]

gravy!, By an oath and an exclamation; a mild disguise of "By God!" [U.S. colloquial, 1800s]

gravy-giver (also **gravy-maker**) **1.** the penis. **2.** the female genitals, specifically the vagina. See GRAVY (sense 1). [both senses, British slang, 1800s, Farmer and Henley]

gray dust stale P.C.P. For synonyms and related subjects see P.C.P. [U.S. drug culture, late 1900s]

grayhound [for a black] to date whites. [U.S., mid 1900s-pres.]

grease 1. opium. *Cf.* DREAM WAX. [U.S. underworld, 1900s or before] **2.** to neck; to MAKE OUT. Probably refers to the bringing on of sexual secretions. [U.S. collegiate, late 1900s, Munro]

greased intoxicated with alcohol. From OILED and WELL-OILED (both *q.v.*). [U.S. slang, early 1900s]

greefo (also **greafa, greapha, greefa, grefa, griefo, griffa, griffo, grifo**) marijuana or a marijuana cigarette. [U.S. underworld and later drug culture, early 1900s-pres.]

green a variety of marijuana. A truncation of CHICAGO GREEN, ILLINOIS GREEN, JERSEY GREEN, VERMONT GREEN (all *q.v.*).

green and yellow fellow a homosexual male. For synonyms see EPICENE. [U.S. slang, mid 1900s]

green dragon 1. an amphetamine capsule or tablet. **2.** a barbiturate capsule or tablet. For synonyms see BARB. [both senses, U.S. drug culture, mid 1900s-pres.]

green goods paper money. [U.S., late 1900s-pres.]

greenie 1. an amphetamine capsule. For synonyms see AMP. [U.S. drug culture, mid 1900s-pres.] **2.** a bottle of Heineken beer, which comes in a green bottle. [U.S. slang, late 1900s]

green queen a homosexual male who is known to prefer sexual experiences in the woods or "bushes." See QUEEN for similar subjects. [U.S. homosexual use, mid 1900s, Farrell]

greens sexual activity; sexual release. *Cf.* AFTER ONE'S GREENS. [British slang and euphemism, 1800s]

green snow the drug P.C.P. (*q.v.*). SNOW (sense 2) is cocaine. [U.S. drug culture, mid 1900s-pres.]

green tea phencyclidine, the drug P.C.P. For synonyms see P.C.P. [U.S. drug culture, late 1900s]

grilled alcohol intoxicated. For synonyms see WOOFLED. [U.S. slang, late 1900s]

grind 1. to coit a woman. Recently, to have sex with anyone. [British and later U.S., late 1500s-pres.] **2.** the movements of the male during copulation. *Cf.* MILL. [British and U.S. use, mid 1900s-pres.] **3.** an act of coition. [British, early 1800s-pres.] **4.** a sex partner; someone who will provide a GRIND (sense 3). [slang and colloquial, 1800s-1900s] **5.** to arouse a woman sexually. For synonyms see FIRKYTOODLE. **6.** to masturbate. [senses 5 and 6 are British, 1900s, *Dictionary of Slang and Unconventional English*]

grind, on the 1. pertaining to a person who is sexually active. **2.** pertaining to a prostitute [slang, 1800s-1900s]

grinning at the daisy roots dead. A variant of PUSHING UP DAISIES (*q.v.*). [British colloquial, late 1800s, Ware]

grip to masturbate. *Cf.* FIST IT, TAKE ONESELF IN HAND. For synonyms see WASTE TIME. [U.S. slang, mid 1900s-pres.]

gripe one's ass to cause someone annoyance. [U.S. slang, mid 1900s-pres.]

gristle the penis. For synonyms see YARD. [British slang, mid 1800s, Farmer and Henley]

grit a cigarette [U.S., late 1900s-pres.]

gritch 1. to complain. A blend of "gripe" and "bitch." [U.S. slang, mid 1900s] **2.** a complainer. [U.S. slang, mid 1900s]

grod (also **groddess**) a sloppy man or woman. **Groddess** is the feminine form. The terms are patterned on "god" and goddess." *Cf.* GROTTY. [U.S. slang, mid 1900s]

grog alcohol; booze. From the nickname for Admiral Vernon ("old Grog"), who diluted the ship's rum with water to discourage or delay his sailors' intoxication. The admiral's nickname is from the grogram coat which he wore. [slang since the early 1700s]

grogan 1. a bowel movement. [U.S., late 1900s-pres.]

grogged 1. intoxicated with alcohol. [slang, mid 1800s-pres.] **2.** really stoned or burnt out on marijuana. For synonyms see TALL. [U.S., late 1900s-pres.]

groggery 1. intoxicated with alcohol. From GROGGY (*q.v.*). [dialect and colloquial, 1800s or before] **2.** a public bar; a tavern. Also **grogmill.** [British and some U.S. use, mid 1800s-1900s]

groggified intoxicated with alcohol. From GROG (*q.v.*). [British slang, early 1800s]

groggy intoxicated with alcohol. For synonyms see WOOFLED. [since the 1700s]

groghound a drunkard. For synonyms see ALCHY. [U.S. slang, 1900s]

groid racially black; Negroid. [U.S. collegiate, mid 1900s]

gronk dirt which collects between the toes. *Cf.* CROTCH-CHEESE, TOE-JAM. Also for any junk or dirt. [U.S. slang, mid 1900s-pres.]

grope 1. to feel a woman; to rudely grasp a woman's private parts, the genitals or the breasts. **2** any sexual foreplay. [both senses, primarily British since the 1300s; sense 1 is current U.S. slang] **3.** a verbal feeler from a homosexual male to a prospective sex partner; a visual groping. *Cf.* EYE SHOP. [U.S. homosexual use, mid 1900s-pres.]

grotbag 1. a dirty or unkempt person. [British, late 1900s-pres.] **2.** a disliked person. For synonyms see SNOKE-HORN. [British, late1900s-pres.]

grotty grotesque; highly undesirable. Attributed to the Beatles. *Cf.* GROD. [British and U.S., mid 1900s]

group-grope a group of people engaged in sexual activities. See GROUP SEX for other similar terms. [U.S. slang, mid 1900s-pres.]

groupie a girl who follows a band and makes herself sexually available to the players. [U.S. slang, mid 1900s-pres.]

group rape the serial rape of a male or female. See GANG-BANG.

group sex a general term covering sexual activities involving more than two persons. Specific activities are: BACK-UP, BUNCH-PUNCH, CHAIN-JERK, CHOO-CHOO, CHUGA-CHUGA, CIRCLE-JERK, CIRCUS LOVE, CLUB SANDWICH, DAISY CHAIN, EVERYTHINGATHON, FUCK-ATHON, GANG-BANG, GANG-SHAG, GANG-

SHAY, GROUP-GROPE, MAZOLA PARTY, MUTUAL MASTURBATION, ORGY, PETTING-PARTY, PULL A TRAIN, PULL-PARTY, RING-JERK, ROUND-POUND, SPINTRIA, SUCKA-THON, SWING PARTY, TEAM-CREAM, THREE-WAY, WESSON PARTY.

grovel to pet and neck. [U.S. collegiate, late 1900s]

growler a toilet. For synonyms see W.C. [U.S., mid 1900s-pres.]

growths the human breasts. For synonyms see BOSOM. [vague euphemism and jocular avoidance; U.S., 1900s]

grub 1. to eat a meal. [U.S. slang, late 1900s] **2.** to kiss and neck. [U.S. collegiate, late 1900s, Eble]

grubble to feel; to GROPE (sense 1). *Cf.* GRABBLE. [British, late 1600s]

grumble and grunt the female genitals. Rhyming slang for CUNT (*q.v.*). *Cf.* GASP AND GRUNT, GROWL (sense 1). [British, 1900s, *Dictionary of Rhyming Slang*]

grump to defecate. For synonyms see EASE ONESELF. [U.S., late 1900s-pres.]

grundle the area between the genitals and the anus. [U.S., late 1900s-pres.]

grundle hair pubic hair. [U.S., late 1900s-pres.]

grunge 1. any nasty substance. *Cf.* CRAP, GRONK, GUNGY. [U.S. slang, mid 1900s-pres.] **2.** an ugly or nasty person. [U.S. slang, mid 1900s-pres.]

grungy 1. sloppy; dirty; untidy. [U.S. slang, mid 1900s-pres.] **2.** a sloppy person. [U.S. collegiate, late 1900s, Eble] See also GRUNGE.

grunt 1. to belch. **2.** to defecate. [euphemistic juvenile, 1900s or before] **3.** an act of defecation. [all senses, U.S. slang or colloquial, 1900s] **4.** dung. For synonyms see DUNG. [U.S. slang, mid 1900s-pres. if not before]

guff to break wind. For synonyms see GURK. [British, mid 1900s-pres.]

gug an extremely unpleasant person. [U.S. slang, mid 1900s, *Current Slang*]

gulf heroin from the Persian Gulf region. For synonyms see HEROIN. [U.S., late 1900s-pres.]

gumf nonsense; rubbish. For synonyms see ANIMAL. [British, late 1900s-pres.]

gummer an act of fellatio done by a toothless person. [British, late 1900s-pres.]

gumshoe (also **gumfoot, gumheel**) a policeman or a detective known for wearing silent, gum-rubber soles. [U.S. slang, early 1900s-pres.]

gun the penis. *Cf.* CUTTY-GUN, PISTOL, SHORT-ARM. [slang and colloquial, mid 1900s and nonce long before] See also GREAT GUNS!

gun, in the intoxicated with alcohol. Because one is almost SHOT (sense 1). [British, 1600s B.E.]

gungeon marijuana. See BLACK GUNGEON.

gungy (also **grungy**) messy, ugly, smelly, old, or ragged. See GRUNGE. [U.S. slang, mid 1900s-pres.]

gunny marijuana; HEMP (*q.v.*). From GUNGEON (*q.v.*) and the "gunny" of a hemp gunny-sack. [U.S. slang, mid 1900s-pres.]

guns the biceps. [U.S., late 1900s-pres.]

gunzel-butt a strange-looking person. Possibly a nickname for a CATAMITE (*q.v.*). *Cf.* GONSEL (senses 2 and 5), GOOSE (sense 5). [U.S. slang, mid 1900s, *Current Slang*]

guppies gay urban professionals; or gay yuppies. [U.S., late 1900s-pres.]

gurk 1. to release intestinal gas audibly. **2.** an audible release of intestinal gas. [both senses, Australian, early 1900s, Baker] Synonyms and related terms for both senses: ANAL APPLAUSE, BACKFIRE, BACK-TALK, BEEF, BEEF-HEARTS, BLAST, BLIND FART, BLOW A FART, BLOW OFF, BLOW THE HORN, BOR-BORYGMUS, BOTCH, BOTCHER, BREAK WIND, BREAK WIND BACKWARDS, BREAK WIND DOWNWARDS, BREEZE, BREEZER, BUCK SNORT, BULLOCK'S HEART, BURN BAD POWDER, BURNT CHEESE, BURST AT THE BROADSIDE, BUSTER, BUTLER'S RE-VENGE, BUZZ, CARMINATE, CHEEZER, CRACK A FART, CREPITATE, CREPITA-TION, CREPITUS, CUT A FART, CUT ONE, D'OYLY CARTE, DROP A ROSE, DROP ASS, DROP ONE, DROP ONE'S GUTS, FART, FARTICK, FARTING SHOT, FARTKIN, FAT-UN, FICE, FIZZLE, FLATULENCE, FLATUS, FLUFF, FOIST, FOYST, GUFF, HINDER-BLAST, HONK, INTESTINAL WINDINESS, JAM TART, LAY A FART, LET ONE, LET ONE GO, MAKE A NOISE, MAKE A RUDE NOISE, MAKE WIND, NOSE-CLOSER, OPEN THE LUNCHBOX, PASS AIR, PASS GAS, PASS WIND, POCKET-THUNDER, POOP, POOT, P.U., PUFF, PUMP, RAISE WIND, RASP-BERRY TART, RASPER, ROUSER, RUMP, SCAPE, SCOTCH WARMING-PAN, SHOOT RABBITS, SNEEZE, STINKER, TAIL-SHOT, TALK GERMAN, THROUGH-COUGH, TOM TART, TROUSER CHUFF, TRUMP, VENT, WET ONE, WHIFFER, WINDER.

gusseteer a whoremonger; a lecher. *Cf.* GUSSET. For synonyms see LECHER. [British, 1800s or before, Farmer and Henley]

gusto 1. beer. From a beer advertising slogan. **2.** to drink beer; to drink beer to inebriation. [both senses, U.S. black use, late 1900s]

gut bucket 1. a CHAMBER POT (*q.v.*), especially one used in a prison cell. [U.S. underworld, early 1900s, Monte-leone] **2.** a toilet. For synonyms see W.C. [U.S. slang and colloquial, early 1900s] **3.** the stomach. [U.S. slang and colloquial, 1900s]

gut-butcher (also **gut-fucker, gut-monger, gut-reamer, gut-scraper, gut-sticker, gut-stretcher, gut-stuffer, gut-vexer**) a PEDERAST (*q.v.*); the IN-SERTOR (*q.v.*). [British and U.S., 1800s-1900s]

gut-rot inferior liquor; ROT-GUT (*q.v.*). For synonyms see EMBALMING FLUID. [British slang, 1900s]

guts 1. courage; masculine valor. **2.** the belly; the intestines. [both senses, Brit-ish and U.S. slang and colloquial, 1900s]

gut-stick the penis. For synonyms see YARD. [British slang, 1800s, Farmer and Henley]

gutter the female genitals. *Cf.* COM-MON SEWER, DRAIN, SCUPPER. [British slang, 1800s, Farmer and Henley]

guttered alcohol intoxicated. For syn-onyms see WOOFLED. [U.S. slang, 1900s, Dickson]

gutter junky (also **gutter hype**) a destitute drug addict. [U.S. drug culture, late 1900s, Kaiser]

gutter slut a low prostitute; a common whore. For synonyms see HARLOT. [U.S., early 1900s]

guttle a drunkard. From the standard word meaning "to make a glutton of oneself." [British slang, 1800s, Farmer and Henley]

guzzled 1. arrested. [U.S., late 1900s-pres.] **2.** alcohol intoxicated. For synonyms see WOOFLED. [U.S., late 1900s-pres.]

guzzle-guts a drunkard. For synonyms see ALCHY. [British slang, 1700s-1800s]

guzzler a drunkard. [since the late 1700s]

gweeb 1. a total JERK; a social outcast. For synonyms see OAF. [U.S. collegiate, late 1900s, Eble] **2.** a studious student. [U.S., late 1900s-pres.]

gweebo contemptible; despicable; pertaining to a GWEEB. [U.S. slang, late 1900s]

gweep a computer nerd. [U.S., late 1900s-pres.]

gym queen a muscular homosexual male who works out in a gym. For synonyms see EPICENE. [British, late 1900s-pres.]

gym shoe a disliked person. For synonyms see SNOKE-HORN. [U.S., late 1900s-pres.]

gyppy tummy diarrhea; an upset stomach. For synonyms see QUICKSTEP. [U.S. slang or colloquial, mid 1900s-pres.]

Gypsy's (kiss) an act of urination. Rhyming slang for PISS. For synonyms see WHIZ. [British, early 1900s-pres.]

gyve marijuana. For synonyms see MARI.

gyve-stick See JIVE-STICK.

H

H. 1. "heroin." [U.S. underworld and drug culture, early 1900s-pres.] **2.** "hell." [euphemistic, 1900s and before]

hacked (**off**) angry; annoyed. [U.S., late 1900s-pres.]

hagalina a very ugly woman. [U.S., late 1900s-pres.]

hagster a very ugly woman. [U.S., late 1900s-pres.]

ha-ha a beer. From BREW-HA-HA (*q.v.* at BREW-HA). [U.S. collegiate, late 1900s, Munro]

hail-fellow-all-wet a jocular reference to a drunkard. Based on "hail-fellow-well-met," where "hail" means "healthy." [U.S., mid 1900s]

hail smiling morn an erection. Rhyming slang on *horn*. For synonyms see ERECTION. [British, mid 1900s-pres.]

hair 1. women considered sexually. From the female pubic hair. *Cf.* AFTER HAIR, BIT OF HAIR. **2.** copulation. [both senses, British slang, 1800s] **3.** virile strength[1] and courage. *Cf.* HAIRY-ASSED. [U.S. slang, mid 1900s-pres.]

hairball 1. (usually **Hairball!**) an exclamation of disgust. From the name of the disgusting mass vomited by a cat. [U.S. slang, late 1900s] **2.** a low person who gets drunk and obnoxious. From sense 1. [U.S. slang, late 1900s]

hairburger 1. the female genitals with reference to CUNNILINGUS (*q.v.*). *Cf.* FURBURGER. [U.S. slang, mid 1900s-pres.] **2.** a homosexual male hairdresser. From sense 1. [U.S. homosexual use, mid 1900s]

hair farmer someone with lush and abundant hair. [U.S., late 1900s-pres.]

hair-pie the female genitals; the female pubic hair. *Cf.* HAIRBURGER. [U.S. slang, mid 1900s-pres.]

hair-splitter the penis. *Cf.* HAIR-DIVIDER. [British slang, early 1800s]

hairy 1. sexually aroused. [said of women, British, mid 1800s; said of men, U.S., mid 1900s-pres.] **2.** covered with hair; crinatory. **3.** virile; masculine. See HAIRY-ASSED. [U.S. slang, mid 1900s-pres.] **4.** difficult; frightening; exciting. [U.S. slang, mid 1900s] See also FEEL HAIRY.

hairy-assed pertaining to a mature, virile, and hairy male. *Cf.* BARE-ASSED (sense 2). [U.S. slang, mid 1900s-pres.]

hairy-fairy an effeminate man; a passive male homosexual. For synonyms see FRIBBLE, EPICENE. [British, mid 1900s-pres.]

half and half 1. half drunk. *Cf.* ARF AN ARF. [British and U.S., early 1700s-pres.] **2.** BISEXUAL (*q.v.*). [U.S. slang, mid 1900s-pres.] Synonyms and related terms for sense 2: A.C.-D.C., AMBIDEXTROUS, AMBISEXTROUS, AMBISEXUAL, AMBOSEXUAL, AMPHIGENOUS INVERSION, BI, BISEXUAL, BISEXUOUS, DOUBLE-GAITED, INTERSEX, KIKI, SWITCH-HITTER. **3.** an act of fellatio followed by sexual intercourse. [U.S. slang, mid 1900s-pres.]

half-assed worthless; stupid; ill-planned; trivial. [U.S. slang, mid 1900s-pres.]

half-blind intoxicated with alcohol. *Cf.* BLIND DRUNK. [U.S. colloquial, mid 1900s-pres.]

half-canned lightly intoxicated with alcohol.

half-cocked intoxicated with alcohol. For synonyms see WOOFLED. [widespread, late 1800s-pres.]

half-crocked alcohol intoxicated. For synonyms see WOOFLED. [U.S., mid 1900s-pres.]

half-cut intoxicated with alcohol. *Cf.*

CUT (sense 2). [widespread slang, mid 1800s-pres.]

half-gone half drunk; mildly intoxicated with alcohol. [British and U.S. slang, 1800s-1900s]

half in the bag intoxicated with alcohol. [U.S. slang, mid 1900s-pres.]

halfling a very short person. [U.S., late 1900s-pres.]

half-lit intoxicated with alcohol. Cf. LIT (sense 1). [U.S. slang, mid 1900s-pres.]

half mast of the state of a partially erect penis. For synonyms see ERECTION. [1900s, if not before]

half-pissed intoxicated with alcohol; partially intoxicated with alcohol. Cf. PISSED. [British and U.S. slang, early 1900s-pres.]

half-rats partially intoxicated with alcohol. Cf. RATS, THE. [British slang, late 1800s, Ware]

half-rinsed partially intoxicated with alcohol. [slang, early 1900s-pres.]

half-screwed partially intoxicated with alcohol. Cf. SCREWED (sense 1). [British and U.S. slang, early 1800s-1900s]

half-seas-over partially intoxicated with alcohol. Like a ship which is washed over by low waves or a ship which is halfway to its destination. [in the mid 1500s, the midpoint of any act; this sense since the 1600s]

half-shaved intoxicated with alcohol. Cf. SHAVED. [colloquial and slang, 1800s or before]

half-shot intoxicated with alcohol. Cf. SHOT (sense 1). [British and U.S. slang, 1900s or before]

half-sprung tipsy; alcohol intoxicated. For synonyms see WOOFLED. [U.S., late 1900s-pres.]

half-stewed tipsy; alcohol intoxicated. For synonyms see WOOFLED. [U.S., late 1900s-pres.]

half-under mildly intoxicated with alcohol; partially under the influence of alcohol. [U.S. slang, early 1900s-pres.]

half up the pole intoxicated with alcohol. Cf. POLE, UP THE.

hambone the penis. Cf. BONE (sense 2). [U.S. slang, 1900s and nonce]

ham-cases (also **hams**) BREECHES (q.v.); trousers. Cf. GAM-CASES. For synonyms see GALLIGASKINS. [British, late 1700s, Grose]

hammer 1. a woman; a girl. Cf. NAIL (sense 1), POUND. [originally black use; U.S. slang, mid 1900s-pres.] **2.** the penis. [Australian and Canadian attestations, 1900s] **3.** to COIT someone. For synonyms see OCCUPY. [British slang, 1900s, McDonald]

hammer a beer (also **pound a beer**) to drink a beer. [U.S. slang, late 1900s]

hammered intoxicated due to drink or drugs. For synonyms see TALL, WOOFLED. [British and U.S. slang, late 1900s-pres.]

hammerhead 1. an oaf; a dullard. Cf. MALLET-HEAD. [since the early 1500s] **2.** a drunkard or a drug user. Cf. HAMMERED. For synonyms see ALCHY. [U.S. collegiate, late 1900s]

hammock for two a brassiere. For synonyms see BRA. [U.S. jocular slang, 1900s]

Hampton Wick (also **Hampton**) the penis. Rhyming slang for "prick." [British, 1800s-1900s, *Dictionary of Rhyming Slang*]

hams 1. the buttocks. Cf. PRESSED-HAM. [colloquial, early 1700s-pres.] **2.** breeches; trousers. See HAM-CASES. [cant, early 1700s]

H. and C. a mixture of "heroin and cocaine." A reinterpretation of the abbreviation for "hot and cold." [U.S. drug culture, mid 1900s-pres.]

hand-jive 1. an act of [male] masturbation. **2.** to masturbate. Said of the male. For synonyms and related subjects see WASTE TIME. [both senses, U.S., late 1900s]

hand-job the masturbation of oneself or of another person. Modeled on BLOW-JOB (q.v.). See JOB (sense 2) for similar "jobs." [U.S. slang, mid 1900s-pres.]

handle 1. to pet; to fondle. [U.S. slang, 1900s and nonce] **2.** to masturbate. [British and U.S. colloquial euphemism, 1800s-1900s] **3.** to copulate. In the sense "manage." **4.** the penis. **5.** a breast. Usually in the plural. [senses 3-5, U.S. slang, 1900s]

handlebars of love the BUTTOCKS. For synonyms see DUFF. [U.S. slang, late 1900s] See also LOVE HANDLES.

handle for the broom the vagina. For synonyms see PASSAGE. [British slang, 1800s, Farmer and Henley]

hands the breasts. Probably an evasive term. For synonyms see BOSOM. *Cf.* EYES. [U.S. collegiate, late 1900s, Munro]

hand shandy masturbation. For synonyms see WASTE TIME. [British, late 1900s-pres.]

handstaff the penis. [British slang or colloquial, mid 1800s, Farmer and Henley]

hand-warmers the breasts, [Australian and U.S., early 1900s-pres.]

hane heinous; HANUS. [U.S., late 1900s-pres.]

hang a B.A. to hang a "bare ass"; to MOON (sense 1), to expose the buttocks for shock or insult. *Cf.* GAUCHO, MOON (sense 1), PRESSED-HAM. [U.S. slang, mid 1900s]

hanging Johnny the penis, espcially when flaccid or diseased. *Cf.* JOHNNY (sense 1). [British slang, 1800s, Farmer and Henley]

hangover 1. an unpleasant period of recovery from heavy alcohol intoxication. [1900s] Synonyms and related terms: BOTTLE-FATIGUE, CRAPULA, LONG STALE DRUNK, SNOZZLE-WOBBLES, WINE-ACHE, WOOFITS. **2.** large buttocks which hang over the chair. **3.** a large belly which hangs over the belt. See also FALL-OUT. Both are from sense 1. [senses 2 and 3 are U.S. slang and colloquial, 1900s]

hank a slut; a sexually loose woman. [U.S. collegiate, late 1900s, Munro]

hanky-panky 1. trickery; deceit. [since the early 1800s] **2.** sexual play; illicit sexual activity; adultery. [British and U.S. slang and colloquial, 1900s]

hanus heinous; really terrible. Mostly a spelling error or a pronunciation variant. [U.S., late 1900s-pres.]

happy mildly intoxicated with alcohol. *Cf.* GLAD, MERRY (sense 2). [since the 1700s]

happy as a pig in shit very contented. [British and U.S., late 1900s-pres.]

happy cap a condom. For synonyms see ELL-SKIN. [U.S., late 1900s-pres.]

happy dust (also **happy powder, happy stuff**) any of the powdered narcotics, specifically morphine or cocaine. [U.S. underworld and drug culture, early 1900s-pres.]

happy juice liquor, beer, and wine. For synonyms see BOOZE. [U.S., late 1900s-pres.]

happy returns vomit; vomitus. *Cf.* RETURN. Also in the catch phrase "many happy returns," said when someone belches. [slang, 1800s-1900s]

happy sticks marijuana cigarettes dusted with P.C.P. For synonyms see MEZZROLL. [U.S. drug culture, late 1900s]

hard as fuck 1. tough and unyielding. [British, late 1900s-pres.] **2.** very difficult. [British and U.S., late 1900s-pres.]

hard-ass 1. a person who has been seasoned or made tough by the ways of the world. A stronger version of "hard-nosed." [U.S. slang, mid 1900s-pres.] **2.** [of a person] tough and unyielding. [British and U.S., late 1900s-pres.]

hard bit 1. the erect penis. For synonyms see ERECTION. **2.** copulation from the woman's point of view. [both senses, British slang, 1800s, Farmer and Henley]

hard case a young person who is difficult to manage. [British and U.S., late 1900s-pres.]

Hard cheese "Tough luck!" [British, late 1900s-pres.]

hard mack a cruel pimp; the same as GORILLA PIMP (*q.v.*) *Cf.* MACK (sense 1. [U.S., 1900s]

hard-nosed 1. erect. Said of the penis. [U.S. slang, late 1900s or before] **2.**

having an erect penis. [U.S. collegiate, late 1900s]

hard-off 1. a woman who cools male lust. [U.S., late 1900s-pres.] **2.** an irritating puff of a marijuana cigarette. [U.S., late 1900s-pres.] **3.** anything or anyone unpleasant. For synonyms see SNOKE-HORN. [U.S., late 1900s-pres.] **4.** a dull and sexless male. The opposite of HARD-ON. [U.S., late 1900s-pres.]

hard-on 1. pertaining to an erect penis. [British, 1800s, Farmer and Henley] **2.** an erect penis. [British and U.S. colloquial, late 1800s-pres]

hard sore a syphilitic chancre as opposed to a SOFT SORE (*q.v.*), which is not from a venereal disease.

hard stuff 1. hard liquor. [British and U.S; slang and colloquial, 1800s-1900s] **2.** strong and addictive drugs, specifically heroin and morphine. For synonyms see COTICS. [U.S. drug culture, mid 1900s-pres.]

hard-up 1. intoxicated with alcohol [since the late 1800s] **2.** very much in need of sexual release. [widespread colloquial; U.S., 1900s] **3.** pertaining to an erect penis. [U.S. slang, 1900s]

harlot 1. a rascal; a knave; a fornicator. [1200s, *Oxford English Dictionary*] **2.** a prostitute. Now with some notion of youth and excitement. [since the early 1400s] Synonyms for sense 2 refer to women unless indicated otherwise: ACADEMICIAN, ALLEY CAT, ANIMAL, ANONYMA, ARTICHOKE, ARTICLE, ASS-PEDDLER, ATHANASIAN WENCH, AUNT, BACHELOR'S WIFE, BADGER, BAG, BAGGAGE, BANGSTER, BARBER'S CHAIR, BARNACLE, BARRACK-HACK, BARREN-JOEY, BAT, BAWDY BASKET, BEAST, BEAT MOLL, BED-FAGGOT, BEEFSTEAK, BELT, BELTER, BICYCLE, BIMMY, BINT, BIRD, BISCUIT, BITCH, BIT OF MEAT, BIT OF MUSLIN, BIT OF MUTTON, BIT OF STUFF, BLACK MEAT, BLIMP, BLINT, BLISTER, BLISTERINE, BLOSS, BLOSY, BLOUSER, BLOUZA-LINDA, BLOUZE, BLOW, BLOWER, BLOWSE, BLOWZY, BLUDGET, BOAT AND OAR, BOB TAIL, BONA ROBA, BOONG-MOLL, BRASS NAIL, BRASS NOB, BRIM, BRIMSTONE, BROAD, BROADWAY BROAD, BROKEN OAR, BROWN BESS, BUCKET-BROAD, BUG, BULKER, BUM, BUN, BUNNY, BUNTER, BURICK, BURLAP SISTER, BUSH-SCRUBBER, BUSINESS GIRL, BUSS BEGGAR, BUTTOCK, BUTT-PEDDLER, CAB-MOLL, CAKE, CALLET, CALL-GIRL, CANNON WOMAN, CANVASBACK, CARRION, CARRY-KNAVE, CASE VROW, CAT, CAT-HOUSE CUTIE, CATTLE, C-GIRL, CHARLIE, CHICK (male), CHIPPY, CHROMO, CLAPTRAP, COCKATRICE, COCK-EYED JENNY, COCKTAIL, COFFEE-GRINDER, COLUMBINE, COMMON-JACK, COMMON SEWER, COMPANY GIRL, CONCILIATRIX, CONVENIENT, COURTESAN, COVENT GARDEN NUN, COVESS-DINGE, COW, CRACK, CRACKED PITCHER, CRACK SALESMAN, CRO, CROSHABELLE, CROW, CRUISER, DANT, DASHER, DAUGHTER, DEADLY NIGHTSHADE, DEAD-MEAT, DEAD-PICKER, DEMIMONDAINE, DEMI-REP, DIRTY PUZZLE, DOG, DOOR-KEEPER, DOXY, DRAB, DRAGON, DRESS FOR SALE, DRIPPER, DUSTY BUTT, DUTCH-WIDOW, EARLY DOOR, EASY VIRTUE, ENDLESS BELT, ENTERTAINER, ERRING SISTER, EWE-MUTTON, FAGGOT, FALLEN WOMAN, FANCY PIECE, FANCY WOMAN, FAST-FANNY, FAST WOMAN, FEN, FERRY, FILLE DE JOIE, FILTH, FIRESHIP, FISH, FLAGABOUT, FLAPPER, FLASH-TAIL, FLAT-BACK, FLATBACKER, FLAT FLOOSIE, FLAX-WENCH, FLEABAG, FLESH-PEDDLER, FLESH-POT, FLING-DUST, FLIPPER, FLOOSEY, FLUZIE, FLY, FLY-BY-NIGHT, FORE-AND-AFTER, FORESKIN-HUNTER, FORGOTTEN WOMAN, FORK, FORTY-FOUR, FRAIL, FRAIL-ONE, FRAIL-SISTER, FREAK TRICK, FREE RIDE, FROW, FUCK-FREAK, GAL, GAME, GAMESTER, GARBAGE CAN, GAY-BIT, GAY-GIRL, GAY-PIECE, GAY-WOMAN, GIGSY, GIN, GINCH, GIRL, GIRL AT EASE, GIVE AND TAKE GIRL, GLUE NECK, GOAT-MILKER, GOB-BLEGOO, GO-BETWEEN, GOOH, GOOK, GOOSE, GREEN-GOODS, GREEN-GOOSE, GRISETTE, GUINEA-HEN, GULL, GUTTER SLUT, GUTTERSNIPE, HACK, HACKNEY, HALF-AND-HALFER, HARPIE, HAT, HAT RACK, HAY, HAY-BAG, HIDE, HIGHWAY HOOKER, HIP-FLIPPER, HIP-PEDDLER, HO, HOBBY-HORSE, HOLER, HOOK, HOOKER, HOP-PICKER, HOT BEEF, HOTEL HOTSY, HOT MEAT, HOT MUTTON, HOT ROCKS, HOUSEKEEPER, HUMP, HUNT-ABOUT, HURRY-WHORE, HUSTLER, HUSTLER (male), HYPE, IMPURE, INCOGNITA, IRON (male), IRON HOOF (male), JACK WHORE, JADE, JA-

GABAT, JANE SHORE, JERKER, JILT, JOY-GIRL, JOY SISTER, JUANITA, JUDY, KID-LEATHER, KIFE, KITTOCK, KNOCK-'EM-DOWN, LACED-MUTTON, LADY, LADY OF EXPANSIVE SENSIBILITY, LADY OF LEISURE, LADY OF PLEASURE, LADY OF THE EVENING, LAY, LEASE-PIECE, LEWD WOMAN, LIFT-SKIRTS, LIONESS, LITTLE BIT, LIVESTOCK, LOON, LOOSE-BODIED GOWN, LOOSE FISH, LOOSE-LOVE LADY, LOST LADY, LOVE-PEDDLER, LOW-HEEL, LOWIE, LUSHER, MAB, MADAM RAN, MADAM VAN, MADGE, MAGGIE, MALLEE ROOT, MARK, MASSEUSE, MAT, MATTRESS, MAUD (male), MAUKS, MEDLAR, MERE-TRICE, MERETRIX, MERMAID, MERRY LEGS, MINX, MISS, MIXER, MOB, MODEL, MOONLIGHTER, MORSEL, MORT, MORT WOP-APACE, MOTH, NAFFGUR, NAFKEH, NAG, NANNY, NAUTCH-BROAD, NECESSARY, NEEDLE-WOMAN, NESTCOCK, NESTLE-coCK, NIGH ENOUGH (male), NIGHT-BIRD, NIGHT-HAWK, NIGHT-HUNTER, NIGHTINGALE, NIGHT-JOBBER, NIGHT-PIECE, NIGHT-SHADE, NIGHT-WALKER, NIT, NOCKS-TRESS, NOCTURNAL, NOCTURNE, NOF-FGUR, NOTCH-BROAD, NOTCH-GIRL, NUN, NYMPH DU PAVE, NYMPH OF DARK-NESS, NYMPH OF THE PAVEMENT, OCCU-PANT, OLD RIP, OLD TIMER, OMNIBUS, OUTLAW, OVERNIGHT-BAG, OWL, PACK, PAGAN, PAINTED-CAT, PAINTED-LADY, PAINTED-WOMAN, PALLIASSE, PAPHIAN, PARTRIDGE, PASTRY, PAVEMENT-POUNDER, PAVEMENT PRINCESS, PED-DLE-SNATCH, PERFECT LADY, PHEAS-ANT, PICKER-UP, PIECE, PIECE OF TRADE, PIG, PINCH-PRICK, PINNACE, PINTLE-FAN-CIER, PINTLE-MERCHANT, PINTLE-MON-GER, PINTLE-TWISTER, PIPER'S WIFE, PLEASURE LADY, PLOVER, POKER-BREAKER, POKER-CLIMBER, POLECAT, PONCESS, PRINCESS OF THE PAVEMENT, PRIVATEER, PRO, PROFESSIONAL, PROSS, PROSSO, PROSSY, PROSTITUTE, PROSTY, PUBLIC LEDGER, PUG, PUG-NASTY, PUNCHABLE NUN, PUNK, PURE, PURITAN, PURSE-FINDER, PUT, PUTA, PUTAIN, PUT-TOCK, PYNNAGE, QUAEDAM, QUAIL, QUAN-DONG, QUIFF, RABBIT-PIE, RAGS, RANNEL, RASPBERRY TART, RATTLE-SNAKE, RECEIVER GENERAL, RED LIGHT, RED-LIGHTER, RED-LIGHT SISTER, REP, RIBALD, ROACH, ROAD, ROMP, RORY O'MORE, RUMPER, SAILOR'S BAIT, SAIL-OR'S DELIGHT, SALES LADY, SAMPLE OF SIN, SARDINE, SCARLET SISTER, SCARLET WOMAN, SCOLOPENDRIA, SCREW, SCROUSHER, SCRUB, SCRUDGE, SCUFFER, SCUPPER, SHAD, SHAKE, SHANK, SHE SAILS, SHIN-GLER, SHOREDITCH-FURY, SHRIMP, SIN-GLE-WOMAN, SINNER, SIN-SISTER, SISTER OF MERCY, SIX-TO-FOUR, SKIRT, SKRUNT, SLOOP OF WAR, SNATCH-PEDDLER, SOILED-DOVE, SOSS-BRANGLE, SPEEDY SISTER, SPINSTER, SPLIT-ARSE MECHANIC, SPOFF-SKINS, SPORTING-GIRL, SPORTSWOMAN, SQUAW, STALE, STALLION, STEM SIREN, STEW, STIFF-QUEAN, STRAM, STREET-MEAT, STREET SISTER, STREETWALKER, STRUM, STRUMPET, SUBURBAN, SUBURB-SINNER, SWALLOW-COCK, TAIL, TAIL-PEDDLER, TARRY ROPE, TART, TENDER-LOIN MADAM, THOROUGHBRED, THRILL DAME, TIGER, TIT, TOBY, TOFFER, TOLL-HOLE, TOMATO, TOTTIE, TRADER, TRAF-FIC, TRAT, TREADLE, TREBLE-CLEFT, TREDDLE, TRICK, TRICK BABE, TRICK-ING-BROAD, TRICKSTER, TRIED VIRGIN, TRIP, TROLLOPS, TROOPER, TRUG, TRUG-MOLDY, TRUGMULLION, TRULL, TUMBLE, TWEAK, TWEAT, TWIDGET, TWIGGER, TWO-BIT HUSTLER, TWO-BY-FOUR, TWOFER, UN-FORTUNATES, UNFORTUNATE WOMAN, VEGETARIAN, VENT-RENTER, VENTURER, VICE-SISTER, VIRTUE AFTER, WAPPING-DELL, WAPPING-MORT, WARM MEMBER, WASP, WEED MONKEY, WHEAT BELT, WHISKER, WHITE-APRON, WHORE, WHORE-BITCH, WINDOW-GIRL, WINDOW-TAPPER, WOMAN, WOMAN ABOUT TOWN, WOMAN OF ACCOMMODATING MORALS, WOMAN OF A CERTAIN CLASS, WOMAN OF LOOSE MORALS, WOMAN OF PLEASURE, WOMAN OF THE TOWN, WOP, WORKING GIRL, WREN, ZOOK.

harp a derogatory nickname for an Irishman. [U.S. slang, early 1900s, Irwin] Synonyms: BARK, BOG-HOPPER, BOG-LANDER, BOG-TROTTER, BOILED DINNER, CHAW, CHAW-MOUTH, CHEAP SHANTY MICK, FLANNEL MOUTH, MICK, MICKY, MIKE, NARROWBACK, PADDY, PAT, PATLANDER, POOKA, SALT-WATER TURKEY, SHAM, SHAMROCK, SHANTY IRISH, SPUD, TERRIER, TURF-CUTTER.

harpie 1. a prostitute. From the "Harpy" of Classical mythology, a nasty creature with the head of a woman on the body of a bird. **2.** a shrewish virago. [U.S. slang, mid 1900s-pres.]

Harry heroin. *Cf.* BIG HARRY [U.S. drug culture, mid 1900s-pres.]

Harry Honkers alcohol intoxicated. An elaboration of HONKERS (*q.v.* at HONKED). For synonyms see WOOFLED. [British slang, late 1900s]

Harry Starkers naked; nude. A personification of nudity. Related to STARK NAKED (*q.v.*) and possibly HAIRY (sense 2). *Cf.* STARKERS. [British, mid 1900s, *Dictionary of Slang and Unconventional English*]

harsh toke 1. a bad or burning puff of a marijuana cigarette. From marijuana smoking. [U.S. drug culture, late 1900s] **2.** any extremely unpleasant thing or person. Originally drug culture use. [U.S. slang, late 1900s]

has marijuana. From HASH (sense 3). [U.S. drug culture, mid 1900s-pres.]

hash 1. vomit; vomitus in FLASH THE HASH (*q.v.*) *Cf.* FLASH (sense 1). **2.** to vomit. [attested as U.S., 1800s, Farmer and Henley] **3.** HASHISH (*q.v.*). Synonyms: BLACK RUSSIAN, BLOND, BLOND HASH, BLOND LEBANESE, CANDY, CAROB CHIPS, CHOCOLATE, FIR, KIF, PAKISTAN HASH, QUARTER MOON, SEALING WAX, SHISHI, SOLES. **4.** any drugs, including marijuana. [senses 3 and 4 are U.S. drug culture, mid 1900s-pres.]

hash head a user of HASHISH (*q.v.*) or marijuana. [U.S. drug culture, mid 1900s-pres.]

hashish (also **hasheesh**) the leaves and flowers of Indian hemp, both raw and in processed form. The term is used in the U.S. for a very strong preparation. [from an Arabic word which is roughly translated as HAY (*q.v.*); in English since the late 1500s.]

hash oil an alcohol extract of CANNABIS SATIVA (*q.v.*). For synonyms see OIL. [U.S. drug culture, mid 1900s-pres.]

hashover a hangover from using HASHISH or some other form of *Cannabis*. [U.S. drug culture, late 1900s]

hat job an act of oral sex. A variant of HEAD JOB. [U.S. slang, 1900s]

haul ass (also **haul tail**) to get out in a hurry. *Cf.* BAG ASS, CUT ASS, DRAG ASS, SHAG ASS. [U.S., World Wars and general slang, early 1900s-pres.]

haul one's ashes to copulate. See GET ONE'S ASHES HAULED. [attested as Canadian, 1800s, *Dictionary of Slang and Unconventional English*]

have 1. to cheat or deceive a person. **2.** to copulate with a woman. [both since the 1600s or before]

have a bad case of the uglies to be extremely ugly. [U.S. slang, late 1900s]

have a bar on (also **have a bar**) to have an erection of the penis. *Cf.* HARD-ON, RAIL. [British slang, 1900s, *Dictionary of Slang and Unconventional English*]

have a beat on to have an erection of the penis. [British slang, 1900s, *Dictionary of Slang and Unconventional English*]

have a bit to copulate, said of males. [British slang, 1800s]

have a bit of bum to copulate, said of the male. See BUM (sense 3), "female genitals." [British, 1800s-1900s]

have a bit of bum-dancing to copulate, said of the male in reference to the male motions of copulation. *Cf.* DANCE THE BUTTOCK JIG. [British slang, 1800s, Farmer and Henley]

have a bit of curly greens to copulate, said of the male. [British, 1800s, Farmer and Henley]

have a bit of fish to coit, said of the male. See FISH (sense 1). [British, 1800s, Farmer and Henley]

have a bit (off with someone) to copulate with someone. For synonyms see OCCUPY. [British, late 1900s-pres.]

have a bit of giblet pie to copulate, said of the male. *Cf.* JOIN GIBLETS. [British, 1800s, Farmer and Henley]

have a bit of rough to copulate, said of the male. *Cf.* ROUGH-AND-TUMBLE. [British slang, 1800s, Farmer and Henley]

have a bit of skirt to copulate, said of the male. Cf. SKIRT. [British slang, 1800s]

have a bit of summer-cabbage to copulate. [British slang, 1800s, Farmer and Henley]

have a bit of the creamstick to copulate, said of the female. Cf. CREAMSTICK, which is the penis. [British slang, 1800s, Farmer and Henley]

have a blow-through to copulate, said of a woman. [British slang, 1800s]

have a bone-on to have an ERECTION of the penis. Cf. BONE, BONE-ON. For synonyms see ERECTION. [U.S. slang, mid 1900s-pres.]

have a brick in one's hat to be drunk. Refers to the swollen feeling in one's head. [British and U.S. slang, 1800s-1900s]

have a brush with the cue to copulate, said of the female. The "cue" here is the penis. [British slang, late 1700s, Grose]

have a bun in the oven to be pregnant. For synonyms see FRAGRANT. [Australian, British, and U.S., late 1900s-pres.]

have a bun on to be drunk. Cf. BUN (sense 5). [U.S. slang and colloquial, 1900s or before]

have a buzz on to be drunk. Cf. BUZZING. For synonyms see WOOFLED. [U.S. slang, 1900s if not before]

have a dumpling on to be pregnant. [British colloquial, late 1800s, Ware]

have a flutter to copulate; to DE-FLOWER (q.v.). [British slang, 1800s, Farmer and Henley]

have a game in the cock-loft to copulate. The cock-loft is the residence of the COCK (senses 1 and 3). [British slang, 1800s, Farmer and Henley]

have a glow on to be mildly intoxicated with alcohol. Cf. LIT. [U.S. slang, mid 1900s-pres.]

have a gutful of piss to be drunk. For synonyms see WOOFLED. [Australian, mid 1900s-pres.]

have a hard-on to have an erection of the penis. See HARD-ON. Cf. HAVE A BAR ON. [slang and colloquial, 1900s]

have a hard-on for someone 1. to have a desire for a particular woman. **2.** to be very angry and intend to do someone harm. [both senses, U.S., late 1900s]

have a hard-up to have an erection of the penis. [British slang and colloquial, 1800s, *Dictionary of Slang and Unconventional English*]

have a hump in the front to be pregnant. [euphemistic and vague; colloquial, 1800s-pres.]

have a jag on to be intoxicated with alcohol. Cf. JAG (sense 1). [U.S. slang, late 1800s-pres.]

have a jug fuck to get drunk. [U.S. military, 1900s, *Soldier Talk*]

have a jump to enjoy an act of copulation. For synonyms see OCCUPY. [British, mid 1900s-pres.]

have all one's marbles to have all one's mental faculties. [U.S., mid 1900s-pres.]

have a load on to be drunk. Cf. LOAD (sense 4). [British and U.S., 1800s-1900s]

have a man by the balls to have rendered a man powerless. Nearly always in a figurative sense. Cf. HAVE A MAN BY THE SHORT HAIRS. [U.S. slang, 1900s]

have a man by the short hairs to have a man in a compromising situation; to have rendered a man powerless to defend himself; the same as HAVE A MAN BY THE BALLS (q.v.). Refers to the pubic hairs, but "short hairs" is also euphemistically defined as "the short hairs at the nape of the neck." [British and U.S. slang, late 1800s-1900s]

have a monkey on one's back to be addicted to a drug; to be burdened by addiction to narcotics. Cf. HAVE AN ORANGUTAN ON ONE'S BACK. [U.S. drug culture, mid 1900s]

have a nine-months dropsy to be pregnant. [British slang, 1800s, Farmer and Henley]

have an orangutan on one's back (also **have a tang on one's back**) to be addicted to a drug; to experience drug withdrawal symptoms. A version of HAVE A MONKEY ON ONE'S BACK with a larger simian. [U.S. drug culture, late 1900s, Kaiser]

have a package on to be intoxicated with alcohol. *Cf.* HAVE A JAG ON, HAVE A LOAD ON. [U.S. slang, 1900s]

have a quickie 1. to have a drink. [British and U.S., mid 1900s-pres.] **2.** to urinate. For synonyms see WHIZ. [British and U.S., mid 1900s-pres.] **3.** to copulate. For synonyms see OCCUPY. [British and U.S., mid 1900s-pres.]

have a roll to perform sexual intercourse. For synonyms see OCCUPY. [British, mid 1900s-pres.]

have a run off to urinate. For synonyms see WHIZ. [British, mid 1900s-pres.]

have a rusty-rifle to have a venereal disease. *Cf.* LONG-ARM INSPECTION, SHORT-ARM INSPECTION. [British military, early 1900s, *Dictionary of Slang and Unconventional English*]

have a shit-fit to have a fit; to throw a temper tantrum. [U.S. slang, late 1900s]

have a skinful [for someone] to contain too much alcohol; to be alcohol intoxicated. For synonyms see WOOFLED. [U.S., mid 1900s-pres.]

have a snoot full to be intoxicated with alcohol. Refers to an elephant's trunk filled with liquid. See ELEPHANT'S TRUNK. [U.S. slang and colloquial, 1900s]

have a spaz to get angry or hysterical. [U.S., late 1900s-pres.]

have a turkey on one's back to be intoxicated with alcohol. [U.S. slang, 1800s]

have a turn on one's back (also **take a turn on one's back**) to copulate, said of a woman. [British slang, 1800s, Farmer and Henley]

have a wipe at the place to copulate. *Cf.* PLACE (sense 2). [British slang, 1800s, Farmer and Henley]

have cobwebs said in describing the length of time one has suffered from the lack of sexual release. [U.S. collegiate, late 1900s, Munro]

have connection to copulate. *Cf.* CONNECTION. [British euphemism, 1800s]

have fifty-up to copulate with a woman. [British slang, 1900s, *Dictionary of Slang and Unconventional English*]

have a gin on the rocks to copulate. "Gin" is an "aborigine." See GIN (sense 3), presumably an aboriginal prostitute or concubine. [Australian, 1900s]

have given pussy a taste of cream to have been deflowered; to have been copulated with, said of a woman. See DEFLOWER. *Cf.* PUSSY (sense 1). CREAM (sense 1) is semen. [British slang, 1800s, Farmer and Henley]

have gravy on one's grits to be rich. [U.S., late 1900s-pres.]

have hot pants (for someone) to be sexually aroused over someone in particular. For synonyms see HUMPY. [U.S., mid 1900s-pres.]

have ink in one's pen to be sexually potent. *Cf.* HAVE LEAD IN ONE'S PENCIL. [jocular and euphemistic colloquial, 1900s]

have it both ways to be BISEXUAL; to desire to copulate with males or females. [U.S. slang, late 1900s]

have it off to coit; to ejaculate. *Cf.* GET IT OFF. [British slang and colloquial, 1900s]

have it on 1. to be experiencing the menses; to have a SANITARY NAPKIN (*q.v.*) on. [British colloquial, 1800s, Farmer and Henley] **2.** to have an erection. [U.S. slang, mid 1900s-pres.]

have lead in one's pencil 1. to be potent, virile, and vigorous. **2.** to be in a state of sexual need. **3.** to have an erection. *Cf.* HAVE INK IN ONE'S PEN. [all senses, colloquial, 1900s]

have live sausage for supper to copulate, said of a woman. *Cf.* LIVE SAUSAGE. [British slang, 1800s, Farmer and Henley]

have no more ink in the pen to be sexually exhausted from ejaculation; to be impotent from advanced age. *Cf.* HAVE INK IN ONE'S PEN, HAVE LEAD IN ONE'S PENCIL. For synonyms see IMPU-

DENT. [colloquial, 1900s and possibly long before]

have one in the oven (also **have one in the box**) to be pregnant; to be pregnant with yet another child. *Cf.* HAVE A BUN IN THE OVEN. [colloquial, 1800s-1900s]

have one's ass in a crack to be in an awkward position. [U.S. slang, late 1900s]

have one's ass in a sling 1. to have suffered unjustly at the hands of another. **2.** to be in an unfortunate predicament. **3.** to complain constantly; to be bitchy. [all senses, U.S. slang, mid 1900s-pres.]

have one's back teeth awash (also **have one's back teeth afloat**) **1.** to be heavily intoxicated with alcohol. [British and U.S., 1900s] **2.** to have a very full bladder. [U.S. colloquial, 1900s]

have one's balls to the walls to be in a bad position; to be [figuratively] pushed to the wall. [U.S. collegiate, late 1900s, Eble]

have one's brain on a leash to be alcohol intoxicated. For synonyms see WOOFLED. [U.S. slang, late 1900s]

have one's cargo aboard to be pregnant. [British slang, 1800s]

have one's cut to copulate; to coit a woman; to have one's share of sexual gratification. *Cf.* CUT. [British, 1800s, *Dictionary of Slang and Unconventional English*]

have one's grandmother in (also **have one's auntie in, have one's friend in**) to experience the menses. [British colloquial, 1800s]

have one's oats to copulate; to sow wild oats. See WILD OATS (sense 1). [British colloquial, late 1800s-1900s]

have one's will of a woman to coit a woman. [euphemistic, 1800s-1900s]

have sex to copulate. See SEX (sense 4), "copulation." [U.S. euphemism, mid 1900s-pres.]

have shit for brains to be exceedingly stupid. [U.S. slang, late 1900s]

have snakes in one's boots to have the DELIRIUM TREMENS (*q.v.*). *Cf.*

SNAKES. [U.S. slang or colloquial, 1800s]

have someone by the short hairs to have someone in an awkward position; to have dominated someone. [1900s or before]

have the flowers to experience the menses. Refers vaguely to the redness of roses and thus to blood. *Cf.* FLOWERS [British euphemism, 1500s-1800s]

have the gate locked and the key lost a catch phrase indicating that one is experiencing the menses. [British colloquial, 1800s, Farmer and Henley]

have the horn to be sexually aroused; to have an erection. *Cf.* HORNY (sense 3). [British slang and colloquial, 1700s-1800s]

have the hots for someone to have strong sexual desire for a specific person. *Cf.* HOT FOR SOMEONE. [U.S. slang, 1900s]

have the pukes to have the feeling of impending vomiting. For synonyms see YORK. [U.S., late 1900s-pres.]

have the rag on to be experiencing the menses. *Cf.* RAG, ON THE. [U.S. colloquial, 1900s]

Hawaiian marijuana. Presumably a Hawaiian variety. *Cf.* KAUI, MAUI. [U.S. drug culture, mid 1900s-pres.]

hawk, the the drug L.S.D. (*q.v.*). *Cf.* CHIEF, THE. [U.S. drug culture, mid 1900s-pres.]

hawk up (also **hawk**) to spit; to cough up and spit phlegm. [U.S. colloquial, 1900s and before]

hay marijuana. *Cf.* HASHISH, INDIAN HAY, STRAW. [translation of the Arabic word "hashish"; U.S. underworld and drug culture, mid 1900s-pres.]

hay-bag a low prostitute whom one lies on like a mattress. [British, mid 1800s]

hay-burner a marijuana smoker. From a nickname for a horse. [U.S. drug culture, mid 1900s-pres.]

hay-butt a marijuana cigarette. *Cf.* GOOF-BUTT. [U.S. underworld and drug culture, mid 1900s]

hay-eater a derogatory nickname for a Caucasian. [some Negro use]

hay-head a marijuana user. *Cf.* HOP-HEAD, [U.S. drug culture, mid 1900s-pres.]

haze the drug L.S.D. (*q.v.*). See PURPLE HAZE. [U.S. drug culture, mid 1900s-pres.]

hazy intoxicated with alcohol. Confused with drink. [British and U.S. slang and colloquial, early 1800s-pres.]

head 1. the HYMEN (*q.v.*). A truncation of MAIDENHEAD (*q.v.*). For synonyms see BEAN. **2.** the toilet on a ship. [colloquial, 1800s-pres.] **3.** any toilet or bathroom. For synonyms see W.C. [U.S. slang, early 1900s-pres.] **4.** the end of the penis, especially the erect penis. [U.S. slang and colloquial, 1900s and nonce long before] Synonyms for sense 4: BELL-END, BLUNT END, CLEAT, END, KNOB, NUT, POINT, POLICEMAN'S HELMET, RED-END. **5.** a drug addict or a drug user. *Cf.* ACID-HEAD, A-HEAD, COKE-HEAD, CUBEHEAD, DRUGHEAD, GOW-HEAD, HOP-HEAD, METH-HEAD, PILL-HEAD, PIN-HEAD. [U.S. drug culture, early 1900s-pres.] See also GIVE HEAD.

headace an act of fellatio. [U.S., late 1900s-pres.]

head-cheese smegma. A reinterpretation of the name for a specific foodstuff. *Cf.* CROTCH-CHEESE. [U.S. slang, mid 1900s]

head-fucked brainwashed. [U.S. slang, late 1900s]

headfucker 1. a disorienting or disruptive person, situation, or object. [U.S. slang, mid 1900s-pres.] **2.** a powerful and disorienting drug. *Cf.* MIND FUCK. [U.S. slang and drug culture, mid 1900s-pres.]

head-job an act of PENILINGUS (*q.v.*); the same as BLOW-JOB (*q.v.*). See HEAD (sense 4). [U.S. slang, mid 1900s-pres.]

headlights the human breasts. From their position and prominence. [Australian and U.S., early 1900s-pres.]

head queen a homosexual male who seeks partners for PENILINGUS (*q.v.*) in public restrooms. See QUEEN for similar topics. *Cf.* HEAD (senses 3 and 4). [U.S. homosexual use, mid 1900s, Farrell]

heart 1. the glans penis. Suggested by its shape or from HARD (*q.v.*). [U.S. slang, mid 1900s, Wentworth and Flexner] **2.** a Benzedrine (trademark) tablet, especially a tablet in the shape of a heart. Also used for other amphetamines. [U.S. drug culture, mid 1900s-pres.]

heart and dart a release of intestinal gas. Rhyming slang for "fart." [British slang, 1800s, Farmer and Henley]

heart-on a volatile substance that is inhaled for a high. [U.S., late 1900s-pres.]

heart starter the first alcoholic drink of the day. For synonyms see BOOZE. [Australian, mid 1900s-pres.]

heat, in sexually aroused, said properly of female mammals. Said jocularly of women and even of men. [U.S. colloquial and slang, 1900s and before]

heat, on sexually aroused. The British equivalent of "in heat." See HEAT, IN.

heater a cigarette. [U.S., late 1900s-pres.]

heave to vomit. See HEAVES. For synonyms see YORK. [colloquial, early 1900s-pres.]

heaven 1. the afterlife for good people. The opposite of hell. [since *c.* 1000, *Oxford English Dictionary*] Synonyms: ABRAHAM'S BOSOM, BEULAH, BEULAH-LAND, BY-AND-BY, CITY OF GOD, ELYSIUM, GREAT UNKNOWN, HAPPY HUNTING-GROUNDS, HAPPYLAND, KINGDOM COME, NEW JERUSALEM, PARADISE, THE GREAT BEYOND. **2.** the female genitals; the same as PARADISE (sense 3). [British, 1800s, Farmer and Henley]

heaven dust cocaine. *Cf.* ANGEL DUST. [U.S. underworld and drug culture, early 1900s-pres.]

heavenly blue 1. the drug L.S.D. (*q.v.*). *Cf.* BLUE HEAVEN (sense 2). **2.** a color variety of morning glory seeds used as a hallucinogenic agent. For synonyms see SEEDS. [both senses, U.S. drug culture, mid 1900s-pres.]

heaves a bout of retching or vomiting. *Cf.* HEAVE. [colloquial, 1900s or before]

heavy hash potent cannabis. For synonyms see MARI. [U.S., late 1900s-pres.]

heavy joint marijuana with the drug P.C.P. added to it. See HEAVIES. [U.S. drug culture, mid 1900s-pres.]

heavy leather refers to BONDAGE, a type of MASOCHISM. [U.S. slang, late 1900s]

H.E. double L. "hell." [U.S. colloquial euphemism, 1900s]

H.E. double toothpicks a jocular avoidance for "hell." [U.S. colloquial euphemism, 1900s]

heeled alcohol intoxicated. For synonyms see WOOFLED. [U.S., late 1900s-pres.]

heesh HASHISH (*q.v.*). A telescoping of "hashish" or "hasheesh." [U.S. underworld, early 1900s]

heifer-dust nonsense. An avoidance for BULLSHIT (*q.v.*); a variant of BULL-DUST (*q.v.*). [Australian and U.S., 1900s]

helium head an oaf; an AIRHEAD. For synonyms see OAF. [U.S., late 1900s-pres.]

hell 1. originally the abode of the dead; later the abode of the dead who were wicked in life; HADES (*q.v.*). [since the 800s, *Oxford English Dictionary*] **2.** an oath or curse. Synonyms and related terms for senses 1 and 2: ABYSS, ALL GET-OUT, AVERN, AVERNUS, BALLYHACK, BALLYWACK, BARATHRUM, B.H., BICKLEBARNEY, BLAZES, BLUE BLAZES, BOTTOMLESS-PIT, CAIN, DING-DONG BELL, FIRE AND DAMNATION, GEHENNA, H., HADES, HAIL COLUMBIA! HOT PLACE, INFERNAL REGIONS, INFERNO, JERICHO, KINGDOM COME, L., LOWER REGIONS, NETHER REGIONS, NETHERWORLD, PERDITION, PIT, SAM HILL, SHEOL, SMACK, THE OTHER PLACE, TOPHET, TUNKET, UNDERWORLD, VERY UNCOMFORTABLE PLACE, YOU-KNOW-WHERE. **3.** the female genitals. *Cf.* BOTTOMLESS-PIT, HEAVEN (sense 2). [British slang, 1800s]

hellacious 1. wild; excellent. [U.S., mid 1900s-pres.] **2.** terrible. [U.S., mid 1900s-pres.]

hell and half of Georgia a great dis-tance; a great amount of space. [U.S. colloquial or regional, 1900s]

hell around to play aimlessly; to waste time or GOOF OFF (*q.v.*). [U.S. slang, mid 1900s-pres.]

hell-bender a drunken spree. See BENDER (sense 1). [U.S. slang, 1900s]

hell bent recklessly determined. [U.S. slang, mid 1900s]

hell-broth inferior whisky; bad liquor. *Cf.* FIREWATER.

hellcat 1. a wild, devil-may-care person. **2.** a witch. **3.** a furious or high-spirited girl or woman. [these and similar senses since the early 1600s]

hell dust any of the powdered narcotics. *Cf.* ANGEL DUST, HEAVEN DUST. [British, 1900s, *Dictionary of the Underworld*]

hell-hole any terrible or hot place. [U.S. colloquial, 1900s or before]

hellpig a fat and ugly girl or woman. A girl FROM HELL. [U.S. collegiate, late 1900s, Munro]

helluva (also **heluva**) a respelling (eye-dialect) of "hell of a." A partial avoidance. *Cf.* MELL OF A HESS. [British and U.S. colloquial, 1900s and before]

hell week the time of a woman's menses. For synonyms see FLOODS. [1900s]

helmet 1. the *glans penis* For synonyms see YARD. [British and U.S., late 1900s-pres.] **2.** a circumcised penis. For synonyms see YARD. [U.S., late 1900s-pres.]

hemispheres the breasts. *Cf.* GLOBES. For synonyms see BOSOM. [British and U.S., 1800s-1900s]

hemp 1. marijuana. *Cf.* GUNNY, ROPE. [U.S. slang, mid 1900s-pres.] **2.** a smelly cigar. [1900s]

hempen fever a jocular term for the "illness" which causes death in an instance of hanging. [British, late 1700s, Grose]

hempy (also **hempie**) a rogue suitable for the gallows. [British, early 1800s]

hen-down fowl feces. *Cf.* COCK'S EGGS (sense 2). For synonyms see DROPPINGS. [U.S. euphemism, 1900s]

hen-hussy an effeminate male. For synonyms see FRIBBLE. [U.S. slang, mid 1900s]

henpicking searching on one's hands and knees for dropped bits of crack. [U.S., late 1900s-pres.]

Henry 1. heroin Cf. H. [U.S. drug culture, mid 1900s-pres.] **2.** one eighth of an ounce of marijuana. From *Henry VIII.* For synonyms see MARI. [U.S., late 1900s-pres.]

her cocaine. Cf. GIRL (sense 9). [U.S. drug culture, mid 1900s-pres.]

herb (also **herbs**) marijuana. Cf. ERB, YERBA. [U.S. drug culture, mid 1900s-pres.]

Herbert a dull oaf. For synonyms see OAF. [British, late 1900s-pres.]

hercules a very powerful type of phencyclidine, the drug P.C.P. For synonyms see P.C.P. [U.S. drug culture, late 1900s]

hermaphrodite 1. one who has both male and female sex organs. From Greek mythology, Hermaphroditos, the son of Hermes and Aphrodite. A blend of the two sexes in one person. [since the 1400s] Synonyms and related terms: AMBOSEXOUS, ANDROGYNE, BISEXUAL, EPICENE, GYNANDROUS, JENNY WILLOCKS, JOHN-AND-JOAN, MOFF, MORPHADITE, MORPHODITE, PANATROPE, SCRAT, WILL-GILL, WILL-JILL. **2.** a person with the psychological characteristics of the opposite sex, an effeminate male or a virago. [since the late 1500s] **3.** a CATAMITE (q.v.); any homosexual male. In this sense, a euphemism for "homosexual." [since the early 1700s]

hermit the penis. Cf. BALD-HEADED HERMIT. For synonyms see YARD. [British slang, 1800s, Farmer and Henley]

heroin a semisynthetic derivative of morphine. A highly addictive opiate. [from the name "Hero" of Classical mythology; discovered and named in 1898] Synonyms: A-BOMB, AITCH, ANTIFREEZE, AUNT HAZEL, BALLOT, BIG DADDY, BIG-H., BIG HARRY, BLANKS, BOY, BROTHER, BROWN, BROWN RINE, BROWN SUGAR, CABALLO, CA-CA, CHINA WHITE, CHINESE RED, CHINESE WHITE, CHIVA, COBICS, COURAGE PILLS, CRAP, DECK, DOGIE, DOJEE, DOJIE, DOOGIE, DOOJEE, DOOJI, DOPE, DOWNTOWN, DUJER, DUJI, DYNAMITE, ESTUFFA, FERRY DUST, FLEA POWDER, FOOLISH POWDER, GLOBETROTTER, GOLD DUST, GOODS, GULF, H., HARD STUFF, HARRY, HEAVY SOUL, HENRY, HERO, HIM, HORSE, JOY POWDER, JUNK, KA-KA, KARACHI, MEXICAN MUD, NOSE-CANDY, NOSE POWDER, PERSIAN BROWN, PERSIAN DUST, POISON, ROCK CANDY, ROCK COCAINE, SALT, SCAG, SCAR, SCAT, SCHMACK, SCHMECK, SCHMECKEN, SCHMEE, SCRAMBLE, SHIT, SHMECK, SMACK, SMECK, SMIZZ, STUFF, TECATA, THING, TRIANGLE STUFF, WHITE, WHITE LADY, WHITE STUFF, WITCH HAZEL, YEN-SHEE.

heroin buzz phencyclidine, potent P.C.P. For synonyms see P.C.P. [U.S. drug culture, late 1900s, Abel]

herp See HERPIE.

herped up infected with herpes. [U.S. slang, late 1900s]

herpie (also **herp**) someone who is infected with herpes. [U.S. slang, late 1900s]

Hershey squirt 1. a wet release of intestinal gas. **2.** to stain one's underwear with a wet release of intestinal gas. **3.** (usually plural) diarrhea. [all senses, U.S., late 1900s]

hesh a HE-SHE (q.v.); an effeminate male or a homosexual male. Cf. SHIM. [U.S. slang, mid 1900s, Berrey and Van den Bark]

he-she a homosexual male. Cf. LADLASS. For synonyms see EPICENE. [U.S. slang, mid 1900s-pres.]

hey-diddle-diddle an act of urination. Rhyming slang on PIDDLE. For synonyms see WHIZ. [British, mid 1900s-pres.]

hicky (also **hickey, hickie**) **1.** mildly intoxicated with alcohol. Probably from HICCIUS-DOCCIUS (q.v.). See HOCKEY (sense 1). [slang, 1700s-1900s] **2.** a pimple. For synonyms see BURBLE. [U.S. colloquial, early 1900s-pres.] **3.** a gadget. Cf. DOHICKY. [U.S. colloquial, mid 1900s-pres.] **4.** the penis, especially that of a child. Cf. PIMPLE. (sense 4). [U.S.

slang or colloquial, 1900s] **5.** a red mark left on the body from kissing, biting, or sucking the skin. *Cf.* MONKEY-BITE. [U.S. slang or colloquial, mid 1900s-pres.]

hiddy hideously drunk; very, very drunk. For synonyms see WOOFLED. [U.S. collegiate, late 1900s, Munro]

hide 1. a prostitute; prostitutes or copulation with prostitutes. See SKIN (sense 4). **2.** a CATAMITE (*q.v.;4s*); catamites. [both senses, U.S. underworld, mid 1900s] **3.** any young woman. *Cf.* LEATHER (sense 1), SKIN (sense 4). [U.S. slang, mid 1900s-pres.]

hide the ferret to copulate. *Cf.* FER-RET. [Australian slang, 1900s]

hide the sausage 1. to copulate. *Cf.* LIVE SAUSAGE. For synonyms see OC-CUPY. [Australian slang, 1900s] **2.** an act of copulation. For synonyms see SMOCKAGE. [U.S. slang, late 1900s] See also PLAY HIDE THE SAUSAGE.

high 1. intoxicated with alcohol. *Cf.* ALTITUDES, IN ONE'S. [since the early 1600s] **2.** intoxicated with drugs. [U.S. underworld and slang, early 1900s-pres.] **3.** a charge or kick from intoxicating drugs; any charge, kick, or elevated sense of well-being. [originally drug culture; U.S. slang, mid 1900s-pres.]

high as a kite intoxicated with alcohol. Rhyming slang for TIGHT (*q.v.*). An elaboration of HIGH (sense 3). [British and U.S. slang, 1800s-1900s]

higher than a kite intoxicated with alcohol. See HIGH AS A KITE. For synonyms see WOOFLED. [U.S. colloquial, mid 1900s-pres.]

high tide the menses. For synonyms see FLOODS. [U.S. slang, mid 1900s]

highty-tighty a wanton girl or woman. [British, 1600s, B.E.]

highway hooker a prostitute who uses citizens band radio to set up customers at truck stops. [U.S. slang, mid 1900s-pres.]

hill, on the pregnant. The hill is the bulging abdomen. [U.S. slang, mid 1900s]

himbo a gigolo, a male BIMBO. [U.S., mid 1900s-pres.]

hippie crack nitrous oxide. [U.S., late 1900s-pres.]

His tang is hongry. "His drug habit demands attention." = He is withdrawing from drugs and needs a dose. *Hongry* is dialect (black) for hungry; the TANG is short for *orangutan,* one of the forms of ape as found in HAVE A MONKEY ON ONE'S BACK. [U.S. drug culture, late 1900s, Kaiser]

hit 1. to coit a woman. *Cf.* SCORE (sense 1). [since the 1500s] **2.** a dose of a drug; a puff of a marijuana cigarette. [U.S. drug culture, mid 1900s-pres.]

hit it and quit it to copulate and then leave. For synonyms see OCCUPY. [U.S., late 1900s-pres.]

hit one home to cause an orgasm in someone. [British, late 1900s-pres.]

hit on someone to make a pass at someone; to make a sexual invitation to someone. [U.S. slang, late 1900s]

hit on the tail to coit a woman. *Cf.* HIT (sense 1). [slang or nonce, early 1500s]

hit some shit to get into trouble; to encounter difficulties. [U.S. black use, late 1900s, Folb]

hit the piss to drink beer. [Australian, mid 1900s-pres.]

H.M.C. a mixture of heroin, morphine, and cocaine. *Cf.* H. AND C. [U.S. underworld, early 1900s]

ho 1. any girl or woman; a girlfriend. **2.** a prostitute; a sexual outlet for males. Both are from WHORE (*q.v.*). For synonyms see HARLOT. [both senses, U.S. black use, 1900s]

hobble to copulate. For synonyms see OCCUPY. [U.S., late 1900s-pres.]

hobeast a disliked female; a whore beast. [U.S., late 1900s-pres.]

hockey 1. intoxicated with alcohol; drunk on hock, "stale beer." [British slang, late 1700s, Grose] **2.** dung; feces. **3.** to defecate. Also **hocky, hookey, hooky.** [U.S. colloquial and dialect, 1900s or before] **4.** semen. For synonyms see METTLE. [U.S. slang, mid 1900s-pres.]

hoe-handle the penis. [U.S. dialect (Ozarks), Randolph and Wilson, 1900s or before]

hog 1. to coit a woman. [British slang, 1800s, Farmer and Henley] **2.** an ugly, overweight young woman. For synonyms see BUFFARILLA. [U.S. slang, mid 1900s-pres.] **3.** the drug P.C.P. (q.v.). Cf. ELEPHANT. [U.S. drug culture, mid 1900s-pres.] **4.** a sexually attractive male. [U.S. collegiate, late 1900s, Eble] **5.** the penis. Cf. BELT ONE'S HOG. For synonyms see GENITALS, YARD. [British slang, late 1900s]

hogans female breasts. For synonyms see BOSOM. [U.S., late 1900s-pres.]

hog eye the female genitals. [U.S. slang, mid 1900s]

hog jaws the human breasts. From the rounded sag of hog jowls. [U.S. slang, 1900s]

hogwash (also **pigwash**) **1.** swill and garbage to be fed to pigs; something worthless. **2.** nonsense. No negative connotations. [U.S. colloquial, 1900s or before] **3.** BULLSHIT (q.v.). A euphemism for "hog shit." [all senses above, U.S. slang and colloquial, 1900s and before] **4.** alcoholic beverages, diluted with water. Cf. SHEEPWASH. [British and U.S. use, 1800s-1900s]

hoitch an unpleasant female; a bitch. A blend of WHORE and BITCH. [U.S. collegiate, late 1900s, Munro]

holding the folding having a supply of cash on one's person. [British, late 1900s-pres.]

hole 1. the anus. [since the 1300s] **2.** the vagina. For synonyms see PASSAGE. [since the 1500s] **3.** to coit; to penetrate the vulva. **4.** copulation. **5.** ejaculation. **6.** women considered sexually. [senses 3-6 are British and U.S. slang and colloquial, 1800s-1900s] **7.** a totally worthless human being; an ASSHOLE. [U.S. slang, late 1900s]

hole in one to copulate on a first date. For synonyms see SMOCKAGE. [British, late 1900s-pres.]

holes and poles sex education classes in college. See HOLE=the vagina,

POLE=the penis. [U.S. collegiate, late 1900s]

hole to hide it in the female genitals, specifically the vagina. [British slang, 1800s, Farmer and Henley]

Holland the anus; the anal area. From "hole land." Cf. LOWLANDS. [from *Henry IV*, Part Two (Shakespeare)]

holy bedlock an extralegal sexual union of a man and a woman. Based on "holy wedlock." [U.S. slang, mid 1900s, Monteleone]

holy deadlock a marriage wherein the battles between the man and wife are hopelessly stagnated. Based on "holy wedlock." Cf. HOLY BEDLOCK. [U.S. slang, early 1900s]

Holy fuck! (also **Holy shit!**) a crude mock oath and an exclamation. [U.S. slang and colloquial, mid 1900s-pres.]

holy week a woman's menstrual period. Comparing sexual abstention during the menses to sexual abstention practiced during religious observances. From the name of the last week in Lent. [British and U.S. slang and colloquial, 1800s-pres.]

home 1. to have or cause an orgasm. **2.** to impregnate a female. Cf. SCORE. [both senses, British slang, 1800s, Farmer and Henley]

home brew semen. Cf. HOMEBREWED. For synonyms see METTLE. [U.S. slang, late 1900s, Lewin and Lewin]

homebrewed semen. From the term used for homemade liquor. [British slang, 1800s, Farmer and Henley]

homegrown 1. marijuana grown privately or secretly at one's residence. **2.** domestic marijuana as opposed to that smuggled from abroad. [both senses, U.S. drug culture, mid 1900s-pres.]

home run an act of successful copulation. Cf. SCORE. For synonyms see SMOCKAGE. [U.S., late 1900s]

homo a truncation of "homosexual." Usually used for a male homosexual. Sometimes used for a LESBIAN (q.v.). [slang, early 1900s-pres.]

hone the female genitals. Cf. GRINDSTONE, WHETING-CORNE. [British, early 1700s]

honey semen. *Cf.* HIVE, WHITE HONEY. [colloquial and slang since the 1800s or before]

honey blunts fat marijuana cigarettes sealed with honey. For synonyms see MEZZROLL. [U.S., late 1900s-pres.]

honey-bucket 1. any mobile tank or container used to carry away the contents of privies or latrines. **2.** the receptacle in a latrine. **3.** a wagon to carry manure used as fertilizer. *Cf.* DANNA-DRAG, HONEY-WAGON. [all senses, slang since the 1800s]

honey-bucket hop a quick trip to the W.C. [U.S. slang, 1900s]

honeydew melons the human breasts. *Cf.* MELONS, ORANGES, WATER-MELONS. For synonyms see BOSOM. [U.S. slang, 1900s]

honey fuck a gentle and loving act of sexual intercourse. For synonyms see SMOCKAGE. [U.S., mid 1900s-pres.]

honey oil ketamine. [U.S., late 1900s-pres.]

honeypot the female genitals. For synonyms see GENITALS, MONOSYLLA-BLE. [1900s or before]

honey-wagon the same as HONEY-BUCKET (*q.v.*). [U.S. slang, mid 1900s-pres.]

honk 1. to vomit. Onomatopoetic. *Cf.* BARF, EARP, RALPH, YORK. [British, early 1900s, *Dictionary of Slang and Unconventional English*] **2.** to blow one's nose loudly. [U.S., 1900s] **3.** to release intestinal gas loudly. [slang, 1900s or before] **4.** to be highly sexually aroused. To be so HORNY, one could HONK. [U.S. collegiate, late 1900s if not before] **5.** a drinking spree; a wild party. [U.S., mid 1900s-pres.] **6.** a bad smell. [British, late 1900s-pres.]

honked (also **honkers**) intoxicated with alcohol. *Cf.* TOOT (senses 1 and 2). [British, mid 1900s, *Dictionary of Slang and Unconventional English*]

honker the penis. For synonyms see GENITALS, YARD. [U.S. slang, late 1900s]

honker helper a breast implant. Based on Hamburger Helper™. [U.S., late 1900s-pres.]

honkers 1. a woman's breasts. Jocular. See also HOOTERS. For synonyms see BOSOM. [U.S., mid 1900s-pres.] **2.** drunk. For synonyms see WOOFLED. [British, mid 1900s-pres.]

honking drunk. For synonyms see WOOFLED. [British, mid 1900s-pres.]

honk (up) to vomit. For synonyms see YORK. [British, late 1900s-pres.]

honk (up) one's ring to vomit in a very bad way. For synonyms see YORK. [British, mid 1900s-pres.]

honky (also **honkey, honkie, hunk, hunky**) a derogatory term for a Caucasian. [U.S. black use, mid 1900s-pres.] 1900s]

hoodie a friend from the neighboorhood. [U.S., late 1900s-pres.]

hood rat a promiscuous girl from the neighbooorhood. For synonyms see BIRD. [U.S., late 1900s-pres.]

hooker 1. one of the nails used in the Crucifixion of Christ. Also a fingernail of Christ. **2.** a prostitute. This hooker is a "fisher, angler, or hooker of men" (Farmer and Henley). Hookers were thieves who used a pole with a hook on the end to snare goods through open windows. For synonyms see HAR-LOT. [ultimately from the cant of the 1500s; by the 1800s, "hooker" meant any thief; U.S. underworld and slang, 1800s-pres.]

hook-nose a derogatory nickname for a Jewish man or woman. For synonyms see FIVE AND TWO. [U.S. slang, 1900s]

hoot to snort cocaine or crank. [U.S., late 1900s-pres.]

hootch (also **hooch**) any alcoholic beverage. *Cf.* HOOCH, SCOOCH. For synonyms see BOOZE. [U.S. slang and colloquial, 1800s-pres.]

hootchee (also **hootchie, hotchie**) **1.** a whoremonger. [U.S. underworld, early 1900s] **2.** the penis. [U.S. slang, mid 1900s-pres.]

hootcher a drunkard. *Cf.* HOOTCH. [U.S. slang, mid 1900s-pres.]

hooted intoxicated with alcohol. *Cf.* HONKED. [U.S. slang, 1900s]

hooter 1. a drink of liquor. [U.S. slang, late 1800s, Green] **2.** cocaine. A slang synonym for *nose*. For synonyms see NOSE-CANDY. [U.S. drug culture, late 1900s] **3.** a marijuana cigarette. For synonyms see MEZZROLL. [U.S. drug culture, late 1900s] **4.** the nose. [British and U.S., mid 1900s-pres.]

hooter helper a breast implant. Based on Hamburger Helper™. [U.S., late 1900s-pres.]

hooters the human breasts. [U.S. slang, mid 1900s-pres.]

hoover to perform FELLATIO on someone. Named after the vacuum cleaner brand. [British slang, mid 1900s-pres.]

hoovering an abortion. [U.S., late 1900s-pres.]

Hooverism an act of FELLATIO (*q.v.*). From the brand name of a vacuum cleaner. [U.S., mid 1900s-pres.]

hop opium; any drug or narcotics, including marijuana. [U.S. underworld, early 1900s]

hop-head (also **hop-fiend, hop-hog, hop-merchant**) an opium addict or seller. *Cf.* HAY-HEAD. [U.S. underworld and slang, late 1800s-early 1900s]

hop-joint an opium den. [U.S. underworld, early 1900s or before]

hopped 1. intoxicated with narcotics. Originally intoxicated with opium. Now with any drug, including marijuana. Also **hopped-up.** [U.S. underworld and drug culture, early 1900s-pres.] **2.** intoxicated with alcohol, especially with beer. From sense 1 and the hops in beer.

hopper 1. a drug addict; originally an opium addict. *Cf.* HOP-HEAD. [U.S. drug culture, 1900s or before] **2.** a toilet; the water-flush basin. [British and U.S. colloquial, 1800s-1900s]

hops (also **hop**) opium or any narcotics. [U.S. underworld, early 1900s]

hopster an opium addict. [U.S. underworld, early 1900s or before]

hop-stick 1. an opium pipe. [U.S. underworld, early 1900s or before] **2.** a marijuana cigarette. From sense 1. [U.S. drug culture, mid 1900s-pres.]

hop-stiff a drug addict. *Cf.* HOP-HEAD. For synonyms see JUNKER. [U.S. underworld, 1900s or before]

horizontal intoxicated with alcohol. [slang, 1900s]

horizontal bop (also **horizontal hula, horizontal mambo**) an act of copulation. For synonyms see SMOCKAGE. [U.S. slang, late 1900s]

horizontal rumble copulation. Possibly in error for *horizontal rumba*. See HORIZONTAL BOP. For synonyms see SMOCKAGE. [U.S. collegiate, late 1900s]

hork 1. to steal something. [U.S., late 1900s-pres.] **2.** to vomit. For synonyms see YORK. [U.S., late 1900s-pres.] **3.** to spit. [U.S., late 1900s-pres.]

horkie a dull and witless male. For synonyms see OAF. [U.S., late 1900s-pres.]

hormone fix a sexual encounter; a period of sexual stimulation. [U.S. collegiate, late 1900s, Munro]

horn 1. to become sexually aroused, said of the male or female. **2.** to CUCKOLD (*q.v.*) someone's spouse; to bedeck someone's spouse, usually the husband, with horns. **3.** the penis, especially the erect penis. [all senses, since the 1400s] **4.** to sniff drugs. [U.S. drug culture, mid 1900s-pres.] **5.** damn in "Gol-horn." See GOL.

horn-colic 1. a normal erection. [British slang or colloquial, late 1700s, Grose] **2.** a persistent erection possibly with pain in the testicles. See PRIAPISM (sense 1). [U.S. dialect (Ozarks), Randolph and Wilson]

hornification an erection of the penis; the erecting of a penis. [British, 1800s or before, Farmer and Henley]

hornify 1. to CUCKOLD (*q.v.*). **2.** to cause a penile erection. [both senses, British, 1800s or before]

horniness lust; sexual arousal, particularly after a period of abstinence. *Cf.* HORNY (sense 1). [U.S. slang, 1900s]

horning sexually aroused; having an erection of the penis. [colloquial and slang since the 1800s or before]

Hornington, old the penis, especially the erect penis. *Cf.* MISS HORNER. [British slang, 1800s, Farmer and Henley]

horn-mad 1. with an erect penis. **2.**

extremely lecherous. **3.** enraged at being cockolded. See CUCKOLD. [possibly apocryphal, since the 1500s]

horn movie a sexually oriented film; a pornographic film. *Cf.* HORN, HORNY. [U.S. collegiate, mid 1900s]

horn-pill an aphrodisiac. [1900s or before]

horn of plenty a husband. From HORN (sense 3) and the notion of a husband as a provider. [U.S. slang, 1900s]

horny 1. sexually aroused especially after a long period of abstinence. For synonyms see HUMPY. **2.** pertaining to a person with a lecherous nature. **3.** with an erect penis. [all senses, slang and colloquial, 1800s-pres.] **4.** virile and capable of copulation, said of a male. *Cf.* HAIRY. [U.S. slang, 1900s]

horrors the DELERIUM TREMENS (*q.v.*). *Cf.* BLUE HORRORS. For synonyms see ORK-ORKS. [British and U.S. slang and colloquial, mid 1800s]

hors d'oeuvres Seconal (trademark) capsules. For synonyms see SEC. [U.S. drug culture, mid 1900s-pres.]

horse 1. to MOUNT (*q.v.*) and coit a woman. [British slang, early 1600s-1800s] **2.** as an exclamation, "Horse!" A euphemism for "Horseshit!" A variation of "bullshit." [U.S. slang, mid 1900s] **3.** heroin. A reinterpretation of "H." for heroin. See CABALLO. [U.S. drug culture, mid 1900s-pres.] **4.** a [Trojan brand] condom. For synonyms see EEL-SKIN. [U.S., late 1900s-pres.]

horse and trap 1. a case of gonorrhea. Rhyming slang for CLAP (*q.v.*). [British slang, late 1800s] **2.** dung; to defecate. Rhyming slang for CRAP (*q.v.*). [British slang, 1900s]

horse apple 1. a formed lump of horse dung. Also **horse dumpling.** *Cf.* ALLEY APPLE, ROAD APPLE. [U.S. slang, mid 1900s] **2.** nonsense; BULLSHIT (*q.v.*). *Cf.* horse (sense 2).

horseback intoxicated with alcohol. For synonyms see WOOFLED. [U.S. slang, early 1900s, Weseen]

horsecock 1. an observation balloon. [U.S., World War I, Lighter] **2.** a sau-

sage. From its phallic shape. *Cf.* LIVE SAUSAGE. [U.S. slang, mid 1900s-pres.]

horse collar the female genitals. A visual image based on the resemblance of a horse collar to the *labia majora*. [British slang, 1800s, Farmer and Henley]

horsed under the influence of heroin. From HORSE (sense 3). [U.S. drug culture, mid 1900s-pres.]

horse's ass an idiot; a fool. [U.S. colloquial, 1900s]

horseshit nonsense; an exclamation of disbelief, a variation of BULLSHIT (*q.v.*). [U.S. slang, 1900s]

horse-shoe the female genitals. *Cf.* HORSE COLLAR. [British, 1800s or before, Farmer and Henley]

horse's hoof a homosexual male. Rhyming slang for POOF (*q.v.*). For synonyms see EPICENE. [British, early 1900s, *Dictionary of Slang and Unconventional English*]

horsh nonsense; a disguise of "horseshit," which is a variant of BULLSHIT (*q.v.*). A blend of "horse" and "shit." [U.S. slang, 1900s]

hose 1. the penis. **2.** to coit a woman; to PHALLICIZE (*q.v.*). **3.** copulation. **4.** to cheat or deceive. [all senses, U.S. slang, early 1900s-pres.] **5.** a sexually loose woman. For synonyms see TAIL. [U.S. slang, late 1900s] **6.** to kill someone, as with a spray of machine gun bullets. [U.S. military and underworld, late 1900s]

hosebag a sexually free and willing female. *Cf.* HOSE. For synonyms see TAIL. [U.S. collegiate, late 1900s, Eble]

hose monster a sexually active woman; a nymphomaniac. For synonyms see TAIL. [U.S. collegiate, late 1900s]

hoser 1. a promiscuous person, often a male. [U.S. slang, late 1900s] **2.** a despised person, often a male. For synonyms see SNOKE-HORN. [U.S. collegiate, late 1900s, Munro]

hosing 1. copulation; an act of copulation from the male point of view. **2.** a cheating; a deception. *Cf.* SCREW (sense 6). [both senses, U.S. slang, 1900s]

hot 1. sexually aroused; lustful; in heat. Cf. ARD. For synonyms see HUMPY. [since the 1500s] **2.** infected with a venereal disease. [colloquial, 1800s-1900s] **3.** intoxicated with alcohol. [U.S. colloquial, 1800s-1900s]

hot air 1. nonsense. **2.** gas from the intestines. Cf. GAS (sense 1). [both senses, colloquial, early 1900s-pres.]

hot and bothered lustful; HORNY (q.v.). See HOT (sense 1). [U.S. slang and colloquial, 1900s or before]

hot and cold heroin and cocaine. Cf. H. AND C. [U.S. drug culture, mid 1900s-pres.] See the following for other drug mixtures: BAM, C. AND H., C. AND M., G.B., H.M.C., M AND C., PEACE PILL, POT-LIQUOR, SET, SPANSULA, SPEEDBALL, WHIZ-BANG.

hot as a red wagon intoxicated with alcohol. [U.S. slang, mid 1900s]

hot-assed sexually aroused. Usually said of a woman. [U.S. slang, late 1900s]

hotcakes crack cocaine. For synonyms see NOSE-CANDY. [U.S., late 1900s-pres.]

hot in the biscuit sexually stimulated; ready to copulate. Cf. BISCUIT, BUN. [U.S. underworld, early 1900s, Goldin, O'Leary, and Lipsius]

hot lay 1. a sexually loose woman. **2.** a passionate act of copulation. [both senses, U.S. slang, early 1900s, Monteleone]

hot meat (also **hot beef, hot mutton**) **1.** a prostitute. **2.** the female genitals. From MEAT (sense 1). [slang since the 1800s] **3.** an expanse of exposed female flesh. [U.S. slang, mid 1900s]

hot member a lascivious man or woman. See HOT NUMBER. MEMBER (sense 1) may have phallic references. [British and U.S., 1800s-1900s]

hot milk semen. Cf. CREAM (sense 1). For synonyms see METTLE. [British slang, 1800s, Farmer and Henley]

hot number a passionate and accessible woman. Possibly refers to her telephone number. From the merchandising

term for an item in great demand. [U.S. slang, mid 1900s-pres.]

hot nuts 1. a nickname for a lascivious man. [U.S. slang, early 1900s-pres.] **2.** testalgia. See HOT ROCKS (sense 2).

hot pants 1. HORNINESS (q.v.); sexual arousal. Cf. ITCHY PANTS. **2.** lust. **3.** the same as HOT NUTS (q.v.); a lecher. **4.** a sexually desirable girl or woman. [all senses, U.S. slang, early 1900s-pres.]

hot rocks 1. a prostitute. [U.S. slang, mid 1900s] **2.** testalgia, pain in the testicles. [U.S. slang and colloquial, mid 1900s-pres.]

hot-rod 1. the penis. **2.** to masturbate. [both senses, U.S. slang, mid 1900s-pres.]

hot roll with cream copulation. HOT (sense 1) is "lustful," ROLL (q.v.) is "copulation," and CREAM (sense 1) is "semen." Cf. BANANAS AND CREAM. [British, 1800s, *Dictionary of Slang and Unconventional English*]

hots, the sexual desire with a special person as its target. Cf. HEAT, IN: HEAT, ON. [U.S. slang, mid 1900s-pres.]

hot shit an arrogant male; a man who thinks he is very important. In expressions such as "he really thinks he's hot shit." [U.S. slang, mid 1900s-pres.]

hot-stick a marijuana cigarette. Cf. HOP-STICK, STICK OF TEA. For synonyms see MEZZROLL. [U.S. drug culture, mid 1900s]

hot stuff 1. a sexually attractive and obliging girl or woman. **2.** the same as HOT SHIT (q.v.); an arrogant male. [both senses, U.S. slang, 1900s]

hot-tailed sexually aroused or eager. For synonyms see HUMPY. [mid 1900spres.]

hottie a sexually attractive female. For synonyms see BIRD. [British and U.S., mid 1900s-pres.]

hot-tongue 1. to kiss passionately and sensually using the tongue. [U.S. slang, early 1900s-pres.] **2.** a sexually aroused woman. A possible reference to PENILINGUS (q.v.). [U.S. slang, early 1900s-pres.]

hot to trot eager for sex. [U.S. slang, mid 1900s-pres.]

hound 1. to COIT a woman. For synonyms see OCCUPY. [U.S. collegiate, late 1900s, Munro] **2.** a lecher. For synonyms see LECHER. [U.S. collegiate, late 1900s, Eble]

house a brothel. [British and U.S., 1800s-1900s] Most of the following brothels retain female prostitutes. Those supplying males for sodomy are so indicated: ACCOMMODATION HOUSE, ASSIGNATION HOUSE, BAND-HOUSE, BAT HOUSE, BAWD'S HOUSE, BAWDYHOUSE, BEDHOUSE, BROTHEL-HOUSE, CALL-HOUSE, CAN HOUSE, CAT-HOUSE, CHIPPY-HOUSE, COUPLING-HOUSE, CRIB-HOUSE, DISORDERLY HOUSE, DOSS HOUSE, DRESS-HOUSE, FANCY HOUSE, FAST HOUSE, FLASH-HOUSE, FRANZY HOUSE, GARDEN-HOUSE, GAY HOUSE, GOAT-HOUSE, GRINDING-HOUSE, HOT-HOUSE, HOUSE IN THE SUBURBS, HOUSE OF ALL NATIONS, HOUSE OF ASSIGNATION, HOUSE OF CALL, HOUSE OF CIVIL RECEPTION, HOUSE OF ENJOYMENT, HOUSE OF ILL-DELIGHT, HOUSE OF ILL-FAME, HOUSE OF ILL-REPUTE, HOUSE OF JOY, HOUSE OF LEWDNESS, HOUSE OF PROFESSION, HOUSE OF RESORT, HOUSE OF SALE, JAG-HOUSE (male), JOY HOUSE, JUKE-HOUSE, KNOCKING-HOUSE, LEAPING-HOUSE, LEWD HOUSE, MEAT HOUSE, MOLLY-HOUSE (male), MONKEY-HOUSE, NANNY-HOUSE, NAUGHTY-HOUSE, NOTCH-HOUSE, NUGGING-HOUSE, OCCUPYING-HOUSE, ONERY-HOUSE, PARLOR HOUSE, PEG-HOUSE (male), PUNCH-HOUSE, RED-LIGHT HOUSE, SLAUGH-TER-HOUSE, SPORTING-HOUSE, VAULT-ING-HOUSE, WHOREHOUSE. See a full list at BROTHEL.

house ape a small child. [U.S., late 1900s-pres.]

housed alcohol intoxicated. Probably short for *shit-housed,* akin to SHIT-FACED. For synonyms see WOOFLED. [U.S. collegiate, late 1900s]

house of many doors a prison. [U.S. slang, late 1900s]

house under the hill the female genitals. The "hill" is the mons veneris. [British slang, 1800s, Farmer and Henley]

How're they hanging? an inquiry calling for a report of the state of a male's testicles, essentially a greeting to another male. [U.S. slang, mid 1900s-pres.]

How's it hanging? an inquiry calling for a report of the state of a male's penis, essentially a greeting to another male. [U.S. slang, mid 1900s-pres.]

How's your hammer hangin'? an inquiry into the state of a male's penis meaning essentially, "How are you?" [British and U.S., late 1900s-pres.]

hubbas CRACK cocaine. For synonyms see NOSE-CANDY. [U.S. drug culture, late 1900s]

hucklefuck a country yokel. For synonyms see OAF. [U.S., late 1900s-pres.]

huddle to hug or embrace a woman; possibly to coit a woman. [British, 1700s]

huevos testicles. Spanish for eggs. For synonyms see WHIRLYGIGS. [U.S., late 1900s-pres.]

huffle to coit a woman. [British, 1800s or before]

hug 1. to embrace a woman; possibly to coit a woman. [since the 1600s] **2.** to garrot a person. [British, mid 1800s]

hughie to vomit. See CRY HUGHIE.

hugsome cuddlesome; sexually attractive, said of a woman. [British, 1800s, Farmer and Henley]

hug the porcelain god to vomit; to vomit while holding on to the toilet seat. *Cf.* KISS THE PORCELAIN GOD. For synonyms see YORK. [U.S. slang, late 1900s]

hug the porcelain goddess to vomit; to vomit while holding on to the toilet seat. For synonyms see YORK. [U.S. slang, late 1900s]

hug the throne to vomit; to vomit while holding onto the toilet seat. For synonyms see YORK. [U.S. collegiate, late 1900s, Eble]

humbug 1. anything false or deceptive. **2.** nonsense. [both senses since the 1700s]

hum-job a type of oral sexual intercourse where sensation is created by placing a part of the body in the mouth and humming. Usually performed on the male genitals. [U.S. slang, mid 1900s-pres.]

humming (also **hummin'**) drug intoxicated. For synonyms see TALL. [U.S. drug culture, late 1900s, Kaiser]

hump 1. to carry a person or a load on one's back. No negative connotations. [attested as Australian, mid 1800s-pres.] **2.** any difficulty; a problem. No negative connotations. **3.** to thrust the pelvis in the manner of a male copulating; to copulate from the male point of view. From the repeated arching or "humping" of the back. [since the mid 1700s] **4.** to copulate, said of either a man or a woman. [since the 1700s] **5.** copulation; an act of copulation. For synonyms see SMOCKAGE. [U.S. slang, mid 1900s-pres.] **6.** a prostitute; a sexually loose woman; women considered sexually. [U.S. slang, mid 1900s-pres.] **7.** a CATAMITE (q.v.). For synonyms see BRONCO. [U.S. underworld, mid 1900s, Goldin, O'Leary, and Lipsius] **8.** to cheat; to SCREW (sense 6). [U.S. underworld, mid 1900s, Goldin, O'Leary, and Lipsius]

humpery copulation. [U.S. slang or nonce, mid 1900s-pres.]

humpy sexually desirable; sexually aroused. [U.S. slang, mid 1900s-pres.] Synonyms and related terms: ACCENSUS LIBIDINE, AFFY, AMATIVE, AMOROUS, APPETENT, BE BLOTTY, BE MUSTARD, BE ON BLOB, BONE-ON, BRIMMING, BULLING, CAGEY, CHUCKED, COCK-HAPPY, COCKISH, CONCUPISCENT, CONSTITUTIONALLY INCLINED TO GALLANTRY, DRIPPING FOR IT (female), FEEL FUZZY, FEEL GAY, FEEL HAIRY, FLAVOUR, FRISKY, FUCKISH, FULL OF FUCK, FULL OF GISM, FULL-ON, GAGGING FOR IT, GAMY, HAIRY, HAVE AN ITCH IN THE BELLY, HAVE HOT PANTS (FOR SOMEONE), HET-UP, HORNING, HORNMAD, HORNY, HOT, HOT AND BOTHERED, HOT-ASSED (female), HOT-BLOODED, HOT IN THE BISCUIT, HOT-TAILED, HUNKY, IN SEASON, IN THE MOOD, ITCHY PANTS, JUICY, LICKERISH, LIQUOROUS, LUST-PROUD, MANISH, MARIS APPENTENS (female), MASHED, METTLED, ON, ONCOMING, ON FOR ONE'S GREENS, OOMPHY, OPEN FLY, PEAS IN THE POT, RIME, PROUD, PROUD BELOW THE NAVEL, PRUNEY, PRURIENT, PURSE-PROUD, RAMMISH, RAMMY, RAMSTUDIOUS, RANDY, RANTING, RED-COMB, ROLLICKY, ROOTY, RUSTY, RUTTISH, SALT, SEXED-UP, TICKLE, TOUCHABLE, TUMBLING-RIPE, TURNED-ON, WET (female), WHISK-TELT.

hunch to copulate. For synonyms see OCCUPY. [U.S., late 1900s-pres.]

hung 1. pertaining to a male with large to very large genitals; pertaining to an older male from the point of view of a younger, immature male. A truncation of WELL-HUNG (q.v.). [widespread colloquial, 1600s-pres.] **2.** a physically WELL-ENDOWED (q.v.) male or female. In the male, either a well-built body or large genitals or both. In the female, a well-built body and large, well-proportioned breasts. A reinterpretation of or a misunderstanding of sense. [U.S. slang, mid 1900s] **3.** a truncation of "hung-over." A mischievous reinterpretation of sense. [U.S. slang, mid 1900s]

hung like a bull pertaining to a male with very large genitals. *Cf.* HUNG (sense 1), WELL-HUNG. [U.S. homosexual use, mid 1900s]

hung like a chicken pertaining to a male with small genitals, possibly having the genitals of an adolescent boy; having virtually no VIRILIA (q.v.) at all. See CHICKEN (sense 2).

hung like a donkey equipped with a large penis. [British and U.S., mid 1900s-pres.]

hung like a horse well endowed with [male] genitals; HUNG LIKE A BULL. [British slang, 1900s, J. Green]

hung like a Tic Tac having a very small penis. [U.S., late 1900s-pres.]

hunk 1. a sexually attractive male or female. [U.S. slang and colloquial, 1900s] **2.** an act of copulation. [U.S. slang, mid 1900s] **3.** a Caucasian. A truncation of HUNKIE or BOHUNK (both q.v.). See HONKY. [U.S. slang, mid 1900s] **4.** a large man; a "hunk of man," not necessarily in a sexual sense. [U.S. colloquial, mid 1900s-pres.]

hunkers the buttocks. For synonyms

see DUFF. [U.S. colloquial, 1900s or before]

hunkie 1. a derogatory nickname for a Hungarian. [U.S. slang, 1900s] **2.** a Caucasian. See HONKY.

hunk of meat 1. a sexually attractive adult person. **2.** the penis. [both senses, U.S. slang, mid 1900s-pres.]

hunk of tail (also **hunk of ass, hunk of butt, hunk of skirt**) copulation; a woman considered sexually. *Cf.* HUNK (sense 2). [U.S. slang, 1900s]

hunky 1. sexually aroused; the same as HORNY (*q.v.*). [U.S. slang, mid 1900s-pres.] **2.** a derogatory nickname for a Hungarian. Also **hunkie.** [U.S. slang and colloquial, 1900s] **3.** an oaf; a dolt. From sense 2. See HONKY. [U.S. slang, early 1900s] **4.** a Caucasian. See HONKY. From sense 2.

hurl to vomit. For synonyms see YORK. [Australian, British, and U.S., late 1900s-pres.]

hurt See HURTING.

hurting (also **hurtin'**) **1.** seriously in need of a dose of drugs; beginning to suffer from drug withdrawal. [U.S. drug culture, late 1900s] **2.** alcohol intoxicated. For synonyms see WOOFLED. [U.S. collegiate, late 1900s, Eble] **3.** (also **hurt**) very ugly. [U.S. black use, late 1900s]

husk to get naked; to remove one's clothes. Compare to SHUCK. [U.S. slang, 1900s]

husker a masturbator. In reference to the action of husking corn. [U.S. dialect

(Boontling), late 1800s-early 1900s, Charles Adams] The following synonyms usually refer to males unless noted otherwise: CANDLE-BASHER (female), CHICKEN-CHOKER, DIDDLER, DOODLE-DASHER, FRIGSTER, FRIGSTRESS (female), FUCK-FINGER (female), FUCK-FIST, JACKER, JAG-OFF, JERK, JERK-OFF, MILKER, MILKMAN, MILK-WOMAN (female), ONANIST, PUSH-PUDDING, WHANKER.

hustle 1. to copulate. [U.S. slang, early 1800s-1900s] **2.** to work as a prostitute. [U.S. underworld, early 1900s-pres.] **3.** to gamble as a profession. [U.S. slang, 1900s] **4.** to steal. [U.S. slang, early 1900s-pres.] **5.** to sell drugs. [U.S. slang and drug culture, mid 1900s-pres.]

hustler 1. a female prostitute. For synonyms see HARLOT. [U.S. slang, early 1900s-pres.] **2.** a homosexual male prostitute. [U.S. slang, mid 1900s-pres.] **3.** a pimp. [U.S. slang, mid 1900s-pres.] **4.** any thief or con man. [U.S. underworld and slang, 1900s] **5.** a sexually successful male. One who can SCORE (*q.v.*) easily. [U.S. slang, mid 1900s-pres.]

hydro(ponic) hydroponically grown marijuana. For synonyms see MARI. [U.S., late 1900s-pres.]

hymenally challenged a virgin. [U.S., late 1900s-pres.]

hype 1. a drug addict, especially a heroin addict. [U.S. underworld and drug culture, 1900s] **2.** under the influence of narcotics. From HYP (*q.v.*) or "hyperactive."

hyped under the influence of narcotics. From HYP (*q.v.*) or "hyperactive." [U.S. drug culture, mid 1900s-pres.]

I

I. and I. 'intoxication and intercourse,' a play on *R. and R.* = "rest and recuperation." [U.S. military, mid 1900s-pres., *Soldier Talk*]

ice-boxed 1. sexually rejected by a woman. [U.S. slang, 1900s] **2.** pertaining to a man who cannot copulate because his sexual partner is menstruating. Also a play on BOX (sense 2), "vagina." [U.S. slang, 1900s]

ice-cream opium. For synonyms see OPE. [U.S. drug culture, early 1900s-pres.]

icer a smoking device for increasing the potency of marijuana. [U.S. drug culture, late 1900s, Kaiser]

ice wagon a frigid woman. *Cf.* ICE-BERG (sense 1). [U.S. slang, early 1900s, Monteleone]

icicles pure cocaine in its crystallized form. For synonyms see NOSE-CANDY. [U.S. drug culture, late 1900s, Kaiser]

idiot pills barbiturate tablets or capsules. For synonyms see BARB. [U.S. drug culture, mid 1900s-pres.]

If that don't fuck all! an exclamation of surprise and amazement. [U.S. slang, mid 1900s-pres.]

If you can't use it, abuse it! a citizens band radio sign-off expression meaning "If you can't copulate, masturbate!" [U.S. slang, mid 1900s-pres.]

Illinois green a type of marijuana. *Cf.* CHICAGO GREEN. For synonyms see MARI. [U.S. drug culture, mid 1900s-pres.]

ill-piece an unattractive male homosexual. [U.S. homosexual use, mid 1900s, Stanley]

illuminated intoxicated with alcohol. An elaboration of LIT (*q.v.*). [U.S. slang, 1900s or before]

IMBARS BIDBIB "I may be a rotten sod, but I don't believe in bullshit."

Cf. DILLIGAF for length and complexity. [British, early 1900s, *Dictionary of Slang and Unconventional English*]

IMFU an immense military blunder, an "imperial military fuck-up." For synonyms see SNAFU. [World War II]

im-fucking-possible totally impossible. [U.S. slang, late 1900s]

impaired physician a physician addicted to alcohol, drugs, or both. [U.S. euphemism, late 1900s]

impudent impotent. An error, jocular or otherwise. [British, early 1600s] Synonyms and related terms: ANANDRIOUS, ANAPHRODISIA, APANDRY, ASTYSIA, ASYNODIA, IMPOTENT, IMPOTENTIA, IMPOTENTIA COEUNDI, IMPOTENTIA ERIGENDI, IMPROCREANT, NO MONEY IN HIS PURSE, ORGIASTIC IMPOTENCE.

impure a prostitute. *Cf.* PURE. [British, late 1700s or early 1800s]

Inca message cocaine. Alludes to Peru, the home of the Incas and the site of cocaine growth and use. For synonyms see NOSE-CANDY. [U.S. collegiate, late 1900s]

incentive cocaine. *Cf.* INITIATIVE. For synonyms see NOSE-CANDY. [U.S. drug culture, late 1900s]

inch boy a male with a small penis. [U.S., late 1900s-pres.]

incident a bastard. *Cf.* ACCIDENT (sense 1). [U.S. colloquial, 1900s]

in-cog intoxicated with alcohol. From "incognito." [British slang, early 1800s, Jon Bee]

inde-goddamn-pendent very independent. [U.S. slang, mid 1900s-pres.]

India the female genitals. For synonyms see MONOSYLLABLE. [British, early 1600s]

Indian hay Indian marijuana; *Cannabis indica*. [U.S. drug culture, 1900s]

Indian hemp marijuana; one of the common names for *Cannabis indica*. *Cf.* INDIAN HAY. For synonyms see MARI. [U.S. underworld and drug culture, early 1900s-pres.]

Indian oil an alcohol extract of *Cannabis sativa*. For synonyms see OIL. [U.S. drug culture, mid 1900s-pres.]

indoor plumbing a bathroom or W.C. as opposed to a privy. *Cf.* OUTDOOR PLUMBING. [U.S. colloquial, early 1900s-pres.]

indorse 1. to commit PEDERASTY (*q.v.*); to commit sadistic acts. Literally "to be behind" someone. Synonyms: COMMIT PEDERASTY, CORN HOLE, GET HUNK, HAVE A BIT OF NAVY CAKE, INGLE, NAVIGATE THE WINDWARD PASSAGE, RIDE THE DECK, SHOOT IN THE TAIL, SNAG, SOD. **2.** to masturbate. Possibly a misunderstanding of sense 1. For synonyms see WASTE TIME. [both senses, British, late 1700s]

indorser 1. a SODOMITE (*q.v.*). [British, late 1700s, Grose] **2.** a sadist; one who flogs the back of another. *Cf.* INDORSE (sense 1). [U.S. underworld, early 1900s, Monteleone]

ineffable 1. the female genitals, specifically the vagina. Literally, "the inexpressible." *Cf.* NAME-IT-NOT, NAMELESS. [British, 1800s] **2.** in the plural, trousers. For synonyms see GALLIGASKINS. [British, mid 1800s]

ingle-nook the female genitals. *Cf.* NOOKER, NOOKY. [British slang, 1800s, Farmer and Henley]

ingler a PEDERAST (*q.v.*). See INGLE. [late 1500s, Florio]

inhale someone's tool to perform fellatio. [U.S., late 1900s-pres.]

initiative cocaine. *Cf.* INCENTIVE. For synonyms see NOSE-CANDY. [U.S. drug culture, late 1900s]

inkypoo intoxicated with alcohol. *Cf.* INKY. [Australian, Baker]

inner itch a craving for drugs. [U.S., late 1900s-pres.]

inside out drunk. For synonyms see WOOFLED. [U.S. slang, late 1900s]

inspector of manholes a male homosexual. For synonyms see PEDER-

AST. [British and U.S., early 1900s-pres.]

inspired intoxicated with alcohol. For synonyms see WOOFLED. [British, 1800s, Farmer and Henley]

instant Zen the drug L.S.D. (*q.v.*). [U.S. drug culture, mid 1900s-pres.]

instrument the penis. *Cf.* GAYING INSTRUMENT, TOOL (sense 1). [British and U.S. euphemism, early 1600s-1900s]

intercourse 1. copulation. Originally "communication and commerce" (late 1400s). A truncation of SEXUAL INTERCOURSE (*q.v.*). [since the late 1700s] **2.** to copulate. A contrived transitive and intransitive verb used as euphemistic jargon and avoidance, *e.g.*, "Intercoursing makes me tired" or "Intercourse you!" [U.S., mid 1900s-pres.]

interesting condition, in an (also **interesting situation, in an**) pregnant. [colloquial, mid 1700s-1900s]

interior decorating copulating; ejaculating into a vagina during copulation. For synonyms see SMOCKAGE. [British and U.S. word play or nonce, 1900s]

internal a drug smuggler who swallows numerous small, rubber packages of a powdered drug. [U.S. drug culture and drug smuggling, late 1900s]

internut someone addicted to the Internet. [U.S., late 1900s-pres.]

in the nick naked. For synonyms see STARKERS. [Australian, mid 1900s-pres.]

in the nuddy naked. For synonyms see STARKERS. [Australian and British, mid 1900s-pres.]

in the poo in trouble. [Australian, mid 1900s-pres.]

in the rude naked. For synonyms see STARKERS. [British, late 1900s-pres.]

into, be 1. to be copulating with a woman. *Cf.* GET INTO. [British and U.S., 1800s-pres.] **2.** to be interested in or involved in something. No negative connotations. [U.S. general slang, mid 1900s-pres.]

intoxed intoxicated with marijuana. For synonyms see TALL. [U.S. drug culture, mid 1900s-pres.]

I.O.F.B. "I only fire blanks," a catch

phrase attributed to a sterile man or a man trying desperately to persuade a woman to copulate.

irre-fucking-sponsible extremely irresponsible. *Cf.* ABSO-FUCKING-LUTELY, IM-FUCKING-POSSIBLE.

irrigated intoxicated with alcohol. [U.S. slang, mid 1800s-1900s]

ishkimmisk intoxicated with alcohol. *Cf.* SKIMISHED. [British, 1800s]

it 1. a CHAMBER POT (*q.v.*). [British, 1800s, Farmer and Henley] **2.** the female genitals. [very old euphemism] **3.** the penis. [very old euphemism] **4.** sex appeal; the ability to sexually stimulate persons of the opposite sex, *i.e.,* turn them on. [U.S., 1900s] **5.** copulation. [widespread avoidance; very old euphemism]

it, in for pregnant. For synonyms see FRAGRANT. [British and U.S. slang, 1900s]

itcher the female genitals, specifically the vagina. *Cf.* ITCHING JENNY. [British slang, 1800s, Farmer and Henley]

itching jenny the female genitals, specifically the vagina. *Cf.* ITCHER. [British slang, 1800s, Farmer and Henley]

itchy eye a case of hemorrhoids. [British, late 1900s-pres.]

itchy pants sexual arousal in expressions such as "have itchy pants." *Cf.* HOT PANTS (sense 1). [U.S. slang, mid 1900s]

it-shay dung; a curse; an oaf or a fool. Pig Latin for "shit." [U.S., 1900s]

ivory-carpenter a dentist. [British slang, 1800s, Farmer and Henley] Synonyms: FANG-CARPENTER, FANG-FAKER, FANG-FARRIER, GUMDIGGER, GUM-PUNCHER, SNAG-CATCHER, SNAG-FENCER, TOOTH-CARPENTER, TOOTH-DOCTOR.

J

J. 1. a marijuana cigarette. From JOINT. (sense 2). [U.S. drug culture, mid 1900s-pres.] **2.** a fool; an oaf. From JAY (sense 1). [British, 1800s]

JAAFU "joint Anglo-American fuck-up," a confused situation caused by American and British military personnel. For synonyms see SNAFU. [World War II]

jab 1. to COIT a female. For synonyms see OCCUPY. [U.S. slang, late 1900s if not before] **2.** an act of copulation, especially if quick. From the male point of view. For synonyms see SMOCKAGE. [U.S. slang, late 1900s if not before]

JACFU "joint American-Chinese fuck-up," a confused situation caused by American military personnel. For synonyms see SNAFU. [World War II]

jack 1. the penis, especially when erect. [British, 1800s] **2.** to copulate. [British slang, 1800s, Farmer and Henley] **3.** a derogatory term for a black man. Possibly from "jackass." See MOKE. [U.S., 1900s] **4.** a prostitute's customer. *Cf.* JOHN.

jackal to masturbate. For synonyms see WASTE TIME. [British, late 1900s-pres.]

Jack and Danny the female genitals. Rhyming slang for FANNY=the vulva and vagina. For synonyms see GENITALS, MONOSYLLABLE. [British, late 1900s-pres.]

jack around to waste time, act childish, or be ineffective, usually said of males. A blend of JACK OFF and PLAY AROUND (both *q.v.*). [U.S. slang and colloquial, mid 1900s-pres.]

jackass 1. an ass; a donkey. Because of "ass," this word is often avoided in the U.S. **2.** a dolt; an oaf. [both senses, British and U.S. colloquial, 1800s-pres.]

Jack Dancer cancer. Rhyming slang. [Australian, mid 1900s-pres.]

jacked intoxicated on a drug; HIGH. As if jacked up "HIGH." For synonyms see TALL. [U.S. collegiate, late 1900s]

jacked it dead; died. For synonyms see DONE FOR. [British slang, late 1800s, Ware]

jacker 1. a male who masturbates frequently. **2.** a derogatory term for a male. *Cf.* JACK OFF. [U.S. dialect (Boontling), late 1800s-early 1900s, Charles Adams]

jack-in-the-box 1. an unborn child in the womb. [British colloquial, 1800s, Farmer and Henley] **2.** the penis. The BOX (sense 2) is the vagina. [British slang, 1800s, Farmer and Henley] **3.** syphilis. Rhyming slang for "pox." [British, late 1800s]

jack nasty-face the female genitals. [British, early 1800s]

jack off 1. to masturbate oneself or another, said of males. From "ejaculate" or JACK (sense 1). *Cf.* JAG OFF. **2.** to waste time; to goof off. **3.** a jerk or incompetent oaf. Usually hyphenated in this sense. *Cf.* JACKER. [all senses, U.S. slang, 1900s and before]

jacks dollars. [U.S., late 1900s-pres.]

jack shit 1. a worthless good-for-nothing. Occasionally capitalized in this sense. **2.** nonsense. **3.** any worthless bit of nothing; a damn; a farthing, as in the phrase "not worth jack shit."

Jacque's 1. a privy. See JAKES for more recent forms. [early 1500s] **2.** the penis. See JAQUES.

jade a rough and contemptible girl or woman; a MINX (*q.v.*). [since the mid 1500s]

jaded jenny (also **cock-eyed jenny**) a prostitute. *Cf.* ITCHING JENNY. For synonyms see HARLOT. [U.S. slang, 1900s, Berrey and Van den Bark]

jadja marijuana. For synonyms see MARI. [U.S. drug culture, late 1900s, Lewin and Lewin]

jag a loser. From JAG OFF. [U.S., late 1900s-pres.]

jag off 1. to masturbate. *Cf.* JACK OFF. See JAG (sense 4). **2.** an incompetent time-waster; a jack-off. Usually hyphenated when written as a noun. [U.S., mid 1900s-pres.]

jagster someone on a drinking spree; a heavy drinker. [U.S., late 1900s-pres.]

jail bait a sexually attractive or flirtatious girl who has not reached the age of consent. *Cf.* BAIT, SAN QUENTIN JAIL-BAIT. [U.S. slang, 1900s]

jake 1. a toilet or W.C., usually for men. From JAKES (*q.v.*). [U.S. colloquial, 1900s or before] **2.** an oaf; a bumpkin. Also **country jake.** [U.S. slang, 1900s]

jam 1. the female genitals. For synonyms see MONOSYLLABLE. [British and U.S. slang, 1800s-1900s] **2.** semen. *Cf.* JELLY (sense 3). [British slang, 1800s, Farmer and Henley] **3.** a pretty young woman. Not necessarily with any sexual connotation. [British slang, mid 1800s, Ware] **4.** pertaining to a nonhomosexual or straight person. [U.S. homosexual use, mid 1900s] **5.** cocaine. [U.S. drug culture, mid 1900s-pres.]

jambled intoxicated with alcohol. For synonyms see WOOFLED. [U.S. slang, early 1700s, Ben Franklin]

jamboree bags, the the female breasts. For synonyms see BOSOM. [British, late 1900s-pres.]

James Earl dog a marijuana cigarette. *Cf.* HOOCH DOG, JIMMY DOG. For synonyms see MEZZROLL. [U.S. collegiate, late 1900s, Eble]

jam-house a house or other place where cocaine is sold and used; a COKE-HOUSE. *Cf.* JAM. For synonyms see NOSE-CANDY. [U.S. drug culture, 1900s]

jammed 1. arrested. [U.S. mid 1900s-pres.] **2.** alcohol intoxicated. For synonyms see WOOFLED. [U.S., late 1900s-pres.] **3.** upset; annoyed. [U.S., late 1900s-pres.]

jammed up full of food or drink. [U.S., late 1900s-pres.]

jammy the penis. For synonyms see YARD. [British and U.S., late 1900s-pres.]

jamoke a victim; a loser. [U.S., late 1900s-pres.]

jam-pot the female genitals. [British, 1800s]

jam-tart 1. one's girlfriend or lover; a mistress. *Cf.* JAM (sense 1), TART. [British, 1800s] **2.** an anal release of intestinal gas. Rhyming slang on FART. For synonyms see GURK. [British, early 1900s-pres.]

Jane a women's restroom; the same as RUTH (*q.v.*). *Cf.* JOHN (sense 1). [U.S. slang, 1900s]

Jane Shore a prostitute. Rhyming slang for "whore." [British, 1800s-1900s, *Dictionary of Rhyming Slang*]

JANFU "joint army-navy-fuck-up," a colossal military blunder with contributions from the Army and the Navy. For synonyms see SNAFU. [U.S. slang, World War II, mid 1900s]

jang the penis. A spelling variant of YANG (*q.v.*). For synonyms see YARD. [U.S. slang, mid 1900s-pres.]

janney to copulate. Possibly from railroad jargon meaning "to couple." [U.S., 1900s, Wentworth and Flexner]

jap's eye the hole at end of penis; the urinary meatus. [British, late 1900s-pres.]

Jaques 1. the penis. [French for the "John" of JOHN THOMAS (*q.v.*); British, 1800s-1900s] **2.** a privy. See JACQUE'S, JAKES.

J. Arthur (Rank) an act of masturbation. Rhyming slang for WHANK = masturbate. For synonyms see WASTE TIME. [British, mid 1900s-pres.]

jay 1. an oaf or a rascal; a frivolous person. See POPINJAY. For synonyms see OAF. [since the late 1500s] **2.** marijuana or a marijuana cigarette. A respelling of the "J" of JOINT (sense 2). [U.S. drug culture, mid 1900s-pres.]

jazz 1. an act of copulation or copulation in general. **2.** to coit a woman. **3.** women considered solely as sexual objects. **4.** the female genitals. **5.** semen. See JIZZ. [all senses, U.S. underworld and later slang; always related to the Negro in America and often etymologized as having an African origin; the first written attestations were in the early 1900s]

jazzed-up (also **jazzed**) intoxicated with alcohol. For synonyms see WOOFLED. [U.S. slang, early 1900s]

jazz it to copulate. *Cf.* JAZZ. [U.S. slang, early 1900s]

jazz joint a house of prostitution. For synonyms see BROTHEL. [U.S., late 1900s-pres.]

jazz mag a pornographic or girlie magazine. [British, late 1900s-pres.]

jazz oneself to masturbate. See JAZZ. [U.S. slang, 1900s]

jazz out to overdose on a drug. [U.S. drug culture, late 1900s]

jazz up to impregnate a woman. [U.S. slang, early 1900s]

J.B. a Negro. From "jet black." Derogatory. See JAYBEE.

J-Bo a marijuana cigarette. *Cf.* J.= joint. For synonyms see MEZZROLL. [U.S. drug culture, late 1900s, Eble]

jean queen 1. a homosexual male who is particularly attracted to males in denim jeans. **2.** a homosexual male who habitually wears denim jeans. See QUEEN for similar terms. [both senses, U.S. homosexual use, mid 1900s]

jeans at half-mast (also **pants at half-mast**) a catch phrase implying that someone has been caught serving as a CATAMITE (*q.v.*). Extended to mean "caught in the act," an elaboration of CAUGHT WITH ONE'S PANTS DOWN (*q.v.*). Based on "flag at half-mast." [U.S. underworld slang, early 1900s, Goldin, O'Leary, and Lipsius]

jeep to copulate in the backseat of a car, especially a jeep. For synonyms see OCCUPY. [U.S., late 1900s-pres.]

jeff a Caucasian. Not necessarily derogatory. For synonyms see PECKERWOOD. [U.S. Negro use, mid 1900s-pres.]

Jefferson airplane a device used to hold the stub of a marijuana cigarette.

Cf. ROACH CLIP. [U.S. drug culture, mid 1900s-pres.]

jelly 1. an attractive, buxom girl. *Cf.* JAM (sense 3), JELLY-ON-SPRINGS. [British slang, early 1800s] **2.** the female genitals. *Cf.* JAM (sense 1), JAM-POT, JELLY-ROLL (sense 1). [U.S. slang, 1900s] **3.** semen. *Cf.* JAM (sense 2). For synonyms see METTLE. [since the early 1600s] **4.** a type of vaginal contraceptive; a vaginal contraceptive jelly. [U.S., mid 1900s-pres.]

jelly baby an amphetamine tablet or capsule. Usually in the plural. See JELLY BEAN. For synonyms see AMP. [U.S. drug culture, mid 1900s]

jelly bag 1. the female genitals. A container for JELLY (sense 3), "semen." *Cf.* JAM-POT. [British, 1600s] **2.** the scrotum. See JELLY (sense 3). From the name of the cloth bag through which jelly is strained. [British, 1800s or before, Farmer and Henley]

jelly bean an amphetamine tablet or capsule. Usually in the plural. [U.S. drug culture, mid 1900s]

jellyfish a timid and ineffectual person. [British, mid 1900s-pres.]

jelly-on-springs a catch phrase describing large, bouncing or quivering female breasts or buttocks. [U.S. slang, 1900s]

jelly-roll 1. the female genitals. **2.** a sexual lover. **3.** a soiled sanitary napkin. [all senses, U.S. slang, 1900s]

jelly sandwich a used sanitary napkin. See JELLY-ROLL. [U.S. black use, 1900s]

jemmison (also **jemsom**) the penis. [U.S. dialect (Ozarks), Randolph and Wilson]

Jenny Hills the testicles. Rhyming slang for "testicles" when pronounced "test-i-kills." [British, 1900s or before, *Dictionary of Rhyming Slang*]

jerk 1. to masturbate. [British, 1800s] **2.** a masturbator. From JERK OFF (sense 2). For synonyms see HUSKER. [U.S. slang, 1800s-pres.] **3.** an oaf or incompetent fool. The connection with sense 1 is rarely recognized. [U.S. slang, 1800s-pres.] **4.** to act like a jerk in expressions such as "jerk around."

[U.S., 1900s] **5.** to coit a woman. [U.S. slang, mid 1900s-pres.]

jerk bumps pimples; acne. From a jocular myth that adolescent masturbation leads to acne. *Cf.* JERK OFF. For synonyms see BURBLE. [colloquial and slang, 1900s]

jerker 1. a CHAMBER POT (*q.v.*). [British, late 1800s] **2.** a prostitute. [British, late 1800s, Farmer and Henley] **3.** a drunkard; a tippler. [British slang, early 1800s] **4.** a male masturbator. See JERK.

jerk off 1. to masturbate oneself or another. See JERK (sense 1). [British and U.S., 1800s-pres.] **2.** a chronic masturbator; an incompetent do-nothing. Usually hyphenated in this sense. [U.S. and British slang, 1900s and before] **3.** a jerk or oaf; a contemptuous term of address. Usually hyphenated in this sense. *Cf.* JACK OFF. [U.S. and British, 1900s or before]

jerk one's gherkin (also **jerk one's gerkin**) to masturbate. Often in the form "jerkin" his gherkin." The gherkin is a type of cucumber which is made into pickles. *Cf.* PUMP ONE'S PICKLE. [U.S. slang, 1900s]

jerk one's mutton to masturbate. See MUTTON, which means "sexual gratification" here. For synonyms see WASTE TIME. [British slang, 1800s, *Dictionary of Slang and Unconventional English*]

jerk the cat to vomit. *Cf.* CAT (sense 7), SHOOT THE CAT, WHIP THE CAT. For synonyms see YORK. [British slang, early 1600s to 1900s]

jerk the turkey to masturbate. Referring to the neck of the turkey. For synonyms and related subjects see WASTE TIME. [British slang, 1900s, McDonald]

jerry 1. a CHAMBER POT (*q.v.*). From JEROBOAM (*q.v.*). [British and U.S. slang, early 1800s] **2.** a German soldier or airplane. Often capitalized. Usually considered derogatory. *Cf.* GERRY. From the pot-shaped German helmet, see JERRY (sense 1), or a respelling of "ger" from "German." [U.S. military, World War II]

Jersey cities the human breasts. Rhyming slang for "titties." Based on BRISTOL CITIES (*q.v.*). For synonyms see BOSOM. [U.S., early 1900s, *Dictionary of Rhyming Slang*]

Jersey green a particular type of marijuana. For synonyms see MARI. [U.S. drug culture, mid 1900s-pres.]

jessie a timid and ineffectual person. [British, late 1900s-pres.]

jesuit 1. a term for a sodomite or a practitioner of disapproved sexual practices. **2.** the penis in BOX THE JESUIT AND GET COCKROACHES (*q.v.*). [both senses, British slang and colloquial, early 1600s-1800s]

jet ketamine hydrochloride, a hallucinogenic drug like L.S.D. [U.S. drug culture, late 1900s, Abel]

jet fuel the drug phencyclidine, P.C.P. For synonyms see P.C.P. [U.S. drug culture, late 1900s, Abel]

jet one's juice to ejaculate. *Cf.* JUICE (sense 1), "semen." For synonyms see MELT. [British slang, 1800s, Farmer and Henley]

Jew-canoe a large, expensive automobile; a Cadillac. Refers to the alleged wealth of Jews. Derogatory. [U.S. slang, mid 1900s]

jewelry 1. the female genitals. *Cf.* JEWELS. **2.** the male genitals. *Cf.* FAMILY JEWELS. [both senses, U.S. slang, 1900s]

jewels the testicles. A truncation of FAMILY JEWELS (*q.v.*). *Cf.* DIAMONDS. For synonyms see WHIRLYGIGS. [U.S. slang, early 1900s-pres.]

Jewish nightcap the foreskin of the penis. [slang, 1900s]

jibs 1. the lips or jaw, and therefore talk or chatter. [U.S. dialect, 1900s and before] **2.** the buttocks. With reference to their projection. [U.S. black use, 1900s]

jick to COIT; to COIT someone. Possibly based on DICK. For synonyms see OCCUPY. [U.S. collegiate, late 1900s, Munro]

jig-a-lig copulation. For synonyms see SMOCKAGE [1900s or before].

jiggady-jig copulation. For synonyms

see SMOCKAGE. [British, mid 1900s-pres.]

jigger 1. the penis. [British and U.S., 1800s-pres.] **2.** the female genitals. [British colloquial, 1800s, Farmer and Henley] **3.** a gadget.

jiggered 1. intoxicated with alcohol. [U.S. slang, early 1900s] **2.** damned. See the following entry. [U.S. colloquial, 1800s-1900s]

jiggle 1. to copulate, said of a man or a woman. **2.** to coit a woman. From the standard meaning (U.S. and British), "rock or move with a jerky motion." [British slang, mid 1800s]

jiggling-bone the penis, especially when erect. Cf. JIGGLE (sense 2). For synonyms see YARD. [British slang, 1800s, Farmer and Henley]

jiggumbob 1. a gadget. [since early 1600s] **2.** the female genitals. For synonyms see MONOSYLLABLE. [British slang, late 1600s] **3.** a testis. See JIGGUMBOBS.

jiggumbobs testicles. For synonyms see WHIRLYGIGS. [British slang, late 1700s, Grose]

jill off to masturbate (female). For synonyms see WASTE TIME. [U.S., late 1900s-pres.]

jim 1. a urinal. Cf. JAKES, JOHN (sense 1). **2.** to urinate. For synonyms see WHIZ. [both senses, U.S. dialect, 1900s and before]

jimbo the penis. For synonyms see YARD. [U.S., late 1900s-pres.]

jimbrowski the penis. See also VAL-BROWSKI. For synonyms see YARD. [U.S., late 1900s-pres.]

jimjams (also **jams**) **1.** the jitters; extreme anxiety or nervousness. **2.** the DELIRIUM TREMENS (q.v.). [both senses, British and U.S. slang, 1800s-1900s]

Jim Jones marijuana laced with cocaine and P.C.P. For synonyms see MARI. [U.S., late 1900s-pres.]

jimmies the DELIRIUM TREMENS (q.v.); the shakes. For synonyms see ORK-ORKS. [U.S. slang, 1900s]

jimmy a penis. For synonyms see YARD. [U.S., late 1900s-pres.]

Jimmy Britts (also **the Jimmys**) diarrhea. Rhyming for the SHITS (q.v.). [Australian, 1900s]

Jimmy dog a marijuana cigarette. Cf. JAMES EARL DOG. For synonyms see MEZZROLL. [U.S. collegiate, late 1900s, Eble]

jimmy hat a condom. Cf. PARTY HAT. For synonyms see EEL-SKIN. [U.S. slang, late 1900s]

Jimmy Riddle urine; to urinate; an act of urination. Rhyming slang for PIDDLE (q.v.). See JERRY RIDDLE (q.v.). [British slang, 1800s]

jinder a fat marijuana cigarette. For synonyms see MEZZROLL. [U.S., late 1900s-pres.]

jingle-berries the testicles. Cf. BERRIES, GOOSEBERRIES. For synonyms see WHIRLYGIGS. [U.S. dialect (Ozarks), Randolph and Wilson]

jingled intoxicated with alcohol. Cf. WHOOPS AND JINGLES. For synonyms see WOOFLED. [from World War I; British and U.S. slang, 1900s]

jingus bogus; false. [U.S., late 1900s-pres.]

jis to ejaculate. From JISM. For synonyms see MELT. [U.S. collegiate, late 1900s, Munro]

jism (also **chism, gism, jizz**) **1.** semen. For synonyms see METTLE. **2.** manly vigor and energy; the same as GISM (sense 4). See also the dialect form CHISM. [both senses, slang, 1900s or before]

jit a derogatory term for a Negro. For synonyms see EBONY. [U.S. slang, 1900s]

jive (also **gyve**) **1.** copulation. For synonyms see SMOCKAGE. [U.S. slang, early 1900s-pres.] **2.** marijuana. For synonyms see MARI. [U.S. drug culture, early 1900s-pres.] **3.** to copulate; to coit a woman. Originally black use. [U.S. slang, mid 1900s-pres.] **4.** to cheat or deceive. **5.** nonsense; idle boasting. [both senses, U.S. slang, mid 1900s-pres.]

jive-ass foolish; annoying. [U.S. black use, late 1900s]

jive-stick (also **gyve-stick**) a marijuana cigarette. [U.S. drug culture, 1900s]

jive turkey a stupid person. For synonyms see OAF. [U.S., mid 1900s-pres.]

jizz 1. semen. **2.** manly vigor. Cf. JISM, METTLE, SPUNK. [both senses, primarily U.S. slang, mid 1900s-pres.]

jizzoint a fat marijuana cigarette. For synonyms see MEZZROLL. [U.S., late 1900s-pres.]

job 1. a drunkard. [Australian, Baker] **2.** a truncation of BLOW-JOB (q.v.), "penilingus." [U.S. slang, 1900s] There are a number of other sexual "jobs": BROWN-JOB, FRAIL-JOB, HAND-JOB, HEAD-JOB, HUM-JOB, KNOB-JOB, PIPE-JOB, PISTON-JOB, RAM-JOB, RIM-JOB, SEX-JOB, SKULL-JOB. **3.** to coit a woman. Cf. DO A WOMAN'S JOB FOR HER, WORK. [slang, early 1500s] **4.** a BOWEL MOVEMENT (sense 1). Cf. DO A JOB (sense 1), JOBBY. For synonyms see EASEMENT. [U.S. colloquial euphemism, 1900s or before] **5.** excrement; feces. [U.S. colloquial and slang, 1900s] **6.** a gadget. See JOBBER.

job, on the in the act of copulating. Cf. DO A JOB. [widespread colloquial, 1900s]

jo-bag a condom. Cf. JOY-BAG. For synonyms see EEL-SKIN. [military, World Wars]

jobbing copulation; coiting a woman. Cf. JOB, WORK. [British, 1700s and before]

jobby a bowel movement. [mostly juvenile; U.S. colloquial, 1900s or before]

jock 1. to copulate with a woman. This is from "jockey," meaning "ride a horse." Also related to "jock," meaning "jolt" in British dialects. [British slang, late 1600s, B.E.] **2.** the penis. From JOCKUM (sense 1). [since the late 1700s and before] **3.** the female genitals. From sense 1. [British slang, late 1700s] **4.** an athletic supporter. Literally, "a strap for the penis." A truncation of JOCK-STRAP (q.v.). [U.S. colloquial, 1900s] **5.** a male athlete, especially if large and stupid. [U.S. slang, 1900s] **6.** a female athlete or sports enthusiast. From sense 5. [U.S., mid 1900s-pres.] **7.** a Scots soldier or any Scotsman. [World War II and before]

8. to cheat or deceive. [British slang, mid 1700s] **9.** a nickname for a bull. Capitalized in this sense. [from Scots colloquial, 1800s or before]

jocker (also **jockey**) a PEDERAST (q.v.) tramp who lives off the begging of his CATAMITE (q.v.). [U.S. underworld, early 1900s]

jockey 1. a PEDERAST (q.v.); the same as JOCKER (q.v.). See also GIN-JOCKEY. **2.** a prostitute's client. [British, mid 1900s-pres.]

jockey-and-boxer a PEDERAST and his CATAMITE (both q.v.). [U.S. slang, mid 1900s-pres.]

jock-itch an itching of the male genitals or of the groin. Associated with the area supported by a JOCK-STRAP (q.v.). Cf. CREEPING CRUD, CROTCH-ROT, GALLOPING KNOB-ROT. [U.S. colloquial, mid 1900s-pres.]

jock-strap (also **jockey-strap**) an athletic supporter for the male genitals. Cf. JOCK (sense 4). [U.S. colloquial, 1900s]

jockstrapper an athlete. Cf. JOCK-STRAP. [U.S. slang, late 1900s]

Jodrell (Bank) masturbation. Rhyming slang for WHANK. For synonyms see WASTE TIME. [British, late 1900s-pres.]

joe (also **Joe**) **1.** a W.C.; a urinal. [U.S. slang, 1900s and before] **2.** to urinate or defecate. [U.S. slang, 1900s and before] **3.** a Schlitz beer. From the name of the Joseph Schlitz Brewing Company. [U.S. collegiate, late 1900s, Eble]

Joe, old 1. syphilis. For synonyms see SPECIFIC STOMACH. [U.S. slang, early 1900s] **2.** any venereal disease. [U.S. slang, mid 1900s-pres.]

Joe Blakes the DELIRIUM TREMENS (q.v.). Rhyming slang for SHAKES (sense 2). [Australian, 1900s]

Joe Buck an act of copulation; to coit a woman. Rhyming slang for FUCK (q.v.). [Australian, early 1900s]

Joe-wad toilet paper. Cf. JOE. For synonyms see T.P. [U.S., 1900s or before]

jog to coit a woman. From the standard sense "move up and down in a heavy, steady motion." [British slang or colloquial, early 1600s]

John (also **john**) **1.** a privy; an out-house. *Cf.* JAKES, JIM, JOE. For synonyms see AJAX. [since the 1600s] **2.** a toilet; a restroom. For synonyms see W.C. [U.S. colloquial, 1900s] **3.** a nickname for a prostitute's customer. Used by both male and female prostitutes. [U.S. slang and underworld, mid 1900s-pres.] **4.** a woman's lover or steady boyfriend. [U.S. slang, mid 1900s-pres.] **5.** a Chinese. *Cf.* JOHN CHINAMAN. [Australian, 1900s or before] **6.** the penis. A truncation of JOHN THOMAS (*q.v.*). [slang, 1900s] **7.** an older male homosexual who supports a young one. *Cf.* SUGAR-DADDY. [U.S. slang, 1900s]

John Barleycorn (also **Sir John Barleycorn**) whisky; a personification of whisky and the evils of drink. Originally ale or beer made from barley. [colloquial, late 1700s-pres.]

John Chinaman (also **John**) the Chinese people; a Chinese. [widespread colloquial, 1800s-1900s] Synonyms: CANARY, CHINAMAN, CHINAMANG, CHINEE, CHINK, CHINKY, CHINO, CHOW-CHOW, COOSIE, DINGBAT, DINK, GOOK, JOHN, JOHNNY, MUSTARD, PADDY, PIGTAIL, PONG, RICE-BELLY, RICEMAN, SLOPIE, YELLOW-BELLY, YELLOW BOY.

John Hall alcohol; liquor. *Cf.* ALCOHOL. [U.S. slang, 1900s]

johnnies the police. For synonyms see FLATFOOT. [U.S., late 1900s-pres.]

Johnny (also **Johnnie, johnnie, johnny**) **1.** a personification of the penis; the diminutive of JOHN (sense 6). Based on JOHN THOMAS (*q.v.*). [British and U.S. slang, 1800s] **2.** a Chinese. *Cf.* JOHN CHINAMAN. [Australian, early 1900s, Baker] **3.** a toilet; a restroom; the W.C. *Cf.* JOHN (sense 1). [1900s] **4.** a condom. [British military, 1900s]

johnny (bag) a condom. For synonyms see EEL-SKIN. [British and U.S. slang, 1900s, McDonald]

Johnny bum euphemistic and jocular for "jackass." See BUM (sense 1). [British slang, late 1700s, Grose]

Johnson 1. the penis; a personification of the penis. *Cf.* DOCTOR JOHNSON, JOHN (sense 6). [attested as British slang, 1800s, *Dictionary of Slang and Unconventional English;* U.S. black use, mid 1900s] See also JOHNSON GRASS. **2.** marijuana; drugs; any contraband. An underworld term meaning "thing." Compare to JONES. *Cf.* JOHNSON GRASS. For synonyms see MARI. [U.S. drug culture, late 1900s]

Johnson Grass (also **Johnson**) marijuana. From a common name for a type of sorghum and also from the release from inhibitions that marijuana provides. *Cf.* JOHNSON. [U.S. drug culture, mid 1900s-pres.]

John Thomas 1. a general nickname for a flunky; a servant. [British slang and colloquial, mid 1800s] **2.** the penis; a personification of the penis. Implies that the penis is the servant of men. [British colloquial, early 1800s-pres.]

John Willie the penis; a personification of the penis. *Cf.* JOHN (sense 6), LITTLE WILLIE. [British colloquial, early 1900s]

join giblets 1. for man and woman to unite in marriage. [British, late 1600s] **2.** to copulate; to copulate casually. [British slang or cant, 1700s, Grose]

joint 1. the penis. For synonyms see YARD. [U.S. slang and underworld, early 1900s-pres.] **2.** a marijuana cigarette. *Cf.* J. (sense 1). [U.S. drug culture, mid 1900s-pres.] **3.** an opium den. Also any establishment where vice is available. [U.S. slang, late 1800s to early 1900s] See also CRYSTAL JOINT.

join the great majority (also **join the ever-increasing majority**) to die. [since the late 1800s]

jollies sexual pleasure; sexual excitement. [U.S. slang, 1900s]

jolly bean an amphetamine tablet or capsule. A play on JELLY BEAN (*q.v.*). [U.S. drug culture, mid 1900s-pres.]

jolt 1. to coit a woman. From a term meaning "move up and down in a jerky manner." [British slang, 1800s, Farmer and Henley] **2.** the kick or charge from an electric shock or a drink of whisky. **3.** the CHARGE (sense

1) or effects of marijuana or other narcotics. [U.S. slang, 1900s]

Jones 1. the penis; a personification of the penis. *Cf.* JOHN (sense 6), JOHNSON. [originally U.S. black use, 1900s] **2.** a drug habit. See SCAG JONES.

jones for someone or something to want someone or something badly; to have an addiction-like yen for someone or something. Literally, to have a thing for someone or something. [U.S. slang, late 1900s]

jonser a drug addict. *Cf.* JONES. [U.S. drug culture, late 1900s]

joog to stab someone. Prisons. [U.S., late 1900s-pres.]

jork a worthless person. A JERK and a DORK. For synonyms see OAF. [U.S., late 1900s-pres.]

joto a male homosexual. From Spanish. For synonyms see EPICENE. [U.S., late 1900s-pres.]

joy-bag a condom; the same as JO-BAG (*q.v.*). For synonyms see EEL-SKIN. [British military, mid 1900s, *Dictionary of Slang and Unconventional English*]

joy-boy 1. a sexually overactive male. [U.S. slang, 1900s] **2.** a homosexual male. [British and U.S. slang, 1900s] **3.** a male drug addict. [U.S. drug culture, 1900s]

joy-buzzer the clitoris. [U.S. slang, 1900s]

joy flakes a powdered narcotic; cocaine or morphine. *Cf.* CALIFORNIA CORNFLAKES. [U.S. underworld, early 1900s]

joy house a brothel. [U.S. slang or colloquial, early 1900s]

joy juice 1. alcohol; liquor. **2.** a liquid substance used for stimulant or narcotic purposes. [both senses, U.S. slang, 1900s]

joy knob the penis, especially the glans penis. *Cf.* GALLOPING KNOB-ROT. [U.S. slang, 1900s, Wentworth and Flexner]

joy-pop a hypodermic injection of narcotics. [U.S. underworld, 1900s]

joy-popper an occasional user of narcotics. *Cf.* CHIPPY (sense 3), JOY-RIDER. [U.S. underworld, mid 1900s]

joy powder one or more of the narcotics used in powder form, *i.e.,* cocaine, heroin, morphine. Originally used for "morphine." [U.S. underworld and later, drug culture, early 1900s-pres.]

joy prong the penis. *Cf.* PRONG. [British and U.S. slang, early 1900s]

joy-ride 1. copulation. *Cf.* RIDE. [U.S. slang, 1900s] **2.** a CHARGE (sense 1) or intoxication from the use of drugs. [1900s] **3.** an execution; a death-ride; a kidnap-murder. [U.S. underworld slang, 1900s]

joy-rider an occasional user of drugs. *Cf.* CHIPPY, JOY-POPPER. [U.S. underworld, early 1900s]

joy sister (also **joy-girl**) a prostitute. [U.S. slang, 1900s]

joy smoke marijuana or a marijuana cigarette. [U.S. slang, mid 1900s-pres.]

joy-stick 1. the penis. [British and U.S. since the 1800s] **2.** a pipe for smoking opium. [U.S. underworld, 1900s] **3.** a marijuana cigarette. [U.S. drug culture, mid 1900s-pres.]

joy-water alcohol; liquor. *Cf.* GIGGLE-WATER. [U.S. slang, early 1900s]

joy-weed marijuana. For synonyms see MARI. [U.S. underworld and drug culture, 1900s]

J-smoke marijuana or a marijuana cigarette, *Cf.* J., JOINT (sense 2). [U.S. drug culture, mid 1900s-pres.]

J-stick a marijuana cigarette. For synonyms see MEZZROLL. [U.S. drug culture, late 1900s]

J.T. JOHN THOMAS (*q.v.*), the penis. [British slang and colloquial, early 1900s-pres.]

juane a truncation of "marijuana." Either marijuana or a marijuana cigarette. [U.S. slang, early 1900s, Wentworth and Flexner]

Juanita 1. marijuana. [U.S. drug culture, 1900s] **2.** a prostitute. [U.S. underworld, 1900s, Goldin, O'Leary, and Lipsius]

Juanita weed marijuana. *Cf.* JUANITA (sense 1). [U.S. drug culture, mid 1900s-pres.]

Juan Valdez marijuana. The Spanish

name of a character who serves as the mascot for a brand of Colombian coffee. For synonyms see MARI. [U.S. drug culture, late 1900s, Abel]

jubbies the female breasts. For synonyms see BOSOM. [British, late 1900s-pres.]

jublies the female breasts. For synonyms see BOSOM. [British, late 1900s-pres.]

jug-bitten intoxicated with alcohol. For synonyms see WOOFLED. [British slang, early 1600s]

jugged-up (also **jugged**) intoxicated with alcohol. [U.S. slang, 1900s]

jugs the breasts. Cf. CREAM-JUGS, NINNY-JUGS. For synonyms see BOSOM. [U.S. and elsewhere, early 1900s-pres.]

jug-steamed intoxicated with alcohol. [U.S. slang, mid 1800s]

juice 1. semen. Cf. JET ONE'S JUICE. For synonyms see METTLE. [widespread nonce use; attested as British slang, 1800s, Farmer and Henley] **2.** vitality; male vigor. Cf. METTLE (sense 1). SPUNK (sense 1). [U.S. colloquial, mid 1900s-pres.] **3.** any alcoholic drink. For synonyms see BOOZE. [U.S. colloquial, early 1900s-pres.] **4.** to drink alcoholic beverages. Usually implying drinking to excess. [U.S. slang, mid 1900s-pres.] **5.** to sexually arouse a woman to the point of producing vaginal lubrication. [attested as U.S. slang, 1900s] See also JUICY (sense 1), which is considerably older. **6.** the animal tranquilizer, P.C.P. For synonyms see P.C.P. [U.S. drug culture, late 1900s] **7.** to ejaculate. For synonyms see MELT. [U.S. slang, late 1900s if not before] **8.** to COIT a female. For synonyms see OCCUPY. [U.S. collegiate, late 1900s, Munro] **9.** power; influence. [U.S., late 1900s-pres.]

juice and beans a narcotic cough syrup taken with Doriden. BEANS = pills. [U.S. drug culture, late 1900s]

juiced copulated with. Said of a woman. [both senses, U.S., late 1900s] See also JUICED-UP.

juiced-up (also **juiced**) **1.** drunk; intoxicated with alcohol. Cf. JUICE (sense 3). [U.S. slang, 1900s] **2.** electrocuted.

Usually in the electric chair. [U.S., early to mid 1900s] **3.** sexually aroused, said of a woman. Cf. JUICE (sense 5).

juice-freak someone whose favorite drug is alcohol. Cf. JUICE (sense 3). [U.S. drug culture, late 1900s]

juicy 1. pertaining to a woman who is sexually aroused. Refers to vaginal lubrication. Cf. JUICE (sense 5), SLICK-CHICK (sense 2). [Slang and colloquial since the late 1600s] **2.** intoxicated with alcohol. Cf. JUICE (sense 3), [colloquial since the early 1700s] **3.** pertaining to something which is bawdy or lewd. [British and some U.S. use, late 1800s-1900s]

juju a marijuana cigarette. [U.S. underworld and slang, early 1900s]

jujubes the female breasts. For synonyms see BOSOM. [British, late 1900s-pres.]

juke (also **juk**) **1.** to coit a woman. **2.** coition in general or an act of coition. [attested in various parts of the Caribbean and the Southern U.S.] **3.** to mess up; to FUCK UP. Extended from sense 1. [U.S. collegiate, late 1900s, Munro]

jump 1. to copulate, usually said of a man, especially in reference to vigorous copulation. Possibly with an element of brutality. See MOTHER-JUMPER at MOTHER-GRABBER. [from *A Winter's Tale* (Shakespeare); currently a U.S. euphemism] **2.** to attack someone, usually by surprise. [U.S. slang, late 1900s]

jump on someone's bones to COIT someone. For synonyms see OCCUPY. [U.S. slang, late 1900s]

jumps the DELIRIUM TREMENS (*q.v.*). Cf. JERKS. [colloquial, late 1800s-pres.]

jungle mouth a case of very bad breath. [U.S., late 1900s-pres.]

junior the penis; one's own penis. One's little man. A recurrent nickname. For synonyms see GENITALS, YARD. [U.S. and probably elsewhere, 1900s or before]

juniper-juice hard liquor, specifically gin. From the juniper berry flavoring of gin. [U.S. slang, 1900s]

junk 1. drugs. [U.S. slang, early 1900s-pres.] **2.** a Caucasian. Derogatory.

[U.S. black use, late 1900s] **3.** semen. For synonyms see METTLE. [U.S. slang, late 1900s and probably recurrent nonce]

junk, on the on drugs; pertaining to a regular drug user. [U.S. underworld and drug culture, mid 1900s]

junker 1. a seller of narcotics, particularly of heroin. [U.S., early 1900s-pres.] **2.** a drug addict or heavy user; the same as JUNKY (*q.v.*). [U.S. underworld and drug culture, early 1900s-pres.] Terms for various types of addicts: ACID-DROPPER, ACID-FREAK, ACID-HEAD, A.D., A-HEAD, BINDLE-STIFF, COKE-FREAK, COKE-HEAD, COKEY, COKOMO, CUBEHEAD, DOPE FIEND, DOPENIK, DOPER, DRUGGY, DRUGHEAD, GONG, GOW-HEAD, GOWSTER, HOP-FIEND, HOP-HEAD, HOP-HOG, HOPPER, HOPPIE, HOPSTER, HOP-STIFF, HORNER, JOY-BOY, JUNK-HOG, JUNK-HOUND, JUNKY, KOKOMO, LOBBY-GOW, MORFIEND, NEEDLE-MAN, SCHMECKER, SMOKEY, SNOWBIRD, SPEED-FREAK, SPOOK, TECATO, TWITCHER, USER.

junky (also **junkie**) a drug addict. [U.S. slang and drug culture, mid 1900s-pres.]

jura the police. For synonyms see FLATFOOT. [U.S., late 1900s-pres.]

just-raped look a clothing style characterized by slovenliness, including holes and other damage. [U.S. slang, late 1900s]

K

K. 1. a homosexual male; "kweer," *i.e.,* QUEER (*q.v.*). [1900s, *Dictionary of the Underworld*] **2.** ketamine hydrochloride, a hallucinogenic drug similar to L.S.D. [U.S. drug culture, late 1900s, Abel]

kack (also **kak**) to vomit. The same as CACK. For synonyms see YORK. [widespread, 1900s]

kaif marijuana. *Cf.* KEEF. [U.S. drug culture, mid 1900s-pres.]

kajoobies the breasts. For synonyms see BOSOM. [U.S. slang, 1900s, Lewin and Lewin]

kak See KACK.

ka-ka 1. a defecation. **2.** feces; dung. [1900s and probably long before] **3.** heroin or counterfeit heroin, literally, SHIT (sense 5); the same as CA-CA (sense 1). [U.S. drug culture, mid 1900s-pres.]

kanakas the testicles. A play on KNACKERS (*q.v.*) and a nickname given to Melanesians brought to Australia to work on the plantations. [from the Hawaiian word *kanaka*, "man"; Australian, 1900s or before, *Dictionary of Slang and Unconventional English*]

kango an Australian. [British, late 1900s-pres.]

kanya marijuana. For synonyms see MARI. [U.S., late 1900s-pres.]

kark to die. See also CARK. For synonyms see DEPART. [Australian, mid 1900s-pres.]

Kaui a variety of marijuana. From the name of one of the Hawaiian Islands. *Cf.* HAWAIIAN, MAUI. [U.S. drug culture, mid 1900s-pres.]

kazoo See GAZOO.

keck to cough or choke; to retch or vomit noisily; to make retching sounds to show disgust. For synonyms see YORK. [onomatopoetic, since the early 1600s]

keef (also **kaif, kef, kief, kif, kiff**) **1.** marijuana or the pleasure derived from smoking it. **2.** HASHISH (*q.v.*) and mixtures of marijuana and tobacco. [both senses are from an Arabic word meaning "pleasure"; in English since the early 1800s; U.S. underworld and drug culture, early 1900s-pres.]

keep the census down 1. to abort a fetus. **2.** to masturbate. *Cf.* HIGHER MALTHUSIANISM, SIMPLE INFANTICIDE. [both senses, British, 1800s, Farmer and Henley]

keester (also **keister, keyster, kiester, kister**) **1.** a valise; a chest or box. **2.** the posteriors or the anus. [U.S. underworld and slang, mid 1900s] **3.** the female genitals. *Cf.* BOX (sense 2). [U.S. underworld, early 1900s]

keg a beer belly. For synonyms see BELLY. [U.S., late 1900s-pres.]

keifer the female genitals. For synonyms see MONOSYLLABLE. [British slang, 1800s, Farmer and Henley]

kelks the testicles. From a word meaning "fish roe." [British dialect, 1800s, Rye]

Kentucky fried alcohol intoxicated. An elaboration of FRIED based on the trade name *Kentucky Fried Chicken.* For synonyms see WOOFLED. [U.S. slang, late 1900s]

kettledrums the breasts. [British slang, late 1700s, Grose]

kevork to kill someone. Based on the name of *Dr. Jack Kevorkian,* the physician who practices assisted suicide. [U.S., late 1900s-pres.]

key 1. the penis. Because "it lets the man in and the maid out" (Farmer and Henley). [British slang, late 1700s] **2.** a kilogram of marijuana. *Cf.* KI. [U.S. drug culture, mid 1900s-pres.]

keyed 1. intoxicated with alcohol. The same as KEYED-UP (sense 2). [U.S. slang, 1900s] **2.** intoxicated with marijuana or with other drugs. *Cf.* KEY (sense 2). [U.S. drug culture, mid 1900s-pres.]

keyed to the roof heavily intoxicated with alcohol. See KEYED (sense 1). [U.S. slang, 1900s]

keyed-up 1. extremely nervous and distraught. **2.** intoxicated with alcohol. *Cf.* KEYED (sense 1). [both senses, U.S. slang, 1900s]

K.G.B. marijuana. From *killer green bud.* For synonyms see MARI. [U.S., late 1900s-pres.]

ki a kilogram of marijuana. *Cf.* KEY. [U.S. drug culture, mid 1900s-pres.]

kick 1. trousers. See KICKS. **2.** a CHARGE (sense 1) from drugs or alcohol; a thrill of any type. [both senses, slang, 1900s]

kick ass 1. (also **kick butt**) to do well; to dominate or manage well. [U.S. slang, late 1900s] **2.** excellent. [U.S., late 1900s-pres.]

kick-ass on someone to dominate someone; to kick someone around. [U.S. slang, late 1900s]

kick butt See KICK ASS.

kick-cloy a pair of breeches. [mid 1800s, Matsell]

kick in the ass 1. shocking or disappointing news. 2. an unwarranted punishment or letdown. [both senses, U.S. colloquial, mid 1900s-pres.]

kick off to die. For synonyms see DEPART. [Australian and U.S., mid 1900s-pres.]

kick some ass (around) to show someone who is in charge; to set someone straight about something; to stir someone into activity. [U.S. slang, late 1900s]

kicksters trousers; breeches. *Cf.* KICKS. [British, early 1800s]

kick-stick marijuana; a marijuana cigarette. [U.S. drug culture, mid 1900s-pres.]

kick the bucket to die. [cant and slang since the 1700s, Grose]

kick the clouds to be hanged. [cant and slang, early 1800s, *Lexicon Balatronicum*]

kick the gong (also **kick the gong around**) to smoke opium or marijuana. [U.S. underworld and drug culture, mid 1900s-pres.]

kidney-buster 1. a rough ride; a rough road. [U.S., mid 1900s-pres.] **2.** an uncomfortable or poorly built seat in a vehicle. [U.S., mid 1900s-pres.]

kidney-scraper (also **kidney-wiper**) the erect penis. *Cf.* LUNG-DISTURBER. For synonyms see ERECTION. [British slang, 1900s, *Dictionary of Slang and Unconventional English*]

kidney-wiper See KIDNEY-SCRAPER.

kiester stash the rectum as a place for concealing illegal drugs. *Cf.* KEESTER (sense 2). [U.S. underworld and drug culture, mid 1900s or before]

kife 1. a prostitute. **2.** a CATAMITE (*q.v.*). **3.** a fellator. [all senses, U.S. underworld, early 1900s]

kike 1. a highly derogatory term for an uncouth Jewish merchant. **2.** a highly derogatory term for any Jewish man or woman. From Yiddish *kikel,* the "circle" which was used by illiterate Jewish immigrants in place of a cross (X) as a signature. For synonyms see FIVE AND TWO. [both senses, U.S. slang, early 1900s-pres.]

kiki BISEXUAL (*q.v.*). *Cf.* CHICHI (sense 3). [U.S. homosexual use, mid 1900s-pres.]

kill a few brain cells to drink (some) beer; to have a beer. Word play on the alleged destruction of brain cells by alcohol. [U.S. slang, late 1900s, Eble]

kill a snake to urinate; a possible reason for leaving the room to urinate. For synonyms see WHIZ. [Australian, early 1900s, Baker]

kill a tree to urinate against a tree, said of males. *Cf.* BURN THE GRASS. [U.S., 1900s]

killed drug intoxicated; marijuana intoxicated. For synonyms see TALL. [U.S. drug culture, late 1900s, Kaiser]

killer a marijuana cigarette. For synonyms see MEZZROLL. [U.S. drug culture, mid 1900s]

killer-weed 1. the drug P.C.P. (*q.v.*). **2.** a mixture of marijuana and P.C.P. (*q.v.*). *Cf.* WEED. [both senses, U.S. drug culture, mid 1900s-pres.]

kilobucks a tremendous sum of money. [U.S., late 1900s-pres.]

Kinell! Fucking hell! For synonyms see 'ZOUNDS. [British, mid 1900s-pres.]

King Kong pills barbiturate tablets or capsules. For synonyms see BARB. [U.S. drug culture, mid 1900s-pres.]

King Lear a male homosexual. Rhyming slang for "queer." [British, early 1900s]

king-member the penis. For synonyms see YARD. [British slang, 1800s, Farmer and Henley]

king's elevator a disguise of the ROYAL SHAFT (*q.v.*). [U.S., mid 1900s]

kink a person who is obsessed with adventuresome or perverse sexual acts. A KINKY person. [U.S. slang, late 1900s]

kinky 1. pertaining to a weird or crooked person. [British and U.S., late 1800s-pres.] **2.** pertaining to a male or female homosexual. [British and U.S., 1900s] **3.** pertaining to deviant or nonorthogenital sexual acts. *Cf.* KINKY-SEX, TWISTY. [U.S. slang, mid 1900s-pres.]

kinky-sex NONORTHOGENITAL (*q.v.*). sex acts. See GROUP SEX. [U.S. slang, mid 1900s]

Kinoath! "My fucking oath!" For synonyms see 'ZOUNDS. [Australian, mid 1900s-pres.]

kipper the female sexual organ. For synonyms see MONOSYLLABLE. [British, late 1900s-pres.]

kip shop a brothel. *Cf.* KIP.

kirp the penis. Backslang for PRICK. For synonyms see YARD. [British, mid 1900s-pres.]

kiss 1. to copulate. **2.** copulation. [both senses, British euphemisms, early 1700s]

kiss-ass 1. to curry favor; to act the sycophant. **2.** flattery; nonsense. **3.** a sycophant. *Cf.* SUCK-ASS. [all senses,

U.S. slang, mid 1900s-pres.] **4.** servile and obsequious. [British and U.S., mid 1900s-pres.]

kisser 1. a homosexual male. [U.S. slang, mid 1900s-pres.] **2.** the face; the mouth. [U.S., early 1900s-pres.]

kissing tackle the lips, as used for kissing. [U.S., late 1900s-pres.]

kiss Mary to smoke marijuana. [U.S. drug culture, mid 1900s-pres.]

Kiss my ass! a curse; also an oath and an exclamation. *Cf.* BASIMECU! [colloquial, 1900s or before]

Kiss my tail! a euphemism for KISS MY ASS! (*q.v.*).

Kiss my tuna! (also **Kiss my squirrel!**) "Kiss my vagina!"; "Kiss my ass!" A general term of derogation. California teens. [U.S. slang, late 1900s] See also TUNA, TUNA TACO, STANKY TUNA.

kiss off 1. to perform PENILINGUS (*q.v.*). [U.S. underworld, early 1900s, Monteleone] **2.** to kill. **3.** death. Usually hyphenated in this sense. [senses 2 and 3 are U.S. underworld, 1900s]

kiss someone's hind tit to be obsequious to someone. [U.S., mid 1900s-pres.]

kiss the dust to die; the same as BITE THE DUST (*q.v.*). [British, 1800s]

kiss the fish to smoke hashish. [U.S. drug culture, mid 1900s-pres., Landy]

kiss the porcelain god to vomit. *Cf.* HUG THE PORCELAIN GOD. For synonyms see YORK. [U.S. slang, late 1900s]

kissy-face 1. kissing; the activity of kissing. **2.** the feeling of wanting to kiss or be kissed. [both senses, U.S., late 1900s]

kit the male genitals. *Cf.* APPARATUS, GEAR.

kitty the female genitals. Named for FUR (sense 1), the pubic hair. *Cf.* CAT (sense 6), PUSSY (sense 1). [British slang, 1800s, Farmer and Henley]

kitty nugget cat dung. For synonyms see DUNG. [U.S., late 1900s-pres.]

K.J. CRYSTAL (krystal) JOINT (*q.v.*); the drug P.C.P. (*q.v.*). [U.S. drug culture, mid 1900s-pres.]

kleenex a promiscuous person, one whom you pick up, blow, and throw away. [U.S., late 1900s-pres.]

Klingons crack addicts. [U.S., late 1900s-pres.]

kluck See CLUCK.

klutz (also **klotz**) an oaf; a clod or a bungler. [from German *Klotz*, "blockhead," via Yiddish; U.S. slang, mid 1900s-pres.]

knackers (also **nackers**) the testicles. For synonyms see WHIRLYGIGS. [British colloquial and slang, 1800s-pres.]

knee deep in shit (also **knee deep**) the state one is in when the lies and boasting have accumulated considerably. *Cf.* OXOMETER. [U.S. slang, mid 1900s]

kneeling at the altar pertaining to the position of a receiving PEDERAST (*q.v.*) during the act of pederasty. [U.S. underworld, early 1900s, Irwin]

knee-trembler an act of copulation accomplished standing up. [British slang, 1800s, Farmer and Henley]

knee-walking alcohol intoxicated. *Cf.* KNEE-WALKING DRUNK. For synonyms see WOOFLED. [U.S. collegiate, late 1900s, Eble]

knee-walking drunk intoxicated with alcohol; so drunk as to have to walk on one's knees. [U.S. regional or nonce, 1900s]

knick-knack 1. a gadget. **2.** the female genitals. **3.** the penis. **4.** a testicle. Usually in the plural. [all senses, British and U.S., 1800s-pres.]

knob (also **nob**) **1.** the penis. **2.** the glans penis. *Cf.* KNOB-JOB. [colloquial since the 1800s or before] **3.** to masturbate. [U.S. slang, mid 1900s-pres.] **4.** an oaf. For synonyms see OAF. [U.S., late 1900s-pres.]

knobber an act of FELLATIO; a KNOB-JOB. [U.S. slang, late 1900s, Munro]

knob gobbler a fellator. For synonyms see PICCOLO-PLAYER. [U.S., late 1900s-pres.]

knob-job an act of PENILINGUS (*q.v.*). See JOB for related subjects. [U.S. slang, mid 1900s-pres.]

knock 1. the penis. See KNOCKER (sense 1). [British, 1700s or before] **2.** an act of copulation. [since the mid 1500s] **3.** to copulate. *Cf.* KNOCK UP. [cant and slang, 1700s-1900s] **4.** a sexually easy young woman. [slang, 1900s]

knock boots with someone to COIT someone; to COIT with someone. For synonyms see OCCUPY. [U.S. slang, late 1900s, Munro]

knock down a prick to bring an end to an erection; to cause a man to have an orgasm. *Cf.* BRING DOWN BY HAND. [British slang, 1800s, Farmer and Henley]

knocked-up 1. experiencing the menses. **2.** pregnant. **3.** intoxicated with alcohol. [all senses, U.S., 1900s]

knocker 1. the penis. **2.** a lecher; a man who copulates frequently. [since c. 1500] **3.** a breast or a testis. See KNOCKERS. **4.** an important or self-important male; a showoff. Pronounced "k'nocker." [Yiddish; U.S., 1900s]

knockers 1. breasts, especially well-shaped breasts. [British and U.S., 1900s] **2.** the testicles. *Cf.* KNACKERS. [British and U.S. slang and colloquial, 1900s or before]

knock it off to copulate. A reinterpretation of an expression meaning "Shut-up!" or "Stop it!" [U.S. slang, 1900s]

knock the shit out of someone to beat someone. *Cf.* TAKE THE PISS OUT OF SOMEONE. [British and U.S. colloquial, 1800s-pres.]

knock up to make pregnant; in British English, "wake someone up by knocking." For synonyms see STORK. [U.S. slang and colloquial, 1900s]

knot the posterior ridge of the glans penis. [British slang or colloquial, 1800s, *Dictionary of Slang and Unconventional English*] See also VIRGINKNOT.

know to have sexual intercourse with someone; to have CARNAL KNOWLEDGE (*q.v.*) of a woman. [since the 1200s]

knowledge copulation. A truncation of CARNAL KNOWLEDGE (*q.v.*). *Cf.*

CARNAL ACQUAINTANCE. [since the 1400s]

know (one's) shit be very competent. [British and U.S., late 1900s-pres.]

know shit about something to know something about something. Often in the negative. [U.S. slang, 1900s]

know shit from shinola to know what's what; to be knowledgeable in the ways of the world. Usually in the negative. Shinola™ is a brand of shoe polish. This refers to brown shoe polish. [U.S. slang, mid 1900s]

know someone's ass from a hole in the ground to be knowledgeable about things; to be discerning. Usually in the negative. [U.S. slang, 1900s]

knuckle-dragger a strong and stupid man. For synonyms see OAF. [U.S., mid 1900s-pres.]

knucklehead a stupid person. For synonyms see OAF. [U.S., late 1900s-pres.]

knuckle oneself to masturbate. For synonyms see WASTE TIME. [U.S., late 1900s-pres.]

knuckle sandwich a blow struck in the teeth or mouth. [U.S., mid 1900s-pres.]

K.O. to die; to "kick off." For synonyms see DEPART. [U.S. collegiate, late 1900s, Eble]

Kojak a police officer. From the television character's name. For synonyms

see FLATFOOT. [U.S. and elsewhere, late 1900s]

kokomo a cocaine user. From COKE (q.v.) and the name of a city in Indiana. [U.S. underworld and drug culture, early 1900s-pres.]

kook an odd person; a weirdo. [U.S. slang, mid 1900s-pres.]

kong strong whisky. From *King Kong.* [U.S. slang, 1900s]

kools the drug phencyclidine, P.C.P. For synonyms see P.C.P. [U.S. drug culture, late 1900s, Abel]

kosher circumcised. [U.S., late 1900s-pres.]

kosher pickle a circumcised penis. Refers to the Jewish practice of circumcision. An inevitable nickname. *Cf.* PICKLE. For synonyms see GENITALS, YARD. [U.S. slang, 1900s and probably recurrent nonce]

Kryptonite crack. For synonyms see NOSE-CANDY. [U.S., late 1900s-pres.]

kucky (also **cucky**) dirty, said of children and animals. See CUCK.

kweef a vaginal fart. [U.S. collegiate, late 1900s]

kweer a homosexual male. A respelling of "queer." *Cf.* K. For synonyms see EPICENE.

KYBO 1. "keep your bowels open," a catch phrase meaning "keep healthy." [U.S. slang, mid 1900s-pres.] 2. a privy. For synonyms see AJAX. [1900s]

L

L. 1. "hell" [U.S., 1900] **2.** the hallucinogenic drug L.S.D. For synonyms see ACID. [U.S. drug culture, late 1900s] **3.** (usually **L.s**) an Elavil antidepressant tablet. [U.S. drug culture, late 1900s, Kaiser]

L7 a total JERK; a social outcast; a SQUARE. For synonyms see OAF. Each of the symbols forms two adjacent sides of a square. [U.S. slang, late 1900s]

labonza the posteriors. For synonyms see DUFF. [U.S. slang, mid 1900s]

lace curtains 1. whiskers, especially false whiskers used in the theater. No negative connotations. [U.S. slang, 1900s, Berrey and Van den Bark] **2.** the foreskin of the uncircumcised penis. [U.S. homosexual use, 1900s]

laced-mutton 1. a prostitute. For synonyms see HARLOT. **2.** any woman. [both senses, British, since the late 1500s]

lackanookie a lack of copulation, from the male point of view. [British, mid 1900s-pres.]

ladder the female genitals, specifically the vagina. Cf. JACOB'S LADDER. [British slang, 1800s, Farmer and Henley]

ladies' delight the penis. Cf. LADIES' LOLLIPOP. [British, 1800s]

ladies' lollipop (also **ladies' lollypop**) the penis. [British jocular euphemism, 1800s]

ladies' tailor a lecher; a whoremonger. Cf. TRIM. [British, 1800s]

ladies' tailoring copulation. See TRIM. [British, early 1800s]

ladies' treasure the penis. For synonyms see YARD. [British, 1800s]

lady in waiting a pregnant woman. [British and U.S. colloquial and nonce, 1900s or before]

Lady Jane the female genitals. For synonyms see MONOSYLLABLE. [British, mid 1800s, Farmer and Henley]

lady-lover a female homosexual; a female lover of ladies. For synonyms see LESBYTERIAN. [U.S. underworld and slang, early 1900s-pres.]

lady's low toupee the female pubic hair. Cf. LOWER-WIG, MERKIN. [British slang, early 1700s]

Lady Snow cocaine. Cf. LADY WHITE, OLD; WHITE LADY.

lady-star the female genitals. [British written nonce, late 1500s]

lady-ware 1. the male genitals, in particular, the penis. [late 1500s] **2.** the female genitals. [British, mid 1600s] See also WARE.

Lady White, old any powdered narcotic. Cf. LADY SNOW, WHITE LADY. [U.S. underworld, early 1900s]

lagging-gage a CHAMBER POT (q.v.). Cf. LAG (sense 2). [British colloquial or cant, 1800s or before]

laid having copulated; having been copulated with; the same as LAYED (sense 1). Originally said of women, now said of both men and women.

laid back drug intoxicated; alcohol intoxicated; MELLOW. For synonyms see TALL, WOOFLED. [U.S. drug culture, late 1900s]

laid-out 1. dead; pertaining to a corpse arranged for a wake. **2.** intoxicated with alcohol. [U.S., early 1900s-pres.] **3.** marijuana intoxicated. From sense 2. [U.S. drug culture, mid 1900s-pres.]

laid to the bone intoxicated with alcohol. For synonyms see WOOFLED. [U.S. colloquial, mid 1900s-pres.]

laid to the natural bone naked. For synonyms see STARKERS. [U.S. black use, late 1900s, Folb]

la-la the BUTTOCKS. For synonyms see DUFF. [U.S. slang, late 1900s]

lamb 1. a CATAMITE (q.v.), especially a much abused and passive one. Cf. CHICKEN (sense 1), KID LAMB. For synonyms see BRONCO. [U.S. underworld, early 1900s and homosexual use, mid 1900s-pres.] **2.** a simpleton; an oaf. [British, mid 1600s]

lamp of life the penis. For synonyms see YARD. [British euphemism, 1800s]

lamp of love the female genitals. Cf. LIGHT THE LAMP. [British euphemism, 1800s]

lance the penis. Cf. BREAK A LANCE WITH. See BRACMARD for similar terms. [widespread nonce use since the 1600s or before]

lap-clap 1. copulation. **2.** conception; a pregnancy. [both senses, British, early 1700s or before]

lapland 1. the female genitals. Cf. LAP, LOW-COUNTRIES, LOWLANDS. [British slang, early 1800s, Farmer and Henley] **2.** women in general; women considered sexually. [British, 1800s]

lapper 1. a heavy drinker, a drunkard. [British colloquial, mid 1800s] **2.** one who performs oral sexual intercourse, primarily PENILINGUS and CUNNILINGUS (both q.v.). [U.S. underworld, early 1900s, Monteleone]

lappy intoxicated with alcohol. For synonyms see WOOFLED. [cant, colloquial, and dialect, 1700s-1800s]

lard 1. to copulate. Refers to inserting fat into meat in preparation for roasting. Reinforced by the sense "fatten," i.e., "make pregnant." [British, 1800s or before, Farmer and Henley] **2.** a police officer. A play on PIG. For synonyms see FLATFOOT. [U.S. black use, late 1900s]

lard ass 1. someone with very fat BUTTOCKS; an obese person. **2.** very large BUTTOCKS. For synonyms and related terms see DUFF. [both senses, U.S., late 1900s]

lardo a fat person. [British and U.S., late 1900s-pres.]

lark to masturbate; to practice PENI-

LINGUS (q.v.). See comments at LARKING. [British, 1800s or before]

larker a frolicking rascal. [U.S. dialect, 1900s or before, Wentworth]

larking possibly FELLATIO but could also be CUNNILINGUS (both q.v.). Farmer and Henley define it as IRRUMATION (q.v.), which means "suck." Partridge suggests cunnilingus. Grose's euphemistic definition is "a lascivious practice that will not bear explanation." From a verb "lark," meaning to trap or catch larks. [British, late 1700s]

larro a homosexual male. Backslang for "oral" with reference to FELLATIO (q.v.). For synonyms see EPICENE. [U.S. slang, mid 1900s-pres.]

larydoodle the penis. For synonyms see YARD. [British colloquial, 1800s or before, Halliwell]

last abode the grave; death. [U.S., 1900s] Synonyms: CHURCH HOLE, COLD MUD, COLD STORAGE, DEEP SIX, DUST-BIN, EARTH-BATH, FINAL RESTING PLACE, GROUND SWEAT, PIT-HOLE.

last home the grave; death; a cemetery. Cf. FINAL RESTING PLACE. [U.S. euphemism, 1900s or before]

last muster death in expressions such as "go to the last muster." Cf. ANSWER THE FINAL SUMMONS, LAST ROUNDUP. [U.S. euphemism, 1900s]

latex 1. a euphemism for a latex condom. For synonyms see EEL-SKIN. [U.S., 1900s] **2.** Later.; See you later. [U.S., late 1900s-pres.]

lather sexual secretions; semen, natural vaginal lubricants, or both. [British, 1800s, Farmer and Henley]

lathered intoxicated with liquor. From an old term meaning "beaten." For synonyms see WOOFLED. [U.S. slang, early 1900s or before]

L.A. turnabouts amphetamine tablets with reference to their use by long-distance truckers. Cf. COASTS-TO-COASTS. [U.S. drug culture, mid 1900s-pres.]

laugh at the carpet to vomit; to vomit on a carpet. For synonyms see YORK. [U.S. slang, late 1900s]

laugh at the lawn to go outside and

vomit. For synonyms see YORK. [Australian, late 1900s-pres.]

laughing soup alcoholic liquor. *Cf.* GIGGLE-WATER. For synonyms see BOOZE. [U.S., 1900s, Wentworth and Flexner]

launching pad a sanitary napkin. For synonyms see MANHOLE COVER. [U.S. slang, late 1900s]

launch (one's lunch) to vomit. For synonyms see YORK. [U.S. slang, late 1900s]

laundry queen a black woman. For synonyms see RAVEN BEAUTY. [U.S. slang, early 1900s]

lav a W.C.A. truncation of "lavatory," which is an old euphemism for "bathroom." *Cf.* LAVO, LAVY. [U.S., 1900s]

lavatory 1. a sink; a wash basin. [since the 1300s] **2.** the bathroom itself. [from Latin *lavatorium*, "place to wash"; since the 1900s]

lavatory roll a roll of toilet paper. *Cf.* BATHROOM ROLL. For synonyms see T.P. [British and U.S. euphemism, 1900s]

lavendar homosexual. For synonyms see EPICENE. [British, mid 1900s-pres.]

lay 1. a job; a deal. A basic cant term for any enterprise (usually illegal) which brings a monetary return. [cant, late 1700s, Grose] **2.** copulation. [U.S. colloquial, since the early 1900s or before] **3.** a woman considered solely as a sexual object. [U.S. colloquial, 1900s] Synonyms and related terms for sense 3: ADULTERA, ADULTRESS, ALLEY CAT, AMORET, AMOROSA, ASS, ATHANASIAN WENCH, BALL-BUSTER, BALONEY, BAND, BANGSTER, BED-BUNNY, BEETLE, BED-BUG, BELLY-LASS, B-GIRL, BIFFER, BIG TWENTY, BIKE, BIMBO, BITER, BIT OF JAM, BLIMP, BLUE GOWN, BOB TAIL, BOMB-SHELL, BROOD, BUMMERKEH, BUNDLE, BUNNY, CAKE, CALICO QUEEN, CHARITY DAME, CHARITY GIRL, CHARITY STUFF, CHIPPY, CLAPTRAP, CLEAVE, CLEAVER, COMING WENCH, COMING WOMAN, CUD-DLE-BUNNY, DANGEROUS CURVES, DEAD EASY, DEB-GENERATE, DIRTY-LEG, DRESS GOODS, DUNKIE, EASY, EASY LAY, EASY MAKE, EASY MARK, EASY MEAT, EASY-RIDER, EASY VIRTUE, FAD-CATTLE, FIZ-GIG, FLAP, FLAPPER, FLIRT-GILL, FLIRTI-GIGGS, FLOOSEY, FLY, FORNICATRESS, FRANION, FREE-FOR-ALL, GASH, GAY, GAY IN THE GROIN, GIG, GIGLER, GIG-LETTING, GIGLOT, GIGSY, GILL, GILL-FLURT, GIXIE, GLUTZ, GOBBLE-PRICK, GOOBER-GRABBER, GOOD GIRL, GOOD LAY, GOOSEBERRY-PUDDING, GRADUATE, GRASSBACK, GRIND, GROUPIE, HAIRY BIT, HAT, HIGHFLYER, HO, HOBBY, HOBBY-HORSE, HOGMINNY, HORNS-TO-SELL, HOT-BOT, HOT LAY, HOT MEMBER, HOT NUM-BER, HOT PANTS, HOT SKETCH, HOT STUFF, HOT TAMALE, HOT TOMATO, HOT-TONGUE, HUMMER, HUMP, HUNK, HUSSY, JAY, JAZZ BABY, KNOCK, LADY-BIRD, LETCHING-PIECE, LIBERTINE, LIGHT FRIGATE, LIGHT HOUSEWIFE, LIGHT O' LOVE, LIGHT SKIRTS, LIGHT WOMAN, LOOSE, LOOSE-KIRTLE, LOOSE WOMAN, LOW RENT, MADAMOIZOOK, MERRY-BIT, MISS HORNER, MUTTON, NESTLE-COCK, NIT, NYSOT, OPEN-ARSE, PARNEL, PEACH, PICK-UP, PIE, PIECE OF ASS, PIECE OF SNATCH, PIECE OF STRAY, PIECE OF TAIL, PIG, PIG-MEAT, PLAYGIRL, PLAYTHING, PLEASER, POKE, POLL, PUSH-OVER, PUTA, QUAIL, QUEAN, QUIFF, RIG-MUTTON, ROUNDHEEL, RUTTER, SCATE, SCUPPER, SEX-JOB, SEXPOT, SHAGSTRESS, SHORT-HEELED WENCH, SHORT-HEELS, SHTUP, SLACK, SLEEPING-PARTNER, SLEEZ, SLOT-TED-JOB, SMOCK-TOY, SNAKE, SNATCH, SOFT-JAW, SOFT LEG, SOFT ROLL, SPLIT, SPLIT-TAIL, STIFF, STROLLOP, SUB, SUB-URB-SINNER, TABLE-GRADE, TAINT, TIB, TICKLE-TAIL, TICKLE-TOBY, TIT, TOMRIG, TOWN PUNCH, TRAMP, TRASH, TROT, TUBE, WAG-TAIL, WALK-UP FUCK, WAN-TON, WARM BIT, WARMING-PAN, WILLING-TIT, YES-GIRL. **4.** to copulate with a woman, possibly by force. [U.S. colloquial, 1900s] **5.** to copulate with a man, said of a woman. [U.S. slang, mid 1900s-pres.] **6.** a prostitute. [U.S. colloquial, 1900s] **7.** a CATAMITE (*q.v.*). From senses 3 and 6. For synonyms see BRONCO. [U.S. underworld, early 1900s] **8.** anal copulation; PEDERASTY (*q.v.*). From sense 2. [U.S. underworld, early 1900s, Goldin, O'Leary, and Lipsius]

layed 1. having been copulated with. From LAY (senses 3 and 4). Also **laid.** [U.S. colloquial, 1900s] **2.** intoxicated with marijuana. From LAY (sense 4);

i.e., SCREWED (*q.v.*). *Cf.* LAID-OUT (sense 3). [U.S. drug culture, mid 1900s-pres.]

lay some pipe to coit a woman. From the act of placing a length of pipe in a trench. *Cf.* PIPE (sense 1). [U.S. slang, mid 1900s-pres.]

lay the hip 1. to copulate. [U.S. slang, early 1900s] **2.** to smoke opium, *i.e.*, to "lie on the hip." *Cf.* HIP-LAYER. [U.S., early 1900s or before]

lay the leg to coit a woman. *Cf.* LIFT ONE'S LEG. [U.S. colloquial, early 1900s]

L.B. a pound of a drug, especially marijuana. For synonyms see MARI. [U.S. drug culture, late 1900s]

lead poisoning death caused by being shot with a lead bullet. [U.S., early 1900s-pres.]

leak 1. the female genitals. [probably written nonce; British slang, early 1700s] **2.** urination; an act of urination. **3.** to urinate. For synonyms see WHIZ. [both colloquial since the 1500s]

leakery (also **leak-house**) a privy or a latrine; a male urinal. [Australian, 1900s]

lean green money. [U.S., late 1900s-pres.]

leap to copulate. Also nominalized in terms such as LEAPING-HOUSE (*q.v.*). *Cf.* JUMP. [slang since the 1500s]

leaping intoxicated with alcohol. For synonyms see WOOFLED. [U.S. slang, early 1900s]

leather 1. the female genitals, specifically the vagina. "Leather" here is synonymous with SKIN (sense 4). [early 1500s] **2.** a homosexual male, especially one who is cruel and sexually sadistic. *Cf.* SADISM. [U.S. slang, mid 1900s-pres.] **3.** pertaining to any sadistic, virile male, homosexual or not. Senses 2 and 3 refer to virile males wearing leather jackets. [U.S. slang, 1900s]

leather-brained stupid. [U.S. colloquial, 1900s]

leather-dresser a lecher; a man who copulates frequently. *Cf.* LEATHER (sense 1). [British slang, 1800s, Farmer and Henley]

leather-head 1. an oaf. Possibly referring to the wearing of a leather cap or to baldness. [colloquial since the late 1600s] **2.** a policeman. Because he "leathers" (beats with a leather strap) people's heads. [U.S., late 1800s, Thornton]

leather lane the female genitals, specifically the vagina. A reinterpretation of a London street name. For synonyms see MONOSYLLABLE. [British, early 1800s or before]

leather queen an aggressive and possibly sadistic male homosexual who wears leather clothing. *Cf.* LEATHER (sense 2). [U.S. homosexual use, mid 1900s-pres.]

leather-stretcher the penis. *Cf.* LEATHER (sense 1), STRETCH LEATHER. For synonyms see YARD. [British, 1800s or before]

leave this world to die. *Cf.* GO ON TO A BETTER WORLD. [euphemistic, 1900s or before]

leaving-shop the female genitals, a place where one's SPENDINGS (*q.v.*) are left. From an old term for "pawn shop." [British slang, mid 1800s]

lech (also **letch**) **1.** a sexual urge; a sexual thought or fantasy. [British and U.S., 1700s-pres.] **2.** to pursue or enjoy sexual matters, especially illicit sex. [from French *lecher;* British and U.S., early 1900s-pres.] **3.** a lewd man; a lecher. [U.S. colloquial, early 1900s-pres.] **4.** to ogle or stare at a woman; to study a woman sexually. [slang, 1900s]

lecher (also **leacher**, **letcher**) **1.** a lewd man; a habitual fornicator. [since the 1100s, *Oxford English Dictionary*] Synonyms and related terms: ADULTERER, ALLEY CAT, AMORIST, AMOROSO, ANIMAL, ASS-MAN, AVOWTERER, BALLOCKER, BALLOCKS, BASHER, BEAVER-RETRIEVER, BED-PRESSER, BELLY-BUMPER, BIRD'S-NESTER, BLUEBEARD, BUCK FITCH, BULL, BUM-FIDDLER, BUST-MAKER, CARNALITE, CASANOVA, CHESTER MOLESTER, CHIMNEY SWEEP, CHIPPY-CHASER, COCK-FIGHTER, COCK-HOUND, COCK OF THE GAME, COCKSMAN, COCKSMITH, CORINTHIAN, DIRTY DOG, DIVER, DOG, DOLLY-MOPPER, D.O.M., DON JUAN, DUNDERING RAKE, EAGER-BEAVER, FAGGO-

TEER, FAGGOT-MASTER, FAGGOTMONGER, FEATHER-BED SOLDIER, FIGURE-MAKER, FISHMONGER, FLEECE-HUNTER, FLEECE-MONGER, FLESH-FLY, FLESH-MAGGOT, FLESH-MONGER, FLOWER-FANCIER, FORBIDDEN FRUIT EATER, FOX-HUNTER, FRANION, FUCKSTER, GAME-COCK, GAP-STOPPER, GASH-HOUND, GAY DOG, GAY-MAN, GETTER, GIN-BURGLAR, GIN-SHEP-HERD, GIRL-TRAP, GOAT, GOER, GROUSER, GULLY-RAKER, GUSSETEER, HAIR-MONGER, HEADHUNTER, HIGH PRIEST OF PAPHOS, HOLER, HOOTCHEE, HORSEMAN, HOT MEMBER, HOT NUTS, HOT PANTS, HOUND, JINKER, JUMBLER, KID-STRETCHER, KING OF CLUBS, KNOCKER, LADIES' TAILOR, LEACHER, LEATHER-DRESSER, LEG-LIFTER, LIBERTINE, LOTHARIO, LOVER, LUSTY-GUTS, LUSTY-LAWRENCE, MAKE-OUT ARTIST, MAKER, MEAT HOUND, MEAT-MONGER, MILLER, MINK, MOLL-HUNTER, MOLROWER, MOR-MON, MOUSE-HUNT, MR. GROIN, MR. HORNER, MUTTON-COVE, MUTTONER, MUTTON-MONGER, NUGGING-COVE, PARISH-BULL, PARISH-PRIG, PARISH-STALLION, PEACH-ORCHARD BOAR, PELTER, PER-FORMER, PHILANDERER, PINCH-BOTTOM, PINCH-BUTTOCK, PINCH-CUNT, POOPSTER, PRIGGER, PUNKER, QUAIL-HUNTER, QUIM-STICKER, RANGER, RATTLE-CAP, RATTLER, RIBALD, RIDER, ROOSTER, ROUNDER, RUMPER, RUMP-SPLITTER, RUTTER, SCOR-TATOR, SERVANT, SEXPERT, SEXUAL ATH-LETE, SHAG, SHARP-SHOOTER, SHIFTER, SKIN-DOG, SKIRT-FOIST, SMELL-SMOCK, SMOCK-SQUIRE, SMOCKSTER, SON OF VENUS, SPORT, SPORTSMAN, SQUIRE OF THE BODY, STALLION, STOAT, STRINGER, STUD, SWINGER, SWIVER, TAD, THRUM-STER, TOMCAT, TOUGH CAT, TOWN BULL, TOWN RAKE, TOWN STALLION, TUG-MUTTON, TUMMY-TICKLER, TWAT-FAKER, TWEAK, TWIGGER, WARM MEMBER, WENCHER, WHISKER-SPLITTER, WHORE-HOPPER, WHORE-HOUND, WHOREMASTER, WOLF, WOMAN-CHASER, WOMANIZER, WOOD-MAN, YENTZER. **2.** to copulate. For synonyms see OCCUPY. [late 1500s]

leerics sexually suggestive song lyrics. [U.S., late 1900s-pres.]

left-handed wife a concubine; the equivalent of a common-law wife. [mid 1600s-1900s]

left-hand son a male bastard. [U.S. underworld, early 1900s]

leg 1. copulation in expressions such as "get some leg." [U.S. slang, mid 1900s-pres.] **2.** a young woman; women considered sexually. [U.S. colloquial, mid 1900s-pres.] **3.** a promiscuous woman; a prostitute. A truncation of DIRTY-LEG (q.v.). [U.S. slang, mid 1900s-pres.]

legless alcohol intoxicated. For synonyms see WOOFLED. [British slang, late 1900s]

leg-lifter a lecher; a male fornicator. Cf. LIFT ONE'S LEG. [British slang, 1700s-1800s]

leg-man a man strongly attracted to women with beautiful legs; a man sexually stimulated by women's legs. From the nickname for a man who does message-carrying and expediting, i.e., "leg-work." Cf. ASS-MAN, TIT-MAN. [U.S. colloquial, mid 1900s-pres.]

leg-opener enough liquor to make a woman agree to copulation. Jocular. Based on eye-opener. [British and U.S. slang, late 1900s]

legume the hallucinogenic substance PEYOTE. A "plant." [U.S. drug culture, late 1900s] See also ORGANIC STUFF.

lem-kee opium. For synonyms see OPE. [Chinese or mock-Chinese; U.S. underworld, early 1900s or before]

lemon tea urine. Rhyming slang on PEE. [British, late 1900s-pres.]

lesbian 1. pliant and accommodating. No negative connotations, but often misunderstood during the 1600s-1700s when the word was used in this sense. [now obsolete] **2.** a woman who is emotionally or sexually and emotionally devoted to members of her own sex; a female homosexual. **3.** pertaining to a female homosexual. [both since the late 1800s]

lesbo a lesbian. For synonyms see LESBYTERIAN. [Australian and U.S., early 1900s]

lesbyterian a jocular nickname for a lesbian. Based on "Presbyterian." Cf. LESBO. [U.S. homosexual use, mid 1900s, Farrell] Synonyms: AMY-JOHN, BEAN FLICKER, BLUFF, BOON-DAGGER, BULL, BULL-DAGGER, BULLDIKE, BULL-

DIKER, BULLDYKE, BULLDYKER, BUTCH, CLAM SMACKERS, CRACK SNACKER, CRESTED HEN, DIESEL DYKE, DIKE, DUFF, DYKE, DYKEY, FAIRY, FAIRY LADY, FEM, FEMME, FLUFF, FLUZZ DYKE, FUTUTRIX, GAL-BOY, GOOSE GIRL, JASPER, LADY-LOVER, LES, LESBINE, LESBO, LESLIE, LEZ, LEZBO, LEZO, LOVER UNDER THE LAP, LUPPIES, MAN, MARGE, MARY, MASON, MINTIE, NELLY, QUEEN, RUFFLE, RUG-MUNCHER, SAPPHIC LOVE, SCREAMING QUEEN, SCREWBALL, SERGEANT, SUCKER, THESPIAN, THIRD-SEXER, TOOTSIE, TOP SERGEANT, WOLF, XENA.

leslie a lesbian. [Australian, early 1900s]

let a fart to release intestinal gas, usually audibly. For synonyms see GURK.

letching-piece a sexually loose woman; a woman considered sexually. For synonyms see LAY. [British slang, 1900s, *Dictionary of Slang and Unconventional English*]

letch-water semen or natural vaginal lubrication, especially as an indication of sexual arousal. [British, 1700s]

let fly 1. to urinate. For synonyms see WHIZ. **2.** to spit. **3.** to break wind. [all senses, U.S. colloquial or slang, 1900s]

let fly a fart to release intestinal gas. [originally "let flee a fart" in "The Miller's Tale" (Chaucer); colloquial since the 1300s]

let go 1. to ejaculate. For synonyms see MELT. [British, 1800s] **2.** to fire; to terminate the employment of someone. [U.S. colloquial, 1900s or before]

let one to release intestinal gas. The "one" is euphemistic for FART (sense 2). For synonyms see GURK. [U.S. colloquial, mid 1900s-pres.]

let one go to release intestinal gas, presumably after a period of avoiding doing so. For synonyms see GURK. [U.S. slang, mid 1900s-pres.]

letter a condom. A truncation of FRENCH LETTER (*q.v.*). *Cf.* ENVELOPE, POST A LETTER. [British, 1800s]

Levi lovin' a dry hump; copulation with the clothes on. [U.S., late 1900s-pres.]

lewd obscene; lascivious. Originally meant "rude." [since the 1300s] Synonyms and related terms: AFTER ONE'S GREENS, ANATOMICAL, APPROACHABLE, BESTIAL, BUCKSOM, CLINICAL, COMING, CRACKISH, DISSOLUTE, EROGENOUS, FAST, FESCENNINE, FILTHY, FOND OF MEAT, FREE-FUCKING, FRENCH, FRUITING, FULL-FLAVORED, GAY, GOATISH, LASCIVIOUS, LENOCINANT, LIBIDINOUS, LICENTIOUS, LIGHT, LIGHT-HEELED, LOOSE, LOOSE IN THE HILT, LOOSE IN THE RUMP, LOOSE-LEGGED, MERRY, PAPHIAN, PERVE, PERVY, PLAYSOME, RADGY, RIBALD, RIG, RIGGISH, RUMP-PROUD, SPICY, SPORTFUL, SPORTIVE, SULTRY, TENTIGINOUS, THICK, TORRID, UNCHASTE, UP-LIFTING, VESTAL, WANTON, WELL-BRED, X-RATED. See also HUMPY.

Lewinsky 1. a vacuum cleaner, something that sucks. [U.S., late 1900s-pres.] **2.** a fellatio. [U.S., late 1900s-pres.]

lez (also **les**) a lesbian. [U.S. slang, mid 1900s-pres.]

lezbo a lesbian. For synonyms see LESBYTERIAN. [U.S. slang, late 1900s]

lezo a lesbian. *Cf.* LESBO. [Australian slang, early 1900s]

lice and fleas someone who carries sexually transmitted diseases. [U.S., late 1900s-pres.]

lick-box a SODOMITE, presumably a fellator. *Cf.* BOX (sense 4). [U.S. underworld, early 1900s]

lickety-split CUNNILINGUS (*q.v.*). "Split" refers to the PUDENDAL CLEAVAGE (*q.v.*) a jocular reapplication of the adverb describing speed in running. [U.S. slang, late 1900s-pres.]

Lick my froth! "Go to hell!"; "Drop dead!"; "Eat me!" Refers to vaginal lubrication. California teens. [U.S. slang, late 1900s]

Lick my love pump! "Perform FELLATIO on me!"; "Suck my prick!" A provocative exclamation. [U.S. collegiate, late 1900s, Munro]

lick-spigot 1. a MOUTH-WHORE (*q.v.*). The spigot is the penis. [British slang, 1700s] **2.** a drunkard who would lick the spigot of a cask to get the alcohol. [British colloquial, 1800s]

lick-twat a CUNNILINGUIST (*q.v.*), presumably a male. [mid 1600s]

licorice stick the penis. For synonyms see GENITALS, YARD. [British homosexual use, 1900s, McDonald]

lid one ounce of marijuana. *Cf.* O.Z., TIN. [U.S. drug culture, mid 1900s-pres.]

lidpoppers amphetamine tablets or capsules. Refers to eyelids. For synonyms see AMP. [U.S. drug culture, mid 1900s-pres.]

lie down 1. to be brought to bed for childbirth. [euphemistic, late 1500s-1700s] **2.** to smoke opium. *Cf.* LAY THE HIP (sense 2). For synonyms see SMOKE. [U.S. underworld, early 1900s]

lifejacket a condom. For synonyms see EEL-SKIN. [U.S. slang, late 1900s]

life-preserver the penis. From the name of a flotation device. [British, 1800s, Farmer and Henley]

lift a leg on a woman to copulate with a woman. *Cf.* LEG-LIFTER. [Scots, late 1700s (Robert Burns)]

lifted drunk. See also HIGH. For synonyms see WOOFLED. [U.S., late 1900s-pres.]

lift one's leg to copulate. *Cf.* LAY THE LEG, LEG-LIFTER, PLAY AT LIFT-LEG. [British euphemistic colloquial, 1700s]

lift up to get an erection. [colloquial and euphemistic, 1900s and before]

light 1. lewd; wanton. [numerous written attestations since the 1300s] **2.** intoxicated with alcohol. [U.S., early 1700s, Ben Franklin]

light bulb a pregnant woman. Describes a woman's shape in late pregnancy. [U.S. slang, mid 1900s]

light-footed pertaining to a homosexual male. *Cf.* LIGHT (sense 1), LIGHT ON HIS FEET. [U.S. slang, 1900s]

light-heeled wanton; pertaining to a sexually loose woman. *Cf.* LIGHT (sense 1), ROUND-HEEL. [since the early 1600s]

lightning 1. gin. *Cf.* CLAP OF THUNDER. For synonyms see RUIN. [British slang, 1700s-1800s] **2.** inferior whisky. *Cf.* WHITE LIGHTNING. [British and U.S., late 1700s-pres.] **3.** amphet-

amines. For synonyms see AMP. [U.S. drug culture, mid 1900s-pres.]

light o' love 1. a wanton woman. *Cf.* LIGHT (sense 1). [late 1500s] **2.** a harmless term of endearment for a girlfriend. [colloquial, 1900s or before]

light on his feet pertaining to an effeminate male. *Cf.* LIGHT (sense 1), LIGHT-FOOTED, possibly referring to a male dancer. [U.S. slang, mid 1900s-pres.]

lights out death. [U.S. underworld, early 1900s]

light the lamp to have sexual intercourse, said of a woman. *Cf.* LAMP OF LOVE. [British euphemism, 1800s]

light troops lice. For synonyms see WALKING DANDRUFF. [British slang, early 1800s]

light up have an orgasm. [British euphemism, mid 1900s]

light wet gin. For synonyms see RUIN. [British slang, early 1800s]

light woman a lewd woman. *Cf.* LIGHT FRIGATE. For synonyms see LAY. [cant or colloquial, late 1600s, B.E.]

like to be fond of someone; to feel the beginnings of love for someone. Occasionally euphemistic for "to desire sexually." [since the 1500s or before]

like a bat out of hell extremely fast. [U.S. colloquial, early 1900s-pres.]

like a fart in a gale insignificant; trivial. [British, late 1900s-pres.]

like a spare prick (at a wedding) to be obviously surplus to requirements. [British and U.S., late 1900s-pres.]

like a tit in a trance as in a dream. [British, late 1900s-pres.]

Like fuck! an exclamation; a disbelieving reply. [British and U.S., 1900s]

Like fun! a disguise of LIKE FUCK! (*q.v.*). [U.S. colloquial, mid 1900s-pres.]

Like hell! a disbelieving reply or exclamation, "The hell you say!" [U.S. colloquial, 1900s]

like pigs in shit with great satisfaction; with great congeniality. [U.S. colloquial, 1900s or before]

like the clappers (of hell) very fast or sudden. [British, late 1900s-pres.]

likkered-up intoxicated with alcohol. See LIQUORED-UP.

lilac effeminate. [British, late 1900s-pres.]

lilies of the valley hemorrhoids. [U.S., late 1900s-pres.]

limb a leg. A term of avoidance for the word "leg," whether human or of furniture. [British and U.S., early 1700s-1800s]

limber intoxicated with alcohol. For synonyms see WOOFLED. [U.S., early 1700s, Ben Franklin]

lime (also **line**) to impregnate a bitch (dog). Cf. LINE. [mid 1500s and obsolete]

limit, the coition. Can also refer to any or all sexual activity except coition. Cf. ALL THE WAY. [U.S. colloquial, 1900s]

limp intoxicated with alcohol. Cf. LIMBER. [U.S. colloquial, 1900s]

limp-wrist an effeminate male or a homosexual male; the same as BROKEN-WRIST (q.v.). [U.S. slang, mid 1900s-pres.]

limpy an impotent man. [U.S., late 1900s-pres.]

linguist a CUNNILINGUIST (q.v.). [slang, mid 1900s-pres.]

lion drunk intoxicated with alcohol. Cf. ROARING-DRUNK. [slang, late 1500s]

lip 1. to kiss intimately. Cf. MOUTH (sense 1). [from *Othello* (Shakespeare)] **2.** a lawyer. [U.S. slang, early 1900s]

lip-clap 1. a kiss. **2.** to kiss. Cf. LAP-CLAP. [both senses, late 1500s]

lip gloss lies and deception; BULLSHIT. For synonyms see ANIMAL. [U.S. slang, late 1900s]

Lipton's a poor grade of marijuana. From "Lipton's Tea" (trademark). [U.S. drug culture, mid 1900s]

liquefied intoxicated with alcohol. For synonyms see WOOFLED. [U.S. slang, early 1900s-pres.]

liquid amber beer. For synonyms see BOOZE. [Australian, mid 1900s-pres.]

liquidate someone to kill someone. [British and U.S., mid 1900s-pres.]

liquid bam injectable amphetamines. Cf. BAM. For synonyms see AMP. [U.S. drug culture, late 1900s, Kaiser]

liquid bread beer. For synonyms see BOOZE. [U.S., late 1900s-pres.]

liquid-fire bad whisky. For synonyms see EMBALMING FLUID. [colloquial, late 1800s-pres.]

liquid-laugh vomitus. For synonyms see YORK. [British and U.S. slang, late 1900s]

liquid lunch a midday repast consisting of alcoholic drink only. [British and U.S., late 1900s-pres.]

liquor 1. any fluid. No negative connotations. [1200s] **2.** alcoholic drink. For synonyms see AMP. [since c. 1300, *Oxford English Dictionary*] **3.** to drink liquor, especially to drink to excess. For synonyms see PLAY CAMELS. [since the early 1800s]

liquorish intoxicated with alcohol. For synonyms see WOOFLED. [U.S. slang, 1900s]

lit 1. intoxicated with alcohol. [U.S. colloquial, 1900s] **2.** intoxicated with marijuana or other drugs. Cf. LIT TO THE GUARDS, LIT-UP. [U.S. slang and drug culture, early 1900s-pres.]

lithper an effeminate male, possibly a homosexual. A lisping pronunciation of LISPER (q.v.). [U.S. slang, 1900s]

little bit copulation. For synonyms see SMOCKAGE. [U.S. colloquial, mid 1900s-pres.]

little boy's room the men's W.C. Cf. LITTLE GIRL'S ROOM. [U.S., early 1900s-pres.]

little brother the penis. Cf. LITTLE SISTER. [British euphemism, 1800s]

little finger the penis. Cf. FOREFINGER, MIDDLE FINGER, POTATO FINGER, THUMB OF LOVE. [originally Biblical (I Kings); since the 1600s]

little friend the menses. For synonyms see FLOODS. [British euphemism, early 1900s-pres.]

little girl's room a women's W.C. Cf. LITTLE BOY'S ROOM. [U.S. colloquial, early 1900s-pres.]

little house (also **littlest house**) a privy; an outhouse. *Cf.* PETTY-HOUSE, SMALLEST ROOM. For synonyms see AJAX. [widespread colloquial, early 1700s-pres.]

little man a small boy's penis. For synonyms see YARD. [British, mid 1900s-pres.]

little man in the boat 1. the clitoris. *Cf.* BOY-IN-THE-BOAT. [British and U.S., 1800s-1900s] **2.** the navel. [British, 1800s-1900s], *Dictionary of Slang and Unconventional English*]

little Mary 1. the female genitals, especially the vagina. [U.S. slang, 1900s] **2.** the stomach. [euphemism, early 1900s, (J.M. Barrie)]

little shit a worthless TWIT of a person; a total JERK. For synonyms see OAF. [U.S. slang, mid 1900s-pres.]

little sister the female genitals. *Cf.* LITTLE BROTHER. [British euphemism, 1800s]

little sister is here a catch phrase indicating that the menses have begun. [euphemistic, 1900s or before]

little visitor the menses. For synonyms see FLOODS. [colloquial, 1900s and before]

little Willie the penis; a personification of the penis. [British, 1900s]

lit-up (also **lit**) **1.** intoxicated with alcohol, especially in expressions such as "lit up like a Christmas tree." [U.S. colloquial, early 1900s-pres.] **2.** drug intoxicated; intoxicated with marijuana. [U.S. drug culture, mid 1900s-pres.]

live sausage the penis. *Cf.* LIVE RABBIT. [mid 1600s (Urquhart)]

living flute See FLUTE.

lizard the penis. *Cf.* STROKE THE LIZARD. [U.S. slang, mid 1900s-pres.]

lizzie a lesbian. For synonyms see LESBYTERIAN. [slang, 1900s]

Lizzie boy (also **Lizzie**) an effeminate male. *Cf.* NAN-BOY. For synonyms see FRIBBLE. [U.S.,1900s]

load 1. semen. For synonyms see METTLE. [late 1500s-pres.] **2.** the weight of a man's body during copulation. **3.** a venereal disease. [slang and euphemistic, 1800s] **4.** sufficient alcohol in the

bloodstream to produce intoxication. *Cf.* HAVE A LOAD ON, JAG. [colloquial or slang since the mid 1700s] **5.** the feces; the fullness of feces in the bowels. *Cf.* DROP ONE'S LOAD (sense 2). For synonyms see DUNG.

loaded 1. intoxicated with alcohol. [U.S. and British colloquial, 1800s-pres.] **2.** drug-intoxicated with marijuana or heroin. [U.S. underworld, colloquial and drug culture, early 1900s-pres.] **3.** pregnant. *Cf.* LOAD (sense 1). [colloquial, 1800s-1900s]

loaded for bear 1. intoxicated with alcohol. [U.S. colloquial, 1800s-1900s] **2.** very angry. [U.S. colloquial, 1900s]

loaded to the earlobes drunk. For synonyms see WOOFLED. [British, mid 1900s-pres.]

loaded to the gills (also **loaded to the barrel, loaded to the guards**) intoxicated with alcohol. [U.S. colloquial, 1900s]

loaded to the gunwales (also **loaded to the gunnels**) intoxicated with alcohol. [U.S. nautical, late 1800s]

loaded to the hat drunk. For synonyms see WOOFLED. [British., mid 1900s-pres.]

loaded to the muzzle drunk. For synonyms see WOOFLED. [British, mid 1900s-pres.]

load of cods (wallop), a nonsense. For synonyms see ANIMAL. [British, early 1900s-pres.]

load of crap, a nonsense. For synonyms see ANIMAL. [British and U.S., early 1900s-pres.]

load of guff, a nonsense. For synonyms see ANIMAL. [British and U.S., early 1900s-pres.]

load of old cobblers, a utter nonsense. For synonyms see ANIMAL. [British, early 1900s-pres.]

loady a drinker or drug user. Also **loadie.** [U.S., late 1900s-pres.]

lob-cock (also **lob**) **1.** a dull oaf; a stupid LUMP (*q.v.*). *Cf.* LOB (sense 1). [colloquial or cant, mid 1500s] **2.** a large, flaccid or semierect penis; the same as LOB (sense 2). *Cf.* LOB-PRICK. From COCK (sense 3). [British colloquial,

1700s, Grose] **3.** a large woodpecker. From COCK (sense 1), no negative connotations. [U.S. colloquial, 1800s]

lob in to insert the penis. [British colloquial, 1900s]

lob-prick a partial erection or an insufficient erection. *Cf.* LOB-COCK (sense 2). [British, late 1800s (Farmer)]

lock 1. the female genitals. The counterpart of KEY (sense 1), "penis." [1600s-1700s] **2.** a person of Polish nationality. Derogatory. [U.S. slang, late 1900s]

locker the female genitals; the vagina. [slang, 1900s or before]

locker-room butyl nitrate sold as a room deodorant stick, the vapors of which are inhaled producing the same effect as amyl nitrite. The term is also used for other drugs. [U.S. drug culture, mid 1900s-pres.]

locks' box (also **lox box**) a van load of Polish cleaning ladies. *Cf.* LOCK. A play on "lox-box." [U.S. slang, late 1900s]

lockjawed intoxicated. For synonyms see WOOFLED. [British, late 1900s-pres.]

locoweed marijuana or a marijuana cigarette. From the common name of a plant which grows in the Southwest U.S. grazing lands and is said to drive cattle mad or "loco." *Cf.* GO LOCO. [U.S. slang, early 1900s-pres.]

locus a W.C. *Cf.* PLACE (sense 1). [from the Latin word for "place"; U.S. slang, 1900s]

log 1. an opium pipe. [U.S. underworld, early 1900s] **2.** the erect penis. *Cf.* POLE (sense 1), RAIL. For synonyms see ERECTION. [widespread jocular nonce]

log in to defecate. For synonyms see EASE ONESELF. [U.S., late 1900s-pres.]

lollos well-proportioned breasts. From the proper name "Gina Lollobrigida" or from "lollopalooza." *Cf.* LULUS (*q.v.*). [British slang, mid 1900s]

lolly money. [Australian, mid 1900s-pres.]

lollypop (also **lollipop**) the penis. *Cf.* LADIES' LOLLIPOP. For synonyms see

YARD. [British slang, 1800s, Farmer and Henley]

long-arm inspection an inspection of the erect penis. Based on SHORT-ARM INSPECTION (*q.v.*). [U.S., 1900s]

long bread money. [U.S., late 1900s-pres.]

long-eye the female genitals. From the configuration of the PUDENDAL CLEAVAGE (*q.v.*). *Cf.* BLIND-EYE (sense 2), SQUINT. [British slang, mid 1800s]

long green money. [U.S., late 1900s-pres.]

long John the penis. *Cf.* JOHNSON, JOHN THOMAS. [U.S. slang, 1900s]

long streak of piss a tall, thin person. [British and U.S., mid 1900s-pres.]

loo a W.C. There are a number of suggested etymologies. Possibly from French *l'eau*, "water"; possibly from GARDY LOO! (*q.v.*); possibly from the numeral "100." The *Lexicon Balatronicum* has an entry "loo," which is "For the good of the loo; for the benefit of the company or community." The word is most likely from "lieu," the "place." *Cf.* LOCUS, PLACE (sense 1). [British colloquial, early 1900s-pres.; recently a part of U.S. vocabulary]

loochie money. From LUCRE. [U.S., late 1900s-pres.]

looking piggy pregnant. For synonyms see FRAGRANT. [U.S. dialect (Ozarks), Randolph and Wilson]

look pricks to OGLE (*q.v.*) and appear to be inviting coition; to make a sexual proposition with the eyes. [British slang, 1800s, Farmer and Henley]

loop-de-loop mutual oral-genital copulation. *Cf.* FLIP-FLOP, SIXTY-NINE. [U.S. slang, mid 1900s]

looped intoxicated with alcohol. From the expression "thrown for a loop." [U.S. slang, early 1900s-pres.]

loop-legged intoxicated with alcohol. For synonyms see WOOFLED. [U.S. slang, 1900s]

loopy drunk. For synonyms see WOOFLED. [U.S., late 1900s-pres.]

loose 1. wanton; lewd; sexually loose and legally unattached. *Cf.* LIGHT (sense 1). [since the late 1400s] **2.** pertaining to laxness in the bowels. See LAX. [since the early 1500s]

loose in the hilt (also **loose in the haft**) **1.** intoxicated with alcohol. [U.S. slang, early 1700s, Ben Franklin] **2.** wanton. [British slang, 1800s, Farmer and Henley] **3.** having diarrhea. [British, 1800s, Farmer and Henley]

loose-love center a brothel. [U.S. slang, 1900s]

loose-love lady a prostitute. [U.S. slang, early 1900s]

looser than a faggot's ass-hole very loose. [U.S. slang, late 1900s]

loose woman a sexually indiscreet female. Cf. LOOSE (sense 1). [U.S. colloquial, 1900s]

lop cock a circumcised penis. For synonyms see YARD. [British, early 1900s-pres.]

Lord love a duck! a mock oath and an exclamation. [colloquial, 1900s]

lorphs BLUE MORPHONE; hydromorphone, a painkiller. Possibly also a blue elixir of morphine sulfate. Cf. BLORPHS, LORDS. [U.S. drug culture, late 1900s, Kaiser]

lose a meal to vomit. For synonyms see YORK. [Australian euphemism, early 1900s, Baker]

lose it 1. to vomit. For synonyms see YORK. [U.S. slang, late 1900s] **2.** to lose control of oneself; to lose one's temper. General slang. [U.S. and elsewhere, late 1900s]

lose one's cookies to vomit. [U.S. slang, mid 1900s-pres.]

lose one's guts to vomit. For synonyms see YORK. [U.S., late 1900s-pres.]

lose one's lunch to vomit. For synonyms see YORK. [U.S. and elsewhere, late 1900s] See also LAUNCH (ONE'S LUNCH).

lost in the sauce alcohol intoxicated and bewildered. For synonyms see WOOFLED. [U.S. slang, late 1900s]

lost lady a prostitute. For synonyms see HARLOT. [U.S. colloquial, 1900s]

love 1. sex; copulation. **2.** to copulate

with. [both senses, euphemistic, since the 1500s or before]

love-apples the testicles. From the colloquial term for an eggplant or a tomato. Cf. APPLES (sense 2). [British, 1800s, Farmer and Henley]

love-begotten child a bastard. For synonyms see ACCIDENT. [colloquial euphemism, 1800s]

love boat phencyclidine, the drug P.C.P. in a form that is to be smoked. For synonyms see P.C.P. [U.S. drug culture, late 1900s]

love-bubbles the breasts, especially well-formed breasts. Cf. BUBBLES. For synonyms see BOSOM. [British, 1900s, *Dictionary of Slang and Unconventional English*]

love chamber the vagina. For synonyms see PASSAGE. [written nonce; U.S. slang, mid 1900s-pres.]

love-child a bastard. [colloquial euphemism, early 1800s]

love-dart (also **dart of love**) the penis. Cf. DARD. [British euphemism, 1800s, Farmer and Henley]

love dust cocaine. For synonyms see NOSE-CANDY. [U.S. drug culture, late 1900s]

love glove a condom. For synonyms see EEL-SKIN. [U.S., late 1900s-pres.]

love-handles fat on the sides of a man or woman held onto during copulation. [U.S. slang, mid 1900s-pres.]

love-juice semen; male or female sexual secretions. [euphemistic nonce, 1800s-pres.]

love-lane the female genitals. For synonyms see MONOSYLLABLE. [British, 1800s, Farmer and Henley]

love-liquor semen. For synonyms see METTLE. [British euphemism, 1800s, Farmer and Henley]

love nuggets marijuana. For synonyms see MARI. [U.S., late 1900s-pres.]

love-nuts pain in the testicles due to sexual excitement. Cf. HOT ROCKS (sense 2), STONE-ACHE. [U.S. slang, 1900s]

love pump the penis; the genitals. Cf. LICK MY LOVE PUMP! For synonyms see

GENITALS, YARD. [U.S. slang, late 1900s]

lover 1. a regular and exclusive sexual lover, heterosexual or homosexual. [since the 1500s or before] **2.** a man found guilty of sexual offenses against a woman. [U.S. underworld slang, early 1900s, Goldin, O'Leary, and Lipsius]

love purse the vagina. For synonyms see GENITALS, MONOSYLLABLE. [U.S., late 1900s-pres.]

lover's nuts pain in the testicles due to sexual excitement; the same as LOVE-NUTS (q.v.).

lover under the lap a lesbian. For synonyms see LESBYTERIAN. [Australian, 1900s]

love sausage the penis. Cf. HIDE THE SAUSAGE. For synonyms see GENITALS, YARD. [U.S. slang, late 1900s]

lovesteak the penis. Cf. MEAT. For synonyms see GENITALS, YARD. [U.S. collegiate, late 1900s, Munro]

love tips the breasts; the nipples. [U.S. slang, mid 1900s-pres.]

love up to fondle and arouse sexually. Cf. RUB UP. For synonyms see FIRKYTOODLE. [colloquial, mid 1900s]

love weed marijuana. From its alleged aphrodisiac qualities. See JOHNSON GRASS. [U.S. drug culture, mid 1900s-pres.]

lower than a snake's armpit despicable; sneaky; underhanded. [Australian, late 1900s-pres.]

L.S.D. 1. "lysergic acid diethylamide," a hallucinogenic drug. Not sold as an ethical drug. For synonyms see ACID. [U.S. drug culture, mid 1900s-pres.] **2.** an abbreviation of "Lake Shore Drive" in Chicago, Illinois. From sense 1. No negative connotations. [U.S., mid 1900s-pres.] **3.** the standard abbreviation of "pounds, shillings, and pence." No negative connotations. **4.** "long, skinny Davy," a nickname for a lanky boy. No negative connotations. [senses 3 and 4 are British, late 1800s-early 1900s]

lubage marijuana. For synonyms see MARI. [U.S., late 1900s-pres.]

lubie a lubricated condom. For synonyms see EEL-SKIN. [U.S. slang, mid 1900s-pres.]

lubricated intoxicated with alcohol. [U.S. slang and colloquial, 1900s]

lubrication alcohol; booze. For synonyms see BOOZE. [British and U.S. slang, late 1900s]

lucci money. From LUCRE. [U.S., late 1900s-pres.]

Lucy the penis. Cf. DUCY. [U.S. dialect, 1900s or before] See also SWEET LUCY.

Lucy in the sky with diamonds a code name for the drug L.S.D. (q.v.). Initials of the name of a rock song. Cf. SWEET LUCY. [U.S. drug culture, mid 1900s-pres.]

lude methaqualone, usually Quaalude (trademark), a tranquilizer. [U.S. drug culture, mid 1900s-pres.]

luggage 1. the male genitals, the VIRILIA (q.v.). Cf. BASKET (sense 3). [British colloquial, 1800s, Farmer and Henley] **2.** the hallucinogenic drug L.S.D. Because you cannot go on a TRIP without it. For synonyms see ACID. [U.S. drug culture, late 1900s] See also BAGGAGE.

lulus 1. the human breasts. See LOLLOS. **2.** two or more of anything good. No negative connotations. [both senses, U.S. slang, 1900s]

lumber stems and other hard chunks found in marijuana. [U.S. drug culture, mid 1900s-pres.]

lumberjack a homosexual. For synonyms see EPICENE. [U.S., late 1900s-pres.]

lumbo (also **limbo**) Colombian marijuana. Cf. COLUMBIAN RED. For synonyms see MARI. [U.S. drug culture, mid 1900s-pres.]

lumpy 1. intoxicated with alcohol. **2.** pregnant. For synonyms see FRAGRANT. [both colloquial since the 1800s]

lum(s) *Cannabis indica* from Colombia. [U.S. drug culture, late 1900s]

lung-butter vomit. For synonyms see YORK. [U.S., late 1900s-pres.]

lung-disturber the penis; the erect penis. [British, 1800s]

lunger a gob of coughed-up mucus. [U.S. and elsewhere, 1900s or before]

lungs the breasts. *Cf.* TONSILS. For synonyms see BOSOM. [U.S. jocular euphemism, 1900s]

lung warts the breasts. For synonyms see BOSOM. [U.S. military, 1900s, *Soldier Talk*]

luppies lesbian urban professionals; lesbian yuppies. For synonyms see LESBYTERIAN. [U.S., late 1900s-pres.]

lush 1. beer or other drink. [British and U.S. since the late 1700s] **2.** a drunkard. [slang and colloquial since the 1800s] **3.** to drink frequently or heavily. For synonyms see PLAY CAMELS. [U.S. slang, 1900s]

lush bint a good-looking or attractive girl or young woman. For synonyms see BIRD. [British, late 1900s-pres., but probably much older]

lushed-up (also **lushed**) **1.** intoxicated with alcohol. For synonyms see WOOFLED. [U.S. colloquial, 1900s or before] **2.** intoxicated with narcotics. From sense 1. For synonyms see TALL. [U.S. drug culture, mid 1900s-pres.]

lusher 1. a prostitute. [U.S. underworld, early 1900s] **2.** a drunkard who "tanks up" quickly. [slang, 1900s]

lushy (also **lushey, lushie**) **1.** intoxicated with alcohol. **2.** a drunkard. [both senses, British and U.S., 1800s-1900s]

lust strong sexual cravings. [since *c.* 1000, *Oxford English Dictionary*] Synonyms and related terms: AMATIVENESS, ARD, ARDOR, ARDOUR, BONE-ON, B.U., BURN, CARNALITY, CONCUPISCENCE, DESIRES OF THE FLESH, GOONA-GOONA, HORNINESS, HOT PANTS, ITCH, NASTIES, NATURE, PRIDE, THE HOTS, THE OLD ADAM. See also HUMPY.

M

mace someone's face to do something drastic to someone, such as spraying mace in the face. [U.S., late 1900s-pres.]

mack (also **mac**) **1.** a pimp; a PONCE (*q.v.*). A truncation of MACKEREL (sense 1). [British and U.S., late 1800s-early 1900s] **2.** an Irishman. Derogatory. For synonyms see HARP. [1500s] **3.** to masturbate. For synonyms see WASTE TIME. [U.S., late 1900s-pres.]

mackerel (also **mac, mack**) **1.** a pimp; a PONCE (*q.v.*). See MACGIMP. **2.** a BAWD (*q.v.*). [both since the early 1400s]

mackerel-snapper a derogatory nickname for a Roman Catholic. *Cf.* FISH-EATER. [U.S. slang, 1900s, Wentworth and Flexner]

macking pimping for a living. *Cf.* MACKEREL. [U.S. slang, mid 1900s-pres.]

macking tackle the lips, as used for kissing. [U.S., late 1900s-pres.]

mack man a pimp; the same as MACKEREL (sense 1). [U.S. slang, mid 1900s-pres.]

madam **1.** a kept woman; a mistress or a concubine. [British, early 1600s] **2.** a wench; a hussy. [British, early 1700s] **3.** the female keeper of a brothel. *Cf.* ABBESS. [since the 1700s] Synonyms: ABBESS, AUNT, BAWD, CASE-KEEPER, COVENT GARDEN ABBESS, FLESH-BROKER, HOUSE-KEEPER, HOUSE-MOTHER, LADY ABBESS, MOTHER, PROVINCIAL, TENDERLOIN MADAM.

mad cheddar lots of money. [U.S., late 1900s-pres.]

Mae West the bosom; a breast. Rhyming slang for "breast." [1900s]

maggot(t)y alcohol intoxicated; very drunk. A play on ROTTEN. For synonyms see WOOFLED. [U.S., late 1900s-pres.]

magic dust (also **magic, magic mist**) the drug phencyclidine, P.C.P. For synonyms see P.C.P. [U.S. drug culture, late 1900s, Abel]

magic flake high-quality cocaine. For synonyms see NOSE-CANDY. [U.S. drug culture, late 1900s]

magic mushroom a species of mushroom containing the hallucinogenic agent psilocybin. [U.S. drug culture, mid 1900s-pres.]

magic pumpkin the hallucinogenic substance, PEYOTE. [U.S. drug culture, late 1900s]

magic wand the penis, especially the erect penis. *Cf.* TWANGER, WAND. [colloquial and nonce, 1900s or before]

magnet the female genitals, that which draws the male. Possibly a play on "magnetic pole." [British, 1700s]

magnum a large penis. For synonyms see YARD. [U.S., late 1900s-pres.]

maharishee marijuana. For synonyms see MARI. [U.S. black use, late 1900s, Folb] See also MARIWEEGEE.

mahogany a mulatto. [U.S., early 1900s] Synonyms: BEIGE, BIRD'S-EYE MAPLE, BLACK AND TAN, BLACKED EBONY, BLEACHED EBONY, BRIGHT MULATTO, BROWN, BROWN GIRL, BROWN MAN, BROWN POLISH, BROWN-SKIN, CAFÉ AU LAIT, CASTE, GRIFANE, GRIFFE, GRIFFIN, GRIFFO, GRIFFONE, GRIFIN, GRIFON, HIGH-BROWN, HIGH-YELLOW, LEMON, LIGHT-BROWN, MUSTARD-YELLOW, PINKY, SEPE, SEPIA, SEPIAN, TAN, TAWNYMOOR, YELLER, YELLOW, YELLOW-BLACK, YELLOW GIRL, YOLA.

mahoska narcotics. *Cf.* MOHASKY, MOSHKY. [U.S. underworld, mid 1900s]

maiden gear **1.** virginity. **2.** the hymen. For synonyms see BEAN. [both senses, British, early 1700s]

maidenhead **1.** virginity. **2.** the

hymen. [both since the 1300s] **3.** newness. [1500s; impolite by the 1600s]

main to inject narcotics directly into a vein; to MAINLINE (*q.v.*). [U.S. drug culture, 1900s]

main-bitch a female MAIN SQUEEZE; one's favorite girl. [U.S. black use, late 1900s]

mainline (also **main**) to inject narcotics directly into a vein. [U.S. drug culture, mid 1900s-pres.]

mainliner a drug addict; someone who injects drugs intravenously. [U.S. slang, mid 1900s-pres.]

main queen 1. a homosexual male who takes the female role; a RECEIVER (*q.v.*). [U.S. slang, mid 1900s] **2.** one's steady girlfriend. [U.S. slang, mid 1900s]

main squeeze 1. one's boss; the head man. No negative connotations. [U.S. colloquial, 1900s] **2.** a steady girlfriend. [originally black use; U.S., mid 1900s-pres.]

main vein 1. the female genitals. For synonyms see MONOSYLLABLE. [British slang, 1900s, *Dictionary of Slang and Unconventional English*] **2.** the penis. For synonyms see YARD. [U.S., late 1900s-pres.]

major need defecation (contrasted to urination). *Cf.* BIG ONE, BIG POTTY. [colloquial euphemism, 1900s or before]

make 1. the copulation of wolves. [late 1600s, B.E.] **2.** copulation. **3.** a sexually loose woman. **4.** to urinate. *Cf.* MAKE WATER. For synonyms see WHIZ. **5.** to seduce; to seduce and copulate. See MAKE IT. [senses 2-5 are U.S., mid 1900s-pres.]

make, on the 1. pertaining to the actions of a sexually promiscuous person. **2.** pertaining to a sexually receptive woman. **3.** pertaining to a person trying to convince someone to copulate. **4.** self-employed as a prostitute. [all senses, U.S. slang, early 1900s-pres.]

make a bog of something to make a mess or muddle of something. [British, late 1900s-pres.]

make a branch to urinate. Refers to a branch of a stream. *Cf.* MAKE (sense 4). [U.S. dialect (Ozarks), Randolph and Wilson]

make a deposit 1. to defecate. **2.** to urinate. See BANK (sense 1). *Cf.* DEPOSIT (sense 2). [both senses, U.S. colloquial, 1900s]

make a fuckup of something to make a complete mess of something. [British, late 1900s-pres.]

make a noise 1. to release intestinal gas audibly. [euphemistic avoidance since the 1800s] **2.** to boast; to give forth hot air. Based on sense 1. [U.S. slang, 1900s]

make a pass at to make a sexual advance toward someone. This may include many activities from flirtation to fondling. [U.S. slang and colloquial, 1900s]

make a piss stop to stop to urinate. A play on MAKE A PIT STOP. For synonyms see WHIZ. [U.S. slang, late 1900s]

make a pit stop to stop to urinate. From the pit stop made by racing cars. For synonyms see WHIZ. [U.S. slang, mid 1900s-pres.]

make a rude noise 1. to release intestinal gas audibly. For synonyms see GURK. **2.** to belch. [both senses since the 1800s]

make a sale to vomit. For synonyms see YORK. [widespread colloquial, 1900s]

make ends meet (also **make both ends meet**) to copulate. *Cf.* FIT END TO END. [since the 1800s or before]

make it to coit, said of a man or a woman or both. [frequent source of double entendre; U.S. slang and colloquial, mid 1900s-pres.]

make love 1. to caress and kiss. **2.** to copulate. A euphemism for "human copulation." [both since the 1600s]

make love to the porcelain goddess to vomit into the toilet. For synonyms see YORK. [U.S. collegiate, late 1900s, Munro]

make Ms and Ws to be drunk; to walk in a zigzag fashion. *Cf.* ZIGZAG.

[British slang, 1800s, Farmer and Henley]

make one's love come down 1. to cause an orgasm. **2.** to copulate. **3.** to cause one to become sexually aroused. [all senses, U.S. black use and slang, mid 1900s-pres.]

make out 1. to kiss and caress. **2.** to copulate. [both senses, U.S. slang, mid 1900s-pres.]

make-out artist a seducer; a lecher. See MAKE OUT. [U.S. slang, mid 1900s-pres.]

make someone scream to bring someone to an orgasm; to have sex with someone, presumably a female. [U.S. collegiate, late 1900s, Munro]

make the chimney smoke to cause a woman to have an orgasm. Cf. CHIMNEY, SMOKE (sense 1). [British slang, 1800s]

make water (also **make**) to urinate. For synonyms see WHIZ. [colloquial since the 1300s]

make wind to break wind; to release intestinal gas. Parallel to MAKE WATER (q.v.). [U.S. slang, 1900s]

making finger pie an act of stimulating the female genitals. [British, late 1900s-pres.]

male 1. a euphemism for a bull, boar, or stallion. [U.S. colloquial, 1900s or before] **2.** male marijuana. In contrast to the female flower tops. The male plants are less desirable because they have less active ingredient. Cf. FEE-TOPS. For synonyms see MARI. [U.S. drug culture, late 1900s, Kaiser]

male member the penis. A translation of *membrum virile* (q.v.).

male-mules the human testicles. For synonyms see WHIRLYGIGS. [British, 1600s]

male prostitute 1. a male, presumably a homosexual male, who provides sexual services to other males. [1800s-1900s] **2.** a male who provides sexual services to women. [1900s or before]

male pudendum the penis. Literally, "that about which a male ought to be modest." Usually seen as "male *puden-*

dum." Patterned on the female PUDEN-DUM (q.v.). [U.S., mid 1900s]

male sheath a condom. For synonyms see EEL-SKIN. Cf. SHEATH (sense 3). [Euphemistic, 1900s or before]

malted intoxicated with alcohol. Refers to the malt in beer. Cf. HOPPED (sense 2). [U.S. slang, mid 1900s]

malt-worm (also **malt-bug, malt-horse**) a beer-drinker. A derogatory nickname for a drunkard. Cf. MALTED. [mid 1500s]

Mama coca cocaine. Cf. COCA. For synonyms see NOSE-CANDY. [U.S. drug culture, late 1900s]

mammy-jammer a despised person; a MOTHER-FUCKER. Partly euphemistic. For synonyms see SNOKE-HORN. [U.S. black use, mid 1900s]

mammy-tapper a despised person; MOTHER-FUCKER. For synonyms see SNOKE-HORN. [U.S. black use, mid 1900s]

man 1. to coit a woman. [since the 1600s or before] **2.** a lesbian in the masculine role. [U.S. slang, mid 1900s-pres.] See also MAN, THE.

man, old 1. the penis. Cf. LADY, OLD (sense 1). [British colloquial, 1800s] **2.** a male; one's husband, boyfriend, or father. [British and U.S. colloquial, 1800s-pres.]

man-balls the testicles. For synonyms see WHIRLYGIGS. [from "I Sing of the Body Electric," *Leaves of Grass* (Walt Whitman)] See also MAN-ROOT.

man box a coffin. [colloquial, 1800s-1900s]

Manchester city a breast. Rhyming slang for TITTY (sense 1.) Often seen in the plural. Cf. BRISTOL CITIES, JERSEY CITIES. [British, 1800s-1900s, *Dictionary of Rhyming Slang*]

Manchesters the human breasts. A truncation of "Manchester cities," which is rhyming slang for "titties." See MANCHESTER CITY. Cf. BRISTOLS. The words "man" and "chest" provided the basis for sexual imagery. [British slang, 1800s]

maneater 1. a FELLATOR or FELLA-TRIX. [euphemistic double entrendre]

2. a woman determined to get a husband. [U.S. slang, 1900s]

man-fat semen. For synonyms see METTLE. [British, late 1900s-pres.]

Manhattan eel a condom. *Cf.* CONEY ISLAND WHITEFISH. For synonyms see EEL-SKIN. [U.S. slang, late 1900s]

Manhattan silver (also **Manhattan white**) white marijuana that is said to have grown from the seeds of the marijuana flushed down New York toilets. For synonyms see MARI. Jocular. [U.S. slang, late 1900s]

manhole 1. the female genitals. *Cf.* MANHOLE COVER, MANTRAP. [colloquial and nonce, 1800s-1900s] **2.** a man's anus in INSPECTOR OF MANHOLES (*q.v.*).

manhole cover a sanitary napkin; a menstrual cloth. [widespread slang, 1900s] Synonyms: AMMUNITION, BANDAGE, CLOUT, CUNT-RAG, DANGERSIGNAL, DIAPER, FANNY RAG, FLAG, GENTLEMAN'S PLEASURE-GARDEN PADLOCK, GRANNY-RAG, LAUNCHING PAD, MENSTRUAL CLOTH, MONTHLY RAG, NAPKIN, PAD, PERINEAL PAD, PERIODICITY RAG, PETER-CHEATER, PLEASUREGARDEN PADLOCK, RAG, RED FLAG, RED RAG, SANITARY, SANITARY NAPKIN, SANITARY TOWEL, SHOE, S.T., WINDOWBLIND, WINDOW-CURTAIN.

manhood 1. the period in the life of a human male after he reaches puberty or the age of majority. **2.** the male genitals; the penis. [euphemistic, 1900s]

man in the boat the clitoris. The "boat" refers to the shape of the *labia minora* and *labia majora.* See BOY-IN-THE-BOAT, LITTLE-MAN-IN-THE-BOAT.

manipulate the member to masturbate. Said of the male. *Cf.* MEMBER. For synonyms and related subjects see WASTE TIME. [U.S. collegiate, late 1900s]

manky dirty; distasteful; yucky. [British, late 1900s-pres.]

man oil semen. Probably from "sperm whale oil," which was called "sperm oil" or "sperm." *Cf.* OIL OF MAN. [U.S. slang, 1900s]

manometer the female genitals, especially the vagina; the vagina considered as a device for measuring manliness as evidenced by penile size. A play on the name of an instrument used to measure air pressure. *Cf.* YARD MEASURE. [slang and nonce, 1900s]

man-root the penis. *Cf.* MAN-BALLS. [from "I Sing of the Body Electric," *Leaves of Grass* (Walt Whitman)]

mantan black a Negro who acts like a Caucasian; an OREO (*q.v.*). From the trademarked brand name of a suntanning agent, "Mantan." Derogatory. [U.S. black use, mid 1900s]

man Thomas, my (also **man Thomas**) the penis. From JOHN THOMAS (*q.v.*). [British colloquial, 1600s-pres.]

mantrap 1. the female genitals. *Cf.* MANHOLE. [British, 1700s] **2.** a woman seeking a husband; a widow; the same as MANEATER (sense 2). [since the 1700s]

manual exercises masturbation. *Cf.* FIVE AGAINST ONE. [military slang, 1900s]

maracas the breasts. From the name of a pair of rounded gourd-rattles used in Latin America. [U.S. slang, early 1900s-pres.]

marble palace a W.C.; a toilet, especially a marble-finished public restroom. [U.S. slang, 1900s]

marbles 1. syphilis; syphilitic buboes. As if the infected person had a pocket full of marbles. [late 1500s] **2.** the testicles. [British and U.S. colloquial and nonce since the 1800s or before] **3.** round, red capsules of Placidyl hypnotic sedative. [U.S. drug culture, late 1900s, Kaiser]

Marge a passive lesbian; the same as MARGERY (*q.v.*). [U.S. homosexual use and slang, mid 1900s-pres.]

Margery an effeminate male; possibly a homosexual male. *Cf.* MARGE. [British slang, 1800s, Ware]

mari marijuana; a marijuana cigarette. *Cf.* MARY (sense 4). [U.S. underworld and drug culture, 1900s] Synonyms and related terms: A-BOMB, ACAPULCO GOLD, AFRICAN BLACK, AQUATIC, ASHES, ATSHITSHI, BABY, BAMBALACHA, BAMMY, BANJI, BEETLE, BHANG, BHANG GANJAH,

BIRDWOOD, BLACK BART, BLACK GUNGEON, BLACK GUNNY, BLACK MO, BLACK MOAT, BLISS, BLONDE, BO, BOB HOPE, BO-BO BUSH, BO JIMMY, BOO, BRICK, BROCCOLI, BUDDAH, BUDLARS, BUDLIES, BULLET THAI, BULL JIVE, BUSH, BUTTER FLOWER, CANADIAN BLACK, CANNABIS INDICA, CANNABIS SATIVA, CESS, CHARAS, CHARGE, CHEESE, CHICAGO GREEN, CHRONIC, CHRONS, CHURRUS, CIGA-WEED, COLI, COLUMBIAN, COLUMBIAN RED, COLUMBIA RED, CONGO HASH, CORNELIUS, CRAB, CREEPER, CREEPERBUD, CRIPS, DA KINE, DAGGA, DEW, DISCIPLINE, DITCH WEED, DOGIE, DONJEM, DOOBAGE, DOPE, DRY HIGH, DUBAGE, DUBICH, ERB, FAGGOT, FEES, FENNEL, FE-OPS, FU, FUNNY STUFF, GAINESVILLE GREEN, GANGSTER, GANJA, GANK, GAUGE, GIGGLE-SMOKE, GIGGLE-WEED, GIZZY, GOLD, GOLD COLUMBIAN, GOLDEN LEAF, GONGA, GOOF, GOOFBALL, GOOF-BUTT, GRASS, GRASS WEED, GREAFA, GREAPHA, GREEFA, GREEFO, GREEN, GREFA, GRIEFO, GRIFFA, GRIFFO, GRIFO, GUNGEON, GUNNY, GYVE, HAS, HAWAIIAN, HAY, HEAVY HASH, HEMP, HENRY, HERB, HOMEGROWN, HOOCH, HOP, HYDRO (PONIC), ILLINOIS GREEN, INDIAN HAY, INDIAN HEMP, JADJA, JERSEY GREEN, JIM JONES, JIVE, JOHNSON, JOHNSON GRASS, JOY-WEED, JUANE, JUANITA, JUANITA WEED, JUAN VALDEZ, KAIF, KANYA, KAUAI, KEEF, KENTUCKY BLUE, K.G.B., KICK-STICK, KIDSTUFF, KIF, L.B., LIPTON'S, LOBO, LOCOWEED, LOVE NUGGETS, LOVE WEED, LUBAGE, LUMBO, M., MACH, MAGGIE, MAHARISHEE, MALE, MANHATTAN SILVER, MANHATTAN WHITE, MARIGUANA, MARIJUANA, MARIWEEGEE, MARJIE, MARY, MARY AND JOHNNIE, MARY ANN, MARY JANE, MARY WARNER, MARY WEAVER, MAUI, MAYO, MEGG, MERRY, MEXICAN BROWN, MEXICAN GREEN, MEXICAN RED, MEZZ, M.J., MOHASKY, MOOCAH, MOON CABBAGE, MOOTAH, MOSHKY, MOTA, MU, MUGGLE, MUSTA, MUTAH, MUTHA, NAM BLACK, NAM WEED, NED, NICKLE, NUG, OREGANO, ORGANIC STUFF, PANAMA GOLD, PANAMA RED, PANATELA, PIG FOOT, POD, POPO ORO, POT, POTIGUAYA, PUKALOLO, PUNA BUTTER, PUNK, QUEEN ANNE'S LACE, RAGWEED, RAINY-DAY WOMAN, RAMA, REAPER, RED, RED-DIRT MARIJUANA, REEFER, REEFER WEED, RIGHTEOUS BUSH, ROPE DOPE, ROUGH STUFF, SALT AND PEPPER, SATIVA, SENSE, SENSE BUD, SHISHI, SHIT, SINSEMILLA, SKINNY, SKUNK, SMOKE, SMOKEY TREAT, SNOP, SPLAY, SPLEEF, SPLIFF, SPLIM, STINK-WEED, STRAW, STUFF, STUM, SUPER COOL, SUPERPOT, SWEET LUCY, SWEET LUNCH, T., TEA, TEDDY PARTY, TEXAS TEA, THAI STICKS, THIRTEEN, TIN, TOPS, TREES, TRIPWEED, TWO-TOKE, TYRONE, UP-POT, VERMONT GREEN, VIPER'S WEED, VONCE, WACKY TABBACKY, WACKY WEED, WANA, WEED, WEED TEA, WHEAT, YERBA, YESCA, ZACATECAS PURPLE, ZELTOIDS, ZIB, ZOL.

maria the police. For synonyms see FLATFOOT. [U.S., late 1900s-pres.]

mariguana marijuana. For synonyms see MARI. [U.S., 1900s]

marijuana CANNABIS SATIVA (*q.v.*). [Mexican Spanish for *Cannabis sativa*; the U.S. word-of-choice for this substance]

marinate to hang out and do nothing. [U.S., late 1900s-pres.]

mariweegee marijuana. For synonyms see MARI. [U.S. black use, late 1900s]

marjie marijuana. For synonyms see MARI. [Australian, mid 1900s]

mark 1. a streetwalking prostitute. [U.S. slang, 1800s] **2.** to geld a lamb. [Australian and U.S. colloquial, 1900s or before] **3.** a dupe; a target for theft or the confidence racket. [underworld, 1900s or before]

mark of the beast the female genitals. [British, early 1700s]

married to Mary Fist accustomed to masturbation rather than coition. [U.S. prison use, mid 1900s, Goldin, O'Leary, and Lipsius]

marrow-bone the penis. *Cf.* MARROW. [British slang, 1800s, Farmer and Henley]

marry one's porcelain mistress to vomit into the toilet. For synonyms see YORK. [U.S. collegiate, late 1900s, Eble]

Marshall Field a reinterpretation of

"M.F.," "mother-fucker." From the name of a Chicago department store. [U.S. black use, mid 1900s]

marshmallow reds barbiturates, specifically red capsules of Seconal (trademark). [U.S. drug culture, mid 1900s-pres.]

marshmallows 1. the breasts. **2.** the testicles. [both senses, U.S. slang, mid 1900s-pres.]

Mary and Johnnie CANNABIS SATIVA (*q.v.*). Rhyming slang for "marijuana." [U.S. slang, 1900s]

Mary Ann 1. a homosexual male; a CATAMITE (*q.v.*). [British and U.S. slang, late 1800s-1900s] **2.** marijuana; a marijuana cigarette. [U.S. drug culture, mid 1900s-pres.]

marygin a device for removing the seeds from marijuana. Based on MARY JANE and *cotton gin*. [U.S. drug culture, late 1900s]

Mary Jane 1. the female genitals. *Cf.* LITTLE MARY (sense 1). [British slang, 1800s, Farmer and Henley] **2.** marijuana. [U.S. drug culture, mid 1900s-pres.]

Mary Warner marijuana; a marijuana cigarette. [U.S. drug culture, mid 1900s-pres.]

Mary Weaver marijuana. [U.S. drug culture, mid 1900s-pres.]

masculine whore a CATAMITE (*q.v.*); a homosexual male; a RECEIVER (*q.v.*). [from *Troilus and Cressida* (Shakespeare)]

mashed intoxicated. For synonyms see WOOFLED. [British, late 1900s-pres.]

masher a male flirt; a philanderer. [U.S. slang and colloquial, 1900s]

mashing courting; flirting. [since the late 1800s]

mason 1. a PEDERAST (*q.v.*); the INSERTOR (*q.v.*). **2.** a lesbian assuming a masculine role. Both refer to the sexual partner who does the "laying." From LAY. From the laying of bricks. [both senses, U.S., mid 1900s]

masturbate 1. to fondle the genitals (male or female) to induce sexual pleasure. Done by oneself or another person of either sex. **2.** to simulate the motions of copulation by hand until orgasm is achieved. Most euphemistic terms refer to male masturbation. See WASTE TIME. [from a Latin word with the same meaning; in English since the 1700s]

matrimonial peacemaker the penis. [British colloquial, late 1700s, Grose]

mattress mambo copulation. For synonyms see SMOCKAGE. [U.S., late 1900s-pres.]

maudlin drunk (also **mawdin drunk**) intoxicated with alcohol and crying. Ultimately based on "Mary Magdalene," who is often portrayed weeping for her sins. [British and U.S. colloquial, 1600s-pres.]

Maui (also **Maui wowie**) a variety of marijuana supposedly grown on the Hawaiian island of Maui. *Cf.* HAWAIIAN, KAUI. [U.S. drug culture, mid 1900s-pres.]

mauled (also **mauld**) intoxicated with alcohol. [British colloquial, 1600s-pres.]

max gin. From "maximum." For synonyms see RUIN. [British slang, early 1800s, *Lexicon Balatronicum*]

maxed out alcohol intoxicated; drug intoxicated. For synonyms see TALL, WOOFLED. [U.S. slang, late 1900s]

may a W.C.; a toilet. [U.S. slang, early 1900s]

mayhem 1. the maiming of a man. [since the late 1400s] **2.** euphemistic for "castration."

May I go to hell! an oath and an exclamation. For synonyms see 'ZOUNDS!

mayo marijuana. For synonyms see MARI. [U.S., late 1900s-pres.]

maypole a large penis. For synonyms see YARD. [U.S., late 1900s-pres.]

Mazola party a form of sexual activity where the participants cover their bodies with liquid cooking oil and perform various sexual activities; the same as WESSON PARTY (*q.v.*). From the trademarked brand name of a cooking oil.

McGimper a pimp. See MACGIMP.

M.D. 1. a physician; a doctor of medicine. **2.** a person who is mentally defective. An ironic reinterpretation of sense 1. **3.** Mogen David™ wine. A reinterpretation of the initials M.D. Cf. MAD DOG. [U.S. drug culture, late 1900s]

M.D.A. "methylenedioxyamphetamine," a recreational drug derived from nutmeg. Elaborated as "mellow drug of America." [U.S. drug culture, 1960s-pres.]

M.D.M.A. the drug ECSTASY, 3,4-methylenedioxymethamphetamine. [U.S. drug culture, late 1900s]

meacocke (also **meacock**) a sissy; an effeminate male. For synonyms see FRIBBLE. [1500s-1600s]

meadow dressing nonsense; a euphemism for BULLSHIT (q.v.). From a term for animal manure used to fertilize the soil of a field. [slang and colloquial, early 1900s]

meadow-mayonnaise nonsense; a euphemism for BULLSHIT (q.v.). Cf. COW-CONFETTI. [Australian slang, early 1900s]

meadow muffin a mass of cow dung. For synonyms see DROPPINGS. [U.S. slang, late 1900s]

mealer a drinker who imbibes only at meals. Cf. AFTER DINNER MAN. [British slang, 1800s, Farmer and Henley]

mean green 1. the drug phencyclidine, P.C.P. For synonyms see P.C.P. [U.S. drug culture, late 1900s, Abel] **2.** money. [U.S., late 1900s-pres.]

meat 1. the female genitals. For synonyms see MONOSYLLABLE. [since the 1500s] **2.** women considered as sexual objects. For synonyms see TAIL. [since the 1500s] **3.** the human breasts. [British and U.S. slang and nonce, 1800s-1900s] **4.** the penis. Cf. BEEF (sense 2). [British and U.S. slang and colloquial, 1800s-pres.] **5.** a strong but stupid male. Cf. BEEF (sense 3). [U.S. slang, 1900s] **6.** males considered as sexual objects by homosexual males. Cf. GOVERNMENT INSPECTED MEAT. [U.S. homosexual use, 1900s]

meat and drink a drunken spree including sexual adventures. [British slang, 1800s, Farmer and Henley]

meatball a stupid oaf. [U.S. slang, early 1900s-pres.]

meat-flasher an exhibitionist, a man who exposes his penis to public view. [British slang, 1800s, Farmer and Henley]

meat for days (also **meat for the poor**) pertaining to a male with large genitals; pertaining to large male genitals. Cf. BASKET FOR DAYS. [U.S. homosexual use, mid 1900s]

meat-grinder (also **meat-cooker**) **1.** the female genitals, specifically the vagina. **2.** a woman considered as a sexual object. For synonyms see TAIL. Refers to MEAT (sense 4). [U.S. slang or nonce]

meat hound 1. a whoremonger. Cf. MEAT (sense 2). **2.** a homosexual male. Cf. MEAT (sense 4), the penis. [both senses, U.S. slang, mid 1900s]

meat injection (also **beef injection**) an act of copulation. For synonyms see SMOCKAGE. [U.S. slang, late 1900s, Lewin and Lewin] See also FOAMING BEEF PROBE.

meat-market 1. a group of prostitutes; the location of a group of prostitutes. **2.** the human breasts. Cf. MEAT (sense 3). **3.** the female genitals. Cf. MEAT (sense 1). [senses 2 and 3 are slang, 1800s-1900s] **4.** an area used by homosexuals to make contacts. [U.S. homosexual use, mid 1900s, Stanley] **5.** a body-building gymnasium. [U.S. slang, mid 1900s]

meat-monger 1. a whoremaster. **2.** a male who is a brothel keeper. [both senses, primarily British slang, 1800s, Farmer and Henley]

meat puppet 1. the penis. For synonyms see YARD. [British, late 1900s-pres.] **2.** a prostitute. For synonyms see HARLOT. [British, late 1900s-pres.]

meat-rack 1. an area where male homosexuals gather to seek partners. [U.S. homosexual use and general slang, mid 1900s] **2.** a body-building gymnasium. [U.S. slang, mid 1900s]

meat-shot a close-up picture of the

male or female genitals. *Cf.* MEAT [British slang, 1900s, J. Green]

meat-wagon an ambulance. *Cf.* BLOOD-WAGON. [British and U.S. slang, World War II]

meat whistle the penis. *Cf.* PICCOLO. For synonyms see GENITALS, YARD. [U.S. slang, late 1900s]

megabitch a really bad person; a very difficult person. Typically a female. [U.S. slang, late 1900s]

megg marijuana. See MARGE, MARGERY. [U.S. drug culture, 1900s]

mell of a hess a deliberate spoonerism for "hell of a mess." *Cf.* FELL OF A HIX. [U.S. slang and colloquial, mid 1900s]

mellow 1. intoxicated with alcohol. [since the 1600s] **2.** peaceful and relaxed due to the use of drugs. From sense 1. [U.S. drug culture, mid 1900s-pres.]

mellow-yellow 1. the skin of a banana dried for smoking. [U.S. drug culture, mid 1900s] **2.** the drug L.S.D. (*q.v.*). [U.S. drug culture, mid 1900s-pres.] **3.** a tablet of Valium™. Named for the 5 milligram yellow tablets. [U.S. drug culture, late 1900s]

melons the human breasts. *Cf.* HONEYDEW MELONS, WATERMELONS. [U.S. slang and colloquial, 1900s]

melt to ejaculate. [euphemistic, early 1600s] Synonyms and related terms: BLOW UP, BUST, BUST ONE'S NUTS, CHEESE, COME, COME OFF, COME ONE'S COCOA, CREAM, DIE IN A WOMAN'S LAP, DISCHARGE, DOUBLE ONE'S MILT, DROP ONE'S LOAD, EASE, EASE ONESELF, EFFECT EMISSION, EJACULATE, EMISSIO, EMISSION, EMISSIO SEMINIS, EMIT, EMPTY THE TRASH, FIRE A SHOT, FIRE IN THE AIR, GET IT OFF, GET OFF, GET OFF THE NUT, GET ONE'S COOKIES OFF, GET ONE'S NUTS OFF, GET ONE'S ROCK OFF, GET THE BUTTON OFF, GET THE DIRTY WATER OFF ONE'S CHEST, GIVE ONE'S GRAVY, GO, GO OFF, HIVE IT, HOLE, JET ONE'S JUICE, JIS, JUICE, LET GO, MILK, NUMBER THREE, PISS ONE'S TALLOW, POP A NUT, POP ONE'S COOKIES, POP ONE'S NUTS, SEMINAL EMISSION, SEMINIS EMISSIO, SEXUAL REFLEX, SHOOT,

SHOOT OFF, SHOOT ONE'S LOAD, SHOOT ONE'S MILT, SHOOT ONE'S ROE, SHOOT ONE'S WAD, SHOOT WHITE, SPEND, SPERMATIZE, SPEW, SPLOOGE, SPOOCH, SPUNK, SQUEEZE UP, SQUIRT, THROW UP, UPSHOOT, WHITE-WASH.

melted intoxicated with alcohol. [U.S. slang, early 1900s]

melted-butter semen. *Cf.* BUTTER, DUCK-BUTTER. [British, 1700s]

melting-pot the female genitals. *Cf.* MELT. [British slang, 1800s, Farmer and Henley]

member 1. the penis. A truncation of MALE MEMBER (*q.v.*). [since the 1300s] **2.** a fellow Negro. [U.S. black use, mid 1900s]

member for the cockshire the penis. *Cf.* PRIVY MEMBER, UNRULY MEMBER, [British, 1800s, Farmer and Henley]

member mug a chamber pot. [British jocular euphemism. 1600s-1700s]

meno the menses. For synonyms see FLOODS. [British, late 1900s-pres.]

mental a deranged person; a mentally deficient person. [British and U.S., early 1900s]

mentulate (also **mentulated**) pertaining to a man with an abnormally large penis. *Cf.* BASKET FOR DAYS, DONKEY-RIGGED, DOUBLE-SHUNG, HUNG, HUNG LIKE A BULL, MEGALOPENIS, MIRACLE-MEAT, TIMBERED, TONS OF BASKET, TONS OF MEAT, WELL-BUILT, WELL-ENDOWED, WELL-FAVORED BY NATURE, WELL-HUNG, WELT. [since the 1700s]

meps (also **mep**) meperdine, probably Demerol™, a painkiller. [U.S. drug culture, late 1900s, Kaiser]

merd dung. Literally, "shit." Widely used in French and used by some speakers of English. Considerably less offensive than "shit." [ultimately from Latin *merda;* English use, 1900s or before]

merkin 1. the female genitals. [British, mid 1600s] **2.** the female pubic hair. *Cf.* LOWER-WIG. [since the mid 1600s] **3.** false female pubic hair. [British, late 1700s-1800s]

merry 1. wanton; without sexual control. Cf. GAY (sense 1). For synonyms see LEWD. [British, 1600s] **2.** intoxicated with alcohol. [British and U.S., early 1700s-pres.] **3.** marijuana. Cf. MARY (sense 4). [U.S. underworld and drug culture, mid 1900s]

mesc a MESCAL BUTTON (q.v.), containing mescaline. Synonyms: BEAN, BIG CHIEF, BUTTON, CACTUS, MESCAL, MESCAL BUTTON, MESCALINE, MOON, PEYOTE, PEYOTE BUTTON, PUMPKIN SEED.

mescal MESCALINE (q.v.) or a MESCAL BUTTON (q.v.). [U.S. drug culture, mid 1900s-pres.]

mescal button the emergent tip of the peyote cactus, which contains MESCALINE (q.v.). See PEYOTE BUTTON. [U.S. drug culture, mid 1900s-pres.]

mescaline the name of the hallucinogenic chemical compound 3,4,5-trimethoxyphenylethylamine. [U.S. underworld and drug culture, mid 1900s-pres.]

mess around to play with sexually; to copulate; to flirt. Said especially of a married person. Cf. MESS (sense 1). [U.S. slang and colloquial, 1900s]

metal mouth someone wearing braces. [U.S., late 1900s-pres.]

meth 1. Methedrine (trademark), an amphetamine, specifically methamphetamine. [U.S. drug culture, mid 1900s-pres.] **2.** METHADONE. [U.S. drug culture, late 1900s, Kaiser]

meth crystal crystallized methamphetamine. [U.S. drug culture, late 1900s]

meth-head (also **meth-freak**) a habitual user of Methedrine (trademark). [U.S. drug culture, mid 1900s-pres.]

meth monster a habitual user of Methedrine (trademark). [U.S. drug culture, mid 1900s]

mettle 1. vigor; masculine vigor; virility. No negative connotations. [since the late 1500s] **2.** semen. Cf. FETCH METTLE, SPUNK. [British, 1600s-pres.] Synonyms and related terms for sense 2: BABY BATTER, BABY-JUICE, BEER, BULLETS, BULL GRAVY, BUTTER, BUTTERMILK, CHISM, CHISSOM, COMINGS, CREAM, CREAM SAUCE, CRUD, DELICIOUS JAM, DICKWAD, DUCK-BUTTER, EFFUSION, FATHER-STUFF, FETCH, FUCK, GISM, GLUE, GRAVY, GUMA, HOCKEY, HOME BREW, HOMEBREWED, HONEY, HOT MILK, JAM, JAZZ, JELLY, JISM, JIZZ, JUICE, JUNK, LETCH-WATER, LEWD INFUSION, LIQUOR SEMINALE, LOAD, LOVE-JUICE, LOVE-LIQUOR, MAN-FAT, MAN OIL, MARROW, MELTED-BUTTER, METTLE OF GENERATION, MILK, MILT, NATURE, OATS, OIL, OIL OF MAN, OINTMENT, OYSTER, PASTE, PECKER TRACKS, PRICK-JUICE, PUDDING, RANCH, REPRODUCTIVE FLUID, SCUM, SEED, SEMEN, SEMEN VIRILE, SEMINAL FILAMENT, SEMINAL FLUID, SEXUAL DISCHARGE, SLIME, SNOWBALL, SOAP, SPEND, SPENDINGS, SPERM, SPERMA, SPERMATIC JUICE, SPEW, SPIRIT, SPLOOGE, SPOO, SPOOCH, SPOOGE, SPUME, SPUNK, STARCH, STUFF, TAIL-JUICE, TAIL-WATER, TALLOW, TREAD, TREASURE, VICTORIA MONK, WHIPPED CREAM, WHITE-BLOW, WHITE HONEY, YOGURT, YORK.

Mex 1. a Mexican. Usually considered derogatory. **2.** pertaining to Mexican things or persons. Derogatory. [both senses, U.S. slang, early 1900s-pres.] Synonyms for sense 1: BEAN, BEAN-EATER, BEANER, BRACERO, BRAVO, BROWN, CHICANO, CHILI, CHILI-CHOMPER, CHILI-EATER, DINO, ENCHILADA-EATER, GREASE-BALL, GREASE GUT, GREASER, HOMBRE, MEX, MEXICAN, MEXICANO, MEXIE, MICK, NEVER-SWEAT, OILER, PAISANO, PEON, PEPPER, PEPPER-BELLY, SHUCK, SPIC, SPIG, SUN-GRINNER, TACO, TACO-BENDER, TAMALE (female), WETBACK.

Mexican brown marijuana; a variety of marijuana grown in Mexico. [U.S. drug culture, mid 1900s-pres.]

Mexican green a variety of marijuana grown in Mexico. [U.S. drug culture, mid 1900s-pres.]

Mexican milk tequila, a Mexican alcoholic beverage. [U.S. slang, mid 1900s-pres.]

Mexican mud heroin. Cf. MUD (sense 3). [U.S. drug culture, mid 1900s-pres.]

Mexican red 1. a variety or grade of marijuana associated with Mexico. Cf. MEXICAN (sense 2). **2.** a homemade barbiturate capsule. See RED (sense 1). Cf. MEXICAN (sense 2). [U.S. drug culture, mid 1900s]

mezz (also **mighty mess**) marijuana or a marijuana cigarette. [U.S. underworld and drug culture, mid 1900-pres.]

mezzroll a fat marijuana cigarette. [U.S. drug culture, mid 1900s-pres.] Synonyms: ACE, BANANA WITH CHEESE, BAZOOKA, BELT, BIFFDA, BLIZZIE, BLUE SAGE, BLUNT, BOMB, BOMBER, BONE, BUDDHA STICK, BURNIE, COCKTAIL, DOOBIE, DOPESTICK, DRAG, DREAMSTICK, DUBEE, DYNAMITE, EARTH, FAT JAY, FAT PAPPY, FATTY, FUNNY CIGARETTE, GANGSTER, GAUGE-BUTT, GOOF-BUTT, GOOFY-BUTT, GOW, HAPPY STICKS, HAY-BUTT, HONEY BLUNTS, HOOCH DOG, HOOTER, HOP-STICK, HOT-STICK, J., JAMES WARNER DOG, JAY, J-BO, JIMMY DOG, JINDER, JIVE STICK, JIZZONT, JOINT, JOLT, JOY SMOKE, JOY-STICK, J-SMOKE, J-STICK, JUANE, JUJU, LOCOWEED, MARY WARNER, MEZZ, MIG, MIGGIES, MUGGLE, NAIL, NUMBER, PIN, PINWHEEL, PRIMO, REEF, REEFER, ROACH, ROCKET, ROOT, ROPE, SAUSAGE, SEED, SKOOFER, SMOKE, SNIPE, SPLEEF, SPLIFF, STENCIL, STICK, STICK OF TEA, STOGIE, TAMPON, THUMB, THUNDER-COOKIE, TOOTHPICK, TORPEDO, TUSKEE, TWIST, WEED, WOOLY, ZEPPELIN, ZONABLES.

M.F. a "mother-fucker." [U.S. slang, mid 1900s-pres.] Synonyms and disguises: MARSHALL FIELD, MOTHER, MOTHER-DANGLER, MOTHER-FUCKER, MOTHER-GRABBER, MOTHER-HUMPER, MOTHER-JUMPER, MOTHER-LOVER, MOTHER-RUCKER, MOTHER-UGLY, MUH-FUH.

M.F.C. "measured for a coffin," near death; dying. Compare to C.T.D. [U.S. slang, late 1900s]

M.F.U. a "military fuck-up." Also occurs as an extreme variety of F.U. (q.v.), a "monstrous fuck-up." For synonyms see SNAFU. [British military, early 1900s]

Mickey Finished intoxicated with alcohol. A play on MICKEY FINN (q.v.). [U.S. slang, mid 1900s]

Mickey Finn 1. a drug, usually chloral hydrate, added to an alcoholic drink for the purpose of rendering the drinker unconscious. **2.** a drink containing chloral hydrate. [both senses, U.S. slang, mid 1900s-pres.]

Mickey Mouse 1. the female genitals.

Cf. MOUSE (sense 2). [U.S., mid 1900s] **2.** pertaining to any useless or worthless thing. [U.S. slang, mid 1900s-pres.] **3.** a derogatory nickname for a Caucasian. [U.S. black use, mid 1900s]

Mickey Mouse mattress a sanitary napkin; a perineal pad. Cf. MICKEY MOUSE (sense 1). [U.S. slang, mid 1900s]

microdots the drug L.S.D. (q.v.). Cf. DOTS, PURPLE MICRODOTS. [U.S. drug culture, mid 1900s-pres.]

middle finger the penis. Cf. FOREFINGER, LITTLE FINGER, THUMB OF LOVE. [British slang, 1800s]

middle-gate the female genitals. For synonyms see MONOSYLLABLE. [British, late 1800s]

middle leg the penis. Cf. BEST LEG OF THREE. [colloquial since the 1800s or before]

miggies marijuana cigarettes. From MIG (sense 2). There is a remote possibility that this is a miscopy.

milk 1. to masturbate a male to ejaculation. [colloquial and slang, 1600s-pres.] **2.** semen. Cf. CREAM (sense 1). HOT MILK. [widespread slang and nonce since the 1600s] **3.** to manipulate the penis in such a way that a whitish fluid will be expressed if its owner is infected with gonorrhea. Done by prostitutes. Cf. FRESH COW. See also LONDON MILK.

milk-bar the female breasts. For synonyms see BOSOM. [British, mid 1900s-pres.]

milk-bottles the human breasts. Cf. CREAM JUGS, DAIRIES, FEEDING-BOTTLES. For synonyms see BOSOM. [widespread slang; attested as Australian and U.S. slang and colloquial, 1900s]

milkers the female breasts. For synonyms see BOSOM. [British, late 1900s-pres.]

milkman 1. a male masturbator. Cf. MILKER (sense 2), MILK-WOMAN. For synonyms see HUSKER. **2.** the penis. [both senses, British slang, 1800s, Farmer and Henley]

milk-pan the female genitals. *Cf.* PAN (sense 2). [British, 1800s]

milk-shop the human breasts. *Cf.* DAIRIES. [British, 1800s or before]

milk the chicken (also **milk the lizard**) to masturbate. Said of the male. Compare to CHOKE THE CHICKEN. For synonyms and related subjects see WASTE TIME. [U.S. slang, late 1900s]

mind fuck to pressure someone to do something that the person would not otherwise do; to confuse or bewilder someone intentionally. [U.S. slang, mid 1900s-pres.]

mind-fuck(er) someone or something that confuses someone or persuades someone to do something. [U.S. slang, late 1900s]

mind in the mud (also **mind in the gutter**) 1. pertaining to a person who thinks vulgar thoughts. 2. pertaining to a person who sees immediately the obscene senses of deliberate or accidental double entendre. [both senses, U.S. slang and colloquial, 1900s]

minibennies amphetamines. For synonyms see AMP. [U.S. drug culture, mid 1900s-pres.]

miniskirt a young woman; a girl. *Cf.* CALICO. [U.S. slang, mid 1900s-pres.]

mink 1. a lecher. Refers to his frequent copulation. [U.S. slang and nonce, 1900s, Wentworth and Flexner] 2. one's girlfriend. [U.S. slang, mid 1900s] 3. a woman. Black. For synonyms see BIRD. [British, late 1900s-pres.]

minks a flirtatious young woman. See MINX. [late 1600s, B.E.]

mintie 1. a homosexual male, especially an effeminate male. Also **minty**. 2. pertaining to a homosexual male. 3. a masculine lesbian. [all senses, U.S. homosexual use and general slang, mid 1900s-pres.]

mint leaf (also **mint weed**) phencyclidine, the drug P.C.P. on a mint leaf. For synonyms see P.C.P. [U.S. drug culture, late 1900s]

minx (also **minks**) 1. a forward woman or girl; a hussy or a harlot. 2. a prostitute; a whore. [both since the late 1500s]

miracle-meat a large penis; a penis which is essentially as large in the flaccid stage as it is in the erect stage. *Cf.* MENTULATE. [U.S. homosexual use, mid 1900s]

miraculous intoxicated with alcohol. [from Scots colloquial; British, 1900s]

miss 1. a high-class prostitute. [British, early 1700s, *New Canting Dictionary*] 2. to fail to have the menses at or soon after the expected time; to miss a period. [U.S. colloquial, mid 1900s-pres.]

Miss Brown the female genitals. For synonyms see MONOSYLLABLE. [British slang, 1700s-1800s]

Miss Emma morphine. Emma is the name of the letter "M" used in signaling. [U.S. underworld, early 1900s-pres.]

Miss Horner 1. the female genitals. *Cf.* HORNINGTON, OLD. [British slang, 1800s, Farmer and Henley] 2. a sexually loose woman. *Cf.* MR. HORNER.

missionary position a position for copulation wherein the man is above the woman, who receives him between her legs; the figura veneris prima. Implies that "natives" to whom missionaries minister in underdeveloped lands copulate in "primitive" ways, *i.e.,* dorsally.

mist the drug P.C.P. (*q.v.*). [U.S. drug culture, mid 1900s-pres.] See also BLUE MIST.

Mister Tom the penis; a personification of the penis. *Cf.* LONG TOM. [U.S. black use, mid 1900s]

misty very ugly. [U.S. collegiate, late 1900s, Munro]

mitten queen a homosexual male who derives special satisfaction from masturbating others. [U.S. homosexual use, mid 1900s-pres.]

mix one's peanut butter to commit pederasty. [U.S. slang, mid 1900s]

mizzled intoxicated with alcohol. For synonyms see WOOFLED. [colloquial, 1900s or before]

M.J. "Mary Jane," marijuana. [U.S. drug culture, mid 1900s-pres.]

M.L.A. "massive lip action"; very active and aggressive kissing. [U.S. collegiate, late 1900s]

mo a homosexual. From HOMO. For synonyms see EPICENE. [U.S., late 1900s-pres.]

modigger the penis [U.S. slang, mid 1900s]

mofo a MOTHER-FUCKER. [U.S. slang, late 1900s, Lewin and Lewin]

mohasky 1. marijuana. **2.** intoxicated with marijuana. Cf. MAHOSKA, MOSHKY. [both senses, U.S. drug culture, mid 1900s-pres.]

moist around the edges intoxicated with alcohol. For synonyms see WOOFLED. [colloquial or slang, 1900s]

mojo narcotics, especially cocaine and morphine. [U.S. underworld and drug culture, mid 1900s-pres.]

M.O.L. the penis, the "muscle of love." For synonyms see YARD. [U.S., late 1900s-pres.]

mola a homosexual male. Cf. MO, NOLA. For synonyms see EPICENE. [U.S. slang, mid 1900s-pres.]

mole the penis. From M.O.L. For synonyms see YARD. [U.S., late 1900s-pres.]

mole-catcher the female genitals; the "mate" of the MOLE (q.v.). [British slang, 1800s, Farmer and Henley]

molehills the human breasts, occasionally implying small breasts. Molehills are the opposite of MOUNTAINS (q.v.). [U.S. slang and nonce, 1900s]

moll 1. a girl. **2.** a thief's accomplice. **3.** a prostitute. **4.** one's girlfriend. "Moll" is a nickname for "Mary." See MALKIN. [in various senses since the 1600s]

moll-hunter a woman-chaser; a lecher. [British slang, late 1800s, Ware]

molly (also **molley, mollie**) **1.** a harlot. Cf. MOLL. [slang since the early 1700s or before] **2.** an effeminate male; a MILKSOP (q.v.); a CATAMITE (q.v.). [British and U.S. underworld, 1800s-early 1900s] **3.** to commit an act of PEDERASTY (q.v.).

mollycoddle 1. to pamper. **2.** an effeminate male; a male who has been

mollycoddled; anyone who has been mollycoddled. [both senses, colloquial, 1800s-1900s]

molly-mop an effeminate male. Cf. DOLLY-MOP. [British, early 1800s, Dictionary of Slang and Unconventional English]

molly's-hole the female genitals. For synonyms see MONOSYLLABLE. [British slang, 1800s, Farmer and Henley]

Molly the monk drunk. Rhyming slang. For synonyms see WOOFLED. [Australian, mid 1900s-pres.]

momzer (also **mamzer**) **1.** an illegitimate child; a BASTARD (sense 1). For synonyms see ACCIDENT. **2.** a wretched and despised person; a BASTARD (sense 2). [Hebrew; attested in Latin as manzer; appears in English in the late 1500s; most of the current U.S. use is from Yiddish]

Monet someone who looks good only from a distance. From the name of the painter. [U.S., late 1900s-pres.]

money the female genitals, a euphemism used with little girls. Patterned on the warning given to children when they are going shopping, i.e., "Don't show your money!" [British, late 1700s, Grose]

Monica a vacuum cleaner, something that sucks. [U.S., late 1900s-pres.]

monkey dust phencyclidine, the drug P.C.P. For synonyms see P.C.P. [U.S. drug culture, late 1900s]

monkey-farting goofing off; wasting time. A blend of "monkeying around" and "farting around." See FIDDLE-FARTING. [British, 1900s]

monkey-house a brothel. Cf. MONKEY (sense 1). [U.S. underworld, mid 1900s]

monosyllable the female genitals. From the monosyllabic word CUNT (q.v.). [British, early 1800s-1900s] Synonyms: A.B.C., ACE, ACE OF SPADES, ADAM'S OWN, AFFAIR, AFFAIRS, ALCOVE, ALMANACH, ALTAR OF HYMEN, ALTAR OF LOVE, APHRODISIACAL TENNIS COURT, ASS, AUNT ANNIE, BABYMAKER, BAG, BANK, BAZOO, BEARDED AXE WOUND, BEARDED CLAM, BEAUTYSPOT, BEAVER, BEE-HIVE, BELLY-DALE,

BELLY-DINGLE, BELLY-ENTRANCE, BERKELEY, BERKELEY HUNT, BERKSHIRE HUNT, bile, BIMBO, BIRD, BIT, BITE, BIT OF JAM, BIT ON A FORK, BLACK BESS, BLACK-HOLE, BLACK-JOCK, BLACK JOKE, BLACK-RING, Bluebeard's CLOSET, BOB-AND-HIT, BOMBO, BOODY, BORE, BOTTOMLESS-PIT, BOX, BOX-UNSEEN, BRAT-GETTING PLACE, BREACH, BREAD, BREAD-WINNER, BROOM, BROWN-JOCK, BROWN MADAM, Brown Miss, BUCKINGER'S BOOT, BUDGET, BULL'S EYE, BUMBO, BUM FIDDLE, BUM-SHOP, BUN, BUNGALOW, BUNNY, BUSH, Bushy Park, BUSINESS, BUTCHER'S SHOP, BUTTER-BOAT, BUTTON-HOLE, C., CABBAGE, CABBAGE-FIELD, CABBAGE-GARDEN, CABBAGE-PATCH, CAKE, CAN, CANDLESTICK, CANYON, Cape Horn, Cape of Good Hope, CARNAL TRAP, CASE, CAT, CATCH-'EM-ALIVE-O, CAT'S-HEAD-CUT OPEN, CAT'S-MEAT, CAULIFLOWER, CAVE, CAVE OF HARMONY, CAZE, CELLAR, CELLAR-DOOR, CENTER OF ATTRACTION, CENTER OF BLISS, CENTRAL FURROW, CENTRAL OFFICE, CERTIFICATE OF BIRTH, Charley, Charley Hunt, CHAT, CHIMNEY, CHINK, CHOCHA, CHUFF BOX, CHUM, CHURN, CIRCLE, CIVET, CLAFF, CLEFT, CLEFT OF FLESH, CLOCK, CLOVEN SPOT, CLOVEN TUFT, COCK, COCK-ALLEY, COCK-HALL, COCKHOLDER, COCK-INN, COCK-LANE, COCK-LOFT, COCKPIT, COCKSHIRE, COCKSHY, COFFEE HOUSE, COFFEE-SHOP, COGIE, COMMODITY, CONCERN, CONTRAPUNCTUM, CONUNDRUM, CONY, COOCH, COOKIE, COOLIE-DO, COOSIE, COOT, COOZ, COOZE, COOZIE, CORNER, CORNUCOPIA, COUPLER, COYOTE, CRACK, CRADLE, CRANNY, CREAM-JUG, CREASE, CREVICE, CRINKUM-CRANKUM, CROTCH, CROWN AND FEATHERS, CRUMPET, CUCKOO'S NEST, CUNNICLE, CUNNIKIN, DAISY, DEAD-END STREET, DEAREST BODILY PART, DEN, DICKY-DIDO, DIDDLE, DIDDLY-POUT, DILBERRY-BUSH, DIMPLE, DIVINE MONOSYLLABLE, DIVINE SCAR, DOODLE-CASE, DOODLE-SACK, DORMOUSE, DOWNY-BIT, DRAIN, DUMB-GLUTTON, DUMB-SQUINT, DUSTER, DYKE, EEL-SKINNER, EVERLASTING WOUND, Eve's CUSTOM-HOUSE, EYE THAT WEEPS MOST WHEN BEST PLEASED, FACTOTUM, FAN, FANCY-BIT, FANNY, FANNY-ARTFUL, FANNY-FAIR, FART-

DANIEL, FAUCET, FEMALE PUDEND, FEMALE PUDENDUM, FEMALE VERENDA, FIDDLE, FIE-FOR-SHAME, FIG, FIRELOCK, FIREPLACE, FISH, FISH POND, FLANGE, FLAP, FLAPDOODLE, FLAT COCK, FLESHLY-IDOL, FLESHLY-PART, FLITTER, FLOWER, FLOWER OF CHIVALRY, FLUSEY, FLY-BY-NIGHT, FLY-CAGE, FLYCATCHER, FLY-TRAP, FOBUS, FOOL-TRAP, FORECASTER, FORECASTLE, FORE-COURT, FOREHATCH, FORE-ROOM, FOREWOMAN, FORNICATOR'S HALL, FORT, Fort Bushy, FORTRESS, FOUNTAIN OF LIFE, FOUNTAIN OF LOVE, FREE-FISHERY, FRONT-ATTIC, FRONT BOTTOM, FRONT-DOOR, FRONT-GARDEN, FRONT-GUT, FRONT-PARLOR, FRONT PASSAGE, FRONT-WINDOW, FRUITFUL VINE, FUCK-HOLE, FUDD, FUNNIMENT, FUNNY BIT, FUR, FUR-PIE, FURROW, FURRY HOOP, FUTY, FUTZ, FUZZY CAP, GALLIMAUFREY, GAP, GAPE, GAPER, GARDEN OF EDEN, GASH, GASP AND GRUNT, GATE, GATE-OF-HORN, GATE-OF-LIFE, GATE-OF-PLENTY, GEAR, GENERATING PLACE, GENTLEMAN'S PLEASURE-GARDEN, GEOGRAPHY, GIG, GIGI, GIMCRACK, GIRL STREET, GOAT-MILKER, GOLDEN DOUGHNUT, GOLDFINCH'S NEST, GRAVY-GIVER, GRAVY-MAKER, GREEN-GROCERY, GREEN MEADOW, GREY-JOCK, GRINDSTONE, GROTTO, GROVE OF EGLANTINE, GROWL, GRUMBLE AND GRUNT, GRUMMET, GULLY, GULLY-HOLE, GUT-ENTRANCE, GUTTER, GYMNASIUM, GYVEL, HAIRBURGER, HAIR-COURT, HAIR-PIE, Hairyfordshire, HAIRY ORACLE, HAIRY-RING, HALF-MOON, HANDLE FOR THE BROOM, HAPPY HUNTING-GROUNDS, HAPPY VALLEY, HARBOUR, HARBOUR OF HOPE, HAT, HATCHWAY, HEY-NONNY-NONNY, HIVE, HOG EYE, HOGSTYE OF VENUS, HOLE, HOLE OF CONTENT, HOLE OF HOLES, HOLLOWAY, Holy of Holies, HOME SWEET HOME, HONE, HONEY-POT, HOOP, HORSE COLLAR, HORSE-SHOE, HORTUS, HOT BEEF, HOT-BOX, HOTEL, HOT MEAT, HOT MUTTON, HOUSE OF SECURITY, HOUSE UNDER THE HILL, HOUSEWIFE, HYPOGASTRIC-CRANNY, INDIA, INEFFABLE, INGLE-NOOK, INSTRUMENT, INTERCRURAL TRENCH, Irish fortune, IT, ITCHER, ITCHING JENNY, IVORY GATE, Jack and Danny, JACK NASTY-FACE, Jack Straw's CASTLE, Jacob's LADDER, JAM, JAM-POT, JAXY, JAZZ, JELLY, JELLY BAG, JELLY-ROLL, JEWEL, JEWELRY, JIG, JIGGER, JIGGUMBOB, JING-JANG, JOCK,

JOE HUNT, KAM, KAZE, KEESTER, KEIFER, KENNEL, KETTLE, KEYHOLE, KEYSTONE OF LOVE, KIPPER, KITCHEN, KITTY, KNICK-KNACK, LADDER, LADY BERKELEY, LADY-FLOWER, LADY JANE, LADY-STAR, LAMP OF LOVE, LAP, LAPLAND, LATHER-MAKER, LEADING ARTICLE, LEAK, LEA-RIGS, LEATHER, LIMBO, LITTLE MARY, LITTLE SISTER, LIVING FOUNTAIN, LOB'S POUND, LOBSTER-POT, LOCK, LOCKER, LONG-EYE, LOVE CHAMBER, LOVE-LANE, LOVE-PAD, LOVE'S CHANNEL, LOVE'S FOUNTAIN, LOVE'S HARBOUR, LOVE'S PARADISE, LOVE'S PAVILLION, LOW-COUNTRIES, LOWER-WIG, LOWLANDS, LUCKY-BAG, LUTE, MACHINE, MAD-DIKIN, MADGE, MAGNET, MAGPIE'S NEST, MAIN AVENUE, MAIN VEIN, MALKIN, MANGLE, MANHOLE, MANTRAP, MARBLE-ARCH, MARK OF THE BEAST, MARY JANE, MASTERPIECE, MATCH, MATE, MA-TRIX, MAWKIN, MEAT, MEAT-COOKER, MEAT-GRINDER, MEAT-MARKET, MED-LAR, MELTING-POT, MERKIN, MICKEY MOUSE, MIDDLE-GATE, MIDDLE KING-DOM, MIDLANDS, MILKER, MILKING-PAIL, MILK-JUG, MILK-PAN, MILL, MILLINER'S SHOP, MILT-MARKET, MILT-SHOP, MINE-OF-PLEASURE, MIRACULOUS-CAIRN, MISS BROWN, MISS HORNER, MISS LAYCOCK, MODESTY, MODICUM, MOLLY'S HOLE, MONEY, MONEY-BOX, MONKEY, MONS MEG, MOOSEY, MORTAR, MOSS-ROSE, MOSSY-CELL, MOTHER OF ALL SAINTS, MOTHER OF ALL SOULS, MOTT, MOUNT PLEASANT, MOUSE, MOUSER, MOUSE-TRAP, MOUTH-THANKLESS, MOUTH-THAT-CANNOT BITE, MOUTH THAT SAYS NO WORDS ABOUT IT, MUFF, MULIEBRIA, MUMBLE-PEG, MUSHROOM, MUSTARD-POT, MUTTON, NAF, NAGGIE, NAME-IT-NOT, NAMELESS, NATURA, NATURALIA, NATURE, NATURE'S TUFTED-TREASURE, NAUGHTY, NAUTCH, NEEDLE-BOOK, NEE-DLE-CASE, NEST, NEST OF SPICERY, NETHER END, NETHER-EYE, NETHER-LANDS, NETHER LIPS, NICHE, NICHE-COCK, NICK, NICK-IN-THE-NOTCH, NICK-NACK, NOCKANDRO, NONESUCH, NONNY-NONNY, NOOKER, NOOKY, NOTCH, NOV-ELTY, NUMBER NIP, NURSERY, OAT-BIN, O.B.H., OLD DING, OLD HAT, OLD LADY, OLD MOSSYFACE, OLD THING, OLD WIFE, OLD WOMAN, OMNIBUS, OPEN C., ORA-CLE, ORANGE, ORCHARD, ORGAN-GRINDER, ORIFICE, ORNAMENT, OVEN, OYSTER, OYSTER-CATCHER, PALACE OF PLEASURE, PAN, PANCAKE, PANNIER, PARADISE, PARENTHESIS, PARLOR, PARS-LEY-BED, PARTS OF SHAME, PATCH, PECULIAR RIVER, PEN, PENWIPER, PERI-WINKLE, PFOTZE, PHOENIX-NEST, PI-GEON-HOLE, PILLICOCK-HILL, PIN-CASE, PIN-CUSHION, PINK PALACE IN THE BLACK, PINTLE-CASE, PIPE, PIPE-CLEANER, PIPKIN, PISSER, PISS-FLAP(PER)S, PIT, PITCHER, PIT-HOLE, PLACKET, PLACKET-BOX, PLACKET-HOLE, PLAYGROUND, PLAYTHING, PLEASURE-BOAT, PLUM-TREE, P-MAKER, POCKET-BOOK, PODY, POGIE, POINT-OF-ATTRACTION, POKE-HOLE, POONOO, POONTANG, POOR MAN'S BLESSING, POOTENANNY, POOZLE, POR-TAL OF VENUS, PORT-HOLE, POSTERN, POT, POUTER, POXBOX, PRANNY, PRATS, PREMISES, PRETTY, PRICK-HOLDER, PRICK-POCKET, PRICK-PURSE, PRICK-SCOURER, PRICK-SKINNER, PRIME CUT, PRINCOCK, PRIVATE PARTS, PRIVATE PLACE, PRIVATES, PRIVY-HOLE, PUDDLE, PUDEND, PUDENDA, PUDENDA MU-LIEBRIS, PUDENDUM, PUDENDUM FEMI-NINUM, PUFFY CLAM, PULPIT, PUMP, PUMP-DALE, PUMPKIN, PUNCE, PUNSE, PURSE, PUSS, PUSSY, QUAINT, QUARRY, QUAVER-CASE, QUEEN-OF-HOLES, QUEM, QUID, QUIFF, QUIM, QUIMMY, QUIMSBY, QUIMSY, QUIN, QUIVER, QUONIAM, RASP, RATTLE-BALLOCKS, RECEIPT-OF-CUSTOM, RECEIVING-SET, RED ONION, REGULATOR, REST-AND-BE-THANKFUL, RING, RINGER-ANGEROO, ROAD, ROAD TO HEAVEN, ROASTING-JACK, ROB-THE-RUFFIAN, ROOST-ER, ROSE, ROUGH-AND-TUMBLE, ROUGH MALKIN, RUFUS, RUMP, SADDLE, SALLY-PORT, SALT-CELLAR, SAMPLER, SATCHEL, SCABBARD, SCUT, SCUTTLE, SEAR, SE-CRET PARTS, SEED-LAND, SEED-PLOT, SEMINARY, SEX, SHADY SPRING, SHAFT, SHAKE-BAG, SHAPE, SHEATH, SHELL, SIR ANTHONY BLUNT, SIR BERKELEY HUNT, SKIN-COAT, SKIN-THE-PIZZLE, SLIP-PER, SLIT, SLOT, SLUICE, SMOCK, SMOCK-ALLEY, SNATCH-BLATCH, SNATCH-BOX, SNIPPET, SOCKET, SOLUTION-OF-CONTINU-ITY, SOUTH POLE, SPENDER, SPERM-SUCKER, SPEW-ALLEY, SPITFIRE, SPLIT-APRICOT, SPORTSMAN'S GAP, SPORTS-MAN'S HOLE, SPOT, SQUANCH, SQUARE PUSH, SQUINT, SQUIRREL, STAR, STENCH-TRENCH, STREAM'S TOWN, STUFF, SUCK-AND-SWALLOW, SUGAR-BASIN, SUGAR DOUGH-

NUT, SUPPER, SWEET-SCENTED HOLE, TAIL, TAIL-BOX, TAIL-GAP, TAIL-GATE, TAIL-HOLE, TAIL-TRIMMER, TARGET, TEAZLE, TEMPLE OF LOW MEN, TEMPLE OF VENUS, TENCH, THAT, THATCH, THATCHED HOUSE UNDER THE HILL, THE ANTIPODES, THE NEVER OUT, THING, THINGAMY, THINGUMBOB, THING-UMMY, TICKLE-THOMAS, TICKLE-TOBY, TILL, TIRLY-WHIRLY, TIT, TIT-MOUSE, TIVVY, TOBY, TOKEN, TOLL-HOLE, TOMBOY, TOOL-CHEST, TOOLSHED, TOUCH-HOLE, TOY, TOY-SHOP, TRAP, TREASURE, TRENCH, TRINKET, TUNA, TUNNEL, TU QUOQUE, TWAT, TWATCHEL, TWIM, TWITCHER, TWITCHET, TWITTLE, TIT-MOSE, UNDER-DIMPLE, UNDERS, UNDER-TAKER, UNT-CAY, UPRIGHT GRIN, UPRIGHT WINK, VACUUM, VALVE, VENERABLE MONO-SYLLABLE, VENT, VENUS FLYTRAP, VENUS'S-CELL, VENUS'S HONEYPOT, VERTICAL SMILE, VICIOUS CIRCLE, VIRGIN-TREASURE, VULVA, WARE, WASTE-PIPE, WATER-BOX, WATER-MILL, WHAT, WHELK, WHERE UNCLE'S DOO-DLE GOES, WHETING-CORNE, WHIM-WHAM, WHISKER BISCUIT, WINKER, WOMANHOOD, WOOKIE, WORKS, WORKSHOP, WOUND, YARD MEASURE, YEAST-POWDER BISCUIT, YONI, YOU-KNOW-WHAT, YUM-YUM, ZIPPER-FISH.

Montezuma's revenge diarrhea. Originated by tourists in Mexico afflicted with diarrhea. *Cf.* AZTEC TWO-STEP. For synonyms see QUICK-STEP. [U.S. slang, mid 1900s-pres.]

monthlies the menses. For synonyms see FLOODS. [British and U.S. colloquial, late 1800s-pres.]

monthly bill a woman's menstrual period. For synonyms see FLOODS. [U.S. collegiate, late 1900s, Munro]

months the menses. *Cf.* MONTHLIES. [since the early 1600s]

moof drunk. For synonyms see WOOFLED. [U.S., late 1900s-pres.]

moolah money. [U.S., early 1900s-pres.]

moon 1. to show one's nude posteriors through a window (usually of an automobile) at someone. *Cf.* HANG A B.A. Derived from, or the source of, sense **4.** [U.S. slang, mid 1900s] **2.** alcohol; whisky. A truncation of MOONSHINE (*q.v.*). [U.S. colloquial, mid 1900s] **3.**

MESCALINE (*q.v.*). [U.S. drug culture, mid 1900s-pres.] **4.** the buttocks. [slang, mid 1900s]

moon beams phencyclidine, the drug P.C.P. For synonyms see P.C.P. [U.S. drug culture, late 1900s]

moon cabbage marijuana. For synonyms see MAIR. [U.S., late 1900s-pres.]

moon cycle, on the [for a woman] to experience the monthly menstrual period. For synonyms see FLOODS. [U.S. slang, 1900s]

mooney intoxicated with alcohol. See MOONY. [1800s]

moon-eyed intoxicated with alcohol. [U.S., early 1700s-pres.]

moonrock a variant form of CRACK cocaine that contains heroin. The same as CROAK (*q.v.*). [U.S. drug culture, late 1900s]

moonshine 1. nonsense; humbug. [since the late 1500s] **2.** homemade whisky; cheap or inferior alcohol; any alcohol. [cant and colloquial, late 1700s-pres.] Synonyms: A-BOMB JUICE, CORN, CORN-JUICE, CORN-MULE, MOUNTAIN-DEW, STUMP-LIKKER, WHITE MULE.

moony (also **mooney**) intoxicated with alcohol. [British and U.S. slang, 1800s-1900s]

moose 1. a derogatory nickname for a woman. [U.S. slang, mid 1900s-pres.] **2.** a big man; an overweight girl; anything big. [U.S. slang, mid 1900s-pres.]

moose beans (also **moose nuggets, moose pecans**) DUNG; bits of dung; moose dung. For synonyms see DROP-PINGS. [U.S. slang, late 1900s, Lewin and Lewin]

mootah (also **mooter, mootie, mota, mu, muta, mutah, mutha**) marijuana or a marijuana cigarette. *Cf.* MOOCAH. [U.S. underworld and drug culture, early 1900s-pres.]

mopped alcohol intoxicated. For synonyms see WOOFLED. [U.S., late 1900s-pres.]

mopper an alcoholic who drinks cheap, fortified wine. [British, late 1900s-pres.]

moppy intoxicated with alcohol. [British and U.S. slang, 1800s-1900s]

mops and brooms (also **all mops and brooms**) intoxicated with alcohol. [slang, 1800s-1900s]

morals tablets of Demerol™ brand of meperdine, a painkiller. From the last two syllables of *Demerols*. [U.S. drug culture, late 1900s, Kaiser]

more in one's belly than ever came through one's mouth pregnant. Found in numerous forms, typically, "There's more in her belly than ever went through her mouth." [colloquial, 1800s-pres.]

morf 1. a hermaphrodite. *Cf.* MOFF, MORPHODITE. [U.S. slang, early 1900s] **2.** morphine. Also **morfo, morph, morpho.** *Cf.* MORPHIE. [U.S. drug culture, mid 1900s-pres.]

morfiend a morphine addict. A blend of "morphine" and "fiend." [U.S. slang, mid 1900s]

morning pride a morning erection. See PRIDE OF THE MORNING. A reinterpretation of the name of a quiet morning rain shower. *Cf.* MATUTINAL ERECTION. [British, 1800s, *Dictionary of Slang and Unconventional English*]

morning wood a morning erection. For synonyms see ERECTION. [British and U.S., late 1900s-pres.]

morph morphine. See MORF. Synonyms: AUNT EMMA, COBY, CUBE, CUBE JUICE, DOPE, EM, EMSEL, FIRST LINE, GLAD STUFF, GOD'S MEDICINE, GOODY, HAPPY DUST, HAPPY POWDER, HAPPY STUFF, HARD STUFF, HOCUS, M., MISS EMMA, MORF, MORPHIA, MORPHIE, MUD, NUMBER THIRTEEN, RED CROSS, SISTER, STUFF, UNKIE, WHITE MERCHANDISE, WHITE NURSE, WHITE STUFF.

morphie (also **morphy**) morphine. See MORF. [U.S. drug culture, 1900s]

morphodite (also **morphydite**) **1.** a sexual pervert; a homosexual male; a hermaphrodite (sense 3). [U.S. underworld, mid 1900s] **2.** a HERMAPHRODITE (sense 1). [U.S. dialect and colloquial, 1900s or before]

mort 1. a girl or woman. [cant, mid 1600s, Harman] **2.** a sexually loose woman; any girl or woman. [British and U.S. underworld with some slang use, 1700s-1900s] **3.** death. **4.** a corpse.

[senses 3 and 4 are British dialect, 1800s or before]

mortal intoxicated with alcohol; dead drunk. *Cf.* MORTALLIOUS. [British slang, early 1800s]

mortar the female genitals. The mate of the PESTLE (sense 1). The penis. [British slang, 1800s, Farmer and Henley]

M.O.S. a "member of the opposite sex." [U.S. collegiate, late 1900s]

moshky a user of marijuana. *Cf.* MAHOSKA, MOHASKY. [U.S. drug culture, mid 1900s-pres.]

mosquito bites (also **bee-bites**) very small breasts. For synonyms see BOSOM. [U.S. slang, late 1900s, Lewin and Lewin]

moss 1. the female pubic hair. For synonyms see DOWNSHIRE. [British slang, 1800s, Farmer and Henley] **2.** a derogatory nickname for a Negro. From the texture of Negroid hair. *Cf.* MOSSHEAD. See also MOSE. [U.S., mid 1900s]

mota marijuana. See MOOTAH. [U.S. drug culture, mid 1900s]

mother 1. a madam. [British slang and cant, 1600s-1700s] **2.** a truncation of MOTHER-FUCKER (*q.v.*). The truncation is in such wide use that its original negative connotation is unknown to many people. [U.S. slang and colloquial, mid 1900s-pres.] **3.** the "leader" of a group of homosexual males. The "sponsor" of a young homosexual in homosexual society. *Cf.* DAUGHTER. [U.S. homosexual use, mid 1900s-pres.] **4.** any homosexual male. *Cf.* FATHER-FUCKER. [U.S. homosexual use, mid 1900s-pres.]

mother-clutcher a MOTHER-FUCKER; a thoroughly despised person, usually a male. For synonyms see SNOKE-HORN. [U.S. slang, late 1900s]

mother-dangler euphemistic for MOTHER-FUCKER (*q.v.*). For synonyms see M.F. [U.S. slang, 1900s]

motherdear Methedrine (trademark), an amphetamine. For synonyms see AMP. [U.S. drug culture, mid 1900s, *Current Slang*]

mother-flunker a euphemism for MOTHER-FUCKER. [U.S. slang, late 1900s]

mother-fouler a euphemism for MOTHER-FUCKER. [U.S. slang, late 1900s]

mother-fucker (also **mother**) **1.** any despicable person or thing. **2.** a superb person or thing. **3.** a male buddy or chum. A term used between males. Cf. FATHER-FUCKER. [all senses, originally U.S. slang, mid 1900s-pres.]

mother-grabber (also **mother-humper, mother-jumper**) a euphemism for MOTHER-FUCKER (q.v.). For synonyms see M.F. [U.S. slang, mid 1900s]

mother-hugger a euphemism for MOTHER-FUCKER. [U.S. slang, late 1900s]

mother-jiver a euphemism for MOTHER-FUCKER. [U.S. slang, late 1900s]

mother-lover a euphemism for MOTHER-FUCKER (q.v.). [U.S. slang, 1900s]

mother-raper a dysphemism for MOTHER-FUCKER. [U.S. slang, late 1900s]

mother-rucker a euphemism of disguise of MOTHER-FUCKER (q.v.). RUCK (q.v.) is a common way of disguising the graffito "fuck." For synonyms see M.F. [U.S. slang, mid 1900s]

mother's milk gin. Cf. LONDON MILK. For synonyms see RUIN. [British slang, early 1800s]

mother-ugly 1. a MOTHER-FUCKER (q.v.). **2.** extremely ugly. [both senses, U.S. slang, mid 1900s]

mott the female sexual organ. For synonyms see MONOSYLLABLE. [1900s or before]

mountain an erection. For synonyms see ERECTION. [U.S., late 1900s-pres.]

mountain climber a drug user who is HIGH. [U.S. drug culture, late 1900s]

mountain-dew 1. a nickname for Scotch whisky. [British and Scots, 1800s] **2.** illicitly brewed whisky; moonshine. Cf. PRAIRIE-DEW. [U.S., 1800s-1900s]

mountain oysters the testicles of a bull, hog, or ram, roasted or fried. Cf. LAMB FRIES. [U.S. dialect and colloquial, 1900s and before]

mountains the human breasts. Cf. MOLEHILLS. [U.S. colloquial and nonce, 1900s]

mount of lilies the human breasts. For synonyms see BOSOM. [euphemism, late 1600s]

mouse 1. the penis. Considered as a burrowing creature. [British slang, 1800s, Farmer and Henley] **2.** the female genitals. The reference is to the soft fur of a mouse. Cf. TIT-MOUSE. [British slang, 1800s, Farmer and Henley] **3.** a girl or a woman. Possibly from sense 2. **4.** to kiss and pet. From MOUTH (sense 1). [senses 3 and 4 are slang, 1900s if not long before]

mouth 1. to kiss passionately, perhaps with the tongue. [since the 1600s] **2.** a lawyer. See MOUTHPIECE. [U.S. underworld, early 1900s]

mouth music oral sex. [British, late 1900s-pres.]

mouth-o a "mouth orgasm." [U.S. collegiate, late 1900s]

mouth-that-cannot-bite the female genitals. [British euphemism, early 1700s]

mouth that says no words about it the female genitals. [British, 1700s]

mouth-to-mouth resuscitation deep or passionate kissing; kissing that goes on and on. [U.S. slang, mid 1900s-pres.]

mouth-whore a prostitute who performs FELLATIO (q.v.), either male or female. [British, 1800s, (Farmer)]

movie queen a vain homosexual male. See QUEEN for similar subjects. [U.S. homosexual use, mid 1900s]

movies diarrhea. From the urgency that makes one move fast. Cf. RUNS, TROTS. [U.S. slang and colloquial, mid 1900s]

Mozart drunk. Rhyming slang for *Mozart and Liszt* = PISSED. For synonyms see WOOFLED. [British, mid 1900s-pres.]

M.P.T.P. a type of DESIGNER DRUG similar to or derived from Demerol™. [U.S. drug culture, late 1900s]

Mr. Groin a nickname for a lecherous male. For synonyms see LECHER. [U.S. collegiate, late 1900s, Munro]

Mr. Happy a penis nickname. For synonyms see YARD. [U.S., late 1900s-pres.]

Mr. Horner a lecher; a whoremonger. *Cf.* MISS HORNER. [British slang, 1800s, Farmer and Henley]

Mr. Sausage a penis nickname. For synonyms see YARD. [British, late 1900s-pres.]

Mrs. Duckett! "Fuck it!" Rhyming slang. [British, 1900s, *Dictionary of Rhyming Slang*]

Mrs. Hand masturbation; the act of masturbation. For synonyms and related subjects see WASTE TIME. [1900s]

Mrs. Jones's place (also **Mrs. Jones, widow Jones**) a W.C.; a toilet. [slang and colloquial, 1800s-1900s]

Mrs. Murphy a W.C.; a bathroom. [U.S. colloquial, 1900s or before]

mu marijuana. See MOOCAH, MOOTAH. [U.S. underworld and drug culture, mid 1900s]

muck 1. anything nasty, *i.e.*, dirt, mud, sweat, feces. [since the 1200s] **2.** a disguise of FUCK (*q.v.*). [British, 1900s and before]

muck about 1. to mess around with a woman; to fondle a woman vaginally. [British slang, late 1800s] **2.** to fuck about; to mess up; to create confusion. [British colloquial, 1900s or before]

muck up a disguise of FUCK UP (*q.v.*). [U.S. slang, mid 1900s]

mud duck an ugly person. [U.S., late 1900s-pres.]

mud flap the scrotum. See also MUD FLAPS. For synonyms see TOOL BAG. [U.S., late 1900s-pres.]

mud flaps the buttocks or the rear end. See also MUD FLAP. For synonyms see DUFF. [U.S., late 1900s-pres.]

mud puppy an ugly female. Named for the fish. [U.S. slang, late 1900s]

muff 1. the female genitals. From the name of a hand-warming muff. In the bawdy verse: "Lost, lost and can't be found; a lady's thing with hair all 'round" (Farmer and Henley). [slang, 1600s-pres.] **2.** a prostitute. For synonyms see HARLOT. [U.S. colloquial, mid 1900s] **3.** any girl or woman. [U.S. slang, early 1900s] **4.** women considered sexually. From a nickname for a cat. For synonyms see TAIL. [British and U.S., 1900s] **5.** an oaf; a fool. [cant, early 1800s, Vaux]

muff-barking CUNNILINGUS (*q.v.*). [U.S. slang, 1900s]

muff-diver (also **diver**) a CUNNILINGUIST (*q.v.*). *Cf.* DIVE A MUFF, DIVER, PEARL-DIVING, SKIN-DIVER. [British and U.S. slang, 1900s]

muffins the human breasts, especially if small. [U.S. slang, 1900s]

muff merchant a pimp. [U.S., late 1900s-pres.]

mugg blotts (also **mug blotto**) intoxicated with alcohol. *Cf.* BLOTTO. [U.S. slang, early 1900s]

mugged up (also **mugged**) intoxicated with alcohol. From a drinking mug. *Cf.* CUP-SHOT. [U.S. slang, mid 1900s]

mugget a false vulva with a pubic wig worn by male homosexual prostitutes in DRAG (*q.v.*). [slang, 1900s]

mugging-up making love; petting; caressing. [U.S. slang, mid 1900s]

muggle-head a user of marijuana. [U.S. underworld and drug culture, mid 1900s-pres.]

muggles (also **muggle**) **1.** marijuana **2.** a marijuana cigarette. [both senses, U.S. underworld, drug culture, early 1900s-pres.]

muggy intoxicated with alcohol. For synonyms see WOOFLED. [British and U.S. slang, 1800s-1900s]

muh-fuh a phonological disguise of MOTHER-FUCKER (*q.v.*). *Cf.* M.F. [primarily black use; U.S. slang, mid 1900s-pres.]

mule 1. an impotent male. [slang or colloquial, 1800s-1900s] **2.** a Caucasian male. *Cf.* MOKE. [U.S. slang, early 1900s, Irwin] See also WHITE MULE. **3.** a drug runner or smuggler. [U.S. drug culture, late 1900s]

mule skinner in drug running or smuggling, the person who recruits and watches over the MULES or runners. *Cf.* MULE. [U.S. drug culture, late 1900s]

mull an oaf; a simpleton. [British colloquial, 1800s]

mulled-up (also **mulled**) intoxicated with alcohol. [U.S. slang, mid 1900s]

munch to perform PENILINGUS (*q.v.*). *Cf.* EAT, GOBBLE, NIBBLE. [U.S. slang, mid 1900s-pres.]

munchasaurus an obese person who is always eating. [U.S., late 1900s-pres.]

muncher-boy (also **muncher**) a fellator; the RECEIVER (*q.v.*). *Cf.* GOBBLER. For synonyms see PICCOLO-PLAYER.

munch out to kiss and MAKE OUT. [U.S. collegiate, late 1900s]

munch the bearded clam to perform CUNNILINGUS (*q.v.*). See BEARD, MUNCH. [slang, 1900s or before]

mungshit a stupid and worthless person; an idiot. [U.S. slang, late 1900s]

munted drunk. For synonyms see WOOFLED. [British, late 1900s-pres.]

mur backslang for "rum." [British, 1800s, Farmer and Henley]

murphies the human breasts. From a nickname for "Irish potatoes." *Cf.* SWEET POTATOES. [U.S. slang, 1900s]

muscle Mary a muscular homosexual male. For synonyms see EPICENE. [British, late 1900s-pres.]

muscle moll a masculine woman; a virago. Based on "gun moll." [U.S. underworld, early 1900s]

muscle of love the penis. [U.S. slang, mid 1900s-pres.]

mush 1. nonsense. [U.S. colloquial, 1900s or before] **2.** romance; lovemaking; kissing. [U.S. colloquial, mid 1900s]

mush mind someone burned out by marijuana smoking. [U.S., late 1900s-pres.]

mushroom 1. the female genitals. For synonyms see MONOSYLLABLE. [British slang, 1800s, Farmer and Henley] **2.** a mushroom containing the hallucinogenic compound psilocybin; the same as MAGIC MUSHROOM (*q.v.*). [U.S. drug culture, mid 1900s-pres.]

musical fruit any variety of beans. Because they produce flatulence. *Cf.* ARS MUSICA, WHISTLE-BERRIES. [U.S. slang and colloquial, 1900s]

muski a cheap brand of wine. From "Muscatel." [U.S. slang, 1900s]

muskra a policeman. For synonyms see FLATFOOT. [U.S., late 1900s-pres.]

musta marijuana. *Cf.* MOOTAH. For synonyms see MARI. [U.S., 1900s]

mustard, be to be sexually attractive; to be as HOT (sense 1) as mustard. [British slang, early 1900s, *Dictionary of Slang and Unconventional English*]

mustard and cress the female pubic hair. See MUSTARD-POT. [British slang, 1800s, Farmer and Henley]

mustard-pot 1. the female genitals, "hot like (English) mustard." [British slang, 1800s, Farmer and Henley] **2.** a CATAMITE (*q.v.*) in a prison. From sense 1. [attested as U.S., mid 1900s]

mustard-yellow a mulatto. *Cf.* HIGH-YELLOW. For synonyms see MAHOGANY. [U.S. slang, early 1900s]

mustn't-mention-'ems trousers. For synonyms see GALLIGASKINS. [British jocular slang, mid 1800s]

mute 1. liquid bird dung; the dung of hawks; the same as muting. Sometimes for any kind of dung. [colloquial, 1500s] **2.** a person hired to mourn at funerals. [British, 1700s-1800s]

mutha 1. marijuana. See MOOTAH. **2.** "mother"; the same as MOTHER-FUCKER (*q.v.*).

mutton 1. a sexually loose woman. For synonyms see LAY. [numerous written attestations; British, 1500s-1800s] **2.** the female genitals. **3.** copulation. **4.** women considered sexually. *Cf.* LACED-MUTTON. [senses 2-4 are British, 1600s] **5.** sexual pleasures. See GREENS. *Cf.* JERK ONE'S MUTTON, where mutton is either sense 5 or the penis.

mutton, in her in the act of copulation with a woman. [British slang, 1800s, Farmer and Henley]

mutton-dagger the penis. *Cf.* PORK-SWORD. For synonyms see YARD. [British slang, 1900s, *Dictionary of the Underworld*]

My bad "It's my fault and I'm sorry." [U.S., late 1900s-pres.]

my man Thomas the penis. See JOHN THOMAS.

mystic biscuit a chunk of peyote cactus. [U.S., late 1900s-pres.]

N

nabbed caught by the police; arrested. [1900s, if not before]

nads testicles. From *gonads*. For synonyms see WHIRLYGIG. [U.S., mid 1900s-pres.]

naffing fucking. [British, mid 1900s-pres.]

Naff off! "Fuck off!" [British, late 1900s-pres.]

nail 1. to copulate with a woman. *Cf.* HAMMER. [U.S. slang, mid 1900s-pres.] **2.** a cigarette. See COFFIN-NAIL. **3.** a "male." Rhyming slang. *Cf.* HAMMER (sense 2). [U.S. black use, mid 1900s-pres.] **4.** a marijuana cigarette. From sense 2. [U.S. drug culture, mid 1900s-pres.]

nail, off the intoxicated with alcohol. For synonyms see WOOFLED. [colloquial, early 1800s-1900s]

naked 1. totally nude; no clothing and no covering over the genitals or breasts. For synonyms see STARKERS. **2.** unclothed, but with the genitals covered. **3.** lacking a shirt, said of the male. In various senses, depending on the sensitivities of the speaker, the audience, and the times. [since before 1000]

Nam black (also **Nam weed**) powerful black marijuana associated with Vietnam. Used there or imported from there. For synonyms see MARI. [U.S. drug culture, late 1900s]

name-it-not the female genitals. An avoidance for CUNT (*q.v.*). *Cf.* INEFFABLE, NAMELESS. [British slang, 1800s, Farmer and Henley]

nameless the female genitals. A jocular avoidance for CUNT (*q.v.*). From a bawdy song. For synonyms see MONOSYLLABLE. [British, 1600s]

Nan-boy (also **Nancy-boy**) **1.** an effeminate male. For synonyms see FRIBBLE. [British, late 1600s] **2.** a CATAMITE

(*q.v.*). For synonyms see BRONCO. [British slang, 1800s or before]

Nance 1. an effeminate male. **2.** a PEDERAST (*q.v.*). [both senses, U.S. slang and colloquial, 1900s or before]

Nancy (also **Nancy-boy**) **1.** a homosexual male, the same as NANCE (*q.v.*). [British and U.S., 1800s-1900s] **2.** the posteriors; the BREECH (sense 2). [British slang, early 1800s]

Nancy Dawson an effeminate male; a homosexual male. Based on the name of a legendary prostitute. [British, late 1800s]

Nancy homey an effeminate male; a homosexual male. [British, 1800s, *Dictionary of Slang and Unconventional English*]

nanny-house (also **nanny-shop**) a brothel. [British, 1700s-1800s]

nap 1. an infection of a venereal disease. **2.** to infect with a venereal disease. [both senses, British, late 1600s, B.E.] **3.** a derogatory nickname for a Negro. From the texture of the hair. *Cf.* NAPS. [U.S., 1900s, Wentworth and Flexner]

napkin ring a COCK RING used to secure an erection. [U.S., late 1900s-pres.]

nards the testicles. A phonological disguise of NERTS or NUTS (both *q.v.*). [U.S. slang, mid 1900s-pres., *Current Slang*]

nark 1. any police spy. [widespread slang, mid 1800s] **2.** a narcotics agent. [1900s] **3.** any unpleasant person; an oaf or jerk. For synonyms see SNOKEHORN. [World War II, Fraser and Gibbons]

Nark it! "Fuck it!" For synonyms see 'ZOUNDS. [British, late 1900s-pres.]

natural, in the naked; nude. *Cf.* au naturel.

natural-child a bastard. *Cf.* NATURAL (sense 2). [since the 1600s]

natural member the penis. *Cf.* MEMBER. [1600s, (Urquhart)]

natural parts (also **natural places**) the genitals, male or female. [mid 1500s]

naturals the genitals, male or female. From NATURAL PARTS (*q.v.*). For synonyms see GENITALS [mid 1600s]

nature 1. the menses. *Cf.* MOTHER-NATURE (sense 2). [since the 1300s] **2.** semen. [euphemism, 1500s] **3.** the genitals, male or female. **4.** the female genitals, especially of a horse. **5.** the libido; male sexual potency. *Cf.* PIONEER OF NATURE. [senses 3-5 since the 1500s]

nature's call the feeling of a need to eliminate wastes; defecation or urination. *Cf.* MOTHER-NATURE (sense 1). [U.S. colloquial, 1900s]

nature's duty copulation. [British, 1700s or earlier]

nature's fonts the breasts. For synonyms see BOSOM. [British euphemism, late 1800s]

nature's garb nakedness. *Cf.* ADAM AND EVE'S TOGS. [British, 1800s, Farmer and Henley]

nature's scythe the penis. For synonyms see YARD. [British, late 1700s]

nature stop a stop (in highway travel) to urinate. *Cf.* COKE-STOP, MOTHER-NATURE (sense 1). [U.S. colloquial, mid 1900s-pres.]

nature's tufted-treasure the female genitals. For synonyms see MONOSYLLABLE. [British, early 1800s]

nature's veil the female pubic hair. *Cf.* NATURE (sense 3). For synonyms see DOWNSHIRE.

naughty copulation. For synonyms see SMOCKAGE. [Australian, mid 1900s-pres.]

naughty bits the genitals of either sex. For synonyms see GENITALS, MONOSYLLABLE, VIRILIA. [British, late 1900s-pres.]

nauticals piles; hemorrhoids. Rhyming slang on nautical miles = *piles*. [British, mid 1900s-pres.]

navel engagement copulation. From

"naval engagement," a battle at sea. *Cf.* JOIN PAUNCHES. [widespread nonce use; attested as Canadian, 1900s, *Dictionary of Slang and Unconventional English*]

navigate the windward passage to copulate anally. The anus is the WINDWARD PASSAGE (*q.v.*).

N.D.B.F. a "needle-dicked bug-fucker," a worthless male. For synonyms see OAF. [U.S. slang, late 1900s]

neanderthal a large and ugly male. For synonyms see OAF. [U.S., mid 1900s-pres.]

neathie-set female underwear. For synonyms see NETHER-GARMENTS. [British slang, early 1900s]

neato (canito) really fine. [U.S., mid 1900s-pres.]

neb a total JERK; a nebbish. For synonyms see OAF. [U.S. slang, late 1900s]

nebbies Nembutal (trademark) capsules, barbiturate capsules. *Cf.* NEMBIES. [U.S. drug culture, mid 1900s-pres.]

Nebraska sign an indication of death. When the line of the EEG monitor is as flat as the Nebraska landscape. *Cf.* FLATLINED. For synonyms see DEMISE. [U.S. medical slang, late 1900s]

Nebuchadnezzar the penis. *Cf.* TAKE NEBUCHADNEZZAR OUT TO GRASS. [British slang, 1800s, Farmer and Henley]

necessaries the VIRILIA (*q.v.*), primarily the testicles. For synonyms see WHIRLYGIGS. [based on *necessariae partes*, Latin for "the necessary parts"; British, early 1900s]

necessary 1. a prostitute; a female companion to be used sexually. For synonyms see HARLOT. [British slang, 1800s, Farmer and Henley] **2.** a privy. A truncation of NECESSARY HOUSE (*q.v.*).

necessary chamber a privy; a W.C. [British, 1600s or before]

necessary house (also **necessary**) a privy. For synonyms see AJAX. [colloquial, early 1600s-1900s]

neck 1. a woman's bosom. [euphemistic and vague; from *Hamlet* (Shakespeare)] **2.** to hang. For synonyms see NUB. [cant or slang, 1700s] **3.** to kiss and pet. [U.S. colloquial, early 1900s-pres.]

necked naked. A regional pronunciation indicated by the spelling. For synonyms see STARKERS. [U.S. rural colloquial, 1900s and before]

neck-oil liquor; BOOZE. For synonyms see BOOZE. [British and U.S. slang, 1900s]

ned marijuana. For synonyms see MARI. [U.S., late 1900s-pres.]

needle the penis. *Cf.* PIN (sense 1), PRICK (sense 1). [British, 1600s]

needle, on the injecting drugs habitually. Pertaining to a drug addict. [U.S. slang, mid 1900s]

needle-book the female genitals. A holder for the NEEDLE (*q.v.*). [British slang, 1800s, Farmer and Henley]

needle-candy a narcotic which is injected. In contrast to narcotics which are sniffed. See NOSE-CANDY. *Cf.* CANDY. [U.S. drug culture, mid 1900s]

needle-case the female genitals. A holder for the NEEDLE (*q.v.*). [British slang, 1800s]

needle dick (also **pencil dick**) **1.** a male with a small penis. **2.** a small penis. For synonyms see GENITALS, YARD. **3.** a worthless male. For synonyms see OAF. [all senses, U.S. slang, late 1900s]

needle-knight a user of injectable drugs. [U.S. drug culture, late 1900s]

needle-man a narcotics addict who uses injected drugs. *Cf.* ARTILLERY MAN. [underworld, 1900s]

Nellie fag an effeminate male homosexual. For synonyms see EPICENE. [U.S. slang, mid 1900s-pres.]

Nelly 1. a lesbian. [U.S. slang, mid 1900s-pres., Underwood] **2.** a homosexual male. [slang, mid 1900s-pres.] **3.** effeminate; pertaining to an effeminate male.

nemish a Nembutal (trademark) capsule. [U.S. drug culture, mid 1900s-pres.]

nemmies (also **nems**) Nembutal (trademark) capsules; the same as NEMBIES (*q.v.*). [U.S. drug culture, mid 1900s-pres.] Synonyms: ABBOT, BLOCK-BUSTER, NEBBIES, NEMISH, NEMS, NIM-BIES, YELLOW, YELLOW ANGEL, YELLOW BULLETS, YELLOW-JACKET.

nerd (also **nurd**) an oaf; an undesirable male. For synonyms see OAF. [U.S. slang and colloquial, mid 1900s-pres.]

nerd magnet a girl or woman who attracts dull males. [U.S. collegiate, late 1900s, Eble]

nerts (also **gnerts, nurts**) **1.** the testicles. A phonological disguise of NUTS (sense 1). *Cf.* NARDS. [U.S., 1900s] **2.** an exclamation of disbelief, "Nerts!" A phonological disguise of NUTS (sense 2). [British and U.S., 1900s]

nervous-cane the penis. *Cf.* VARNISH ONE'S CANE. [mid 1600s (Urquhart)]

net-head someone addicted to using the Internet. [U.S., late 1900s-pres.]

nether-eye the female genitals or the anus. [1300s, "The Miller's Tale," *The Canterbury Tales* (Chaucer)]

nether eyebrow (also **nether eyelashes, nether whiskers**) the female pubic hair. [British slang, 1800s]

nether garments 1. underwear. Synonyms: BRIEFS, DRAWERS, FRILLERY, IN-SIDE CLOTHES, SKIVVIES, SMALLCLOTHES, SMALLS, SMALL SNOW, SNOW, STEP-INS, SUB-TROUSERS, UNDERCLOTHING, UNDERGAR-MENTS, UNDERS, UNDERWARDROBE, UNDIES, UNHINTABLES, UNMENTION-ABLES, UNWHISPERABLES, U-TROU, U-WEAR, WHEREABOUTS, WHITE SEWING, WHITE WORK, WOOLENS, WOOLIES. **2.** trouser. [both senses, euphemistic, 1800s-1900s]

Netherlands 1. the male genitals. **2.** the female genitals. *Cf.* LOW-COUN-TRIES, LOWLANDS. [both senses, British, 1800s, Farmer and Henley]

nether-limbs the legs. *Cf.* LIMB. [classic euphemism of the 1800s]

nethers the genitals. For synonyms see GENITALS. [British, late 1900s-pres.]

new magic phencyclidine, the drug P.C.P. For synonyms see P.C.P. [U.S. drug culture, late 1900s]

newted drunk; PISSED AS A NEWT. For

synonyms see WOOFLED. [British slang, late 1900s if not before]

N.H.O. hard nipples; a "nipple hard-on." [U.S., late 1900s-pres.]

Niagara Falls the testicles. Rhyming slang for "balls." For synonyms see WHIRLYGIGS. [British, 1900s, *Dictionary of Rhyming Slang*]

nibble 1. to steal, cheat, or deceive. [cant, 1600s-1800s] **2.** to copulate. **3.** copulation. [both senses, British slang, 1800s, Farmer and Henley]

nibbler a RECEIVER (*q.v.*). Cf. GOBBLER, MOUSER, MUNCHER-BOY. For synonyms see PICCOLO-PLAYER. [U.S. underworld, early 1900s, Goldin, O'Leary, and Lipsius].

nice Nellie 1. a prudish man or woman. Cf. NICE-NELLYISM. [U.S. colloquial, 1900s and before] **2.** an effeminate male, probably a homosexual male. Cf. NELLY (sense 2). [U.S. slang, early 1900s]

nice-Nellyism any euphemism; a euphemism. [U.S. colloquial, 1900s and before]

nick 1. to arrest someone. [U.S., mid 1900s-pres.] **2.** to steal something. [U.S., mid 1900s-pres.] **3.** to get or take something. [U.S., mid 1900s-pres.]

nicked arrested. [U.S., mid 1900s-pres.]

nickel (also **nickel bag**) five dollars worth of marijuana. Cf. DIME. [U.S. drug culture, mid 1900s-pres.]

nick-nacks 1. the male genitals; the human testicles; the same as BAUBLES (*q.v.*). [colloquial, 1700s or before] **2.** the human breasts. [slang, 1900s and probably long before]

nigger (also **niger, niggar, niggur**) **1.** a derogatory term for a Negro. For synonyms see EBONY. Currently one of the most contemptible terms for a Negro. See also BAD NIGGER, BUCK NIGGER, CHARCOAL NIGGER, FIELD NIGGER, HOUSE NIGGER, INTERNATIONAL NIGGER, NIGGAR, NIGGERBRAND, NIGGERDOM, NIGGER-DRIVER, NIGGER-FISHING, NIGGER-GAL, NIGGER-GIN, NIGGERHEAD, NIGGER-HEAVEN, NIGGER-HEEL, NIGGER-JOCKY, NIGGER-LIPPING, NIGGER-LOVER, NIGGER-LUCK, NIGGER-NIGHT, NIGGER-POT, NIGGER-RICH, NIGGER-SHOOTER, NIGGERS-IN-A-SNOWSTORM, NIGGER'S KNACKERS, NIGGER-SHOOTER, NIGGER-SPECIAL, NIGGER-SPIT, NIGGER-STEAK, NIGGER-TIP, NIGGER-TOE, NIGGERTOWN, NIGGER-WOOL, NIGGERY, SHOWCASE NIGGER, WHITE NIGGER. **2.** a fellow black, a chum or an intimate friend. [used among blacks; from Latin *niger*, "black, sable, dark, dusky," via the romance languages; in various spellings since the late 1500s]

nigger-fishing fishing from the bank of a river or pond. Derogatory. [U.S. colloquial, 1900s or before]

nigger-gin bad gin or bad liquor in general. Derogatory. [U.S. colloquial, 1900s]

niggerhead 1. a black boulder or dark coral-head partially submerged in the water. Derogatory. [widespread colloquial, mid 1800s-early 1900s] **2.** a prune. Derogatory. [U.S. slang, early 1900s, Goldin, O'Leary, and Lipsius] **3.** a plug of black tobacco; the same as NEGRO-HEAD (sense 2). At one time, a brand name of chewing tobacco. Derogatory. [U.S., 1800s-1900s]

nigger-heaven 1. the upper balcony in a movie theater. Derogatory. Cf. ETHIOPIAN PARADISE. [attested as U.S. (Boston), late 1800s, Thornton] **2.** the roof of a freight train. Derogatory. [U.S., 1900s]

niggers-in-a-snowstorm stewed prunes and rice. Cf. HEADLIGHT TO A SNOWSTORM. More jocular than derogatory. [British, 1800s-early 1900s]

nigger-spit lumps in cane sugar. Based in part on the legendary practice of slaves spitefully spitting in the master's soups or stew. [colloquial since the 1800s]

nigger-toe 1. a Brazil nut. Cf. NIGGER-HEEL. Derogatory. [U.S. colloquial, 1800s-1900s] **2.** a small potato. Derogatory. [U.S. colloquial, mid 1900s]

niggertown the Negro district of a town. Derogatory. Cf. BLACK BELT, LAND OF DARKNESS. [U.S. colloquial, 1900s]

niggra (also **nigra**) a Negro. The Southern pronunciation of "Negro" or "nigger." This word is particularly offensive to some blacks. [U.S., 1800s-pres.]

night baseball copulation. *Cf.* BALL. For synonyms see SMOCKAGE. [U.S. slang, late 1900s]

nightcap a condom. For synonyms see EEL-SKIN. [U.S. slang, 1900s]

night-glass a CHAMBER POT (*q.v.*); the same as BED-GLASS (*q.v.*). *Cf.* VASE DU NUIT. [Caribbean (Jamaican), Cassidy and Le Page]

nimbies amphetamines, specifically Nembutal (trademark) capsules. See NEMBIES. [U.S. drug culture, mid 1900s-pres.]

nimrod 1. the penis. Named for the son of Cush, the great-grandson of Noah who was known to be a great hunter. [British slang, 1800s, Farmer and Henley] **2.** a total JERK; a GEEK. For synonyms see OAF. [U.S. collegiate, late 1900s]

nine-eyed alcohol intoxicated. For synonyms see WOOFLED. [U.S. slang, late 1900s]

nineteenth hole a place to buy an alcoholic beverage after a golf game. Likely to be filled with golfers who have played eighteen holes of golf. [U.S., late 1900s-pres.]

ninnies the human breasts. See NINNY, NINNY-JUGS. For synonyms see BOSOM. [U.S. slang and colloquial, 1900s]

nip 1. a derogatory nickname for a Japanese. [from "Nippon," the Japanese name for Japan; widespread slang, 1900s] **2.** a nipple. See NIPS. **3.** a small drink of whisky or other liquor. [1900s and before] **4.** to take small drinks of whisky or other liquor; to TIPPLE. [U.S. colloquial, mid 1900s]

nip factor the outside temperature when the weather is cold. See also NIPPLY. [U.S., late 1900s-pres.]

nipped alcohol intoxicated. For synonyms see WOOFLED. [U.S., late 1900s-pres.]

nippen an erect nipple. [U.S., late 1900s-pres.]

nipple count the degree to which a newspaper exploits bare breasts. [British, late 1900s-pres.]

nipples the protuberances on the foremost part of the human breasts of the female or the undeveloped breasts of the male. Most euphemistic references are to the female nipples. Synonyms (singular and plural): CHERRY, CHERRYLETS, DUBS, NIPS, PAP-HEAD, PAPILLA MAMMAE, TEAT, THELIUM, TIT.

nipply [of weather] cold. From *nippy [weather]* and what the cold may do to the human nipples. [U.S., late 1900s-pres.]

nippy the penis, especially a child's penis, a nickname for the penis. [British slang, 1800s, Farmer and Henley]

nips the nipples. A truncation. [U.S. slang, mid 1900s-pres.]

nob 1. a total JERK; a social outcast. *Cf.* DICK-HEAD. For synonyms see OAF. [U.S. slang, late 1900s] **2.** See KNOB.

no-brainer an easy question that takes no thinking to answer; a simple problem that requires no intellect to solve; a dilemma that requires no pondering to resolve. [U.S., late 1900s-pres.]

no-brow a stupid person. Patterned on LOWBROW. For synonyms see OAF. [U.S., late 1900s-pres.]

nocks narcotics. Possibly a pronunciation variant. For synonyms see COTICS. [U.S. slang, 1900s]

nodded out in a heroin euphoria; under the influence of heroin. [U.S. drug culture, late 1900s]

no hitter a virgin. [U.S. late 1900s-pres.]

noid a *paranoid* person. [U.S., late 1900s-pres.]

noisy as a dunny door in a storm very noisy [Australian, mid 1900s-pres.]

nola a homosexual male. *Cf.* MOLA. [U.S. slang, early 1900s]

no money in his purse impotent. For synonyms see IMPUDENT. [British slang, 1800s, Farmer and Henley]

no more, be to die. [euphemistic and colloquial, 1900s and before]

non compos poopoo alcohol intoxicated. From *non compos.* For synonyms see WOOFLED. [1900s, Dickson]

no-neck a muscular male athlete. For synonyms see OAF. [U.S., late 1900s-pres.]

nonesuch (also **nonsuch**) the female genitals. Something unrivaled and unequaled. [British slang, late 1700s, Grose]

nong an oaf; an idiot. For synonyms see OAF. [Australian, mid 1900s-pres.]

nooker copulation; the same as NOOKY (*q.v.*). For synonyms see SMOCKAGE. [U.S. slang, mid 1900s, *Current Slang*]

nooky (also **nooker, nookie**) **1.** the female genitals, specifically the vagina. **2.** copulation. **3.** women considered solely as sexual objects; the equivalent of PUSSY (sense 3). [all senses, U.S. slang, early 1900s-pres.]

nooner See FUNCH.

norgies (also **norgs, norks, norkers**) the breasts. From an Australian brand name for butter, "Norco," which pictures a cow's udder on the wrapper. *Cf.* BUTTER-BAGS. [Australian, mid 1900s, *Dictionary of Slang and Unconventional English*]

nose 1. the penis. [nonce; from *Antony and Cleopatra* (Shakespeare)] **2.** the clitoris. [colloquial and nonce] **3.** cocaine. A truncation of NOSE-CANDY (*q.v.*). [U.S. drug culture, 1900s] **4.** heroin. See NOSE HABIT. [U.S. drug culture, 1900s]

nose-candy cocaine. [U.S. underworld and drug culture, early 1900s-pres.] Synonyms: ANGEL, ANGIE, APPLEJACKS, BAZOOKA, BEAUTIFUL BOULDERS, BEBE, BELUSHI, BERNICE, BIG BLOKE, BIG-C., BLACK ROCK, BLIPS, BLOKE, BLORT, BLOW, BOLIVIAN MARCHING POWDER, BONECRUSHER, BONES, BOOGER JUICE, BOULDER, BOUNCING-POWDER, BURESE, C., CADILLAC, CALIFORNIA CORNFLAKES, CANDY, CANDYCANE, CANE, CARRIE, CASPER THE GHOST, CAVIAR, CECIL, CEE, CHARLES, CHARLEY COKE, CHARLIE, CHOLLY, C-JAM, COCA, COCAINE, COCANUTS, COCOA PUFFS, COCONUTS, COOKIE, CORINE, CRACK, CREEDLE, CROAK, CRUNCH AND MUNCH, DEVIL'S DANDRUFF, DOCTOR WHITE, DREAM, DUST, DYNAMITE, FAMOUS DIMES, FISH SCALES, FLAKE, FLORIDA SNOW, FRENCH FRIES, FRISKY POWDER, GERKS, GIBRALTAR, GIN, GIRL, GLAD STUFF, GOLD DUST, GO POWDER, HAPPY DUST, HAPPY POWDER, HAPPY STUFF, HER, HOOTER, HOTCAKES, HUBBAS, ICICLES, INCA MESSAGE, INCENTIVE, INITIATIVE, JAM, JAMHOUSE, JOY FLAKES, JOY POWDER, KRYPTONITE, LADY, LADY SNOW, LOVE DUST, MAGIC FLAKE, MAMA COCA, NOSE, NOSE POWDER, NUMBER THREE, PARADISE, PERUVIAN FLAKE, PIMP DUST, POGO-POGO, PONY, POWDERED DIAMOND, RAILS, REINDEER DUST, ROCK CANDY, ROCK COCAINE, SCHOOL BOY, SEA, SLUDGE, SNORT, SNOW, SNOWBALL, SNOWBIRD, SNOWCAINE, SNOW STUFF, SPANISH FLY, STARDUST, SUPERBLOW, SUPERFLY, THE LEAF, TOOT, TOOTONIUM, TOOTUNCOMMON, UPTOWN, WHITE, WHITE CROSS, WHITE DRUGS, WHITE GIRL, WHITE MOSQUITOES, WHITE STUFF, WINGS, WRECKING CREW, YIMYON.

nose-closer a release of intestinal gas, especially if very bad smelling. For synonyms see GURK. [U.S. slang, 1900s]

nose habit drug addiction or use; the practice or habit of sniffing drugs. *Cf.* NOSE (sense 4). [U.S. drug culture, mid 1900s, *Current Slang*]

nose hit marijuana smoke taken through the nose from the burning end of the cigarette. [U.S., mid 1900s-pres.]

nose-hole a nostril. [colloquial since the early 1500s]

nose-lunger a glob of nasal mucus. *Cf.* LUNGER. [U.S. slang, late 1900s]

nose powder powdered narcotics. Primarily cocaine, but also morphine and heroin. *Cf.* NOSE (senses 3 and 4). From "face powder." [U.S. drug culture, mid 1900s-pres.]

nose rag a handkerchief. *Cf.* SNOTRAG. [colloquial since the early 1800s]

nose-wipe a handkerchief. Milder than NOSE RAG or SNOT-RAG (both *q.v.*). [colloquial since the 1800s]

No shinola! "NO SHIT!" *Cf.* KNOW SHIT FROM SHINOLA. [U.S. slang, late 1900s]

No shit! 1. an exclamatory assurance of truthfulness, "I'm not bullshitting you!" [U.S. slang, mid 1900s-pres.] **2.** "You are kidding me, aren't you." For synonyms see 'ZOUNDS. [U.S., mid 1900s-pres.]

Not! "Not really so!" A phrase added to the end of a statement, changing it from affirmative to negative [U.S., late 1900s-pres.]

not give a monkey's (fuck) to not care at all. [British, late 1900s-pres.]

not know one's arse from one's elbow to be incompetent. [British, mid 1900s-pres.]

not know one's ass from a hole in the ground not to be knowledgeable; not to be alert and effective. [U.S., mid 1900s-pres.]

not know shit from Shinola to not know what's what; not to be intelligent and aware. [U.S., mid 1900s-pres.]

not tell shit from Shinola to not know what's what; not to be intelligent and aware. [U.S., late 1900s-pres.]

no toothpaste in the tube a catch-phrase said of a man who is impotent. [U.S. slang, late 1900s, Lewin and Lewin]

no wuckers no wucking furries = no fucking worries. [Autralian, late 1900s-pres.]

no wucking furries no fucking worries. [Australian, mid 1900s-pres.]

nub 1. to hang by the neck until dead. "Nub" is a cant word for "neck." [cant, late 1600s] Synonyms and related terms: CARNIFICATE, CLIMB THE STALK, DANCE UPON NOTHING, DANGLE, DIE IN ONE'S SHOES, GO UP A LADDER TO BED, IN DEADLY SUSPENSE, JERK TO JESUS, KICK THE CLOUDS, LEAP FROM THE LEAFLESS, NECK, PATIBULATE, SCRAG, SHAKE A CLOTH IN THE WIND, STRETCH, TOP, TOTTER, TRINE, TUCK, TWIST. **2.** copulation. [British, 1700s-1800s] **3.** an ugly young woman. For synonyms see BUFFARILLA. [U.S., mid 1900s-pres.]

nubbies the breasts. [Australian, 1900s or before, Baker]

nudger the penis. For synonyms see YARD. [British, mid 1900s-pres.]

nug a marijuana bud. From *nugget.* For synonyms see MARI. [U.S., late 1900s-pres.]

nuggets 1. amphetamine capsules. For synonyms see AMP. [U.S. drug culture, mid 1900s-pres.] **2.** the testicles. Also **nuggies, nugs.** [U.S. colloquial and nonce] **3.** the breasts. [U.S. slang, 1900s] **4.** crack cocaine. For synonyms see NOSE-CANDY. [U.S., late 1900s-pres.]

nuggies See under NUGGETS.

nuisance, the the menses. For synonyms see FLOODS. [colloquial and nonce]

num to perform a fellatio on someone. [U.S., late 1900s-pres.]

numbed out nearly paralyzed by P.C.P. For synonyms see TALL. [U.S. drug culture, late 1900s, Abel]

number 1. a girl; a sexually attractive girl, especially a "cute little number." [U.S. slang, 1900s] **2.** a marijuana cigarette. For synonyms see MEZZROLL. [U.S. drug culture, mid 1900s-pres.] See also DO A NUMBER ON.

number eight heroin. From "H," which is the eighth letter of the alphabet. [U.S. drug culture, mid 1900s]

number nip the female genitals. For synonyms see MONOSYLLABLE. [British slang, 1800s, Farmer and Henley]

number one to urinate. Spoken or indicated with finger signals. [colloquial and juvenile, 1800s-pres.]

number thirteen morphine. From "M," which is the thirteenth letter of the alphabet. [U.S. drug culture, mid 1900s]

number three 1. an ejaculation of semen. An extension of NUMBER ONE and NUMBER TWO (both *q.v.*). [British, 1900s, *Dictionary of Slang and Unconventional English*] **2.** cocaine. From "C," which is the third letter of the alphabet. [U.S. drug culture, mid 1900s]

number two a bowel movement. Can be either spoken or indicated with finger signals. *Cf.* NUMBER ONE. [colloquial and juvenile, 1800s-pres.]

numbnuts an oaf. For synonyms see OAF. [U.S., mid 1900s-pres.]

nunya "none of your business" [U.S., late 1900s-pres.]

nurd (also **nerd**) an oaf; a jerk. [U.S. slang and colloquial, mid 1900s-pres.]

nurts (also **nerts**) nonsense. A phonological disguise of NUTS (sense 2). See NERTS (sense 2). [U.S. slang, early 1900s-pres.]

nut 1. an odd or strange person; an insane person. [U.S. colloquial, 1900s] **2.** to copulate; the same as BALL (sense 2). [U.S. slang, mid 1900s-pres.] **3.** the glans penis. [from Latin *glans*, meaning "acorn"] **4.** to castrate. *Cf.* KNACKER (sense 1). [U.S. underworld, mid 1900s, Goldin, O'Leary, and Lipsius] **5.** a testicle. See NUTS (sense 1). **6.** to ejaculate semen. [U.S., late 1900s-pres.]

nut, off one's 1. crazy. [colloquial, late 1800s-pres.] **2.** intoxicated with alcohol. From sense 1. [British, late 1800s, Farmer and Henley]

nut-cracker 1. the pillory. [cant or slang, 1600s, B.E.] **2.** an ugly young woman; an aggressive and castrating woman. [U.S. slang, 1900s]

nuthouse (also **nut factory, nut-foundry, nut-hatch**) an insane asylum. [U.S. colloquial, early 1900s-pres.]

nutmegs the testicles. Probably from

the size and shape of the nutmeg. For synonyms see WHIRLYGIGS. [British, 1600s]

nuts 1. the testicles. See NUTMEGS. [since the 1700s] **2.** as an exclamation, "Nuts!" Slightly euphemistic for BALLS! (sense 4) and considered taboo in some quarters. [U.S. colloquial, 1900s] **3.** confused about; crazy about, as in "nuts about someone." [U.S. colloquial, 1900s]

nutsac the scrotum. For synonyms see TOOL BAG. [U.S., late 1900s-pres.]

nut scrinch a powerful itch in the male groin. [U.S., late 1900s-pres.]

nutter a crazy person. [British, later 1900s-pres.]

nuttery an insane asylum. From the literal meaning, "a place for storing nuts." [U.S. slang, mid 1900s, Goldin, O'Leary, and Lipsius] Synonyms: BOOBY HATCH, BUGHOUSE, FUNNY FARM, LOONY BIN, NUT-FOUNDRY, NUT-HATCH, NUTHOUSE, NUTTERY.

nut up to go crazy; to go NUTS. [U.S., late 1900s-pres.]

N.W.A.B. "necks with anybody." An initialism describing someone who will kiss and pet indiscriminately. [U.S., 1900s]

nympho a woman with an insatiable sex drive. A truncation of nymphomaniac. [colloquial and slang, early 1900s-pres.]

O

O. "opium." *Cf.* C. (sense 1), M. For synonyms see OPE. [U.S. underworld, early 1900s or before]

oaf (also **auf, aufe, auph, oaph, ouph**) originally the child of an elf. Now the term embraces all of the negative characteristics of "dullard," "fool," "bumpkin," and "lummox." Such terms almost always refer to males. [since the early 1600s] Synonyms: ACE, ADDLE-BRAIN, ADDLE-HEAD, ANIMAL, AP-SAY, ARS-WORM, ASS, ASS-MASTER, BAMA, BABOON, BAKE-HEAD, BALATRON, BALLOONHEAD, BANANA-HEAD, BAWCOCK, BEANHEAD, BEEF-HEAD, BEETLE-BRAIN, BEETLE-HEAD, BEN, BESOM-HEAD, B.F., BIRD-BRAIN, BIRDSHIT, BIRD-TURD, BIRK, BITE, BLOB, BLOCK, BLOCKHEAD, BLOKE, BLUB-BERBRAIN, BLUBBERHEAD, BLUDGER, BLUNDERBUSS, BLUNDERHEAD, BOEO-TIAN, BOHUNK, BONEHEAD, BONETOP, BOOB, BOOBERKIN, BOOBUS AMERI-CANUS, BOOBY, BOOFA, BOOFHEAD, BOOR, BOSTHORN, BOTTLE-HEAD, BUF-FLE, BUFFLE-HEAD, BUFFOON, BUG-FUCKER, BUGGER, BULLET-HEAD, BULL-FINCH, BUM, BUMPKIN, BUN-HEAD, BUT-TER BACK, BUTTERBALL, BUTTERHEAD, BUTTLICK, CABBAGEHEAD, CAKEY, CALF, CALF-LOLLY, CALF'S HEAD, CALM, CHAWBACON, CHEESE-HEAD, CHICKEN-HEAD, CHOWDER-HEAD, CHUCKLE-HEAD, CHUFF, CHUMP, CHUMP-HEAD, CHURL, CLABBER-HEAD, CLINCHPOOP, CLOD, CLOD-HEAD, CLOWN, CLUCK, CLUCK-HEAD, CLUMPERTON, CLUNCH, CLUNK, CLUNKHEAD, CLYDE, COCKSCOMB, COD, COD'S HEAD, COKES, CONGEON, COOT, COUNTRY JAKE, COUSIN BETTY, CRACK-BRAIN, CRUMB BUM, CUCKOO, CUDDEN, CULVER-HEAD, DASTARD, DAWKIN, DAW-PATE, DEADHEAD, DEADNECK, DEAD-SHIT, DICK, DICK-HEAD, DICKSPLASH, DICKSPLAT, DICKWAD, DICKWEED, DICKY-DIDO, DIDDLE-HEAD, DIL, DILLYPOT, DIM-BLEFUCK, DIMBO, DIM BULB, DIMWIT, DING-A-LING, DINGBAT, DING-DONG, DINK, DIPHEAD, DIPSHIT, DIPSTICK, DIZZARD, DOBBY, DODDYPATE, DODDYPOLL, DODE, DODO, DODUNK, DOLDRUM, DOLT, DOLT-HEAD, DONK, DONKEY, DOODLE, DOOF, DOPE, DOR, DORBEL, DORF, DORK, DOR-KMEIER, DORKMUNDER, DORKUS MAX-IMUS, DOTARD, DOUGH-FACE, DOUGH-HEAD, DOWCOCK, DOYBURGER, DRIP, DROMEDARY, DRONGO, DROOB, DROUD, DRUBE, DRUMBLE, DUB, DUCK, DUFFER, DULLARD, DULL-HEAD DULL PICKLE, DULLY, DUMBARD, DUMBASSKISS, DUMB BUNNY, DUMB CLUCK, DUMB-DUMB, DUMBELL, DUMB FUCK, DUMBFUCK, DUMB-HEAD, DUMBKOPF, DUMBNUTS, DUMBO, DUMB OX, DUMBSKI, DUMBSOCKS, DUM-DUM, DUMMEL, DUMMY, DUNCE, DUNDER-HEAD, DUNDERPATE, DUNDER-WHELP, DWEEB, ELROD, FART-BLOSSOM, FART HOLE, FAT-HEAD, FEATHERBRAIN, FEATHERHEAD, FEEB, FINK, FISH, FLAKE, FLAPDOODLE, FLAT, FLATHEAD, FLAT TIRE, FLEGMATIC FELLOW, FOGAY, FOLT, FOLTHEAD, FON, FONKIN, FOO-FOO, FOP, FOP-DOODLE, FRIP, FUCK-HEAD, FUCK-NUT, FUCK-PIG, FUCKWIT, GAAPUS, GABEY, GALLOOT, GANDER-HEAD, GANEY, GAUM, GAWBY, GAW-GAW, GAWK, GAWNEY, GAZ-IZZEY, GAZOB, GAZOOK, GECK, GEEK, GEEKAZOID, GERK, GIDDYHEAD, GIG, GILLY, GILLY-GAUPUS, GIMCRACK, GIMP, GINK, GLEEP, GLOIK, GLOM, GNATBRAIN, GOBBIN, GOBSHITE, GOLLUMPUS, GOM-ERAL, GOMUS, GONES, GONEY, GONIF, GONUS, GOO-BRAIN, GOOBY, GOOF, GOOF-BALL, GOOFUS, GOOG, GOOK, GOON, GOOP, GOOPUS, GOOSE, GOOSEBERRY, GOOSECAP, GOOSEY-GANDER, GOUP, GOURD, GOWK, GREENHEAD, GROBIAN, GROUTNOLL, GROWTNOLL, GUFFIN, GUF-FOON, GULL, GULL-FINCH, GULPIN, GUMMY, GUMP, GUMSUCKER, GWEEB, HAIRBRAIN, HAMMERHEAD, HANKTELO, HARDHEAD, HAREBRAIN, HAWBUCK, HAWSEED, HELIUM HEAD, HERBERT, HERKIMER JERKIMER, HERKLE, HICK, HICKJOP, HICKORYHEAD, HICKSAM, HILLBILLY, HIND, HOBALL, HOBB, HOB-

BIL, HOBBY, HOB-CLUNCH, HOBGOBLIN, HODDY-NODDY, HODDY-PEAK, HODDY-POLL, HODGE, HOMO BOOBUS, HOMO SAP, HONYOCK, HORKIE, HUCKLEFUCK, HULVERHEAD, HUNKY, IDIOT, IGNATZ, IGNORAMUS, IMBECILE, INNOCENT, INSIPID, IRONHEAD, IVORY DOME, J., JABBERNOL, Jack Adams, JACKASS, JACK OFF, Jack-sauce, Jacob, JAKE, JARHEAD, JAY, JERK, JERK OFF, JIVE TURKEY, JOBBERNOLL, Joe Cunt, Joe Erk, JOLTERHEAD, JOLTHEAD, JORK, JOSH, JOSHER, JOSKIN, JUGGINS, JUGHEAD, KLOTZ, KLUCK, KNOB, KNOBHEAD, KNOCK-SOFTLY, KNOTHEAD, KNUCKLE-DRAGGER, KNUCKLEHEAD, L7, LACK-BRAIN, LACK-WIT, LALDRUM, LAMB, LAMEBRAIN, LARDHEAD, LEADENPATE, LEAD-HEAD, LEATHER-HEAD, LERICOM-POOP, LIGHTS, LIRRIPOOP, LITTLE SHIT, LOB, LOBBUS, LOBCOCK, LOBLOLLY LOBSCOUSE, LOBSTER, LOGGERHEAD, LOOBY, LOOGAN, LOON, LOPLOLLY, LOPPUS, LORG, LOSER, LOUT, LOW-BROW, LUBBER, LUBBERHEAD, LUBBY, LUG, LUG-LOAF, LUMMAKIN, LUMMOX, LUMP, LUMPKIN, LUMPUS, LUNK, LUNKER, LUNKHEAD, LURDAN, LUSK, LUSKARD, MALLET-HEAD, MARBLE-DOME, MARCROON, MEAT, MEATBALL, MEATHEAD, MELON, MELONHEAD, MESS, MOBARD, MOKE, MOME, MOONCALF, MOONLING, MOONRAKER, MOP, MOPE, MOP STICK, MOREPORK, MORON, MUD, MUDDLEHEAD, MUD-HEAD, MUFF, MUFFIN, MUG, MUGGINS, MULL, MULLET-HEAD, MUSCLEHEAD, MUSHHEAD, MUTANT, MUT-HEAD, MUTT, MUTTONHEAD, NARK, NAZOLD, N.D.B.F., NEANDERTHAL, NEB, Neddy, Ned-fool, NEEDLE DICK, NERD, NEWT, NIAS, NICK-NINNY, NICKUMPOOP, NIDICOCK, NIDDIPOL, NIDIOT, NIGMENOG, NIG-NOG, NIKIN, NIMROD, NIMSHI, NINCOMPOOP, NING-NONG, NINNY, NINNYHAMMER, NIT, NITWIT, NIZY, NIZZIE, NOB, NOBBY, NO-BROW, NOCKY, NOCKY BOY, NODCOCK, NODDIPOL, NODDY, NODDY-PATE, NODDY-PEAK, NODDY-POLE, NODDY-POLL, NODGECOCK, NOGGERHEAD, NOG-HEAD, NOGMAN, NOKES, NOLE, NOLL, NOLT, NO-NECK, NONG, NOODLE, NOODLEHEAD, NOSE-PICKER, NUMBHEAD, NUMB-NUTS, NUMBSKULL, NUMPS, NUMSKULL, NUNNY-FUDGY, NUPSON, NURD, NUT, NYAS, OOFUS, OOLFOO, PALOOKA, PASTE EATER, PEAGOOSE, PEAHEAD, PENCIL DICK, PENIS WRINKLE, PESTLE-HEAD, PIGHEAD, PIGSCONCE, PINHEAD, PISHER, PISS-ASS, PLAT, PLUMP-PATE, POON, POOP, POOPHEAD, POTATO-HEAD, POTHEAD, PRICK, PROW, PUDDINGHEAD, PUMPKINHEAD, PUNKINHEAD, PUT, PUTTYHEAD, PUTZ, QUEER, QUEERE-CULL, QUIMP, QUINCE, QUOIT, Ralph, Ralph Spooner, RATTLEHEAD, REDNECK, REJECT, REMO, Reuben, ROCKHEAD, ROLY- POLY, Rube, RUM-DUMB, RUSTIC, Sammy, Sammy-Soft, SAP, SAP-HEAD, SAPSKULL, SATE-POLL, SAUSAGE, SAWDUST-BRAINED, SAWDUST-HEAD, SAWNEY, SCATTERBRAIN, SCHLEMIEL, SCHLUB, SCHLUMP, SCHMEKEL, SCHMENDRICH, SCHMENDRICK, SCHMOE, SCHMUCK, SCHNOOK, SHALLOW-PATE, SHANNY, SHATTERBRAIN, SHEEPSHAGGER, SHEEP'S-HEAD, SHIT BREATH, SHIT FACE, SHIT-HEAD, SHITSKY, SHMO, SHMUCK, SHNOOK, SHOHIZA, SHOON, SHUTTLE-BRAIN, SHUTTLE-HEAD, SHUTTLE-WIT, SIDE SIM, SIMKIN, SIMON, SIMP, SINGLETON, SKITTER-BRAIN, SKRIMSHANKER, SKYTE, SLANGAM, SLANGRILL, SLOUCH, SLUBBERDEGULLION, SOAP, SOD, SOFTHEAD, SONKY, SOP, SOT, SOUSE-CROWN, SOZZLE, SPARE PRICK, SPASTIC, SPAZ, SPLODGER, SPOON, SPOONY, SPOOPS, SQUID, STICK, STOCK, STOOP, STOOPNAGEL, STOT, STROKER, STUB, STUMBLE-BUM, STUMP, STUPE, STUPEHEAD, SUB, SUCKA, SUMPH, SWAD, TACKHEAD, THICK, TIMDOODLE, TITLESS WONDER, Tom Coney, Tom Doodle, Tom-Farthing, Tommy, Tommy Noddy, Tom Noddy, Tom Towly, TONK, Tony, TOOT, TOOTLEDUM-PATTICK, TOSSER, TROG(LODYTE), TRUNK, TUCK, TURKEY, TWILLE, TWIMBLE, TWINK, TWIRP, TWIT, TWO-FOOT RULE, ULLAGE, UM-BAY, UMP-CHAY, UNDERWIT, WAFFLES, WAG, WAG-WIT, WANK, WANT-WIT, WARB, WEENIE, WET, WET-GOOSE, WETHER-HEAD, WET-SOCK, WHACK, WHIMP, WHITLING, WIDGEON, WIMP, WISEACRE, WISE GUY, WONK, WOODCOCK, WOODENHEAD, WOODENSPOON, YACK, YAHOO, YAP, YAWNEY, YOB, YOCK, YOKEL, YOLD, YO-YO, YUCKEL, YULD, YUTZ, ZAMMY, ZANY, ZERK, ZERO, ZHLUB, ZIZ, ZOMBIE, ZONE, ZONK, ZONKO, ZOTY, ZOUCH.

oats semen, as what is sowed. For synonyms see METTLE. [British, late 1900s-pres.]

obli-goddamn-ation an emphatic form of "obligation" based on "goddamn" and "obligation."

obliterated alcohol intoxicated. For synonyms see WOOFLED. [U.S. slang, late 1900s if not before]

obno(c) obnoxious; disgusting. [U.S. collegiate, late 1900s]

obscene lewd; pertaining to a thing, person, or word representing sexual or excremental matters. Synonyms and related terms: BARNYARD, BAWDY, BLUE, FILTHY, HARD-CORE, HIGH-KILTED, INDECENT, MEATY, NASTY, OFF-COLOR, PAW-PAW, PORNY, QUISI, RAUNCHY, RUDE, SMUTTY, SPICY, UNPARLIAMENTARY. See also LEWD.

occupant 1. a prostitute, a woman who is occupied by a man. *Cf.* OCCUPY. A resident of an OCCUPYING-HOUSE (*q.v.*). [late 1500s] **2.** a brothel. [British, 1700s or before, Farmer and Henley]

occupy to coit a woman; to take sexual possession of a woman. This word was avoided in polite company during the period [1400s-1600s] when it was used in this sense. The following synonyms and related terms refer to males or both males and females except as indicated. Both transitive and intransitive senses are included: ACCOMMODATE, ADAM AND EVE IT, ADAMIZE, BAG, BALL, BALLOCK, BANG, BATTER, BEAT SOMEONE WITH AN UGLY STICK, BEEF, BE FAMILIAR WITH, BE IN A WOMAN'S BEEF, BELT, BLOCK, BLOW OFF ON THE GROUNSILLS, BLOW OFF THE LOOSE CORNS, BOARD, BOB, BOIL BANGERS, BOINK, BONE, BONK, BOOST, BOP, BORE, BOTTLE, BOUNCE, BOSH, BOX, BREAK A LANCE WITH, BREAK A LEG, BREED, BROWN BAG IT, BRUSH, BULL, BUMBASTE, BUMBLE, BUMP MONKIES, BUMP TUMMIES, BUNNY-FUCK, BURDEN, BURY ONE'S WICK, BURY THE WEENIE, BUZZ THE BRILLO, CANE, CANOE, CARESS, CARNALIZE, CATTLE, CAULK, CAVAULT, CHAFER, CHANGE ONE'S LUCK, CHARGE, CHUCK, CHUCK A TREAD, CLIMB, CLUB, COCK, COCK SOMEONE UP, COCK UP, COHABIT, COIT, COME ABOUT, COME ABOUT A WOMAN, COME ACROSS, COME ALOFT, COME OVER, COMPRESS, CONJUGATE, CONSUMMATE, COOL OUT, CORRESPOND, COUCH, COUPLE, COUPLE WITH, COVER, CRACK IT, CRAM, CRAWL, CREAM, CROSS, CUDDLE, DANCE THE BUTTOCK JIG, DANCE THE GOAT'S JIG, DANCE THE MARRIED MAN'S COTILLION, DANCE THE MARRIED MAN'S JIG, DANCE THE MATRIMONIAL POLKA, DANCE THE MATTRESS JIG, DEHORN, DIBBLE, DICK, DIDDLE, DIP ONE'S WICK, DO, DQ A BIT, DO A BOTTOM-WETTER, DO A DIVE IN THE DARK, DO A FLOP, DO A GOOD TURN TO SOMEONE, DO A GRIND, DO A GROUSE, DO A KINDNESS TO, DO AN INSIDE WORRY, DO A PUSH, DO A PUT, DO A RUDENESS TO, DO A SHOOT UP THE STRAIGHT, DO A SLIDE UP THE BOARD, DO A SPREAD, DO A WOMAN'S JOB FOR HER, DOCK, DOG, DO ILL TO, DOINK, DO IT, DO ONE'S OFFICE, DO OVER, DORK, DORSE WITH, DO SOME GOOD FOR ONESELF, DO THE BONE THROW, DO THE BUSINESS, DO THE CHORES, DO THE DO, DO THE HORIZONTAL BOOGIE, DO THE LATERAL LAMBADA, DO THE NAUGHTY (female), DO THE STORY WITH, DO THE TRICK, DRAG THE SHAG, DRILL FOR VEGEMITE, DRIVE HOME, DRIVE INTO, DRY RUN, DUNK, EASE, EASE NATURE, EFFECT INTROMISSION, EMBRACE, ENJOY, ENJOY A WOMAN, EXCHANGE SPITS, FAGGOT, FAN, FEED THE DUMB-GLUTTON, FEED THE DUMMY, FREEZE, FERRET, FETTLE, FIDDLE, FIRK, FIT ENDS, FIT END TO END, FIX HER PLUMBING, FIX SOMEONE UP, FLAP, FLESH, FLESH IT, FLIMP, FLOP IN THE HAY, FLURGLE, FOIN, FONDLE, FOOT, FORAMINATE, FOREGATHER, FORNICATE, FOYST, FRIG, FUCK, FUCKLE, FUGLE, FULKE, FUMBLE, FUTUERE, FUTUO, FUTY, FUTZ, GAFFER, GAY IT, GEAR, GENDER, GEORGE, GET A BELLY FULL OF MARROW-PUDDING (female), GET ABOUT HER, GET A CRUMPET, GET AMONG IT, GET A PAIR OF BALLS AGAINST ONE'S BUTT (female), GET A SHOVE IN ONE'S BLIND-EYE (female), GET DOWN TO IT, GET FIXED-UP, GET HILT AND HAIR (female), GET HOME, GET HULLED BETWEEN WIND AND WATER (female), GET IN, GET INTO, GET INTO HER, GET INTO HER PANTS, GET IT ON, GET JACK IN THE ORCHARD, GET LAYED, GET OFF THE GUN, GET ONE'S ASHES HAULED, GET ONE'S CHIM-

NEY SWEPT OUT (female), GET ONE'S END AWAY, GET ONE'S END IN. GET ONE'S END WET, GET ONE'S GREENS, GET ONE'S HAIR CUT, GET ONE'S END AWAY, GET ONE'S LEATHER STRETCHED (female), GET ONE'S LEG ACROSS, GET ONE'S LEG LIFTED (female), GET ONE'S NUTS CRACKED, GET ONE'S OATS FROM SOMEONE, GET ONE'S OIL CHANGED, GET ON TOP OF, GET OUTSIDE IT (female), GET OUTSIDE OF (female), GET OVER SOMEONE, GET SOME, GET SOME ACTION, GET SOME ASS, GET SOME COLD COCK, GET SOME CUNT, GET THERE, GET THE UPSHOT (female), GET THROUGH, GET UP THE POLE (female), GINICOMTWIG, GIRL, GIVE A HOLE TO HIDE IT IN (female), GIVE A WOMAN A SHOT, GIVE HARD FOR SOFT, GIVE HER A FRIGGING, GIVE HER A HOSING, GIVE HER A PAST, GIVE HER A SCREWING, GIVE HER THE BUSINESS, GIVE IT TO SOMEONE, GIVE JUICE FOR JELLY, GIVE MUTTON FOR BEEF (female), GIVE NATURE A FILLIP, GIVE ONE A STAB, GIVE ONESELF (female), GIVE ONE THE WORKS, GIVE STANDING-ROOM FOR ONE (female), GIVE THE DOG A BONE, GIVE WAY (female), GO, GO BALLOCKING, GO BEDPRESSING, GO BIRD'S-NESTING, GO BUMFAKING, GO BUM-TICKLING, GO BUMWORKING, GO BUSH-RANGING, GO BUTTOCKING, GO COCK-FIGHTING, GO CUNNY-CATCHING, GO DOODLING, GO DOWN (female), GO DRABBING, GO FISHING, GO FLASHING IT, GO FOR THE DRAG OFF, GO GOOSING, GO IN UNTO, GO JOTTLING, GO LEATHER-STRETCHING, GO LIKE A BELT FED MOTOR, GO LIKE A RAT UP A DRAIN PIPE, GO LIKE A RAT UP A RHODODENDRON, GOOSE, GO RUMPING, GO RUMP-SPLITTING, GO STAR-GAZING ON ONE'S BACK (female), GO THE LIMIT, GO THROUGH A WOMAN, GO TO BED WITH, GO TO IT, GO TO TOWN, GO TO WORK WITH, GO TWAT-FAKING, GO VAULTING, GO WENCHING, GO WITH, GO WOMANIZING, GRANT THE FAVOR (female), GREASE, GREASE THE WHEEL, GRIND, GRIND ONE'S TOOL, HAMMER, HANDLE, HAUL ONE'S ASHES, HAVE, HAVE A BIT, HAVE A BIT OF BUM, HAVE A BIT OF BUM-DANCING, HAVE A BIT OF COCK, HAVE A BIT OF CUNT, HAVE A BIT OF CURLY GREENS, HAVE A BIT (OFF WITH SOMEONE), HAVE A BIT OF FISH,

HAVE A BIT OF GIBLET PIE, HAVE A BIT OF GUTSTICK (female), HAVE A BIT OF MEAT, HAVE A BIT OF MUTTON, HAVE A BIT OF PORK, HAVE A BIT OF ROUGH, HAVE A BIT OF SKIRT, HAVE A BIT OF SPLIT-MUTTON, HAVE A BIT OF STUFF, HAVE A BIT OF SUGAR-STICK (female), HAVE A BIT OF SUMMER-CABBAGE, HAVE A BIT OF THE CREAMSTICK (female), HAVE A BLOW-THROUGH, HAVE A BRUSH WITH THE CUE, HAVE A BUN IN THE OVEN, HAVE A FLUTTER, HAVE A FUCK, HAVE A GAME IN THE COCK-LOFT, HAVE A JUMP, HAVE A LEAP UP THE LADDER, HAVE A NORTHWEST COCKTAIL, HAVE A POKE, HAVE A RIDE, HAVE A ROLL, HAVE A TURN ON ONE'S BACK (female), HAVE A WIPE AT THE PLACE, HAVE CONNECTION, HAVE FIFTY-UP, HAVE GIN ON THE ROCKS, HAVE GIVEN PUSSY A TASTE OF CREAM (female), HAVE HOT PUDDING FOR SUPPER (female), HAVE IT OFF, HAVE IT UP, HAVE LIVE SAUSAGE FOR SUPPER (female), HAVE ONE'S CUT, HAVE ONE'S OATS, HAVE ONE'S WILL OF A WOMAN, HIDE THE FERRET, HIDE THE SALAMI, HIDE THE SAUSAGE, HIT, HIT IT AND QUIT IT, HIT IT OFF, HIT ON THE TAIL, HIVE IT, HOBBLE, HOG, HOIST, HOME, HONEYFUCK, HOOPER'S HIDE, HOP ON, HORIZONTALIZE, HORSE, HOSE, HOUND, HUDDLE, HUFFLE, HUMP, HUNCH, HUSBAND, HUSTLE, IMPALE, INFEMURATE, INTERCOURSE, INTRODUCE CHARLEY, INVADE, JAB, JACK, JANNEY, JAPE, JAZZ, JAZZ IT, JEEP, JERK, JICK, JIGGLE, JIG-JIG, JINK, JOB, JOCK, JOCKUM, JOG, JOIN GIBLETS, JOIN PAUNCHES, JOLT, JOTTLE, JOUNCE, JUICE, JUKE, JUMBLE, JUMM, JUMP, JUMP ON SOMEONE'S BONES, KISS, KNOCK, KNOCK BOOTS WITH SOMEONE, KNOCK IT OFF, KNOW, LABOR LEATHER, LABOUR-LEA, LALLY-GAG, LARD, LAY, LAY OFF WITH, LAY OUT, LAY SOME PIPE, LAY THE HIP, LAY THE LEG, LEAP, LERICOMPOOP, LIB, LIBERATE, LIE FEET UPPERMOST (female), LIE ON, LIE UNDER (female), LIE WITH, LIFT A LEG ON A WOMAN, LIFT ONE'S LEG, LIGHT THE LAMP (female), LINE, LOB IN, LOOK AT THE CEILING OVER A MAN'S SHOULDER (female), LOSE THE MATCH AND POCKET THE STAKE (female), LOVE, LUBRICATE, MAKE, MAKE ENDS MEET, MAKE FEET FOR CHILDREN'S SHOES,

MAKE HER GRUNT, MAKE IT, MAKE LOVE, MAKE ONE'S LOVE COME DOWN, MAKE THE CHIMNEY SMOKE, MAKE THE SCENE, MAN, MATE, MEDDLE, MESS AROUND, MINGLE BLOODS, MINGLE LIMBS, MIX ONE'S PEANUT BUTTER, MOUNT, MUDDLE, MUG, MUMP, MUSS, NAIL, NAIL TWO BELLIES TOGETHER, NAUGHTY, NIBBLE, NICK, NIDGE, NIG, NIGGLE, NOCKANDRO, NODGE, NUG, NUT, NYGLE, OBLIGE, OEDIPUS REX, OFF, OPEN UP TO (female), PALLIARDIZE, PARALLEL PARK, PASH ON, PEEL ONE'S BEST END, PEG, PERFORM, PESTLE, PHALLICIZE, PHEEZE, PILE, PIN, PIZZLE, PLANK, PLANT, PLANT A MAN, PLANT THE OATS, PLAY, PLAY AT ALL-FOURS, PLAY AT COCK-IN-COVER, PLAY AT COUPLE-YOUR-NAVELS, PLAY AT IN-AND-OUT, PLAY AT ITCH-BUTTOCK, PLAY AT LEVEL-COIL, PLAY AT LIFT-LEG, PLAY AT PICKLE-ME-TICKLE-ME, PLAY AT PULLY-HAULLY, PLAY AT THE FIRST-GAME-EVER PLAYED, PLAY AT TOPS-AND-BOTTOMS, PLAY AT TOP-SAWYER, PLAY BOUNCY-BOUNCY, PLAY CARS AND GARAGES, PLAY DOCTOR, PLAY HIDE THE SALAMI, PLAY HIDE THE SAUSAGE, PLAY HIDE THE WEENIE, PLAY HOSPITAL, PLAY ONE'S ACE (female), PLAY THE GOAT, PLAY THE ORGAN, PLAY TIDDLYWINKS, PLEASE, PLEASURE, PLOOK, PLOUGH, PLOW, PLOWTER, PLUCK, PLUG, PLUKE, POCKET THE RED, POKE, POKE A HONTAS, POKE SQUID, POLE, POOP, POP, POP IT IN, PORK, POSSESS, POSSESS CARNALLY, POST A LETTER, POUND, PRANG, PRAY WITH THE KNEES UPWARDS (female), PRIAPIZE, PRIG, PROD, PRONG, PUMP, PUNCH, PUSH, PUSH ON, PUSH-PIN, PUT, PUT FOUR QUARTERS ON THE SPIT, PUT IT IN, PUT IT TO HER, PUT THE BLOCKS TO, PUT THE BOOTS TO, PUT THE DEVIL INTO HELL, QUALIFY, QUIFF, QUIM, RABBIT, RAKE, RAKE OUT, RAM, RASP, RASP AWAY, RIDE, RIDE BELOW THE CRUPPER, RIDE THE HOBBY HORSE, RIDE THE HOG, RIFLE, RIP OFF, ROCK, ROD, ROGER, ROLLER SKATE, ROMP, ROOT, ROOTLE, ROUST, ROUT, RUB BACONS, RUB UP, RUDDER, RUMBUSTICATE, RUMMAGE, RUMP, RUMPLE, SACRIFICE TO VENUS, SALT, SARD, SAW OFF A CHUNK, SCALE, SCORE, SCOUR, SCRAPPING, SCREW, SCROG, SCROMP, SCROUPERIZE, SCUTTLE, SCUTZ AROUND, SEASON, SEE, SEE A MAN, SERVE, SERVICE, SEW UP, SEX, SHACK UP WITH SOMEONE, SHAFT, SHAG, SHAKE, SHAKE A SKIN-COAT, SKROGG, SHAKE A TART, SHARE THE SEXUAL EMBRACE, SHARGE, SHEG, SHOOT BETWEEN WIND AND WATER, SHOOT IN THE TAIL, SHOOT ONE'S WAD, SHOVE, SHTUP, SIN, SINK IN, SINK THE SOLDIER, SKLOOK, SLAG, SLAM, SLAP SKINS, SLEEP WITH, SLIP HER A LENGTH, SLIP INTO, SLIP IT ABOUT, SLIP SOMEONE A FATTY, SLIP SOMEONE A LENGTH, SLIP SOMEONE THE HOT BEEF INJECTION, SMOCK, SMOCK-SERVICE, SMOKE, SNABBLE, SNAG, SNIB, SNUG, SOLACE, SPEAR THE BEARDED CLAM, SPIT, SPLICE, SPLIT, SPOIL, SPOON, SPOT, SQUARE SOMEONE'S CIRCLE, STAB, STAB A WOMAN IN THE THIGH, STABLE-MY-NAGGIE, STAIN, STAND THE PUSH, STAND UP, STICK, STITCH, STRAIN, STRAP, STRETCH LEATHER, STRIKE, STRIP ONE'S TARSE IN, STROKE, STROP ONE'S BEAK, STRUM, SUBAGITATE, SUCCEED AMOROUSLY, SUCK THE SUGAR-STICK, SUPPLE BOTH ENDS OF IT, SWING, SWINGE, SWITCH, SWITCHEL, SWIVE, TAIL, TAKE A TURN IN THE STUBBLE, TAKE A TURN ON SHOOTER'S HILL, TAKE IN AND DO FOR, TAKE IN BEEF, TAKE IN CREAM, TAKE NEBUCHADNEZZAR OUT TO GRASS, TAKE THE STARCH OUT OF (female), TASTE, TAX, TEAR OFF A PIECE, TEST THE SHOCKS, TETHER ONE'S NAG, THREAD, THREAD THE NEEDLE, THROW A LEG OVER, THROW ONE A HUMP, THRUM, THUMB, THUMP, TICKLE, TICK-TACK, TIE THE TRUE LOVER'S KNOT, TIFF, TIP, TIP THE LONG ONE, TO BE INTIMATE, TOM, TONYGLE, TOP, TOUCH, TOUZE, TRIM, TRIM THE BUFF, TROT OUT ONE'S PUSSY (female), TROUNCE, TUMBLE, TUMP, TURN UP, TWIDDLE, TWIGLE, TWIST, UP, USE, VARNISH ONE'S CANE, VAULT, WAG ONE'S BUM, WANK, WAP, WAX, WAX THE KNOB, WET A BOTTOM (female), WET ONE'S WICK, WHACK IT UP, WHAT MOTHER DID BEFORE ME, WHEEL, WHITEWASH, WIND UP THE CLOCK, WOMANIZE, WOMP ON SOMEONE, WORK, WORK OUT, WORK THE DUMB ORACLE, WORK THE HAIRY ORACLE, WRIGGLE NAVELS, YARD, YENTZ, YIELD ONE'S FAVORS, ZIGZAG.

occupying-house a brothel; a bawdy-house. [late 1500s]

O.D. 1. an "overdose" of drugs. **2.** to take an overdose of drugs; to be hospitalized because of an overdose of drugs. [both senses, U.S. drug culture, mid 1900s-pres.]

oddish intoxicated with alcohol. For synonyms see WOOFLED. [British slang, 1800s]

odious maximus of a very bad stink. Said about something that is disliked. [U.S., late 1900s-pres.]

Oedipus Rex to copulate. Rhyming slang on *sex*. For synonyms see OC-CUPY. [British, late 1900s-pres.]

off 1. to die. [British, World War II] **2.** to kill. [U.S.. slang, mid 1900s] **3.** to coit a woman. *Cf.* BRING OFF. See also JERK OFF.

off-color 1. out of health; looking ill. [British and U.S. colloquial, 1800s-1900s] **2.** slightly obscene or indecent. [U.S. colloquial, mid 1900s-pres.]

off like a bride's nightie 1. [departing] quickly. [Australian, late 1900s-pres.] **2.** rotten and smelly. [Australian, late 1900s-pres.]

off like a bucket of prawns in the hot sun 1. [departing] quickly. [Australian, late 1900s-pres.] **2.** rotten and smelly. [Australian, late 1900s-pres.]

off one's face drunk. For synonyms see WOOFLED. [Australian, mid 1900s-pres.]

oil 1. semen. See MAN OIL. For synonyms see METTLE. **2.** an alcohol extract of hashish or CANNABIS SATIVA (*q.v.*). *Cf.* RED OIL. [U.S. drug culture, mid 1900s-pres.] Synonyms: AFGANI, BLACK OIL, CHERRY LEB, HASH OIL, HONEY OIL, INDIAN OIL, RED OIL, SMASH, SON OF ONE, THE ONE.

oil change an act of copulation. *Cf.* OIL OF MAN. For synonyms see SMOCK-AGE. [U.S. slang, late 1900s, Lewin and Lewin]

oiled intoxicated with alcohol. *Cf.* WELL-OILED. [primarily U.S. slang, early 1700s-pres., Ben Franklin]

oiler 1. a drunkard who is frequently OILED (*q.v.*). For synonyms see ALCHY.

[slang, 1900s] **2.** a derogatory nickname for a Mexican. *Cf.* GREASER (sense 1). For synonyms see MEX. [U.S. slang, 1900s] **3.** a smoker of hashish oil. [U.S. drug culture, mid 1900s-pres.]

oil of barley (also **oyle of barley**) beer. *Cf.* BARLEY BROTH. [British, 1600s]

oil of giblets (also **oil of horn**) a woman's vaginal secretions; natural vaginal lubricant. For synonyms see FEMALE SPENDINGS. [British slang, 1800s, Farmer and Henley]

oil of horn the same as OIL OF GIB-LETS (*q.v.*). *Cf.* HORN (sense 3), the penis.

oil of man semen. A play on "sperm oil" or "sperm whale oil." *Cf.* MAN OIL. Possibly a play on the "Isle of Man." For synonyms see METTLE. [British slang, 1800s, Farmer and Henley]

oinker a very fat person. Refers to the fatness of the pig. [U.S. slang, late 1900s if not before]

old fella the penis. For synonyms see YARD. [Australian and British, mid 1900s-pres.]

olds one's parents. [Australian, mid 1900s-pres.]

on 1. sexually aroused. *Cf.* TURNED ON (sense 2). For synonyms see HUMPY. **2.** intoxicated with alcohol. [both senses, British, 1800s or before]

one-bagger a very ugly person, typically an ugly female. Someone whose facial ugliness can be concealed by a [single] paper bag. [U.S. slang, late 1900s] See also TWO-BAGGER.

one, the old the devil; Satan. For synonyms see FIEND. [since *c.* 1000]

one-eyed Bob the penis. For synonyms see YARD. [British and U.S., late 1900s-pres.]

one-eyed brother the penis. For synonyms see GENITALS, YARD. [British slang, late 1900s]

one-eyed milkman the penis. *Cf.* MILK, MILKMAN (sense 2). For synonyms see YARD. [British, 1900s, *Dictionary of Slang and Unconventional English*]

one-eyed monster (also **one-eyed**

wonder) the penis. For synonyms see GENITALS, YARD. [U.S. slang, Lewin and Lewin]

one-eyed pants mouse the penis. For synonyms see GENITALS, YARD. [U.S. and elsewhere, late 1900s]

one-eyed trouser snake the penis. For synonyms see GENITALS, YARD. [British slang, late 1900s]

one-eyed wonder the penis. For synonyms see YARD. [U.S., late 1900s-pres.]

one-eyed worm the penis. For synonyms see YARD. [U.S. nonce, mid 1900s]

one-eyed zipper snake the penis. For synonyms see GENITALS, YARD. [U.S. military, 1900s, *Soldier Talk*]

one-finger exercise digital stimulation of the genitals of a woman. From "five-finger (piano) exercise." *Cf.* DIGITATE.

one-finger salute an obscene gesture; the FINGER (*q.v.*). [U.S. slang, mid 1900s-pres.]

one-holed flute See FLUTE.

one in the bush is worth two in the hand "an act of copulation is worth two acts of masturbation." The bush refers to the female genitals and the pubic hair. [Australian, 1900s, *Dictionary of Slang and Unconventional English*]

one-legged race male masturbation. For synonyms and related subjects see WASTE TIME. [British slang, 1900s]

one of the Brown family a CATAMITE (*q.v.*). Refers to PEDERASTY (*q.v.*). *Cf.* BROWN (sense 3). For synonyms see BRONCO. [U.S. slang and underworld, mid 1900s]

one of the faithful a drunkard; a man always seen at the same tavern or bar. *Cf.* RELIGIOUS. [since the early 1600s]

one of those a homosexual male. For synonyms see EPICENE. [British and U.S. slang and colloquial, 1900s]

one-piece overcoat a condom. *Cf.* RAINCOAT. For synonyms see EEL-SKIN. [British, mid 1900s, *Dictionary of Slang and Unconventional English*]

one's ear, on 1. angry. **2.** broke; bankrupt. [both senses, U.S. slang, 1900s] **3.** intoxicated with alcohol. [all senses, euphemistic for "on one's ass"; sense 3 is slang, early 1900s-pres.]

one's ease, at intoxicated with alcohol. For synonyms see WOOFLED. [colloquial, 1900s]

one's flag is out one is intoxicated with alcohol. [British slang, 1800s, Farmer and Henley]

one's greens, on for sexually aroused. *Cf.* GREENS. For synonyms see HUMPY. [British slang, 1800s, Farmer and Henley]

one-shot a woman who agrees to a ONE-NIGHT STAND (*q.v.*). *Cf.* SHOT (sense 2). [U.S. slang, 1900s]

one's Sunday best, in with an erect penis. For synonyms see ERECTION. [British slang, 1800s, Farmer and Henley]

on the horse under the effects of heroin. For synonyms see TALL. [Australian, mid 1900s-pres.]

on the nose smelling badly. [British, mid 1900s-pres.]

On your bike! "Get the hell out of here!"; "Get on your motorcycle and get out!" [U.S. slang, late 1900s]

oojahs the female breasts. For synonyms see BOSOM. [British, late 1900s-pres.]

oomphy sexually aroused; sexy. For synonyms see HUMPY. [U.S., mid 1900s-pres.]

oozy alcohol intoxicated. For synonyms see WOOFLED. [1900s, Dickson]

ope (also **op**) "opium." [U.S. underworld and slang, early 1900s or before] Synonyms: BIG-O., BLACK PILLS, BLACK SILK, BLACK SMOKE, BLACK STUFF, BRICK, BRICK GUM, BROWN STUFF, BUTTON, CHINESE TOBACCO, COOLIE MUD DOPIUM, DREAM BEADS, DREAM GUM, DREAMS, DREAMSTICK, DREAM WAX, ELEVATION, GLAD STUFF, GOMA, GONG, GONGER, GOW, GREASE, GREAT TOBACCO, GUM, HOP, HOPS, JUNK, LEM-KEE, MIDNIGHT OIL, MUD, O., PEN YEN, PIN-YON, POPPY TRAIN, SHELL OF HOP, SKA-

MAS, TAR, YAM-YAM, YEN-CHEE, YEN-SHEE.

open ass of a very bad smell or taste. [U.S., late 1900s-pres.]

open fly eager for sex. For synonyms see HUMPY. [U.S., late 1900s-pres.]

open the lunchbox to break wind. For synonyms see GURK. [U.S., late 1900s-pres.]

open (up) one's kimono to reveal what one is planning. [U.S., late 1900s-pres.]

oral oral sex. [British and U.S., mid 1900s-pres.]

oranges the human breasts. *Cf.* GRAPEFRUITS, MELONS. [U.S. slang, 1900s]

orange sunshine the drug L.S.D. (*q.v.*). *Cf.* YELLOW SUNSHINE. [U.S. drug culture, mid 1900s-pres.]

orange wedges the drug L.S.D. (*q.v.*). [U.S. drug culture, mid 1900s-pres.]

orchard the female genitals. In the expression GET JACK IN THE ORCHARD (*q.v.*). [British slang, 1800s, Farmer and Henley]

orchestra a homosexual male who will perform anything sexual with any object or body part. [U.S. homosexual use, mid 1900s]

orchestra stalls (also **orchestras**) the testicles. Rhyming slang for "balls." [British, 1800s, *Dictionary of Rhyming Slang*]

oregano marijuana. From the name of the herb. For synonyms see MARI. [U.S. drug culture, late 1900s]

oreo a Negro who thinks and acts like a Caucasian; a derogatory nickname for a Negro who is black on the outside and white on the inside. From the trademarked brand name of a cookie. [U.S. slang, mid 1900s-pres.] See also AFRO-SAXON, AUNT JANE, CHALKER, COOKIE, FADE, FADED BOOGIE, FROSTY.

org to experience a drug RUSH. From *orgasm*. [U.S. drug culture, late 1900s]

organ the penis. *Cf.* FAMILY ORGAN. [colloquial, 1900s]

organ donor a bicyle or motorcycle rider who does not wear a helmet. [U.S., late 1900s-pres.]

organ-grinder 1. a derogatory nickname for an Italian. [slang and colloquial, 1900s] **2.** the female genitals, specifically the vagina. **3.** a prostitute; a sexually loose woman.

organic stuff marijuana. As opposed to chemicals as found in pills. For synonyms see MARI. [U.S. collegiate, late 1900s, Eble] See also LEGUME, PLANTS.

organism a contrived euphemism for ORGASM (*q.v.*). [widespread, recurrent, jocular nonce; attested as U.S., 1900s]

organized intoxicated with alcohol. For synonyms see WOOFLED. [U.S. slang and colloquial, early 1900s]

organ recital 1. a recital of one's medical history. [U.S., late 1900s-pres.] **2.** a sex education class. [U.S., late 1900s-pres.]

organ music (also **organ recital**) **1.** growling or gurgling in the stomach or intestines. [U.S. colloquial, 1900s or before] **2.** the audible release of intestinal gas, [U.S. colloquial, 1900s]

ork-orks the DELIRIUM TREMENS (*q.v.*). [U.S. colloquial, early 1900s] Synonyms: ABSTINENCE DELIRIUM, ALCOHOL DEMENTIA, ALCOHOLIC SEIZURE, ALCOHOLISMUS ACUTUS, BARREL-FEVER, BLACK DOG, BLUE DEVILS, BLUE HORRORS, BLUE JOHNNIES, BLUES, BOTTLEACHE, CLANKS, DELIRIUM TREMENS, DIDDLEUMS, DINGBATS, DITHERS, DRUNKEN HORRORS, D.T.s, DYSPEPSIA, ELEPHANTS, ENOMANIA, GALLON DISTEMPER, HAVE SNAKES IN ONE'S BOOTS, HORRORS, JERKS, JIM-JAMS, JIMMIES, JOE BLAKES, JUMPS, MANIA A POTU, PINK-SPIDERS, QUART-MANIA, SCREAMING-MEANIES, SCREAMING-MEEMIES, SHAKES, SNAKES, THE RAMS, THE RATS, TREMENS, TRIANGLES, UGLIES, WHOOPS AND JINGLES, WOOLIES.

orks the testicles. A truncation of "orchestras" or ORCHESTRA STALLS (*q.v.*), "balls." [British slang, early 1900s, *Dictionary of Slang and Unconventional English*]

ornament the female genitals. For synonyms see MONOSYLLABLE. [British slang, 1800s, Farmer and Henley]

orthogenital pertaining to sexual copulation. Describing acts of copulation optimally suitable for procreation, *i.e.*, acts leading directly to an ejaculation of semen in the vagina. The term is used in avoidance of "normal" or "biologically normal."

orts 1. any leavings, droppings, or crumbs. [early 1400s] **2.** mouse droppings. **3.** fish innards. [senses 2 and 3 are colloquial, 1800s-1900s]

oscar 1. a homosexual male. Often capitalized in this sense. For synonyms see EPICENE. **2.** to commit PEDERASTY (*q.v.*). From the proper name "Oscar Wilde." [British, 1800s]

oscarize to act as a PEDERAST (*q.v.*). See OSCAR.

O-sign a sign of death as represented by a dead person's mouth hanging open. *Cf.* Q-SIGN. For synonyms see DEMISE. [U.S. mock medical, late 1900s]

ossified intoxicated with alcohol; turned into bone by alcohol. *Cf.* PETRIFIED. [U.S. slang, early 1900s]

Otis 1. alcohol intoxicated. From the character Otis in the Andy Griffith television series. For synonyms see WOOFLED. **2.** a drunkard; a drunk. [both senses, U.S. collegiate, late 1900s]

O.T.R. 1. expecting the menses; "on the rag." See RAG, ON THE. [U.S. slang, 1900s] **2.** being grouchy or BITCHY. From *on the rag.* Said of males or females. [U.S. slang, late 1900s] See RAG, ON THE.

out 1. intoxicated with alcohol; unconscious from alcohol. [British and U.S. colloquial, 1700s-1900s] **2.** drug intoxication. [U.S. drug culture, mid 1900s-pres.] **3.** homosexual; out of the closet; pertaining to a person who practices homosexual acts and is a recognized member of the homosexual community. *Cf.* COME OUT OF THE CLOSET. [U.S. homosexual use, mid 1900s-pres.]

outer 1. the drug L.S.D. Possibly from *outer limits.* For synonyms see ACID. **2.** MESCALINE. [both senses, U.S. drug culture, late 1900s, Abel]

outfit the male genitals. *Cf.* APPARATUS, EQUIPMENT, GEAR, KIT. [euphemistic]

outlaw a prostitute who works independently from a pimp.

out of one's brain (also **out of one's skull**) drunk; drug intoxicated. For synonyms see TALL, WOOFLED. [widespread, late 1900s]

out of order experiencing the menses. From a common expression describing anything which will not work. *Cf.* STREET UP FOR REPAIRS. [U.S. slang, 1900s]

out of this world experiencing the menses. For synonyms see FLOODS. [U.S. slang, 1900s]

out on the roof intoxicated with alcohol. [U.S. slang or nonce, mid 1900s]

out someone 1. to reveal someone to be homosexual. [U.S., late 1900s-pres.] **2.** to sack someone. [British, mid 1900s-pres.] **3.** to suspend someone from membership of a club, society, etc. [British, late 1900s-pres.]

out to it intoxicated with alcohol. *Cf.* OUT (sense 1). [Australian, 1800s-1900s]

oval office a bedroom. A post-Clinton comment. [U.S., late 1900s-pres.]

overboard intoxicated with alcohol. For synonyms see WOOFLED. [U.S. slang, 1900s]

overcome intoxicated with alcohol. For synonyms see WOOFLED. [British and U.S. slang, 1800s-1900s]

overseen intoxicated with alcohol. For synonyms see WOOFLED. [late 1400s-1600s]

overserved having to do with a drunk person in a bar; alcohol intoxicated. Euphemistic. *Cf.* SERVED UP. For synonyms see WOOFLED. [U.S. slang, late 1900s]

oversexed See HIGHLY-SEXED.

overshot intoxicated with alcohol. *Cf.* CUP-SHOT, GRAPE-SHOT, POT-SHOT. [since the early 1600s]

overtaken intoxicated with alcohol. [slang, 1500s-1600s]

over the bay intoxicated with alcohol. *Cf.* OVERSEAS. [U.S. slang and colloquial, early 1800s-1900s]

over the mark intoxicated with alcohol. See LOADED TO THE PLIMSOLL MARK, of which this is a paraphrase. [British slang, early 1800s]

over-the-shoulder-boulder-holder a brassiere. *Cf.* BOULDERS. For synonyms see BRA. [U.S. jocular slang, mid 1900s-pres.]

owled intoxicated with alcohol. See DRUNK AS A BOILED OWL. For synonyms see WOOFLED. [U.S. slang, early 1900s]

owly-eyed (also **owl-eyed**) intoxicated with alcohol. *Cf.* ORIE-EYED. [U.S. slang and colloquial, early 1900s]

oyster 1. a gob of phlegm. [since the late 1700s, Grose] Senses 1-3 are from the slimy nature of the oyster. **2.** the female genitals. [British, 1800s, Farmer and Henley] **3.** semen; an ejaculation of semen. [British, 1800s, Farmer and Henley] **4.** a testicle used for food. See MOUNTAIN OYSTERS.

oyster-catcher the female genitals, specifically the vagina. *Cf.* OYSTER (sense 3). [British slang, 1800s, Farmer and Henley]

O.Z. one ounce of marijuana. Occasionally used for other drugs. *Cf.* LID, TIN, Z. From "oz.," the abbreviation of "ounce." [U.S. drug culture, mid 1900s-pres.]

ozone phencyclidine, the drug P.C.P. For synonyms see P.C.P. [U.S. drug culture, late 1900s]

ozone, in the intoxicated with marijuana. For synonyms see TALL. [U.S. drug culture, mid 1900s-pres.]

P

P. 1. urine; to urinate; an act of urination. From PISS (q.v.). **2.** PEYOTE. [U.S. drug culture, late 1900s] **3.** phencyclidine, the drug P.C.P. For synonyms see P.C.P. [U.S. drug culture, late 1900s]

package a cute girl; a sexually attractive woman. Cf. BUNDLE (sense 2). [U.S. colloquial and slang, 1900s]

packaged intoxicated with alcohol. Cf. BOXED-UP. [U.S. slang and colloquial, late 1800s-1900s]

packet the male genitals. For synonyms see GENITALS, VIRILIA. [British, late 1900s-pres.]

pack (fudge) (also **pack peanut butter**) to perform PEDERASTY. Cf. FUDGE-PACKER. For related subjects see PEDERASTY. [U.S. slang, late 1900s]

pack of poo tickets toilet paper. [Australian, late 1900s-pres.]

pack one's nose to use (SNORT) cocaine. [U.S. drug culture, late 1900s]

paddle the pickle to masturbate. Said of the male. Cf. PICKLE. For synonyms and related subjects see WASTE TIME. [U.S. slang, late 1900s]

paddling the pink canoe female masturbation. For synonyms see WASTE TIME. [U.S., late 1900s-pres.]

padlock the penis. Rhyming slang on COCK. For synonyms see YARD. [British, late 1900s-pres.]

pain in the ass (also **pain in the derrière, pain in the rear**) **1.** an obnoxious person. Cf. PAIN. **2.** a difficult or unpleasant task or subject. Cf. PAIN. [both senses, U.S. colloquial, 1900s]

pain in the neck a bothersome person or thing. Euphemistic for PAIN IN THE ASS (q.v.). [U.S. colloquial, 1900s]

painkiller any alcoholic drink. Cf. MEDICINE (sense 2). SNAKEBITE MEDICINE. For synonyms see BOOZE. [U.S. colloquial and slang, 1900s]

painted-Willie a CATAMITE (q.v.). For synonyms see BRONCO.

paint the town red to go on a drinking spree; to celebrate wildly. [U.S. slang and colloquial, 1900s]

pair the breasts, especially large and shapely breasts. [U.S. colloquial, mid 1900s-pres.]

Pakistani hash a type of HASHISH, presumably from Pakistan. For synonyms see HASH. [U.S. drug culture, late 1900s]

Panama gold (also **Panama**) a variety of marijuana said to be grown in Panama. [U.S. drug culture, mid 1900s-pres.]

Panama red (also **Panamanian red**) a potent variety of marijuana supposedly grown in Panama. [U.S. drug culture, mid 1900s-pres.]

panatela (also **panatella**) a potent type of marijuana. From the cigar name. [U.S. drug culture, mid 1900s]

pansy 1. a weakling; an effeminate male. For synonyms see FRIBBLE. **2.** a homosexual male, especially a RECEIVER (q.v.). For synonyms see EPICENE. [both senses, U.S. slang, early 1900s-pres.]

pansy-ball a dance attended by homosexual males. [U.S. slang, mid 1900s]

pansy up to doll oneself up, said of a male. Not necessarily a homosexual male. Cf. PIMP UP, QUEER UP. [British, 1900s, Dictionary of the Underworld]

panters the breasts. Cf. HEAVER. For synonyms see BOSOM. [British slang, 1800s, Farmer and Henley]

panther juice any alcoholic beverage. [U.S. slang and colloquial, 1900s or before]

panther piss (also **panther's piss**) an inferior grade of alcohol; any strong alcoholic drink. *Cf.* COUGAR-MILK. [Australian and U.S. slang, 1900s]

panther pizen strong or inferior alcohol. *Cf.* PIZEN. For synonyms see EMBALMING FLUID. [U.S. slang, 1900s]

panther sweat any alcoholic drink. *Cf.* NANNY-GOAT SWEAT, PIG SWEAT. [U.S. slang, early 1900s]

pantry shelves the human breasts. *Cf.* BALCONY (sense 1). [British, late 1800s]

pants rabbits lice. *Cf.* SEAM-SQUIRREL. For synonyms see WALKING DANDRUFF. [U.S. slang, early 1900s]

panty-stretcher a well-built young lady. [U.S. slang, mid 1900s-pres.]

paper money. [U.S., late 1900s-pres.]

paper acid the drug L.S.D. (*q.v.*). *Cf.* BLOTTER (sense 2). [U.S. drug culture, mid 1900s-pres.]

paper bag case a very ugly person. A person who is a ONE-BAGGER, DOUBLE-BAGGER, TRIPLE-BAGGER, or even COYOTE-UGLY. [U.S. collegiate, late 1900s, Eble]

paper tiger an impotent penis; a limp penis. For synonyms see GENITALS, YARD. [U.S. slang, late 1900s]

paperweight a serious student; a hard-working student. [U.S., late 1900s-pres.]

parallel park to copulate. Refers to the bodies of two people parallel to each other. For synonyms see OCCUPY. [U.S. slang, late 1900s]

paralytic extremely drunk. For synonyms see WOOFLED. [Australian and U.S., mid 1900s-pres.]

parboiled alcohol intoxicated. For synonyms see WOOFLED. [U.S., mid 1900s-pres.]

pardon my hard-on a catch phrase used simply to be rude or in reference to a sexually stimulating situation, person, or object. Refers to an erection at an inappropriate time or place. *Cf.* RISE IN ONE'S LEVIS. [U.S. slang, 1900s]

parenthesis the female genitals. From the image of the vulva suggested by ( ). [British euphemism, late 1800s, Farmer and Henley]

park a custard to vomit. For synonyms see YORK. [British slang, late 1900s]

parking place the BUTTOCKS. For synonyms see DUFF. [British slang or colloquial, 1900s, J. Green]

parsley 1. pubic hair, especially female pubic hair. For synonyms see PLUSH. [British, 1700s-1800s] 2. nonsense; a worthless and extraneous bit of nothing. [colloquial, 1900s] 3. phencyclidine, the animal tranquilizer P.C.P. For synonyms see P.C.P. [U.S. drug culture, late 1900s]

part that went over the fence last 1. the rump of an animal (whether or not the animal jumps over fences). 2. the human posteriors. [both senses, U.S. colloquial, 1900s or before]

party 1. drinking; sexual play. Used in expressions to refer to certain kinds of activity carried on in groups or in pairs. *Cf.* PETTING-PARTY, WESSON PARTY. [U.S. slang, 1900s] 2. to drink; to smoke marijuana. Occasionally, the term may include additional illicit activities. [U.S. euphemistic slang, mid 1900s-pres.]

party animal a person who celebrates wildly at a party; a person who acts like a beast at parties. [U.S. slang, late 1900s]

party favors drugs, especially those used or distributed at a party. [U.S. slang, late 1900s]

party hat a condom. *Cf.* JIMMY HAT. For synonyms see EEL-SKIN. [U.S. collegiate, late 1900s, Munro]

party hats hard nipples, visible through a female's clothing. [U.S. late 1900s-pres.]

party-in-a-can beer; a can of beer. [U.S. collegiate, late 1900s, Eble]

party out to use drugs in a group. [U.S. drug culture, late 1900s]

pash on (also **pash**) to be in a state of sexual arousal. Patterned on HARD-ON (*q.v.*) and "passion." [U.S. slang, mid 1900s]

passage the vagina. [colloquial euphemism, 1900s and before] See also WINDWARD PASSAGE. Synonyms: LIT-

TLE MARY, NOOKER, NOOKY, PEE HOLE, SNAPPER, STINK-POT, VENUS' GLOVE. See MONOSYLLABLE for related terms.

pass air (also **pass wind**) to release intestinal gas; euphemistic for PASS GAS (*q.v.*). For synonyms see GURK. [U.S. colloquial, 1900s]

pass away to die. *Cf.* PASS ON. [colloquial, 1900s and before]

passed died; dead. For synonyms see DONE FOR. [Euphemism, 1900s if not before]

pass gas to release intestinal gas; to break wind. *Cf.* PASS AIR. For synonyms see GURK. [U.S. colloquial, 1900s]

pass in one's chips (also **pass in one's checks**) to die; to leave the game and turn in one's playing pieces. [U.S. colloquial, 1800s-pres.]

pass in one's marble to die. [Australian colloquial, 1900s, Wilkes]

passion boat a big car or a van, used for copulation. [U.S., late 1900s-pres.]

passion flower a sexually passionate woman. From the name of the flower. [U.S. colloquial, mid 1900s]

passion pit a drive-in movie where a considerable amount of "necking" is supposed to take place. Also for any location where necking takes place. [U.S. slang, mid 1900s]

passion wagon a SIN-BIN; a van fitted out as a portable bedroom for sex; any vehicle where hot passion is experienced. [British slang, late 1900s, J. Green]

pass on to die. *Cf.* PASS AWAY. [U.S. colloquial, 1900s]

pass out 1. to faint. [colloquial, 1900s or before] **2.** to die. [British, World War I, Fraser and Gibbons] **3.** to lose consciousness due to intoxication with alcohol or drugs. An extension of sense 1. [U.S. slang, mid 1900s-pres.]

pass over to die. *Cf.* CROSS OVER, PASS ON. For synonyms see DEPART. [colloquial, 1900s or before]

paste semen. For synonyms see MET-TLE. [U.S. slang, late 1900s]

paste eater a total JERK; a social out-

cast. *Cf.* PASTE = semen. For synonyms see OAF. [U.S. slang, late 1900s]

pasted 1. intoxicated with alcohol. **2.** intoxicated with drugs. [both senses, U.S. slang, mid 1900s-pres.]

Pat and Mick the penis. Rhyming slang for "prick." [British, 1800s, *Dictionary of Rhyming Slang*]

pause that refreshes a rest break including an opportunity to use the restroom. From an advertising slogan for Coca-Cola (trademark). [U.S. slang and nonce, mid 1900s-pres.]

pavement pizza a mass of vomit on the sidewalk. For synonyms see YORK. [Australian, late 1900s-pres.]

pavement-pounder 1. a policeman. **2.** a prostitute. [both senses, U.S. slang, mid 1900s]

paw to fondle; to caress a woman against her will. *Cf.* GROPE, MAUL. [U.S. slang and colloquial, mid 1900s-pres.]

paw-paw tricks masturbation in expressions such as "play paw-paw tricks." This is a special application of a general term for "naughty tricks." [British slang, 1800s]

pay a visit to retire to the W.C. For synonyms see RETIRE. [U.S. colloquial, 1900s]

P.C.O.D. "pussy cut off date," four or five weeks before leaving for home. This allows sufficient time for venereal disease to become evident and be treated before departure for home. [U.S. military, 1900s, *Soldier Talk*]

P.C.P. "phencyclidine," an animal tranquilizer and anesthetic used as a hallucinogenic drug. [U.S. drug culture, mid 1900s-pres.] Synonyms: AMOEBA, ANGEL DUST, ANGEL HAIR, ANGEL MIST, ANGEL PUKE, ANIMAL, ANIMAL TRANQUILIZER, AURORA BOREALIS, BLACK WHACK, BUSY-BEE, CADILLAC, CANNABINOL, C.J., COZMOS, CRAZY-COKE, CRYSTAL JOINT, DEATH WISH, DETROIT PINK, DEVIL DUST, D.O.A., DUMMY DUST, ELEPHANT, ELEPHANT TRANQUILIZER, ENERGIZER, ERTH, FUEL, GOOD DUST, GOON, GORILLA TABS, GRAY DUST, GREEN SNOW, GREEN TEA, HERCULES, HERMS, HEROIN BUZZ, HOG,

HORSE TRANK, HORSE TRANQUILIZER, JET FUEL, JUICE, KAPS, KILLER-WEED, K.J., KOOLS, LOVE BOAT, LOVELY, MAGIC, MAGIC DUST, MAGIC MIST, MEAN GREEN, MINT LEAF, MINT WEED, MIST, MONKEY DUST, MOON BEAMS, NEW MAGIC, NIEBLA, OZONE, P., PARSLEY, PAZ, PEACE PILL, PEACEWEED, PEEP, PHENCYCLIDINE, PIG KILLER, PIG TRANQUILIZER, PUFFY, ROCKET-FUEL, SCAFFLE, SCUFFLE, SHEETS, SKUFFLE, SNORTS, SOMA, STARDUST, SUPERGRASS, SUPERWEED, SURFER, SNYTHETIC MARIJUANA, T-BUZZ, T-TAB, WEED, WHITE DUST, WOBBLE WEED, WOLF, ZOMBIE BUZZ.

p-crutch a police car. [U.S., late 1900s-pres.]

P'd off PISSED-OFF (*q.v.*); extremely angry. [U.S. euphemism, mid 1900s-pres.]

peacemaker the penis. *Cf.* MATRIMONIAL PEACEMAKER. For synonyms see YARD. [British slang, late 1700s, Grose]

peace pill 1. a mixture of L.S.D. (*q.v.*) and Methedrine (trademark). **2.** the drug P.C.P. (*q.v.*). *Cf.* PEP PILL. [both senses, U.S. drug culture, mid 1900s-pres.]

peaceweed the drug phencyclidine, P.C.P. For synonyms see P.C.P. [U.S. drug culture, late 1900s]

peaches 1. the breasts. *Cf.* ORANGES. [U.S. slang, mid 1900s] **2.** amphetamine tablets, especially peach-colored tablets or capsules. [U.S. drug culture, mid 1900s-pres.]

peanut a barbiturate tablet. For synonyms see BARB. [U.S. drug culture, mid 1900s-pres.]

peanut smuggling an imaginary activity done by women, evidenced by the visibility of the outlines of erect nipples through their clothing. See also GRAPE SMUGGLING. [British, late 1900s-pres.]

pearl (also **pearly**) **1.** a syphilitic sore. [U.S. slang, mid 1900s] **2.** an amyl nitrite ampule. *Cf.* POPPER, SNAPPER (sense 5). [U.S. drug culture, mid 1900s-pres.]

pearl-diving CUNNILINGUS (*q.v.*). *Cf.* MUFF-DIVER. [U.S. slang, mid 1900s]

pearly gate 1. morning glory seeds. From the color variety name. **2.** the drug L.S.D. (*q.v.*). [both senses, U.S. drug culture, mid 1900s-pres.]

pearly whites morning glory seeds used as a hallucinogenic agent. From the color variety name. [U.S. drug culture, mid 1900s]

peas in the pot sexually aroused. Rhyming slang for "hot." [British slang, late 1800s]

pebbles the testicles. *Cf.* GOOLIES, ROCKS, STONES. For synonyms see WHIRLYGIGS. [British slang, 1800s, Farmer and Henley]

peck a derogatory nickname for a Caucasian. From PECKERWOOD (*q.v.*). [U.S. Southern Negro use, 1900s or before]

pecker 1. the "chin" in the British expression KEEP YOUR PECKER UP! (*q.v.*). No negative connotations in this sense. [British slang and colloquial, 1800s-pres.] **2.** the penis. For synonyms see YARD. [primarily U.S. slang and colloquial, 1800s-pres.]

pecker-checker 1. a doctor who examines men's genitals for signs of venereal disease. [U.S. military, late 1900s, *Soldier Talk*] **2.** a urologist [U.S., late 1900s-pres.]

peckerhead 1. the head or end of the penis. For synonyms see YARD. [U.S., mid 1900s-pres.] **2.** a stupid and ignorant male. For synonyms see OAF. [U.S., mid 1900s-pres.]

pecker tracks 1. dribbles of urine on one's pants. [U.S. slang, late 1900s] **2.** dribbled semen. For synonyms see METTLE. [U.S. slang, late 1900s, Lewin and Lewin]

peckerwood (also **peckawood**) a derogatory nickname for a Caucasian. From the common name of a species of woodpecker. The term may be an elaboration of PECKER (sense 2). [from Southern black dialect; U.S. black use and slang, early 1900s-pres.] Synonyms: BALL-FACE, BEAST, BLANCO, BLUE-EYED DEVIL, BRIGHT SKIN, BUCKRA, CHARLES, CHARLIE, CHUCK, CRACKER, DAP, DEVIL, DOG, FACE, FADE, FAY, FROSTY, GEORGIA CRACKER, GRAY,

GRAY BOY, GREY BOY, HAY-EATER, HIN-KTY, HONKY, HOOPLE, HUNKY, JEFF, KELTCH, KU KLUXER, LILY-WHITE, LONG KNIFE, MARSHMALLOW, MEAN WHITE, MISTER CHARLIE, MONKEY, MULE, OFAY, OOFAY, PADDY, PADDY BOY, PALE, PALEFACE, PECK, PEEK A WOODS, PINK, PINKY, RED-NECK, RIDGERUNNER, ROUNDEYE, SHITKICKER, SILK, SNAKE, THE MAN, WHITE MEAT, WHITE PADDY, WHITEY.

pederast 1. a man who performs anal copulation upon boys. **2.** a man who performs anal copulation upon males of any age. Synonyms and related terms: ACTIVE SODOMIST, ANAL ASTRO-NAUT, ANGEL, ANGELINA, ARSE BANDIT, ARSE-KING, ASS PIRATE, BACKGAM-MONER, BACKGAMMON-PLAYER, BAR-DACHE, BIRDIE, BIRD-TAKER, BOTTY BOY, BROWN-HATTER, BROWNIE, BROWNIE KING, BUD SALLOGH, BUG, BUGGAH, BUGGER, BUM BANDIT, BUMHOLE ENGINEER, BUNKER, BURGLAR, CAPON, CHOCO-LATE-BANDIT, CHUTNEY FERRET, CINAE-DUS, COLON COWBOY, CORN-HOLDER, CORVETTE, DADDY, ENEMA BANDIT, EYE DOCTOR, EYE-OPENER, FATHER-FUCKER, GENTLEMAN OF THE BACK DOOR, GOOSER, GUT-BUTCHER, GUT-FUCKER, GUT-MONGER, GUT-REAMER, GUT-SCRAPER, GUT-STICKER, GUT-STRETCHER, GUT-STUFFER, GUT-VEXER, INDORSER, IN-GLER, INSERTEE, INSERTOR, INSPECTOR OF MANHOLES, JESUIT, JOCKER, JOCKEY, JOEY, LICK-BOX, LIMP-WRIST, MASON, POO-JABBER, PRUSSIAN, PUFF, REAMER, RING-SNATCHER, SAUSAGE JOCKEY, SHEEP-HERDER, SHITFUCKER, SHIT-HUNTER, SHIT-STABBER, SHIT-STIRRER, SOD, SOD-OMIST, SODOMITE, STERN-CHASER, STIR-SHIT, STUFFER, TURD BURGLAR, TURK, UNCLE, UNNATURAL DEBAUCHEE, UP-HILL GARDENER, USHER, VERT, WOLF.

pederasty (also **paederasty**) **1.** anal copulation where the INSERTOR (*q.v.*) is an adult male and the RECEIVER (*q.v.*) is an adolescent or preadolescent boy. [since the 1300s] **2.** anal copula-tion involving males of any age. Ex-tended from sense 1. Synonyms and related terms: ASS-FUCK, BACK-DOOR-WORK, BACK-SCUTTLE, BIT OF BROWN, BOODY, BOTTLE, BROWN-EYE, BROWN HOLE, BROWNING, BUCKLEBURY, BUG-GERY, BUNG HOLE, BUTT-FUCK, COITUS IN ANO, COITUS PER ANUM, CONCUBITUS CUM PERSONA EJUSDEM SEXUS, DAUB OF THE BRUSH, DIP IN THE FUDGE POT, GREEK, GREEK LOVE, GREEK WAY, HIGHER MALTHUSIANISM, ITALIAN MAN-NER, KIESTER STAB, KNEELING AT THE ALTAR, LAY, PAEDICATIO, PEDICATION, PIG-STICKING, RAM-JOB, SHIP'S, SHIT-FUCK, SODOMY, UNMENTIONABLE VICE, UNNATURAL CONNECTION, UNNATURAL OFFENSE, UNNATURAL PURPOSES, UN-NATURAL SEXUAL INTERCOURSE, UN-NATURAL VICE.

pee 1. urine. **2.** to urinate. [both senses, widespread colloquial, 1800s-pres.]

pee'd off extremely angry. A variety of "pissed-off." *Cf.* P'D OFF. [U.S. slang and colloquial, 1900s]

pee-eyed intoxicated with alcohol. From the P.I. of PISSED (*q.v.*). For syn-onyms see WOOFLED.

pee-pee (also **pee**) **1.** urine. **2.** to uri-nate. Both are from the initial letter of "piss." The reduplicated form is usu-ally considered to be juvenile. [both since the late 1700s]

peer-queer a homosexual male who derives special pleasure from watching others participate in sexual acts. See QUEEN for similar subjects. *Cf.* PEEK-FREAK, VOYEUR, WATCH-QUEEN. [U.S. homosexual use, mid 1900s]

pee-wee 1. the penis, especially that of a child. *Cf.* PEENIE. [primarily Brit-ish juvenile] **2.** the female genitals. **3.** to urinate. *Cf.* WEE-WEE. [all senses, British and U.S. use, 1800s-1900s]

peg boy a CATAMITE (*q.v.*). See PEGO. One etymology states that this was a catamite who belonged to a sailor who kept the boy sitting on a large peg to dilate his anus for PEDERASTY (*q.v.*). For synonyms see BRONCO. [U.S., 1900s]

pegger a drunkard. For synonyms see ALCHY. [British slang, 1800s]

peg house a house of prostitution. For synonyms see BROTHEL. [British, mid 1900s-pres.]

pellets 1. the human breasts, espe-cially if very small. [U.S. slang or colloquial, 1900s] **2.** rabbit, deer, or goat dung. [colloquial and euphemistic, 1900s or before]

pen 1. the penis. One of the etymologically correct nicknames for this organ. [from Latin *peniculus,* an "artist's brush"; British, 1500s and widespread nonce] See also PIN (sense 1). **2.** the female genitals, primarily of sows. [British, 1800s or before] **3.** a state "penitentiary."

pencil 1. the penis. *Cf.* PEN (sense 1). [from Latin *peniculus,* an "artist's brush"; British and U.S. slang, 1800s-1900s] **2.** a small penis. [U.S: homosexual use, mid 1900s]

pencil and tassel the male genitals, especially those of a little boy. [British and U.S. slang, 1900s]

pencil dick See NEEDLE DICK.

pencil-squeezer a male masturbator. *Cf.* PENCIL. [British slang, 1900s]

penile size the size of the male organ. The following are related to or are synonymous with penile size: BASKET FOR DAYS, DONKEY-RIGGED, DOUBLE-SHUNG, HUNG, HUNG LIKE A BULL, MEGALOPENIS, MENTULATE, MICROCAULIA, MICROGENITALISM, MICROPENIS, MICROPHALLUS, MIRACLE-MEAT, TIMBERED, TONS OF BASKET, TONS OF MEAT, WELL-BUILT, WELL-ENDOWED, WELL-FAVORED BY NATURE, WELL-HUNG, WELT.

penilingus the use of the tongue or lips to stimulate the penis of a male; the same as FELLATIO (*q.v.*). See also BAGPIPE, B.J., BLOW, BLOW-JOB, FELLATIO, FRENCH TRICKS, FRENCH WAY, GOBBLE, HEAD-JOB, HOOVERISM, IRRUMATION, JOB, KNOB-JOB, MUNCH, ORAL SERVICE, PIPE-JOB, PISTON-JOB, SERVE HEAD, SIXTY-NINE, SMOKE, SODOMY, SUCK, SUCK OFF, SUCK THE SUGAR-STICK, SUCKY-FUCKY, TITTY-OGGY, TONGUE-FUCK.

penis the male sexual and urinary organ. [from Latin *peniculus,* "artist's brush"] See list at YARD.

penis breath a negative term of address or an epithet. [U.S. slang, late 1900s]

penis machinist a doctor who examines men's genitals for signs of vene-

real disease; a PECKER-CHECKER. [U.S. military, 1900s, *Soldier Talk*]

penis wrinkle a total JERK; a social outcast. For synonyms see OAF. [U.S. collegiate, late 1900s, Munro]

pen yen (also **pinyon**) opium. For synonyms see OPE. [Chinese or mock-Chinese; U.S. underworld, 1900s or before]

pepper-belly (also **chili-belly, pepper-gut**) a derogatory nickname for a Mexican. For synonyms see MEX. [U.S. slang, 1900s]

per a prescription for drugs. [U.S. slang and drug culture, 1900s]

Perce the penis. See PERCY (sense 1). For synonyms see YARD.

perch the penis. Possibly the erect penis as a perch for a bird. [U.S. homosexual use, mid 1900s, Farrell]

percolate to sweat. [U.S. slang, mid 1900s]

Percy (also **Perce**) **1.** the penis; a personification of the penis. *Cf.* POINT PERCY AT THE PORCELAIN. **2.** an effeminate male; a nickname for an effeminate male. [both senses, British and U.S. colloquial, 1900s]

periodicity rag a menstrual cloth. [British slang, 1800s, Farmer and Henley]

perish 1. to die. [since the 1200s] **2.** to kill. [U.S. slang, 1900s]

perisher a drunken SPREE (sense 2), a "killer" of a drunken spree. See synonyms at SPREE. [Australian, 1900s, Baker]

periwinkle the female genitals. [British slang, 1800s, Farmer and Henley]

perk to vomit. Based on the image of a percolating coffee pot. [Australian, early 1900s, Baker]

perked intoxicated with alcohol. [British, World War 1, Fraser and Gibbons]

permafried high all the time. For synonyms see TALL. [U.S., late 1900s-pres.]

perma-grin the grin stuck on one's face while one is high. [U.S., late 1900s-pres.]

perp a criminal; the doer or perpetrator of something, especially of a crime. [U.S. police jargon, late 1900s]

Persian brown (also **Persian dust**) a brownish heroin from Iran or elsewhere in the Middle East. For synonyms see HEROIN. [U.S. drug culture, late 1900s]

person, the the genitals; the breasts. Occasionally refers to any part of the body which is not normally exposed in public. Cf. EXPOSURE OF THE PERSON.

Peruvian (flake) high-quality cocaine from Peru. Cf. FLAKE. For synonyms see NOSE-CANDY. [U.S. drug culture, late 1900s]

perve (also **perv**) 1. a sexual pervert. A truncation of "pervert," usually in reference to a homosexual male. [slang, early 1900s-pres.] 2. to be perverted; to behave in a perverted manner. 3. erotic; sexually arousing. 4. to OGLE (q.v.) at a woman. [senses 2-4 are Australian, 1900s]

perved drunk. For synonyms see WOOFLED. [U.S., late 1900s-pres.]

perve on, to to stare lustfully at a woman. Cf. OGLE, PERVE (sense 4). [Australian, 1900s, Baker]

pervert 1. a person who practices any nonorthogenital sexual act. 2. a person whose libido is directed at any thing, cause, or person other than a member of the opposite sex. 3. a homosexual male. Usually considered a rude epithet. [U.S. colloquial and slang, 1900s]

perverted a euphemism for "buggered" in expressions such as "I'll be perverted!" See BUGGER. [British, early 1900s, *Dictionary of Slang and Unconventional English*]

perve show a striptease show. Cf. PERVE (sense 3). [Australian, 1900s]

pervy 1. erotic. Cf. PERVE (sense 3). 2. the anus. Probably related in some way to PEDERASTY (q.v.). [U.S. underworld (tramps), early 1900s]

pestle 1. the penis; the mate of the MORTAR (q.v.). For synonyms see YARD. 2. to coit a woman. Implies pelvic thrusting, as with the pestle into the mortar. For synonyms see OCCUPY. [both senses, British slang, 1800s, Farmer and Henley]

pet to kiss and caress; to fondle the breasts and genitals of a woman. [U.S. colloquial, early 1900s-pres.]

petal an effeminate male. Cf. FLOWER (sense 4). For synonyms see FRIBBLE. [British military, World War II]

peter the penis. Occasionally capitalized. Cf. SAINT PETER. [primarily U.S., 1800s-pres.]

peter-cheater a sanitary napkin for use during a woman's monthly menstrual cycle. Cf. PETER = the penis. For synonyms see MANHOLE COVER. [U.S. slang, late 1900s]

peter-eater someone who performs oral sex on the penis. Cf. PETER. For synonyms see PICCOLO-PLAYER. [U.S. slang, late 1900s]

peter out to give out; to wear out. As a nonce term, to lose an erection; to become impotent in the act of copulating. Based on PETER (q.v.). [U.S. colloquial nonce, 1900s or before]

Peter Pan P.C.P. [U.S., late 1900s-pres.]

peter pansy a homosexual male; one who practices FELLATIO (q.v.). See PETER. [U.S. slang, mid 1900s]

peter-puffer someone who performs oral sex on a penis; a homosexual male. Cf. PETER. For synonyms see EPICENE, PICCOLO-PLAYER. [U.S. slang, late 1900s]

petrified intoxicated with alcohol. For synonyms see WOOFLED. [U.S. slang, early 1900s]

petticoat a woman, especially one considered as a sex object. [slang and colloquial since the 1600s]

petticoat-merchant 1. a pimp. 2. a prostitute. 3. a lecher. [all senses, British, 1600s-1800s]

petting-party a session of kissing, caressing, and fondling involving one or more couples. [U.S. slang, mid 1900s]

petty-house privy; an outhouse. Cf. LITTLE HOUSE, SMALLEST ROOM. For synonyms see AJAX. [British colloquial, 1800s]

pet up to arouse by petting and fondling. Cf. PET, RUB UP. [U.S. slang, mid 1900s]

peyote the tip of the peyote cactus, which contains MESCALINE (*q.v.*). [U.S. drug culture, mid 1900s-pres.]

peyote button the tip of the peyote cactus, which contains MESCALINE (*q.v.*), a hallucinogenic substance. Sometimes the tips are dried to be transported or sold, and look like shriveled buttons. [U.S. drug culture, mid 1900s-pres.]

P.F.M. "pure fucking magic"; absolutely astounding. [British, late 1900s-pres.]

P.G. 1. "pregnant." For synonyms see FRAGRANT. [U.S. colloquial euphemism, 1900s] **2.** "paregoric." *Cf.* PROCTER & GAMBLE. [U.S. drug culture, mid 1900s-pres.]

phallicize to coit a woman; to move the erect penis in and out of the vagina. [British slang, 1800s, Farmer and Henley]

phallic thimble a condom. A jocular play on PHALLIC SYMBOL (*q.v.*). For synonyms see EEL-SKIN. [British, early 1900s, *Dictionary of Slang and Unconventional English*]

PHAT 1. good; excellent. This is essentially a respelling of FAT, and can have all the senses that FAT has. [U.S., late 1900s-pres.] **2.** "pretty hips and thighs," said of a woman. [U.S., late 1900s-pres.] **3.** "pretty, hot, and tempting," said of a woman. [U.S., late 1900s-pres.]

phat-phree not cool; not PHAT. A play on *fat free*. [British, late 1900s-pres.]

phazed (also **phased**) intoxicated with marijuana. For synonyms see TALL. [U.S. drug culture, mid 1900s-pres.]

pheasant plucker a disliked person. For synonyms see SNOKE-HORN. [U.S., late 1900s-pres.]

phennies capsules of phenobarbital. *Cf.* BENNY. [U.S. drug culture, mid 1900s-pres.]

phumfed drug intoxicated. For synonyms see TALL. [U.S., late 1900s-pres.]

phungky cool. Another spelling for *funky*. [U.S., late 1900s-pres.]

Phyllis "syphilis." From the feminine name. For synonyms see SPECIFIC STOMACH. [British, 1900s]

physic 1. copulation. *Cf.* NIGHT-PHYSIC. For synonyms see SMOCKAGE. [since the early 1600s] **2.** a laxative; a purgative. [since the early 1600s] **3.** any strong alcoholic drink. From sense 2. For synonyms see BOOZE. [British slang, 1800s, Farmer and Henley]

P.I. a pimp. From "pimp." For synonyms see PIMP. [U.S. underworld, mid 1900s]

piano a CHAMBER POT (*q.v.*). From "pee-ano." Related semantically to TINKLE (*q.v.*). For synonyms see POT. [British slang, 1900s, *Dictionary of Slang and Unconventional English*]

pianoing using the fingers to find lost crack crystals on the floor. [U.S., late 1900s-pres.]

piccolo the penis, especially when used in FELLATIO (*q.v.*). *Cf.* BAGPIPE, FLUTE, SILENT FLUTE. [U.S. slang, 1900s]

piccolo-player a man or woman who performs PENILINGUS (*q.v.*). *Cf.* FLUTER. [U.S. slang, 1900s] The following synonyms refer to males unless indicated otherwise: BLOW-BOY, BLOW MONKEY, CANNIBAL, CATCH, CHOAD SMOKER, COCKSMOKER, COCKSUCKER, C–R, DICK-SUCKER, DICKY-LICKER, FLAKE, FUCKSAUCE GOBBLER, GOOT-GOBBLER, KNOB GOBBLER, LAPPER, LICK-SPIGOT, MOUTH-WHORE, MUNCHER-BOY, NEPHEW, NIBBLER, PANSY, PETER-EATER, PETER-PUFFER, PIECE OF SNATCH, PINK PANTS, PIPE SMOKER, PUNK, QUEEN, RECEIVER, SKIN-DIVER, SMOKER (female), SPIGOT-SUCKER, STAND, SUCKSTER, SUCKSTRESS (female).

pick a daisy to retire to urinate or defecate. For synonyms see RETIRE. [British colloquial euphemism, 1900s]

pick fruit to seek out homosexual males for sexual purposes or to rob them. From FRUIT (sense 4). See FRUIT-PICKER. [U.S. underworld, mid 1900s, Goldin, O'Leary, and Lipsius]

pick her cherry to DEFLOWER (*q.v.*) a woman. *Cf.* CHERRY (sense 1). [U.S. slang, mid 1900s-pres.]

pickle the penis; the same as GHERKIN. See PADDLE THE PICKLE and JERK ONE'S GHERKIN. [widespread, old and recurrent nonce]

pickle, in infected with a venereal disease. [cant, 1600s, B.E.]

pickled intoxicated with alcohol. Cf. CORNED, PRESERVED, SALTED-DOWN. [slang and colloquial, 1900s or before]

pickle-paddling male masturbation. From PADDLE THE PICKLE. For synonyms and related subjects see WASTE TIME. [U.S. slang, late 1900s, Lewin and Lewin]

picklock the penis. Cf. KEY (sense 1). For synonyms see YARD. [British slang, 1800s, Farmer and Henley]

pick up 1. to seek out and find a sexually loose woman. **2.** a sexually loose and available man or woman. Usually hyphenated in this sense. [widespread slang, 1800s-pres.] **3.** to meet a seller or MULE and take delivery of drugs. [U.S. drug culture, late 1900s] **4.** a successful act of taking delivery of drugs, as in *make a pickup*. [U.S. drug culture, 1900s] **5.** a dose or shot of drugs. [U.S. drug culture, early 1900s-pres.] **6.** a sudden burst of drug euphoria. [U.S. drug culture, early 1900s]

picnic 1. anything which is obtained easily. **2.** easily obtained sex or petting. **3.** a sexually available girl or woman. [all senses, U.S. slang and colloquial, 1900s]

piddle 1. urine. **2.** to urinate. For synonyms see WHIZ. [colloquial and slang, late 1700s-pres.] **3.** to waste time. A euphemism for PISS (sense 5). [colloquial, 1900s and before]

pie and mash an act of urination. Rhyming slang on *slash*. For synonyms see WHIZ. [U.S., late 1900s-pres.]

piece 1. any person. [1200s] **2.** a girl or a woman. Cf. ARTICLE (sense 1). [British and U.S. colloquial, 1300s-pres.] **3.** a harlot. [slang and colloquial, 1800s-pres.] **4.** a woman considered sexually. See the entries beginning with PIECE OF—. [slang, late 1800s-1900s] **5.** an orgasm; an act of copulation. Extended from sense 4. [U.S. slang, mid 1900s-pres.] **6.** An ounce of heroin. [U.S. drug culture, mid 1900s-pres.] **7.** a gun. [U.S. underground, late 1900s]

piece of ass 1. a woman considered as a sexual object. **2.** an act of copulation. [both senses, U.S. slang, mid 1900s-pres.]

piece of piss very easy. [Australian, mid 1900s-pres.]

piece of shit 1. a piece of junk. **2.** a lie; a deceptive story. **3.** a bad performance; a task done badly. **4.** a piece of bad luck. Cf. PILE OF SHIT. [all senses, U.S. slang, mid 1900s-pres.]

piece of snatch 1. a sexually loose woman; a woman who is known to copulate. Cf. SNATCH (sense 3). **2.** a homosexual male, especially a RECEIVER (*q.v.*). [both senses, U.S. underworld and slang, mid 1900s]

piece of stuff a woman considered as a sexual object. Cf. STUFF (sense 3). For synonyms see TAIL. [since the 1700s]

piece of tail 1. a woman considered as a sexual object. For synonyms see TAIL. **2.** an act of copulation. Cf. TAIL. For synonyms see SMOCKAGE. [both senses, U.S. slang, mid 1900s-pres.]

piece of trade a prostitute. Cf. TRADE (sense 1). [U.S. slang, mid 1900s]

pie-eyed (also **pye-eyed**) intoxicated with alcohol. For synonyms see WOOFLED. [U.S. slang, late 1800s-pres.]

piffed 1. dead; killed. Also **pifted.** For synonyms see DONE FOR. [U.S., 1900s] **2.** intoxicated with alcohol. [U.S. slang and colloquial, early 1900s-pres.]

piffled intoxicated with alcohol. For synonyms see WOOFLED. [U.S. slang and colloquial, early 1900s-pres.]

pifflicated (also **pifficated**) intoxicated with alcohol. [U.S. colloquial and slang, early 1900s-pres.]

pig 1. an officer, a police officer or a military officer. For synonyms see FLATFOOT. [originally cant; widespread slang, early 1800s-pres.; U.S. underworld or revolutionary use, mid 1900s-pres.] **2.** a prostitute. [U.S. underworld, mid 1900s, Goldin, O'Leary, and Lipsius] **3.** an ugly young woman, especially if fat or dirty. For synonyms see BUFFARILLA. [U.S. slang, mid 1900s-pres.] **4.** a promiscuous girl or woman; one who will WALLOW (q.v.) readily. [U.S. slang, mid 1900s-pres.] **5.** any dirty or slovenly person. [U.S. colloquial, 1900s or before]

piggies large female breasts. For synonyms see BOSOM. [U.S., late 1900s-pres.]

pig foot marijuana. For synonyms see MARI. [U.S. drug culture, 1900s, Abel]

pig killer the drug phencyclidine, P.C.P. Cf. HOG (sense 3). For synonyms see P.C.P. [U.S. drug culture, late 1900s-pres.]

pig-meat a sexually loose woman; a prostitute. Cf. PIG (sense 2). For synonyms see LAY. [originally black use; U.S. slang, mid 1900s-pres.]

pigmobile a police car. [U.S., late 1900s-pres.]

pig-party an act of group rape; a GANG BANG. [British slang, 1900s, McDonald]

pig's bum wrong. [Australian, late 1900s-pres.]

pig's knockers pig's testicles. Cf. KNACKERS, KNOCKERS (sense 2). [U.S. rural colloquial, 1900s or before]

pigwash See HOGWASH.

pike the penis, especially the erect penis. [widespread nonce; from *Much Ado About Nothing* (Shakespeare)]

piker 1. a petty thief. [1300s] **2.** a coward; a quitter. **3.** a cheapskate. [both senses, U.S. slang and colloquial, early 1900s-pres.]

pikestaff the penis. For synonyms see YARD. [the standard meaning since the 1300s; this sense, British nonce, 1700s]

pile to copulate. For synonyms see OCCUPY. [U.S. black use, mid 1900s-pres.]

pile-driver the penis, especially the erect penis. Cf. SCREWDRIVER. [colloquial and nonce, 1800s-pres.]

pile-driving copulation. Cf. PILE. For synonyms see SMOCKAGE. [colloquial, 1800s-1900s]

pile of shit 1. junk; anything worthless. **2.** a worthless person. **3.** nonsense; lies; a deceptive story. Cf. PIECE OF SHIT. [all senses, U.S. slang, mid 1900s-pres.]

pilfered intoxicated with alcohol. For synonyms see WOOFLED. [U.S., 1900s]

pill 1. a pill or pellet of opium. [U.S. underworld, early 1900s or before] **2.** an obnoxious person; a PAIN IN THE NECK (q.v.). [U.S. colloquial, mid 1900s-pres.] **3.** a birth control pill, "the pill." [U.S. colloquial, mid 1900s-pres.]

pill-head someone who takes drugs illicitly in tablet or capsule form. [U.S. drug culture, mid 1900s-pres.]

pillow biter the RECEIVER in an act of PEDERASTY. [British slang, 1900s, McDonald]

pillowed pregnant. As if a woman were wearing a pillow over her abdomen. For synonyms see FRAGRANT. [U.S. slang, mid 1900s]

pillowy large-breasted. From the softness of a pillow and "billowy." Cf. BABY PILLOWS. [euphemistic, 1900s, *Dictionary of Slang and Unconventional English*]

pill-pusher (also **pill-roller**) **1.** a physician. [U.S. slang and colloquial, early 1900s-pres.] **2.** a doctor who is known to be willing to supply narcotics illegally. [U.S. drug culture, mid 1900s-pres.]

pimp 1. a man who secures customers for one or more prostitutes. **2.** a man who lives off the earnings of one or more prostitutes. Cf. PONCE (q.v.). [both since the 1600s] **3.** to secure customers for one or more prostitutes. **4.** to live off the earnings of one or more prostitutes. [both since the 1600s] Synonyms: ALPHONSE, APPLE-SQUIRE, APRON-SQUIRE, ASS-PEDDLER, BELSWAGGER, BLUDGEONER, BOSS PIMP, BROTHER OF THE GUSSET, BUTTOCK-BROKER, BUTT-PEDDLER, CADET, COCK-BAWD, COCK-PIMP, CRACK SALESMAN, EASTMAN, ECNOP, FAG, FAKER, FANCY MAN, FISH AND SHRIMP, FISH-MONGER, FLESH-BROKER, FLESH-PEDDLER, GAGGER, GO-BETWEEN, GORILLA, GORILLA PIMP, HONEY MAN, HOON, HUSTLER, ICEBERG SLIM, JACK-GAGGER, JOE RONCE, JOHNNIE RONCE, MAC-

GIMP, MACK, MACKEREL, MACK MAN, MCGIMPER, MISSIONARY, PANDER, PANDERER, PEE-EYE, PETTICOAT-MERCHANT, P.I., PIMPLE, PONCE, PROCURER, PROSSER, RONI, RUFFIAN, RUNNER, RUSTLER, SILVER SPOON, SKIRT-MAN, SOUTENEUR, SPORTING-GIRL'S MANAGER, STABLEBOSS, SUGAR PIMP, TOUTE, WELFARE PIMP, WHISKIN. **5.** a male prostitute for homosexual males. From senses 1 and 2. [U.S., mid 1900s]

pimp dust cocaine. For synonyms see NOSE-CANDY. [U.S. black use, late 1900s, Folb]

pimple 1. a swelling on the skin. From an accumulation of material in a sebaceous gland. For synonyms see BURBLE. **2.** syphilis; a syphilitic pimple or rash. **3.** a PIMP (q.v.) or procurer. A dysphemism for "pimp." [U.S. slang, early 1900s, Monteleone] **4.** a baby's penis. [British slang or colloquial, 1800s, *Dictionary of Slang and Unconventional English*]

pimpmobile (also **pimp ride**) a big gaudy car, as driven by a PIMP. [U.S. black use, late 1900s]

pimp steak a frankfurter. [primarily black use; U.S. slang, mid 1900s or before, Major]

pimp stick a cigarette. [U.S. underworld and World War I, early 1900s]

pimp talk the speech used by pimps and procurers. [U.S. slang and black use, mid 1900s-pres.]

pimp up to doll up; to fix oneself up like a fancy-dressed pimp. A dysphemism based on "primp up." See PANSY UP, QUEER UP.

pin 1. the penis. [colloquial and nonce, early 1600s-pres.] **2.** to copulate with a woman; to use a PIN (sense 1) on a woman. [British, 1900s or before] **3.** a thin marijuana cigarette. Also **pinner.** [U.S. drug culture, mid 1900s-pres.] **4.** (also **pin gun**) a hypodermic syringe and needle; a pin (sewing needle, safety pin, etc.) and medicine dropper used to inject drugs. [U.S. drug culture, late 1900s] **5.** a drug seller. Probably from *kingpin*. [U.S. drug culture, late 1900s]

pinch-fart (also **pinch-gut**) a stingy person, a man so stingy that he tries to retain intestinal gas. [British colloquial, 1600s to the 1800s]

pinch hitter someone who is hired by a debilitated addict to inject drugs. From the baseball expression. [U.S. drug culture, late 1900s, Kaiser]

pinch one off to defecate. For synonyms see EASE ONESELF. [British, late 1900s-pres.]

pinch-prick 1. a prostitute. **2.** a wife who demands copulation; a wife who insists on receiving all of her husband's sexual attention. [both senses, British slang, 1800s, Farmer and Henley]

pineapple a male homosexual. For synonyms see EPICENE. [British, late 1900s-pres.]

pinga the penis. [attested as Spanish slang, late 1800s, Farmer and Henley; U.S. slang, mid 1900s-pres.]

pink elephants the DELIRIUM TREMENS (q.v.), especially in the expression "see pink elephants." Visions of BLUE DEVILS (sense 2), red spiders, and red monkeys are typical of the hallucinations experienced while having the D.T.s (q.v.). For synonyms see ORKORKS. [U.S. slang and colloquial, mid 1900s-pres.]

Pink Floyd a nickname for a whale's penis. A recent interest in close-up whale watching has drawn attention to this enormous appendage. From the name of the rock group. [U.S., late 1900s]

pink lady a Seconal (trademark) capsule. *Cf.* PINK (sense 3). For synonyms see SEC. [U.S. drug culture, mid 1900s-pres.]

pinko 1. intoxicated with alcohol. [Australian slang, early 1900s] **2.** a communist. [U.S. slang, mid 1900s]

pink oboe a penis; the penis [of a Caucasian]. For synonyms see GENITALS, YARD. [British slang, 1900s, McDonald]

pink palace in the black forest, the the vagina. For synonyms see GENITALS, MONOSYLLABLE. [U.S., late 1900s-pres.]

pink pants a CATAMITE (q.v.); an effeminate male homosexual. For synonyms see BRONCO. [U.S. underworld, mid 1900s, Goldin, O'Leary, and Lipsius]

pink-spiders the DELIRIUM TREMENS (*q.v.*). [slang, late 1800s-1900s]

pink swirl (also **pink**) the drug L.S.D. (*q.v.*). [U.S. drug culture, mid 1900s-pres.]

pint pot 1. a beer merchant. [colloquial, late 1500s] 2. a drunkard. Rhyming slang for SOT (sense 2). [British, 1900s, *Dictionary of Rhyming Slang*]

pin-up girl 1. a girl or woman who appears partially clothed on posters and calendars. 2. a girl or woman who is appealing enough to appear on posters and calendars. [both senses, U.S. slang and colloquial, mid 1900s]

pinwheel a fat marijuana cigarette. For synonyms see MEZZROLL. [U.S., late 1900s-pres.]

pioneer of nature the penis. See GARGANTUA'S PENIS. [mid 1600s (Urquhart)]

pip, the syphilis. For synonyms see SPECIFIC STOMACH. [late 1500s-1600s]

pipe 1. the penis. *Cf.* WATER-PIPE (sense 2). [colloquial and nonce since the 1600s] 2. the female genitals. Comparing the vagina to the inside of a pipe. *Cf.* WATER-PIPE. [British slang, 1800s, Farmer and Henley] 3. the urethra of the male or female. [slang and colloquial, 1800s-1900s] 4. a user of marijuana. From WATER-PIPE (sense 1). [U.S. drug culture, mid 1900s-pres.]

pipe-cleaner 1. the vagina. For synonyms see PASSAGE. 2. a woman considered as a sexual object. The PIPE (sense 1) is the penis. [both senses, slang, 1900s or before]

pipe-hitter 1. an opium smoker. [U.S. underworld, mid 1900s or before] 2. a marijuana smoker. *Cf.* PIPE (sense 4). [U.S. drug culture, mid 1900s-pres.]

pipe-job an act of FELLATIO (*q.v.*). Usually a request made of a prostitute. *Cf.* BLOW-JOB, PIPE (sense 1). [U.S. slang, mid 1900s-pres.]

piper a drug user who smokes a drug

in a pipe. [U.S. drug culture, late 1900s]

pipe smoker a fellator. For synonyms see PICCOLOPLAYER. [U.S., late 1900s-pres.]

pirate's dream a flat chest on a woman. Word play for "sunken [treasure] chest." [U.S. slang, mid 1900s-pres.]

piss 1. urine. 2. to urinate. In some parts of the English-speaking world this term can be used in polite conversation without giving offense. [onomatopoetic, from Vulgar Latin; both since the 1200s] Disguises: COUSIN SIS, MICKEY 'BLISS, MIKE BLISS, RATTLE AND HISS, SNAKE'S HISS, THAT AND THIS. 3. an exclamation, "Piss!" 4. any weak beer or alcoholic drink. *Cf.* PANTHER PISS, PISS-MAKER, SQUAW PISS, TIGER PISS, WITCH-PISS. [slang, 1900s] 5. to waste time.

piss and vinegar energy; vigor. [U.S. colloquial, 1900s or before]

piss and wind nonsense; lies and deceit. Apparently in avoidance of BULL SHIT (*q.v.*). [early 1900s, *Dictionary of Slang and Unconventional English*]

pissant around to waste time; to goof off, a way to express "piss around" by using the non-taboo term PIS-ANT (*q.v.*). [Australian, mid 1900s, Baker]

piss artist a drunkard. For synonyms see ALCHY. [British slang, late 1900s]

piss-ass 1. a worthless JERK. For synonyms see OAF. 2. worthless; piddling. [both senses, U.S., 1900s]

piss blood to work very hard. [slang and colloquial, 1800s-1900s; other senses since the 1600s]

piss-bowl a CHAMBER POT (*q.v.*). For synonyms see POT. [mid 1500s]

piss call a waking up of people before the latrines are to be closed for cleaning or some other purpose. [U.S. military, 1900s, *Soldier Talk*]

piss-can a toilet or a chamber pot. *Cf.* CAN (sense 1). [U.S. colloquial, 1900s or before]

piss-cutter a very excellent thing, person, or situation. Someone who can do the impossible. *Cf.* PISS-WHIZ. [U.S. slang, 1900s]

pissed 1. intoxicated with alcohol. *Cf.* PISSED-UP. For synonyms see WOOFLED. [British and U.S. slang, early 1900s-pres.] **2.** very angry. A truncation of PISSED-OFF (*q.v.*). [U.S. slang, 1900s]

pissed as a fart very drunk. For synonyms see WOOFLED. [British slang, late 1900s]

pissed as a newt drunk. *Cf.* NEWTED. For synonyms see WOOFLED. [British slang, 1900s and probably before]

pissed as a parrot drunk. For synonyms see WOOFLED. [Australian, late 1900s-pres.]

pissed-off (also **pissed**) very angry. *Cf.* P'D OFF. [U.S. slang, mid 1900s-pres.]

pissed-up (also **pissed**) intoxicated with alcohol. [British slang, wartime]

pissed up to the eyebrows intoxicated with alcohol. An elaboration of PISSED (sense 1). [British military, early 1900s, *Dictionary of Slang and Unconventional English*]

piss-elegant quite elegant; pretentious. *Cf.* PISS-POOR. [U.S. slang, mid 1900s-pres.]

pisser 1. the penis. For synonyms see YARD. **2.** the female genitals. For synonyms see MONOSYLLABLE. [both senses, colloquial and nonce, 1800s-pres.] **3.** any difficult task or situation; a task which is likely to make you angry or PISSED (sense 2). **4.** a urinal. [British and U.S. colloquial and nonce, 1800s-pres.] **5.** a really superb party or spree. *Cf.* PISS-ELEGANT. [U.S. slang, mid 1900s-pres.] **6.** a joke funny enough to make one wet one's pants. [British slang, late 1900s]

piss-factory a tavern. Refers to the diuretic properties of beer. [British and U.S. slang, 1800s-1900s]

piss-flap(pers)s the labia. For synonyms see MONOSYLLABLE. [British, late 1900s-pres.]

piss freak one who derives sexual pleasure from urine. [U.S. slang, mid 1900s-pres.]

piss hard-on a morning erection; a

urinary erection. *Cf.* PISS-PROUD. [colloquial, 1900s or before]

piss-head 1. an oaf; a foolish jerk. [U.S. slang, 1900s] **2.** a heavy drinker; a drunkard. *Cf.* PISSED (sense 1). [slang, 1900s]

piss-hole a urinal; any place as unpleasant as a urinal. [British slang, 1900s]

pisshouse 1. a police station. **2.** a W.C.; a privy. *Cf.* PISSER (sense 4). [both senses, U.S. slang, mid 1900s]

pissing minimal; worthless; brief. [since the 1500s]

pissing-drunk heavily intoxicated with alcohol. For synonyms see WOOFLED. [British slang, 1800s or before]

pissing-match 1. a hopeless waste of time; a competition of no consequence. [U.S. slang, 1900s] **2.** an argument. [U.S., mid 1900s-pres.]

pissing-while a minimal amount of time; the amount of time it takes to urinate; the amount of time it takes a drink of fluid to be assimilated and expelled as urine. *Cf.* FARTING-SPELL, PISSING. [colloquial, early 1500s]

piss in someone's pocket to attempt to ingratiate oneself with someone. [British slang, mid 1900s-pres.]

piss-maker 1. a heavy drinker. [since the 1700s] **2.** alcoholic drink; beer. [U.S. slang, 1900s]

piss off 1. to depart in a hurry. Also used as an order meaning "beat it!" *Cf.* DRAG ASS. [British slang, 1900s or before] **2.** to make someone very angry. Also **piss someone off.** [U.S. slang, mid 1900s-pres.]

piss oneself laughing to laugh so hard that one wets one's pants. [British, late 1900s-pres.]

Piss on it! "To hell with it!" For synonyms see 'ZOUNDS. [U.S., late 1900s-pres.]

piss on someone or something 1. to urinate on someone or something. For synonyms see WHIZ. [old] **2.** to degrade or denigrate someone or something [1900s, if not before]

piss on someone's parade to ruin

someone's event or plans for something. An extension of general slang *rain on someone's parade.* [British slang, late 1900s]

piss pins and needles to have gonorrhea. From the pain experienced in urinating. Usually said of males. [British slang, late 1700s, Grose]

pisspiration a dysphemism for "sweat." [U.S. jocular colloquial and nonce, early 1900s]

piss-poor really terrible; low-quality or ineffectual. *Cf.* PISS-ELEGANT. [British and U.S. slang, early 1900s-pres.]

piss-pot 1. a CHAMBER POT (*q.v.*). [colloquial, 1400s to the 1900s] **2.** a physician; an early urologist. A medical man who diagnosed diseases by studying urine. [1500s] **3.** a rotten rascal; a real stinker. For synonyms see SNOKE-HORN. [British slang, 1800s and nonce elsewhere]

piss-proud pertaining to a morning erection. *Cf.* PISS·HARD-ON. [British, early 1800s or before, *Lexicon Balatronicum*]

piss something away to waste all of something, such as time or money. [1900s]

piss-ugly very ugly. [U.S. slang, late 1900s]

piss-up a drinking spree; a BENDER (*q.v.*). [British slang, 1900s]

piss-warm warm; lukewarm; the temperature of new urine. [1900s]

piss wet soaked. [British, late 1900s-pres.]

piss-whiz very excellent. *Cf.* PISS-CUTTER. [U.S. slang, early 1900s]

pissy 1. small [Australian, mid 1900s-pres.] **2.** weak; diluted. [British, late 1900s-pres.]

piss(y)-faced drunk. For synonyms see WOOFLED. [U.S. and elsewhere, 1900s]

pistol the penis. See GUN. [from *Henry IV, Part Two* (Shakespeare)]

piston-job an act of PENILINGUS (*q.v.*).

piston rod (also **piston**) the penis. *Cf.*

CYLINDER. For synonyms see YARD. [slang, late 1900s]

pit 1. the female genitals. *Cf.* BOTTOM-LESS-PIT. [British slang, late 1600s] **2.** hell, especially as "the pit." [U.S. colloquial, 1900s and before]

PITA [a] "pain in the ass." [U.S., late 1900s-pres.]

pitch 1. the INSERTOR in PEDERASTY or PENILINGUS (all *q.v.*). The opposite of CATCH (sense 1). [U.S. slang, mid 1900s-pres.] **2.** a fat or ugly young woman; an undesirable woman. A blend of "pig" and "bitch." [U.S. college slang, mid 1900s-pres., Underwood] **3.** to ejaculate [U.S., late 1900s-pres.]

pitch a bitch to complain about something; to present a complaint. [U.S. slang, late 1900s]

pitch a tent to get an erection underneath clothing or bedsheets. [U.S., late 1900s-pres.]

pitch a tent in one's shorts to get an erection in one's pants. [British, late 1900s-pres.]

pit-hole 1. a grave. For synonyms see LAST ABODE. [British, early 1600s] **2.** the female genitals. See PIT (sense 1). [British, 1800s, Farmer and Henley]

pito the penis. For synonyms see YARD. [U.S., late 1900s-pres.]

pits, the 1. the armpits. **2.** anything really bad. [both senses, U.S. slang, mid 1900s-pres.]

pit stop 1. a pause to urinate. From the name of the refueling stop in automobile racing. [U.S. slang, mid 1900s-pres.] **2.** an underarm deodorant. Because it stops armpit odor. [U.S. slang and nonce, mid 1900s-pres.] **3.** a departure to the toilet. Based on sense 1. For synonyms see RETIRE.

pitty-tink the color pink. From "titty-pink," a deliberate spoonerism. [U.S. slang, mid 1900s]

pity fuck an act of copulation permitted by a woman who feels sorry for a man. Probably nonce. For synonyms see SMOCKAGE. [U.S. slang, late 1900s]

pity party a session of feeling sorry for oneself. [U.S., late 1900s-pres.]

pixilated intoxicated with alcohol; silly from alcohol. From a term meaning "daffy." [U.S. slang, mid 1800s]

pizen whisky. A dialect form of the word "poison." *Cf.* PANTHER PIZEN. [U.S. slang and colloquial, late 1800s-1900s]

pizened (also **poisoned**) pregnant. *Cf.* STUNG BY A SERPENT. [U.S. dialect (Ozarks), Randolph and Wilson]

pizza face See CRATER-FACE.

pizza man a derogatory nickname for an Italian. [U.S. slang, late 1900s]

pizza-puss See CRATER-FACE.

pizzle (also **peezel, pissel, pizell**) 1. the penis of an animal, especially that of a bull. [since the 1500s] 2. the penis. For synonyms see YARD. [since the 1600s] 3. to coit a woman; to copulate. For synonyms see OCCUPY. [British colloquial, 1600s-1800s]

place 1. a privy. *Cf.* LOCUS. For synonyms see AJAX. [euphemistic, 1800s-1900s] 2. the male or female genitals or pubic areas. *Cf.* AREA, PARTS. [euphemistic and nonce, 1700s-pres.]

place where you cough the bathroom; a W.C. Because when you are there, you cough to warn an approaching person of your presence. This practice includes sneezing, whistling, shuffling, and clearing the throat. [attested as British, early 1900s, *Dictionary of Slang and Unconventional English*]

planted alcohol intoxicated. For synonyms see WOOFLED. [U.S. slang, late 1900s]

plants the hallucinogenic substance PEYOTE. Plants as opposed to chemicals such as P.C.P. and L.S.D. [U.S. drug culture, late 1900s] See also LEGUME, ORGANIC STUFF.

plant the oats to coit a woman. *Cf.* HAVE ONE'S OATS, OAT-BIN, SOW ONE'S WILD OATS. "Oats" refers to semen. [U.S. colloquial and euphemistic, early 1900s]

plasma coffee; caffeine. [U.S., late 1900s-pres.]

plass (also **plac**) Placidyl™, a sedative. [U.S. drug culture, late 1900s, Kaiser]

plastered intoxicated with alcohol. *Cf.* STUCCOED. [British and U.S. slang, early 1900s-pres.]

plate someone to perform oral sex on someone. [British, late 1900s-pres.]

play to copulate. For synonyms see OCCUPY. [euphemistic since the late 1300s]

play around 1. to court or copulate with a number of members of the opposite sex. 2. to have extramarital sexual intercourse. 3. to tease and trifle with members of the opposite sex. [all senses, U.S. colloquial, mid 1900s-pres.]

play bouncy-bouncy to copulate [with] someone. For synonyms see OCCUPY. [British, mid 1900s-pres.]

play camels to get drunk; to see how much drink one can store up; to guzzle beverage alcohol. [British slang, late 1800s, Ware] Synonyms: BARREL, BEEZZLE, BELT THE GRAPE, BEVVY, BIBBLE, COP THE BREWERY, CRAPULATE, DEBAUCH, GUZZLE, SPREE, TIPPLE.

play cars and trucks to coit. Rhyming slang for "fucks." Refers to driving in and out. [Australian slang, 1900s] See also PUSH IN THE TRUCK.

played having to do with a portion of marijuana (cigarette or other) that has had all of the active principle smoked out of it. Short for *played out*. *Cf.* CASHED. [U.S. drug culture, late 1900s]

player 1. a drug user. 2. a drug seller. [both senses, U.S. drug culture, late 1900s] 3. a sexually promiscuous person; someone obsessed with copulation. [U.S. slang, mid 1900s-pres.]

play funny buggers to deceive or cheat someone. [Australian, mid 1900s-pres.]

play grab-ass to fool around sexually; to pet; to feel someone up. For synonyms see FIRKYTOODLE. [widespread, late 1900s]

play hide the salami (also **bury the weenie, play hide the sausage, play hide the weenie**) to copulate. For synonyms see OCCUPY. [U.S. slang, late 1900s]

play hospital to copulate *Cf.* PLAY DOCTOR (sense 2). [Australian, 1900s]

play house 1. to copulate; to play at being man and wife. [U.S. colloquial, early 1900s-pres.] **2.** for an unmarried man and woman to live together. [U.S. colloquial, mid 1900s-pres.]

play lighthouses to have an erection while in the bathtub. [British, mid 1900s-pres.]

play monopoly to smoke marijuana. [U.S., late 1900s-pres.]

play off to masturbate. For synonyms see WASTE TIME. [British, 1800s or before, Farmer and Henley]

play one's ace to coit; said of a woman. *Cf.* ACE (sense 2). [British slang, 1800s, Farmer and Henley]

play the organ to copulate. *Cf.* FAMILY ORGAN, ORGAN. [colloquial and jocular, 1900s or before]

plaything 1. the penis. *Cf.* BAUBLE (sense 1), TOY (sense 4), TRIFLE (sense 3). [British and U.S. colloquial, 1800s-pres.] **2.** the female genitals. *Cf.* TOY (sense 2). [British and U.S. colloquial, 1800s-pres.] **3.** a sexually easy woman. For synonyms see LAY. [U.S. slang, early 1900s-pres.]

play tonsil hockey to kiss deeply; to French kiss. [U.S. collegiate and general slang. late 1900s] See also BOX TONSILS, GIVE SOMEONE A TONSILLECTOMY, SWAB SOMEONE'S TONSILS, TONSIL-SWABBING.

pleasantly plastered intoxicated with alcohol. *Cf.* PLASTERED, STUCCOED. [U.S. slang, early 1900s pres.]

plink a cheap and inferior local wine. Based on PLONK (sense 1). [Australian, 1900s, Baker]

ploll-cat a prostitute. Possibly a typographical error for POLECAT (*q.v.*). [attested by Farmer and Henley and Halliwell]

plonk 1. a cheap grade of alcohol or hard liquor. Also **plunk.** [originally Australian; from the French *vin blanc;* slang, World War II] **2.** a bore; a jerk. [U.S. slang, mid 1900s]

plonk-dot a wine-drinker; a WINO (*q.v.*). DOT (*q.v.*) is the anus. [Australian, 1900s]

plonked intoxicated with alcohol, done in by PLONK (sense 1). [U.S. slang, mid 1900s]

plonker the penis. For synonyms see GENITALS, YARD. [British slang, 1900s, McDonald]

plonko a drunkard. *Cf.* PLONK (sense 1). [Australian, early 1900s]

plootered intoxicated with alcohol. For synonyms see WOOFLED. [British and U.S. slang, 1900s]

ploughed intoxicated with alcohol. *Cf.* PLOWED (sense 1).

plow to copulate [with] someone aggresivly. For synonyms see OCCUPY. [British and U.S., mid 1900s-pres.]

plowed (also **ploughed**) **1.** intoxicated with alcohol. [British and U.S. slang and colloquial, 1800s-pres.] **2.** having been copulated with. *Cf.* PLOW (sense 3).

plow the back forty to copulate. Possibly a reference to anal copulation. For synonyms see SMOCKAGE. [U.S. slang, late 1900s, probably recurrent nonce]

pluck 1. to coit; to deflower; to pluck a girl's FLOWER (sense 2). [British euphemism, 1600s] **2.** to coit. A disguise of "fuck." Also **plook.** See SKLOOK. [U.S., mid 1900s or before] **3.** cheap wine. Possibly related to PLONK (*q.v.*). [U.S. slang, mid 1900s-pres.]

pluck a rose to retire to a garden privy or to a W.C. *Cf.* DROP A ROSE. [colloquial since the 1700s]

plug 1. to coit a woman. [slang since the 1700s] **2.** a tampon. [U.S. colloquial or slang, mid 1900s] **3.** the penis. [widespread nonce and slang]

plug in both ways [for a male] to be bisexual. [British, mid 1900s-pres.]

plug-tail the penis. For synonyms see YARD. [British, 1700s-1900s, Grose]

pluke to copulate. For synonyms see OCCUPY. [U.S., late 1900s-pres.]

plums the human testicles. From their shape. [U.S., 1900s]

plunger the penis. For synonyms see GENITALS, YARD. [U.S. slang, late 1900s]

plurry bloody. For synonyms see BLOODY. [from the aboriginal pronunciation of "bloody"; Australian, 1800s, *Dictionary of Slang and Unconventional English*]

plush the pubic hair. *Cf.* FUR (sense 1). [British slang, 1800s, Farmer and Henley] Synonyms: BRAKES, BUSH, FUD, PUBES, SCRUBBING-BRUSH, SHORT AND CURLY, SPORRAN, TUFT. See also DOWNSHIRE.

P-maker the male or female genitals. Euphemistic for PISS-MAKER (*q.v.*). For synonyms see GENITALS. [British slang, 1800s, Farmer and Henley] See also PISS-MAKER.

P.M.S. monster a menstruating woman. *Cf.* P.M.S. [U.S. collegiate, late 1900s, Munro]

P.O. 1. a "piss-off," an oaf or a jerk. **2.** to make someone very angry or PISSED-OFF (*q.v.*). [both senses, U.S. slang, mid 1900s]

pockes syphilis. An early spelling of POX (*q.v.*). [1500s or before]

pocket billiards [for a male] to play with one's genitals with a hand in a pocket. [British, mid 1900s-pres.]

pocket-book the female genitals. *Cf.* MONEY. [U.S. black use, 1900s]

pocket-pool (also **pocket-billiards**) the act of a male playing with his genitals through his trouser pockets. *Cf.* STICK AND BANGERS. [U.S. slang, mid 1900s]

pocket-rocket the penis. For synonyms see YARD. [U.S., late 1900s-pres.]

pocket the red to coit a woman; to penetrate a woman. From billiards. [British slang, 1800s, *Dictionary of Slang and Unconventional English*]

pocket-thunder an audible breaking of wind. *Cf.* THUNDER-BOX. [British slang, 1800s, Farmer and Henley]

P.O.d very angry and upset; PISSED-OFF. Partially euphemistic. [widespread, mid 1900s-pres.]

pod 1. marijuana or a marijuana ciga-

rette. *Cf.* POT. [U.S. drug culture, mid 1900s-pres.] **2.** the posteriors; the anus.

pod, in pregnant. For synonyms see FRAGRANT. [British, late 1800s]

poddy 1. pregnant. *Cf.* POD, IN. [British, 1800s] **2.** intoxicated with alcohol. *Cf.* POTTED (sense 1). [British and U.S. slang, late 1800s-1900s]

poet's corner a toilet; a W.C. [U.S. slang, early 1900s]

poger a CATAMITE (*q.v.*). Possibly connected with some sense of ROGER (*q.v.*). For synonyms see BRONCO. [U.S. underworld, mid 1900s, Goldin, O'Leary, and Lipsius]

poggled (also **puggled**) crazy; intoxicated with alcohol. [British, Fraser and Gibbons]

pogie (also **pody**) the vagina. For synonyms see MONOSYLLABLE. [U.S. slang, 1900s]

pogo-pogo cocaine. For synonyms see NOSE-CANDY. [U.S. drug culture, late 1900s, Abel]

pogy (also **pogey**) intoxicated with alcohol; mildly drunk. [British and U.S. colloquial, 1800s-1900s]

point the penis, especially the glans penis. *Cf.* LANCE. [colloquial and nonce since the 1600s or before]

pointer the penis. For synonyms see YARD. [British slang, 1800s, Farmer and Henley]

point-of-attraction the female genitals. *Cf.* CENTER OF ATTRACTION. For synonyms see MONOSYLLABLE. [British, late 1700s]

point Percy at the porcelain to urinate. PERCY (*q.v.*) is the penis. *Cf.* TRAIN TERRENCE ON THE TERRACOTTA. For synonyms see WHIZ. [contrived jocular euphemism; Australian, 1900s or before]

points the nipples; the breasts; conical and pointed breasts. Heard in the ambiguous catch phrase "Well, she has her points." [U.S. colloquial and slang, 1900s]

poke 1. to copulate with a woman. Also **poge, pogh, pogue.** [colloquial since the early 1700s or before] **2.** copulation; an act of copulation. [British and U.S., 1800s-1900s] **3.** a sexually loose woman; a mistress; a concubine. [slang, 1800s-1900s] **4.** a lazy person. From "slow-poke." [U.S. colloquial, 1800s-1900s] **5.** the scrotum. In the dialect sense "sack." [attested as dialect (Ozarks), Randolph and Wilson] **6.** a puff of a marijuana cigarette; the same as TOKE (sense 2). [U.S. drug culture, mid 1900s-pres.]

poke a hontas to copulate. For synonyms see OCCUPY. [U.S., late 1900s-pres.]

poke-hole the female genitals. For synonyms see MONOSYLLABLE. [British slang, 1800s, Farmer and Henley]

poker the penis, especially the erect penis. *Cf.* RED-HOT POKER. [slang and nonce since the 1700s]

poker-breaker (also **poker-climber**) **1.** a prostitute. **2.** a wife. For synonyms see WARDEN. [both senses, British slang, 1800s, Farmer and Henley]

poke squid to copulate. For synonyms see OCCUPY. [U.S., late 1900s-pres.]

poking through the whiskers copulating. [U.S. collegiate, late 1900s]

polack a derogatory nickname for a Polish man or woman. From the nonderogatory Polish word for a Polish male. [since the 1600s]

pole 1. the penis, especially the erect penis. [widespread recurrent nonce; British and U.S. slang and colloquial, 1800s-1900s and certainly long before] **2.** to coit a woman. [British and U.S. slang and colloquial, 1800s-pres.]

pole, up the 1. pregnant. Also **stick, up the.** The "pole" is a vague reference to the penis. *Cf.* GET UP THE POLE. [widespread slang, 1900s] **2.** intoxicated with alcohol. *Cf.* HALF UP THE POLE. [slang, late 1800s-1900s]

polecat a mean and deceitful person, usually male. For synonyms see SNOKE-HORN. [U.S., early 1900s-pres.]

polished-up (also **polished**) intoxicated with alcohol. For synonyms see WOOFLED. [U.S. slang, early 1900s]

polluted 1. intoxicated with alcohol. [U.S. slang, early 1900s-pres.] **2.** intoxicated with drugs or marijuana. [U.S. drug culture and slang, mid 1900s-pres.]

ponce 1. a pimp; a solicitor for a prostitute. **2.** to solicit for a prostitute. [both senses, British and U.S., 1800s-1900s] **3.** any man supported by a woman. From sense 1. [colloquial, 1800s] **4.** a young and vigorous lover of an older woman. [U.S. underworld, early 1900s, Irwin]

ponce on to live on the earnings of a prostitute. [British, 1800s]

pond scum 1. a disliked person. For synonyms see SNOKE-HORN. [U.S., late 1900s-pres.] **2.** hair dressing. [U.S., late 1900s-pres.]

pong 1. to smell. [Australian, mid 1900s-pres.] **2.** a smell. [Australian, mid 1900s-pres.]

pony and trap dung; to defecate; junk. Rhyming slang for CRAP (*q.v.*). British, 1900s, *Dictionary of Rhyming Slang*]

poo 1. dung; feces. For synonyms see DUNG. [1900s and probably long before] **2.** nonsense. *Cf.* PHOOEY. See also POO-POO. **3.** champagne. From SHAMPOO. [1900s, Janssen]

poof (also **pouf, pouffe, puff**) an effeminate male; a homosexual male. *Cf.* FOOP, POOFTER. [Australian and British, early 1900s-pres.]

poof-rorting the robbing or mugging of homosexual males. *Cf.* POOF, POOFTER-RORTER. [attested as British, early 1900s, *Dictionary of Slang and Unconventional English*]

poofter 1. a homosexual male. **2.** a pimp for a male prostitute. [both senses, Australian and British, 1900s or before]

poofter-rorter a male procurer for homosexual male prostitutes. *Cf.* POOF-RORTING. [Australian slang, mid 1900s, Baker]

poohead an obnoxious person. For synonyms see SNOKE-HORN. [U.S. collegiate, late 1900s]

poo-jabber a pederast. For synonyms see PEDERAST. [Australian, mid 1900s-pres.]

poon a truncation of POONTANG *(q.v.)*.

poontang 1. copulation with a black woman. **2.** a black woman considered as a source of sexual gratification; the genitals of a black woman. [both senses, U.S. slang and colloquial, late 1800s-pres.] **3.** an act of copulation, either heterosexual or homosexual. [all are from French *putain,* "prostitute"; U.S. slang, 1900s]

poontanger the penis. From POONTANG (sense 3). [attested as Canadian, 1900s, *Dictionary of Slang and Unconventional English*]

poontang palace a brothel. For synonyms see BROTHEL. [U.S. slang, late 1900s]

poop 1. the posteriors. For synonyms see DUFF. **2.** to coit a woman. [both senses, British, 1600s] **3.** to defecate. [colloquial, 1600s-pres.] **4.** to release intestinal gas. For synonyms see GURK. [slang and colloquial, early 1700s-pres.] **5.** a stupid oaf; a dullard. *Cf.* POOP-HEAD. **6.** to infect with a venereal disease. [used in the past tense in *Pericles* (Shakespeare)] **7.** feces; human feces. [U.S. juvenile and colloquial, 1900s]

poop-chute See DIRT-CHUTE.

pooper the BUTTOCKS. For synonyms see DUFF. [U.S. and elsewhere, 1900s if not before]

poopied intoxicated with alcohol. See SHIT-FACED. For synonyms see WOOFLED. [U.S. slang, mid 1900s, *Current Slang*]

poo-poo (also **poo, pooh**) **1.** to defecate. **2.** feces; an act of defecation. [both senses, U.S. juvenile and colloquial, 1900s] **3.** to deride an idea. [U.S. colloquial, 1900s or before]

poorlander a poor Caucasian; POOR WHITE TRASH *(q.v.)*. [U.S. colloquial, 1900s or before]

poor man's blessing the female genitals; copulation. [British slang, 1800s, Farmer and Henley]

poor man's cocaine methamphetamine. [U.S. drug culture, late 1900s]

poor white trash (also **po white trash, white trash**) Caucasians of very low status; a Southern white who ranks below slaves. [U.S. colloquial, early 1800s-pres.]

poot 1. an audible release of intestinal gas. **2.** to release intestinal gas audibly. *Cf.* POOP (sense 4). [both senses, rural colloquial, 1800s]

pootenanny the female genitals. For synonyms see GENITALS, MONOSYLLABLE. [U.S., late 1900s-pres.]

poozle the vagina. For synonyms see MONOSYLLABLE. [U.S. slang, probably nonce, late 1900s]

pop to coit a woman. *Cf.* POP IT IN. [U.S. slang, mid 1900s-pres.]

pop a nut (also **pop one's nuts**) to ejaculate. *Cf.* GET ONE'S NUTS CRACKED. For synonyms see MELT. [U.S. slang, mid 1900s-pres.]

popcorn pimp a pimp who runs a small operation. *Popcorn* here means small. [U.S., late 1900s-pres.]

popeye the police. For synonyms see FLATFOOT. [U.S., late 1900s-pres.]

pop-eyed alcohol intoxicated, with bulging eyes. For synonyms see WOOFLED. [U.S., late 1900s-pres.]

pop junk to gossip; to DIS someone. [U.S. slang, late 1900s]

po-po to police. For synonyms see FLATFOOT. [U.S., late 1900s-pres.]

pop off 1. to die. See POP OFF THE HOOKS. [slang and colloquial, mid 1700s-pres.] **2.** to kill someone. [U.S. slang, early 1900s]

pop off the hooks to die. For synonyms see DEPART. [British, 1800s]

pop one's cookies to ejaculate. Probably could also be interpreted to mean "to vomit." For synonyms see MELT. [U.S. slang, late 1900s]

popper an ampule of amyl nitrite. *Cf.* PEARL (sense 2). POPSIE, SNAPPER (sense 5). [U.S. drug culture, mid 1900s-pres.]

poppycock nonsense. For synonyms see ANIMAL. [U.S. colloquial, mid 1800s-pres.]

popsicle a penis. For synonyms see YARD. [U.S., late 1900s-pres.]

popsie an ampule of amyl nitrite. *Cf.* PEARL (sense 2). POPPER, SNAPPER (sense 5). [U.S. drug culture, mid 1900s-pres.]

pop (some) tops to drink beer. [U.S. collegiate, late 1900s]

pork 1. a woman considered as a sexual object. Cf. MUTTON (sense 4). [British slang, 1700s] **2.** the penis. Cf. PORK-SWORD. [British slang, 1800s, Farmer and Henley] **3.** to coit a woman. [attested as British slang, 1800s, Farmer and Henley; U.S. slang, mid 1900s-pres.] **4.** a derogatory nickname for a Jewish man or woman. Cf. PORKY. [U.S. slang, mid 1900s] **5.** a corpse. U.S. slang, 1900s] **6.** the police in general. A variation of PIG. Cf. BACON, HOG, OINK. For synonyms see FLAT-FOOT. [U.S. drug culture, late 1900s, Kaiser]

porked copulated with; devirginated. [attested as U.S., late 1900s]

porker 1. a derogatory nickname for a Jewish man or woman. Cf. PORK (sense 4), PORKY. [slang since the 1700s] **2.** an ugly young woman, especially a fat, ugly young woman. Cf. HOG (sense 2), PIG (sense 3). For synonyms see BUFFARILLA. [U.S. slang, mid 1900s] **3.** one who copulates; a fornicator. [U.S. slang, 1900s] **4.** a fat person. [U.S., late 1900s-pres.]

porking copulating. For synonyms see SMOCKAGE. [British and U.S., late 1900s-pres.]

pork-sword the penis. Cf. MUTTON-DAGGER, PIG-STICKING, PORK (sense 2). [British, 1900s, *Dictionary of the Underworld*]

porky 1. a derogatory nickname for a Jewish man or woman. Cf. PORKER (sense 1). [British slang, late 1800s, Ware] **2.** a very fat person. Also a term of address and a nickname. Supported by the cartoon character named Porky Pig. [widespread, 1900s]

Port Said garter a condom. For synonyms see EEL-SKIN. [British Army, World War II]

Portugoose 1. a jocular and derogatory nickname for a Portuguese. **2.** an imaginary and jocular singular form of "Portuguese." [U.S. slang, 1900s]

Portuguese pump masturbation; an

act of masturbation. Cf. PUMP (sense 3). [British nautical slang, late 1800s, Ware]

position a truncation of "sexual position." Frequently heard as double entendre. See BREAD AND BUTTER, CHINESE-FASHION, COIT DORSALLY, CO-ITION A POSTERIORI, COITUS À LA VACHE, DOG-FASHION, DOG-STYLE, DOG-WAYS, DRAGON UPON SAINT GEORGE, FIGURA VENERIS PRIMA, MATRIMONIAL, MISSIONARY POSITION, PENDULA VENUS.

post 1. the penis. Cf. STERN-POST. [colloquial and nonce] **2.** copulation; an act of copulation. Probably related to sense 1. Cf. POLE (senses 1 and 2). [British slang, 1800s, Farmer and Henley] **3.** an autopsy, a postmortem examination. [U.S. medical slang, 1900s]

post a letter 1. to copulate. For synonyms see OCCUPY. [British slang, 1800s] **2.** to retire to defecate. For synonyms see RETIRE. [primarily British use, late 1800s-pres.]

postern 1. the female genitals. For synonyms see MONOSYLLABLE. **2.** the posteriors; the anus. [both senses, British, 1700s]

pot 1. the female genitals, a pot for MEAT (sense 4). [British slang, 1600s] **2.** a urinal; a CHAMBER POT (q.v.); later, a water-flush toilet bowl. A truncation of "chamber pot." [colloquial, 1600s-pres.] Synonyms: ALTAR, ARTICLE, BED-GLASS, BISHOP, CHAMBER OF COM-MERCE, CHAMBER POT, CHAMBER UTEN-SIL, CHAMBER VESSEL, CHANTIE, CHARMBER, CLOSE STOOL, COMMODE, CONVENIENCE, CROCK, DAISY, GASH-BUCKET, GAUGE, GUT-BUCKET, GU-ZUNDER, IT, JEMIMA, JERKER, JERO-BOAM, JERRY, JEWEL CASE, JOCK-UM-GAGE, JORDAN, JUG, LAG-GING-GAGE, LOOKING-GLASS, MASTER-CAN, MEMBER MUG, MINGO, NIGHT-GLASS, NIGHT-STOOL. **3.** a drunkard; a sot, a truncation of POTHEAD (q.v.). [U.S. slang, mid 1900s-pres.] **4.** marijuana. [from a Mexican Indian term, *potaguaya;* U.S. drug culture and slang, mid 1900s-pres.]

potato-finger 1. the penis. From the name for a medical condition wherein a finger is elongated and thickened. Cf.

FOREFINGER. [from *Troilus and Cressida* (Shakespeare)] **2.** a DILDO (sense 2).

potatohead a stupid person. For synonyms see OAF. [U.S., mid 1900s-pres.]

pot-fury 1. a drunkard. Also **potknight. 2.** intoxication with alcohol. [both senses, late 1500s]

potsed drunk. For synonyms see WOOFLED. [U.S. slang, 1900s, Lewin and Lewin]

pot-shot intoxicated with alcohol. A reinterpretation of a term for a shot taken at game with the goal of providing something for the cooking pot. See POTTED. *Cf.* CUP-SHOT, GRAPE-SHOT. [British slang, 1800s, Farmer and Henley]

potted 1. intoxicated with alcohol; having been POT-SHOT (*q.v.*). *Cf.* POT-HEAD (sense 2). [U.S. slang, early 1900s-pres.] **2.** intoxicated with drugs; intoxicated with marijuana. Reinforced by POT (sense 4). For synonyms see TALL. [U.S. slang and drug culture, 1900s]

potty 1. a CHAMBER POT (*q.v.*); a W.C.; a water-flush toilet bowl. *Cf.* POT (sense 2). [U.S. juvenile and colloquial, 1900s] **2.** to urinate or defecate; to use the POTTY (sense 1). [U.S. juvenile, 1900s]

potty mouth a person who uses obscene or profane language in all or most social settings; the same as TOILET MOUTH (*q.v.*). [U.S. slang, mid 1900s-pres.]

pot-valiant (also **pot-sure**) intoxicated with alcohol and brave because of it. *Cf.* DUTCH COURAGE, POT-SURE. [slang and colloquial, early 1600s-pres.]

pouch out [for a male] to sit around in his underwear. [U.S. slang, late 1900s]

poultry women in general; women considered as sexual objects. *Cf.* QUAIL. [British, 1600s]

poultry-show a group inspection of penes for venereal disease. Poultry refers to COCK (sense 3), the penis. *Cf.* DANGLE-PARADE, SHORT-ARM INSPECTION, SMALL-ARM INSPECTION, TOOLCHECK. [British military, 1900s]

pound to coit a woman. *Cf.* HAMMER. [U.S. slang, late 1800s-pres.]

pound a beer See HAMMER A BEER.

pound-cake queen a male, usually described as homosexual, who derives special sexual pleasure from being defecated on. See QUEEN for similar subjects. [U.S. homosexual use, mid 1900s, Farrell]

pounders the testicles. For synonyms see WHIRLYGIGS. [British slang, late 1600s]

pound off to masturbate. *Cf.* BEAT OFF, JACK OFF, JAG OFF, JERK OFF. [U.S. slang, mid 1900s-pres.]

pound one's pud to masturbate. Said of the male. *Cf.* PULL ONE'S PUD. For synonyms and related subjects see WASTE TIME. [U.S. slang, late 1900s]

Pound salt up your ass! a curse; an order to go to hell. [U.S. slang, mid 1900s]

pound the meat to masturbate. *Cf.* BEAT THE MEAT, POUND OFF. For synonyms see WASTE TIME. [U.S. slang, mid 1900s-pres.]

pouter the female genitals. From the standard term meaning "poke" or "stir." [British, early 1800s]

powder monkey a drug seller. [drug culture, late 1900s]

powder one's nose (also **powder one's face**) to retire to the W.C. Usually said by women or jocularly by men. [British and U.S. slang and colloquial, early 1900s-pres.]

powder puff 1. a silly girl or woman. **2.** an effeminate male. *Cf.* POOF. For synonyms see FRIBBLE. [both senses, U.S. slang, early 1900s]

powerbarf pwerful or projectile vomiting. For synonyms see YORK. [U.S., late 1900s-pres.]

power-boot to vomit with great force. *Cf.* BOOT. For synonyms see YORK. [U.S. slang, late 1900s]

power drinker a very heavy drinker. Probably patterned on "power user" in computer jargon. For synonyms see ALCHY. [U.S. slang, late 1900s]

power sludge strong coffee. [U.S., late 1900s-pres.]

power tool a student who studies most of the time. An elaboration of TOOL, meaning studious student. [U.S., late 1900s-pres.]

pratfall a fall on the buttocks, especially an exaggerated fall on the buttocks on stage. [U.S. slang and colloquial, early 1900s-pres.]

prats (also **prat, pratts**) 1. the buttocks. For synonyms see DUFF. [since the 1500s] 2. to strike or beat on the buttocks. [1500s] 3. the female genitals. Cf. ASS (sense 3). For synonyms see MONOSYLLABLE. [British slang, 1800s, Farmer and Henley]

prayerbones the knees. [1900s, if not before]

pray to the enamel god to vomit into an enameled basin. For synonyms see YORK. [U.S. slang, late 1900s]

pray to the porcelain god to vomit into a toilet. For synonyms see YORK. [U.S. slang, late 1900s]

pray with the knees upwards to copulate, said of a woman. [British slang, late 1700s, Grose]

precious juice alcohol; BOOZE. For synonyms see BOOZE. [U.S. collegiate, late 1900s, Munro]

preeze to urinate. For synonyms see WHIZ. [British colloquial dialect, 1800s, Farmer and Henley] See also FEEZE.

preggers pregnant. For synonyms see FRAGRANT. [originally British collegiate; slang, 1900s]

preggy pregnant. [British slang, early 1900s, Dictionary of Slang and Unconventional English]

preserved intoxicated with alcohol. Cf. CORNED; PICKLED, SALTED-DOWN. For synonyms see WOOFLED. [U.S. slang, early 1900s-pres.]

pressed-ham the buttocks in the act of "mooning." See MOON. [U.S. slang, mid 1900s]

Pressie (also **Presbo**) a Presbyterian. [Australian, 1900s]

press whore someone who will do anything to get press attention. [U.S., late 1900s-pres.]

prick 1. the penis; the erect penis. [since the 1500s or before] 2. an oaf; an offensive male. [U.S. slang, mid 1900s-pres.] 3. a hard taskmaster. [U.S. slang, early 1900s]

prick-chinking copulating. [British slang, 1600s]

prick-juice semen. Cf. CUNT-JUICE. [slang, 1900s or before]

prickle the penis. For synonyms see YARD. [slang, early 1600s]

prick-parade a group inspection for venereal disease in the military. Cf. POULTRY-SHOW. [British military, early 1900s, Dictionary of Slang and Unconventional English]

prick-pocket 1. the vagina. For synonyms see PASSAGE. 2. a woman considered sexually. A play on "pickpocket."

prick-pride an erection. For synonyms see ERECTION. [British, 1500s-1800s]

prick-skinner the female genitals. Cf. EEL-SKINNER. [British slang, 1600s]

prick-smith a military medical officer. From his treatment of venereal disease or from his giving hypodermic injections. Cf. PINTLE-SMITH. [British, early 1900s, Dictionary of Slang and Unconventional English]

prick-teaser a woman who leads a man on sexually but who refuses to copulate; a COCK-TEASER (q.v.). Cf. P.T. [U.S. slang, mid 1900s-pres.]

pride and joy one's penis. From the term for one's newborn baby or spouse. Cf. PRIDE (sense 1).

pride of the morning a morning erection. A reinterpretation of the Irish term for a morning shower of rain. Cf. MORNING PRIDE. [British, 1800s, Dictionary of Slang and Unconventional English]

prides 1. the male genitals. 2. the genitals, male or female; the reproductive system of either sex. [both senses, British and U.S. rural colloquial, 1800s-1900s]

primed 1. intoxicated with alcohol. For synonyms see WOOFLED. [British and U.S. slang, 1800s-pres.] 2. pertaining to a woman readied for copulation. [U.S. collegiate, late 1900s]

prime someone's pump to excite someone sexually. [British slang, 1900s]

primo a marijuana cigarette with cocaine added. For synonyms see MEZZ-ROLL. [U.S. drug culture, late 1900s]

Princeton rub male homosexual hugging and petting to orgasm. Cf. FLAT-FUCK, TUMMY-FUCK.

private office a privy; a W.C. Cf. HOUSE OF OFFICE. [U.S. slang, mid 1900s]

privy-hole the female genitals, specifically the vagina, a "private hole." [British, 1800s, Farmer and Henley]

privy member the penis; a "private member." Cf. MEMBER FOR THE COCKSHIRE, UNRULY MEMBER. [euphemistic since the 1600s]

prize bull prizewinning nonsense. A partial disguise of the "bull" of BULL-SHIT (q.v.). For synonyms see ANIMAL. [U.S. slang, mid 1900s-pres.]

pro 1. a prostitute. From "professional." For synonyms see HARLOT. [U.S. slang, early 1900s-pres.] 2. a prophylactic condom. [U.S. slang, mid 1900s-pres.]

prod 1. the penis, especially the erect penis. 2. to copulate. [both senses, British and U.S. slang, 1800s-pres.]

Proddo (also **Prod**) a Protestant. [Australian, 1900s] Related terms: BAPPO, BIBLE-BELTER, BLUESKIN, CONGO, DIPPER, HOLY-ROLLER, JESUS-SCREAMER, METHO, PLUNGER, PRESBO, PRESSIE.

prod the peepee to masturbate. For synonyms and related subjects see WASTE TIME. [U.S. collegiate, late 1900s]

profane 1. to utter or write irreverence to God, holy matters, or things. [since the 1300s] 2. pertaining to that which is not consecrated. [since the 1400s] 3. obscene; smutty. [U.S. colloquial, 1900s]

prong 1. the penis. Cf. JOY PRONG. For synonyms see YARD. [slang, mid 1900s-pres.] 2. to coit a woman. [slang, mid 1900s]

prostitute 1. a woman who sells her sexual services. For synonyms see HARLOT. [since the 1500s] 2. a catamite; a male prostitute who sells his sexual services in PEDERASTY (q.v.). [since the 1600s] 3. to sell oneself cheaply; to do something which is beneath one.

prostitution the occupation or profession of selling sexual acts; indiscriminate sexual intercourse exchanged for money. Usually thought of as feminine but the term applies to both men and women. Synonyms: BITCHERY, BORDEL, BOTTLE, BUTTOCK BANQUETTING, FAST LIFE, LOVE-FOR-SALE, MRS. WARREN'S PROFESSION, OLD PATROL, PALLIARDY, PUTAGE, SACKING, SOCIAL E., SOCIAL EVIL, STREET OF SHAME, SUBURB TRADE, TAIL-TRADING, THE TRADE, VICE, WHOREDOM.

proud desirous of copulation; sexually excited; with swollen genitals. Often said of animals, especially of a bitch in heat. See PRIDES. [colloquial since the late 1500s]

proud below the navel sexually aroused. Refers to the swelling of the genitals. [British, early 1600s]

prushun (also **preshen**) a CATAMITE (q.v.); a tramp's catamite. From PRUSSIAN (q.v.). [U.S. underworld (tramps), 1900s or before]

Prussian an active PEDERAST (q.v.); the INSERTOR (q.v.). Cf. PRUSHUN. Probably from "Prussian Blue," a term of endearment (like "true blue") in the mid 1800s. [U.S., 1900s]

P.T. a PRICK-TEASER (q.v.); a woman who leads a man on sexually but who refuses to copulate. [U.S. slang, mid 1900s-pres.]

pubehead a person with short curly hair like pubic hair. [U.S. collegiate, late 1900s, Munro]

pud 1. the penis. Rhymes with "wood." Cf. PULL ONE'S PUDDING. [U.S. slang, 1900s] 2. a jerk; a PRICK (sense 2). For synonyms see OAF. [U.S. slang, 1900s]

pudding 1. the penis. Probably from PUDENDUM (q.v.). Cf. PULL ONE'S PUDDING. For synonyms see YARD. [since the 1600s] 2. copulation. For synonyms see SMOCKAGE. [British, 1600s-1700s]

3. semen. For synonyms see METTLE. [British, late 1600s] **4.** innards; guts; stuffing. Sometimes in the plural. [British colloquial, 1700s and before]

pudding club, in the pregnant. [British colloquial, 1800s]

pudendum* the genitals. Usually the female genitals but occasionally the penis. (See MALE PUDENDUM.) Occasionally in the plural, *i.e., pudenda,* referring to the "things about which one should be modest." [from Latin; since the late 1300s] See MONOSYLLABLE.

pud wacker a masturbator. For synonyms see WASTE TIME. [U.S., late 1900s-pres.]

puff 1. to release intestinal gas. *Cf.* POOP (sense 4). [colloquial and nonce, 1800s-1900s] **2.** a fop; an effeminate male; a homosexual male. A variant of POOF (*q.v.*). [British slang, 1800s-1900s]

puffy the drug phencyclidine, P.C.P. For synonyms see P.C.P. [U.S. drug culture, late 1900s, Abel]

puffy clam the vulva. For synonyms see MONOSYLLABLE. [U.S., late 1900s-pres.]

puggled intoxicated with alcohol; crazy drunk. *Cf.* POGGLED.

puggy-drunk intoxicated with alcohol. *Cf.* POGY. [British slang, 1800s]

pugnasty a nasty slut; a dirty prostitute. From a nickname for a monkey. *Cf.* PUG. [British, 1600s, B.E.]

pug-ugly 1. pertaining to a very ugly person. **2.** a very ugly person. [both senses, U.S. slang and colloquial, 1900s]

pukalolo marijuana. For synonyms see MARI. [U.S. drug culture, late 1900s]

puke 1. to vomit. **2.** vomit. [both since the 1600s] **3.** an obnoxious person; a real pest. [British and U.S. slang, early 1800s-pres.]

puke hole 1. a tavern. **2.** toilet, especially for vomiting. For synonyms see W.C. **3.** the mouth. [all senses, U.S., late 1900s]

pukes nausea; vomiting.

pukish nauseated. [colloquial since the 1500s]

pukoid disgusting. [U.S., late 1900s-pres.]

pull a train for a woman to have sexual intercourse with a succession of males. See GROUP SEX for similar topics. [U.S. slang, mid 1900s-pres.]

pull a trick to perform an act of FELLATIO or PEDERASTY (both *q.v.*). *Cf.* TRICK (sense 1). [U.S. slang, mid 1900s, Goldin, O'Leary, and Lipsius]

pull jive to drink alcohol; to drink beer. [U.S. slang, late 1900s]

pull oneself off to masturbate. *Cf.* PLAY OFF. For synonyms see WASTE TIME. [slang, 1900s or before]

pull one's pud to masturbate. *Cf.* PUD (sense 1), the penis. [U.S. slang, mid 1900s-pres.]

pull one's pudding to masturbate. *Cf.* PUDDING (sense 1). [slang, 1900s]

pull one's wire to masturbate. *Cf.* WIRE. For synonyms see WASTE TIME. [British and some U.S. use, 1800s-1900s]

pull someone's dick to tease or attempt to deceive someone. *Cf.* PULL SOMEONE'S PISSER. [U.S. slang, late 1900s]

pull someone's pisser to tease someone. Compare to PULL SOMEONE'S DICK. [British slang, late 1900s]

pull the pin to masturbate. As with pulling the pin of a grenade before the explosion. For synonyms see WASTE TIME. [British, late 1900s-pres.]

pull the plug to commit suicide. [British, late 1900s-pres.]

pull the plug (on someone or something) to put an end to someone or something as a problem. [British and U.S., late 1900s-pres.]

pull tubes to smoke marijuana from a bong. [U.S., late 1900s-pres.]

Pull your finger out! a command to "hurry up!" "Pull your finger out of your ass-hole so that you can run!" *Cf.* DEDIGITATE! [British and U.S. military and general slang, 1900s]

pulpit the female genitals. For synonyms see MONOSYLLABLE. [British, mid 1600s]

pulpit-cuffer a Bible-pounding preacher. [British colloquial, 1800s, Halliwell]

pummelled alcohol intoxicated. For synonyms see WOOFLED. [U.S., late 1900s-pres.]

pump 1. the female genitals. *Cf.* PUMPDALE, PUMPKIN. For synonyms see MONOSYLLABLE. [British, 1600s] **2.** to vomit. *Cf.* PUMP SHIP (sense 2). For synonyms see YORK. [British slang, 1800s] **3.** to masturbate. See PUMP ONESELF OFF. [primarily British, 1800s] **4.** to coit a woman. *Cf.* PUMPED. [colloquial or slang, 1800s-pres.] **5.** a breaking of wind. For synonyms see GURK. [British slang, 1800s, Farmer and Henley] **6.** the penis. See PUMP-HANDLE. **7.** to urinate. *Cf.* PUMP SHIP (sense 1). [British and U.S. slang, 1800s-pres.] **8.** a breast. See PUMPS.

pumped pregnant. *Cf.* PUMP (sense 4). For synonyms see FRAGRANT. [U.S. slang, mid 1900s-pres.]

pump-handle (also **pump**) the penis. *Cf.* PUMP (sense 1). [British, early 1700s]

pumpkin seed a tablet of MESCALINE (*q.v.*). [U.S. drug culture, mid 1900s-pres.]

pump oneself off to masturbate. [British and some U.S. use, 1800s-1900s]

pump one's nads to send surges of sexual excitement to the testicles or gonads. [British, late 1900s-pres.]

pump one's pickle to masturbate. Based on JERK ONE'S GHERKIN (*q.v.*). [attested as Canadian, 1900s, *Dictionary of Slang and Unconventional English*]

pump one's python to masturbate. *Cf.* PUMP (sense 3), PYTHON. For synonyms see WASTE TIME. [U.S. slang, mid 1900s-pres.]

pumps the human breasts. For synonyms see BOSOM. [U.S. slang, early 1900s]

pump ship 1. to urinate. For synonyms see WHIZ. [originally nautical, 1700s-pres.] **2.** to vomit. For synonyms see YORK. [since the 1700s]

puna butter a potent variety of Hawaiian marijuana. For synonyms see MARI. [U.S. drug culture, late 1900s]

punce 1. an effeminate male; a homosexual male; a CATAMITE (*q.v.*). [Australian slang, 1900s, Baker] **2.** the female genitals. *Cf.* PUNSE. [Australian and British slang, 1900s]

punch 1. to coit and DEFLOWER (*q.v.*) a woman. [since the 1800s or before] **2.** to copulate. [U.S. slang, mid 1900s-pres.] **3.** women considered as sexual objects. From senses 1 and 2. [slang since the 1700s]

punchable pertaining to a woman who desires copulation. *Cf.* BEDWORTHY, FUCKABLE, FUCKSOME, ROMPWORTHY, SHAFTABLE. [since the 1700s, Grose]

punk 1. a prostitute; a sexually loose woman. Also **punck, puncke, punque.** [British, late 1500s-1700s] **2.** to procure customers for a prostitute. [British, 1600s] **3.** a CATAMITE (*q.v.*). For synonyms see BRONCO. [U.S. underworld and slang, early 1900s] **4.** a homosexual male. [U.S. slang, mid 1900s-pres.] **5.** a woman who performs PENILINGUS (*q.v.*). [U.S. underworld, mid 1900s, Goldin, O'Leary, and Lipsius] **6.** any male; a chum; a young fellow. [U.S. slang and colloquial, mid 1900s-pres.] **7.** a weak person; a useless jerk, usually a male. [U.S. slang, mid 1900s-pres.] **8.** inferior marijuana. [U.S. drug culture, mid 1900s-pres.]

punker a whoremonger. From PUNK (sense 1). For synonyms see LECHER. [British slang, 1600s-1700s]

punk kid 1. a CATAMITE (*q.v.*). *Cf.* PUNK (sense 3). [U.S. slang, mid 1900s] **2.** any adolescent male. [U.S. slang, mid 1900s-pres.]

punk pills any tranquilizer taken illicitly. [U.S. drug culture, mid 1900s-pres.]

pup 1. the penis, especially in the expression BEAT THE PUP (*q.v.*). [attested as U.S., mid 1900s, Goldin, O'Leary, and Lipsius] **2.** an oaf; a dummy. [U.S. slang, mid 1900s, Goldin, O'Leary, and Lipsius]

pup, in pregnant, as with dogs. [British colloquial, mid 1800s, *Dictionary of Slang and Unconventional English*]

puppy's mamma a euphemism for BITCH (*q.v.*). [since the early 1800s]

pure silk pertaining to a homosexual male. [U.S. slang, mid 1900s-pres.] See also SILK.

purge 1. to remove undesirable substances from the body. **2.** to give an enema. [both since the 1400s] **3.** beer. [British slang, 1800s] **4.** to expurgate. **5.** to vomit. For synonyms see YORK. [senses 4 and 5 are U.S. colloquial, 1900s]

purple pornographic; grossly pornographic. Even more extreme than BLUE (sense 1). [U.S. slang, mid 1900s]

purple flats (also **purple**) the drug L.S.D. (*q.v.*). Cf. FLATS. [U.S. drug culture, mid 1900s-pres.]

purple haze (also **haze**) the drug L.S.D. (*q.v.*). [U.S. drug culture, mid 1900s-pres.]

purple heart a Dexedrine (trademark) tablet. A reinterpretation of the name of a U.S. military decoration. [U.S. drug culture, 1900s]

purple microdots the drug L.S.D. (*q.v.*). Cf. MICRODOTS. [U.S. drug culture, mid 1900s-pres.]

purse a condom. For synonyms see EEL-SKIN. [U.S. slang, 1900s or before]

push 1. to copulate. Cf. DO A PUSH, STAND THE PUSH. [slang and colloquial, 1600s-1900s] **2.** to sell narcotics. [U.S. underworld and drug culture, 1900s]

pushed intoxicated with alcohol. For synonyms see WOOFLED. [British slang, 1800s, Farmer and Henley]

pusher a seller of narcotics and heroin. Cf. DEALER. [U.S. drug culture, mid 1900s-pres.] Synonyms: BAG LADY, BAGMAN, BINGLE, BROKER, CANDY MAN, DEALER, ICE-CREAM MAN, JUNK-PEDDLER, SWING MAN, TEN-TWO THOUSAND, TRAFFIKER.

pushing up daisies dead and buried. Cf. DAISY-PUSHING. [British and U.S. wartime and general slang, 1900s]

push in the bush is worth two in the hand a catch phrase signifying that "one act of coition is worth two

acts of masturbation." [British, 1900s, *Dictionary of Slang and Unconventional English*]

push in the truck an act of copulation; to coit a woman. Rhyming slang for "fuck." [British, early 1900s, *Dictionary of Rhyming Slang*]

push on to copulate with; to coit. Said of a male. Cf. PUSH (sense 1). [colloquial, 1700s-1900s]

push-over a woman who yields easily to sexual propositions. Cf. PULL-OVER. [U.S. slang and colloquial, early 1900s-pres.]

push-pin to coit. For synonyms see OCCUPY. [British slang, 1600s]

puss 1. a cat; a nickname for a cat. No negative connotations. [since the early 1500s] **2.** a woman; a nickname for a woman. [since the late 1500s] **3.** the female genitals. Cf. PUSSY (sense 1). [colloquial, 1600s-pres.] **4.** a hare. [British colloquial, 1600s] **5.** copulation. Cf. PUSSY (sense 4). [U.S. slang mid 1900s-pres.] **6.** an effeminate male. Cf. CUT PUSS, PUSSYCAT. [U.S. slang, 1900s] **7.** a face; an ugly face. [U.S. slang and colloquial, mid 1900s-pres.]

pussy 1. the female genitals. Cf. PUSS (sense 3). [slang and colloquial, 1800s-pres.] **2.** an effeminate male. Cf. CUT PUSS. For synonyms see FRIBBLE. [U.S. slang, early 1900s-pres.] **3.** women considered sexually. For synonyms see TAIL. [U.S. slang, mid 1900s-pres.] **4.** copulation. [U.S. slang, mid 1900s]

pussy-bumping meaning uncertain. Most likely some type of lesbian sexual activity. Definitions include CUNNILINGISM, LESBIANISM, and SODOMY (all *q.v.*). See FLAT-FUCK. [U.S. slang mid 1900s-pres.]

pussy butterfly a birth control device; an I.U.D. (*q.v.*) of a specific design. [U.S. colloquial, mid 1900s-pres.]

pussycat 1. a girl, one's girlfriend. **2.** a timid male. [both senses, U.S. slang and colloquial, 1900s]

pussyfart (also **cunt-fart**) a sometimes audible release of air trapped in the vagina by the penis at the time of penetration.

pussy pelmet a very short miniskirt. [British, late 1900s-pres.]

pussy posse the police prostitution squad; the vice squad. [U.S. slang, mid 1900s-pres.]

pussy-simple crazy or obsessed with copulation, said of a man. *Cf.* KID-SIMPLE, TWITCHET-STRUCK. [U.S. dialect (Ozarks), 1900s or before, Randolph and Wilson]

pussy-struck totally obsessed with the sexual possibilities of one woman or of all women. A milder and more recent version of CUNT-STRUCK (*q.v.*). *Cf.* PUSSY-SIMPLE. [1900s]

pussy-wagon a fancy or gaudy automobile used by a PIMP; a PIMPMOBILE. [U.S. slang, late 1900s]

pussy-whipped henpecked; dominated by a demanding wife. Based on "horse-whipped." [U.S. slang, mid 1900s]

Put a sock in it! See STUFF A SOCK IN IT!

put balls on something to make something more masculine or powerful. [British and U.S., mid 1900s-pres.]

put birdie to vomit. For synonyms see YORK. [U.S. slang, early 1900s]

put it to her to coit a woman. For synonyms see OCCUPY. [U.S. slang, 1900s]

put lipstick on his dipstick to perform FELLATIO (*q.v.*) on a man, said of a woman. *Cf.* DIPSTICK (sense 2). [U.S. slang, mid 1900s, *Current Slang*]

put one's ass on the line to take a great risk. [U.S. slang, late 1900s]

put out 1. to kill. From the extinguishing of a candle or a fire. [British, late 1800s, Ware] **2.** to permit kissing and caressing readily, usually said of a co-operative date. [U.S. slang, mid 1900s-pres.]

putrid drunk; STINKING DRUNK. For

synonyms see WOOFLED. [1900s if not much earlier]

put the blocks to to coit a woman. *Cf.* BLOCK (sense 2) [U.S. slang, mid 1900s-pres.]

put the boots to to coit a woman; to RIDE (sense 2) a woman. [U.S. slang, early 1900s or before, Irwin]

put the eye on someone to flirt with a member of the opposite sex. [U.S. slang and colloquial, 1900s]

put the hard word on her to proposition a woman; to attempt to persuade a woman to copulate. [Australian and U.S. slang, 1900s]

put the make on (also **put the move on**) to flirt with a woman; to proposition a woman or a man. [U.S. slang, mid 1900s-pres.]

put to bed with a shovel 1. buried. [British and U.S. colloquial, 1800s-1900s] **2.** intoxicated with alcohol. For synonyms see WOOFLED. [U.S. slang, 1900s]

puttock 1. a prostitute; a common whore. **2.** a greedy person; a glutton. [both senses, British, 1500s-1600s]

put to sleep to kill something or someone, often used for killing a pet. *Cf.* GO TO SLEEP. [U.S. euphemism, 1900s]

putz 1. a fool; an oaf. **2.** the penis. More rude than SCHMUCK (sense 1). [from Yiddish; both senses, U.S. slang, mid 1900s-pres.]

putz around to waste time; to do something ineffectually. [U.S. slang, mid 1900s-pres.]

pye-eyed intoxicated with alcohol. See PIE-EYED.

python the penis in PUMP ONE'S PYTHON, ROCK PYTHON, SYPHON THE PYTHON (all *q.v.*). For synonyms see YARD.

pythons large, muscular biceps. [U.S., late 1900s-pres.]

Q

Q. an abbreviation of "queer," a male homosexual. For synonyms see EPICENE. [British slang, early 1900s, *Dictionary of Slang and Unconventional English*]

Q.B. a cigarette; a "quick butt." High school use. [U.S. slang, late 1900s]

Q-sign the mouth of a person hanging open in death with the tongue hanging out like the tail of a Q. *Cf.* O-SIGN. For synonyms see DEMISE. [U.S. mock medical, late 1900s]

quack 1. a fraudulent physician; a seller of patent medicines; a derogatory term for any physician. [since the late 1600s] 2. a methaqualone tablet. [U.S. drug culture, mid 1900s-pres.]

quad a methaqualone tablet. [U.S. drug culture, mid 1900s-pres.]

quail 1. a prostitute. For synonyms see HARLOT. [since the early 1600s] 2. a spinster. No negative connotations. Also an early term for "co-ed." [U.S. underworld, 1800s-1900s] 3. any sexually loose woman. [U.S. slang, 1900s] 4. any girl or woman. [U.S. slang, 1900s] Synonyms: BIDDY, BIRD, CANARY, CHICK, DUCK, GOOSE, GROUSE, GUINEA-HEN, GULL, LOON, NESTLECOCK, PARTRIDGE, PELICAN, PHEASANT, PIGEON, PLOVER, POULTRY, WREN.

quail-hunter a woman-chaser; a whoremonger. *Cf.* QUAIL (sense 1). [U.S. slang, 1900s]

qualify to succeed in copulating. *Cf.* SCORE. [British slang, 1800s, Farmer and Henley]

quarter moon HASHISH (*q.v.*). For synonyms see HASH. [U.S. drug culture, mid 1900s-pres.]

quartzed alcohol intoxicated. Probably a play on *quarts* or a play on STONED. For synonyms see WOOFLED. [U.S. slang, late 1900s]

quas the plural of "qua." A truncation of "methaqualone," specifically Quaalude (trademark), a tranquilizer. [U.S. drug culture, mid 1900s-pres.]

quean 1. a sexually loose woman; a prostitute. [since *c.* 1000] 2. an effeminate male. *Cf.* COTQUEAN (sense 1). For synonyms see FRIBBLE. 3. a homosexual male. [both senses, Australian, 1800s-1900s]

queanie pertaining to effeminacy or softness in males. [Australian, early 1900s]

queen 1. an effeminate male, not necessarily a homosexual male. *Cf.* QUEENIE. [U.S. slang, early 1900s] 2. an effeminate male homosexual, especially one who prefers virile men. 3. a type of male homosexual with specific preferences as to types of lovers and NONORTHOGENITAL (*q.v.*) behavior or other matters. There are numerous terms for queens, many of them are of a jocular nature. A few of the following list refer to personality traits rather than sexual appetite. *Cf.* BODY QUEEN, BROWNIE QUEEN, BUTTERFLY QUEEN, CHICKEN QUEEN, CLOSET QUEEN, DINGE QUEEN, DISH QUEEN, DRAG QUEEN, FACE QUEEN, FELCH QUEEN, FIRE QUEEN, FLAMING QUEEN, FOOT QUEEN, GOLDEN SHOWER QUEEN, GREEN QUEEN, HEAD QUEEN, JEAN QUEEN, MAIN QUEEN, MITTEN QUEEN, MOVIE QUEEN, POUNDCAKE QUEEN, SHOWER QUEEN, SHRIMP QUEEN, SIZE QUEEN, SNOWBALL QUEEN, SUCK QUEEN, TEAROOM QUEEN, TOE QUEEN, VIRGIN QUEEN, WATCHQUEEN. 4. any homosexual male. [U.S. slang, 1900s] 5. a fellator; a male who performs FELLATIO (*q.v.*). [U.S. underworld, early 1900s] 6. a lovely young woman. No negative connotations. [colloquial since the 1700s or before] 7. a beautiful lesbian. [U.S., 1900s]

Queen Anne's lace marijuana. For synonyms see MARI [U.S., late 1900s-pres.]

queenie 1. an effeminate male. For synonyms see FRIBBLE. **2.** a charming and attractive young woman. *Cf.* QUEEN. [both senses, U.S., 1900s]

queening courting women or girls; flirting. [U.S. slang, early 1900s, Weseen]

queer (also **queere, quire**) **1.** pertaining to a thing or a person which is odd, naughty, eccentric, counterfeit, or worthless. [originally cant; since the 1600s] **2.** to spoil; to make bad or worthless, as in "queer the deal" [originally cant; since the late 1700s] **3.** pertaining to a male or female homosexual. [U.S., 1900s] **4.** a homosexual male. Usually considered to be a highly derogatory term. [U.S. underworld and general slang, early 1900s-pres.] **5.** a female homosexual; a lesbian. For synonyms see LESBYTERIAN. [U.S. slang, mid 1900s-pres.] **6.** intoxicated with alcohol. From sense 1. **7.** a fool. [underworld slang and colloquial, 1900s]

queer as a nine bob note 1. odd; unusual. [British, late 1900s-pres.] **2.** homosexual. For synonyms see EPICENE. [British, late 1900s-pres.]

queer beer beer with low alcohol content, *e.g.*, three-two beer, (3.2 percent alcoholic content). Rhyming with NEAR BEER (*q.v.*). *Cf.* SISSY BEER, SQUAW PISS. [U.S. slang, mid 1900s-pres.]

queered intoxicated with alcohol. *Cf.* QUEER (sense 6). For synonyms see WOOFLED. [British slang, early 1800s]

queer queen a masculine woman; a lesbian. [U.S. slang, early 1900s]

queer up to primp, said of a man, not necessarily an effeminate man. [Australian, 1900s, Baker]

queervert a homosexual male. A blend of QUEER and PERVERT (both *q.v.*). [U.S. slang, early 1900s]

quickstep diarrhea. From the name of a dance step. [U.S. colloquial, early 1900s] Synonyms: AZTEC TWO-STEP, BACK-DOOR TROTS, BARLEY-CORN SPRINTS, B.D.T.s, BLATTS, BOWEL OFF, COCKTAILS, CRAPS, DELHI BELLY, FLUXES, FLYING HANDICAP, GASTROINTESTINAL TROUBLES, G.I.s, G.I. SHITS, GURR, GYPPY TUMMY, JIMMY BRITTS, JOE-TROTS, LASK, LAX, LOOSE, LOOSE-ENDED, LOOSE IN THE HILT, LOOSENESS IN THE BELLY, LOOSENESS IN THE BOWELS, LURKIES, MONTEZUMA'S REVENGE, MOVIES, PURGE, QUICK-SHITS, RUNNING-BELLY, RUN OFF, RUNS, SCATE, SCATTERS, SCOOTS, SCOURS, SCREAMING SHITS, SHITS, SHITTERS, SHOOT, SHORTS, SKIT, SKITTER, SQUIRTS, SUMMER COMPLAINT, THREEPENNY BITS, TOURISTAS, TREY-BITS, TROTS, WILD SQUIRT, WOG GUT.

quicky (also **quickie**) a very brief copulation. *Cf.* FLYER. [U.S. slang, mid 1900s-pres.]

quid the female genitals. *Cf.* QUIM. [British, 1800s]

quiff 1. the female genitals. *Cf.* QUIM. [slang, 1700s-1900s] **2.** women considered solely as sexual objects. **3.** a sexually loose woman; a slut. For synonyms see LAY. [slang, early 1900s-pres.] **4.** a cheap and low prostitute. [slang, 1900s or before] **5.** to copulate. [British slang or cant, 1700s]

quim (also **quem, queme, quimsbox, quimsby, quimsy, quin, quint**) **1.** the female genitals. **2.** copulation. **3.** to copulate. [originally British, 1600s-pres.]

quim-bush the female pubic hair. For synonyms see DOWNSHIRE. [British slang, 1800s]

quimby a weak and ineffectual male. For synonyms see FRIBBLE, EPICENE. [British, late 1900s-pres.]

quim nuts labia hanging so low as to be confused with a scrotum. [British, late 1900s-pres.]

quimp a total JERK; a social outcast. For synonyms see OAF. [U.S. slang, late 1900s]

quimsby (also **quimmy**) the female genitals. See QUIM. [British, 1800s or before]

quim-stake the penis. For synonyms see YARD. [British, 1800s or before]

quim-sticker a lecher; a whoremonger. [British, 1800s or before]

quim-sticking copulating. In expressions such as "go quim-sticking." *Cf.* QUIM. [British, 1800s or before]

quimsy 1. the female genitals. **2.** copulation. Both are in expressions such as "bit of quimsy." *Cf.* QUIM. [both British, 1800s or before]

quin the female gentials. See QUIM. [British, 1800s or before]

R

rack 1. a bed. [U.S., late 1900s-pres.] **2.** a pair of [female] breasts. For synonyms see BOSOM. [U.S., late 1900s-pres.]

rackdate a sexually free female. Rack = bed. [U.S. collegiate, late 1900s, Eble]

racked (also **racked-up**) **1.** intoxicated with alcohol. For synonyms see WOOFLED. [U.S. slang, 1900s] **2.** intoxicated with marijuana. For synonyms see TALL. [U.S. drug culture, mid 1900s-pres.] **3.** struck in the testicles. [U.S. slang, late 1900s]

racks the human breasts. From "racks of meat" or "meat racks." For synonyms see BOSOM. [U.S. slang, 1900s]

rag a sanitary napkin; a PERINEAL PAD (*q.v.*). *Cf.* RIDING THE RAG. For synonyms see MANHOLE COVER. [U.S. colloquial, 1900s] See also RAGS.

rag, on the 1. menstruating. Abbreviated as O.T.R. (*q.v.*). [U.S. colloquial, mid 1900s-pres.] **2.** acting bitchy. From sense 1. Not limited to women. [U.S. slang, mid 1900s-pres.]

rag doll a slovenly woman. For synonyms see TROLLYMOG. [British and U.S. slang, mid 1800s-1900s]

ragged intoxicated with alcohol. For synonyms see WOOFLED. [U.S. slang, early 1700s-pres.]

Raggedy Ann L.S.D. solution on blotter paper stamped with a picture of Raggedy Ann. For synonyms see ACID. [U.S. drug culture, late 1900s, Abel]

ragging having the menstrual period. From RAG, ON THE (*q.v.*). [U.S. slang, mid 1900s-pres.]

ragging it having the menses. For synonyms see FLOODS. [U.S., late 1900s-pres.]

ragtime the menses. From the name of a popular music style in the early 1900s. For synonyms see FLOODS. [U.S. slang, mid 1900s-pres.]

ragweed a low grade of marijuana. From the common name of a weed. *Cf.* WEED (sense 1).

rail an erection of the penis. For synonyms see ERECTION. [slang, mid 1900s-pres.]

railroad (tracks) rows of needle scars along the main vein of the arms. [U.S. drug culture, late 1900s, Kaiser]

rails lines of cocaine ready for snorting. For synonyms see NOSE-CANDY. [U.S. drug culture, late 1900s]

rainbow 1. a nickname for a bow-legged person. [colloquial, 1900s] **2.** a Tuinal (trademark) capsule. [U.S. drug culture, mid 1900s-pres.] **3.** to have coition with a person of another race. From the bands of colors in the rainbow. [U.S. slang, mid 1900s-pres.]

raincoat a condom. *Cf.* DIVING SUIT, ONE-PIECE OVERCOAT. For synonyms see EEL-SKIN. [U.S. slang, mid 1900s]

rainy-day woman marijuana; a marijuana cigarette. [U.S. drug culture, mid 1900s-pres.]

raise a gallop to get an erection. [British, early 1900s-pres.]

ralph 1. a fool; an oaf. See RALPH SPOONER. [colloquial since the 1700s] **2.** to vomit. *Cf.* BARF, EARP, YORK. [U.S. slang, mid 1900s-pres.] **3.** VOMITUS. For synonyms see YORK. [U.S. slang, late 1900s] **4.** a nickname for the penis. For synonyms see GENITALS, YARD. [U.S. collegiate, late 1900s, Munro]

ralph something up to vomit something up. For synonyms see YORK. [U.S. slang, late 1900s]

ram 1. an act of copulation. [colloquial and nonce, 1600s-pres.] **2.** to copulate with a female, from the male point of view. [colloquial since the 1800s or before] **3.** to perform PEDERASTY (*q.v.*). *Cf.* RAM-JOB. **4.** the penis, especially the erect penis. [colloquial, 1900s or before]

ram-bam a rapid and harsh act of copulation. From "Ram-bam, thank you, ma'am." [U.S. slang, mid 1900s]

Ram it! a derisive exclamation, "Ram it up your ass!"; the same as SHOVE IT! (*q.v.*). [U.S. slang, mid 1900s]

ram-job an act of anal intercourse. *Cf.* RAM (sense 3). [U.S. slang, mid 1900s-pres.]

rammer the penis, especially the erect penis. *Cf.* RAM (sense 4). [colloquial and nonce, 1800s or before]

ramped drunk. For synonyms see WOOFLED. [British, late 1900s-pres.]

ramrod the penis, especially the erect penis. *Cf.* RAMMER. [colloquial and nonce, 1600s-pres.]

rams, the the DELIRIUM TREMENS (*q.v.*). For synonyms see ORK-ORKS. [U.S. slang, 1800s] See also RATS, THE.

ramstudious lustful. [U.S. colloquial, 1900s, Berrey and Van den Bark]

ranch 1. semen. Similar in appearance and consistency to Ranch [salad] dressing. For synonyms see METTLE. [U.S., late 1900s-pres.] **2.** to ejaculate. [U.S., late 1900s-pres.]

randy 1. coarse, rude, and violent. [colloquial, 1600s] **2.** lewd, salacious, and lustful; later sexy-looking. [colloquial, 1700s-pres.] **3.** a penis. For synonyms see YARD. [late 1900s]

rank ugly; unpleasant; vile; rotten. The standard sense of the word used in slang contexts. [U.S., late 1900s]

rank on someone to attack someone verbally; to gossip about someone. [U.S. collegiate, late 1900s]

ran the good race died. [U.S. colloquial, 1900s or before]

ranting sexually aroused and lustful. *Cf.* RANDY. [British, 1800s or before]

rape fluid perfume. [U.S. slang, 1900s]

Raquel Welch a belch. Rhyming slang. [British, late 1900s-pres.]

rare 1. to inhale powdered narcotics,

e.g., cocaine. [U.S. drug culture, mid 1900s-pres.] **2.** a drink of an alcoholic beverage. [U.S., 1900s, Berrey and Van den Bark]

rare as rocking horse shit very rare; very unusual. [Australian, mid 1900s-pres.]

rasp 1. the female genitals. For synonyms see MONOSYLLABLE. **2.** to coit a woman; to copulate. **3.** coition as in the expression "do a rasp." [all senses, British slang, 1800s, Farmer and Henley]

raspberries a woman's nipples, especially if erect. [U.S. slang, late 1900s]

raspberry tart 1. a release of intestinal gas. Rhyming slang for FART (*q.v.*). For synonyms see GURK. **2.** the heart. Rhyming slang. [both senses, British, 1800s]

rasper a loud release of intestinal gas. For synonyms see GURK. [British slang, 1900s, *Dictionary of Slang and Unconventional English*]

rasty having to do with a harsh-looking young woman. [U.S., late 1900s-pres.]

rat 1. a drunken man or woman arrested in the night by the authorities. [British, 1600s, B.E.] **2.** an extremely detestable person, usually a male. [U.S. slang, 1900s or before]

rat-arsed drunk. For synonyms see WOOFLED. [British, late 1900s-pres.]

ratbag a despised person. For synonyms see SNOKE-HORN. [Australian and British, late 1900s-pres.]

rat-bastard a really wretched or despised person. For synonyms see SNOKE-HORN. [U.S. slang, late 1900s]

rat-fink an extremely unpleasant person, usually a male; a detestable variety of FINK (*q.v.*). [U.S. slang, mid 1900s-pres.]

Rat-fuck! an expletive and exclamation, somewhat milder than "Fuck!" Based on RAT-FINK (*q.v.*). [U.S. slang, mid 1900s-pres.]

ratfuck to break up with someone, unpleasantly; to discard a lover. [U.S. slang, late 1900s]

Rats! an exclamation of despair or

disapproval. [colloquial since the late 1800s]

rats, the the DELIRIUM TREMENS (*q.v.*). Cf. RAMS, THE. For synonyms see ORK-ORKS. [colloquial, 1800s-1900s]

ratted alcohol intoxicated. [British slang, late 1900s, J. Green]

rattle and hiss urine; to urinate; a urination. Rhyming slang for PISS (*q.v.*). [U.S., 1900s, *Dictionary of Rhyming Slang*]

rattle beads to express aggravation. Cf. DROP ONE'S BEADS. [U.S. homosexual use, 1900s, Stanley]

rattled heavily intoxicated with alcohol; distraught; with one's senses impaired. Cf. RADDLED. [colloquial, 1800s-pres.]

rattler a man who copulates athletically. See FUCK LIKE A RATTLESNAKE. [British slang, 1900s, *Dictionary of Slang and Unconventional English*]

rattlesnake a prostitute. Because of the way she shakes her tail. Cf. FUCK LIKE A RATTLESNAKE. [Australian, Baker]

rat-trap a bustle. From the shape of the frame. [British slang, 1800s, Farmer and Henley]

raunch someone out to offend by using bad language or referring to disgusting things. [U.S. collegiate, late 1900s, Eble]

raunchy (also **ronchie**) **1.** dirty, sloppy, and bad-smelling. **2.** racy, obscene, or off-color. **3.** intoxicated with alcohol. [all senses, U.S. slang, mid 1900s-pres.]

raven beauty a beautiful black woman. From the blackness of a raven and a play on "raving beauty." [U.S. slang, early 1900s] Synonyms: BANANA, BIT OF EBONY, BLACK DOLL, BLACK MEAT, BLACK VELVET, BROWN-SKIN BABY, BROWN SUGAR, CHARCOAL BLOSSOM, CHARCOAL LILY, COVESS-DINGE, CULLUD GAL, DANGE BROAD, DARK MEAT, FEMMOKE, HOT CHOCOLATE, LAUNDRY QUEEN, LIZA, MULATTO MEAT, NIGGER-GAL, NIGGER-WENCH, PIECE OF DARK MEAT, REDBONE, SAPPHIRE, SEAL, SHADY LADY.

raw, in the nude; naked. For synonyms see STARKERS. [U.S. and elsewhere, 1900s]

raw dog [copulating] without a condom. [U.S., late 1900s-pres.]

raw meat 1. the penis. Cf. MEAT (sense 4). For synonyms see YARD. [colloquial and nonce, 1700s-pres.] **2.** a naked person, usually a naked woman. [British and U.S. slang, 1800s-1900s]

R.D. a "red devil," a capsule of Seconal (trademark). For synonyms see SEC. [U.S. drug culture, mid 1900s-pres.]

reach around an act of masturbation performed on a RECEIVER by an INSERTOR during an act of PEDERASTY. For synonyms and related subjects see WASTE TIME. [U.S. slang, late 1900s]

readies cash; ready cash. [British, late 1900s-pres.]

ready to spit on the verge of ejaculating, said of the male when highly sexually aroused. Cf. DRIPPING FOR IT. [British slang, 1900s, *Dictionary of Slang and Unconventional English*]

ream 1. to stick something up someone's rectum. Cf. GOOSE (sense 6). **2.** to commit ANILINGUS (*q.v.*). **3.** anilingus. Cf. REAM-JOB, RIM. **4.** to commit PEDERASTY (*q.v.*). **5.** to cheat. Cf. SCREW (sense 6). [all senses, U.S. slang, 1900s]

reamer 1. the penis, especially the erect penis. **2.** a PEDERAST (*q.v.*). [both sense, U.S. underworld, early 1900s]

ream-job ANILINGUS (*q.v.*). See REAM (sense 3).

reaper marijuana. From REEFER (*q.v.*). [U.S., mid 1900s, *Current Slang*]

rear 1. a privy; an outhouse; the same as BACK (*q.v.*). For synonyms see AJAX. [British colloquial, late 1800s-1900s] **2.** the posteriors. For synonyms see DUFF. [U.S. colloquial, 1900s]

receiving-set 1. the female genitals. **2.** a toilet or chamber pot. Both are from a term for a radio receiver. [U.S., 1900s, Berrey and Van den Bark]

red 1. a Seconal (trademark) capsule. A truncation of RED DEVIL (*q.v.*). [U.S. drug culture, mid 1900s-pres.] **2.** red wine; cheap red wine. [slang, 1900s] **3.** a communist. [U.S., mid 1900s] **4.** marijuana. A truncation of PANAMA RED (*q.v.*). [U.S. drug culture, mid 1900s-pres.]

red and blue a Tuinal (trademark) capsule. [U.S. drug culture, mid 1900s-pres.]

red-assed very angry. From "red-faced." [U.S. slang, mid 1900s-pres.]

redbird a Seconal (trademark) capsule. *Cf.* BLACKBIRD, BLUEBIRD. [U.S. drug culture, mid 1900s-pres.]

red bumpies a sexually transmitted disease. [U.S., late 1900s-pres.]

red-cap the penis; the *glans penis.* [British, early 1900s, *Dictionary of Slang and Unconventional English*]

red cross morphine. From its common use in wartime. *Cf.* WHITE CROSS. [U.S., early 1900s or before]

red devil a capsule of Seconal (trademark), a barbiturate. *Cf.* BLACKBIRD, BLUEBIRD. [U.S. drug culture, mid 1900s-pres.]

red-dirt marijuana marijuana which grows freely in the wild. [U.S. drug culture, mid 1900s-pres.]

red-end the *glans penis. Cf.* RED-CAP. [British, 1900s, *Dictionary of Slang and Unconventional English*]

red flag 1. a sanitary napkin; a PERINEAL PAD (*q.v.*). *Cf.* DANGER-SIGNAL. **2.** the menses. *Cf.* FLAGGING. [both senses, 1800s-1900s]

red-handed in the act of copulating. The "red" is a play on the heat of passion and RED-END (*q.v.*). From an expression referring to taking someone by surprise and, in the minds of some, the redness of the erect penis.

red-hot poker the penis, especially the erect penis. *Cf.* POKER. [colloquial and nonce, 1800s-pres.]

red-jacket a capsule of Seconal (trademark). *Cf.* YELLOW-JACKET. [U.S. drug culture, mid 1900s-pres.]

red lamp a brothel. *Cf.* RED LIGHT (sense 2). [British, early 1900s, *Dictionary of Slang and Unconventional English*]

red light 1. a prostitute. **2.** a brothel.

3. pertaining to brothels or to prostitution. [all senses, U.S. slang, early 1900s-pres.]

red-light district an area where prostitution is available; the "low" part of town. [U.S. colloquial, 1900s]

red-lighter a prostitute. *Cf.* RED LIGHT (sense 1). [U.S. slang, 1900s]

red-light house a brothel. [U.S., mid 1900s]

red-light sister a prostitute. For synonyms see HARLOT. [U.S. slang, early 1900s]

red rag a sanitary napkin; a perineal pad. For synonyms see MANHOLE COVER. [British slang, late 1800s, Farmer and Henley]

reds amphetamine capsules. For synonyms see AMP. [U.S. drug culture, mid 1900s-pres.]

red sails in the sunset the menses. For synonyms see FLOODS. [jocular euphemism, 1900s]

red tummy-ache the menses. For synonyms see FLOODS. [U.S., 1900s]

reeb backslang for "beer." For synonyms see SUDS. [British and U.S. slang, 1800s-1900s]

reefer 1. marijuana or a marijuana cigarette. [U.S., early 1900s-pres.] **2.** a marijuana smoker. See GREEFO. [U.S. drug culture, early 1900s-pres.]

reefer man a seller of marijuana. [U.S. slang, mid 1900s-pres.]

reefer weed marijuana or a marijuana cigarette. *Cf.* WEED (sense 1). [U.S. drug culture, mid 1900s-pres.]

reeking intoxicated with alcohol; stinking drunk. For synonyms see WOOFLED. [U.S. slang, 1900s]

reeling ripe (also **reeling**) intoxicated with alcohol. [British and U.S., 1800s-1900s]

reely intoxicated with alcohol. *Cf.* REELING RIPE. [British slang, early 1900s, *Dictionary of Slang and Unconventional English*]

reesch gross; vile; nasty. [U.S. collegiate, late 1900s, Munro]

reindeer dust a powdered narcotic, specifically cocaine. *Cf.* SNOW (sense

2). [underworld, mid 1900s, *Dictionary of the Underworld*]

relief station a W.C.; a privy. [U.S. euphemism, early 1900s-pres.]

relieve oneself 1. to defecate. **2.** to urinate. [both senses, widespread euphemism, 1800s-1900s] **3.** to ejaculate; to achieve sexual satisfaction, said of the male. For synonyms see MELT. [British, 1800s, Farmer and Henley]

religious intoxicated with alcohol. *Cf.* ONE OF THE FAITHFUL. [U.S. slang, early 1700s, Ben Franklin]

rent (also **renter**) a homosexual male who charges for his services rather than provide them free. *Cf.* TRADE. [British, late 1800s-1900s, *Dictionary of Slang and Unconventional English*]

rep a prostitute. From "reputation." *Cf.* DEMI-REP. [British, late 1700s, Grose]

repeaters beans. [U.S., late 1900s-pres.]

respond 1. to respond sexually, usually said of women. **2.** to respond sexually with an erection, said of men. [both senses, colloquial, 1800s-1900s]

reproductive fluid semen. For synonyms see METTLE. [U.S. euphemism, late 1900s, Lewin and Lewin]

rest, at 1. intoxicated with alcohol. [British and U.S. euphemism, 1800s-1900s] **2.** dead. [U.S. euphemism, 1900s]

rest-and-be-thankful the female genitals. [British slang, 1800s, Farmer and Henley]

restroom a W.C. found in a public building. Bathing facilities are rarely included. The word-of-choice for a public bathroom. [U.S., 1900s]

resurrection-cove a body-stealer; a RESURRECTIONIST (*q.v.*). [cant, 1800s or before, Vaux]

resurrection doctor a doctor who buys corpses which are stolen from graves or has people murdered and delivered to him. [British, 1800s]

resurrectionist (also **resurrection man**) a body-stealer. [British, late 1700s]

reswort trousers. Backslang for "trou-

ser." For synonyms see GALLIGASKINS. [British, 1800s]

retire to depart from the immediate premises to urinate. [euphemistic since the 1800s] Synonyms and related terms: ANSWER NATURE'S CALL, BOG, BURN THE GRASS, CHECK THE SKI RACK, COKE-STOP, DRAIN THE SPUDS, FIND A HAVEN OF REST, GIVE THE CHINAMAN A MUSIC LESSON, GO AND CATCH A HORSE, GO AND LOOK AT THE CROPS, GO AND SEE IF THE HORSE HAS KICKED OFF HIS BLANKET, GONE FOR A SLASH, GO TO EGYPT, NATURE STOP, PAY A VISIT, PLUCK A ROSE, POST A LETTER, POWDER ONE'S NOSE, SEE A MAN ABOUT A DOG, SEE A MAN ABOUT A HORSE, SEE JOHNNY, SEE MRS. MURPHY, VISIT THE SAND-BOX, WASH, WASH ONE'S HANDS, WASH UP.

retiring room a restroom, bathroom, or W.C. [U.S. euphemism, 1900s or before]

revenant the ghost of a dead person returning from the dead to haunt the living. [since the mid 1800s] Related terms: APPARITION, BANSHEE, BARGHEST, BOGEY, BOGGARD, BOGY, BOODIE, BOOGER MAN, BUGBEAR, BUGGER, BULL-BEAR, BULL-BEGGAR, DIBBUK, DUPPY, DYBBUK, EMPUSA, EPHIALTES, EVILS, FANTASM, FEAR-BABE, FEARIN', FETCH, GHOUL, HANTS, IMP, INCUBUS, JINNI, SPECTER, SPOOK, WILL O' THE WISP, WRAITH.

reverse gears to vomit. For synonyms see YORK. [U.S. slang, late 1900s]

revved up HIGH on methamphetamine. For synonyms see TALL. [U.S. drug culture, late 1900s]

R.F. 1. a ROYAL FUCKING (*q.v.*). **2.** a RAT-FINK (*q.v.*). **3.** RAT-FUCK! (*q.v.*). [all senses, U.S. slang, mid 1900s-pres.]

Rhea sisters (also **rhea brothers, rheas, rhea twins**) a jocular term for leucorrhea, gonorrhea, diarrhea, and pyorrhea.

rhoid a bothersome person. A *hemorrhoid*. For synonyms see SNOKE-HORN. [U.S., late 1900s-pres.]

rhythms amphetamines or amphetamine capsules. For synonyms see

AMP. [U.S. drug culture, mid 1900s-pres.]

rib a girl, woman, or wife. Based on "Adam's rib." [colloquial and slang, 1700s-pres.]

rib cushions the breasts. For synonyms see BOSOM. [late 1900s]

rib joint a house of prostitution. For synonyms see BROTHEL. [U.S., late 1900s-pres.]

rice queen a gay man who prefers Asian males. For synonyms see EPICENE. [U.S., late 1900s-pres.]

ricockulous ridiculous. Word play based on dick = cock. [U.S., late 1900s-pres.]

ride 1. an act of coition. Refers to the motions of coition. **2.** to copulate, said of a man or a woman. Cf. PRIG (sense 1). [colloquial since the 1500s or before]

rider a sexually aroused male; one who is ready to RIDE (sense 2); a lecher or a whoremonger. [British, 1700s]

ride the Buick to vomit. Cf. BUICK. For synonyms see YORK. [U.S. collegiate, late 1900s, Munro]

ride the cotton pony to have the menses. For synonyms see FLOODS. [U.S., late 1900s-pres.]

ride the Hershey Highway to perform an act of PEDERASTY. For related subjects see PEDERASTY. [U.S. collegiate, late 1900s, Munro]

ride the hobby horse to copulate; to COIT someone. For synonyms see OCCUPY. [U.S. collegiate, late 1900s]

ride the hog to copulate. For synonyms see OCCUPY. [U.S., late 1900s-pres.]

ride the porcelain bus (also **ride the porcelain Honda, ride the porcelain train**) to sit on the toilet having diarrhea. [U.S. slang, late 1900s]

riding the cotton bicycle the menses. See RIDING THE RAG. [1900s]

riding the rag 1. having one's menstrual period. For synonyms see FLOODS. [U.S., 1900s] **2.** a catch phrase explaining why someone is in a bad humor; the same as RAG, ON THE

(sense 2). Said of women and men. [U.S. slang, 1900s]

riding the white horse having one's menstrual period. "White" refers here to the PERINEAL PAD (q.v.). [U.S. slang, 1900s]

righteous bush marijuana. Cf. BUSH (sense 6). [U.S. slang, mid 1900s-pres.]

rigid 1. intoxicated with alcohol. **2.** very angry; stiff with rage. [both senses, U.S. slang, mid 1900s]

rim 1. ANILINGUS (q.v.); the same as REAM (sense 3). **2.** to commit ANILINGUS (q.v.). [both senses, U.S. slang, 1900s] **3.** to reach ejaculation through masturbation. [U.S. slang, mid 1900s, Dahlskog] **4.** to coit a woman anally. [British slang, 1900s, *Dictionary of Slang and Unconventional English*] **5.** pertaining to a female who is ready and eager for copulation. Reminiscent of BRIM (sense 3). [U.S. dialect (Ozarks), 1900s or before, Randolph and Wilson]

rimadonna a homosexual male who prefers to perform or receive ANILINGUS (q.v.). A jocular play on "prima donna." [U.S. homosexual use, mid 1900s, Farrell]

rim-job an act of ANILINGUS (q.v.). See REAM-JOB.

ring 1. the female genitals, specifically the vagina. Cf. CIRCLE, HOOP. [slang, late 1500s] **2.** the anus. [slang, 1800s-pres.] **3.** a contraceptive diaphragm. [U.S. slang, 1900s]

ring-jerk See CIRCLE-JERK.

ring someone's chimes to excite someone sexually; to give someone an orgasm. [U.S. slang, mid 1900s-pres.]

ring-tail 1. a derogatory nickname for an Italian. [U.S., 1900s] **2.** a derogatory nickname for a Japanese. [World War II] **3.** a coward. [Australian slang, 1900s, Baker] **4.** a CATAMITE (q.v.). [U.S. underworld, early 1900s]

ring-tailed polecat, I'll be a a jocular oath or an exclamation of surprise. [stereotypical cowboy jargon; U.S., 1900s or before]

ring-tail wife a CATAMITE (q.v.). Cf.

RING (sense 2). RING-TAIL (sense 4). [U.S. underworld, early 1900s]

ringtum the anus. For synonyms see ANUS. [British, late 1900s-pres.]

rip, old 1. a jaded old man. **2.** an aged prostitute. Cf. GASH (sense 2), REP, SLIT. [both senses, British and U.S., late 1800s-1900s]

ripe intoxicated with alcohol. For synonyms see WOOFLED. [colloquial and slang, 1800s-1900s]

ripped 1. intoxicated with alcohol. For synonyms see WOOFLED. **2.** drug intoxicated. Cf. TORE-UP. For synonyms see TALL. [both senses, U.S. slang, mid 1900s]

ripped to the tits heavily alcohol intoxicated. Cf. STONED TO THE TITS. An elaboration of RIPPED. For synonyms see WOOFLED. [U.S. slang, 1900s, Rodgers]

ripples for nipples small or nonexistent breasts. For synonyms see BOSOM. [U.S., late 1900s-pres.]

rise to get an erection of the penis. Cf. GET A RISE. [since the 1600s]

rise, a an erection. For synonyms see ERECTION. [British, late 1900s-pres.]

rise in one's Levi's an erection, especially in the expression "I'm wise to the rise in your Levi's." [U.S., mid 1900s]

rise to the occasion to get an erection. [nonce and double entendre; British and U.S. colloquial, 1900s]

rites of love copulation. For synonyms see SMOCKAGE. [euphemistic, 1600s]

rits tablets of Ritalin, a stimulant. [U.S. drug culture, late 1900s, Kaiser]

roach 1. a cockroach. A truncation of "cockroach." [U.S., 1800s-1900s] **2.** a low prostitute. Based on "cockroach." [U.S., 1900s] **3.** the stub of a marijuana cigarette. The stub is highly valued because it contains accumulated deposits of T.H.C. (q.v.), the active ingredient in marijuana. See ROACH CLIP. [U.S. drug culture, mid 1900s-pres.] **4.** a girl, especially an unattractive girl. From the insect name. For synonyms see BUFFARILLA. [U.S. slang, 1900s] **5.** a

policeman. [U.S. underworld, early-mid 1900s, Weseen]

roach clip a holder for smoking the butt of a marijuana cigarette. Cf. ROACH (sense 3). [U.S. drug culture, mid 1900s-pres.] See also JEFFERSON AIRPLANE.

roach coach a truck whose driver sells sandwiches and other prepared food. [U.S., late 1900s-pres.]

roached hung over; exhausted. [U.S., late 1900s-pres.]

road apple a formed lump of horse excrement; the same as ALLEY APPLE and HORSE APPLE (both q.v.). [U.S. colloquial, 1900s]

road brew (also **road sauce**) beer. [U.S. collegiate, late 1900s]

road dog one's best friend. [U.S., late 1900s-pres.]

road dope amphetamines. Refers to the use of amphetamines by cross-country truck drivers. For synonyms see AMP. [U.S. drug culture, late 1900s, Abel]

road hash roadkill; an animal killed on the road. [U.S., late 1900s-pres.]

road kid a CATAMITE (q.v.); a tramp's catamite. [U.S. underworld, early 1900s]

road pizza a dead animal on the road. [U.S. slang, late 1900s]

road whore a sexually free female; a SLUT. Derogatory. For synonyms see TAIL. [U.S. slang, late 1900s]

roaring-drunk (also **roaring**) heavily intoxicated with alcohol. Cf. LION DRUNK. [U.S. slang, 1900s]

roaring horn a very hard erection. For synonyms see ERECTION. [Australian, 1800s, *Dictionary of Slang and Unconventional English*]

roasted alcohol intoxicated. For synonyms see WOOFLED. [U.S., late 1900s-pres.]

rock 1. to coit a woman. From the motions of coition. [U.S. slang, mid 1900s] **2.** (also **rock candy, rock cocaine**) a smokable, crystallized form of cocaine. For synonyms see NOSE-CANDY. **3.** a crystallized form of heroin used for smoking. For synonyms see

HEROIN. [both senses, U.S. drug culture, late 1900s] **4.** a well-built male. [U.S., late 1900s-pres.]

rock cocaine See ROCK.

rocked to sleep dead. Refers to rocking in the bosom of Abraham. See ABRAHAM'S BOSOM. [U.S. euphemism, late 1800s, Ware]

rocket 1. a marijuana cigarette. Because it sends one on a HIGH (sense 3). Cf. ROCKET-FUEL, SKYROCKET. [U.S. underworld and drug culture, 1900s] **2.** a sanitary tampon. For synonyms see MANHOLE COVER. [U.S. slang, late 1900s]

rocket-fuel phencyclidine, the drug P.C.P. (q.v.). Cf. ROCKET, SKYROCKET. [U.S. drug culture, mid 1900s-pres.]

rockette a female crack user. [U.S., late 1900s-pres.]

rock-house a place where rock cocaine is made, sold, and used. A CRACK HOUSE. Often an abandoned house. [U.S. drug culture, late 1900s]

rockman a drug dealer who specializes in crystallized cocaine. [U.S. drug culture, late 1900s]

rock out 1. to pass out from the use of marijuana or other drugs. Cf. CAP OUT, STONED (sense 2). [U.S. drug culture, mid 1900s-pres.] **2.** to overdose on a drug, especially CRACK cocaine. [U.S. drug culture, late 1900s]

rock python the erect penis. From the common name of a snake. Cf. SYPHON THE PYTHON. [British slang, mid 1900s-pres.]

rocks the testicles. Cf. GOOLIES, PEBBLES, STONES (sense 2). For synonyms see WHIRLYGIGS. [slang and colloquial, 1900s or before]

rocky intoxicated with alcohol. Related to instability and "rocking." [U.S. slang, early 1700s, Ben Franklin]

rod 1. to coit a woman. [colloquial, 1800s-1900s] **2.** the penis, especially the erect penis. [British and U.S., 1800s-1900s] **3.** a gun. [U.S. underworld and stereotypical gangster jargon, early 1900s-pres.]

rod of love the penis; the erect penis.

Cf. ROD. For synonyms see ERECTION, YARD. [U.S. slang, late 1900s]

rod-walloper a male masturbator. Cf. ROD. [British slang, late 1900s, J. Green]

roger 1. the penis. For synonyms see YARD. [British, mid 1600s-1800s] **2.** the nickname for a bull and occasionally for a ram. [rural colloquial, 1700s-1800s] **3.** to copulate with a cow, said of a bull. **4.** to coit a woman. From sense 3. [British, 1700s-1900s; various senses are attested in U.S. dialects, 1800s-1900s] **5.** to rape a woman. [U.S. dialect, 1900s, Wentworth]

roid rage aggressive behavior caused by excessive steroid use. A play on *road rage*. [U.S. late 1900s-pres.]

rolf to vomit; to RALPH. A spelling variant. For synonyms see YORK. [U.S. slang, late 1900s]

roll copulation; coition as enjoyed by the male. See JELLY-ROLL (sense 1). [U.S. slang, early 1900s-pres.]

roller 1. a prostitute who specializes in robbing (rolling) drunks. [U.S., 1900s] **2.** a police car; a police officer in a police car. Refers to the police car that "rolls" on wheels. [U.S. drug culture, late 1900s, Kaiser]

roller skate to coit. [U.S. slang, mid 1900s, *Current Slang*]

rolling buzz a long-lasting drug high. [U.S., mid 1900s-pres.]

rolling-drunk (also **rulling-drunk**) intoxicated with alcohol. [colloquial and slang, 1900s and before]

rolling-pin the penis. From the shape. See ROLL. [colloquial and nonce, 1800s-pres.]

roll in the hay (also **toss in the hay**) copulation; a spontaneous or secret act of copulation performed in a .barn or a haystack; any spontaneous or casual act of copulation. Cf. ROLL. [U.S. slang, early 1900s-pres.]

rollocks the testicles. From TOMMY ROLLOCKS (q.v.). Cf. ROLLIES. [British, 1900s]

rolls tablets of Ecstacy. [U.S., late 1900s-pres.]

roof, off the experiencing the menses. *Cf.* FALL OFF THE ROOF. [U.S. slang, mid 1900s-pres.]

rooster 1. the penis. A jocular and euphemistic avoidance of COCK (sense 3). [U.S., 1800s] **2.** to cock a gun. An aviodance of "cock." [U.S. jocular euphemism, 1900s] **3.** a lascivious man. Refers to a rooster and his harem of hens. For synonyms see LECHER. [U.S. colloquial, 1900s or before] **4.** the female genitals. In avoidance of "cock." See COCK (sense 6). [British slang, 1800s, Farmer and Henley]

roostered intoxicated with alcohol. See COCKED (sense 1). [U.S. euphemism of avoidance, 1900s or before]

root 1. the penis. [since the 1600s] **2.** to coit a woman. Also **root around**. From sense 1. *Cf.* ROOTLE. [colloquial, 1900s] **3.** a marijuana cigarette. [U.S. drug culture, mid 1900s-pres.] **4.** amphetamines or an amphetamine tablet or capsule. [U.S. drug culture, mid 1900s-pres.] **5.** copulation; a session of sexual activity. For synonyms see SMOCKAGE. [Australian, mid 1900s-pres.]

rope marijuana or a marijuana cigarette. Refers to a "hemp" rope. *Cf.* GUNNY, HEMP. [U.S. drug culture, mid 1900s-pres.]

rope dope low-quality marijuana from hemp. For synonyms see MARI. [U.S., late 1900s-pres.]

rose 1. the female genitals. **2.** the maidenhead; the hymen. *Cf.* BUD. [both senses, British, 1800s, or before] See also ROSES.

rosebuds a woman's nipples, especially if erect. *Cf.* RASPBERRIES. [U.S. slang, 1900s]

roses 1. the menses. *Cf.* FLOWERS. [British euphemism, 1800s] **2.** amphetamines; amphetamine tablets or capsules. For synonyms see AMP. [U.S. drug culture, mid 1900s-pres.]

rosy intoxicated with alcohol; reddened from drink. [U.S. slang, late 1800s-mid 1900s]

rosy about the gills intoxicated with alcohol. See GILLS, UP TO THE. [U.S. slang, early 1900s]

rot 1. nonsense. See TOMMY-ROT. [slang and colloquial, mid 1800s-pres.] **2.** inferior liquor. A truncation of ROT-GUT (*q.v.*). For synonyms see EMBALMING FLUID. See also DAD, DOD.

rot-gut weak beer; inferior liquor; strong homebrewed liquor. *Cf.* GUT-ROT, POP-SKULL. [colloquial and slang since the late 1500s] Synonyms: CONK-BUSTER, GNAT'S PISS, GREEK FIRE, PAINT-REMOVER, POP-SKULL, SNEAKY PETE, VARNISH-REMOVER, WILD MARE'S MILK.

roto-rooter the penis. From the trade name of a sewer-cleaning firm. For synonyms see GENITALS, YARD. [U.S. slang, mid 1900s-pres.]

rotten intoxicated with alcohol. [widespread slang, 1800s-pres.]

rough as a badger's arse very rough. [British, mid 1900s-pres.]

rough as a badger's bum very rough. [British, mid 1900s-pres.]

rough rider a ribbed condom. For synonyms see EEL-SKIN. [U.S., late 1900s-pres.]

rough-riding copulation without a condom. From the male point of view. *Cf.* BAREBACK. [British slang, 1900s, *Dictionary of Slang and Unconventional English*]

rough stuff marijuana containing an excess of roots, stems, and seeds. *Cf.* LUMBER. [U.S. drug culture, mid 1900s-pres.]

rough trade a cruel and physically abusive male homosexual partner. He may beat or rob after sexual relations. *Cf.* LEATHER (sense 2), SISSY-BEATER. [U.S. homosexual use, mid 1900s-pres.]

roundeye 1. a CATAMITE (*q.v.*). For synonyms see BRONCO. [U.S. underworld, early 1900s, Goldin, O'Leary, and Lipsius] **2.** the anus. *Cf.* BLIND-EYE (sense 1). [U.S. slang, mid 1900s-pres.] **3.** a Caucasian. From the point of view of an Oriental. [U.S. slang, mid 1900s]

roundhead a circumcised penis. For synonyms see YARD. [British, late 1900s-pres.]

roundheel 1. (also **roundheels**) a woman who permits sexual intercourse without much fuss; a pushover. Her heels are round and she just falls over. **2.** a prizefighter who is knocked out easily. [both senses, U.S. slang, early 1900s-pres.]

round-pound a type of mutual masturbation; the same as CIRCLE-JERK (*q.v.*). [U.S. slang, mid 1900s]

rounds trousers; pants. From rhyming slang, "round-the-houses." [slang, 1800s]

round-the-houses (also **round-me-houses, round-my-houses**) trousers; pants. Rhyming slang for "trousers." [British slang, mid 1800s]

rouser a very loud release of intestinal gas. *Cf.* TRUMP. For synonyms see GURK. [slang since the early 1700s]

roust 1. to coit a woman. **2.** coition. [both senses, British, late 1500s]

rout to copulate with a woman. *Cf.* ROOT (sense 2). From the standard sense of "carve" or "scoop out." [U.S. slang, mid 1900s-pres.]

royal blue the drug L.S.D. (*q.v.*). [U.S. drug culture, mid 1900s-pres.]

R.T.F.M. "Read the fucking manual!" [British and U.S., late 1900s-pres.]

rubber a condom. For synonyms see EEL-SKIN. [U.S.colloquial, mid 1900s-pres.]

rubber boot a condom. For synonyms see EEL-SKIN. [U.S. slang, 1900s]

rubber cookie a contraceptive diaphragm. [U.S. slang, late 1900s]

rubber duckie a condom. For synonyms see EEL-SKIN. [U.S., late 1900s-pres.]

rubber johnny a condom. For synonyms see EEL-SKIN. [British slang, 1900s, McDonald]

ruck a disguise of "fuck." Seen primarily as a camouflage of the graffito "fuck." See MOTHER-RUCKER.

rudder 1. the penis. **2.** to copulate. [both senses, British, early 1600s-1700s]

ruddy a disguise of "bloody." [British and U.S., late 1800s-1900s]

rude bits the genitals. For synonyms see GENITALS. [British, late 1900s-pres.]

rudery a rude remark. [British, late 1900s-pres.]

rug 1. a wig of any type. No negative connotations. **2.** the female pubic hair. *Cf.* MERKIN, TWAT-RUG. For synonyms see DOWNSHIRE. [both senses, U.S. colloquial and slang, 1900s or before]

rug-muncher a lesbian. *Cf.* RUG. For synonyms see LESBYTERIAN. [(U.S. slang, late 1900s]

ruin 1. to DEFLOWER (*q.v.*) a woman; to ruin a woman's reputation. [euphemistic, 1700s-1900s] **2.** gin. From BLUE RUIN (*q.v.*). [British and U.S. slang, 1800s-1900s] Synonyms for sense 2: BATHTUB GIN, BLUE RIBBON, BLUE RUIN, BLUE STONE, BLUE TAPE, BOB, BRIAN O'LINN, CAT'S WATER, CLAP OF THUNDER, DIDDLE, DRAIN, EYE-WATER, FLASH OF LIGHTNING, JACKY, LIGHTNING, LIGHT WET, LONDON MILK, MAX, MISERY, MOTHER'S MILK, NIG, OLD TOM, RIGHT-SORT, SATIN, SKY BLUE, STARK NAKED, STINKIOUS, STREAK OF LIGHTNING, STRIP-ME-NAKED, STRONG AND THIN, TANGLE-LEG, TAPE, TITTERY, TWANKAY, UNSWEETENED, WATER OF LIFE, WHITE, WHITE PORT, WHITE SATIN, WHITE TAPE, WHITE VELVET, WHITE WINE, YARD OF SATIN.

ruin a woman's shape See SPOIL A WOMAN'S SHAPE.

ruined drunk. For synonyms see WOOFLED. [U.S., late 1900s-pres.]

rule-of-three 1. the VIRILIA (*q.v.*), *i.e.*, one penis and two testicles. [British, early 1700s] **2.** copulation. For synonyms see SMOCKAGE. [British slang, 1800s, Farmer and Henley]

rum-bag a drunkard. For synonyms see ALCHY. [U.S., mid 1900s]

rumble-seat the posteriors. May include a reference to the audible breaking of wind. [U.S., 1900s]

rummed-up (also **rummed**) intoxicated with alcohol. [U.S. slang, early 1900s]

rummy a drunkard. For synonyms see ALCHY. [U.S. colloquial, mid 1800s-pres.]

rump 1. the hindquarters; the buttocks; the posteriors. [since the mid 1400s] **2.** the female genitals. [primarily

British, since the mid 1600s] **3.** to coit a woman. [British slang, 1800s, Farmer and Henley] **4.** to copulate with a woman (vaginally) from the rear. [British, 1800s] **5.** to flog someone on the buttocks. [British, cant or colloquial early 1800s] **6.** to defecate on someone. **7.** to break wind at someone. [senses 6 and 7 are British slang, 1800s, Farmer and Henley]

rump-cleft the fissure between the buttocks. [British, 1900s]

rumper 1. a prostitute. **2.** a whoremonger. [both senses, British slang, 1800s]

Rumpleforeskin the penis. Based on the name of the fairy-tale character *Rumplestiltskin.* Cf. RUMP. For synonyms see GENITALS, YARD. [U.S. slang, late 1900s, Lewin and Lewin]

rump-shaker an act of sexual intercourse. For synonyms see SMOCKAGE. [British, mid 1900s-pres.]

rump-splitter 1. the penis, especially the erect penis. [British slang, mid 1600s] **2.** a whoremonger. For synonyms see LECHER. [1600s (Urquhart)]

rumpus the posteriors. An elaboration of RUMP (sense 1). [U.S., mid 1900s]

rump-work copulation. For synonyms see SMOCKAGE. [British slang, 1800s, Farmer and Henley]

rumpy-pumpy copulation. For synonyms see SMOCKAGE. [British, late 1900s-pres.]

running-belly diarrhea; dysentery. For synonyms see QUICKSTEP. [Caribbean]

running-off at the mouth talking too much. Cf. DIARRHEA OF THE MOUTH. [U.S. colloquial, 1900s]

run off 1. to have diarrhea. **2.** the effluvium of diarrhea. Usually hyphenated in this sense. [both senses, U.S. colloquial, 1900s or before] **3.** a urination; a stop at the W.C. Usually hyphenated in this sense. [British, early 1900s, *Dictionary of Slang and Unconventional English*]

run one's tail to work as a prostitute. [British slang, 1800s, Farmer and Henley]

runs diarrhea. Cf. MOVIES, SCOOTS, TROTS, For synonyms see QUICKSTEP. [colloquial, 1800s-1900s]

run to seed (also **gone to seed**) pregnant. See SEED (sense 1). For synonyms see FRAGRANT. [British jocular slang, 1800s]

Rupert the penis. For synonyms see GENITALS, YARD. [British slang, 1900s, McDonald]

Russian duck to coit a woman; an act of copulation. Rhyming slang for "fuck." [British, early 1900s, *Dictionary of Rhyming Slang*]

Ruth 1. a women's restroom. Cf. JANE, JOHN (sense 1). [U.S. slang and colloquial, early-mid 1900s] **2.** to vomit. Cf. CRY RUTH. For synonyms see YORK. [widespread, late 1900s]

S

SABU "self-adjusting balls-up," a military blunder. *Cf.* BALLS-UP. For synonyms see SNAFU. [British military slang, 1900s]

sacking prostitution. *Cf.* BAG (sense 4), BURLAP SISTER. [slang, 1500s]

sacks 1. trousers. *Cf.* BAGS (sense 1). For synonyms see GALLIGASKINS. **2.** the human breasts. [U.S. slang, 1900s and nonce elsewhere]

saddie-maisie (also **sadie-maisie**) a practitioner of sadism and masochism. *Cf.* S. AND M. [U.S. slang, mid 1900s-pres.]

safe 1. a condom. *Cf.* SAFETY. For synonyms see EEL-SKIN. [British and U.S. colloquial, late 1800s-pres.] **2.** good; excellent. [British, late 1900s-pres.]

safe period the time of the month where conception is least likely to take place because of the nature of the menstrual cycle. An important concept in the RHYTHM METHOD (*q.v.*) of birth control.

safety a condom *Cf.* SAFE. For synonyms see EEL-SKIN. [U.S. slang, mid 1900s]

safety-sheath a condom. *Cf.* MALE SHEATH. [British and U.S., 1900s]

sailor's bait a prostitute; any girl or woman. [U.S. slang, early 1900s]

sailor's delight a prostitute. [U.S. slang, mid 1900s]

Saint Peter the penis. *Cf.* PETER. [British slang, 1800s, Farmer and Henley]

salt 1. sexually aroused; lewd and lecherous. Said of bitches in heat, *i.e.*, "salt bitch," and extended to humans. *Cf.* FLAVOUR. [British, 1500s-1800s] **2.** copulation. **3.** to copulate. [senses 2 and 3 are 1600s] **4.** intoxicated with alcohol. A truncation of SALT JUNK (*q.v.*), "drunk." [British, late 1800s,

Ware] **5.** powdered heroin. [U.S. drug culture, mid 1900s-pres.]

salt and pepper an inferior grade of marijuana. [U.S. drug culture, early 1900s]

salt cellar the female genitals. See SALT (sense 2). For synonyms see MONOSYLLABLE.

salted-down (also **salted**) **1.** intoxicated with alcohol. See SALT (sense 4). *Cf.* CORNED, PICKLED. [slang since the 1800s] **2.** dead. [U.S. slang, 1900s or before]

saltine a white person. A play on *cracker,* which is a derogatory term for a white person. [U.S., late 1900s-pres.]

SAM a "sorry-ass motherfucker." [U.S., late 1900s-pres.]

SAMFU a "self-adjusting military fuck-up," a military mess which will straighten itself out in time. For synonyms see SNAFU. [British, World War II]

sample 1. to fondle a woman sexually. **2.** to coit a virgin or to experience copulation with a particular woman for the first time. *Cf.* TASTE. [both senses, colloquial and nonce, 1800s-pres.]

sample of sin a prostitute. For synonyms see HARLOT. [British euphemism, mid 1700s]

sampler the female genitals. [British slang, 1800s, Farmer and Henley]

sandbagged blocked out of one's own room, as if by sandbags, while one's roommate is having sex. [U.S. collegiate, late 1900s, Eble]

sand-box 1. a box prepared in such a way that most cats can be trained to use it for elimination. **2.** a W.C. A jocular extension of sense 1. [both senses, colloquial, 1900s]

S. and M. 1. sadism and masochism. **2.** any type of nonorthogenital sexual activity. **3.** any practitioner of nonorthogenital sexual activity. Senses 2 and 3 are an extension of or a misunderstanding of sense 1. [all senses, U.S. slang, mid 1900s-pres.]

sanitary napkin a PERINEAL PAD (*q.v.*); the U.S. word-of-choice for an absorbent menstrual pad. [U.S. colloquial, 1900s]

San Quentin jail-bait a girl under the legal age for copulation even without consent. [U.S. slang, mid 1900s-pres.]

San Quentin quail an underage girl; a girl under the legal age for copulation even without consent. *Cf.* QUAIL. [U.S. slang, mid 1900s-pres.]

Santa Marta gold Colombian marijuana. [U.S. drug culture, mid 1900s-pres.]

sap a jerk; an oaf. [British and later, U.S. slang and colloquial, early 1800s-pres.]

SAPFU a military blunder "surpassing all previous fuck-ups"; the greatest military blunder to date. For synonyms see SNAFU. [U.S. military, World War II]

sap happy intoxicated with alcohol. "Sap" refers to alcohol. Patterned on "slap happy." [U.S. slang, mid 1900s]

satchel the female genitals. *Cf.* TWATCHEL. [U.S. dialect (Ozarks), 1900s or before, Randolph and Wilson]

satchel-crazy obsessed with the sexual prospects of a specific woman or of all women. Possibly from TWATCHEL (*q.v.*). See SATCHEL.

satin gin. *Cf.* WHITE SATIN, YARD OF SATIN. For synonyms see RUIN. [colloquial, 1800s]

saturated alcohol intoxicated. For synonyms see WOOFLED. [U.S. slang, 1900s]

sauce 1. a venereal disease. Probably refers to the secretions associated with gonorrhea. [British, late 1600s] **2.** alcohol; booze. [U.S. slang, early 1900s-pres.] **3.** to perform sexual intercourse. For synonyms see OCCUPY. [British, late 1900s-pres.]

sauced (out) drunk. For synonyms

see WOOFLED. [British, late 1900s-pres.]

sauce, on the 1. drinking regularly; drinking in the manner of an alcoholic. **2.** intoxicated with alcohol. [both senses, U.S. slang, mid 1900s-pres.]

sauced intoxicated with alcohol. For synonyms see WOOFLED. [U.S. slang, early 1900s-pres.]

sauced out drunk. For synonyms see WOOFLED. [British, late 1900s-pres.]

sausage 1. the penis; the erect penis. *Cf.* LIVE SAUSAGE. [widespread recurrent nonce, since the mid 1600s or before] **2.** a derogatory nickname for a German or a German soldier. [U.S. slang, World War II] **3.** a stupid person; an oaf. [U.S. slang, mid 1900s-pres.] **4.** a marijuana cigarette, especially a fat one. [U.S. drug culture, mid 1900s-pres.]

sausage-grinder 1. the vagina. **2.** a prostitute. For synonyms see HARLOT. **3.** women considered sexually. See SAUSAGE (sense 1). For synonyms see TAIL.

sausage jockey a pederast. For synonyms see PEDERAST. [British, late 1900s-pres.]

sausage sandwich 1. a sexual act involving one man and two women. [British, late 1900s-pres.] **2.** a kind of masturbation where the penis is sandwiched between a woman's breasts. [British, late 1900s-pres.]

sausage sling men's bikini underpants or very brief swimming suit. [U.S., late 1900s-pres.]

save someone's ass to save someone's life, neck, reputation, or sense of well-being. [U.S. and elsewhere, late 1900s]

saw off a chunk (also **saw off a piece**) to copulate; to coit a woman. *Cf.* CHUNK, PIECE (sense 5). [attested as Canadian, early 1900s, *Dictionary of Slang and Unconventional English;* U.S. slang, early 1900s-pres.]

S.B.D. "silent but deadly." Refers to an inaudible release of intestinal gas which has a very potent odor. [U.S. slang, mid 1900s]

scab a repellent person. For synonyms see SNOKE-HORN. [1900s]

scaffle (also **scuffle, skuffle**) the drug phencyclidine, P.C.P., an animal tranquilizer. For synonyms see P.C.P. [U.S. drug culture, late 1900s]

scag (also **skag**) **1.** an ugly young woman. For synonyms see BUFFARILLA. [U.S. slang, early 1900s-pres.] **2.** hero in. From sense 1. Cf. GIRL (sense 9). [U.S. drug culture, mid 1900s-pres.]

scag-hag a heterosexual woman who associates with homosexual males. Cf. FAG-BAG, FRUIT-FLY. [U.S. homosexual use, mid 1900s, Stanley]

scag Jones a heroin addiction. [U.S. drug culture, mid 1900s]

scalded infected with venereal disease. Synonyms: CLAPPED, CLAWED-OFF, FRENCHIFIED, GLUED, HOT, IN PICKLE, PEPPERED, PEPPERED-OFF, PLACKET-STUNG, SUNBURNT, SWINGED-OFF, UPHOLSTERED.

scalder a venereal disease, especially gonorrhea. [British slang, early 1800s, *Lexicon Balatronicum*]

scallywag the penis. For synonyms see YARD. [British, mid 1900s-pres.]

scammered intoxicated with alcohol. [colloquial and slang, 1800s-1900s]

scamper juice low-quality alcohol which is likely to send one scampering to the W.C. Cf. BARLEYCORN SPRINTS. [U.S. slang, early 1900s]

scank an ugly young woman; a scraggly and underdeveloped young woman. [U.S. slang, mid 1900s-pres.]

scar heroin. Cf. SCAG (sense 2). [U.S. drug culture, mid 1900s-pres.] See also DIVINE SCAR.

scarce as rocking horse shit very rare; very unusual. [Australian, mid 1900s-pres.]

scared shitless (also **scared spitless**) very frightened; extremely worried; frightened enough to defecate. Cf. SHIT-SCARED. [slang, mid 1900-pres.]

scarf a joint to swallow a marijuana cigarette to avoid detection and arrest. See SCOFF. [U.S. drug culture, mid 1900s-pres.]

scatters diarrhea, especially in animals. Possibly cognate with "shit." [rural colloquial, 1900s or before]

scavenger 1. an emptier of privies. Cf. TOM TURDMAN. [U.S. colloquial, 1900s or before] **2.** a garbageman; a collector of refuse. [U.S. colloquial euphemism, mid 1900s-pres.]

sceptre the penis. In the phrase "Cyprian sceptre." Cf. WAND. [widespread recurrent nonce, mid 1600s-1900s]

scharn cow dung. For synonyms see DROPPINGS.

schicker (also **shikker**) **1.** a drunkard. Cf. SHICKER. **2.** intoxicated with alcohol. See SHICKER. [from Hebrew *shikor*, via Yiddish]

schizzed drunk; drug intoxicated. For synonyms see TALL, WOOFLED. [U.S. slang, 1900s]

schizzing out acting schizoid because of methamphetamine use. [U.S. drug culture, late 1900s]

schlange (also **schlang**) the penis. Cf. SCHLONG. [from the German word for "snake" via Yiddish; U.S. slang, mid 1900s-pres.]

schlock narcotics. For synonyms see COTICS. [from a Yiddish word for "junk"; U.S. underworld, mid 1900s]

schlockkered alcohol intoxicated. For synonyms see WOOFLED. [U.S. slang, late 1900s, Dickson]

schlong the penis. See SCHLANGE. [from the German word for "snake" via Yiddish; U.S. slang, 1900s]

schlub (also **shlub**) an oaf. [from Yiddish; U.S. slang, mid 1900s-pres.] See also ZHLUB.

schmack heroin. See SCHMECK. [U.S. underworld and drug culture, early 1900s-pres.]

schmeck (also **schmack, schmee, shmeck, smeck**) **1.** heroin. **2.** any narcotics. [ultimately from the German word for "taste" via Yiddish; both senses, U.S. underworld and drug culture, early 1900s-pres.]

schmee (also **shmee**) heroin. See SCHMECK. [U.S. drug culture, mid 1900s-pres.]

schmekel 1. the diminutive of

SCHMUCK (*q.v.*), "penis." **2.** an oaf. [U.S. drug culture, mid 1900s-pres.]

schmendrich (also **shmendrick**) **1.** an oaf; a dummy; an immature male; a nonvirile male. **2.** the penis. "Used derisively by women" (Rosten). [both senses are Yiddish; both senses, U.S. slang, 1900s]

schmuck 1. the penis. **2.** a fool; an oaf. Both are the same as SCHMUCK (*q.v.*).

schmuck (also **shmuck**) **1.** the penis. **2.** an oaf; a jerk; a dullard. [if this form comes from German *Schmuck,* "jewel" or "ornament," via Yiddish, it does so without obeying the usual German and Yiddish sound correspondences; both senses, U.S. slang, mid 1900s-pres.]

schnockered (also **shnockered**) alcohol or drug intoxicated. *Cf.* SNOCKERED. For synonyms see TALL, WOOFLED. [British and U.S. slang, late 1900s]

schnorrer a beggar; a worthless fellow. [from Yiddish; since the late 1800s]

school boy 1. codeine as found in cough syrups. Considered as a "starter" drug. *Cf.* KID-STUFF. [U.S. drug culture, mid 1900s] **2.** cocaine or a user of cocaine. [attested as mid 1900s-pres., Landy]

schtoonk a rotten fellow; a real stinker. [from Yiddish; U.S. slang, mid 1900s-pres.]

schwanz (also **shvance, schvontz**) the penis. [ultimately from the German word for "tail"; also German slang for "penis"; U.S. slang, 1900s]

schween the penis. Possibly a blend of SCHMUCK and WEENIE (both *q.v.*). [U.S., mid 1900s]

Schwing! "How exciting!"; "How stimulating!"; Said on seeing an extremely sexually attractive girl. The word is onomatopoeic for the imaginary whishing sound of an instant erection. [British, late 1900s-pres.]

scoff (also **scarf, scorf**) to commit an oral sex act. See SCARF A JOINT. [from a cant word meaning "eat" or "drink"; U.S. slang, mid 1900s]

scooch 1. rum; any hard liquor. *Cf.*

HOOTCH. [British military, early 1900s] **2.** to kiss. Similar to *smooch.* [U.S. collegiate, late 1900s, Eble]

scoop to kiss someone. [U.S., late 1900s-pres.]

scooped intoxicated with alcohol. For synonyms see WOOFLED. [U.S. slang, mid 1900s, Berrey and Van den Bark]

scorched 1. intoxicated with alcohol. [U.S. slang, mid 1900s-pres.] **2.** drug intoxicated. *Cf.* FRIED (sense 2). [U.S. drug culture, mid 1900s-pres.]

score 1. to achieve coition, said of a male. Said especially among males who are interested in keeping track of the number of copulations they have performed. [U.S. slang, mid 1900s-pres.] **2.** an act of copulation. For synonyms see SMOCKAGE. [U.S. slang, mid 1900s-pres.] **3.** a client of a male or female prostitute. *Cf.* TRICK (sense 4). See COUNTER. [U.S. slang and underworld, mid 1900s-pres.] **4.** to make a connection and purchase illegal narcotics. [U.S. drug culture, mid 1900s-pres.]

Scotch mist intoxicated with alcohol. Rhyming slang for "pissed." [British, early 1900s, *Dictionary of Rhyming Slang*]

Scotch warming-pan 1. a female bed companion; a chambermaid. [British, 1700s, Grose] **2.** a release of intestinal gas. For synonyms see GURK. [British, 1800s, Farmer and Henley]

scours diarrhea. From a verb meaning "purge" (1300s). [British and U.S. slang and colloquial, early 1900s]

scrag 1. to hang a person. [cant, mid 1700s if not much earlier] **2.** an ugly young woman. *Cf.* SCAG (sense 1). [U.S. slang, mid 1900s] **3.** a professor in college; any general collegiate bother. [U.S. slang, early 1900s, Berrey and Van den Bark] **4.** to kill. Probably from sense 1. [U.S. slang, mid 1900s-pres. and probably much older] Synonyms for sense 4: BUMP OFF, CREAM, CROAK, DO AWAY WITH, DO FOR, HUSH, JUGULATE, KNOCK OVER, LIQUIDATE, OFF, PERISH, PUT AWAY, PUT DOWN, PUT ONE OUT OF ONE'S MISERY, PUT OUT, PUT OUT OF THE WAY, PUT TO SLEEP,

RUB OUT, TAKE FOR A RIDE, WASTE, WIPE OFF, WIPE OUT, ZAP.

scramble heroin. For synonyms see HEROIN. [U.S. drug culture, late 1900s]

scrambled intoxicated with alcohol. For synonyms see WOOFLED. [U.S. slang, mid 1900s]

scrapping copulating. For synonyms see OCCUPY. [U.S., late 1900s-pres.]

scratched intoxicated with alcohol. [since the early 1600s]

scraunched (also **scranched, scronched**) intoxicated with alcohol. [U. S. slang, mid 1900s]

screaming fairy a very obvious homosexual male. [U.S. slang, mid 1900s-pres.]

screaming-meemies (also **screaming-meanies**) the DELIRIUM TREMENS (*q.v.*). From a term for nonspecific nervous upset. [U.S. slang, early 1900s]

screaming queen 1. an obvious homosexual. See SCREAMING FAIRY. [U.S. slang, 1900s] **2.** a lesbian. For synonyms see LESBYTERIAN. [attested as U.S. college slang, Underwood]

screaming shits diarrhea. [originally military; British and U.S. slang, 1900s]

screw 1. to coit a woman. **2.** copulation. **3.** a prostitute. [senses 1-3 since the 1700s] **4.** a woman considered sexually. [British and U.S. slang, 1800s-1900s] **5.** to permit copulation; to actively copulate with a male, said of a woman. [U.S. slang, mid 1900s-pres.] **6.** to cheat; to deceive. [U.S. slang, mid 1900s-pres.] **7.** to mess up. Cf. SCREW UP.

screw around to waste time. From SCREW (sense 7), but not strongly taboo. [U.S. slang, mid 1900s-pres.]

screwdriver the penis. Cf. PILE-DRIVER, TOOL (sense 1). [U.S. slang and nonce, 1900s]

screwed 1. intoxicated with alcohol. Also **screwed tight.** [British and U.S. slang, early 1800s-pres.] **2.** copulated with. **3.** cheated; deceived. [senses 2 and 3 are slang, 1900s] **4.** confused; messed-up. Also **screwed-up.** [U.S. colloquial, mid 1900s-pres.]

screwed, blued, and tattooed 1.

cheated very badly. [U.S. slang, 1900s] **2.** heavily intoxicated with alcohol. [U.S. slang, mid 1900s]

screw off 1. to mess around; to goof off. Cf. SCREW AROUND. **2.** to masturbate. A milder version of FUCK OFF (sense 1). [both senses, U.S. slang, mid 1900s-pres.]

screw up (also **screw**) **1.** to mess up. **2.** a mess; utter confusion. Usually hyphenated. [both senses, slang, 1900s]

screwy 1. crazy. **2.** intoxicated with alcohol. From sense 1. [both senses, slang, early 1800s-pres.]

Screw you! "To hell with you!" Euphemistic for FUCK YOU! [U.S. and elsewhere, late 1900s]

scrilla money. See also SKRILLA. [U.S., late 1900s-pres.]

scrog 1. to COIT someone. For synonyms see OCCUPY. **2.** to cheat or deceive someone. [both senses, U.S., late 1900s]

scromp to copulate. For synonyms see OCCUPY. [U.S., late 1900s-pres.]

scronched alcohol intoxicated. For synonyms see WOOFLED. [U.S., late 1900s-pres.]

scrote the scrotum. For synonyms see TOOL SACK. [British, late 1900s-pres.]

scrump. 1. to COIT someone. For synonyms see OCCUPY. **2.** copulation. For synonyms see SMOCKAGE. [both senses, late 1900s]

scrump queen a sexually free female; a SLUT. [U.S. collegiate, late 1900s, Eble]

scuffer a prostitute. Possibly from the noisy way some prostitutes walk to get attention. [U.S. slang, mid 1900s-pres.]

scuffle 1. to identify and PICK UP (sense 1) someone for sexual purposes. [U.S. slang, mid 1900s] **2.** the drug P.C.P. (*q.v.*). [U.S. drug culture, mid 1900s-pres.] **3.** See SCAFFLE.

scum semen. Cf. SCUMBAG. For synonyms see METTLE. [U.S. slang, mid 1900s-pres.]

scumbag 1. a condom. Cf. SCUM. [U.S. slang, mid 1900s-pres.] **2.** a thoroughly disgusting person. Cf. DOUCHE BAG. [U.S. slang, mid 1900s-pres.]

scumsucker 1. someone who performs oral sex on a penis. For synonyms see PICCOLO-PLAYER. **2.** a totally despicable person of either sex. For synonyms see SNOKE-HORN. [both senses, U.S., late 1900s]

scum-sucking "semen-sucking," totally disgusting; pertaining to a disgusting person. *Cf.* SCUM. [U.S. slang, late 1900s]

scungies swimming trunks. [Australian, late 1900s-pres.]

scupper 1. a sexually loose woman. **2.** a prostitute. From the term for the opening used to drain a ship's deck. *Cf.* COMMON SEWER, DRAIN. [both senses, U.S. slang, 1900s, Wentworth and Flexner]

scut 1. the tail of an animal, especially that of a rabbit or a deer. No negative connotations. *Cf.* BUN. [rural colloquial, 1500s-1900s] **2.** the posteriors. From sense 1. **3.** the female genitals. [late 1500s-1700s] **4.** the female pubic hair. [1500s] **5.** a contemptible person. [U.S. slang, mid 1900s]

scuttle 1. the female genitals. Literally, "trap door." [British slang, 1800s, Farmer and Henley] **2.** to coit. *Cf.* BACK-SCUTTLE. [U.S. slang, mid 1900s] **3.** to DEFLOWER (*q.v.*) a woman. [British slang, 1800s, Farmer and Henley] **4.** a derogatory nickname for a Negro. From the blackness of a coal scuttle. [U.S. slang, early 1900s or before]

scutz a young male interested in girls for copulation only. See SCUZZ. [U.S. slang, mid 1900s-pres.]

scutz around to coit; to be sexually promiscuous. [U.S. slang, mid 1900s-pres.]

scuzz (also **scuz**) a scraggly or ugly person. [U.S. slang, mid 1900s-pres.]

sea cocaine. A respelling of the initial C of cocaine. For synonyms see NOSE-CANDY [U.S. drug culture, late 1900s]

seafood 1. a sailor considered as a sexual object by a homosexual male. *Cf.* GOVERNMENT INSPECTED MEAT, MEAT, SHORE DINNER. [U.S. underworld and homosexual use, mid 1900s-pres.] **2.** CUNNILINGUS; an act of CUNNILINGUS. *Cf.* FISH. For synonyms see CUNNILINGUS. [U.S. slang, late 1900s or before]

sea hag a very ugly woman. [U.S., late 1900s-pres.]

secret vice masturbation. *Cf.* SOLITARY SIN. [euphemistic, 1800s]

secret works the male or female genitals. For synonyms see GENITALS. [U.S. slang, mid 1900s]

see 1. to coit. Euphemistic for the act of copulation. [British slang, 1800s, Farmer and Henley] **2.** to consort with someone; to date someone; to copulate with someone. [U.S. colloquial, 1900s]

see a man 1. to have a drink of an alcoholic beverage. [British colloquial, late 1800s, Ware] **2.** to copulate.

see a man about a dog (also **see a man about a horse**) to depart to urinate. [U.S. colloquial, 1900s]

seedling a man's erect penis. Refers to a small tree. For synonyms see ERECTION. [U.S., late 1900s-pres.]

seeds 1. the testicles. *Cf.* SEED (sense 2). [U.S. slang, mid 1900s] **2.** morning glory seeds. [U.S. drug culture, mid 1900s-pres.] See BLUE STAR, FLYING SAUCERS, GLORY SEEDS, PEARLY GATE, PEARLY WHITES, SUMMER SKIES.

seeing snakes 1. having the DELIRIUM TREMENS (*q.v.*). [British and U.S. slang, 1800s-1900s] **2.** intoxicated with alcohol. *Cf.* SNAKES. [U.S. slang, early 1900s-pres.]

seeing-things drunk heavily intoxicated with alcohol; drunk and hallucinating. [U.S. colloquial or mock-colloquial, 1900s]

see Johnny to retire to go to the toilet; to visit the JOHN (sense 2). For synonyms see RETIRE. [U.S. colloquial, mid 1900s]

see Mrs. Murphy to retire to urinate. MRS. MURPHY (*q.v.*) is the bathroom. [U.S. slang and colloquial, mid 1900s-pres.]

see Mrs. Murray to retire to the W.C. [Australian, 1900s, Baker]

seen more ass than a toilet seat said of a sexually promiscuous male. [U.S. slang, late 1900s]

seen more pricks than a dartboard

said of a sexually promiscuous female. [British, late 1900s, J. Green]

see oneself off to commit suicide; to DO AWAY WITH ONESELF (*q.v.*). [colloquial, 1900s or before]

see pink elephants 1. to be heavily intoxicated with alcohol. **2.** to have the DELIRIUM TREMENS (*q.v.*). *Cf.* SEEING SNAKES. [both senses, U.S. slang and colloquial, 1900s]

see two moons to be drunk. [U.S. slang, early 1700s, Ben Franklin]

seg 1. a bull castrated after it is full-grown [British colloquial, 1600s] **2.** any castrated animal. [British colloquial, 1800s, Rye]

seggy a Seconal (trademark) capsule, a barbiturate. *Cf.* SECCY. [U.S. drug culture, mid 1900s-pres.]

seldom see underwear; men's underpants. Rhyming slang for B.V.D. (*q.v.*). Usually in the plural. For synonyms see NETHER GARMENTS. [U.S., 1900s, *Dictionary of Rhyming Slang*]

self-destruction suicide. [euphemistic since the late 1500s] Synonyms and related terms; DO AWAY WITH ONESELF, DUTCH ACT, DUTCH CURE, FELO-DE-SE, HARA-KIRI, SEE ONESELF OFF, SELF-VIOLENCE.

sell Buicks to vomit. *Cf.* BUICK. For synonyms see YORK. [U.S. collegiate, late 1900s, Eble]

sell one's bacon (also **sell one's flesh, sell one's hip**) to be a prostitute. From the MEAT (sense 2) theme. [U.S. slang, mid 1900s]

sell out to vomit; the same as MAKE A SALE (*q.v.*). For synonyms see YORK. [Australian slang, early 1900s, Baker]

S'elp me God! an oath and an exclamation, "So help me God!" [since the 1300s]

seminary the female genitals. A play on "semen-ary." *Cf.* LADIES' COLLEGE. [British slang, 1800s, Farmer and Henley]

sent 1. intoxicated with alcohol. **2.** drug intoxicated. From sense 1. [both senses, U.S. slang, early 1900s-pres.]

sent to the skies dead; killed. For synonyms see DONE FOR. [British, late 1800s, Ware]

septic-stick a formed rod of excrement. [U.S. jocular slang, mid 1900s]

sergeant a lesbian; a masculine lesbian. For synonyms see LESBYTERIAN. [U.S. slang, mid 1900s]

serpent the penis. See SNAKE. For synonyms see GENITALS, YARD. [1900s and recurrent nonce]

servant's entrance the anus. A play on BACKDOOR. For synonyms see ANUS. [U.S. slang, 1900s]

serve to copulate and impregnate. Originally said of a stallion and later of a man. [since the late 1500s]

served-up intoxicated with alcohol. *Cf.* BOILED, FRIED (sense 1). [U.S. slang, early 1900s]

serve head to perform PENILINGUS (*q.v.*). *Cf.* GIVE HEAD. [U.S. homosexual use, mid 1900s-pres.]

set a dose of drugs consisting of two Seconal (trademark) capsules and one amphetamine capsule. [U.S. drug culture, mid 1900s-pres.]

sew to masturbate, presumably said of the male. For synonyms and related subjects see WASTE TIME. [U.S. slang, 1900s]

sewed-up 1. intoxicated with alcohol. *Cf.* STITCHED. [colloquial and slang, early 1800s-pres.] **2.** pregnant. *Cf.* SEW UP. [British slang, 1800s, Farmer and Henley]

sewer the anus. *Cf.* DIRT-CHUTE. [U.S. slang, mid 1900s]

sewermouth one who uses vile language constantly. *Cf.* LATRINE LIPS. [U.S. slang, mid 1900s-pres.]

sew up to coit and impregnate a woman. [British slang, 1800s, Farmer and Henley]

sex 1. the quality or character of maleness or femaleness. [since the 1300s] **2.** the female genitals. [British slang, 1800s, Farmer and Henley] **3.** the pleasure associated with the stimulation of the genitals. **4.** copulation. [colloquial, 1900s] **5.** Seconal barbiturate capsules. The same as SECS. For synonyms see BARB. [U.S. drug culture, late 1900s,

Kaiser] **6.** to copulate. For synonyms see OCCUPY. [U.S. slang, late 1900s-pres.]

sexed-up 1. sexually aroused. For synonyms see HUMPY. [U.S. slang and colloquial, mid 1900s-pres.] **2.** made sexier; made SPICY (q.v.) as in a sexed-up movie or song. [U.S. slang, mid 1900s-pres.]

sexile sexual exile from one's room while one's roommate is "entertaining" a member of the opposite sex. [U.S. late 1900s-pres.]

sex-juice a drug, presumably a liquid, used to stimulate a person sexually. Cf. LOVE DRUG. [U.S. slang, late 1900s]

sex-machine a sexually aggressive male or female. [U.S. slang, late 1900s]

sexpot a sexually attractive woman; a very sexy woman who labors to be nothing but a SEX OBJECT (q.v.). [U.S. slang, mid 1900s-pres.]

sex ring 1. organized prostitution. **2.** organized group sex activity. [both senses, U.S. slang, mid 1900s-pres.]

sex something up 1. to add sex to something; to put sexual scenes into a movie or a novel. See SEXED-UP. **2.** to JAZZ (q.v.) something up; to give it some cleverness or sparkle. [both senses, U.S. slang and colloquial, mid 1900s-pres.]

sexual deviation a form (or forms) of sexual behavior which differs markedly from those considered NORMAL. (q.v.) for a society. In the U.S. this includes PENILINGISM, CUNNILINGISM, ANILINGISM, SADISM, MASOCHISM, EXHIBITIONISM, PEDERASTY, PEDOPHILIA, and ZOOERASTY (all q.v.).

sexual discharge 1. semen. **2.** natural vaginal lubrication. [both senses, late 1800s-1900s]

sexual intercourse 1. penetration followed by pelvic movement which usually leads to orgasm in one or both partners. The U.S. word-of-choice for coition. **2.** PEDERASTY (q.v.). **3.** any type of sexual act which involves two or more people and which leads to orgasm for at least one of them.

sexy pertaining to persons or objects which are sexually stimulating or basically of a sexual nature. [colloquial, 1900s]

S.F. alcohol intoxicated. From SHIT-FACED. For synonyms see WOOFLED. [U.S. euphemistic slang, late 1900s]

S.F.W. "So fucking what?" [U.S. late 1900s-pres.]

shack 1. a really worthless man; a tramp or a vagabond. Also **shackaback.** [since the early 1700s] **2.** a privy. For synonyms see AJAX. [U.S. slang, early 1900s or before] **3.** a mistress; a resident concubine. [U.S. slang, mid 1900s]

shacked-up 1. living with a woman or a concubine, said of a man. **2.** living together unmarried, said of a man and a woman. [both senses, U.S. slang, mid 1900s-pres.]

shack up with someone 1. to set up housekeeping with a person of the opposite sex to whom one is not married. Cf. SHACK (sense 3). [U.S. slang, mid 1900s-pres.] **2.** to copulate in a temporary relationship, said of heterosexual and homosexual couples. See ONE-NIGHT STAND. [U.S. slang, mid 1900s-pres.]

shad a prostitute. Cf. FISH (sense 2). [U.S. slang, 1800s, Farmer and Henley]

shaft 1. the penis, especially the erect penis. Anatomically, the body of the penis as opposed to the glans. [U.S. slang, 1900s] **2.** to copulate with a woman. For synonyms see TAIL. [1900s] **3.** women considered sexually. [U.S. slang, mid 1900s-pres.] **4.** an imaginary pole which is thrust up someone's anus. **5.** to thrust (in one's imagination) a pole up someone's anus; essentially, to stop a person short; to punish or treat very badly. Cf. ROYAL SHAFT. [senses 4 and 5 are U.S. slang, mid 1900s-pres.]

shaftable pertaining to a woman who is so SEXY (q.v.) that she immediately makes a man think of copulation. Also pertaining to a woman known to permit copulation readily. Cf. PUNCHABLE. From SHAFT (senses 2 and 3).

shag 1. to wiggle; to shake; to toss about. Also the name for a U.S. dance. No negative connotations. [since the

1300s] **2.** a low rascal; the same as SHACK (sense 1). [British, early 1600s] **3.** to copulate; to coit a woman. **4.** copulation [both senses, British and U.S. slang, 1800s-pres.] **5.** a lecher. [1900s and before] **6.** to masturbate. [British slang, 1800s, Farmer and Henley] See also GANG-SHAG.

shag ass to depart in a hurry. *Cf.* CUT ASS, DRAG ASS, HAUL ASS. [U.S. slang, mid 1900s-pres.]

shag-bag (also **shag-rag**) a low, shabby fellow. See SHACK (sense 1). [slang, 1500s-1600s]

shaggin' wagon a car or van used for copulation. [British and U.S., late 1900s-pres.]

shag oneself to masturbate. For synonyms see WASTE TIME. [British, late 1900s-pres.]

shake 1. to coit a woman. *Cf.* ROCK. [British, 1600s] **2.** a prostitute. **3.** copulation. **4.** to masturbate. [senses 2-4 are British with some U.S. use, 1800s-1900s] See also SHAKES.

shake a cloth in the wind 1. to hang in chains. [British slang, late 1700s, Grose] **2.** to be intoxicated and shaking. See SHAKES. For synonyms see WOOFLED. [possibly nautical in origin; slang, mid 1800s-pres.]

shake a skin-coat to coit a female. *Cf.* SHAKE (sense 1), SKIN-COAT (sense 1). [mid 1600s (Urquhart)]

shake a sock to urinate. *Cf.* WRING ONE'S SOCK OUT. For synonyms see WHIZ. [U.S. slang, mid 1900s]

shake hands with the governor to masturbate. For synonyms see WASTE TIME. [U.S., late 1900s-pres.]

shake hands with wife's best friend (also **shake hand's with one's best friend**) to urinate. The "friend" is the penis. [slang, World War II]

shaker a drunkard, especially one with the DELIRIUM TREMENS (*q.v.*). [U.S. slang, 1900s]

shakes 1. a nervous condition; nerves jangled from fear. **2.** the DELIRIUM TREMENS (*q.v.*). [both senses, U.S. slang, mid 1800s-pres.]

shake the dew off the lily (also

shake the lily) to urinate. *Cf.* WRING THE DEW OFF THE BRANCH. [U.S. slang, early 1900s-pres.]

shake up to masturbate. *Cf.* SHAKE (sense 4). [British slang, 1800s, Farmer and Henley]

shaking of the sheets copulation. For synonyms see SMOCKAGE. [British, 1600s]

shallows, on the naked; half-naked. [slang or cant, early 1800s, Matsell]

sham 1. champagne. [slang, 1800s] **2.** an Irishman. More jocular than derogatory. From SHAMROCK (*q.v.*). For synonyms see HARP. [U.S. slang, 1900s or before] **3.** a policeman. From sense 1 or from SHAMUS (*q.v.*). For synonyms see FLATFOOT. [U.S. slang, early 1900s]

shampoo champagne. From the bubbles. *Cf.* SHAM. [U.S. slang, 1900s]

shamrock a nickname for an Irishman. *Cf.* SHAM (sense 2). [U.S. slang, 1900s or before]

shank 1. a prostitute. See LEG (sense 3). [U.S. slang, mid 1900s-pres.] **2.** a venereal CHANCRE (sense 2).

shanker (also **chancre**) a BUBO (*q.v.*); a venereal CHANCRE (sense 2). [since the 1600s]

shark biscuit a novice surfer. [Australian, late 1900s-pres.]

shat a past tense of SHIT (*q.v.*). Also somewhat euphemistic for "shit." [dialect and slang, 1800s-1900s]

shat-off angered; PISSED-OFF (*q.v.*). [Australian slang, mid 1900s, *Dictionary of Slang and Unconventional English*]

shaved intoxicated with alcohol. *Cf.* HALF-SHAVED. For synonyms see WOOFLED. [late 1500s-pres.]

she 1. the penis. [nonce, 1900s] **2.** the pronoun "he" in homosexual use.

sheath 1. the vagina. [since the 1800s or before] **2.** the foreskin of the penis. [British slang, 1800s. Farmer and Henley] **3.** a condom. *Cf.* MALE SHEATH, SAFETY-SHEATH. For synonyms see EEL-SKIN. [originally medical]

she-bop to masturbate. Said of the male. *Cf.* BOP. For synonyms and related subjects see WASTE TIME. [U.S. slang, late 1900s]

shed a tear to urinate. For synonyms see WHIZ. [British, late 1900s-pres.]

she-devil 1. a female devil. See DEVIL. **2.** a vile and evil woman. A SPITFIRE (sense 1).

she-dog 1. a bitch; a female dog. *Cf.* LADY-DOG. [colloquial, 1800s if not long before] **2.** to complain. [U.S. slang and colloquial, 1900s or before]

Shee-it! the exclamation "SHIT!" prolonged and emphasized. [U.S. slang, 1900s]

sheepdog a brassiere. Because it "rounds them up and points them in the right direction." See also COWBOY BRA. [U.S., late 1900s-pres.]

sheepshagger a rustic oaf; a country bumpkin. See SHAG. For synonyms see OAF. [British, late 1900s-pres.]

sheet a jocular disguise of SHIT (*q.v.*). *Cf.* SHOOT (sense 3). [U.S. slang, mid 1900s]

sheg 1. to annoy someone **2.** to seduce and coit a woman. Both senses, from SHAG (*q.v.*).

she-he an effeminate male; a homosexual male. See SHIM. *Cf.* HERMAPHRODITE (sense 3). [U.S. slang, mid 1900s, Berrey and Van den Bark]

shekels dollars; money. [U.S., late 1900s-pres.]

shellac head a person wearing a hairdo thick with stiffener and shellac. [U.S., late 1900s-pres.]

shemale a hateful woman; a BITCH (sense 5). [British and U.S. slang, late 1800s-early 1900s]

she-man an effeminate male; possibly a homosexual male. [U.S. slang, mid 1900s, Berrey and Van den Bark]

sherman (also **sherm**) **1.** a device for smoking marijuana. [U.S. drug culture, late 1900s] **2.** a tobacco or marijuana cigarette soaked in a solution of phencyclidine, P.C.P. For related subjects see MEZZROLL. [U.S. drug culture, late 1900s]

shermed HIGH on P.C.P. For synonyms see TALL. [U.S. drug culture, late 1900s]

shicer (also **shice**) **1.** a rotten cheat; a contemptible male. Cognate with SHIT (*q.v.*). **2.** intoxicated with alcohol. See SHICKER. For synonyms see WOOFLED. [both senses, British slang, 1800s]

shick 1. intoxicated with alcohol. See SHICKED, SHICKER, SHICKERED. **2.** a drunkard. [both senses are from Yiddish; Australian slang, 1900s]

shicked (also **shick, shickery**) intoxicated with alcohol. [Australian and U.S. slang, mid 1800s-pres.]

shicker (also **shikker**) **1.** liquor; booze. **2.** intoxicated with alcohol. Also **on the shicker. 3.** a drunkard. [all are Yiddish; since the late 1800s]

shickered intoxicated with alcohol. *Cf.* SHICK (sense 1). [U.S. slang, early 1900s-pres.]

shifter 1. a worthless man; a shiftless man. [colloquial since the 1600s] **2.** a lecher; a man who specializes in SHIFT-WORK (*q.v.*), "copulation." [British slang, 1500s-1800s] **3.** a drunkard. [slang, 1800s]

shim a homosexual male; a she-him. *Cf.* HESH, HE-SHE. [U.S. slang, mid 1900s-pres.]

shipwrecked intoxicated with alcohol. For synonyms see WOOFLED. [British slang, late 1800s, Ware]

shirt lifter a male homosexual. Patterned on *skirt lifter*. For synonyms see EPICENE. [British slang, 1900s, McDonald]

shishi marijuana; hashish. From "hashishi." [U.S. drug culture, mid 1900s-pres.] See also CHICHI.

shit (also **sh**, s***, s--t**) **1.** diarrhea in cattle. *Cf.* SCATTERS. [c. 1000] **2.** to defecate. For synonyms see EASE ONESELF. [since the 1300s or before] **3.** fecal excrement. [since the 1500s] **4.** any unwanted junk; nonsense; rubbish. [U.S. slang, mid 1900s-pres.] **5.** heroin; marijuana; illicit drugs. *Cf.* GONG (sense 3). [U.S. drug culture, mid 1900s-pres.] **6.** to vomit. For synonyms see YORK. [British slang, late 1800s, *Dictionary of Slang and Unconventional English*] **7.** to lie. A truncation of BULLSHIT (*q.v.*). [U.S. slang, mid 1900s-pres.] **8.** as an exclamation,

"Shit!" **9.** a rotten man; a hateful rascal. Disguises for the word SHIT: BIT HIT, IT-SHAY, SHEET, SHOOT, SKITE, SUGAR, TOM-TIT.

shit, in the in trouble; in a real sticky mess. [British and later U.S. slang, 1800s-1900s]

shit a brick 1. to defecate an extremely hard stool as after a period of constipation. [British and U.S., 1800s-1900s] **2.** to do something that is recognized to be impossible, especially to show amazement, as in the expression "I could have shit a brick!" [U.S. slang, mid 1900s-pres.]

shit-ass 1. a contemptible person, usually a male. [U.S. slang, mid 1900s-pres.] **2.** pertaining to an undesirable person or matter. [U.S. slang, mid 1900s-pres.]

shit-ass luck very bad luck. [British and U.S. slang, 1900s]

shit-bag 1. the abdomen; the belly; in the plural, the intestines. [slang or colloquial, 1800s-1900s] **2.** a totally worthless person. [U.S. slang, 1900s] **3.** a large amount; a SHIT LOAD OF SOMETHING. [U.S. slang, late 1900s]

shitbox any worthless thing or person; especially a car. [U.S. slang, late 1900s]

shit breath a total JERK. Cf. PENIS BREATH. For synonyms see OAF. [U.S. slang, late 1900s]

shitburger a totally worthless and disgusting person; any worthless thing. [U.S. slang, late 1900s]

shitcan 1. a trash or garbage can. **2.** to gossip about a person; to inform on a person. An elaboration of SHIT (sense 7). [both senses, U.S. slang, mid 1900s-pres.] **3.** to discard or throw away. [U.S. slang, 1900s] **4.** a toilet; an outhouse. For synonyms see W.C. [U.S. slang, mid 1900s-pres.]

shit creek a bad place or a rotten situation; the stream named in the expression "Up shit creek without a paddle." [U.S. slang, mid 1900s-pres.]

shit-eating pertaining to a really wretched or disgusting person. [U.S. slang, late 1900s if not before]

shit face an oaf; a fool. Cf. CUNT FACE. [U.S. slang, mid 1900s-pres.]

shit-faced intoxicated with alcohol. Cf. POOPIED. [U.S. slang, mid 1900s-pres.]

shit-fire a bully; a mean rascal; based on SPITFIRE (sense 1); the same as CACAFUEGO (q.v.). [British slang, 1800s, Farmer and Henley]

shit-fit a temper tantrum; a display of anger. [U.S. slang, late 1900s]

shit-for brains 1. an idiot. Also a term of address. [U.S. slang, late 1900s] **2.** what a stupid-acting person has in the head. [U.S. slang, late 1900s]

shit for the birds nonsense. An elaboration of the expression "for the birds." [U.S. slang, mid 1900s]

shit-fuck 1. to copulate anally. **2.** an act of anal copulation. [both senses, 1900s or before]

shitfucker a pederast. For synonyms see PEDERAST. [U.S., late 1900s-pres.]

Shit happens. "Things just happen"; "Bad things just happen—too bad." [U.S. slang, late 1900s]

shit-head a stupid jerk. For synonyms see OAF. [widespread slang and colloquial, 1900s]

shit-heap any disgusting thing, person, or place. [U.S. slang, 1900s]

shitheel a scoundrel; a despised person. For synonyms see SNOKE-HORN. [U.S. and elsewhere, 1900s]

shit-hole 1. the anus. **2.** a privy; a latrine. [both senses, British slang, 1800s, Farmer and Henley]

shit-hooks the fingers. Cf. CUNT-HOOKS.

shit-hot 1. very exciting or excited; powerful and effective. **2.** very hot. Probably a misunderstanding of sense 1. [both senses, U.S., 1900s]

shit-house a privy. For synonyms see AJAX. [slang and colloquial, late 1700s-pres.]

shit-house poet 1. someone who writes on the walls of outhouses or public restrooms. **2.** any very bad poet. From sense 1. [1900s or before]

Shitlaw! "Oh, damn!" [U.S. collegiate, late 1900s, Munro]

shit list a list of people at whom one is angry. [U.S. slang, late 1900s]

shit load of something a large amount of something. [U.S. slang, mid 1900s-pres.]

shit locker the bowels; the stomach. *Cf.* SHIT-BAG. [U.S. and elsewhere, 1900s if not before]

shit on a shingle a meal of creamed chipped beef on toast. *Cf.* S.O.S. [U.S. military, World War II]

shit on a stick a really grand person or thing. Usually used sarcastically for someone or something highly overrated. [U.S. slang, late 1900s]

shit on one's own doorstep to do something that causes oneself trouble. [U.S., late 1900s-pres.]

shit on someone from a great height to abuse someone severely. Often in the passive. [U.S. slang, late 1900s]

Shit on it! a rude exclamation; an exclamation of extreme disgust. [U.S. slang, mid 1900s-pres.]

shit on wheels a male who thinks he is the best that there is; a HOT SHIT (*q.v.*). [U.S. slang, mid 1900s]

shit or bust [persisting] no matter what it takes. [British, late 1900s-pres.]

shit order, in in bad order; in disarray. [U.S. slang, 1900s]

Shit or get off the pot! a command for someone to act affirmatively and immediately accomplish the assigned task or give up and let someone else do it. Subject to elaborate euphemism, "If one does not intend to wash up, one should not monopolize the ablution facilities." [slang and colloquial, 1900s or before]

shit out of luck luckless; having only bad luck. *Cf.* S.O.L. [slang, mid 1900s-pres.]

shit parade a SHIT LIST; a list of people at whom one is angry. A play on "hit parade." [U.S. slang, late 1900s]

shit-pot a deceitful and worthless person. [slang, 1800s, Farmer and Henley]

shitrag toilet paper. [U.S., late 1900s-pres.]

shitsky a totally worthless JERK. For synonyms see OAF. [U.S. slang, late 1900s]

shits, the (also **shits**) diarrhea. For synonyms see QUICKSTEP. [U.S. colloquial, mid 1900s-pres.]

shit-sack a really rotten rascal. [British slang, late 1700s, Grose]

shit-scared terribly frightened; frightened enough to defecate in one's pants. *Cf.* SCARED SHITLESS. [British and U.S. slang, 1900s]

shit-shark the man who empties the CESSPIT (*q.v.*); a cleaner of privies. *Cf.* HONEY-DIPPER, TOM TURDMAN. [British slang, 1800s, Farmer and Henley]

shit-stabber a pederast. For synonyms see PEDERAST. [British, late 1900s-pres.]

shitstain a disliked person. For synonyms see SNOKE-HORN. [British, late 1900s-pres.]

shit-stick 1. a worthless oaf; a real jerk. **2.** a stick or cylinder of fecal material; the same as SEPTIC-STICK (*q.v.*). [both senses, U.S. slang, mid 1900s-pres.]

shitsure very, very sure. Also an exclamation. [U.S. slang, mid 1900s-pres.]

shitter 1. a toilet; a W.C. *Cf.* CRAPPER (sense 1). **2.** a BULLSHITTER (*q.v.*); a liar or a braggart. *Cf.* CRAPPER (sense 2). For synonyms see BULLER. [both senses, U.S. slang, mid 1900s-pres.]

shitty 1. lousy; really bad. [U.S. slang, mid 1900s-pres.] **2.** alcohol intoxicated. *Cf.* S.F. For synonyms see WOOFLED. [U.S. slang, mid 1900s-pres.]

shitty end of the stick the bad side of a bargain; the troublesome part of a transaction. [U.S. slang, mid 1900s-pres.]

shit-word a dirty word; a term of abuse. [since the 1200s]

shitwork menial work; hard labor. [U.S. slang, late 1900s]

Shiver my timbers! a mild, mock oath and an exclamation. [U.S. slang, 1900s or before]

shlong monster a male with a large penis. [U.S., late 1900s-pres.]

shock absorbers the female breasts. For synonyms see BOSOM. [1900s, recurrent nonce]

shoot 1. to ejaculate. Cf. SHOOT OFF, SHOOT WHITE. For synonyms see MELT. [colloquial and slang, since the 1800s or before] **2.** to have a wet dream. [since the late 1800s] **3.** a euphemism for SHIT! (sense 8). [British and U.S. slang, 1900s or before] **4.** to have diarrhea.

shoot a bishop to have a wet dream. The bishop's miter resembles the glans penis. Cf. POLICEMAN'S HELMET. [British slang, 1800s, Farmer and Henley]

shooting submarines defecating. As if one were bombing imaginary submarines in the toilet bowl. [mostly juvenile use; U.S., mid 1900s]

shoot in the bush to ejaculate prematurely. Cf. FIRE IN THE AIR. [British slang, 1700s]

shoot in the tail 1. to coit a woman. **2.** to commit PEDERASTY (q.v.). [both senses, British slang, 1800s, Farmer and Henley]

shoot off to ejaculate. Cf. SHOOT (sense 1). [U.S. slang, mid 1900s-pres.]

shoot one's cookies (also **shoot one's breakfast, shoot one's dinner, shoot one's lunch, shoot one's supper**) to vomit. For synonyms see YORK. [U.S. slang, early 1900s-pres.]

shoot one's load to ejaculate. [British and U.S., late 1900s-pres.]

shoot one's wad 1. to ejaculate. **2.** to copulate. [both senses, U.S. slang, mid 1900s-pres.]

shoot over the stubble to ejaculate prematurely. Cf. SHOOT IN THE BUSH. [British slang, 1800s, Farmer and Henley]

shoot rabbits to release intestinal gas. For synonyms see GURK. [colloquial euphemism, 1900s]

shoot the bull (also **shoot the crap, shoot the shit**) to chat and gossip. [U.S. slang, early 1900s-pres.]

shoot the cat to vomit. Cf. CAT, JERK THE CAT, WHIP THE CAT. [British and U.S. slang, early 1800s-1900s]

shoot the works to vomit. For synonyms see YORK. [U.S. slang, early 1900s]

shoot (up) 1. to inject drugs. [U.S. drug culture, late 1900s] **2.** (usually **shoot-up**) an injection of drugs. [U.S. drug culture, late 1900s]

short 1. a SHORT SNORT (q.v.) of a drug, usually cocaine. **2.** to sniff or snort heroin or cocaine. Cf. SNORT (sense 2). [both senses, U.S. drug culture, mid 1900s-pres.]

short and curly the pubic hair. Cf. CURLIES, SHORT HAIRS.

short-arm the penis. Cf. CUTTY-GUN, GUN, PISTOL, SHORT-ARM INSPECTION. [U.S. military, World War II and general slang, mid 1900s-pres.]

short-arm drill a penile inspection for venereal disease. Probably also used to mean "copulation." See SHORT-ARM PRACTICE. [U.S. slang, mid 1900s]

short-arm heist rape. [U.S. underworld, mid 1900s, Goldin, O'Leary, and Lipsius]

short-arm inspection a penile inspection for venereal disease. Cf. DANGLE-PARADE. [British and U.S. slang, World Wars]

short-arm practice copulation. Based on an expression for target practice with a pistol. Cf. SHORT-ARM. [U.S. military slang, mid 1900s]

shortarse a small person. [British, late 1900s-pres.]

short hairs the pubic hairs. Euphemistically defined as "the short hairs at the nape of the neck." Cf. SHORT AND CURLY. [British and U.S. slang, 1900s]

short out of luck a euphemism for SHIT OUT OF LUCK (q.v.). Cf. S.O.L. [U.S., 1900s]

short-skirted pregnant. The swelling makes skirts appear to be shorter. Cf. APRON-UP. For synonyms see FRAGRANT. [British slang, 1800s, Farmer and Henley]

short snort a dose of a drug taken by

inhalation. Usually cocaine. [U.S. drug culture, 1900s]

shot full of holes heavily intoxicated with alcohol. An elaboration of SHOT (sense 1). [widespread slang, 1900s or before]

shotgun 1. a pipe designed to aid a person in blowing marijuana smoke into someone else's mouth. [U.S. collegiate and drug culture, late 1900s] **2.** to blow a puff of marijuana smoke into someone else's mouth. [U.S. drug culture, late 1900s] **3.** someone who accompanies a drug smuggler and observes the practice of a man riding shotgun as an armed guard for an overland shipment in the Old West. *Cf.* MULE SKINNER. [U.S. drug culture, late 1900s] **4.** a "brand name" for amyl nitrite. [U.S. drug culture, late 1900s, Abel]

shot in the neck intoxicated with alcohol. [U.S. slang, 1800s-1900s]

shot tower a toilet. For synonyms see W.C. [U.S. slang, early 1900s]

shot-up 1. intoxicated with alcohol. **2.** intoxicated with narcotics. [both senses, U.S., mid 1900s-pres.]

shouse a privy. A blend of "shit" and "house." [Australian slang, mid 1900s-pres.]

shout at one's shoes to vomit [on one's shoes]. For synonyms see YORK. [U.S., late 1900s-pres.]

shove 1. an act of copulation. **2.** to copulate; the same as PUSH (sense 1). [slang since the 1600s]

Shove it! a curse, "Shove it up your ass!" [widespread slang, mid 1900s-pres.]

shovel the shit to lie or boast excessively; to bring on loads of BULLSHIT (*q.v.*). [U.S. slang, early 1900s-pres.]

show 1. the appearance of blood at the onset of the menses. [British and U.S. colloquial, 1800s-1900s] **2.** a small mass of blood-tinged mucus indicating the onset of labor. [colloquial, 1500s and before]

show-and-tell pants very tightly fitting men's pants which reveal the outlines of the genitals. *Cf.* BASKET DAYS. [U.S. slang, mid 1900s]

shower-cap 1. a condom. For synonyms see EEL-SKIN. **2.** a birth control diaphragm. For synonyms see B.C. [both senses, U.S. slang, mid 1900s-pres.]

shower queen See GOLDEN SHOWER QUEEN.

shower scum a total JERK; a despised person. *Cf.* POND SCUM. For synonyms see SNOKE-HORN. [U.S. slang, late 1900s]

(shower) spank to masturbate. Said of the male. For synonyms and related subjects see WASTE TIME. [U.S. collegiate, late 1900s, Munro]

shrapnel loose change. [British, late 1900s-pres.]

shredded (also **shreaded**) alcohol intoxicated. For synonyms see WOOFLED. [British and U.S. slang, late 1900s]

shrimp to lick, suck, and kiss the toes for sexual gratification. [British and U.S., late 1900s-pres.]

shrimp queen a male who derives special pleasure from fondling or kissing someone's feet. "Shrimp" refers to the shape of the toes, the odor of unclean feet, or both. *Cf.* FOOT QUEEN, TOE QUEEN. See QUEEN for similar subjects. [U.S. homosexual use, mid 1900s]

shrink a psychoanalyst or psychotherapist. [U.S. slang and colloquial, 1900s] Synonyms: ANALYST, BUG, BUG DOCTOR, COUCH-DOCTOR, COUCH-JOB, DOME-DOCTOR, HEAD-SHRINKER, NUTPUCK.

shroom to use a hallucinogenic substance; to use SHROOMS. [U.S. drug culture, late 1900s]

shroom dog a user of SHROOMS. [U.S. drug culture, late 1900s]

shrooms tips of the PEYOTE cactus containing MESCALINE. This is a cactus, not a mushroom. May also be used to refer to any hallucinogenic substance, specifically PSILOCYBIN. [U.S. drug culture, late 1900s]

shrubbery the pubic hair, especially the female pubic hair. [slang or colloquial, 1800s-1900s]

shtup 1. to coit; to fornicate; to copulate. Literally, "push." **2.** copulation. **3.** a sexually easy woman. *Cf.* FUCK-STRESS. [all senses, from Yiddish; U.S. slang, mid 1900s-pres.]

shuck 1. a derogatory nickname for a Mexican. [U.S. slang, mid 1900s] **2.** a euphemism for BULLSHIT (*q.v.*). See SHUCKS! [U.S. slang, mid 1900s-pres.] **3.** to strip off one's clothes. Compare to HUSK. [U.S. slang, 1900s]

Shucks! (also **Aw shucks!**) a mild exclamation; possibly a euphemism for "Shit!" This has become a stereotypical expression used by a shy, awkward rustic. [U.S. colloquial, mid 1800s-pres.]

shufflebutt a fidgety person. [British, late 1900s-pres.]

shuffle off this mortal coil (also **shuffle off**) to die. [U.S. colloquial, early 1900s-pres.]

shuttle-butt a female with extremely large posteriors. A play on "scuttle-butt." [U.S. slang, mid 1900s-pres., Underwood]

Shut your face! a rude request for someone to "Shut up!" [U.S. slang, 1900s]

shvance the penis. See SCHWANZ.

shy-cock a coward. From COCK (sense 3 or 5). [British slang, late 1700s, Grose]

sick 1. having the menses. *Cf.* UNWELL. For synonyms see FLOODS. **2.** to vomit. *Cf.* SICK UP. [U.S. colloquial, 1900s] **3.** mentally ill; pertaining to a delight in horror, sexual perversions, or the plight of the physically handicapped. [U.S. slang and colloquial, mid 1900s-pres.]

sick up (also **sick**) to vomit. For synonyms see YORK. [U.S. colloquial, 1900s and before]

sid (also **delysid, Sid**) the hallucinogenic drug L.S.D. From the second syllable of ACID. For synonyms see ACID. [U.S. drug culture, late 1900s]

side dish a mistress, in the sense of "something extra." *Cf.* DISH (sense 2). [U.S. slang, mid 1900s]

side ho a mistress. [U.S., late 1900s-pres.]

sideways drug intoxicated. For synonyms see WOOFLED. [U.S., late 1900s-pres.]

siege 1. a privy. For synonyms see AJAX. [1400s] **2.** to defecate. [mid 1400s] **3.** dung; feces. [mid 1500s] **4.** the anus. [mid 1500s] All are from an obsolete sense of "siege," meaning "seat." *Cf.* STOOL.

sieg-heil someone to show homage to someone; to salute and obey someone. From German. Use caution with this reminder of Nazi Germany. [U.S., mid 1900s-pres.]

siff (also **siph, syph**) syphilis. For synonyms see SPECIFIC STOMACH. [U.S. slang, mid 1900s-pres.]

silent flute the penis with a reference to FELLATIO (*q.v.*). *Cf.* FLUTE, PICCOLO, SKIN FLUTE, all of which mean "penis." [British slang, late 1700s, Grose]

silicone carne breast implants. From *chili con carne.* [U.S., late 1900s-pres.]

silk a Caucasian. For synonyms see PECKERWOOD. [U.S. black use, mid 1900s-pres.]

silo drippings real or imaginary alcohol obtained by tapping the base of a silo containing fermenting corn. [U.S. rural colloquial]

simoleon a dollar. [U.S., early 1900s-pres.]

simple infanticide masturbation. *Cf.* HIGHER MALTHUSIANISM. [British slang, 1800s, Farmer and Henley]

sinbad the penis. For synonyms see YARD. [U.S., late 1900s-pres.]

sin-bin (also **cock-wagon**) a van, especially one fitted with bedding as a place for necking and copulation. [U.S. slang, mid 1900s]

sin bosun a ship's chaplain. [British, mid 1900s-pres.]

sin-hiders trousers. Because they conceal the private parts. [British, early 1900s, *Dictionary of the Underworld*]

sink some piss to drink beer. [Australian, mid 1900s-pres.]

sink the soldier to coit a woman. [British slang, 1900s, *Dictionary of Slang and Unconventional English*]

sinner 1. anyone who commits a sin [since the 1300s, *Oxford English Dictionary*] **2.** a prostitute. For synonyms see HARLOT. [British, early 1600s]

sinse (also **sense, sense bud**) seedless marijuana. A truncation of SINSEMILLA. For synonyms see MARI. [U.S. drug culture, late 1900s]

sinsemilla marijuana; seedless marijuana. [U.S. drug culture, mid 1900s-pres.]

sin-sister a prostitute. For synonyms see HARLOT. [U.S. slang, early 1900s]

siph syphilis. *Cf.* SIFF. [U.S. slang, mid 1900s-pres.]

sip some suds to drink beer. [U.S. slang, late 1900s]

Sir Anthony Blunt the female genitals. Rhyming slang for CUNT. For synonyms see MONOSYLLABLE. [British, mid 1900s-pres.]

Sir Berkeley Hunt the female genitals. Rhyming slang for "cunt." An elaboration of BERKELEY HUNT (*q.v.*). [British slang, 1800s]

Sir Harry a chamber pot; a covered chamber pot. *Cf.* CLOSE STOOL. [British slang or colloquial, 1800s]

Sir John the penis. For synonyms see YARD. [British, late 1900s-pres.]

Sir John Barleycorn See JOHN BARLEYCORN.

Sir Martin Wagstaff the erect penis personified. *Cf.* STAFF. For synonyms see ERECTION. [mid 1600s (Urquhart)]

Sir Walter Scott 1. a CHAMBER POT (*q.v.*). Rhyming slang for "pot." [British slang with some U.S. use, 1800s] **2.** a vessel of beer. Rhyming slang for "pot." [British slang, 1800s, Farmer and Henley]

sis 1. a nickname for one's sister. No negative connotations. [U.S. colloquial, 1900s] **2.** a weak or effeminate boy; a cry baby. [U.S. slang and colloquial, 1900s] **3.** a homosexual male. For synonyms see EPICENE. [U.S. slang, mid 1900s-pres.] **4.** urine. Rhyming slang for "piss." [U.S. juvenile, 1900s]

sissified effeminate or homosexual. [British and U.S., 1900s]

sissy 1. a coward. **2.** a weak or effemi-nate boy. **3.** a homosexual male. [all since the late 1800s]

sissy-beater a sadistic male who derives special pleasure from beating up homosexual males. *Cf.* LEATHER (sense 2), ROUGH TRADE. [U.S. homosexual use, mid 1900s-pres., Farrell]

sissy beer beer with very low alcohol content. *Cf.* NEAR BEER, SQUAW PISS. [U.S. slang, early 1900s]

sissy-britches an effeminate male; a SISSY (sense 2). For synonyms see FRIBBLE. [U.S. slang or colloquial, 1900s]

sister 1. a prostitute. *Cf.* SIN-SISTER. [British, early 1600s] **2.** among homosexual males, one's pal or fellow. See SHE (sense 2). [U.S. homosexual use, mid 1900s-pres.] **3.** a black woman. [U.S. black use, mid 1900s-pres.] **4.** a supporter of women's movements; from the viewpoint of women's movements, any woman. [U.S. slang, mid 1900s-pres.] **5.** morphine. *Cf.* BROTHER (sense 1). For synonyms see MORPH. [U.S. drug culture, mid 1900s-pres.]

Sit and spin! (also **Sit on it and rotate!**) a catchphrase uttered while giving someone the finger, the upraised middle finger. [U.S. slang, late 1900s]

Sit on it and rotate! See SIT AND SPIN!

sit on someone's face to provide access to one's [female] genitals by sitting on someone's face or approximating such a position. [U.S. slang, mid 1900s-pres.]

sitter the posteriors. For synonyms see DUFF. [U.S. colloquial euphemism, 1900s]

six-pack to pass time or accompany some other act while consuming approximately six beers. Can also refer to the similar consumption of other alcoholic drinks.

six sheets to the wind very drunk; drunker than THREE SHEETS IN THE WIND. For synonyms see WOOFLED. [U.S. slang, late 1900s]

sixty-nine (also **soixanteneuf, 69**) mutual PENILINGUS or CUNNILINGUS (both *q.v.*); simultaneous penilingus and cunnilingus. Used for both heterosexual and homosexual acts. *Cf.* FLIP-FLOP,

LOOP-DE-LOOP. From the interlocking image of the numerals, 69. [U.S. slang, mid 1900s-pres.]

sixty-three a nonorthogenital sex act; a "sexual variant" (Monteleone). Similar to SIXTY-NINE (*q.v.*), but the exact nature of the act cannot be determined. Possibly in error for SIXTY-NINE (*q.v.*). [attested as U.S. underworld, mid 1900s, Monteleone]

size queen a homosexual male who is particularly attracted to men with large penes, or to the penes themselves. Possibly from "queen size," a bed and mattress size designation. See QUEEN for similar topics. [U.S. homosexual use, mid 1900s-pres.]

sizzlechest a woman with fantastic breasts. [U.S., late 1900s-pres.]

skag an ugly and unpleasant young woman. For synonyms see BUFFARIL-LA. See SCAG (sense 1).

skagged out drug intoxicated; very HIGH. SKAG = a hard drug. For synonyms see TALL. [U.S. drug culture, late 1900s]

skank 1. a whore, a slut. [U.S. black use, late 1900s] **2.** an ugly girl or woman. [U.S. collegiate, late 1900s]

skanky a sluttish, sexually loose woman. [U.S. collegiate, late 1900s]

skanky box a sexually loose woman. *Cf.* BOX. [U.S. collegiate, late 1900s, Munro]

skat a formed mass of feces. A word used when a word like "turd" is required but forbidden. Also in compounds like "bear-skat" and "dog-skat." [from the Greek combining form *skatos*, "dung"; U.S., 1900s]

skee whisky. From "whiskee." See SKY (sense 3). [U.S. slang, early 1900s]

skeet a glob of nasal mucus. [U.S. collegiate, late 1900s]

skeet-shooting blowing the nose into the air with the thumb. [U.S. collegiate, late 1900s]

skeevy sleazy and disgusting. [U.S., late 1900s-pres.]

skeezer 1. a sexually loose woman. [U.S. collegiate, late 1900s] **2.** a flirta-

tious or seductive person. [U.S. black use, late 1900s]

skid lid a helmet for riding a bicycle or motor cycle. [U.S., mid 1900s-pres.]

skid mark 1. an American black of African descent. As with the black marks left from rubber tires in a skid. Derogatory. For synonyms see EBONY. **2.** an unclean, brownish mark on one's underpants. [British and U.S., late 1900s-pres.]

skin 1. the prepuce of the penis. A truncation of "foreskin." [British, 1800s] **2.** to remove one's clothing; to strip. [British and U.S. colloquial, mid 1800s-pres.] **3.** a condom. *Cf.* EEL-SKIN, FROG-SKIN. [U.S. slang, mid 1900s-pres.] **4.** sexually attractive women; women considered sexually, as in "some skin." **5.** an act of copulation. [senses 4 and 5 are U.S. slang, 1900s]

skin a goat to vomit. Partly from the odor of vomitus. [U.S. colloquial, 1900s]

skin-coat 1. the female genitals, in the expression SHAKE A SKIN-COAT (*q.v.*). [1600s (Urquhart)] **2.** one's skin; the epidermis. [U.S. colloquial, 1900s or before]

skin-diver 1. a male copulating; the penis. [U.S. slang, mid 1900s-pres.] **2.** a fellator or fellatrix. *Cf.* MUFF-DIVER. [U.S. slang, mid 1900s-pres.]

skin-dog a lecher. See CUNT-HOUND. *Cf.* SKIN (sense 4). [attested as Canadian slang, mid 1900s, *Dictionary of Slang and Unconventional English*]

skin-flick a movie focusing on nudity or sex; a movie with nude scenes; a pornographic film or an X-rated film. [U.S. slang, mid 1900s-pres.]

skin flute the penis; the erect penis in reference to FELLATIO (*q.v.*). *Cf.* FLUTE, PICCOLO. [U.S. slang, mid 1900s]

skin-heist a rape. From SKIN (sense 5). *Cf.* SHORT-ARM HEIST. [U.S. underworld slang, mid 1900s, Goldin, O'Leary, and Lipsius]

skin-house a movie theatre featuring films of nude women or pornographic films. [U.S. slang, mid 1900s-pres.]

skin-mag (also **skin-magazine**) a magazine featuring male or female nudes. [U.S. slang, mid 1900s-pres.]

skin-popping shooting drugs; injecting narcotics. [U.S. drug culture and slang, mid 1900s-pres.]

skin the live rabbit 1. to retract the prepuce of the uncircumcised male, presumably in copulation. See LIVE RABBIT. *Cf.* PEEL ONE'S BEST END. [British slang, 1800s, Farmer and Henley] **2.** to undress; to undress someone; to take the clothing off a child. No negative connotations. [U.S. slang, 1900s]

skin-the-pizzle the female genitals, specifically the vagina. The PIZZLE (sense 2) is the penis. [British slang, 1800s, Farmer and Henley]

skinz a sexually attractive woman. For synonyms see BIRD. [U.S., late 1900s-pres.]

skip out to die. [British slang and colloquial, early 1900s]

skippy 1. an Oriental prostitute. From SKIBBY (sense 2). [U.S. slang, 1900s] **2.** a homosexual male. [U.S. black use, 1900s, Major]

skirt 1. a woman; women considered sexually; a sexually loose woman. **2.** a prostitute. [both since the 1500s]

skirt-foist a lecher, a lifter of skirts. [British, mid 1600s]

skirt-man 1. a pimp; a seller of skirts. See SKIRT (sense 2). [U.S. underworld, early 1900s] **2.** a man who prefers women in skirts rather than in trousers. [U.S. slang, mid 1900s-pres.]

skirt-patrol the search for a woman for romantic or sexual purposes. [military and later general slang, 1900s]

skit 1. diarrhea, especially that in animals. Cognate with SHIT (*q.v.*). *Cf.* SCATTERS. [British rural colloquial, 1400s-1800s] **2.** beer. From the gastrointestinal problems resulting from drinking bad beer. For synonyms see SUDS. [British military, early 1900s, Fraser and Gibbons]

skizzled alcohol intoxicated. For synonyms see WOOFLED. [U.S. slang, late 1900s]

sklook (also **plook**) to copulate. For syn-

onyms see OCCUPY. [U.S. slang, early 1900s]

skoofer (also **skoofus, skrufer, skrufus**) a marijuana cigarette. *Cf.* SKAMAS. [U.S. drug culture, mid 1900s-pres.]

skrill(a) money. [U.S., late 1900s-pres.]

skrogg to copulate. For synonyms see OCCUPY. [U.S., late 1900s-pres.]

skrungy disgusting. [U.S., late 1900s-pres.]

skuffle See SCAFFLE.

skull to perform fellatio. [U.S., late 1900s-pres.]

skull-job an act of CUNNILINGUS (*q.v.*). *Cf.* HEAD-JOB. [U.S. slang, mid 1900s-pres.]

skunk an odorous form of marijuana from Afghanistan. For synonyms see MARI. [U.S., late 1900s-pres.]

skunk-drunk (also **skunked**) alcohol intoxicated. For synonyms see WOOFLED. [U.S. slang, 1900s if not before]

sky 1. an unpleasant person; one's enemy. Possibly from SKITE (*q.v.*). [British slang, mid 1800s, Hotten] **2.** a derogatory nickname for an Italian. [Australian, early 1900s, Baker] Synonyms for sense 2: DINGBAT, DINO, EYTIES, EYTO, GHIN, GINGO, GINNEY, GINZO, GREASER, GUIN, GUINEA, GUINIE, GUINNEE, HIKES, ITE, ORGANGRINDER, RING-TAIL, SPAGHETTI, SPAGHETTI-BENDER, SPIC, WALLIYO, WOP, ZOOL. **3.** whisky. From "whisky." *Cf.* SKEE. [widespread slang, 1900s]

sky-pilot a preacher; a chaplain; an evangelist or a missionary. [British and U.S. slang, late 1800s-pres.] Synonyms: AMEN SNORTER, BIBLE-BANGER, BIBLE-BASHER, BIBLE-POUNDER, BIBLE-PUNCHER, BIBLE-THUMPER, BISH, BLACK COAT, CHIMNEY SWEEP, CHRISTER, CUSHION-THUMPER, DEVIL-CATCHER, DEVIL-CHASER, DEVIL-DODGER, DEVIL-DRIVER, DEVIL-PITCHER, DEVIL-SCOLDER, DEVIL-TEASER, DIVINE, DOMINIE, FIRE ESCAPE, FIRE INSURANCE AGENT, GLUEPOT, GOD-BOTHERER, GOSPEL-COVE, GOSPEL-GRINDER, GOSPEL-POSTILION, GOSPEL-PUSHER, GOSPEL-SHARK, GOSPEL-SHARP, GOSPEL-SHOOTER, GOSPEL-WHANGER, HAUL-DEVIL, HEAD CLERK OF

THE DOXOLOGY-WORKS, HOLY-JOE!, JESUS-SCREAMER, JESUS-SHOUTER, MAN-IN-BLACK, MAN OF THE CLOTH, PADRE, PARISH-BULL, PARISH-PRIG, PARSON, POUND-TEXT, PULPIT-CUFFER, PUZZLE-TEXT, SALVATION-RANCHER, SIN-HOUND, SKY-RIDER, SKY-SCOUT, SNUB-DEVIL, SOUL-AVIATOR, SOUL-DOCTOR, SOUL-DRIVER, SPIRITUAL FLESH-BROKER, TICKLE-TEXT.

skyrocket an amphetamine tablet or capsule. *Cf.* ROCKET, ROCKET-FUEL. For synonyms see AMP. [U.S. drug culture, mid 1900s-pres.]

slack 1. to urinate. [British slang, 1800s, Farmer and Henley] **2.** a slovenly man or woman; a sexually loose woman. [Caribbean (Jamaican). Cassidy and Le Page]

slacks trousers. For synonyms see GALLIGASKINS. [U.S. colloquial, 1900s]

slag 1. (also **slagheap**) a sexually loose woman. [U.S. collegiate, late 1900s, Munro] **2.** to copulate. For synonyms see OCCUPY. [U.S., late 1900s-pres.]

slam to COIT someone, presumably a woman. For synonyms see OCCUPY. [U.S. slang, late 1900s]

slammed alcohol intoxicated. For synonyms see WOOFLED [U.S. slang, late 1900s]

slam some beers to drink beer; to drink a number of beers. [U.S. slang, late 1900s]

slanging selling drugs. [U.S., late 1900s-pres.]

slant a derogatory nickname for any Oriental. From the shape of the Oriental eyes. *Cf.* SRANT. [U.S. slang, mid 1900s-pres.]

slant-eye (also **slant-eyes**) a derogatory nickname for an Oriental. [U.S. underworld and slang, early 1900s-pres.]

slapper a woman who is cheap and ugly but sexually active. [British, late 1900s-pres.]

slap skins to copulate. For synonyms see OCCUPY. [U.S., late 1900s-pres.]

slap the salami to masturbate (male). For synonyms see WASTE TIME. [U.S., late 1900s-pres.]

slash 1. to urinate. *Cf.* SPLASH. For synonyms see WHIZ. **2.** urination; an act of urination. [both senses, British slang, 1900s, *Dictionary of Slang and Unconventional English*] **3.** women considered as sexual objects. [U.S. slang, 1900s]

slashers the testicles. For synonyms see WHIRLYGIGS. [British slang, mid 1900s, *Dictionary of Slang and Unconventional English*] **3.** women considered as sexual objects. [U.S. slang, 1900s]

slaughtered alcohol or drug intoxicated. For synonyms see TALL, WOOFLED. [U.S. slang, 1900s]

sleep around to be sexually promiscuous. [somewhat euphemistic; U.S. slang, mid 1900s-pres.]

sleeper a barbiturate or nonbarbiturate capsule or tablet. [U.S. slang and drug culture, mid 1900s-pres.]

sleep with to copulate with someone; to copulate with someone illicitly. This may or may not involve a period of time as long as a night and may or may not involve sleep. *Cf.* GO TO BED WITH. [U.S. colloquial euphemism, mid 1900s-pres.]

sleez a slut; a woman of very low character. From the adjective "sleazy." [U.S. slang, mid 1900s, *Current Slang*]

sleighride a cocaine party; the act of taking cocaine and being under its influence. From the SNOW (sense 2) theme. [U.S. drug culture, early 1900s-pres.]

slewed (also **slewy, slued**) intoxicated with alcohol. From a nautical term applied to a ship changing her tack. [British and U.S. slang, early 1800s-pres.]

slick-chick 1. an attractive and cute young woman. [U.S. slang, mid 1900s-pres.] **2.** a sexually aroused woman. [U.S. slang, mid 1900s-pres.]

slightly-tightly mildly intoxicated with alcohol. For synonyms see WOOFLED. [British slang, late 1800s-early 1900s, Ware]

slim good-looking; sexually attractive. [U.S. slang, late 1900s]

slim-dilly a girl or woman. [Australian, 1900s, Baker]

slime 1. semen. For synonyms see METTLE. [British slang, 1800s, *Dictionary of Slang and Unconventional English*] **2.** a worthless person; a low and wretched person. [U.S. slang, mid 1900s-pres.] **3.** pornography; low entertainment; degrading matters.

slimy, old the penis. For synonyms see YARD. [British, 1800s, Farmer and Henley]

sling a cat to vomit. *Cf.* CAT (sense 7), JERK THE CAT, WHIP THE CAT. [British and U.S. slang, 1800s-1900s]

sling a snot (also **sling**) to blow one's nose without a handkerchief. [British and U.S. slang and colloquial, mid 1800s-1900s]

sling one's jelly (also **sling one's juice**) to masturbate. *Cf.* JELLY (sense 3), JUICE (sense 1). [British slang, 1800s, Farmer and Henley]

sling the crap (also **sling the bull**) to tell tall tales or to lie; to BULLSHIT (*q.v.*). [U.S. slang, mid 1900s-pres.]

slip her a length to copulate with a woman. The "length" is the penis. [widespread slang, 1800s-1900s]

slip into to coit; to penetrate a woman. [British and U.S. colloquial, 1900s and before]

slip someone a fatty to copulate [with] someone. For synonyms see OCCUPY. [British, mid 1900s-pres.]

slip someone a length to copulate [with] someone. For synonyms see OCCUPY. [British and U.S., mid 1900s-pres.]

slip someone the hot beef injection to COIT a woman. *Cf.* MEAT INJECTION. For synonyms see OCCUPY. [U.S. collegiate, late 1900s, Munro]

slit the female genitals; the clitoris (possibly in error); the PUDENDAL CLEAVAGE (*q.v.*). *Cf.* GASH (sense 1). [widespread recurrent nonce; slang since the mid 1600s]

slithery copulation. For synonyms see SMOCKAGE. [British slang, 1900s, *Dictionary of Slang and Unconventional English*]

slobberchops someone who produces lots of saliva. [British, late 1900s-pres.]

slop-chute the anus. *Cf.* DIRT-CHUTE. [U.S. slang, mid 1900s]

sloppy-drunk (also **sloppy**) intoxicated with alcohol. *Cf.* DIRTY-DRUNK. [U.S. slang, late 1800s-1900s]

sloppy seconds an act of copulation wherein the vagina of the woman still contains the spendings of a previous copulation. *Cf.* BUTTERED BUN. [U.S. slang, mid 1900s]

sloppy sex casual sex; nonorthogenital sex. [U.S. slang, mid 1900s-pres.]

slosh alcohol; a drink of alcohol. [British and U.S. slang, late 1800s-1900s]

sloshed intoxicated with alcohol. For synonyms see WOOFLED. [U.S. slang since the early 1900s or before]

sloshed to the ears intoxicated with alcohol. [U.S. slang, mid 1900s]

sloshy drunk. For synonyms see WOOFLED. [U.S., late 1900s-pres.]

slot the female genitals; the PUDENDAL CLEAVAGE (*q.v.*). [widespread recurrent nonce; slang, 1800s-1900s]

sloughed intoxicated with alcohol. See SLEWED. [U.S. slang and colloquial, mid 1900s]

slow 1. slow to become sexually interested or aroused. *Cf.* FAST. [British and U.S. colloquial, 1800s-pres.] **2.** stupid. [colloquial since the 1800s]

sludgeball a despicable and repellent person. For synonyms see SNOKEHORN. [British, late 1900s-pres.]

slug the penis. For synonyms see YARD. [Australian, late 1900s-pres.]

slugged intoxicated with alcohol. For synonyms see WOOFLED. [U.S. slang, mid 1900s-pres.]

slugos men's brief swimming trunks. See SLUG. [Australian, late 1900s-pres.]

slurks a drunkard. For synonyms see ALCHY.

slushed-up (also **slushed**) intoxicated with alcohol. [U.S. slang, mid 1900s]

slusher (also **slush**) a drunkard. [colloquial, 1800s-1900s]

slush hog a heavy drinker; a drunkard. For synonyms see ALCHY. [U.S. slang, late 1900s]

slut 1. a nasty slattern; a sexually loose woman. [since the mid 1400s] **2.** to work as a servant. [British and U.S. colloquial, early 1800s] **3.** a bitch; a female dog; a rude woman. [British, mid 1800s] **4.** a promiscuous homosexual male. From sense 1. [U.S. homosexual use, mid 1900s-pres., Farrell]

slut hut a house of prostitution. For synonyms see BROTHEL. [British, late 1900s-pres.]

S.M. SADISM and MASOCHISM (both *q.v.*); a "sado-masochist." [U.S. slang, mid 1900s-pres.]

smack 1. a kiss, especially a noisy one. [U.S. slang, early 1900s-pres.] **2.** heroin. *Cf.* SHMECK. [U.S. drug culture, 1900s]

small-arm the penis. A reinterpretation of the expression meaning "small gun" or "pistol." See SMALL-ARM INSPECTION. [military, early 1900s]

small-arm inspection visual inspection of the male genitals for signs of venereal disease or for lice. *Cf.* DANGLE-PARADE, POULTRY-SHOW, SHORT-ARM INSPECTION. [military, early 1900s]

smart-ass (also **smart-arse**) a smart aleck; a know-it-all. [widespread slang, mid 1900s-pres.]

smarty-pants 1. a smart aleck. [U.S. colloquial, 1900s] **2.** a young male who is beginning to feel strong sexual desire. [U.S. slang, mid 1900s]

smash 1. an alcohol extract of CANNABIS SATIVA (*q.v.*). Probably related to SMASHED (sense 2). [U.S. drug culture, mid 1900s-pres.] **2.** wine. Because it is "smashed" out of grapes. [U.S. black use, late 1900s]

smashed 1. intoxicated with alcohol. [British and U.S. slang, mid 1900s-pres.] **2.** drug intoxicated. [U.S. drug culture, mid 1900s-pres.]

smashing kissing; petting. *Cf.* MASH. [U.S. slang, mid 1900s]

smear an American black of African descent. Derogatory. For synonyms see EBONY. [U.S. slang, late 1900s]

smeared 1. intoxicated with alcohol.

[U.S. slang, mid 1900s-pres.] **2.** drug intoxicated. [U.S. drug culture, mid 1900s-pres.]

smeck heroin. See SCHMECK. [U.S. underworld and drug culture, early 1900s-pres.]

smecker any drug except marijuana. *Cf.* SCHMECKER. [U.S. underworld, mid 1900s]

smeg something disgusting. From *smegma.* [U.S., late 1900s-pres.]

smegma 1. a soap or detergent substitute. No negative connotations. [British, 1600s-1800s] **2.** a thick, cheesy, or soapy substance which collects beneath the foreskin and around the clitoris. [since the early 1800s] Synonyms for sense 2: CHEESE, COCK-CHEESE, CROTCH-CHEESE, DUCK-BUTTER, GNAT-BREAD, HEAD-CHEESE.

smeg-head a disliked person. From *smegma.* [British, late 1900s-pres.]

Smell me! a rude curse or exclamation; a command to smell one's pubic or anal area. [U.S., mid 1900s]

smell the place up (also **stink the place up**) to defecate; to use the BATHROOM (*q.v.*) for defecation. [U.S. slang, mid 1900s-pres.]

smizz heroin. For synonyms see HEROIN. [British drug culture, late 1900s]

smock 1. a woman; women considered sexually; the same as SKIRT (*q.v.*). [around the 1600s] **2.** to make womanish. [early 1600s] **3.** to coit a woman. **4.** to chase women; to act as a lecher. **5.** the female genitals. [senses 3-5 are British, 1700s-1800s]

smockage chasing women; copulating with women; copulation. [British slang, early 1600s] Synonyms and related terms: ACTION, ACT OF ANDROGYNATION, ACT OF DARKNESS, ACT OF GENERATION, ACT OF KIND, ACT OF LOVE, ACT OF PLEASURE, ACT OF SHAME, ACT OF SPORT, ALL THE WAY, AMOROUS CONGRESS, AMOUROUS RITES, APHRODISIA, BANANAS AND CREAM, BANG, BASKET-MAKING, BATE-UP, BAWDY BANQUET, BED-RITE, BEDTIME STORY, BEDWARD BIT, BEEF INJECTION, BEE IS IN THE HIVE, BEHIND-DOOR WORK, BELLY-BUMPING, BELLY-RIDE, BELLY TO BELLY, BELLY-

WARMER, BELT, BEST AND PLENTY OF IT, BIG TIME, BITCH, BIT OF FRONT DOOR WORK, BIT OF FUN, BIT OF HAIR, BIT OF HARD, BIT OF HARD FOR A BIT OF SOFT, BIT OF JAM, BIT OF MEAT, BIT OF NIFTY, BIT OF QUIMSY, BIT OF ROUGH, BIT OF SNUG, BIT OF SNUG FOR A BIT OF STIFF, BIT OF THE GOOSE'S-NECK, BIT OF THE OTHER, BIT ON A FORK, BLANKET, BLANKET DRILL, BLANKET HORNPIPE, BOFFING, BONE DANCE, BOODY, BOOLY-DOG, BOOM-BOOM, BOOZLE, BOP, BOTTOM-WETTER, BOUNCY-BOUNCY, BOXING, BRIM, BRUSH, BUNK-UP, BURLAP, BUSH PATROL, BUSINESS, BUTT, BUTTOCK-BALL, BUTTOCK-STIRRING, CARNAL ACQUAINTANCE, CARNAL CONNECTION, CARNAL COPULATION, CARNAL ENGAGEMENT, CARNAL INTERCOURSE, CARNAL KNOWLEDGE, CAULIFLOWER, CAVAULTING, CHAWS, CHIVALRY, CHUNK, COCKING, COITION, COITURE, CONCUBITUS, CONJUGAL ACT, CONJUGAL EMBRACE, CONJUGAL RELATIONS, CONJUGAL RITES, CONJUGALS, CONNECTION, CONNUBIAL RITES, CONSUMMATION, CONVERSATION, COOT, COPULATION, COUNTER, CRACK, CRUMPET, CULBUTIZING EXERCISE, CULLY-SHANGY, DAUB OF THE BRUSH, DEED OF KIND, DEED OF PLEASURE, DICKY-DUNK, DIRTY WORK AT THE CROSSROADS, DONALD DUCK, FEATHER-BED JIG, FEDERATING, FLESH SESSION, FLOP, FORE AND AFT, FORNICATION, FOUR-LEGGED FROLIC, FRAIL-JOB, FRIGGING, FRISK, FRUIT THAT MADE MEN WISE, FUCK, FUCKATHON, FUCKING, FUN AND GAMES, FUNCH, FUTTER, GALLANTRY, GINCH, GOAT'S JIG, GREENS, GROUND RATIONS, GRUMBLE AND GRUNT GRUMMET, HAIR, HAIR-COURT, HANDY-DANDY, HANKY-PANKY, HIDE THE SAUSAGE, HOGMAGUNDY, HOLE, HOLE IN ONE, HOME RUN, HONEY FUCK, HORIZONTAL EXERCISE, HORIZONTAL HULA, HORIZONTAL MAMBO, HORIZONTAL REFRESHMENT, HORIZONTAL RUMBLE, HORSEMANSHIP, HOSE, HOSING, HOT LAY, HOT ROLL WITH CREAM, HUMP, HUMPERY, HUNK, HUNK OF ASS, HUNK OF BUTT, HUNK OF HYMIE, HUNK OF SKIRT, HUNK OF TAIL, HYMENEAL-SWEETS, HYMIE, IMPROPER INTERCOURSE, IN ACTUS COITU, INCOITU, INTERCOURSE, INTERIOR DECORATING, IRISH WHIST, IT, JAB, JAPE, JAZZ, JIG, JIG-A-GIG, JIG-A-LIG, JIGGADY-JIG, JING-JANG, JIVE, JOBBING, JOCKUM-CLOY, JOY-RIDE, JUMBLE-GIBLETS, KINDNESS, KISS, KNOCK, KNOCKING, KNOWLEDGE, LADIES' TAILORING, LADY-FEAST, LAP-CLAP, LAST COMPLIMENT, LAY, LEG-BUSINESS, LEWD INFUSION, LING-GRAPPLING, LISTS OF LOVE, LITTLE BIT, LITTLE BIT OF KEG, LOOSE-COAT GAME, LOVE-LIFE, MAKE, MARITAL DUTY, MATTRESS MAMBO, MEAT, MEAT INJECTION, MEDICINE, MERRY BOUT, MOTTING, MOW, MUTTON, MYRTLE, NATTUM, NATURE'S DUTY, NAUGHTY, NAVEL ENGAGEMENT, NETHER-WORK, NIFTY, NIGHT BASEBALL, NIGHT-PHYSIC, NIGHT-WORK, NOOKY, NOONER, NOSE-PAINTING, NUB, NUBBING, NUBBING-CHEAT, NUGGING, NUPTIAL RITES, NURTLE, OCCUPY, OIL CHANGE, ONE WITH T'OTHER, ON THE JOB, PASSION, PENETRATION, PHYSIC, PIECE, PIECE OF FLESH, PIECE OF TAIL, PILE-DRIVING, PITY FUCK, PLOW THE BACK FORTY, POKE, POLE-WORK, POON-TANG, POOP-NODDY, PORKING, POST, POST-CONNUBIAL, PRANKS, PRICK-CHINKING, PROD, PRONE POSITION, PUDDING, PULLY-HAWLY, PUSS, PUSSY, PUT AND TAKE, QUIFFING, QUIM, QUIMING, QUIM-STICKING, RAM, RANTUM-SCANTUM, RELATIONS, RELISH, REM-IN-RE, RITES OF LOVE, RITES OF VENUS, ROLL, ROLL IN THE HAY, ROMP, ROOT, ROOTLE, ROUST, RUB-BELLY, RULE-OF-THREE, RUMBLE, RUMP-SHAKER, RUMP-WORK, RUMPY-PUMPY, RUN-OFF, RUT, RUTTING, SALT, SCORE, SCREW, SCRUMP, SECRET SERVICES, SETTLEMENT-IN-TAIL, SEX, SEX ACT, SEX-JOB, SEXUAL COMMERCE, SEXUAL CONGRESS, SEXUAL CONJUNCTION, SEXUAL CONNECTION, SEXUAL EMBRACE, SEXUAL INTERCOURSE, SEXUAL INTIMACY, SEXUAL RELATIONS, SEXUAL UNION, SHAG, SHAKE, SHAKING OF THE SHEETS, SHEETS, SHIFT-SERVICE, SHIFT-WORK, SHINES, SHORT-ARM PRACTICE, SHOVE, SHTUP, SLITHERY, SNIBBET, SNIPPET, SOME, SOUL ROLL, SPORT, SPORT OF VENUS, SQUEEZE AND A SQUIRT, STUFF, SUBAGITATION, TAIL, TAIL-TICKLING, TAIL-TWITCHING, TAIL-WAGGING, TAIL-WORK, TARGET PRACTICE, THE ACT, THE FAVOR, THE LIMIT, THE ULTIMATE FAVOR, TOPS-AND-BOTTOMS, TRIP UP THE RHINE, TROMBONING, TUP, TURN,

TWAT-RAKING, TWATTING, TWO-HANDED PUT, UGLY, UH-HUH, UPTAILS-ALL, UP TO ONE'S BALLS, USE OF THE SEX, USSY-PAY, VALVE JOB, VENEREAL ACT, VENERY, VENUS, VENUS'S HONYPOT, WET-'UN, WHAT EVE DID WITH ADAM, WIE-NERING, WORKS.

smockster 1. a madam or a pimp. [British, early 1600s] **2.** a whoremonger; a lecher. [British slang, 1600s-1700s]

smoke 1. to coit a woman. Cf. CHIMNEY, MAKE THE CHIMNEY SMOKE. [British slang, 1800s] **2.** a derogatory nickname for a Negro. For synonyms see EBONY. [U.S. slang, early 1900s] **3.** to perform an act of PENILINGUS (q.v.). [British and U.S. slang, 1900s] **4.** to smoke marijuana; to smoke any drugs. [U.S. drug culture and slang, mid 1900s-pres.] Various types of drug smoking: BANG A REEFER (marijuana), BEAT THE GONG (opium), BLAST (marijuana), BLOW A STICK (marijuana), BLOW GAGE (marijuana), BLOW HAY (marijuana), BLOW JIVE (marijuana), BLOW ONE'S ROOF (marijuana), BLOW POT (marijuana), BLOW TEA (marijuana), GO LOCO (marijuana), HIT THE FLUTE (opium), HIT THE GONGER (opium), HIT THE GOW (opium), HIT THE PIPE (opium), KICK THE GONG (opium), KISS MARY (marijuana), KISS THE FISH (hashish), LIE DOWN (opium), SUCK BAMBOO (opium), SUCK THE BAMBOO (opium), TOKE (marijuana), TORCH UP (marijuana). **5.** marijuana; a marijuana cigarette. [U.S. drug culture, mid 1900s-pres.]

smoked intoxicated with alcohol. Cf. CORNED, SALTED-DOWN. [U.S. slang or colloquial, 1800s, Wentworth and Flexner]

smokey treat marijuana. For synonyms see MARI. [U.S., late 1900s-pres.]

Smoley hoke! a deliberate spoonerism for "Holy Smoke!" [not widely known; 1900s]

smooch (also **smoodge, smooge, smouch, smouge**) **1.** to kiss; to kiss and pet. [widespread colloquial, 1800s-pres.] **2.** a kiss. Also **smoucher.** [collo-

quial, 1800s-pres.] **3.** to act like a sycophant. Cf. ASS-KISSER. [Australian, 1900s, Baker] See also SMOUSE.

smooth as a baby's bottom (also **soft as a baby's bottom**) pertaining to something which is very smooth or soft. [colloquial, 1900s]

smouse (also **smouch, smous, smoutch**) a derogatory nickname for a Jewish man. [British colloquial or slang, early 1700s-1800s] See also SMOOCH.

smuckered alcohol intoxicated. For synonyms see WOOFLED. [U.S. slang, late 1900s]

SNAFU (also **snafu**) **1.** "situation normal, all fucked-up" or "situation normal, all fouled-up." [originally military use; U.S. slang, mid 1900s-pres.] **2.** to mess up; to make a blunder; to ruin something. The original meaning is unknown to many users of this acronym. Frequently appears in lower case in this sense. [U.S. slang, mid 1900s-pres.] Similar forms: COMMFU, FUBAR, FUBB, FUMTU, G.F.U., IMFU, JAAFU, JACFU, JANFU, M.F.U., NABU, SABU, SAMFU, SAPFU SNEFU, SNRAFU, SUSFU, TABU, TA-FUBAR, TARFU, TASFUIRA, T.C.C.FU.

snaffle to steal. [U.S., late 1900s-pres.]

snag 1. to copulate; to rape. [U.S. slang, 1900s] **2.** to commit PEDERASTY (q.v.). [U.S. underworld, early 1900s] **3.** an ugly girl or woman. Cf. SCAG (sense 1). [U.S. slang, mid 1900s]

snag-fencer (also **snag-catcher**) a nickname for a dentist. [British slang, 1800s or before]

snail mail the U.S. mail, compared to E-mail. [widespread, late 1900s-pres.]

snake 1. the penis. Cf. BLACKSNAKE, ROCK PYTHON, SNAKE IN THE GRASS. [widespread recurrent nonce] **2.** inferior whisky. A truncation of SNAKE-BITE MEDICINE (q.v.). For synonyms see EMBALMING FLUID. [U.S. slang, early 1900s] **3.** a girl, especially an ugly girl or a promiscuous girl. [U.S. slang, mid 1900s] **4.** a derogatory nickname for a Caucasian. [U.S. black use, mid 1900s] **5.** a marijuana. [U.S. underworld, mid 1900s or before, Goldin, O'Leary, and Lipsius]

snakebite medicine (also **snake medicine**) whisky; any strong alcoholic drink; the same as MEDICINE (sense 2), SNAKE (sense 2). [U.S. colloquial, 1900s or before]

snake-charmer someone who is interested in the penis; someone who plays with the penis. [U.S. slang, late 1900s]

snake in the grass 1. a sneaky and despised person; a lurking danger. [colloquial since the 1600s] **2.** the penis and the pubic hair. A reinterpretation of sense 1. [recurrent nonce]

snake-juice inferior alcohol; bad whisky; alcohol as potent as snake's venom. *Cf.* SNAKEBITE MEDICINE. [Australian, 1900s or before]

snake-poison inferior alcohol; bad whisky; the same as SNAKE-JUICE (*q.v.*). [U.S. slang or colloquial, late 1800s]

snake ranch a brothel. *Cf.* SNAKE. For synonyms see BROTHEL. [U.S. slang, 1900s]

snakes the DELIRIUM TREMENS (q.v.). *Cf.* SEEING SNAKES. [U.S. slang or colloquial, late 1800s-mid 1900s]

snake's hiss urine; to urinate; an act of urination. Rhyming slang for "piss." [Australian, 1900s, *Dictionary of Rhyming Slang*]

snap one's cookies to vomit; to regurgitate. *Cf.* TOSS ONE'S COOKIES. [U.S. slang, mid 1900s-pres.]

snapped (also **schnapped**) intoxicated with alcohol. [U.S. slang, mid 1800s-1900s]

snapped-up intoxicated with narcotics. For synonyms see TALL. [U.S. drug culture, mid 1900s]

snapper 1. the penis. [British slang, 1800s, Farmer and Henley] **2.** the foreskin of the penis. [U.S. slang, mid 1900s-pres.] **3.** the vagina. [U.S. slang, mid 1900s-pres.] **4.** a very attractive girl; a very sexy girl. Probably from sense 2. [U.S. slang, mid 1900s-pres.] **5.** an ampule of amyl nitrite. A vasodilator sold in ampules which are crushed

to release amyl nitrite vapor. *Cf.* PEARL (sense 2). POPPER. [U.S. drug culture, mid 1900s-pres.]

snapping log a crocodile. [Australian, late 1900s-pres.]

snaps money. [U.S., late 1900s-pres.]

snatch 1. a very rapid act of copulation. [British, early 1600s] **2.** the female genitals. [British and U.S. slang, mid 1900s-pres.] **3.** women considered sexually; women of loose sexual control. *Cf.* PIECE OF SNATCH (sense 1). [U.S. slang, mid 1900s-pres.] **4.** the posteriors. **5.** catamites. See CATAMITE. From senses 2 and 4. [senses 4 and 5 are U.S. underworld, mid 1900s, Goldin, O'Leary, and Lipsius] See also DAD.

snatch-box the female genitals, a play on "matchbox." *Cf.* BOX (sense 2), SNATCH (sense 2). [British slang, 1900s or before]

snatched arrested. [U.S., late 1900s-pres.]

snatcher a police officer; a detective. For synonyms see FLATFOOT. [U.S., late 1900s-pres.]

snatch-peddler (also **peddle-snatch**) **1.** a prostitute, either male or female. **2.** a CATAMITE (*q.v.*). For synonyms see BRONCO. [both senses, U.S. underworld, mid 1900s, Goldin, O'Leary, and Lipsius]

snaved in drug intoxicated. For synonyms see WOOFLED. [U.S., late 1900s-pres.]

sneeze a release of intestinal gas, especially if forceful. *Cf.* THROUGH-COUGH. For synonyms see GURK. [U.S. euphemism, 1900s]

sneeze in the basket an act of CUNNILINGUS (*q.v.*). [U.S. slang, 1900s]

SNEFU "situation normal, everything fucked-up," describing a situation where everything is as confused as usual. A variation of SNAFU (*q.v.*). [nonce or synthetic military slang]

snipcock a Jewish male. Referring to circumcision. [British, late 1900s-pres.]

snob nasal mucus. See SNOT (sense 1). For synonyms see BOOGIE. [British colloquial, 1800s]

snockered intoxicated with alcohol.

From a term for "sock" or "knock." [U.S. slang, mid 1900s-pres.]

snoke-horn a sneak; a devious rascal. "Snoke" is from "sneak." [mid 1400s] Synonyms: A.H., ANIMAL, ANTI-BOD, APE, ASS-HOLE, ASS-WIPE, BAD EGG, BATHTUB SCUM, BEZONIAN, BITE, BLACKGUARD, BLIGHTER, BLODGIE, BLOOD OF A BITCH, BOB SQUIRT, BOB TAIL, BRIGAND, BUCKEEN, BUFU, BULLY, BUSTA, CAD, CAITIFF, CATSO, CHIT, CHUFFER, CLAPPERDUDGEON, CLOWES, COCKAPERT, COCKSUCKER, COISTRELL, COKIN, CONGEON, COVE, COWSON, CRAP-BRAIN, CRAPHEAD, CREEP, CRUMB, CUNT-BALL, DAMBER, DASTARD, DICKBREATH, DOUCHE, DOUCHE BAG, DROOP, FAT-ASSED, FLID, FOUR-LETTER MAN, FUCK-PIG, FURBALL, GEECH, GEEK, GOODMAN-TURD, GROD, GROTBAG, GRUBBER, GRUNGE, GUG, GULLION, GUNZEL-BUTT, GUTTER PUP, GYM SHOE, HARD-OFF, HARLOT, HASKARD, HEANLING, HEMPIE, HOOD, HOODLUM, HOOLIGAN, HOSER, ICK, JACK NASTY, JACK SHIT, LADRONE, LARRIKIN, LOON, LOUSE, LOUSE-BAG, LOWLIFE, LURCHER, LURKER, MAMMY-JAMMER, MAMMY-TAPPER, MISCREANT, MOMZER, MOTHER-CLUTCHER, MUCK-SPOUT, MUDSNOOT, NITHING, PAIN IN THE ASS, PALTRY FELLOW, PHEASANT PLUCKER, PICAROON, PICCOLO-PLAYER, PILL, POLECAT, POND SCUM, POOHEAD, PRICK, PUKE, PUP, QUEERE-COVE, RAFF, RATBAG, RAT-BASTARD, RHOID, ROGER, ROGUE, ROPE-RIPE, SCAB, SCADGER, SCHTOONK, SCUBBADO, SCUMSUCKER, SCUT, SCUTZ, SHAB, SHABAROON, SHAG-BAG, SHAG-NASTY, SHAKE-BAG, SHICER, SHIT-ASS, SHITE-POKE, SHIT-FIRE, SHIT-HEEL, SHIT-POT, SHIT-SACK, SHITSTAIN, SHIT-STICK, SHOWER SCUM, SIWASH, SKA-LAWAG, SKUNK, SLUDGEBALL, SLUM-BUM, SLYBOOTS, SNAKE IN THE GRASS, SNARGE, SNIDE, SON-OF-A-BEE, SON-OF-A-BISCUIT-EATER, SON OF A FEMALE CA-NINE, SON OF A SEA COOK, SON OF A SOW, SON OF A WHORE, SONUVABITCH, STINKARD, STINKER, STITCHEL, TATTER-DEMALLION, THUG, TITIVIL, TOSSBAG, TROLL, TROLLY-BAGS, TURD FACE, TURD POODLE, VARLET, VILLAIN, WANKSTAIN, WARLOCK, WART, WEINER, WEISENHEI-MER, WHANG, WORM, YAZZIHAMPER, YELLOW-DOG, YERNT, ZARF, ZOD.

snolly-goster a devious lawyer; a shyster. [U.S. slang and colloquial, mid 1800s-1900s] Synonyms: AMBU-LANCE-CHASER, LIP, MOUTH, MOUTH-PIECE, PHILADELPHIA LAWYER, SHARK, SHYSTER.

snooted intoxicated with alcohol. See HAVE A SNOOTFUL.

snooter a cocaine user; someone who SNORTS cocaine. [U.S. drug culture, late 1900s]

snoozamorooed alcohol intoxicated. For synonyms see WOOFLED. [U.S. slang, late 1900s]

snop marijuana. For synonyms see MARI. [U.S. drug culture, mid 1900s-pres.]

snorbs the breasts. For synonyms see BOSOM. [U.S. slang, mid 1900s, *Current Slang*]

snork to smoke marijuana or hashish. [U.S., late 1900s-pres.]

snort 1. a drink; a swig of alcohol. [U.S. slang and colloquial, 1900s or before] **2.** to sniff cocaine or other drugs. [U.S. drug culture, mid 1900s-pres.] **3.** cocaine. "Some snort" is a portion of cocaine. From sense 2. [U.S. drug culture, mid 1900s-pres.] **4.** powdered drugs including P.C.P. [U.S. drug culture, mid 1900s-pres.]

snorter 1. a drink of undiluted whisky. *Cf.* SNORT. [U.S. slang, late 1800s] **2.** a drunkard. *Cf.* SNORT. For synonyms see ALCHY. [U.S. slang, mid 1900s] **3.** a drug user who typically takes drugs nasally. [U.S. drug culture, late 1900s] **4.** a device for snorting cocaine. [U.S. drug culture, late 1900s]

snorts the drug P.C.P. (*q.v.*). From SNORT (sense 4). [U.S. drug culture, mid 1900s-pres.]

snot 1. nasal mucus. [since the 1400s] **2.** to blow the nose or wipe mucus from the nose. [since the 1500s; no longer in polite use] **3.** a term of contempt for a person. [since the early 1600s]

snot balls rubber cement rolled into balls and burned for the vapors. [U.S., late 1900s-pres.]

snot-box the nose. [British with some U.S. use, 1800s-1900s]

snot-rag a handkerchief. [widespread slang and colloquial, 1800s-1900s]

snot rocket mucus blown from the nose. [U.S., late 1900s-pres.]

snots 1. gobs of nasal mucus. [U.S. colloquial, 1900s] **2.** oysters. [U.S. slang and colloquial, 1900s]

snotted intoxicated with alcohol. For synonyms see WOOFLED. [U.S. slang, early 1900s]

snowball queen a homosexual male who practices snowballing. See SNOW-BALL (sense 4) for details and see QUEEN for similar subjects.

snow-bank a place for consuming cocaine. *Cf.* SNOW (sense 2). [U.S. underworld and drug culture, mid 1900s]

snowbird 1. a cocaine user. **2.** a heroin addict or an illicit user of any powdered drug. **3.** cocaine. [all senses, U.S. underworld and drug culture, early 1900s-pres.]

snow-caine cocaine. SNOW (sense 2) and "cocaine." [U.S. underworld slang and drug culture, mid 1900s-pres.]

snow-drifter 1. a cocaine user. **2.** a cocaine seller. See SNOW (sense 2). Both are from "snowdrift." [both senses, U.S. underworld, early 1900s]

snowed-under (also **snowed-in, snowed up**) **1.** under the influence of cocaine. **2.** under the influence of any narcotic. Both are from the standard expression meaning "buried." [both senses, U.S. underworld, early 1900s]

snow queen a gay black man who prefers white males. For synonyms see EPICENE. [U.S., late 1900s-pres.]

snow snorter a cocaine addict. [U.S. drug culture, late 1900s, Lewin and Lewin]

snow-storm 1. a large amount of cocaine or other powdered drugs. **2.** a party where abundant cocaine is available. *Cf.* CAUGHT IN A SNOWSTORM. [both senses, U.S. underworld and drug culture, mid 1900s-pres.]

snow-stuff cocaine. *Cf.* WHITE STUFF. [U.S. drug culture, mid 1900s-pres.]

snozzled intoxicated with alcohol. For synonyms see WOOFLED. [U.S. slang and colloquial, early 1900s]

SNRAFU "situation normal, really all fucked-up." a variant of SNAFU (*q.v.*). [nonce or synthetic military slang]

snubbed intoxicated with alcohol. For synonyms see WOOFLED. [U.S. slang, Wentworth and Flexner]

snuff it to die. Refers to snuffing out a candle. [British slang, early 1900s]

snuffy intoxicated with alcohol. For synonyms see WOOFLED. [British and U.S. slang, early 1800s-1900s]

snug 1. to coit; to copulate with a woman. *Cf.* BIT OF SNUG. [British slang, 1800s, Farmer and Henley] **2.** intoxicated with alcohol. [British and U.S. slang, 1800s-1900s]

snuggle to cuddle and kiss. *Cf.* SMUGGLE. [U.S. colloquial, 1900s]

so 1. intoxicated with alcohol. Also **so-so.** *Cf.* HOW-CAME-YOU-SO? (sense 1). [British euphemism, early 1800s] **2.** menstruating. Also **so-so.** [British colloquial euphemism, 1800s, Farmer and Henley] **3.** pregnant. *Cf.* HOW-CAME-YOU-SO? (sense 2). [British, 1800s] **4.** homosexual. [euphemistic slang, late 1800s-1900s]

soak 1. a drinking bout. **2.** a drunkard. **3.** to drink to intoxication. [senses 1-3 since the 1800s or before] **4.** to linger in coition after ejaculation. [British slang and nonce elsewhere, 1800s-1900s, *Dictionary of Slang and Unconventional English*]

soaked intoxicated with alcohol. [U.S. slang and colloquial, early 1700s-pres.]

soaker a heavy drinker; a drunkard. [British slang, 1700s or before]

soap 1. semen. For synonyms see METTLE. [British slang, 1800s, Farmer and Henley] **2.** a simpleton; a fool. For synonyms see OAF. [Australian slang, mid 1900s, Baker] **3.** a methaqualone tablet. Also **sope.** *Cf.* SUPER-SOAPER. [U.S. drug culture, mid 1900s-pres.]

soapy-eyed intoxicated with alcohol. [U.S. slang, early 1900s]

S.O.B. 1. "son of a bitch," a highly despised person. Synonyms: BLOOD OF

A BITCH, COW-SON, DASTARD, SON-OF-A-BEE, SON-OF-A-BISCUIT-EATER, SON OF A FEMALE CANINE, SON OF A SEA COOK, SON OF A SOW, SON OF A WHORE, SONUVABITCH. [widespread slang, 1900s] **2.** "silly old bugger"; "silly old blighter." **3.** "shit or bust." [senses 2 and 3 are British slang, 1900s]

social disease venereal disease; syphilis or gonorrhea or both. [U.S. colloquial, 1900s] Synonyms: BAD BLOOD, BAD DISEASE, BAD DISORDER, BLOOD DISEASE, BLUE BALLS, BLUE BOAR, BLUE FEVER, BONE-AGUE, BURNER, CLAP, COVENT GARDEN AGUE, CRINKUMS, CRUD, DELICATE DISEASE, DELICATE TAINT, DOSE, DOUBLE-EVENT, FLAME, FLAP DRAGON, FORGET-ME-NOT, FULL HAND, FULL HOUSE, GARDEN-GOUT, GENITO-URINARY DISEASE, GOOSE, GOUT, GRINCUMS, KERTERVER-CARTZO, LOAD, LOBSTER TAILS, NAP, NOLI-ME-TANGERE, PINTLE-FEVER, PLAGUE, PREVENTABLE DISEASE, RHEA SISTERS, SAUCE, SCALDER, SCRUD, SEXUAL DISEASE, STICK, TOKEN, VENEREAL, VENEREAL DISEASE, VENUS'S CURSE, VICE DISEASE. Terms for "syphilis" are at SPECIFIC STOMACH.

socked alcohol intoxicated. For synonyms see WOOFLED. [U.S. collegiate, late 1900s]

sod 1. a SODOMITE (q.v.). [British and U.S., 1800s-1900s] **2.** to commit sodomy; to commit PEDERASTY (q.v.). A truncation of "sodomy." [British slang, 1900s] **3.** a derogatory term of address. Based on sense 1 or perhaps sense 4. Sometimes used in fun. [British, 1800s-1900s] **4.** a drunkard. From SOT (sense 2) or "sodden." [U.S. slang, early 1900s-pres.]

sodden bum a drunkard; a soggy and worthless wretch. [U.S. slang, mid 1900s-pres.]

sodomite (also **sodomist**) a PEDERAST (q.v.); a man who habitually commits NONORTHOGENITAL (q.v.) sexual acts. From the ancient city of Sodom. [since the late 1700s] Synonyms: BARDACHE, BIRDIE, BIRD-TAKER, BROWN-HATTER, BROWNIE, BROWNIE KING, BUD SALLOGH, BUG, BUGGAH, BUGGER, BUM-FUCKER, BUNKER, BURGLAR, CAPON, CORN-HOLER, CORVETTE, DADDY, EYE DOCTOR, EYE-OPENER, GENTLEMAN OF THE BACK DOOR, GOOSER, GUT-BUTCHER, GUT-FUCKER, GUT-MONGER, GUT-REAMER, GUT-SCRAPER, GUT-STICKER, GUT-STRETCHER, GUT-STUFFER, GUT-VEXER, INDORSER, INGLER, INSERTEE, IN-SERTOR, INSPECTOR OF MANHOLES, JE-SUIT, JOCKER, JOCKEY, JOEY, LICK-BOX, LIMP-WRIST, MASON, PRUSSIAN, PUFF, REAMER, RING-SNATCHER, SHEEP-HERDER, SHIT-HUNTER, SHIT-STIRRER, SOD, SODOMITE, STERN-CHASER, STIR-SHIT, STUFFER, TURK, UNCLE, UNNATURAL DEBAUCHEE, USHER, VERT, WOLF.

sodomy 1. NONORTHOGENITAL (q.v.) sexual acts, especially those between males. [since the 1200s, *Oxford English Dictionary*] **2.** anal copulation between males; pederasty. [1800s-1900s] **3.** sexual perversions; nonorthogenital sexual acts proscribed by law. Whether or not the following acts are sodomy depends on the wording of the various state (U.S.) sodomy laws and the legal precedents set in the past: pederasty or any anal copulation, bestiality, fellation, cunnilingus, lesbian acts, mutual masturbation, anilingus, exhibitionism, and taking indecent liberties with a minor. Related terms for all senses: ASS-FUCK, BACK-DOOR WORK, BACK-SCULL, BACK-SCUTTLE, BIT OF BROWN, BOODY, BOTTLE, BROWN-EYE, BROWN HOLE, BROWNING, BUCKLEBURY, BUGGERY, BUNG HOLE, BUTT-FUCK, COITUS IN ANO, COITUS PER ANUM, CONCUBITUS CUM PERSONA EJUSDEM SEXUS, CRIME AGAINST NATURE, CRIMEN INNOMINATUM, DAUB OF THE BRUSH, DIP IN THE FUDGE POT, GREEK, GREEK LOVE, GREEK WAY, HIGHER MALTHUSIANISM, ITALIAN MANNER, KIESTER STAB, KNEELING AT THE ALTAR, LAY, NAMELESS CRIME, PAEDICATIO, PEDICATION, PIG-STICKING, RAM-JOB, SEXUAL ANOMALY, SEXUAL PERVERSION, SHIP'S, SHIT-FUCK, UNMENTIONABLE VICE, UNNATURAL CONNECTION, UNNATURAL OFFENSE, UNNATURAL PURPOSES, UNNATURAL SEXUAL INTERCOURSE, UNNATURAL VICE.

sods' holiday, a a bad muddle or state of confusion. [British, mid 1900s-pres.]

Sod this for a game of soldiers! "Enough of this!" [British, mid 1900s-pres.]

sofa-spud a lazy person, a COUCH-POTATO. [U.S. slang, late 1900s]

soft-ass(ed) easy; compliant. Compare to CANDY-ASS(ED). [U.S. slang, late 1900s]

soft-core 1. pornography where sexual acts are simulated. *Cf.* HARD-CORE. Softness is often understood to refer to the state of the penis in such portrayals. [U.S. slang and colloquial, mid 1900s-pres.] **2.** pertaining to anything mild compared to something extreme. [U.S. slang, mid 1900s-pres.]

S.O.L. "shit out of luck." Euphemized as "short of luck" or "soldier out of luck." A reinterpretation of "Sol.," an abbreviation of "soldier." [military, World War I]

soldier's home, old the W.C. A DEAD SOLDIER (sense 1) is "dung." [U.S. colloquial, 1900s]

soles HASHISH (*q.v.*). For synonyms see HASH. [U.S. drug culture, mid 1900s-pres.]

solitary sin masturbation. *Cf.* SECRET VICE. A dysphemism of avoidance.

soma the drug P.C.P. (*q.v.*). From the name of an intoxicating drink. [U.S. drug culture, mid 1900s-pres.]

son 1. a truncation of SON OF A BITCH (*q.v.*). [U.S., 1900s] **2.** a term of contempt for a male. A truncation of "son of a bitch" and a play on the term of endearment for a young male. Usually pronounced derisively. [both senses, U.S., mid 1900s]

son of a bachelor a bastard; an illegitimate child. *Cf.* BACHELOR'S BABY. [since the 1600s]

son-of-a-biscuit-eater an avoidance for SON OF A BITCH (*q.v.*). [U.S. colloquial, 1900s]

son of a bitch 1. a bastard; an illegitimate child. **2.** a rotten fellow; a contemptible male. [both senses, since the mid 1700s] **3.** a very difficult task. [U.S. slang, mid 1900s-pres.] **4.** an exclamation, "Son of a bitch!" A truncation of "I'll be a son of a bitch!" [U.S. slang, mid 1900s-pres.]

son of a female canine "son of a bitch!" A contrived avoidance. *Cf.* PUPPY'S MAMMA. [U.S., mid 1900s]

son of a gun 1. a soldier's bastard. This literal interpretation is no longer extant. [attested as British, early 1800s, Jon Bee] **2.** a pal; a fellow; a chum. A mild avoidance for SON OF A BITCH (*q.v.*). [British and U.S. slang and colloquial, early 1800s-pres.] **3.** an oath from "I'll be a son of a gun!" [U.S. colloquial, 1900s]

son of a sea cook a bastard; a contrived avoidance for SON OF A BITCH (*q.v.*). [British and U.S. slang and colloquial, 1800s-1900s]

sonuvabitch a phonetic respelling of SON OF A BITCH (*q.v.*). Seen often in print, especially direct quotes. [U.S. slang and colloquial, mid 1900s-pres.]

sorry-ass(ed) 1. sad and depressed. [U.S., mid 1900s-pres.] **2.** worthless; poor quality. [U.S., mid 1900s-pres.]

S.O.S. the best-known interpretation is "shit on a shingle," creamed chipped beef on toast. An initialism for "same old shit," euphemized as "same old slumgullion" or "same old stew." *Cf.* CREAMED FORESKINS. [U.S. military and general slang, early 1900s-pres.]

soshed intoxicated with alcohol. For synonyms see WOOFLED. [U.S. slang, early 1900s]

S.O.T. a "son of temperance"; a drunkard. [U.S. ironic slang, mid 1900s]

sot 1. an oaf; a dolt. [c. 1000, *Oxford English Dictionary*] **2.** a drunkard. [slang and colloquial since the late 1500s]

soul roll passionate and loving copulation. *Cf.* ROLL, SOFT ROLL. [primarily black use; U.S. slang, mid 1900s-pres.]

soundproof bra a padded brassiere. *Cf.* FALSIES. [U.S. slang, mid 1900s-pres.]

soupy drunk, sick, and vomiting. For synonyms see WOOFLED. [U.S. slang, late 1900s]

soused (also **soust**) heavily intoxicated with alcohol; the same as PICKLED (*q.v.*). For synonyms see WOOFLED. [slang since the 1600s]

southern-fried alcohol intoxicated. An elaboration of FRIED. For synonyms see WOOFLED. [U.S. slang, late 1900s]

sow-drunk intoxicated with alcohol. *Cf.* DRUNK AS DAVID'S SOW. [British colloquial, mid 1800s or before]

sow one's wild oats 1. to get youthful play out of one's system, said of the male. [British and later U.S. colloquial, 1600s-pres., B.E.] **2.** to lose one's virginity; to copulate in an unrestrained manner. Said of a male. There is a notion that such behavior will result in more mature and more faithful males. The oats here are the SEED (sense 1), "semen." [U.S. colloquial, 1900s or before]

sozzle 1. excrement. Also **sorzle**. For synonyms see DUNG. [British dialect, 1800s, Rye] **2.** to mix into a confused mess; to confuse. [British dialect] **3.** a slattern; a very sloppy woman. For synonyms see TROLLYMOG. [U.S. colloquial, mid 1800s] **4.** an oaf; a blockhead. [British, 1800s, Farmer and Henley] **5.** to drink to excess. [since the 1800s]

sozzled intoxicated with alcohol. For synonyms see WOOFLED. [British and U.S. slang, late 1800s-pres.]

sozzly intoxicated with alcohol. [U.S. slang, mid 1900s]

spaced-out 1. silly; giddy. **2.** intoxicated with drugs. [both senses, U.S. slang and drug culture, mid 1900s-pres.]

Spanish letter See FRENCH LETTER.

Spanish-pox syphilis. For synonyms see SPECIFIC STOMACH. [British, 1800s]

spank to masturbate. *Cf.* (SHOWER SPANK.) For synonyms and related subjects see WASTE TIME. [U.S. collegiate, late 1900s, Munro] See also (SHOWER) SPANK.

spanking excellent. [U.S., late 1900s-pres.]

spank the monkey to masturbate

(male). For synonyms see WASTE TIME. [U.S., late 1900s-pres.]

spanners a sexually attractive woman or girl. Because a spanner (a wrench) is used to tighten "nuts," the testes. [Australian, mid 1900s, *Dictionary of Slang and Unconventional English*]

spar the penis. A nautical reference. For synonyms see GENITALS, YARD. [British slang, 1900s, McDonald]

spare part a useless man; an uneeded man on a work crew. See SPARE PRICK, for which this is a euphemism. [British and U.S. wartime, 1900s]

spare prick a totally useless man; a lazy or incompetent man on a work crew. From the expression "as useless as a spare prick." See PRICK. [British and U.S. slang, early 1900s-pres.]

spare rib (also **sperrib**) a married man's mistress. Ware defines this as "wife." A reinterpretation of the term for lean cuts of pork ribs. *Cf.* RIB. [slang and nonce, U.S. and elsewhere, 1900s] Synonyms and related terms: BACHELOR'S WIFE, BELLY-LASS, BELLY-PIECE, BLOWEN, BROAD, CONVENIENT, DOLLY-MOP, FAIR LADY, FANCY WOMAN, FLAME, GALLIMAUFREY, GIRL, HONEY-STAR, INAMORATA, JAM-TART, JOMER, JUG, KEPT WOMAN, LADY-BIRD, LEV-ERET, LIE-A-SIDE, LIGBY, LINDA-BRIDES, LORETTE, LOTEBY, LYERBY, MADAM, MISTRESS, NATURAL, PECU-LIAR, PELLEX, PIECE OF STRAY, PINTLE-BIT, PINTLE-MAID, POKE, SIDE DISH, SLEEPING-DICTIONARY, SMIG, SMOCK-SERVANT, TACKLE, WIFE.

spare tongue the clitoris. [U.S. slang, late 1900s, Lewin and Lewin]

spark to court; to kiss and utter terms of endearment. See SPUNK UP. *Cf.* FIR-KYTOODLE. [U.S. colloquial, late 1700s-pres.]

sparkle plenty an amphetamine tablet. From the name of a character in *Dick Tracy,* a comic strip by Chester Gould. [U.S. drug culture, mid 1900s-pres.]

sparrow-fart 1. daybreak; a play on "cockcrow." *Cf.* CROW-PEE. [British, 1800s] **2.** a worthless pipsqueak; an

OAF. *Cf.* FART (sense 3). [1900s (James Joyce)]

sparrow's cough a euphemism for SPARROW-FART (*q.v.*).

spaz 1. a SPASTIC (sense 1); a jerk; a totally uncoordinated person. **2.** a fit; an attack; a strong reaction to a bad or a funny situation. [both senses, U.S. slang, mid 1900s-pres.]

S.P.C.H. the "Society for the Prevention of Cruelty to Homosexuals." A jocular term for an imaginary society patterned on "S.P.C.A.," the "Society for the Prevention of Cruelty to Animals." [U.S. slang, mid 1900s-pres.]

spear the bearded clam to COIT a woman. *Cf.* BEARDED CLAM. For synonyms see OCCUPY. [Australian, late 1900s]

Special K ketamine. [U.S., late 1900s-pres.]

specialities condoms. A euphemism used in publicly available printed matter. For synonyms see EEL-SKIN. [British, 1800s, Farmer and Henley]

specific stomach syphilis. [vague euphemism; U.S., 1900s] Synonyms and related terms: BAD BLOOD, BAD DISEASE, BAND-IN-THE-BOX, BANG AND BIFF, BLOOD DISEASE, BONE-ACHE, BOOGIE, CLAP, COACHMAN ON THE BOX, COALS, DELICATE DISEASE, DELICATE TAINT, ENVIABLE DISEASE, FIRE, FOUL DISEASE, FOUL DISORDER, FRENCH-CROWN, FRENCH-DISEASE, FRENCH GOODS, FRENCH GOUT, FRENCH POX, GOODYEAR, IRISH MUTTON, JACK-IN-THE-BOX, LADIES' FEVER, LUES VENEREA, MALA DE FRANZOS, MALADY OF FRANCE, MARBLES, MEASLES, MESO-SYPHILIS, MORBUS GALLICUS, MORBUS HISPANICUS, MORBUS INDICUS, MOR-BUS NEOPOLITANUS, NEAPOLITAN, NE-APOLITAN CONSOLATION, NEAPOLITAN DISEASE, NEAPOLITAN FAVOR, NEO-POLITAN BONE-ACHE, NOLI-ME-TAN-GERE, OLD JOE, PHYLLIS, PIMPLE, PISS OUT OF A DOZEN HOLES, POCKES, POX, SCABBADO, SECONDARY, SYPHILIS, SE-CRET DISEASE, SIFF, SIGMA PHI, SPAN-ISH-GOUT, SPANISH-NEEDLE, SPANISH-POX, SPECIFIC ULCER, SYPH, SYPHO, THE OLD DOG, THE PIP, THE RAHL, V.D.S., WINTER COALS.

speckled bird an amphetamine capsule. *Cf.* BLACKBIRD. [U.S. drug culture, mid 1900s-pres.]

sped a stupid person. From "*special education.*" [U.S. slang, late 1900s]

speed amphetamines; Methedrine (trademark). For synonyms see METH. [U.S. drug culture, mid 1900s-pres.]

speedball a mixture of drugs injected with a syringe. May be heroin and cocaine, cocaine and morphine, or heroin and amphetamines. [underworld and drug culture, early 1900s-pres.]

speed-freak 1. a person who swallows or injects amphetamines. **2.** a drug addict or user. [both senses, U.S. drug culture, mid 1900s-pres.]

spend 1. to ejaculate semen; to have an orgasm. [British, 1600s-1800s] **2.** semen; sexual spendings. [slang, 1800s-1900s]

spender the female genitals. That which causes the male to SPEND (*q.v.*). [British slang, 1800s or before]

spendings semen which has been ejaculated. *Cf.* COMINGS. [British, late 1500s-1800s]

spew (also **spue**) **1.** to ejaculate. [British, 1600s] **2.** to vomit. [British and U.S. slang and colloquial, late 1600s-pres.] **3.** a dysphemism for "stew." For synonyms see DOG'S VOMIT. [British juvenile, 1900s (Opie and Opie)] **4.** semen; ejaculated semen. [slang or nonce, 1800s-1900s]

spew-up to vomit. For synonyms see YORK. [British, late 1900s-pres.]

spice-island 1. the anus. **2.** a privy. [both senses, British slang or colloquial, early 1800s, *Lexicon Balatronicum*]

spicy sexy; smutty; slightly sexually oriented. [slang since the early 1800s]

spifflicated (also **spificated**) intoxicated with alcohol; confused with drink. From a verb meaning "dumbfound." [slang, late 1700s-1900s]

spifflo intoxicated with alcohol. From SPIFFLICATED (*q.v.*). [U.S. slang, mid 1900s, Berrey and Van den Bark]

spike 1. an erection of the penis. For synonyms see ERECTION. [widespread recurrent nonce; attested as British slang, 1800s, Farmer and Henley] **2.** to copulate. *Cf.* SPIT (sense 1). [British slang, 1800s]

spike-faggot the penis. FAGGOT (sense 3) is a prostitute. [British slang, 1800s, Farmer and Henley]

spill one's breakfast to vomit. For synonyms see YORK. [1900s]

spill the blue groceries to vomit. For synonyms see YORK. [U.S. collegiate, late 1900s, Eble]

spirit semen. An elaboration of "vital principle." *Cf.* METTLE, SPUNK. [vague and euphemistic, 1600s]

spiritual flesh-broker a parson; a clergyman. [colloquial, 1900s or before]

spit 1. to coit a woman; to penetrate a woman sexually. [British slang, 1800s, Farmer and Henley] **2.** spittle. Synonyms for both senses: CONSPUTE, EXPECTORATE, GOB, LET FLY, SALIVA. **3.** the penis. **4.** to ejaculate semen. [slang, 1900s]

spit beef to vomit. For synonyms see YORK. [U.S. collegiate, late 1900s, Eble]

spitfire 1. a hot-tempered person; a spirited woman. [since the late 1600s] **2.** the female genitals. Possibly infected with a venereal disease. [British slang, 1800s, Farmer and Henley] **3.** a condom. [British naval slang, mid 1900s, *Dictionary of Slang and Unconventional English*]

spit-swapping kissing; lingual kissing. [U.S. slang, early 1900s-pres.]

splash 1. to urinate, said of the male; to make a splash by urinating. *Cf.* SLASH, TINKLE. [slang, 1900s] **2.** amphetamines. [U.S. drug culture, mid 1900s-pres.]

splash one's boots to urinate. For synonyms see WHIZ. [British, late 1900s-pres.]

spleef (also **shpleef**) marijuana; a marijuana cigarette. The same as SPLIFF. For synonyms see MARI, MEZZROLL. [U.S. drug culture, late 1900s]

spliff marijuana or a marijuana cigarette, especially a large cigarette. Often

refers to Jamaican marijuana. [U.S. drug culture, mid 1900s-pres.]

splim marijuana. For synonyms see MARI. [U.S. drug culture, mid 1900s-pres.]

split 1. to coit a woman; to penetrate a woman. [British slang, 1700s] **2.** a woman. See SPLIT-TAIL. [U.S. slang, mid 1900s]

split-apricot the female genitals. From the image of a cross section of an apricot with the pit removed. [British slang, 1800s, Farmer and Henley]

split beaver 1. the image of a woman's genitals when a woman sits with her legs spread. A real or imagined view. *Cf.* BEAVER (sense 1). **2.** a stripper. [both senses, U.S. slang, mid 1900s-pres.]

split-stuff women viewed as sexual objects. [Australian slang, early 1900s, Baker]

split-tail a woman; a crude term for a young woman or a girl. [U.S. slang, mid 1900s-pres.]

splooge 1. to ejaculate. For synonyms see MELT. **2.** semen. *Cf.* SPOOCH. For synonyms see METTLE. [both senses, U.S. collegiate, late 1900s, Munro]

splosh 1. women in general. For synonyms see TAIL. [British, late 1900s-pres.] **2.** copulation. For synonyms see SMOCKAGE. [British, late 1900s-pres.]

sponge (also **spunge**) **1.** a drunkard, one who soaks up drink. [slang and colloquial since the late 1500s] **2.** to drink heavily at someone else's expense. [British, late 1600s, B.E.] **3.** to beg or borrow from people constantly. **4.** someone who begs and borrows constantly. [senses 3 and 4 are U.S. colloquial, 1900s or before] **5.** the penis. [British slang, 1800s, Farmer and Henley]

spoo sperm; ejaculant. *Cf.* SPEW. For synonyms see METTLE. [U.S. collegiate, late 1900s, Munro]

spooch 1. to ejaculate. For synonyms see MELT. **2.** semen. *Cf.* SPLOOGE. For synonyms see METTLE. [both senses, U.S. collegiate, late 1900s, Munro]

spooge semen. For synonyms see METTLE. [U.S., late 1900s-pres.]

spook 1. a ghost. [British and U.S. slang and colloquial, 1800s-pres.] **2.** a derogatory nickname for a Negro. [U.S. Caucasian use, 1900s] **3.** a derogatory nickname for a Caucasian. [U.S. Negro use, 1900s]

spoon 1. an oaf; a simpleton. [slang since the late 1700s] **2.** to pet or neck; to SPARK (q.v.). [U.S. colloquial, early 1800s-pres.] **3.** to perform sexual foreplay. Possibly the same as sense 2. [British slang, 1800s, Farmer and Henley] **4.** to copulate. **5.** a spoonful or approximately two grams of heroin. **6.** a spoon used for heating drugs which are to be injected. **7.** a spoon used for sniffing cocaine. [senses 5-7 are U.S. drug culture, mid 1900s-pres.] **8.** to lie together (and possibly copulate) like two spoons stacked bowl-in-bowl. [U.S., late 1800s, Farmer and Henley] **9.** a tonguing technique used in CUNNILINGUS (q.v.). Possibly related to sense 8. [U.S. slang, mid 1900s-pres.]

sport a woody to have an erection. Cf. WOODY. [U.S. collegiate, late 1900s, Munro]

sport blubber to expose the breasts. Cf. BLUBBERS. [British slang, 1800s]

sporter a brothel; a SPORTING-HOUSE (q.v.). [attested as Caribbean (Jamaican), Cassidy and Le Page]

spout the penis. [widespread recurrent nonce; colloquial and slang, 1800s-pres.]

spray someone's tonsils to ejaculate into someone's mouth as in FELLATIO. For synonyms see MELT. [U.S. homosexual use, 1900s]

spread 1. to spread one's legs for copulation, said of a woman. [colloquial, late 1600s-pres.] **2.** to position or lay out a woman for copulation, said of a man. Cf. FLOP A WOMAN, LAY DOWN, PUT DOWN (sense 1). [British, 1600s] **3.** the posteriors. [U.S. slang, mid 1900s]

spread beaver a glance at a woman's genitals; a photograph showing a woman's genitals. Also **spread shot**. See SPLIT BEAVER (sense 1). [U.S. slang, mid 1900s-pres.] **2.** pertaining to the posture of a woman sitting with her legs spread. [U.S. slang, mid 1900s-pres.]

spread the good news to share a marijuana cigarette. [U.S. drug culture, 1900s, Abel]

spree 1. to drink to excess in the company of others; to DEBAUCH. **2.** a wild, drunken time; an orgy of drink. [both senses, British and U.S. slang and colloquial, early 1800s-pres.] Synonyms for sense 2: BAT, BENDER, BINGE, BLINDO, BLOW, BUM, BUN, BUST, COMUS, DEBAUCH, FUDDLE, GUZZLE, JAG, MEAT AND DRINK, PAINT THE TOWN RED, PERISHER, PISS-UP, SOAK, TEAR, TOOT, TOPE, TWIST, WHING-DING.

spreeing drinking; consorting with women. [U.S. colloquial, 1800s-1900s]

sproutsy a vegetarian. [U.S., late 1900s-pres.]

sprunch to engage in sexual play; possibly to copulate. [U.S. dialect (Ozarks), 1900s or before, Randolph and Wilson]

sprung 1. intoxicated with alcohol. [British and U.S. slang or colloquial, early 1800s-1900s] **2.** pregnant, as in "sprung out of shape." [U.S. dialect (Ozarks), 1900s or before, Randolph and Wilson]

spule to vomit. Cf. SPEW. Possibly a Southern version of SPEW. For synonyms see YORK. [U.S. collegiate, late 1900s, Eble]

spunk 1. METTLE (q.v.); SPIRIT (q.v.); vigor. [late 1700s-pres.] **2.** semen. [British, 1800s, Farmer and Henley] **3.** to ejaculate. From sense 2. [British, 1900s, Dictionary of Slang and Unconventional English]

spunk-bound pertaining to a man without vigor. Cf. SPUNK (sense 1). [British colloquial, 1800s, Dictionary of Slang and Unconventional English]

spunk-holders the testicles. Cf. SPUNK (sense 2). For synonyms see WHIRLYGIGS. [British, 1800s, Farmer and Henley]

spunk rat a sexually attractive male. [U.S., late 1900s-pres.]

spunk up to fondle a woman sexually;

to attempt to arouse a woman sexually. "Spunk" refers here to tinder or other stuff from which a fire can be built. [U.S. colloquial, mid 1800s] See also ROTTENLOGGING.

squanch 1. the female genitalia. For synonyms see GENITALS, MONOSYLLABLE. [U.S., late 1900s-pres.] **2.** a rotten smell. [U.S., late 1900s-pres.]

square 1. a straitlaced person; someone who probably does not smoke, drink, use drugs, or appreciate hard rock music. **2.** pertaining to a prude. [both senses, U.S. slang and colloquial, mid 1900s-pres.]

square someone's circle to COIT someone; to have sex with someone. For synonyms see OCCUPY. [U.S. collegiate, late 1900s, Munro]

squashed drunk. For synonyms see WOOFLED. [U.S. slang, late 1900s]

squatter's rites defecation; a jocular play on "squatter's rights." [U.S., mid 1900s-pres.]

squatter's writes writing done on the wall of a public restroom; graffiti produced while a person is seated and eliminating. A jocular play on "squatter's rights." [U.S., mid 1900s-pres.]

squaw piss beer with a low alcohol content. Cf. NEAR BEER, SISSY BEER, TIGER PISS. For synonyms see SUDS. [U.S. slang, mid 1900s]

squeeze liquor; wine. Cf. SMASH. [U.S. black use, late 1900s]

squeeze and a squirt copulation from the point of view of the male. [British slang, 1800s, Farmer and Henley]

squeeze-'em-close copulation; the sexual embrace. [British slang, 1800s, Farmer and Henley]

squeeze the cheese to defecate. For synonyms see EASE ONESELF. [Australian, late 1900s-pres.]

squeeze the lemon 1. to urinate, said of the male. [slang, 1800s-1900s] **2.** to masturbate, said of the male. [U.S. slang, mid 1900s-pres.]

squid 1. a slimy JERK. For synonyms see OAF. [U.S. slang, late 1900s] **2.** an earnest student. [U.S., late 1900s-pres.]

squiffed intoxicated with alcohol. [British and U.S. slang, late 1800s-pres.]

squiffy 1. intoxicated with alcohol. [British and U.S. slang, late 1800s-pres.] **2.** stupid. [Australian, 1900s, Baker] **3.** sick; nauseated. [Australian and U.S. slang or colloquial, 1900s]

squill 1. a diuretic drug. **2.** an expectorant drug. Both are from the name of a plant. [since the 1500s]

squint the female genitals. From the PUDENDAL CLEAVAGE (q.v.). Cf. DUMB-SQUINT, LONG-EYE. [British slang, 1800s, Farmer and Henley]

squirrel 1. the female genitals. **2.** the female pubic hair. Both senses are from FUR (q.v.). **3.** women in general; women considered as sexual objects. See BUNNY (sense 2), CONY. **4.** a psychoanalyst; a psychotherapist. Because each patient is a NUT (sense 1). [all senses, U.S. slang, mid 1900s-pres.]

squirt 1. a small person; a young child, especially a young boy. Cf. BOB SQUIRT. [U.S. colloquial, 1900s] **2.** to urinate. [U.S. slang and nonce, 1900s or before] **3.** to ejaculate semen. [widespread recurrent nonce; colloquial, 1900s and before]

squirts diarrhea. [in various forms since the 1500s]

S.S. 1. the "screaming shits," diarrhea. [British with some U.S. use, mid 1900s] **2.** a warning that one has one's "shimmy showing," said by one (little) girl to another concerning a visible slip. Cf. P.P. [U.S. jocular and contrived, 1900s]

stacked pertaining to a woman with a sexually attractive body. Also used to describe a muscular male. [U.S. slang, mid 1900s-pres.]

stacked like a brick shit-house 1. pertaining to a woman with a sexually attractive body. One with many curves as might be found in the walls of a homemade brick privy. An elaboration of STACKED (q.v.). Cf. BUILT LIKE A BRICK SHIT-HOUSE. **2.** pertaining to a strong and muscular male. [U.S. colloquial, mid 1900s]

staff the penis. For synonyms see

YARD. [widespread recurrent nonce; slang and colloquial, 1600s-pres.]

staff of life the penis. [widespread recurrent nonce; since the 1800s or before]

stag 1. pertaining to gatherings which are for men only. **2.** pertaining to a man who attends a gathering for couples without a female companion. [both senses, U.S. slang, mid 1900s-pres.]

staggerish intoxicated with alcohol. For synonyms see WOOFLED. [slang, 1900s]

stagger-juice strong alcoholic beverage. [Australian and U.S. slang, 1900s]

stagger-water (also **stagger-soup**) alcoholic liquor. [British and U.S. slang, mid 1900s]

stag-mag a magazine featuring nude women. Cf. FAG-MAG, STAG. [U.S. slang, mid 1900s]

stag movie 1. a privately shown movie for groups of men. Usually pornographic, SOFT-CORE or HARD-CORE (both q.v.). [U.S., early 1900s-pres.] **2.** any pornographic film. [U.S. slang, mid 1900s-pres.]

stake the penis. For synonyms see YARD. [recurrent nonce; since the 1600s or before]

stale 1. a very low prostitute. [late 1500s-1600s] **2.** urine. **3.** to urinate. Now said only of quadrupeds. [British rural colloquial, 1400s-1800s]

stale drunk intoxicated with alcohol; an intoxication lingering from the night before. [colloquial, 1800s]

stalk an erection. For synonyms see ERECTION. [British, late 1900s-pres.]

stallion 1. a male horse used for breeding purposes. Cf. STONE-HORSE. [since the 1300s] **2.** a lascivious man; a whoremonger; a man who copulates notoriously frequently or well. [since the early 1600s] **3.** a prostitute's customer. This may be the same as sense 2. [attested as British slang, 1800s, Barrère and Leland] **4.** a man kept by a woman for sexual purposes. [British cant, late 1700s, Grose] **5.** a beautiful and sexually attractive black woman.

For synonyms see RAVEN BEAUTY. [U.S. black use, mid 1900s-pres.] **6.** the penis. [U.S. black use, 1900s]

stand 1. to erect the penis. [1500s-1600s] **2.** an erection of the penis. [colloquial, 1500s-1800s] **3.** a MOUTH-WHORE (q.v.). For synonyms see PICCOLO-PLAYER. [British slang, 1800s, Farmer and Henley]

stand, on the pertaining to the erect penis. [British colloquial, 1800s, Farmer and Henley]

standing too long in the sun intoxicated with alcohol. Cf. SUN, IN THE. [British colloquial, 1800s]

stand out like a dog's balls to appear very obvious. [Australian, mid 1900s-pres.]

stank 1. the anus, the pubic region. Refers to odor. From *stink*. For synonyms see ANUS. [U.S. black use, late 1900s] **2.** ugly. [U.S. collegiate, late 1900s, Munro]

stanky nasty. Said especially of a woman. [U.S. collegiate, late 1900s]

stanky tuna a sexually loose woman; a promiscuous woman. Cf. TUNA. [U.S. collegiate, late 1900s, Munro)

starch 1. semen in the expression TAKE THE STARCH OUT OF (q.v.). Cf. SPUNK. [British slang, 1800s] **2.** vigor; SPIRIT (q.v.); SPUNK (q.v.). [U.S. colloquial, mid 1900s-pres.] **3.** an adulterated drug. [U.S. drug culture, mid 1900s]

starched alcohol intoxicated. From STIFF. For synonyms see WOOFLED. [U.S., late 1900s-pres.]

starchy alcohol intoxicated. From STIFF. For synonyms see WOOFLED. [U.S., late 1900s-pres.]

stardust 1. cocaine. Cf. ANGEL DUST, HEAVEN DUST. [U.S. drug culture, mid 1900s-pres.] **2.** the drug phencyclidine, P.C.P. For synonyms see P.C.P. [U.S. drug culture, late 1900s, Abel]

star-fucker someone, usually a teenage female, who follows performers, especially rock performers, from town to town, offering herself sexually. [U.S. slang, late 1900s]

stark-ballock-naked naked. Cf.

BALLOCK-NAKED. [British, 1900s or before]

stark-ballux naked. A truncation of STARK-BALLOCK-NAKED (*q.v.*). [attested as Australian, late 1800s, *Dictionary of Slang and Unconventional English*]

starkers naked. [originally British; slang, early 1900s-pres.] Synonyms and related terms: ABRAM, ADAMATICAL, ALL FACE, AU NATUREL, BALLOCK-NAKED, BALLOCKY, BOLLOCKY STARKERS, BARE-ASSED, BARE-NAKED, BARE-POLES, BELLY-NAKED, BIRTH-NAKED, BLEAT, BLETE, BODY-NAKED, BUCK-NAKED, BUFF-BARE, BUTT NAKED, FRONTAL NUDITY, HARRY STARKERS, IN CUERPO, IN MOROCCO, IN PURIS NATURALIBUS, IN STAG, IN THE ALTOGETHER, IN THE BUFF, IN THE NATURAL, IN THE NICK, IN THE NUDDY, IN THE RAW, IN THE RUDE, LAID TO THE NATURAL BONE, MOTHER-NAKED, NAKED, NAKED AS MY NAIL, NAKED BUFF, NECKED, NUDDY, NUDE, ON THE SHALLOWS, PEELED, SKUDDY, STARBOLIC NAKED, STAR-BOLLOCK-NAKED, STARK-BALLOCK-NAKED, STARK-BALLUX, STARK NAKED, STARKO, STAR-NAKED, START-BONE-NAKED, START-BORN-NAKED, START-MOTHER-NAKED, START NAKED, STATE OF NATURE, SUNDAY SUIT, UNCLAD, UNCLOTHED, WEARING A SMILE, WHOLLY NAKED.

stark naked 1. nude; naked with the genitals uncovered. *Cf.* HARRY STARKERS. [since the early 1500s] **2.** gin. Because of its clearness. For synonyms see RUIN. [British slang and colloquial, early 1800s]

start-born-naked (also **start-bone-naked, start-mother-naked**) naked. [U.S. colloquial, 1800s]

starter marriage a first marriage. Sarcastic. [U.S., late 1900s-pres.]

stash a supply of marijuana or drugs; a cache of drugs. *Cf.* KIESTER STASH. [U.S. drug culture, mid 1900s-pres.]

state house a toilet; a privy. For synonyms see AJAX. [U.S. slang, early 1900s]

stay to maintain an erection for the completion of an act of copulation. [U.S. slang, mid 1900s-pres.]

S.T.D. sexually transmitted disease. [British and U.S., late 1900s-pres.]

steady bone one's habitual sex partner. [U.S., late 1900s-pres.]

steady-lapper a drunkard; a tippler. [Australian, 1900s]

steamboats very intoxicated due to drink. For synonyms see WOOFLED. [British, late 1900s-pres.]

steamed-up (also **steamed**) **1.** angry. [U.S. slang and colloquial, 1900s] **2.** intoxicated with alcohol. [U.S. slang, early 1900s] **3.** drug intoxicated. [U.S. underworld, early 1900s]

steeped intoxicated with alcohol. For synonyms see WOOFLED. [U.S. slang, early 1900s]

stemmer the penis. For synonyms see YARD. [U.S. slang, mid 1900s-pres.]

stem siren a prostitute. *Cf.* STEM (sense 2). [U.S. slang, mid 1900s, Monteleone]

stench-trench the vagina. For synonyms see MONOSYLLABLE. [British slang, late 1900s]

stencil a long, thin marijuana cigarette. [U.S. drug culture, mid 1900s-pres.]

step into one's last bus to die. For synonyms see DEPART. [British, 1800s]

step on to dilute powdered drugs by one-half. This can be repeated a number of times. See CUT. [U.S. drug culture, late 1900s]

step on a frog to make the sound of the release of intestinal gas; to FART. *Cf.* BARKING SPIDER. [U.S. slang, late 1900s]

stepped on having to do with diluted drugs; having to do with overly diluted drugs. [U.S. drug culture, late 1900s] *Cf.* STEP ON.

stepping-high intoxicated with drugs. *Cf.* HIGH (sense 2). For synonyms see TALL. [U.S. underworld, mid 1900s]

stern the posteriors. For synonyms see DUFF. [since the early 1600s]

stew 1. a brothel or an area of brothels; the same as, THE STEWS (*q.v.*). [since the 1300s] **2.** a prostitute. From sense 1. [British slang, 1600s-1800s]

3. intoxicated with alcohol. *Cf.* STEWED. [U.S. slang, mid 1900s, Deak] **4.** a drunkard; a STEWIE (*q.v.*). [U.S. slang, early 1900s-pres.]

stew bum a drunken tramp; any drunkard. [U.S. underworld and slang, early 1900s-pres.]

stewed intoxicated with alcohol; very drunk. *Cf.* STEW (sense 3). For synonyms see WOOFLED. [slang, early 1700s pres., Ben Franklin]

stewed as a prune drunk. Contrived. For synonyms see WOOFLED. [British slang, 1900s]

stewie -(also **stewy**) a drunkard, especially a low drunkard or a WINO (*q.v.*). [U.S. slang, mid 1900s-pres.]

stews, the a brothel or a street of brothels. From a nickname for a public bathhouse which grew to be associated with prostitution. *Cf.* BAGNIO. Halliwell defines "stews" as "strumpet." [since the 1300s]

stick 1. a venereal disease. [British, late 1800s, Farmer and Henley] **2.** an oaf; a dullard. [British colloquial, early 1800s-1900s] **3.** the penis. [widespread recurrent nonce; attested as U.S. slang, mid 1900s] **4.** to coit a woman. [widespread recurrent nonce; attested as British, 1800s, Farmer and Henley] **5.** a marijuana cigarette. For synonyms see MEZZROLL. [U.S. drug culture, mid 1900s-pres.]

stick, up the pregnant; the same as POLE, UP THE (sense 1). *Cf.* STICK (sense 3). [British slang, early 1900s]

stick and bangers the penis and testicles; the male genitals. From billiard jargon. *Cf.* POCKET-POOL. [British slang, late 1800s-early 1900s, Ware]

Stick it in your ear! "Go to hell!"; "Drop dead!" [U.S. slang, late 1900s]

stick of tea a marijuana cigarette. *Cf.* HOT-STICK, STICK (sense 5). [U.S. drug culture, mid 1900s-pres.]

stick one's spoon in the wall to die. *Cf.* LAY DOWN THE KNIFE AND FORK. [British slang, 1800s, Farmer and Henley]

sticks 1. a person's legs. No negative connotations. **2.** a woman's legs. Either

very shapely legs or skinny and ugly legs. [U.S. slang, 1900s, Goldin, O'Leary, and Lipsius] **3.** a truncation of THAI STICKS (*q.v.*).

sticks like shit to a shovel See CLINGS LIKE SHIT TO A SHOVEL.

stickybeak a nosy person. [Australian, mid 1900s-pres.]

sticky-fingered 1. liable to steal something. [British and U.S., late 1900s-pres.] **2.** having semen on one's fingers from ejaculation, presumably masturbation. For synonyms see WASTE TIME. [U.S., late 1900s-pres.]

stiff 1. an erection of the penis. **2.** pertaining to the erectness of the penis. [both senses, colloquial since the early 1700s] **3.** intoxicated with alcohol. [U.S. slang, early 1700s-pres.] **4.** pertaining to a sexually loose person. [British slang, 1800s, Farmer and Henley] **5.** a drunkard. [U.S. slang, 1900s and before] **6.** a corpse. [widespread slang, late 1800s-pres.] **7.** a tramp; a hobo. [U.S. underworld and slang, 1900s] **8.** any male. [U.S. slang, mid 1900s-pres.]

stick and stout the erect penis. For synonyms see ERECTION. [mid 1600s (Urquhart)]

stiff-arsed 1. constipated. [British, late 1900s-pres.] **2.** uncompromising. [British, late 1900s-pres.]

stiffed intoxicated with alcohol. *Cf.* STIFF (sense 3). [U.S. slang, mid 1900s-pres.]

stiffeners pornography; materials used by males to cause erections; inspiration for sexual fantasies during masturbation. [U.S. slang, mid 1900s-pres.]

stiffo heavily intoxicated with alcohol. [U.S. slang, mid 1900s]

stiff one 1. an erection of the penis. [colloquial and nonce since the 1800s] **2.** a corpse. *Cf.* STIFF (sense 6). [U.S. slang, 1900s and before]

stiff prick 1. an erection of the penis. [widespread colloquial] **2.** a strict boss; a hard taskmaster. [U.S. slang, mid 1900s]

stiff-stander an erection of the penis.

For synonyms see ERECTION. [U.S. slang, late 1900s]

stiffy 1. an erection or partial erection. *Cf.* STIFF (sense 1). [slang, 1800s-1900s] **2.** a corpse. *Cf.* STIFF (sense 6).

sting the penis. *Cf.* STUNG BY A SERPENT. [British and elsewhere, 1800s, *Dictionary of Slang and Unconventional English*]

stinker 1. a rotten person; a SKUNK (sense 1). [since the 1600s] **2.** a small child; an infant. A jocular term for a baby with soiled diapers. [U.S. colloquial, 1900s] **3.** a release of intestinal gas. [U.S. slang, mid 1900s-pres.]

stinking (drunk) very drunk; DRUNK AS A SKUNK. For synonyms see WOOFLED. [1900s if not before]

stinko 1. smelling very badly. [U.S. slang, 1900s] **2.** intoxicated with alcohol. [widespread slang, early 1900s-pres.]

stink on ice to be really rotten. So rotten as to reek even when frozen. [U.S., late 1900s-pres.]

stink-pot 1. the vagina. *Cf.* PLAY AT STINK-FINGER. For synonyms see PASSAGE. [U.S. slang, mid 1900s] **2.** a juvenile term of contempt. [U.S., mid 1900s] **3.** a jocular nickname for a smelly baby. [U.S. colloquial, 1900s]

stink-weed marijuana. [U.S. underworld and drug culture, mid 1900s-pres.]

stir-shit a PEDERAST (*q.v.*); the INSERTOR (*q.v.*). *Cf.* BUTTOCK-STIRRING. [British slang, 1800s, Farmer and Henley]

stitch to coit a woman. See SEW UP. [British slang, 1800s, Farmer and Henley]

stitched intoxicated with alcohol. *Cf.* SEWED-UP (sense 1). [slang, early 1700s-1900s]

stogie 1. a large, fat marijuana cigarette. From the slang term for a large cigar. [U.S. drug culture, mid 1900s] **2.** a tobacco cigarette. [U.S. black use, late 1900s]

stone-ache pain in the testicles. *Cf.* BLUE BALLS, HOT ROCKS. [U.S. dialect (Ozarks), 1900s or before, Randolph and Wilson]

stone blind heavily intoxicated with alcohol. From a term meaning "completely blind." [U.S. slang, mid 1900s]

stoned 1. intoxicated with alcohol. [U.S. slang, mid 1900s-pres.] **2.** intoxicated with drugs or marijuana. [U.S. drug culture, mid 1900s-pres.]

stone fox an attractive woman; a very sexy girl. [U.S. slang, mid 1900s-pres.]

stone-horse a stallion; a male horse kept for breeding purposes. *Cf.* SEEDHORSE, STABLE-HORSE. [colloquial, 1600s-1700s]

stones 1. kidney stones; gall stones. [since *c.* 1000] **2.** the testicles. *Cf.* GOOLIES, PEBBLES, ROCKS. For synonyms see WHIRLYGIGS. [since the 1100s]

stonkered killed; dead. For synonyms see DONE FOR. [U.S. military, early 1900s, *Soldier Talk*]

stonkers the female breasts. For synonyms see BOSOM. [U.S., late 1900s-pres.]

stony blind intoxicated with alcohol; the same as STONE BLIND (*q.v.*). [British slang]

stool 1. an act of defecation. **2.** to defecate. [both since the early 1500s] **3.** feces; a mass of dung. [medical] **4.** the toilet; the water-flush toilet bowl.

stork 1. to give birth. **2.** the process of giving birth. [both senses, U.S. slang, mid 1900s, Berrey and Van den Bark] **3.** to impregnate. From senses 1 and 2. [U.S. slang, mid 1900s-pres.] Synonyms for sense 3: BEGET, BOOM THE CENSUS, BUMP, COCK UP, DO A JOB, DO THE TRICK, DOUBLE-EVENT, FECUNDATE, FILL IN, FIX SOMEONE UP, GET WITH CHILD, GRAVIDATE, IMPREGNATE, INGRAVIDATE, INSEMINATE, JAZZ UP, KNOCK UP, PROGENERATE, RING THE BELL, SEMINATION, SEW UP, SIRE, SPERMATIZE, SPOIL A WOMAN'S SHAPE, TIE UP. **4.** a penile erection. For synonyms see ERECTION. [British, late 1900s-pres.]

storked pregnant. *Cf.* STORK (sense 3). For synonyms see FRAGRANT. [U.S. slang, early 1900s]

stork-mad 1. pregnant. **2.** eager to become pregnant; wanting to have a child. Said of women. [both senses, U.S. slang, mid 1900s, Berrey and Van den Bark]

stormy dick the penis. Rhyming slang for "prick." [U.S., 1900s, *Dictionary of Rhyming Slang*]

stozzled intoxicated with alcohol. *Cf.* SOZZLED. [U.S. slang, 1800s]

S.T.P. a stimulant and pseudo-hallucinogenic drug; the chemical compound 2,5-Dimethoxy-4-methylamphetamine. Also called D.O.M. (*q.v.*). From the trademarked name of a motor-oil additive reinterpreted as "serenity, tranquility, and peace." [U.S. drug culture, mid 1900s-pres.]

strain 1. offspring; children. No negative connotations. [1100s] **2.** to copulate. The *Oxford English Dictionary* defines this as "embrace tightly." [1300s (Chaucer)] **3.** to apply force in an attempt to defecate; to strain at the stool. [since the mid 1600s] **4.** gonorrhea. The particular "strain" or species of microbes. [British euphemism, 1900s, *Dictionary of the Underworld*]

strain one's taters to urinate; an excuse to leave the room (to urinate) as if one were going to drain the water from boiled potatoes. *Cf.* DRAIN THE SPUDS. For synonyms see RETIRE. [British slang, late 1800s]

strap 1. to coit a woman; to copulate with a whore. [slang, colloquial, or nonce since the 1600s] **2.** the penis. *Cf.* YANK ONE'S STRAP. [U.S. slang, mid 1900s-pres.]

straw marijuana. *Cf.* HAY. [U.S. drug culture, mid 1900s-pres.]

strawberry fields the drug L.S.D. (*q.v.*). From the Beatles' song "Strawberry Fields Forever." [U.S. drug culture, mid 1900s-pres.]

streak 1. for a person to leave in a great hurry; to move very rapidly. No negative connotations. [colloquial since the 1600s] **2.** to run around; to run around wildly. [attested as U.S. slang, 1970, *Current Slang*] **3.** to run about in public places totally nude. [U.S., late 1973-pres.] **4.** a wild party; a wild and

exciting time. From sense 3. [U.S. slang, current]

street-meat a street-walking prostitute; a STREETWALKER. For synonyms see HARLOT. [U.S. slang, late 1900s]

street of sin (also **street of shame**) prostitution; the world of prostitutes. [U.S. euphemism, mid 1900s]

street pimp a pimp who works the streets with his prostitutes in order to be present when finances are arranged. [U.S. underworld, mid 1900s-pres.]

street sister a prostitute. [U.S. slang, mid 1900s]

street up for repairs the menses. See ROAD UP FOR REPAIRS. [British slang, 1800s, Farmer and Henley]

streetwalker a prostitute who solicits customers in the streets. [British and U.S. colloquial, 1800s-pres.]

stretch to cut or dilute a drug. [U.S. drug culture, late 1900s]

stretched drunk. For synonyms see WOOFLED. [U.S. slang, late 1900s]

stretcher 1. a large penis. *Cf.* LEATHER-STRETCHER. [possibly written nonce; attested as British, mid 1700s] **2.** something used to dilute or STRETCH a drug. [U.S. drug culture, 1900s, Abel]

stretch the rubber to be unfaithful to one's wife or mistress. *Cf.* SNAP THE RUBBER. [U.S. underworld, mid 1900s, Goldin, O'Leary, and Lipsius]

strike 1. to coit a woman. For synonyms see OCCUPY. [British, 1600s] **2.** a dose of drugs in any form. A synonym of HIT. [U.S. drug culture, late 1900s] **3.** to move from bar to bar; to "hit" or visit a bar. [U.S. military, late 1900s]

striped intoxicated with alcohol. [U.S. slang, mid 1900s, Wentworth and Flexner]

stroke 1. to coit a woman. [slang, late 1700s-pres.] **2.** to fondle; to caress a woman. For synonyms see FIRKY-TOODLE. [British colloquial, 1800s and nonce elsewhere] **3.** to praise or compliment a person. [U.S. colloquial, mid 1900s-pres.] **4.** to masturbate; to masturbate a male. For synonyms and related subjects see WASTE TIME. [U.S. slang, late 1900s]

stroke book a book or magazine with lewd contents used to stimulate masturbation fantasies. Cf. STROKE. For synonyms and related subjects see WASTE TIME. [widespread, late 1900s]

stroker 1. a male masturbator; someone who masturbates a male. **2.** a stupid JERK; a stupid or incompetent oaf. Primarily used for males. For synonyms see OAF. [both senses, U.S., late 1900s]

stroke the lizard to masturbate. Cf. LIZARD. [U.S. slang, mid 1900s-pres.]

strop one's beak to coit a woman. Cf. BEAK. [British slang, 1800s, Farmer and Henley]

structural engineering the breasts; the bust. For synonyms see BOSOM. [Australian, mid 1900s.]

strung-out 1. intoxicated with drugs. See LINE (sense 5). **2.** addicted to drugs. [both senses, U.S. drug culture, mid 1900s-pres.]

strut-fart a person, usually a male, who struts around looking very important. Cf. FART (sense 3). [U.S. colloquial, 1900s]

stubbed intoxicated with alcohol. For synonyms see WOOFLED. [U.S. slang, early 1700s, Ben Franklin]

stubble the female pubic hair. Cf. TAKE A TURN IN THE STUBBLE. [British, 1700s]

stub one's toe to experience the menses; to have one's period. For synonyms see FLOODS. [U.S. euphemism, 1900s, Rawson]

stuccoed intoxicated with alcohol. A play on PLASTERED (q.v.). [U.S. slang, early 1900s]

stud 1. a male horse used for breeding purposes. [U.S. colloquial, 1800s-1900s] **2.** a human male emphasizing one or more of the following characteristics: virility, stylishness, sex appeal, sexual success with women. [U.S. slang and colloquial, early 1900s-pres.]

studhammer a male who is very busy with women; a sexually successful male. [U.S. slang, mid 1900s]

studmuffin a good-looking, sexually attractive male. Cf. STUD. [U.S. collegiate, late 1900s]

studola very masculine. Cf. STUD. [U.S. collegiate, late 1900s, Munro]

stud out to luck out, as with getting some sexual activity. [U.S. collegiate, late 1900s, Munro]

stuff 1. to coit a woman; to penetrate a woman. **2.** semen. [senses 1 and 2 are colloquial 1600s-1900s] **3.** women considered as sexual objects. Also stuff in the sense of "cloth." See DRESS GOODS, DRY GOODS. Cf. SPLIT-STUFF. [British and U.S. slang and colloquial, late 1800s-pres.] **4.** copulation; an act of copulation. **5.** the female genitals. [senses 4 and 5 are U.S. slang, mid 1900s-pres.] **6.** the penis; the VIRILIA (q.v.). [U.S. slang and colloquial, mid 1900s-pres.] **7.** marijuana. [U.S. drug culture, mid 1900s-pres.] **8.** heroin. Cf. WHITE STUFF. [U.S. underworld and drug culture, mid 1900s-pres.] **9.** morphine, Demerol (trademark), or other hard drugs. [U.S. underworld and slang, early 1900s-pres.]

Stuff a sock in it! (also **Put a sock in it!**) "Shut up!"; "Stuff a sock in your mouth!" The it is ambiguous, however, and may be interpreted as any orifice. [U.S. and elsewhere, late 1900s]

stuffer a SODOMITE (q.v.); a PEDERAST (q.v.); the INSERTOR (q.v.). See the entries under GUT-BUTCHER. Cf. STUFF (sense 4). [U.S. slang, mid 1900s, Monteleone]

stum 1. marijuana. **2.** a sleeping pill; a barbiturate tablet or capsule. Because it makes a person stumble. Cf. STUMBLER. [both senses, U.S. drug culture, mid 1900s-pres.]

stumbler a barbiturate capsule or tablet, usually Seconal (trademark). Cf. STUM (sense 2). For synonyms see BARB. [U.S. drug culture, mid 1900s-pres.]

stump 1. the penis. Cf. CARNAL STUMP. [British, 1600s] **2.** an oaf; a fool. [British slang, 1800s, Farmer and Henley]

stung intoxicated with alcohol. [Australian slang, early 1900s-pres.]

stung by a serpent pregnant. *Cf.* PIZENED, POISONED, STING. [slang, 1800s or before]

stunned intoxicated with alcohol. For synonyms see WOOFLED. [widespread slang and colloquial, early 1900s-pres.]

stupehead an oaf; a blockhead. [U.S. colloquial, 1900s]

stupid 1. a blockhead; an oaf. From the literal meaning. [since the 1800s] Synonyms: AIR-BRAINED, ASS-BRAINED, AS THICK AS PIGSHIT, BARMYBRAINED, BEEF-HEADED, BEEF-WITTED, BESOM-HEADED, BIRD-BRAINED, BLOCKHEADED, BLOCKY, BLUBBER-BRAINED, BLUBBER-HEADED, BLUNDERHEADED, BOG-IGNORANT, BONE-HEADED, BOOF, BOTTLE-HEADED, BUFFLEBRAINED, BUFFLE-HEADED, BULLET-HEADED, BULLHEAD, BUTT-HEADED, CLAY-BRAINED, CLODPOLISH, CLOD-SKULLED, CLOUTER-HEADED, COCK-BRAIN, COCK-BRAINED, CULVER-HEADED, DICK-BRAINED, DORKY, EMPTY-SKULLED, FEATHER-BRAINED, FEATHERHEADED, FUCK-BRAINED, HALF-HARD, HAMMER-HEADED, HARE-BRAINED, IDLEHEADED, LEATHER-BRAINED, LOBBER-HEADED, LOGGER-HEADED, MAGGOT-BRAINED, RUM-DUMB, SCRAMBLE-BRAINED, SHIT-BRAINED, SLOW, SQUIFFY, THICK, TIMBER-HEADED. **2.** heavily intoxicated with alcohol. [widespread slang, 1800s-1900s]

suck 1. strong alcoholic beverages. [British slang, 1600s-1700s] **2.** a sycophant. *Cf.* BUM-SUCKER, EGG-SUCKER, SUCK-ASS. [British and U.S. slang, 1900s] **3.** to toady; to act the sycophant. [U.S. slang, early 1900s-pres.] **4.** special influence with a person; "pull" with a person or an organization. [U.S. slang, mid 1900s] **5.** to perform PENILINGUS or CUNNILINGUS (both *q.v.*). *Cf.* SUCK OFF. [British and U.S. slang, 1800s-1900s] **6.** an act of penilingus. [U.S. slang, 1900s and before]

sucka a sucker; a dupe. For synonyms see OAF. [U.S., late 1900s-pres.]

suckabuck greedy; exhibiting greed. [British, late 1900s-pres.]

Suck a fatty! "Go suck a big fat penis!" [British, late 1900s-pres.]

suck-and-swallow the female genitals, specifically the vagina. *Cf.* SWAL-LOW-COCK. [British slang, 1800s, Farmer and Henley]

suck-ass a sycophant. *Cf.* KISS-ASS. [U.S. slang, mid 1900s-pres.]

suckathon group sex where the principal activity is oral sex. See similar subjects at GROUP SEX. [U.S., mid 1900s-pres.]

suck bamboo (also **suck the bamboo**) to smoke opium. For synonyms see SMOKE. [U.S. underworld, early 1900s or before]

suck-bottle (also **suck-spigot**) a drunkard. [colloquial, mid 1600s]

sucked intoxicated with alcohol. For synonyms see WOOFLED. [British slang, 1800s, *Sinks of London Laid Open*]

sucker 1. the penis. *Cf.* LADIES' LOLLI-POP. [British slang, 1700s-1800s] **2.** a baby. [British slang, early 1800s, Jon Bee] **3.** a woman or a prostitute who performs penilingus; a COCKSUCKER (sense 1). *Cf.* MOUTH-WHORE. [British and later U.S. slang, 1800s-1900s] **4.** a dupe; a gullible person.

suck face to kiss; to FRENCH KISS. See CHEW FACE. [U.S. slang, late 1900s]

suck heads to kiss. [U.S. collegiate, late 1900s, Eble]

suck off to perform CUNNILINGUS or PENILINGUS (both *q.v.*). [British and U.S. slang, 1800s-pres.]

suck out a few heads to drink a few beers. [U.S. slang, late 1900s]

suck queen a homosexual male who prefers PENILINGUS (*q.v.*). See QUEEN for similar subjects. [(U.S. homosexual use, mid 1900s, Farrell]

sucks!, It a rude exclamation, "It is extremely bad." [U.S. slang, mid 1900s-pres.]

suck someone's hind tit to kowtow or toady to someone; to be obsequious to someone. [U.S. slang, mid 1900s-pres.]

suckster a male performer of PENILIN-GUS (*q.v.*). *Cf.* SUCKSTRESS. [British slang, 1800s, Farmer and Henley]

suckstress a female performer of PEN-ILINGUS (*q.v.*). *Cf.* SUCKSTER. [British slang, 1800s, Farmer and Henley]

suck the bamboo to smoke opium. See SUCK BAMBOO.

suck the sugar-stick to copulate, said of a woman. Perhaps to perform PENILINGUS (q.v.). Cf. SUGAR-STICK. [British slang, 1800s, Farmer and Henley]

sucky 1. (also **suckey**) intoxicated with alcohol. For synonyms see WOOFLED. [British slang, 1600s-1700s] **2.** awful. [U.S. slang, late 1900s]

sucky-fucky 1. an act of PENILINGUS (q.v.) followed by orthogenital copulation. **2.** an act of PENILINGUS (q.v.). [both senses, U.S. slang, mid 1900s-pres.]

suction influence; "pull"; the same as SUCK (sense 4). [U.S. slang, mid 1900s]

sudds, in the (also **suds, in the**) intoxicated with alcohol; intoxicated with beer or ale. [U.S. slang, early 1700s, Ben Franklin]

suds beer. [British and U.S. slang, 1900s] Synonyms: BARLEY BROTH, BARLEY JUICE, BARLEY WATER, BELCH, BELSH, BERPS, BEVVY, BUB, BUCKET OF SUDS, COCK-ALE, COLD COFFEE, COLORADO COOLAID, FAR AND NEAR, GROWLER, KOOL-AID, LUBE, LUSH, NEAR BEER, NEVER-FEAR, OIL OF BARLEY, PIG SWEAT, PISS, PONG, PONGELOW, PURGE, QUEER BEER, REEB, SISSY BEER, SKIT, SQUAW PISS, SUPER SUDS, SWIPES, TANGLE-LEG, WITCH-PISS.

sugar 1. shit. Partridge suggests this is a blend of SHIT and BUGGER (both q.v.). [British and U.S. slang, 1900s] **2.** heroin. [U.S. drug culture, mid 1900s-pres.] **3.** the drug L.S.D. (q.v.). From the use of sugar cubes in its ingestion. [U.S. drug culture, mid 1900s-pres.]

sugar-daddy 1. an older man who keeps a young girl. [U.S. slang, early 1900s-pres.] **2.** an elderly homosexual male who keeps a younger homosexual male. [U.S. homosexual use, mid 1900s-pres.]

sugar doughnut the female genitals; the vagina. [U.S. slang, mid 1900s-pres.]

sugar lump (also **sugar**) the drug L.S.D. (q.v.). [U.S. drug culture, mid 1900s-pres.]

sugar-stick the penis, especially the erect penis. [British slang, early 1800s]

summer complaint diarrhea, especially that experienced in the summer. For synonyms see QUICKSTEP. [colloquial, mid 1800s-pres.]

sun, in the intoxicated with alcohol. Cf. STANDING TOO LONG IN THE SUN. [slang, 1800s-1900s]

Sunday suit nakedness. Cf. BIRTHDAY SUIT; ONE'S SUNDAY BEST, IN. [U.S. slang, mid 1900s-pres.]

sun in the eyes intoxication with alcohol. [British and U.S. slang or colloquial, 1800s-1900s]

sunshine the drug L.S.D. (q.v.). Cf. ORANGE SUNSHINE, YELLOW SUNSHINE. [U.S. drug culture, mid 1900s-pres.]

superblow cocaine. Cf. BLOW (sense 5). [U.S. drug culture, mid 1900s-pres.]

super C. ketamine hydrochloride. [U.S. drug culture, 1900s, Abel]

supercharged 1. intoxicated with alcohol. [British and U.S. slang, 1900s] **2.** intoxicated with drugs. Cf. CHARGE (sense 1). [U.S. drug culture, mid 1900s-pres.]

super cool very strong marijuana. For synonyms see MARI. [U.S. drug culture, late 1900s]

superdroopers large breasts; pendulous breasts. Cf. DROOPERS. [U.S. slang, mid 1900s-pres.]

superfly cocaine. For synonyms see NOSE-CANDY. [U.S. drug culture, late 1900s, Eble]

supergrass (also **superweed**) the drug P.C.P. (q.v.). Sometimes sold deceptively as T.H.C. (q.v.), the active ingredient in marijuana. Cf. GRASS (sense 1), WEED (sense 1). [U.S. drug culture, mid 1900s-pres.]

superpot marijuana mixed with other drugs. [U.S. drug culture, mid 1900s-pres.]

super-soaper methaqualone. Cf. SOAP (sense 3). [U.S. drug culture, mid 1900s-pres.]

super suds beer; Coors (trademark) beer. Cf. SUDS. [U.S. slang, mid 1900s-pres.]

supper the female genitals. From the expression GIVE THE OLD MAN HIS SUPPER (*q.v.*). [British, 1800s]

surfboard 1. a girl possessing tiny or very flat breasts. [British, late 1900s-pres.] **2.** a sexually willing girl or woman. For synonyms see BIRD. [British, late 1900s-pres.]

surfer the drug P.C.P. (*q.v.*). [U.S. drug culture, mid 1900s-pres.]

SUSFU "situation unchanged, still fucked-up," pertaining to a situation which is perpetually messed-up. [U.S. slang, mid 1900s]

swabler a dirty fellow. Possibly related to "swabber," a common laborer. [attested at 1800s, Matsell]

swab someone's tonsils to neck; to kiss deeply with the tongue. Named after the medical treatment. [U.S. slang, early 1900s-pres.]

swacked intoxicated with alcohol. For synonyms see WOOFLED. [U.S. slang, early 1900s]

swacko drunk. See SWACKED. For synonyms see WOOFLED. [U.S. slang, 1900s]

SWAK "sealed with a kiss." *Cf.* SWANK. [originally military; widespread slang, 1900s]

swallow-cock a prostitute. *Cf.* SUCK-AND-SWALLOW. [British slang, 1800s, Farmer and Henley]

swallowed a watermelon seed pregnant. For synonyms see FRAGRANT. [U.S. colloquial, 1900s]

swallower 1. a drunkard; a tippler. For synonyms see ALCHY. [British colloquial, 1800s] **2.** a person who is hired to smuggle drugs by swallowing rubber packages of powdered drugs and retrieving the packages from excreted stools. [U.S. drug culture, late 1900s]

swallow hit a puff of marijuana smoke that is swallowed. [U.S. drug culture, late 1900s]

swamped (also **swampt**) intoxicated with alcohol. [slang since the early 1700s]

SWANK "sealed with a nice kiss." *Cf.* SWAK. [British military, Fraser and Gibbons]

swap slops to kiss in a messy fashion; to FRENCH KISS. See SWAP SPIT(s). [U.S. slang, late 1900s]

swap spit (also **swap spits**) **1.** to kiss deeply using the tongue. [U.S. and British, slang, 1900s] **2.** to perform mutual PENILINGUS (*q.v.*). [U.S. underworld, mid 1900s, Goldin, O'Leary, and Lipsius]

swattled intoxicated with alcohol. [British and U.S. slang, 1800s-1900s]

swazzled intoxicated with alcohol. A spelling variant of SWOZZLED (*q.v.*). [U.S. slang, 1900s]

sweater a condom. For synonyms see EEL-SKIN. [U.S., late 1900s-pres.]

sweater full a full and ample bosom; a large pair of breasts. For synonyms see BOSOM. [U.S. slang, 1900s, Lewin and Lewin]

sweaty-toe cheese inferior, soft cheese. *Cf.* CROTCH-CHEESE. [British slang, 1800s]

sweep (also **sweep with both barrels**) to SNORT a line of cocaine. [U.S. drug culture, late 1900s]

sweet 1. intoxicated with alcohol. *Cf.* HAPPY. [Caribbean (Jamaican), Cassidy and Le Page] **2.** pertaining to a homosexual male; pertaining to male homosexuality. *Cf.* SWEETIE. [U.S. slang, mid 1900s-pres.] **3.** an amphetamine tablet or capsule. Usually in the plural. [U.S. drug culture, mid 1900s-pres.]

sweetbriar the female pubic hair. For synonyms see DOWNSHIRE. [British slang, 1800s, Farmer and Henley]

sweet-by-and-by heaven; death; the afterlife. [U.S. colloquial, 1900s or before]

sweet cheesecake a jocular disguise of "Sweet Jesus." [U.S. colloquial, 1900s] Synonyms and oaths: CHEESE AND CRUST!, CHRISTMAS!, CHRISTOPHER COLUMBUS!, CRIPES!, CRIPUS!, GEEKUS CROW!, GEEZ!, GEMMENIE!, GREASE-US TWICE!, J.C. JEANSRICE!, JEE!, JEEPERS!, JERUSALEM SLIM, JIMINY!, LAMB, LAMB OF GOD, MESSIAH, SON OF RIGHTEOUSNESS, THE ANOINTED, THE ANOINTED ONE, THE DIVINITY, THE LORD, THE NAZARENE, THE

REDEEMER, THE SAVIOUR, X., XPC, XS.

sweet chocolate a sexually attractive black woman. *Cf.* CHOCOLATE DROP, HOP CHOCOLATE. [U.S. slang, mid 1900s]

sweet fuck all not much; virtually nothing. [Australian, 1900s, if not before]

sweetie a homosexual male. *Cf.* SWEET (sense 2). For synonyms see EPICENE. [U.S. slang, mid 1900s-pres.]

sweet Lucy marijuana. *Cf.* LUCY IN THE SKY WITH DIAMONDS. [U.S. slang, mid 1900s-pres.]

sweet-meat 1. the penis. *Cf.* MEAT (sense 4). [British slang, 1800s, Farmer and Henley] **2.** a young girl kept as a mistress. [British slang, 1800s, Farmer and Henley] **3.** any young girl or woman. [U.S. slang, mid 1900s-pres.]

sweet potatoes the human breasts. *Cf.* MURPHIES. [U.S. slang, 1900s]

sweets the testicles. For synonyms see WHIRLYGIGS. [British, late 1900s-pres.]

sweet stuff any powdered narcotic. *Cf.* WHITE STUFF (sense 3). [U.S. underworld, mid 1900s]

swerved drunk. For synonyms see WOOFLED. [U.S., late 1900s-pres.]

swig 1. to drink. [British, 1600s] **2.** a drink, especially a drink of an alcoholic beverage. Also **swiggle.** [since the 1600s or before]

swigged intoxicated with alcohol. *Cf.* SWIG. [British colloquial, 1800s]

swiggled intoxicated with alcohol. From the colloquial term "swiggle," meaning "drink." [British and U.S. colloquial, 1800s-pres.]

swill 1. to drink heavily. [since the early 1500s] **2.** alcoholic beverages. From a colloquial term for "hogwash." [since the early 1600s]

swilled-up (also **swilled**) intoxicated with alcohol. [British and U.S. slang, 1800s-1900s]

swine-drunk heavily intoxicated with alcohol. *Cf.* SOW-DRUNK. [colloquial, late 1500s-1900s]

swing 1. to copulate. [colloquial, early 1500s-1600s] **2.** to hang; to be hanged. [colloquial since the early 1500s] **3.** the gallows. [British colloquial, 1700s or before] **4.** to neck and pet. [U.S. slang, early 1900s, Weseen] **5.** to engage in homosexual activities. [U.S., mid 1900s] **6.** to be involved in sexual fads, group sex, or the swapping of sexual partners. [U.S. slang, mid 1900s-pres.]

swing a free leg to be unmarried. [British, mid 1900s-pres.]

swing both ways to be bisexual; to practice homosexual and heterosexual sexual activities indiscriminately. [U.S. slang, mid 1900s-pres.]

swinge (also **swynge**) to copulate; the same as SWING (sense 1).

swinger 1. a person who participates in swinging. See SWING (sense 6). **2.** a youthful, socially active, and knowledgeable person. Not necessarily with sexual connotations. [both senses, U.S. slang, mid 1900s-pres.] **3.** a person who uses all forms of drugs. [U.S. drug culture, mid 1900s-pres.]

swingers 1. the testicles. For synonyms see WHIRLYGIGS. [colloquial and nonce, 1800s-pres.] **2.** breasts; breasts which jiggle and bounce when a woman is walking. For synonyms see BOSOM. [widespread colloquial and nonce, 1900s]

swinging-steak animal testicles considered as food. Probably also used for human testicles in the oral sex sense. [U.S. slang, late 1900s, Lewin and Lewin]

swing man a drug dealer. *Cf.* BAGMAN. [U.S. drug culture, mid 1900s-pres.]

swing party a group sex party. See GROUP SEX for similar terms. From SWING (sense 6). [U.S. slang, mid 1900s-pres.]

swish 1. absent without leave. Onomatopoetic for the sound of a rapid departure. *Cf.* A.W.O.L. [Australian military, early 1900s, Baker] **2.** a homosexual male. [U.S. slang, mid 1900s] **3.** pertaining to a homosexual or effeminate male; pertaining to homosexuality. *Cf.* SWISHY. [U.S. slang, mid

1900s-pres.] **4.** to walk in an effeminate manner; to flaunt homosexual or effeminate characteristics. [U.S. slang, mid 1900s]

swishy effeminate; homosexual. [U.S. slang, mid 1900s]

Swiss purple a type of high-quality L.S.D. Refers to Sandoz Laboratories in Switzerland where L.S.D. was developed. For synonyms see ACID. [U.S. drug culture, late 1900s, Abel]

switch-hitter a bisexual person. From the baseball term. [U.S. slang, mid 1900s-pres.]

swive (also **swhyve, swyfe**) to coit a woman; to copulate. [1300s or before (Chaucer)]

swively intoxicated with alcohol. From the oscillations of a swivel. [British and U.S. slang, 1800s-1900s]

swizzle 1. to drink; to drink alcohol. [British slang, mid 1800s] **2.** alcohol; beer or ale, or a mixture of the two. [British and U.S. slang, mid 1800s-pres.]

swizzled intoxicated with alcohol. *Cf.* SWIZZLE. [British and U.S. slang, mid 1800s-pres.]

swizzle-guts a drunkard. For synonyms see ALCHY. [British and U.S. slang, 1800s-1900s]

swizzle-stick the penis. From the name of the stick used to stir a mixed drink. For synonyms see GENITALS, YARD. [U.S. slang, late 1900s if not before]

swoop on someone to make a pass at someone. [U.S. slang, late 1900s]

swoozled (also **swozzled**) alcohol intoxicated. For synonyms see WOOFLED. [U.S. slang, 1900s]

sword the penis. *Cf.* BRACMARD, CUTLASS, DIRK, PORK-SWORD. [widespread recurrent nonce]

S-word the word "SHIT." *Cf.* F-WORD. [U.S. euphemism, late 1900s]

swozzled intoxicated with alcohol. *Cf.* SWAZZLED. [U.S. slang, mid 1900s, Wentworth and Flexner]

synthetic grass synthetic marijuana, the chemical compound T.H.C. (*q.v.*). *Cf.* GRASS (sense 1). [U.S. drug culture, mid 1900s-pres.]

synthetic marijuana the drug P.C.P. or T.H.C. (both *q.v.*). [U.S. drug culture, mid 1900s-pres.]

syphon off to urinate. *Cf.* DRAW OFF. For synonyms see WHIZ. [U.S. slang, mid 1900s, Berrey and Van den Bark]

syphon the python to urinate. *Cf.* ROCK PYTHON. [Australian slang, 1900s]

T

T. 1. an abbreviation of TEA (sense 3), "marijuana." [U.S. drug culture, mid 1900s-pres.] **2.** Tuinal (trademark), a barbiturate. *Cf.* TOOIE, TUIE. [U.S. drug culture, mid 1900s-pres.] **3.** (also **tee**) T.H.C. (*q.v.*). [U.S. drug culture, late 1900s] **4.** a tablet of some sort (i.e., saccharine) with a dot of L.S.D. on it. Short for *tablet.* For synonyms see ACID. [U.S. drug culture, late 1900s]

table-grade pertaining to a sexually attractive female who looks good enough to eat. Refers to CUNNILINGUS (*q.v.*). *Cf.* BARBECUE, EATING-STUFF, GOOD-EATING.

TABU "typical army balls-up"; "typical army box-up," a typical army mess. Reinforced by "taboo." See SNAFU for similar expressions. [British military, World War II]

tac T.H.C. (*q.v.*). [U.S. drug culture, late 1900s]

tackle the male genitals. For synonyms see GENITALS, VIRILIA. [British, late 1900s-pres.]

TAFUBAR "things are fucked-up beyond all recognition," said of an extremely bad situation. See SNAFU for similar expressions. [military, World War II]

tagnuts fecal matter that adheres to anal hairs. [British, late 1900s-pres.]

tag the lawn to urinate in the open. For synonyms see WHIZ. [U.S., late 1900s-pres.]

tail 1. the female genitals. **2.** the posteriors; the buttocks; occasionally, the anus. [euphemistic and widespread] **3.** the penis. [senses 1-3 since the 1300s] **4.** to coit a woman. [since the 1700s] **5.** copulation. [U.S., early 1900s-pres.] **6.** a prostitute. [British and U.S., early 1800s-pres., *Lexicon Balatronicum*] **7.** women considered solely as sexual objects. [U.S. slang, 1900s or before] Synonyms for sense 7: ARTICLE, ASS, BEDDY, BIT OF GOODS, BIT OF ROUGH, BRUSH, BUSH, BUTT, C., CALICO, CATTLE, CAVE, CHUNK OF MEAT, COCK, COOLER, COOT, COVER GIRL, CRUMPET, DUNKIE, FISH, FUCK, GASH, GIRL, GIRL STREET, GOOSE, GROUSE, GUSSET, HAIR, HAT, HOLE, HOSE, HOSE BAG, HOSE MONSTER, JAZZ, KIPPY-DOPE, MAKE, MEAT, MUFF, NOOKY, PIECE, PIECE OF EVE'S FLESH, PIECE OF MUTTON, PIECE OF STUFF, PIECE OF TAIL, PLACKET, PORK, PUNCH, PUSSY, RABBIT-PIE, ROAD WHORE, SADDLE, SCREW, SHAFT, SKIRT, SNATCH, SPLIT, SPLIT-ARSE MECHANIC, SPLIT-MUTTON, SPLIT-STUFF, SPLIT-TAIL, SPLOSH, STUFF, TIT, TRIM, WHISKER, WOMAN-FLESH.

tail-pipe the penis. [slang and nonce, 1800s-pres.]

tail-shot an audible release of intestinal gas. For synonyms see GURK. [British, 1600s]

tail-water 1. semen. **2.** urine.

tail-work copulation. [British slang, 1800s or before]

taint 1. a very dirty slattern. [British, 1800s or before] **2.** the PERINEUM (*q.v.*) of a woman. Properly spelled " 'tain't" because the perineum " 'tain't cunt and 'tain't ass." [U.S. slang, mid 1900s]

take 1. to allow a man to intromit his penis. [British, late 1600s, Farmer and Henley] **2.** to become pregnant, usually said of animals. *Cf.* CATCH (sense 2), KETCHED. [British and U.S. colloquial, 1800s-1900s] **3.** to receive the penis into the mouth or anus, said of a CATAMITE or fellator. From sense 2. *Cf.* CATCH (sense 1), RECEIVER. [slang, 1900s or before]

take a crap to defecate. Somewhat milder than TAKE A SHIT (*q.v.*), for which it is euphemistic. *Cf.* CRAP. [U.S. colloquial, 1900s]

take a dump to defecate. See DUMP (sense 2). For synonyms see EASE ONE-SELF.]U.S. slang, 1900s]

take a leak to urinate. For synonyms see WHIZ. [U.S., colloquial, 1900s]

take a shit to defecate. [U.S. colloquial, 1900s or before]

take a turn in the stubble to copulate. STUBBLE (q.v.) is the female pubic hair. [British slang, 1800s]

take his commission to castrate a man. [U.S., 1900s or before]

take in beef to receive a man sexually, said of a woman. BEEF (sense 2) refers to the penis.

take in cargo (also **take on cargo**) to get drunk. [British, early 1800s (Pierce Egan)]

take in cream for a woman to permit copulation. CREAM (sense 1) refers to semen. [British slang, 1800s, Farmer and Henley]

take it out in trade for a person to permit copulation in payment of a debt. [U.S. slang, early 1900s-pres., Monteleone]

taken intoxicated or unconscious due to narcotics. For synonyms see TALL. [U.S. underworld, early 1900s]

take oneself in hand to masturbate, said of a male. For synonyms see WASTE TIME. [U.S. slang, mid 1900s-pres.]

take one's snake for a gallop to urinate. Cf. BLACKSNAKE, ROCK PYTHON, SYPHON THE PYTHON. [British military, 1900s, *Dictionary of Slang and Unconventional English*]

take on fuel to drink alcohol to excess. For synonyms see PLAY CAMELS. [U.S. colloquial, 1900s]

take the piss out of someone (also **knock the piss out of someone**) to deflate someone; to make a person (almost always a male) behave with less boasting and bravado. Cf. KNOCK THE SHIT OUT OF SOMEONE. [British and U.S., 1900s]

take the starch out of for a woman to copulate with a man. STARCH (sense 1) refers to stiffness and to semen. [British, 1800s, Farmer and Henley]

talk German to break wind audibly. Refers to the "guttural" sounds in German. For synonyms see GURK.

talking-load intoxication with alcohol; a degree of alcoholic intoxication marked by talkativeness.

talk into the porcelain telephone to vomit. Cf. TELEPHONE. For synonyms see YORK. [U.S. collegiate, late 1900s, Eble]

talk on the big white phone (also **talk on the great white telephone**) to vomit. For synonyms see YORK. [U.S. collegiate, late 1900s]

talk to Earl to vomit. "Earl" is onomatopoetic. For synonyms see YORK. [U.S. slang, late 1900s]

talk to Ralph on the big white phone to vomit. For synonyms see YORK. [U.S. slang, late 1900s]

talk to the canoe driver to perform CUNNILINGUS (q.v.). The "canoe driver" is the clitoris. "Canoe" refers to the shape of the vulva or the *labia minora*. Based on "talk to the (bus) driver." Cf. LITTLE MAN IN THE BOAT. [U.S. slang, mid 1900s-pres.]

talk to the mike to perform FELLATIO. [U.S. collegiate, late 1900s, Munro]

talk turkey to perform oral sex. [U.S., late 1900s-pres.]

tall intoxicated with marijuana; under the effects of any RECREATIONAL DRUG (q.v.). Based on HIGH (sense 3). [U.S. drug culture, early 1900s] Similar terms: ALED(-UP), AMPED, ANNIHILATED, ATE UP, BACKED-UP, BAKED, BASTED, BATTERED, BEAMING, BELTED, BENNY, BENT, BLASTED, BLAZED, BLIND, BLISSED OUT, BLITZED, BLIXED, BLOCKED, BLOWED-AWAY, BLOWN-AWAY, BLOWN OUT, BLUNTED, BLUNTED OUT, BOGGY, BOMBED, BOXED-UP, BRIGHTENED, BROKE, BUZZ, BUZZED, CANED, CAUGHT IN A SNOWSTORM, CLUCKED, COASTING, COCAINIZED, COCK-EYED, COKED, COKED OUT, CONKED UP, COMATOSED, CRISP, DEAD, DOOBIOUS, DRAGGED, ENHANCED, ETHEREAL, FADED, FLOATING, FLYING, FREAKED, FREAKED-OUT, FRENCH-FRIED, FRIED, FROST, FROSTED, FROSTY, GASSED (up), GEEKED, GEEZED, GEEZED-UP, GIRKED,

GEEKED, GOOFED-UP, GOWED-UP, GROGGED, HAMMERED, HIGH, HOPPED, HORSED, HUMMIN', HUMMING, JACKED, JOY-RIDE, KEYED, KIF, KILLED, LAID BACK, LAID-OUT, LAYED, LIT, LOADED, MAXED OUT, MOHASKY, NUMBED OUT, ON THE HORSE, OUT, OUT OF ONE'S BRAIN, OUT OF ONE'S SKULL, PASTED, PERMAFRIED, PHAZED, PHUMFED, POLLUTED, POTS-VILLE, POTTED, RACKED, RACKED-UP, REVVED UP, RIPPED, SCHIZZED, SENT, SHERMED, SHNOCKERED, SHOT-UP, SKAGGED OUT, SLAUGHTERED, SMASHED, SMEARED, SNAPPED-UP, SNOWED-UNDER, SPACED-OUT, STEAMED-UP, STEPPING-HIGH, STRUNG-OUT, TAKEN, TATTERED, TEAD-UP (marijuana), TRIPPED-OUT, TRIP-PING, TROLLEYED, TURNED-ON, TWEAKED, TWEEKED, TWISTED, UNDER, UP, WASTED, WIPED, WIPED-OUT, WIRED-UP, WRECKED, ZAPPED, ZERKED OUT, ZIPPED, ZONED, ZONKED, ZONKED-OUT, ZOOTED, ZOO-TIED, ZOOTY, ZOUNKED (OUT), ZONKED.

tallywhacker the penis. Cf. BUSH-WHACKER. [U.S. colloquial, late 1800s-pres.]

tampon a fat marijuana cigarette. For synonyms see MEZZROLL. [U.S., late 1900s-pres.]

T. and A. "tits and ass." pertaining to magazines or any publicly available material showing exposed or promi-nent breasts and buttocks. Cf. B. and B., SOFT-CORE (sense 1). [U.S., mid 1900s-pres.]

tang drug addiction; one's drug habit. From *orangutan*. [U.S. drug culture, late 1900s, Kaiser]

tanglefoot any alcoholic drink. Refers to the effect alcohol can have on one's ability to walk. From the common name of a vining weed. For synonyms see BOOZE. [colloquial, mid 1800s-pres.]

tanglefooted intoxicated with alco-hol. For synonyms see WOOFLED. [Brit-ish and U.S., mid 1800s-pres.]

tangle-leg any alcoholic drink. Used specifically at various times and places for beer, gin, rum, and whisky. [British and U.S., mid 1800s]

tanked-up (also **tanked**) intoxicated with alcohol. [U.S. slang, early 1900s-pres.]

tanky alcohol intoxicated. For syn-onyms see WOOFLED. [U.S., late 1900s-pres.]

tanned drunk. Preserved like a tanned hide of an animal. For synonyms see WOOFLED. [U.S., late 1900s-pres.]

tape liquor, especially gin. Cf. BLUE RIBBON, BLUE TAPE, WHITE TAPE. [cant, early 1700s]

tap out to die; to expire. For syn-onyms see DEPART. [U.S. slang, late 1900s]

tap-shackled intoxicated with alco-hol; chained to a cask of drink. [slang, early 1600s]

tarantula-juice very strong or infe-rior liquor; rot-gut. For synonyms see EMBALMING FLUID. [U.S. slang, 1900s, Berrey and Van den Bark]

TARFU "things are really fucked-up," said when everything is in a state of confusion. See SNAFU for similar expressions. [British and U.S., World War II]

target practice copulation; sexual in-tercourse. For synonyms see SMOCK-AGE. [U.S. and probably elsewhere, 1900s]

tart 1. a wanton young woman; a pros-titute. [British and later U.S., 1500s-pres.] **2.** any girl, especially a sweet girl. Cf. CAKE (sense 3), PIE. [collo-quial, 1800s-pres.]

TASFUIRA "things are so fucked-up it's really amazing," said when ev-erything is in an amazingly confused mess. A contrived acronym. See SNAFU for similar expressions. [World War II]

tassel 1. a child's penis. [British, 1900s] **2.** the scrotum. [U.S., 1900s]

taste 1. to coit. Cf. FLAVOUR, SALT. [from *Othello* (Shakespeare)] **2.** copu-lation. Similar to BIT OF -- or SOME (both q.v.). [U.S., mid 1900s-pres.]

taste bud the clitoris. With reference to oral sex. [1900s]

tattered drunk; drug intoxicated. For

synonyms see TALL, WOOFLED. [U.S. collegiate, late 1900s]

taverned intoxicated with alcohol. For synonyms see WOOFLED. [British, 1800s or long before]

tax to copulate. For synonyms see OC-CUPY. [U.S., late 1900s-pres.]

taxi (cab) a pubic louse. Rhyming slang on CRAB. [British, late 1900s-pres.]

T.B. 1. "tired butt," said when one has grown tired of sitting. [U.S. slang, mid 1900s-pres.] **2.** "two beauts," said of well-proportioned or large breasts. Both are based on the abbreviation of "tuberculosis." [Australian, early 1900s, *Dictionary of Slang and Unconventional English*]

T-buzz phencyclidine, the drug P.C.P. For synonyms see P.C.P. [U.S. drug culture, late 1900s]

T.C.C.FU "typical coastal command fuck-up," the type of slip-up typically created by the coastal command. A mixture of initialism and acronym. See SNAFU for similar expressions. [British, World War II]

tea 1. alcoholic drink. [British, late 1600s, *Oxford English Dictionary*] **2.** urine. From its color. [euphemistic colloquial and slang, early 1700s-pres.] Synonyms for sense 2: ADDLE, APPLE AND PIP, CHAMBER-LYE, COUSIN SIS, EMICTION, GOLDEN SHOWER, LANT, LONG TEA, LYE, MICKEY BLISS, MIKE BLISS, NETTING, PEE-PEE, PIDDLE, PISS, SALT-WATER, SIG, SIS, STALE, TAIL-JUICE, TAIL-WATER, URINA, URINE, WASTE, WEE-WEE, YOU AND ME, ZIGG. **3.** marijuana. [U.S. drug culture, mid 1900s-pres.] **4.** marijuana brewed and drunk like tea. [U.S. drug culture, mid 1900s-pres.]

teacups small human breasts. [U.S. slang, mid 1900s]

tead-up 1. intoxicated with marijuana. *Cf.* TEA (sense 3). [U.S. drug culture, mid 1900s] **2.** intoxicated with alcohol. *Cf.* TEA (sense 1). [U.S. slang, early 1900s]

teahound a marijuana smoker. [U.S. drug culture, mid 1900s-pres.]

tea-man 1. a seller of marijuana. **2.** a

marijuana smoker. [both senses, U.S. drug culture, mid 1900s]

team-cream any type of group sex involving ejaculation; a "gang-rape." *Cf.* BUNCH-PUNCH, GANG-BANG. [U.S. slang and male homosexual use, 1900s]

tea party a party where marijuana is smoked or any occasion marked by the smoking of marijuana. *Cf.* PARTY. [U.S. slang and drug culture, mid 1900s-pres.]

teapot 1. a child's penis, from which comes TEA (sense 2). [U.S. dialect, 1800s, Green] **2.** a Negro. Possibly from the color black. Derogatory. For synonyms see EBONY. [British, 1800s] See also TEAPOT LID.

tear off a piece to copulate with a female. The "piece" is PIECE (sense 4), a woman considered as a source of sexual gratification. [widespread colloquial, 1800s-pres.]

tearoom a men's restroom, particularly a public restroom where homosexual activity is known to take place. *Cf.* COFFEE HOUSE. [U.S. homosexual use, mid 1900s-pres.]

tearoom queen a homosexual male who specializes in having sexual relations in public restrooms. See similar terms at QUEEN. *Cf.* HEAD QUEEN. [U.S. homosexual use, mid 1900s-pres.]

teaser a sexually loose female; a VAMP (sense 1). *Cf.* COCK-TEASER. [U.S. slang, mid 1900s-pres.]

teat the nipple. Either one of those on the breasts or (later) a rubber one on a baby's bottle. [since before 1000, *Oxford English Dictionary*]

tecata (also **tecaba**) heroin. From the name of a town in Mexico. [U.S. drug culture, mid 1900s-pres.]

tecato a heroin or morphine addict. [U.S. drug culture, mid 1900s-pres., *Current Slang*]

ted alcohol intoxicated. From WASTED (*q.v.*) For synonyms see WOOFLED. [U.S. collegiate, late 1900s, Eble]

Teddies and Betties a mixture of Talwin and Pyribenzamine. [U.S. drug culture, late 1900s, Abel]

Teddy party marijuana. Origin unknown. For synonyms see MARI. [U.S. drug culture, late 1900s, Abel]

teed-up (also **teed**) intoxicated with alcohol; the same as TEAD-UP (sense 2). For synonyms see WOOFLED. [U.S. slang, mid 1900s-pres.]

teeny weeny 1. a small penis. For synonyms see YARD. [U.S., late 1900s-pres.] **2.** a male with a small penis. [U.S., mid 1900s-pres.]

telephone a toilet. Especially in reference to vomiting. Perhaps because toilets are often found in booths, as are telephones. See TALK INTO THE PORCELAIN TELEPHONE, TALK ON THE BIG WHITE PHONE, TALK ON THE GREAT WHITE TELEPHONE, TALK TO RALPH ON THE BIG WHITE PHONE. For synonyms see W.C. [U.S. collegiate, late 1900s]

temple a privy; a bathroom. *Cf.* CHAPEL OF EASE. [U.S. slang, 1900s]

temple of convenience a privy. For synonyms see AJAX. [euphemistic, 1800s or before]

temple of low men the female genitals, especially the vagina. A play on "the temple of high men" (hymen). [British, 1800s, *Dictionary of Slang and Unconventional English*]

ten–one hundred urination; a stop along a highway to urinate. Mock-citizens band radio slang based on the "ten-code." [U.S., mid 1900s-pres.]

tent-peg the penis. [British slang, 1800s, Farmer and Henley]

tenuc backslang for CUNT (*q.v.*). [British slang, 1800s, Farmer and Henley]

terms the menses; a woman's period. *Cf.* MONTHLY TERMS. For synonyms see FLOODS. [medical]

testicles 1. the male gonads. The medical word-of-choice for these glands. [since the early 1400s, *Oxford English Dictionary*] **2.** oysters. A play on MOUNTAIN OYSTERS (*q.v.*), which refers to testicles eaten as food. [U.S. slang, early 1900s, Monteleone]

testimonials the testicles. An intentional malapropism for a cognate of "testicles." *Cf.* CREDENTIALS. For synonyms see WHIRLYGIGS. [British military, early 1900s]

Texas tea marijuana. *Cf.* OIL, RED OIL, TEA (sense 3). [U.S. drug culture, mid 1900s-pres.]

T.F.A. "totally fucking awesome." [U.S. slang, late 1900s]

T.G.I.F. "Thank God it's Friday!" or, in a milder form "Thank goodness it's Friday!"

T.G.I.F.-O.T.M.W.D.U.M. "Thank God it's Friday, only two more work days until Monday." An elaboration of T.G.I.F. (*q.v.*).

Thai a THAI STICK; THAI STICKS in general. [U.S. drug culture, late 1900s]

Thai sticks. 1. a marijuana cigarette coated with opium; marijuana. **2.** a grade of marijuana; the type of marijuana typically consumed by smoking. [both senses, U.S. drug culture, mid 1900s-pres.]

thang (also **theng**) a drug addiction. Southern (black) pronunciation of *thing*. Possibly a play on TANG. Essentially the same as JONES and JOHNSON. [U.S. drug culture, late 1900s, Kaiser]

that 1. the penis. **2.** the female genitals. For both, *cf.* IT (sense 2), THING (sense 2). [colloquial euphemism, 1800s-pres.] **3.** the hymen. For synonyms see BEAN [British, 1800s]

that and this urine; an act of urination; to urinate. Rhyming slang for "piss." [British, 1800s, *Dictionary of Rhyming Slang*]

That bites! "That is bad!" [U.S., late 1900s-pres.]

thatch 1. the pubic hair. For synonyms see PLUSH. **2.** the female genitals. [both senses, British slang, late 1700s]

thatched house under the hill the female genitals. From a song title. [British slang, late 1700s]

that crime SODOMY (*q.v.*); sexual perversion. [U.S., 1900s, Berrey and Van den Bark]

That's so suck! That's so awful! [U.S., mid 1900s-pres.]

that time the menses; the same as HER TIME (sense 2). [colloquial, 1900s or before]

that way 1. having one's menstrual period. **2.** homosexual. **3.** intoxicated with alcohol. **4.** pregnant. [all senses, 1900s]

thawed intoxicated with alcohol. From the dripping of melting ice. [U.S. slang, early 1700s, Ben Franklin]

T.H.C. 1. TETRAHYDROCANNABINOL (*q.v.*), the active ingredient in marijuana. A highly desirable substance among marijuana smokers. **2.** erroneously for the drug P.C.P. (*q.v.*), which is sometimes sold as T.H.C. [both senses, U.S. drug culture, mid 1900s-pres.]

the day the eagle shits pay day. [Australian and U.S., mid 1900s-pres.]

(the) full monty the full amount. Used as the title of a movie to indicate the complete exposure of male genitals. [British, mid 1900s-pres.]

thespian a lesbian. A pun. For synonyms see LESBYTERIAN. [British slang, 1900s]

thing 1. the penis or the male genitals. **2.** the female genitals. See THINGSTABLE. *Cf.* IT, THAT. [senses 1 and 2 since the early 1600s or before] **3.** a homosexual male or an effeminate male. [U.S. slang, early 1900s] **4.** an illicit romance; an affair. [U.S., euphemism, 1900s] **5.** heroin. [U.S. drug culture, mid 1900s-pres.]

thing, old the female genitals. *Cf.* THING (sense 2). [British, 1800s, *Dictionary of Slang and Unconventional English*]

thing, the the menses. For synonyms see FLOODS A euphemism of avoidance. See also THING.

thingamabob 1. a gadget. **2.** the penis. [both senses, slang, mid 1900s-pres.]

thingamy 1. the female genitals. **2.** the penis. **3.** a gadget. [all senses, colloquial, 1800s-1900s]

thingstable a "constable," an officer of the law. A jocular play on the British pronunciation "cunt-stable." *Cf.* THING (sense 2). [British slang, late 1700s, Grose]

third leg the penis. *Cf.* BEST LEG OF THREE. [U.S. slang, 1900s]

third sex 1. homosexuals; homosexual

males. [U.S. slang, 1900s] **2.** eunuchs; males who have been neutered or who have not developed sexually. [early 1800s-pres.]

third-sexer a male or female homosexual. [U.S. slang, early 1900s]

thirstington a drunkard. *Cf.* LUSHINGTON, SWIPPINGTON. [British slang, 1800s]

thirteen marijuana. "M" is the thirteenth letter of the alphabet. [U.S. drug culture, mid 1900s-pres.]

thithy an effeminate male. A lisping pronunciation of "sissy." For synonyms see FRIBBLE. [U.S. slang, 1900s]

Thomas the penis; a personification of the penis. From JOHN THOMAS (*q.v.*), a stereotypical name for a manservant. [British and some U.S. use, late 1700s-1900s, Grose]

thorn the penis *Cf.* PRICK (sense 1), PRICKLE, THISTLE. [literary euphemism and widespread recurrent nonce]

thorn-in-the-flesh the penis. *Cf.* PRICKLE, THORN. [British, 1800s, Farmer and Henley]

those days of the month the menses. *Cf.* MONTHLIES. For synonyms see FLOODS.

thousand pities the human breasts. Rhyming slang for "titties." [British, 1800s, *Dictionary of Slang and Unconventional English*]

three-dollar bill a homosexual male. Related to the expression "queer as a three-dollar bill." "Queer" in the 1600s-1800s meant "counterfeit." [U.S. slang, 1900s, Wentworth and Flexner]

three-legged beaver a homosexual male. In citizens band radio slang, a "beaver" is a "woman." The THIRD LEG (*q.v.*) is the penis. [U.S., mid 1900s-pres.]

three-letter man a homosexual male. From FAG. See FAG (sense 2). *Cf.* FOUR-LETTER MAN. [U.S. slang, 1900s]

three-piece suite the male sexual organs. For synonyms see GENITALS. [British and U.S., late 1900s-pres.]

three sheets in the wind (also **three sheets to the wind**) intoxicated with alcohol. [originally nautical; British and U.S. slang, 1800s-pres.]

three-way sexual activity involving three people in any combination of sexes. *Cf.* CLUB SANDWICH. [attested as U.S. homosexual use, mid 1900s, Farrell]

three-way girl (also **three-way woman**) a woman who practices ORTHOGENITAL copulation, anal copulation, and FELLATIO. [U.S. slang, early 1900s-pres.]

thrill pills barbiturate tablets. [U.S. drug culture, mid 1900s-pres.]

throg to drink lots of alcohol. [U.S. collegiate, late 1900s, Munro]

throne 1. a CHAMBER POT (*q.v.*). *Cf.* TIN THRONE. **2.** a toilet; a toilet seat. [both senses, U.S. colloquial, 1900s]

throw to castrate a quadruped, usually a colt. [Australian and U.S. euphemism, 1900s or before]

throw a bird to give someone the FINGER (*q.v.*). *Cf.* FLIP THE BIRD. [U.S. slang, mid 1900s-pres.]

throw a leg over to coit a woman. *Cf.* BOARD, MOUNT. [British, 1700s-1800s]

throw a map to vomit. For synonyms see YORK. [Australian, 1900s or before, Baker]

throw mud to defecate. For synonyms see EASE ONESELF, [U.S., late 1900s-pres.]

thrown down to gobble down one's food; to eat; the opposite of THROW UP. [U.S. slang, late 1900s]

throw one a hump to coit a woman, said of a male; to permit coition, said of a female. *Cf.* HUMP. [U.S. underworld, early 1900s, Goldin, O'Leary, and Lipsius]

throw one's voice to vomit. Jocular. For synonyms see YORK. [Australian and U.S., late 1900s]

throw up 1. to vomit. [colloquial since the early 1700s] **2.** vomitus. Usually hyphenated. [colloquial since the 1800s or before] **3.** to ejaculate. [British slang, 1800s, *Dictionary of Slang and Unconventional English*]

throw up one's accounts (also **cast up one's accounts**) to vomit. [British

and some U.S. use, mid 1700s-early 1900s]

throw up one's toenails to vomit a lot. [U.S. slang, 1900s]

thrust 1. a pelvic thrust, said in reference to the movements of the male in copulation. The term is generally used in reference to any copulatory movements. [since the early 1600s or before] **2.** amphetamine tablets. See THRUSTERS. [U.S. drug culture, mid 1900s-pres.]

thrusters amphetamine tablets. From the space jargon term for a rocket engine. *Cf.* ROCKET, ROCKET-FUEL. [U.S. drug culture, mid 1900s-pres.]

thuggettes female thugs. [U.S., late 1900s-pres.]

thumb 1. to coit a woman. [British slang, 1700s] **2.** to feel or grope a woman. *Cf.* FINGER (senses 1 and 2). [British, 1800s, Farmer and Henley] **3.** a fat marijuana cigarette. [U.S. drug culture, mid 1900s-pres.]

thumb of love the penis. *Cf.* FOREFINGER, LITTLE FINGER, MIDDLE FINGER. This is one of the very few entries which Farmer and Henley mark "obscene." [euphemistic, 1800s]

thump to coit a woman. [from *The Winter's Tale* (Shakespeare)]

thunder-thighs 1. someone who is grossly overweight. [British and U.S., late 1900s-pres.] **2.** fattening food capable of enlarging the thighs. [U.S., late 1900s-pres.] **3.** big or fat thighs. [U.S., late 1900s-pres.]

thwip onomatopoetic for the sound of snorting cocaine. For related subjects see SNORT. [U.S. drug culture, late 1900s]

tic (also **tich, tick**) T.H.C. (*q.v.*), the active element in *Cannabis*. [U.S. drug culture, late 1900s]

ticket the drug L.S.D. (*q.v.*), a ticket for a TRIP (sense 3). [U.S. drug culture, mid 1900s-pres.]

tickle 1. sexually aroused. *Cf.* FLAVOUR, SALT. [1300s] **2.** to coit a woman. [slang, late 1500s] **3.** to feel or grope a woman. *Cf.* FINGER (sense 1). [colloquial and nonce, 1700s-pres.]

tickle-brain 1. strong alcoholic drink. [from *Henry IV*, Part One (Shakespeare)] **2.** a drunkard. [British slang, 1800s, Farmer and Henley]

tickle one's crack to masturbate, said of a woman. [British slang, 1800s, Farmer and Henley]

tickle one's pickle to masturbate. *Cf.* PICKLE = penis; JERK THE GHERKIN. For synonyms and related subjects see WASTE TIME. [U.S. slang, 1900s]

tickle-pitcher a drunkard. [British colloquial, 1800s or before]

tickler the penis. [British slang, 1800s, Farmer and Henley]

tickle-tail 1. a rod used for punishment, *i.e.*, for striking the buttocks. [British slang, late 1700s, Grose] **2.** the penis. [British slang, early 1800s, *Lexicon Balatronicum*] **3.** a wanton woman. [British slang, early 1800s or before]

tickle-text a clergyman. For synonyms see SKY-PILOT. [British colloquial, 1800s or before]

tickle the tack to masturbate (female) For synonyms see WASTE TIME. [U.S., late 1900s-pres.]

tickle-Thomas the female genitals. "Thomas" is JOHN THOMAS (*q.v.*), "penis." [British slang, 1800s, Farmer and Henley]

tickle-toby 1. a wanton woman. [British slang, 1600s] **2.** the female genitals. [British slang, 1800s, Farmer and Henley]

tickle-your-fancy a homosexual male; an effeminate male. Rhyming slang for NANCY (*q.v.*), a male homosexual. [British, 1900s, *Dictionary of Rhyming Slang*]

tiddled intoxicated with alcohol. Perhaps only slightly. [British slang, early 1900s, *Dictionary of Slang and Unconventional English*]

tiddly intoxicated with alcohol. [British and U.S., 1800s-1900s]

tie one on 1. to spree; to become intoxicated with alcohol. Also **tie the bag on.** [U.S. slang, 1900s] **2.** to become intoxicated with marijuana. [U.S. drug culture, mid 1900-pres.]

tie the true lover's knot to copulate.

Cf. KNOT, VIRGIN-KNOT. [euphemistic, 1800s-1900s]

tie up 1. to impregnate a woman. For synonyms see STORK. [British, 1800s, *Dictionary of Slang and Unconventional English*] **2.** to render one constipated. [colloquial, 1800s-1900s]

tiffled intoxicated with alcohol. [U.S. slang, 1900s]

tig bitties large breasts. A spoonerism. For synonyms see BOSOM. [U.S., late 1900s-pres.]

tiger juice strong alcoholic drink. Euphemistic for TIGER PISS (*q.v.*). *Cf.* PANTHER JUICE. [U.S., 1900s]

tiger milk strong alcohol, drink; any alcoholic drink. See TIGER JUICE. [U.S. slang, 1900s]

tiger piss inferior or weak beer or any alcoholic drink. *Cf.* SQUAW PISS. [slang, 1900s]

tiger sweat strong alcoholic drink; whisky. Euphemistic for TIGER PISS (*q.v.*). [U.S., slang, 1900s]

tight intoxicated with alcohol. Refers to being full enough to burst. [colloquial since the 1800s]

tight-arsed (also **tight-assed**) **1.** pertaining to a chaste woman. [British, 1800s, Farmer and Henley] **2.** prudish and overly alarmed by subjects like sex. [U.S. slang, 1900s]

tight as a badger's bum very tight. [British, late 1900s-pres.]

tight as a brassiere intoxicated with alcohol, as drunk as a brassiere is tight. [U.S. slang, mid 1900s]

tight as a drum intoxicated with alcohol. The expression pertains to anything tight. [U.S. slang, 1900s]

tight as a fart intoxicated with alcohol. Refers to the tension required to prevent the breaking of wind. [British slang, early 1900s, *Dictionary of Slang and Unconventional English*]

tight as a goat intoxicated with alcohol. A mixture of "tight as a drum" and "stinking (drunk) as a goat." *Cf.* GOAT-DRUNK. [U.S. slang, 1900s]

tight as a mink intoxicated with alcohol. [U.S. slang, 1900s]

tight as a ten-day drunk intoxicated with alcohol; very drunk indeed. [U.S. slang, 1900s]

tight as a tick intoxicated with alcohol; as full of drink as a tick engorged with blood. *Cf.* DRUNK AS A TICK, FULL AS A TICK. For synonyms see WOOFLED. [British and U.S., 1900s]

tight-ass(ed) having to do with an overly rigid person who is uptight about moral matters. [U.S. slang, late 1900s]

tight as the bark on a tree very drunk. [U.S. slang, 1900s]

tighter than a nun's cunt very tight. [U.S. slang, late 1900s]

tight skirt a drunken woman. From TIGHT (*q.v.*) meaning "drunk" and SKIRT (*q.v.*) meaning "woman." [U.S. slang, 1900s, Berrey and Van den Bark]

till the female genitals. Directly from MONEY-BOX (*q.v.*). [British slang, 1800s, Farmer and Henley]

timbered 1. pertaining to a WELL-BUILT (sense 1) male. [colloquial, 1400s] 2. MENTULATE (*q.v.*); pertaining to a male with large genitals. *Cf.* WELL-BUILT (sense 2).

timothy 1. the penis, especially that of a child; a personification of the penis. Sometimes capitalized. *Cf.* PETER. [British colloquial dialect, 1800s] 2. a brothel. [Australian, early 1900s]

tin 1. one ounce (one tobacco tin) of marijuana. *Cf.* O.Z. [U.S. drug culture, 1900s] 2. a can of beer. [U.S. slang, late 1900s or before]

tin grin a smile showing metal braces on the teeth. [U.S., late 1900s-pres.]

tin hat (Also **tin hats**) intoxicated with alcohol. Implying that one is wearing a tin hat that someone is beating on. Also a slang term for a military helmet. [British military, late 1800s-mid 1900s]

tinhorn 1. a cheap gambler [U.S. slang, 1900s or before] 2. pertaining to an insignificant and inexperienced person, usually a male. The HORN (sense 3) is a veiled reference to the penis.

Cf. GREENHORN. [British and U.S., late 1800s-pres.]

tink the penis. For synonyms see YARD. [U.S., late 1900s-pres.]

tinkerbelle a male homosexual For synonyms see EPICENE. [British and U.S., late 1900s-pres.]

tinkle 1. urine. For synonyms see TEA. 2. to urinate. Based on the sound of urination into a vessel of water. For synonyms see WHIZ. [originally and primarily juvenile; both senses, British and U.S., 1900s or before]

tinkler the penis. For synonyms see YARD. [British, late 1900s-pres.]

tinkle-tinkle an effeminate male. For synonyms see FRIBBLE. [Australian, World War II, Baker]

tinned intoxicated with liquor. [British slang, 1900s]

tinnie a can of cold beer. For synonyms see BOOZE. [Australian, mid 1900s-pres.]

tinsel teeth someone wearing metal braces on the teeth. [U.S., late 1900s-pres.]

tin throne a CHAMBER POT (*q.v.*). *Cf.* CAN (sense 1), THRONE. [U.S. prison slang, 1900s]

tipple 1. any alcoholic beverage. 2. to drink an alcoholic beverage, especially to sip a little bit every now and then. [both colloquial since the 1500s]

tippler 1. a tavern-keeper. [1300s] 2. a drunkard or a person who sips drink all day. [since the mid 1500s]

tipsified intoxicated with alcohol. For synonyms see WOOFLED. [British slang, early 1800s]

tipsy (also **tipsey**) intoxicated with alcohol, not necessarily deeply intoxicated. [colloquial since the 1500s]

tit 1. a horse, *i.e.*, a filly. No negative connotations. [British, mid 1500s-1800s] 2. a young woman. From sense 1. *Cf.* TITTER (sense 1). [since the late 1500s] 3. a harlot or a prostitute. This is probably an overstatement of sense 2. [late 1500s] 4. a nipple. Based on "titty," which dates from the 1700s. 5. a human breast. Usually in the plural. [U.S. slang and colloquial, 1800s-pres.]

Synonyms for sense 5: BRACE AND BIT, BUB, BUBBY, DIDDY, MAMMA, TITTY, TRACY-BIT. See BOSOM for a complete list. **6.** human milk. *Cf.* TITTY (sense 2). **7.** to milk a cow. [U.S. colloquial, 1900s or before] **8.** the female genitals. [never in wide use, 1900s] **9.** an exclamation. See TITS! **10.** a teat or nipple. [old] **11.** a foolish or insignificant person. For synonyms see FRIBBLE. [British, late 1900s-pres.]

tit-bag a brassiere. A play on "kitbag." For synonyms see BRA. [widespread slang, 1900s]

tit-hammock a brassiere; the same as TIT-BAG (*q.v.*). For synonyms see BRA. [British, early 1900s, *Dictionary of Slang and Unconventional English*]

titiculture the appreciation of well-shaped human breasts; breast worship. Patterned on "agriculture." Partly jocular. See TIT-MAN. [1900s or before]

tit job surgical breast augmentation. [U.S. slang, late 1900s or before]

titley alcoholic drink. For synonyms see BOOZE. [British slang, mid 1800s]

titless wonder 1. a flat-chested woman. [British and U.S., mid 1900s-pres.] **2.** an oafish or awkward person. For synonyms see OAF. [U.S., mid 1900s-pres.]

tit-mag a magazine featuring female nudity. To be used to stimulate masturbation fantasies. [late 1900s]

tit-man a male who is attracted to women's breasts; a TITTER (sense 3). *Cf.* LEG-MAN. [British and U.S. slang, early 1900s-pres.]

tits for days pertaining to a woman with large or immensely large breasts. *Cf.* DOUBLE-DUGGED. [U.S. slang, mid 1900s-pres.]

titskis the female breasts; tits. For synonyms see BOSOM. [U.S., late 1900s-pres.]

tit-sling a brassiere. [British, late 1900s-pres.]

tits up upside down; on its or someone's back. [U.S., mid 1900s-pres.]

titter 1. a young woman or girl. [slang since the 1800s] **2.** an animal's teat. [British colloquial, 1800s or before] **3.**

a man who spends much time with girls or is highly attracted to them. *Cf.* TIT-MAN. [U.S. slang, early 1900s]

titty (also **diddy**) **1.** the human breast. Usually in the plural. *Cf.* DIDDIES, TIT. [since the mid 1700s] **2.** human breast milk. [colloquial, 1700s-early 1900s] **3.** a girl or a woman. [since the late 1700s]

titty fuck masturbation by placing the penis between the breasts. For synonyms see WASTE TIME. [British, late 1900s-pres.]

T.N.T "two nifty tits." A reinterpretation of the initialism for "trinitrotoluene." [U.S. slang]

toast and butter (also **toast**) a drunkard. For synonyms see ALCHY. [1500s-1600s]

toasted drunk. For synonyms see WOOFLED. [U.S. slang, late 1900s] See also BAKED.

tocks the posteriors. A truncation of "buttocks." [U.S. slang, mid 1900s, *Current Slang*]

todger the penis. For synonyms see YARD. [British, late 1900s-pres.]

toe-jam (also **toe-punk**) a real or imagined nasty substance found between the toes. *Cf.* GRONK. [U.S. slang, 1900s]

toe queen a homosexual male who obtains gratification through playing with the feet of another person. See related subjects at QUEEN. *Cf.* FOOT QUEEN, SHRIMP QUEEN. [U.S. homosexual use, 1900s]

toilet mouth a person who uses obscene language illegally on citizens band radio. *Cf.* POTTY MOUTH. [U.S., mid 1900s-pres.]

toke (also **toak**) **1.** to smoke a marijuana cigarette. **2.** a puff of a marijuana cigarette. [both senses, U.S. drug culture, mid 1900s-pres.] **3.** a cigarette made of tobacco. All senses are from "token." [U.S. slang, mid 1900s-res.]

toke a number to smoke a marijuana cigarette. The number is probably THIRTEEN (*q.v.*). [U.S. drug culture, late 1900s]

token 1. the female genitals. [early

1500s] **2.** the plague. [British, late 1600s, B.E.] **3.** venereal disease. [British slang or cant, late 1700s, Grose]

toker **1.** a smoker of marijuana. **2.** a water pipe for smoking marijuana. [both senses, U.S. drug culture, late 1900s]

tokus (also **dokus, tochas, tockus, tokis**) **1.** the posteriors; the buttocks. **2.** the anus or rectum. [from Yiddish; both senses, British and U.S. since the early 1800s]

tolley the solvent toluene, used for sniffing by teenagers. [U.S. drug culture, late 1900s]

toll-hole the vagina of a prostitute; a prostitute. [U.S. nonce or synthetic slang, 1900s]

tom **1.** the male of certain animals; a tomcat, tom turkey, or the male of other animals. Sometimes for a human male. No negative connotations. **2.** an UNCLE TOM (*q.v.*). Usually capitalized. [U.S., 1900s or before] **3.** a prostitute. [British and U.S.] **4.** to coit a woman. *Cf.* MAN (sense 1). [British slang, 1800s] **5.** a chamber pot; a close stool. [British colloquial, 1800s or before] **6.** a virago; a lesbian. [British, late 1800s, Ware] **7.** a gin. See TOM, OLD. For synonyms see RUIN. **8.** a girl or woman. [Australian and U.S., 1900s] **9.** the penis. See LONG TOM, MISTER TOM.

Tom, old gin. For synonyms see RUIN. [British slang, early 1800s]

tomas a penis. For synonyms see YARD. [U.S., late 1900s-pres.]

tomcat **1.** a sexually active male; a whoremonger. **2.** to prowl around searching for sex, said of a male. [Both senses, U.S. slang, 1900s]

Tommy Rollocks the testicles. Rhyming slang for BALLOCKS (sense 1). [British slang, late 1800s, *Dictionary of Slang and Unconventional English*]

Tom Tart **1.** one's girlfriend. Rhyming slang for "sweetheart." [Australian, late 1800s-1900s, Wilkes] **2.** a sexually loose woman. Rhyming slang for "tart." **3.** a release of intestinal gas. Rhyming slang for FART (*q.v.*). [senses 2 and 3 are U.S., 1900s]

Tom Thumb rum; a glass of rum.

Rhyming slang for "rum." [British, 1900s, Fraser and Gibbons]

tom-tit dung; to defecate. Rhyming slang for SHIT (*q.v.*). [British slang, 1800s]

Tom Turdman (also **turdman**) the man who hauls away excrement; a cleaner of privies. *Cf.* HONEY-DIPPER, SHIT-SHARK. [British slang, late 1700s, Grose]

tongue bath a sexual act or the prelude to a sexual act wherein the genitals and the genital area are licked with the tongue; an act of licking the entire body. [1900s]

tongue-fuck **1.** CUNNILINGUS (*q.v.*). **2.** PENILINGUS (*q.v.*). **3.** ANILINGUS (*q.v.*). [all senses, slang, 1900s or before]

tongue washing (also **tongue lashing**) an act of oral sex. [1900s and probably before]

tongue wrestling deep kissing. [U.S., late 1900s-pres.]

tonsil bath a drink of an alcoholic beverage. [U.S. slang, mid 1900s]

tonsil hockey **1.** an act of oral sex performed on the penis; FELLATIO. (Refers to the tonsils being struck with semen.) **2.** an act of French kissing. [both senses, U.S., late 1900s]

tonsil paint an alcoholic drink. [U.S. slang, mid 1900s]

tonsils the human breasts. *Cf.* LUNGS. [U.S. jocular euphemism, 1900s]

tonsil-swabbing kissing and necking. See SWAB SOMEONE'S TONSILS.

tons of basket pertaining to extremely large male genitals. *Cf.* BASKET (sense 3), BASKET FOR DAYS. [U.S. homosexual use, mid 1900s, Farrell]

tons of meat pertaining to extremely large male genitals, especially a large penis. See MEAT (sense 4). *Cf.* BASKET FOR DAYS, MENTULATE, MIRACLE-MEAT. [U.S. homosexual use, mid 1900s]

too big for her clothes pregnant. Based on "too big for his britches," an expression describing an arrogant male. [U.S. colloquial, 1900s]

tool **1.** the penis. In the plural, the male genitals. [since the early 1600s] **2.**

a dupe; someone easily tricked. [British and later, U.S., mid 1600s-pres.]

tool bag the scrotum or the scrotum and its contents. [colloquial and nonce] Synonyms: BAG, BALLOCK-COD, BALLOCKS, BALLSACK, BASKET, BURSA VIRILIS, BURSULA TESTICUM, COD, JELLY BAG, LURN, MUD FLAP, NUTSAC, POKE, PURSE, SACK, SCROTE, TASSEL.

tool-check a military inspection of the male genitals for venereal disease. Cf. POULTRY-SHOW. [British military, early 1900s, *Dictionary of Slang and Unconventional English*]

tool-chest the female genitals, especially the vagina. A place for the TOOL (sense 1).]British slang, 1800s, Farmer and Henley]

too many cloths in the wind intoxicated with alcohol. Nautically, a "sheet" is a rope. Cf. THREE SHEETS IN THE WIND. [British and U.S., 1800s]

too numerous to mention. intoxicated with alcohol. [British, late 1800s, Ware]

toot 1. to drink copiously. [British slang, late 1600s] **2.** a binge or a drinking spree. [U.S., late 1800s-pres.] **3.** a fool; an oaf. [British slang, late 1800s] **4.** the devil. Usually capitalized. [British, 1800s, Farmer and Henley] **5.** a W.C. Cf. THUNDER-BOX. [Australian, 1900s, *Dictionary of Slang and Unconventional English*] **6.** a breaking of wind. [U.S., 1900s] **7.** cocaine. A LINE (sense 5) of cocaine. [U.S. drug culture, mid 1900s-pres.] **8.** to inhale or SNORT (sense 2) cocaine. [U.S. drug culture, mid 1900s-pres.] **9.** dung; fecal material. For synonyms see DUNG. [British, mid 1900s-pres.]

tooter 1. a drunkard who frequently goes on a TOOT (sense 2). [British slang, early 1900s] **2.** a cocaine user; a cocaine addict. See TOOT. [U.S. drug culture, late 1900s]

toothache an erection of the penis. From IRISH TOOTHACHE (q.v.). [British slang, 1800s]

tooth-carpenter a dentist. [British slang, 1800s, Farmer and Henley]

tooth-doctor a dentist. [U.S. colloquial, 1900s or before]

toothead a cocaine user. [U.S. drug culture, late 1900s]

toothpick a long thin marijuana cigarette. For synonyms see MEZZROLL. [U.S. black use, 1900s]

tootonium a fabled, potent type of cocaine. A play on *titanium*. Cf. TOOTUNCOMMON. For synonyms see NOSE-CANDY. [U.S. drug culture, late 1900s, Abel]

tootoo dung; fecal material. For synonyms see DUNG. [British, mid 1900s-pres.]

tootsie 1. a Tuinal (trademark) capsule. [U.S. drug culture, mid 1900s-pres.] **2.** a lesbian. For synonyms see LESBYTERIAN. [Australian, 1900s, Baker]

tootuncommon very high-quality cocaine. A play on (King) *Tutankhamen*. For synonyms see NOSE-CANDY. [U.S. drug culture, late 1900s]

top-heavy 1. intoxicated with alcohol. Refers to a swollen head, the inability to stand up, and a fullness in the stomach. [slang since the late 1600s] **2.** heavy-breasted; pertaining to a woman with large or pendulous breasts. [U.S. slang, 1900s]

toppy (also **topy**) intoxicated with alcohol. Cf. TOP-HEAVY (sense 1). [British slang, late 1800s]

tops 1. PEYOTE. The tops of a small cactus. **2.** marijuana tops. For synonyms see MARI. [both senses, U.S. drug culture, late 1900s]

tops-and-bottoms 1. copulation in expressions such as "play at tops-and-bottoms." [British slang, 1800s, Farmer and Henley] **2.** a mixture of Talwin™ painkiller and Pyribenzamine™. An elaboration or disguise of T.s AND BLUES. [U.S. drug culture, late 1900s]

top sergeant a lesbian who takes the masculine role, literally, "on top." [U.S. slang, mid 1900s]

topsy-boozy intoxicated with alcohol. [British and U.S. slang, late 1800s]

topsy-turvy 1. head over heels. [since the 1700s or before] **2.** intoxicated with alcohol. From sense 1. [U.S. slang, early 1700s, Ben Franklin]

tora-loorals a woman's breast. For

synonyms see BOSOM. [British, late 1800s, Ware]

torch of Cupid the penis. From the heat generated by passion. For synonyms see GARGANTUA'S PENIS. Cf. CUPID'S TORCH. [mid 1600s (Urquhart)]

torch up to smoke marijuana. [U.S. drug culture, mid 1900s]

tore-up (also **torn-up**) intoxicated with alcohol. [U.S. slang, mid 1900s-pres.]

torpedo 1. a marijuana cigarette. Cf. BOMBER. [U.S. drug culture, 1900s] **2.** a female human breast. Usually plural. Looking like an oncoming torpedo. For synonyms see BOSOM. [U.S. slang, 1900s]

torqued drunk. Akin to TWISTED (q.v.) For synonyms see WOOFLED. [U.S. slang, late 1900s]

torrid 1. intoxicated with alcohol. [British, late 1700s] **2.** lustful, ardent, or passionate.

tosh the penis. [British, late 1800s, *Dictionary of Slang and Unconventional English*]

toss to vomit. See HURL. For synonyms see YORK. [U.S. slang, late 1900s]

toss a tiger on the carpet to vomit. For synonyms see YORK. [Australian, late 1900s-pres.]

tossbag a contemptible person. For synonyms see SNOKE-HORN. [British, mid 1900s-pres.]

tossed intoxicated with alcohol. [British slang, 1800s, Farmer and Henley]

tosselberry the penis. For synonyms see YARD. [U.S. slang, late 1900s]

tosser an oaf; a disliked person. For synonyms see OAF. [British, mid 1900s-pres.]

toss in the hay an act of copulation; the same as ROLL IN THE HAY (q.v.).

toss off (also **toss**) to masturbate. [slang, late 1700s-pres.]

toss one's cookies (also **toss one's lunch**) to vomit. Cf. SNAP ONE'S COOKIES. [U.S., 1900s]

toss one's tacos to vomit. For syn-

onyms see YORK. [U.S. collegiate, late 1900s]

toss-pot a drunkard. [slang and colloquial, mid 1500s-1900s]

toss someone's salad to lick someone's anus. [U.S., late 1900s-pres.]

tostificated (also **tosticated**) intoxicated with alcohol. A corruption of "intoxicated." [British and U.S. slang, 1700s-early 1900s]

totalled intoxicated with alcohol; very drunk. From the term used to describe an automobile which has been demolished in a collision. [U.S. slang, mid 1900s-pres.]

totalled out alcohol intoxicated. For synonyms see WOOFLED. [U.S. collegiate, late 1900s, Eble]

touched (also **teched**) crazy or slightly crazy. [since the early 1600s]

touch-up 1. sexual foreplay; stimulation in preparation for copulation. Cf. RUB-UP. [British, 1700s] **2.** masturbation. [British 1800s]

Tough shit! "Tough luck!" or "Too bad!" [U.S., 1900s]

Tough titty! (also **Hard titty!**) a catch phrase meaning "Tough luck!" [slang, mid 1900s-pres.]

toupee 1. the female pubic hair. [British, 1700s] **2.** a MERKIN (sense 2). For both, see LADY'S LOW TOUPEE.

touristas (also **turistas**) diarrhea, especially when it occurs in American tourists in Mexico. Cf. AZTEC TWO-STEP. [U.S. slang, mid 1900s-pres.]

town bike a sexually available woman who can be "ridden" by anyone. For synonyms see BIRD. [1900s or before]

town pump a sexually loose woman; a woman who is known to copulate with anyone without much persuasion. A reinterpretation of the name of a water supply held in common by townspeople, similar to TOWN BULL (q.v.). [colloquial, 1900s and before]

town punch a sexually loose woman who permits copulation with any males who ask. Cf. PUNCHABLE [U.S. slang, mid 1900s-pres.]

towns and cities the breasts. Rhyming slang for "titties." Cf. BRISTOLS.

For synonyms see BOSOM. [British, 1900s, *Dictionary of Rhyming Slang*]

toy 1. to play sexually; to engage in sexual foreplay. [since the early 1500s] **2.** the female genitals. [British and U.S., 1800s-pres.] **3.** the HYMEN (sense 2). [British, 1800s] **4.** the penis. *Cf.* TRIFLE (sense 3). [1800s-pres.]

toy cop a private security officer. For synonyms see FLATFOOT. [U.S., late 1900s-pres.]

toy-shop the female genitals, especially the vagina. *Cf.* TOY (sense 2). [British, 1800s, Farmer and Henley]

toy-toy to urinate. For synonyms see WHIZ. [U.S. juvenile, 1900s or before]

T.P. 1. "toilet paper." [U.S., 1900s and before] Synonyms: AMMUNITION, ARMY FORM BLANK, ASS-WIPE, BATHROOM ROLL, BIMPH, BUMF, BUM-FODDER, BUM WAD, BUNG-FODDER, BUTT-WIPE, CANPAPER, FODDER, JOE-WAD, LAVATORY ROLL, SANITARY PAPER, SIX-BY-FOUR, TAIL-TIMBER, TOILET TISSUE, TORCHECUL. **2.** to festoon the trees and shrubbery of a residential yard with toilet paper. A teenage prank. Also **teepee.** [U.S. slang, mid 1900s-pres.]

trade 1. a man or a woman considered sexually in a commercial sense. [U.S. slang, 1900s and probably considerably older] **2.** the occupation of prostitute, pimp, or bawd. **3.** to look for some type of sexual activity or ACTION (*q.v.*). **4.** a male (presumably homosexual) who is seeking another male as a sex partner. [U.S. homosexual use, mid 1900s-pres., Farrell]

trade, the prostitution. See TRADE (sense 2). [U.S. euphemism, 1900s]

traf a release of intestinal gas; FART spelled backwards. [U.S. and probably elsewhere, 1900s]

traffic 1. a prostitute. [1500s] **2.** coition. [1600s or before]

traffiker (also **trafficer**) a drug peddler. [U.S. drug culture, mid 1900s-pres.]

train Terrence on the terracotta to urinate, said of a male. *Cf.* POINT PERCY AT THE PORCELAIN. [Australian, 1900s]

trammeled intoxicated with alcohol. [U.S. slang, early 1700s, Ben Franklin]

tramp a sexually loose woman. For synonyms see LAY. [U.S. slang, early 1900s-pres.]

trams a woman's legs, especially if shapely. Rhyming slang for "gams." [British, early 1800s]

trance, in a intoxicated with alcohol. [U.S. slang, early 1700s, Ben Franklin]

trancs (also**1 tranks, tranx**) tranquilizer tablets or capsules. [U.S. drug culture and now general slang, mid 1900s-pres.]

tranzie a transsexual. [U.S., late 1900s-pres.]

trap the female genitals. Primarily in CARNAL TRAP (*q.v.*). [1600s]

trap-stick the penis. *Cf.* TRAP. [British slang, late 1600s]

trash 1. a slut; a sexually loose female who is worse than a TRAMP (*q.v.*).

trashed drunk. For synonyms see WOOFLED. [U.S., late 1900s-pres.]

trashmire. [since the early 1600s] **2.** a promiscuous homosexual male. From sense 1. [U.S. homosexual use, mid 1900s, Farrell] **3.** to gossip; to slander. [U.S. slang, mid 1900s-pres.] See also POOR WHITE TRASH.

trat 1. an old lady. [1300s (Chaucer)] **2.** backslang for TART (*q.v.*). *Cf.* TROT (sense 2). [British slang, late 1800s]

tree hugger an environmental activist. [U.S., late 1900s-pres.]

trees marijuana. For synonyms see MARI. [U.S., late 1900s-pres.]

tremblers large and quaking breasts. For synonyms see BOSOM. [U.S. slang, late 1900s]

trench the female genitals, particularly the PUDENDAL CLEAVAGE (*q.v.*). [written nonce; British, late 1700s]

trey bits 1. the breasts. Rhyming slang for "tits." [Australian, 1900s, Baker] **2.** diarrhea. Rhyming slang for "shits." Also **treys.** [Australian, mid 1900s, Wilkes]

triangles the DELIRIUM TREMENS (*q.v.*). Named for the ringing in the ears which accompanies this disorder. Cf. CLANKS. [British slang, mid 1800s]

triangle stuff heroin from the golden triangle: Burma, Laos, Thailand. For synonyms see HEROIN. [U.S. drug culture, late 1900s, Kaiser]

trichet the female genitals. See TWITCHET. For synonyms see MONOSYLLABLE. [U.S. colloquial, 1900s or before]

trick 1. copulation [since the 1600s] **2.** an unpopular or disliked person. [U.S. slang, 1900s] **3.** a sexually attractive girl, as in "cute trick." [U.S. slang, 1900s] **4.** a sexual customer of a prostitute. [U.S., mid 1900s-pres.] **5.** a casual (nonpaying) male homosexual partner. Cf. TRADE. [U.S. homosexual use, mid 1900s-pres.] **6.** to seek out a male homosexual partner.

trick babe a prostitute. Cf. TRICK (sense 1). [U.S. slang, mid 1900s-pres.]

trick-flick a pornographic movie which depicts some type of sexual activity or copulation. [U.S. homosexual use, 1900s]

tricking-broad a prostitute. [U.S. underworld, early 1900s]

trickster a prostitute. [U.S. slang, 1900s]

trigger the penis. Cf. GUN. [slang, 1800s-1900s]

trim 1. to DEFLOWER (q.v.) a woman. Cf. UNTRIMMED. [British, 1500s-1700s] **2.** to copulate with a woman. [slang, 1500s-pres.] **3.** copulation, as in "get some trim." [U.S., 1900s and before] **4.** women considered sexually. For synonyms see TAIL. [U.S., 1900s] **5.** to castrate. See CUT (sense 1). [U.S. dialect and colloquial, 1800s-1900s] **6.** to cheat or beat. [cant and slang, early 1800s-1900s]

trim and buff 1. to deflower a woman. For synonyms see DEFLOWER. **2.** to copulate with a woman. Cf. TRIM (sense 2). [both senses, British, late 1700s]

trinket the female genitals or an act of copulation; a sexual toy or favor. Cf. TOY (sense 2). [recurrent nonce; British, early 1700s]

trip 1. a bastard in "make a trip," i.e.,

"have a bastard." [British, late 1700s, Grose] **2.** a prostitute. [cant, 1800s] **3.** a period of intoxication from drugs. [U.S. drug culture, mid 1900s-pres.]

triple-W a "warm, wet womb," a deeply satisfying act of copulation or a sexually obliging woman. [U.S. slang, mid 1900s, Current Slang]

tripped alcohol intoxicated. For synonyms see WOOFLED. [U.S. slang, late 1900s]

tripped-out intoxicated with alcohol or drugs or both. Cf. TRIP (sense 3). [U.S. drug culture, mid 1900s-pres.]

tripping 1. intoxicated with drugs. **2.** in the process of becoming drug intoxicated. **3.** enjoying drug intoxication; in a daze from intoxicants. [all senses, U.S. drug culture, mid 1900s-pres.]

tripple-bagger someone who is so ugly that it takes three paper bags over the head to contain the ugliness. [U.S. slang, late 1900s] See also COYOTE-UGLY.

tripsit to sit with someone who is experiencing an L.S.D. trip. [U.S. drug culture, late 1900s]

trizzer a men's urinal; a W.C. Cf. WHIZ-STAND. [onomatopoetic; Australian, early 1900s]

trog(lodyte) a very stupid person. For synonyms see OAF. [British, late 1900s-pres.]

troll 1. an ugly person; a grouchy person. [1900s or before] **2.** an Internet user who sends inflammatory or provocative messages designed to start an argument. [U.S. and worldwide, late 1900s to the pres.] **3.** a message sent by a TROLL as in sense 2. [U.S., and worldwide, late 1900s-pres.]

troller a male exhibitionist; a FLASHER. As a fisherman might cast out his line and drag it around to catch something. [U.S. slang, late 1900s]

trolley and truck to coit a woman; copulation. Rhyming slang for "fuck." [British, early 1900s, Dictionary of Rhyming Slang]

trolleyed intoxicated on drink or

drugs. For synonyms see TALL, WOOFLED. [British, late 1900s-pres.]

trolling a prostitute's prowling the streets for a customer. From the fishing technique. *Cf.* HOOKER. [British, early 1900s, *Dictionary of Slang and Unconventional English*]

trollymog a slovenly woman; a slattern. [British, 1900s or before] Synonyms: BRUM, CLAMMUX, DAGGLE-TAIL, DANGUS, DAWKIN, DIRTY PUZZLE, DISH-CLOUT, DOLLOP, DOLLUMS, DRABBLE-TAIL, DRAGGLE-TAIL, DRAP, DRAPSOCK, DRASSOCK, DRATCHELL, DROOPY-DRAWERS, DROSSEL, DROZEL, DROZZLE-TAIL, DULLYTRIPE, FEAGUE, FEAK, FLAMTAG, FLOMMAX, GAD-ABOUT, HAGGAGE, MAB, MAUKS, MAUNSEL, MAWKIN, MIDDEN, MOPSY, MOX, MUCK-HEAP, MUCK-SCUTCHEON, MUCK-SUCKLE, MULLOCKS, RAG DOLL, RUBBACROCK, SLACK-TRACE, SLACKUM-TRANS, SLAMKIN, SLAMMERKIN, SLATTERN, SLOMMOCKS, SLUMMOCKS, SLURRUP, SLUT, SOSS-BRANGLE, SOZZLE, STREEL, SWASH-BUCKET, SWATCHEL, TRAPES, TRASHMIRE, TROLLOPS, TRUB.

tromboning copulating. From the action of a trombone slide. Reinforced by BONE (senses 2 and 3). [British slang, late 1800s, Farmer and Henley]

trot (also **trat**) 1. a base and ugly old woman. *Cf.* TRAT (sense 1). [early 1500s or before] 2. a bawd; a harlot; an old whore. A narrowing of sense 1. [1500s-1600s] See also TROTS

trot out one's pussy (also **feed one's pussy**) to receive a man sexually, said of a woman. As one might trot out a horse for approval. [British, 1800s, Farmer and Henley]

trots diarrhea. *Cf.* BACK-DOOR TROTS, MOVIES, RUNS. [British and U.S., late 1800s-pres.]

trouble, in pregnant and unmarried. *Cf.* DUTCH, IN. [colloquial, 1800s-pres.]

trouble-giblets (also **trouble-gusset**) the penis. *Cf.* GIBLETS (sense 2). [mid 1600s (Urquhart)] See also JOIN GIBLETS.

trounce to coit a woman. From the meaning "beat." [British, 1800s, Farmer and Henley]

trouser chuff 1. an anal release of

intestinal gas. For synonyms see GURK. [British, late 1900s-pres.] 2. the smell of a release of intestinal gas. For synonyms see GURK. [British, late 1900s-pres.]

trouser snake the penis. For synonyms see YARK. [British, and U.S., 1900s-pres.]

trouser trout the penis. For synonyms see YARD. late 1900s-pres.]

truck-driver 1. a masculine homosexual, either male or female. *Cf.* COWBOY. [U.S. homosexual use, mid 1900s] 2. a straight male, a nonhomosexual male. [U.S. underworld, early 1900s, Goldin, O'Leary, and Lipsius] 3. an amphetamine tablet or capsule. From the use of amphetamines by cross-country truck drivers. [U.S. drug culture, mid 1900s-pres.]

trump a breaking of wind. *Cf.* ARS MUSICA, BLOW THE HORN, TOOT (sense 6). For synonyms see GURK. [British slang, late 1700s]

trumpet spider See BARKING SPIDER.

try to get even for a man to switch from being a CATAMITE (*q.v.*) to acting as the inserting PEDERAST (*q.v.*). [U.S. underworld, early 1900s, Goldin, O'Leary, and Lipsius]

T.S. an abbreviation of "tough shit." Also euphemized as "tough situation." [from World War II; U.S. slang, mid 1900s-pres.]

T.s and blues a mixture of Talwin™ painkiller and Pyribenzamine.™ This combination is usually injected. [U.S. drug culture, late 1900s]

tsup catsup. [U.S., late 1900s-pres.]

T-tab phencyclidine, the drug P.C.P. For synonyms see P.C.P. [U.S. drug culture, late 1900s]

tubby a fat person. [British and U.S., early 1900s-pres.]

tube 1. a very promiscuous girl. The "tube" is the vagina. [U.S. slang, mid 1900s, *Current Slang*] 2. the penis. [nonce, 1900s and before]

tubed 1. alcohol intoxicated. For synonyms see WOOFLED. [U.S., late 1900s-pres.] 2. dead. Medical. For synonyms see DONE FOR. [U.S., late 1900s-pres.]

tube-steak 1. a frankfurter or a wiener. Based on "cube-steak." [U.S., 1900s] **2.** the penis. *Cf.* MEAT (sense 4). [U.S. slang, mid 1900s-pres.]

tubesteak of love the penis. An elaboration of TUBE-STEAK. Based on an old slang term for a wiener. *Cf.* WEENIE. For synonyms see GENITALS, YARD. [U.S. collegiate, late 1900s, Munro]

tub of guts (also **tub of lard**) a fat person. [U.S. colloquial, 1900s or before]

tucked-away dead and buried. From an expression meaning "put to bed." [1900s]

tuie a Tuinal (trademark) capsule, a specific barbiturate. For synonyms see BARB. [U.S. drug culture, mid 1900s-pres.]

TUIFU "the ultimate in fuck-ups," the worst conceivable confused mess. See SNAFU for similar expressions. [U.S., mid 1900s]

tulip-sauce kissing. Based on "two lips." [British slang, 1800s]

tumble 1. to fondle or grope. [1600s] **2.** to coit a female. [since the early 1600s] **3.** a prostitute. [British slang, 1800s, Farmer and Henley]

tumble-down-the-sink (also **tumble-down**) a glass of gin, beer, or other alcoholic beverage. Rhyming slang for an alcoholic "drink." [Australian and British, late 1800s]

tumble in 1. to get into bed, presumably for sexual purposes. **2.** to copulate; to penetrate a woman. [both senses, British, 1800s, Farmer and Henley]

tumble-turd a dung beetle. [U.S. colloquial, 1900s and before]

tumbling-drunk intoxicated with alcohol; drunk and willing to copulate. See TUMBLE (sense 2). [British, 1800s or before]

tumbling-ripe pertaining to a female who is sufficiently aroused for copulation. *Cf.* BED-WORTHY, TOUCH-ABLE, TUMBLE (sense 2). [British, early 1600s]

tummy the stomach. For synonyms see BELLY. [colloquial, 1800s-1900s]

tummy banana the penis. For synonyms see GENITALS, YARD. [British slang, McDonald]

tummy-fuck simulated coition between males. *Cf.* PRINCETON RUB. [U.S. homosexual use, 1900s, Farrell]

tummy-tickler a lecher; a whoremonger. *Cf.* TICKLE (sense 2). [British slang, 1800s, Farmer and Henley]

tump to PUSH (sense 1); to copulate. Similar to "tamp." [British slang, 1800s, Farmer and Henley]

tum-tum the stomach. *Cf.* TUMMY. [U.S. juvenile, 1800s-1900s]

tuna 1. a disliked person. [U.S. slang, mid 1900s] **2.** a girl or young woman; a sexually attractive woman. *Cf.* FISH (sense 1). [U.S. slang, mid 1900s] **3.** the female genitals. For synonyms see GENITALS, MONOSYLLABLE.

tuna taco an act of cunnilingus. For synonyms see CUNNILINGUS. [U.S. slang, late 1900s, Lewin and Lewin]

tuned tipsy; drunk. For synonyms see WOOFLED. [U.S. slang, 1900s]

tunnel the female genitals, specifically the vagina. *Cf.* CAVE OF HARMONY.

tup 1. a ram. No negative connotations. [1300s-1800s] **2.** the ram's copulation with a ram. [British, early 1600s-1800s] **3.** to seek copulation, said of ewes and of human males. [British, early 1600s] **4.** human copulation. CF. TIP (sense 1), TOP (sense 1). [British slang, early 1800s] **5.** a CUCKOLD (*q.v.*). [British, early 1800s]

tup cat a tomcat. Literally, RAM CAT (*q.v.*). *Cf.* TUP (sense 1). [British dialect, 1800s or before, Holland]

turbobitch a really bitchy female. From *turbo,* meaning powerful. [U.S. collegiate, late 1900s]

turboslut a real slut; a sleazy girl. [U.S. collegiate, late 1900s, Munro]

turd 1. a lump of excrement; a formed lump of excrement. This is one of the few terms for dung which can be made plural. **2.** a rude nickname for a disliked person. From sense 1. [both senses, Anglo-Saxon; both since *c.* 1000]

turd burglar a pederast. For synonyms see PEDERAST. [Australian and U.S., late 1900s-pres.]

turd face a totally despised person; a real JERK. For synonyms see SNOKE-HORN. [U.S. and elsewhere, late 1900s]

turd-packer See FUDGE-PACKER.

turd poodle a disagreeable person; a despised person. For synonyms see SNOKE-HORN. [U.S. collegiate, late 1900s, Eble]

turd-walloper the man who carts away dung from privies. [British, 1900s or before, *Dictionary of Slang and Unconventional English*]

turn an act of copulation *Cf.* TAKE A TURN IN THE STUBBLE.

turnabouts amphetamine tablets. See L.A. TURNABOUTS. [U.S. drug culture, mid 1900s-pres.]

turn a trick 1. to commit a crime of any type. **2.** to practice prostitution; to perform an act of male or female prostitution with a customer. **3.** to perform a homosexual act. *Cf.* TRICK. [all senses, U.S. underworld, early 1900s]

turned-on 1. intoxicated with marijuana or other drugs. [U.S. colloquial, 1900s] **2.** sexually aroused. See TURN ON (sense 1). *Cf.* TURN OFF. [U.S. colloquial, mid 1900s-pres.] **3.** interested, alerted to, or made enthusiastic by some thing or person. [U.S. current slang]

turn gay 1. to become a prostitute, said of a woman *Cf.* GAY [British, late 1800s] **2.** to become homosexual. [slang, mid 1900s-pres.]

turn off to prevent or terminate sexual desire or arousal. *Cf.* TURN ON. [U.S., mid 1900s-pres.]

turn on 1. to arouse someone sexually or to become sexually aroused; to turn someone on or to become turned on oneself. *Cf.* BRING ON. **2.** to excite or entice. **3.** to experience drug intoxication. *Cf.* TURNED-ON. **4.** to persuade someone

to use drugs. To "turn someone on to L.S.D." (*q.v.*) [all senses, U.S. slang and drug culture, mid 1900s-pres.]

turns the menses. *Cf.* COURSES. For synonyms see FLOODS. [U.S. colloquial, 1900s]

turn up to coit a woman. [British, 1800s, Farmer and Henley]

turn up one's toes (also **turn one's toes up**) to die. [British and U.S., mid 1800s]

turps (also **terps**) any alcoholic drink. From a nickname for turpentine. [slang, 1900s]

turtle 1. the female genitals. [British, 1800s] **2.** women considered sexually. *Cf.* NURTLE. **3.** a prostitute. For synonyms see HARLOT. [both senses, Australian, 1900s or before, Baker]

turtleneck the foreskin. [U.S., late 1900s-pres.]

turtlenecked uncircumcised. [U.S., late 1900s-pres.]

tus (also **twos**) capsules of Tuinal™, a barbiturate. Pronounced *twos*. For synonyms see BARB. [U.S. drug culture, late 1900s, Kaiser]

tussey a low drunkard. *Cf.* TUZZY. [British, 1800s, Farmer and Henley]

tuzzy intoxicated with alcohol. This is most likely related to MUZZY (*q.v.*), and probably to TUZZY-MUZZY (*q.v.*), in its dialect sense, "nosegay." [British dialect, 1800s or before, Rye]

tuzzy-muzzy the female genitals. From an old term for "nosegay." [British slang, early 1700s-mid 1800s]

twack a twelve-pack of beer. [U.S. collegiate, late 1900s, Munro]

twaddle 1. to utter nonsense. **2.** nonsense. [both since the late 1700s]

twammy (also **twam**) the female genitals. For synonyms see MONOSYLLABLE. [British slang, 1900s, *Dictionary of Slang and Unconventional English*]

twang 1. to coit a female. *Cf.* STRUM. **2.** a term of contempt. [since the late 1500s] **3.** opium. [Australian, late 1800s-1900s, Wilkes]

twanger the penis. [slang since the 1500s]

twang one's wire to masturbate. Said of the male. *Cf.* WHIP ONE'S WIRE. For synonyms and related subjects see WASTE TIME. [Australian, late 1900s]

twank 1. an effeminate male. For synonyms see FRIBBLE. **2.** a homosexual male. *Cf.* TWINK (sense 2). [early 1900s, *Dictionary of the Underworld*]

twat (also **twot**) **1.** the female genitals. Occasionally the British pronunciation rhymes with "sat"; the U.S. pronunciation rhymes with "sot." [widespread, mid 1600s-pres.] **2.** the buttocks. Not widely known. [U.S. slang, 1900s]

twatchel (also **twachel, twachylle, twatchil, twatchit, twitchet, twittle**) the female genitals. For synonyms see MONOSYLLABLE. [British and some U.S. dialect use, 1600s-1900s]

twat-faker a lecher; a whoremonger; a pimp; a whore's bully. ["fake" is probably from a Gypsy word meaning "mend"; British, 1800s-1900s, Farmer and Henley]

twat-raking copulating; copulation. [British, 1600s]

twat-rug the female pubic hair. For synonyms see DOWNSHIRE. [British, late 1800s-1900s]

tweak 1. a prostitute. [British colloquial, 1600s] **2.** a whoremonger. For synonyms see LECHER. [British colloquial, 1700s] **3.** to wobble around, drunk or HIGH on drugs. [U.S. collegiate, late 1900s]

tweaked (also **tweeked**) drunk; drug intoxicated. For synonyms see TALL, WOOFLED. [U.S. collegiate, late 1900s]

tweaker a crack user searching for a bit of crack on the floor. [U.S., 1900s-pres.]

tweak mission a search for lost bits of crack on the floor. [U.S., late 1900s-pres.]

tweased alcohol intoxicated. For synonyms see WOOFLED. [U.S. collegiate, late 1900s]

tweeked alcohol intoxicated. For synonyms see WOOFLED. [U.S., late 1900s-pres.]

tweek out to use drugs; to get HIGH on a drug. [U.S. drug culture, late 1900s]

twiddle to copulate. *Cf.* DIDDLE. [British slang, 1800s]

twiddle-diddles the testicles. [British slang, late 1700s, Grose]

twidget 1. a prostitute. **2.** a CATAMITE (*q.v.*). From sense 1. [both senses, U.S. underworld, mid 1900s, Goldin, O'Leary, and Lipsius]

twig and berries the penis and testicles of a child. *Cf.* PENCIL AND TASSEL. [British and U.S., 1900s]

twigle to copulate. *Cf.* NIGGLE (sense 1). For synonyms see OCCUPY. [British slang, 1800s, Farmer and Henley]

twille an oaf. For synonyms see OAF. [U.S., late 1900s-pres.]

twink an oaf; a loser. For synonyms see OAF. [U.S., late 1900s-pres.]

twin lovelies the human breasts. [euphemistic, 1900s or before]

twins 1. the testicles. [U.S. slang, 1900s] **2.** the human breasts. [U.S. 1900s]

twirl 1. a woman; a girl. From TWIST AND TWIRL (*q.v.*). [U.S. slang, 1900s] **2.** to sell drugs, especially heroin. [U.S. drug culture, late 1900s, Kaiser]

twirler a drug seller; a seller of heroin. See TWIRL. This twirler can get you TWISTED. [U.S. drug culture, late 1900s, Kaiser]

twiss a CHAMBER POT (*q.v.* at the bottom of which appeared the face of one Richard Twiss, who had published derogatory remarks about the Irish. The expression "Let everyone piss on lying Dick Twiss" was inscribed with the portrait of Twiss. [Irish use, late 1700s]

twist 1. to hand a man. [cant, early 1800s, Egan's Grose] **2.** a girl, especially a wanton girl; a SCREW (sense 4). From rhyming slang TWIST AND TWIRL (*q.v.*). [U.S. slang, early 1900s] **3.** a passive lesbian. [U.S. homosexual use, mid 1900s, Stanley] **4.** a drunken spree. [U.S., 1900s, Wentworth and Flexner] **5.** marijuana or a marijuana cigarette. [U.S. drug culture, mid 1900s-pres.] **6.** to copulate; to SCREW (sense 1). [U.S. slang, mid 1900s-pres.]

twist and twirl one's sweetheart; any woman. Rhyming slang for "girl." *Cf.* TWIRL, TWIST (sense 2).

twisted alcohol or drug intoxicated. For synonyms see TALL, WOOFLED. [U.S. slang, late 1900s if not before]

twister a sexually perverted person; a TWISTY (sense 1) person. [slang, mid 1900s-pres.]

twisty 1. perverted; pertaining to a "perverted" person. **2.** a person who has a "perverted" sexual appetite. Both are from KINKY (sense 3). [both senses, slang, mid 1900s-pres.]

twitcher 1. a drug addict. From the trembling and twitching. *Cf.* SHAKER. [British, early 1900s, *Dictionary of the Underworld*] **2.** the female genitals; the vagina. *Cf.* SNAPPER (sense 3). [slang, mid 1900s]

twitchet (also **twitchit**) the female genitals. *Cf.* TRICHET, TWATCHEL. For synonyms see MONOSYLLABLE. [U.S. dialect or slang, 1800s-1900s]

twitchet-struck woman-crazy; enamored of females and sexual matters. *Cf.* PUSSY-SIMPLE. [U.S. dialect]

twitters (also **twitteration**) **1.** sexual excitement, especially that of a woman. [British, 1600s] **2.** excitement of any kind. [U.S. slang, 1900s]

twitters, the the menstruation. For synonyms see FLOODS. [British, late 1900s-pres.]

twittle the female genitals. *Cf.* TWATCHEL [British slang, 1800s, Farmer and Henley]

two-bagger (also **double-bagger**) a very ugly person; someone whose facial ugliness requires two paper bags for total concealment. See TRIPLE-BAGGER, which is the next degree of ugliness. [U.S. slang, late 1900s]

two sheets to the wind intoxicated with alcohol. *Cf.* BOTH SHEETS IN THE WIND, FOUR SHEETS TO THE WIND, THREE SHEETS IN THE WIND, TOO MANY CLOTHS IN THE WIND.

two stone underweight castrated. The STONES (sense 2) are the testicles. Body weight in Britain is measured in "stones." A stone is equal to fourteen pounds. *Cf.* UNPAVED. [British, 1800s, Farmer and Henley]

two-time to be (sexually) unfaithful to one's lover, as in "Don't you two-time me, buster!" [U.S. slang, 1900s]

two tin fucks a worthless bit of nothing in expressions such as "I don't give two tin fucks." *Cf.* FLYING-FUCK (sense 1). [British slang, 1900s, *Dictionary of Slang and Unconventional English*]

two-toke a potent batch of marijuana that produces results after only two puffs. For synonyms see MARI. [U.S. drug culture, late 1900s, Abel]

tyrone marijuana. For synonyms see MARI. [U.S., late 1900s-pres.]

U

uck-fay Pig Latin for "fuck." [U.S. slang, 1900s]

uglies the DELIRIUM TREMENS (*q.v.*). For synonyms see ORK-ORKS. [British and U.S., late 1800s-1900s]

ugly fornication, especially in "the ugly." *Cf.* NAUGHTY. [U.S. dialect (Southern), 1900s]

uh-huh (also **some uh-huh, the uh-huh**) copulation. For synonyms see SMOCKAGE. [U.S. slang, early 1900s, Rose]

uke See YUKE.

ultimate favor, the copulation; the same as the FAVOR (*q.v.*). [literary euphemism; British, late 1600s]

umbrella a condom. For synonyms see EEL-SKIN. [U.S., late 1900s-pres.]

ums Valium™ tablets. [U.S. drug culture, late 1900s, Kaiser]

uncle 1. a privy. Especially in expressions such as "visit one's uncle." *Cf.* AUNT (sense 5). [British slang, late 1700s, Grose] **2.** a PEDERAST or a FELLATOR who is interested in young boys. *Cf.* AUNTIE, CHICKEN-HAWK. [U.S. underworld, early 1900s, Goldin, O'Leary, and Lipsius]

Uncle (Dick) 1. sick. Rhyming slang. [British, mid 1900s-pres.] **2.** the penis. Rhyming on PRICK. For synonyms see YARD. [British, mid 1900s-pres.]

Uncle Milty a depressant. Probably from *Miltown*. [U.S., late 1900s-pres.]

Uncle nab a police officer. For synonyms see FLATFOOT. [U.S. black use, late 1900s]

uncles and aunts trousers; pants. Rhyming slang for "pants." *Cf.* BULL ANTS.

Uncle Tom a Negro who is a traitor to racial causes. From the book *Uncle Tom's Cabin*, by Harriet Beecher Stowe, 1852. Derogatory. *Cf.* AUNT TOM. [U.S. slang, mid 1900s-pres.]

Uncle Tommyhawk an American Indian who is a traitor to militant Indian causes. Derogatory. Based on UNCLE TOM (*q.v.*). [U.S. slang, mid 1900s-pres.]

uncut 1. unedited; not shortened by editing. [British and U.S., mid 1900s-pres.] **2.** not circumcised. [British and U.S., mid 1900s-pres.]

undamaged goods a virgin female. The opposite of DAMAGED GOODS (*q.v.*). *Cf.* CANNED GOODS. [U.S. slang, 1900s, Berrey and Van den Bark]

under 1. unconscious due to anesthesia. No negative connotations. [U.S., 1900s] **2.** intoxicated with narcotics. For synonyms see TALL. [drug culture, 1900s] **3.** intoxicated with alcohol. For synonyms see WOOFLED. [U.S. slang, 1900s] See also GONE UNDER.

undercover man a homosexual male. Refers to his secrecy and is reinforced by a reference to bed-covers. [U.S. underworld, early 1900s, Monteleone]

undercrackers underpants [British, mid 1900s-pres.]

underdaks underpants. [Australian, mid 1900s-pres.]

under-dimple the female genitals. For synonyms see MONOSYLLABLE. [British, 1800s, Farmer and Henley]

underfug underclothes. [British, mid 1900s-pres.]

underkecks underpants. [British, mid 1900s-pres.]

underparts the genitals, either male or female. See BACK PARTS, PARTS BELOW. [colloquial, 1800s or before]

unders 1. the female genitals. *Cf.* UNDERPARTS. [British colloquial, 1800s] **2.** underpants. For synonyms see NETHER GARMENTS. [U.S. slang, 1900s]

underside 1. death; the grave. [colloquial euphemism, 1800s] **2.** the posteriors; the bottom. For synonyms see DUFF. [colloquial since the 1800s or before]

undertaker 1. someone who operates a funeral parlor; a man who makes his livelihood by performing burials. [British and U.S., early 1800s-pres.] Synonyms: BLACK COAT, BODY-SNATCHER, CARRION-HUNTER, COLD COOK, DEATH-HUNTER, GRAVE-DIGGER, LAND-BROKER, PLANTER. **2.** the female genitals. Cf. UNDERS (sense 1). [British slang, 1800s, Farmer and Henley]

under the affluence of incohol alcohol intoxicated. A deliberate spoonerism on *under the influence of alcohol*. For synonyms see WOOFLED. [British and U.S. colloquial, 1900s if not before]

under the influence a truncation of "under the influence of alcohol." Euphemistic for "drunk." [U.S., 1900s]

under the table intoxicated with alcohol. Implying that someone has slid under the table. [U.S. slang, early 1900s-pres.]

under the weather 1. intoxicated with alcohol or having a hangover. [1800s-pres.] **2.** pertaining to a woman who is menstruating. [U.S. slang, 1900s] **3.** pertaining to any sick person. [U.S. colloquial, 1900s or before]

undy-grundy a poke or goose in the anus that soils the victim's underwear. [U.S. slang, late 1900s]

unfeed to defecate. For synonyms see EASE ONESELF. [U.S. dialect, 1900s or before]

unflushable an outdoor privy compared to a water-flush toilet bowl. [U.S. slang, early 1900s or before, *Current Slang*] See also OUTDOOR PLUMBING.

un-fucking-conscious totally unconscious. [U.S., 1900s]

un-fucking-sociable extremely unsociable. [U.S., 1900s]

unhinged without mental control; mentally unstable. [British and U.S., mid 1900s-pres.]

unisex pertaining to a lack of distinc-

tion between the sexes. A fad (late 1960s, U.S.) and an occasional theme in the women's movements. The goals include (in varying degrees) identical dress, rights, and a dissolution of the traditional male-female division of labor.

unit 1. a gadget; a nameless object. **2.** the penis. For synonyms see YARD. [both senses, U.S. slang, 1900s]

unkie morphine. For synonyms see MORPH. [U.S. drug culture, 1900s]

unknown birth, of illegitimate; bastard. [euphemistic]

unk-pay a chump or a dupe. Pig Latin for "punk." Cf. UMP-CHAY. [U.S. underworld, early 1900s]

unlawfully begotten pertaining to a bastard.

unload 1. to defecate. For synonyms see EASE ONESELF. [British and U.S., mid 1900s-pres.] **2.** to release intestinal gas anally. For synonyms see GURK. [British and U.S., mid 1900s-pres.]

unmentionable vice SODOMY (*q.v.*) in general; an act of sexual perversion; the CRIMEN INNOMINATUM (*q.v.*). [euphemistic, 1800s-1900s]

unnatural connection SODOMY (*q.v.*), primarily PEDERASTY (*q.v.*). Cf. CARNAL CONNECTION. [euphemistic, 1800s-pres.]

unnatural sexual intercourse SODOMY (*q.v.*), in particular, PEDERASTY (*q.v.*). Includes any nonorthogenital sexual intercourse. [euphemistic, 1800s-pres.]

unnatural vice any nonorthogenital sexual act, including solitary masturbation; a euphemism for SODOMY. [1800s or before]

unpaved castrated. Literally, "without stones," *i.e.,* "without testicles." Cf. TWO STONE UNDERWEIGHT. [from *Cymbeline* (Shakespeare)]

unruly member the penis. Cf. MEMBER (sense 1), MEMBER FOR THE COCKSHIRE, PRIVY MEMBER. [British slang, late 1800s]

upspit to vomit. [British euphemism, late 1800s]

unswallow to vomit. [British and U.S., early 1900s]

unt-cay the vagina; the female genitals. Pig Latin for CUNT. For synonyms see GENITALS, MONOSYLLABLE. [U.S. slang, early 1900s-pres.]

unwell experiencing the menses. Cf. SICK (sense 1), UNDER THE WEATHER (sense 2). [U.S. colloquial, 1900s]

up 1. to coit a woman. [British and U.S. slang, 1800s-pres.] **2.** pertaining to the erect penis. Cf. GET IT UP. [U.S., 1900s or before] **3.** pertaining to the state of one who has consumed or abused drugs, especially amphetamines. A variation of HIGH (sense 3). [U.S. drug culture, mid 1900s-pres.] **4.** an amphetamine capsule or tablet; an UPPER (q.v.). [U.S. drug culture, mid 1900s-pres.]

up-and-coming pregnant. For synonyms see FRAGRANT. [U.S. dialect (Ozarks), Randolph and Wilson]

upchuck 1. to vomit. Cf. CHUCK UP. **2.** vomitus. [both senses, U.S. colloquial, 1900s]

up high a stimulating rather than a relaxing HIGH. *Up* is an adjective here. [U.S. drug culture, late 1900s, Kaiser]

uphill gardener a pederast. For synonyms see PEDERAST. [British, late 1900s-pres.]

upholstered 1. infected with venereal disease. [U.S. underworld, early 1900s] **2.** intoxicated with alcohol. [U.S. slang, 1900s]

Up it! a curse directing the cursed person to shove something up his anus, or her vagina or anus.

upper amphetamine. Cf. UP (sense 4). For synonyms see AMP. (U.S. drug culture, mid 1900s-pres.]

upper-deck the human breasts. For synonyms see BOSOM. [widespread slang; attested as Australian, 1900s, *Dictionary of Slang and Unconventional English*]

upper-works the human breasts. In contrast to the underparts. [British slang, late 1800s]

uppie an amphetamine tablet or cap-

sule. Cf. UP (sense 4), UPPER. [U.S. drug culture, mid 1900s-pres.]

uppish intoxicated with alcohol. For synonyms see WOOFLED. [British slang, early 1700s-1900s]

up-pot stimulating marijuana. In contrast to marijuana that sedates. Cf. UP HIGH. For synonyms see MARI. [U.S. drug culture, late 1900s, Kaiser]

up-Quaalude FREE BASE. For synonyms see FREE BASE. [U.S. drug culture, late 1900s, Abel]

upright an act of copulation performed standing up. [British, 1700s] Synonyms and related terms: FAST-FUCK, KNEE-TREMBLER, PERPENDICULAR, PERPENDICULAR CONJUNCTION, QUICKY, THREEPENNY UPRIGHT, UPRIGHT GRAND.

upright grin the female genitals. From the image of the PUDENDAL CLEAVAGE (q.v.). Cf. FLASH THE UPRIGHT GRIN, LONG-EYE. For synonyms see MONOSYLLABLE. [British slang, 1800s, Farmer and Henley]

upright wink the female genitals. From the image of the PUDENDAL CLEAVAGE (q.v.). Cf. LONG-EYE, SQUINT, UPRIGHT GRIN. [British euphemism, late 1800s (Farmer)]

upshoot an ejaculation of semen. Cf. GET THE UPSHOOT. For synonyms see MELT. [from *Love's Labour's Lost* (Shakespeare)]

upside down drunk. For synonyms see WOOFLED. [1900s if not before]

up the butt (also **up the ying-yang**) in excess; to an excessive degree. [U.S. slang, late 1900s]

up the creek (also **up a creek**) See SHIT CREEK.

up the duff pregnant. For synonyms see FRAGRANT. [Australian and British, mid 1900s-pres.]

up the spout pregnant. For synonyms see FRAGRANT. [Australian and British, mid 1900s-pres.]

up the yin-yang in abundance; up to the anus. [U.S., late 1900s-pres.]

up to one's arse in alligators in serious trouble. [British and U.S., mid 1900s-pres.]

uptown cocaine. For synonyms see NOSE-CANDY. [U.S. drug culture, late 1900s]

Up yours! an oath meaning "Go to hell!"; "Stick it up your ass!" [widespread, 1900s]

urge to purge the need to throw up. [U.S. slang, late 1900s if not recurrent nonce]

urinal of the planets a derogatory nickname for Ireland. Refers to the frequent rains. [British slang, 1600s]

urp 1. to vomit. **2.** vomit. See EARP.

use to copulate with, usually to coit a woman. See USE OF THE SEX. [since the 1500s]

use to use drugs. An intransitive verb; parallel to CONSUME = to drink alcohol. *Cf.* DO. [widespread drug culture and drug treatment jargon, late 1900s]

used-beer department a toilet; a W.C., especially one in a tavern or saloon. For synonyms see W.C. [slang, 1900s]

used-up dead; killed in battle. For synonyms see DONE FOR. [U.S. slang, World War I]

use of the sex copulation. [British euphemism, 1800s, Farmer and Henley]

user someone who takes "hard" drugs, *i.e.* cocaine, morphine, heroin, L.S.D., and P.C.P. [U.S. underworld and drug culture, 1900s] Similar terms; GHOST, HAY-BURNER, HAY-HEAD, HEAD, JOY-POPPER, JOY-RIDER, KOKOMO, METH-FREAK, METH-HEAD, METH MONSTER, OPIUM-EATER, PILL-HEAD, PINHEAD, SCHNOZZLER, SCHOOL BOY, SNIFFER, SNOWDRIFTER, SNOW-FLOWER, SPEED-FREAK, ZONKER.

usher a PEDERAST (*q.v.*). Primarily the INSERTOR, but also the RECEIVER (both *q.v.*). From GENTLEMAN OF THE BACK DOOR (*q.v.*). *Cf.* BACK-DOOR WORK, BURGLAR (sense 1). [British slang, late 1700s-late 1800s]

ussy-pay an act of copulation; PUSSY, or sexual release. Pig Latin. Attested in a homosexual (prison) context. For synonyms see SMOCKAGE. [U.S. slang, mid 1900s, Rodgers]

V

vacuum the female genitals; the vagina. NATURE (sense 5), the male libido abhors a vacuum and seeks to fill it. [British, 1800s, Farmer and Henley]

vagina the sheath of flesh in the female which receives the penis. From the Latin word for "sheath." It is this sheath which receives the "gladius," the "sword" or penis. This is the word-of-choice for this organ. See PUDENDUM. For synonyms see PASSAGE. [from Latin; in English since the late 1600s]

vagina-juice See CUNT-JUICE.

valbowski the penis. From the name of a wrestler, Val Valbowski or Val Venis. For synonyms see YARD. [U.S., late 1900s-pres.]

vals tablets of Valium™, a tranquilizer. [U.S. drug culture, late 1900s, Kaiser]

valve the female genitals. A confusion of "vulva" and "valve," a synonym of "cock." [slang and nonce, 1800s-1900s]

valve job copulation in a car. For synonyms see SMOCKAGE. [U.S., late 1900s-pres.]

vapors 1. a sickness; a fainting spell; nausea. [colloquial euphemism, 1900s and before] **2.** the menses. [U.S. colloquial, 1900s]

varf to vomit. See BARF. [from German *werfen*, "throw," via Yiddish, 1900s]

varnished intoxicated with alcohol. *Cf.* SHELLACKED

varnish one's cane to copulate. From the male point of view. *Cf.* CANE (sense 2). [attested as Canadian, 1900s, *Dictionary of Slang and Unconventional English*]

varnish-remover (also **paint-remover**) an inferior grade of whisky or homemade whisky. [U.S. slang, 1900s or before]

Vatican roulette a jocular or sarcastic nickname for the RHYTHM METHOD (*q.v.*) of birth control. "Vatican" refers to "Vatican City," the seat of the Roman Catholic Church. Based on "Russian roulette." [U.S. slang, mid 1900s-pres.]

vault to copulate, especially when done illicitly. A literal translation of the Latin FORNIX (*q.v.*). [slang, late 1500s]

vegetable garden a place where comatose patients are kept. [U.S., late 1900s-pres.]

vegetarian a prostitute who does not perform FELLATIO; a prostitute who does not eat MEAT. For synonyms see HARLOT. [U.S. slang, 1900s]

veiled twins the breasts. For synonyms see BOSOM. [British, 1800s]

Velcro head an American black of African descent. Derogatory. Intended as jocular. Refers to tightly curled hair. For synonyms see EBONY. [U.S. slang, late 1900s]

velvet the tongue in expressions such as TIP THE VELVET (*q.v.*). [cant, late 1600s, B.E.]

vent-renter a prostitute. See VENT (sense 3). U.S. synthetic slang or nonce, 1900s]

venturer a prostitute. [British, 1800s, Farmer and Henley]

Venus flytrap the vagina. A contrived play on *Venus,* the goddess of love, and the reference to the male trouser-fly. For synonyms see MONOSYLLABLE. [U.S. slang, late 1900s, Lewin and Lewin]

Venus' glove the vagina. For synonyms see PASSAGE. [from *Troilus and Cressida* (Shakespeare)]

Venus's-cell the female genitals; the vagina. [early 1500s]

Venus's curse (also **Venus' curse**) a venereal disease, syphilis or gonorrhea. [British and U.S., 1800s-1900s]

Venus's honypot (also **Venus's honeypot**) 1. the female genitals. 2. copulation. [both senses, British, early 1700s] See also HONEY-POT.

verbal diarrhea non-stop talking. [Australian, mid 1900s-pres.]

verge 1. the penis. [from Latin VIRGA (q.v.), 1400s] 2. the male copulatory organ of certain insects.

Vermont green local variety of marijuana. For synonyms see MARI. [U.S. drug culture, mid 1900s-pres.]

vert 1. a sexual pervert. [British and U.S., 1800s-pres.] 2. to practice sexual perversion. [U.S. slang] See also PERVE.

vertical bathtub a wall-mounted men's urinal. [U.S. jocular slang, mid 1900s]

verticle smile the vulva. For synonyms see MONOSYLLABLE. [U.S., late 1900s-pres.]

vestry-man the penis. For synonyms see YARD. [British slang, 1800s, Farmer and Henley]

vic (also **vick**) 1. a victim. [U.S. streets, late 1900s] 2. to victimize, to rob, etc. [U.S. streets, primarily black, late 1900s] 3. a convict. [U.S., late 1900s-pres.]

vice sister a prostitute. For synonyms see HARLOT. [U.S. slang, 1900s]

vicious circle the vagina. For synonyms see MONOSYLLABLE. [British slang, 1900s, McDonald] See also RING.

vick to victimize someone; to mug someone. [U.S., late 1900s-pres.]

Vickie a [Ford] Crown Victoria police car; the police in a Crown Victoria car. [U.S., late 1900s-pres.]

vinegar stroke the final stroke of an act of masturbation, which brings on [off] ejaculation, as compared to shaking a shot of vinegar from a bottle of vinegar. [British, late 1900s-pres.]

vipe to crave a marijuana cigarette. [U.S. underworld, early 1900s, Deak]

viper 1. a dealer in marijuana. [U.S.

drug culture, 1900s] 2. a marijuana smoker, especially one who has been at it for some years. [U.S. drug culture, early 1900s]

viper's weed marijuana. [U.S. drug culture, mid 1900s-pres.]

virgin queen a homosexual male who will not engage in coition until after MARRIAGE (sense 2). Based on the well-known nickname for Queen Elizabeth I. [U.S. homosexual use, 1900s, Farrell]

virgin-treasure the female genitals. For synonyms see MONOSYLLABLE. (British slang, early 1600s]

virile 1. masculine, said of men or women. 2. pertaining to the male sex. [both since the late 1400s]

virile member the penis; the erect penis. [translation of the Latin *membrum virile*; since the 1700s]

virilia the external male genitals, the penis and the scrotum containing the testicles. [Latin; medical] Synonyms: ADAM'S ARSENAL, AFFAIR, AFFAIRS, APPARATUS, BAG OF TRICKS, BALLS AND BAT, BASKET, BAT AND BALLS, BOX, BUSINESS, CODPIECE, CONCERN, COOKIES, CREDENTIALS, CROTCH, CROWN JEWELS, DINGBATS, DOHICKIES, DOJIGGERS, EQUIPMENT, FAMILY JEWELS, FANCY PARTS, FANCY-WORK, GEAR, HAIRY WHEEL, JEWELRY, KIT, LADYWARE, LOINS, LOT, LUGGAGE, MANLINESS, MATCH, MATE, MEAT AND TWO VEGETABLES, NATURA, NATURALIA, NECESSARIES, NETHERLANDS, OUTFIT, PACKET, PENCIL AND TASSEL, POPERINE PEAR, PRACK, PRIDES, PRIVATE PARTS, PRIVATE PROPERTY, PRIVATES, PRIVITIES, RULE-OF-THREE, SHAPE, STICK AND BANGERS, TACKLE, THREE-PIECE SUIT, TOODLES, TOOLS, VITALS, WARE, WATCH-AND-SEALS, WEDDING-KIT, WEDDING TACKLE, WORKS.

virtue 1. female chastity. [since the late 1500s] 2. jocular for "vice," *i.e.*, drinking and womanizing. [British slang, 1800s, Farmer and Henley]

viscera the intestines or inner organs. Used euphemistically for "guts." [since the mid 1600s] Synonyms: ALIMENTARY CANAL, ARSE-ROPES, BOWEL,

CHITTERLINGS, GUT, INNARDS, INSIDES, INTESTINAL FORTITUDE, INWARDS, PUDDING, TRANKLEMENTS, TRIPES, TROLLYBAGS.

visit from Flo a menstrual period. See AUNT FLO. For synonyms see FLOODS. [U.S. euphemism, late 1900s]

visitors (also **visitor**) the menses. [U.S. slang, early 1900s or before, Monteleone]

visit the sand-box to retire to urinate. With reference to a box of sand used for elimination by a cat. *Cf.* SAND-BOX. [jocular euphemism, 1900s]

vitals the genitals of both sexes; the male genitals; the testicles. [euphemistic, 1900s]

vital zone the male pubic area; the groin. [1900s]

vivor a survivor; a street person who manages to survive. [U.S., late 1900s-pres.]

volume Valium™, a muscle relaxant. [U.S. drug culture, late 1900s]

vomatose very sick, especially from drinking; vomiting and comatose. [U.S. collegiate, late 1900s, Eble]

vomick 1. to vomit. **2.** VOMITUS (*q.v.*). [U.S. dialect, 1900s or before]

vomit 1. to eject or release the contents of the stomach through the mouth. [since the 1300s] **2.** the contents of the stomach when brought up. See list at YORK.

vomitive (also **vomitory**) **1.** pertaining to VOMIT (sense 2) or the act of vomiting. **2.** an emetic; an agent causing vomiting. [both since the late 1500s]

vomitus the contents of the stomach when brought up; VOMIT (sense 2).

vomity nasty; rude and unpleasant. [U.S. slang, late 1900s]

vonce marijuana. For synonyms see MARI. [U.S. drug culture, mid 1900s-pres.]

vons capsules of Darvon™, a painkiller. [U.S. drug culture, late 1900s, Kaiser]

voos the breasts. [U.S. slang, 1900s, Wentworth and Flexner]

V.T.P. "voluntary termination of pregnancy," an abortion; a therapeutic abortion. [U.S. euphemism, 1970-1980]

vulcanized intoxicated. For synonyms see WOOFLED. [U.S. slang, early 1900s]

W

wacker crazy. For synonyms see DAFT. [Australian, late 1900s-pres.]

wacky tabbacky marijuana. [U.S. drug culture and slang, mid 1900s-pres.]

wacky weed marijuana. *Cf.* WEED (sense 1). [U.S. drug culture and slang, mid 1900s-pres.]

wad 1. accumulated semen, as in SHOOT ONE'S WAD (*q.v.*). [U.S. slang, 1900s] **2.** an unpopular or disliked person. [U.S., 1900s] See also BUM WAD.

waddy contemptible; undesirable. From WAD (sense 2). *Cf.* BUM WAD. [U.S. slang, 1900s]

waffle to talk nonsense. [Australian, late 1900s-pres.]

waffles an idle loafer; a good-for-nothing. [British slang, 1800s, Farmer and Henley]

wag 1. a buffoon; a jester; a joker. [slang since the late 1500s] **2.** the penis, especially that of a child. Also **wiggle.** [U.S., 1900s]

wagon, on the abstaining totally from alcohol. [U.S., 1900s and before]

waiter a male who waits in a public restroom for another male who has agreed to come there and perform a homosexual act. An extension of the TEAROOM (*q.v.*) theme. [U.S., 1900s]

wake-up an amphetamine tablet. Usually plural. *Cf.* EYE-OPENER. For synonyms see AMP. [U.S. drug culture, mid 1900s-pres.]

walking dandruff lice. [U.S., 1900s or before] Synonyms both singular and plural: ACTIVE CITIZEN, BOSOM CHUMS, BOSOM FRIEND, CHATTS, CHUM, COOTIES, CRABS, CREEPERS, FAMILIARS, GENTLEMAN'S COMPANION, LIGHT TROOPS, PANTS RABBITS. SCOTCH GREYS, SCOTCHMEN, SEAM-SQUIRREL.

walking hard-on a male who is very

much sexually aroused or sexually frustrated. [U.S. slang, late 1900s]

walking on rocky socks drunk. For synonyms see WOOFLED. [U.S. slang, late 1900s]

walk-up a brothel. [U.S., 1900s]

wall, off the pertaining to a strange or improbable person or situation. [U.S. slang, mid 1900s-pres.]

wall-eyed intoxicated with alcohol. [U.S. slang, 1900s]

walliyo a derogatory term for an Italian. For synonyms see SKY. [U.S., 1900s]

wallopies large breasts, not necessarily shapely ones. [U.S. slang, mid 1900s-pres.]

wallow to copulate. [U.S. slang, 1900s]

wamba money. [British, late 1900s-pres.]

wammers the female breasts. The same as WHAMMERS. For synonyms see BOSOM. [British and U.S.]

wana marijuana. For synonyms see MARI. [U.S. black drug culture, late 1900s]

wand the penis, especially in MAGIC WAND (*q.v.*). [attested as British slang, 1800s, Farmer and Henley]

wand-waver an exhibitionist; a FLASHER. [U.S. slang, late 1900s]

wang the penis. See WHANG, WONG. For synonyms see YARD.

wang(er) the penis. For synonyms see YARD. [British and U.S., mid 1900s-pres.]

wank 1. a simpleton; an oaf. [British colloquial] **2.** to coit a woman. **3.** to masturbate. *Cf.* LEVY AND FRANK, WHANK OFF. [British slang, 1900s]

wanker 1. a serious problem; a great annoyance. **2.** a masturbator. [both senses, U.S., late 1900s]

wankered drunk. For synonyms see WOOFLED. [British and U.S., late 1900s-pres.]

wank mag a pornographic magazine used as an aid in masturbation. [British, late 1900s-pres.]

wank off masturbate. See WHANK OFF. For synonyms see WASTE TIME.

wankstain a worthless and disliked person. For synonyms see SNOKEHORN. [British, late 1900s-pres.]

wank trade the pornography industry. [British, late 1900s-pres.]

wannabe raped look wearing slovenly, holey clothing. Said of a woman who seems to be inviting rape or molestation. See JUST-RAPED LOOK. [U.S. collegiate, late 1900s, Munro]

wapsed down intoxicated with alcohol. For synonyms see WOOFLED. [U.S. slang, 1900s]

warden a wife. [U.S. slang, 1900s] Synonyms: BALL AND CHAIN, BEST PIECE, BETTER HALF, BIT OF TRIPE, BITTER HALF, BRIDE, CARVING-KNIFE, CHEESE AND KISSES, COWS AND KISSES, DRUM AND FIFE, DUCHESS OF FIFE, FORK AND KNIFE, JOY OF MY LIFE, LAWFUL BLANKET, LAWFUL JAM, MARE, O.L., OLD LADY, O.W., PLATES AND DISHES, POKER-BREAKER, SQUAW, STRUGGLE AND STRIFE, TROUBLE AND STRIFE, WAR AND STRIFE, WEDDED-WENCH, WORRY AND STRIFE.

wardrobe 1. a privy. See GARDEROBE. [1300s (Chaucer)] **2.** a bathroom. [vague and euphemistic]

ware 1. a general term for male and female genitals. [1400s-1900s] **2.** the female genitals. [British slang, 1800s] **3.** the male genitals; the VIRILIA (*q.v.*). Cf. LADY-WARE, STANDING-WARE. [British slang, 1700s] **4.** the breasts or other sexual characterics. Also **wares.** [British, 1700s]

warm bit (also **warm-baby**) a sexually attractive and COMING (*q.v.*) woman. Ware has "vigorous woman," which may be euphemistic. [British and U.S., 1800s-1900s]

warm member 1. a prostitute. [British slang, 1800s] **2.** a lecher or whore-

monger. [British slang, 1800s] **3.** a wanton man or woman. [British, 1800s]

war paint makeup; facial cosmetics. [U.S., early 1900s-pres.]

wash one's hands to retire to the bathroom; to eliminate waste. [widespread colloquial euphemism]

washroom a W.C.; a bathroom; a place to wash one's hands. For synonyms see W.C. [U.S. euphemism, 1800s or before]

wash up (also **wash**) to wash one's hands; to eliminate. Cf. WASHROOM. [British and U.S.]

WASP "white Anglo-Saxon Protestant," a stereotype of the white, middle-class, conservative bigot. Usually derogatory. [U.S., mid 1900s-pres.]

wasp a prostitute with venereal disease, especially gonorrhea, *i.e.*, a prostitute with a sting in her tail. [British slang, 1800s]

wass to urinate. For synonyms see WHIZ. [British, mid 1900s-pres.]

wassailer a heavy drinker or a drunkard. For synonyms see ALCHY. [since the early 1600s]

waste 1. products of elimination; urine and feces. **2.** to kill. [U.S. slang, mid 1900s-pres.]

wasted 1. dead. **2.** intoxicated with alcohol. [both senses, U.S. slang, mid 1900s-pres.] **3.** intoxicated with marijuana. [U.S. drug culture, mid 1900s-pres.]

waste-pipe the female genitals. For synonyms see MONOSYLLABLE. [British slang, 1800s, Farmer and Henley]

waste time to masturbate. [euphemistic, 1900s] These synonyms and related terms refer to males unless indicated otherwise: ABUSE, ABUSE ONESELF, ARM THE CANNON, AUDITION THE FINGER PUPPETS, AUTOBATE, BALL OFF, BANANAS AND CREAM, BARCLAY, BAT, BEAT OFF, BEAT ONE'S HOG, BEAT ONE'S MONGREL, BEAT THE BISHOP, BEAT THE DUMMY, BEAT THE MEAT, BEAT THE PUP, BELT ONE'S HOG, BISHOP-BEATING, BLANKET DRILL, BLOOCH, BOB, BOFF, BOP, BOP ONE'S BALONEY, BOP THE BOLOGNA, BOX THE JESUIT, BOX THE JESUIT AND

GET COCKROACHES, BRANDLE, BRING DOWN BY HAND, BRUSH THE BEAVER, BUFF THE HELMET, BURP ONE'S BABY, BURP ONE'S WORM, CHECK ONE'S OIL, CHICKEN-MILKING, CHOKE THE CHICKEN, CHUFF, COAX THE COJONES, COME ONE'S MUTTON, COME ONE'S TURKEY, CROTCH PONG, CUFF ONE'S GOVERNOR, DIDDLE, DO-IT-YOURSELF, DONG-FLOGGING, EAT COCKROACHES, EXPRESS A SECRET VICE, FAIRE ZAGUE-ZAGUE, FETCH METTLE, FIGHT ONE'S TURKEY, FIST-FUCK, FIVE AGAINST ONE, FIVE KNUCKLE SHUFFLE, FLOG, FLOG ONE'S DONG, FLOG ONE'S DONKEY, FLOG ONE'S LOG, FLOG ONE'S MEAT, FLOG ONE'S SAUSAGE, FLOG THE BISHOP, FLOG THE DUMMY, FLOG THE LOG, FLONG ONE'S DONG, FLUFF ONE'S DUFF, FONDLE ONE'S FIG, FRIG, FRIGGLE, FRIG ONESELF, FUCK MARY FIST, FUCK OFF, FUCK ONE'S FIST, GALLOP ONE'S ANTELOPE, GALLOP ONE'S MAGGOT, GET A HOLD OF ONESELF, GET COCKROACHES, GET ONE'S NUTS OFF, GHERKIN-JERKING, GRIND, GRIP, HAND-JIVE, HAND-JOB, HANDLE, HAND SHANDY, HOT-ROD, JACKAL, JACK OFF, JAG OFF, J. ARTHUR (Rank), JAZZ ONESELF, JERK OFF, JERK ONE'S GHERKIN, JERK ONE'S MUTTON, JERK THE TURKEY, JILL OFF, JODRELL (Bank), KEEP THE CENSUS DOWN, KNOB, KNUCKLE ONESELF, LARK, LEVY AND FRANK, LIZARD-MILKING, MACK, MANIPULATE ONE'S MANGO, MANIPULATE THE MEMBER, MANUAL EXERCISE, MANUAL POLLUTION, MANUSTUPRATION, MASTURBATE, MEANS OF WEAKNESS AND DEBILITY, MILK THE CHICKEN, MILK THE LIZARD, MOUNT A CORPORAL AND FOUR, MRS. HAND, ONANISM, ONE-LEGGED RACE, PADDLE THE PICKLE, PADDLING THE PINK CANOE, PAW-PAW TRICKS, PICKLE-PADDLING, PLAY OFF, PLAY WITH ONESELF, PLUNK ONE'S TWANGER, POLLUTE, POLLUTION, PORTUGUESE PUMP, POUND OFF, POUND ONE'S POMEGRANATE, POUND ONE'S PUD, POUND THE MEAT, PROD THE PEEPEE, PUD WACKER, PULL ABOUT, PULL ONSELF OFF, PULL ONE'S PUD, PULL ONE'S PUDDING, PULL ONE'S WIRE, PULL THE PIN, PUMP, PUMP ONESELF OFF, PUMP ONE'S PICKLE, PUMP ONE'S PYTHON, REACH AROUND, RUB-OFF, RUB UP, SCREW OFF, SECRET VICE, SELF-ABUSE, SELF-POLLUTION, SEW, SHAG, SHAG ONESELF, SHAKE, SHAKE UP, SHAKING HANDS WITH THE GOVERNOR, SHE-BOP, SHOWER SPANK, SIMPLE INFANTICIDE, SLAP THE SALAMI, SLING ONE'S JELLY, SLING ONE'S JUICE, SNAP THE RUBBER, SNAP THE WHIP, SOLDIER'S JOY, SOLITARY SIN, SPANK, SPANK THE MONKEY, SQUEEZE THE LEMON, STROKE, STROKE THE LIZARD, TAKE ONESELF IN HAND, TICKLE ONE'S CRACK (female), TICKLE ONE'S PICKLE, TICKLE THE TACK, TITTY FUCK, TOSS OFF, TOUCH-UP, TWANG ONE'S WIRE, WANK OFF, WAX THE DOLPHIN, WHACK OFF, WHACK THE BISHOP, WHANG OFF, WHANK OFF, WHIP OFF, WHIP ONE'S WIRE, WHIP THE DUMMY, WORK OFF, YANK, YANK ONE'S STRAP, YANK ONE'S YAM.

watch-and-seals the penis and testicles. Gentlemen would often attach to their watch fobs objects used to seal letters. *Cf.* DUMB WATCH, SEALS. [British, 1800s, Farmer and Henley]

watchqueen. 1. a peeper; a voyeur. *Cf.* PEEK-FREAK, PEER-QUEER. The nickname for a lookout in a public restroom where homosexual activities are performed. See TEAROOM. [both senses, U.S. homosexual use, mid 1900s]

water buffalo to vomit; to vomit a lot. See comments at YAK. To WATER BUFFALO is worse [bigger] than to YAK. For synonyms see YORK. [U.S. collegiate, late 1900s, Munro]

water-logged intoxicated with alcohol; absolutely saturated. For synonyms see WOOFLED. [British and U.S. slang, early 1900s-pres.]

watermelons the human breasts, especially if large. *Cf.* HONEYDEW MELONS, MELONS. [U.S. slang, 1900s]

water-mill the female genitals. See WATER-BOX for similar terms. [British slang, 1800s]

water of life gin. For synonyms see RUIN. [British slang, early 1800s]

water one's pony (also **water one's nag**) to urinate; to retire to urinate. A variant of WATER THE HORSES (*q.v.*). For synonyms see RETIRE. [British slang, 1800s]

water-pipe 1. a pipe used for smoking marijuana, hashish, or opium. [U.S. drug culture, mid 1900s] **2.** the male or female urethra. *Cf.* WATER-BOX. [U.S. slang, 1900s or before]

waterspout the penis, especially if flaccid. *Cf.* SPOUT. [widespread slang, 1900s or before]

water tank the bladder. [U.S. colloquial, 1900s or before]

water the dragon for a male to urinate; the same as DRAIN THE DRAGON (*q.v.*). *Cf.* WATER THE HORSES. [slang, 1700s-1900s]

water the horses for a male to retire to urinate. An excuse for leaving the room. For synonyms see RETIRE. [widespread slang since the 1800s]

water the plants to urinate in the open. For synonyms see WHIZ. [U.S., late 1900s-pres.]

waterworks 1. the male or female urinary organs. *Cf.* PLUMBING, WATER-BOX. [British slang, 1800s, Farmer and Henley] **2.** the eyes when used for crying. No negative connotations.

wax to copulate. For synonyms see OC-CUPY. [U.S., late 1900s-pres.]

waxed alcohol intoxicated, See also POLISHED (UP). For synonyms see WOOFLED. [U.S., late 1900s-pres.]

wax the dolphin to masturbate. For synonyms see WASTE TIME. [British, late 1900s-pres.]

wax the knob to copulate. For synonyms see OCCUPY. [U.S., late 1900s-pres.]

way, on the pregnant. For synonyms see FRAGRANT. [since the 1600s or before]

wazoo 1. the penis; the anus or any unnamed area which can be tantalizingly hinted about. *Cf.* BAZOO. [U.S. slang, 1900s] **2.** the mouth. No negative connotations.

wazz to urinate. For synonyms see WHIZ. [British, late 1900s-pres.]

wazzocked drunk. For synonyms see WOOFLED. [British slang, late 1900s, J. Green]

W.C. a "water closet," a bathroom or toilet [originally British; colloquial,

mid 1800s-pres.] Synonyms: ALTAR, ALTAR ROOM, BATH, BIF, BIFFY, BOG, CABINET D'AISANCE, CARSEY, CASA, CASE, CHAMBER OF COMMERCE, CLOAK-ROOM, CLOSET OF DECENCY, CLOSET OF EASE, CLOSET STOOL, COLFABIAS, COM-FORT ROOM, COMFORT STATION, CONVE-NIENCE, CRYSTAL, CUZ, DOMUS, DUBBY, EGYPT, GAB ROOM, GENTLEMEN'S ROOM, GENTLEMEN'S WALK, GROWLER, GULF, GUTTER-ALLEY, GUTTER-LANE, HEAD, HOLY OF HOLIES, HOUSE OF LORDS, INDOOR PLUMBING, JAKE, JAKE-HOUSE, JAKES, JANE, JIM, JOE, JOHN, JOHN-NIE, LADIES', LADIES' ROOM, LADIES' WALK, LAST RESORT, LAT, LAV, LAVA-TORY, LAVO, LAVVY, LAVY, LEAKERY, LIBRARY, LITTLE BOY'S ROOM, LITTLE GIRL'S ROOM, LOB, LOCUS, LOO, LULU, MARBLE PALACE, MAY, MEN'S JOHN, MEN'S ROOM, MINOR, MRS. JONES, MRS. JONES'S PLACE, MRS. MURPHY, NECES-SARY CHAMBER, OLD SOLDIER'S HOME, PISSER, PISSHOUSE, PISSING-POST, PLACE, PLUMBING, POET'S CORNER, POT, POTTY, POWDER ROOM, PRIVATE OFFICE, PUB-LIC COMFORT STATION, PUBLIC CONVE-NIENCE, PUKE HOLE, RECEIVING-SET, RESTROOM, RETIRING ROOM, ROUND HOUSE, RUTH, SAND-BOX, SHITCAN, SHIT-TER, SHOT TOWER, SMALLEST ROOM, STATE HOUSE, TEAROOM, TELEPHONE, TEMPLE, THE EXCUSE ME, THE GENT'S, THE GENT'S ROOM, THRONE, THUNDER-BOWL, THUNDER-BOX, TOOT, TRIZZER, TWILIGHT, USED-BEER DEPARTMENT, W., WASHROOM, WATER CLOSET, WEST-CENTRAL, WHERE THE QUEEN GOES ON FOOT, WHIZ-STAND, WIDOW JONES, WIZ-ZER, X.

weaker-vessel a woman; females in general. [from *Love's Labour's Lost* (Shakespeare)]

weak-jointed intoxicated with alcohol. *Cf.* TANGLEFOOTED. [U.S., 1900s]

weak sister 1. a weakling or a coward. **2.** an effeminate male, possibly a homosexual male. [both senses, U.S., 1900s or before]

weapon the penis. *Cf.* CLUB. (sense 1). GUN. [widespread nonce; since c. 1000, *Oxford English Dictionary*]

wearing a smile (also **wearing nothing but a smile**) to be completely naked. Refers to both sexes. May be from the UPRIGHT GRIN (*q.v.*). [U.S. slang, 1900s]

wearing beer goggles not able to see or perceive things well owing to having drunk too much beer. For synonyms see WOOFLED. [U.S., late 1900s-pres.]

wedding-kit the male genitals. [British military, early 1900s, *Dictionary of Slang and Unconventional English*]

wedding tackle the male genitals. See FAMILY JEWELS. For synonyms see GENITALS, VIRILIA. [Australian and British, mid 1900s-pres.]

wedge 1. the penis. For synonyms see YARD [slang since the 1800s] **2.** back-slang for "Jew." Usually considered derogatory. [British slang, 1800s] See also WEDGES.

wedged-up pregnant. *Cf.* WEDGE (sense 1). For synonyms see FRAGRANT. [British slang, 1800s, Farmer and Henley]

wedges (also **wedgies**) the drug L.S.D. (*q.v.*). *Cf.* CUBE (sense 2). [U.S. drug culture, mid 1900s-pres.]

weed 1. marijuana or a marijuana cigarette. From a term for tobacco. [U.S. slang and drug culture, 1900s] **2.** the drug P.C.P. (*q.v.*). sold as T.H.C. See T.H.C. [U.S. drug culture, mid 1900s-pres.]

weed monkey a cheap and lewd prostitute. See MONKEY (sense 1), the female genitals. [U.S. slang, 1900s]

weed tea marijuana. Sometimes in reference to a tea brewed from marijuana. [U.S. drug culture, 1900s]

weekend ho a "weekend whore," a part-time prostitute who usually only works on weekends or during conventions. [U.S. black use, mid 1900s-pres.]

weekend warrior 1. a "weekend" or occasional prostitute; a WEEKEND HO (*q.v.*). From the nickname for members of the U.S. military reserves. [U.S., mid 1900s-pres.] **2.** a person who uses drugs only occasionally or on weekends. [U.S. drug culture, late 1900s]

weenie 1. the penis, particularly if small or that of a child. *Cf.* PEENIE. [U.S. slang, 1900s] **2.** a jerk or an oaf. From sense 1. [U.S. slang, 1900s]

weenie-wagger a male exhibitionist. *Cf.* FLASHER, WEENIE. [U.S. slang, late 1900s]

wee-wee 1. to urinate. *Cf.* PEE-WEE (sense 3). **2.** urine. [both senses, juvenile euphemism; British and U.S., 1800s-pres.]

weiner a jerk or an oaf. *Cf.* WEENIE (sense 2). [U.S. slang, mid 1900s-pres.]

weird pertaining to a homosexual male. [U.S. slang, 1900s]

weirdo (also **weirdy**) **1.** any unpleasant person, usually male; an oaf or jerk. [U.S. slang, mid 1900s] **2.** a homosexual male. See WEIRD. [both senses, U.S. slang, mid 1900s-pres.]

well-built 1. pertaining to a well-proportioned woman or a well-proportioned and well-muscled man. [colloquial, 1800s-pres.] **2.** euphemistic for "having large male genitals." *Cf.* MENTULATE. [British and U.S., 1800s-pres.]

well-developed 1. pertaining to a woman with qualities such as large, well-proportioned breasts and prominent hips and buttocks; pertaining to a woman who has reached sexual maturity. **2.** pertaining to a man with fully developed or large genitals, slim hips, broad shoulders, and a muscular body. **3.** pertaining to primary sexual characteristics.

well-endowed 1. pertaining to a woman with large or very large breasts or any other significantly large primary or secondary sexual characteristic. **2.** pertaining to a man with large or very large genitals or some other significant sexual characteristic. [both senses, British and U.S., 1900s or before]

well-favored by nature 1. having large male genitals, said of a man. **2.** having large breasts, said of a woman. [both senses, British euphemism, late 1800s (Farmer)]

well-hung pertaining to a man with large or very large genitals. *Cf.* MENTULATE. [colloquial since the early 1800s] See also HUNG.

wellie a condom. From *Wellington boot.* For synonyms see EEL-SKIN. [British, late 1900s-pres.]

well-oiled intoxicated with alcohol. See OILED. [British and U.S. military, early 1900s-pres.]

well-sprung intoxicated with alcohol. For synonyms see WOOFLED. [British and U.S. slang, 1900s]

well-stacked [of a woman] well built. [mid 1900s-pres.]

well-under intoxicated with alcohol. *Cf.* UNDER (sense 3). [Australian, 1900s]

(well-)upholstered fat; chubby; plump. [U.S., mid 1900s-pres.]

welly a condom. From *Wellington boot.* See WILLIE-WELLIE. For synonyms see EEL-SKIN. [British, late 1900s-pres.]

wenchy pertaining to a cruel or mean woman. [U.S. collegiate, late 1900s]

Wesson party a form of sexual contact where the participants cover their bodies with liquid cooking oil and then perform various sexual activities; the same as MAZOLA PARTY (*q.v.*). From the trademarked brand name of a cooking oil. See GROUP SEX for related subjects. [U.S. slang, mid 1900s-pres.]

West Coast turnarounds amphetamines; the same as L.A. TURNABOUTS (*q.v.*). [U.S. drug culture, 1900s]

wet 1. intoxicated with alcohol. [slang since the early 1700s] **2.** pertaining to a woman who is sufficiently sexually aroused to produce vaginal lubrication. *Cf.* DRIPPING FOR IT, JUICY (sense 1), SLICK-CHICK. [since the 1700s] **3.** to urinate, especially in "wet one's pants," as said of a child. *Cf.* MAKE WATER. [U.S. slang, 1900s or before] **4.** a fool; an oaf, as in WET NOODLE (*q.v.*) or "wet behind the ears." [Australian, Baker] **5.** backward, dull, and stupid; nerdy. [U.S. colloquial, late 1900s]

wet dream a nocturnal seminal emission. [British and U.S., 1800s-pres.]

wet duck the same as WET DECK (*q.v.*).

wet-goose an oaf or simpleton. For synonyms see OAF. [British, 1800s, Farmer and Henley]

wet-hand a drunkard. For synonyms see ALCHY. [British slang, late 1800s]

wet one (also **wet fart**) a strong breaking of wind containing fecal matter. [British slang, 1800s]

wet one's pants to urinate in one's pants from fear or other uncontrolled emotional situations. [colloquial, 1900s or before]

wet one's wick (also **wet one's end**) to copulate, from the male point of view. *Cf.* DIP ONE'S WICK, WICK, [U.S. slang, 1900s]

wet stuff sex or violence in a movie. [U.S., late 1900s-pres.]

wet-subject a drunkard. The opposite of a dry or dull subject. [British and U.S. slang, 1800s-1900s]

wet-'un 1. coition; an act of coition. **2.** a drunkard. See also WET ONE. This entry is eye-dialect and could be spelled "wet-one" just as well [both senses, British slang, 1800s, Farmer and Henley]

whack 1. to cut or dilute a drug such as heroin or cocaine. [U.S. drug culture, mid 1900s-pres.] **2.** a JERK; a male who does nothing but masturbate. For synonyms see OAF. [U.S. collegiate, late 1900s, Munro]

whacker 1. the penis. *Cf.* BUSH-WHACKER (sense 2). **2.** a gadget. [both senses, U.S., 1900s]

whack it up to copulate. For synonyms see OCCUPY. [British slang, 1800s]

whack off (also **wack off**) to masturbate, said of a male. *Cf.* WHANK OFF. For synonyms see WASTE TIME. [U.S. slang, 1900s]

whack the bishop to masturbate. Said of the male. *Cf.* BEAT THE BISHOP. For synonyms and related subjects see WASTE TIME. [U.S. slang, late 1900s]

wham-bam-thank-you-ma'am a catch phrase used in reference to real or imagined extremely rapid copulation. *Cf.* BIP-BAM-THANK-YOU-MA'AM. [U.S. slang, late 1800s-pres.]

whamdanglers the breasts. For synonyms see BOSOM. [late 1900s]

whammer a female drug smuggler who transports containers of drugs (typically cocaine) in her vagina. [U.S. drug culture, late 1900s]

whammers the female breasts. The same as WAMMERS. For synonyms see BOSOM. [Britishand U.S., late 1900s-pres.]

whang (also **wang**) 1. the penis. Also **whangbone**. [British and U.S., 1900s] 2. an oaf; a contemptible person. [U.S. slang, 1900s]

whanger the penis. For synonyms see YARD. [slang, 1900s]

whank off (also **wank, wank off, whang off, whank**) to masturbate, said of a male. *Cf.* WHACK OFF. [primarily British slang, 1800s-pres.]

whank-pit a bed; the place where a male "whanker" masturbates. See WHANK OFF.

what 1. the penis. For synonyms see YARD. 2. the female genitals in expressions such as "What's-her-name?", "What's-its-name?", "The Lord-knows-what." [both senses, British euphemisms, 1800-pres.]

what Eve did with Adam copulation. *Cf.* ADAM-AND-EVE IT. [British euphemism, 1800s]

What (in) the fucking hell! an angry and surprised elaboration of *"What?"* [U.S., mid 1900s-pres.]

what mother did before me copulation. [British euphemism, 1800s]

what-nosed intoxicated with alcohol. For synonyms see WOOFLED. [British and U.S. slang, 1800s]

whazzod (also **waa-zooed**) intoxicated with alcohol. From a slang term meaning "beat" or "worn down." [U.S. slang, mid 1900s-pres.] See also WAZOO.

wheat marijuana. For synonyms see MARI. [U.S. drug culture, mid 1900s-pres.]

wheeze to vomit. Partly onomatopoetic. For synonyms see YORK. [U.S. collegiate, late 1900s, Eble]

whennymegs the testicles. From a colloquial term for "trinkets." [British dialect, 1800s or before]

where the queen goes on foot the W.C.; the bathroom. [British euphemism, 1800s]

where the sun don't shine the anus. Often with *put it . . . . shove it . . . ,* etc. Part of the answer to the question "Where shall I put it?" For synonyms see ANUS. [U.S. slang, mid 1900s-pres.]

where uncle's doodle goes the vagina; the female genitals in general. *Cf.* DOODLE (sense 3). [British slang, 1800s, Farmer and Henley]

Whickerbill 1. a worthless oaf or bumpkin. [U.S. slang, 1900s or before, Berrey and Van den Bark] 2. the foreskin of the penis. [U.S. dialect (Ozarks), Randolph and Wilson]

whiffenpopper an ampule of amyl nitrite. [U.S. drug culture, late 1900s, Lewin and Lewin] See also POPPER.

whiffer 1. the nose. [U.S. slang, 1900s] 2. a bad-smelling breaking of wind. *Cf.* BURNT CHEESE, S.B.D. [U.S. slang, 1900s]

whiffled intoxicated with alcohol. [British slang, early 1900s]

whiffles a relaxation of the scrotum. [British slang, late 1700s]

whim-wham (also **whim**) the female genitals. [British slang, early 1700s]

whin-bush the female pubic hair. [British slang, 1800s, Farmer and Henley]

whingding 1. a drunken spree; any wild time. [U.S., 1900s or before] 2. a gadget. [U.S. colloquial, 1900s]

whip the penis. For synonyms see YARD. [slang, mid 1900s]

Whip it to me! 1. catch phrase encouraging the continuation of sexual advances or performance. 2. a proposition for sexual intercourse. *Cf.* SOCK IT TO ME! [both senses, U.S. slang, mid 1900s-pres.]

whip off to masturbate. For synonyms see WASTE TIME. [U.S. slang, mid 1900s-pres.]

whip one's wire to masturbate. *Cf.* PULL ONE'S WIRE, YANK ONE'S STRAP. [U.S. slang, 1900s]

whipped intoxicated with alcohol. For synonyms see WOOFLED. [U.S. slang, 1800s]

whipped cream semen. *Cf.* CREAM. For synonyms see METTLE. [U.S. slang, late 1900s if not recurrent nonce]

whippets nitrous oxide (for inhalation purposes) dispensed from a pressurized can of whipped cream. [U.S. drug culture, late 1900s, Abel]

whipsey intoxicated with alcohol. [U.S. slang, 1900s]

whip the cat to vomit; the same as JERK THE CAT, SHOOT THE CAT (both *q.v.*). [British slang, 1600s]

whip the dummy to masturbate. *Cf.* DUMMY. [slang, 1900s]

whirlygigs the human testes. [British slang, 1600s-1700s] Synonyms: ACHERS, ACRES, AGOTS, ALLS-BAY, APPLES, APRICOTS, BALLICKS, BALLOCKS, BALLOCKSTONES, BALLS, BANGERS, BAUBLES, BEECHAM'S PILLS, BERRIES, BIRD'S-EGGS, BOBBLES, BOOBOOS, BULLETS, BUM-BALLS, BUTTONS, CALLIBISTERS, CANNON BALLS, CHARLIES, CHESTNUTS, CHONES, CHOOMS, CLANGERS, CLAPPERS, CLOCK-WEIGHTS, CLUSTER, COBBLER'S, COBBLER'S AWLS, COBBLER'S STALLS, COBS, CODS, COFFEE STALLS, CO-JONES, CRYSTAL, CUBES, CULLION, CULLS, DANGLERS, DIAMONDS, DODAD, DOHICKY, DUSTERS, FAMILY JEWELS, FLOWERS AND FROLICS, FRICK AND FRACK, FUN AND FROLICS, FUTURE, GIN-GAMBOLS, GLANDS, GONADS, GOOLIES, GOOSEBERRIES, GROIN, HUEVOS, JENNY HILLS, JEWELS, JIGGUMBOBS, JINGLE-BERRIES, KANAKAS, KELKS, KNACKERS, KNOCKERS, LES ACCESSORIES, LOVE-APPLES, MALE-MULES, MAN-BALLS, MARBLES, MARSHMALLOWS, MOUNTAIN OYSTERS, NACKERS, NADS, NAGS, NARDS, NERTS, NIAGARA FALLS, NICKNACKS, NUGGETS, NUTMEGS, NUTS, ORCHESTRA STALLS, ORKS, OYSTER, PEBBLES, PLUMS, POUNDERS, ROCKS, ROLLIES, ROLLOCKS, SEALS, SEEDS, SEX GLANDS, SLASHERS, SPUNK-HOLDERS, STONES, SWEETS, SWINGERS, TALLYWAGS, TARRIWAYS, TESTICLES, TESTICULUS, TESTIMONIALS, THINGUM-BOBS, THINGUMMY, TOMMY ROLLOCKS, TWIDDLE-DIDDLES, TWINS, VITALS, WHENNYMEGS.

whisker biscuit the vulva. For synonyms see MONOSYLLABLE. [U.S., late 1900s-pres.]

whisky dick 1. an impotent penis due to too much alcohol. For synonyms see GENITALS, YARD. **2.** a male too drunk to get an erection of the penis. [both senses, U.S. collegiate, late 1900s]

whiskyfied intoxicated with alcohol. [U.S. slang, mid 1800s-pres.]

whisky-frisky intoxicated with alcohol. From an older term meaning "flighty." [U.S. slang, early 1900s]

whistle the penis, especially that of a child. Essentially a small FLUTE (sense 1). [British colloquial, 1800s, *Dictionary of Slang and Unconventional English*]

whistle-berries beans. *Cf.* ARS MUSICA, MUSICAL FRUIT. [U.S. slang, 1900s or before]

whistling in the dark performing CUNNILINGUS. [British slang, 1900s, McDonald]

white 1. gin or any alcoholic beverage. *Cf.* WHITE MULE. [U.S. drug culture, 1900s] **2.** one of the powerful powdered narcotics, heroin or cocaine. [U.S. drug culture 1900s] **3.** a Caucasian.

white-boy butt the cleavage at the top of the buttocks appearing when a man bends over and his pants scoot down. [U.S., late 1900s-pres.]

white-boy crack the cleavage at the top of the buttocks appearing when a man bends over and pants scoot down. [U.S., late 1900s-pres.]

white coffee illicit (bootleg) alcohol. [U.S. underworld, early 1900s]

white cross 1. cocaine. *Cf.* RED CROSS. (U.S. slang, 1900s] **2.** an amphetamine tablet. *Cf.* CARTWHEEL. [U.S. drug culture, mid 1900s-pres.]

white drugs cocaine. *Cf.* WHITE, WHITE STUFF. [U.S. drug culture, mid 1900s-pres.]

white dust the animal tranquilizer, P.C.P. For synonyms see P.C.P. [U.S. drug culture, late 1900s]

white girl cocaine. *Cf.* GIRL (sense 9). [U.S. drug culture, 1900s]

white honey semen. *Cf.* HIVE, HONEY. [British, late 1800s]

white lady cocaine. The "white" is from SNOW (sense 2). *Cf.* LADY SNOW. [U.S. drug culture, 1900s]

white lightning 1. whisky. *Cf.* LIGHTNING (sense 2). [U.S. colloquial, 1900s] **2.** the drug L.S.D. (*q.v.*) or L.S.D. mixed with other drugs, such as Methedrine (trademark). [U.S. drug culture, mid 1900s-pres.] **3.** a substance which produces a shock or a charge: alcohol or amphetamines. See LIGHTNING (sense 1)

white line alcohol. [U.S. slang, 1900s, Berrey and Van den Bark]

white meat 1. a white woman considered sexually by a non-white male. *Cf.* DARK MEAT. **2.** a white woman's genitals. Both are from the term used to describe the breast meat of the domestic chicken. [both are U.S. slang, 1900s]

white nurse morphine or other drugs secretly passed to an inmate of a prison or a hospital. [U.S. underworld, 1900s or before]

whites 1. Benzedrine (trademark) tablets. [U.S. drug culture, mid 1900s-pres.] **2.** amphetamines in general. [U.S. drug culture, mid 1900s-pres.] **3.** LEUKORRHEA (*q.v.*). [British and U.S. colloquial, 1800s-pres.]

white satin (also **satin**) gin. For synonyms see RUIN. [British slang, 1800s or before]

white stuff 1. alcohol, especially illegal whisky. *Cf.* WHITE MULE. [U.S., 1900s] **2.** cocaine. From a nickname for SNOW (sense 2). *Cf.* SNOW STUFF. [U.S. underworld, early 1900s] **3.** various hard drugs. The exact definition varies in time and place: heroin, morphine, and others. *Cf.* BLACK STUFF, SNOW STUFF. [U.S. drug culture, mid 1900s-pres.]

white tape gin. Similar to BLUE RIBBON and BLUE TAPE (both *q.v.*). [British slang, early 1700s-1800s]

white tornado FREE BASE cocaine. For synonyms see FREE BASE. [U.S. drug culture, late 1900s, Abel]

white velvet gin. *Cf.* WHITE SATIN. [U.S. underworld, 1800s]

whitewash 1. to coit a female. *Cf.* LIME. [British slang, 1900s] **2.** liquor. [U.S., 1900s] **3.** to ejaculate. For synonyms see MELT. [U.S. slang, late 1900s]

white whisky PEYOTE. [U.S. drug culture, late 1900s]

whittled intoxicated with alcohol. *Cf.* CUT (sense 2). [British and U.S., late 1500s-1700s]

whiz 1. to urinate. **2.** "urination" in expressions such as "take a whiz." Euphemistic for PISS (sense 2). *Cf.* WHIZ-STAND, WIZZER. [both senses, U.S. slang, mid 1900s-pres.] Synonyms and related terms for both senses: BURN THE GRASS, DICKY-DIDDLE, DO A RURAL, DRAIN, DRAIN ONE'S RADIATOR, DRAIN ONE'S SNAKE, DRAIN THE CRANKCASE, DRAIN THE DRAGON, DRAIN THE LIZARD, DRAIN THE MAIN VEIN, DRAIN THE SPUDS, DRAIN THE SUDS, DRAW OFF, EMICTION, EVACUATE THE BLADDER, GO TO PAY THE WATER BILL, GO TO THE BATHROOM, GYPSY'S (KISS), HAVE A QUICKIE, HAVE A RUN OFF, HAVE A RUN-OUT, HEY-DIDDLE-DIDDLE, HIT AND MISS, JERRY RIDDLE, JIM, JIMMY RIDDLE, KILL A SNAKE, KILL A TREE, LAG, LANT, LEAK, LET FLY, LOOK UPON A HEDGE, MAKE, MAKE A BRANCH, MAKE A PISS STOP, MAKE A PIT STOP, MAKE WATER, MICTURATE, NATURE STOP, NUMBER ONE, PASS URINE, PASS WATER, PEE-WEE, PERFORM THE WORK OF NATURE, PICK A DAISY, PIDDLE, PIE AND MASH, PISS, PISS ON SOMEONE OR SOMETHING, POINT PERCY AT THE PORCELAIN, POTTY, PREEZE, PUMP, PUMP SHIP, RACK OFF, RUN OFF, SAY, SCATTER, SHAKE A SOCK, SHAKE HANDS WITH AN OLD FRIEND, SHAKE HANDS WITH THE BLOKE ONE ENLISTED WITH, SHAKE

HANDS WITH WIFE'S BEST FRIEND, SHAKE THE DEW OFF THE LILY, SHED A TEAR, SHOOT A LION, SLACK, SPLASH, SPLASH ONE'S BOOTS, SPRING A LEAK, SQUEEZE THE LEMON, SQUIRT, STIMBLE, STRAIN ONE'S TATERS, SYPHON OFF, SYPHON THE PYTHON, TAG THE LAWN, TAKE A LEAK, TAKE A PISS, TAKE ONE'S SNAKE FOR A GALLOP, TAP A KIDNEY, TINKLE, TOY-TOY, TRAIN TERRENCE ON THE TERRACOTTA, URINATE, VOID, WASS, WATER ONE'S NAG, WATER ONE'S PONY, WATER THE DRAGON, WATER THE HORSES, WATER THE PLANTS, WAZZ, WEE-WEE, WET, WIDDLE, WRING ONE'S SOCK OUT, WRING THE DEW OFF THE BRANCH, WRING THE RATTLESNAKE, WRITE ONE'S NAME (IN THE SNOW).

whiz-bang a mixture of cocaine and morphine or other drugs. [U.S. drug culture, mid 1900s]

whiz-stand a urinal, usually a male urinal. [U.S. slang, mid 1900s-pres.]

Who cut the dog in half? "Who broke wind?" [Australian, late 1900s-pres.]

whoopee-water champagne or other liquor. [U.S. slang, 1900s] Synonyms: BUBBLE-WATER, BUBBLY, CHAM, FIZZ, SHAMPOO.

whoopsie excrement; a fecal mass. For synonyms see DUNG. [British, mid 1900s-pres.]

whooshed intoxicated with alcohol. [U.S. slang, mid 1900s]

whore 1. a prostitute. [since the 1100s, *Oxford English Dictionary*] **2.** to utilize prostitutes; to consort with harlots. **3.** the queen in chess and playing cards. *Cf.* BITCH (sense 7). **4.** a promiscuous homosexual male. **5.** a term of contempt from one male to another. [1800s-1900s]

whore-bitch a prostitute. For synonyms see HARLOT. [U.S. colloquial dialect, 1900s and before]

whore-hopper a user of prostitutes; a whoremonger. [U.S. slang, 1900s]

whoremaster 1. a user of whores; a whoremonger. [since the 1500s] **2.** a

pimp; a procurer. Possibly in error. [both senses, British, early 1500s-1800s]

wick the penis. Especially in the expressions, BURY ONE'S WICK, DIP ONE'S WICK, WET ONE'S WICK (all *q.v.*). [slang, 1900s]

widdle to urinate, usually said of a child. *Cf.* PIDDLE. [British, 1900s, *Dictionary of Slang and Unconventional English*]

wide on the state of the female genitals, ready for copulation. [U.S., late 1900s-pres.]

wide open alcohol intoxicated. For synonyms see WOOFLED. [U.S. collegiate, late 1900s, Eble]

widget a gadget. Recently, a generic term for a real or imaginary manufactured product. [U.S. colloquial, 1900s]

widow Jones a privy; a W.C. *Cf.* MRS. JONES'S PLACE. [U.S. dialect and slang, 1900s]

wienering copulation. *Cf.* WEENIE. For synonyms see SMOCKAGE. [U.S. slang, late 1900s]

wiener wrap a condom. For synonyms see EEL-SKIN. [U.S., late 1900s-pres.]

wife 1. a mistress or concubine. [slang, 1800s-1900s] **2.** a passive homosexual partner; a CATAMITE or FLUFF (both *q.v.*). [British and U.S. slang, 1800s-1900s] **3.** the more feminine partner in a homosexual marriage.

wigga-wagga the penis. Named for a flexible walking cane (Partridge). [British slang, early 1900s]

wild hair the imaginary cause of impassioned or violent behavior. A truncation of "have a wild hair up one's asshole." [U.S. slang, mid 1900s-pres.]

wild mare's milk rot-gut liquor. [U.S. slang, 1900s, Berrey and Van den Bark]

wild oats 1. excitement and energy in youth. Usually considered to be sexual in the male. **2.** a youth; a male who sows wild oats. [both since the 1500s]

willie-wellie a condom. See WELLIE. From *Wellington boot*. For synonyms see EEL-SKIN. [British, late 1900s-pres.]

willy the penis. For synonyms see YARD. [Australian and British, early 1900s-pres.]

willy warmer an (imaginary) item of clothing designed to keep the penis warm. [British, late 1900s-pres.]

wimble the penis. From a term for an auger. Cf. TOOL (sense 1). [British slang, 1800s]

wimpish weak; inept. [British and U.S., mid 1900s-pres.]

wimpy weak; inept. [British and U.S., mid 1900s-pres.]

wind, in the intoxicated with alcohol. Cf. BOTH SHEETS IN THE WIND. [British slang, 1800s]

winder a breaking of wind. For synonyms see GURK. [U.S. slang, 1900s]

wind-mill the anus. Refers to the breaking of wind. Cf. WATER-MILL. [British slang, early 1800s. *Lexicon Balatronicum*]

window pane the drug L.S.D. (*q.v.*). [U.S. drug culture, mid 1900s-pres.]

wind-pills beans. [British, mid 1900s-pres.]

wind up with one's joint in one's hand to be put in jail with no sexual outlet but masturbation. Cf. JOINT (sense 1). [U.S. underworld, early 1900s, Goldin, O'Leary, and Lipsius]

windward passage the anus with reference to the breaking of wind. "To navigate the windward passage" is to commit PEDERASTY (*q.v.*). [British slang, late 1700s, Grose]

windy-puffs flatulence. For synonyms see GURK. [British colloquial, 1900s or before]

wineache a hangover from wine; severe intestinal pain resulting from overindulging in wine, especially cheap wine. [U.S., 1900s]

wine-bag a drunkard. For synonyms see ALCHY. [British slang, 1800s, Farmer and Henley]

wine jockey a WINO. [U.S. slang, late 1990s]

wine mopper an alcoholic who drinks cheap, fortified wine. [British, late 1900s-pres.]

winey intoxicated with alcohol. [British and U.S. slang, 1800s-1900s]

wing-ding (also **whing-ding**) 1. a gadget. 2. a drinking spree. 3. an affair or sexual encounter. [all senses, U.S., 1900s]

wing-heavy intoxicated with alcohol to the degree that one is unable to move or navigate. [U.S. slang, 1900s, Wentworth and Flexner]

wings cocaine. Cf. ROCKET-FUEL, SKYROCKET. [U.S. underworld, early 1900s]

winker the female sexual organ. For synonyms see MONOSYLLABLE. [British, late 1900s-pres.]

winkie the penis. The same as WINKLE (*q.v.*). For synonyms see GENITALS, YARD. [widespread juvenile, 1900s if not before]

winkle a child's penis. [British juvenile, 1800s, *Dictionary of Slang and Unconventional English*]

winky a device for smoking FREE BASE. [U.S. drug culture, late 1900s, Abel]

wino someone who is a drunkard on wine. [U.S., 1900s]

wiped-out (also **wiped**) drug or alcohol intoxicated. Cf. ELIMINATED. [U.S. slang and drug culture, 1900s]

wiped-over intoxicated with alcohol. For synonyms see WOOFLED. See WIPED-OUT.

wipe off to kill. See WIPE OUT.

wipe out (also **wipe off**) 1. to kill a person. Also **rub out.** [U.S. underworld, early 1900s] 2. to cleanse oneself after excreting. [U.S. slang, 1900s]

wire the penis. In expressions such as PULL ONE'S WIRE and WHIP ONE'S WIRE (both *q.v.*). [British and U.S. slang, 1900s or before]

wired-up (also **wired**) drug or alcohol intoxicated. [U.S. slang and drug culture, mid 1900s-pres.]

witch hazel heroin. From the medicine name. [U.S. drug culture, 1900s]

witch-piss inferior liquor; weak beer. *Cf.* SQUAW PISS. [British slang, early 1900s]

without a paddle being in a very bad situation. A euphemism for "up shit creek without a paddle." *Cf.* SHIT CREEK [U.S. slang, 1900s]

with squirrel pregnant. For synonyms see FRAGRANT. [U.S. dialect (Ozarks), Randolph and Wilson]

wizzer (also **wizzy**) an act of urination. Probably developed independently from WHIZ (*q.v.*). [Scots juvenile (Partridge); British, 1800s]

wobble weed the drug phencyclidine, P.C.P. WEED refers to marijuana, a substance often used with P.C.P. For synonyms see P.C.P. [U.S. drug culture, late 1900s, Abel]

wobbly intoxicated with alcohol. For synonyms see WOOFLED. [U.S. slang, 1900s]

wog-box a portable stereo radio and tape player combination; a COON-BOX. Essentially derogatory. [British slang, late 1900s]

wog gut diarrhea. For synonyms see QUICKSTEP. [Australian military, early 1900s, *Dictionary of Slang and Unconventional English*]

WOGS a derogatory term for "natives" of various countries, *e.g.*, Indians, Arabs, Australian aborigines. Said to be based on "Wonderful Oriental Gentleman," "Westernized Oriental Gentleman," or "Wily Oriental Gentleman." These are all reinterpretations of the acronym printed on WOGS' work uniforms, which stands for "Working on Government Services." There is also a tradition that "wog" is from "golliwog" or "polliwog." See GOLLY. [attested in some form in both World Wars and the Vietnamese War]

wolf 1. a chaser or seducer of women; a flirt. [U.S. slang, early 1900s-pres.] **2.** an aggressive or masculine lesbian. From sense 1. [U.S. mid 1900s] **3.** an active PEDERAST (*q.v.*); an INSERTOR (*q.v.*). The combative opposite of LAMB (sense 1), a CATAMITE (*q.v.*).

From sense 1. [U.S., early 1900s] **4.** the drug phencyclidine, P.C.P. For synonyms see P.C.P. [U.S. drug culture, late 1900s]

wolfess jocular for a "seductress," a female flirt. [U.S. slang, mid 1900s]

womanhood the female genitals. Based on MANHOOD (sense 2), the male genitals. [U.S., mid 1900s]

womanize to chase women for sexual purposes; to coit women. [1800s-pres.]

womanizer a lecher; a woman-chaser; a whoremonger. [since the late 1800s or before]

woman of loose morals a sexually loose woman; a harlot. [U.S., 1900s]

woman's home companion the menses. From the name of a women's magazine. For synonyms see FLOODS. [U.S., 1900s]

womb 1. the belly. [c. 800s, *Oxford English Dictionary*] **2.** the belly and the bowels. [c. 1000, *Oxford English Dictionary*] **3.** the uterus.

womble-ty-cropt (also **womble-cropped, womblety-cropt**) intoxicated with alcohol and very sick; hung over. From an old term meaning "uncertain" or "uncomfortable." *Cf.* WAMBLE-CROPPED. [British slang, 1700s, *New Canting Dictionary*]

womp on someone to copulate with someone; to COIT someone. For synonyms see OCCUPY. [U.S. collegiate, late 1900s, Munro]

wong the penis. One of a number of spelling variants of WHANG (sense 1). For synonyms see YARD. [U.S. slang, mid 1900s-pres.]

wonk (also **wank**) **1.** a simpleton; an oaf. [slang, 1900s] **2.** a homosexual male. [Australian, mid 1900s-pres., Wilkes]

wood the penis, especially the erect penis. See WOODMAN. For synonyms see ERECTION. [colloquial since the 1700s]

wooden-kimona (also **wooden-kimono**) a coffin. [U.S. underworld, early 1900s]

wooden-overcoat a coffin. [underworld, mid 1800s-pres.]

wooden-suit a coffin. *Cf.* WOODEN-COAT, WOODEN-OVERCOAT. [U.S. dialect and slang, 1900s and before]

woodpecker of Mars the AMANITA MUSCARIA (*q.v.*), a hallucinogenic mushroom. [U.S. drug culture, mid 1900s-pres.]

woods-colt 1. a colt sired by an unknown stallion. No negative connotations. **2.** a bastard. Partly euphemistic. *Cf.* CATCH-COLT. [both senses, U.S. colloquial, late 1800s-1900s]

woody an erection of the penis. For synonyms see ERECTION. [U.S. collegiate, late 1900s] See also SPORT A WOODY.

woof to vomit. Onomatopoeic. For synonyms see YORK. [U.S. collegiate, late 1900s, Eble]

woof cookies to vomit. *Cf.* BLOW (ONE'S) COOKIES, DROP ONE'S COOKIES, SNAP ONE'S COOKIES. For synonyms see YORK. [U.S. collegiate, late 1900s, Eble]

woofits a hangover, especially if notably unpleasant. [U.S. slang, 1900s]

woofled intoxicated with alcohol. [U.S. slang, 1900s] Synonyms: A BIT HIGH, A BIT LIT, A BIT ON, A BIT UNDER, ABOUT DRUNK, ABOUT FULL, ABOUT GONE, ABOUT HAD IT, ABOUT HALF DRUNK, ABOUT RIGHT, ABOUT SHOT, ABOUT TO CAVE IN, ABOUT TO GO UNDER, A-BUZZ, ACED, ACTIVATED, ADDLED, ADRIP, AFFLICTED, AFLOAT, AGLOW, ALCOHOLIZED, ALECIED, ALED(-UP), ALIGHT, ALKEYED, ALKEYED UP, ALKIED, ALKIED UP, ALKY-SOAKED, ALL AT SEA, ALL FUCKED UP, ALL GEEZED UP, ALL GONE, ALL HET UP, ALL IN, ALL KEYHOLE, ALL MOPS AND BROOMS, ALL OUT, ALL PINK ELEPHANTS, ALL SCHNOZZLED UP, ALL THERE, ALL WET, ALMOST FROZE, ALTOGETHERY, AMONG THE PHILISTINES, AMUCK, ANCHORED IN SOT'S BAY, ANNIHILATED, ANTIFREEZED, ANTISEPTIC, APED, A PEG TOO LOW, APE WILD, ARF ARF AN ARF, ARSEHOLED, AS FULL AS A FAIRY'S PHONE BOOK, AS GOOD CONDITIONED AS A PUPPY, A SHEET OR TWO TO THE WIND, AT REST, AWASH, AWRY-EYED, BACCHI PLENUS, BAGGED, BAG

(IN THE), BAKED, BALL-DOZED, BALMED (IN THE), BALMY, BAMBOOZLED, BANGED UP TO THE EYES, BANJAXED, BAPTIZED, BARLEY SICK, BARMY, BARRELED, BARRELED UP, BARRELHOUSE DRUNK, BASHED, BASTED, BATS, BATTED, BATTERED, BATTY BEARGERED, BEARING THE ENSIGN, BEEN AMONG THE PHILIPPIANS, BEEN AMONG THE PHILISTINES, BEEN AT AN INDIAN FEAST, BEEN AT A PLOUGHING MATCH, BEEN AT BARBADOS, BEEN AT GENEVA, BEEN BEFORE GEORGE, BEEN BITTEN BY A BARN MOUSE, BEEN CROOKING THE ELBOW, BEEN DROWNING THE SHAMROCK, BEEN FLYING RATHER HIGH, BEEN HAVING THE EYES OPENED, BEEN IN THE BIBBING PLOT, BEEN IN THE CELLAR, BEEN IN THE SAUCE, BEEN IN THE SUN, BEEN LAPPING IN THE GUTTER, BEEN LIFTING THE LITTLE FINGER, BEEN LOOKING THROUGH A GLASS, BEEN MAKING FUN, BEEN ON SENTRY, BEEN TALKING TO JAMIE MOORE, BEEN TO A FUNERAL, BEEN TO FRANCE, BEEN TO JERICHO, BEEN TO MEXICO, BEEN TOO FREE WITH SIR JOHN STRAWBERRY, BEEN TOO FREE WITH THE CREATURE, BEEN TO THE SALT WATER, BEEN TRYING TAYLOR'S BEST, BEEN WITH SIR JOHN GOA, BEERIFIED, BEERILY, BEERMUDDLED, BEER-SOAKED, BEERY, BEHIND JUICE, BEHIND THE CORK, BELLIGERENT, BELLY UP, BELOW THE MAHOGANY, BELTED, BEMUSED, BENT, BENT AND BROKEN, BENT OUT OF SHAPE, BESOTTED, BEVVIED, BEWILDERED, BEWITCHED, BEWOTTLED, BEZZLED, BIBULOUS, BIFFY, BIGGY, BILED, BILED AS AN OWL, BINGED, BINGO'D, BINGOED, BIT BY A BARN WEASEL, BLACKJACKED, BLADDERED, BLAH, BLANK-ED, BLANKED, BLASTED, BLEARY-EYED, BLEWED, BLIMPED, BLIND, BLIND AS A BAT, BLIND AS A BEETLE, BLIND AS A MOLE, BLIND AS AN OWL, BLIND AS CHLOE, BLIND DRUNK, BLINDED, BLINDERS, BLINDO, BLINDO-BLOTTO, BLISSED OUT, BLITHERED, BLITZED, BLITZKRIEGED, BLOATED, BLOCK AND BLOCK, BLOCK AND FALL, BLOCKED, BLOOEY, BLOOTERED, BLOTTED, BLOTTO, BLOWED, BLOWED AWAY, BLOWN, BLOWN AWAY, BLOWN OUT, BLOWN UP, BLOWZY, BLUE, BLUED, BLUE-EYED, BOBO, BOFFED, BOILED, BOILED AS AN OWL, BOILING

DRUNK, BOKOO SOUSED, BOMBED, BOMBED OUT, BONED, BONGO, BONGO'D, BONGOED, BONKERS, BOOED AND HISSED, BOOSED, BOOSY, BOOZEBLIND, BOOZED, BOOZED AS THE GAGE, BOOZED UP, BOOZEY, BOOZIFIED, BOOZY, BOOZY-WOOZY, BORACCHIO, BOSCO ABSOLUTO, BOSHY, BOSKO ABSOLUTO, BOSKY, BOTH SHEETS IN THE WIND, BOTTLED, BOTTLED UP, BOUSY, BOWZED, BOXED, BOXED UP, BRAHMS AND LISZT, BREATH STRONG ENOUGH TO CARRY COAL WITH, BREEZY, BREWED, BRIDGEY, BRIGHT-EYED, BRIGHT IN THE EYE, BRUISED, BUBBED, BUBBLED, BUBBY, BUDGY, BUFFY, BULLDOZED, BULLETPROOFED, BUMPSIE, BUMPSY, BUNG, BUNGED, BUNGEY, BUNG-EYED, BUNGY, BUNNED, BUOYANT, BUOYED, BURDOCKED, BURIED, BURN WITH A LOW BLUE FLAME, BUSKEY, BUSKY, BUSTED, BUSTED IN, BUZZED, BUZZED UP, BUZZEY, BUZZING, BUZZY, CACHED, CACKO, CAGED, CAGRINED, CANDY, CANED, CANNED, CANNED UP, CANNON, CANON, CAN'T SEE, CAN'T SEE A HOLE IN A LADDER, CAN'T SEE THROUGH A LADDER, CAPABLE, CAPERNOITED, CAP SICK, CARGOED, CARRY BALLAST, CARRYING A HEAVY LOAD, CARRYING A LOAD, CARRYING SOMETHING HEAVY, CARRYING THREE RED LIGHTS, CARRYING TOO MUCH SAIL, CARRYING TWO RED LIGHTS, CAST, CASTING UP ONE'S ACCOUNTS, CAT, CATCHED, CATSOOD, CAUGHT, CHÂTEAUED, CHAP-FALLEN, CHARGED UP, CHEERIO, CHERRY-MERRY, CHERUBIMICAL, CHICE, CHICKERY, CHICKORY, CHIPPER, CHIRPING MERRY, CHUCKED, CLEAR, CLINCHED, CLIPPING THE KING'S ENGLISH, CLOBBERED, CLUCKED, COAGULATED, COCKED, COCKED AS A LOG, COCKED TO THE GILLS, COCK-EYED, COCK-EYED DRUNK, COGEY, COGNACKED, COGUY, COMATOSED, COMBOOZELATED, COMFORTABLE, COMMODE-HUGGING DRUNK, CONCERNED, CONFLUMMOXED, CONFOUNDEDLY CUT, CONTENDING WITH THE PHARAOH, COO-COO, COOKED, COPEY, CORKED, CORKED UP, CORKSCREWED, CORKSCREWED UP, CORKY, CORNED, CORNY, COUNTRY DRUNK, COXY-LOXY, CRACKED, CRAMPED, CRAPSICK, CRAPULOUS, CRASHED, CRAZED, CRAZY, CRAZY-DRUNK, CREAMED, CRISPY, CROCKED CROCKO, CROCUS,

CRONK, CROPSICK, CROSS-EYED, CROSS-EYED DRUNK, CRUMPED OUT, CRUMP-FOOTED, CRUSHED, CRYING DRUNK, CUCKOO, CUCKOOED, CUPPED, CUPSHOT, CURVED, CUSHED, CUT, CUT IN THE BACK, CUT IN THE LEG, CUT ONE'S CAPERS, D., DAGGED, DAMAGED, DAMP, D. AND D., DEAD, DEAD DRUNK, DEADO, DEAD-OH, DEADS, DEAD TO THE WORLD, DECAYED, DECKS AWASH, DEEP CUT, DINGED OUT, DING-SWIZZLED, DINGY, DINKY, DIPPED HIS BILL, DIPPED RATHER DEEP, DIPPED TOO DEEP, DIRTY DRUNK, DISCOMBOBULATED, DISCOMBOOBULATED, DISCOURAGED, DISCUMFUDDLED, DISGUISED, DISGUISED IN LIQUOR, DISORDERLY, DITHERED, DIZZY, DIZZY AS A COOT, DIZZY AS A DAME, DIZZY AS A GOOSE, DOG DRUNK, DOING THE EMPEROR, DOING THE LORD, DONE OVER, DOUBLED UP, DOUBLE-HEADED, DOUBLE-TONGUED, DOWN, DOWN AMONG THE DEAD MEN, DOWN WITH BARREL FEVER, DOWN WITH THE FISH, DRAGGED, DRAPED, DRENCHED, DRINKATIVE, DRINKY, DRIPPING TIGHT, DRONED, DRUFFEN, DRUNK, DRUNK AS A BADGER, DRUNK AS A BASTARD, DRUNK AS A BAT, DRUNK AS A BEGGAR, DRUNK AS A BESOM, DRUNK AS A BIG OWL, DRUNK AS A BILED OWL, DRUNK AS A BOILED OWL, DRUNK AS A BREWER'S FART, DRUNK AS A BROOM, DRUNK AS A COOK, DRUNK AS A COON, DRUNK AS A COOT, DRUNK AS A COOTER, DRUNK AS A COOTIE, DRUNK AS A CUNT, DRUNK AS A DOG, DRUNK AS A DUTCHMAN, DRUNK AS A FIDDLE, DRUNK AS A FIDDLER, DRUNK AS A FIDDLER'S BITCH, DRUNK AS A FISH, DRUNK AS A FLY, DRUNK AS A FOOL, DRUNK AS A FOWL, DRUNK AS A GOAT, DRUNK AS A GOSPORT FIDDLER, DRUNK AS A HOG, DRUNK AS A KETTLEFISH, DRUNK AS A KING, DRUNK AS A KITE, DRUNK AS A LITTLE RED WAGON, DRUNK AS A LOG, DRUNK AS A LOON, DRUNK AS A LORD, DRUNK AS A MONKEY, DRUNK AS A MOUSE, DRUNK AS AN EARL, DRUNK AS AN EMPEROR, DRUNK AS A NEWT, DRUNK AS AN OWL, DRUNK AS A PERRANER, DRUNK AS A PIG, DRUNK AS A PIPER, DRUNK AS A PISSANT, DRUNK AS A POET, DRUNK AS A PRINCE, DRUNK AS A RAT, DRUNK AS A ROLLING FART, DRUNK AS A SAILOR,

DRUNK AS A SKUNK, DRUNK AS A SKUNK IN A TRUNK, DRUNK AS A SOW, DRUNK AS A SWINE, DRUNK AS A TAPSTER, DRUNK AS A TICK, DRUNK AS A TOP, DRUNK AS A WHEELBARROW, DRUNK AS BACCHUS, DRUNK AS BLAZES, DRUNK AS BUGGERY, DRUNK AS CHLOE, DRUNK AS COOTER BROWN, DRUNK AS DAVID'S SOW, DRUNK AS DAVY'S SOW, DRUNK AS FLOEY, DRUNK AS HELL, DRUNK AS HOOT, DRUNK AS MICE, DRUNK AS MUCK, DRUNK AS POLONY, DRUNK AS THE DEVIL, DRUNK AS ZEUS, DRUNK BACK, DRUNKER THAN WHISKEY, DRUNKULENT, DRUNKY, DRUNOK, DRY, DULL-EYED, DULL IN THE EYE, EAT A PUDDING BAG, EATEN A TOAD AND A HALF FOR BREAKFAST, EAT OPIUM, EDGED, ELECTRIFIED, ELEPHANT'S, ELEPHANTS, ELEPHANT'S TRUNK, ELEVATED, ELIMINATED, EMBALMED, ENTERED, ETHEREAL, EXALTED, EXTRACTED, FACED, FADED, FAINT, FALLING-DOWN DRUNK, FARAHEAD, FAR GONE, FARMED, FAR OUT, FEARS NO MAN, FEATURED, FEAVOURISH, FEELING ACES, FEELING DIZZY, FEELING EXCELLENT, FEELING FRISKY, FEELING FUNNY, FEELING GLORIOUS, FEELING GOOD, FEELING HAPPY, FEELING HIGH, FEELING HIS ALCOHOL, FEELING HIS BOOZE, FEELING HIS CHEERIOS, FEELING HIS DRINK, FEELING HIS LIQUOR, FEELING HIS OATS, FEELING HIS ONIONS, FEELING IT, FEELING NO PAIN, FEELING PRETTY GOOD, FEELING REAL WELL, FEELING RIGHT, FEELING RIGHT ROYAL, FEELING THE EFFECT, FESHNUSHKIED, FETTERED, FETTLED, FIDDLED, FIGHTING DRUNK, FIGHTING TIGHT, FIRED, FIRED UP, FISHY, FISHY ABOUT THE GILLS, FITSHACED, FIXED UP, FIZZED UP, FLABBERGASTED, FLAKED OUT, FLAKO, FLAKY, FLARING DRUNK, FLAW'D, FLAWED, FLOATING, FLOODED, FLOOEY, FLOORED, FLOPPY, FLORID, FLUFFED, FLUFFY, FLUMMOXED, FLUMMUXED, FLUSH, FLUSHED, FLUSTERED, FLUSTICATED, FLUSTRATED, FLY BLOWN, FLY-BY-NIGHT, FLYING HIGH, FLYING THE ENSIGN, FOG BOUND, FOGGED, FOGGY, FOLDED, FOOZLIFIED, FORTIFIED, FOSSILIZED, FOU, FOUR SHEETS, FOUR SHEETS IN THE WIND, FOUR SHEETS TO THE WIND, FOW, FOX DRUNK, FOXED, FOXY, FRACTURED, FRAZZLED, FRESH, FRESHISH, FRIED,

FRIED ON BOTH SIDES, FRIED TO THE EYEBROWS, FRIED TO THE EYES, FRIED TO THE GILLS, FRIED TO THE HAT, FROZE HIS MOUTH, FROZEN, FUCKED OUT, FUCKED OVER, FUCKED UP, FUDDLE, FUDDLED, FULL, FULL AS A BOOT, FULL AS A BULL, FULL AS A BULL'S BUM, FULL AS A FART, FULL AS A FIDDLE, FULL AS A GOAT, FULL AS A GOOG, FULL AS A GOOSE, FULL AS A LORD, FULL AS AN EGG, FULL AS A PISS-ANT, FULL AS A PO, FULL AS A TICK, FULL AS THE FAMILY PO, FULL-COCKED, FULL-FLAVORED, FULL OF COURAGE, FULL OF DUTCH COURAGE, FULL OF HOPS, FULL TO THE BRIM, FULL TO THE BUNG, FULL TO THE GILLS, FULL TO THE GUARDS, FULL UP, FUNKY-DRUNK, FUNNY, FUZZED, FUZZLED, FUZZY, GAGED, GALVANIZED, GASSED, GASSED UP, GAUGED, GAY, GAYED, GEARED UP, GEED UP, GEESED, GEEZED, GEEZED UP, GENEROUS, GIDDY, GIFFED, GIGGLED, GIGGLED UP, GILDED, GINGERED UP, GINNED, GINNED UP, GINNIFIED, GINNY, GIN SOAKED, GLAD, GLASSY-EYED, GLAZED, GLAZED DRUNK, GLAZED OVER, GLOBULAR, GLORIOUS, GLOWING, GLUED, GOAT DRUNK, GOGGLE-EYED, GOING TO JERUSALEM, GOLDHEADED, GONE, GONE BORNEO, GONE UNDER, GONGED, GOOFY, GOOGLY-EYED, GOONED, GORDONED, GOREY-EYED, GORY-EYED, GOT A BRASS EYE, GOT A BUN ON, GOT A DROP IN THE EYE, GOT A GLOW ON, GOT BY THE HEAD, GOT CORNS IN HIS HEAD, GOT HIS TOP GALLANT SAILS OUT, GOT KIBBED HEELS, GOT ON HIS LITTLE HAT, GOT THE BACK TEETH WELL AFLOAT, GOT THE GLANDERS, GOT THE GOUT, GOT THE GRAVEL RASH, GOT THE HORNS ON, GOT THE INDIAN VAPORS, GOT THE NIGHTMARE, GOT THE POLE EVIL, GOWED, GOWED UP, GRAPE SHOT, GRAVELLED, GREASED, GRILLED, GROATABLE, GROGGED, GROGGED UP, GROGGIFIED, GROGGY, GUTTERED, GUYED OUT, GUZZLED, HAD A FEW, HAD A KICK IN THE GUTS, HAD A THUMP OVER THE HEAD WITH SAMSON'S JAWBONE, HAD ENOUGH, HAD ONE OR TWO, HAD ONE TOO MANY, HAD TOO MUCH, HALF AND HALF, HALF BLIND, HALF BULLED, HALF CANNED, HALF COCKED, HALF CORNED, HALF-CROCKED, HALF CUT, HALF-DOPED, HALF

GONE, HALF-HIGH, HALF HOT, HALF IN THE BAG, HALF IN THE BOOT, HALF IN THE TANK, HALF LIT, HALF-LOOPED, HALF NELSON, HALF ON, HALF-OUT, HALF-PICKLED, HALF PISSED, HALF RATS, HALF RINSED, HALF SCREWED, HALF SEAS OVER, HALF SEAS UNDER, HALF SHAVED, HALF SHOT, HALF-SLAMMED HALF SLEWED, HALF-SLOPPED, HALF SNAPPED, HALF-SOBER, HALF-SOUSED, HALF SPRUNG, HALF STEWED, HALF-STIFF, HALF-STOUSED, HALF-TANKED, HALF THE BAY OVER, HALF THERE, HALF UNDER, HALF UP THE POLE, HALFWAY OVER, HALFWAY TO CONCORD, HAMMERED, HAMMERISH, HANCED, HAPPY, HARD UP, HARDY, HARRY FLAKERS, HARRY HONKERS, HARRY SCREECHERS, HARTY, HAS BEEN IN THE BIBBING PLOT, HAS BOOZED THE GAGE, HAS DIPPED HIS BILL, HAS DRUNK MORE THAN HE HAS BLED, HAS HEAT HIS COPPER, HAS HET HIS KETTLE, HAS SCALT HIS HEAD PAN, HAS STOLEN A MANCHET OUT OF THE BREWER'S BASKET, HAS TAKEN HIPPOCRATES' GRAND ELIXIR, HAS WET BOTH EYES, HAUNTED WITH EVIL SPIRITS, HAVE A BRICK IN ONE'S HAT, HAVE A BUN ON, HAVE A BUZZ ON, HAVE A CAB, HAVE A CUP TOO MUCH, HAVE A CUT LEG, HAVE A FULL CARGO ABOARD, HAVE A GLOW ON, HAVE A GUEST IN THE ATTIC, HAVE A GUTFUL OF PISS, HAVE A JAG ON, HAVE A KEG ABOARD, HAVE A LOAD ON, HAVE AN EDGE ON, HAVE A PACKAGE ON, HAVE A POT IN THE PATE, HAVE A ROSY GLOW ON, HAVE A SKATE ON, HAVE A SKINFUL, HAVE A SLANT ON, HAVE AS MUCH AS ONE CAN CARRY, HAVE A SNOOTFULL, HAVE A SWOLLEN HEAD, HAVE A TALKING LOAD, HAVE A THICK HEAD, HAVE A TOUCH OF BOSKINESS, HAVE A TURKEY ON ONE'S BACK, HAVE BEEN DIPPING RATHER DEEP, HAVE BEEN PAID, HAVE BURNT ONE'S SHOULDER, HAVE CUT ONE'S LEG, HAVE EATEN SOME HULL CHEESE, HAVE GOT A DISH, HAVE GOT A SKINFULL, HAVE GROG ON BOARD, HAVE HAD ONE OVER THE EIGHT, HAVE KNOCKED ONE'S LINK OUT, HAVE ONE OVER THE EIGHT, HAVE ONE'S BACK TEETH AFLOAT, HAVE ONE'S BACK TEETH WELL AFLOAT, HAVE ONE'S BRAIN ON A LEASH, HAVE ONE'S FLAG OUT, HAVE ONE'S NUFF, HAVE ONE'S POTS ON, HAVE PUNCH ABOARD, HAVE RAISED ONE'S MONUMENTS, HAVE SOLD ONE'S SENSES, HAVE SWALLOWED A HAIR, HAVE SWALLOWED A HARE, HAVE THE BIGHEAD, HAVE THE HEAD FULL OF BEES, HAVE THE SUN IN ONE'S EYES, HAVE YELLOW FEVER, HAZY, HEAD IS FULL OF BEES, HEARTY, HEATED, HEATED HIS COPPER, HEELED, HEELED OVER, HELPLESS, HEPPED, HEPPED UP, HET UP, HICCIUS-DOCCIUS, HICKEY, HICKIE, HICKSIUS-DOXIUS, HICKY, HICTIUS-DOCTIUS, HIDDEY, HIDDY, HIGH, HIGH AS A CAT'S BACK, HIGH AS A FIDDLER'S FIST, HIGH AS A GEORGIA PINE, HIGH AS A KITE, HIGH AS A STEEPLE, HIGH AS LINDBERGH, HIGH AS THE SKY, HIGHER THAN A KITE, HIGHER THAN GILROY'S KITE, HIGH IN THE SADDLE, HIPPED, HIT UNDER THE WING, HOARY-EYED, HOCKEY, HOCUS, HOCUS-POCUS, HONKED, HONKERS, HONKING, HOOCHED, HOOCHED UP, HOODMAN, HOODMAN BLIND, HOOTED, HOPPED, HOPPED UP, HORIZONTAL, HORSEBACK, HOT, HOT AS A RED WAGON, HOTTER THAN A BILED OWL, HOTTER THAN A BOILED OWL, HOTTER THAN A SKUNK, HOUSED, HOW CAME YOU SO?, HOWLING, HOWLING DRUNK, HURTIN', ILLUMINATED, IMPAIRED, IMPIXLO-CATED, IN A BAD WAY, IN A FIX, IN A FUDDLE, IN A HEAP, IN A MUDDLE, IN ARMOUR, IN A STATE OF ELEVATION, IN A STEW, IN A TRANCE, IN BAD SHAPE, IN BEER, IN BOOZE, INCOG, INCOGNITIBUS, INCOGNITO, IN COLOR, IN DRINK, IN FINE FETTLE, IN GOOD FETTLE, INJUN DRUNK, INKED, INKY, INKYPOO, IN LIQUOR, IN ONE'S AIRS, IN ONE'S ALTITUDES, IN ONE'S ARMOUR, IN ONE'S CUPS, IN ONE'S ELEMENT, IN ONE'S POTS, IN ONE'S PROSPERITY, IN POTS, IN RARE FORM, INSIDE OUT, IN SOAK, INSPIRED, IN THE ALTITUDES, IN THE BAG, IN THE BLUES, IN THE GRIP OF THE GRAPE, IN THE GUN, IN THE GUTTER, IN THE OZONE, IN THE PINK, IN THE SHAKES, IN THE SUDS, IN THE SUN, IN THE SUNSHINE, IN THE WIND, INTOX, INTOXED, INTOXICATED, INUNDATED, IN VERY GOOD HUMOR, IRRIGATED, ISHKIMMISK, IT IS A DARK DAY WITH HIM, JAGGED, JAGGED UP, JAMBLED, JAMMED, JAZZED, JAZZED UP, JIGGERED, JINGLED, JOCULAR, JOLLY, JUG-BITTEN, JUGGED, JUGGED UP, JUG-STEAMED, JUICED, JUICED TO THE GILLS,

JUICED UP, JUICY, JUMBO'S TRUNK, JUN-
GLED, JUNKED UP, KANURD, KENNURD,
KENTUCKY FRIED, KENURD, KETTLED,
KEYED, KEYED UP, KEYED UP TO THE
ROOF, KEYHOLED, KILLED HIS DOG,
KILLED OFF, KISKY, KISSED BLACK
BETTY, KITED, KNAPPED, KNAPT, KNEE-
WALKING, KNEE-WALKING DRUNK,
KNOCKED OUT, KNOCKED UP, KNOWS
NOT THE WAY HOME, LAID BACK, LAID
OUT, LAID TO THE BONE, LAPPING IN
THE GUTTER, LAPPY, LATHERED, LEAP-
ING, LEARY, LEERY, LEGLESS, LIFTED,
LIGHT, LIKE A RAT IN TROUBLE, LIK-
KERED, LIKKERED UP, LIKKERISH, LIK-
KER SOAKED, LIMBER, LIMP, LINED, LION
DRUNK, LIQUEFIED, LIQUORED, LI-
QUORED UP, LIQUORISH, LIQUOR STRUCK,
LIT, LIT TO THE GILLS, LIT TO THE
GUARDS, LIT TO THE GUNNELS, LIT UP, LIT
UP LIKE A CATHEDRAL, LIT UP LIKE A
CATHOLIC CHURCH, LIT UP LIKE A
CHRISTMAS TREE, LIT UP LIKE A
CHURCH, LIT UP LIKE A CHURCH WIN-
DOW, LIT UP LIKE A HIGH MASS, LIT UP
LIKE A KITE, LIT UP LIKE A LIGHTHOUSE,
LIT UP LIKE A SKYSCRAPER, LIT UP LIKE
A STORE WINDOW, LIT UP LIKE BROAD-
WAY, LIT UP LIKE MAIN STREET, LIT UP
LIKE THE COMMONWEALTH, LIT UP LIKE
THE SKY, LIT UP LIKE TIMES SQUARE,
LOADED, LOADED FOR BEAR, LOADED
HIS CART, LOADED TO THE BARREL,
LOADED TO THE EARLOBES, LOADED TO
THE GILLS, LOADED TO THE GUARDS,
LOADED TO THE GUNNELS, LOADED TO
THE GUNWALES, LOADED TO THE HAT,
LOADED TO THE MUZZLE, LOADED TO
THE PLIMSOLL MARK, LOCKJAWED,
LOGGED, LOOKING LIVELY, LOONY,
LOOPED, LOOPED TO THE EYEBALLS,
LOOP-LEGGED, LOOPY, LOOSE, LOOSE IN
THE HILTS, LORDLY, LOST HIS RUDDER,
LOST IN THE SAUCE, LUBED, LUBRI-
CATED, LUMPY, LUSH, LUSHED, LUSHED
UP, LUSHED UP TO THE NUTS, LUSHEY,
LUSHY, MADE AN EXAMPLE, MAGGOTTY,
MAKES VIRGINIA FENCE, MAKING MS
AND WS, MAKING SCALLOPS, MALTED,
MALTY, MASHED, MAUDLIN, MAUDLIN
DRUNK, MAUL'D, MAULED, MAWDLIN,
MAXED OUT, MELLOW, MELTED, MERRY,
MERRY AS A GREEK, MESSED UP, METH-
ODISTCONATED, MICKEY FINISHED, MID-
DLING, MILLED, MIRACULOUS, MIXED,
MIXED UP, MIZZLED, MOCCASINED, MOIST
AROUND THE EDGES, MOKUS, MOLLY,
MOLLY THE MONK, MOLO, MOOF, MOO-
NEY, MOON-EYED, MOONLIT, MOONY,
MOORED IN SOT'S BAY, MOPPED, MOPPY,
MOPS AND BROOMS, MORTAL, MORTAL
DRUNK, MORTALLIOUS, MORTALLY DRUNK,
MOUNTOUS, MUCKIBUS, MUDDLED, MUD-
DLED UP, MUDDY, MUG BLOT, MUG
BLOTTO, MUG BLOTTS, MUGG BLOTTS,
MUGGED, MUGGED UP, MUGGY, MULLED,
MULLED UP, MUY TOSTADO, MUZZY,
NAPPY, NASE, NAZY, NAZZIE, NAZZY, NEED
A REEF TAKEN IN, NEGRO DRUNK,
NEWTED, NIMPTOPSICAL, NINE-EYED,
NIPPED, NODDY-HEADED, NOGGY, NOLO,
NON COMPOS, NON COMPOS POOPOO,
NUTS, NUTTY, N.Y.D., OBFUSCATED, OB-
FUSTICATED, OBLITERATED, OCKSE-
CROTIA, ODDISH, OFF, OFF AT THE NAIL,
OFF ONE'S FACE, OFF ONE'S NUT, OFF
THE NAIL, OILED, ON, ON A JAG, ONE
OVER EIGHT, ONE OVER THE EIGHT, ON
ONE'S ASS, ON ONE'S EAR, ON ONE'S
FOURTH, ON SENTRY, ON THE BATTER,
ON THE BEER, ON THE BEND, ON THE
BLINK, ON THE FRITZ, ON THE FUDDLE, ON
THE GROG, ON THE KIP, ON THE LOOSE,
ON THE MUDDLE, ON THE RANTAN, ON
THE REE-RAW, ON THE RE-RAW, ON THE
SAUCE, ON THE SCOOP, ON THE SCOOT, ON
THE SHICKER, ON THE SHIKKER, ON THE
SKYTE, ON THE SPREE, OOZY, ORGANIZED,
ORIE-EYED, ORRY-EYED, OSSIFIED, OTIS,
OUT, OUTASIGHT, OUT COLD, OUT LIKE A
LIGHT, OUT OF FUNDS, OUT OF HERE, OUT
OF IT, OUT OF ONE'S BRAIN, OUT OF ONE'S
GOURD, OUT OF ONE'S SKULL, OUT OF
SIGHT, OUT OF THE WAY, OUT ON THE
FUDDLE, OUT ON THE ROOF, OUT TO IT,
OVERBOARD, OVERCOME, OVERSEAS,
OVERSEEN, OVERSERVED, OVERSET, OVER-
SHOT, OVER-SPARRED, OVERTAKEN, OVER
THE BAR, OVER THE BAY, OVER THE
EIGHT, OVER THE MARK, OVER-WINED,
OWES NO MAN A FARTHING, OWLED,
OWL-EYED, OWLY-EYED, OXYCROCIUM,
PACKAGED, PAFISTICATED, PAID, PA-
LATIC, PALLED, PARALYSED, PARA-
LYTIC, PARALYZED, PARBOILED, PASSED
OUT, PASSED OUT COLD, PASSED OUT OF
THE PICTURE, PASTED, PECKISH, PEE'D,
PEE-EYED, PEONIED, PEPPED, PEPPED UP,
PEPPY, PERKED, PERVED, PETRIFICATED,
PETRIFIED, PHFFT, PICKLED, PIED, PIE-
EYED, PIFFED, PIFFICATED, PIFFLED, PIF-
FLICATED, PIGEON-EYED, PILFERED,

PINKED, PINKO, PIPED, PIPED UP, PIPER DRUNK, PIPER FOU', PIPER MERRY, PIPPED, PIPPED UP, PISSED, PISSED AS A FART, PISSED AS A FIDDLER'S BITCH, PISSED AS A NEWT, PISSED AS A PARROT, PISSED IN THE BROOK, PISSED OUT OF ONE'S MIND, PISSED UP, PISSED UP TO THE EYEBALLS, PISSED UP TO THE EYEBROWS, PISSING DRUNK, PISSING FOU', PISSY-ARSED, PISSY-FACED, PIXILATED, PIXOLATED, PIZZ, PIZZICATO, PLANTED, PLASTERED, PLEASANTLY PLASTERED, PLONK, PLONKED, PLONKED UP, PLOOTERED, PLOUGHED, PLOUGHED UNDER, PLOWED, PLOWED UNDER, PODDY, PODGY, POFFERED, POGEY, POGGLED, POGY, POLISHED, POLISHED UP, POLITE, POLLED OFF, POLLUTED, POOPED, POOPED OUT, POOPIED, POP-EYED, POPPED, POT-EYED, POTSED, POT SHOT, POT SICK, POTTED, POTTED OFF, POTTED UP, POTULENT, POT VALIANT, POWDERED, POWDERED UP, PRESERVED, PRESTONED, PRETTY WELL ENTER'D, PRIDDY, PRIMED, PRIMED TO THE BARREL, PRIMED TO THE EARS, PRIMED TO THE MUZZLE, PRIMED TO THE NUTS, PRIMED TO THE TRIGGER, PRINCE EUGENE, PRUNED, PSYCHED OUT, PUGGLED, PUGGY DRUNK, PUMMELLED, PUNGEY, PUSHED, PUSHED OUT, PUTRID, PUT TO BED WITH A SHOVEL, PYE-EYED, QUARRELSOME, QUARTZED, QUEER, QUEERED, QUICK-TEMPERED, QUISBY, RACKED, RACKED UP, RADDLED, RAGGED, RAISED, RAMMAGED, RAMPED, RAMPING MAD, RAT-ARSED, RATTED, RATTLED, RATTY, RAUNCHY, REEKING, REELING, REELING RIPE, REELY, RELIGIOUS, RICH, RIFFED, RIGHT BEFORE THE WIND WITH ALL HIS STUDDING SAIL OUT, RIGID, RILEYED, RIPE, RIPPED, RIPPED OFF, RIPPED TO THE TITS, RIPPED UP, ROARING, ROARING DRUNK, ROARING FOU', ROASTED, ROCKY, RONCHIE, ROOSTERED, RORTY, ROSEY, ROSIE, ROSINED, ROSY, ROSY ABOUT THE GILLS, ROTTEN, ROTTEN DRUNK, ROUND THE BEND, ROYAL, RUINED, RUM-DUM, RUMMED, RUMMED UP, RUMMY, SALT, SALTED, SALTED DOWN, SALT JUNK, SALUBRIOUS, SAP HAPPY, SATURATED, SAUCED, SAWED, SCAMMERED, SCHICE, SCHIZZED, SCHLOCKERED, SCHNOCKERED, SCHNOGGERED, SCOOPED, SCORCHED, SCOTCH MIST, SCRAMBLED, SCRANCHED, SCRATCHED, SCRAUNCHED, SCREAMING, SCREAMING DRUNK, SCREECHERS, SCREECHING, SCREECHING DRUNK, SCREWED, SCREWED TIGHT, SCREWY, SCRONCHED, SCROOCHED, SCROOCHED UP, SEAFARING, SEEING PINK ELEPHANTS, SEEING PINK SPIDERS, SEEING SNAKES, SEEING-THINGS DRUNK, SEEING TWO MOONS, SEEN A FLOCK OF MOONS, SEEN THE DEVIL, SEEN THE FRENCH KING, SEEN THE YELLOW STAR, SEES THE BEARS, SEES THE SUN, SEES TWO MOONS, SENT, SERVED UP, SEWED UP, SEWN UP, S.F., SHAGGED, SHAKING A CLOTH IN THE WIND, SHAKING LIKE CLOTH IN THE WIND, SHAKY, SHAVED, SHELLACKED, SHICE, SHICER, SHICERY, SHICK, SHICKED, SHICKERED, SHICKERY, SHIKKER, SHIKKERED, SHIKKUR, SHINED, SHINNY, SHINY, SHIPWRECKED, SHISE, SHIT-FACED, SHITTY, SHNOCKERED, SHOT, SHOT-AWAY, SHOT DOWN, SHOT FULL OF HOLES, SHOT IN THE NECK, SHOT UP, SHREADED, SHREDDED, SIDEWAYS, SIX SHEETS TO THE WIND, SIZZLED, SKEW-WHIFF, SKIMISHED, SKIMMISHED, SKIZZLED, SKUNK-DRUNK, SKUNKED, SLAMMED, SLATHERED, SLAUGHTERED, SLEEPY, SLEWED, SLEWY, SLIGHTLY DAMAGED, SLIGHTLY DAMP, SLIGHTLY ELEVATED, SLIGHTLY RATTLED, SLIGHTLY-TIGHTLY, SLOPPED, SLOPPED OVER, SLOPPED TO THE EARS, SLOPPED UP, SLOPPY, SLOPPY DRUNK, SLOSHED, SLOSHED TO THE EARS, SLOSHY, SLOUGHED, SLOUGHED UP, SLUED, SLUGGED, SLUSHED, SLUSHED UP, SMASHED, SMEARED, SMEEKIT, SMELLING OF THE CORK, SMELT OF AN ONION, SMOKED, SMUCKERED, SNACKED, SNAPED, SNAPPED, SNOCKERED, SNOCKERED TO THE GILLS, SNOGGERED, SNOOTED, SNOOZAMOROOED, SNOTFLINGING DRUNK, SNOTTED, SNOZZLED, SNUBBED, SNUFFY, SNUG, SO, SOAKED, SOAPY-EYED, SOCKED, SODDEN, SOFT, SOGGY, SOMEBODY STOLE HIS RUDDER, SOPPING, SOPPING WET, SOPPY, SOREFOOTED, SOSHED, SO-SO, SOSSLED, SOTTISH, SOUFFLED, SOUPY, SOUSED, SOUSED TO THE EARS, SOUSED TO THE GILLS, SOUST, SOUTHERN-FRIED, SOW DRUNK, SOZZLED, SOZZLY, SPEECHLESS, SPIFFED, SPIFFLICATED, SPIFFLO, SPIFICATED, SPIFLICATED, SPIKED, SPOKE WITH HIS FRIEND, SPOONY, SPOONY DRUNK, SPREEISH, SPRUNG, SQUASHED, SQUIFFED, SQUIFFY, STAGGERISH, STALE DRUNK, STANDING TOO LONG IN THE

SUN, STARCHED, STARCHY, STEADY, STEAMBOATS, STEAMED, STEAMED UP, STEEPED, STEPPING HIGH, STEW, STEWED, STEWED AS A PRUNE, STEWED TO THE EARS, STEWED TO THE GILLS, STEWED UP, STIBBED, STIFF, STIFF AS A BOARD, STIFF AS A GOAT, STIFF AS A PLANK, STIFF AS A RING-BOLT, STIFFED, STIFFO, STIMU-LATED, STINKING, STINKING DRUNK, STINKO, STITCHED, STOLLED, STOLLING, STONE BLIND, STONED, STONED TO THE TITS, STONKERED, STONY BLIND, STOVE IN, STOZZLED, STRETCHED, STRIPED, STRONG, STUBBED, STUCCOED, STUNG, STUNNED, SUCKED, SUCKEY, SUCKY, SUPER-CHARGED, SWACKED, SWACKO, SWAL-LOWED A TAVERN TOKEN, SWAMPED, SWAMPT, SWATCHED, SWATTLED, SWAZ-ZLED, SWERVED, SWIGGED, SWIGGLED, SWILLED, SWILLED UP, SWINED, SWINE DRUNK, SWINNY, SWIPED, SWIPEY, SWIPY, SWIVELLY, SWIZZLED, SWOOZLED, SWOZZLED, TACKY, TAKEN A CHIRRIP-ING GLASS, TAKEN A CUP TOO MUCH, TAKING IT EASY, TANGLED, TANGLE-FOOTED, TANGLE-LEGGED, TANKED, TANKED UP, TANKY, TANNED, TAP SHACKLED, TATTERED, TAVERNED, TEA'D UP, TEAD UP, TED, TEED, TEE'D TO THE TITS, TEED UP, TEETH UNDER, TEMULENT, THAT WAY, THAWED, THERE, THERE WITH BOTH FEET, THE SUN HAS SHONE ON THEM, THIRSTY, THREE SHEETS, THREE SHEETS IN THE WIND, THREE SHEETS TO THE WIND, TIDDLED, TID-DLEY, TIDDLY, TIFFLED, TIGHT, TIGHT AS A BOILED OWL, TIGHT AS A BRASSIERE, TIGHT AS A DRUM, TIGHT AS A FART, TIGHT AS A GOAT, TIGHT AS A LORD, TIGHT AS A MINK, TIGHT AS A NEWT, TIGHT AS AN OWL, TIGHT AS A TEN-DAY DRUNK, TIGHT AS A TICK, TIGHT AS THE BARK ON A TREE, TIGHTER THAN A DRUM, TIGHTER THAN A GOAT, TIGHTER THAN A MINK, TIGHTER THAN A SCOTCHMAN, TIGHTER THAN A TICK, TIGHTER THAN DICK'S HATBAND, TIN HATS, TINNED, TIPIUM GROVE, TIP MERRY, TIPPED, TIPPLING, TIPPLY, TIP-SEY, TIPSIFIED, TIPSY, TIP-TOP, TIRED, TISHY, TITE, TOASTED, TONGUE-TIED, TOOK HIS DROPS, TOO MANY CLOTHS IN THE WIND, TOO NUMEROUS TO MEN-TION, TOP HEAVY, TOPPED, TOPPLED, TOPPY, TOPSY-BOOSY, TOPSY-BOOZY, TOPSY-TURVEY, TOPY, TORE, TORE DOWN, TORE UP, TORN UP, TORQUED, TORRID, TOSSED, TOSTICATED, TOSTIFI-CATED, TOTALLED, TOTALLED OUT, TOTTY, TOUCHED, TOUGH AS A BOILED OWL, TOW-ROW, TOXED, TOXICATED, TOXY, TRAMMELED, TRANSLATED, TRASHED, TRIMMED DOWN, TRIPPED, TROLLEYED, TUBED, TUMBLING, TUM-BLING DRUNK, TUNED, TUNED UP, TUZZY, TWEAKED, TWEASED, TWEEKED, TWISTED, TWO SHEETS TO THE WIND, UN-ABLE TO SCRATCH HIMSELF, UNDER, UNDER THE AFFLUENCE OF INCOHOL, UNDER THE INFLUENCE, UNDER THE TABLE, UNDER THE WEATHER, UNK-DRAY, UP A TREE, UPHOLSTERED, UP-PISH, UPPITY, UPSEY, UPSIDE DOWN, UP THE POLE, UP TO THE EARS, UP TO THE GILLS, VALIANT, VARNISHED, VEGETA-BLE, VERY WEARY, VULCANIZED, WAA-ZOOED, WALKING ON ROCKY SOCKS, WALL-EYED, WAM-BAZZLED, WAMBLE-CROPPED, WANKERED, WAPSED-DOWN, WASTED, WATER LOGGED, WATER SOAKED, WAXED, WAZZOCKED, WEAK-JOINTED, WEARING BEER GOGGLES, WEARY, WELL-AWAY, WELL-BOTTLED, WELL-FIXED, WELL-HEELED, WELL IN FOR IT, WELL-LIT, WELL-LUBRICATED, WELL-OILED, WELL-PRESERVED, WELL-PRIMED, WELL-SOAKED, WELL-SPRUNG, WELL TO LIVE, WELL-UNDER, WET, WET BOTH EYES, WET-HANDED, WHACKED, WHAT-NOSED, WHAZOOD, WHAZOOED, WHIFFLED, WHIPPED, WHIPSEY, WHISKY-FRISKY, WHISKIFIED, WHISTLED, WHIS-TLE DRUNK, WHITTLED, WHITTLED AS A PENGUIN, WHOOSHED, WHOOZY, WIDE OPEN, WIGGED WIGGED OUT, WIGGY, WILTED, WINEY, WING'D, WINGED, WING HEAVY, WIPED, WIPED OUT, WIPED OVER, WIRED, WIRED UP, WISE, WITH MAIN BRACE WELL SPLICED, WOBBLY, WOMBLETY-CROPT, WOODY, WOOFY, WOOZEY, WOOZY, WRECKED, WRENCHED, YAPPISH, YAPPY, YAUPISH, YAUPY, ZAGGED, ZAPPED, ZIGZAG, ZIG-ZAGGED, ZISSFIED, ZONED, ZONK, ZONKED, ZONKED OUT, ZOOBANG, ZOOED, ZOOTED, ZORKED, ZOSTED, ZOUNK, ZOUNKED (OUT), ZOZ-ZLED, ZULUED, ZUNKED.

Woof one's custard to vomit. For synonyms see YORK. [British, late 1900s-pres.]

woofy alcohol intoxicated. For synonyms see WOOFLED. [U.S. collegiate, late 1900s]

wookie the vagina. For synonyms see GENTIALS, MONOSYLLABLE. [U.S., late 1900s-pres.]

wooly a marijuana cigarette with cocaine mixed into it. For synonyms see MEZZROLL. [U.S., late 1900s-pres.]

wooly bear 1. a woman; a woman considered sexually. **2.** a female police officer. [both senses, citizens band radio slang, U.S., mid 1900s-pres.]

woozy (also **woozey**) intoxicated with alcohol. [U.S. slang, late 1800s-1900s]

work 1. to coit a woman. *Cf.* DO A WOMAN'S JOB FOR HER. **2.** copulation. [senses 1 and 2 are both U.S. slang, 1900s] **3.** a euphemism for any sexual activity. [colloquial, 1900s or before] **4.** to solicit and perform sexual acts, as in "work an area" in prostitution. [U.S. underworld, mid 1900s or before]

working girl (also **working broad, working woman**) a euphemism for "prostitute." *Cf.* BUSINESS GIRL. [U.S. slang, mid 1900s or before]

work off to masturbate. For synonyms see WASTE TIME. [British colloquial or slang, 1800s or before]

work out to coit. Borrowed from an athletic "workout." [U.S. slang, mid 1900s]

works 1. either the male or female genitals. In the sense of WATERWORKS (*q.v.*). **2.** copulation, "the works." From the male point of view. Referring to "giving" the female his WORKS (sense 1). **3.** the "third degree," a prolonged and supposedly violent period of questioning by the police. [all senses, slang, 1900s]

workshop the female genitals. See WORK (sense 1). [British slang, late 1800s, Farmer and Henley]

work the dumb oracle (also **work the hairy oracle**) to coit a woman. *Cf.* MOUTH-THANKLESS, MOUTH-THAT-CANNOT-BITE. [British slang, 1800s, Farmer and Henley]

worm 1. a low creep or jerk. From the lowness and sliminess of a worm. [U.S. slang, 1900s or before] **2.** the penis. [widespread nonce, 1800s-1900s]

worms spaghetti. For similar terms see DOG'S VOMIT. [colloquial since the early 1900s or before]

worms in blood spaghetti in tomato sauce. [U.S. jocular dysphemism, 1900s]

worship the porcelain god (also **worship the porcelain goddess**) to vomit. For synonyms see YORK. [U.S. collegiate, late 1900s]

worship the throne to vomit. *Cf.* THRONE. For synonyms see YORK. [U.S. collegiate, late 1900s, Eble]

wound the female genitals. *Cf.* CUT, GASH, SLIT. [from *Cymbeline* (Shakespeare)]

wrecked alcohol or drug intoxicated. [U.S. slang and drug culture, mid 1900s-pres.]

wrecking crew crack cocaine. For synonyms see NOSE-CANDY. [U.S., late 1900s-pres.]

wrenched drunk. For synonyms see WOOFLED. [U.S., late 1900s-pres.]

wriggle navels to copulate. [British slang, 1800s, Farmer and Henley]

wring one's sock out to urinate. There is an implication that one has waited too long to urinate. *Cf.* SHAKE A SOCK. For synonyms see WHIZ. [British slang, 1900s, *Dictionary of Slang and Unconventional English*]

wring the dew off the branch to urinate. A confusion of WRING ONE'S SOCK OUT (*q.v.*) and SHAKE THE DEW OFF THE LILY (*q.v.*). [U.S. slang, 1900s]

wring the rattlesnake to urinate. *Cf.* BLACKSNAKE, ROCK PYTHON. [Australian, 1900s or before]

write one's name (in the snow) to urinate in the open, especially in the snow. Male. For synonyms see WHIZ. [U.S., mid 1900s-pres.]

W.T.T. "white trailer trash." For synonyms see PECKERWOOD. [U.S., late 1900s-pres.]

wuk copulation. For synonyms see SMOCKAGE. [British, late 1900s-pres.]

wurst the penis. The German word for sausage. The same as FRANKFURTER, SAUSAGE, WEENIE. For synonyms see GENITALS, YARD. [U.S. slang, 1900s]

wuss(y) a weak, wishy-washy person. [U.S. slang, late 1900s]

X

X. 1. a toilet or privy. For synonyms see AJAX. [U.S., 1900s] **2.** ecstasy, the drug. [U.S., late 1900s-pres.]

Xena a lesbian. For synonyms see LES-BYTERIAN. [U.S., late 1900s-pres.]

X.L. "ex-lady" friend; former lady friend. *Cf.* X.Y.L. [U.S. slang, mid 1900s-pres.]

X-out to use drugs; to become drug intoxicated. [U.S. collegiate, late 1900s, Eble]

X-rated the extreme end of a rating scale of sexual content and violence in the motion picture industry. X-rated films usually contain explicit sex acts. *Cf.* ADULT, FRANK. [U.S., mid 1900s-pres.]

X.Y.L. "ex-young lady," former girl-friend or former wife.

X.Y.Z. "examine your zipper," a catch phrase reminding a male that he has forgotten to zip up his trousers. [U.S. slang, 1900s] Synonyms: COWS AND HORSES WILL GET OUT, ONE O'CLOCK, ONE O'CLOCK AT THE WATER-WORKS, YOUR MEDALS ARE SHOWING, YOUR NOSE IS BLEEDING.

Y

yack (also **yock, yuck, yuk**) a stupid fellow; an oaf. For synonyms see OAF. [U.S. slang, 1900s]

yak 1. a derogatory nickname for a Pole or a person of Polish descent. *Cf.* YACK. [U.S. slang, 1900s] **2.** to vomit. Onomatopoetic. Also interpreted as the animal name. This theme is extended to more severe vomiting as represented by WATER BUFFALO and BISON. For synonyms see YORK. [U.S. collegiate, late 1900s, Munro]

yakky-dak (also **yocky-dock**) any intoxicant: pills, hard drugs, or liquor. [U.S. slang, mid 1900s-pres.]

yank 1. to vomit. For synonyms see YORK. [U.S. collegiate, late 1900s] **2.** to masturbate. For synonyms and related subjects see WASTE TIME. [U.S. slang, mid 1900s-pres.]

yang the penis. *Cf.* JANG, YING-YANG. [U.S., 1900s]

yank to masturbate. For synonyms see WASTE TIME. [British, late 1900s-pres.]

yank one's strap (also **fondle one's fig, manipulate one's mango, pound one's pomegranate, yank, yank one's yam**) to masturbate. *Cf.* STRAP (sense 2). For synonyms see WASTE TIME. [slang, mid 1900s-pres.]

yank someone's crank 1. to tease a male sexually. As if tugging his penis. *Cf.* PULL SOMEONE'S PISSER. [U.S. slang, late 1900s] **2.** to tease anyone; to attempt to anger or get a rise out of someone, male or female. [U.S. general slang, late 1900s]

yank-tank a large American car. [British, late 1900s-pres.]

yap 1. an easy victim; a dupe. [U.S., 1900s] **2.** a fool or oaf; a hillbilly or bumpkin. [U.S. slang and dialect, 1900s]

3. a Japanese. [1900s] **4.** nonsense. *Cf.* YAWP. [U.S. colloquial, 1900s] **5.** to vomit. Onomatopoetic. For synonyms see YORK. [U.S. slang, late 1900s] See also YAK.

yard 1. a one-hundred-dollar bill. Underworld. [U.S., late 1900s-pres.] **2.** the penis. The word-of-choice for the penis between 1400s-1800. [primarily British, but also used in U.S. regional dialect and for literary effect, 1300s-pres.] Synonyms: AARON'S ROD, ABRAHAM, AFFAIR, ALMOND, ALMOND ROCK, ANGLE, ARBOR VITAE, ARM, ARSE-OPENER, ARSE-WEDGE, ATHENAEUM, AULD HORNIE, BABY-MAKER, BALD-HEADED HERMIT, BALD-HEADED MOUSE, BALONEY, BALONEY-PONY, BANANA, BAT, BATTERING-PIECE, BAUBLE, BAYONET, BAZOOKA, BEAK, BEAN, BEAN-TOSSER, BEEF, BEEF BAYONET, BELL-ROPE, BELLY, BELLY-RUFFIAN, BEST LEG OF THREE, BICHO, BIG DADDY, BIG WILLY, BINGY, BIRD, BISHOP, BLACKSNAKE, BLADE, BLOW-TORCH, BLUDGEON, BLUESKIN, BLUE-VEINED CUSTARD CHUCKER, BOB (AND DICK), BOB TAIL, BODKIN, BONE, BONFIRE, BOW, BOWSPRIT, BOZACK, BRACMARD, BROOM-HANDLE, BROOMSTICK, BUG-FUCKER, BUM-TICKLER, BURRITO, BUSH-BEATER, BUSHWHACKER, BUSK, BUTTER-KNIFE, BUTTON-HOLE WORKER, CADULIX, CALLIBISTRIS, CANDLE, CANE, CARK, CARNAL STUMP, CARROT, CATSO, CHANTICLEER, CHERRY-PICKER, CHICKEN, CHILD-GETTER, CHINGUS, CHINK-STOPPER, CHOAD, CHOPPER, CHORIZA, CHUB, CHUBSTER, CHUM, CLAVA, CLOTHES PROP, CLUB, COBRA, COCK, CODPIECE, COPPERSTICK, CORAL BRANCH, COREY, CRACK-HAUNTER, CRACK-HUNTER, CRACKSMAN, CRANK, CRANNY-HUNTER, CREAMSTICK, CRIMSON-CHITTERLING, CROOK, CROTCH-COBRA, CUCKOO, CUCUMBER, CULTY-GUN, CURP, DADADDY, DAGGER,

DANG, DANGLER, DANGLING PARTICI-
PLE, DANK, DARD, DART OF LOVE,
DEAREST MEMBER, DIBBLE, DICK, DICK-
ORY DOCK, DICKY, DIDDLE, DILDO, DIN-
GBAT, DING-DONG, DINGER, DINGLE,
DINGLE-DANGLE, DINGUS, DINK, DIP-
STICK, DIRK, DITTY, DIVINING ROD, DI-
ZACK, DOCTOR JOHNSON, DODAD,
DOFUNNY, DOHICKY, DOHINGER, DOJIG-
GER, DOJE, DOJOHNNIE, DOLLY, DONG,
DONG(ER), DOODLE, DOOFLICKER, DOO-
VER, DORK, DOWN-LEG, DRAGON, DRIB-
BLING DART OF LOVE, DROPPING
MEMBER, DRUMSTICK, DUCKELBERRY,
DUCY, DUMMY, EEL, ELEVENTH FINGER,
END, ENEMY, ENOB, EYE-OPENER, FAG,
FAMILY ORGAN, FATHER-CONFESSOR,
FIDDLE-BOW, FIREBRAND, FISH, FISHING
ROD, FLAPDOODLE, FLAPPER, FLIP-FLAP,
FLOATER, FOAMING BEEF PROBE, FOOL-
STICKER, FOREFINGER, FOREMAN, FOR-
NICATING-ENGINE, FORNICATING-MEM-
BER, FORNICATING-TOOL, FORNICATOR,
FRANKFURTER, FRIGAMAJIG, FUCKER,
FUCKSTICK, GADGET, GADSO, GAP-STOP-
PER, GARDEN-ENGINE, GARDENER, GAYING
INSTRUMENT, GENERATION TOOL, GENTLE-
TITTLER, GIGGLE-STICK, GIGGLING-PIN,
GIRLOMETER, GLADIUS, GOOBER, GOOSER,
GOOSE'S-NECK, GOOT, GRAVY-GIVER,
GRAVY-MAKER, GRINDING-TOOL, GRIS-
TLE, GULLY-RAKER, GUN, GUT-STICK,
HAIR-DIVIDER, HAIR-SPLITTER, HAM-
BONE, HAMMER, HAMPTON WICK, HAND-
STAFF, HANGING JOHNNY, HELMET,
HERMIT, HOE-HANDLE, HOG, HOLY
POKER, HONEY-POT CLEAVER, HONKER,
HOOTCHEE, HORN, HOSE, HOT-ROD,
HUNK OF MEAT, HUSBANDMAN OF NA-
TURE, IMPUDENCE, INSTRUMENT, INTRO-
MITTENT ORGAN, IRISH ROOT, IT, JACK,
JACK-IN-THE-BOX, JACK ROBINSON,
JACOB, JACQUE'S, JAMMY, JANG, JAQUES,
JERK-
ING-IRON, JEZEBEL, JIG, JIGGER, JIG-
GLING-BONE, JIMBO, JIMBROWSKI, JIMMY,
JING-JANG, JOCK, JOCKAM, JOCKUM,
JOCKY, JOCUM, JOHN, JOHNNIE, JOHNSON,
JOHN THOMAS, JOHN WILLIE, JOINT,
JONES, JOY KNOB, JOY PRONG, JOY-
STICK, J.T., JULIUS CAESAR, JUNIOR,
JUSTUM, KEY, KIDNEY-SCRAPER, KID-
NEY-WIPER, KING-MEMBER, KIRP, KNOB,
KNOCK, KNOCKER, KORI, KORO, KOSHER
PICKLE, LABOURER OF NATURE, LADIES'

DELIGHT, LADIES' LOLLIPOP, LADIES'
TREASURE, LAMP OF LIFE, LANCE,
LANCE OF LOVE, LANGOLEE, LARY-
DOODLE, LICORICE STICK, LIFE-PRE-
SERVER, LITTLE BROTHER, LITTLE
DAVY, LITTLE FINGER, LITTLE MAN, LIT-
TLE WILLIE, LIVE RABBIT, LIVER-
TURNER, LIVE SAUSAGE, LIZARD, LOB,
LOB-COCK, LOBSTER, LOLLYPOP, LONG
JOHN, LONG TOM, LOP COCK, LOVE-
DART, LOVE MUSCLE, LOVE PUMP, LOVE
SAUSAGE, LOVE'S PICKLOCK, LOVE-
STEAK, LUCY, LULLABY, LUNG-DIS-
TURBER, MACHINE, MAD MICK, MAGIC
WAND, MAGNUM, MAIN VEIN, MALE GEN-
ITAL ORGAN, MALE MEMBER, MALE PU-
DENDUM, MAN-ROOT, MAN THOMAS,
MARROW-BONE, MARROW-BONE-AND-
CLEAVER, MARROW-PUDDING, MASCU-
LINE PART, MASTER JOHN THURSDAY,
MASTER MEMBER, MASTER OF CEREMON-
IES, MATRIMONIAL PEACEMAKER, MAY-
POLE, MEAT, MEAT WHISTLE, MEMBER,
MEMBER FOR THE COSKSHIRE, MEMBRUM,
MEMBRUM VIRILE, MENTULA, MENTULE,
MERRYMAKER, MICKEY, MIDDLE FINGER,
MIDDLE LEG, MIDDLE STUMP, MILKMAN,
MISTER TOM, MODIGGER, MOL, MOLE,
MOUSE, MOWDIEWART, MR. HAPPY, MR.
SAUSAGE, MUSCLE OF LOVE, MUTTON-
DAGGER, MY BODY'S CAPTAIN, MY MAN
THOMAS, NAG, NATURAL MEMBER, NA-
TURE'S SCYTHE, NEBUCHADNEZZAR,
NEEDLE, NEEDLE DICK, NERVOUS-CANE,
NIMROD, NINE-INCH KNOCKER, NIPPY,
NOONEY, NOSE, NUDGER, NUDINNUDO,
OL' DAMOCLES, OLD BLIND BOB, OLD
FELLA, OLD HORNINGTON, OLD HORNY,
OLD MAN, OLD SLIMY, ONE-EYED BOB,
ONE-EYED BROTHER, ONE-EYED MILK-
MAN, ONE-EYED MONSTER, ONE-EYED
PANTS MOUSE, ONE-EYED TROUSER
SNAKE, ONE-EYED WONDER, ONE-EYED
WORM, ONE-EYED ZIPPER SNAKE,
ORGAN, PADLOCK, PAPER TIGER, PAT
AND MICK, PAX-WAX, PEACEMAKER,
PECKER, PECKERHEAD, PECNOSTER,
PEENIE, PEE-WEE, PEEZEL, PEGO, PEN,
PENCIL, PENCIL DICK, PENDULUM, PENIS,
PENIS DEPENDENS, PERCE, PERCH,
PERCY, PESTLE, PETER, PICCOLO, PICK-
LOCK, PIKE, PIKESTAFF, PILE-DRIVER,
PILGRIM'S STAFF, PILLICOCK, PIMPLE,
PIN, PINGA, PINK OBOE, PINKY, PINTLE,

PIONEER OF NATURE, PIPE, PISSER, PIS-
TOL, PISTON, PISTON ROD, PITO, PIZELL,
PIZZLE, PLACKET-RACKET, PLAYTHING,
PLENIPO, PLONKER, PLOWSHARE, PLUG,
PLUGTAIL, PLUM-TREE, PLUNGER, P-
MAKER, POCKET-ROCKET, POINT,
POINTER, POKER, POLE, POLL-AXE, POL-
YPHEMUS, PONDSNIPE, PONY, POON-
TANGER, POPERINE PEAR, POPSICLE,
PORK, PORK-SWORD, POST, POTATO-FIN-
GER, POTENT REGIMENT, POWER, PRIA-
PUS, PRICK, PRICKLE, PRIDE AND JOY,
PRINCOCK, PRIVY MEMBER, PRONG, PUD,
PUDDING, PULSE, PUMP, PUMP-HANDLE,
PUP, PUTZ, QUARTER-MASTER, QUICK-
ENING-PEG, QUIM-STAKE, QUIM-WEDGE,
RADISH, RALPH, RAM, RAMMER, RAM-
ROD, RANDY, RANGER, RAW MEAT,
REAMER, RECTOR OF THE FEMALES,
RED-CAP, RED-HOT POCKER, RHUBARB,
ROD, ROD OF LOVE, ROGER, ROGERRY,
ROLLING-PIN, ROLY-POLY, ROOSTER,
ROOT, ROTO-ROOTER, ROUNDHEAD, RUB-
IGO, RUDDER, RUFFIAN, RUMPLEFORE-
SKIN, RUMP-SPLITTER, RUPERT, SAINT
PETER, SCALLYWAG, SCEPTRE, SCHLANGE,
SCHLONG, SCHMOCK, SCHMUCK, SCHVANCE,
SCHVONTZ, SCHWEEN, SCREWDRIVER, SEN-
SITIVE PLANT, SENSITIVE-TRUNCHEON, SER-
PENT, SEXING-PIECE, SHAFT OF CUPID,
SHAKER, SHE, SHORT-ARM, SHORT-ARM
TRAIL, SHOVE-DEVIL, SHOVE-STRAIGHT,
SILENT FLUTE, SINBAD, SIR JOHN, SIR
MARTIN WAGSTAFF, SKIN FLUTE, SKY-
SCRAPER, SLUG, SMALL-ARM, SMELL-
SMOCK, SNAKE, SNAKE IN THE GRASS,
SNAPPER, SOLICITOR-GENERAL, SPAR,
SPIGOT, SPIKE-FAGGOT, SPINDLE, SPIT,
SPLIT-ARSE MECHANIC, SPLIT-MUTTON,
SPLIT-RUMP, SPONGE, SPOUT, STAFF,
STALLION, STAR-GAZER, STEMMER,
STERN-POST, STICK, STING, STORMY DICK,
STRAP, STRETCHER, STRUNT, STUFF,
STUMP, SUCKER, SUGAR-STICK, SWEET-
MEAT, SWIPE, SWIVER, SWIZZLE-STICK,
SWORD, TACKET, TACKLE, TADGER, TAIL,
TAIL-PIKE, TAIL-PIN, TAIL-PIPE, TAIL-
TACKLE, TAIL-TREE, TALLY-WHACKER,
TANTRUM, TARSE, TASSEL, TEAPOT,
TEENY WEENY, TENANT-IN-TAIL, TENT,
TENT-PEG, TENTUM, THAT, THE BOY, THE
OLD ADAM, THE OLD ROOT, THING,
THINGAMBOB, THINGAMY, THINGUMMY,
THIRD LEG, THISTLE, THOMAS, THORN,
THORN-IN-THE-FLESH, THUMB OF LOVE,

TICKLE-GIZZARD, TICKLER, TICKLE-
TAIL, TIMOTHY, TINK, TINKLER, TODGER,
TOMAS, TOMMY, TONGE, TOOL, TORCH
OF CUPID, TOSH, TOSSELBERRY, TOUCH-
TRAP, TOY, TRAP-STICK, TRIFLE, TRIG-
GER, TROUBLE-GIBLETS, TROUSER
SNAKE, TROUSER TROUT, TUBE, TUBE-
STEAK, TUBESTEAK OF LOVE, TUG-MUT-
TON, TUMMY BANANA, UNCLE DICK,
UNIT, UNRULY MEMBER, VALBOWSKI,
VERGE, VESTRY-MAN, VIRGA, VIRILE
MEMBER, VOMER, WAG, WAND, WANG,
WANG(ER), WATER-SPOUT, WAZOO,
WEAPON, WEDGE, WEENIE, WHACKER,
WHANG, WHANG-BONE, WHANGER, WHAT,
WHIP, WHISKY DICK, WHISTLE, WHORE-
PIPE, WICK, WIGGA-WAGGA, WILLIE, WIM-
BLE, WINKIE, WINKLE, WIRE, WONG,
WORM, WRIGGLING-POLE, WURST, YANG,
YARD MEASURE, YING-YANG, YOSH,
YUM-YUM, ZUBRICK.

yard measure 1. the female genitals,
specifically the vagina. From a name
for a one-yard measuring stick (yard-
stick). A jocular reference to the
penis and to the length implications
of "yard." *Cf.* GIRLOMETER. [British
slang, 1800s] **2.** the penis. [British,
late 1800s-1900s]

Yasser an erection. From Yasser Ar-
afat = Crackafat. For synonyms see
ERECTION. [British, late 1900s-pres.]

yawn in technicolor to vomit. For
synonyms see YORK. [U.S., late
1900s-pres.]

yeaster a beer-drinker. [U.S., mid
1900s-pres.]

yeast-powder biscuit the female
genitals, especially when swollen due
to sexual stimulation. *Cf.* BISCUIT.
[U.S. dialect (Boontling), late 1800s-
early 1900s, Charles Adams]

yellow angel a barbiturate, Nembutal (trademark). [U.S. drug culture,
1900s]

yellow-back a gob of phlegm. [Aus-
tralian, 1900s, Baker]

yellow bullets Nembutal (trademark)
capsules; any barbiturate tablets or capsules. [U.S. drug culture, mid 1900s-
pres.]

yellow-dog 1. a coward. [U.S. slang,

1900s] Synonyms: CANDY-ASS, CHICKEN, CHICKEN-HEART, COW-BABY, CRADDON, CRAVEN, DAFF, DASTARD, FUNKER, JELLY BELLY, LILY-LIVER, MILQUE-TOAST, MUDGER, PANSY, PANTYWAIST, PIKER, POLTROON, PUSSYCAT, QUAKEBUTTOCK, RABBIT, RECREANT, RING-TAIL, SHY-COCK, SISSY, SOOK, SOP, SQUIB, WEAK SISTER, WHEYFACE, YELLOWBELLY, YELLOW HEEL, YELLOW LIVER. **2.** a term of contempt. [both senses, U.S., 1800s-pres.]

yellow-jacket a barbiturate tablet or capsule, usually Nembutal (trademark). From the common name of the insect. [U.S. drug culture, mid 1900s-pres.]

yellow sunshine the drug L.S.D. (q.v.). Cf. ORANGE SUNSHINE, SUNSHINE. [U.S. drug culture, mid 1900s-pres.]

yen 1. sexual arousal or desire. [colloquial, 1900s] **2.** a craving for addictive drugs, especially opium or heroin. See PEN YEN. [U.S. drug culture, 1900s] **3.** money. [U.S., late 1900s-pres.]

yench to swindle someone; to victimize someone. Underworld. [U.S., late 1900s-pres.]

yenta a gossip, usually a woman. From yiddish. [U.S., mid 1900s-pres.]

yentz 1. to copulate or screw (q.v.). **2.** to cheat or deceive, i.e., screw. [both senses, Yiddish, 1900s]

yentzer a man or woman who copulates frequently or obsessively. See YENTZ (sense 1).

yerba marijuana. [the Spanish cognate of HERB (q.v.); U.S. drug culture, mid 1900s-pres.]

yernt a despised person, an outcast. For synonyms see SNOKE-HORN. [U.S. collegiate, late 1900s, Eble]

yesca marijuana. [U.S. drug culture, 1900s]

yield one's favors for a female to agree to coition. [British euphemism, 1800s, Farmer and Henley]

yimyon crack cocaine. For synonyms see NOSE-CANDY. [U.S., late 1900s-pres.]

ying-yang the penis. Cf. JING-JANG. [U.S. slang, 1900s]

yodel 1. to commit SODOMY (q.v.), possibly COITUS PER ANUM (q.v.). More likely FELLATIO (q.v.) with repeated movement of the tongue. Cf. CANYON-YODELING. [U.S. underworld, Berrey and Van den Bark] **2.** to vomit. For synonyms see YORK. [British, late 1900s-pres.]

yodeling in a canyon talking aimlessly. [U.S., late 1900s-pres.]

yodel in the canyon to perform CUNNILINGUS. [U.S. slang, late 1900s]

yodel in the gully to perform an act of CUNNILINGUS; an act of CUNNILINGUS. For synonyms see CUNNILINGUS. [U.S. slang, mid 1900s-pres.] See also YODEL IN THE CANYON.

yogurt semen. For synonyms see METTLE. [U.S. collegiate, late 1900s]

yoke semen. Possibly confusing the yolk of an egg with the albumin. For synonyms see METTLE. [U.S., late 1900s-pres.]

yoked having well-marked abdominal muscles. [U.S., late 1900s-pres.]

yokel 1. a bumpkin or an oaf. [British and U.S., 1800s-pres.] **2.** a black term of contempt for Caucasians. [U.S., mid 1900s]

yola a female mulatto. For synonyms see MAHOGANY.

yoni the female sexual organ. For synonyms see GENITALS, MONOSYLLABLE. [British and U.S., late 1900s-pres.]

york 1. to vomit. **2.** vomitus. [both senses, U.S. slang and dialect, 1900s] Synonyms for both senses: ACCOUNTS, AIR ONE'S BELLY, BARF, BE AT THE CURB, BECOME ILL, BISON, BLOW BEETS, BLOW CHOW, BLOW GRITS, BLOW LUNCH, BLOW ONE'S COOKIES, BLOW ONE'S DOUGHNUTS, BLOW ONE'S GROCERIES, BOAG, BOFF, BOW TO THE PORCELAIN ALTAR, BOW TO THE PORCELAIN GOD, BRACK, BRAKE, BRING UP, BUICK, CACK, CALL EARL, CALL FOR HUGHIE, CALL RUTH, CASCADE, CAST, CAST UP, CAT, CHEESE, CHEW THE CHEESE, CHUCK, CHUCK A DUMMY,

CHUCK UP, CHUMMY, CHUM THE FISH, CHUNDER, CHUNK, CRY HUGHIE, CRY RALPH, CRY RUTH, decorate one's shoes, DEFOOD, DRAIN THE BILGE, DRIVE FRENCH HORSES, DRIVE THE PORCELAIN BUS, DROP ONE'S COOKIES, DUKE, DUMP, DUMP ONE'S LOAD, EARL, EARP, EASE ONESELF, FEED THE FISHES, FEED THE KIPPERS, FETCH UP, FLASH, FLASH THE HASH, FLAY THE FOX, FLING UP, FRED, GIP, GO TO EUROPE WITH RALPH AND EARL IN A BUICK, HAPPY RETURNS, HASH, HAVE THE PUKES, HONK, HONK (UP) ONE'S RING, HORK, HUG THE PORCELAIN GOD, HUG THE PORCELAIN GODDESS, HUG THE THRONE, HURL, JERK THE CAT, KACK, KAK, KECK, KISS THE PORCELAIN GOD, LAUGH AT THE CARPET, LAUGH AT THE LAWN, LAUNCH ONE'S LUNCH, LIQUID-LAUGH, LOSE A MEAL, LOSE IT, LOSE ONE'S COOKIES, LOSE ONE'S GUTS, LOSE ONE'S LUNCH, LUNG-BUTTER, MAKE A SALE, MAKE LOVE TO THE PORCELAIN GODDESS, MARRY ONE'S PORCELAIN MISTRESS, PARBREAK, PARK A CUSTARD, PAVEMENT PIZZA, PERK, POWERBARF, POWER-BOOT, PRAY TO THE ENAMEL GOD, PRAY TO THE PORCELAIN GOD, PUKE, PUMP, PUMP SHIP, PURGE, PUT, PUT BIRDIE, QUOCKEN, RALPH, RALPH SOMETHING UP, REECH, REGURGITATE, RETCH, REVERSE GEARS, RIDE THE BUICK, RIDE THE PORCELAIN BUS, RIDE THE PORCELAIN HONDA, RIDE THE PORCELAIN TRAIN, ROLF, RUTH, SELL BUICKS, SELL OUT, SHIT, SHOOT ONE'S COOKIES, SHOOT THE CAT, SHOOT THE WORKS, SHOUT AT ONE'S SHOES, SICK, SICKS, SICK UP, SKIN A GOAT, SLING A CAT, SNAP ONE'S COOKIES, SPEW, SPEW-UP, SPILL ONE'S BREAKFAST, SPILL THE BLUE GROCERIES, SPIT BEEF, SPULE, TALK INTO THE PORCELAIN TELEPHONE, TALK ON THE BIG WHITE PHONE, TALK ON THE GREAT WHITE TELEPHONE, TALK TO EARL, TALK TO RALPH ON THE BIG WHITE PHONE, THROW A MAP, THROW ONE'S VOICE, THROW UP, THROW UP ONE'S ACCOUNTS, THROW UP ONE'S TOENAILS, TOSS, TOSS A TIGER ON THE CARPET, TOSS ONE'S COOKIES, TOSS ONE'S LUNCH, TOSS ONE'S TACOS, UKE, UNSPIT, UNSWALLOW, UPCHUCK, URP, VARF, VOMICK, VOMIT, VOMITUS, WATER BUFFALO, WHEEZE, WHIP THE CAT, WOOF, WOOF COOKIES, WOOF ONE'S CUSTARD, WORSHIP THE PORCELAIN GOD, WORSHIP THE PORCELAIN GODDESS, WORSHIP THE THRONE, YAK, YANK, YAP, YAWN IN TECHNICOLOR, YODEL, YUKE, ZUKE.

yosh the penis. For synonyms see YARD. [U.S. slang, 1900s]

you and me urine; an act of urination; to urinate. Rhyming slang for "pee," *i.e.*, urine. [British, 1900s]

You (can) bet your (sweet) ass! "You can be sure about that!"; "You are right!" [U.S. slang, colloquial, mid 1900s-pres.]

You must have been vaccinated with a gramophone needle! "You talk too much!" [Australian, mid 1900s-pres.]

your brown!, Up a curse the equivalent of "Up your ass!" *Cf.* BROWN (sense 1). [U.S. slang, 1900s]

your medals are showing a disguised warning that one's fly is undone. The medals are fly buttons. See TURKISH MEDAL. For synonyms see X.Y.Z. [British slang, 1900s or before]

Your place or mine? an inquiry meant to determine the site of a sexual encounter. [U.S. and elsewhere, late 1900s]

yours!, Up the same as UP IT! (*q.v.*). [U.S., 1900s]

yuckie nuk nuks bad food. [U.S., late 1900s-pres.]

yuke (also **uke**) **1.** to vomit. Both entry forms are pronounced the same. For synonyms see YORK. See also ZUKE. **2.** VOMITUS. For synonyms see YORK. [both senses, U.S., late 1900s]

yummy pants a sexually attractive female. For synonyms see BIRD. [U.S., late 1900s-pres.]

yum-yum 1. the female genitals. **2.** the penis. [both senses, British slang, 1800s, Farmer and Henley]

yuppie flu the respiratory effects of cocaine use. [U.S., late 1900s-pres.]

Z

Z. one ounce of a narcotic or marijuana. From "oz.," the abbreviation of "ounce." *Cf.* LID, O.Z. [U.S. drug culture, 1900s]

Zacatecas purple marijuana from Zacatecas, Mexico. [U.S. drug culture, mid 1900s-pres.]

zagged intoxicated with alcohol. *Cf.* ZIG-ZAG. [U.S. slang, 1900s]

zapped 1. tired; exhausted. [U.S., late 1900s-pres.] **2.** alcohol or drug intoxicated. For synonyms see TALL, WOOFLED. *[U.S., late 1900s-pres.]*

zarf an ugly and undesirable male. [U.S. slang, mid 1900s]

zazzle 1. sexual desire. **2.** exaggerated sexuality; sex appeal [both senses, U.S. slang, 1900s]

zebra someone who is racially half black and half white. Rude. [U.S., late 1900s-pres.]

zeltoids marijuana. For synonyms see MARI. [U.S., late 1900s-pres.]

Zen the drug L.S.D. (*q.v.*). [U.S. drug culture, mid 1900s-pres.]

zent a pimple. See ZIT. For synonyms see BURBLE.

zeppelin a large marijuana cigarette. For synonyms see MEZZROLL. [U.S., late 1900s-pres.]

zerked out drug intoxicated; heavily drug intoxicated; very high on marijuana. For synonyms see TALL. [U.S. drug culture, late 1900s, Kaiser]

zero an insignificant person; a dull nobody. For synonyms see OAF. [U.S. slang, mid 1900s-pres.]

Z-head someone who is oblivious to everything; a person who is completely out of it; a ZONE. [U.S. collegiate, late 1900s, Eble]

zib marijuana. For synonyms see MARI. [U.S., late 1900s-pres.]

zig-zig 1. to copulate. **2.** copulation.

[both are widespread military slang; 1800s-1900s]

zimmer a girl; an attractive woman. [U.S. slang, late 1900s]

zings the DELIRIUM TREMENS (*q.v.*). [U.S. slang, early 1900s]

zipped drug intoxicated. For synonyms see TALL. [U.S., late 1900s-pres.]

zipperfish the female genitals. For synonyms see GENITALS, MONOSYLLABLE. [U.S., late 1900s-pres.]

zipper morals loose sexual morals, said of a man or a woman. [U.S. slang, mid 1900s-pres.]

zissified drunk. *Cf.* WHISKYFIED. [U.S. slang, 1900s, Berrey and Van den Bark]

zit a pimple. Usually in the plural. For synonyms see BURBLE. [U.S. slang, mid 1900s-pres.]

zob a worthless person; a nobody. See ZIB. [U.S. slang, 1900s]

zod 1. any repellent thing or person. **2.** a studious person. [U.S., late 1900s-pres.]

zol marijuana. For synonyms see MARI. [U.S., late 1900s-pres.]

zombie 1. a very stupid person; a dunce. **2.** a weird and frightening person. **3.** a dead body made to live by magic or some other force. The word and concepts are ultimately West African via West Indian voodoo. [all senses, U.S., 1900s] **4.** a drug addict; a drug or marijuana user who is debilitated from drug use. [U.S. drug culture, late 1900s]

zombie buzz a variety of the drug phencyclidine, P.C.P. For synonyms see P.C.P. [U.S. drug culture, late 1900s, Abel]

zonables marijuana cigarettes. For

synonyms see MEZZROLL. [U.S., late 1900s-pres.]

zone a detached and giddy person; someone who is SPACED-OUT (*q.v.*). [U.S. slang, mid 1900s-pres.]

zoned drug or alcohol intoxicated. [U.S. drug culture and slang, mid 1900s-pres.]

zoned (out) 1. alcohol or drug intoxicated. For synonyms see WOOFLED. [U.S., late 1900s-pres.] 2. exhausted [U.S., late 1900s-pres.]

zonk an oaf; a totally incompetent person. [U.S. slang, mid 1900s-pres.]

zonked-out (also **zonked**) 1. asleep or very sleepy. [U.S. slang, mid 1900s-pres.] 2. drug or alcohol intoxicated. [U.S. drug culture and slang, mid 1900s-pres.]

zonker a frequent user of drugs or a marijuana smoker. Based on ZONK (*q.v.*). Cf. ZONKED-OUT. [U.S. drug culture, mid 1900s-pres.]

zoo 1. a brothel with women of various types and nationalities. 2. a prison, especially if racially mixed. [both senses, U.S. underworld, 1900s]

zoobang intoxicated with alcohol. For synonyms see WOOFLED. [U.S. slang, late 1900s]

zooed alcohol intoxicated. For synonyms see WOOFLED. [U.S. slang, late 1900s, Eble] See also ZOOBANG.

zook (also **zucke**) a wretched and dilapidated prostitute. Cf. MADAMOI-ZOOK. [U.S. underworld, 1900s]

zoom amphetamines, specifically Methedrine (trademark). [U.S. drug culture, mid 1900s-pres.]

zooted 1. high on cocaine. For synonyms see TALL. [U.S., late 1900s-pres.] 2. extremely intoxicated. For synonyms see TALL, WOOFLED. [U.S., late 1900s-pres.]

zootied (also **zooty**) intoxicated with drugs; HIGH. For synonyms see TALL. [U.S. collegiate, late 1900s]

zoozled drunk. For synonyms see WOOFLED. [U.S. slang, 1900s]

zorked alcohol intoxicated. For synonyms see WOOFLED. [U.S. slang, late 1900s]

zosted drunk. For synonyms see WOOFLED. [U.S., late 1900s-pres.]

zot nothing; zero. [U.S., late 1900s-pres.]

zotz 1. zero; nothing. [U.S., late 1900s-pres.] 2. to kill someone or something. [U.S., late 1900s-pres.]

'Zounds! an old oath and an exclamation now used primarily for effect, "By His wounds!" Perhaps the most widely known of the ancient oaths. [late 1600s-pres.] Other oaths: ADAD!, ADOD!, ADZOOKS!, AGAD!, BEDAD!, BEGAD!, BEGORRA!, BEGOSH!, BEGUM!, BEJABERS!, BEJESUS!, BELEAKINS!, BLI-MEY!, BLIND ME!, BLOOD-AN'-'OUNS!, BLOW ME DOWN!, BLUE-BOTTLES!, BLURT, BOB!, BODI-KIN!, BODKINS!, BUDKIN!, BUDLINKINS!, BUGGER ME BACKWARDS!, BUGGER ME!, BUGGER ME DEAD!, BUMFAY!, BURBAGE!, BURN YOU!, BY CHRISAMIGHTY!, BY CHRIST'S FOOT!, BY COB'S BODY!, BY COCK-AND PIE!, BY CORPUS BONES!, BY CRACKY!, BY CRICKETY!, BY CRICKY!, BY DINGY!, BY GAD'S BUD!, BY GAR!, BY GARY!, BY GEE AND JAY!, BY GINGER!, BY GIS!, BY GODFREY!, BY GOD'S ARMS!, BY GOD'S BODIKEN!, BY GOD'S BODIKIN!, BY GOD'S CORPUS!, BY GOD'S DIG-GERS!, BY GOD'S DIGNITY!, BY GOD'S PITTIKINS!, BY GOD'S SANTY!, BY GOG!, BY GOG'S WOUNS!, BY GOLLY!, BY GORRAM!, BY GOSH!, BY GOSHDANG!, BY GRABS!, BY GRACIOUS!, BY GRANNY!, BY GRAVY!, BY GUINEA!, BY GUM!, BY GYS!, BY HOKEY!, BY JEHOSHAPHAT!, BY JERPS!, BY JINGO!, BY JINKS!, BY JOCK-IES!, BY JOCKS!, BY JOE BEESWAX!, BY JOVE!, BY JUCKIES!, BY JUDAS!, BY JU-PITER!, BY JYSSE!, BY KING!, BY MY CABBAGE-TREE!, BY MY FAY!, BY MY SAINTED AUNT!, BY NAILS AND BY BLOOD!, BY OUR LADY!, BY THE BLOOD OF CHRIST!, BY THE CROSS!, BY THE ELEVENS!, BY THE ETERNAL GOD!, BY THE FATHER OF LIGHT!, BY THE GREAT FATHER!, BY THE GREAT HORN SPOON!, BY THE GREAT JEHOVAH!, BY THE HOLY CROSS!, BY THE HOLY SACRAMENT!, BY THE LORD OF HEAVEN!, BY THE MASS!, BY THE MOUSE-FOOT!, BY THE SAINTS ABOVE!, BY THUNDER!, CARAMBA!, CAT'S NOUNS!, CATSO!, CHEESE AND CRUST!, CHRIST-ALL-BLEEDING-MIGHTY!, CHRIST-

ALL-JESUS!, CHRIST-ALMIGHTY-WONDER!, CHRISTMAS!, CHRIST-ON-A-CRUTCH!, CODS-FISH!, COKKES BODY!, COKKES BONES!, CONSARN!, CONSARN YE!, COO LUMMY!, CORKS!, CORKSCREW!, COR LUMMIE!, COT, COTZOOKS!, CREEPING JESUS!, CRIMENY SAKES ALIVE!, CRIMINEY!, CRIMINITLY!, CRIPES!, CRIPUS!, DAMMIT TO HELL!, DAMN YOUR EYES!, DEAR GUSSIE!, DEAR ME!, DIG SWIGGER IT!, DING BUST IT!, DOB DARN!, DOG BITE ME!, DOG-BLINE-ME!, DOG'S WOUNDS!, DOG TAKE!, DONNER UND BLITZEN!, D'RAB-BIT!, DRAT!, DRAT IT!, ECOD!, EDOD!, EGAD!, FEGS!, FISH!, FOR CHRISAKE!, FOR COCK'S BONES!, FOR CRIMP'S SAKE!, FOR CRYING OUT LOUD!, FOR GOSH SAKE!, FOR JESUS' FOOT!, FORSOOTH!, FOR THE LOVE OF MIKE!, FOR THE LOVE OF MUD!, FRICK!, FUCKNAYE!, FUCK ME!, GAD'S BUD!, GADSO!, GADSOBS!, GADZOOKS!, GARDENIA!, GARN IT!, GAW BLIMEY!, GAWDFER!, GEE-HOLLI-KENS!, GEE-WHILLICATS!, GEE-WHILLI-GINS!, GEE-WHILLIKERS!, GEE-WHISKERS!, GEE-WHITTAKERS!, GEE-WHIZ!, GEE-WHIZZARD!, GEE-WHOLLIKER!, GEEZ!, GODAMERCY!, GODAMIGHTY!, GOD BLESS AMERICA!, GOD BLIND ME, GOD BURN!, GOD DAMN ME!, GOD FORBID!, GODFREY DORMAN!, GODFREY MIGHTY!, GOD'S DEATH!, GOD'S HOOKS!, GODSO!, GOD SWORBET!, GOLBLAST!, GOM!, GONNOWS!, GOOD CHRISTMAS!, GOOD GOD!, GOOD GODFREY!, GOOD GODFREY DANIEL!, GOOD GRACIOUS!, GOOD GRIEF!, GOODNESS GRACIOUS!, GOODY GOODY GODDAMN!, GOODY GOODY GUMDROP!, GORAMITY!, GOR-BLIMEY!, GORDELPUS!, GOSH-ALL-LIGHT-NING!, GOSH ALMIGHTY!, GOSH-AMIGHTY!, GOSHDAL!, GOSHWALADER!, GO TO BUGGERY!, GREAT CAESAR'S GHOST!, GREAT GUNS!, GREAT SCOTT!, GREAT SNAKES!, HANG IT!, HOLY CATS, HOLY CHRIST!, HOLY COW!, HOLY DOG CRAP!, HOLY DOG SHIT!, HOLY FUCK!, HOLY GEE!, HOLY GOD!, HOLY GUM-DROPS!, HOLY JERUSALEM!, HOLY JUMP-ING MOTHER OF JESUS!, HOLY JUMPING MOTHER OF MOSES!, HOLY KERIST!, HOLY MACKEREL!, HOLY MITHER!, HOLY MOLY!, HOLY MOSES!, HOLY SMOKES!, HOLY SNOOKS!, HOLY SOCKS!, HOLY SUF-FERING SNAKES!, HOLY SWISS CHEESE!, HOLY TOLEDO!, HONEST TO GOD!, HON-EST-TO-GOODNESS!, HONEST-TO-GOTHAM!, HOT ALMIGHTY!, HOT-DAMN!, I DO VUM!, IGAD!, I'LL BE A DIRTY WORD!, I'LL BE A RING-TAILED POLECAT!, I'LL BE DING-BUSTED!, I'LL BE DUM SQUIZZLED!, I'LL BE FLABBERGASTED!, I'LL BE HANGED!, I'LL BE JIGGERED!, I'LL BE JIG-SWIGGERED!, I'LL BE JIM-SWIGGLED!, I'LL BE SWITCHED!, I SNOW!, I SNUM!, I SWAN!, I SWANNY!, I SWOW!, I VUM!, JEE!, JEES!, JEE-WHILLIK-INS!, JEE-WHISKERS!, JEEZ!, JEEZE!, JEHOS-HAPHAT!, JEMIMA!, JEMINY!, JERUSALEM!, JESUS!, JESUS H. CHRIST!, JEWHILLIKENS!, JIMINITLY!, JIMINY CRICKETS!, JUDAS PRIEST!, JUMPING JEHOSHAPHAT!, JUMP-ING JEW'S-HARPS!, JUMPING MOSES!, KE-RIST!, KINELL!, KINOATH!, LAND OF GOS-HEN!, LAND SAKES, LAWDY SAKES ALIVE!, LAWKS!, LAW'S SAKES!, LAWSY!, LAWSY'S SAKES!, LIKE FUCK!, LIKE FUN!, LIKE HELL!, LIKE SIN!, LOD-A-MASSY!, LORD LOVE A DUCK, LORD SAKES ALIVE!, LORDY!, LORGAMIGHTY!, LORS!, MAY GOD BLIND ME!, MAY I GO TO HELL!, MERCY!, MIST ALCRITY!, MON DIEU!, MRS. DUCKETT!, MY ASS, MY BLOOD!, MY FOOT!, MY GAY!, MY GOD!, MY GOOD-NESS!, MY KING OATH!, MY OATH!, MYST ALL CRIKEY!, MYST ALL CRITEY!, MYST ALL KRITEY!, MY STARS ALIVE!, NARK IT!, NICK TAKE ME!, NIGGERS!, NIGGERS-NOG-GERS!, NO SHIT!, NOUNS, O CRIMES!, 'ODDS BOB!, 'ODDS BONES!, 'ODDS FISH!, 'ODDS WUCKS AND TAR!, 'O ROT IT!, 'ODS BLOOD!, 'ODS-BODIKINS, 'ODS BODKINS!, 'ODSFLESH!, 'ODS FOOT!, 'ODS HARICOTS AND CUTLETS!, 'ODSKILDERKINS!, 'OD-SOONS!, 'ODS WOOKERS!, ON MY TROTH!, PAR-DEE!, PERDITION!, PISS ON IT!, SAKES ALIVE!, 'SBLID!, 'SBLOOD!, 'SBOBS, 'SBOD-KINS!, 'SBODY!, 'SBORES!, 'SBUD!, 'SDEATH!, 'SDEYNES!, 'SDIGGERS!, S'ELP ME GOD!, S'ELP ME GREENS!, S'FIRE!, 'SFLESH!, 'SFOOT!, S'GAD!, 'SHEART!, SHIDDLE-CUM-SHITE!, SHIT!, SHITTLE-CUM-SHAW!, SHITTLETIDEE!, SHIVER MY TIM-BERS!, 'SLID!, 'SLIDIKINS!, 'SLIFE!, 'SLIGHT!, 'SLOOD!, 'SLUCK!, 'SLUD!, SMOLEY HOKE!, 'SNAILS!, 'SNEAKS!, 'SNIGGERS!, 'SNIGS!, 'SNOWNS!, SO 'ELP ME!, SO HELP ME GOD!, S'OONDS!, SPLIT MY WINDPIPE!, 'STREWTH!, STRIKE ME DEAD!, STRIKE ME DUMB!, STRIKE ME HANDSOME!, 'STRUTH!, SUF-FERING CATS!, SUFFERING CHRIST!, SUF-FERING SAINTS!, SUFFERING SASSAFRAS!, SUFFERING SEASERPENTS!, SUFFERING

SEAWEED!, SUFFERING SNAKES!, 'SWILL!, SWOGGLE MY EYES!, 'SWORBOTE!, 'SWOUNDS!, THE HELL!, THE HELL YOU SAY!, THE MISCHIEF YOU SAY!, THE PODY CODY!, THUNDERATION!, UPON MY SOUL!, UPON MY WORD!, WOUNDS!, YE GODS!, YE GODS AND LITTLE FISHES!, 'ZBLOUD!, 'ZBUD!, 'ZDEATH!, Z-DZ!, ZOODIKERS!, ZOOKERS!, 'ZOOKS!, ZOWKS!

zounked (out) 1. alcohol or drug intoxicated. For synonyms see TALL, WOOFLED. [U.S., late 1900s-pres.] 2. exhausted; asleep. [U.S., late 1900s-pres.]

zozzled drunk. For synonyms see WOOFLED. [U.S., late 1900s-pres.]

zubrick the penis. For synonyms see YARD. [Australian, 1900s, *Dictionary of Slang and Unconventional English*]

zuke to vomit. For synonyms see YORK. [U.S. collegiate, late 1900s, Munro] See also YUKE.

Zulued alcohol intoxicated. For synonyms see WOOFLED. [U.S. collegiate, late 1900s, Eble]

zunked alcohol or drug intoxicated. For synonyms see TALL, WOOFLED. [U.S., late 1900s-pres.]

WORKS CONSULTED

Reference Works

The American College Dictionary. New York: Random House, 1957.

The American Heritage Dictionary of the English Language. Boston: Houghton Mifflin Company, 1976.

The Concise Oxford Dictionary. Sixth edition. Oxford, England: The Clarendon Press, 1976.

Dorland's Pocket Medical Dictionary. Philadelphia: W.B. Saunders Company, 1959.

Oxford English Dictionary. Oxford, England: Oxford University Press, 1933, and supplements.

Physicians' Desk Reference. Thirty-second edition. Oradell, New Jersey: Medical Economics Co., 1978.

The Random House Dictionary of the English Language. New York: Random House, 1966.

The Scribner-Bantam English Dictionary. New York: Charles Scribner's Sons, 1977.

Stedman's Medical Dictionary. Twenty-first edition. Baltimore, Maryland: The Williams & Wilkins Company, 1966.

Taber's Cyclopedic Medical Dictionary. Philadelphia: F.A. Davis Company, 1973.

Webster's New International Dictionary. Springfield, Massachusetts: G. & C. Merriam Company, 1881; second edition, 1934; third edition, 1961.

Webster's New Collegiate Dictionary. Seventh edition. Springfield, Massachusetts: G. & C. Merriam Company, 1963.

Other Works Consulted

Abel, Ernest. *A Dictionary of Drug Abuse Terms.* Westport, Connecticut: Greenwood, 1984.

Adams, Charles C. *Boontling, An American Lingo.* Austin: University of Texas Press, 1971.

Adams, Ramon F. *Western Words*. Second edition. Norman: University of Oklahoma Press, 1968.

Anderson, Dennis. *The Book of Slang*. Middle Village, New York: Jonathan David Publishers, Inc., 1975.

Andrews, William. *Old Time Punishments*. Hull, England: W. Andrews and Company, 1890.

Anglicus, Ducange (pseud.). *The Vulgar Tongue*. London: Bernard Quaritch, 1857.

Anonymous. *Dictionary of Love*. 1733.

——. *New Canting Dictionary*. London, 1725.

——. *Sinks of London Laid Open*. London: J. Duncombe, 1848.

Axley, Lowry. " 'Drunk' again." *American Speech*, Volume IV, Number 6, (1929).

Axon, W.E.A. *English Dialect in the Eighteenth Century*. Publication Number 41. English Dialect Society, 1883.

Babbitt, E. H. "College Words and Phrases." *Dialect Notes*, Volume II, Part I (1900).

Badcock, Jon (Jon Bee). *Dictionary*. 1823.

Bailey, Nathan. *Dictionarium Britannicum: Universal Etymological English Dictionary*. 1730. Reprinted by Georg Olms Verlag, 1969.

Baker, Sidney J. *The Australian Language*. Sydney: Angus and Robertson, Ltd., 1945.

——. *Australia Speaks*. Sydney: Shakespeare Head Press, 1953.

——. *The Drum*. Sydney: Currawong, 1959.

——. *A Popular Dictionary of Australian Slang*. Melbourne: Robertson and Mullens Limited, 1943.

——. *New Zealand Slang*. Christchurch: Whitcombe and Tombs Limited, 1941.

Baring-Gould, William S. *The Lure of the Limerick*. New York: Clarkson N. Potter, Inc., 1967.

Barrère. Albert, and Charles G. Leland. *A Dictionary of Slang, Jargon, and Cant*. Two volumes. London: The Ballantyne Press, 1889-90.

Bartlett, John Russell. *Americanisms*. Boston: Little, Brown and Co., 1884.

B.E. *A New Dictionary of the Canting Crew*. 1690-1700.

Beale, Paul, editor. *A Concise Dictionary of Slang and Unconventional English*. London: Routledge, 1989.

Beath, Paul Robert. "More Crook Words." *American Speech*, Volume VI, Number 2 (1930).

Berger, Morroe. "Army Language." *American Speech*, Volume XX, Number 4 (1945).

Berrey, Lester V., and Melvin Van den Bark. *The American Thesaurus of Slang.* Second edition. New York: Thomas Y. Crowell Company, 1953.

Bierce, Ambrose. *The Devil's Dictionary.* New York: World Publishing Company, 1942.

Billups, Norman F. *American Drug Index.* Philadelphia: J. B. Lippincott Company, 1977.

Black, Henry Campbell. *Black's Law Dictionary.* Revised fourth edition. St. Paul, Minnesota: West Publishing Company, 1968.

Bolwell, Robert. "College Slang Words and Phrases." *Dialect Notes,* Volume IV, Part III (1915).

Brackbill, Hervey. "Midshipman Jargon." *American Speech,* Volume III, Number 6 (1928).

Brewer, E. Cobham. *The Dictionary of Phrase and Fable.* 1894. Reprinted by Avenel Books, 1978.

Brophy, John, and Eric Partridge. *The Long Trail.* New York: London House and Maxwell, 1965.

Carey, James T. *The College Drug Scene.* Englewood Cliffs, New Jersey: Prentice-Hall, Inc., 1968.

Cassidy, Frederic, G. *Jamaica Talk.* London: Macmillan & Co. Ltd., 1961.

Cassidy, F.G., and R.B. Le Page. *Dictionary of Jamaican English.* London: Cambridge University Press, 1967.

Chaplin, J.P. *Dictionary of Psychology.* New York: Dell Publishing Company, Inc., 1975.

Chapman, Robert L., editor. *New Dictionary of American Slang.* New York: Harper & Row, 1986.

Claerbaut, David. *Black Jargon in White America.* Grand Rapids, Michigan: William B. Eerdman's Publishing Company, 1972.

Coles, Elisha. *An English Dictionary.* London, 1696.

Cope, William H. *Hampshire Words and Phrases.* Publication Number 40. English Dialect Society, 1883.

Craigie, W.L., and R.J. Hulbert. *Dictionary of American English.* Chicago: University of Chicago Press, 1942.

Crowley, Ellen T., and Robert C. Thomas. *Reverse Acronyms, Initialisms, and Abbreviations Dictionary.* Fifth edition. Detroit, Michigan: Gale Research Company, 1976.

Dahlskog, Helen, editor. *A Dictionary of Contemporary and Colloquial Usage.* Chicago: The English-Language Institute of America, 1972.

Dartnell, G.E. *A Glossary of Wiltshire Words.* Publication Number 69, English Dialect Society, 1893.

Deak, Etienne, and Simone Deak. *Grand Dictionnaire d'Américanismes.* Paris: Editions Du Dauphin, 1956.

Dekker, Thomas, *The Gull's Hornbook*. 1609.

De Lannoy, William C., and Elizabeth Masterson. "Teen-Age Hophead Jargon." *American Speech,* Volume XXVII, Number 1 (1952).

Dennis, Paul, and Carolyn Barry. *The Marijuana Catalogue.* Chicago: Playboy Press, 1978.

DeSola, Ralph. *Crime Dictionary*. New York: Facts on File, 1982.

Dickson, Paul. *Words*. New York: Dell, 1982.

Dill, Stephen H., and Donald E. Bebeau. *Current Slang*. Six volumes. Vermillion: University of South Dakota, 1966-1971.

Dillard, J.L. *All-American English*. New York: Random House, 1975.

——. *Black English*. New York: Random House, 1972.

Dills, Lanie. *CB Slanguage Language Dictionary*. Nashville, Tennessee: Lanie Dills, Publisher, 1976.

Dingus, L.R. "A Word-List from Virginia." *Dialect Notes,* Volume IV, Part III (1915).

Douglas, Norman. *Some Limericks*. Originally privately printed, 1928. Reprinted by Grove Press, Inc., 1967.

Easther, A., and Thomas Lees. *A Glossary of the Dialect of Almondbury and Huddersfield.* Publication Number 39. English Dialect Society, 1883.

Eble, Connie. *College Slang 101*. Georgetown, Conn.: Spectacle Lane, 1989.

Edwards, Gillian. *Uncumber and Pantaloons*. New York: E.P. Dutton, 1969.

Eliason, Norman E. *Tarheel Talk*. Chapel Hill: University of North Carolina Press, 1956.

Elting, John R. *et al. A Dictionary of Soldier Talk*. New York: Scribner's. 1984.

English, Horace B., and Ava Champney English. *A Comprehensive Dictionary of Psychological and Psychoanalytical Terms*. New York: David McKay Co., Inc., 1958.

Espy, Willard R. *The Game of Words*. New York: Bramhall House, 1972.

——. *O Thou Improper, Thou Uncommon Noun*. New York: Charkson N. Potter, Inc., 1978.

Evans, A.B. *The Dialect of Leicestershire*. Publication Number 31. English Dialect Society, 1881.

Evans, Bergen. *Comfortable Words*. New York: Random House, 1962.

Evans, Bergen, and Cornelia Evans. *A Dictionary of Contemporary American Usage*. New York: Random House, 1957.

Fairchild, Henry Pratt. *Dictionary of Sociology and Related Sciences*. Paterson, New Jersey: Littlefield Adams and Co., 1961.

Farb, Peter. *Word Play.* New York: Alfred A. Knopf, 1974.

Farmer, John S. *Americanisms.* London: Thomas Poulter and Sons, 1889.

Farmer, John Stephen, and W. E. Henley. *Slang and Its Analogs.* Seven volumes, 1890-1904. Reprinted by Kraus Reprint Col., 1974.

Farmer, John. *Vocabula Amatoria.* 1896. Secaucus, New Jersey: Reprinted by University Books, 1966.

Farrell, Ronald A. "The Argot of the Homosexual Subculture." *Anthropological Linguistics,* Volume 14, Number 3 (1972).

Flexner, Stuart Berg. *I Hear America Talking.* New York: Van Nostrand Reinhold, 1976.

Florio, John. *A Worlde of Words.* 1598.

Folb, Edith A. *A Comparative Study of Urban Black Argot.* Arlington, Virginia: ERIC Document Reproduction Service, 1972.

——. *Runnin' Down Some Lines.* Cambridge: Harvard University Press, 1980.

Fowler, H. W. *A Dictionary of Modern English Usage.* London: Oxford University Press, 1937.

Franklin, Benjamin. "The Drinker's Dictionary." *Pennsylvania Gazette,* January 6, 1737.

Franklyn, Julian. *Dictionary of Nicknames.* London: Hamish Hamilton, 1962.

——. *A Dictionary of Rhyming Slang.* London: Routledge & Kegan Paul, 1961.

——. *Which Witch?* Boston: Houghton Mifflin Co., 1966.

Fraser, Edward, and John Gibbons. *Soldier and Sailor Words and Phrases.* London: George Routledge and Sons, Ltd., 1925.

Fuller, Robert Sevier. *Duppies Is.* Georgetown, Cayman Islands: Cayman Authors Limited, 1967.

Funk, Wilfred. *Word Origins.* New York: Grosset and Dunlap, 1950.

Gibson, Walter B., and Litzka R. Gibson. *The Complete Illustrated Book of Divination and Prophesy.* Garden City, New York: Doubleday and Company, Inc., 1973.

Goldin, Hyman E., Frank O'Leary, and Morris Lipsius. *Dictionary of American Underworld Lingo.* New York: Twayne Publishers, Inc., 1950.

Granville, Wilfred. *Dictionary of Sailor's Slang.* London: Andre Deutsch, 1962.

Green, B.W. *World-Book of Virginia Folk-Speech.* Richmond, Virginia: Wm. Ellis Jones, Inc., 1899.

Green, Jonathon. *The Dictionary of Contemporary Slang.* London: Pan Books, 1984.

Grose, Francis. *A Classical Dictionary of the Vulgar Tongue.* 1785; second edition, 1788; third edition, 1796.

——. *A Classical Dictionary of the Vulgar Tongue.* Edited by Pierce Egan. London: Sherwood, Neely, and Jones, 1823.

——. *A Classical Dictionary of the Vulgar Tongue.* Edited by Eric Partridge. London: The Scholartis Press, 1931.

——. *Lexicon Balatronicum.* Edited by H. Clarke. London, 1811.

——. *Provincial Glossary.* London: E. Jeffery, 1811.

Hall, B.H. *A Collection of College Words and Customs.* Cambridge, Massachusetts: John Bartlett, 1856.

Halliwell, James Orchard. *A Dictionary of Archaic and Provincial Words.* Fifth edition. London: Gibbings and Company, Limited, 1901.

Hamilton, Delbert W. "Pacific War Language." *American Speech,* Volume XXII, Number 1 (1947).

Hardin, Achsah. "Volstead English." *American Speech,* Volume IV, Number 2 (1931).

Hardy, Richard E., and John G. Cull. *Drug Language and Lore.* Springfield, Illinois: Charles C. Thomas, 1975.

Harman, Thomas. *A Caveat.* 1567.

Hayden, M.G. "Terms of Disparagement." *Dialect Notes,* Volume IV, Part III (1915).

Haywood, Charles. *Yankee Dictionary.* Lynn, Massachusetts: Jackson and Phillips, Inc., 1963.

Heifetz, Josefa. *Mrs. Byrne's Dictionary.* Secaucus, New Jersey: Citadel Press, 1976.

Heslop, R. Oliver. *Northumberland Words.* Publication Number 66, 68, 71. English Dialect Society. 1892-1894.

Hills, E.C. "Exclamations in American English." *Dialect Notes,* Volume V, Part III (1924).

Holland, Robert. *Glossary of Cheshire Words.* Publication Number 44 and 46. English Dialect Society, 1884-1885.

Hotten, John Camden. *The Slang Dictionary.* London, 1859; second edition, 1860; third edition, 1864; fourth edition, 1870; fifth edition, 1874.

Humphreys, Laud. *Tearoom Trade.* Chicago: Aldine Publishing Co., 1970.

Irwin, Godfrey. *American Tramp and Underworld Slang.* London: Scholartis Press, 1931.

James, Jennifer. "Two Domains of Streetwalker Argot." *Anthropological Linguistics,* Volume 14, Number 5 (1972).

Jamieson, John. *Dictionary of the Scottish Language.* Edited by John Johnstone. London: William P. Nimmo, 1885.

Joffe, Natalie. "The Vernacular of Menstruation." *Word,* Volume 4, Number 3 (1948).

Kaiser, Jay W. Personal Communications.

Kane, Elisha K. "The Jargon of the Underworld." *Dialect Notes,* Volume V, Part X (1927).

Keller, Mark, and Mairi McCormick. *A Dictionary of Words About Alcohol.* New Brunswick, New Jersey: Rutgers Center for Alcohol Studies, 1968.

Kirshenblatt-Gimblett, Barbara, editor. *Speech Play.* Philadelphia: University of Pennsylvania Press, 1976.

Klein, Nicholas. "Hobo Lingo." *American Speech,* Volume I, Number 12 (1926).

Kolin, Philip C. "The Language of Nursing." *American Speech,* Volume 48, Numbers 3-4 (1973).

Kuethe, J. Louis. "Prison Parlance." *American Speech,* Volume IX, Number 1 (1934).

Lambton, Lucinda. *Temples of Convenience.* New York: St. Martin's Press, 1978.

Landy, Eugene E. *The Underground Dictionary.* New York: Simon and Schuster, 1971.

Lawrence, Jeremy. *Unmentionables and Other Euphemisms.* London: Gentry Books, 1973.

Leeds, Winifred. *Herefordshire Speech.* n.d.

Legman, G. *Rationale of the Dirty Joke: An Analysis of Sexual Humor.* New York: Dell Publishing Company, 1975.

Lester, David. *Unusual Sexual Behavior.* Springfield, Illinois: Charles C. Thomas, 1975.

Lewin, Esther, and Alber E. Lewin. *The Thesaurus of Slang.* New York: Facts on File, 1988.

Liddell, H. G., and Robert Scott. *A Greek-English Lexicon.* Oxford, England: Clarendon Press, 1940.

Lighter, Jonathan. "The Slang of the American Expeditionary Forces in Europe, 1917-1919." *American Speech,* Volume 47 (1972).

Lingeman, Richard R. *Drugs From A To Z: A Dictionary.* Second edition. New York: McGraw-Hill Book Company, 1974.

Fruit, J.P. "Kentucky Words." *Dialect Notes,* Volume I, Part V (1891).

Major, Clarence. *Dictionary of Afro-American Slang.* New York: International Publishers, 1970.

Manchon, Joseph. *Le Slang, Lexique de l'Anglais Familier et Vulgaire.* Paris, 1923.

Marckwardt, Albert H. *An Introduction to the English Language.* New York: Oxford University Press, 1942.

Marples, Morris. *University Slang.* London: Williams and Norgate, 1950.

Marshall, Mary. *Bozzimacoo: Origins and Meanings of Oaths and Swearwords.* London: M. & J. Hobbs, 1975.

Matsell, George W. *Vocabulum; or The Rogue's Dictionary.* New York: George W. Matsell & Co., 1859.

Matthews, Mitford M. *A Dictionary of Americanisms on Historical Principles.* Chicago: University of Chicago Press, 1951.

Maurer, David W. "The Argot of the Underworld." *American Speech,* Volume VII, Number 2 (1931).

——. "Argot of the Underworld Narcotics Addict." *American Speech,* Volume XI, Number 2, Part 1 (1936); Volume XIII, Number 3, Part 2 (1938).

——. " 'Australian' Rhyming Argot in the American Underworld." *American Speech,* Volume XIX, Number 3 (1944).

——. *Language of the Underworld.* Lexington: University of Kentucky Press, 1981.

——. "The Lingo of the Good-People." *American Speech,* Volume X, Number 1 (1935).

Mawson, C.O. Sylvester. *Dictionary of Foreign Terms.* New York: Thomas Y. Crowell Company, 1934.

Mayhew, Henry. *Mayhew's London, Selections From "London Labour and the London Poor."* Edited by P. Quennell. London: Spring Books, 1949.

McCulloch, Walter F. *Woods Words.* Corvallis: Oregon State College, Champoeg Press, 1958.

McDonald, James. *A Dictionary of Obscenity, Taboo, and Euphemism.* London: Sphere, 1988.

Mead, W.E., and G.D. Chase. "A Central Connecticut Word-List." *Dialect Notes,* Volume III, Part I (1905).

Mencken, H.L. *The American Language.* New York: Alfred A. Knopf, 1921.

——. *The American Language.* Supplement One. New York: Alfred A. Knopf, 1945.

——. *The American Language.* Supplement Two. New York: Alfred A. Knopf, 1948.

Monteleone, Vincent J. *Criminal Slang.* Revised edition. Boston: The Christopher Publishing House, 1949.

Montagu, Ashley. *The Anatomy of Swearing.* New York: Macmillan Publishing Company, 1967.

Morris, William, and Mary Morris. *Morris Dictionary of Word and Phrase Origins.* New York: Harper & Row, Publishers, 1977.

Mueller, Gerhard O.W. *Legal Regulation of Sexual Conduct.* New York: Oceana Publications, Inc., 1961.

Munro, Pamela *et al. U.C.L.A. Slang.* UCLA Occasional Papers in Linguistics 8, Los Angeles, 1989.

Nares, Robert. *A Glossary of Words, Phrases, Names, and Allusions in Works of English Authors.* London: Reeves and Turner, 1888.

Neaman, Judith S., and Carole G. Silver. *Kind Words: A Thesaurus of Euphemisms.* New York: Facts on File, 1983.

Nicholson, Margaret. *A Dictionary of American-English Usage.* New York: Oxford University Press, 1957.

Niemoeller, A.F. "A Glossary of Homosexual Slang." *Fact,* Volume 2, Number 1 (1965).

Nodal, J.H., and George Milner. *Glossary of the Lancashire Dialect.* Publication Number 35. English Dialect Society, 1882.

Northall, G.F. *A Warwickshire Word-Book.* Publication Number 79. English Dialect Society, 1896.

Opie, I., and P. Opie. *Children's Games in Street and Playground.* Oxford, England: Clarendon Press, 1969.

——. *The Lore and Language of School Children.* Oxford, England: Clarendon Press, 1959.

Orkin, Mark M. *Speaking Canadian English.* Toronto: General Publishing Company Limited, 1970.

Ottley, C.R. *Creole Talk, Trinibaganese.* Trinidad, Victory Printers, 1971.

Partridge, Eric. *A Dictionary of Catch Phrases.* New York: Stein and Day, 1977.

——. *Dictionary of Forces Slang.* London: Secker & Warburg, 1948.

——. *A Dictionary of R.A.F. Slang.* London: Michael Joseph Ltd., 1945.

——. *A Dictionary of Slang and Unconventional English.* Seventh edition. New York: Macmillan Publishing Co., 1970.

——. *A Dictionary of Slang and Unconventional English.* Edited by Paul Beale. New York: Macmillan, 1984.

——. *A Dictionary of the Underworld.* New York: Macmillan Publishing Col., 1968.

——. *Origins.* London: Routledge and Kegan Paul, 1958.

——. *Shakespeare's Bawdy.* London: Routledge & Kegan Paul, 1968.

——. *Slang Today and Yesterday.* Fourth edition. New York: Barnes and Noble, Inc., 1970.

——. *Smaller Slang Dictionary.* London: Routledge and Kegan Paul, 1964.

Pederson, Lee. "An Approach to Urban Word Geography." *American Speech,* Volume 46, Numbers 1-2 (1971).

——. "Chicago Words: The Regional Vocabulary." *American Speech,* Volume 46, Numbers 3-4 (1971).

Pegge, Samuel. *Two Collections of Derbicisms.* Publication Number 78. English Dialect Society, 1896.

Pei, Mario, and Salvatore Ramondino. *Dictionary of Foreign Terms.* New York: Dell Publishing Company, Inc., 1974.

Potter, Stephen, and Laurens Sargent. *Pedigree: The Origins of Words From Nature.* New York: Taplinger Publishing Company, 1974.

Pound, Louise. "American Euphemisms for Dying, Death, and Burial." *American Speech,* volume XI, Number 3 (1936).

——. "Dialect Speech of Nebraska." *Dialect Notes,* Volume III, Part I (1905).

Pratt, Jane, editor. *Harrap's Slang Dictionary.* London: Harrap, 1984.

Prenner, Manuel. "Slang Synonyms for Drunk." *American Speech,* Volume IV, Number 2 (1928).

Pudney, John. *The Smallest Room.* London: Michael Joseph, 1954.

Pyles, Thomas. *The Origin and Development of the English Language.* Second edition. New York: Harcourt, Brace, Jovanovich Inc., 1971.

Randolph, Vance. "Verbal Modesty in the Ozarks." *Dialect Notes,* Volume VI, Part I (1928).

——. "Wet Words in Kansas." *American Speech,* Volume IV, Number 5, (1929).

Randolph, Vance, and Carl Pingry. "Kansas University Slang." *American Speech,* Volume III, Number 3 (1928).

Randolph, Vance, and George P. Wilson. *Down in the Holler.* Norman: University of Oklahoma Press, 1953.

Rawson, Hugh. *A Dictionary of Euphemisms & Other Doubletalk.* New York: Crown, 1981.

Read, Allen Walker. "An Obscenity Symbol." *American Speech,* Volume IX (1934).

——. *Lexical Evidence from Folk Epigraphy in Western North America.* Printed privately in Paris in 1935. Reprinted as *Classical American Graffiti.* Waukesha, Wisconsin: Maledicta Press, 1977.

——. "Noah Webster as a Euphemist." *Dialect Notes,* Volume VI, Part VIII (1934).

Reynolds, Reginald. *Cleanliness and Godliness.* Garden City, New York: Doubleday and Company, Inc., 1943.

Roback, A.A. *A Dictionary of International Slurs.* Cambridge, Massachusetts: Sci-Art Publishers, 1944.

Rodgers, Bruce. *The Queen's Vernacular: A Gay Lexicon.* San Francisco: Straight Arrow Books, 1972.

Rose, Howard N. *A Thesaurus of Slang*. New York: The Macmillan Company, 1934.

Ross, Alan S.C., and A.W. Moverley. *The Pitcairnese Language*. London: Andre Deutsch, 1964.

Rosten, Leo. *The Joys of Yiddish*. New York: McGraw-Hill Book Company, 1968.

Rye, Walter. *East Anglian Glossary*. Publication Number 75. English Dialect Society, 1895.

Sabbath, Dan, and Mandel Hall. *End Product: The First Taboo*. New York: Urizen Books, 1977.

Sagarin, Edward. *The Anatomy of Dirty Words*. New York: Lyle Stuart, Publisher, 1962.

Samolar, Charlie. "The Argot of the Vagabond." *American Speech,* Volume II, Number 9 (1927).

Saul, Vernon W. "The Vocabulary of Bums." *American Speech,* Volume IV, Number 5 (1929).

Schur, Norman W. *British Self-taught with Comments in American*. New York: Macmillan Publishing Company, Inc., 1973.

Seymour, Richard K. "Collegiate Slang: Aspects of Word Formation and Semantic Change." *Publication of the American Dialect Society,* Number 51 (April, 1969).

Shipley, Joseph T. *Dictionary of Early English*. New York: Philosophical Library, 1955.

Simons, Hi. "A Prison Dictionary (Expurgated)." *American Speech,* Volume VIII, Number 3 (1933).

Skeat, Walter, editor. *Fitzherbert's Book of Husbandry, 1534*. Publication Number 37. English Dialect Society, 1882.

Skeat, Walter. *Nine Specimens of English Dialect*. Publication Number 76. English Dialect Society.

Skinner, Henry Alan. The Origin of Medical Terms. Second edition. New York: Hafner Publishing Co., 1970.

Slovenko, Ralph. *Sexual Behavior and the Law*. Springfield, Illinois: Charles C. Thomas, 1965.

Spears, Richard A. *Forbidden American English*. Lincolnwood, Illinois: Passport Books, 1990.

——. *NTC's Dictionary of American Slang and Colloquial Expressions*. Lincolnwood, Illinois: NTC Publishing Group, 1989.

——. *The Slang and Jargon of Drugs and Drink*. Metuchen, New Jersey: Scarecrow Press, 1986.

Sperling, Susan Kelz. *Poplollies and Bellibones: A Celebration of Lost Words*. New York: Clarkson N. Potter, 1977.

Stanley, Julia P. "Homosexual Slang." *American Speech,* Volume 45 (1970).

Steadman, J.M. "A Study of Verbal Taboos." *American Speech,* Volume X, Number 2, (1935).

Tak, Montie, *Truck Talk.* Philadelphia: Chilton Book Co., 1971.

Taylor, A. Marjorie. *The Language of World War II.* New York: H.W. Wilson Co., 1944.

Taylor, Sharon Henderson. "Terms for Low Intelligence." *American Speech,* Volume 49, Numbers 3-4 (1974).

Thornton, Richard H. *An American Glossary.* Philadelphia: J.B. Lippincott, 1912.

Underwood, Gary. "Razorback Slang." *American Speech,* Volume 50 (1975).

Untermeyer, Louis. *Lots of Limericks.* New York: Dell Publishing Company, 1959.

Ward, Harvey E. *Down Under Without Blunder.* Rutland, Vermont: Charles E. Tuttle Co., 1967.

Ware, J. Redding. *Passing English of the Victorian Era.* London: George Routledge & Sons, Limited, 1909.

Warnock, E.L. "Terms of Approbation and Eulogy." *Dialect Notes,* Volume IV, Part I (1913).

Weingarten, Joseph. *An American Dictionary of Slang and Colloquial Speech.* New York: 1954.

Wentworth, Harold. *American Dialect Dictionary.* New York: Thomas Y. Crowell Company, 1944.

Wentworth, Harold, and Stuart Berg Flexner. *Dictionary of American Slang.* Second supplemented edition. New York: Thomas Y. Crowell Company, 1975.

Weseen, Maurice H. *Dictionary of American Slang.* New York: Thomas Y. Crowell Company, 1934.

Whitman, Walt. *Leaves of Grass.* First published in 1855. Revised and expanded in various editions until 1891.

Wilkes, Gerald Alfred. *A Dictionary of Australian Colloquialisms.* London: Routledge & Kegan Paul, 1978.

Wilson, David. *Staffordshire Dialect Words.* Stafford, England: Moorland Publishing Co., 1974.

Wolfenstein, Martha. *Children's Humor: A Psychological Analysis.* Glencoe, Illinois: The Free Press, 1954.

Wright, Joseph, editor. *The English Dialect Dictionary.* 6 vols. London: Henry Frowde, 1898-1905.

Wright, Lawrence. *Clean and Decent.* London: Routledge & Kegan Paul, 1960.

Wright, Peter. *The Language of British Industry.* London: Macmillan Publishing Company, 1974.

Yenne, Herbert. "Prison Lingo." *American Speech,* Volume II, Number 6 (1927).

Young, Lawrence A., *et al. Recreational Drugs.* New York: Collier Macmillan Publishers, 1977.

Zandvoort, R.U. *Wartime English.* Groningen: J.B. Wolters, 1957.

Various works of the following authors were consulted:

Joseph Addison, Francis Beaumont, James Boswell, Robert Burns, Truman Capote, Thomas Carew, Thomas Carlyle, George Chapman, Geoffrey Chaucer, Samuel Clemens (Mark Twain), William Congreve, James Fenimore Cooper, Randle Cotgrave, Daniel Defoe, Charles Dickens, John Dryden, Thomas D'Urfrey, Pierce Egan, Henry Fielding, John Fletcher, Sigmund Freud, George Gordon (Lord Byron), Robert Graves, Zane Grey, Joseph Heller, William Ernest Henley, Robert Herrick, Washington Irving, James Joyce, Rudyard Kipling, William Langland, D.H. Lawrence, Jack London, Thomas Babington Macaulay, Thomas Malory, Thomas Middleton, John Stuart Mill, John Milton, Peter Anthony Motteux, Vladimir Nabokov, Thomas Nashe, George Orwell, Samuel Pepys, Alexander Pope, Philip Roth, J.D. Salinger, Sir Walter Scott, William Shakespeare, George Bernard Shaw, Tobias George Smollett, Edmund Spenser, Richard Steele, Jonathan Swift, William Makepeace Thackeray, Anthony Trollope, Nicholas Udall, Sir Thomas Urquhart, Edward (Ned) Ward, John Webster, Walt Whitman.

READ THE TOP 25 SIGNET CLASSICS

Signet

A world of reference at your fingertips

❑ *THE NEW ROBERT'S RULES OF ORDER* *(2ND EDITION)*
   MARY A. DE VRIES 195175 / $6.99
Long considered the bible of parliamentary procedures, this new edition updates the archaic prose of the original into easy-to-follow, contemporary English while maintaining the work's original order and content.

❑ *THE NEW AMERICAN ROGET'S COLLEGE THESAURUS*
   (REVISED & EXPANDED) *PHILIP D. MOREHEAD*, ED.
                                    151674 / $6.50
Extensively revised and expanded to include: 15,000 new words; 1,500 additional entries; improved cross-referencing; alphabetical listings of synonyms and antonyms; and the latest colloquial terms and slang expressions.

❑ *THE NEW AMERICAN WEBSTER HANDY COLLEGE*
   DICTIONARY *(3RD EDITION)* *PHILIP D. MOREHEAD*, ED.
                                    181662 / $5.99
This all-new, enlarged edition contains over 1,500 new words—including hundreds not found in any other pocket dictionary, an indispensible tool for a better mastery of the English language!